The Majestic Quran

The Majestic
Quran

A Plain English Translation

Third Edition

Translated by Dr Musharraf Hussain, Al-Azhari, OBE, DL, D.Univ

Helpful tips for studying the Majestic Quran effectively

Our goal is to convey the meaning of the Quran accurately. This translation is easy to read and understand. Here are some useful tips to help you enjoy and benefit from reading the Majestic:

1. The Quran is a book of guidance, that impresses the reader, drives home the message deep into the heart and mind. It moulds the attitude and inspires you. Every Surat develops its central theme from the beginning to the end logically, there is a gradual move to completion, sometimes it seems disjointed, but these are digressions, Divine comments. The pattern seems to be: Some surats open with the mysterious broken letters, others with praise and glorification of the Lord. Followed by arguments for the Lords majesty, reference to His creative power in nature, or description of hell and heaven, rewards, punishment, or reference to human history of disobedience. This form helps in achieving the original goal, which is to impress the reader. So, read the introduction of the Surat.

2. The Quran gives direct instructions, it doesn't speak in abstract terms, often uses the imperative for example: *Anfiqu*, give charity; *Aqeemu-salah*, pray regularly; *Athu-zakah*, pay zakah. When you carry out these Divine orders you will experience a change. Look for Allah's orders.

3. The Quran routinely keeps things brief, with minimum details, It's concise. Minimalism is the Quranic style. For example, it leaves out names of people and towns, as though it's in a hurry to get to the message, and pronounce the moral and spiritual lessons, pay special notice to this.

4. The Quran is a useful manual not a textbook, it persuades, dissuades, pricks the conscience, flips from present to future and back to the past, reasons using evidence from nature, human experience, and history. Just follow its guidance.

5. The Quran demands the reader's full attention: Applying one's mind, being focused. This leads to reflection and asking pertinent questions; who is the Creator? What does He expect from me? Answer these questions.

6. The Quran persuades through reason. So, when reading, ask yourself: What's the message for me? What does the Majestic Quran want me to believe, accept or do? What does it expect me to learn and understand about Allah? It's teaching you the bigger picture, so you may understand the deceptive nature of worldly life.

O Allah, the Loving and Caring Lord, open our hearts and minds to Your beautiful speech. We ask You to make our global village peaceful and safe. Kind Lord, bless our Master Muhammed, his companions and wonderful family.

What Readers Say

"... it's a beautiful and rich English language work with new aspects and comments (especially in the side margins), which are tremendously insightful and inspired"

Yusuf Islam (Cat Stevens), Singer/Songwriter

"The Majestic Quran is an excellent translation in contemporary English, its faithful to the original text and presents the meaning and the message thematically."

Imam Qari Asim, MBE, Chairman MINAB

"... an excellent translation, revealing the clear message of the Holy Qur'an in plain language and style. The Introduction to Surat is a summary of the subject matter and highlights the central theme. Giving separate headings to a set of verses is commendable, a unique feature of this translation."

Allama M. Masood Ahmed, Global Islamic Mission, New York

"Dr Hussain was inspired to translate the Quran to share his love of its 'breathtaking beauty'. In attempting to avoid the 'old-fashioned English' of Pickthall and Yusuf Ali, he has avoided such 'old' terminology as much as possible, while still retaining the original meaning of the Majestic Quran. As if to underscore the point, his sub-title is 'A Plain English Translation.'"

Professor Akbar Ahmed, American University, Washington DC

"Dr Hussain's new translation combines deep piety with philological accuracy, conveying the complexity of the text with admirable simplicity... in plain English. This new translation invites us all to appreciate the Islamic scripture in a new way and will enrich experienced readers as well as beginners."

Dr Holger Zellentin, Lecturer in Classical Rabbinic Judaism, University of Cambridge

"This translation of the Quran is commendable for its successful attempt at conveying the meaning and message. The lucid translation ... will advance readers' understanding of the Quran."

Professor Abdur Raheem Kidwai, Aligarh University

"It often requires much effort on the part of the reader to understand the message of the Quran and in particular where the language used is sometimes unfamiliar from the normal reading experience. This translation has strived to make the Quran accessible and effortless for the contemporary reader. I believe the Majestic Quran has made an original contribution to the existing translations of the Quran and will come to be used widely."

Shaykh Amer Jamil, Director iSyllabus

"Dr Hussain's translation is a beautiful rendering of the divine message, aiding our understanding ... It is a wonderful addition to the field of Quran translation."

Ustadh Yasrab Daud Shah, Special Programmes Manager, Muslim Hands

"The Majestic Qur'an in Plain English is an inspirational, forward-thinking, new way of presenting Qur'anic translation accessibly to a modern audience."

Dr Asam Latif, NIHR Clinical-Academic Lecturer, University of Nottingham

"... I thoroughly enjoyed its simple thematic structure and relevance to our times/cultural landscape. I must congratulate you on this excellent effort and years of toil and hard work mashaAllah tabrakAllah. I made and continue to make dua to Allah (swt) that he accepts this as a means of achieving greater understanding, peace, guidance, tranquillity and transformation in the world, Ameen."

Maulana Waqaus Ali, Chief Executive ILM 2 AMAL, Bolton

"The translation presents the message of the Quran with clarity, reveals how the genuine Believer lives a lofty life of morality and spiritual yearning. Everyone should have this."

Maulana Abdul Hai Shami, Imam and Qari, Karimia Institute

12-1-2017

To Whom it May Concern

Egypt's Dar Aliftaa, the premier institution for Islamic Legal Interpretation in the Muslim World, is pleased to inform you that your translation of the glorious Qur'an has been approved by the board.

It affirms that this new valuable translation reflects the original beautiful message of the glorious Qur'an in plain English, its language is contemporary and an accurate interpretation of the meanings of the Quran according to the classical Muslim commentators.

Dr Musharraf Hussain's translation is accessible and readable in English, and it is an excellent addition to the field of Quran translations.

On behalf of Egypt's Dar AlIftaa

Dr. Ibrahim Negm

The Senior Advisor to His Excellency the Grand Mufti of Egypt

E-mail : mofti.office@dar-alifta.org
Site : www.dar-alifta.org

العنوان : حديقة الخالدين - الدراسة - القاهرة - ص.ب : ١١٦٧٥
تليفون : ٢٥٨٨٧٠١٣ - ٢٥٨٨٧٠٢٦ - ٢٥٨٨٧٠١٠ (٢٠٢+)
فاكس : ٢٥٨٩٩٦٥٢ (٢٠٢+)

The Majestic Quran – A Plain English Translation

First edition published March 2018
Reprinted with corrections June 2018
Second edition May 2019
Third edition July 2020
Reprinted with corrections July 2021
Reprinted with corrections January 2023

INVITATION PUBLISHING,
512 Berridge Road West
Nottingham
NG7 5JU
E-mail: info@invitationpublishing.co.uk
https://majesticquran.co.uk

Distributed by
INVITATION PUBLISHING.
Tel: +44[0] 115 855 0961

Cataloguing-in-Publication Data is available
from the British Library

ISBN: 978-1902248-85-1

Typeset in Minion Pro.
Cover design and typesetting by Sajhd Hussain.
Printed by Mega Basim (Istanbul, Türkiye).

Contents

Introduction

My Objectives and Methodology

I have under taken this translation because I owe so much to the Quran; it has given me meaning and purpose in life. I feel indebted, and this translation is a labour of love that I believe will offer fresh insights and understanding for readers living in a global village in an exciting age of science and information technology. The purpose of this translation is to convey the meanings of the Majestic Quran clearly, concisely and in a clear tone of voice, making this 'majestic reading' the most readable and appealing translation of the Quran in English.

I have been a serious student of the Quran for more than fifty years, during this time I have memorised the Quran, and studied the Arabic language, the science of Tafsir and Hadith at Al-Azhar University, Cairo. Prior to this I was a research scientist for more than ten years.

For the past fourteen centuries, Muslim scholars worked hard to understand the Majestic Quran as accurately as possible. My own understanding of the Quran is based on these works of honourable sages, and this translation is underpinned by the accumulated treasury of classical Islamic wisdom. It would not be an exaggeration to say that this translation and the introductions to the Surahs is the crystallisation of the traditional understanding of the divine words.

Although I have been guided by the past English translations of the Majestic Quran, I hope I have taken the work of those renowned scholars a bit further. I have learnt a lot from my predecessors and I have tried my best to avoid some of the pitfalls, biases, and inaccuracies they made. However, the most widely read and circulated translations of the Quran were unfortunately published in 'old-fashioned' English: Marmaduke Pickthall, Abdullah Yusuf Ali and the Sahih International version, which makes the Quran appear an outdated book that is nothing to do with contemporary society. In this translation, I have attempted to avoid such 'old' terminology as much as possible, while still retaining the original meaning of the Majestic Quran.

I hope this 'majestic reading' will be widely read the world over. The Quran is a living book, its message: Islam is a living message; a message of hope, providing spiritual and material prosperity and a happy life. Muslims are a young community that needs guidance, and is there any guidance better than the guidance of Allah? That's why this 'majestic reading' must once again be presented with clarity, and this translation attempts to give clarity to the message of the Majestic Qur'an in plain English; it's to the point, easy to understand and readable in contemporary English.

1. Plain and Contemporary English

My goal has been to translate the meaning of the divine message, all the time being faithful and accurate in expressing the exact meaning of the Quranic words; by using the root meanings of the words rather than freer interpretation. Mine is an authentic translation, neither liberal nor free, however, I have used interpretation to join ideas together. I believe this is the best way to give readers a true taste of the Quran, so that it can speak for itself. I have used plain English: simple words and avoiding archaic words and turns of phrase. Instead of translating Arabic idioms, I have used English idioms wherever possible. I have aimed for an accurate translation by relying on classical Arabic dictionaries and Quranic commentaries. How successful I have been in providing a meaning that is clear, plain and contemporary is for you, the reader to judge.

2. The Topical Section Headings

A distinct feature of this translation is the use of section headings for the sake of clarity. These headings correspond to the main themes and subject matter presented in the text. The headings of each section are not just attention-grabbing, but reflect its contents, themes and specific topics that will help the reader to understand the "bursts of revelation" as the Quran was revealed according to the needs of the time. However, this is only an attempt at clarity for the sake of understanding the divine text. They are not there to dictate the interpretation of these verses, although they may possibly give a particular interpretation to some readers. Their main purpose is to join ideas in the section, so helping to contextualise the passages. This allows the Quran to speak for itself. In brief, the headings are a useful device for unlocking the meaning and the purpose of the Quran and to help to make its teachings fully transparent. I believe this is a very convincing way for the reader to get a true taste of the Majestic Quran.

3. Introduction to the Surahs

The surahs, or chapters, in the Quran are divided into sections, based on where the subject begins or at the seam between two subjects. These act as 'hinge passages', which are separate units that can be attached to a preceding or following narrative block. These narrative blocks can be very fluid, particularly those that act as buffer zones which allow one passage to merge into the next.

The surahs highlight the period of revelation, the major themes and shed some light on the socio-economic, political, historical and cultural environment of the Arabian Peninsula at the time of revelation, the seventh century.

4. The Footnotes

I have used footnotes sparingly to add value to the communicative process of translation, where their absence could lead to misunderstandings. I have used them to explain metaphors and the figurative language of the Quran, and to describe circumstances of revelation that will help the reader to understand the background and the context of the events.

5. The Quranic Lessons

The short lessons in the margin of the Arabic page aim to encourage the reader to reflect on Quranic teachings; think deeply about the section/verse; and contemplate on its meanings using reason, emotion and spiritual insights. Just like the car indicator shows other road users that you're about to change direction, I hope the reader will use the Quranic lessons to change the direction of their lives. Intense focus is going on during the *Tilawat*; this is a great spiritual activity, worship and getting close to the Lord. Its purpose is to gain inspiration from reading the Quran. The Messenger, peace be upon him, said: "a moment's reflection is better than sixty years of worship." This makes the Quran reader more certain of the revelation; s/he will experience the revelation as one focuses on a single point, whether this is an object or an idea.

6. Presentation and Layout of the Translation

- The Quran is full of dialogue, sometimes between the Messenger, peace be upon him, and the Quraysh, with the People of The Book, and sometimes with all of humanity, etc. By using quotation marks I have endeavoured to convey the conversation in the original text. This has also been useful for identifying the start and end of sections.
- I have paid special attention to verses concerned with the Majesty of Allah and to honour the Messenger I have avoided using irreverent words. This also applies to anthropomorphic terms used for Allah in the Quran, including references to Allah's face, eyes, hands and expressions of Allah's response to human folly, like mocking, deception, etc. In places, these have been in interpreted and in others I have used English equivalents, as recommended by orthodox commentators.
- Arabic names of the prophets have been used instead of the biblical, for example Ibrahim, not Abraham, and Musa, not Moses. I have also kept some Arabic and Islamic words for their accuracy and emotional charge.

- Capitalisation has been used when reference is made to Allah; the pronouns, titles, the beautiful names of Allah, and the major concepts and terms in Islamic studies.
- I have used italics rather than brackets for any extra words inserted for the sake of explanation. The reason is that the omission of words and phrases is a common feature of the Quranic style, where things are left unsaid.
- For clarity, ayah (verse) numbers are mentioned at start in this English translation but are usually placed at the end in Arabic.

I am grateful to the Almighty loving Lord who gave me the opportunity to serve his wonderful book. I pray that Allah accepts this humble effort. However, it is a fact that no translation of the Quran no matter how accurate it is can express all the meanings of the Divine text, my translation is an attempt to understand the meanings of the Quran, it is not possible to fully translate and grasp the inimitable and powerful words of Allah. Therefore, it is likely that there will be shortcomings and even mistakes in the translation, so I request my readers to point them out so, they can be corrected in the next edition.

Dr Musharraf Hussain, Al-Azhari, OBE, DL, D.Univ

Acknowledgements

I would like to thank all of the people who have helped in this wonderful and sacred project, from those who gave moral support to those who provided finance, may Allah reward them plenty. My team, who ensured that the translation is accurate and accessible, were: Dr Roderic Vassie, Shaikh Yasrab Shah, Maulana Asif Ali, Mufti M Ismael, Hafiz Naveed MA, and my students at the Karimia Institute. May Allah bless them abundantly. Keith Devereux for the extensive proofreading. My typesetter and layout designer, Sajhd Hussain, deserves a special mention for his tireless work. I wish to pay a special thanks to the Dar Al-Ifta of Cairo, Egypt for approving the translation.

1. Surat Al-Fatihah
The Opening

The opening surat of the Majestic Quran summarises the major themes and topics of the Quran: shaping a world view through the belief system; faith in Allah, His messengers and the Hereafter; the Angels; Predestination and the Day of Resurrection; challenging idolatry and materialism; practising the five pillars; emphasis on obeying the laws: halal and haram; an invitation to embrace spiritual ideals: mindfulness and alertness, reliance on Allah; the promotion of moral teachings; the condemnation of moral vices; social obligations; the life and beautiful character of the Messenger ﷺ; the history of human disobedience; Satan the arch enemy, how he misleads and his snares and traps; human diversity and pluralism; the awe-inspiring nature; vivid descriptions of Heaven and Hell. This is the essence of the Quran.

It is read dozens of time daily in the prayers and is a plea, a prayer that the devout servant makes to the Caring Lord. The rest of the Quran is a response to this, and the blessed Messenger ﷺ praised its virtue: "by Him in whose hand is my life, nothing like this was ever revealed in the Torah, or the Psalms or the Gospel" (Ahmed). A concise prayer that is life transforming, no wonder the Messenger ﷺ described it as: *al-fatihah*, the door to the treasury of wisdom; Umm al-Quran, the Fountain of Quranic wisdom; *al-shifa*, the healing for moral, spiritual and social diseases.

2. Surat Al-Baqarah
The Cow

Historical Background

This, the longest surat in the Quran, was revealed in Madinah after the migration of the Prophet ﷺ in 622 CE (Common Era). It was completed in two years, by now two-thirds of the Quran had been revealed in Makkah, under a tense social and political environment. In Madinah, settling down in a new city with Arabs and Jews, Muslims faced new challenges. There were two main Arab tribes: the Aus and the Khazraj, both with a long history of rivalry and bloodshed, and three main Jewish tribes. The Jewish tribes had moved to Madinah after they were expelled from Jerusalem by the Romans, and were literate, skilled and affluent compared to the Arabs. The Jews also believed that they were "chosen people".

The first action of The Prophet ﷺ, to develop trust in his new home city, was to make a treaty with the Jewish and Arab tribes. The treaty stated all the communities were one community and would protect each other, they were guaranteed freedom to practise their religions.

The Main Themes of the Surat

- The surat opens by describing the inhabitants of Madinah and dividing them into three groups: the pious believers, the disbelievers and the hypocrites. Imam Razi, in *The Great Commentary*, states:

  > The believer is the one whose heart and conscience are religiously clear and good; the disbeliever is one who stubbornly refuses to believe, the hypocrite is the one who pretends to believe but whose conscience is against it.

- The Five Pillars of Islam: belief in the Oneness of Allah, the five daily prayers, Zakat, Ramadan, and pilgrimage to Makkah.
- The unity of the Abrahamic faiths: the surat repeatedly points out that Islam is not a new religion but instead a system which verifies and continues the original teachings of Judaism and Christianity, which also taught belief in one God and of serving humanity. Islam replaces Judaism and Christianity as the final religion of Allah, and the Quran is The Final Revelation.
- Family matters: the surat covers various aspects of marital laws and means of resolving family disputes and addressing divorce.
- The social, spiritual and economic principles of a just society.

New Laws Established

In Madinah, Muslims were able to practise Islam with a freedom they had not been allowed in Makkah. There is a lot of emphasis on developing a civil society that is not defined by blood, but instead by a belief system, by spiritual and moral teachings, and by social and political values. The surat establishes a clear legal context to support this spiritual and moral social structure and to tackle the sickness of an uncaring society. In addition, political and economic principles are laid out within a legal framework. These include:

- The change of the direction of prayer from Jerusalem to Makkah (verse 142).
- The four forbidden foods (172).
- The obligation to fast during the month of Ramadan (183).
- The morals and rules of Hajj and Umrah (197).

- Family laws: the law of retribution (178); writing down one's will (180); the prohibition of marriage with non-Muslims (222); divorce and marital discord (228–32); the duty of fathers to pay maintenance expenses (233), and the rules and manners of giving charity (261–74).
- Commercial transactions: the prohibition of earning interest (275); business contracts; commercial transactions, and guarantees for loans (282–3).
- The permissibility for Muslims to fight against others in defence (190).

The Story of the Cow

What is the relevance of this story? In a surat that lays down many laws, it is important to point out that a human society is not just based on laws. A balanced civil society is one which respects moral and social values and spiritual ideals. A legal system is only one part of a flourishing civilisation, and the Story of the Cow highlights the idea that attitudes and values lie at the heart of a just society.

Key Concepts

Salvation Lies in Submission to Allah

An overview of the surat reveals an important thread woven throughout: "Human salvation lies in complete submission and commitment to the Lord of the Worlds". This is comprised of the following principles:
- Firm faith in Allah, the One God.
- Belief in His majestic rule and power.
- Belief in Allah as the Sole Creator of The Universe.
- Belief in His messengers sent to guide humanity, and to make clear the straight path that will help creation to achieve the pleasure of the Creator.

Such belief helps us to live a righteous life: a good life pleasing to the Lord, and conducive to both our own healthy living and the well-being of people. This is not a mechanical performance of ritual exercises. Instead, it is conscious awareness of and attentiveness to The Divine, in such a way that one feels His presence everywhere. A natural outcome of this way of living is a belief in a resurrection and Judgement Day, signifying that this life is an opportunity to gain the pleasure of Allah, and therefore to secure a place near Him in Paradise.

Diversity in the Existence of Various Faiths and Ways of Living

The Quran presents this variety as "Allah's way" and nothing unusual or strange:

> Say, "We believe in Allah and what is revealed to us, and what was revealed to Ibrahim, Ismael, Ishaq, Yaqub and the Tribes, as well as what was given to Musa and Isa, and what was given to all The Messengers from their Lord: we make no distinction between any one of them, we are Muslims (136)".

Some Key Questions

The new community in Madinah faced many challenges, hence, this surat addressed the following questions:

- How should Muslims relate to the Jews in Madinah?
- What is Ibrahim to Muslims? Ibrahim's prayer for Prophet Muhammad ﷺ was:

> Our Lord, raise among them a noble messenger who will recite your verses unto them and teach them The Book and The Wisdom, and will purify them; You are The Almighty, The Wise (129).

In other words, the religion of Islam is the fulfilment of the prayer of Ibrahim.

- Should Muslims take up arms against an enemy?

> Fighting is compulsory for you although you dislike it. Sometimes you dislike something that is good for you; and sometimes you like something that is bad for you. Only Allah knows the truth but you do not know (216).

In Madinah, Muslims were given permission for the first time to take up arms against an enemy to defend themselves. This contrasted with the policy in Makkah, where they could not physically retaliate against aggression.

- What is the nature of a Muslim's relationship with Allah?

> When My servants ask you about Me, tell them I am near; I answer the prayer of the prayerful whenever he prays to Me. Therefore, obey Me and believe in Me so that you may be guided (186).

In the name of Allah, the Kind, the Caring.

The key to the Quran

¹ All praises are for Allah, the Lord of the worlds.ᵃ ² The Kind, the Caring, ³ the Master of Judgement Day. ⁴ We worship You alone and from You alone we seek help. ⁵ Guide us on the straight path, ⁶ the path of those You favoured, not those who are condemnedᵇ nor the misguided ones.

ᵃ An alternative meaning is "praise be to Allah".
ᵇ *"Maghdoob"* literally means "with anger on them", or "those who have failed to win your favour".

In the name of Allah, the Kind, the Caring.

[1] *Alif Lam Meem.*[a]

A description of The Faithful

[2] This is the *Majestic* book, there is no doubt in it, guidance for the pious, [3] who believe in the unseen, perform prayer and spend in charity from what We have provided them. [4] They believe in what is revealed to you and what was revealed before you, and they have firm faith in the Hereafter.

---

[a]   These are three letters of the Arabic alphabet, and there are twenty-nine surats that begin with such letters. They are described as "*Muqatta'at*", detached letters or acronyms, whose meaning is known to Allah and His Messenger ﷺ.

أُولٰٓئِكَ عَلٰى هُدًى مِّنْ رَّبِّهِمْ ۖ وَأُولٰٓئِكَ هُمُ الْمُفْلِحُوْنَ ۟

اِنَّ الَّذِيْنَ كَفَرُوْا سَوَآءٌ عَلَيْهِمْ ءَاَنْذَرْتَهُمْ اَمْ لَمْ

تُنْذِرْهُمْ لَا يُؤْمِنُوْنَ ۟ خَتَمَ اللّٰهُ عَلٰى قُلُوْبِهِمْ وَعَلٰى

سَمْعِهِمْ ۗ وَعَلٰٓى اَبْصَارِهِمْ غِشَاوَةٌ ۖ وَّلَهُمْ عَذَابٌ

عَظِيْمٌ ۟ وَمِنَ النَّاسِ مَنْ يَّقُوْلُ اٰمَنَّا بِاللّٰهِ وَ

بِالْيَوْمِ الْاٰخِرِ وَمَا هُمْ بِمُؤْمِنِيْنَ ۟ يُخٰدِعُوْنَ اللّٰهَ

وَالَّذِيْنَ اٰمَنُوْا ۚ وَمَا يَخْدَعُوْنَ اِلَّا اَنْفُسَهُمْ وَمَا

يَشْعُرُوْنَ ۟ فِيْ قُلُوْبِهِمْ مَّرَضٌ ۙ فَزَادَهُمُ اللّٰهُ مَرَضًا ۚ

وَّلَهُمْ عَذَابٌ اَلِيْمٌ ۢ ۙ بِمَا كَانُوْا يَكْذِبُوْنَ ۟ وَاِذَا

قِيْلَ لَهُمْ لَا تُفْسِدُوْا فِى الْاَرْضِ ۙ قَالُوْٓا اِنَّمَا نَحْنُ

مُصْلِحُوْنَ ۟ اَلَآ اِنَّهُمْ هُمُ الْمُفْسِدُوْنَ وَلٰكِنْ لَّا

يَشْعُرُوْنَ ۟ وَاِذَا قِيْلَ لَهُمْ اٰمِنُوْا كَمَآ اٰمَنَ النَّاسُ

قَالُوْٓا اَنُؤْمِنُ كَمَآ اٰمَنَ السُّفَهَآءُ ۗ اَلَآ اِنَّهُمْ هُمُ السُّفَهَآءُ

وَلٰكِنْ لَّا يَعْلَمُوْنَ ۟ وَاِذَا لَقُوا الَّذِيْنَ اٰمَنُوْا قَالُوْٓا

اٰمَنَّا ۖ وَاِذَا خَلَوْا اِلٰى شَيٰطِيْنِهِمْ ۙ قَالُوْٓا اِنَّا مَعَكُمْ ۙ اِنَّمَا

نَحْنُ مُسْتَهْزِءُوْنَ ۟ اَللّٰهُ يَسْتَهْزِئُ بِهِمْ وَيَمُدُّهُمْ فِيْ

طُغْيَانِهِمْ يَعْمَهُوْنَ ۟ اُولٰٓئِكَ الَّذِيْنَ اشْتَرَوُا الضَّلٰلَةَ

بِالْهُدٰى ۖ فَمَا رَبِحَتْ تِّجَارَتُهُمْ وَمَا كَانُوْا مُهْتَدِيْنَ ۟

مَثَلُهُمْ كَمَثَلِ الَّذِى اسْتَوْقَدَ نَارًا ۚ فَلَمَّآ اَضَآءَتْ

مَا حَوْلَهُ ذَهَبَ اللّٰهُ بِنُوْرِهِمْ وَتَرَكَهُمْ فِيْ ظُلُمٰتٍ لَّا

The believers are serious but hypocrites consider religion a joke.

[5] Those are the ones who follow their Lord's guidance and those are the successful.

The locked minds of disbelievers

[6] Those who disbelieve, it is all the same for them whether you warn or not, they will not believe. [7] Allah sealed their hearts and hearing; laid a blindfold over their eyes, and they will have a painful punishment.[a]

They are deceivers and liars

[8] Some people say: "We believe in Allah and the Hereafter", but they aren't believers. [9] They try to deceive Allah and the believers, but they are unwittingly deceiving themselves. [10] There's a disease in their hearts, and Allah has increased their disease, and they shall have a painful punishment because of the lies they told.

They mock and make trouble

[11] When they are told *for their own good*: "Don't make trouble in the land", they say: "We are the peacemakers". [12] Beware! They are the troublemakers, but they don't realise it. [13] When they are told: "Believe like other people believed", they say: "Shall we believe like the fools?" It is they who are the fools, but they don't know. [14] And, when they meet the believers, they say: "We believe", but when they are alone with their devilish friends, they say: "We are with you, we were just joking with them". [15] Allah will punish them for mocking,[b] and He extends their wandering around blindly in their disobedience.

They are ignorant and misguided

[16] They have chosen error instead of guidance; their bargain is without profit, and they aren't rightly guided. [17] They are like the one who lights a fire, and when everything is bright, suddenly Allah takes away their light and leaves them in pitch darkness so they cannot see.

---

[a]   This is explained as follows; everyone is given the ability to know right and wrong, they have free choice in adopting either one. A person who persists in falsehood and refuses to accept the truth, gradually loses the ability to see it - this is the meaning of "Allah sealed their hearts..."

[b]   Literally translated as: "Allah mocks them". However, this is too negative a quality for the Lord, therefore I have translated it to express the holiness of Allah.

يُبْصِرُوْنَ ⑭ صُمٌّ بُكْمٌ عُمْىٌ فَهُمْ لَا يَرْجِعُوْنَ ⑱

اَوْ كَصَيِّبٍ مِّنَ السَّمَآءِ فِيْهِ ظُلُمٰتٌ وَّرَعْدٌ وَّبَرْقٌ

يَجْعَلُوْنَ اَصَابِعَهُمْ فِيْٓ اٰذَانِهِمْ مِّنَ الصَّوَاعِقِ حَذَرَ

الْمَوْتِ ۛ وَاللّٰهُ مُحِيْطٌۢ بِالْكٰفِرِيْنَ ⑲ يَكَادُ الْبَرْقُ

يَخْطَفُ اَبْصَارَهُمْ ؕ كُلَّمَآ اَضَآءَ لَهُمْ مَّشَوْا فِيْهِ ۙ وَاِذَآ

اَظْلَمَ عَلَيْهِمْ قَامُوْا ؕ وَلَوْ شَآءَ اللّٰهُ لَذَهَبَ بِسَمْعِهِمْ

وَاَبْصَارِهِمْ ؕ اِنَّ اللّٰهَ عَلٰى كُلِّ شَىْءٍ قَدِيْرٌ ⑳ يٰٓاَيُّهَا

Why worship, adore, obey and love Allah?

النَّاسُ اعْبُدُوْا رَبَّكُمُ الَّذِيْ خَلَقَكُمْ وَالَّذِيْنَ مِنْ

قَبْلِكُمْ لَعَلَّكُمْ تَتَّقُوْنَ ㉑ الَّذِيْ جَعَلَ لَكُمُ الْاَرْضَ

فِرَاشًا وَّالسَّمَآءَ بِنَآءً ۪ وَّاَنْزَلَ مِنَ السَّمَآءِ مَآءً فَاَخْرَجَ

بِهٖ مِنَ الثَّمَرٰتِ رِزْقًا لَّكُمْ ۚ فَلَا تَجْعَلُوْا لِلّٰهِ اَنْدَادًا وَّ

اَنْتُمْ تَعْلَمُوْنَ ㉒ وَاِنْ كُنْتُمْ فِيْ رَيْبٍ مِّمَّا نَزَّلْنَا عَلٰى

عَبْدِنَا فَاْتُوْا بِسُوْرَةٍ مِّنْ مِّثْلِهٖ ۪ وَادْعُوْا شُهَدَآءَكُمْ

مِّنْ دُوْنِ اللّٰهِ اِنْ كُنْتُمْ صٰدِقِيْنَ ㉓ فَاِنْ لَّمْ تَفْعَلُوْا

وَلَنْ تَفْعَلُوْا فَاتَّقُوا النَّارَ الَّتِيْ وَقُوْدُهَا النَّاسُ

وَالْحِجَارَةُ ۖ اُعِدَّتْ لِلْكٰفِرِيْنَ ㉔ وَبَشِّرِ الَّذِيْنَ اٰمَنُوْا

وَعَمِلُوا الصّٰلِحٰتِ اَنَّ لَهُمْ جَنّٰتٍ تَجْرِيْ مِنْ تَحْتِهَا

الْاَنْهٰرُ ؕ كُلَّمَا رُزِقُوْا مِنْهَا مِنْ ثَمَرَةٍ رِّزْقًا ۙ قَالُوْا

هٰذَا الَّذِيْ رُزِقْنَا مِنْ قَبْلُ وَاُتُوْا بِهٖ مُتَشَابِهًا ؕ وَلَهُمْ

فِيْهَآ اَزْوَاجٌ مُّطَهَّرَةٌ ۙ وَّهُمْ فِيْهَا خٰلِدُوْنَ ㉕ اِنَّ اللّٰهَ

[18] Deaf, dumb and blind, they will not return to *the straight path*.

They are disorientated and fearful

[19] Or they are like a raincloud in a sky full of darkness, thunder and lightning. They stick their fingers in their ears for fear of death by thunderbolts. Allah has the disbelievers surrounded. [20] The lightning nearly blinds them; whenever it lights up they walk *about* in it, and when it falls dark they stand still. If Allah wanted, He could take their hearing and sight. Allah controls all things.

The Quran's challenge to the hypocrites

[21] People, worship your Lord Who created you and those before you, so that you may guard yourselves *against evil*. [22] Who spread out the Earth for you and made the sky a roof, and sent down rain by which He produces fruits to provide for you. So, do not knowingly make any rivals equal with Allah. [23] If you have doubts about what We have revealed to Our servant, then produce a surat like it and call all your witnesses and supporters besides Allah; *that is* if you are truthful[a]. [24] If you have not done so – and you will never be able to do so – then fear the Fire whose fuel is people and brimstone, prepared for the disbelievers.

Paradise is an amazing reward

[25] And to those who believe and carry out good works, give them good news of gardens with running streams beneath them. Each time they are given a fruit to eat from there, they say: "We used to eat this before". They will be given something like it, and they will have chaste spouses and live there forever.

---

[a] The message of The Majestic Quran is brief, inspirational and factual. It's portrayal of the reality. That's why it is free of doubt.

لَا يَسْتَحْىٓ اَنْ يَّضْرِبَ مَثَلًا مَّا بَعُوْضَةً فَمَا فَوْقَهَا ط

فَاَمَّا الَّذِيْنَ اٰمَنُوْا فَيَعْلَمُوْنَ اَنَّهُ الْحَقُّ مِنْ رَّبِّهِمْ ج

وَاَمَّا الَّذِيْنَ كَفَرُوْا فَيَقُوْلُوْنَ مَا ذَاۤ اَرَادَ اللّٰهُ بِهٰذَا

مَثَلًا ط يُضِلُّ بِهٖ كَثِيْرًا لا وَّيَهْدِىْ بِهٖ كَثِيْرًا ط وَمَا يُضِلُّ

بِهٖۤ اِلَّا الْفٰسِقِيْنَ ۙ الَّذِيْنَ يَنْقُضُوْنَ عَهْدَ اللّٰهِ مِنْ

بَعْدِ مِيْثَاقِهٖ ۪ وَيَقْطَعُوْنَ مَاۤ اَمَرَ اللّٰهُ بِهٖۤ اَنْ يُّوْصَلَ

وَيُفْسِدُوْنَ فِى الْاَرْضِ ط اُولٰٓئِكَ هُمُ الْخٰسِرُوْنَ ۲۶

Why are some people guided and others not?

كَيْفَ تَكْفُرُوْنَ بِاللّٰهِ وَكُنْتُمْ اَمْوَاتًا فَاَحْيَاكُمْ ج ثُمَّ

يُمِيْتُكُمْ ثُمَّ يُحْيِيْكُمْ ثُمَّ اِلَيْهِ تُرْجَعُوْنَ ۲۸ هُوَ الَّذِىْ

خَلَقَ لَكُمْ مَّا فِى الْاَرْضِ جَمِيْعًا ثُمَّ اسْتَوٰۤى اِلَى السَّمَاۤءِ

فَسَوّٰىهُنَّ سَبْعَ سَمٰوٰتٍ ط وَهُوَ بِكُلِّ شَىْءٍ عَلِيْمٌ ۲۹ وَاِذْ

قَالَ رَبُّكَ لِلْمَلٰٓئِكَةِ اِنِّىْ جَاعِلٌ فِى الْاَرْضِ خَلِيْفَةً ط

قَالُوْۤا اَتَجْعَلُ فِيْهَا مَنْ يُّفْسِدُ فِيْهَا وَيَسْفِكُ الدِّمَاۤءَ ۚ

وَنَحْنُ نُسَبِّحُ بِحَمْدِكَ وَنُقَدِّسُ لَكَ ط قَالَ اِنِّىْۤ اَعْلَمُ

مَا لَا تَعْلَمُوْنَ ۳۰ وَعَلَّمَ اٰدَمَ الْاَسْمَاۤءَ كُلَّهَا ثُمَّ عَرَضَهُمْ

عَلَى الْمَلٰٓئِكَةِ ۙ فَقَالَ اَنْۢبِئُوْنِىْ بِاَسْمَاۤءِ هٰٓؤُلَاۤءِ اِنْ كُنْتُمْ

صٰدِقِيْنَ ۳۱ قَالُوْا سُبْحٰنَكَ لَا عِلْمَ لَنَاۤ اِلَّا مَا عَلَّمْتَنَا ط اِنَّكَ

اَنْتَ الْعَلِيْمُ الْحَكِيْمُ ۳۲ قَالَ يٰۤاٰدَمُ اَنْۢبِئْهُمْ بِاَسْمَاۤئِهِمْ ج

فَلَمَّاۤ اَنْۢبَاَهُمْ بِاَسْمَاۤئِهِمْ ۙ قَالَ اَلَمْ اَقُلْ لَّكُمْ اِنِّىْۤ اَعْلَمُ

غَيْبَ السَّمٰوٰتِ وَالْاَرْضِ ۙ وَاَعْلَمُ مَا تُبْدُوْنَ وَمَا كُنْتُمْ

Only the disobedient are misguided

²⁶ Allah is not embarrassed to give the example of a mosquito or something even smaller. Those who believe know that this is the truth from their Lord, but those who disbelieve say: "What does Allah mean by this example?" He allows many to be misguided by it and others to be guided; *yet* only the disobedient are misguided by it, ²⁷ those who break their ties with Allah after it has been agreed; they break *the ties* that Allah has ordered to be joined, and they make trouble in the land: these are the losers.^a ²⁸ How can you deny Allah when you were dead and He brought you to life, then He will cause you to die and give you life once more, and to Him you shall be returned. ²⁹ It is He who created everything on Earth for you, then He turned to the sky^b and completed the seven Heavens; He has knowledge of all things.

The Story of Adam's creation

³⁰ Remember when Your Lord told the Angels: "I am creating a representative on Earth". They replied: "Are You creating someone who will make trouble there and shed blood? Is it not enough that we glorify You with praises and proclaim Your Holiness?" He said: "I know what you don't know".

Prophet Adam's knowledge and Satan's arrogance

³¹ He taught Adam the names of all things, then presented them to the Angels and asked: "Tell Me the names of these things, if you are right". ³² They said, "Glory be to You! We only know what You have taught us. You are the Knower and Wise". ³³ He said, "Adam, tell them their names". So, when *Adam* told them *all* of the names, *Allah* said: "Did I not tell you that I know the secrets of the Heavens and the Earth, and that I know what you show and what you hide?"

---

^a A person goes astray because of their attitude and stubbornness not to listen. So, it is a consequence of their choice, Allah knows the person's choice, so He lets them go astray.

^b "Turned to the sky" does not imply Allah physically turning in a direction, but turning His attention to the next phase of His creation.

تَكْتُمُونَ ۝ وَإِذْ قُلْنَا لِلْمَلٰٓئِكَةِ اسْجُدُوْا لِاٰدَمَ فَسَجَدُوْۤا

إِلَّاۤ إِبْلِيْسَ ط أَبٰى وَاسْتَكْبَرَ ۙ وَكَانَ مِنَ الْكٰفِرِيْنَ ۝ وَقُلْنَا

يٰاٰدَمُ اسْكُنْ أَنْتَ وَزَوْجُكَ الْجَنَّةَ وَكُلَا مِنْهَا رَغَدًا

حَيْثُ شِئْتُمَا ۪ وَلَا تَقْرَبَا هٰذِهِ الشَّجَرَةَ فَتَكُوْنَا مِنَ

الظّٰلِمِيْنَ ۝ فَأَزَلَّهُمَا الشَّيْطٰنُ عَنْهَا فَأَخْرَجَهُمَا مِمَّا

كَانَا فِيْهِ ۪ وَقُلْنَا اهْبِطُوْا بَعْضُكُمْ لِبَعْضٍ عَدُوٌّ ۚ وَلَكُمْ

فِى الْأَرْضِ مُسْتَقَرٌّ وَّمَتَاعٌ إِلٰى حِيْنٍ ۝ فَتَلَقّٰى اٰدَمُ مِنْ

رَّبِّهٖ كَلِمٰتٍ فَتَابَ عَلَيْهِ ط إِنَّهٗ هُوَ التَّوَّابُ الرَّحِيْمُ ۝

قُلْنَا اهْبِطُوْا مِنْهَا جَمِيْعًا ۚ فَإِمَّا يَأْتِيَنَّكُمْ مِّنِّىْ هُدًى

فَمَنْ تَبِعَ هُدَاىَ فَلَا خَوْفٌ عَلَيْهِمْ وَلَا هُمْ يَحْزَنُوْنَ ۝

وَالَّذِيْنَ كَفَرُوْا وَكَذَّبُوْا بِاٰيٰتِنَاۤ أُولٰٓئِكَ أَصْحٰبُ النَّارِ ۚ

هُمْ فِيْهَا خٰلِدُوْنَ ۝ يٰبَنِىْۤ إِسْرَآءِيْلَ اذْكُرُوْا نِعْمَتِىَ

الَّتِىْۤ أَنْعَمْتُ عَلَيْكُمْ وَأَوْفُوْا بِعَهْدِىْۤ أُوْفِ بِعَهْدِكُمْ ۚ

وَإِيَّاىَ فَارْهَبُوْنِ ۝ وَاٰمِنُوْا بِمَاۤ أَنْزَلْتُ مُصَدِّقًا لِّمَا

مَعَكُمْ وَلَا تَكُوْنُوْۤا أَوَّلَ كَافِرٍ بِهٖ ۪ وَلَا تَشْتَرُوْا بِاٰيٰتِىْ

ثَمَنًا قَلِيْلًا ۙ وَّإِيَّاىَ فَاتَّقُوْنِ ۝ وَلَا تَلْبِسُوا الْحَقَّ

بِالْبَاطِلِ وَتَكْتُمُوا الْحَقَّ وَأَنْتُمْ تَعْلَمُوْنَ ۝ وَأَقِيْمُوا

الصَّلٰوةَ وَاٰتُوا الزَّكٰوةَ وَارْكَعُوْا مَعَ الرّٰكِعِيْنَ ۝ أَتَأْمُرُوْنَ

النَّاسَ بِالْبِرِّ وَتَنْسَوْنَ أَنْفُسَكُمْ وَأَنْتُمْ تَتْلُوْنَ

الْكِتٰبَ ط أَفَلَا تَعْقِلُوْنَ ۝ وَاسْتَعِيْنُوْا بِالصَّبْرِ وَ

What are the signs of mindfulness, of being awake?

[34] Then We commanded the Angels to prostrate to Adam, they all prostrated except Iblis, Satan[a]; he disobeyed, acted arrogantly and was ungrateful.

Adam and Eve are tempted

[35] We said: "Adam, live with your wife in Paradise and eat freely from wherever you want, but don't go near this tree, or you will be wrongdoers". [36] But Satan tempted them and had them expelled from where they were. We told them: "Go down as enemies of each other on Earth, you will have a place to live and things to enjoy for a fixed term".[b] [37] *Then*, Adam received words *of inspiration* from his Lord, so He accepted his repentance; He is Forgiving, Kind. [38] We said: "Go down from here, you all! When the guidance comes from Me, whoever follows it will have nothing to fear, nor to grieve". [39] Those who disbelieved and denied Our verses, these are the people of the Fire, and they will be there forever.

The Jews are invited to believe in The Messenger ﷺ

[40] Children of Israel, remember My gifts I gave you, and fulfil My contract, and I will fulfil your contract. Fear Me! [41] Believe what I have revealed, it confirms what you *already* have, and don't be the first to deny it or to sell My verses cheaply. Be mindful of Me.[c]

How to become pious

[42] Do not mix the truth with falsehood, nor knowingly hide the truth. [43] Perform prayer, pay Zakat, and bow down with those who bow *in prayer*. [44] You tell people to be righteous but forget yourselves, although you read The Book? Don't you understand?

---

[a]   Iblis, is the name of the devil, he is the rebel, the one who refuses the command of Allah to prostrate. He is from the Jinns, an invisible creation of Allah made from the Fire.

[b]   Shaytan, the name of the devil when he acts as a tempter, the one who tempted Adam and Eve.

[c]   *Taqwa* is translated as "be mindful": be aware of Allah's creative power, be conscious of your dependency on Him, and of your shortcomings.

الصَّلٰوةِ ط وَاِنَّهَا لَكَبِيْرَةٌ اِلَّا عَلَى الْخٰشِعِيْنَ ۞ الَّذِيْنَ يَظُنُّوْنَ اَنَّهُمْ مُّلٰقُوْا رَبِّهِمْ وَاَنَّهُمْ اِلَيْهِ رٰجِعُوْنَ ۞ يٰبَنِيْٓ اِسْرَآءِيْلَ اذْكُرُوْا نِعْمَتِيَ الَّتِيْٓ اَنْعَمْتُ عَلَيْكُمْ وَ اَنِّيْ فَضَّلْتُكُمْ عَلَى الْعٰلَمِيْنَ ۞ وَاتَّقُوْا يَوْمًا لَّا تَجْزِيْ نَفْسٌ عَنْ نَّفْسٍ شَيْئًا وَّلَا يُقْبَلُ مِنْهَا شَفَاعَةٌ وَّلَا يُؤْخَذُ مِنْهَا عَدْلٌ وَّلَا هُمْ يُنْصَرُوْنَ ۞ وَاِذْ نَجَّيْنٰكُمْ مِّنْ اٰلِ فِرْعَوْنَ يَسُوْمُوْنَكُمْ سُوْٓءَ الْعَذَابِ يُذَبِّحُوْنَ اَبْنَآءَكُمْ وَيَسْتَحْيُوْنَ نِسَآءَكُمْ ط وَفِيْ ذٰلِكُمْ بَلَآءٌ مِّنْ رَّبِّكُمْ عَظِيْمٌ ۞ وَاِذْ فَرَقْنَا بِكُمُ الْبَحْرَ فَاَنْجَيْنٰكُمْ وَ اَغْرَقْنَآ اٰلَ فِرْعَوْنَ وَاَنْتُمْ تَنْظُرُوْنَ ۞ وَاِذْ وٰعَدْنَا مُوْسٰٓى اَرْبَعِيْنَ لَيْلَةً ثُمَّ اتَّخَذْتُمُ الْعِجْلَ مِنْ بَعْدِهٖ وَاَنْتُمْ ظٰلِمُوْنَ ۞ ثُمَّ عَفَوْنَا عَنْكُمْ مِّنْ بَعْدِ ذٰلِكَ لَعَلَّكُمْ تَشْكُرُوْنَ ۞ وَاِذْ اٰتَيْنَا مُوْسَى الْكِتٰبَ وَ الْفُرْقَانَ لَعَلَّكُمْ تَهْتَدُوْنَ ۞ وَاِذْ قَالَ مُوْسٰى لِقَوْمِهٖ يٰقَوْمِ اِنَّكُمْ ظَلَمْتُمْ اَنْفُسَكُمْ بِاتِّخَاذِكُمُ الْعِجْلَ فَتُوْبُوْٓا اِلٰى بَارِئِكُمْ فَاقْتُلُوْٓا اَنْفُسَكُمْ ط ذٰلِكُمْ خَيْرٌ لَّكُمْ عِنْدَ بَارِئِكُمْ ط فَتَابَ عَلَيْكُمْ ط اِنَّهٗ هُوَ التَّوَّابُ الرَّحِيْمُ ۞ وَاِذْ قُلْتُمْ يٰمُوْسٰى لَنْ نُّؤْمِنَ لَكَ حَتّٰى نَرَى اللّٰهَ جَهْرَةً فَاَخَذَتْكُمُ الصّٰعِقَةُ وَاَنْتُمْ تَنْظُرُوْنَ ۞ ثُمَّ بَعَثْنٰكُمْ مِّنْ بَعْدِ مَوْتِكُمْ لَعَلَّكُمْ تَشْكُرُوْنَ ۞ وَظَلَّلْنَا

The boundless favours of Allah on some people.

15

⁴⁵ Seek help through patience and prayer; these are burdensome virtues except for the humble, ⁴⁶ who believe they will meet their Lord. *In the end,* they will return to Him.

Allah's favours on the Israelites after Pharaoh's oppression

⁴⁷ Children of Israel, remember the *great* gifts that I gave you when I favoured you above all other people; ⁴⁸ and fear the day when no one will be willing to pay even a small ransom for another person, and no intercession will be accepted from *the disbelievers* nor any compensation allowed, and nor will they be helped. ⁴⁹ *Remember* when We saved you from the people of Pharaoh who punished you severely, killing your sons and sparing your women; that was a tremendous test from your Lord. ⁵⁰ *And remember* also when We parted the sea for you, rescuing you but drowning the people of Pharaoh before your very eyes.

The Israelites worship a calf

⁵¹ *Remember* when We invited Musa for forty nights, but you began worshipping the *golden* calf, *becoming* wrongdoers. ⁵² Afterwards We pardoned you so that you might be grateful. ⁵³ Then We gave Musa The Book and told him how to judge right from wrong so that you may be guided. ⁵⁴ Remember when Musa said to his people: "My people, you have committed a major sin by worshipping the *golden* calf; so repent to your Maker and *punish the culprits* among yourselves.ᵃ That is better for you in the sight of your Maker so that He may accept your repentance: indeed, He is Relenting and Kind". ⁵⁵ *Remember* when you said: "Musa, we won't believe you until we openly see Allah", and a thunderbolt struck you as you watched. ⁵⁶ We then resurrected you after death so you might be thankful.

ᵃ Qadi Abdul Jabbar, said that the words "kill yourselves" should not be understood literally, but mean "mortify" or "punish yourselves" (Razi).

16

عَلَيْكُمُ الْغَمَامَ وَاَنْزَلْنَا عَلَيْكُمُ الْمَنَّ وَالسَّلْوٰى ط كُلُوْا

مِنْ طَيِّبٰتِ مَا رَزَقْنٰكُمْ ط وَمَا ظَلَمُوْنَا وَلٰكِنْ كَانُوْٓا

اَنْفُسَهُمْ يَظْلِمُوْنَ ۵۶ وَاِذْ قُلْنَا ادْخُلُوْا هٰذِهِ الْقَرْيَةَ

فَكُلُوْا مِنْهَا حَيْثُ شِئْتُمْ رَغَدًا وَّادْخُلُوا الْبَابَ

سُجَّدًا وَّقُوْلُوْا حِطَّةٌ نَّغْفِرْ لَكُمْ خَطٰيٰكُمْ ط وَسَنَزِيْدُ

الْمُحْسِنِيْنَ ۵۷ فَبَدَّلَ الَّذِيْنَ ظَلَمُوْا قَوْلًا غَيْرَ الَّذِيْ

قِيْلَ لَهُمْ فَاَنْزَلْنَا عَلَى الَّذِيْنَ ظَلَمُوْا رِجْزًا مِّنَ

السَّمَآءِ بِمَا كَانُوْا يَفْسُقُوْنَ ۵۸ وَاِذِ اسْتَسْقٰى مُوْسٰى

لِقَوْمِهِ فَقُلْنَا اضْرِبْ بِّعَصَاكَ الْحَجَرَ ط فَانْفَجَرَتْ مِنْهُ

اثْنَتَا عَشْرَةَ عَيْنًا ط قَدْ عَلِمَ كُلُّ اُنَاسٍ مَّشْرَبَهُمْ ط

كُلُوْا وَاشْرَبُوْا مِنْ رِّزْقِ اللهِ وَلَا تَعْثَوْا فِى الْاَرْضِ

مُفْسِدِيْنَ ۵۹ وَاِذْ قُلْتُمْ يٰمُوْسٰى لَنْ نَّصْبِرَ عَلٰى طَعَامٍ

وَّاحِدٍ فَادْعُ لَنَا رَبَّكَ يُخْرِجْ لَنَا مِمَّا تُنْۢبِتُ الْاَرْضُ

مِنْۢ بَقْلِهَا وَقِثَّآئِهَا وَفُوْمِهَا وَعَدَسِهَا وَبَصَلِهَا ط قَالَ

اَتَسْتَبْدِلُوْنَ الَّذِيْ هُوَ اَدْنٰى بِالَّذِيْ هُوَ خَيْرٌ ط اِهْبِطُوْا

مِصْرًا فَاِنَّ لَكُمْ مَّا سَاَلْتُمْ ط وَضُرِبَتْ عَلَيْهِمُ الذِّلَّةُ

وَالْمَسْكَنَةُ وَبَآءُوْ بِغَضَبٍ مِّنَ اللهِ ط ذٰلِكَ بِاَنَّهُمْ

كَانُوْا يَكْفُرُوْنَ بِاٰيٰتِ اللهِ وَيَقْتُلُوْنَ النَّبِيّٖنَ بِغَيْرِ

الْحَقِّ ط ذٰلِكَ بِمَا عَصَوْا وَّكَانُوْا يَعْتَدُوْنَ ۶۰ اِنَّ

الَّذِيْنَ اٰمَنُوْا وَالَّذِيْنَ هَادُوْا وَالنَّصٰرٰى وَالصّٰبِـِٔيْنَ

Do you accept the differences in the practices and customs of others?

Allah continued to bless the Israelites

⁵⁷We sent clouds to give you shade, We sent Manna and quails for you, *saying:*ᵃ "Eat the pure provision We have provided you". They didn't harm Us, but they harmed themselves. ⁵⁸When We said: "Enter this town and eat from wherever you like, and enter the gate with humility saying: 'Forgive us'ᵇ so We forgive your sins and increase the reward of the righteous". ⁵⁹The wrongdoers altered the words to *something* other than what they were taught. So, We sent down a plague from the sky for their wickedness.

Musa's miracle of the twelve springs

⁶⁰When Musa prayed for water for his people. We said: "Strike the rock with your staff", twelve springs gushed out, and each tribe recognised its drinking place. "Eat and drink Allah's provision, and don't go around making trouble in the land". ⁶¹When you said: "Musa, we are weary of eating the same meal *every day*, so ask your Lord to produce for us, herbs, cucumbers, garlic, lentil and onions". He said: "Why are you swapping something superior for something less? Go back to Egypt, if that's what you want". So, they were disgraced and humiliated, and brought on themselves Allah's anger because they denied His signs, killed the prophets unjustly, disobeyed and often broke the rules.

Only faith and good deeds guarantee success

⁶²The believers,ᶜ the Jews, Christians and Sabians,ᵈ whoever believed in Allah,ᵉ the Hereafter and did righteous works, shall have reward from their Lord. They shall not fear nor grieve.

ᵃ "Manna and quails": Manna is a special type of food, like honey, that was graciously provided by Allah to the Israelites, along with quails, a type of small game bird.
ᵇ Instead of saying *hittah* ("forgive us"), they used a meaningless irreverent word.
ᶜ This refers to the followers of the Prophet Muhammad ﷺ.
ᵈ Sabians were a monotheistic sect of Christianity.
ᵉ It has always been a perfectly natural and common practice for Arabic-speaking Jews and Christians to use the name Allah in their prayers and everyday speech.

مَنْ اٰمَنَ بِاللّٰهِ وَالْيَوْمِ الْاٰخِرِ وَعَمِلَ صَالِحًا فَلَهُمْ اَجْرُهُمْ عِنْدَ رَبِّهِمْ ۚ وَلَا خَوْفٌ عَلَيْهِمْ وَلَا هُمْ يَحْزَنُوْنَ ۝ وَاِذْ اَخَذْنَا مِيْثَاقَكُمْ وَرَفَعْنَا فَوْقَكُمُ الطُّوْرَ ؕ خُذُوْا مَا اٰتَيْنٰكُمْ بِقُوَّةٍ وَّاذْكُرُوْا مَا فِيْهِ لَعَلَّكُمْ تَتَّقُوْنَ ۝ ثُمَّ تَوَلَّيْتُمْ مِّنْ بَعْدِ ذٰلِكَ ۚ فَلَوْلَا فَضْلُ اللّٰهِ عَلَيْكُمْ وَرَحْمَتُهُ لَكُنْتُمْ مِّنَ الْخٰسِرِيْنَ ۝ وَلَقَدْ عَلِمْتُمُ الَّذِيْنَ اعْتَدَوْا مِنْكُمْ فِى السَّبْتِ فَقُلْنَا لَهُمْ كُوْنُوْا قِرَدَةً خٰسِئِيْنَ ۝ فَجَعَلْنٰهَا نَكَالًا لِّمَا بَيْنَ يَدَيْهَا وَمَا خَلْفَهَا وَمَوْعِظَةً لِّلْمُتَّقِيْنَ ۝ وَاِذْ قَالَ مُوْسٰى لِقَوْمِهٖٓ اِنَّ اللّٰهَ يَاْمُرُكُمْ اَنْ تَذْبَحُوْا بَقَرَةً ؕ قَالُوْٓا اَتَتَّخِذُنَا هُزُوًا ؕ قَالَ اَعُوْذُ بِاللّٰهِ اَنْ اَكُوْنَ مِنَ الْجٰهِلِيْنَ ۝ قَالُوا ادْعُ لَنَا رَبَّكَ يُبَيِّنْ لَّنَا مَا هِيَ ؕ قَالَ اِنَّهٗ يَقُوْلُ اِنَّهَا بَقَرَةٌ لَّا فَارِضٌ وَّلَا بِكْرٌ ؕ عَوَانٌ بَيْنَ ذٰلِكَ ؕ فَافْعَلُوْا مَا تُؤْمَرُوْنَ ۝ قَالُوا ادْعُ لَنَا رَبَّكَ يُبَيِّنْ لَّنَا مَا لَوْنُهَا ؕ قَالَ اِنَّهٗ يَقُوْلُ اِنَّهَا بَقَرَةٌ صَفْرَآءُ ۙ فَاقِعٌ لَّوْنُهَا تَسُرُّ النّٰظِرِيْنَ ۝ قَالُوا ادْعُ لَنَا رَبَّكَ يُبَيِّنْ لَّنَا مَا هِيَ ۙ اِنَّ الْبَقَرَ تَشٰبَهَ عَلَيْنَا ؕ وَاِنَّآ اِنْ شَآءَ اللّٰهُ لَمُهْتَدُوْنَ ۝ قَالَ اِنَّهٗ يَقُوْلُ اِنَّهَا بَقَرَةٌ لَّا ذَلُوْلٌ تُثِيْرُ الْاَرْضَ وَلَا تَسْقِى الْحَرْثَ ۚ مُسَلَّمَةٌ لَّا شِيَةَ فِيْهَا ؕ قَالُوا الْـٰٔنَ جِئْتَ

When asked to do something, don't dither, don't nit-pick. Do as you are told.

[63] With the mountain towering over you, We took your contract, *saying:* "Hold firmly to what We have given you and remember what it teaches so you become mindful of Allah". [64] But you turned away. If it hadn't been for the grace and Allah's favour, you would be losers. [65] You knew those who broke the law of Sabbath; We said to them: "Be *like* apes, shunned and rejected". [66] So, We made their fate an example for their generation and those who followed them, and a clear lesson for the God-fearing.

The story of the cow

[67] *Remember* when Musa said to his people: "Allah commands you to slaughter a cow". They said: "Are you joking with us?" He replied: "Allah forbids that I should be so bad-mannered". [68] They said: "Then ask your Lord to explain what sort of cow it is". He answered: "He says she is neither old nor young but in-between, so do as instructed". [69] They said: "Ask your Lord to clarify what colour she is". He said: "Allah says it is a light-yellow coloured cow, pleasing to the onlookers". [70] They again *repeated*: "Ask your Lord to spell out for us what she looks like, as all cows look similar to us; then, if Allah wills, we shall be guided". [71] *Musa* said: "He says she is a cow that has not been yoked for ploughing or watering the fields, a healthy cow with no scars". They then said: "Now you have given us the exact description". Eventually they slaughtered it though they disliked doing so.

بِالْحَقِّ ۖ فَذَبَحُوهَا وَمَا كَادُوا يَفْعَلُونَ ۝ وَإِذْ قَتَلْتُمْ

نَفْسًا فَادّٰرَءْتُمْ فِيهَا ۖ وَاللّٰهُ مُخْرِجٌ مَّا كُنْتُمْ تَكْتُمُونَ ۝

فَقُلْنَا اضْرِبُوهُ بِبَعْضِهَا ۚ كَذٰلِكَ يُحْيِ اللّٰهُ الْمَوْتٰى ۙ

وَيُرِيكُمْ اٰيٰتِهٖ لَعَلَّكُمْ تَعْقِلُونَ ۝ ثُمَّ قَسَتْ قُلُوبُكُمْ

مِّنْ بَعْدِ ذٰلِكَ فَهِيَ كَالْحِجَارَةِ أَوْ أَشَدُّ قَسْوَةً ۚ

وَإِنَّ مِنَ الْحِجَارَةِ لَمَا يَتَفَجَّرُ مِنْهُ الْأَنْهٰرُ ۚ وَإِنَّ

مِنْهَا لَمَا يَشَّقَّقُ فَيَخْرُجُ مِنْهُ الْمَآءُ ۚ وَإِنَّ مِنْهَا

لَمَا يَهْبِطُ مِنْ خَشْيَةِ اللّٰهِ ۗ وَمَا اللّٰهُ بِغَافِلٍ عَمَّا

What might soften your heart?

تَعْمَلُونَ ۝ أَفَتَطْمَعُونَ أَنْ يُّؤْمِنُوا لَكُمْ وَقَدْ كَانَ

فَرِيقٌ مِّنْهُمْ يَسْمَعُونَ كَلٰمَ اللّٰهِ ثُمَّ يُحَرِّفُونَهٗ مِنْ

بَعْدِ مَا عَقَلُوهُ وَهُمْ يَعْلَمُونَ ۝ وَإِذَا لَقُوا الَّذِيْنَ

اٰمَنُوا قَالُوا اٰمَنَّا ۖ وَإِذَا خَلَا بَعْضُهُمْ إِلٰى بَعْضٍ

قَالُوا أَتُحَدِّثُونَهُمْ بِمَا فَتَحَ اللّٰهُ عَلَيْكُمْ لِيُحَآجُّوكُمْ بِهٖ

عِنْدَ رَبِّكُمْ ۗ أَفَلَا تَعْقِلُونَ ۝ أَوَلَا يَعْلَمُونَ أَنَّ اللّٰهَ

يَعْلَمُ مَا يُسِرُّونَ وَمَا يُعْلِنُونَ ۝ وَمِنْهُمْ أُمِّيُّونَ لَا

يَعْلَمُونَ الْكِتٰبَ إِلَّا أَمَانِيَّ وَإِنْ هُمْ إِلَّا يَظُنُّونَ ۝

فَوَيْلٌ لِّلَّذِيْنَ يَكْتُبُونَ الْكِتٰبَ بِأَيْدِيهِمْ ثُمَّ

يَقُولُونَ هٰذَا مِنْ عِنْدِ اللّٰهِ لِيَشْتَرُوا بِهٖ ثَمَنًا قَلِيلًا ۖ

فَوَيْلٌ لَّهُمْ مِّمَّا كَتَبَتْ أَيْدِيهِمْ وَوَيْلٌ لَّهُمْ مِّمَّا

يَكْسِبُونَ ۝ وَقَالُوا لَنْ تَمَسَّنَا النَّارُ إِلَّا أَيَّامًا

A murdered man is resurrected.

⁷² *Remember* when you killed a person, and you quarrelled about it; Allah exposed what you were hiding. ⁷³ So, We told them: "Touch with a piece of the cow's meat *the corpse of the dead* person". That is how Allah brings the dead to life, and He shows you His signs so you might understand.

Hardened hearts refuse to understand

⁷⁴ Afterwards, your hearts became hard like rocks or even harder. There are some rocks from which streams flow, and there are others when split open, water flows from them, and yet other rocks which tumble down out of fear of Allah, He is not unaware of what you do. ⁷⁵ Do you expect them to believe you when a group of them hears the words of Allah and, after understanding them, deliberately changes them?

Be wary of inventing lies

⁷⁶ When *such people* meet those who believe, they tell them: "We believe". However, when they are alone, they say: "Why tell them about what Allah has granted you so they use it as evidence against you before your Lord. Don't you have any sense?" ⁷⁷ Do they not realise, Allah knows what they hide and what they publicise? ⁷⁸ Some of them are illiterate; their knowledge of The Book is *based on* false hopes, and mere guess. ⁷⁹ What misery awaits those who rewrite The Book with their own hands and then claim: "This is from Allah", just to earn a little money! What misery awaits them for what their hands have written, and what misery awaits them for what they have earned!

مَّعْدُوْدَةً ۗ قُلْ اَتَّخَذْتُمْ عِنْدَ اللّٰهِ عَهْدًا فَلَنْ يُّخْلِفَ
اللّٰهُ عَهْدَهٗٓ اَمْ تَقُوْلُوْنَ عَلَى اللّٰهِ مَا لَا تَعْلَمُوْنَ ۝
بَلٰى مَنْ كَسَبَ سَيِّئَةً وَّاَحَاطَتْ بِهٖ خَطِيْٓئَتُهٗ فَاُولٰٓئِكَ
اَصْحٰبُ النَّارِ ۚ هُمْ فِيْهَا خٰلِدُوْنَ ۝ وَالَّذِيْنَ اٰمَنُوْا
وَعَمِلُوا الصّٰلِحٰتِ اُولٰٓئِكَ اَصْحٰبُ الْجَنَّةِ ۚ هُمْ فِيْهَا
خٰلِدُوْنَ ۝ وَاِذْ اَخَذْنَا مِيْثَاقَ بَنِيْٓ اِسْرَآئِيْلَ لَا
تَعْبُدُوْنَ اِلَّا اللّٰهَ ۟ وَبِالْوَالِدَيْنِ اِحْسَانًا وَّذِى الْقُرْبٰى
وَالْيَتٰمٰى وَالْمَسٰكِيْنِ وَقُوْلُوْا لِلنَّاسِ حُسْنًا وَّاَقِيْمُوا
الصَّلٰوةَ وَاٰتُوا الزَّكٰوةَ ۗ ثُمَّ تَوَلَّيْتُمْ اِلَّا قَلِيْلًا مِّنْكُمْ
وَاَنْتُمْ مُّعْرِضُوْنَ ۝ وَاِذْ اَخَذْنَا مِيْثَاقَكُمْ لَا تَسْفِكُوْنَ
دِمَآءَكُمْ وَلَا تُخْرِجُوْنَ اَنْفُسَكُمْ مِّنْ دِيَارِكُمْ ثُمَّ
اَقْرَرْتُمْ وَاَنْتُمْ تَشْهَدُوْنَ ۝ ثُمَّ اَنْتُمْ هٰٓؤُلَآءِ
تَقْتُلُوْنَ اَنْفُسَكُمْ وَتُخْرِجُوْنَ فَرِيْقًا مِّنْكُمْ مِّنْ دِيَارِهِمْ ۡ
تَظٰهَرُوْنَ عَلَيْهِمْ بِالْاِثْمِ وَالْعُدْوَانِ ۗ وَاِنْ يَّأْتُوْكُمْ
اُسٰرٰى تُفٰدُوْهُمْ وَهُوَ مُحَرَّمٌ عَلَيْكُمْ اِخْرَاجُهُمْ ۗ
اَفَتُؤْمِنُوْنَ بِبَعْضِ الْكِتٰبِ وَتَكْفُرُوْنَ بِبَعْضٍ ۚ فَمَا
جَزَآءُ مَنْ يَّفْعَلُ ذٰلِكَ مِنْكُمْ اِلَّا خِزْيٌ فِى الْحَيٰوةِ
الدُّنْيَا ۚ وَيَوْمَ الْقِيٰمَةِ يُرَدُّوْنَ اِلٰٓى اَشَدِّ الْعَذَابِ ۗ
وَمَا اللّٰهُ بِغَافِلٍ عَمَّا تَعْمَلُوْنَ ۝ اُولٰٓئِكَ الَّذِيْنَ
اشْتَرَوُا الْحَيٰوةَ الدُّنْيَا بِالْاٰخِرَةِ ۡ فَلَا يُخَفَّفُ عَنْهُمُ

What pledge have you made with Allah?

The false claim of a light punishment

[80] They claim: "The Fire will only burn us for a few days". Ask them: "Have you taken a pledge from Allah; He never breaks His pledge, or are you making a claim about Allah, ignorantly?" [81] Rather, the evildoers are occupied in their sins, these are the people of the Fire, there forever. [82] But those who believed and did righteous works, these are the people of Paradise, there forever.

The contract of the Israelites with Allah

[83] *Remember* when We took the contract from the Israelites: worship Allah alone, care for parents, relatives, orphans and the needy; speak kindly to people; perform the prayer and give Zakat. Unfortunately, you turned away, objecting to it except a few of you. [84] We took the contract that you would not shed one another's blood or expel one another from their homes; you accepted and witnessed.

Injustice and oppression are unacceptable

[85] You were killing one another, one group forcing the other out of their homes, or helping one side *to commit* sin and *sow* enmity against the other. When you took them prisoners, you demanded a ransom for them, although it was forbidden to evict them *in the first place*. Do you believe in some parts of The Book and reject others? The only fitting punishment for those who commit such crimes is disgrace in this life, and on Judgement Day will be dispatched to the severest punishments. Allah is not unaware of what you do. [86] Such people have chosen this worldly life instead of The Hereafter; their punishment will not be lessened nor will they be helped.

الْعَذَابُ وَلَا هُمْ يُنْصَرُوْنَ ۝ وَلَقَدْ اٰتَيْنَا مُوْسَى الْكِتٰبَ وَقَفَّيْنَا مِنْ بَعْدِهٖ بِالرُّسُلِ وَاٰتَيْنَا عِيْسَى ابْنَ مَرْيَمَ الْبَيِّنٰتِ وَاَيَّدْنٰهُ بِرُوْحِ الْقُدُسِ ؕ اَفَكُلَّمَا جَآءَكُمْ رَسُوْلٌ بِمَا لَا تَهْوٰۤى اَنْفُسُكُمُ اسْتَكْبَرْتُمْ ۚ فَفَرِيْقًا كَذَّبْتُمْ ۫ وَفَرِيْقًا تَقْتُلُوْنَ ۝ وَ قَالُوْا قُلُوْبُنَا غُلْفٌ ؕ بَلْ لَّعَنَهُمُ اللّٰهُ بِكُفْرِهِمْ فَقَلِيْلًا مَّا يُؤْمِنُوْنَ ۝ وَلَمَّا جَآءَهُمْ كِتٰبٌ مِّنْ عِنْدِ اللّٰهِ مُصَدِّقٌ لِّمَا مَعَهُمْ ۙ وَكَانُوْا مِنْ قَبْلُ يَسْتَفْتِحُوْنَ عَلَى الَّذِيْنَ كَفَرُوْا ۚ فَلَمَّا جَآءَهُمْ مَّا عَرَفُوْا كَفَرُوْا بِهٖ ۫ فَلَعْنَةُ اللّٰهِ عَلَى الْكٰفِرِيْنَ ۝ بِئْسَمَا اشْتَرَوْا بِهٖۤ اَنْفُسَهُمْ اَنْ يَّكْفُرُوْا بِمَاۤ اَنْزَلَ اللّٰهُ بَغْيًا اَنْ يُّنَزِّلَ اللّٰهُ مِنْ فَضْلِهٖ عَلٰى مَنْ يَّشَآءُ مِنْ عِبَادِهٖ ۚ فَبَآءُوْ بِغَضَبٍ عَلٰى غَضَبٍ ؕ وَلِلْكٰفِرِيْنَ عَذَابٌ مُّهِيْنٌ ۝ وَ اِذَا قِيْلَ لَهُمْ اٰمِنُوْا بِمَاۤ اَنْزَلَ اللّٰهُ قَالُوْا نُؤْمِنُ بِمَاۤ اُنْزِلَ عَلَيْنَا وَيَكْفُرُوْنَ بِمَا وَرَآءَهٗ ۗ وَهُوَ الْحَقُّ مُصَدِّقًا لِّمَا مَعَهُمْ ؕ قُلْ فَلِمَ تَقْتُلُوْنَ اَنْبِيَآءَ اللّٰهِ مِنْ قَبْلُ اِنْ كُنْتُمْ مُّؤْمِنِيْنَ ۝ وَلَقَدْ جَآءَكُمْ مُّوْسٰى بِالْبَيِّنٰتِ ثُمَّ اتَّخَذْتُمُ الْعِجْلَ مِنْ بَعْدِهٖ وَاَنْتُمْ ظٰلِمُوْنَ ۝ وَاِذْ اَخَذْنَا مِيْثَاقَكُمْ وَرَفَعْنَا فَوْقَكُمُ الطُّوْرَ ؕ خُذُوْا مَاۤ اٰتَيْنٰكُمْ بِقُوَّةٍ وَّاسْمَعُوْا ؕ

Why do people ignore the truth even after seeing miracles?

The Israelites denied and killed Prophets

[87] We gave Musa The Book and sent messengers *afterwards* to succeed him. We gave miracles to Isa, son of Maryam, and supported him with the Spirit of the Holy One.[a] Is it not *true* that whenever a messenger came to you with a message that you did not like you became arrogant, refusing to believe some *of them* and killing others. [88] They said: "Our hearts are covered". Indeed, Allah cursed them because of their disbelief. How little they believe!

Jealousy breeds double standards

[89] When a book from Allah came to them, the Majestic Quran, confirming what they already have – they used to pray for victory over the disbelievers – when what they recognise *as true* comes to them, they deny it. So, Allah's curse *falls* on the disbelievers. [90] What a miserable price they have sold themselves for, denying rudely what Allah has revealed, because Allah sends down His favour on anyone of His Servants He wills! *That is why* they have brought down on themselves wrath upon wrath; for *such* disbelievers is humiliating punishment. [91] And when they are told: "Believe in what Allah has sent", they say: "We believe in what was sent to us". However, they deny what came afterwards, even though it is the truth confirming that which they already have. Ask them: "Why then, if you were believers, did you kill the previous prophets of Allah?"

Exposing those who love this world more than the Hereafter

[92] Musa came to you with miracles, *but* you started worshipping the calf *soon* afterwards, and became wrongdoers.

---

[a]   *Ruh ul-Qudus* refers to the Archangel Jibreel.

قَالُوا سَمِعْنَا وَعَصَيْنَا وَأُشْرِبُوا فِي قُلُوبِهِمُ الْعِجْلَ بِكُفْرِهِمْ ۚ قُلْ بِئْسَمَا يَأْمُرُكُم بِهِ إِيمَانُكُمْ إِن كُنتُم مُّؤْمِنِينَ ٩٣ قُلْ إِن كَانَتْ لَكُمُ الدَّارُ الْأَخِرَةُ عِندَ اللَّهِ خَالِصَةً مِّن دُونِ النَّاسِ فَتَمَنَّوُا الْمَوْتَ إِن كُنتُمْ صَادِقِينَ ٩٤ وَلَن يَتَمَنَّوْهُ أَبَدًا بِمَا قَدَّمَتْ أَيْدِيهِمْ ۚ وَاللَّهُ عَلِيمٌ بِالظَّالِمِينَ ٩٥ وَلَتَجِدَنَّهُمْ أَحْرَصَ النَّاسِ عَلَىٰ حَيَوٰةٍ ۚ وَمِنَ الَّذِينَ أَشْرَكُوا ۚ يَوَدُّ أَحَدُهُمْ لَوْ يُعَمَّرُ أَلْفَ سَنَةٍ ۚ وَمَا هُوَ بِمُزَحْزِحِهِ مِنَ الْعَذَابِ أَن يُعَمَّرَ ۗ وَاللَّهُ بَصِيرٌ بِمَا يَعْمَلُونَ ٩٦ قُلْ مَن كَانَ عَدُوًّا لِّجِبْرِيلَ فَإِنَّهُ نَزَّلَهُ عَلَىٰ قَلْبِكَ بِإِذْنِ اللَّهِ مُصَدِّقًا لِّمَا بَيْنَ يَدَيْهِ وَهُدًى وَبُشْرَىٰ لِلْمُؤْمِنِينَ ٩٧ مَن كَانَ عَدُوًّا لِّلَّهِ وَمَلَائِكَتِهِ وَرُسُلِهِ وَجِبْرِيلَ وَمِيكَالَ فَإِنَّ اللَّهَ عَدُوٌّ لِّلْكَافِرِينَ ٩٨ وَلَقَدْ أَنزَلْنَا إِلَيْكَ آيَاتٍ بَيِّنَاتٍ ۖ وَمَا يَكْفُرُ بِهَا إِلَّا الْفَاسِقُونَ ٩٩ أَوَكُلَّمَا عَاهَدُوا عَهْدًا نَّبَذَهُ فَرِيقٌ مِّنْهُم ۚ بَلْ أَكْثَرُهُمْ لَا يُؤْمِنُونَ ١٠٠ وَلَمَّا جَاءَهُمْ رَسُولٌ مِّنْ عِندِ اللَّهِ مُصَدِّقٌ لِّمَا مَعَهُمْ نَبَذَ فَرِيقٌ مِّنَ الَّذِينَ أُوتُوا الْكِتَابَ كِتَابَ اللَّهِ وَرَاءَ ظُهُورِهِمْ كَأَنَّهُمْ لَا يَعْلَمُونَ ١٠١ وَاتَّبَعُوا مَا تَتْلُو الشَّيَاطِينُ عَلَىٰ مُلْكِ سُلَيْمَانَ ۖ وَمَا كَفَرَ

What made these people deny their prophets and teachers?

٢٧

[93] We took a contract from you, near the Mount Sinai towering over you, *and We said*: "Hold on firmly to what We gave you and listen", *but your forefathers* said: "We hear and we disobey", swallowing *love of* the calf *deep* into their hearts because they were unthankful. Tell them: "How wrong is what your faith tells you to do, if you are believers!" [94] Say: "If the Final Abode with Allah is reserved solely for you and no one else, then *why do you not* wish for death, if you are truthful?" [95] However, they will never wish for it since *they know well* what their hands have stockpiled, and Allah knows well *who the wrongdoers are.* [96] You will find them and some of the idolators among the most eager of people for *the pleasures of* this worldly life. Every single one of them would love to live a thousand years, even though living so long would not save them from the punishment. Allah sees what they do.

Pretending to not know the truth

[97] Ask: "Who is the enemy of Jibreel?" He brought the Quran down into your heart by Allah's authority, confirming what came before it, and as guidance and good news for the believers. [98] Whoever is an enemy of Allah, His Angels, His Messengers, and Jibreel and Mikaeel, *should know* that Allah is the enemy of *such* disbelievers. [99] We have sent down to you clear verses, and only the wicked deny them. [100] Every time they enter an agreement, a group of them breaks it; in fact, most of them do not believe. [101] When a messenger from Allah came to them, confirming what they already had, a group of the People of The Book refused to accept it, pretending that they had never heard of it.

سُلَيْمٰنُ وَلٰكِنَّ الشَّيٰطِيْنَ كَفَرُوْا يُعَلِّمُوْنَ النَّاسَ

السِّحْرَ وَمَاۤ اُنْزِلَ عَلَى الْمَلَكَيْنِ بِبَابِلَ هَارُوْتَ

وَمَارُوْتَ ۗ وَمَا يُعَلِّمٰنِ مِنْ اَحَدٍ حَتّٰى يَقُوْلَاۤ

اِنَّمَا نَحْنُ فِتْنَةٌ فَلَا تَكْفُرْ ۖ فَيَتَعَلَّمُوْنَ مِنْهُمَا

مَا يُفَرِّقُوْنَ بِهٖ بَيْنَ الْمَرْءِ وَزَوْجِهٖ ۗ وَمَا هُمْ

بِضَآرِّيْنَ بِهٖ مِنْ اَحَدٍ اِلَّا بِاِذْنِ اللّٰهِ ۗ وَيَتَعَلَّمُوْنَ

مَا يَضُرُّهُمْ وَلَا يَنْفَعُهُمْ ۗ وَلَقَدْ عَلِمُوْا لَمَنِ

اشْتَرٰىهُ مَا لَهٗ فِى الْاٰخِرَةِ مِنْ خَلَاقٍ ۗ وَلَبِئْسَ

مَا شَرَوْا بِهٖۤ اَنْفُسَهُمْ ۗ لَوْ كَانُوْا يَعْلَمُوْنَ ۝ وَلَوْ

They split up husband and wife and broke up families with their magic.

اَنَّهُمْ اٰمَنُوْا وَاتَّقَوْا لَمَثُوْبَةٌ مِّنْ عِنْدِ اللّٰهِ خَيْرٌ ۗ

لَوْ كَانُوْا يَعْلَمُوْنَ ۝ يٰۤاَيُّهَا الَّذِيْنَ اٰمَنُوْا لَا تَقُوْلُوْا

رَاعِنَا وَقُوْلُوا انْظُرْنَا وَاسْمَعُوْا ۗ وَلِلْكٰفِرِيْنَ عَذَابٌ

اَلِيْمٌ ۝ مَا يَوَدُّ الَّذِيْنَ كَفَرُوْا مِنْ اَهْلِ الْكِتٰبِ

وَلَا الْمُشْرِكِيْنَ اَنْ يُّنَزَّلَ عَلَيْكُمْ مِّنْ خَيْرٍ مِّنْ

رَّبِّكُمْ ۗ وَاللّٰهُ يَخْتَصُّ بِرَحْمَتِهٖ مَنْ يَّشَآءُ ۗ وَاللّٰهُ

ذُو الْفَضْلِ الْعَظِيْمِ ۝ مَا نَنْسَخْ مِنْ اٰيَةٍ اَوْ نُنْسِهَا

نَأْتِ بِخَيْرٍ مِّنْهَاۤ اَوْ مِثْلِهَا ۗ اَلَمْ تَعْلَمْ اَنَّ اللّٰهَ

عَلٰى كُلِّ شَيْءٍ قَدِيْرٌ ۝ اَلَمْ تَعْلَمْ اَنَّ اللّٰهَ لَهٗ

مُلْكُ السَّمٰوٰتِ وَالْاَرْضِ ۗ وَمَا لَكُمْ مِّنْ دُوْنِ اللّٰهِ

مِنْ وَّلِيٍّ وَّلَا نَصِيْرٍ ۝ اَمْ تُرِيْدُوْنَ اَنْ تَسْـَٔلُوْا

The blind quest for worldly power

¹⁰²They *blindly* followed the devilish people who had fabricated about the kingdom of Sulayman. Sulayman did not disbelieve; rather, it was the devilish people who became disbelievers by teaching people magic and what had been given to the two *angels*, Harut and Marut, in Babylon. These two angels did not teach anyone until they had warned them: "We are *sent as* a test, so do not disbelieve". From these two *angels*, they learned how to create conflict between husband and wife, but they couldn't harm anyone without Allah's permission. So, people studied what harmed them rather than what benefitted them, knowing that anyone who gained this *knowledge of magic* will have no share in the Hereafter. How wretched is what they have sold themselves for! If only they knew! ¹⁰³Had they believed and feared *Allah*, the reward would have been far better, if they knew!

The proper manner of addressing the Messenger ﷺ

¹⁰⁴Believers,ᵃ do not say: "Ra'ina," but *instead* say: "Look at us,ᵇ and listen carefully *to him*". As for the disbelievers, a painful punishment awaits. ¹⁰⁵Neither the disbelievers among the People of The Book nor the idolaters desire that anything good should come from your Lord; Allah chooses for his favour anyone who wants to please Him, He is Gracious.

The dangers of questioning Allah's power

¹⁰⁶If ever We abrogate or postpone any verse, We replace it with something better or similar. Do you not know that Allah has power over all things? ¹⁰⁷Do you not know that the Kingdom of Heaven and Earth belongs to Allah; there is no protector and helper for you besides Him.

ᵃ The vocative phrase "O believers" occurs eighty-eight times in the Quran, and this is the first time it is used.

ᵇ The word *"Ra'ina"* has two meanings: "look at us", and "attend to our need". However, by a slight twist of the tongue, it has an insulting meaning (carry on deceiving us). That's why it was banned from being used to address the Messenger ﷺ, and the clearer term *"unzurna"* is recommended.

رَسُوْلَكُمْ كَمَا سُئِلَ مُوْسٰى مِنْ قَبْلُ ؕ وَمَنْ يَّتَبَدَّلِ الْكُفْرَ بِالْاِيْمَانِ فَقَدْ ضَلَّ سَوَآءَ السَّبِيْلِ ۞ وَدَّ كَثِيْرٌ مِّنْ اَهْلِ الْكِتٰبِ لَوْ يَرُدُّوْنَكُمْ مِّنْ بَعْدِ اِيْمَانِكُمْ كُفَّارًا ۖ حَسَدًا مِّنْ عِنْدِ اَنْفُسِهِمْ مِّنْ بَعْدِ مَا تَبَيَّنَ لَهُمُ الْحَقُّ ۚ فَاعْفُوْا وَاصْفَحُوْا حَتّٰى يَأْتِيَ اللّٰهُ بِاَمْرِهٖ ؕ اِنَّ اللّٰهَ عَلٰى كُلِّ شَيْءٍ قَدِيْرٌ ۞ وَاَقِيْمُوا الصَّلٰوةَ وَاٰتُوا الزَّكٰوةَ ؕ وَمَا تُقَدِّمُوْا لِاَنْفُسِكُمْ مِّنْ خَيْرٍ تَجِدُوْهُ عِنْدَ اللّٰهِ ؕ اِنَّ اللّٰهَ بِمَا تَعْمَلُوْنَ بَصِيْرٌ ۞ وَقَالُوْا لَنْ يَّدْخُلَ الْجَنَّةَ اِلَّا مَنْ كَانَ هُوْدًا اَوْ نَصٰرٰى ؕ تِلْكَ اَمَانِيُّهُمْ ؕ قُلْ هَاتُوْا بُرْهَانَكُمْ اِنْ كُنْتُمْ صٰدِقِيْنَ ۞ بَلٰى ۗ مَنْ اَسْلَمَ وَجْهَهٗ لِلّٰهِ وَهُوَ مُحْسِنٌ فَلَهٗ اَجْرُهٗ عِنْدَ رَبِّهٖ ۖ وَلَا خَوْفٌ عَلَيْهِمْ وَلَا هُمْ يَحْزَنُوْنَ ۞ وَقَالَتِ الْيَهُوْدُ لَيْسَتِ النَّصٰرٰى عَلٰى شَيْءٍ ۖ وَّقَالَتِ النَّصٰرٰى لَيْسَتِ الْيَهُوْدُ عَلٰى شَيْءٍ ۙ وَّهُمْ يَتْلُوْنَ الْكِتٰبَ ؕ كَذٰلِكَ قَالَ الَّذِيْنَ لَا يَعْلَمُوْنَ مِثْلَ قَوْلِهِمْ ۚ فَاللّٰهُ يَحْكُمُ بَيْنَهُمْ يَوْمَ الْقِيٰمَةِ فِيْمَا كَانُوْا فِيْهِ يَخْتَلِفُوْنَ ۞ وَمَنْ اَظْلَمُ مِمَّنْ مَّنَعَ مَسٰجِدَ اللّٰهِ اَنْ يُّذْكَرَ فِيْهَا اسْمُهٗ وَسَعٰى فِيْ خَرَابِهَا ؕ اُولٰٓئِكَ مَا كَانَ لَهُمْ اَنْ يَّدْخُلُوْهَا اِلَّا خَآئِفِيْنَ ؕ لَهُمْ فِي الدُّنْيَا خِزْيٌ وَّلَهُمْ فِي الْاٰخِرَةِ عَذَابٌ عَظِيْمٌ ۞

Submission to the will of Allah is the key to success. Have you committed yourself?

[108] Or do you want to ask your Messenger what Musa was asked *by others* before?[a] *We hope not, because* whoever swaps faith for disbelief has wandered far from the straight path. [109] Many of the People of The Book would dearly love to change you into disbelievers after you have believed; *this is* out of jealousy inside themselves *even* after truth has become clear to them. So, *believers*, pardon and be forgiving until Allah fulfils His command. Allah has control over all things.

Paradise is for anyone who submits to Allah

[110] And perform prayer and give Zakat; whatever good you send ahead for yourselves, you will find it with Allah. Allah sees all that you do. [111] They claim that only the Jews, or only the Christians, will enter Paradise; this is their wishful thinking. Say: "If you are telling the truth, prove it". [112] On the contrary, anyone who submits to Allah and is righteous, their reward shall be with their Lord, and they shall neither fear nor grieve.

Respecting freedom of religion

[113] The Jews say: "The Christians are misguided", and the Christians say: "The Jews are misguided", yet all read the *same* Book the Bible. Similarly, those who know nothing say the same thing as them. Allah will decide between them on Judgement Day regarding their differences. [114] Who can be more wicked than the one who stops people from glorifying Allah's name in His Mosques,[b] and who tries to destroy them? Yet they should only enter them in the fear *of Allah*. They shall suffer disgrace in this world and severe punishment in the Hereafter.

---

[a]   This refers to verse 55 above, when the Israelites demanded: "Musa, we will not believe you until we openly see Allah".

[b]   *Zikr ul-llah* here refers to Salah, study, spiritual retreat and all kinds of worship.

وَلِلّٰهِ الْمَشْرِقُ وَالْمَغْرِبُ ۚ فَاَيْنَمَا تُوَلُّوْا فَثَمَّ وَجْهُ اللّٰهِ ۗ اِنَّ اللّٰهَ وَاسِعٌ عَلِيْمٌ ۝ وَقَالُوا اتَّخَذَ اللّٰهُ وَلَدًا ۙ سُبْحٰنَهٗ ۗ بَلْ لَّهٗ مَا فِى السَّمٰوٰتِ وَالْاَرْضِ ۗ كُلٌّ لَّهٗ قٰنِتُوْنَ ۝ بَدِيْعُ السَّمٰوٰتِ وَالْاَرْضِ ۗ وَاِذَا قَضٰٓى اَمْرًا فَاِنَّمَا يَقُوْلُ لَهٗ كُنْ فَيَكُوْنُ ۝ وَقَالَ الَّذِيْنَ لَا يَعْلَمُوْنَ لَوْلَا يُكَلِّمُنَا اللّٰهُ اَوْ تَأْتِيْنَآ اٰيَةٌ ۗ كَذٰلِكَ قَالَ الَّذِيْنَ مِنْ قَبْلِهِمْ مِثْلَ قَوْلِهِمْ ۗ تَشَابَهَتْ قُلُوْبُهُمْ ۗ قَدْ بَيَّنَّا الْاٰيٰتِ لِقَوْمٍ يُّوْقِنُوْنَ ۝ اِنَّآ اَرْسَلْنٰكَ بِالْحَقِّ بَشِيْرًا وَّنَذِيْرًا ۙ وَّلَا تُسْئَلُ عَنْ اَصْحٰبِ الْجَحِيْمِ ۝ وَلَنْ تَرْضٰى عَنْكَ الْيَهُوْدُ وَلَا النَّصٰرٰى حَتّٰى تَتَّبِعَ مِلَّتَهُمْ ۗ قُلْ اِنَّ هُدَى اللّٰهِ هُوَ الْهُدٰى ۗ وَلَئِنِ اتَّبَعْتَ اَهْوَآءَهُمْ بَعْدَ الَّذِيْ جَآءَكَ مِنَ الْعِلْمِ ۙ مَا لَكَ مِنَ اللّٰهِ مِنْ وَّلِيٍّ وَّلَا نَصِيْرٍ ۝ اَلَّذِيْنَ اٰتَيْنٰهُمُ الْكِتٰبَ يَتْلُوْنَهٗ حَقَّ تِلَاوَتِهٖ ۗ اُولٰٓئِكَ يُؤْمِنُوْنَ بِهٖ ۗ وَمَنْ يَّكْفُرْ بِهٖ فَاُولٰٓئِكَ هُمُ الْخٰسِرُوْنَ ۝ يٰبَنِيْٓ اِسْرَآءِيْلَ اذْكُرُوْا نِعْمَتِيَ الَّتِيْٓ اَنْعَمْتُ عَلَيْكُمْ وَاَنِّيْ فَضَّلْتُكُمْ عَلَى الْعٰلَمِيْنَ ۝ وَاتَّقُوْا يَوْمًا لَّا تَجْزِيْ نَفْسٌ عَنْ نَّفْسٍ شَيْئًا وَّلَا يُقْبَلُ مِنْهَا عَدْلٌ وَّلَا تَنْفَعُهَا شَفَاعَةٌ وَّلَا هُمْ يُنْصَرُوْنَ ۝ وَاِذِ ابْتَلٰٓى اِبْرٰهٖمَ رَبُّهٗ بِكَلِمٰتٍ

The People of The Book meddled with their religion. Will you avoid that?

33

The vastness of Allah's creation is proof of His existence

[115]The East and the West belong to Allah, so wherever you turn, Allah's Presence will be there. Indeed, Allah is Boundlessly Vast, the Knowing. [116]They claim Allah has adopted a son. Glory be to Him! The Heavens and the Earth belong to Him; everything obeys Him, [117]The Creator of The Heavens and the Earth. When He decides on any matter, He only says: "Be!" And *there* it is. [118]The ignorant say: "If Allah spoke to us, or sent us a sign, we would believe." People before them said similar things; they think alike. We have made Our signs *abundantly* clear for those who firmly believe.

You cannot please both Allah and the disbelievers

[119]*Prophet*, We sent you with the truth, as the bearer of good news and a warner; you will not be asked about the people of the blazing fire. [120]The Jews and the Christians will never be satisfied with you until you follow their religion. Tell them: "Allah's guidance is the only guidance". If you *Muslims* follow their wishes after the knowledge has come to you, then you will have no one to protect you from Allah and to help you[a]. [121]Those given The Book, recite as it ought to be recited,[b] they are the true believers. Anyone who disbelieves in it, they are the losers.

Do not take Allah's favours for granted

[122]Children of Israel, remember My gifts to you; I preferred you over all other people. [123]So, fear a day when no one will be able to compensate for anyone else; no ransom will be accepted, and no one's intercession will benefit, and they will not be helped.

---

[a] "If you follow" is an address to the followers of the Prophet ﷺ. The Prophet ﷺ is making the announcement.

[b] "Reciting" here means combining reading with understanding and action.

فَٱتَّمَّهُنَّ ۚ قَالَ إِنِّى جَاعِلُكَ لِلنَّاسِ إِمَامًا ۖ قَالَ وَمِن ذُرِّيَّتِى ۖ قَالَ لَا يَنَالُ عَهْدِى ٱلظَّٰلِمِينَ ۝ وَإِذْ جَعَلْنَا ٱلْبَيْتَ مَثَابَةً لِّلنَّاسِ وَأَمْنًا ۖ وَٱتَّخِذُوا مِن مَّقَامِ إِبْرَٰهٖمَ مُصَلًّى ۖ وَعَهِدْنَآ إِلَىٰٓ إِبْرَٰهٖمَ وَإِسْمَٰعِيلَ أَن طَهِّرَا بَيْتِىَ لِلطَّآئِفِينَ وَٱلْعَٰكِفِينَ وَٱلرُّكَّعِ ٱلسُّجُودِ ۝ وَإِذْ قَالَ إِبْرَٰهٖمُ رَبِّ ٱجْعَلْ هَٰذَا بَلَدًا

Ibrahim was a symbol of true submission to Allah – truly committed. A Muslim.

ءَامِنًا وَٱرْزُقْ أَهْلَهُ مِنَ ٱلثَّمَرَٰتِ مَنْ ءَامَنَ مِنْهُم بِٱللّٰهِ وَٱلْيَوْمِ ٱلْءَاخِرِ ۖ قَالَ وَمَن كَفَرَ فَأُمَتِّعُهُ قَلِيلًا ثُمَّ أَضْطَرُّهُۥٓ إِلَىٰ عَذَابِ ٱلنَّارِ ۖ وَبِئْسَ ٱلْمَصِيرُ ۝ وَإِذْ يَرْفَعُ إِبْرَٰهٖمُ ٱلْقَوَاعِدَ مِنَ ٱلْبَيْتِ وَإِسْمَٰعِيلُ رَبَّنَا تَقَبَّلْ مِنَّا ۖ إِنَّكَ أَنتَ ٱلسَّمِيعُ ٱلْعَلِيمُ ۝ رَبَّنَا وَٱجْعَلْنَا مُسْلِمَيْنِ لَكَ وَمِن ذُرِّيَّتِنَآ أُمَّةً مُّسْلِمَةً لَّكَ ۖ وَأَرِنَا مَنَاسِكَنَا وَتُبْ عَلَيْنَآ ۖ إِنَّكَ أَنتَ ٱلتَّوَّابُ ٱلرَّحِيمُ ۝ رَبَّنَا وَٱبْعَثْ فِيهِمْ رَسُولًا مِّنْهُمْ يَتْلُوا عَلَيْهِمْ ءَايَٰتِكَ وَيُعَلِّمُهُمُ ٱلْكِتَٰبَ وَٱلْحِكْمَةَ وَيُزَكِّيهِمْ ۚ إِنَّكَ أَنتَ ٱلْعَزِيزُ ٱلْحَكِيمُ ۝ وَمَن يَرْغَبُ عَن مِّلَّةِ إِبْرَٰهٖمَ إِلَّا مَن سَفِهَ نَفْسَهُ ۚ وَلَقَدِ ٱصْطَفَيْنَٰهُ فِى ٱلدُّنْيَا ۖ وَإِنَّهُۥ فِى ٱلْءَاخِرَةِ لَمِنَ ٱلصَّٰلِحِينَ ۝ إِذْ قَالَ لَهُۥ رَبُّهُۥٓ أَسْلِمْ ۖ قَالَ أَسْلَمْتُ لِرَبِّ ٱلْعَٰلَمِينَ ۝ وَوَصَّىٰ بِهَآ إِبْرَٰهٖمُ بَنِيهِ وَيَعْقُوبُ ۖ

Ibrahim prays for his descendants and for Makkah

¹²⁴ *Remember* when Ibrahim was put to *all kinds* of tests by His Lord, he achieved them. His Lord said: "I will make you a leader of humanity", so he asked: "And what about my children?" Allah said: "My pledge will not benefit the evildoers *amongst them*". ¹²⁵ We made The *Ancient* House a safe and much frequented place, *saying*: "Take *the place where* Ibrahim stood as a place of prayer". And We told Ibrahim and Ismael: "Keep My House clean for those who circle it, those who stay there to worship, to bow and to prostrate". ¹²⁶ *Remember* when Ibrahim prayed: "Lord, make this a city of sanctuary, and sustain with fruits those who believe in Allah and The Last Day". *Allah* said: "The disbelievers, We shall let them enjoy themselves a little, then drive them towards the punishment of Fire. What a terrible destination!"

Ibrahim's prayer for a special messenger

¹²⁷ *Remember* when Ibrahim and Ismael were raising the foundations of The House, they prayed: "Our Lord, accept *this* from us. You are the Listener, the Knower. ¹²⁸ Our Lord, keep us committed to You,ᵃ and make our children a community that submits to You, and teach us our rites, and be relenting towards us: indeed, You accept repentance, the Kind. ¹²⁹ Our Lord, send them a messenger from their people, who will teach your signs, the Book, the wisdom, and purify them. You are the Almighty, the Wise".

Ibrahim's religion is for all generations

¹³⁰ Only a fool can turn away from the religion of Ibrahim; We chose him in this world, and in the next life he will be among the Righteous. ¹³¹ *Remember* when His Lord said to him: "Submit", and he replied: "I submit myself to the Lord of the Universe".

ᵃ The Arabic uses "Muslims", referring to people who have chosen to submit and commit to the will of Allah and to enjoy a living relationship with Allah.

يٰبَنِىَّ اِنَّ اللّٰهَ اصْطَفٰى لَكُمُ الدِّيْنَ فَلَا تَمُوْتُنَّ اِلَّا

وَ اَنْتُمْ مُّسْلِمُوْنَ ۞ اَمْ كُنْتُمْ شُهَدَآءَ اِذْ حَضَرَ

يَعْقُوْبَ الْمَوْتُ ۚ اِذْ قَالَ لِبَنِيْهِ مَا تَعْبُدُوْنَ مِنْ

بَعْدِىْ ؕ قَالُوْا نَعْبُدُ اِلٰهَكَ وَ اِلٰهَ اٰبَآئِكَ اِبْرٰهٖمَ

وَ اِسْمٰعِيْلَ وَ اِسْحٰقَ اِلٰهًا وَّاحِدًا ۚ وَّ نَحْنُ لَهٗ

مُسْلِمُوْنَ ۞ تِلْكَ اُمَّةٌ قَدْ خَلَتْ ۚ لَهَا مَا كَسَبَتْ وَ

لَكُمْ مَّا كَسَبْتُمْ ۚ وَ لَا تُسْـَٔلُوْنَ عَمَّا كَانُوْا يَعْمَلُوْنَ ۞

وَ قَالُوْا كُوْنُوْا هُوْدًا اَوْ نَصٰرٰى تَهْتَدُوْا ؕ قُلْ بَلْ مِلَّةَ

What is the colour of Allah? (Think of His beautiful names.)

اِبْرٰهٖمَ حَنِيْفًا ؕ وَ مَا كَانَ مِنَ الْمُشْرِكِيْنَ ۞ قُوْلُوْا

اٰمَنَّا بِاللّٰهِ وَ مَآ اُنْزِلَ اِلَيْنَا وَ مَآ اُنْزِلَ اِلٰٓى اِبْرٰهٖمَ

وَ اِسْمٰعِيْلَ وَ اِسْحٰقَ وَ يَعْقُوْبَ وَ الْاَسْبَاطِ وَ مَآ اُوْتِىَ

مُوْسٰى وَ عِيْسٰى وَ مَآ اُوْتِىَ النَّبِيُّوْنَ مِنْ رَّبِّهِمْ ۚ

لَا نُفَرِّقُ بَيْنَ اَحَدٍ مِّنْهُمْ ۖ وَ نَحْنُ لَهٗ مُسْلِمُوْنَ ۞

فَاِنْ اٰمَنُوْا بِمِثْلِ مَآ اٰمَنْتُمْ بِهٖ فَقَدِ اهْتَدَوْا ۚ وَ اِنْ

تَوَلَّوْا فَاِنَّمَا هُمْ فِىْ شِقَاقٍ ۚ فَسَيَكْفِيْكَهُمُ اللّٰهُ ۚ

وَ هُوَ السَّمِيْعُ الْعَلِيْمُ ؕ ۞ صِبْغَةَ اللّٰهِ ۚ وَ مَنْ اَحْسَنُ

مِنَ اللّٰهِ صِبْغَةً ۫ وَّ نَحْنُ لَهٗ عٰبِدُوْنَ ۞ قُلْ

اَتُحَآجُّوْنَنَا فِى اللّٰهِ وَ هُوَ رَبُّنَا وَ رَبُّكُمْ ۚ وَ لَنَآ اَعْمَالُنَا

وَ لَكُمْ اَعْمَالُكُمْ ۚ وَ نَحْنُ لَهٗ مُخْلِصُوْنَ ۞ اَمْ

تَقُوْلُوْنَ اِنَّ اِبْرٰهٖمَ وَ اِسْمٰعِيْلَ وَ اِسْحٰقَ وَ يَعْقُوْبَ

[132] He advised his children to *submit*, and *later* Yaqub *also* did the same, saying: "My children, Allah has chosen your religion for you, so till you die remain as true Muslims".

Yaqub's final advice to his children

[133] Were you witness when death came to Yaqub? *Remember* when he asked his children: "What will you worship after me?" *And* they replied: "We will worship Your God and the God of our forefathers, Ibrahim, Ismael and Ishaq, the One God, and we submit to Him". [134] That community has passed away; they will reap the reward of what they did, and so will you, and you will not be asked about what they did.

Muslims do not pick and choose from the prophets

[135] They say *to you*: "Become Jews…", or: "Become Christians and you will be guided". Tell them: "In fact *our religion is* the religion of Ibrahim, *who was a true* Hanif,[a] and was not an idolater".[b] [136] Say: "We believe in Allah and in what is revealed to us, and in what was revealed to Ibrahim, Ismael, Ishaq, Yaqub and the Tribes, and in what was given to Musa and Isa, and in what was given to *all* the prophets from their Lord: we make no distinction between any one of them, we submit to Him".

True faith in Allah affects the whole of a believer's life

[137] If they *decide to* believe in the same *God* as you believe, then they will be guided, but if they turn away, they will be divided. Allah will be sufficient for you against them. He is the Listener, the Knower. [138] The dye of Allah *is the best*, whose dye is better than Allah's at colouring *our whole being*?[c] We worship Him *alone*. [139] Say: "Do you argue with us about Allah, when He is Our Lord as well as Yours, when we have our deeds and you have yours, we are absolutely committed to Him?"

---

[a] *Hanif* describes a person who believes in One God and rejects all forms of idolatry.

[b] What is idolatry? None of us would dream of worshipping an idol, but succumbing to things that have no eternal value, pleasures, power and possessions? Isn't this a form of idolatry? Anything we put before Allah, which dilutes our trust in Him, becomes an idol.

[c] "Dye of Allah" refers to the natural state of humans. This natural state is mentioned in *Surat Al-Rum: 30* as *"Fitra"*: the original and good nature of humanity that is instinctively receptive to moral virtues and spiritual values.

وَالْاَسْبَاطِ كَانُوْا هُوْدًا اَوْ نَصٰرٰى ۭ قُلْ ءَاَنْتُمْ

اَعْلَمُ اَمِ اللّٰهُ ۭ وَمَنْ اَظْلَمُ مِمَّنْ كَتَمَ شَهَادَةً

عِنْدَهٗ مِنَ اللّٰهِ ۭ وَمَا اللّٰهُ بِغَافِلٍ عَمَّا تَعْمَلُوْنَ ۝

تِلْكَ اُمَّةٌ قَدْ خَلَتْ ۚ لَهَا مَا كَسَبَتْ وَلَكُمْ

مَّا كَسَبْتُمْ ۚ وَلَا تُسْـَٔلُوْنَ عَمَّا كَانُوْا يَعْمَلُوْنَ ۝

سَيَقُوْلُ السُّفَهَاءُ مِنَ النَّاسِ مَا وَلّٰىهُمْ عَنْ

قِبْلَتِهِمُ الَّتِىْ كَانُوْا عَلَيْهَا ۭ قُلْ لِّلّٰهِ الْمَشْرِقُ وَ

الْمَغْرِبُ ۭ يَهْدِىْ مَنْ يَّشَآءُ اِلٰى صِرَاطٍ مُّسْتَقِيْمٍ ۝

وَكَذٰلِكَ جَعَلْنٰكُمْ اُمَّةً وَّسَطًا لِّتَكُوْنُوْا شُهَدَآءَ عَلَى

النَّاسِ وَيَكُوْنَ الرَّسُوْلُ عَلَيْكُمْ شَهِيْدًا ۭ وَمَا جَعَلْنَا

الْقِبْلَةَ الَّتِىْ كُنْتَ عَلَيْهَآ اِلَّا لِنَعْلَمَ مَنْ يَّتَّبِعُ

الرَّسُوْلَ مِمَّنْ يَّنْقَلِبُ عَلٰى عَقِبَيْهِ ۭ وَاِنْ كَانَتْ

لَكَبِيْرَةً اِلَّا عَلَى الَّذِيْنَ هَدَى اللّٰهُ ۭ وَمَا كَانَ اللّٰهُ

لِيُضِيْعَ اِيْمَانَكُمْ ۭ اِنَّ اللّٰهَ بِالنَّاسِ لَرَءُوْفٌ رَّحِيْمٌ ۝

قَدْ نَرٰى تَقَلُّبَ وَجْهِكَ فِى السَّمَآءِ ۚ فَلَنُوَلِّيَنَّكَ

قِبْلَةً تَرْضٰىهَا ۠ فَوَلِّ وَجْهَكَ شَطْرَ الْمَسْجِدِ الْحَرَامِ ۭ

وَحَيْثُ مَا كُنْتُمْ فَوَلُّوْا وُجُوْهَكُمْ شَطْرَهٗ ۭ وَاِنَّ

الَّذِيْنَ اُوْتُوا الْكِتٰبَ لَيَعْلَمُوْنَ اَنَّهُ الْحَقُّ مِنْ

رَّبِّهِمْ ۭ وَمَا اللّٰهُ بِغَافِلٍ عَمَّا يَعْمَلُوْنَ ۝ وَلَىِٕنْ

اَتَيْتَ الَّذِيْنَ اُوْتُوا الْكِتٰبَ بِكُلِّ اٰيَةٍ مَّا تَبِعُوْا

The prayer direction also defines the direction of your life journey, your heart should be set on it

[140] Or do you claim that Ibrahim, Ismail, Ishaq, Yaqub and the Tribes[a] were "Jews" or "Christians?" Say: "Who knows better, you or Allah? And who can be more sinful than the one who tries to hide evidence from Allah? Indeed, Allah is not unaware of what you do". [141] That community has passed away; they will reap the reward of what they did, and so will you, and you will not be questioned about what they did.

The reason for change in the direction of prayer

[142] Some foolish people will ask: "What has turned them away from the direction they used to pray in?" Say: "The East and The West belong to Allah. He guides to the straight path anyone who wants to be guided". [143] So We made you a well-balanced nation,[b] to be witnesses against humanity, and the Messenger will be your witness. We only established your previous prayer direction *towards Aqsa Mosque* to distinguish[c] those who follow the Messenger from those who turn on their heels. This was indeed a difficult test, except for those whom Allah has guided; Allah will never allow your prayer[d] to go to waste. Indeed, Allah is Most Kind and Gracious to people. [144] We saw you turning your face towards the Heaven, and We shall turn you towards a direction of the prayer that will please you. So, now turn your face towards The Sacred Mosque. Wherever you are, turn your faces towards it. Those who were given The Book know *well* that this is the truth from their Lord, and Allah is aware of what they do.

---

[a]   Since these prophets, and The Twelve Tribes until the time of Musa, lived before the revelation of the Torah, they could not have been Jews.

[b]   The phrase *"Ummatan wastan"* means "a middle nation" a metaphor for "moderate people", far from extremism.

[c]   The primary meaning is "to know", but since Allah knows everything, it is not an appropriate term to use here so we have used the term "distinguish".

[d]   The phrase *"Li-eemanikum"* literally means "your faith". However, commentators translate this as "prayer".

قِبْلَتَكَ ۚ وَمَآ اَنْتَ بِتَابِعٍ قِبْلَتَهُمْ ۚ وَمَا بَعْضُهُمْ

بِتَابِعٍ قِبْلَةَ بَعْضٍ ط وَلَئِنِ اتَّبَعْتَ اَهْوَآءَهُمْ

مِّنْۢ بَعْدِ مَا جَآءَكَ مِنَ الْعِلْمِ لا اِنَّكَ اِذًا لَّمِنَ

الظّٰلِمِيْنَ ﴿۱۴۵﴾ اَلَّذِيْنَ اٰتَيْنٰهُمُ الْكِتٰبَ يَعْرِفُوْنَهٗ كَمَا

يَعْرِفُوْنَ اَبْنَآءَهُمْ ط وَاِنَّ فَرِيْقًا مِّنْهُمْ لَيَكْتُمُوْنَ الْحَقَّ

وَهُمْ يَعْلَمُوْنَ ﴿۱۴۶﴾ اَلْحَقُّ مِنْ رَّبِّكَ فَلَا تَكُوْنَنَّ مِنَ

الْمُمْتَرِيْنَ ۠ ﴿۱۴۷﴾ وَلِكُلٍّ وِّجْهَةٌ هُوَ مُوَلِّيْهَا فَاسْتَبِقُوا

الْخَيْرٰتِ ط اَيْنَ مَا تَكُوْنُوْا يَاْتِ بِكُمُ اللّٰهُ جَمِيْعًا ط اِنَّ

اللّٰهَ عَلٰى كُلِّ شَيْءٍ قَدِيْرٌ ﴿۱۴۸﴾ وَمِنْ حَيْثُ خَرَجْتَ فَوَلِّ

وَجْهَكَ شَطْرَ الْمَسْجِدِ الْحَرَامِ ط وَاِنَّهٗ لَلْحَقُّ مِنْ رَّبِّكَ ط

وَمَا اللّٰهُ بِغَافِلٍ عَمَّا تَعْمَلُوْنَ ﴿۱۴۹﴾ وَمِنْ حَيْثُ خَرَجْتَ

فَوَلِّ وَجْهَكَ شَطْرَ الْمَسْجِدِ الْحَرَامِ ط وَحَيْثُ مَا

كُنْتُمْ فَوَلُّوْا وُجُوْهَكُمْ شَطْرَهٗ ۙ لِئَلَّا يَكُوْنَ لِلنَّاسِ

عَلَيْكُمْ حُجَّةٌ ۙ اِلَّا الَّذِيْنَ ظَلَمُوْا مِنْهُمْ ۗ فَلَا

تَخْشَوْهُمْ وَاخْشَوْنِيْ ۙ وَلِاُتِمَّ نِعْمَتِيْ عَلَيْكُمْ وَلَعَلَّكُمْ

تَهْتَدُوْنَ ﴿۱۵۰﴾ۙ كَمَآ اَرْسَلْنَا فِيْكُمْ رَسُوْلًا مِّنْكُمْ يَتْلُوْا

عَلَيْكُمْ اٰيٰتِنَا وَيُزَكِّيْكُمْ وَيُعَلِّمُكُمُ الْكِتٰبَ وَالْحِكْمَةَ

وَيُعَلِّمُكُمْ مَّا لَمْ تَكُوْنُوْا تَعْلَمُوْنَ ﴿۱۵۱﴾ؕ فَاذْكُرُوْنِيْۤ

اَذْكُرْكُمْ وَاشْكُرُوْا لِيْ وَلَا تَكْفُرُوْنِ ﴿۱۵۲﴾ يٰٓاَيُّهَا الَّذِيْنَ

اٰمَنُوا اسْتَعِيْنُوْا بِالصَّبْرِ وَالصَّلٰوةِ ط اِنَّ اللّٰهَ مَعَ

Which way is your life going? What is your goal?

41

Don't try to please others at the expense of Allah

[145] Even if you were to produce conclusive evidence for the People of The Book, they will not adopt your direction of prayer, nor will you adopt their direction of prayer; *in fact,* they do not even follow each other's direction. If anyone were to follow their desires after the knowledge has come to you then they would be wrongdoers. [146] Those Jews given the Book recognise *The Messenger* just as they recognise their sons, *yet* a group of them deliberately tries to hide the truth. [147] The truth has come from your Lord. *Listener,* don't be among those who have doubts *about it.*

Each person has a goal and a direction

[148] Everyone has a direction to which they turn, so compete in doing good works. Wherever you happen to be, Allah will bring you together. Allah has power over everything. [149] By whichever direction you go out of *Madinah,* turn to face the Sacred Mosque *in prayer;* that is the truth from your Lord, and Allah is not unaware of what you do. [150] In whichever direction you go always turn to face the Sacred Mosque. All of you, wherever you are, always turn your faces towards it, so that people do not have any evidence *of disunity* against you except, *of course,* the wrongdoers among them. Don't be afraid of them, but fear Me, so I will complete My favours on you, and ensure you are guided.

The functions of The Messenger ﷺ

[151] For example, We sent to you a *noble* Messenger from amongst you; he recites Our verses for you, purifies you, teaches you the Book and wisdom, and teaches you what you didn't know. [152] So, remember Me, and I shall remember you. Be thankful to Me, and don't be unthankful to Me.

Patience: Coping with life's tests

[153] Believers, find strength through patience and prayer – Allah is with those who are patient.

الصّٰبِرِينَ ۝ وَلَا تَقُولُوا لِمَنْ يُقْتَلُ فِى سَبِيلِ اللهِ

اَمْوَاتٌ ۚ بَلْ اَحْيَاءٌ وَّلٰكِنْ لَّا تَشْعُرُونَ ۝ وَلَنَبْلُوَنَّكُمْ

بِشَىْءٍ مِّنَ الْخَوْفِ وَالْجُوعِ وَنَقْصٍ مِّنَ الْاَمْوَالِ

وَالْاَنْفُسِ وَالثَّمَرٰتِ ۗ وَبَشِّرِ الصّٰبِرِينَ ۝ الَّذِينَ اِذَآ

اَصَابَتْهُمْ مُّصِيبَةٌ ۙ قَالُوٓا اِنَّا لِلهِ وَاِنَّآ اِلَيْهِ

رٰجِعُونَ ۝ اُولٰٓئِكَ عَلَيْهِمْ صَلَوٰتٌ مِّنْ رَّبِّهِمْ وَ

رَحْمَةٌ ۗ وَاُولٰٓئِكَ هُمُ الْمُهْتَدُونَ ۝ اِنَّ الصَّفَا وَ

الْمَرْوَةَ مِنْ شَعَآئِرِ اللهِ ۚ فَمَنْ حَجَّ الْبَيْتَ اَوِ اعْتَمَرَ

فَلَا جُنَاحَ عَلَيْهِ اَنْ يَّطَّوَّفَ بِهِمَا ۗ وَمَنْ تَطَوَّعَ

خَيْرًا ۙ فَاِنَّ اللهَ شَاكِرٌ عَلِيمٌ ۝ اِنَّ الَّذِينَ يَكْتُمُونَ

مَآ اَنْزَلْنَا مِنَ الْبَيِّنٰتِ وَالْهُدٰى مِنْ بَعْدِ مَا بَيَّنّٰهُ

لِلنَّاسِ فِى الْكِتٰبِ ۙ اُولٰٓئِكَ يَلْعَنُهُمُ اللهُ وَيَلْعَنُهُمُ

اللّٰعِنُونَ ۝ اِلَّا الَّذِينَ تَابُوا وَاَصْلَحُوا وَبَيَّنُوا

فَاُولٰٓئِكَ اَتُوبُ عَلَيْهِمْ ۚ وَاَنَا التَّوَّابُ الرَّحِيمُ ۝ اِنَّ

الَّذِينَ كَفَرُوا وَمَاتُوا وَهُمْ كُفَّارٌ اُولٰٓئِكَ عَلَيْهِمْ

لَعْنَةُ اللهِ وَالْمَلٰٓئِكَةِ وَالنَّاسِ اَجْمَعِينَ ۝ خٰلِدِينَ

فِيهَا ۚ لَا يُخَفَّفُ عَنْهُمُ الْعَذَابُ وَلَاهُمْ يُنْظَرُونَ ۝

وَاِلٰهُكُمْ اِلٰهٌ وَّاحِدٌ ۚ لَآ اِلٰهَ اِلَّا هُوَ الرَّحْمٰنُ الرَّحِيمُ ۝

اِنَّ فِى خَلْقِ السَّمٰوٰتِ وَالْاَرْضِ وَاخْتِلَافِ الَّيْلِ

وَالنَّهَارِ وَالْفُلْكِ الَّتِى تَجْرِى فِى الْبَحْرِ بِمَا

Patience: being cool in times of difficulty.

[154]Don't speak *irreverently* of those who were killed *fighting* in Allah's way, *that they are* "dead"; rather, they are living, though you don't sense *it*. [155]We will certainly test you: with fear, hunger, loss of wealth, health and harvests. Give good news to the patient [156]and who, when they are struck by misfortune, *softly* say: "We belong to Allah and are returning to Him". [157]These are the ones who shall be blessed and will be taken care of by their Lord; they are the guided.

A tribute to Hajar's patience

[158]The hills of Safa and Marwa are Symbols of Allah;[a] whoever comes to *Allah's* House to perform the Hajj or Umrah, *let him know that* there is no objection in walking between them. Whoever works voluntarily will be rewarded by Allah, the Knower of all things.

Allah's teachings are not secrets to be hidden away

[159]Those who hide the clear signs and the guidance We have revealed, after We have clearly explained it in The Book for people, they are the ones whom Allah curses, as do those who *have the authority to* curse, [160]but if they repent, reform themselves and openly declare faith then I shall accept their repentance; I am the Accepter of repentance and the Kind. [161]Those who disbelieve and die as disbelievers will be cursed by Allah, the angels and *the rest* of humanity, [162]dwelling therein forever, and their punishment will be neither reduced nor delayed.

The signs of Allah's creative power

[163]Your God is one God; there is no God beside Him, the Kind, the Caring. [164]In the creation of The Heavens and the Earth, in the cycle of night and day, and in the ships which sail the seas for people's profit; in the rain Allah sends down from the skies, bringing the dead Earth to life, and causing it to abound with all kinds of animals; in the movements of the winds, and in the clouds which float between Heaven and Earth: *in all these things,* there are signs for people who understand.

---

[a] The Quran pays a special tribute to the patience of Lady Hajar, the wife of Prophet Ibrahim, as she frantically searched for water between these two hillocks. Making these symbols of Allah teaches the reward of patience.

يَّنْفَعُ النَّاسَ وَمَآ اَنْزَلَ اللهُ مِنَ السَّمَآءِ مِنْ
مَّآءٍ فَاَحْيَا بِهِ الْاَرْضَ بَعْدَ مَوْتِهَا وَبَثَّ فِيْهَا
مِنْ كُلِّ دَآبَّةٍ ۖ وَّتَصْرِيْفِ الرِّيٰحِ وَ السَّحَابِ
الْمُسَخَّرِ بَيْنَ السَّمَآءِ وَالْاَرْضِ لَاٰيٰتٍ لِّقَوْمٍ
يَّعْقِلُوْنَ ۝ وَمِنَ النَّاسِ مَنْ يَّتَّخِذُ مِنْ دُوْنِ
اللهِ اَنْدَادًا يُّحِبُّوْنَهُمْ كَحُبِّ اللهِ ۖ وَالَّذِيْنَ اٰمَنُوْٓا
اَشَدُّ حُبًّا لِّلّٰهِ ۖ وَلَوْ يَرَى الَّذِيْنَ ظَلَمُوْٓا اِذْ يَرَوْنَ
الْعَذَابَ ۙ اَنَّ الْقُوَّةَ لِلّٰهِ جَمِيْعًا ۙ وَّاَنَّ اللهَ شَدِيْدُ
الْعَذَابِ ۝ اِذْ تَبَرَّاَ الَّذِيْنَ اتُّبِعُوْا مِنَ الَّذِيْنَ اتَّبَعُوْا
وَرَاَوُا الْعَذَابَ وَتَقَطَّعَتْ بِهِمُ الْاَسْبَابُ ۝ وَقَالَ
الَّذِيْنَ اتَّبَعُوْا لَوْ اَنَّ لَنَا كَرَّةً فَنَتَبَرَّاَ مِنْهُمْ كَمَا
تَبَرَّءُوْا مِنَّا ۚ كَذٰلِكَ يُرِيْهِمُ اللهُ اَعْمَالَهُمْ حَسَرٰتٍ
عَلَيْهِمْ ۖ وَمَا هُمْ بِخٰرِجِيْنَ مِنَ النَّارِ ۝ يٰٓاَيُّهَا
النَّاسُ كُلُوْا مِمَّا فِى الْاَرْضِ حَلٰلًا طَيِّبًا ۖ وَّلَا
تَتَّبِعُوْا خُطُوٰتِ الشَّيْطٰنِ ۚ اِنَّهُ لَكُمْ عَدُوٌّ مُّبِيْنٌ ۝
اِنَّمَا يَاْمُرُكُمْ بِالسُّوْٓءِ وَالْفَحْشَآءِ وَاَنْ تَقُوْلُوْا
عَلَى اللهِ مَا لَا تَعْلَمُوْنَ ۝ وَاِذَا قِيْلَ لَهُمُ اتَّبِعُوْا
مَآ اَنْزَلَ اللهُ قَالُوْا بَلْ نَتَّبِعُ مَآ اَلْفَيْنَا عَلَيْهِ
اٰبَآءَنَا ۗ اَوَلَوْ كَانَ اٰبَآؤُهُمْ لَا يَعْقِلُوْنَ شَيْئًا
وَّلَا يَهْتَدُوْنَ ۝ وَمَثَلُ الَّذِيْنَ كَفَرُوْا كَمَثَلِ

Love: Allah should be in first position

٢٠
ع
٤

45

Regrets about wasted life on Judgement Day

[165] Some people take idols[a] beside Allah, loving them as much as *they* love Allah, *whereas* those who believe, love Allah passionately. If only the wrongdoers could see the punishment, they would realise that Allah possesses all power, and that Allah's punishment is severe. [166] *On Judgement Day*, the followers *of idols* will be disowned by the idols they served, and they will see the punishment, and their ties *with these idols* torn to shreds. [167] Then the followers will say: "If only we had another chance so we could disown them as they have disowned us *today*". That is how Allah will show them their deeds, which they will bitterly regret, and they will never get out of the Fire *of Hell*.

How Satan influences people

[168] People, eat of what is lawful and wholesome on Earth, and do not follow the footsteps of Satan; he is your open enemy. [169] He will direct you to evil, indecency and saying things about Allah which you don't know. [170] When *the disbelievers* are told, "Follow what Allah has revealed," they say: "No! We follow what we found our ancestors doing", even though their ancestors lacked both basic understanding and guidance. [171] The disbelievers are like the bleating *sheep being called* loudly *by the shepherd,* they hear nothing but crying and screaming; deaf, dumb and blind, they *simply* don't understand.

---

[a] "Idols" refers not only to physical statues that people worship, but any material thing in which one puts trust instead of Allah. This can include wealth, career, family, technological gadgets and even gangs.

الَّذِیْ یَنْعِقُ بِمَا لَا یَسْمَعُ اِلَّا دُعَآءً وَّنِدَآءً ؕ صُمٌّۢ بُكْمٌ عُمْیٌ فَهُمْ لَا یَعْقِلُوْنَ ۝ یٰۤاَیُّهَا الَّذِیْنَ اٰمَنُوْا كُلُوْا مِنْ طَیِّبٰتِ مَا رَزَقْنٰكُمْ وَ اشْكُرُوْا لِلّٰهِ اِنْ كُنْتُمْ اِیَّاهُ تَعْبُدُوْنَ ۝ اِنَّمَا حَرَّمَ عَلَیْكُمُ الْمَیْتَةَ وَ الدَّمَ وَ لَحْمَ الْخِنْزِیْرِ وَ مَاۤ اُهِلَّ بِهٖ لِغَیْرِ اللّٰهِ ۚ فَمَنِ اضْطُرَّ غَیْرَ بَاغٍ وَّلَا عَادٍ فَلَاۤ اِثْمَ عَلَیْهِ ؕ اِنَّ اللّٰهَ غَفُوْرٌ رَّحِیْمٌ ۝ اِنَّ الَّذِیْنَ یَكْتُمُوْنَ مَاۤ اَنْزَلَ اللّٰهُ مِنَ الْكِتٰبِ وَ یَشْتَرُوْنَ بِهٖ ثَمَنًا قَلِیْلًا ۙ اُولٰٓئِكَ مَا یَاْكُلُوْنَ فِیْ بُطُوْنِهِمْ اِلَّا النَّارَ وَ لَا یُكَلِّمُهُمُ اللّٰهُ یَوْمَ الْقِیٰمَةِ وَ لَا یُزَكِّیْهِمْ ۖ وَ لَهُمْ عَذَابٌ اَلِیْمٌ ۝ اُولٰٓئِكَ الَّذِیْنَ اشْتَرَوُا الضَّلٰلَةَ بِالْهُدٰی وَ الْعَذَابَ بِالْمَغْفِرَةِ ۚ فَمَاۤ اَصْبَرَهُمْ عَلَی النَّارِ ۝ ذٰلِكَ بِاَنَّ اللّٰهَ نَزَّلَ الْكِتٰبَ بِالْحَقِّ ؕ وَ اِنَّ الَّذِیْنَ اخْتَلَفُوْا فِی الْكِتٰبِ لَفِیْ شِقَاقٍۭ بَعِیْدٍ ۝

لَیْسَ الْبِرَّ اَنْ تُوَلُّوْا وُجُوْهَكُمْ قِبَلَ الْمَشْرِقِ وَ الْمَغْرِبِ وَ لٰكِنَّ الْبِرَّ مَنْ اٰمَنَ بِاللّٰهِ وَ الْیَوْمِ الْاٰخِرِ وَ الْمَلٰٓئِكَةِ وَ الْكِتٰبِ وَ النَّبِیّٖنَ ۚ وَ اٰتَی الْمَالَ عَلٰی حُبِّهٖ ذَوِی الْقُرْبٰی وَ الْیَتٰمٰی وَ الْمَسٰكِیْنَ وَ ابْنَ السَّبِیْلِ ۙ وَ السَّآئِلِیْنَ وَ فِی الرِّقَابِ ۚ وَ اَقَامَ الصَّلٰوةَ وَ اٰتَی الزَّكٰوةَ ۚ وَ الْمُوْفُوْنَ بِعَهْدِهِمْ اِذَا عٰهَدُوْا ۚ

Religion isn't only about carrying out rituals, it's about giving your best to others.

Meat which is unlawful to eat

[172] Believers, eat the wholesome foods We provide you and thank Allah, if you truly worship Him. [173] The *few* things He has made unlawful for you are carrion, blood, pork, and animals slaughtered in any name other than Allah's. However, if anyone is compelled *by circumstance*,[a] not because he desires it or wishes to disobey *Allah*, then he commits no sin. Allah is the Forgiving, the Kind.

It is wrong to use religion for worldly gains

[174] Anyone who hides what Allah has revealed in the Book, or sells it for a small sum *of money* are filling their stomachs with Hellfire. Allah will neither speak to them nor purify them on Judgement Day; they shall have a painful punishment. [175] They have chosen *for themselves* error over guidance and punishment over forgiveness. How will they endure Hellfire? [176] That is because Allah has sent The Book with the truth, *but* those who differ about The Book have digressed with farfetched heresy.

What is righteousness?

[177] Righteousness is not simply turning your face towards The East or The West *in prayer*, rather, righteousness is believing in Allah, The Last Day, the angels, the *revealed* books and the prophets; spending wealth for the love of Allah on relatives, orphans, the needy, travellers, beggars and freeing slaves; performing prayer and paying Zakat; fulfilling any contracts one has entered; and being patient in illness, misfortune and in times of hardship. Those *who do these things* are the truthful people, and they are mindful of Allah.

---

[a] For example, if you hate the thought but are dying of hunger or thirst, are being force-fed by a captor, or told you will be killed if you refuse to do so, then consuming such meat is not a sin.

وَالصّٰبِرِيْنَ فِى الْبَاْسَاءِ وَالضَّرَّاءِ وَحِيْنَ الْبَاْسِ ط

اُولٰٓئِكَ الَّذِيْنَ صَدَقُوْا ط وَاُولٰٓئِكَ هُمُ الْمُتَّقُوْنَ ۝

يٰٓاَيُّهَا الَّذِيْنَ اٰمَنُوْا كُتِبَ عَلَيْكُمُ الْقِصَاصُ فِى

الْقَتْلٰى ط اَلْحُرُّ بِالْحُرِّ وَالْعَبْدُ بِالْعَبْدِ وَالْاُنْثٰى

بِالْاُنْثٰى ط فَمَنْ عُفِيَ لَهٗ مِنْ اَخِيْهِ شَىْءٌ فَاتِّبَاعٌ

بِالْمَعْرُوْفِ وَاَدَاءٌ اِلَيْهِ بِاِحْسَانٍ ط ذٰلِكَ تَخْفِيْفٌ

مِّنْ رَّبِّكُمْ وَرَحْمَةٌ ط فَمَنِ اعْتَدٰى بَعْدَ ذٰلِكَ

فَلَهٗ عَذَابٌ اَلِيْمٌ ۝ وَلَكُمْ فِى الْقِصَاصِ حَيٰوةٌ

يٰٓاُولِى الْاَلْبَابِ لَعَلَّكُمْ تَتَّقُوْنَ ۝ كُتِبَ عَلَيْكُمْ اِذَا

حَضَرَ اَحَدَكُمُ الْمَوْتُ اِنْ تَرَكَ خَيْرَۨا الْوَصِيَّةُ

لِلْوَالِدَيْنِ وَالْاَقْرَبِيْنَ بِالْمَعْرُوْفِ ۚ حَقًّا عَلَى

الْمُتَّقِيْنَ ۝ فَمَنْ بَدَّلَهٗ بَعْدَ مَا سَمِعَهٗ فَاِنَّمَاۤ اِثْمُهٗ

عَلَى الَّذِيْنَ يُبَدِّلُوْنَهٗ ط اِنَّ اللّٰهَ سَمِيْعٌ عَلِيْمٌ ۝

فَمَنْ خَافَ مِنْ مُّوْصٍ جَنَفًا اَوْ اِثْمًا فَاَصْلَحَ

بَيْنَهُمْ فَلَاۤ اِثْمَ عَلَيْهِ ط اِنَّ اللّٰهَ غَفُوْرٌ رَّحِيْمٌ ۝

يٰٓاَيُّهَا الَّذِيْنَ اٰمَنُوْا كُتِبَ عَلَيْكُمُ الصِّيَامُ كَمَا كُتِبَ

عَلَى الَّذِيْنَ مِنْ قَبْلِكُمْ لَعَلَّكُمْ تَتَّقُوْنَ ۝ اَيَّامًا

مَّعْدُوْدٰتٍ ط فَمَنْ كَانَ مِنْكُمْ مَّرِيْضًا اَوْ عَلٰى سَفَرٍ

فَعِدَّةٌ مِّنْ اَيَّامٍ اُخَرَ ط وَعَلَى الَّذِيْنَ يُطِيْقُوْنَهٗ

فِدْيَةٌ طَعَامُ مِسْكِيْنٍ ط فَمَنْ تَطَوَّعَ خَيْرًا فَهُوَ

Being fair is a sign of being mindful and fearful of Allah.

The law of taking revenge for justice

[178] Believers, retribution is prescribed for you in the case of victims of murderers: a free man for a free man, a slave for a slave, and a woman for a woman. *However*, if the *culprit* is pardoned by his *aggrieved* brother, this will be adhered to in accordance with best practice, *the culprit* paying *the next of kin* what is due. This represents a *lightening of the burden* and an act of kindness from your Lord. After this *day* if anyone goes beyond *these limits,* they will suffer a painful punishment. [179] The people of understanding *will appreciate* that in the law of retribution there is *a means for preserving* life, so you're stopped from being unfair.

Instructions for writing a will

[180] *Also* prescribed for you *is the writing of a will*: when death approaches any of you, who is leaving behind wealth, let him prepare a will in favour of parents and close relatives in accordance with best practice; this is a duty upon those who are mindful *of Allah.* [181] If any *witness*, after hearing *the terms*, alters them then they – and they alone – has committed a sin. Allah is the Hearer, the Knower. [182] Anyone who suspects that a testator[a] has made a mistake intentionally or unintentionally, and tries to put things right between the parties, commits no sin in doing so. Allah is the Forgiving, the Kind.

The purpose of fasting in Ramadan

[183] Believers, fasting has been compulsory for you as it was made compulsory for those before you so you become mindful *of Allah.* [184] *Fast* for a fixed number of days, but if any of you is ill or on a journey then *let him fast* an *equivalent* number of days *later.* The obligatory compensation on those who *do not fast,* is to feed a needy person, *if they* can afford it. However, anyone who voluntarily does good will benefit from that, *but* to fast would be better for you, if you knew.

---

[a] The testator is the person who has made the will.

خَيْرٌ لَّهٗ ط وَاَنْ تَصُوْمُوْا خَيْرٌ لَّكُمْ اِنْ كُنْتُمْ
تَعْلَمُوْنَ ۞ شَهْرُ رَمَضَانَ الَّذِىْٓ اُنْزِلَ فِيْهِ
الْقُرْاٰنُ هُدًى لِّلنَّاسِ وَبَيِّنٰتٍ مِّنَ الْهُدٰى وَ
الْفُرْقَانِ ج فَمَنْ شَهِدَ مِنْكُمُ الشَّهْرَ فَلْيَصُمْهُ ط
وَمَنْ كَانَ مَرِيْضًا اَوْ عَلٰى سَفَرٍ فَعِدَّةٌ مِّنْ اَيَّامٍ
اُخَرَ ط يُرِيْدُ اللّٰهُ بِكُمُ الْيُسْرَ وَلَا يُرِيْدُ بِكُمُ الْعُسْرَ ز
وَلِتُكْمِلُوا الْعِدَّةَ وَلِتُكَبِّرُوا اللّٰهَ عَلٰى مَا هَدٰىكُمْ وَ
لَعَلَّكُمْ تَشْكُرُوْنَ ۞ وَاِذَا سَاَلَكَ عِبَادِىْ عَنِّىْ
فَاِنِّىْ قَرِيْبٌ ط اُجِيْبُ دَعْوَةَ الدَّاعِ اِذَا دَعَانِ ۙ
فَلْيَسْتَجِيْبُوْا لِىْ وَلْيُؤْمِنُوْا بِىْ لَعَلَّهُمْ يَرْشُدُوْنَ ۞
اُحِلَّ لَكُمْ لَيْلَةَ الصِّيَامِ الرَّفَثُ اِلٰى نِسَآئِكُمْ ط هُنَّ
لِبَاسٌ لَّكُمْ وَاَنْتُمْ لِبَاسٌ لَّهُنَّ ط عَلِمَ اللّٰهُ اَنَّكُمْ
كُنْتُمْ تَخْتَانُوْنَ اَنْفُسَكُمْ فَتَابَ عَلَيْكُمْ وَعَفَا عَنْكُمْ ج
فَالْـٰٔنَ بَاشِرُوْهُنَّ وَابْتَغُوْا مَا كَتَبَ اللّٰهُ لَكُمْ ۪ وَ
كُلُوْا وَاشْرَبُوْا حَتّٰى يَتَبَيَّنَ لَكُمُ الْخَيْطُ الْاَبْيَضُ مِنَ
الْخَيْطِ الْاَسْوَدِ مِنَ الْفَجْرِ ۪ ثُمَّ اَتِمُّوا الصِّيَامَ اِلَى
الَّيْلِ ۚ وَلَا تُبَاشِرُوْهُنَّ وَاَنْتُمْ عٰكِفُوْنَ ۙ فِى
الْمَسٰجِدِ ط تِلْكَ حُدُوْدُ اللّٰهِ فَلَا تَقْرَبُوْهَا ط كَذٰلِكَ
يُبَيِّنُ اللّٰهُ اٰيٰتِهٖ لِلنَّاسِ لَعَلَّهُمْ يَتَّقُوْنَ ۞ وَلَا
تَاْكُلُوْٓا اَمْوَالَكُمْ بَيْنَكُمْ بِالْبَاطِلِ وَتُدْلُوْا بِهَآ اِلَى

The Majestic Quran:
Divine directives,
recipe for success and
happiness.

The Quran was revealed in Ramadan

¹⁸⁵ The Quran was revealed in the month of Ramadan; *the Quran* is a guidance for people, it contains clear teachings and distinguishes *right from wrong*; whoever is present in the month must fast in it, but, if anyone is ill or on a journey, then *let them fast* an *equivalent* number of days *later*. Allah wants ease for you, not difficulty, and wants to see you complete the *compulsory* number *of fasts. So,* glorify Allah for guiding you, and be ever-thankful.

Allah answers our prayers

¹⁸⁶ If My servants ask you about Me, *tell them that* I am near, I answer *the* prayer of the prayerful whenever he prays to Me. So, let them obey Me, and believe in Me so they may be guided.

A rule for married couples in Ramadan

¹⁸⁷ It is permissible for you to sleep with your wives during the nights of the fast – they are *like* a garment for you, as you are for them.ᵃ Allah knew that you were deceiving yourselves *by what you were doing in secret*, and He has relented towards you and pardoned you. So now be intimate with them, and desire whatever Allah has allowed you, and eat and drink until the white streak of dawn is distinct from the blackness of the night, then complete the fast until the nightfall.ᵇ However, do not be intimate with your wives *on those nights* when you are engaged in a *spiritual* retreat in the Mosque. These are Allah's boundaries, so do not breach them. This is how Allah explains His verses for people, so they are mindful.

Bribery, fraud and squandering one's wealth are all immoral

¹⁸⁸ Do not misuse your wealth *by spending it* amongst yourselves for wrong purpose, or by deliberately bribing judges to misuse a part of other people's wealth wrongfully.

ᵃ   Literally translated as: "they are your garments and you are their garments". In other words, the sexual intimacy that husbands and wives enjoy helps cover them both in public like clothing, preventing them from acting indecently.

ᵇ   The white streak of dawn refers to the daybreak when the light is spread horizontally as the sun is 18° below the horizon.

٢٣
ع
٧

الْحُكَّامِ لِتَأْكُلُوْا فَرِيْقًا مِّنْ اَمْوَالِ النَّاسِ بِالْاِثْمِ وَاَنْتُمْ تَعْلَمُوْنَ ۞ يَسْئَلُوْنَكَ عَنِ الْاَهِلَّةِ ؕ قُلْ هِىَ مَوَاقِيْتُ لِلنَّاسِ وَالْحَجِّ ؕ وَلَيْسَ الْبِرُّ بِاَنْ تَأْتُوا الْبُيُوْتَ مِنْ ظُهُوْرِهَا وَلٰكِنَّ الْبِرَّ مَنِ اتَّقٰى ۚ وَأْتُوا الْبُيُوْتَ مِنْ اَبْوَابِهَا ۚ وَاتَّقُوا اللهَ لَعَلَّكُمْ تُفْلِحُوْنَ ۞

وَقَاتِلُوْا فِىْ سَبِيْلِ اللهِ الَّذِيْنَ يُقَاتِلُوْنَكُمْ وَلَا تَعْتَدُوْا ؕ اِنَّ اللهَ لَا يُحِبُّ الْمُعْتَدِيْنَ ۞ وَاقْتُلُوْهُمْ حَيْثُ ثَقِفْتُمُوْهُمْ وَاَخْرِجُوْهُمْ مِّنْ حَيْثُ اَخْرَجُوْكُمْ وَالْفِتْنَةُ اَشَدُّ مِنَ الْقَتْلِ ۚ وَلَا تُقٰتِلُوْهُمْ عِنْدَ الْمَسْجِدِ الْحَرَامِ حَتّٰى يُقٰتِلُوْكُمْ فِيْهِ ۚ فَاِنْ قٰتَلُوْكُمْ فَاقْتُلُوْهُمْ ؕ كَذٰلِكَ جَزَآءُ الْكٰفِرِيْنَ ۞ فَاِنِ انْتَهَوْا فَاِنَّ اللهَ غَفُوْرٌ رَّحِيْمٌ ۞ وَقٰتِلُوْهُمْ حَتّٰى لَا تَكُوْنَ فِتْنَةٌ وَّيَكُوْنَ الدِّيْنُ لِلهِ ؕ فَاِنِ انْتَهَوْا فَلَا عُدْوَانَ اِلَّا عَلَى الظّٰلِمِيْنَ ۞ اَلشَّهْرُ الْحَرَامُ بِالشَّهْرِ الْحَرَامِ وَالْحُرُمٰتُ قِصَاصٌ ؕ فَمَنِ اعْتَدٰى عَلَيْكُمْ فَاعْتَدُوْا عَلَيْهِ بِمِثْلِ مَا اعْتَدٰى عَلَيْكُمْ ۪ وَاتَّقُوا اللهَ وَاعْلَمُوْا اَنَّ اللهَ مَعَ الْمُتَّقِيْنَ ۞ وَاَنْفِقُوْا فِىْ سَبِيْلِ اللهِ وَلَا تُلْقُوْا بِاَيْدِيْكُمْ اِلَى التَّهْلُكَةِ ۛ ۚ وَاَحْسِنُوْا ۛ ؕ اِنَّ اللهَ يُحِبُّ الْمُحْسِنِيْنَ ۞ وَاَتِمُّوا الْحَجَّ وَالْعُمْرَةَ لِلهِ ؕ فَاِنْ اُحْصِرْتُمْ فَمَا

Fighting is allowed in self-defence, not offensively. Peace is the goal.

Examining supersitious practices

[189] They ask you about the crescent moon, say: "It is *to help* people keep track of time, *not least* for the pilgrimage". There is no virtue in entering homes from the back, but virtue lies in piety. Enter homes from front doors, and be mindful of Allah so you may be successful.

Fighting is only permitted in self-defence

[190] Fight in Allah's way those who fight you, but do not attack first. Allah does not like aggressors.[a] [191] *When in battle,* fight them wherever you find them, and expel them from where they expelled you. *A prolonged campaign of* persecution is far worse than *a decisive battle involving* killing. Do not attack them near the Sacred Mosque until they attack you. If they attack you, fight back; that is the way to deal with the disbelievers. [192] If they cease fighting, Allah is the Forgiving, the Kind.

Just retaliation to end persecution is allowed

[193] Fight them until there is no more persecution, and people are free to worship Allah. If they cease fighting, then let there be no hostility except against wrong-doers. [194] A sacred month always remains a sacred month; therefore, any violation of what Allah has forbidden calls for retaliation. If someone is hostile to you, respond in equal measure, and be mindful of Allah, and know *for certain* that Allah is with the pious. [195] Spend generously in Allah's way, but do not cast yourselves into *the jaws of* destruction by your own hands, and do your best. Allah loves those who do good[b].

---

[a] This verse and others which permit fighting are giving permission for self-defence only. This is an agreed opinion of all commentators and jurists. Fighting can only be authorised by legitimately elected governments, not self-proclaimed leaders. This passage was revealed when Muslims were performing the Umrah and were anxious about what to do if they were attacked by the Makkans.

[b] These six verses have four prohibitions; seven restrictions...The prevalent message of the Quran is one of peace and tolerance it allows self-defence (Abdal Haleem).

اسْتَيْسَرَ مِنَ الْهَدْيِ ۚ وَلَا تَحْلِقُوْا رُءُوْسَكُمْ حَتّٰى

يَبْلُغَ الْهَدْيُ مَحِلَّهٗ ؕ فَمَنْ كَانَ مِنْكُمْ مَّرِيْضًا اَوْ

بِهٖٓ اَذًى مِّنْ رَّاْسِهٖ فَفِدْيَةٌ مِّنْ صِيَامٍ اَوْ صَدَقَةٍ

اَوْ نُسُكٍ ۚ فَاِذَآ اَمِنْتُمْ ۚ فَمَنْ تَمَتَّعَ بِالْعُمْرَةِ

اِلَى الْحَجِّ فَمَا اسْتَيْسَرَ مِنَ الْهَدْيِ ۚ فَمَنْ لَّمْ

يَجِدْ فَصِيَامُ ثَلٰثَةِ اَيَّامٍ فِى الْحَجِّ وَ سَبْعَةٍ اِذَا

رَجَعْتُمْ ؕ تِلْكَ عَشَرَةٌ كَامِلَةٌ ؕ ذٰلِكَ لِمَنْ لَّمْ يَكُنْ

اَهْلُهٗ حَاضِرِى الْمَسْجِدِ الْحَرَامِ ؕ وَ اتَّقُوا اللّٰهَ

وَ اعْلَمُوْٓا اَنَّ اللّٰهَ شَدِيْدُ الْعِقَابِ ۞ اَلْحَجُّ اَشْهُرٌ

مَّعْلُوْمٰتٌ ۚ فَمَنْ فَرَضَ فِيْهِنَّ الْحَجَّ فَلَا رَفَثَ

وَلَا فُسُوْقَ ۙ وَلَا جِدَالَ فِى الْحَجِّ ؕ وَمَا تَفْعَلُوْا مِنْ

خَيْرٍ يَّعْلَمْهُ اللّٰهُ ؕ وَ تَزَوَّدُوْا فَاِنَّ خَيْرَ الزَّادِ

التَّقْوٰى ۫ وَ اتَّقُوْنِ يٰٓاُولِى الْاَلْبَابِ ۞ لَيْسَ عَلَيْكُمْ

جُنَاحٌ اَنْ تَبْتَغُوْا فَضْلًا مِّنْ رَّبِّكُمْ ؕ فَاِذَآ اَفَضْتُمْ

مِّنْ عَرَفٰتٍ فَاذْكُرُوا اللّٰهَ عِنْدَ الْمَشْعَرِ الْحَرَامِ ۪

وَ اذْكُرُوْهُ كَمَا هَدٰىكُمْ ۚ وَ اِنْ كُنْتُمْ مِّنْ قَبْلِهٖ

لَمِنَ الضَّآلِّيْنَ ۞ ثُمَّ اَفِيْضُوْا مِنْ حَيْثُ اَفَاضَ

النَّاسُ وَ اسْتَغْفِرُوا اللّٰهَ ؕ اِنَّ اللّٰهَ غَفُوْرٌ رَّحِيْمٌ ۞

فَاِذَا قَضَيْتُمْ مَّنَاسِكَكُمْ فَاذْكُرُوا اللّٰهَ كَذِكْرِكُمْ

اٰبَآءَكُمْ اَوْ اَشَدَّ ذِكْرًا ؕ فَمِنَ النَّاسِ مَنْ يَّقُوْلُ

What's the best preparation for life? Being mindful, awake and attentive to Allah!

٢٤
ع
٨

How to compensate for an incomplete pilgrimage

[196] Perform Hajj and Umrah for the sake of Allah. If you are prevented *from performing Umrah*, then *make* whatever sacrificial offering you can afford. Do not shave your heads until your offering has reached the place of sacrifice *in Mina*. If anyone of you is ill or has a disease of the scalp then he should fast, give in charity or make a sacrifice in compensation. When you are safe, then anyone wishing to combine Hajj and Umrah *must make* whatever sacrificial offering he can afford, *and* anyone who lacks the means to do so should fast for three days during the pilgrimage and seven days after returning home – that is ten days in all. This applies to those whose families do not live near the Sacred Mosque. Be mindful of Allah, and remember Allah's punishment is severe.

The rites of Hajj

[197] Hajj takes place in the specified months, and anyone undertaking this duty must not: engage in sexual intimacy *with one's spouse*; commit sin nor quarrel with each other. Whatever good you do, Allah knows it. Prepare yourselves *for Hajj*, and the best preparation is being mindful *of Allah*. People of understanding, be mindful of Me. [198] There is no sin in seeking your Lord's bounty *by offering a service whilst performing your Hajj*. When you leave Mount Arafat, remember Allah at the sacred place *of Muzdalifa*. Remember Him, because He guided you when, in the past, you were misguided. [199] Then set off from where *other* people set off, and seek Allah's forgiveness. Indeed, Allah is the Forgiving, the Compassionate.

The pilgrims' prayer

[200] Once you have completed your rites, remember Allah as you used to remember your ancestors, and even more. There are people who pray: "Our Lord, grant us *wealth* in this world", they will have no share in the Hereafter.

رَبَّنَاۤ اٰتِنَا فِي الدُّنْيَا وَمَا لَهٗ فِي الْاٰخِرَةِ مِنْ

خَلَاقٍ ۞ وَمِنْهُمْ مَّنْ يَّقُوْلُ رَبَّنَاۤ اٰتِنَا فِي

الدُّنْيَا حَسَنَةً وَّفِي الْاٰخِرَةِ حَسَنَةً وَّقِنَا عَذَابَ

النَّارِ ۞ اُولٰٓئِكَ لَهُمْ نَصِيْبٌ مِّمَّا كَسَبُوْا ط

وَاللهُ سَرِيْعُ الْحِسَابِ ۞ وَاذْكُرُوا اللهَ فِيْ اَيَّامٍ

مَّعْدُوْدٰتٍ ط فَمَنْ تَعَجَّلَ فِيْ يَوْمَيْنِ فَلَاۤ اِثْمَ

عَلَيْهِ ۚ وَمَنْ تَاَخَّرَ فَلَاۤ اِثْمَ عَلَيْهِ ۙ لِمَنِ اتَّقٰى ط

وَاتَّقُوا اللهَ وَاعْلَمُوْۤا اَنَّكُمْ اِلَيْهِ تُحْشَرُوْنَ ۞

وَمِنَ النَّاسِ مَنْ يُّعْجِبُكَ قَوْلُهٗ فِي الْحَيٰوةِ الدُّنْيَا

وَيُشْهِدُ اللهَ عَلٰى مَا فِيْ قَلْبِهٖ ۙ وَهُوَ اَلَدُّ

الْخِصَامِ ۞ وَاِذَا تَوَلّٰى سَعٰى فِي الْاَرْضِ لِيُفْسِدَ فِيْهَا

وَيُهْلِكَ الْحَرْثَ وَالنَّسْلَ ط وَاللهُ لَا يُحِبُّ الْفَسَادَ ۞

وَاِذَا قِيْلَ لَهُ اتَّقِ اللهَ اَخَذَتْهُ الْعِزَّةُ بِالْاِثْمِ

فَحَسْبُهٗ جَهَنَّمُ ط وَلَبِئْسَ الْمِهَادُ ۞ وَمِنَ النَّاسِ

مَنْ يَّشْرِيْ نَفْسَهُ ابْتِغَاۤءَ مَرْضَاتِ اللهِ ط وَاللهُ

رَءُوْفٌۢ بِالْعِبَادِ ۞ يٰۤاَيُّهَا الَّذِيْنَ اٰمَنُوا ادْخُلُوْا فِي

السِّلْمِ كَاۤفَّةً ۪ وَلَا تَتَّبِعُوْا خُطُوٰتِ الشَّيْطٰنِ ط اِنَّهٗ

لَكُمْ عَدُوٌّ مُّبِيْنٌ ۞ فَاِنْ زَلَلْتُمْ مِّنْۢ بَعْدِ مَا

جَاۤءَتْكُمُ الْبَيِّنٰتُ فَاعْلَمُوْۤا اَنَّ اللهَ عَزِيْزٌ حَكِيْمٌ ۞

هَلْ يَنْظُرُوْنَ اِلَّاۤ اَنْ يَّاْتِيَهُمُ اللهُ فِيْ ظُلَلٍ مِّنَ

Are you a full-time or a part-time Muslim? Have you fully committed yourself to Allah?

التَّغَابُن

[201] But others pray: "Our Lord, grant us good in this world and good in the Hereafter, and protect us from the punishment of the Fire". [202] Such *people* will have a *full* share of what they earned, and Allah is swift in calculating *good and bad deeds.* [203] Continue remembering Allah till specified days, but if anyone is in a hurry to leave after two days, *he can,* he will not have sinned, nor will anyone who delays his departure have sinned, so long as he is mindful *of Allah.* Be mindful of Allah, and know that you will be gathered before Him.

The troublemaker

[204] There is a *type of* person whose speech will please you, and he even calls on Allah as a witness to what is in his heart, yet he is the bitterest of opponents. [205] As soon as he turns away, he makes mischief in the land, destroying crops and cattle[a]. Allah detests mischief. [206] When he is told: "Fear Allah!" His pride leads him to sin. Hell will be enough for him. A dreadful place.

The peacemaker: committed to Allah

[207] Yet there is *another type* of person who would give away his life to gain Allah's pleasure; Allah is Compassionate to *His* servants. [208] Believers, submit and dedicate fully, and do not follow in the footsteps of Satan; he is your sworn enemy. [209] If you should turn back after clear signs have come to you, then know that Allah is the Almighty and the Wise. [210] What are they waiting for? Allah and the angels to come down in the shade of the clouds? By then, *their* fate will have been sealed. *In the end,* all matters will return to Allah.

---

[a] *"Al-hars wanasl"* is an idiom for human civilisation (Hans Wher), so they raid villages and towns destroying them.

الْغَمَامُ وَالْمَلَٰٓئِكَةُ وَقُضِيَ الْأَمْرُ ۖ وَإِلَى اللهِ تُرْجَعُ الْأُمُورُ ۝ سَلْ بَنِيٓ اِسْرَآئِيلَ كَمْ اٰتَيْنٰهُمْ مِنْ اٰيَةٍ بَيِّنَةٍ ۗ وَمَنْ يُبَدِّلْ نِعْمَةَ اللهِ مِنْ بَعْدِ مَا جَآءَتْهُ فَاِنَّ اللهَ شَدِيدُ الْعِقَابِ ۝ زُيِّنَ لِلَّذِينَ كَفَرُوا الْحَيٰوةُ الدُّنْيَا وَيَسْخَرُونَ مِنَ الَّذِينَ اٰمَنُوا ۘ وَالَّذِينَ اتَّقَوْا فَوْقَهُمْ يَوْمَ الْقِيٰمَةِ ۗ وَاللهُ يَرْزُقُ مَنْ يَشَآءُ بِغَيْرِ حِسَابٍ ۝ كَانَ النَّاسُ اُمَّةً وَّاحِدَةً ۫ فَبَعَثَ اللهُ النَّبِيّٖنَ مُبَشِّرِينَ وَمُنْذِرِينَ ۠ وَاَنْزَلَ مَعَهُمُ الْكِتٰبَ بِالْحَقِّ لِيَحْكُمَ بَيْنَ النَّاسِ فِيمَا اخْتَلَفُوا فِيهِ ۗ وَمَا اخْتَلَفَ فِيهِ اِلَّا الَّذِينَ اُوتُوهُ مِنْ بَعْدِ مَا جَآءَتْهُمُ الْبَيِّنٰتُ بَغْيًا بَيْنَهُمْ ۚ فَهَدَى اللهُ الَّذِينَ اٰمَنُوا لِمَا اخْتَلَفُوا فِيهِ مِنَ الْحَقِّ بِاِذْنِهِ ۗ وَاللهُ يَهْدِي مَنْ يَشَآءُ اِلَى صِرَاطٍ مُّسْتَقِيمٍ ۝ اَمْ حَسِبْتُمْ اَنْ تَدْخُلُوا الْجَنَّةَ وَلَمَّا يَأْتِكُمْ مَّثَلُ الَّذِينَ خَلَوْا مِنْ قَبْلِكُمْ ۗ مَسَّتْهُمُ الْبَأْسَآءُ وَ الضَّرَّآءُ وَزُلْزِلُوا حَتّٰى يَقُولَ الرَّسُولُ وَالَّذِينَ اٰمَنُوا مَعَهُ مَتٰى نَصْرُ اللهِ ۗ اَلَآ اِنَّ نَصْرَ اللهِ قَرِيبٌ ۝ يَسْئَلُونَكَ مَا ذَا يُنْفِقُونَ ۗ قُلْ مَآ اَنْفَقْتُمْ مِّنْ خَيْرٍ فَلِلْوَالِدَيْنِ وَالْاَقْرَبِينَ وَالْيَتٰمٰى وَالْمَسٰكِينِ

Do you think you will go to Paradise without paying for it? What is the payment?

Success in this life is no guarantee of success in the next

²¹¹ Ask the Israelites how many clear signs We gave them. Anyone who exchanges a gift of Allah *for something else* after it has been granted to him, *beware*; Allah is severe in *His* punishment. ²¹² The worldly life is attractive for the disbelievers; they may mock some believers *now*, but the pious *will rise* above them on Judgement Day. Allah will provide abundantly to those who He wishes.

Gaining knowledge prompts some people to argue

²¹³ Humanity was once a single nation. Then Allah sent prophets, who brought good news and warnings, and He sent with them the Book containing the truth, providing rulings to help people solve their differences. This was due to the rivalry that arose from differences *of interpretation* after clear signs had come to the People *of The Book*. However, Allah, by His authority, guided the believers to the truth regarding the point of disagreement. Allah guides to the straight path anyone who wants to be guided.

Every generation of believers has been tested

²¹⁴ Did you think of going to Paradise without experiencing the difficulties of those *who* came before you? They were struck by misfortune and hardships, and were subjected to Earthquakes, even the messenger *of that time* and those who believed him cried out: "When will Allah's help come?" Beware, the help of Allah is near. ²¹⁵ They ask you what they should spend *their wealth* on; tell them: "Spend on your parents, relatives, orphans, the needy and the travellers". Whatever good you have done Allah is the Knower *and is fully aware* of it.

وَابْنِ السَّبِيلِ ط وَمَا تَفْعَلُوا مِنْ خَيْرٍ فَإِنَّ اللّٰهَ

بِهِ عَلِيمٌ ۝ كُتِبَ عَلَيْكُمُ الْقِتَالُ وَهُوَ كُرْهٌ لَّكُمْ ج

وَعَسٰى أَنْ تَكْرَهُوا شَيْئًا وَّهُوَ خَيْرٌ لَّكُمْ ج وَعَسٰى

أَنْ تُحِبُّوا شَيْئًا وَّهُوَ شَرٌّ لَّكُمْ ط وَاللّٰهُ يَعْلَمُ وَ

أَنْتُمْ لَا تَعْلَمُونَ ۝ يَسْئَلُونَكَ عَنِ الشَّهْرِ الْحَرَامِ

قِتَالٍ فِيهِ ط قُلْ قِتَالٌ فِيهِ كَبِيرٌ ط وَصَدٌّ

عَنْ سَبِيلِ اللّٰهِ وَكُفْرٌ بِهِ وَالْمَسْجِدِ الْحَرَامِ

وَإِخْرَاجُ أَهْلِهِ مِنْهُ أَكْبَرُ عِنْدَ اللّٰهِ ج وَالْفِتْنَةُ

أَكْبَرُ مِنَ الْقَتْلِ ط وَلَا يَزَالُونَ يُقَاتِلُونَكُمْ حَتّٰى

يَرُدُّوكُمْ عَنْ دِينِكُمْ إِنِ اسْتَطَاعُوا ط وَمَنْ

يَّرْتَدِدْ مِنْكُمْ عَنْ دِينِهِ فَيَمُتْ وَهُوَ كَافِرٌ

فَأُولٰئِكَ حَبِطَتْ أَعْمَالُهُمْ فِي الدُّنْيَا وَالْأٰخِرَةِ ج

وَأُولٰئِكَ أَصْحَابُ النَّارِ ج هُمْ فِيهَا خٰلِدُونَ ۝

إِنَّ الَّذِينَ أٰمَنُوا وَالَّذِينَ هَاجَرُوا وَجَاهَدُوا فِي

سَبِيلِ اللّٰهِ لَا أُولٰئِكَ يَرْجُونَ رَحْمَتَ اللّٰهِ ط وَاللّٰهُ

غَفُورٌ رَّحِيمٌ ۝ يَسْئَلُونَكَ عَنِ الْخَمْرِ وَالْمَيْسِرِ ط

قُلْ فِيهِمَا إِثْمٌ كَبِيرٌ وَّمَنَافِعُ لِلنَّاسِ ز وَإِثْمُهُمَا

أَكْبَرُ مِنْ نَّفْعِهِمَا ط وَيَسْئَلُونَكَ مَا ذَا يُنْفِقُونَ ەؕ

قُلِ الْعَفْوَ ط كَذٰلِكَ يُبَيِّنُ اللّٰهُ لَكُمُ الْأٰيٰتِ لَعَلَّكُمْ

تَتَفَكَّرُونَ ۝ فِي الدُّنْيَا وَالْأٰخِرَةِ ط وَيَسْئَلُونَكَ عَنِ

The warriors of Allah: migrate, work hard for goodness and stand up for justice.

۲٦
ع
١٠

61

Jihad is compulsory

²¹⁶ War is ordained though you dislike it. *Sometimes,* you may dislike something that is good for you, and sometimes you may like something that is bad for you. Only Allah knows *the whole truth,* not you. ²¹⁷ They ask you about the sacred months, and *specifically* fighting in them; say: "Fighting in them is a major sin, but blocking the way of Allah and rejecting Him, *barring* access to the Sacred Mosque and expelling its residents from it – these are even greater *offences* in Allah's sight. *A prolonged campaign of* persecution is a far greater sin than *a decisive battle involving* killing". The *disbelievers* will go on fighting until they achieve what they want: that you give up your religion. *But beware.* If any of you gives up his religion and dies as a disbeliever, such people's deeds will come to nothing in this world and in the Hereafter. These are people of the Fire, where they will stay forever. ²¹⁸ The believers, who migrated and struggled in Allah's way, have *full* hope in Allah's Kindness. Allah is the Forgiving, the Kind.

Questions on alcohol, gambling, charity and orphans

²¹⁹ They ask you about wine and gambling; say: "Both are major sins, there is a small benefit for people, but the sin in them by far outweighs any benefits". They ask you what they should spend *in charity,* say: "Whatever you can spare". This is how Allah explains His verses to you so that you may reflect, ²²⁰ in this world, and the next. They also ask you about orphans, say: "Keeping *their affairs and accounts in order* is best. If you mix *your investments* with theirs, *remember that* they are your brothers and sisters, and Allah knows well who is straight and who is dishonest". If Allah so wished, He could put you in *all kinds* of difficulties. He is the Almighty, the Wise.

الْيَتٰمٰى ط قُلْ اِصْلَاحٌ لَّهُمْ خَيْرٌ ط وَاِنْ تُخَالِطُوْهُمْ فَاِخْوَانُكُمْ ط وَاللّٰهُ يَعْلَمُ الْمُفْسِدَ مِنَ الْمُصْلِحِ ط وَلَوْ شَآءَ اللّٰهُ لَاَعْنَتَكُمْ ط اِنَّ اللّٰهَ عَزِيْزٌ حَكِيْمٌ ۝ وَلَا تَنْكِحُوا الْمُشْرِكٰتِ حَتّٰى يُؤْمِنَّ ط وَلَاَمَةٌ مُّؤْمِنَةٌ خَيْرٌ مِّنْ مُّشْرِكَةٍ وَّلَوْ اَعْجَبَتْكُمْ ج وَلَا تُنْكِحُوا الْمُشْرِكِيْنَ حَتّٰى يُؤْمِنُوْا ط وَلَعَبْدٌ مُّؤْمِنٌ خَيْرٌ مِّنْ مُّشْرِكٍ وَّلَوْ اَعْجَبَكُمْ ط اُولٰٓئِكَ يَدْعُوْنَ اِلَى النَّارِ ج وَاللّٰهُ يَدْعُوْا اِلَى الْجَنَّةِ وَالْمَغْفِرَةِ بِاِذْنِهٖ ج

وَيُبَيِّنُ اٰيٰتِهٖ لِلنَّاسِ لَعَلَّهُمْ يَتَذَكَّرُوْنَ ۝ وَ يَسْئَلُوْنَكَ عَنِ الْمَحِيْضِ ط قُلْ هُوَ اَذًى ۙ فَاعْتَزِلُوا النِّسَآءَ فِي الْمَحِيْضِ ۙ وَلَا تَقْرَبُوْهُنَّ حَتّٰى يَطْهُرْنَ ج فَاِذَا تَطَهَّرْنَ فَأْتُوْهُنَّ مِنْ حَيْثُ اَمَرَكُمُ اللّٰهُ ط اِنَّ اللّٰهَ يُحِبُّ التَّوَّابِيْنَ وَيُحِبُّ الْمُتَطَهِّرِيْنَ ۝ نِسَآؤُكُمْ حَرْثٌ لَّكُمْ ۠ فَأْتُوْا حَرْثَكُمْ اَنّٰى شِئْتُمْ ۠ وَقَدِّمُوْا لِاَنْفُسِكُمْ ط وَاتَّقُوا اللّٰهَ وَاعْلَمُوْٓا اَنَّكُمْ مُّلٰقُوْهُ ط وَبَشِّرِ الْمُؤْمِنِيْنَ ۝ وَلَا تَجْعَلُوا اللّٰهَ عُرْضَةً لِّاَيْمَانِكُمْ اَنْ تَبَرُّوْا وَتَتَّقُوْا وَتُصْلِحُوْا بَيْنَ النَّاسِ ط وَاللّٰهُ سَمِيْعٌ عَلِيْمٌ ۝ لَا يُؤَاخِذُكُمُ اللّٰهُ بِاللَّغْوِ فِيْٓ اَيْمَانِكُمْ وَلٰكِنْ يُّؤَاخِذُكُمْ بِمَا كَسَبَتْ قُلُوْبُكُمْ ط وَاللّٰهُ غَفُوْرٌ حَلِيْمٌ ۝ لِلَّذِيْنَ

Going to Paradise or Hell may be determined by who one marries
²²¹ Do not marry disbelieving women[a] until they believe; a female slave who believes is better than an idolatress, even if the idolatress pleases you more. *Similarly*, do not marry *believing women to* any idolater until they believe; a male slave who believes is better than an idolater, even if the idolater is more pleasing. These *idolaters* invite you to the Fire, whereas Allah, by His grace, invites you to Paradise and forgiveness; and He explains His verses for people to remind them.

An answer to a question about menstruation and sexual intimacy
²²² They ask you about menstruation, say: "It is a sore state *that women go through*, so stay away from *sexual intimacy with* women during menstruation, and do not approach them *for that purpose* until they are clean again. However, once they are clean, come to them as Allah has allowed you. Allah loves those who repent, and He loves those who maintain cleanliness". ²²³ Your women are like pastures for you, so enter your pastures as you wish, and prepare for yourselves *good deeds*. Be mindful of Allah, remember you will meet Him, and you, *Muhammad, continue to* give good news to the believers".

Ruling about settling marital disputes
²²⁴ Do not make your oaths in the name of Allah an excuse to stop you from doing good, being mindful, and reconciling people *who are undergoing some marital dispute*; Allah is the Hearer, the Knower. ²²⁵ Allah will not hold your thoughtless oaths against you, but He will take you to task over your heart's *intentions*. Allah is The Forgiving, The Gentle.

---

[a] *"Mushrik"* refers to the idolaters and idol worshippers, and therefore refers to a special kind of disbelief.

يُؤْلُوْنَ مِنْ نِّسَآئِهِمْ تَرَبُّصُ اَرْبَعَةِ اَشْهُرٍ ۚ

فَاِنْ فَآءُوْ فَاِنَّ اللّٰهَ غَفُوْرٌ رَّحِيْمٌ ۞ وَاِنْ عَزَمُوا

الطَّلَاقَ فَاِنَّ اللّٰهَ سَمِيْعٌ عَلِيْمٌ ۞ وَالْمُطَلَّقٰتُ

يَتَرَبَّصْنَ بِاَنْفُسِهِنَّ ثَلٰثَةَ قُرُوْءٍ ۚ وَلَا يَحِلُّ لَهُنَّ

اَنْ يَّكْتُمْنَ مَا خَلَقَ اللّٰهُ فِيْٓ اَرْحَامِهِنَّ اِنْ كُنَّ

يُؤْمِنَّ بِاللّٰهِ وَالْيَوْمِ الْاٰخِرِ ۚ وَبُعُوْلَتُهُنَّ اَحَقُّ

بِرَدِّهِنَّ فِيْ ذٰلِكَ اِنْ اَرَادُوْٓا اِصْلَاحًا ۚ وَلَهُنَّ

مِثْلُ الَّذِيْ عَلَيْهِنَّ بِالْمَعْرُوْفِ ۚ وَلِلرِّجَالِ عَلَيْهِنَّ

درَجَةٌ ۗ وَاللّٰهُ عَزِيْزٌ حَكِيْمٌ ۞ اَلطَّلَاقُ مَرَّتٰنِ ۖ

فَاِمْسَاكٌ بِمَعْرُوْفٍ اَوْ تَسْرِيْحٌ بِاِحْسَانٍ ۗ وَلَا يَحِلُّ

لَكُمْ اَنْ تَأْخُذُوْا مِمَّآ اٰتَيْتُمُوْهُنَّ شَيْئًا اِلَّآ اَنْ

يَّخَافَآ اَلَّا يُقِيْمَا حُدُوْدَ اللّٰهِ ۚ فَاِنْ خِفْتُمْ اَلَّا

يُقِيْمَا حُدُوْدَ اللّٰهِ ۙ فَلَا جُنَاحَ عَلَيْهِمَا فِيْمَا

افْتَدَتْ بِهٖ ۗ تِلْكَ حُدُوْدُ اللّٰهِ فَلَا تَعْتَدُوْهَا ۚ وَ

مَنْ يَّتَعَدَّ حُدُوْدَ اللّٰهِ فَاُولٰٓئِكَ هُمُ الظّٰلِمُوْنَ ۞

فَاِنْ طَلَّقَهَا فَلَا تَحِلُّ لَهٗ مِنْۢ بَعْدُ حَتّٰى تَنْكِحَ

زَوْجًا غَيْرَهٗ ۗ فَاِنْ طَلَّقَهَا فَلَا جُنَاحَ عَلَيْهِمَآ اَنْ

يَّتَرَاجَعَآ اِنْ ظَنَّآ اَنْ يُّقِيْمَا حُدُوْدَ اللّٰهِ ۗ وَتِلْكَ

حُدُوْدُ اللّٰهِ يُبَيِّنُهَا لِقَوْمٍ يَّعْلَمُوْنَ ۞ وَاِذَا طَلَّقْتُمُ

النِّسَآءَ فَبَلَغْنَ اَجَلَهُنَّ فَاَمْسِكُوْهُنَّ بِمَعْرُوْفٍ

Be kind and caring even during the divorce proceedings.

٢٨
ع
١٢

65

[226] For those who take an oath to *separate from* their wives, the waiting period is four months, but if they go back on their oath, then they will find Allah Forgiving, Most Kind. [227] However, if they are determined to divorce, then Allah is the Hearer and the Knower.

The rights and responsibilities of married couples and of divorcees

[228] Divorced women must wait for three menstrual cycles *before they can marry*; it is not lawful for them to keep secret what Allah has created in their womb if they believe in Allah and the Last Day. Their husbands have the right to take them back during this period, if they wish to be reconciled. Women too have rights and responsibilities in equal measure, according to the custom. However, men have an *additional* degree *of rights and responsibilities* over them. Allah is The Almighty, The Wise.

What to do if marriage guidance and reconciliation fail

[229] A revokable divorce *may be pronounced* twice only; after that *a wife* must either be kept honourably or allowed to leave honourably. It is not lawful for you *husbands* to take back anything that you have given them, except when both parties fear that they may not be able to live within Allah's boundaries. However, if, *after attempting reconciliation*, you believe that the couple may not be able to live within the bounds set by Allah, then there will be no blame on either if *the woman* chooses to give back part of her settlement. These are Allah's boundaries, so do not overstep them. Only the wrongdoers overstep Allah's boundaries.

Third time divorce

[230] If *the husband* divorces her *a third time*; she will no longer be lawful for him *to remarry* until she marries another husband. Then, if *the second husband* divorces her, there will be no blame on either of them to return to each other, provided they feel confident that they will keep within Allah's boundaries. These are Allah's boundaries which He has explained for people who understand.

أَوْ سَرِّحُوْهُنَّ بِمَعْرُوْفٍ ۪ وَّلَا تُمْسِكُوْهُنَّ ضِرَارًا
لِّتَعْتَدُوْا ۚ وَمَنْ يَّفْعَلْ ذٰلِكَ فَقَدْ ظَلَمَ نَفْسَهٗ ؕ
وَلَا تَتَّخِذُوْٓا اٰيٰتِ اللّٰهِ هُزُوًا ۫ وَّاذْكُرُوْا نِعْمَتَ اللّٰهِ
عَلَيْكُمْ وَمَآ اَنْزَلَ عَلَيْكُمْ مِّنَ الْكِتٰبِ وَالْحِكْمَةِ
يَعِظُكُمْ بِهٖ ؕ وَاتَّقُوا اللّٰهَ وَاعْلَمُوْٓا اَنَّ اللّٰهَ بِكُلِّ
شَيْءٍ عَلِيْمٌ ﴿٢٣١﴾ وَاِذَا طَلَّقْتُمُ النِّسَآءَ فَبَلَغْنَ
ع ٢٩ ٣ ١٣ الثلثة
اَجَلَهُنَّ فَلَا تَعْضُلُوْهُنَّ اَنْ يَّنْكِحْنَ اَزْوَاجَهُنَّ
اِذَا تَرَاضَوْا بَيْنَهُمْ بِالْمَعْرُوْفِ ؕ ذٰلِكَ يُوْعَظُ بِهٖ
مَنْ كَانَ مِنْكُمْ يُؤْمِنُ بِاللّٰهِ وَالْيَوْمِ الْاٰخِرِ ؕ
ذٰلِكُمْ اَزْكٰى لَكُمْ وَاَطْهَرُ ؕ وَاللّٰهُ يَعْلَمُ وَاَنْتُمْ
لَا تَعْلَمُوْنَ ﴿٢٣٢﴾ وَالْوَالِدٰتُ يُرْضِعْنَ اَوْلَادَهُنَّ
حَوْلَيْنِ كَامِلَيْنِ لِمَنْ اَرَادَ اَنْ يُّتِمَّ الرَّضَاعَةَ ؕ
وَعَلَى الْمَوْلُوْدِ لَهٗ رِزْقُهُنَّ وَكِسْوَتُهُنَّ بِالْمَعْرُوْفِ ؕ
لَا تُكَلَّفُ نَفْسٌ اِلَّا وُسْعَهَا ۚ لَا تُضَآرَّ وَالِدَةٌۢ
بِوَلَدِهَا وَلَا مَوْلُوْدٌ لَّهٗ بِوَلَدِهٖ ۗ وَعَلَى الْوَارِثِ
مِثْلُ ذٰلِكَ ۚ فَاِنْ اَرَادَا فِصَالًا عَنْ تَرَاضٍ مِّنْهُمَا
وَتَشَاوُرٍ فَلَا جُنَاحَ عَلَيْهِمَا ؕ وَاِنْ اَرَدْتُّمْ اَنْ
تَسْتَرْضِعُوْٓا اَوْلَادَكُمْ فَلَا جُنَاحَ عَلَيْكُمْ اِذَا سَلَّمْتُمْ
مَّآ اٰتَيْتُمْ بِالْمَعْرُوْفِ ؕ وَاتَّقُوا اللّٰهَ وَاعْلَمُوْٓا اَنَّ
اللّٰهَ بِمَا تَعْمَلُوْنَ بَصِيْرٌ ﴿٢٣٣﴾ وَالَّذِيْنَ يُتَوَفَّوْنَ

Concern for children's welfare during divorce. Who will take care of them?

Don't be unjust when going through divorce

²³¹ When you divorce women, and they reach the end of the waiting period, either keep them honourably or allow them to leave honourably. Don't hold on to them to cause harm or to transgress Allah's boundaries; whoever does so has wronged himself. Do not play with the commands of Allah. Remember His favours on you and what He has revealed to you of the Book and wisdom, through which He teaches you. So be mindful of Allah, and know that He is the Knower. ²³² When you divorce women, and they reach the end of the waiting period, do not prevent them remarrying their *former* husbands, if they choose to do so by mutual consent *and* according to the custom. Anyone who sincerely believes in Allah and the Last Day is instructed to do this. This is a purer and cleaner *way* for you by far. Allah knows that which you don't know.

A father will pay maintenance expenses for his children

²³³ *Divorced* mothers may breastfeed their children up to full two years; that is if they wish to complete the full term. The father of the child is responsible for *the mother's* food and clothing in accordance with the best practice. *However,* no one is to be burdened over and above their means. Neither should the mother be harmed because of her child, nor the father. The same goes for the *father's* heirs. No one shall be to blame if *the father or the mother* wishes to wean the child, and it is agreed by mutual consent after proper consultation. *Likewise,* if you wish to employ a nanny for your children, you can't be blamed, if you pay as agreed in accordance with the best practice. *Always* be mindful of Allah, and know that He sees what you do.

مِنْكُمْ وَيَذَرُوْنَ أَزْوَاجًا يَّتَرَبَّصْنَ بِأَنْفُسِهِنَّ

أَرْبَعَةَ أَشْهُرٍ وَّعَشْرًا ۚ فَإِذَا بَلَغْنَ أَجَلَهُنَّ

فَلَا جُنَاحَ عَلَيْكُمْ فِيْمَا فَعَلْنَ فِيْ أَنْفُسِهِنَّ

بِالْمَعْرُوْفِ ط وَاللّٰهُ بِمَا تَعْمَلُوْنَ خَبِيْرٌ ۝ وَلَا

جُنَاحَ عَلَيْكُمْ فِيْمَا عَرَّضْتُمْ بِهٖ مِنْ خِطْبَةِ

النِّسَآءِ أَوْ أَكْنَنْتُمْ فِيْ أَنْفُسِكُمْ ط عَلِمَ اللّٰهُ أَنَّكُمْ

سَتَذْكُرُوْنَهُنَّ وَلٰكِنْ لَّا تُوَاعِدُوْهُنَّ سِرًّا إِلَّا أَنْ

تَقُوْلُوْا قَوْلًا مَّعْرُوْفًا ط وَلَا تَعْزِمُوْا عُقْدَةَ النِّكَاحِ

حَتّٰى يَبْلُغَ الْكِتٰبُ أَجَلَهٗ ط وَاعْلَمُوْٓا أَنَّ اللّٰهَ يَعْلَمُ

مَا فِيْ أَنْفُسِكُمْ فَاحْذَرُوْهُ ۚ وَاعْلَمُوْٓا أَنَّ اللّٰهَ غَفُوْرٌ

Marriage is the preferred state to be in, so Allah encourages "get married again after the divorce".

حَلِيْمٌ ۝ لَا جُنَاحَ عَلَيْكُمْ إِنْ طَلَّقْتُمُ النِّسَآءَ مَالَمْ

تَمَسُّوْهُنَّ أَوْ تَفْرِضُوْا لَهُنَّ فَرِيْضَةً ۖ وَّمَتِّعُوْهُنَّ ۚ

عَلَى الْمُوْسِعِ قَدَرُهٗ وَعَلَى الْمُقْتِرِ قَدَرُهٗ ۚ مَتَاعًا

بِالْمَعْرُوْفِ ۚ حَقًّا عَلَى الْمُحْسِنِيْنَ ۝ وَإِنْ طَلَّقْتُمُوْهُنَّ

مِنْ قَبْلِ أَنْ تَمَسُّوْهُنَّ وَقَدْ فَرَضْتُمْ لَهُنَّ

فَرِيْضَةً فَنِصْفُ مَا فَرَضْتُمْ إِلَّآ أَنْ يَّعْفُوْنَ أَوْ

يَعْفُوَا الَّذِيْ بِيَدِهٖ عُقْدَةُ النِّكَاحِ ط وَأَنْ تَعْفُوْٓا

أَقْرَبُ لِلتَّقْوٰى ط وَلَا تَنْسَوُا الْفَضْلَ بَيْنَكُمْ ط إِنَّ

اللّٰهَ بِمَا تَعْمَلُوْنَ بَصِيْرٌ ۝ حَافِظُوْا عَلَى الصَّلَوٰتِ

وَالصَّلٰوةِ الْوُسْطٰى ۙ وَقُوْمُوْا لِلّٰهِ قٰنِتِيْنَ ۝ فَإِنْ

The waiting period for widows, and encouragement to remarry
234 Those who die, leaving behind widows, *their widows* should wait for four months and ten *days* then, once they have reached *the end of* this period, there is no blame on you regarding whatever they choose to do with themselves in accordance with the best practice. Allah is aware of what you do. 235 There is no blame on you if you propose engagement to *these* women *before the end of the waiting period*, or you keep *your feelings* to yourself. Allah knows that you intend to propose to them. However, do not make them any promises unless you speak to them in a respectful way, and do not confirm contracting the marriage until the prescribed *waiting* term has ended. Remember that Allah knows what is in your hearts, so beware. Allah is the Forgiving, The Gentle.

What to do if divorce occurs before a marriage is consummated
236 There is no blame on you if you divorce a woman before either consummating the marriage or paying the marriage gift. Let the rich and the poor each give them generously according to their means; this is a duty on the righteous. 237 If you divorce them before consummation but after fixing the marriage gift, then let them have half of what you had previously settled on, unless *the women* agree to waive their right or the one contracting the marriage tie waives his right, and waiving one's right is nearer to piety. So, do not forget to be gracious to each other, *because* Allah sees all that you do.

Never neglect your prayers under any circumstances
238 Make sure to perform your *daily* prayers, particularly the middle prayer *Asr*, and stand devoutly before Allah.

خِفْتُمْ فَرِجَالًا اَوْ رُكْبَانًا ۚ فَاِذَآ اَمِنْتُمْ فَاذْكُرُوا

اللّٰهَ كَمَا عَلَّمَكُمْ مَّا لَمْ تَكُوْنُوْا تَعْلَمُوْنَ ۝ وَ

الَّذِيْنَ يُتَوَفَّوْنَ مِنْكُمْ وَيَذَرُوْنَ اَزْوَاجًا ۖ

وَّصِيَّةً لِّاَزْوَاجِهِمْ مَّتَاعًا اِلَى الْحَوْلِ غَيْرَ

اِخْرَاجٍ ۚ فَاِنْ خَرَجْنَ فَلَا جُنَاحَ عَلَيْكُمْ فِيْ مَا

فَعَلْنَ فِيْٓ اَنْفُسِهِنَّ مِنْ مَّعْرُوْفٍ ۗ وَاللّٰهُ عَزِيْزٌ

حَكِيْمٌ ۝ وَلِلْمُطَلَّقٰتِ مَتَاعٌۢ بِالْمَعْرُوْفِ ۗ حَقًّا

عَلَى الْمُتَّقِيْنَ ۝ كَذٰلِكَ يُبَيِّنُ اللّٰهُ لَكُمْ اٰيٰتِهٖ

Give freely, just as you have received freely.

لَعَلَّكُمْ تَعْقِلُوْنَ ۝ اَلَمْ تَرَ اِلَى الَّذِيْنَ خَرَجُوْا

مِنْ دِيَارِهِمْ وَهُمْ اُلُوْفٌ حَذَرَ الْمَوْتِ ۙ

فَقَالَ لَهُمُ اللّٰهُ مُوْتُوْا ۖ ثُمَّ اَحْيَاهُمْ ۗ اِنَّ اللّٰهَ

لَذُوْ فَضْلٍ عَلَى النَّاسِ وَلٰكِنَّ اَكْثَرَ النَّاسِ

لَا يَشْكُرُوْنَ ۝ وَقَاتِلُوْا فِيْ سَبِيْلِ اللّٰهِ وَاعْلَمُوْٓا

اَنَّ اللّٰهَ سَمِيْعٌ عَلِيْمٌ ۝ مَنْ ذَا الَّذِيْ يُقْرِضُ

اللّٰهَ قَرْضًا حَسَنًا فَيُضٰعِفَهٗ لَهٗٓ اَضْعَافًا كَثِيْرَةً ۗ

وَاللّٰهُ يَقْبِضُ وَيَبْصُۜطُ ۖ وَاِلَيْهِ تُرْجَعُوْنَ ۝ اَلَمْ

تَرَ اِلَى الْمَلَاِ مِنْۢ بَنِيْٓ اِسْرَآءِيْلَ مِنْۢ بَعْدِ مُوْسٰى ۘ

اِذْ قَالُوْا لِنَبِيٍّ لَّهُمُ ابْعَثْ لَنَا مَلِكًا نُّقَاتِلْ

فِيْ سَبِيْلِ اللّٰهِ ۗ قَالَ هَلْ عَسَيْتُمْ اِنْ كُتِبَ

عَلَيْكُمُ الْقِتَالُ اَلَّا تُقَاتِلُوْا ۗ قَالُوْا وَمَا لَنَآ اَلَّا

²³⁹ If you are fearful *of an enemy*, then pray standing or in the saddle; then, when you are safe and secure once more, then remember Allah, as He taught you what you didn't know.

Further rulings on maintenance for widows and divorcees
²⁴⁰ Those who die, leaving behind widows, should make a will for their maintenance for one year: they should not be expelled *from the family home*. However, if they *choose to* leave *the family home*, then you can't be blamed with regards to what they have chosen to do in line with custom. Allah is the Almighty and Wise. ²⁴¹ Divorced women are entitled to maintenance[a] in line with custom; this is a duty on the pious. ²⁴² This is how Allah explains His verses for you, so that you might understand.

The story of the Jewish King Talut
²⁴³ Haven't you seen those who left their homes in their thousands for fear of death, and Allah said to them: "Die!" And then He brought them back to life?[b] Allah is very gracious to people, but they are ungrateful. ²⁴⁴ Fight in the cause of Allah, and remember He is the Hearer, the Knower. ²⁴⁵ Who will offer Allah a loan, a beautiful loan, He will multiply its reward many times over. Allah withholds *His favour*, or He gives plenty, and to Him you will return.

The Israelites demand a king
²⁴⁶ Have you not considered the Jewish leaders *who came after* Musa. They said to a prophet of theirs: "Appoint a king so that we may fight in Allah's way". He said to them: "When fighting is ordained for you, will you fight?" They said: "Why would we not fight in the way of Allah when we and our children have been expelled from our homes?" When fighting was ordained for them, they turned away except for a few of them. Allah knows the disobedient.

---

[a] Mata'un is the post-divorce financial support a woman receives. According to Tabari it is an obligation on the husband: "Mut'ah is mandatory for all divorced women".

[b] This refers to the story below of a community of the Jews who refused to take part in Jihad as ordered by their king, Talut, known as Saul in the Bible.

نُقَاتِلَ فِيْ سَبِيْلِ اللهِ وَقَدْ أُخْرِجْنَا مِنْ دِيَارِنَا

وَأَبْنَآئِنَا ۖ فَلَمَّا كُتِبَ عَلَيْهِمُ الْقِتَالُ تَوَلَّوْا

اِلَّا قَلِيْلًا مِّنْهُمْ ۗ وَاللهُ عَلِيْمٌۢ بِالظّٰلِمِيْنَ ۝

وَقَالَ لَهُمْ نَبِيُّهُمْ اِنَّ اللهَ قَدْ بَعَثَ لَكُمْ

طَالُوْتَ مَلِكًا ۚ قَالُوْٓا اَنّٰى يَكُوْنُ لَهُ الْمُلْكُ

عَلَيْنَا وَنَحْنُ اَحَقُّ بِالْمُلْكِ مِنْهُ وَلَمْ يُؤْتَ

سَعَةً مِّنَ الْمَالِ ۚ قَالَ اِنَّ اللهَ اصْطَفٰهُ عَلَيْكُمْ

وَزَادَهٗ بَسْطَةً فِى الْعِلْمِ وَالْجِسْمِ ۗ وَاللهُ يُؤْتِيْ

مُلْكَهٗ مَنْ يَّشَآءُ ۗ وَاللهُ وَاسِعٌ عَلِيْمٌ ۝ وَقَالَ

لَهُمْ نَبِيُّهُمْ اِنَّ اٰيَةَ مُلْكِهٖٓ اَنْ يَّاْتِيَكُمُ التَّابُوْتُ

فِيْهِ سَكِيْنَةٌ مِّنْ رَّبِّكُمْ وَبَقِيَّةٌ مِّمَّا تَرَكَ اٰلُ

مُوْسٰى وَاٰلُ هٰرُوْنَ تَحْمِلُهُ الْمَلٰٓئِكَةُ ۗ اِنَّ فِيْ

ذٰلِكَ لَاٰيَةً لَّكُمْ اِنْ كُنْتُمْ مُّؤْمِنِيْنَ ۝ فَلَمَّا

فَصَلَ طَالُوْتُ بِالْجُنُوْدِ ۙ قَالَ اِنَّ اللهَ مُبْتَلِيْكُمْ

بِنَهَرٍ ۚ فَمَنْ شَرِبَ مِنْهُ فَلَيْسَ مِنِّيْ ۚ وَمَنْ

لَّمْ يَطْعَمْهُ فَاِنَّهٗ مِنِّيْٓ اِلَّا مَنِ اغْتَرَفَ غُرْفَةً

بِيَدِهٖ ۚ فَشَرِبُوْا مِنْهُ اِلَّا قَلِيْلًا مِّنْهُمْ ۗ فَلَمَّا

جَاوَزَهٗ هُوَ وَالَّذِيْنَ اٰمَنُوْا مَعَهٗ ۙ قَالُوْا لَا طَاقَةَ

لَنَا الْيَوْمَ بِجَالُوْتَ وَجُنُوْدِهٖ ۗ قَالَ الَّذِيْنَ يَظُنُّوْنَ

اَنَّهُمْ مُّلٰقُوا اللهِ ۙ كَمْ مِّنْ فِئَةٍ قَلِيْلَةٍ غَلَبَتْ

Don't be critical, show respect for authority and listen.

Talut is the King

[247] Their prophet said to them: "Allah has appointed Talut to be your king". They said: "How can he be our king, when we have more right to kingship than him, he is not wealthy enough?" He replied: "Allah has selected him for you, given him vast knowledge and phyiscal strength. Allah gives His kingship to anyone He finds suitable. Allah is boundlessly Vast, He is The Knower". [248] And their Prophet said to them: "The sign of his kingship is The Ark *of the Contract,* which will be brought to you by the angels,[a] a source of tranquillity from your Lord which contains relics left behind by families of Musa and Harun. In this there are signs for you, if you believe".

Talut's soldiers fail the test

[249] When Talut set out with his army, he said: "Allah will test you near the river. Anyone who drinks from it will no longer be my *soldier,* but whoever does not taste it will be mine, except those who scoop it up in the palm of their hands". So, they all drank from it, except a few of them. When he crossed *the river* along with those who had believed him, they said: "We have no strength today to fight Jalut and his army". But those who believed that they would meet their Lord said: "How many times have small forces defeated large forces with the help of Allah, and Allah is with the patient".

---

[a] The Ark was a wooden chest containing the two stone tablets with the Ten Commandments. The Israelites treasured it as a sacred sign of God's presence among them.

فِئَةً كَثِيْرَةً بِإِذْنِ اللّٰهِ ۖ وَاللّٰهُ مَعَ الصّٰبِرِيْنَ ۞

وَلَمَّا بَرَزُوْا لِجَالُوْتَ وَ جُنُوْدِهٖ قَالُوْا رَبَّنَا

اَفْرِغْ عَلَيْنَا صَبْرًا وَّ ثَبِّتْ اَقْدَامَنَا وَانْصُرْنَا

عَلَى الْقَوْمِ الْكٰفِرِيْنَ ۞ فَهَزَمُوْهُمْ بِإِذْنِ اللّٰهِ ۙ

وَقَتَلَ دَاوٗدُ جَالُوْتَ وَ اٰتٰىهُ اللّٰهُ الْمُلْكَ وَ الْحِكْمَةَ

وَعَلَّمَهٗ مِمَّا يَشَآءُ ۗ وَلَوْ لَا دَفْعُ اللّٰهِ النَّاسَ

بَعْضَهُمْ بِبَعْضٍ ۙ لَّفَسَدَتِ الْاَرْضُ وَلٰكِنَّ

اللّٰهَ ذُوْ فَضْلٍ عَلَى الْعٰلَمِيْنَ ۞ تِلْكَ اٰيٰتُ اللّٰهِ

نَتْلُوْهَا عَلَيْكَ بِالْحَقِّ ۗ وَاِنَّكَ لَمِنَ الْمُرْسَلِيْنَ ۞

Spend generously to gain Allah's pleasure before it's too late.

تِلْكَ الرُّسُلُ فَضَّلْنَا بَعْضَهُمْ عَلٰى بَعْضٍ ۘ

مِنْهُمْ مَّنْ كَلَّمَ اللّٰهُ وَ رَفَعَ بَعْضَهُمْ دَرَجٰتٍ ۗ وَ

اٰتَيْنَا عِيْسَى ابْنَ مَرْيَمَ الْبَيِّنٰتِ وَ اَيَّدْنٰهُ بِرُوْحِ

الْقُدُسِ ۗ وَلَوْ شَآءَ اللّٰهُ مَا اقْتَتَلَ الَّذِيْنَ مِنْ

بَعْدِهِمْ مِّنْ بَعْدِ مَا جَآءَتْهُمُ الْبَيِّنٰتُ وَلٰكِنِ

اخْتَلَفُوْا فَمِنْهُمْ مَّنْ اٰمَنَ وَمِنْهُمْ مَّنْ كَفَرَ ۚ

وَلَوْ شَآءَ اللّٰهُ مَا اقْتَتَلُوْا ۙ وَلٰكِنَّ اللّٰهَ يَفْعَلُ مَا

يُرِيْدُ ۞ يٰٓاَيُّهَا الَّذِيْنَ اٰمَنُوْٓا اَنْفِقُوْا مِمَّا رَزَقْنٰكُمْ

مِّنْ قَبْلِ اَنْ يَّاْتِيَ يَوْمٌ لَّا بَيْعٌ فِيْهِ وَلَا خُلَّةٌ وَّلَا

شَفَاعَةٌ ۗ وَالْكٰفِرُوْنَ هُمُ الظّٰلِمُوْنَ ۞ اَللّٰهُ لَآ اِلٰهَ

اِلَّا هُوَ ۚ اَلْحَيُّ الْقَيُّوْمُ ۚ لَا تَاْخُذُهٗ سِنَةٌ وَّلَا

The faithful Israelites are victorious

²⁵⁰ When they advanced to face Jalut and his army, they prayed: "Our Lord, shower patience on us, keep our feet firm *on the ground*, and help us against the disbelievers". ²⁵¹ So, by the help of Allah they defeated them, and Dawud killed Jalut, and Allah gave Dawud kingship and wisdom, and taught him what it pleased Him to teach. If Allah did not repel one group of people with another there would be a lot of conflict on Earth, but Allah is Most Gracious to His creatures. ²⁵² These are the exact verses of Allah that We recite to you, and you are one of the Messengers.

Allah has placed the Prophets in ranks

²⁵³ Of these prophets We ranked some above others; Allah spoke with some, and others He raised *many* degrees. *For example*, We gave Isa, son of Maryam, many miracles, and supported him with the Spirit of the Holy One. If Allah had so wanted, *the Christians* would not have fought each other after the miracles had come to them, but they disputed. Some of them believed and others disbelieved. If Allah wanted, they would not have divided into sects, but Allah does what is just. ²⁵⁴ Believers, spend *in charity* from what We provided you before that day comes when there will be no buying and selling, no friendship and no intercession; the disbelievers are wicked people.

العربية

نَوْمٌ ط لَهُ مَا فِي السَّمٰوٰتِ وَمَا فِي الْأَرْضِ ط مَنْ ذَا

الَّذِيْ يَشْفَعُ عِنْدَهُ إِلَّا بِإِذْنِهِ ط يَعْلَمُ مَا بَيْنَ

أَيْدِيْهِمْ وَمَا خَلْفَهُمْ ج وَلَا يُحِيْطُوْنَ بِشَيْءٍ مِّنْ

عِلْمِهِ إِلَّا بِمَا شَاءَ ج وَسِعَ كُرْسِيُّهُ السَّمٰوٰتِ

وَالْأَرْضَ ج وَلَا يَئُوْدُهُ حِفْظُهُمَا ج وَهُوَ الْعَلِيُّ

الْعَظِيْمُ ۲۵۵ لَا إِكْرَاهَ فِي الدِّيْنِ قلى قَدْ تَّبَيَّنَ الرُّشْدُ

مِنَ الْغَيِّ ج فَمَنْ يَّكْفُرْ بِالطَّاغُوْتِ وَيُؤْمِنْ بِاللهِ

فَقَدِ اسْتَمْسَكَ بِالْعُرْوَةِ الْوُثْقٰى لَا انْفِصَامَ لَهَا ط

وَاللهُ سَمِيْعٌ عَلِيْمٌ ۲۵۶ اَللهُ وَلِيُّ الَّذِيْنَ اٰمَنُوْا لا

يُخْرِجُهُمْ مِّنَ الظُّلُمٰتِ إِلَى النُّوْرِ ط وَالَّذِيْنَ كَفَرُوْۤا

أَوْلِيٰٓئُهُمُ الطَّاغُوْتُ لا يُخْرِجُوْنَهُمْ مِّنَ النُّوْرِ إِلَى

الظُّلُمٰتِ ط أُولٰٓئِكَ أَصْحٰبُ النَّارِ ج هُمْ فِيْهَا

خٰلِدُوْنَ ۲۵۷ أَلَمْ تَرَ إِلَى الَّذِيْ حَاۤجَّ إِبْرٰهٖمَ فِيْ

رَبِّهٖٓ أَنْ اٰتٰهُ اللهُ الْمُلْكَ ج اِذْ قَالَ إِبْرٰهٖمُ رَبِّيَ

الَّذِيْ يُحْيٖ وَيُمِيْتُ لا قَالَ أَنَا أُحْيٖ وَأُمِيْتُ ط

قَالَ إِبْرٰهٖمُ فَإِنَّ اللهَ يَأْتِيْ بِالشَّمْسِ مِنَ الْمَشْرِقِ

فَأْتِ بِهَا مِنَ الْمَغْرِبِ فَبُهِتَ الَّذِيْ كَفَرَ ط

وَاللهُ لَا يَهْدِي الْقَوْمَ الظّٰلِمِيْنَ ۲۵۸ أَوْ كَالَّذِيْ

مَرَّ عَلٰى قَرْيَةٍ وَّهِيَ خَاوِيَةٌ عَلٰى عُرُوْشِهَا ج قَالَ

أَنّٰى يُحْيٖ هٰذِهِ اللهُ بَعْدَ مَوْتِهَا ج فَأَمَاتَهُ اللهُ

Diversity of faith: people are free to choose what religion they follow.

77

The Throne Verse: a glorious portrayal of Allah

²⁵⁵ Allah, there is no god but Him! *He is* The Living, The Everlasting. Neither tiredness nor sleep overwhelm Him. All that is in The Heavens and on Earth belongs to Him. Who dares to intercede without His permission? He knows what they have achieved and what they have failed to do,ᵃ but they can only grasp what He wishes of His knowledge. His *Majestic* Throne extends over the Heavens and the Earth, and He never tires of protecting them both. He is The Exalted, The Majestic.

Freedom of religion is a fundamental human right

²⁵⁶ There is no compulsion in religion. Guidance is clearly distinct from error.ᵇ Whoever rejects false godsᶜ and believes *solely* in Allah has grasped the most trustworthy handhold, which will never break. Allah is the Hearing, the Knowing.

Allah is the friend of the believers

²⁵⁷ Allah is the friend of believers, taking them out of darkness into light. As for the disbelievers, their friends are the false gods, who take them out of light into darkness; these are people of the Fire, where they will stay forever.

Examples of Allah's guidance

Ibrahim defeats the tyrant Namrood

²⁵⁸ Have you not considered the one who Allah made King, when he argued with Ibrahim about his Lord? Ibrahim said to him: "It is my Lord Who gives life and death". He replied: "I too give life and death". Ibrahim replied: "Allah brings the Sun from the East, so why not bring it from the West, *if you can*?" The disbeliever was speechless, Allah does not guide the wicked people.

Uzair is shown Allah's power over life and death

²⁵⁹ Or take *the example of* the one who passed through a town, its buildings razed to the ground; he *asked himself*: "How can Allah bring these *ruins* to life once they are dead?" So, Allah made him die for hundred years and then brought him back to life. *Allah* asked him: "How long did you remain *dead* in such way?" He replied: "Possibly a day or part of a day". Allah told him: "In fact you remained dead for

---

ᵃ I have used Ibn Abbas interpretation "what they have achieved" as what happened to them in this world, while "what they failed to do" points to what will happen to them in the Hereafter.

ᵇ The occasion for its revelation is: some Ansar whose children died young would take an oath to devote their children to Judaism if they remained alive, so some of them converted to Judaism. After the Jewish tribe Banu Nadhir was expelled from Madinah, they wanted to convert them to Islam.

ᶜ All manner of things can be *"Taghut"*, including an unhealthy appetite for money, power and unjust governments etc.

مِائَةَ عَامٍ ثُمَّ بَعَثَهُ ط قَالَ كَمْ لَبِثْتَ ط قَالَ

لَبِثْتُ يَوْمًا اَوْ بَعْضَ يَوْمٍ ط قَالَ بَل لَّبِثْتَ مِائَةَ

عَامٍ فَانْظُرْ اِلٰى طَعَامِكَ وَشَرَابِكَ لَمْ يَتَسَنَّهْ ج

وَانْظُرْ اِلٰى حِمَارِكَ وَلِنَجْعَلَكَ اٰيَةً لِّلنَّاسِ وَانْظُرْ

اِلَى الْعِظَامِ كَيْفَ نُنْشِزُهَا ثُمَّ نَكْسُوهَا لَحْمًا ط

فَلَمَّا تَبَيَّنَ لَهُ ۙ قَالَ اَعْلَمُ اَنَّ اللهَ عَلٰى كُلِّ

شَيْءٍ قَدِيرٌ ۝ وَاِذْ قَالَ اِبْرٰهٖمُ رَبِّ اَرِنِيْ كَيْفَ

تُحْيِ الْمَوْتٰى ط قَالَ اَوَلَمْ تُؤْمِنْ ط قَالَ بَلٰى وَلٰكِنْ

لِّيَطْمَئِنَّ قَلْبِيْ ط قَالَ فَخُذْ اَرْبَعَةً مِّنَ الطَّيْرِ

فَصُرْهُنَّ اِلَيْكَ ثُمَّ اجْعَلْ عَلٰى كُلِّ جَبَلٍ مِّنْهُنَّ

جُزْءًا ثُمَّ ادْعُهُنَّ يَاْتِيْنَكَ سَعْيًا ط وَاعْلَمْ اَنَّ اللهَ

عَزِيْزٌ حَكِيْمٌ ۝ مَثَلُ الَّذِيْنَ يُنْفِقُوْنَ اَمْوَالَهُمْ

فِيْ سَبِيْلِ اللهِ كَمَثَلِ حَبَّةٍ اَنْبَتَتْ سَبْعَ سَنَابِلَ

فِيْ كُلِّ سُنْبُلَةٍ مِّائَةُ حَبَّةٍ ط وَاللهُ يُضٰعِفُ لِمَنْ

يَّشَاءُ ط وَاللهُ وَاسِعٌ عَلِيْمٌ ۝ اَلَّذِيْنَ يُنْفِقُوْنَ

اَمْوَالَهُمْ فِيْ سَبِيْلِ اللهِ ثُمَّ لَا يُتْبِعُوْنَ مَا اَنْفَقُوْا

مَنًّا وَّلَا اَذًى ۙ لَّهُمْ اَجْرُهُمْ عِنْدَ رَبِّهِمْ ج وَلَا

خَوْفٌ عَلَيْهِمْ وَلَا هُمْ يَحْزَنُوْنَ ۝ قَوْلٌ مَّعْرُوْفٌ

وَّمَغْفِرَةٌ خَيْرٌ مِّنْ صَدَقَةٍ يَّتْبَعُهَا اَذًى ط وَاللهُ

غَنِيٌّ حَلِيْمٌ ۝ يٰاَيُّهَا الَّذِيْنَ اٰمَنُوْا لَا تُبْطِلُوْا

The rewards for charity are enormous, so give generously.

a hundred years! Look at your food and drink, they have not gone off; but look at your donkey. We *have done all* this to make you a sign for people, look at the *donkey's* bones, how We put them back together and covered them with flesh". When it had *all* become clear to him, he said: "I now know that Allah has power over all things".

Ibrahim witnesses the resurrection of dead birds

260 *Remember* when Ibrahim said: "My Lord, show me how you bring the *dead* back to life", *Allah* said: "Do you not believe?" He said: "Yes, of course, but I want my heart to be at peace". He told him: "Take four birds and *tame them first,* then cut them into pieces and put a piece of each of them on different hilltops and call them; they will come hurrying back to you. Know that Allah is the Almighty, the Wise."

Those who spend in the way of Allah

Parable of a single grain

261 Those people who spend their wealth in Allah's way are like a grain that sprouts into seven ears, each ear has a hundred seeds, and Allah will multiply it for them many times more as He pleases.[a] Allah is The Vast, The Knowing.

Parable of the soil-covered rock: do not seek favours in return

262 Those who spend their wealth in the way of Allah and do not follow it up by reminding the recipients of the favour, or causing them offence, shall have reward from their Lord: they shall neither fear nor grieve. 263 A kind word and forgiveness are far better than charity that is followed by an insult. Allah is Self-Sufficient and Most Gentle.

---

[a]   Allah multiplies the reward according to the sincerity and the donors love of Allah.

صَدَقْتِكُمْ بِالْمَنِّ وَالْاَذٰى ۙ كَالَّذِىْ يُنْفِقُ

مَالَهٗ رِئَآءَ النَّاسِ وَلَا يُؤْمِنُ بِاللّٰهِ وَالْيَوْمِ الْاٰخِرِ ؕ

فَمَثَلُهٗ كَمَثَلِ صَفْوَانٍ عَلَيْهِ تُرَابٌ فَاَصَابَهٗ وَابِلٌ

فَتَرَكَهٗ صَلْدًا ؕ لَا يَقْدِرُوْنَ عَلٰى شَىْءٍ مِّمَّا

كَسَبُوْا ؕ وَاللّٰهُ لَا يَهْدِى الْقَوْمَ الْكٰفِرِيْنَ ۞ وَمَثَلُ

الَّذِيْنَ يُنْفِقُوْنَ اَمْوَالَهُمُ ابْتِغَآءَ مَرْضَاتِ اللّٰهِ

وَتَثْبِيْتًا مِّنْ اَنْفُسِهِمْ كَمَثَلِ جَنَّةٍۭ بِرَبْوَةٍ اَصَابَهَا

وَابِلٌ فَاٰتَتْ اُكُلَهَا ضِعْفَيْنِ ۚ فَاِنْ لَّمْ يُصِبْهَا

وَابِلٌ فَطَلٌّ ؕ وَاللّٰهُ بِمَا تَعْمَلُوْنَ بَصِيْرٌ ۞ اَيَوَدُّ

اَحَدُكُمْ اَنْ تَكُوْنَ لَهٗ جَنَّةٌ مِّنْ نَّخِيْلٍ وَّاَعْنَابٍ

تَجْرِىْ مِنْ تَحْتِهَا الْاَنْهٰرُ ۙ لَهٗ فِيْهَا مِنْ كُلِّ

الثَّمَرٰتِ ۙ وَاَصَابَهُ الْكِبَرُ وَلَهٗ ذُرِّيَّةٌ ضُعَفَآءُ ۖ

فَاَصَابَهَآ اِعْصَارٌ فِيْهِ نَارٌ فَاحْتَرَقَتْ ؕ كَذٰلِكَ

يُبَيِّنُ اللّٰهُ لَكُمُ الْاٰيٰتِ لَعَلَّكُمْ تَتَفَكَّرُوْنَ ۞

يٰٓاَيُّهَا الَّذِيْنَ اٰمَنُوْٓا اَنْفِقُوْا مِنْ طَيِّبٰتِ مَا

كَسَبْتُمْ وَمِمَّآ اَخْرَجْنَا لَكُمْ مِّنَ الْاَرْضِ ۪ وَلَا

تَيَمَّمُوا الْخَبِيْثَ مِنْهُ تُنْفِقُوْنَ وَلَسْتُمْ بِاٰخِذِيْهِ

اِلَّآ اَنْ تُغْمِضُوْا فِيْهِ ؕ وَاعْلَمُوْٓا اَنَّ اللّٰهَ غَنِىٌّ

حَمِيْدٌ ۞ اَلشَّيْطٰنُ يَعِدُكُمُ الْفَقْرَ وَيَأْمُرُكُمْ

بِالْفَحْشَآءِ ۚ وَاللّٰهُ يَعِدُكُمْ مَّغْفِرَةً مِّنْهُ وَفَضْلًا ؕ

Give charity for one reason only: to please Allah!

²⁶⁴Believers, do not invalidate your charity by reminders *of favours done* or by insulting, like the one who spends his wealth to show off in front of people and does not *truly* believe in Allah and the Last Day; he is like a rock with a layer of soil on the top, when heavy rain comes, it is left clean and bare. They will get nothing from their efforts. Allah does not guide the disbelievers.

Parable of the orchard that produces fruit regardless of the rain
²⁶⁵Those who spend their wealth seeking Allah's pleasure, and for strengthening their faith, are like an orchard on a hilltop; if it rains, it produces double yield, and if there is no rain the dew is enough. Allah sees all that you do.

Parable of the orchard destroyed by stinginess
²⁶⁶Would any of you wish to have an orchard of date palms and grape vines beneath which streams flow, producing all kinds of fruits? Then suppose he grows old whilst his children are still small, then *out of the blue* comes a hurricane with lightening and fire that burns *his orchard* to ashes? This is how Allah makes clear His signs, so that you may reflect.

Give the best you have in charity
²⁶⁷Believers, give in charity of the good things that you have earned and that We have brought forth for you from the soil. Do not pick out the least attractive things to give in charity, things you wouldn't readily accept yourselves. Know that Allah is Self-Sufficient, Worthy of all praise. ²⁶⁸The Satan scares you of poverty, and he urges you to behave indecently, *but* Allah promises you *a share of* His forgiveness and bounty. Allah is the Vast, the Knowing.

وَاللّٰهُ وَاسِعٌ عَلِيمٌ ۞ يُؤْتِى الْحِكْمَةَ مَنْ يَّشَاءُ ۚ
وَمَنْ يُّؤْتَ الْحِكْمَةَ فَقَدْ اُوْتِىَ خَيْرًا كَثِيْرًا ؕ
وَمَا يَذَّكَّرُ اِلَّاۤ اُولُوا الْاَلْبَابِ ۞ وَمَاۤ اَنْفَقْتُمْ
مِّنْ نَّفَقَةٍ اَوْ نَذَرْتُمْ مِّنْ نَّذْرٍ فَاِنَّ اللّٰهَ
يَعْلَمُهٗ ؕ وَمَا لِلظّٰلِمِيْنَ مِنْ اَنْصَارٍ ۞ اِنْ تُبْدُوا
الصَّدَقٰتِ فَنِعِمَّا هِىَ ۚ وَاِنْ تُخْفُوْهَا وَتُؤْتُوْهَا
الْفُقَرَآءَ فَهُوَ خَيْرٌ لَّكُمْ ؕ وَيُكَفِّرُ عَنْكُمْ مِّنْ
سَيِّاٰتِكُمْ ؕ وَاللّٰهُ بِمَا تَعْمَلُوْنَ خَبِيْرٌ ۞ لَيْسَ عَلَيْكَ
هُدٰىهُمْ وَلٰكِنَّ اللّٰهَ يَهْدِىْ مَنْ يَّشَاءُ ؕ وَمَا
تُنْفِقُوْا مِنْ خَيْرٍ فَلِاَنْفُسِكُمْ ؕ وَمَا تُنْفِقُوْنَ اِلَّا
ابْتِغَآءَ وَجْهِ اللّٰهِ ؕ وَمَا تُنْفِقُوْا مِنْ خَيْرٍ يُّوَفَّ
اِلَيْكُمْ وَاَنْتُمْ لَا تُظْلَمُوْنَ ۞ لِلْفُقَرَآءِ الَّذِيْنَ
اُحْصِرُوْا فِىْ سَبِيْلِ اللّٰهِ لَا يَسْتَطِيْعُوْنَ ضَرْبًا
فِى الْاَرْضِ ۫ يَحْسَبُهُمُ الْجَاهِلُ اَغْنِيَآءَ مِنَ
التَّعَفُّفِ ۚ تَعْرِفُهُمْ بِسِيْمٰهُمْ ۚ لَا يَسْئَلُوْنَ النَّاسَ
اِلْحَافًا ؕ وَمَا تُنْفِقُوْا مِنْ خَيْرٍ فَاِنَّ اللّٰهَ بِهٖ
عَلِيْمٌ ۞ اَلَّذِيْنَ يُنْفِقُوْنَ اَمْوَالَهُمْ بِالَّيْلِ وَالنَّهَارِ
سِرًّا وَّعَلَانِيَةً فَلَهُمْ اَجْرُهُمْ عِنْدَ رَبِّهِمْ ۚ وَلَا
خَوْفٌ عَلَيْهِمْ وَلَا هُمْ يَحْزَنُوْنَ ۞ اَلَّذِيْنَ يَأْكُلُوْنَ
الرِّبٰوا لَا يَقُوْمُوْنَ اِلَّا كَمَا يَقُوْمُ الَّذِىْ يَتَخَبَّطُهُ

Charity benefits the donor; one becomes strong, determined and generous.

Wisdom is the greatest gift of all

[269] He gives wisdom to whom He pleases, and whoever is given wisdom has received great goodness, but only understanding people are mindful *of this fact.*[a]

Whether you give openly or secretly, do it to please Allah

[270] Whatever you give in charity or vow you make, Allah knows it. Evildoers will have no helpers. [271] If you give charity openly, that is wonderful, but giving it secretly to the needy is *even* better; *in both cases* it will compensate for your sins. Allah is fully aware of what you do. [272] It is not for you, *Muhammad,* to guide them, rather Allah guides *anyone who wants to be guided.* Whatever good things you give in charity will benefit yourselves; that is, if you give, seeking only Allah's pleasure. Whatever good things you give in charity will be rewarded, and you will not be short-changed in the least.

How to recognise the genuinely needy

[273] *Give charity* to the poor who are completely absorbed working in the way of Allah, unable to travel about the land *to earn their livelihood.* Because of their modest behaviour *some* ignorant *people* consider them wealthy. You can recognise them from their facial expression and the fact that they do not make demands on people. Whatever good things you give in charity, Allah knows it well. [274] People who give their wealth in charity by night or by day, secretly or openly, shall have their reward from their Lord: they shall neither fear nor grieve.

[a] Wisdom is Allah's gift to those who make the right choices, who make constant effort to better themselves by practicing moral, social and spiritual values.

الشَّيْطٰنُ مِنَ الْمَسِّ ط ذٰلِكَ بِاَنَّهُمْ قَالُوْٓا اِنَّمَا

الْبَيْعُ مِثْلُ الرِّبٰوا � وَاَحَلَّ اللهُ الْبَيْعَ وَحَرَّمَ

الرِّبٰوا ؕ فَمَنْ جَآءَهٗ مَوْعِظَةٌ مِّنْ رَّبِّهٖ فَانْتَهٰى فَلَهٗ

مَا سَلَفَ ؕ وَاَمْرُهٗٓ اِلَى اللهِ ؕ وَمَنْ عَادَ فَاُولٰٓئِكَ

اَصْحٰبُ النَّارِ ۚ هُمْ فِيْهَا خٰلِدُوْنَ ۝ يَمْحَقُ اللهُ

الرِّبٰوا وَيُرْبِى الصَّدَقٰتِ ؕ وَاللهُ لَا يُحِبُّ كُلَّ كَفَّارٍ

اَثِيْمٍ ۝ اِنَّ الَّذِيْنَ اٰمَنُوْا وَعَمِلُوا الصّٰلِحٰتِ وَاَقَامُوا

الصَّلٰوةَ وَاٰتَوُا الزَّكٰوةَ لَهُمْ اَجْرُهُمْ عِنْدَ رَبِّهِمْ ۚ

وَلَاخَوْفٌ عَلَيْهِمْ وَلَا هُمْ يَحْزَنُوْنَ ۝ يٰٓاَيُّهَا الَّذِيْنَ

اٰمَنُوا اتَّقُوا اللهَ وَذَرُوْا مَا بَقِيَ مِنَ الرِّبٰوٓا اِنْ

كُنْتُمْ مُّؤْمِنِيْنَ ۝ فَاِنْ لَّمْ تَفْعَلُوْا فَاْذَنُوْا بِحَرْبٍ

مِّنَ اللهِ وَرَسُوْلِهٖ ۚ وَاِنْ تُبْتُمْ فَلَكُمْ رُءُوْسُ

اَمْوَالِكُمْ ۚ لَا تَظْلِمُوْنَ وَلَا تُظْلَمُوْنَ ۝ وَاِنْ كَانَ ذُوْ

عُسْرَةٍ فَنَظِرَةٌ اِلٰى مَيْسَرَةٍ ؕ وَاَنْ تَصَدَّقُوْا خَيْرٌ لَّكُمْ

اِنْ كُنْتُمْ تَعْلَمُوْنَ ۝ وَاتَّقُوْا يَوْمًا تُرْجَعُوْنَ فِيْهِ

اِلَى اللهِ �َّ ثُمَّ تُوَفّٰى كُلُّ نَفْسٍ مَّا كَسَبَتْ وَهُمْ

لَا يُظْلَمُوْنَ ۝ يٰٓاَيُّهَا الَّذِيْنَ اٰمَنُوْٓا اِذَا تَدَايَنْتُمْ

بِدَيْنٍ اِلٰٓى اَجَلٍ مُّسَمًّى فَاكْتُبُوْهُ ؕ وَلْيَكْتُبْ

بَّيْنَكُمْ كَاتِبٌۢ بِالْعَدْلِ ۙ وَلَا يَاْبَ كَاتِبٌ اَنْ

يَّكْتُبَ كَمَا عَلَّمَهُ اللهُ فَلْيَكْتُبْ ۚ وَلْيُمْلِلِ الَّذِىْ

Allah expects kindness in all matters including dealings with money. That's why interest is forbidden.

Stark warning to loan sharks who exploit the poor

²⁷⁵ Those who deal in usuryᵃ will stand *on the Day of Judgement* like the one who is demented by Satan's touch; that is because they claim: "Trading and usury are alike", whereas Allah has made trading lawful and forbidden usury. So, whoever takes heed of his Lord's warning and gives up *usurious lending*, he can have *the capital* that he lent back, and his case rests with Allah. However, whoever goes back *to usury*, then such people will be the companions of the Fire, remaining in it forever. ²⁷⁶ Allah wipes out *the benefits of* usury, but multiplies *those of* acts of charity. Allah dislikes every ungrateful sinner. ²⁷⁷ *As for* those who believe, do righteous deeds, perform the prayer and pay Zakat, they shall have reward from their Lord: neither shall they fear, nor grieve.

Allah declares a war on usurers and offers a way out

²⁷⁸ Believers, be mindful of Allah and give up any outstanding usury *on debts owed to you*, if you are true believers. ²⁷⁹ If you do not do so, then heed this declaration of war from Allah and His Messenger. However, if you repent you may keep the capital of your wealth so that you neither wrong others nor are yourselves wronged. ²⁸⁰ If *the debtor* is in difficulty, allow him time to repay when it is easier for him, but to write off the debt out of charity would be better for you, if only you knew. ²⁸¹ Be fearful of the day you will return to Allah; then every soul will receive exactly what it has earned, and no one will be wronged.

ᵃ Usury is the exploitation of the weak by charging interest on money borrowed.

عَلَيْهِ الْحَقُّ وَلْيَتَّقِ اللهَ رَبَّهُ وَلَا يَبْخَسْ مِنْهُ

شَيْئًا ط فَاِنْ كَانَ الَّذِىْ عَلَيْهِ الْحَقُّ سَفِيْهًا اَوْ

ضَعِيْفًا اَوْ لَا يَسْتَطِيْعُ اَنْ يُّمِلَّ هُوَ فَلْيُمْلِلْ

وَلِيُّهُ بِالْعَدْلِ ط وَاسْتَشْهِدُوْا شَهِيْدَيْنِ مِنْ

رِّجَالِكُمْ ۚ فَاِنْ لَّمْ يَكُوْنَا رَجُلَيْنِ فَرَجُلٌ وَّامْرَاَتٰنِ

مِمَّنْ تَرْضَوْنَ مِنَ الشُّهَدَآءِ اَنْ تَضِلَّ اِحْدٰىهُمَا

فَتُذَكِّرَ اِحْدٰىهُمَا الْاُخْرٰى ط وَلَا يَاْبَ الشُّهَدَآءُ

اِذَا مَا دُعُوْا ط وَلَا تَسْئَمُوْۤا اَنْ تَكْتُبُوْهُ صَغِيْرًا اَوْ

كَبِيْرًا اِلٰۤى اَجَلِهٖ ط ذٰلِكُمْ اَقْسَطُ عِنْدَ اللهِ وَاَقْوَمُ

لِلشَّهَادَةِ وَاَدْنٰۤى اَلَّا تَرْتَابُوْۤا اِلَّاۤ اَنْ تَكُوْنَ تِجَارَةً

حَاضِرَةً تُدِيْرُوْنَهَا بَيْنَكُمْ فَلَيْسَ عَلَيْكُمْ جُنَاحٌ

اَلَّا تَكْتُبُوْهَا ط وَاَشْهِدُوْۤا اِذَا تَبَايَعْتُمْ ۪ وَلَا يُضَآرَّ

كَاتِبٌ وَّلَا شَهِيْدٌ ط وَاِنْ تَفْعَلُوْا فَاِنَّهُ فُسُوْقٌۢ

بِكُمْ ط وَاتَّقُوا اللهَ ط وَيُعَلِّمُكُمُ اللهُ ط وَاللهُ بِكُلِّ

شَىْءٍ عَلِيْمٌ ۝ وَاِنْ كُنْتُمْ عَلٰى سَفَرٍ وَّلَمْ تَجِدُوْا

كَاتِبًا فَرِهٰنٌ مَّقْبُوْضَةٌ ط فَاِنْ اَمِنَ بَعْضُكُمْ

بَعْضًا فَلْيُؤَدِّ الَّذِى اؤْتُمِنَ اَمَانَتَهُ وَلْيَتَّقِ

اللهَ رَبَّهُ ط وَلَا تَكْتُمُوا الشَّهَادَةَ ط وَمَنْ يَّكْتُمْهَا

فَاِنَّهُ اٰثِمٌ قَلْبُهُ ط وَاللهُ بِمَا تَعْمَلُوْنَ عَلِيْمٌ ۝

لِلّٰهِ مَا فِى السَّمٰوٰتِ وَمَا فِى الْاَرْضِ ط وَاِنْ تُبْدُوْا

Always write down monetary contracts and agreements; verbal agreement isn't enough.

Instructions for loans and business contracts

Recording loan terms to prevent fraud

[282] Believers, when you enter into a loan agreement for a fixed period, then write it down, and let a scribe write it down accurately. A scribe should never refuse to write down *the truth*, as Allah has taught him. So, let *the scribe* write, and let the debtor be mindful of Allah his Lord and dictate without any subtraction *the exact terms of what he has borrowed.*

Witnesses are required to protect those liable to exploitation

If the debtor has learning difficulties, is feeble or otherwise incapable of dictating by himself, then let his guardian dictate accurately *on his behalf;* and let two men amongst you witness *the agreement.* If two men are not available, then a man and two women of whom you approve can be witnesses so that, if one of *the women* makes a mistake, the other can remind her. Witnesses should never refuse to attend when they are called upon.

All commercial deals should be recorded, with one exception

Do not consider recording the terms of small amounts and its due date as insignificant compared to large ones; that is fairer in the sight of Allah. However, an exception exists for on-the-spot transactions which you arrange amongst yourselves, and for which there is no blame on you if you do not record *the details*, but make sure witnesses are present when you exchange the goods. No pressure should be brought to bear on either a scribe or a witness *to any transaction*; if you do so, you will be guilty of wrongdoing. So be mindful of Allah, and follow Allah's instructions. Allah knows all things.[a]

The place of securities and trust in business deals

[283] If you are on a journey and unable to find a scribe then pledge something as a security. However, if you decide to trust one another, then let the trustee fulfil his trust, and let him be mindful of his Lord. Let none of you hide the truth; whoever does so, his heart is sinful. Allah is fully aware of what you do.

---

[a] Why two women witnesses giving witness is not a 'right' it's a duty, real responsibility. The Quran here is not obliging women to take this duty; they can have another woman with them. So, a woman is not being deprived of a right.

مَا فِيٓ أَنْفُسِكُمْ أَوْ تُخْفُوهُ يُحَاسِبْكُمْ بِهِ اللّٰهُ ۚ

فَيَغْفِرُ لِمَنْ يَّشَآءُ وَيُعَذِّبُ مَنْ يَّشَآءُ ۗ وَاللّٰهُ

عَلٰى كُلِّ شَيْءٍ قَدِيرٌ ۞ اٰمَنَ الرَّسُوْلُ بِمَآ اُنْزِلَ

اِلَيْهِ مِنْ رَّبِّهٖ وَالْمُؤْمِنُوْنَ ۚ كُلٌّ اٰمَنَ بِاللّٰهِ وَ

مَلٰٓئِكَتِهٖ وَكُتُبِهٖ وَرُسُلِهٖ ۚ لَا نُفَرِّقُ بَيْنَ اَحَدٍ

مِّنْ رُّسُلِهٖ ۚ وَقَالُوْا سَمِعْنَا وَاَطَعْنَا ۖ غُفْرَانَكَ

رَبَّنَا وَاِلَيْكَ الْمَصِيْرُ ۞ لَا يُكَلِّفُ اللّٰهُ نَفْسًا اِلَّا

وُسْعَهَا ۚ لَهَا مَا كَسَبَتْ وَعَلَيْهَا مَا اكْتَسَبَتْ ۗ

رَبَّنَا لَا تُؤَاخِذْنَآ اِنْ نَّسِيْنَآ اَوْ اَخْطَأْنَا ۚ رَبَّنَا وَلَا

تَحْمِلْ عَلَيْنَآ اِصْرًا كَمَا حَمَلْتَهٗ عَلَى الَّذِيْنَ مِنْ

قَبْلِنَا ۚ رَبَّنَا وَلَا تُحَمِّلْنَا مَا لَا طَاقَةَ لَنَا بِهٖ ۚ

وَاعْفُ عَنَّا ۗ وَاغْفِرْ لَنَا ۗ وَارْحَمْنَا ۗ اَنْتَ مَوْلٰىنَا

فَانْصُرْنَا عَلَى الْقَوْمِ الْكٰفِرِيْنَ ۞

Allah doesn't burden anyone beyond their capacity.

Allah's knowledge of all things visible and invisible

[284] Allah owns everything in the Heavens and on Earth. Whether you reveal your innermost thoughts or you hide them, Allah will hold you to account for them; then He will forgive whomever He pleases and punish whomever He pleases. Allah has control over all things.

The articles of faith

[285] The Messenger accepts as truth what has been revealed to him by his Lord, as do the believers; all of them believe in Allah, His angels, His books and His messengers. *They say*: "We make no distinction between any of His messengers"[a]. And they say: "We hear and obey. Forgive us, our Lord, to You is the final return".

A prayer for consolation, justice and kindness

[286] Allah does not burden anyone beyond their capacity; they will receive the *reward* they earned, and will suffer the consequences of whatever *evil* they committed. *So, pray in this way*: "Our Lord, when we forget and make a mistake do not punish us. Our Lord, do not *make things* hard for us, as you did with those before us. Our Lord, do not burden us with more than we can bear, pardon us, forgive us and be kind to us. You are our Protector, so help us against the disbelievers".

---

[a] All the Messengers are equal in their Prophethood but differ in ranks.

3. Surat Ale 'Imran

The Family of Imran

This surat was revealed after the battle of Uhud, which took place in Shawwal 3 AH (Anno Hegirae, "in the year of the Hijra"). Its title, 'The family of Imran,' refers to Imran, the father of Maryam, the mother of Prophet Isa. Three major themes of the surat are:

- Allah's Oneness, *tawhid*, and His unique power and majesty.
- Criticism of certain Jewish and Christian doctrines and practices, especially sectarianism. There follows an invitation to the Jews and Christians to follow the Prophet Muhammad ﷺ who is praised for his brilliant leadership.
- The last part of the surat deals with the battle of Uhud.

The surat opens by proclaiming that Allah's revelation has been continuous from the beginning of time, and that it includes the Torah of the Jewish Scriptures, the scrolls revealed to many other prophets and the Gospel of Isa. The Quran is a continuation of that chain and therefore the final revelation. So, the People of The Book are invited to embrace this final testament, and to follow it. The Quran warns against erraneous intrepretation of metaphorical passages and making interpretations that go against the spirit of the divine message, thus sowing the seeds of conflict, even though, "Only Allah knows their exact meaning" (7). This kind of 'stretching' the meanings of divine scripture was the root of sectarianism rampant among the Jews and Christians. The Christian doctrine of the divinity of Jesus and the "son ship of God," is an example of this arbitrary interpretation of the message of Jesus. The Quran challenges the Christian doctrine of Jesus being either one with Allah or the "son" of Allah. Instead it asserts that "Isa is like Adam; *Allah* created him from dust then said to him 'Be!' And he was" (59).

The story of Maryam's childhood is beautifully told through the miracles that occurred around her. Upon seeing these miracles, the Prophet Zakariyya, Maryam's guardian, prayed to Allah for a child of his own. His prayer was heard, and he was blessed with a son: Yahya. This is followed by an account of Maryam's virgin conception and the birth of Isa.

The Battle of Uhud

Since their defeat at the Battle of Badr, the Makkans had been planning to avenge their dead. Within a year, they mustered an army of some 3,000 men to attack Madinah. When the Prophet ﷺ learnt of this, he held a war council. The overwhelming opinion was to leave the city and meet the enemy in the open field. To begin with Muslims numbered about 1,000. However, by the time this army reached mount Uhud, 300 men led by Abdullah ibn Ubayy, the hypocrite, had deserted.

> Having fewer than 700 men with him, the Prophet ﷺ arrayed the bulk of his forces with their backs to Mount Uhud, and posted fifty archers on the nearby hill, to provide cover against outflanking manoeuvres by the enemy cavalry. These archers were ordered not to leave their post under any circumstances. In their subsequent, death-defying assault upon the numerically superior forces of the Makkan idolaters, the Muslims gained a decisive advantage over the former, who turned to flee. At that moment, believing that the battle had been won and fearing lest they lose their share of the spoils, most of the archers abandoned their covering position and joined the skirmish around the encampment of the Quraysh. Seeing this opportunity, the Makkan cavalry, under the command of Khalid ibn Walid, veered round in a wide arc and attacked the Muslim forces from the rear. Deprived of the cover of the archers and caught between two fires, the Muslims retreated in disorder, with the loss of many lives (Asad).

Amidst all this mayhem, a rumour quickly spread that the Prophet ﷺ had been killed, and this caused some Muslims to flee. However, Omar and some other companions dispelled the rumour and regrouped to defend the Prophet ﷺ. When the other Muslims learnt that the Prophet was alive, they rallied and attacked the enemy once more, so that the Quraysh fled in the direction of Makkah. The Muslim army was so exhausted and wounded that they could not pursue the enemy any further, and the battle ended as a draw. The Muslims had incurred heavy losses, with seventy men martyred.

This was a devastating blow for them, due to sloppy discipline and disobeying the command of the Prophet ﷺ. The lesson was learned: "Obey your leader." The Quran provided a detailed analysis of what went wrong: "When you were defeating them with His permission, until the moment when you lost courage, argued about the order you had been given and disobeyed it, even after He had shown you what you wanted – the fact is that some of you long for the world, whilst others among you long for the Hereafter" (152). A harsh criticism, but Allah reassures the Muslims, "Do not be disheartened or sad, you will come out on top if you are true believers" (139).

بِسْمِ اللهِ الرَّحْمٰنِ الرَّحِيْمِ

الٓمّٓ ۟ اللهُ لَاۤ اِلٰهَ اِلَّا هُوَ ۙ الْحَیُّ الْقَیُّوْمُ ۟ نَزَّلَ

عَلَیْكَ الْكِتٰبَ بِالْحَقِّ مُصَدِّقًا لِّمَا بَیْنَ یَدَیْهِ

وَ اَنْزَلَ التَّوْرٰىةَ وَ الْاِنْجِیْلَ ۟ مِنْ قَبْلُ هُدًی

لِّلنَّاسِ وَ اَنْزَلَ الْفُرْقَانَ ۟ اِنَّ الَّذِیْنَ كَفَرُوْا

بِاٰیٰتِ اللهِ لَهُمْ عَذَابٌ شَدِیْدٌ ۟ وَ اللهُ عَزِیْزٌ

ذُو انْتِقَامٍ ۟ اِنَّ اللهَ لَا یَخْفٰی عَلَیْهِ شَیْءٌ فِی الْاَرْضِ

وَ لَا فِی السَّمَاءِ ۟ هُوَ الَّذِیْ یُصَوِّرُكُمْ فِی الْاَرْحَامِ

كَیْفَ یَشَاءُ ۟ لَاۤ اِلٰهَ اِلَّا هُوَ الْعَزِیْزُ الْحَكِیْمُ ۟ هُوَ

الَّذِیْۤ اَنْزَلَ عَلَیْكَ الْكِتٰبَ مِنْهُ اٰیٰتٌ مُّحْكَمٰتٌ

هُنَّ اُمُّ الْكِتٰبِ وَ اُخَرُ مُتَشٰبِهٰتٌ ۟ فَاَمَّا الَّذِیْنَ

فِیْ قُلُوْبِهِمْ زَیْغٌ فَیَتَّبِعُوْنَ مَا تَشَابَهَ مِنْهُ ابْتِغَاءَ

الْفِتْنَةِ وَ ابْتِغَاءَ تَاْوِیْلِهِ ۚ وَ مَا یَعْلَمُ تَاْوِیْلَهُ اِلَّا

اللهُ ۘ وَ الرّٰسِخُوْنَ فِی الْعِلْمِ یَقُوْلُوْنَ اٰمَنَّا بِهٖ ۙ

كُلٌّ مِّنْ عِنْدِ رَبِّنَا ۚ وَ مَا یَذَّكَّرُ اِلَّاۤ اُولُوا الْاَلْبَابِ ۟

رَبَّنَا لَا تُزِغْ قُلُوْبَنَا بَعْدَ اِذْ هَدَیْتَنَا وَ هَبْ لَنَا

مِنْ لَّدُنْكَ رَحْمَةً ۚ اِنَّكَ اَنْتَ الْوَهَّابُ ۟ رَبَّنَاۤ

اِنَّكَ جَامِعُ النَّاسِ لِیَوْمٍ لَّا رَیْبَ فِیْهِ ۟ اِنَّ

اللهَ لَا یُخْلِفُ الْمِیْعَادَ ۟ اِنَّ الَّذِیْنَ كَفَرُوْا لَنْ

*Read and study the
Quran with faith and
hope of guidance.*

In the name of Allah, the Kind, the Caring.

¹*Alif Lam Meem.*

The Quran is the absolute standard for goodness
²Allah is the only God, the Living, the Everlasting. ³Truly He has revealed to you the Book, confirming what *scriptures* already existed, and He revealed the Torah and the Gospel ⁴before that as a guidance for people, and He sent the criterion *for distinguishing right from wrong*. Those who deny Allah's verses will be severely punished. Allah is the Almighty, the Avenger. ⁵Nothing on Earth and in the Heavens is hidden from Allah. ⁶He is the one who forms you in *mothers'* wombs as He pleases; there is no God besides Him, the Almighty, the Wise.

Searching for hidden meanings of the Quran could mislead
⁷He is the one Who revealed the Book to you: some of its verses are precise in meaning, they are the foundation stone of the Book, whilst others are metaphorical. The people whose minds are sick chase after what is metaphorical, they want to stir up disagreement and to concoct their own interpretations; yet only Allah knows their exact meaning, and those firmly grounded in knowledge say, "We believe in it, *since* all of it is from Our Lord," only those with understanding pay heedᵃ. ⁸"Our Lord, let not our hearts waver *from the truth* after You have guided us, and take care of us. You are the Giver of gifts. ⁹Our Lord, You will gather people on for a day in which there is no doubt." Allah never breaks His promise.

ᵃ   Some verses are more direct than others, the less direct ones are metaphorical. They convey multiple meanings or ambiguous meanings. A metaphor compares one aspect of an idea with another to illuminate the idea. So, a metaphor takes you beyond one meaning and opens the mind to many possible meanings.

تُغْنِىْ عَنْهُمْ اَمْوَالُهُمْ وَلَاۤ اَوْلَادُهُمْ مِّنَ اللّٰهِ
شَيْئًا ۭ وَاُولٰٓئِكَ هُمْ وَقُوْدُ النَّارِ ﴿١٠﴾ كَدَاْبِ اٰلِ
فِرْعَوْنَ ۙ وَالَّذِيْنَ مِنْ قَبْلِهِمْ ۭ كَذَّبُوْا بِاٰيٰتِنَا ۚ
فَاَخَذَهُمُ اللّٰهُ بِذُنُوْبِهِمْ ۭ وَاللّٰهُ شَدِيْدُ الْعِقَابِ ﴿١١﴾
قُلْ لِّلَّذِيْنَ كَفَرُوْا سَتُغْلَبُوْنَ وَتُحْشَرُوْنَ اِلٰى
جَهَنَّمَ ۭ وَبِئْسَ الْمِهَادُ ﴿١٢﴾ قَدْ كَانَ لَكُمْ اٰيَةٌ فِىْ
فِئَتَيْنِ الْتَقَتَا ۭ فِئَةٌ تُقَاتِلُ فِىْ سَبِيْلِ اللّٰهِ

Avoiding worldly traps and pleasures will lead to enjoyment of Paradise.

وَاُخْرٰى كَافِرَةٌ يَّرَوْنَهُمْ مِّثْلَيْهِمْ رَأْىَ الْعَيْنِ ۭ
وَاللّٰهُ يُؤَيِّدُ بِنَصْرِهٖ مَنْ يَّشَاءُ ۭ اِنَّ فِىْ ذٰلِكَ
لَعِبْرَةً لِّاُولِى الْاَبْصَارِ ﴿١٣﴾ زُيِّنَ لِلنَّاسِ حُبُّ
الشَّهَوٰتِ مِنَ النِّسَاۤءِ وَالْبَنِيْنَ وَالْقَنَاطِيْرِ
الْمُقَنْطَرَةِ مِنَ الذَّهَبِ وَالْفِضَّةِ وَالْخَيْلِ
الْمُسَوَّمَةِ وَالْاَنْعَامِ وَالْحَرْثِ ۭ ذٰلِكَ مَتَاعُ الْحَيٰوةِ
الدُّنْيَا ۚ وَاللّٰهُ عِنْدَهٗ حُسْنُ الْمَاٰبِ ﴿١٤﴾ قُلْ
اَؤُنَبِّئُكُمْ بِخَيْرٍ مِّنْ ذٰلِكُمْ ۭ لِلَّذِيْنَ اتَّقَوْا عِنْدَ
رَبِّهِمْ جَنّٰتٌ تَجْرِىْ مِنْ تَحْتِهَا الْاَنْهٰرُ خٰلِدِيْنَ
فِيْهَا وَاَزْوَاجٌ مُّطَهَّرَةٌ وَّرِضْوَانٌ مِّنَ اللّٰهِ ۭ وَاللّٰهُ
بَصِيْرٌ بِالْعِبَادِ ﴿١٥﴾ اَلَّذِيْنَ يَقُوْلُوْنَ رَبَّنَاۤ اِنَّنَاۤ
اٰمَنَّا فَاغْفِرْ لَنَا ذُنُوْبَنَا وَقِنَا عَذَابَ النَّارِ ﴿١٦﴾ اَلصّٰبِرِيْنَ وَ
الصّٰدِقِيْنَ وَالْقٰنِتِيْنَ وَالْمُنْفِقِيْنَ وَالْمُسْتَغْفِرِيْنَ

Worldly wealth and power is not a guarantee of victory

[10] As for the disbelievers, their wealth and their children will not benefit them in the least against Allah; they will be fuel of the Fire, [11] just like the people of Pharaoh and those before them who denied Our signs, so Allah punished them for their sins. Allah is severe in punishment. [12] Tell the disbelievers: "You will soon be defeated and be herded into Hell." What a miserable place of rest! [13] A sign for you was the meeting *at Badr*; one army fought in the path of Allah, *and* the others were disbelievers, they saw *the Muslims* as twice as many as themselves. Allah strengthens with His help anyone He pleases; for those of insight, it had a lesson.

Worldly luxuries and the delights of Paradise

[14] People's love of worldly pleasures has been made attractive to them: women, children, heaps of gold and silver, well-bred horses, animals and farmland, such are delights of this worldly life, but Allah has the best place of return. [15] Say: "Shall I tell you of something far better than these? To those who are mindful, their Lord will give them gardens beneath which rivers flow where they will live forever, and pure spouses and the pleasure of Allah." Allah watches over His servants [16] who *pray*, "Our Lord, we believe, so forgive us our sins and save us from the punishment of Hellfire," [17] *they are* patient, truthful, obedient, charitable, and seek forgiveness at dawn.

بِالْأَسْحَارِ ۞ شَهِدَ اللّٰهُ أَنَّهُ لَا إِلٰهَ إِلَّا هُوَ لا وَ الْمَلٰٓئِكَةُ وَ أُولُوا الْعِلْمِ قَآئِمًا بِالْقِسْطِ ۚ لَا إِلٰهَ إِلَّا هُوَ الْعَزِيْزُ الْحَكِيْمُ ۞ إِنَّ الدِّيْنَ عِنْدَ اللّٰهِ الْإِسْلَامُ ۖ وَمَا اخْتَلَفَ الَّذِيْنَ أُوْتُوا الْكِتٰبَ إِلَّا مِنْۢ بَعْدِ مَا جَآءَهُمُ الْعِلْمُ بَغْيًۢا بَيْنَهُمْ ۗ وَمَنْ يَّكْفُرْ بِاٰيٰتِ اللّٰهِ فَإِنَّ اللّٰهَ سَرِيْعُ الْحِسَابِ ۞ فَإِنْ حَآجُّوْكَ فَقُلْ أَسْلَمْتُ وَجْهِيَ لِلّٰهِ وَمَنِ اتَّبَعَنِ ۗ وَقُلْ لِّلَّذِيْنَ أُوْتُوا الْكِتٰبَ وَالْأُمِّيّٖنَ ءَأَسْلَمْتُمْ ۚ فَإِنْ أَسْلَمُوْا فَقَدِ اهْتَدَوْا ۚ وَّإِنْ تَوَلَّوْا فَإِنَّمَا عَلَيْكَ الْبَلٰغُ ۗ وَاللّٰهُ بَصِيْرٌۢ بِالْعِبَادِ ۞ إِنَّ الَّذِيْنَ يَكْفُرُوْنَ بِاٰيٰتِ اللّٰهِ وَيَقْتُلُوْنَ النَّبِيّٖنَ بِغَيْرِ حَقٍّ ۙ وَّيَقْتُلُوْنَ الَّذِيْنَ يَأْمُرُوْنَ بِالْقِسْطِ مِنَ النَّاسِ ۙ فَبَشِّرْهُمْ بِعَذَابٍ أَلِيْمٍ ۞ أُولٰٓئِكَ الَّذِيْنَ حَبِطَتْ أَعْمَالُهُمْ فِي الدُّنْيَا وَالْاٰخِرَةِ ۖ وَمَا لَهُمْ مِّنْ نّٰصِرِيْنَ ۞ أَلَمْ تَرَ إِلَى الَّذِيْنَ أُوْتُوْا نَصِيْبًا مِّنَ الْكِتٰبِ يُدْعَوْنَ إِلٰى كِتٰبِ اللّٰهِ لِيَحْكُمَ بَيْنَهُمْ ثُمَّ يَتَوَلّٰى فَرِيْقٌ مِّنْهُمْ وَهُمْ مُّعْرِضُوْنَ ۞ ذٰلِكَ بِأَنَّهُمْ قَالُوْا لَنْ تَمَسَّنَا النَّارُ إِلَّآ أَيَّامًا مَّعْدُوْدٰتٍ ۖ وَّغَرَّهُمْ فِيْ دِيْنِهِمْ مَّا كَانُوْا يَفْتَرُوْنَ ۞ فَكَيْفَ إِذَا جَمَعْنٰهُمْ لِيَوْمٍ لَّا

Islam is a religion of submission to Allah's laws.

97

¹⁸ Allah bears witness that there is no god beside Him, as do the angels and those whose knowledge *is used* to uphold fairness; there is no god but Him, the Almighty, the Wise.

Religion means submission and commitment to the will of Allah

¹⁹ Islam is the *only* religion acceptable to Allah. Those given the Book began to disagree amongst themselves out of sheer rebelliousness after knowledge had come to them. Whoever denies Allah's signs, *let him remember that* Allah is swift in settling accounts. ²⁰ If they argue with you, then say, "I have submitted myself to Allah, as have those who follow me", then ask those given the Book and the *Arabs* without any scripture: "Have you submitted *to Allah*?" If they submit *to Allah*, they will be guided, but if they turn away, you will have done your job of delivering the message. Allah watches over His servants.

The disobedient will be punished

²¹ Those who reject Allah's verses, unlawfully killed the prophets and killed those who enjoined justice, give them the good news of painful punishment. ²² Their deeds will prove to be worthless in this world and the Hereafter, and they'll have no one to help them. ²³ Haven't you seen those who have been given a share of the Book? When they are referred to the Book of Allah to judge between themselves, a group turns away, stubbornly resisting. ²⁴ That is because they said, "We will be in Hellfire only for a few days." The lies they used to make about their religion have deceived them. ²⁵ How will it be when We gather them on *the* Day that is certain to come, and everyone is paid in full what they've earned without being wronged *in the least*?

رَيْبَ فِيْهِ ۚ وَوُفِّيَتْ كُلُّ نَفْسٍ مَّا كَسَبَتْ وَهُمْ لَا

يُظْلَمُوْنَ ۝ قُلِ اللّٰهُمَّ مٰلِكَ الْمُلْكِ تُؤْتِى الْمُلْكَ

مَنْ تَشَاءُ وَتَنْزِعُ الْمُلْكَ مِمَّنْ تَشَاءُ ۖ وَتُعِزُّ مَنْ

تَشَاءُ وَتُذِلُّ مَنْ تَشَاءُ ۗ بِيَدِكَ الْخَيْرُ ۗ إِنَّكَ

عَلٰى كُلِّ شَيْءٍ قَدِيْرٌ ۝ تُوْلِجُ الَّيْلَ فِى النَّهَارِ وَ

تُوْلِجُ النَّهَارَ فِى الَّيْلِ ۖ وَتُخْرِجُ الْحَىَّ مِنَ الْمَيِّتِ وَ

تُخْرِجُ الْمَيِّتَ مِنَ الْحَىِّ ۖ وَتَرْزُقُ مَنْ تَشَاءُ بِغَيْرِ

Love of Allah is shown by obeying the Messenger ﷺ.

حِسَابٍ ۝ لَا يَتَّخِذِ الْمُؤْمِنُوْنَ الْكٰفِرِيْنَ أَوْلِيَاءَ

مِنْ دُوْنِ الْمُؤْمِنِيْنَ ۚ وَمَنْ يَّفْعَلْ ذٰلِكَ فَلَيْسَ

مِنَ اللّٰهِ فِى شَيْءٍ إِلَّا أَنْ تَتَّقُوْا مِنْهُمْ تُقٰةً ۗ

وَيُحَذِّرُكُمُ اللّٰهُ نَفْسَهٗ ۗ وَإِلَى اللّٰهِ الْمَصِيْرُ ۝

قُلْ إِنْ تُخْفُوْا مَا فِى صُدُوْرِكُمْ أَوْ تُبْدُوْهُ يَعْلَمْهُ

اللّٰهُ ۗ وَيَعْلَمُ مَا فِى السَّمٰوٰتِ وَمَا فِى الْأَرْضِ ۗ وَ

اللّٰهُ عَلٰى كُلِّ شَيْءٍ قَدِيْرٌ ۝ يَوْمَ تَجِدُ كُلُّ نَفْسٍ

مَّا عَمِلَتْ مِنْ خَيْرٍ مُّحْضَرًا ۚ وَّمَا عَمِلَتْ مِنْ

سُوْءٍ ۚ تَوَدُّ لَوْ أَنَّ بَيْنَهَا وَبَيْنَهٗ أَمَدًا بَعِيْدًا ۗ

وَيُحَذِّرُكُمُ اللّٰهُ نَفْسَهٗ ۗ وَاللّٰهُ رَءُوْفٌ بِالْعِبَادِ ۝

قُلْ إِنْ كُنْتُمْ تُحِبُّوْنَ اللّٰهَ فَاتَّبِعُوْنِىْ يُحْبِبْكُمُ اللّٰهُ

وَيَغْفِرْ لَكُمْ ذُنُوْبَكُمْ ۗ وَاللّٰهُ غَفُوْرٌ رَّحِيْمٌ ۝

قُلْ أَطِيْعُوا اللّٰهَ وَالرَّسُوْلَ ۖ فَإِنْ تَوَلَّوْا فَإِنَّ اللّٰهَ

A prayer of submission to Allah's will

²⁶ Say, "Allah! Master of all power, You give power to anyone You want, and You take it away from anyone You want; You bestow honour and You humiliate anyone You please. All goodness is in Your hands. You have power over all things. ²⁷ You *gradually* merge the night in to the day, and You *gradually* merge the day into the night. You create the living from the dead, and You cause the living to die. You provide without bounds to anyone You want."

Evidence of Allah's love: obeying the Messenger ﷺ

²⁸ The believers should not make the disbelievers their allies in preference to the believers, and whoever does so will receive no *help* from Allah unless they have done so to protect themselves out of fear[a]. Allah cautions you to be mindful of Him, and the final return is to Allah. ²⁹ Say, "Whether you reveal what is in your minds or you conceal it, Allah knows it. In fact, He knows whatever is in the Heavens and on the Earth and Allah has power over all things." ³⁰ Every person that day will find *in front of them* whatever good and whatever evil they had done. They will wish that they had not done their bad deeds. Allah warns you to be mindful of Him, He is kind to His servants. ³¹ Say: "If you love Allah then follow me, and Allah will love you and forgive your sins. Allah is the Forgiver, the Kind." ³² Say: "Obey Allah and the Messenger." If they turn away, *remember that* Allah does not love the disbelievers.

---

[a] Ubaidah ibn Samat a prominent disciple of the Prophet ﷺ had a treaty with the Jews of Madinah. At the battle of trenches, he said to the Prophet ﷺ "I have five hundred of the Jews who will fight alongside me against the enemy." These verses were revealed on that occasion (al Sabuni).

لَا يُحِبُّ الْكٰفِرِيْنَ ۞ اِنَّ اللّٰهَ اصْطَفٰٓى اٰدَمَ وَ نُوْحًا

وَّاٰلَ اِبْرٰهِيْمَ وَاٰلَ عِمْرٰنَ عَلَى الْعٰلَمِيْنَ ۞ ذُرِّيَّةً

بَعْضُهَا مِنْ بَعْضٍ ؕ وَاللّٰهُ سَمِيْعٌ عَلِيْمٌ ۞ اِذْ

قَالَتِ امْرَاَتُ عِمْرٰنَ رَبِّ اِنِّيْ نَذَرْتُ لَكَ

مَا فِيْ بَطْنِيْ مُحَرَّرًا فَتَقَبَّلْ مِنِّيْ ۚ اِنَّكَ اَنْتَ

السَّمِيْعُ الْعَلِيْمُ ۞ فَلَمَّا وَضَعَتْهَا قَالَتْ رَبِّ

اِنِّيْ وَضَعْتُهَآ اُنْثٰى ؕ وَاللّٰهُ اَعْلَمُ بِمَا وَضَعَتْ ؕ وَ

لَيْسَ الذَّكَرُ كَالْاُنْثٰى ۚ وَاِنِّيْ سَمَّيْتُهَا مَرْيَمَ وَاِنِّيْٓ

اُعِيْذُهَا بِكَ وَذُرِّيَّتَهَا مِنَ الشَّيْطٰنِ الرَّجِيْمِ ۞

Sometimes Allah gives in mysterious and miraculous ways.

فَتَقَبَّلَهَا رَبُّهَا بِقَبُوْلٍ حَسَنٍ وَّاَنْۢبَتَهَا نَبَاتًا

حَسَنًا ۙ وَّكَفَّلَهَا زَكَرِيَّا ؕ كُلَّمَا دَخَلَ عَلَيْهَا زَكَرِيَّا

الْمِحْرَابَ ۙ وَجَدَ عِنْدَهَا رِزْقًا ۚ قَالَ يٰمَرْيَمُ اَنّٰى

لَكِ هٰذَا ؕ قَالَتْ هُوَ مِنْ عِنْدِ اللّٰهِ ؕ اِنَّ اللّٰهَ

يَرْزُقُ مَنْ يَّشَآءُ بِغَيْرِ حِسَابٍ ۞ هُنَالِكَ دَعَا

زَكَرِيَّا رَبَّهٗ ۚ قَالَ رَبِّ هَبْ لِيْ مِنْ لَّدُنْكَ ذُرِّيَّةً

طَيِّبَةً ۚ اِنَّكَ سَمِيْعُ الدُّعَآءِ ۞ فَنَادَتْهُ الْمَلٰٓئِكَةُ

وَهُوَ قَآئِمٌ يُّصَلِّيْ فِى الْمِحْرَابِ ۙ اَنَّ اللّٰهَ يُبَشِّرُكَ

بِيَحْيٰى مُصَدِّقًۢا بِكَلِمَةٍ مِّنَ اللّٰهِ وَسَيِّدًا وَّحَصُوْرًا

وَّنَبِيًّا مِّنَ الصّٰلِحِيْنَ ۞ قَالَ رَبِّ اَنّٰى يَكُوْنُ

لِيْ غُلٰمٌ وَّقَدْ بَلَغَنِيَ الْكِبَرُ وَامْرَاَتِيْ عَاقِرٌ ؕ

The story of Maryam and her son Isa

[33] From all the creation, Allah chose Adam, Noah, the families of Ibrahim and of Imran, [34] each generation related to the other. Allah is the Hearer, the Knower. [35] When Imran's wife said, "Lord, I vow to dedicate whatever is in my womb to Your service, so accept *this vow* from me. You are the Hearer, the Knower." [36] Once she had given birth to her, she *complained*, "Lord, I gave birth to a girl" – Allah knew well what she had given birth to, the male is not like the female[a] – *then she added*, "I have named her Maryam, and I place her and her offspring in Your protection from the accursed Satan."

Zakariyya takes the responsibility of raising Maryam

[37] Her Lord accepted her and raised her in the best way, and He entrusted her to the care of Zakariyya. Whenever Zakariyya entered the prayer room, he found fruits around her; so *one day* he asked her, "Where do you get these from Maryam?" She replied, "It's from Allah. Indeed, Allah provides boundlessly to whomever He pleases."

Zakariyya prays for a child and receives a sign

[38] Standing there *in a state of bliss*, Zakariyya prayed to his Lord, saying, "My Lord, kindly grant me a righteous child. You are the Hearer of prayers." [39] The angels called out to him as he stood praying in the prayer room, "Allah gives you good news of Yahya, confirming a Word from Allah, a chaste and distinguished person, a Prophet from among the righteous." [40] He asked, "Will I have a boy, I have reached old age and my wife is infertile." *The angel* replied, "It will be so. Allah does what He pleases."

---

[a] 'The male is not like the female' is a paranthesis that explained to Mary's mother "the male child she had prayed for could not have been like the female she was granted." This implies that Mary's excellence would go far beyond any hopes, which her mother had ever entertained (Asad).

قَالَ كَذٰلِكِ اللّٰهُ يَفْعَلُ مَا يَشَآءُ ﴿٤٠﴾ قَالَ رَبِّ

اجْعَلْ لِّيْ اٰيَةً ؕ قَالَ اٰيَتُكَ اَلَّا تُكَلِّمَ النَّاسَ

ثَلٰثَةَ اَيَّامٍ اِلَّا رَمْزًا ؕ وَاذْكُرْ رَّبَّكَ كَثِيْرًا وَّ

سَبِّحْ بِالْعَشِيِّ وَالْاِبْكَارِ ﴿٤١﴾ وَاِذْ قَالَتِ الْمَلٰٓئِكَةُ

يٰمَرْيَمُ اِنَّ اللّٰهَ اصْطَفٰىكِ وَطَهَّرَكِ وَاصْطَفٰىكِ

عَلٰى نِسَآءِ الْعٰلَمِيْنَ ﴿٤٢﴾ يٰمَرْيَمُ اقْنُتِيْ لِرَبِّكِ

وَاسْجُدِيْ وَارْكَعِيْ مَعَ الرّٰكِعِيْنَ ﴿٤٣﴾ ذٰلِكَ مِنْ

اَنْۢبَآءِ الْغَيْبِ نُوْحِيْهِ اِلَيْكَ ؕ وَمَا كُنْتَ لَدَيْهِمْ

اِذْ يُلْقُوْنَ اَقْلَامَهُمْ اَيُّهُمْ يَكْفُلُ مَرْيَمَ ۪

وَمَا كُنْتَ لَدَيْهِمْ اِذْ يَخْتَصِمُوْنَ ﴿٤٤﴾ اِذْ قَالَتِ

الْمَلٰٓئِكَةُ يٰمَرْيَمُ اِنَّ اللّٰهَ يُبَشِّرُكِ بِكَلِمَةٍ

مِّنْهُ ۖ اسْمُهُ الْمَسِيْحُ عِيْسَى ابْنُ مَرْيَمَ وَجِيْهًا

فِى الدُّنْيَا وَالْاٰخِرَةِ وَمِنَ الْمُقَرَّبِيْنَ ﴿٤٥﴾ وَيُكَلِّمُ

النَّاسَ فِى الْمَهْدِ وَكَهْلًا وَّمِنَ الصّٰلِحِيْنَ ﴿٤٦﴾

قَالَتْ رَبِّ اَنّٰى يَكُوْنُ لِيْ وَلَدٌ وَّلَمْ يَمْسَسْنِيْ

بَشَرٌ ؕ قَالَ كَذٰلِكِ اللّٰهُ يَخْلُقُ مَا يَشَآءُ ؕ اِذَا قَضٰٓى

اَمْرًا فَاِنَّمَا يَقُوْلُ لَهٗ كُنْ فَيَكُوْنُ ﴿٤٧﴾ وَيُعَلِّمُهُ

الْكِتٰبَ وَالْحِكْمَةَ وَالتَّوْرٰىةَ وَالْاِنْجِيْلَ ﴿٤٨﴾ وَ

رَسُوْلًا اِلٰى بَنِيْٓ اِسْرَآءِيْلَ ۬ اَنِّيْ قَدْ جِئْتُكُمْ

بِاٰيَةٍ مِّنْ رَّبِّكُمْ ۙ اَنِّيْٓ اَخْلُقُ لَكُمْ مِّنَ الطِّيْنِ

The virgin Maryam has a son in a miraculous way.

⁴¹*Zakariyya* asked, "My Lord, give me a sign." He said, "The sign is that for three days, you will only speak by sign language to people. So, remember your Lord constantly, glorifying Him in the morning and the evening."

Maryam is chosen above all the women of her time
⁴²*Remember* when the angels said to Maryam: "Maryam, Allah has chosen you and purified you from all the women of the world. ⁴³Maryam, worship your Lord, prostrate and bow with those who bow." ⁴⁴This is from the reports of the unseen which We revealed to you. You weren't there among them when they cast lots to determine who would be Maryam's guardian; nor were you there with them when they argued *about the virgin conception.*

Maryam learns of the birth and the miracles of Isa
⁴⁵*Remember* when the angels said: "Maryam, Allah gives you good news of a Word from Him, his name will be the Messiah, Isa son of Maryam, honoured in this world and in the Hereafter, and among *those nearest to Allah.* ⁴⁶He will speak to people from *his* cradle and as a grown-up, and he will be righteous." ⁴⁷She asked, "Lord, how can I have a son when no man has touched me?" *The angel* said, "That is how Allah is; He creates whatever He pleases. If He decides something, He *simply* says, 'Be!' And *there* it is. ⁴⁸And *Allah* will teach him the Book, wisdom, Torah and the Gospel." ⁴⁹And, as a messenger to the Israelites, *he will tell them:* "I have come to you with miracles from your Lord. I will create for you a model of a bird from clay, and with Allah's approval, when I blow on it, it will become a *living* bird. With Allah's approval, I will heal the blind, the leper, and I will bring the dead back to life, and I will tell you what you ate and what you stockpile in your homes. In that there is a sign for you, if you are believers.

كَهَيْئَةِ الطَّيْرِ فَاَنْفُخُ فِيْهِ فَيَكُوْنُ طَيْرًا بِاِذْنِ

اللّٰهِ ۚ وَاُبْرِئُ الْاَكْمَهَ وَالْاَبْرَصَ وَاُحْىِ الْمَوْتٰى

بِاِذْنِ اللّٰهِ ۚ وَاُنَبِّئُكُمْ بِمَا تَاْكُلُوْنَ وَمَا تَدَّخِرُوْنَ ۙ

فِيْ بُيُوْتِكُمْ ؕ اِنَّ فِيْ ذٰلِكَ لَاٰيَةً لَّكُمْ اِنْ كُنْتُمْ

مُّؤْمِنِيْنَ ۚ۲۹ وَمُصَدِّقًا لِّمَا بَيْنَ يَدَىَّ مِنَ

التَّوْرٰىةِ وَلِاُحِلَّ لَكُمْ بَعْضَ الَّذِيْ حُرِّمَ عَلَيْكُمْ

وَجِئْتُكُمْ بِاٰيَةٍ مِّنْ رَّبِّكُمْ قف فَاتَّقُوا اللّٰهَ وَ

اَطِيْعُوْنِ ۝ اِنَّ اللّٰهَ رَبِّيْ وَرَبُّكُمْ فَاعْبُدُوْهُ ؕ هٰذَا

صِرَاطٌ مُّسْتَقِيْمٌ ۝ فَلَمَّاۤ اَحَسَّ عِيْسٰى مِنْهُمُ

الْكُفْرَ قَالَ مَنْ اَنْصَارِيْ اِلَى اللّٰهِ ؕ قَالَ الْحَوَارِيُّوْنَ

نَحْنُ اَنْصَارُ اللّٰهِ ۚ اٰمَنَّا بِاللّٰهِ ۚ وَاشْهَدْ بِاَنَّا

مُسْلِمُوْنَ ۝ رَبَّنَاۤ اٰمَنَّا بِمَاۤ اَنْزَلْتَ وَاتَّبَعْنَا الرَّسُوْلَ

فَاكْتُبْنَا مَعَ الشّٰهِدِيْنَ ۝ وَمَكَرُوْا وَمَكَرَ اللّٰهُ ؕ

وَاللّٰهُ خَيْرُ الْمٰكِرِيْنَ ۝ اِذْ قَالَ اللّٰهُ يٰعِيْسٰۤى اِنِّيْ

مُتَوَفِّيْكَ وَرَافِعُكَ اِلَىَّ وَمُطَهِّرُكَ مِنَ الَّذِيْنَ

كَفَرُوْا وَجَاعِلُ الَّذِيْنَ اتَّبَعُوْكَ فَوْقَ الَّذِيْنَ كَفَرُوْۤا

اِلٰى يَوْمِ الْقِيٰمَةِ ۚ ثُمَّ اِلَىَّ مَرْجِعُكُمْ فَاَحْكُمُ بَيْنَكُمْ

فِيْمَا كُنْتُمْ فِيْهِ تَخْتَلِفُوْنَ ۝ فَاَمَّا الَّذِيْنَ

كَفَرُوْا فَاُعَذِّبُهُمْ عَذَابًا شَدِيْدًا فِى الدُّنْيَا

وَالْاٰخِرَةِ ۡ وَمَا لَهُمْ مِّنْ نّٰصِرِيْنَ ۝ وَاَمَّا الَّذِيْنَ

The disciples of Isa were helpers of Allah and were Muslims.

⁵⁰ I shall confirm what came before me in the Torah, and I will make lawful some things that were *previously* unlawful for you. I have come to you with a sign from your Lord, so fear Allah and obey me. ⁵¹ Allah is mine and your Lord, so worship Him: this is the straight path."

Isa calls his disciples, and they confirm they are Muslims

⁵² When Isa sensed rejection from them, he called out, "Who will be my helper for the sake of Allah?" The disciples replied, "We are Allah's helpers. We believe in Allah and bear witness that we submit *to His will*. ⁵³ Our Lord, we believe in what You have revealed and we follow the messenger, so include us among witnesses *to the truth*."

Isa is told what lies in store for those who deny him

⁵⁴ *The hypocrites among the Israelites* plotted, and Allah prepared a counterplan. Allah is the Best of the planners. ⁵⁵ *Remember* when Allah said: "Isa, I will receive you,ᵃ then raise you up to Me, and I will acquit you of *all the charges invented by* those who deny *the truth*. I will place your followers above those who denied *the truth* until the Day of Judgement; *but for now* you shall return to Me, and I will make judgement about their differences concerning you. ⁵⁶ The deniers, I will punish them severely in this world and the Hereafter, and they will have no helpers."

ᵃ   Tabari said "this phrase is back to front, it means Isa I will raise you up to Me then after your second coming let you die as fixed." This reflects the belief Isa ﷺ will return before the world ends, he will establish Islamic guidance before his death.

اٰمَنُوا وَ عَمِلُوا الصّٰلِحٰتِ فَيُوَفِّيهِمْ أُجُورَهُمْ ط

وَاللّٰهُ لَا يُحِبُّ الظّٰلِمِينَ ۵۷ ذٰلِكَ نَتْلُوهُ عَلَيْكَ

مِنَ الْاٰيٰتِ وَ الذِّكْرِ الْحَكِيمِ ۵۸ اِنَّ مَثَلَ عِيْسٰى

عِنْدَ اللّٰهِ كَمَثَلِ اٰدَمَ ط خَلَقَهٗ مِنْ تُرَابٍ ثُمَّ قَالَ

لَهٗ كُنْ فَيَكُونُ ۵۹ اَلْحَقُّ مِنْ رَّبِّكَ فَلَا تَكُنْ مِّنَ

الْمُمْتَرِينَ ۶۰ فَمَنْ حَآجَّكَ فِيهِ مِنْ بَعْدِ مَا جَآءَكَ

مِنَ الْعِلْمِ فَقُلْ تَعَالَوْا نَدْعُ اَبْنَآءَنَا وَ اَبْنَآءَكُمْ

*Invitation to Jews and
Christians to accept
worship of One God.*

وَ نِسَآءَنَا وَ نِسَآءَكُمْ وَاَنْفُسَنَا وَاَنْفُسَكُمْ قف ثُمَّ

نَبْتَهِلْ فَنَجْعَلْ لَّعْنَتَ اللّٰهِ عَلَى الْكٰذِبِينَ ۶۱

اِنَّ هٰذَا لَهُوَ الْقَصَصُ الْحَقُّ ج وَ مَا مِنْ اِلٰهٍ

اِلَّا اللّٰهُ ط وَاِنَّ اللّٰهَ لَهُوَ الْعَزِيزُ الْحَكِيمُ ۶۲ فَاِنْ

تَوَلَّوْا فَاِنَّ اللّٰهَ عَلِيمٌۢ بِالْمُفْسِدِينَ ۶۳ قُلْ يٰاَهْلَ

الْكِتٰبِ تَعَالَوْا اِلٰى كَلِمَةٍ سَوَآءٍ بَيْنَنَا وَ بَيْنَكُمْ

اَلَّا نَعْبُدَ اِلَّا اللّٰهَ وَلَا نُشْرِكَ بِهٖ شَيْئًا وَّلَا يَتَّخِذَ

بَعْضُنَا بَعْضًا اَرْبَابًا مِّنْ دُونِ اللّٰهِ ط فَاِنْ تَوَلَّوْا

فَقُولُوا اشْهَدُوا بِاَنَّا مُسْلِمُونَ ۶۴ يٰاَهْلَ الْكِتٰبِ

لِمَ تُحَآجُّونَ فِيۡ اِبْرٰهِيمَ وَمَاۤ اُنْزِلَتِ التَّوْرٰةُ

وَالْاِنْجِيلُ اِلَّا مِنْ بَعْدِهٖ ط اَفَلَا تَعْقِلُونَ ۶۵

هٰاَنْتُمْ هٰؤُلَآءِ حَاجَجْتُمْ فِيمَا لَكُمْ بِهٖ عِلْمٌ

فَلِمَ تُحَآجُّونَ فِيمَا لَيْسَ لَكُمْ بِهٖ عِلْمٌ ط وَاللّٰهُ

⁵⁷The believers who do righteous deeds, He will reward them in full, but Allah dislikes the wrongdoers. ⁵⁸That is what We recite to you of *Our* verses from the wise Reminder.

Isa's nature explained in response to Christian misunderstandings

⁵⁹In the sight of Allah, Isa is like Adam; He created him from dust then said to him "Be!" And he became. ⁶⁰This is the truth from Your Lord, so listener, don't be among the doubters.⁶¹Whoever argues with you over this once *the* knowledge has come to you, say to them: "Come! Let us call our sons and your sons, our women and your women, ourselves and yourselves; then let us call on Allah's curse on the liars." ⁶²This is the true account. There is no god but Allah, and Allah is the Almighty, the Wise. ⁶³If they turn away, *so what*, Allah knows the troublemakers.

Judaism, Christianity and Islam: convergence and divergence

⁶⁴Say: "People of The Book, let us agree on a common statement *that exists* between us: We worship no one except Allah; we associate nothing with Him; and we shall not adopt anyone else as lord besides Allah." Then if they turn away *from this*, say: "Be witnesses that we submit *to Allah's will*."

Ibrahim was neither a Jew nor a Christian

⁶⁵"People of The Book, why do you argue over Ibrahim, given that the Torah and the Gospel were not revealed until after him? Why don't you think? ⁶⁶Here you are arguing over something that you know well, but why must you argue over something you don't know?ᵃ Allah knows but you don't know.

ᵃ This verse helps explain what was mentioned in verse 7, the question of the reason for all the friction and disunity.

يَعْلَمُ وَ اَنْتُمْ لَا تَعْلَمُوْنَ ۝ مَا كَانَ اِبْرٰهِيْمُ

يَهُوْدِيًّا وَّلَا نَصْرَانِيًّا وَّلٰكِنْ كَانَ حَنِيْفًا مُّسْلِمًا ؕ

وَمَا كَانَ مِنَ الْمُشْرِكِيْنَ ۝ اِنَّ اَوْلَى النَّاسِ

بِاِبْرٰهِيْمَ لَلَّذِيْنَ اتَّبَعُوْهُ وَهٰذَا النَّبِيُّ وَالَّذِيْنَ

اٰمَنُوْا ؕ وَاللّٰهُ وَلِيُّ الْمُؤْمِنِيْنَ ۝ وَدَّتْ طَّآئِفَةٌ

مِّنْ اَهْلِ الْكِتٰبِ لَوْ يُضِلُّوْنَكُمْ ؕ وَمَا يُضِلُّوْنَ

اِلَّا اَنْفُسَهُمْ وَمَا يَشْعُرُوْنَ ۝ يٰٓاَهْلَ الْكِتٰبِ لِمَ

تَكْفُرُوْنَ بِاٰيٰتِ اللّٰهِ وَاَنْتُمْ تَشْهَدُوْنَ ۝ يٰٓاَهْلَ

الْكِتٰبِ لِمَ تَلْبِسُوْنَ الْحَقَّ بِالْبَاطِلِ وَتَكْتُمُوْنَ

الْحَقَّ وَاَنْتُمْ تَعْلَمُوْنَ ۝ وَقَالَتْ طَّآئِفَةٌ مِّنْ

اَهْلِ الْكِتٰبِ اٰمِنُوْا بِالَّذِيْٓ اُنْزِلَ عَلَى الَّذِيْنَ اٰمَنُوْا

وَجْهَ النَّهَارِ وَاكْفُرُوْٓا اٰخِرَهٗ لَعَلَّهُمْ يَرْجِعُوْنَ ۝ وَلَا

تُؤْمِنُوْٓا اِلَّا لِمَنْ تَبِعَ دِيْنَكُمْ ؕ قُلْ اِنَّ الْهُدٰى هُدَى

اللّٰهِ ۙ اَنْ يُّؤْتٰٓى اَحَدٌ مِّثْلَ مَآ اُوْتِيْتُمْ اَوْ يُحَآجُّوْكُمْ

عِنْدَ رَبِّكُمْ ؕ قُلْ اِنَّ الْفَضْلَ بِيَدِ اللّٰهِ ۚ يُؤْتِيْهِ مَنْ

يَّشَآءُ ؕ وَاللّٰهُ وَاسِعٌ عَلِيْمٌ ۝ يَّخْتَصُّ بِرَحْمَتِهٖ مَنْ

يَّشَآءُ ؕ وَاللّٰهُ ذُو الْفَضْلِ الْعَظِيْمِ ۝ وَمِنْ اَهْلِ الْكِتٰبِ

مَنْ اِنْ تَاْمَنْهُ بِقِنْطَارٍ يُّؤَدِّهٖٓ اِلَيْكَ ۚ وَمِنْهُمْ مَّنْ

اِنْ تَاْمَنْهُ بِدِيْنَارٍ لَّا يُؤَدِّهٖٓ اِلَيْكَ اِلَّا مَا دُمْتَ

عَلَيْهِ قَآئِمًا ؕ ذٰلِكَ بِاَنَّهُمْ قَالُوْا لَيْسَ عَلَيْنَا فِيْ

Never exploit others or take advantage of their weakness.

٨ع
١٥

109

[67] Ibrahim was neither a Jew nor a Christian, but a person of true faith who submitted *to the will of Allah*; he certainly was not from among the idolaters. [68] The closest of people to Ibrahim are those who followed him *at that time*, and this Prophet and those who believe *in his Message*. Allah is the Protector of the believers."

Clever arguments and tricks are no substitute for Divine guidance

[69] Some People of The Book would love to mislead you, not realising that they are only misleading themselves. [70] "People of The Book, why do you deny Allah's signs when you are eyewitnesses *to their revelation?* [71] People of The Book, why do you dress up the truth with falsehood and knowingly hide the truth?" [72] A group of People of The Book say: "*Go ahead and* believe what has been revealed to the believers early in the day then, at the end of the day, deny it; this way, *the believers may give up their faith.*" [73] And they say: "Only believe in those who follow your religion." Say: "Allah's guidance is the only guidance *to rely on that has been given to like.* So why do they dispute with you before your Lord?" Say: "All grace is in Allah's hand, to give to anyone who wants it. Allah is Vast, the Knower. [74] He selects for His kindness anyone He pleases." Allah is Most Gracious, the Almighty.

Warning against changing Allah's words or their meanings

[75] Among the People of The Book are those who, if you entrust them with a heap of gold, they will return it to you. But there are others who, if you entrust them with a single gold coin, they will not return it to you unless you stand over them *until they give it back*; this is because they claim, "We are under no contract when it comes to non-Jews,"[a] and *in this way* they knowingly tell lies against Allah.

---

[a]   Literally, the verse says "illiterate", in the sense of having no scripture or revelation from Allah.

الْاُمِّيّٖنَ سَبِيلٌ ۚ وَيَقُوْلُوْنَ عَلَى اللّٰهِ الْكَذِبَ وَهُمْ

يَعْلَمُوْنَ ۞ بَلٰى مَنْ اَوْفٰى بِعَهْدِهٖ وَاتَّقٰى فَاِنَّ اللّٰهَ

يُحِبُّ الْمُتَّقِيْنَ ۞ اِنَّ الَّذِيْنَ يَشْتَرُوْنَ بِعَهْدِ اللّٰهِ

وَاَيْمَانِهِمْ ثَمَنًا قَلِيْلًا اُولٰٓئِكَ لَا خَلَاقَ لَهُمْ فِى

الْاٰخِرَةِ وَلَا يُكَلِّمُهُمُ اللّٰهُ وَلَا يَنْظُرُ اِلَيْهِمْ يَوْمَ

الْقِيٰمَةِ وَلَا يُزَكِّيْهِمْ ۖ وَلَهُمْ عَذَابٌ اَلِيْمٌ ۞ وَاِنَّ

مِنْهُمْ لَفَرِيْقًا يَّلْوٗنَ اَلْسِنَتَهُمْ بِالْكِتٰبِ لِتَحْسَبُوْهُ

Allah's Prophets could not possibly invite to idolatry.

مِنَ الْكِتٰبِ وَمَا هُوَ مِنَ الْكِتٰبِ ۚ وَيَقُوْلُوْنَ هُوَ مِنْ

عِنْدِ اللّٰهِ وَمَا هُوَ مِنْ عِنْدِ اللّٰهِ ۚ وَيَقُوْلُوْنَ عَلَى اللّٰهِ

الْكَذِبَ وَهُمْ يَعْلَمُوْنَ ۞ مَا كَانَ لِبَشَرٍ اَنْ يُّؤْتِيَهُ

اللّٰهُ الْكِتٰبَ وَالْحُكْمَ وَالنُّبُوَّةَ ثُمَّ يَقُوْلَ لِلنَّاسِ

كُوْنُوْا عِبَادًا لِّيْ مِنْ دُوْنِ اللّٰهِ وَلٰكِنْ كُوْنُوْا رَبَّانِيّٖنَ

بِمَا كُنْتُمْ تُعَلِّمُوْنَ الْكِتٰبَ وَبِمَا كُنْتُمْ تَدْرُسُوْنَ ۞

وَلَا يَأْمُرَكُمْ اَنْ تَتَّخِذُوا الْمَلٰٓئِكَةَ وَالنَّبِيّٖنَ اَرْبَابًا ۗ

اَيَأْمُرُكُمْ بِالْكُفْرِ بَعْدَ اِذْ اَنْتُمْ مُّسْلِمُوْنَ ۞ وَ

اِذْ اَخَذَ اللّٰهُ مِيْثَاقَ النَّبِيّٖنَ لَمَا اٰتَيْتُكُمْ مِّنْ

كِتٰبٍ وَّحِكْمَةٍ ثُمَّ جَاۤءَكُمْ رَسُوْلٌ مُّصَدِّقٌ لِّمَا

مَعَكُمْ لَتُؤْمِنُنَّ بِهٖ وَلَتَنْصُرُنَّهٗ ؕ قَالَ ءَاَقْرَرْتُمْ

وَاَخَذْتُمْ عَلٰى ذٰلِكُمْ اِصْرِيْ ؕ قَالُوْٓا اَقْرَرْنَا ؕ قَالَ

فَاشْهَدُوْا وَاَنَا مَعَكُمْ مِّنَ الشّٰهِدِيْنَ ۞ فَمَنْ تَوَلّٰى

⁷⁶ Not so! Whoever fulfils his pledge and is mindful *let him know that* Allah loves the mindful. ⁷⁷ Those who sell Allah's contract and their own vows in return for a small sum of money will have no share in the Hereafter. Allah will not speak to them nor look at them nor purify them on Judgement Day, *instead* they will have a painful punishment. ⁷⁸ Some of them twist their tongues *when reciting* from the Book to make you think it is from the Book, even though it forms no part of the Book, and they say: "This is from Allah," even though it is not from Allah, and they knowingly tell lies against Allah.

How to test the validity of controversial doctrines

⁷⁹ It is inconceivable for a man who has been given the Book, authority and prophethood by Allah to then tell people: "Worship me instead of Allah." Rather he will say, "Be godly, seeing as you used to teach the Book and study it." ⁸⁰ *Likewise* he would never command you to adopt the angels and prophets as lords. Would he command you to disbelieve after you have submitted *yourselves to the will of Allah*?

The conference of the Prophets

⁸¹ *Remember the time* when Allah took a pledge from *all* the prophets, saying, "Whatever I give you of *the* Book and wisdom, and later *the final* messenger comes to you confirming what you have, then you must believe in him and lend him your support.ᵃ" *They were then asked*, "Do you affirm and accept my pledge as it is?" They replied, "We do." So, *Allah* said, "So be witnesses, and I am a witness with you. ⁸² So, whoever turns away now, these are the sinners.

ᵃ "The final Messenger" here is our Beloved Prophet Muhammad 鬱. So, Allah took a pledge from all the Prophets to believe in him. This pledge was affirmed when all the Prophets prayed behind him in Masjid al Aqsa on the occassion of Ascension (Zia ul Quran).

بَعْدَ ذٰلِكَ فَاُولٰٓئِكَ هُمُ الْفٰسِقُوْنَ ۝ اَفَغَيْرَ دِيْنِ

اللّٰهِ يَبْغُوْنَ وَلَهٗٓ اَسْلَمَ مَنْ فِى السَّمٰوٰتِ وَالْاَرْضِ

طَوْعًا وَّ كَرْهًا وَّ اِلَيْهِ يُرْجَعُوْنَ ۝ قُلْ اٰمَنَّا بِاللّٰهِ

وَمَآ اُنْزِلَ عَلَيْنَا وَمَآ اُنْزِلَ عَلٰٓى اِبْرٰهِيْمَ وَاِسْمٰعِيْلَ

وَاِسْحٰقَ وَيَعْقُوْبَ وَالْاَسْبَاطِ وَمَآ اُوْتِىَ مُوْسٰى

وَعِيْسٰى وَالنَّبِيُّوْنَ مِنْ رَّبِّهِمْ ۙ لَا نُفَرِّقُ بَيْنَ

اَحَدٍ مِّنْهُمْ ۫ وَنَحْنُ لَهٗ مُسْلِمُوْنَ ۝ وَمَنْ يَّبْتَغِ

Islam is surrendering to the will of Allah: a commitment.

غَيْرَ الْاِسْلَامِ دِيْنًا فَلَنْ يُّقْبَلَ مِنْهُ ۚ وَهُوَ فِى

الْاٰخِرَةِ مِنَ الْخٰسِرِيْنَ ۝ كَيْفَ يَهْدِى اللّٰهُ قَوْمًا

كَفَرُوْا بَعْدَ اِيْمَانِهِمْ وَشَهِدُوْٓا اَنَّ الرَّسُوْلَ حَقٌّ وَّ

جَآءَهُمُ الْبَيِّنٰتُ ۭ وَاللّٰهُ لَا يَهْدِى الْقَوْمَ الظّٰلِمِيْنَ ۝

اُولٰٓئِكَ جَزَآؤُهُمْ اَنَّ عَلَيْهِمْ لَعْنَةَ اللّٰهِ وَالْمَلٰٓئِكَةِ

وَالنَّاسِ اَجْمَعِيْنَ ۝ خٰلِدِيْنَ فِيْهَا ۚ لَا يُخَفَّفُ عَنْهُمُ

الْعَذَابُ وَلَا هُمْ يُنْظَرُوْنَ ۝ اِلَّا الَّذِيْنَ تَابُوْا مِنْ

بَعْدِ ذٰلِكَ وَاَصْلَحُوْا ۫ فَاِنَّ اللّٰهَ غَفُوْرٌ رَّحِيْمٌ ۝ اِنَّ

الَّذِيْنَ كَفَرُوْا بَعْدَ اِيْمَانِهِمْ ثُمَّ ازْدَادُوْا كُفْرًا لَّنْ

تُقْبَلَ تَوْبَتُهُمْ ۚ وَاُولٰٓئِكَ هُمُ الضَّآلُّوْنَ ۝ اِنَّ

الَّذِيْنَ كَفَرُوْا وَمَاتُوْا وَهُمْ كُفَّارٌ فَلَنْ يُّقْبَلَ مِنْ

اَحَدِهِمْ مِّلْءُ الْاَرْضِ ذَهَبًا وَّلَوِ افْتَدٰى بِهٖ ط

اُولٰٓئِكَ لَهُمْ عَذَابٌ اَلِيْمٌ وَّمَا لَهُمْ مِّنْ نّٰصِرِيْنَ ۝

Submission to Allah is the only true religion

[83] Are they seeking something other than Allah's religion, while all things in the Heavens and on Earth willingly and unwillingly submit to Him, and to Him they will return? [84] Say: "We believe in Allah and everything revealed to us and to Ibrahim, Ismael, Ishaq, Yaqub[a] and *his* children, and in what Musa and Isa and *other* prophets were given by their Lord. We do not discriminate between any of them, and *we bear witness that* we submit and commit ourselves to Him." [85] Whoever seeks a religion other than Islam,[b] it will never be accepted from him, and in the Hereafter he will be among the losers.

Look out for words and actions that lead to apostasy

[86] Why should Allah guide people who rejected *faith* after believing? They witnessed that the messenger *sent to them* was genuine and came to them with clear proofs. Allah will not guide such wrongdoers. [87] The reward for such *people* is the curse of Allah, the angels and all humanity. [88] They will remain in *Hell* forever; neither will the torment be lightened nor will they be given any respite, [89] except those who later repent and reform themselves. Allah is the Forgiver, the Kind. [90] Those who disbelieve after believing will increase in *their* disbelief, their repentance will never be accepted; such people are utterly misguided. [91] Those who disbelieve and then die as disbelievers, even if one of them were to offer as a ransom enough gold to cover the Earth, it would not be accepted. For such people, a painful punishment is *in store*, and they will have no helpers.

---

[a] Israel is a name which was given to Yaqub later in life, so it is his sons who were the first of the twelve tribes, or the children, of Israel.

[b] Islam means to surrender oneself, commit to the teachings of Allah; Religion of Islam.

لَنْ تَنَالُوا الْبِرَّ حَتّٰى تُنْفِقُوْا مِمَّا تُحِبُّوْنَ ۬

وَمَا تُنْفِقُوْا مِنْ شَيْءٍ فَاِنَّ اللّٰهَ بِهٖ عَلِيْمٌ ۝

كُلُّ الطَّعَامِ كَانَ حِلًّا لِّبَنِيْ اِسْرَآءِيْلَ اِلَّا مَا

حَرَّمَ اِسْرَآءِيْلُ عَلٰى نَفْسِهٖ مِنْ قَبْلِ اَنْ تُنَزَّلَ

التَّوْرٰىةُ ۬ قُلْ فَأْتُوْا بِالتَّوْرٰىةِ فَاتْلُوْهَآ اِنْ كُنْتُمْ

صٰدِقِيْنَ ۝ فَمَنِ افْتَرٰى عَلَى اللّٰهِ الْكَذِبَ مِنْ

بَعْدِ ذٰلِكَ فَاُولٰٓئِكَ هُمُ الظّٰلِمُوْنَ ۝ قُلْ صَدَقَ

اللّٰهُ ۬ فَاتَّبِعُوْا مِلَّةَ اِبْرٰهِيْمَ حَنِيْفًا ۬ وَمَا كَانَ مِنَ

الْمُشْرِكِيْنَ ۝ اِنَّ اَوَّلَ بَيْتٍ وُّضِعَ لِلنَّاسِ لَلَّذِيْ

بِبَكَّةَ مُبٰرَكًا وَّ هُدًى لِّلْعٰلَمِيْنَ ۝ فِيْهِ اٰيٰتٌ

بَيِّنٰتٌ مَّقَامُ اِبْرٰهِيْمَ ۬ وَمَنْ دَخَلَهٗ كَانَ اٰمِنًا ۬

وَلِلّٰهِ عَلَى النَّاسِ حِجُّ الْبَيْتِ مَنِ اسْتَطَاعَ اِلَيْهِ

سَبِيْلًا ۬ وَمَنْ كَفَرَ فَاِنَّ اللّٰهَ غَنِيٌّ عَنِ الْعٰلَمِيْنَ ۝

قُلْ يٰٓاَهْلَ الْكِتٰبِ لِمَ تَكْفُرُوْنَ بِاٰيٰتِ اللّٰهِ ۬

وَاللّٰهُ شَهِيْدٌ عَلٰى مَا تَعْمَلُوْنَ ۝ قُلْ يٰٓاَهْلَ

الْكِتٰبِ لِمَ تَصُدُّوْنَ عَنْ سَبِيْلِ اللّٰهِ مَنْ اٰمَنَ

تَبْغُوْنَهَا عِوَجًا وَّاَنْتُمْ شُهَدَآءُ ۬ وَمَا اللّٰهُ

بِغَافِلٍ عَمَّا تَعْمَلُوْنَ ۝ يٰٓاَيُّهَا الَّذِيْنَ اٰمَنُوْٓا اِنْ

تُطِيْعُوْا فَرِيْقًا مِّنَ الَّذِيْنَ اُوْتُوا الْكِتٰبَ يَرُدُّوْكُمْ

بَعْدَ اِيْمَانِكُمْ كٰفِرِيْنَ ۝ وَكَيْفَ تَكْفُرُوْنَ وَاَنْتُمْ

A lesson from the Israelites: not to invent beliefs and practices

[92] You will never achieve goodness until you spend *in charity* from what you dearly love, and whatever you spend, Allah Knows it. [93] *Initially* all foods were lawful for the Israelites except what Yaqub outlawed for himself before the Torah was revealed. Say: "Bring the Torah and read it, if you are telling the truth." [94] After this, whoever makes up lies against Allah, such people are wrongdoers. [95] Say: "Allah has spoken the truth," so together follow the religion of Ibrahim, a man of firm faith; he was not an idolater.

The first place of worship on Earth

[96] The first house founded for people *to worship in* was that in Bakka,[a] as a blessing and *source* of guidance for all people. [97] There are clear signs in it, *for example* the place where Ibrahim stood. Anyone entering it will be given sanctuary. Pilgrimage to the *Ancient* House is compulsory for People who can make the journey, in order to seek Allah's pleasure. Anyone who denies *this duty should know that* Allah is Self-Sufficient, *independent* of all the creation.

A warning not to deny obvious signs of Allah's favour

[98] Say: "People of The Book, why do you deny Allah's signs, *knowing that* Allah is a witness to all that you do?" [99] Say: "People of The Book, why do you stop believers from Allah's path, seeking to make *those signs* appear to be a deviation, even though you are eyewitnesses *to them*. Allah is not unaware of what you do?" [100] Believers, if you pay heed to *the teachings of* any sect of the People of The Book, they will urge you to revert to disbelief after having believed.

---

a   Bakka is the old name of Makkah.

تُتْلٰى عَلَيْكُمْ اٰيٰتُ اللّٰهِ وَفِيْكُمْ رَسُوْلُهٗ ط وَمَنْ يَّعْتَصِمْ بِاللّٰهِ فَقَدْ هُدِيَ اِلٰى صِرَاطٍ مُّسْتَقِيْمٍ ۞ يٰٓاَيُّهَا الَّذِيْنَ اٰمَنُوا اتَّقُوا اللّٰهَ حَقَّ تُقٰتِهٖ وَلَا تَمُوْتُنَّ اِلَّا وَاَنْتُمْ مُّسْلِمُوْنَ ۞ وَاعْتَصِمُوْا بِحَبْلِ اللّٰهِ جَمِيْعًا وَّلَا تَفَرَّقُوْا ص وَاذْكُرُوْا نِعْمَتَ اللّٰهِ عَلَيْكُمْ اِذْ كُنْتُمْ اَعْدَآءً فَاَلَّفَ بَيْنَ قُلُوْبِكُمْ فَاَصْبَحْتُمْ بِنِعْمَتِهٖٓ اِخْوَانًا ج وَكُنْتُمْ عَلٰى شَفَا حُفْرَةٍ مِّنَ النَّارِ فَاَنْقَذَكُمْ مِّنْهَا ط كَذٰلِكَ يُبَيِّنُ اللّٰهُ لَكُمْ اٰيٰتِهٖ لَعَلَّكُمْ تَهْتَدُوْنَ ۞ وَلْتَكُنْ مِّنْكُمْ اُمَّةٌ يَّدْعُوْنَ اِلَى الْخَيْرِ وَيَاْمُرُوْنَ بِالْمَعْرُوْفِ وَيَنْهَوْنَ عَنِ الْمُنْكَرِ ط وَاُولٰٓئِكَ هُمُ الْمُفْلِحُوْنَ ۞ وَلَا تَكُوْنُوْا كَالَّذِيْنَ تَفَرَّقُوْا وَاخْتَلَفُوْا مِنْ بَعْدِ مَا جَآءَهُمُ الْبَيِّنٰتُ ط وَاُولٰٓئِكَ لَهُمْ عَذَابٌ عَظِيْمٌ ۞ يَّوْمَ تَبْيَضُّ وُجُوْهٌ وَّتَسْوَدُّ وُجُوْهٌ ج فَاَمَّا الَّذِيْنَ اسْوَدَّتْ وُجُوْهُهُمْ ۙ اَكَفَرْتُمْ بَعْدَ اِيْمَانِكُمْ فَذُوْقُوا الْعَذَابَ بِمَا كُنْتُمْ تَكْفُرُوْنَ ۞ وَاَمَّا الَّذِيْنَ ابْيَضَّتْ وُجُوْهُهُمْ فَفِيْ رَحْمَةِ اللّٰهِ ط هُمْ فِيْهَا خٰلِدُوْنَ ۞ تِلْكَ اٰيٰتُ اللّٰهِ نَتْلُوْهَا عَلَيْكَ بِالْحَقِّ ط وَمَا اللّٰهُ يُرِيْدُ ظُلْمًا لِّلْعٰلَمِيْنَ ۞ وَلِلّٰهِ مَا فِي السَّمٰوٰتِ وَمَا فِي الْاَرْضِ ط وَاِلَى اللّٰهِ

Community cohesion comes from unity and a sense of belonging.

¹⁰¹ How could you possibly disbelieve when Allah's verses are being recited to you and His Messenger lives among you? Anyone who holds firmly to *faith in* Allah will be guided to a straight path.

Unity among believers is a sign of Allah's favour

¹⁰² Believers, fear Allah as He deserves to be feared, and do not die except in a state of submission *to Him.* ¹⁰³ Hold tightly to Allah's rope altogether, let nothing divide you, and remember Allah's favour on you when you were enemies and He joined your hearts together *in mutual love* so that, by His favour, you became brothers. You were on the edge of a pit of fire when He saved you from *falling into* it. This is how Allah makes clear His signs for you, so you may be rightly guided. ¹⁰⁴ There should *always* be a group among you that calls *people* to what is best, enjoins the common good and forbids evil; *these people* are the successful.

Sectarianism is condemned

¹⁰⁵ Don't be like those who differed and became divided among themselves after clear signs came to them; severe punishment awaits such people, ¹⁰⁶ on a day when some faces will be bright whilst others will be gloomy. As for those whose faces are gloomy, *they will be asked,* "Did you disbelieve after having believed? So taste the punishment for your disbelief!" ¹⁰⁷ Those whose faces shine joyfully *will be* in Allah's care, where they will remain forever. ¹⁰⁸ These truly are Allah's verses that We recite to you, and Allah does not want to be unjust to His creation. ¹⁰⁹ All things in the Heavens and on Earth belong to Allah, and He determines the outcome of all things.

تُرْجَعُ الْاُمُوْرُ ۞ كُنْتُمْ خَيْرَ اُمَّةٍ اُخْرِجَتْ لِلنَّاسِ

تَاْمُرُوْنَ بِالْمَعْرُوْفِ وَتَنْهَوْنَ عَنِ الْمُنْكَرِ وَتُؤْمِنُوْنَ

بِاللّٰهِ ۭ وَلَوْ اٰمَنَ اَهْلُ الْكِتٰبِ لَكَانَ خَيْرًا لَّهُمْ ۭ

مِنْهُمُ الْمُؤْمِنُوْنَ وَاَكْثَرُهُمُ الْفٰسِقُوْنَ ۞ لَنْ

يَّضُرُّوْكُمْ اِلَّا اَذًى ۭ وَاِنْ يُّقَاتِلُوْكُمْ يُوَلُّوْكُمُ

الْاَدْبَارَ ۣ ثُمَّ لَا يُنْصَرُوْنَ ۞ ضُرِبَتْ عَلَيْهِمُ

الذِّلَّةُ اَيْنَ مَا ثُقِفُوْٓا اِلَّا بِحَبْلٍ مِّنَ اللّٰهِ وَحَبْلٍ

مِّنَ النَّاسِ وَبَآءُوْ بِغَضَبٍ مِّنَ اللّٰهِ وَضُرِبَتْ

عَلَيْهِمُ الْمَسْكَنَةُ ۭ ذٰلِكَ بِاَنَّهُمْ كَانُوْا يَكْفُرُوْنَ

بِاٰيٰتِ اللّٰهِ وَيَقْتُلُوْنَ الْاَنْبِيَآءَ بِغَيْرِ حَقٍّ ۭ ذٰلِكَ

بِمَا عَصَوْا وَّكَانُوْا يَعْتَدُوْنَ ۞ لَيْسُوْا سَوَآءً ۭ مِنْ

اَهْلِ الْكِتٰبِ اُمَّةٌ قَآئِمَةٌ يَّتْلُوْنَ اٰيٰتِ اللّٰهِ اٰنَآءَ

الَّيْلِ وَهُمْ يَسْجُدُوْنَ ۞ يُؤْمِنُوْنَ بِاللّٰهِ وَالْيَوْمِ

الْاٰخِرِ وَيَاْمُرُوْنَ بِالْمَعْرُوْفِ وَيَنْهَوْنَ عَنِ

الْمُنْكَرِ وَيُسَارِعُوْنَ فِي الْخَيْرٰتِ ۭ وَاُولٰٓئِكَ مِنَ

الصّٰلِحِيْنَ ۞ وَمَا يَفْعَلُوْا مِنْ خَيْرٍ فَلَنْ يُّكْفَرُوْهُ ۭ

وَاللّٰهُ عَلِيْمٌۢ بِالْمُتَّقِيْنَ ۞ اِنَّ الَّذِيْنَ كَفَرُوْا لَنْ

تُغْنِيَ عَنْهُمْ اَمْوَالُهُمْ وَلَاۤ اَوْلَادُهُمْ مِّنَ اللّٰهِ

شَيْئًا ۭ وَاُولٰٓئِكَ اَصْحٰبُ النَّارِ ۚ هُمْ فِيْهَا خٰلِدُوْنَ ۞

مَثَلُ مَا يُنْفِقُوْنَ فِيْ هٰذِهِ الْحَيٰوةِ الدُّنْيَا كَمَثَلِ

Social responsibilities of a Muslim: standing up for justice and supporting the needy.

119

The special role of the Muslim community
¹¹⁰You are the best community to emerge for humanity, *so long as* you enjoin the common good, forbid evil and believe in Allah.

Disgrace for those who disobey Allah's commands
Had the People of The Book believed, it would be better for them. Some of them believe, but most of them are evildoers. ¹¹¹They will never do you *any* major harm even if they were to fight you, they would soon turn their backs and then no one would help them. ¹¹²They will be disgraced wherever they go, *unless they are loyal to Allah or loyal to the people*. They have incurred the wrath of Allah, and they are disgraced. All because they denied Allah's signs, killed prophets unjustly, were disobedient and overstepped *Allah's boundaries*.

Do not stereotype people because of religion and race
¹¹³All of them are not alike; a group among the People of The Book upholds the *teachings of the scripture*, reciting Allah's verses throughout the night as they prostrate *to Him*. ¹¹⁴They believe in Allah and the Last Day, enjoin common good and forbid evil, and always rush to perform good deeds; such people are the righteous. ¹¹⁵Whatever good they do, it will never go unrewarded *by Allah*, Allah knows the pious.

The good deeds of disbelievers will be of no value
¹¹⁶Neither the wealth nor the children of the disbelievers shall benefit them in the least before Allah. They are companions of the Fire, remaining therein forever.

رِيحٌ فِيهَا صِرٌّ اَصَابَتۡ حَرۡثَ قَوۡمٍ ظَلَمُوٓا اَنۡفُسَهُمۡ
فَاَهۡلَكَتۡهُ ؕ وَمَا ظَلَمَهُمُ اللّٰهُ وَلٰكِنۡ اَنۡفُسَهُمۡ
يَظۡلِمُوۡنَ ۱۱۷ يٰٓاَيُّهَا الَّذِيۡنَ اٰمَنُوۡا لَا تَتَّخِذُوۡا
بِطَانَةً مِّنۡ دُوۡنِكُمۡ لَا يَاۡلُوۡنَكُمۡ خَبَالًا ؕ وَدُّوۡا
مَا عَنِتُّمۡ ۚ قَدۡ بَدَتِ الۡبَغۡضَآءُ مِنۡ اَفۡوَاهِهِمۡ ۚ
وَمَا تُخۡفِيۡ صُدُوۡرُهُمۡ اَكۡبَرُ ؕ قَدۡ بَيَّنَّا لَكُمُ
الۡاٰيٰتِ اِنۡ كُنۡتُمۡ تَعۡقِلُوۡنَ ۱۱۸ هٰٓاَنۡتُمۡ اُولَآءِ

Fellowship and friendship with righteous people is beneficial for self-improvement.

تُحِبُّوۡنَهُمۡ وَلَا يُحِبُّوۡنَكُمۡ وَتُؤۡمِنُوۡنَ بِالۡكِتٰبِ كُلِّهٖ ۚ
وَاِذَا لَقُوۡكُمۡ قَالُوٓا اٰمَنَّا ۖ وَاِذَا خَلَوۡا عَضُّوۡا عَلَيۡكُمُ
الۡاَنَامِلَ مِنَ الۡغَيۡظِ ؕ قُلۡ مُوۡتُوۡا بِغَيۡظِكُمۡ ؕ اِنَّ
اللّٰهَ عَلِيۡمٌۢ بِذَاتِ الصُّدُوۡرِ ۱۱۹ اِنۡ تَمۡسَسۡكُمۡ
حَسَنَةٌ تَسُؤۡهُمۡ ۫ وَاِنۡ تُصِبۡكُمۡ سَيِّئَةٌ يَّفۡرَحُوۡا
بِهَا ؕ وَاِنۡ تَصۡبِرُوۡا وَتَتَّقُوۡا لَا يَضُرُّكُمۡ كَيۡدُهُمۡ
شَيۡئًا ؕ اِنَّ اللّٰهَ بِمَا يَعۡمَلُوۡنَ مُحِيۡطٌ ۱۲۰ وَاِذۡ
غَدَوۡتَ مِنۡ اَهۡلِكَ تُبَوِّئُ الۡمُؤۡمِنِيۡنَ مَقَاعِدَ
لِلۡقِتَالِ ؕ وَاللّٰهُ سَمِيۡعٌ عَلِيۡمٌ ۱۲۱ اِذۡ هَمَّتۡ طَّآئِفَتٰنِ
مِنۡكُمۡ اَنۡ تَفۡشَلَا ۙ وَاللّٰهُ وَلِيُّهُمَا ؕ وَعَلَى اللّٰهِ
فَلۡيَتَوَكَّلِ الۡمُؤۡمِنُوۡنَ ۱۲۲ وَلَقَدۡ نَصَرَكُمُ اللّٰهُ بِبَدۡرٍ وَّ
اَنۡتُمۡ اَذِلَّةٌ ۚ فَاتَّقُوا اللّٰهَ لَعَلَّكُمۡ تَشۡكُرُوۡنَ ۱۲۳ اِذۡ
تَقُوۡلُ لِلۡمُؤۡمِنِيۡنَ اَلَنۡ يَّكۡفِيَكُمۡ اَنۡ يُّمِدَّكُمۡ رَبُّكُمۡ

[117] In this life anything they spend *in charity* is like a biting wind that blows and destroys the crops of the wrongdoers. Allah did not wrong them but it was themselves.

Choose friends wisely

[118] Believers, don't take as your closest friends others apart from fellow believers, they will cause you grief and they'd like to cause you distress. Their hatred is obvious from their mouths, but what they hide in their hearts is even worse. We have clearly explained to you *Our* signs, if you reflect.[a] [119] This is how you are, you love them, but they don't love you *though* you believe in their whole Book. When they meet you, they say: "We believe," but when they are alone they bite their fingertips out of rage. Say, "Die in your rage!" Allah knows well *people's* innermost feelings. [120] When you have good time, they are saddened, but when you have hard time, they are happy. As long as you are patient and guard yourselves *against them*, their plotting will not harm you. Allah is aware of what they do.

The story of the Battle of Uhud

[121] *Remember* that morning, when you left your home to align the believers in their fighting position. Allah is the Hearer, the Knower. [122] When your two parties considered giving up *the fight*, though Allah was their protector; so let the believers put their trust in Allah. [123] Allah had helped you in *the battle of* Badr, when you were weak, be mindful of Allah so that you are thankful *to Him*.

---

[a] The early Muslims of Madinah were cautioned to befriend the People of the Book who could mislead them.

بِثَلٰثَةِ اٰلٰفٍ مِّنَ الْمَلٰٓئِكَةِ مُنْزَلِيْنَ ۝ بَلٰٓ

اِنْ تَصْبِرُوْا وَتَتَّقُوْا وَيَأْتُوْكُمْ مِّنْ فَوْرِهِمْ هٰذَا

يُمْدِدْكُمْ رَبُّكُمْ بِخَمْسَةِ اٰلٰفٍ مِّنَ الْمَلٰٓئِكَةِ

مُسَوِّمِيْنَ ۝ وَمَا جَعَلَهُ اللّٰهُ اِلَّا بُشْرٰى لَكُمْ

وَلِتَطْمَئِنَّ قُلُوْبُكُمْ بِهٖ ۗ وَمَا النَّصْرُ اِلَّا مِنْ

عِنْدِ اللّٰهِ الْعَزِيْزِ الْحَكِيْمِ ۝ لِيَقْطَعَ طَرَفًا مِّنَ

الَّذِيْنَ كَفَرُوْٓا اَوْ يَكْبِتَهُمْ فَيَنْقَلِبُوْا خَآئِبِيْنَ ۝

لَيْسَ لَكَ مِنَ الْاَمْرِ شَيْءٌ اَوْ يَتُوْبَ عَلَيْهِمْ اَوْ

Why interest is
forbidden; people should
be generous to one
another.

يُعَذِّبَهُمْ فَاِنَّهُمْ ظٰلِمُوْنَ ۝ وَلِلّٰهِ مَا فِى السَّمٰوٰتِ

وَمَا فِى الْاَرْضِ ۗ يَغْفِرُ لِمَنْ يَّشَآءُ وَيُعَذِّبُ

مَنْ يَّشَآءُ ۗ وَاللّٰهُ غَفُوْرٌ رَّحِيْمٌ ۝ يٰٓاَيُّهَا الَّذِيْنَ

اٰمَنُوْا لَا تَأْكُلُوا الرِّبٰٓوا اَضْعَافًا مُّضٰعَفَةً ۪ وَاتَّقُوا

اللّٰهَ لَعَلَّكُمْ تُفْلِحُوْنَ ۝ وَاتَّقُوا النَّارَ الَّتِيْٓ

اُعِدَّتْ لِلْكٰفِرِيْنَ ۝ وَاَطِيْعُوا اللّٰهَ وَالرَّسُوْلَ

لَعَلَّكُمْ تُرْحَمُوْنَ ۝ وَسَارِعُوْٓا اِلٰى مَغْفِرَةٍ مِّنْ

رَّبِّكُمْ وَجَنَّةٍ عَرْضُهَا السَّمٰوٰتُ وَالْاَرْضُ ۙ

اُعِدَّتْ لِلْمُتَّقِيْنَ ۝ الَّذِيْنَ يُنْفِقُوْنَ فِى السَّرَّآءِ

وَالضَّرَّآءِ وَالْكٰظِمِيْنَ الْغَيْظَ وَالْعَافِيْنَ عَنِ

النَّاسِ ۗ وَاللّٰهُ يُحِبُّ الْمُحْسِنِيْنَ ۝ وَالَّذِيْنَ

اِذَا فَعَلُوْا فَاحِشَةً اَوْ ظَلَمُوْٓا اَنْفُسَهُمْ ذَكَرُوا

News of an army of Angels strengthens the believers' resolve

[124] *Remember* when you were motivating the believers: "Aren't you glad your Lord helped you with three thousand angels sent down *as reinforcement*?" [125] Of course, Allah will send five thousand angels swooping down if you are steadfast and mindful, even if the enemy attacks suddenly. [126] Allah did so to raise your spirits and to reassure you, help comes from Allah the Almighty, the Wise. [127] *It was done* to cut off one of the flanks of the disbelievers' army or to weaken them so much that they fled in disarray. [128] It isn't your concern whether Allah forgives them or punishes them; they are wrongdoers. [129] All things in the Heavens and on Earth belong to Allah; He forgives anyone He pleases, and He punishes anyone He pleases. Allah is the Forgiver, the Kind.

The taking of compound interest is forbidden

[130] Believers, do not take compound interest,[a] *increasing your wealth unjustly*, and fear Allah so that you may prosper; [131] protect yourselves from the Fire prepared for the disbelievers, [132] and obey Allah and the Messenger so you are treated kindly.

Believers always try to put things right

[133] Rush towards your Lord's forgiveness and towards Paradise, which is *as* wide as the Heavens and the Earth, prepared for those who are mindful *of Allah*: [134] who spend *in charity* in good and bad times, *can control* their anger and pardon people.

---

[a] Compound interest is a type of usurious practice, where the borrower is forced to pay interest on any accumulated interest as well as on the capital. It is different from simple interest which is interest paid on the capital sum only. It was practised by rich Arabs before the advent of Islam to exploit the poor, who had to borrow money to survive. See *Surat Al-Baqarah* 275-278 for more on the prohibition of usury.

اللّٰهَ فَاسْتَغْفَرُوْا لِذُنُوْبِهِمْ ۗ وَمَنْ يَّغْفِرُ
الذُّنُوْبَ اِلَّا اللّٰهُ ۚ وَلَمْ يُصِرُّوْا عَلٰى مَا فَعَلُوْا
وَهُمْ يَعْلَمُوْنَ ۞ اُولٰٓئِكَ جَزَآؤُهُمْ مَّغْفِرَةٌ مِّنْ
رَّبِّهِمْ وَجَنّٰتٌ تَجْرِيْ مِنْ تَحْتِهَا الْاَنْهٰرُ
خٰلِدِيْنَ فِيْهَا ۗ وَنِعْمَ اَجْرُ الْعٰمِلِيْنَ ۞ قَدْ خَلَتْ
مِنْ قَبْلِكُمْ سُنَنٌ ۙ فَسِيْرُوْا فِى الْاَرْضِ فَانْظُرُوْا
كَيْفَ كَانَ عَاقِبَةُ الْمُكَذِّبِيْنَ ۞ هٰذَا بَيَانٌ
لِّلنَّاسِ وَهُدًى وَّمَوْعِظَةٌ لِّلْمُتَّقِيْنَ ۞ وَلَا تَهِنُوْا

Try to be upbeat,
confident and brave in
the face of adversity.

وَلَا تَحْزَنُوْا وَاَنْتُمُ الْاَعْلَوْنَ اِنْ كُنْتُمْ مُّؤْمِنِيْنَ ۞
اِنْ يَّمْسَسْكُمْ قَرْحٌ فَقَدْ مَسَّ الْقَوْمَ قَرْحٌ مِّثْلُهٗ ۗ
وَتِلْكَ الْاَيَّامُ نُدَاوِلُهَا بَيْنَ النَّاسِ ۚ وَلِيَعْلَمَ اللّٰهُ
الَّذِيْنَ اٰمَنُوْا وَيَتَّخِذَ مِنْكُمْ شُهَدَآءَ ۗ وَاللّٰهُ
لَا يُحِبُّ الظّٰلِمِيْنَ ۞ وَلِيُمَحِّصَ اللّٰهُ الَّذِيْنَ اٰمَنُوْا
وَيَمْحَقَ الْكٰفِرِيْنَ ۞ اَمْ حَسِبْتُمْ اَنْ تَدْخُلُوا
الْجَنَّةَ وَلَمَّا يَعْلَمِ اللّٰهُ الَّذِيْنَ جٰهَدُوْا مِنْكُمْ
وَيَعْلَمَ الصّٰبِرِيْنَ ۞ وَلَقَدْ كُنْتُمْ تَمَنَّوْنَ الْمَوْتَ
مِنْ قَبْلِ اَنْ تَلْقَوْهُ ۫ فَقَدْ رَاَيْتُمُوْهُ وَاَنْتُمْ
تَنْظُرُوْنَ ۞ وَمَا مُحَمَّدٌ اِلَّا رَسُوْلٌ ۚ قَدْ خَلَتْ
مِنْ قَبْلِهِ الرُّسُلُ ۗ اَفَاِنْ مَّاتَ اَوْ قُتِلَ انْقَلَبْتُمْ
عَلٰٓى اَعْقَابِكُمْ ۗ وَمَنْ يَّنْقَلِبْ عَلٰى عَقِبَيْهِ فَلَنْ

¹³⁵Allah loves those who strive to do good. If *by mistake* they act indecently or wrong themselves, at once they remember Allah and seek forgiveness for their sins – can anyone except Allah forgive sins? – And never continue doing *the wrong* knowingly. ¹³⁶The reward for them is forgiveness from their Lord and gardens beneath which rivers flow, where they'll live forever. What an excellent reward for those who act *righteously!* ¹³⁷*Many different* ways of life have existed before you, so travel the Earth and see *for yourselves* what became of those who denied *Allah's signs.* ¹³⁸This is an explanation for humanity, a guidance and warning for those mindful *of Allah.*

Hard lessons learnt from the Battle of Uhud

¹³⁹Do not be disheartened or sad; you will come out on top when you are *true* believers. ¹⁴⁰If you were injured, they were injured too. We cause such days to alternate between people, so that Allah may mark out the true believers among you, and select some as martyrs. *Even if they sometimes win,* Allah does not love the wrongdoers. ¹⁴¹*Furthermore,* Allah *may do this* to put the believers to the test and wipe out the disbelievers. ¹⁴²Or did you think you would go to Paradise without Allah marking out those of you who had struggled *in His path* and those among you who are steadfast? ¹⁴³Before coming face to face with it, you were eager to fight,ᵃ but now you have seen it with your own eyes.

The spoils of war are never the real prize

¹⁴⁴Muhammad is a *noble* messenger, many Messengers came and went before him. If he should die or be martyred, would you turn on your heels *and head back to the old ways*? Whoever turns back will not harm Allah in the slightest. Allah rewards the thankful.

ᵃ   This alludes to the eagerness of some of the Muslims to go to battle.

يَضُرَّ اللّٰهَ شَيْئًا ۚ وَسَيَجْزِى اللّٰهُ الشّٰكِرِيْنَ ۝

وَمَا كَانَ لِنَفْسٍ اَنْ تَمُوْتَ اِلَّا بِاِذْنِ اللّٰهِ

كِتٰبًا مُّؤَجَّلًا ۗ وَمَنْ يُّرِدْ ثَوَابَ الدُّنْيَا نُؤْتِهٖ

مِنْهَا ۚ وَمَنْ يُّرِدْ ثَوَابَ الْاٰخِرَةِ نُؤْتِهٖ مِنْهَا ۗ

وَسَنَجْزِى الشّٰكِرِيْنَ ۝ وَكَاَيِّنْ مِّنْ نَّبِيٍّ قٰتَلَ ۙ

مَعَهٗ رِبِّيُّوْنَ كَثِيْرٌ ۚ فَمَا وَهَنُوْا لِمَاۤ اَصَابَهُمْ فِىْ

سَبِيْلِ اللّٰهِ وَمَا ضَعُفُوْا وَمَا اسْتَكَانُوْا ۗ وَاللّٰهُ

يُحِبُّ الصّٰبِرِيْنَ ۝ وَمَا كَانَ قَوْلَهُمْ اِلَّاۤ اَنْ

قَالُوْا رَبَّنَا اغْفِرْ لَنَا ذُنُوْبَنَا وَاِسْرَافَنَا فِىْ

اَمْرِنَا وَثَبِّتْ اَقْدَامَنَا وَانْصُرْنَا عَلَى الْقَوْمِ

الْكٰفِرِيْنَ ۝ فَاٰتٰهُمُ اللّٰهُ ثَوَابَ الدُّنْيَا وَحُسْنَ

ثَوَابِ الْاٰخِرَةِ ۗ وَاللّٰهُ يُحِبُّ الْمُحْسِنِيْنَ ۝

يٰۤاَيُّهَا الَّذِيْنَ اٰمَنُوْۤا اِنْ تُطِيْعُوا الَّذِيْنَ كَفَرُوْا

يَرُدُّوْكُمْ عَلٰۤى اَعْقَابِكُمْ فَتَنْقَلِبُوْا خٰسِرِيْنَ ۝

بَلِ اللّٰهُ مَوْلٰىكُمْ ۚ وَهُوَ خَيْرُ النّٰصِرِيْنَ ۝ سَنُلْقِىْ

فِىْ قُلُوْبِ الَّذِيْنَ كَفَرُوا الرُّعْبَ بِمَاۤ اَشْرَكُوْا بِاللّٰهِ

مَا لَمْ يُنَزِّلْ بِهٖ سُلْطٰنًا ۚ وَمَأْوٰىهُمُ النَّارُ ۗ وَ

بِئْسَ مَثْوَى الظّٰلِمِيْنَ ۝ وَلَقَدْ صَدَقَكُمُ اللّٰهُ

وَعْدَهٗۤ اِذْ تَحُسُّوْنَهُمْ بِاِذْنِهٖ ۚ حَتّٰۤى اِذَا فَشِلْتُمْ

وَتَنَازَعْتُمْ فِى الْاَمْرِ وَعَصَيْتُمْ مِّنْۢ بَعْدِ مَاۤ

[145] No one dies without Allah's knowledge, but dies at the appointed time, as approved by Allah. Anyone who wants riches of this world, We shall give him some, and whoever wants riches of the Hereafter We shall give him all; and We will reward the thankful.

Believers always stood firm in battle

[146] *Muhammad is* like many other prophets alongside whom masses of *devout men* have fought; they were neither disheartened nor weakened, nor did they surrender in face of their sufferings. Allah loves the patient. [147] They prayed, "Our Lord, forgive our sins and any extravagance of ours, make us steadfast, and help us against the disbelievers." [148] Allah granted them both the rewards of this world and an excellent reward in the Hereafter. Allah loves those who strive to do good. [149] Believers, if you obey the disbelievers, they will make you turn on your heels and go back *to your previous ways* as losers. [150] Rather, Allah is your Protector, and He is the Best of helpers. [151] We will cast terror into the hearts of the disbelievers because *of* all that they associated with Allah without any revealed authority. Their home is the Fire. What an evil resting place for the wrongdoers!

A bitter lesson for the archers who disobeyed Prophet's ﷺ order

[152] Allah fulfilled His promise of help, so you defeated them, then you lost courage, argued about the order *you had been given* and disobeyed, even after He had shown you what you desired – *the fact is that* some of you long for the world, whilst others among you long for the Hereafter – and then He saved you from them in order to test you *further*. Now He has pardoned you. Allah is Gracious to the believers.

اَرٰىكُمْ مَّا تُحِبُّوْنَ ط مِنْكُمْ مَّنْ يُّرِيْدُ الدُّنْيَا وَ

مِنْكُمْ مَّنْ يُّرِيْدُ الْاٰخِرَةَ ج ثُمَّ صَرَفَكُمْ عَنْهُمْ

لِيَبْتَلِيَكُمْ ج وَلَقَدْ عَفَا عَنْكُمْ ط وَاللّٰهُ ذُوْ فَضْلٍ

عَلَى الْمُؤْمِنِيْنَ ۝ اِذْ تُصْعِدُوْنَ وَلَا تَلْوٗنَ عَلٰى

اَحَدٍ وَّالرَّسُوْلُ يَدْعُوْكُمْ فِيْٓ اُخْرٰىكُمْ فَاَثَابَكُمْ

غَمًّا بِغَمٍّ لِّكَيْلَا تَحْزَنُوْا عَلٰى مَا فَاتَكُمْ وَلَا مَآ

اَصَابَكُمْ ط وَاللّٰهُ خَبِيْرٌۢ بِمَا تَعْمَلُوْنَ ۝ ثُمَّ اَنْزَلَ

عَلَيْكُمْ مِّنْ بَعْدِ الْغَمِّ اَمَنَةً نُّعَاسًا يَّغْشٰى

طَآئِفَةً مِّنْكُمْ ۙ وَطَآئِفَةٌ قَدْ اَهَمَّتْهُمْ اَنْفُسُهُمْ

يَظُنُّوْنَ بِاللّٰهِ غَيْرَ الْحَقِّ ظَنَّ الْجَاهِلِيَّةِ ط يَقُوْلُوْنَ

هَلْ لَّنَا مِنَ الْاَمْرِ مِنْ شَىْءٍ ط قُلْ اِنَّ الْاَمْرَ

كُلَّهٗ لِلّٰهِ ط يُخْفُوْنَ فِيْٓ اَنْفُسِهِمْ مَّا لَا يُبْدُوْنَ

لَكَ ط يَقُوْلُوْنَ لَوْ كَانَ لَنَا مِنَ الْاَمْرِ شَىْءٌ مَّا

قُتِلْنَا هٰهُنَا ط قُلْ لَّوْ كُنْتُمْ فِيْ بُيُوْتِكُمْ لَبَرَزَ

الَّذِيْنَ كُتِبَ عَلَيْهِمُ الْقَتْلُ اِلٰى مَضَاجِعِهِمْ ۚ

وَلِيَبْتَلِيَ اللّٰهُ مَا فِيْ صُدُوْرِكُمْ وَلِيُمَحِّصَ مَا

فِيْ قُلُوْبِكُمْ ط وَاللّٰهُ عَلِيْمٌۢ بِذَاتِ الصُّدُوْرِ ۝

اِنَّ الَّذِيْنَ تَوَلَّوْا مِنْكُمْ يَوْمَ الْتَقَى الْجَمْعٰنِ ۙ

اِنَّمَا اسْتَزَلَّهُمُ الشَّيْطٰنُ بِبَعْضِ مَا كَسَبُوْا ج

وَلَقَدْ عَفَا اللّٰهُ عَنْهُمْ ط اِنَّ اللّٰهَ غَفُوْرٌ حَلِيْمٌ ۝

Disobedience of the Messenger ﷺ will cause you hardships.

۱۶
ع

129

[153] *Remember* how you fled uphill *in panic* without concern for anyone, yet the Messenger was calling you from behind; so He gave you a lot of anguish so that *afterwards you don't* grieve over your loss and sufferings. Allah is aware of what you did.

Doubts are means of testing courage

[154] Then, after the anguish, He gave you a sense of security, drowsiness overwhelmed some of you, whilst others were absorbed in their private thoughts, entertaining false ideas about Allah, ideas only fit for the Age of Ignorance. They were saying *to themselves*, "Do we have any say in this?" Tell them, *Muhammad*: "All of this rests with Allah." They conceal in their hearts what they will not reveal to you, saying, "If we had a say in this, we would not have been killed in this spot." Say: "Even if you had stayed at home, those who were fated to be killed would still have come out here to their graves. Allah did this to test your courage and to prove what is in your hearts." Allah knows well *people's* innermost feelings.

Allah pardoned the archers who disobeyed

[155] Those of you who fled on the day the two armies met did so because Satan made some of them err, but Allah has pardoned them; Allah is the Forgiver, the Gentle.

يٰٓاَيُّهَا الَّذِيْنَ اٰمَنُوْا لَا تَكُوْنُوْا كَالَّذِيْنَ كَفَرُوْا وَ

قَالُوْا لِاِخْوَانِهِمْ اِذَا ضَرَبُوْا فِى الْاَرْضِ اَوْ كَانُوْا

غُزًّى لَّوْ كَانُوْا عِنْدَنَا مَا مَاتُوْا وَمَا قُتِلُوْا ۚ

لِيَجْعَلَ اللّٰهُ ذٰلِكَ حَسْرَةً فِىْ قُلُوْبِهِمْ ۗ وَاللّٰهُ

يُحْىٖ وَيُمِيْتُ ۗ وَاللّٰهُ بِمَا تَعْمَلُوْنَ بَصِيْرٌ ۝ وَلَئِنْ

قُتِلْتُمْ فِىْ سَبِيْلِ اللّٰهِ اَوْ مُتُّمْ لَمَغْفِرَةٌ مِّنَ اللّٰهِ

وَرَحْمَةٌ خَيْرٌ مِّمَّا يَجْمَعُوْنَ ۝ وَلَئِنْ مُّتُّمْ اَوْ

قُتِلْتُمْ لَاِلَى اللّٰهِ تُحْشَرُوْنَ ۝ فَبِمَا رَحْمَةٍ مِّنَ

اللّٰهِ لِنْتَ لَهُمْ ۚ وَلَوْ كُنْتَ فَظًّا غَلِيْظَ الْقَلْبِ

لَانْفَضُّوْا مِنْ حَوْلِكَ ۖ فَاعْفُ عَنْهُمْ وَاسْتَغْفِرْ

لَهُمْ وَشَاوِرْهُمْ فِى الْاَمْرِ ۚ فَاِذَا عَزَمْتَ فَتَوَكَّلْ

عَلَى اللّٰهِ ۗ اِنَّ اللّٰهَ يُحِبُّ الْمُتَوَكِّلِيْنَ ۝ اِنْ

يَّنْصُرْكُمُ اللّٰهُ فَلَا غَالِبَ لَكُمْ ۚ وَاِنْ يَّخْذُلْكُمْ

فَمَنْ ذَا الَّذِىْ يَنْصُرُكُمْ مِّنْۢ بَعْدِهٖ ۗ وَعَلَى اللّٰهِ

فَلْيَتَوَكَّلِ الْمُؤْمِنُوْنَ ۝ وَمَا كَانَ لِنَبِيٍّ اَنْ يَّغُلَّ ۗ

وَمَنْ يَّغْلُلْ يَأْتِ بِمَا غَلَّ يَوْمَ الْقِيٰمَةِ ۚ ثُمَّ تُوَفّٰى

كُلُّ نَفْسٍ مَّا كَسَبَتْ وَهُمْ لَا يُظْلَمُوْنَ ۝ اَفَمَنِ

اتَّبَعَ رِضْوَانَ اللّٰهِ كَمَنْۢ بَآءَ بِسَخَطٍ مِّنَ اللّٰهِ وَ

مَأْوٰىهُ جَهَنَّمُ ۗ وَبِئْسَ الْمَصِيْرُ ۝ هُمْ دَرَجٰتٌ عِنْدَ

اللّٰهِ ۗ وَاللّٰهُ بَصِيْرٌۢ بِمَا يَعْمَلُوْنَ ۝ لَقَدْ مَنَّ اللّٰهُ

The Messenger ﷺ was an exemplary leader: gentle, forgiving and trustworthy.

131

¹⁵⁶Believers, do not be like the disbelievers who say of their brothers who *die* on a journey or in battle: "Had they stayed with us they wouldn't have died nor been killed." This is how Allah sows regret in their hearts. Allah gives life, and He takes it away, He sees all you do. ¹⁵⁷Whether you are killed for Allah's cause or you die, Allah's forgiveness and kindness are far better than what they can gather. ¹⁵⁸If you die or get killed, you will certainly be gathered before Allah.

Your setback will lead to your comeback

¹⁵⁹Allah made you kind, so you are lenient with them; had you been harsh and hardhearted they would have deserted you, so pardon, seek forgiveness and consult them. Once you have made up your mind, put trust in Allah. Allah loves those who put their trust *in Him*. ¹⁶⁰If Allah helps you, no one can defeat you, but if He humiliates you, then who will be your helper? The believers put their trust in Allah. ¹⁶¹A prophet does not cheat *anyone*. Whoever cheats will *be forced to* produce what he gained by cheating on the Day of Judgement; then everyone will be paid their due in full, and they will not be wronged. ¹⁶²How can a person who seeks Allah's pleasure be compared with one who earned His anger, and whose destination is Hell? What a wretched end! ¹⁶³For each of them, Allah has *prepared* different ranks. Allah sees what they do.

عَلَى الۡمُؤۡمِنِيۡنَ اِذۡ بَعَثَ فِيۡهِمۡ رَسُوۡلًا مِّنۡ اَنۡفُسِهِمۡ يَتۡلُوۡا عَلَيۡهِمۡ اٰيٰتِهٖ وَيُزَكِّيۡهِمۡ وَيُعَلِّمُهُمُ الۡكِتٰبَ وَالۡحِكۡمَةَ ۚ وَاِنۡ كَانُوۡا مِنۡ قَبۡلُ لَفِىۡ ضَلٰلٍ مُّبِيۡنٍ ﴿۱۶۴﴾ اَوَلَمَّآ اَصَابَتۡكُمۡ مُّصِيۡبَةٌ قَدۡ اَصَبۡتُمۡ مِّثۡلَيۡهَا ۙ قُلۡتُمۡ اَنّٰى هٰذَا ؕ قُلۡ هُوَ مِنۡ عِنۡدِ اَنۡفُسِكُمۡ ؕ اِنَّ اللّٰهَ عَلٰى كُلِّ شَىۡءٍ قَدِيۡرٌ ﴿۱۶۵﴾ وَمَآ اَصَابَكُمۡ يَوۡمَ الۡتَقَى الۡجَمۡعٰنِ فَبِاِذۡنِ اللّٰهِ وَلِيَعۡلَمَ الۡمُؤۡمِنِيۡنَ ﴿۱۶۶﴾ وَلِيَعۡلَمَ الَّذِيۡنَ نَافَقُوۡا ۚ وَقِيۡلَ لَهُمۡ تَعَالَوۡا قَاتِلُوۡا فِىۡ سَبِيۡلِ اللّٰهِ اَوِ ادۡفَعُوۡا ؕ قَالُوۡا لَوۡ نَعۡلَمُ قِتَالًا لَّاتَّبَعۡنٰكُمۡ ؕ هُمۡ لِلۡكُفۡرِ يَوۡمَئِذٍ اَقۡرَبُ مِنۡهُمۡ لِلۡاِيۡمَانِ ۚ يَقُوۡلُوۡنَ بِاَفۡوَاهِهِمۡ مَّا لَيۡسَ فِىۡ قُلُوۡبِهِمۡ ؕ وَاللّٰهُ اَعۡلَمُ بِمَا يَكۡتُمُوۡنَ ﴿۱۶۷﴾ اَلَّذِيۡنَ قَالُوۡا لِاِخۡوَانِهِمۡ وَقَعَدُوۡا لَوۡ اَطَاعُوۡنَا مَا قُتِلُوۡا ؕ قُلۡ فَادۡرَءُوۡا عَنۡ اَنۡفُسِكُمُ الۡمَوۡتَ اِنۡ كُنۡتُمۡ صٰدِقِيۡنَ ﴿۱۶۸﴾ وَلَا تَحۡسَبَنَّ الَّذِيۡنَ قُتِلُوۡا فِىۡ سَبِيۡلِ اللّٰهِ اَمۡوَاتًا ؕ بَلۡ اَحۡيَآءٌ عِنۡدَ رَبِّهِمۡ يُرۡزَقُوۡنَ ﴿۱۶۹﴾ فَرِحِيۡنَ بِمَآ اٰتٰهُمُ اللّٰهُ مِنۡ فَضۡلِهٖ ۙ وَيَسۡتَبۡشِرُوۡنَ بِالَّذِيۡنَ لَمۡ يَلۡحَقُوۡا بِهِمۡ مِّنۡ خَلۡفِهِمۡ ۙ اَلَّا خَوۡفٌ عَلَيۡهِمۡ وَلَا هُمۡ يَحۡزَنُوۡنَ ﴿۱۷۰﴾ يَسۡتَبۡشِرُوۡنَ بِنِعۡمَةٍ مِّنَ اللّٰهِ وَفَضۡلٍ ۙ وَّاَنَّ اللّٰهَ لَا يُضِيۡعُ اَجۡرَ الۡمُؤۡمِنِيۡنَ ﴿۱۷۱﴾

Martyrdom: dying for the cause of Allah; truth and justice and common good.

133

The Messenger ﷺ is the greatest favour of Allah for the believers

[164] Allah favoured the believers when He sent them a messenger from among themselves, reciting His verses, purifying them, and teaching them the Book and wisdom, before that they were misguided.

The defeat at Uhud distinguished the hypocrites from the believers

[165] *Strangely*, when a tragedy struck you, after you had inflicted twice as much *damage on your enemies*, you said, "Where did this come from?" Tell them: "It came from yourselves." Allah has power over all things. [166] What happened to you that day when the two armies met happened with Allah's permission, and to mark out the believers, [167] and to mark out the hypocrites; when they were told: "Come and fight in Allah's way, or at least defend yourselves," they answered, "If only we knew how to fight we would have followed you." That day, they were far nearer to disbelief than ever they were to faith, saying with their mouths what wasn't in their hearts. Allah knows well what they hide. [168] Those who told their brothers to remain behind with them, *and then said*, "If only they had listened to us, they would not have been killed." Say *to them*: "Ward off death from yourselves, if you are telling the truth."

The martyrs of Uhud; the dead don t die

[169] Don't consider dead those killed in Allah's way; they're alive *eating and drinking*, in their Lord's presence. [170] Delighting in that portion of grace which Allah has given them and rejoicing at those who have yet to join them *as martyrs* in succession, *saying* that they should have no fear nor should they grieve. [171] They rejoice in Allah's gifts and favours, Allah will not lower the value of the believer's reward.

اَلَّذِيْنَ اسْتَجَابُوْا لِلّٰهِ وَالرَّسُوْلِ مِنْۢ بَعْدِ مَاۤ

اَصَابَهُمُ الْقَرْحُ ۛ لِلَّذِيْنَ اَحْسَنُوْا مِنْهُمْ وَاتَّقَوْا

اَجْرٌ عَظِيْمٌ ۚ۝ اَلَّذِيْنَ قَالَ لَهُمُ النَّاسُ اِنَّ النَّاسَ

قَدْ جَمَعُوْا لَكُمْ فَاخْشَوْهُمْ فَزَادَهُمْ اِيْمَانًا ۖ

وَّقَالُوْا حَسْبُنَا اللّٰهُ وَنِعْمَ الْوَكِيْلُ ۝ فَانْقَلَبُوْا

بِنِعْمَةٍ مِّنَ اللّٰهِ وَفَضْلٍ لَّمْ يَمْسَسْهُمْ سُوْٓءٌ ۙ

وَّاتَّبَعُوْا رِضْوَانَ اللّٰهِ ۗ وَاللّٰهُ ذُوْ فَضْلٍ عَظِيْمٍ۝ اِنَّمَا

ذٰلِكُمُ الشَّيْطٰنُ يُخَوِّفُ اَوْلِيَآءَهٗ ۪ فَلَا تَخَافُوْهُمْ

وَخَافُوْنِ اِنْ كُنْتُمْ مُّؤْمِنِيْنَ ۝ وَلَا يَحْزُنْكَ

الَّذِيْنَ يُسَارِعُوْنَ فِى الْكُفْرِ ۚ اِنَّهُمْ لَنْ يَّضُرُّوا

اللّٰهَ شَيْئًا ۗ يُرِيْدُ اللّٰهُ اَلَّا يَجْعَلَ لَهُمْ حَظًّا فِى

الْاٰخِرَةِ ۚ وَلَهُمْ عَذَابٌ عَظِيْمٌ۝ اِنَّ الَّذِيْنَ اشْتَرَوُا

الْكُفْرَ بِالْاِيْمَانِ لَنْ يَّضُرُّوا اللّٰهَ شَيْئًا ۚ وَلَهُمْ

عَذَابٌ اَلِيْمٌ۝ وَلَا يَحْسَبَنَّ الَّذِيْنَ كَفَرُوْۤا اَنَّمَا نُمْلِيْ

لَهُمْ خَيْرٌ لِّاَنْفُسِهِمْ ۗ اِنَّمَا نُمْلِيْ لَهُمْ لِيَزْدَادُوْۤا

اِثْمًا ۚ وَلَهُمْ عَذَابٌ مُّهِيْنٌ ۝ مَا كَانَ اللّٰهُ لِيَذَرَ

الْمُؤْمِنِيْنَ عَلٰى مَاۤ اَنْتُمْ عَلَيْهِ حَتّٰى يَمِيْزَ

الْخَبِيْثَ مِنَ الطَّيِّبِ ۗ وَمَا كَانَ اللّٰهُ لِيُطْلِعَكُمْ

عَلَى الْغَيْبِ وَلٰكِنَّ اللّٰهَ يَجْتَبِيْ مِنْ رُّسُلِهٖ مَنْ

يَّشَآءُ ۖ فَاٰمِنُوْا بِاللّٰهِ وَرُسُلِهٖ ۚ وَاِنْ تُؤْمِنُوْا وَ

Don't lose hope even after a severe loss.

¹⁷²Those *believers* who rallied to the call of Allah and the Messenger after getting injured will get a great reward, for striving to do good and being mindful *of Allah*. ¹⁷³When they were told: "The people *of Makkah* have gathered against you, so fear them," their faith increased, and they said: "Allah's *help* is enough for us. What an Excellent Guardian!" ¹⁷⁴So they returned *home* with Allah's blessing and favour, without being harmed since they had sought Allah's pleasure. Allah is Most Gracious.

Consolation following the defeat at Battle of Uhud

¹⁷⁵That was Satan, making *you* fear his cronies. Don't be afraid of them but fear Me, if you are *true* believers. ¹⁷⁶*Muhammad*, do not be distressed by those who rush headlong into disbelief; they will never harm Allah in the slightest. Allah wishes to give them no share in the Hereafter, but their punishment will be severe. ¹⁷⁷They have traded their faith for disbelief,^a they can never harm Allah in the slightest; for them is a painful punishment.

The wealth of the ungodly is not blessing but a test

¹⁷⁸The disbelievers shouldn't consider Our prolonging their lives as a good thing for them; We prolong their lives so they increase in their sinfulness; for them is a shameful punishment. ¹⁷⁹Allah will not leave *you* believers as you are now until He has separated the good from the bad; nor will Allah inform *all of* you about the unseen realm, but Allah picks out anyone He pleases from His messengers. So, believe in Allah and His Messenger, and if you believe and are mindful *of Allah*, then you shall have a great reward.

---

^a Literally translated as: "bought disbelief instead of faith".

تَتَّقُوْا فَلَكُمْ اَجْرٌ عَظِيْمٌ ۝ وَلَا يَحْسَبَنَّ الَّذِيْنَ

يَبْخَلُوْنَ بِمَآ اٰتٰىهُمُ اللّٰهُ مِنْ فَضْلِهٖ هُوَ خَيْرًا

لَّهُمْ ط بَلْ هُوَ شَرٌّ لَّهُمْ ط سَيُطَوَّقُوْنَ مَا بَخِلُوْا بِهٖ

يَوْمَ الْقِيٰمَةِ ط وَلِلّٰهِ مِيْرَاثُ السَّمٰوٰتِ وَالْاَرْضِ ط

وَاللّٰهُ بِمَا تَعْمَلُوْنَ خَبِيْرٌ ۝ لَقَدْ سَمِعَ اللّٰهُ قَوْلَ

الَّذِيْنَ قَالُوْۤا اِنَّ اللّٰهَ فَقِيْرٌ وَّ نَحْنُ اَغْنِيَآءُ ۘ

سَنَكْتُبُ مَا قَالُوْا وَقَتْلَهُمُ الْاَنْبِيَآءَ بِغَيْرِ حَقٍّ ۙ

وَّنَقُوْلُ ذُوْقُوْا عَذَابَ الْحَرِيْقِ ۝ ذٰلِكَ بِمَا قَدَّمَتْ

Beware of the deceptions of the world.

اَيْدِيْكُمْ وَ اَنَّ اللّٰهَ لَيْسَ بِظَلَّامٍ لِّلْعَبِيْدِ ۝

اَلَّذِيْنَ قَالُوْۤا اِنَّ اللّٰهَ عَهِدَ اِلَيْنَآ اَلَّا نُؤْمِنَ

لِرَسُوْلٍ حَتّٰى يَاْتِيَنَا بِقُرْبَانٍ تَاْكُلُهُ النَّارُ ط قُلْ

قَدْ جَآءَكُمْ رُسُلٌ مِّنْ قَبْلِيْ بِالْبَيِّنٰتِ وَبِالَّذِيْ

قُلْتُمْ فَلِمَ قَتَلْتُمُوْهُمْ اِنْ كُنْتُمْ صٰدِقِيْنَ ۝ فَاِنْ

كَذَّبُوْكَ فَقَدْ كُذِّبَ رُسُلٌ مِّنْ قَبْلِكَ جَآءُوْ

بِالْبَيِّنٰتِ وَالزُّبُرِ وَالْكِتٰبِ الْمُنِيْرِ ۝ كُلُّ نَفْسٍ

ذَآئِقَةُ الْمَوْتِ ط وَاِنَّمَا تُوَفَّوْنَ اُجُوْرَكُمْ يَوْمَ

الْقِيٰمَةِ ط فَمَنْ زُحْزِحَ عَنِ النَّارِ وَاُدْخِلَ الْجَنَّةَ

فَقَدْ فَازَ ط وَمَا الْحَيٰوةُ الدُّنْيَآ اِلَّا مَتَاعُ الْغُرُوْرِ ۝

لَتُبْلَوُنَّ فِيْۤ اَمْوَالِكُمْ وَاَنْفُسِكُمْ ۗ وَلَتَسْمَعُنَّ مِنَ

الَّذِيْنَ اُوْتُوا الْكِتٰبَ مِنْ قَبْلِكُمْ وَمِنَ الَّذِيْنَ

[180] Don't let those who are stingy with what Allah has given them of His favours imagine for a moment that it is good for them; rather it is bad for them. On Judgement Day they will be made to wear the wealth they hoarded as collars round their necks. Everything in the Heavens and Earth belongs to Allah. Allah is aware of what you do.

They have denied, mocked and killed Prophets
[181] Allah has heard the words of those who said, "Allah is poor, and we are rich." We shall write down what they said. They killed the Prophets unlawfully, and We shall say to them, "Taste the punishment of the blazing Fire, [182] this is for the misdeeds committed by your hands." Allah is not unjust to *His* servants, [183] who say, "Allah has taken our pledge not to believe in a messenger until he comes to you with a burnt offering."[a] Say: "Many messengers came to you before me with clear proofs, and practised what you mention. Why did you kill them, if you are telling the truth?" [184] If they accuse you of lying, many messengers before you were also accused of lying, *even though* they came with miracles, scriptures and the enlightening Book.

Tests are a part of life
[185] Everyone will have the taste of death, and on Judgement Day you will be given your full reward. Anyone who is saved from the Fire and is admitted to Paradise will be the winner. This worldly life is no more than a deception. [186] You will certainly be tested through your wealth and persons and you will hear many insults from the idolaters and those given the Book before you. If you are patient and mindful *of Allah*, that is real resolve.

---

[a] "A burnt offering" refers to "conforming to the Mosaic Law, which prescribes burnt offerings as an essential part of Divine services." (Asad).

أَشْرَكُوٓا أَذًى كَثِيرًا ۚ وَإِن تَصْبِرُوا وَتَتَّقُوا فَإِنَّ

ذٰلِكَ مِنْ عَزْمِ الْأُمُورِ ۝ وَإِذْ أَخَذَ اللّٰهُ مِيثَاقَ

الَّذِينَ أُوتُوا الْكِتٰبَ لَتُبَيِّنُنَّهُ لِلنَّاسِ وَلَا

تَكْتُمُونَهُ ۗ فَنَبَذُوهُ وَرَآءَ ظُهُورِهِمْ وَاشْتَرَوْا بِهِ

ثَمَنًا قَلِيلًا ۚ فَبِئْسَ مَا يَشْتَرُونَ ۝ لَا تَحْسَبَنَّ

الَّذِينَ يَفْرَحُونَ بِمَآ أَتَوْا وَيُحِبُّونَ أَن يُحْمَدُوا

بِمَا لَمْ يَفْعَلُوا فَلَا تَحْسَبَنَّهُم بِمَفَازَةٍ مِّنَ الْعَذَابِ

وَلَهُمْ عَذَابٌ أَلِيمٌ ۝ وَلِلّٰهِ مُلْكُ السَّمٰوٰتِ وَ

Who are intelligent people? Devout, thoughtful and disciplined.

الْأَرْضِ ۗ وَاللّٰهُ عَلَىٰ كُلِّ شَيْءٍ قَدِيرٌ ۝ إِنَّ فِي

خَلْقِ السَّمٰوٰتِ وَالْأَرْضِ وَاخْتِلَافِ الَّيْلِ وَالنَّهَارِ

لَآيٰتٍ لِّأُولِي الْأَلْبَابِ ۝ الَّذِينَ يَذْكُرُونَ اللّٰهَ

قِيٰمًا وَّقُعُودًا وَّعَلَىٰ جُنُوبِهِمْ وَيَتَفَكَّرُونَ فِي

خَلْقِ السَّمٰوٰتِ وَالْأَرْضِ ۚ رَبَّنَا مَا خَلَقْتَ هٰذَا

بَاطِلًا ۚ سُبْحٰنَكَ فَقِنَا عَذَابَ النَّارِ ۝ رَبَّنَآ إِنَّكَ

مَن تُدْخِلِ النَّارَ فَقَدْ أَخْزَيْتَهُ ۗ وَمَا لِلظّٰلِمِينَ

مِنْ أَنصَارٍ ۝ رَبَّنَآ إِنَّنَا سَمِعْنَا مُنَادِيًا يُّنَادِي

لِلْإِيمَانِ أَنْ آمِنُوا بِرَبِّكُمْ فَآمَنَّا ۚ رَبَّنَا فَاغْفِرْ

لَنَا ذُنُوبَنَا وَكَفِّرْ عَنَّا سَيِّئَاتِنَا وَتَوَفَّنَا مَعَ

الْأَبْرَارِ ۝ رَبَّنَا وَآتِنَا مَا وَعَدتَّنَا عَلَىٰ رُسُلِكَ وَلَا

تُخْزِنَا يَوْمَ الْقِيٰمَةِ ۗ إِنَّكَ لَا تُخْلِفُ الْمِيعَادَ ۝

139

Do not hide the message

[187] *Remember,* Allah made a contract with those given the Book: "Proclaim it to the people and do not hide it." So, they threw it behind them[a] and sold it for a small sum of money. How evil was their bargaining! [188] *Prophet,* do not consider those who delight at what they have done and wish to be praised for what they failed to do; don't think they've escaped the punishment; they shall have a painful punishment. [189] Control of the Heavens and the Earth belong to Allah. Allah has power over all things.

The prayer of intelligent people

[190] In the creation of the Heavens and the Earth and the cycle of night and day, there are signs for smart people, [191] who remember Allah standing, sitting and lying down, and think about the creation of the Heavens and the Earth, *prayerfully saying,* "Our Lord, You haven't created this in vain, Glory be to You! Save us from the punishment of the Fire. [192] Our Lord, anyone You assign to the Fire is humiliated; the evildoers shall have no helpers. [193] Our Lord, we heard a crier calling to faith; 'Believe in your Lord,' so we believed. Our Lord, forgive our sins, delete our evil deeds, and when we die count us among the righteous. [194] Our Lord, give us what You've promised us through Your messengers and do not humiliate us on the Day of Judgement; indeed, You do not break *Your* promise."

---

[a]   Literally translated as: "threw it behind their backs".

فَاسْتَجَابَ لَهُمْ رَبُّهُمْ اَنِّىْ لَا اُضِيْعُ عَمَلَ

عَامِلٍ مِّنْكُمْ مِّنْ ذَكَرٍ اَوْ اُنْثٰى ۚ بَعْضُكُمْ مِّنْ

بَعْضٍ ۚ فَالَّذِيْنَ هَاجَرُوْا وَ اُخْرِجُوْا مِنْ دِيَارِهِمْ

وَ اُوْذُوْا فِىْ سَبِيْلِىْ وَ قَاتَلُوْا وَ قُتِلُوْا لَاُكَفِّرَنَّ

عَنْهُمْ سَيِّاٰتِهِمْ وَلَاُدْخِلَنَّهُمْ جَنّٰتٍ تَجْرِىْ مِنْ

تَحْتِهَا الْاَنْهٰرُ ۚ ثَوَابًا مِّنْ عِنْدِ اللهِ ۗ وَاللهُ عِنْدَهٗ

حُسْنُ الثَّوَابِ ۝ لَا يَغُرَّنَّكَ تَقَلُّبُ الَّذِيْنَ كَفَرُوْا

فِى الْبِلَادِ ۝ مَتَاعٌ قَلِيْلٌ ۗ ثُمَّ مَأْوٰىهُمْ جَهَنَّمُ ۗ

وَبِئْسَ الْمِهَادُ ۝ لٰكِنِ الَّذِيْنَ اتَّقَوْا رَبَّهُمْ لَهُمْ

جَنّٰتٌ تَجْرِىْ مِنْ تَحْتِهَا الْاَنْهٰرُ خٰلِدِيْنَ فِيْهَا نُزُلًا

مِّنْ عِنْدِ اللهِ ۗ وَمَا عِنْدَ اللهِ خَيْرٌ لِّلْاَبْرَارِ ۝

وَ اِنَّ مِنْ اَهْلِ الْكِتٰبِ لَمَنْ يُّؤْمِنُ بِاللهِ وَمَآ

اُنْزِلَ اِلَيْكُمْ وَمَآ اُنْزِلَ اِلَيْهِمْ خٰشِعِيْنَ لِلهِ ۙ

لَا يَشْتَرُوْنَ بِاٰيٰتِ اللهِ ثَمَنًا قَلِيْلًا ۗ اُولٰٓئِكَ لَهُمْ

اَجْرُهُمْ عِنْدَ رَبِّهِمْ ۗ اِنَّ اللهَ سَرِيْعُ الْحِسَابِ ۝

يٰٓاَيُّهَا الَّذِيْنَ اٰمَنُوا اصْبِرُوْا وَصَابِرُوْا وَرَابِطُوْا ۚ

وَاتَّقُوا اللهَ لَعَلَّكُمْ تُفْلِحُوْنَ ۝

Don't be impressed with the pomp and prosperity of disbelievers; it's fleeting.

141

The Lord answers their prayer

¹⁹⁵ Their Lord answered the prayer, *saying*, "I will not allow the deeds of any of you, male or a female, to go to waste; you will both get the same reward. As for those who migrated, those expelled from their homes, those who suffered in My way, those who fought, and those who were killed, I will certainly delete their evil deeds, and I will certainly admit them into gardens beneath which rivers flow. This is their reward from Allah; and Allah gives the best reward.

What is true success?

¹⁹⁶ Don't be deceived by the disbelievers' commercial trade through the land; ¹⁹⁷ it's a temporary provision, and their final home will be Hell. What a wretched place! ¹⁹⁸ However, those who are mindful of their Lord will have gardens beneath which rivers flow, where they will live forever, a resting place provided by Allah. Most wonderful is that which Allah has *prepared* for the righteous. ¹⁹⁹ Among the People of The Book are those who believe in Allah and what has been revealed to you and to them; they are humble towards Allah, not selling Allah's verses for a small sum of money; such people shall *find* their reward with their Lord. Allah is swift in settling accounts. ²⁰⁰ Believers, be patient, encourage each other to be patient, be disciplined,ᵃ and be mindful of Allah so that you may prosper.

ᵃ To serve Allah and to defend yourself, like a soldier who stands guard at a border post.

4. Surat An-Nisa'

The Women

This surat was revealed in Madinah over a period of eighteen months after the Battle of Uhud, in 3 AH/625 CE. Nearly a third of the surat discusses family issues, since seventy Muslim men were martyred, leaving behind them orphans, widows and creating a crisis in families. There was a dire need for clear guidance on how to deal with the crisis. The surat lays out a series of laws concerning: the status of women, marriage, marital discord, inheritance, capital punishment for murder, prohibition of praying under the influence of alcohol, and the rights of orphans. It provides instructions on settling family disputes arising out of what is now called "post-traumatic stress disorder". It lays out clear rulings to ensure justice is done, but still emphasises the need to be caring and loving towards orphans and one's family. In this way, a safe space is created for the nurturing of children.

The surat sheds light on the tension between Muslims and the Jews, whose persistent mockery of the Muslims is condemned. They are reminded of their iniquities, rebellion, and disobedience against their prophets, and their hostility towards the Prophet Isa. The Christians are also censured for tampering with Scripture and adopting Trinity as the foundation of Christianity. In the case of the claims of many Jews at that time, the Quran makes it clear that: "They neither killed him nor crucified him but it appeared like that to them." (157)

Regarding jihad, the Muslims "who are willing to swap this worldly life for the Hereafter" are urged to "fight in the way of Allah" (74). It goes on to explain that jihad is not about fighting and killing people, but standing up for justice against the persecution of those who pray, "Our Lord, take us out of this town with its tyrannical people and, out of Your kindness, give us protectors and helpers" (75).

A portion of the surat discusses the problem of the hypocrites: people who profess Islam while secretly disbelieving. This was – and remains – the most challenging and troublesome group, sitting on the fence that separates faith from disbelief, and described as "dithering between *this and* that, *they are* neither with these *believers* nor with those *disbelievers*" (143). They were a real menace for the Muslims, an enemy within, always plotting, spreading rumours and sowing doubts.

The hypocrites felt there were sufficient grounds to raise doubts about the truthfulness of Islam whenever the Muslims faced hardship. Their characteristic traits have already been mentioned in *Surat Al-Baqarah*: troublemakers, sick at heart, and spreaders of corruption. More are mentioned: they obstruct people from believing, and engaged in scheming against the Muslims. By describing their traits, the Quran is cautioning Muslims to beware of them. After all, hypocrisy can creep in when a person fails to obey the Shariah; although he may remain a believer, his conduct is disliked by Allah. By enumerating these negative qualities, the surat stresses the need to adopt values opposite to those of the hypocrites: sincerity, loyalty, kindness and generosity towards fellow citizens and the authorities.

Obedience to the Messenger ﷺ is a Source of Blessing

Good leadership is a powerful glue that holds a society together: "Believers, obey Allah, the Messenger and those in authority amongst you, if you disagree amongst yourselves over anything, then refer it to Allah and the Messenger" (59). A later verse gives further reason why the leadership of the Prophet ﷺ was so important, explaining that: "We haven't sent a single messenger for any purpose except he should be obeyed by the will of Allah. If only, when they wronged themselves, they were to come to you and seek Allah's forgiveness and the Messenger too would seek forgiveness for them" (64). Those who obey the Messenger are blessed: "Whoever obeys Allah and the Messenger, such people shall be with those whom Allah has favoured: the Prophets, the truthful, the martyrs and the righteous. What wonderful companions!" (69).

The advice to counter hypocrisy is: be honest, sincere and genuine to oneself; secondly, care for and serve others, particularly members of one's family; and thirdly, show love and respect for the leadership of the community. These three principles form the basis of a peaceful, harmonious and just society as described in this blessed surat.

بِسْمِ اللهِ الرَّحْمٰنِ الرَّحِيْمِ

یٰۤاَیُّهَا النَّاسُ اتَّقُوْا رَبَّكُمُ الَّذِیْ خَلَقَكُمْ مِّنْ نَّفْسٍ وَّاحِدَةٍ وَّخَلَقَ مِنْهَا زَوْجَهَا وَبَثَّ مِنْهُمَا رِجَالًا كَثِيْرًا وَّنِسَآءً ۚ وَاتَّقُوا اللهَ الَّذِیْ تَسَآءَلُوْنَ بِهٖ وَالْاَرْحَامَ ؕ اِنَّ اللهَ كَانَ عَلَيْكُمْ رَقِيْبًا ۝

وَاٰتُوا الْيَتٰمٰۤى اَمْوَالَهُمْ وَلَا تَتَبَدَّلُوا الْخَبِيْثَ بِالطَّيِّبِ ۪ وَلَا تَاْكُلُوْۤا اَمْوَالَهُمْ اِلٰۤى اَمْوَالِكُمْ ؕ اِنَّهٗ كَانَ حُوْبًا كَبِيْرًا ۝

وَاِنْ خِفْتُمْ اَلَّا تُقْسِطُوْا فِی الْيَتٰمٰى فَانْكِحُوْا مَا طَابَ لَكُمْ مِّنَ النِّسَآءِ مَثْنٰى وَثُلٰثَ وَرُبٰعَ ۚ فَاِنْ خِفْتُمْ اَلَّا تَعْدِلُوْا فَوَاحِدَةً اَوْ مَا مَلَكَتْ اَيْمَانُكُمْ ؕ ذٰلِكَ اَدْنٰۤى اَلَّا تَعُوْلُوْا ۝ وَاٰتُوا النِّسَآءَ صَدُقٰتِهِنَّ نِحْلَةً ؕ فَاِنْ طِبْنَ لَكُمْ عَنْ شَیْءٍ مِّنْهُ نَفْسًا فَكُلُوْهُ هَنِیْۤئًا مَّرِیْۤئًا ۝ وَلَا تُؤْتُوا السُّفَهَآءَ اَمْوَالَكُمُ الَّتِیْ جَعَلَ اللهُ لَكُمْ قِیٰمًا وَّارْزُقُوْهُمْ فِيْهَا وَاكْسُوْهُمْ وَقُوْلُوْا لَهُمْ قَوْلًا مَّعْرُوْفًا ۝ وَابْتَلُوا الْيَتٰمٰى حَتّٰۤى اِذَا بَلَغُوا النِّكَاحَ ۚ فَاِنْ اٰنَسْتُمْ مِّنْهُمْ رُشْدًا فَادْفَعُوْۤا اِلَيْهِمْ اَمْوَالَهُمْ ۚ وَلَا تَاْكُلُوْهَاۤ اِسْرَافًا وَّبِدَارًا اَنْ يَّكْبَرُوْا ؕ وَمَنْ كَانَ غَنِيًّا فَلْيَسْتَعْفِفْ ۚ وَمَنْ كَانَ فَقِيْرًا

Social responsibilities: take care of orphans, respect your relatives.

145

In the name of Allah, the Kind, the Caring

Maintain family ties, as they connect you to Allah

[1] People, be mindful of your Lord, He created you from a single person and created his partner from him, and then from the pair He spread countless men and women *throughout the world*. Be mindful of Allah in Whose name you make demands from each other, and take care of the relatives. Allah watches over you.

Taking care of the orphans

[2] Give the orphans *in your care* their belongings, and do not swap *their quality belongings* for worthless ones, nor misuse their wealth *by merging it* with yours; this is a major sin. [3] If you're afraid that you may be unfair to *female* orphans *by marrying them*, you may marry other women as you like: two, three or four. However, if you fear you may be unfair *by marrying two or more*, then *marry just* one or what your right hands possess;[a] that is just, so don't deviate *from the right path*. [4] Give women their dowers as a marriage gift; however, if they are kind and give you some of it back, then take it and use it as you wish.

Advice to trustees of orphans' property

[5] Do not give your wealth, which Allah has given you for your use, to those with learning disabilities, but provide for them, clothe them, and treat them kindly. [6] Assess the orphans to see if they are ready to be married; then, if you find them to be mature enough, hand over their wealth to them, and do not squander it hastily before they have grown up. If *their guardian* is wealthy, he should not take *any of the orphans' wealth*, but if he's poor, let him take what is a fair *compensation*. When you hand over their wealth, have it witnessed. Allah is a sufficient Reckoner.

---

[a]   The phrase "what your right hands possess" refers to slaves. The Prophet ﷺ received the revelation at a time when slavery was widespread. Although Islam encouraged the freeing of slaves, this was not possible to achieve all at once, therefore rules were revealed on how to treat slaves in the best possible way. *See Surat Al-Nur p688.*

فَلْيَأْكُلْ بِالْمَعْرُوفِ ط فَاِذَا دَفَعْتُمْ اِلَيْهِمْ اَمْوَالَهُمْ

فَاَشْهِدُوْا عَلَيْهِمْ ط وَكَفٰى بِاللهِ حَسِيْبًا ۞ لِلرِّجَالِ

نَصِيْبٌ مِّمَّا تَرَكَ الْوَالِدَانِ وَالْاَقْرَبُوْنَ ۙ وَلِلنِّسَآءِ

نَصِيْبٌ مِّمَّا تَرَكَ الْوَالِدَانِ وَالْاَقْرَبُوْنَ مِمَّا قَلَّ

مِنْهُ اَوْ كَثُرَ ط نَصِيْبًا مَّفْرُوْضًا ۞ وَاِذَا حَضَرَ

الْقِسْمَةَ اُولُوا الْقُرْبٰى وَالْيَتٰمٰى وَالْمَسٰكِيْنُ فَارْزُقُوْهُمْ

مِّنْهُ وَقُوْلُوْا لَهُمْ قَوْلًا مَّعْرُوْفًا ۞ وَلْيَخْشَ

الَّذِيْنَ لَوْ تَرَكُوْا مِنْ خَلْفِهِمْ ذُرِّيَّةً ضِعٰفًا خَافُوْا

عَلَيْهِمْ ۪ فَلْيَتَّقُوا اللهَ وَلْيَقُوْلُوْا قَوْلًا سَدِيْدًا ۞

اِنَّ الَّذِيْنَ يَأْكُلُوْنَ اَمْوَالَ الْيَتٰمٰى ظُلْمًا اِنَّمَا

يَأْكُلُوْنَ فِيْ بُطُوْنِهِمْ نَارًا ط وَسَيَصْلَوْنَ سَعِيْرًا ۞

يُوْصِيْكُمُ اللهُ فِيْ اَوْلَادِكُمْ ۗ لِلذَّكَرِ مِثْلُ حَظِّ

الْاُنْثَيَيْنِ ۚ فَاِنْ كُنَّ نِسَآءً فَوْقَ اثْنَتَيْنِ فَلَهُنَّ

ثُلُثَا مَا تَرَكَ ۚ وَاِنْ كَانَتْ وَاحِدَةً فَلَهَا النِّصْفُ ط

وَلِاَبَوَيْهِ لِكُلِّ وَاحِدٍ مِّنْهُمَا السُّدُسُ مِمَّا تَرَكَ

اِنْ كَانَ لَهٗ وَلَدٌ ۚ فَاِنْ لَّمْ يَكُنْ لَّهٗ وَلَدٌ وَّوَرِثَهٗ

اَبَوٰهُ فَلِاُمِّهِ الثُّلُثُ ۚ فَاِنْ كَانَ لَهٗ اِخْوَةٌ فَلِاُمِّهِ

السُّدُسُ مِنْ بَعْدِ وَصِيَّةٍ يُّوْصِيْ بِهَآ اَوْ دَيْنٍ ط

اٰبَآؤُكُمْ وَاَبْنَآؤُكُمْ ۚ لَا تَدْرُوْنَ اَيُّهُمْ اَقْرَبُ لَكُمْ

نَفْعًا ط فَرِيْضَةً مِّنَ اللهِ ط اِنَّ اللهَ كَانَ عَلِيْمًا

Law of inheritance ensures fair distribution of parent's wealth.

The law of inheritance

[7] Men receive a share of what parents and relatives leave behind, and women receive a share in what parents and relatives leave behind, whether *the estate* is small or big, there are fixed shares. [8] If relatives, orphans and the needy are present at the time of distribution, then offer them something from *the estate* and speak kindly to them, [9] and let those who fear leaving their own vulnerable offspring behind show concern *for the orphans*. They should be mindful of Allah and say what is right. [10] Those who misuse the wealth of orphans are feeding their bellies fire, and will burn in a blazing Fire.

Men and women have different shares

[11] Allah commands you regarding your children: a son's share is equal to the share of two daughters. If there are more than two female heirs, *they will receive* two-thirds of what *the deceased* leaves behind, and if there is only one female she will have one half. Each of *the deceased's* parents shall receive a sixth of what he leaves behind if he had children; *but* if he had no children and his parents are sole heirs then his mother gets one third. If he had siblings, then his mother will get a sixth; *and the above is calculated* after settling any bequest[a] or debt. You do not know which of them are more deserving; your parents or your children. This is an essential *requirement* from Allah. Allah is the Knower, the Wise.

---

[a] *Wasiyya*: Bequest is the written will.

حَكِيْمًا ۝ وَلَكُمْ نِصْفُ مَا تَرَكَ اَزْوَاجُكُمْ اِنْ لَّمْ

يَكُنْ لَّهُنَّ وَلَدٌ ۚ فَاِنْ كَانَ لَهُنَّ وَلَدٌ فَلَكُمُ

الرُّبُعُ مِمَّا تَرَكْنَ مِنْ بَعْدِ وَصِيَّةٍ يُّوْصِيْنَ بِهَآ

اَوْ دَيْنٍ ۗ وَلَهُنَّ الرُّبُعُ مِمَّا تَرَكْتُمْ اِنْ لَّمْ يَكُنْ

لَّكُمْ وَلَدٌ ۚ فَاِنْ كَانَ لَكُمْ وَلَدٌ فَلَهُنَّ الثُّمُنُ مِمَّا

تَرَكْتُمْ مِّنْ بَعْدِ وَصِيَّةٍ تُوْصُوْنَ بِهَآ اَوْ دَيْنٍ ۗ وَ

اِنْ كَانَ رَجُلٌ يُّوْرَثُ كَلَالَةً اَوِ امْرَاَةٌ وَّلَهٗٓ اَخٌ

اَوْ اُخْتٌ فَلِكُلِّ وَاحِدٍ مِّنْهُمَا السُّدُسُ ۚ فَاِنْ كَانُوْٓا

Keep within the boundaries of Allah, sexual laxity is forbidden.

اَكْثَرَ مِنْ ذٰلِكَ فَهُمْ شُرَكَآءُ فِي الثُّلُثِ مِنْ بَعْدِ

وَصِيَّةٍ يُّوْصٰى بِهَآ اَوْ دَيْنٍ ۙ غَيْرَ مُضَآرٍّ ۚ وَصِيَّةً

مِّنَ اللّٰهِ ۗ وَاللّٰهُ عَلِيْمٌ حَلِيْمٌ ۝ تِلْكَ حُدُوْدُ اللّٰهِ ۗ

وَمَنْ يُّطِعِ اللّٰهَ وَرَسُوْلَهٗ يُدْخِلْهُ جَنّٰتٍ تَجْرِيْ مِنْ

تَحْتِهَا الْاَنْهٰرُ خٰلِدِيْنَ فِيْهَا ۗ وَذٰلِكَ الْفَوْزُ الْعَظِيْمُ ۝

وَمَنْ يَّعْصِ اللّٰهَ وَرَسُوْلَهٗ وَيَتَعَدَّ حُدُوْدَهٗ يُدْخِلْهُ

نَارًا خَالِدًا فِيْهَا ۖ وَلَهٗ عَذَابٌ مُّهِيْنٌ ۝ وَالّٰتِيْ

يَاْتِيْنَ الْفَاحِشَةَ مِنْ نِّسَآئِكُمْ فَاسْتَشْهِدُوْا

عَلَيْهِنَّ اَرْبَعَةً مِّنْكُمْ ۚ فَاِنْ شَهِدُوْا فَاَمْسِكُوْهُنَّ

فِي الْبُيُوْتِ حَتّٰى يَتَوَفّٰهُنَّ الْمَوْتُ اَوْ يَجْعَلَ اللّٰهُ

لَهُنَّ سَبِيْلًا ۝ وَالَّذٰنِ يَاْتِيٰنِهَا مِنْكُمْ فَاٰذُوْهُمَا ۚ

فَاِنْ تَابَا وَاَصْلَحَا فَاَعْرِضُوْا عَنْهُمَا ۗ اِنَّ اللّٰهَ

The inheritance of husbands, wives and distant relatives

¹² Half of what your wives leave behind is yours, provided they had no children; if they had children, then a quarter of their estate is yours. *This is calculated* after settling any bequest or debt. Wives shall receive a quarter of what you leave behind, if you had no children; but if you had children, then *wives* will get an eighth of what you leave behind. *This is calculated* after settling any bequest you have made or any debt. If a man or a woman's only heir is a distant relative who has a brother or a sister, then each one of them shall receive a sixth; but if they are more *than two*, then they shall be partners in one third. *This is calculated* after settling any bequest or debt, if *the bequest* is not detrimental.[a] This is a command from Allah. Allah is the Knower, the Gentle.

The reward for adhering to Allah's boundaries

¹³ These are the boundaries set by Allah. Anyone who obeys Allah and His Messenger will have gardens beneath which rivers flow, living in them forever; that is a great victory. ¹⁴ Anyone who disobeys Allah and His Messenger and oversteps His boundaries will be cast into Fire, remaining in a humiliating punishment forever.

Penalty for adultery

¹⁵ If any of your women commit adultery, and there is testimony of four men against them, then keep them under house arrest until death, or else Allah provides another way out for them. ¹⁶ *Likewise,* if a man and a woman commit adultery among you, punish them both. However, if they repent and reform themselves, then leave them alone. Allah is the Relenting, Kind.[b]

---

[a] In Shariah, the maximum that can be bequeathed is a third of the estate.
[b] Verses 15 and 16 describe the penalty for adultery and fornication, respectively; this was later changed by the ruling mentioned in *Surat Al-Nur*: 1.

كَانَ تَوَّابًا رَّحِيمًا ۞ اِنَّمَا التَّوْبَةُ عَلَى اللّٰهِ لِلَّذِيْنَ يَعْمَلُوْنَ السُّوْٓءَ بِجَهَالَةٍ ثُمَّ يَتُوْبُوْنَ مِنْ قَرِيْبٍ فَاُولٰٓئِكَ يَتُوْبُ اللّٰهُ عَلَيْهِمْ ط وَ كَانَ اللّٰهُ عَلِيْمًا حَكِيْمًا ۞ وَلَيْسَتِ التَّوْبَةُ لِلَّذِيْنَ يَعْمَلُوْنَ السَّيِّاٰتِ ۚ حَتّٰٓى اِذَا حَضَرَ اَحَدَهُمُ الْمَوْتُ قَالَ اِنِّيْ تُبْتُ الْـٰٔنَ وَلَا الَّذِيْنَ يَمُوْتُوْنَ وَهُمْ كُفَّارٌ ط اُولٰٓئِكَ اَعْتَدْنَا لَهُمْ عَذَابًا اَلِيْمًا ۞ يٰٓاَيُّهَا الَّذِيْنَ اٰمَنُوْا لَا يَحِلُّ لَكُمْ اَنْ تَرِثُوا النِّسَآءَ كَرْهًا ط وَلَا تَعْضُلُوْهُنَّ لِتَذْهَبُوْا بِبَعْضِ مَآ اٰتَيْتُمُوْهُنَّ اِلَّآ اَنْ يَّاْتِيْنَ بِفَاحِشَةٍ مُّبَيِّنَةٍ ۚ وَ عَاشِرُوْهُنَّ بِالْمَعْرُوْفِ ۚ فَاِنْ كَرِهْتُمُوْهُنَّ فَعَسٰٓى اَنْ تَكْرَهُوْا شَيْئًا وَّيَجْعَلَ اللّٰهُ فِيْهِ خَيْرًا كَثِيْرًا ۞ وَاِنْ اَرَدْتُّمُ اسْتِبْدَالَ زَوْجٍ مَّكَانَ زَوْجٍ ۙ وَّاٰتَيْتُمْ اِحْدٰىهُنَّ قِنْطَارًا فَلَا تَاْخُذُوْا مِنْهُ شَيْئًا ط اَتَاْخُذُوْنَهٗ بُهْتَانًا وَّاِثْمًا مُّبِيْنًا ۞ وَكَيْفَ تَاْخُذُوْنَهٗ وَقَدْ اَفْضٰى بَعْضُكُمْ اِلٰى بَعْضٍ وَّاَخَذْنَ مِنْكُمْ مِّيْثَاقًا غَلِيْظًا ۞ وَلَا تَنْكِحُوْا مَا نَكَحَ اٰبَآؤُكُمْ مِّنَ النِّسَآءِ اِلَّا مَا قَدْ سَلَفَ ط اِنَّهٗ كَانَ فَاحِشَةً وَّمَقْتًا ط وَسَآءَ سَبِيْلًا ۞ حُرِّمَتْ عَلَيْكُمْ اُمَّهٰتُكُمْ وَبَنٰتُكُمْ وَاَخَوٰتُكُمْ وَ

Men and women have equal rights, respect and responsibilities.

۳
ع
۸
۱۴

When is repentance acceptable?

[17] Those who do wrong ignorantly then repent immediately can expect Allah to accept their repentance, and Allah will relent towards them. Allah is the Knower, Wise. [18] There is no repentance for those who keep on doing evil deeds until death is near, then they say: "Now I repent," nor for those who die as disbelievers. For such We've prepared a painful punishment.

Men are urged to be kind to their wives

[19] Believers, it is not lawful for you to inherit women against their will,[a] nor to prevent them from marrying so that you may make off with part of what you have given them, that is unless they have committed a clear act of gross indecency. Live with them in a good way. If you *hate* them, it may be that you *hate* something in which Allah has placed much goodness. [20] If you wish to change one wife for another wife after having given the former heap of gold, do not withhold anything from it. Would you invent a slanderous accusation and an open sin to take it *from her*? [21] How could you possibly take it after having enjoyed intimacy with each other? They took a solemn pledge from you.

Women relatives forbidden for marriage

[22] Do not marry women who your fathers married, except *if such a marriage* has already taken place; *from now on* it would count as gross indecency, vile, and leading to evil consequences.

---

[a] A pre-Islamic Arab custom: a man could inherit a male relative's widow without her consent or the need to renew the marriage.

عَمَّٰتُكُمْ وَخَٰلَٰتُكُمْ وَبَنَاتُ الْأَخِ وَبَنَاتُ الْأُخْتِ وَ
أُمَّهَٰتُكُمُ الَّٰتِىٓ أَرْضَعْنَكُمْ وَأَخَوَٰتُكُم مِّنَ الرَّضَٰعَةِ
وَأُمَّهَٰتُ نِسَآئِكُمْ وَرَبَٰٓئِبُكُمُ الَّٰتِى فِى حُجُورِكُم
مِّن نِّسَآئِكُمُ الَّٰتِى دَخَلْتُم بِهِنَّ فَإِن لَّمْ تَكُونُوا۟
دَخَلْتُم بِهِنَّ فَلَا جُنَاحَ عَلَيْكُمْ وَحَلَٰٓئِلُ أَبْنَآئِكُمُ
الَّذِينَ مِنْ أَصْلَٰبِكُمْ وَأَن تَجْمَعُوا۟ بَيْنَ الْأُخْتَيْنِ
إِلَّا مَا قَدْ سَلَفَ إِنَّ اللَّهَ كَانَ غَفُورًا رَّحِيمًا ۝

وَالْمُحْصَنَٰتُ مِنَ النِّسَآءِ إِلَّا مَا مَلَكَتْ أَيْمَٰنُكُمْ
كِتَٰبَ اللَّهِ عَلَيْكُمْ وَأُحِلَّ لَكُم مَّا وَرَآءَ ذَٰلِكُمْ أَن
تَبْتَغُوا۟ بِأَمْوَٰلِكُم مُّحْصِنِينَ غَيْرَ مُسَٰفِحِينَ فَمَا
اسْتَمْتَعْتُم بِهِ مِنْهُنَّ فَـَٔاتُوهُنَّ أُجُورَهُنَّ فَرِيضَةً
وَلَا جُنَاحَ عَلَيْكُمْ فِيمَا تَرَٰضَيْتُم بِهِ مِنۢ بَعْدِ
الْفَرِيضَةِ إِنَّ اللَّهَ كَانَ عَلِيمًا حَكِيمًا ۝ وَ

مَن لَّمْ يَسْتَطِعْ مِنكُمْ طَوْلًا أَن يَنكِحَ الْمُحْصَنَٰتِ
الْمُؤْمِنَٰتِ فَمِن مَّا مَلَكَتْ أَيْمَٰنُكُم مِّن فَتَيَٰتِكُمُ
الْمُؤْمِنَٰتِ وَاللَّهُ أَعْلَمُ بِإِيمَٰنِكُم بَعْضُكُم مِّنۢ
بَعْضٍ فَانكِحُوهُنَّ بِإِذْنِ أَهْلِهِنَّ وَءَاتُوهُنَّ
أُجُورَهُنَّ بِالْمَعْرُوفِ مُحْصَنَٰتٍ غَيْرَ مُسَٰفِحَٰتٍ
وَلَا مُتَّخِذَٰتِ أَخْدَانٍ فَإِذَآ أُحْصِنَّ فَإِنْ أَتَيْنَ
بِفَٰحِشَةٍ فَعَلَيْهِنَّ نِصْفُ مَا عَلَى الْمُحْصَنَٰتِ مِنَ

The close relatives you can't marry.

153

²³ It is forbidden for you to marry: your mothers; your daughters; your sisters; your maternal aunts; your paternal aunts; nieces from the brother's or sister's side; your foster mothers who have suckled you, and your foster sisters; your mothers-in-law; the stepdaughters who are in your care from women with whom you have consummated marriage, but if you have not consummated your marriage with them then there's no blame. *Also, forbidden are*: the wives of your sons; and marrying two sisters *at the same time*, except *if such a marriage* has already taken place. Allah is the Forgiver, the Kind.

The enjoyment of sex is only lawful in marriage

²⁴ *Also forbidden are* women who are already married, except your slaves.ᵃ *These prohibited marriages* are Allah's commandment *to be obeyed*. Whatever falls outside the above-mentioned *prohibitions* is lawful for you to desire, using your wealth to become married men, not fornicators. Whichever of them you wish to enjoy *in lawful marriage* you must give them their bridal gift; there is no blame on you, after fulfilling that obligation, in whatever you may mutually agree to do with *the marriage gift*. Allah is the Knower, the Wise.

Marrying a believing woman is best

²⁵ If anyone lacks the means to marry chaste believing freewomen then *let him marry* from the believing slave girls you own. Allah knows best your faith. You are all of the same *origin*; so, marry them with the permission of their owners and give them their marriage gifts according to custom, as with chaste freewomen, not as fornicators or taken as lovers. If, after they are married, they commit an act of gross indecency then their punishment is half that of a chaste freewoman. That *permission* is for those of you who fear *falling into* sin. It is, *of course*, best for you to be patient *and exercise restraint*. Allah is Forgiving, and Kind.

ᵃ The custom of war in Arabia and elsewhere at the time was that women and children captured on the battlefield were not to be killed or left to die, but taken as hostages or slaves. Their previous marriage became void.

الْعَذَابِ ۖ ذٰلِكَ لِمَنْ خَشِيَ الْعَنَتَ مِنْكُمْ ۚ وَاَنْ تَصْبِرُوْا خَيْرٌ لَّكُمْ ۗ وَاللّٰهُ غَفُوْرٌ رَّحِيْمٌ ۝ يُرِيْدُ اللّٰهُ لِيُبَيِّنَ لَكُمْ وَيَهْدِيَكُمْ سُنَنَ الَّذِيْنَ مِنْ قَبْلِكُمْ وَيَتُوْبَ عَلَيْكُمْ ۗ وَاللّٰهُ عَلِيْمٌ حَكِيْمٌ ۝ وَاللّٰهُ يُرِيْدُ اَنْ يَّتُوْبَ عَلَيْكُمْ ۙ وَيُرِيْدُ الَّذِيْنَ يَتَّبِعُوْنَ الشَّهَوٰتِ اَنْ تَمِيْلُوْا مَيْلًا عَظِيْمًا ۝ يُرِيْدُ اللّٰهُ اَنْ يُّخَفِّفَ عَنْكُمْ ۚ وَخُلِقَ الْاِنْسَانُ ضَعِيْفًا ۝ يٰٓاَيُّهَا الَّذِيْنَ اٰمَنُوْا لَا تَاْكُلُوْٓا اَمْوَالَكُمْ بَيْنَكُمْ بِالْبَاطِلِ اِلَّآ اَنْ تَكُوْنَ تِجَارَةً عَنْ تَرَاضٍ مِّنْكُمْ ۚ وَلَا تَقْتُلُوْٓا اَنْفُسَكُمْ ۗ اِنَّ اللّٰهَ كَانَ بِكُمْ رَحِيْمًا ۝ وَمَنْ يَّفْعَلْ ذٰلِكَ عُدْوَانًا وَّظُلْمًا فَسَوْفَ نُصْلِيْهِ نَارًا ۗ وَكَانَ ذٰلِكَ عَلَى اللّٰهِ يَسِيْرًا ۝ اِنْ تَجْتَنِبُوْا كَبَآئِرَ مَا تُنْهَوْنَ عَنْهُ نُكَفِّرْ عَنْكُمْ سَيِّاٰتِكُمْ وَنُدْخِلْكُمْ مُّدْخَلًا كَرِيْمًا ۝ وَلَا تَتَمَنَّوْا مَا فَضَّلَ اللّٰهُ بِهٖ بَعْضَكُمْ عَلٰى بَعْضٍ ۗ لِلرِّجَالِ نَصِيْبٌ مِّمَّا اكْتَسَبُوْا ۗ وَلِلنِّسَآءِ نَصِيْبٌ مِّمَّا اكْتَسَبْنَ ۗ وَسْـَٔلُوا اللّٰهَ مِنْ فَضْلِهٖ ۗ اِنَّ اللّٰهَ كَانَ بِكُلِّ شَيْءٍ عَلِيْمًا ۝ وَلِكُلٍّ جَعَلْنَا مَوَالِيَ مِمَّا تَرَكَ الْوَالِدٰنِ وَالْاَقْرَبُوْنَ ۗ وَالَّذِيْنَ عَقَدَتْ اَيْمَانُكُمْ فَاٰتُوْهُمْ نَصِيْبَهُمْ ۗ اِنَّ اللّٰهَ كَانَ عَلٰى كُلِّ شَيْءٍ شَهِيْدًا ۝ اَلرِّجَالُ

Allah wants to make our lives smooth and peaceful.

155

Allah makes allowances for human weaknesses

²⁶ Allah explains and guides you in the traditions of those *believers* who came before you, and to forgive you. Allah is the Knower, the Wise. ²⁷ Allah wishes to accept your repentance, whereas people who pursue their lusts want you to deviate far from the course. ²⁸ Allah wishes to ease your burden, since humans were created weak.

Honesty is the best policy

²⁹ Believers, don't use one another's wealth dishonestly, rather only for a business venture through agreement, and do not ruin yourself.ᵃ Allah treats you Kindly. ³⁰ Whoever *disobeys Allah* out of hostility and injustice, shall be thrown in the Fire, that's easy for Allah. ³¹ If you avoid major sins that are forbidden, then We shall delete your *minor* sins, and grant you an honourable entry *into Paradise.*

Be content with your share of the deceased's estate

³² Do not wish *to get that* which Allah has favoured others with. Men *get* a share of what they've earned, and women *get* a share of what they've earned, and ask Allah for a share of His favour. Allah knows all things. ³³ What parents and relatives leave behind, We have appointed beneficiaries for them, and those whom your right hands have contractedᵇ *should be beneficiaries of your wills*, give them their shares. Allah Witnesses all things.

ᵃ Literally "don't eat one another's wealth" but here it is metaphorical, as we might say, "don't kill yourself," to someone who is throwing all their effort into getting a job done, for example, or saving up money to buy something. Others say it refers to suicide, or it is an order not to kill each other.

ᵇ In Arabia, contracts like wills became binding not by a signature, but by a solemn oath.

قَوّٰمُوْنَ عَلَى النِّسَآءِ بِمَا فَضَّلَ اللّٰهُ بَعْضَهُمْ عَلٰى بَعْضٍ وَّبِمَاۤ اَنْفَقُوْا مِنْ اَمْوَالِهِمْ ؕ فَالصّٰلِحٰتُ قٰنِتٰتٌ حٰفِظٰتٌ لِّلْغَيْبِ بِمَا حَفِظَ اللّٰهُ ؕ وَالّٰتِيْ تَخَافُوْنَ نُشُوْزَهُنَّ فَعِظُوْهُنَّ وَاهْجُرُوْهُنَّ فِى الْمَضَاجِعِ وَاضْرِبُوْهُنَّ ۚ فَاِنْ اَطَعْنَكُمْ فَلَا تَبْغُوْا عَلَيْهِنَّ سَبِيْلًا ؕ اِنَّ اللّٰهَ كَانَ عَلِيًّا كَبِيْرًا ۝

وَاِنْ خِفْتُمْ شِقَاقَ بَيْنِهِمَا فَابْعَثُوْا حَكَمًا مِّنْ اَهْلِهٖ وَحَكَمًا مِّنْ اَهْلِهَا ۚ اِنْ يُّرِيْدَاۤ اِصْلَاحًا يُّوَفِّقِ اللّٰهُ بَيْنَهُمَا ؕ اِنَّ اللّٰهَ كَانَ عَلِيْمًا خَبِيْرًا ۝

وَاعْبُدُوا اللّٰهَ وَلَا تُشْرِكُوْا بِهٖ شَيْئًا وَّبِالْوَالِدَيْنِ اِحْسَانًا وَّبِذِى الْقُرْبٰى وَالْيَتٰمٰى وَالْمَسٰكِيْنِ وَالْجَارِ ذِى الْقُرْبٰى وَالْجَارِ الْجُنُبِ وَالصَّاحِبِ بِالْجَنْۢبِ وَابْنِ السَّبِيْلِ ۙ وَمَا مَلَكَتْ اَيْمَانُكُمْ ؕ اِنَّ اللّٰهَ لَا يُحِبُّ مَنْ كَانَ مُخْتَالًا فَخُوْرَاۨ ۝

الَّذِيْنَ يَبْخَلُوْنَ وَيَأْمُرُوْنَ النَّاسَ بِالْبُخْلِ وَيَكْتُمُوْنَ مَاۤ اٰتٰىهُمُ اللّٰهُ مِنْ فَضْلِهٖ ؕ وَاَعْتَدْنَا لِلْكٰفِرِيْنَ عَذَابًا مُّهِيْنًا ۝ وَالَّذِيْنَ يُنْفِقُوْنَ اَمْوَالَهُمْ رِئَآءَ النَّاسِ وَلَا يُؤْمِنُوْنَ بِاللّٰهِ وَلَا بِالْيَوْمِ الْاٰخِرِ ؕ وَمَنْ يَّكُنِ الشَّيْطٰنُ لَهٗ قَرِيْنًا فَسَآءَ قَرِيْنًا ۝ وَمَا ذَا عَلَيْهِمْ لَوْ اٰمَنُوْا بِاللّٰهِ وَالْيَوْمِ

Religion is both worship and service to others.

157

Dealing with marital discord

³⁴Men are guardian-carers of women, Allah granted some more favours then others, because they spend money on their wives. Honourably acting wives are pious and they guard *their chastity* as Allah expects them to guard it. Those whose ill-conduct[a] you are afraid of, *first gently* warn them, *then* leave them alone in the bed and for a while live separately from them, *if all else fails*, apply *a minimum of* force on them.[b] If, *after taking these steps*, they obey you, then don't behave unjustly in any way against them. Allah is Most High, the Great.

Mediation for resolving marital disputes will work

³⁵If you fear hostility between husband and wife, then appoint a mediator from his family and one from her family. When both try *sincerely* to reconcile them, Allah will certainly bring about reconciliation between them. Allah is the Knower, the Aware.

The purpose of religion is Allah's worship and kindness to others

³⁶Worship Allah and don't associate anything with Him; be kind to parents, to relatives, to orphans, to the needy, to those neighbours you know well and those you don't, to travellers and to *the slaves* you own. Allah dislikes the arrogant and the boastful; ³⁷*and* those who are miserly and advise others to be miserly, hiding His favours that Allah has blessed them with – for the disbelievers – We have prepared a humiliating punishment. ³⁸Those who spend their wealth to show off; they don't believe in Allah and the Last Day. Anyone who has made a close friend of Satan has taken an evil friend!

---

[a]   See also verse 128 for advice to women on how to deal with such ill-conduct and high-handedness of husbands.

[b]   There is an alternative meaning of the word 'Wadrebuhunna'; apply force on them. When asked to explain this phrase, the Prophet ﷺ took his miswak (a teeth cleaning twig, a traditional alternative to the modern toothbrush) and lightly prodded the Companion sat next to him; a purely symbolic act, like not sharing the bed, which represents the husband's displeasure but does not cause any physical harm. Violence of any kind against women is forbidden.

الْاٰخِرِ وَ اَنْفَقُوْا مِمَّا رَزَقَهُمُ اللهُ ط وَكَانَ اللهُ بِهِمْ

عَلِيْمًا ۝ اِنَّ اللهَ لَا يَظْلِمُ مِثْقَالَ ذَرَّةٍ ۚ وَاِنْ

تَكُ حَسَنَةً يُّضٰعِفْهَا وَيُؤْتِ مِنْ لَّدُنْهُ اَجْرًا

عَظِيْمًا ۝ فَكَيْفَ اِذَا جِئْنَا مِنْ كُلِّ اُمَّةٍ بِشَهِيْدٍ

وَّجِئْنَا بِكَ عَلٰى هٰٓؤُلَآءِ شَهِيْدًا ۝ط يَوْمَئِذٍ يَّوَدُّ

الَّذِيْنَ كَفَرُوْا وَعَصَوُا الرَّسُوْلَ لَوْ تُسَوّٰى بِهِمُ

الْاَرْضُ ط وَلَا يَكْتُمُوْنَ اللهَ حَدِيْثًا ۝ يٰٓاَيُّهَا الَّذِيْنَ

اٰمَنُوْا لَا تَقْرَبُوا الصَّلٰوةَ وَاَنْتُمْ سُكٰرٰى حَتّٰى تَعْلَمُوْا

مَا تَقُوْلُوْنَ وَلَا جُنُبًا اِلَّا عَابِرِيْ سَبِيْلٍ حَتّٰى

تَغْتَسِلُوْا ط وَاِنْ كُنْتُمْ مَّرْضٰٓى اَوْ عَلٰى سَفَرٍ اَوْ جَآءَ

اَحَدٌ مِّنْكُمْ مِّنَ الْغَآئِطِ اَوْ لٰمَسْتُمُ النِّسَآءَ فَلَمْ

تَجِدُوْا مَآءً فَتَيَمَّمُوْا صَعِيْدًا طَيِّبًا فَامْسَحُوْا

بِوُجُوْهِكُمْ وَاَيْدِيْكُمْ ط اِنَّ اللهَ كَانَ عَفُوًّا غَفُوْرًا ۝

اَلَمْ تَرَ اِلَى الَّذِيْنَ اُوْتُوْا نَصِيْبًا مِّنَ الْكِتٰبِ

يَشْتَرُوْنَ الضَّلٰلَةَ وَيُرِيْدُوْنَ اَنْ تَضِلُّوا السَّبِيْلَ ط ۝

وَاللهُ اَعْلَمُ بِاَعْدَآئِكُمْ ط وَكَفٰى بِاللهِ وَلِيًّا ۙ وَّكَفٰى

بِاللهِ نَصِيْرًا ۝ مِنَ الَّذِيْنَ هَادُوْا يُحَرِّفُوْنَ

الْكَلِمَ عَنْ مَّوَاضِعِهٖ وَيَقُوْلُوْنَ سَمِعْنَا وَعَصَيْنَا

وَاسْمَعْ غَيْرَ مُسْمَعٍ وَّرَاعِنَا لَيًّا بِاَلْسِنَتِهِمْ وَطَعْنًا

فِى الدِّيْنِ ط وَلَوْ اَنَّهُمْ قَالُوْا سَمِعْنَا وَ اَطَعْنَا

The Messenger ﷺ will be the witness on Judgement Day

³⁹ What harm would it do them if they believed in Allah and the Last Day and spent *in charity* from what Allah has provided them? Allah knows them well. ⁴⁰ Allah wrongs *no one*, not even an atom's weight; and if it is a good deed, He multiplies it and gives an immense reward. ⁴¹ How *will they react* when We bring a witness from every nation and then We bring you, *Muhammad*, as a witness against them all? ⁴² That day the disbelievers and those who disobeyed the Messenger will wish that the Earth would swallow them up; and they won't be able to hide from Allah anything they had spoken.

Rules on what invalidates prayer

⁴³ Believers, don't come to the prayer whilst you are drunk *stay away* until you know what you are saying;^a nor when you are in the state of major ritual impurity, and when on a journey,^b until you have bathed yourselves. *However*, if you are ill or on a journey, or if you have relieved yourself or had sexual intercourse with *your spouse*, and you cannot find water, then purify yourselves with some clean sand, wiping your faces and forearms.^c Allah is Pardoner, Forgiver.

Exposing the petty rudeness of some Jews of Madinah

⁴⁴ Haven't you seen those given a portion of the Book, *how* they swap it for error, wishing you stray from the path? ⁴⁵ Allah is aware of your enemies; and Allah is sufficient as a Protector and a Helper. ⁴⁶ Some of the Jews *deliberately* misquote the words *of revelation*, saying, "We hear and disobey," and, "Listen like a deaf man," and, "Look to us,"^d twisting *the words* with their tongues to insult the religion. If only they had said: "We hear and obey," and, "Listen and look out for us," that would be far better and proper for them. However, Allah deprives them of his kindness because of their disbelief, and only a few of *them truly* believe.

---

^a In the early days of Islam alcoholic drink was not banned, it was forbidden by the revelation of *Al-Ma'idah: 90*

^b In the Hanafi school, a person is a traveller when he sets off on a journey of fifty four miles or more, and intends to stay fewer than fifteen days in any one place, in which case he can shorten the prayer.

^c This is known as *"tayammum"*, a symbolic way of purifying oneself, in lieu of wudu, ablution.

^d See *Al-Baqarah* 2: 104 for an explanation.

وَاسْمَعْ وَانْظُرْنَا لَكَانَ خَيْرًا لَّهُمْ وَاَقْوَمَ ۙ

وَلٰكِنْ لَّعَنَهُمُ اللّٰهُ بِكُفْرِهِمْ فَلَا يُؤْمِنُوْنَ اِلَّا

قَلِيْلًا ۝ يٰٓاَيُّهَا الَّذِيْنَ اُوْتُوا الْكِتٰبَ اٰمِنُوْا بِمَا

نَزَّلْنَا مُصَدِّقًا لِّمَا مَعَكُمْ مِّنْ قَبْلِ اَنْ نَّطْمِسَ

وُجُوْهًا فَنَرُدَّهَا عَلٰٓى اَدْبَارِهَا اَوْ نَلْعَنَهُمْ كَمَا

لَعَنَّا اَصْحٰبَ السَّبْتِ ؕ وَكَانَ اَمْرُ اللّٰهِ مَفْعُوْلًا ۝

اِنَّ اللّٰهَ لَا يَغْفِرُ اَنْ يُّشْرَكَ بِهٖ وَيَغْفِرُ مَا دُوْنَ

ذٰلِكَ لِمَنْ يَّشَآءُ ۚ وَمَنْ يُّشْرِكْ بِاللّٰهِ فَقَدِ

افْتَرٰٓى اِثْمًا عَظِيْمًا ۝ اَلَمْ تَرَ اِلَى الَّذِيْنَ يُزَكُّوْنَ

اَنْفُسَهُمْ ؕ بَلِ اللّٰهُ يُزَكِّيْ مَنْ يَّشَآءُ وَلَا يُظْلَمُوْنَ

فَتِيْلًا ۝ اُنْظُرْ كَيْفَ يَفْتَرُوْنَ عَلَى اللّٰهِ الْكَذِبَ ؕ

وَكَفٰى بِهٖٓ اِثْمًا مُّبِيْنًا ۝ اَلَمْ تَرَ اِلَى الَّذِيْنَ اُوْتُوْا

نَصِيْبًا مِّنَ الْكِتٰبِ يُؤْمِنُوْنَ بِالْجِبْتِ وَالطَّاغُوْتِ

وَيَقُوْلُوْنَ لِلَّذِيْنَ كَفَرُوْا هٰٓؤُلَآءِ اَهْدٰى مِنَ

الَّذِيْنَ اٰمَنُوْا سَبِيْلًا ۝ اُولٰٓئِكَ الَّذِيْنَ لَعَنَهُمُ

اللّٰهُ ؕ وَمَنْ يَّلْعَنِ اللّٰهُ فَلَنْ تَجِدَ لَهٗ نَصِيْرًا ۝

اَمْ لَهُمْ نَصِيْبٌ مِّنَ الْمُلْكِ فَاِذًا لَّا يُؤْتُوْنَ

النَّاسَ نَقِيْرًا ۝ اَمْ يَحْسُدُوْنَ النَّاسَ عَلٰى

مَآ اٰتٰىهُمُ اللّٰهُ مِنْ فَضْلِهٖ ۚ فَقَدْ اٰتَيْنَآ اٰلَ اِبْرٰهِيْمَ

الْكِتٰبَ وَالْحِكْمَةَ وَاٰتَيْنٰهُمْ مُّلْكًا عَظِيْمًا ۝

Don't be overwhelmed by the wizardry of modern technology and the power of leaders.

ع
۴

An invitation to Jews and Christians to accept the truth

[47] You who received the Book, believe in what We revealed, it confirms what you already have, before We turn *your* faces back to front, or else We curse you as We cursed the People of the Sabbath. Allah's command is always fulfilled. [48] Allah does not forgive those who associate anything with Him, but He forgives anything less than that for whomever He pleases. Whoever associates anything with Allah has invented a great sin. [49] Haven't you seen those who regard themselves as pure? Rather it is Allah Who purifies whomever He pleases, and not an ounce of injustice will be done to them.[a] [50] Look how they make up lies about Allah. That is a blatant sin. [51] Haven't you seen those who were given a portion of the Book and they continue to believe in idols and false gods, saying to the disbelievers that they are more on the right track than the believers? [52] Allah has cursed them; and anyone Allah curses, you will find no helper for him. [53] Or do they have a share in *Allah's* sovereignty? If so, they would never give people even a tiny bit.[b]

Why are they jealous?

[54] Or do they envy *other* people for what Allah has given them from His grace? We gave Ibrahim's family the Book, wisdom, and a vast country *to rule over*.

---

[a] The word *"fateel"* refers to the thin film covering a date stone, a metaphor for an insignificant weight or amount.

[b] *"Naqeer"* refers to the little groove in date stones, and means the same as *"fateel"* in this context.

فَمِنْهُمْ مَّنْ اٰمَنَ بِهٖ وَمِنْهُمْ مَّنْ صَدَّ عَنْهُ ط وَكَفٰى بِجَهَنَّمَ سَعِيْرًا ۝ اِنَّ الَّذِيْنَ كَفَرُوْا بِاٰيٰتِنَا سَوْفَ نُصْلِيْهِمْ نَارًا ط كُلَّمَا نَضِجَتْ جُلُوْدُهُمْ بَدَّلْنٰهُمْ جُلُوْدًا غَيْرَهَا لِيَذُوْقُوا الْعَذَابَ ط اِنَّ اللّٰهَ كَانَ عَزِيْزًا حَكِيْمًا ۝ وَالَّذِيْنَ اٰمَنُوْا وَعَمِلُوا الصّٰلِحٰتِ سَنُدْخِلُهُمْ جَنّٰتٍ تَجْرِيْ مِنْ تَحْتِهَا الْاَنْهٰرُ خٰلِدِيْنَ فِيْهَا اَبَدًا ط لَهُمْ فِيْهَا اَزْوَاجٌ مُّطَهَّرَةٌ ز وَّنُدْخِلُهُمْ ظِلًّا ظَلِيْلًا ۝ اِنَّ اللّٰهَ يَاْمُرُكُمْ اَنْ تُؤَدُّوا الْاَمٰنٰتِ اِلٰى اَهْلِهَا لا وَاِذَا حَكَمْتُمْ بَيْنَ النَّاسِ اَنْ تَحْكُمُوْا بِالْعَدْلِ ط اِنَّ اللّٰهَ نِعِمَّا يَعِظُكُمْ بِهٖ ط اِنَّ اللّٰهَ كَانَ سَمِيْعًا بَصِيْرًا ۝ يٰٓاَيُّهَا الَّذِيْنَ اٰمَنُوْٓا اَطِيْعُوا اللّٰهَ وَاَطِيْعُوا الرَّسُوْلَ وَاُولِى الْاَمْرِ مِنْكُمْ ۚ فَاِنْ تَنَازَعْتُمْ فِيْ شَيْءٍ فَرُدُّوْهُ اِلَى اللّٰهِ وَالرَّسُوْلِ اِنْ كُنْتُمْ تُؤْمِنُوْنَ بِاللّٰهِ وَالْيَوْمِ الْاٰخِرِ ط ذٰلِكَ خَيْرٌ وَّ اَحْسَنُ تَاْوِيْلًا ۝ اَلَمْ تَرَ اِلَى الَّذِيْنَ يَزْعُمُوْنَ اَنَّهُمْ اٰمَنُوْا بِمَآ اُنْزِلَ اِلَيْكَ وَمَآ اُنْزِلَ مِنْ قَبْلِكَ يُرِيْدُوْنَ اَنْ يَّتَحَاكَمُوْٓا اِلَى الطَّاغُوْتِ وَقَدْ اُمِرُوْٓا اَنْ يَّكْفُرُوْا بِهٖ ط وَيُرِيْدُ الشَّيْطٰنُ اَنْ يُّضِلَّهُمْ ضَلٰلًۢا بَعِيْدًا ۝ وَاِذَا قِيْلَ لَهُمْ

Respect for authority is part of faith in Allah.

163

⁵⁵Some of them believe in *the Prophet*, and others block the way to him. Hell, with its blazing fire will be enough *for them*. ⁵⁶Those who deny Our signs will soon roast in Fire. Whenever their skin falls off, We will replace it with fresh skin so they may taste the torment.^a Allah is Almighty, Wise. ⁵⁷As for those who believe and do righteous deeds, We will take them to gardens under which rivers flow, living in them forever; there they'll have pure spouses, and We'll let them enter the cool shade.

Advice on obeying authority

⁵⁸Allah commands you to return trusts to their rightful owners, and when you judge between people, be just, Allah reminds you gently! Allah is the Hearer, the Seeing. ⁵⁹Believers, obey Allah, the Messenger and those among you in authority. If you disagree over something, then refer it to Allah and the Messenger, that is if you believe in Allah and the Last Day: that's the best solution.

The deceptions of hypocrites

⁶⁰Haven't you seen those who claim to believe in what is revealed to you and what was revealed before you, yet they turn to false gods for judgements despite having been ordered to reject them. Satan wants to lead them far from the right way.

---

^a The nerves that sense pain are in the skin, without the skin there would be no pain. So, this terrible and painful description shows the nature of that suffering.

تَعَالَوْا اِلٰى مَآ اَنْزَلَ اللّٰهُ وَ اِلَى الرَّسُوْلِ رَاَيْتَ

الْمُنٰفِقِيْنَ يَصُدُّوْنَ عَنْكَ صُدُوْدًا ۞ فَكَيْفَ اِذَآ

اَصَابَتْهُمْ مُّصِيْبَةٌۢ بِمَا قَدَّمَتْ اَيْدِيْهِمْ ثُمَّ

جَآءُوْكَ يَحْلِفُوْنَ ۙ بِاللّٰهِ اِنْ اَرَدْنَآ اِلَّآ اِحْسَانًا

وَّ تَوْفِيْقًا ۞ اُولٰٓئِكَ الَّذِيْنَ يَعْلَمُ اللّٰهُ مَا فِيْ

قُلُوْبِهِمْ ۗ فَاَعْرِضْ عَنْهُمْ وَعِظْهُمْ وَقُلْ لَّهُمْ فِيْٓ

اَنْفُسِهِمْ قَوْلًۢا بَلِيْغًا ۞ وَمَآ اَرْسَلْنَا مِنْ رَّسُوْلٍ اِلَّا

لِيُطَاعَ بِاِذْنِ اللّٰهِ ط وَلَوْ اَنَّهُمْ اِذْ ظَّلَمُوْٓا اَنْفُسَهُمْ

Obey the Messenger ﷺ unconditionally, follow his orders wholeheartedly.

جَآءُوْكَ فَاسْتَغْفَرُوا اللّٰهَ وَاسْتَغْفَرَ لَهُمُ الرَّسُوْلُ

لَوَجَدُوا اللّٰهَ تَوَّابًا رَّحِيْمًا ۞ فَلَا وَرَبِّكَ لَا يُؤْمِنُوْنَ

حَتّٰى يُحَكِّمُوْكَ فِيْمَا شَجَرَ بَيْنَهُمْ ثُمَّ لَا يَجِدُوْا فِيْٓ

اَنْفُسِهِمْ حَرَجًا مِّمَّا قَضَيْتَ وَيُسَلِّمُوْا تَسْلِيْمًا ۞ وَلَوْ

اَنَّا كَتَبْنَا عَلَيْهِمْ اَنِ اقْتُلُوْٓا اَنْفُسَكُمْ اَوِ اخْرُجُوْا مِنْ

دِيَارِكُمْ مَّا فَعَلُوْهُ اِلَّا قَلِيْلٌ مِّنْهُمْ ط وَلَوْ اَنَّهُمْ

فَعَلُوْا مَا يُوْعَظُوْنَ بِهٖ لَكَانَ خَيْرًا لَّهُمْ وَاَشَدَّ

تَثْبِيْتًا ۞ وَّ اِذًا لَّاٰتَيْنٰهُمْ مِّنْ لَّدُنَّآ اَجْرًا عَظِيْمًا ۞

وَّلَهَدَيْنٰهُمْ صِرَاطًا مُّسْتَقِيْمًا ۞ وَمَنْ يُّطِعِ اللّٰهَ

وَالرَّسُوْلَ فَاُولٰٓئِكَ مَعَ الَّذِيْنَ اَنْعَمَ اللّٰهُ عَلَيْهِمْ

مِّنَ النَّبِيّٖنَ وَالصِّدِّيْقِيْنَ وَالشُّهَدَآءِ وَالصّٰلِحِيْنَ ۚ

وَ حَسُنَ اُولٰٓئِكَ رَفِيْقًا ط ۞ ذٰلِكَ الْفَضْلُ مِنَ اللّٰهِ ط

⁶¹ If they are told, "Come *along* to *listen to* what Allah has revealed to the Messenger, you will see the hypocrites turning to face in the opposite direction from you." ⁶² But when a disaster strikes them because of what they have done, they turn to you swearing by Allah: "We only want what is best and *to maintain* harmony." ⁶³ Allah knows what is in these peoples' hearts, so, forgive them, warn them, and speak eloquently with them so it penetrates their minds.

The sinner who comes to the Messenger ﷺ is forgiven

⁶⁴ We haven't sent a single messenger except that he should be obeyed as commanded by Allah. If anyone who wronged themselves came to you seeking Allah's forgiveness, Messenger, seek forgiveness for them! They will find Allah Relenting, Most Kind. ⁶⁵ By your Lord, they aren't believers until they make you the judge in their disputes, accept your decision without reservation, and commit themselves *to your decision.*

The rewards of obeying the Prophet ﷺ

⁶⁶ If We had ordered them: "Lay down your lives," or "Leave your homes," for the sake of Allah only a few of them would have done so.ᵃ Had they done what they were *told*, that would have been better for them and *put them* on a far firmer footing; ⁶⁷ We would have given them a great reward, ⁶⁸ and guided them on the straight path. ⁶⁹ Anyone who obeys Allah and the Messenger shall be with those Allah favoured: the Prophets, the truthful, the martyrs and the righteous. What a wonderful fellowship! ⁷⁰ Such is Allah's grace; and Allah is sufficient, the Knower.

ᵃ This introduces verse 71, encouraging *Jihad* for the defence of faith and freedom.

وَكَفٰى بِاللّٰهِ عَلِيْمًا ۞ يٰٓاَيُّهَا الَّذِيْنَ اٰمَنُوْا خُذُوْا

حِذْرَكُمْ فَانْفِرُوْا ثُبَاتٍ اَوِ انْفِرُوْا جَمِيْعًا ۞ وَاِنَّ

مِنْكُمْ لَمَنْ لَّيُبَطِّئَنَّ ۚ فَاِنْ اَصَابَتْكُمْ مُّصِيْبَةٌ قَالَ

قَدْ اَنْعَمَ اللّٰهُ عَلَيَّ اِذْ لَمْ اَكُنْ مَّعَهُمْ شَهِيْدًا ۞

وَلَئِنْ اَصَابَكُمْ فَضْلٌ مِّنَ اللّٰهِ لَيَقُوْلَنَّ كَاَنْ لَّمْ

تَكُنْ بَيْنَكُمْ وَبَيْنَهٗ مَوَدَّةٌ يّٰلَيْتَنِيْ كُنْتُ مَعَهُمْ

فَاَفُوْزَ فَوْزًا عَظِيْمًا ۞ فَلْيُقَاتِلْ فِيْ سَبِيْلِ اللّٰهِ

الَّذِيْنَ يَشْرُوْنَ الْحَيٰوةَ الدُّنْيَا بِالْاٰخِرَةِ ؕ وَمَنْ

يُّقَاتِلْ فِيْ سَبِيْلِ اللّٰهِ فَيُقْتَلْ اَوْ يَغْلِبْ فَسَوْفَ

نُؤْتِيْهِ اَجْرًا عَظِيْمًا ۞ وَمَا لَكُمْ لَا تُقَاتِلُوْنَ فِيْ

سَبِيْلِ اللّٰهِ وَالْمُسْتَضْعَفِيْنَ مِنَ الرِّجَالِ وَالنِّسَآءِ وَ

الْوِلْدَانِ الَّذِيْنَ يَقُوْلُوْنَ رَبَّنَاۤ اَخْرِجْنَا مِنْ هٰذِهِ

الْقَرْيَةِ الظَّالِمِ اَهْلُهَا ۚ وَاجْعَلْ لَّنَا مِنْ لَّدُنْكَ

وَلِيًّا ۙ وَّاجْعَلْ لَّنَا مِنْ لَّدُنْكَ نَصِيْرًا ۞ اَلَّذِيْنَ

اٰمَنُوْا يُقَاتِلُوْنَ فِيْ سَبِيْلِ اللّٰهِ ۚ وَالَّذِيْنَ كَفَرُوْا

يُقَاتِلُوْنَ فِيْ سَبِيْلِ الطَّاغُوْتِ فَقَاتِلُوْۤا اَوْلِيَآءَ

الشَّيْطٰنِ ۚ اِنَّ كَيْدَ الشَّيْطٰنِ كَانَ ضَعِيْفًا ۞ اَلَمْ

تَرَ اِلَى الَّذِيْنَ قِيْلَ لَهُمْ كُفُّوْۤا اَيْدِيَكُمْ وَاَقِيْمُوا

الصَّلٰوةَ وَاٰتُوا الزَّكٰوةَ ۚ فَلَمَّا كُتِبَ عَلَيْهِمُ الْقِتَالُ

اِذَا فَرِيْقٌ مِّنْهُمْ يَخْشَوْنَ النَّاسَ كَخَشْيَةِ اللّٰهِ

War is sometimes necessary to protect the weak and stand up against injustice.

Jihad for worldly gains is condemned

⁷¹Believers, take all precautions and let the battle-hardened march out *in front* or else march out together. ⁷²There are some of you who lag behind and if you suffered a setback, will say, "It was Allah's favour on me that I wasn't there with them." ⁷³When Allah favours you, he will say, "If only I had been with them, I would have gained a great victory," as though there was no love lost between you and him. ⁷⁴So those who are willing to swap this worldly life for the Hereafter, let them fight in the way of Allah. Whoever fights in the way of Allah and is either killed or victorious, We will give him a great reward.

The purpose of Jihad is to fight injustice

⁷⁵What is the matter with you that you do not fight in the way of Allah when the weak – men, women and children – are saying, "Our Lord, out of Your graciousness, take us out of this town of cruel people, give us a protector and a helper!" ⁷⁶The believers fight for the sake of Allah, whilst the disbelievers fight for the sake of false gods; so, fight the supporters of Satan. Satan's scheming is weak. ⁷⁷Haven't you seen those who were told: "Hold back your hands *from wrongdoing*, and *instead* perform the prayer and pay zakat"? Since fighting was prescribed for them, a group of them fears men as they fear Allah, or even more.ᵃ They say, "Our Lord, why have You prescribed fighting for us? Couldn't You have delayed it for a while?" Say: "The delights of this world are little, while the Hereafter is far better for the mindful, you will not be treated unjustly in the slightest."

ᵃ   The pagans used to plunder to enrich their tribe, violence wasn't for defence or a moral cause as in Islam. The Quran repeatedly speaks of war as a means of putting an end to the persecution of the weak by the strong. They were told: "Hold back your hands" from wrongdoing, since they would pick only on weak groups, which tended to run away, leaving their goods behind for the taking.

اَوْ اَشَدَّ خَشْيَةً ۚ وَقَالُوْا رَبَّنَا لِمَ كَتَبْتَ عَلَيْنَا

الْقِتَالَ ۚ لَوْلَا اَخَّرْتَنَا اِلٰٓى اَجَلٍ قَرِيْبٍ ؕ قُلْ

مَتَاعُ الدُّنْيَا قَلِيْلٌ ۚ وَالْاٰخِرَةُ خَيْرٌ لِّمَنِ اتَّقٰى

وَلَا تُظْلَمُوْنَ فَتِيْلًا ۝ اَيْنَ مَا تَكُوْنُوْا يُدْرِكُّكُمُ

الْمَوْتُ وَلَوْ كُنْتُمْ فِيْ بُرُوْجٍ مُّشَيَّدَةٍ ؕ وَاِنْ تُصِبْهُمْ

حَسَنَةٌ يَّقُوْلُوْا هٰذِهٖ مِنْ عِنْدِ اللّٰهِ ۚ وَاِنْ تُصِبْهُمْ

سَيِّئَةٌ يَّقُوْلُوْا هٰذِهٖ مِنْ عِنْدِكَ ؕ قُلْ كُلٌّ مِّنْ

عِنْدِ اللّٰهِ ؕ فَمَالِ هٰٓؤُلَآءِ الْقَوْمِ لَا يَكَادُوْنَ يَفْقَهُوْنَ

Good is from Allah and bad is from ourselves: so be careful and cautious.

حَدِيْثًا ۝ مَآ اَصَابَكَ مِنْ حَسَنَةٍ فَمِنَ اللّٰهِ ۚ وَمَآ

اَصَابَكَ مِنْ سَيِّئَةٍ فَمِنْ نَّفْسِكَ ؕ وَاَرْسَلْنٰكَ

لِلنَّاسِ رَسُوْلًا ؕ وَكَفٰى بِاللّٰهِ شَهِيْدًا ۝ مَنْ يُّطِعِ

الرَّسُوْلَ فَقَدْ اَطَاعَ اللّٰهَ ۚ وَمَنْ تَوَلّٰى فَمَآ اَرْسَلْنٰكَ

عَلَيْهِمْ حَفِيْظًا ۝ وَيَقُوْلُوْنَ طَاعَةٌ ۖ فَاِذَا بَرَزُوْا

مِنْ عِنْدِكَ بَيَّتَ طَآئِفَةٌ مِّنْهُمْ غَيْرَ الَّذِيْ

تَقُوْلُ ؕ وَاللّٰهُ يَكْتُبُ مَا يُبَيِّتُوْنَ ۚ فَاَعْرِضْ عَنْهُمْ وَ

تَوَكَّلْ عَلَى اللّٰهِ ؕ وَكَفٰى بِاللّٰهِ وَكِيْلًا ۝ اَفَلَا يَتَدَبَّرُوْنَ

الْقُرْاٰنَ ؕ وَلَوْ كَانَ مِنْ عِنْدِ غَيْرِ اللّٰهِ لَوَجَدُوْا فِيْهِ

اخْتِلَافًا كَثِيْرًا ۝ وَاِذَا جَآءَهُمْ اَمْرٌ مِّنَ الْاَمْنِ اَوِ

الْخَوْفِ اَذَاعُوْا بِهٖ ؕ وَلَوْ رَدُّوْهُ اِلَى الرَّسُوْلِ وَاِلٰٓى

اُولِي الْاَمْرِ مِنْهُمْ لَعَلِمَهُ الَّذِيْنَ يَسْتَنْبِطُوْنَهٗ

There is no escape from death when its time comes

[78] Death will catch up wherever you may be, even if you are in strong forts.[a] When good things happen to them, they say, "This is from Allah," and, when bad things happen to them, they say, "This is your fault, *Muhammad*." Say: "All is from Allah." What is the matter with these people that they hardly understand what they are told? [79] Whatever good things happen to you they're from Allah, and whatever evil happens to you it's from yourselves. We sent you as a Messenger to people; Allah is sufficient witness. [80] Whoever obeys the Messenger has obeyed Allah, but whoever turns away, We didn't send you as a guardian over them.

Hypocrites will always find excuses in the Shariah

[81] They say, "We will obey." However, when they leave your presence, a group of them spend the night plotting against what you said. Allah writes down how they spend the night, so, ignore them and put your trust in Allah. Allah suffices as a Protector. [82] Don't they reflect on the Quran? Had it come from anyone beside Allah, they would have found many inconsistencies in it.

Don't be disheartened by the rumours spread by the hypocrites

[83] Whenever a report of war or peace comes to them they broadcast it loudly; whereas, if they had referred it to the Messenger or to those in authority, its significance could be determined by those best suited to interpret it. If it had not been for Allah's grace and kindness, most of you would have followed Satan.

---

[a] The Bedouins were used to raids, which they won by a mere show of strength, rather than actual fighting.

مِنْهُمْ ۚ وَلَوْ لَا فَضْلُ اللّٰهِ عَلَيْكُمْ وَرَحْمَتُهُ لَاتَّبَعْتُمُ

الشَّيْطٰنَ اِلَّا قَلِيْلًا ۞ فَقَاتِلْ فِىْ سَبِيْلِ اللّٰهِ ۚ لَا

تُكَلَّفُ اِلَّا نَفْسَكَ وَحَرِّضِ الْمُؤْمِنِيْنَ ۚ عَسَى اللّٰهُ

اَنْ يَّكُفَّ بَأْسَ الَّذِيْنَ كَفَرُوْا ۗ وَاللّٰهُ اَشَدُّ بَأْسًا وَّ

اَشَدُّ تَنْكِيْلًا ۞ مَنْ يَّشْفَعْ شَفَاعَةً حَسَنَةً يَّكُنْ لَّهٗ

نَصِيْبٌ مِّنْهَا ۚ وَمَنْ يَّشْفَعْ شَفَاعَةً سَيِّئَةً يَّكُنْ لَّهٗ

كِفْلٌ مِّنْهَا ۗ وَكَانَ اللّٰهُ عَلٰى كُلِّ شَىْءٍ مُّقِيْتًا ۞ وَ

اِذَا حُيِّيْتُمْ بِتَحِيَّةٍ فَحَيُّوْا بِاَحْسَنَ مِنْهَآ اَوْ رُدُّوْهَا ۗ

اِنَّ اللّٰهَ كَانَ عَلٰى كُلِّ شَىْءٍ حَسِيْبًا ۞ اَللّٰهُ لَآ اِلٰهَ

اِلَّا هُوَ ۚ لَيَجْمَعَنَّكُمْ اِلٰى يَوْمِ الْقِيٰمَةِ لَا رَيْبَ فِيْهِ ۗ

وَمَنْ اَصْدَقُ مِنَ اللّٰهِ حَدِيْثًا ۞ فَمَا لَكُمْ فِى

الْمُنٰفِقِيْنَ فِئَتَيْنِ وَاللّٰهُ اَرْكَسَهُمْ بِمَا كَسَبُوْا ۗ

اَتُرِيْدُوْنَ اَنْ تَهْدُوْا مَنْ اَضَلَّ اللّٰهُ ۗ وَمَنْ يُّضْلِلِ

اللّٰهُ فَلَنْ تَجِدَ لَهٗ سَبِيْلًا ۞ وَدُّوْا لَوْ تَكْفُرُوْنَ كَمَا

كَفَرُوْا فَتَكُوْنُوْنَ سَوَآءً فَلَا تَتَّخِذُوْا مِنْهُمْ اَوْلِيَآءَ

حَتّٰى يُهَاجِرُوْا فِىْ سَبِيْلِ اللّٰهِ ۗ فَاِنْ تَوَلَّوْا فَخُذُوْهُمْ

وَاقْتُلُوْهُمْ حَيْثُ وَجَدْتُّمُوْهُمْ ۖ وَلَا تَتَّخِذُوْا

مِنْهُمْ وَلِيًّا وَّلَا نَصِيْرًا ۞ اِلَّا الَّذِيْنَ يَصِلُوْنَ

اِلٰى قَوْمٍ بَيْنَكُمْ وَبَيْنَهُمْ مِّيْثَاقٌ اَوْ جَآءُوْكُمْ

حَصِرَتْ صُدُوْرُهُمْ اَنْ يُّقَاتِلُوْكُمْ اَوْ يُقَاتِلُوْا

التقوى   ع ١١   ٨

Initiating good works or making suggestions for them makes you a shareholder in them.

⁸⁴So, *Muhammad*, fight in the way of Allah – you are only answerable for yourself – and encourage the believers. It may be that Allah will curb the power of disbelievers. Allah is stronger in might and more severe in punishment.

Always be courteous
⁸⁵Whoever speaks out for a worthy cause will have a share in its benefits, and whoever speaks out for a wrong cause will share its burden, Allah is Watchful over everything. ⁸⁶When anyone greets you, respond with a better greeting or *at least* return it *in kind*. Allah keeps account of everything. ⁸⁷Allah is the only God, He will gather you all on Judgement Day, there is no doubt about that. Who is more truthful in speech than Allah?

The rules of engagement with prowling bands of hypocrites
⁸⁸Why are you divided in two groups concerning the hypocrites? Allah has driven them back into *disbelief* for what they did. Do you want to guide those who Allah has allowed to go astray? Anyone who Allah allows to go astray, you will never find a way out for him. ⁸⁹They would love to see *all of* you disbelieve as they have disbelieved, so that you become equal. Don't ally yourselves to any of them until they migrate for the sake of Allah. If they turn away, seize them and slay them wherever you find them, and take none of them as an ally or a helper, ⁹⁰except for those who are related to a people with whom you have a treaty, or who come over to you because their hearts are wary of fighting you or of fighting their own people. Had Allah wished, He would have given them power over you, so they would have fought you. If they withdraw and do not fight you but make you an offer of peace, then Allah gives you no excuse *to fight* against them.

قَوْمَهُمْ ط وَلَوْ شَآءَ اللّٰهُ لَسَلَّطَهُمْ عَلَيْكُمْ فَلَقَاتَلُوْكُمْ ۚ

فَإِنِ اعْتَزَلُوْكُمْ فَلَمْ يُقَاتِلُوْكُمْ وَ الْقَوْا اِلَيْكُمُ

السَّلَمَ ۙ فَمَا جَعَلَ اللّٰهُ لَكُمْ عَلَيْهِمْ سَبِيْلًا ۞

سَتَجِدُوْنَ اٰخَرِيْنَ يُرِيْدُوْنَ اَنْ يَّأْمَنُوْكُمْ وَ

يَأْمَنُوْا قَوْمَهُمْ ط كُلَّمَا رُدُّوْٓا اِلَى الْفِتْنَةِ اُرْكِسُوْا

فِيْهَا ۚ فَاِنْ لَّمْ يَعْتَزِلُوْكُمْ وَ يُلْقُوْٓا اِلَيْكُمُ السَّلَمَ

وَ يَكُفُّوْٓا اَيْدِيَهُمْ فَخُذُوْهُمْ وَ اقْتُلُوْهُمْ حَيْثُ

ثَقِفْتُمُوْهُمْ ط وَ اُولٰٓئِكُمْ جَعَلْنَا لَكُمْ عَلَيْهِمْ سُلْطٰنًا

مُبِيْنًا ۞ وَ مَا كَانَ لِمُؤْمِنٍ اَنْ يَّقْتُلَ مُؤْمِنًا

اِلَّا خَطَأً ۚ وَ مَنْ قَتَلَ مُؤْمِنًا خَطَأً فَتَحْرِيْرُ

رَقَبَةٍ مُّؤْمِنَةٍ وَّدِيَةٌ مُّسَلَّمَةٌ اِلٰٓى اَهْلِهٖٓ اِلَّآ

اَنْ يَّصَّدَّقُوْا ط فَاِنْ كَانَ مِنْ قَوْمٍ عَدُوٍّ لَّكُمْ

وَ هُوَ مُؤْمِنٌ فَتَحْرِيْرُ رَقَبَةٍ مُّؤْمِنَةٍ ط وَ اِنْ

كَانَ مِنْ قَوْمٍ بَيْنَكُمْ وَ بَيْنَهُمْ مِّيْثَاقٌ فَدِيَةٌ

مُّسَلَّمَةٌ اِلٰٓى اَهْلِهٖ وَ تَحْرِيْرُ رَقَبَةٍ مُّؤْمِنَةٍ ۚ

فَمَنْ لَّمْ يَجِدْ فَصِيَامُ شَهْرَيْنِ مُتَتَابِعَيْنِ ۫ تَوْبَةً

مِّنَ اللّٰهِ ط وَ كَانَ اللّٰهُ عَلِيْمًا حَكِيْمًا ۞ وَ مَنْ يَّقْتُلْ

مُؤْمِنًا مُّتَعَمِّدًا فَجَزَآؤُهٗ جَهَنَّمُ خٰلِدًا فِيْهَا وَ

غَضِبَ اللّٰهُ عَلَيْهِ وَ لَعَنَهٗ وَ اَعَدَّ لَهٗ عَذَابًا

عَظِيْمًا ۞ يٰٓاَيُّهَا الَّذِيْنَ اٰمَنُوْٓا اِذَا ضَرَبْتُمْ فِيْ

When the opportunity for peace arises don't miss it.

۱۲
ع
۹

⁹¹There are others whom you will find wanting to be on good terms with both you and their own people, but whenever they are put to the test, they return to *fighting*. So, if they don't withdraw or make you an offer of peace, and cease hostility, seize them and slay them wherever you encounter them, We've given you clear authority against such people.

Penalty for accidental death and murder

⁹²It is forbidden for a believer to kill another believer, except by mistake. Anyone who kills a believer by mistake must free a believing slave and pay compensation to the *victim's* family, unless they waive it as an act of charity. If *the victim* belonged to an enemy tribe but was himself a believer, then free a believing slave and if he was from a tribe with which you have a treaty, then pay compensation to their family and free a believing slave. Whoever cannot find the means *to pay compensation* let him fast two consecutive months to gain Allah's forgiveness. Allah is the Knower, Wise. ⁹³The penalty of intentionally killing a believer is Hell, living there for a long time; Allah's anger and curse will fall on him, and He has prepared for him a terrible punishment.

سَبِيلِ اللهِ فَتَبَيَّنُوْا وَلَا تَقُوْلُوْا لِمَنْ اَلْقٰى اِلَيْكُمُ

السَّلٰمَ لَسْتَ مُؤْمِنًا ۚ تَبْتَغُوْنَ عَرَضَ الْحَيٰوةِ

الدُّنْيَا ۫ فَعِنْدَ اللهِ مَغَانِمُ كَثِيْرَةٌ ؕ كَذٰلِكَ

كُنْتُمْ مِّنْ قَبْلُ فَمَنَّ اللهُ عَلَيْكُمْ فَتَبَيَّنُوْا ؕ

اِنَّ اللهَ كَانَ بِمَا تَعْمَلُوْنَ خَبِيْرًا ﴿۹۴﴾ لَا يَسْتَوِى

الْقٰعِدُوْنَ مِنَ الْمُؤْمِنِيْنَ غَيْرُ اُولِى الضَّرَرِ وَ

الْمُجٰهِدُوْنَ فِيْ سَبِيْلِ اللهِ بِاَمْوَالِهِمْ وَاَنْفُسِهِمْ ؕ

فَضَّلَ اللهُ الْمُجٰهِدِيْنَ بِاَمْوَالِهِمْ وَ اَنْفُسِهِمْ

عَلَى الْقٰعِدِيْنَ دَرَجَةً ؕ وَكُلًّا وَّعَدَ اللهُ الْحُسْنٰى ؕ

وَ فَضَّلَ اللهُ الْمُجٰهِدِيْنَ عَلَى الْقٰعِدِيْنَ اَجْرًا

عَظِيْمًا ﴿۹۵﴾ دَرَجٰتٍ مِّنْهُ وَمَغْفِرَةً وَّرَحْمَةً ؕ وَ

كَانَ اللهُ غَفُوْرًا رَّحِيْمًا ﴿۹۶﴾ اِنَّ الَّذِيْنَ تَوَفّٰهُمُ

الْمَلٰٓئِكَةُ ظَالِمِيْٓ اَنْفُسِهِمْ قَالُوْا فِيْمَ كُنْتُمْ ؕ

قَالُوْا كُنَّا مُسْتَضْعَفِيْنَ فِى الْاَرْضِ ؕ قَالُوْٓا اَلَمْ

تَكُنْ اَرْضُ اللهِ وَاسِعَةً فَتُهَاجِرُوْا فِيْهَا ؕ

فَاُولٰٓئِكَ مَأْوٰىهُمْ جَهَنَّمُ ؕ وَسَآءَتْ مَصِيْرًا ﴿۹۷﴾

اِلَّا الْمُسْتَضْعَفِيْنَ مِنَ الرِّجَالِ وَ النِّسَآءِ وَ

الْوِلْدَانِ لَا يَسْتَطِيْعُوْنَ حِيْلَةً وَّلَا يَهْتَدُوْنَ

سَبِيْلًا ﴿۹۸﴾ فَاُولٰٓئِكَ عَسَى اللهُ اَنْ يَّعْفُوَ عَنْهُمْ ؕ

وَكَانَ اللهُ عَفُوًّا غَفُوْرًا ﴿۹۹﴾ وَمَنْ يُّهَاجِرْ فِيْ

A wake up call for those satisfied with evil in their society. Challenge the evil.

۱۳
ع
۵
۱۰

Do not be judgemental or dismissive

[94] Believers, when you set out on patrol in the path of Allah, be cautious. When someone gives you a greeting of peace,[a] do not say: "You are not a believer," seeking worldly gains, Allah has many *other* rewards. That is how you used to behave in the past until Allah favoured you *with Islam*, so be open and honest. Allah is aware of what you do.

Believers are rewarded according to their efforts

[95] The believers who stayed behind – apart from those who were physically or financially incapable – are not equal to those who strive with their lives and their wealth in the path of Allah. Allah has favoured by degrees those who strive with their wealth and lives above those who stayed behind. Allah has promised both goodness; *however*, Allah has favoured those who strive over those who stayed behind with a great reward, [96] high ranks, forgiveness and kindness. Allah is Forgiving, Most Kind.

Migration for the sake of saving

[97] The *Muslims* whose souls the angels take while they were doing wrong to themselves *since they didn't migrate*,[b] will be asked: "What *state* were you in?" They will say, "We were weak and vulnerable in the land." *Then* the Angels will ask: "Wasn't Allah's Earth spacious enough for you to migrate?" For such people, their refuge will be Hell. What a wretched destination! [98] Except for the weak among the men, women and children who were unable to come up with a strategy or to find a way out. [99] They may be pardoned by Allah. Indeed, Allah is Pardoning, Forgiving.

---

[a] *Salam*, meaning "peace", a customary greeting of Arab Jews, Christians and Muslims. The verse was revealed after a Muslim had killed someone who had greeted him with *"as-salam 'alaykum"*. Rather than give the stranger the benefit of the doubt, he thought this person was pretending to be a Muslim to save his life. His action was condemned.

[b] A reference to Muslims who stayed behind in Makkah, choosing not to migrate although they had the means, but instead hid their faith and lived an oppressed life. Is this threat of Hell a veiled wake-up call for those who are comfortable with their material life? Muslim by name not by conviction?

سَبِيْلِ اللّٰهِ يَجِدْ فِى الْاَرْضِ مُرَاغَمًا كَثِيْرًا

وَّسَعَةً ط وَمَنْ يَّخْرُجْ مِنْۢ بَيْتِهٖ مُهَاجِرًا اِلَى

اللّٰهِ وَرَسُوْلِهٖ ثُمَّ يُدْرِكْهُ الْمَوْتُ فَقَدْ وَقَعَ

اَجْرُهٗ عَلَى اللّٰهِ ط وَكَانَ اللّٰهُ غَفُوْرًا رَّحِيْمًا ۞ وَاِذَا

ضَرَبْتُمْ فِى الْاَرْضِ فَلَيْسَ عَلَيْكُمْ جُنَاحٌ اَنْ

تَقْصُرُوْا مِنَ الصَّلٰوةِ ۖ اِنْ خِفْتُمْ اَنْ يَّفْتِنَكُمُ

الَّذِيْنَ كَفَرُوْا ط اِنَّ الْكٰفِرِيْنَ كَانُوْا لَكُمْ عَدُوًّا

مُّبِيْنًا ۞ وَاِذَا كُنْتَ فِيْهِمْ فَاَقَمْتَ لَهُمُ الصَّلٰوةَ

فَلْتَقُمْ طَآئِفَةٌ مِّنْهُمْ مَّعَكَ وَلْيَاْخُذُوْۤا

اَسْلِحَتَهُمْ فَاِذَا سَجَدُوْا فَلْيَكُوْنُوْا مِنْ وَّرَآئِكُمْ

وَلْتَاْتِ طَآئِفَةٌ اُخْرٰى لَمْ يُصَلُّوْا فَلْيُصَلُّوْا مَعَكَ

وَلْيَاْخُذُوْا حِذْرَهُمْ وَاَسْلِحَتَهُمْ ۚ وَدَّ الَّذِيْنَ

كَفَرُوْا لَوْ تَغْفُلُوْنَ عَنْ اَسْلِحَتِكُمْ وَاَمْتِعَتِكُمْ

فَيَمِيْلُوْنَ عَلَيْكُمْ مَّيْلَةً وَّاحِدَةً ط وَلَا جُنَاحَ

عَلَيْكُمْ اِنْ كَانَ بِكُمْ اَذًى مِّنْ مَّطَرٍ اَوْ كُنْتُمْ

مَّرْضٰۤى اَنْ تَضَعُوْۤا اَسْلِحَتَكُمْ ۚ وَخُذُوْا حِذْرَكُمْ ط

اِنَّ اللّٰهَ اَعَدَّ لِلْكٰفِرِيْنَ عَذَابًا مُّهِيْنًا ۞ فَاِذَا

قَضَيْتُمُ الصَّلٰوةَ فَاذْكُرُوا اللّٰهَ قِيَامًا وَّقُعُوْدًا وَّعَلٰى

جُنُوْبِكُمْ ۚ فَاِذَا اطْمَاْنَنْتُمْ فَاَقِيْمُوا الصَّلٰوةَ ۚ اِنَّ

الصَّلٰوةَ كَانَتْ عَلَى الْمُؤْمِنِيْنَ كِتٰبًا مَّوْقُوْتًا ۞

Prayer is compulsory all the time, even in the midst of a battle!

177

[100] Whoever migrates in the path of Allah will find a place of refuge *somewhere* in the land and worldly abundance and whoever sets out from home to migrate for the sake of Allah and His Messenger, and dies *on the way*, Allah will grant him his reward. Allah is Forgiving, Kind.

Shortening the prayer when travelling

[101] When you are travelling in the land, you can shorten the prayer without feeling guilty,[a] if you fear being attacked by the disbelievers; the disbelievers are your open enemies.

The prayer in the state of fear

[102] *Messenger*, when you are among them and leading them in prayer, let a group of them stand with you carrying their weapons; then, when they have prostrated, they may *cover* you from behind while another group who hasn't yet prayed come and pray with you, *again* with due precaution and with their weapons. The disbelievers would love to see you neglect your weapons and your possessions so they could descend on you all at once. Nor is there any blame on you if some hardship such as rain or illness makes you put down your weapons, but remain on your guard. Indeed, Allah has prepared humiliating punishment for the disbelievers. [103] When you have completed the prayer, *continue nevertheless to* remember Allah, be it standing, sitting or lying down. Then, whenever you feel safe again, perform the prayer. The prayer is compulsory for the believers at fixed times.

---

a   The shortening of the prayer refers to shortening the 4 *Fardh* of *Dhur*, *Asr* and *Isha* to two units only. This is a special concession when travelling a minimum of fifty four miles away from home and staying there for less than fifteen days.

وَلَا تَهِنُوْا فِى ابْتِغَآءِ الْقَوْمِ ط اِنْ تَكُوْنُوْا تَأْلَمُوْنَ

فَاِنَّهُمْ يَأْلَمُوْنَ كَمَا تَأْلَمُوْنَ ج وَتَرْجُوْنَ مِنَ اللّٰهِ

مَا لَا يَرْجُوْنَ ط وَكَانَ اللّٰهُ عَلِيْمًا حَكِيْمًا ۞ اِنَّآ

اَنْزَلْنَآ اِلَيْكَ الْكِتٰبَ بِالْحَقِّ لِتَحْكُمَ بَيْنَ النَّاسِ

بِمَآ اَرٰىكَ اللّٰهُ ط وَلَا تَكُنْ لِّلْخَآئِنِيْنَ خَصِيْمًا ۞

وَّاسْتَغْفِرِ اللّٰهَ ط اِنَّ اللّٰهَ كَانَ غَفُوْرًا رَّحِيْمًا ۞

وَلَا تُجَادِلْ عَنِ الَّذِيْنَ يَخْتَانُوْنَ اَنْفُسَهُمْ ط اِنَّ

اللّٰهَ لَا يُحِبُّ مَنْ كَانَ خَوَّانًا اَثِيْمًا ۞ يَّسْتَخْفُوْنَ

Loyalty to leadership and community is essential.

مِنَ النَّاسِ وَلَا يَسْتَخْفُوْنَ مِنَ اللّٰهِ وَهُوَ مَعَهُمْ

اِذْ يُبَيِّتُوْنَ مَا لَا يَرْضٰى مِنَ الْقَوْلِ ط وَكَانَ اللّٰهُ

بِمَا يَعْمَلُوْنَ مُحِيْطًا ۞ هٰٓاَنْتُمْ هٰٓؤُلَآءِ جٰدَلْتُمْ

عَنْهُمْ فِى الْحَيٰوةِ الدُّنْيَا قف فَمَنْ يُّجَادِلُ اللّٰهَ

عَنْهُمْ يَوْمَ الْقِيٰمَةِ اَمْ مَّنْ يَّكُوْنُ عَلَيْهِمْ وَكِيْلًا ۞

وَمَنْ يَّعْمَلْ سُوْٓءًا اَوْ يَظْلِمْ نَفْسَهٗ ثُمَّ يَسْتَغْفِرِ

اللّٰهَ يَجِدِ اللّٰهَ غَفُوْرًا رَّحِيْمًا ۞ وَمَنْ يَّكْسِبْ اِثْمًا

فَاِنَّمَا يَكْسِبُهٗ عَلٰى نَفْسِهٖ ط وَكَانَ اللّٰهُ عَلِيْمًا

حَكِيْمًا ۞ وَمَنْ يَّكْسِبْ خَطِيْٓئَةً اَوْ اِثْمًا ثُمَّ يَرْمِ

بِهٖ بَرِيْٓئًا فَقَدِ احْتَمَلَ بُهْتَانًا وَّاِثْمًا مُّبِيْنًا ۞

وَلَوْ لَا فَضْلُ اللّٰهِ عَلَيْكَ وَرَحْمَتُهٗ لَهَمَّتْ

طَّآئِفَةٌ مِّنْهُمْ اَنْ يُّضِلُّوْكَ ط وَمَا يُضِلُّوْنَ اِلَّآ

¹⁰⁴ *So* do not be half-hearted in seeking out the *hostile, disbelieving* people. If you are suffering, then they are suffering just like you, however *there is difference,* while you have hope in Allah they have no such hope. Allah is the Knower, Wise.

There is no excuse for treachery

¹⁰⁵ We sent down to you the Book containing the truth so that you may judge between people the way Allah has shown you. So, don't support the traitors, ¹⁰⁶ but seek Allah's forgiveness. Allah is Forgiving, Kind. ¹⁰⁷ And do not argue about those who deceive themselves. Allah dislikes anyone who is treacherous and sinful. ¹⁰⁸ They try to hide from people, but they can't hide from Allah; He is with them as they talk late into the night about things that displease Him. Allah is aware of what they do. ¹⁰⁹ *Believers,* here you are defending them in this worldly life, but who will defend them against Allah on Judgement Day, or be their lawyer?

The case of a Muslim who lied to avoid punishment

¹¹⁰ Whoever does an evil deed or wrongs himself but then seeks Allah's forgiveness, he will find Allah Forgiving, Kind. ¹¹¹ Whoever commits a sin will reap its reward. Allah is All-Knowing, Wise. ¹¹² Whoever does wrong or commits a sin then blames *someone else* for it, he has burdened himself with a slander and an open sin.[a]

To avoid Hell, Muslims must follow the path of Allah's pleasure

¹¹³ If it wasn't for Allah's grace and kindness towards you, a group amongst them would have misled you, but as it is they only misled themselves, doing you no harm. Allah has revealed to you the Book and wisdom, and has taught you what you didn't know. Allah's favour on you is great.

---

[a] This refers to an incident of theft by a Muslim who blamed a Jew, so his family asked the Prophet ﷺ to punish the Jew. However, these verses were revealed clarifying the innocence of the Jew.

اَنْفُسَهُمْ وَمَا يَضُرُّوْنَكَ مِنْ شَيْءٍ ط وَاَنْزَلَ اللّٰهُ

عَلَيْكَ الْكِتٰبَ وَالْحِكْمَةَ وَعَلَّمَكَ مَا لَمْ تَكُنْ

تَعْلَمُ ط وَكَانَ فَضْلُ اللّٰهِ عَلَيْكَ عَظِيْمًا ۝ لَا خَيْرَ

فِيْ كَثِيْرٍ مِّنْ نَّجْوٰىهُمْ اِلَّا مَنْ اَمَرَ بِصَدَقَةٍ اَوْ

مَعْرُوْفٍ اَوْ اِصْلَاحٍ بَيْنَ النَّاسِ ط وَمَنْ يَّفْعَلْ

ذٰلِكَ ابْتِغَآءَ مَرْضَاتِ اللّٰهِ فَسَوْفَ نُؤْتِيْهِ اَجْرًا

عَظِيْمًا ۝ وَمَنْ يُّشَاقِقِ الرَّسُوْلَ مِنْ بَعْدِ مَا

تَبَيَّنَ لَهُ الْهُدٰى وَيَتَّبِعْ غَيْرَ سَبِيْلِ الْمُؤْمِنِيْنَ

نُوَلِّهٖ مَا تَوَلّٰى وَ نُصْلِهٖ جَهَنَّمَ ط وَسَآءَتْ مَصِيْرًا ۝

اِنَّ اللّٰهَ لَا يَغْفِرُ اَنْ يُّشْرَكَ بِهٖ وَ يَغْفِرُ مَا دُوْنَ

ذٰلِكَ لِمَنْ يَّشَآءُ ط وَمَنْ يُّشْرِكْ بِاللّٰهِ فَقَدْ ضَلَّ

ضَلٰلًا بَعِيْدًا ۝ اِنْ يَّدْعُوْنَ مِنْ دُوْنِهٖ اِلَّا اِنَاثًا ج

وَاِنْ يَّدْعُوْنَ اِلَّا شَيْطٰنًا مَّرِيْدًا ۝ لَّعَنَهُ اللّٰهُ ۚ

وَ قَالَ لَاَتَّخِذَنَّ مِنْ عِبَادِكَ نَصِيْبًا مَّفْرُوْضًا ۝

وَّلَاُضِلَّنَّهُمْ وَلَاُمَنِّيَنَّهُمْ وَلَاٰمُرَنَّهُمْ فَلَيُبَتِّكُنَّ

اٰذَانَ الْاَنْعَامِ وَلَاٰمُرَنَّهُمْ فَلَيُغَيِّرُنَّ خَلْقَ اللّٰهِ ط

وَمَنْ يَّتَّخِذِ الشَّيْطٰنَ وَلِيًّا مِّنْ دُوْنِ اللّٰهِ فَقَدْ

خَسِرَ خُسْرَانًا مُّبِيْنًا ۝ يَعِدُهُمْ وَيُمَنِّيْهِمْ ط وَمَا

يَعِدُهُمُ الشَّيْطٰنُ اِلَّا غُرُوْرًا ۝ اُولٰٓئِكَ مَأْوٰىهُمْ

جَهَنَّمُ ۚ وَ لَا يَجِدُوْنَ عَنْهَا مَحِيْصًا ۝ وَالَّذِيْنَ

Be wary of Satan's strategies to mislead. They can be clever.

¹¹⁴ There's very little good in most of their secret meetings, except when they enjoin acts of charity or do common good or reconcile between people. Whoever does these things seeking Allah's pleasure, We will give them a great reward. ¹¹⁵ Whoever opposes the Messenger after the guidance has been made clear to him and follows a path other than that of the believers, We will let him continue down his chosen path, until We burn him in Hell. What an evil destination!

Satan's way of misleading people

¹¹⁶ Allah will not forgive idolatry, but He forgives whatever is less than that to whomever He pleases. Whoever associates anything with Allah has wandered far, far astray. ¹¹⁷ What they call on apart from Him are nothing but *fabricated* goddesses and *ultimately* what they call on is only a rebellious demon. ¹¹⁸ Allah has cursed him for saying: "I will take an allotted share of Your servants; ¹¹⁹ and I will lead them astray and give them false hopes and I will order them to slit the ears of cattle and to tinker with Allah's creation." Whoever takes Satan as a protector beside Allah will clearly be a loser. ¹²⁰ He promises them and gives them hopes, but Satan's promises are mere deception. ¹²¹ Their home is Hell, and they will find no way out of it.

اٰمَنُوْا وَعَمِلُوا الصّٰلِحٰتِ سَنُدْخِلُهُمْ جَنّٰتٍ تَجْرِیْ

مِنْ تَحْتِهَا الْاَنْهٰرُ خٰلِدِیْنَ فِیْهَاۤ اَبَدًا ؕ وَعْدَ

اللّٰهِ حَقًّا ؕ وَمَنْ اَصْدَقُ مِنَ اللّٰهِ قِیْلًا ۱۲۲ لَیْسَ

بِاَمَانِیِّکُمْ وَلَاۤ اَمَانِیِّ اَهْلِ الْکِتٰبِ ؕ مَنْ یَّعْمَلْ

سُوْٓءًا یُّجْزَ بِهٖ ۙ وَلَا یَجِدْ لَهٗ مِنْ دُوْنِ اللّٰهِ وَلِیًّا

وَّلَا نَصِیْرًا ۱۲۳ وَمَنْ یَّعْمَلْ مِنَ الصّٰلِحٰتِ مِنْ ذَکَرٍ

اَوْ اُنْثٰی وَهُوَ مُؤْمِنٌ فَاُولٰٓئِکَ یَدْخُلُوْنَ الْجَنَّةَ

وَلَا یُظْلَمُوْنَ نَقِیْرًا ۱۲۴ وَمَنْ اَحْسَنُ دِیْنًا مِّمَّنْ

اَسْلَمَ وَجْهَهٗ لِلّٰهِ وَهُوَ مُحْسِنٌ وَّاتَّبَعَ مِلَّةَ

إِبْرٰهِیْمَ حَنِیْفًا ؕ وَاتَّخَذَ اللّٰهُ اِبْرٰهِیْمَ خَلِیْلًا ۱۲۵

وَلِلّٰهِ مَا فِی السّمٰوٰتِ وَمَا فِی الْاَرْضِ ؕ وَکَانَ اللّٰهُ

بِکُلِّ شَیْءٍ مُّحِیْطًا ۱۲۶ وَیَسْتَفْتُوْنَکَ فِی النِّسَآءِ ؕ

قُلِ اللّٰهُ یُفْتِیْکُمْ فِیْهِنَّ ۙ وَمَا یُتْلٰی عَلَیْکُمْ

فِی الْکِتٰبِ فِیْ یَتٰمَی النِّسَآءِ الّٰتِیْ لَا تُؤْتُوْنَهُنَّ

مَا کُتِبَ لَهُنَّ وَتَرْغَبُوْنَ اَنْ تَنْکِحُوْهُنَّ وَ

الْمُسْتَضْعَفِیْنَ مِنَ الْوِلْدَانِ ۙ وَاَنْ تَقُوْمُوْا لِلْیَتٰمٰی

بِالْقِسْطِ ؕ وَمَا تَفْعَلُوْا مِنْ خَیْرٍ فَاِنَّ اللّٰهَ کَانَ

بِهٖ عَلِیْمًا ۱۲۷ وَاِنِ امْرَاَةٌ خَافَتْ مِنْ بَعْلِهَا

نُشُوْزًا اَوْ اِعْرَاضًا فَلَا جُنَاحَ عَلَیْهِمَاۤ اَنْ یُّصْلِحَا

بَیْنَهُمَا صُلْحًا ؕ وَالصُّلْحُ خَیْرٌ ؕ وَاُحْضِرَتِ الْاَنْفُسُ

Allah made Ibrahim his friend. Who are your friends?

١٨
١١
١٥

183

Submission is the spirit and the heart of Islam

[122] Those who believe and do good works, We will admit them into gardens beneath which rivers flow, living there forever. *This is* Allah's true promise, and whose word is more truthful than Allah's? [123] It is neither according to your wishes nor to the wishes of the People of The Book; anyone who does evil will be repaid in kind, but will not find any protector or helper besides Allah. [124] A believer who does good works whether male or female will enter Paradise and will not be wronged in the least. [125] Can anyone have a better religion than the one who surrenders himself *completely* to Allah, performs good works and, out of a natural inclination,[a] follows Ibrahim's way of worshipping? Allah made Ibrahim a close friend. [126] Whatever is in the Heavens and on Earth belongs to Allah. Allah has full control of all things.

Safeguarding orphans and children in care

[127] They asked you concerning women. Say: "Allah instructs you concerning them – in addition to what was recited to you in the Book[b] – about female orphans from whom you withhold what is prescribed for them *regarding their inheritance because* you wish to marry them," and likewise helpless children, deal fairly with orphans. Allah knows whatever good you do.

Dealing with marital disputes

[128] If a woman is afraid of her husband's ill-conduct or alienation, both should *try* to reconcile with each other without feeling guilty. Reconciliation is the best *policy*, but humans tend to be selfish.[c] So if you are righteous and mindful *of Allah, remember that* Allah is aware of what you do.

---

[a] *"Hanif"* refers to one who believes in one true God and rejects all false gods, which comes naturally to him or her.

[b] This refers to verses 2–10.

[c] *"Shuh"* implies greed, avarice, self-centredness and egotism.

الشُّحَّ ط وَاِنْ تُحْسِنُوْا وَتَتَّقُوْا فَاِنَّ اللّٰهَ كَانَ بِمَا

تَعْمَلُوْنَ خَبِيْرًا ۝ وَلَنْ تَسْتَطِيْعُوْا اَنْ تَعْدِلُوْا بَيْنَ

النِّسَآءِ وَلَوْ حَرَصْتُمْ فَلَا تَمِيْلُوْا كُلَّ الْمَيْلِ فَتَذَرُوْهَا

كَالْمُعَلَّقَةِ ط وَاِنْ تُصْلِحُوْا وَتَتَّقُوْا فَاِنَّ اللّٰهَ كَانَ

غَفُوْرًا رَّحِيْمًا ۝ وَاِنْ يَّتَفَرَّقَا يُغْنِ اللّٰهُ كُلًّا مِّنْ

سَعَتِهٖ ط وَكَانَ اللّٰهُ وَاسِعًا حَكِيْمًا ۝ وَلِلّٰهِ مَا فِي

السَّمٰوٰتِ وَمَا فِي الْاَرْضِ ط وَلَقَدْ وَصَّيْنَا الَّذِيْنَ اُوْتُوا

الْكِتٰبَ مِنْ قَبْلِكُمْ وَاِيَّاكُمْ اَنِ اتَّقُوا اللّٰهَ ط وَاِنْ

تَكْفُرُوْا فَاِنَّ لِلّٰهِ مَا فِي السَّمٰوٰتِ وَمَا فِي الْاَرْضِ ط

وَكَانَ اللّٰهُ غَنِيًّا حَمِيْدًا ۝ وَلِلّٰهِ مَا فِي السَّمٰوٰتِ

وَمَا فِي الْاَرْضِ ط وَكَفٰى بِاللّٰهِ وَكِيْلًا ۝ اِنْ يَّشَأْ

يُذْهِبْكُمْ اَيُّهَا النَّاسُ وَيَأْتِ بِاٰخَرِيْنَ ط وَكَانَ

اللّٰهُ عَلٰى ذٰلِكَ قَدِيْرًا ۝ مَنْ كَانَ يُرِيْدُ ثَوَابَ

الدُّنْيَا فَعِنْدَ اللّٰهِ ثَوَابُ الدُّنْيَا وَالْاٰخِرَةِ ط وَكَانَ

اللّٰهُ سَمِيْعًا بَصِيْرًا ۝ يٰٓاَيُّهَا الَّذِيْنَ اٰمَنُوْا كُوْنُوْا

قَوّٰمِيْنَ بِالْقِسْطِ شُهَدَآءَ لِلّٰهِ وَلَوْ عَلٰٓى اَنْفُسِكُمْ

اَوِ الْوَالِدَيْنِ وَالْاَقْرَبِيْنَ ۚ اِنْ يَّكُنْ غَنِيًّا اَوْ فَقِيْرًا

فَاللّٰهُ اَوْلٰى بِهِمَا ۟ فَلَا تَتَّبِعُوا الْهَوٰٓى اَنْ تَعْدِلُوْا ۚ

وَاِنْ تَلْوٗٓا اَوْ تُعْرِضُوْا فَاِنَّ اللّٰهَ كَانَ بِمَا تَعْمَلُوْنَ

خَبِيْرًا ۝ يٰٓاَيُّهَا الَّذِيْنَ اٰمَنُوْٓا اٰمِنُوْا بِاللّٰهِ وَرَسُوْلِهٖ

Do not cling on to difficult marriages; separate amicably, Allah will help you both.

¹²⁹ You will never be able to be *strictly* just *when dealing* with your wives, however hard you try, but do not lean so much towards one that you leave the other as though suspended *between marriage and divorce*. If you can reconcile and be mindful, Allah is Forgiving, Most Kind. ¹³⁰ If they separate, Allah will provide for each of them from His abundance. Allah is the Vast, Wise.

Everything belongs to Allah; He gives as He likes

¹³¹ Whatever is in the Heavens and the Earth belongs to Allah. We commanded you and the People of The Book before you: "Be mindful of Allah." Even if you deny it, whatever is in the Heavens and the Earth belongs to Allah. Allah is Self-Sufficient, Worthy of praise. ¹³² Whatever is in the Heavens and the Earth belongs to Allah, and He is sufficient as a Guardian. ¹³³ If He wishes, people, He can get rid of you altogether and replace you with others. Allah has the power to do that. ¹³⁴ Whoever desires the reward of this world *only*, then *let him know that* the reward of this world and of the Hereafter are with Allah. Allah is the Hearer, the Seeing.

Stand up for justice and struggle against prejudice

¹³⁵ Believers, stand up as Allah's witnesses for justice even if it's against yourselves, parents or relatives, and *regardless of* whether a person is wealthy or poor, Allah has more right *to your loyalty* than they. Therefore, do not follow *your* desire instead of being just. If you distort *the truth* or refuse *to give testimony*, Allah is aware of what you do.

وَالْكِتٰبِ الَّذِيْ نَزَّلَ عَلٰى رَسُوْلِهٖ وَالْكِتٰبِ الَّذِيْ
اَنْزَلَ مِنْ قَبْلُ ۗ وَمَنْ يَّكْفُرْ بِاللّٰهِ وَمَلٰٓئِكَتِهٖ وَ
كُتُبِهٖ وَرُسُلِهٖ وَالْيَوْمِ الْاٰخِرِ فَقَدْ ضَلَّ ضَلٰلًۢا
بَعِيْدًا ۞ اِنَّ الَّذِيْنَ اٰمَنُوْا ثُمَّ كَفَرُوْا ثُمَّ اٰمَنُوْا ثُمَّ
كَفَرُوْا ثُمَّ ازْدَادُوْا كُفْرًا لَّمْ يَكُنِ اللّٰهُ لِيَغْفِرَ لَهُمْ
وَلَا لِيَهْدِيَهُمْ سَبِيْلًا ۞ بَشِّرِ الْمُنٰفِقِيْنَ بِاَنَّ
لَهُمْ عَذَابًا اَلِيْمًا ۞ الَّذِيْنَ يَتَّخِذُوْنَ الْكٰفِرِيْنَ
اَوْلِيَآءَ مِنْ دُوْنِ الْمُؤْمِنِيْنَ ۚ اَيَبْتَغُوْنَ عِنْدَهُمُ
الْعِزَّةَ فَاِنَّ الْعِزَّةَ لِلّٰهِ جَمِيْعًا ۞ وَقَدْ نَزَّلَ عَلَيْكُمْ
فِى الْكِتٰبِ اَنْ اِذَا سَمِعْتُمْ اٰيٰتِ اللّٰهِ يُكْفَرُ بِهَا وَ
يُسْتَهْزَاُ بِهَا فَلَا تَقْعُدُوْا مَعَهُمْ حَتّٰى يَخُوْضُوْا فِيْ
حَدِيْثٍ غَيْرِهٖٓ ۖ اِنَّكُمْ اِذًا مِّثْلُهُمْ ۗ اِنَّ اللّٰهَ جَامِعُ
الْمُنٰفِقِيْنَ وَالْكٰفِرِيْنَ فِيْ جَهَنَّمَ جَمِيْعًا ۞ الَّذِيْنَ
يَتَرَبَّصُوْنَ بِكُمْ ۚ فَاِنْ كَانَ لَكُمْ فَتْحٌ مِّنَ اللّٰهِ قَالُوْٓا
اَلَمْ نَكُنْ مَّعَكُمْ ۖ وَاِنْ كَانَ لِلْكٰفِرِيْنَ نَصِيْبٌ ۙ قَالُوْٓا
اَلَمْ نَسْتَحْوِذْ عَلَيْكُمْ وَنَمْنَعْكُمْ مِّنَ الْمُؤْمِنِيْنَ ۗ فَاللّٰهُ
يَحْكُمُ بَيْنَكُمْ يَوْمَ الْقِيٰمَةِ ۗ وَلَنْ يَّجْعَلَ اللّٰهُ لِلْكٰفِرِيْنَ
عَلَى الْمُؤْمِنِيْنَ سَبِيْلًا ۞ اِنَّ الْمُنٰفِقِيْنَ يُخٰدِعُوْنَ
اللّٰهَ وَهُوَ خَادِعُهُمْ ۚ وَاِذَا قَامُوْٓا اِلَى الصَّلٰوةِ
قَامُوْا كُسَالٰى ۙ يُرَآءُوْنَ النَّاسَ وَلَا يَذْكُرُوْنَ

Be decisive, don't dither once you've decided to do something.

١٤
ع
٢٠

187

¹³⁶ Believers, believe *firmly* in Allah and His Messenger and in the Book that He has sent down to His Messenger and in the Book He sent before. Whoever rejects Allah, His Angels, His books, His messengers and the Last Day has gone far astray.

The hypocrites are waiting until a victor emerges

¹³⁷ Those who believed then disbelieved, then believed *again*, then disbelieved, then increased *yet further* in disbelief, Allah will not forgive nor guide them towards *His* way. ¹³⁸ Give glad tidings of painful punishment to the hypocrites, ¹³⁹ who have taken disbelievers as their allies instead of the believers. Do they seek strength from them, when strength is Allah's? ¹⁴⁰ Allah revealed in the Book, when you hear Allah's verses being rejected or mocked, do not sit with them till they turn to another topic of conversation; otherwise you will be like them. Allah will gather all the hypocrites and disbelievers in Hell. ¹⁴¹ They are waiting to see what happens to you; if victory from Allah comes to you they will say: "Were we not with you?" And if the disbelievers gain some success, they will say to them: "Didn't we encourage you and protect you against the believers?" Allah will decide between you on the Day of Judgement; however, Allah will never give the disbelievers a way *to a conclusive victory* over the believers.

Hypocrites make a show of praying

¹⁴² The hypocrites try to deceive Allah, but He leaves them in their deception; *thus* whenever they stand up for the prayer, they do so lazily, making a show for the people and they remember Allah little;

اللّٰهِ اِلَّا قَلِيْلًا ۩ مُّذَبْذَبِيْنَ بَيْنَ ذٰلِكَ ۖ لَا اِلٰى

هٰٓؤُلَآءِ وَلَآ اِلٰى هٰٓؤُلَآءِ ؕ وَمَنْ يُّضْلِلِ اللّٰهُ فَلَنْ

تَجِدَ لَهٗ سَبِيْلًا ۩ يٰٓاَيُّهَا الَّذِيْنَ اٰمَنُوْا لَا

تَتَّخِذُوا الْكٰفِرِيْنَ اَوْلِيَآءَ مِنْ دُوْنِ الْمُؤْمِنِيْنَ ؕ

اَتُرِيْدُوْنَ اَنْ تَجْعَلُوْا لِلّٰهِ عَلَيْكُمْ سُلْطٰنًا مُّبِيْنًا ۩

اِنَّ الْمُنٰفِقِيْنَ فِى الدَّرْكِ الْاَسْفَلِ مِنَ النَّارِ ۚ

وَلَنْ تَجِدَ لَهُمْ نَصِيْرًا ۩ اِلَّا الَّذِيْنَ تَابُوْا وَ

اَصْلَحُوْا وَاعْتَصَمُوْا بِاللّٰهِ وَاَخْلَصُوْا دِيْنَهُمْ لِلّٰهِ

فَاُولٰٓئِكَ مَعَ الْمُؤْمِنِيْنَ ؕ وَسَوْفَ يُؤْتِ اللّٰهُ

الْمُؤْمِنِيْنَ اَجْرًا عَظِيْمًا ۩ مَا يَفْعَلُ اللّٰهُ بِعَذَابِكُمْ

اِنْ شَكَرْتُمْ وَاٰمَنْتُمْ ؕ وَكَانَ اللّٰهُ شَاكِرًا عَلِيْمًا ۩

لَا يُحِبُّ اللّٰهُ الْجَهْرَ بِالسُّوْٓءِ مِنَ الْقَوْلِ اِلَّا

مَنْ ظُلِمَ ؕ وَكَانَ اللّٰهُ سَمِيْعًا عَلِيْمًا ۩ اِنْ تُبْدُوْا

خَيْرًا اَوْ تُخْفُوْهُ اَوْ تَعْفُوْا عَنْ سُوْٓءٍ فَاِنَّ اللّٰهَ كَانَ

عَفُوًّا قَدِيْرًا ۩ اِنَّ الَّذِيْنَ يَكْفُرُوْنَ بِاللّٰهِ وَ

رُسُلِهٖ وَيُرِيْدُوْنَ اَنْ يُّفَرِّقُوْا بَيْنَ اللّٰهِ وَرُسُلِهٖ وَ

يَقُوْلُوْنَ نُؤْمِنُ بِبَعْضٍ وَّنَكْفُرُ بِبَعْضٍ ۙ وَّيُرِيْدُوْنَ

اَنْ يَّتَّخِذُوْا بَيْنَ ذٰلِكَ سَبِيْلًا ۩ اُولٰٓئِكَ هُمُ

الْكٰفِرُوْنَ حَقًّا ۚ وَاَعْتَدْنَا لِلْكٰفِرِيْنَ عَذَابًا مُّهِيْنًا ۩

وَالَّذِيْنَ اٰمَنُوْا بِاللّٰهِ وَرُسُلِهٖ وَلَمْ يُفَرِّقُوْا بَيْنَ

The rights of victims to speak out publicly. Give them sympathy and support.

189

^{143} dithering between *this and* that, *they are* neither with these *believers* nor with those *disbelievers*. Whoever Allah allows to go astray, you can't ever guide him.

Hypocrites will be in Hell

^{144} Believers don't take disbelievers as allies instead of the believers. Do you wish to give Allah clear proof against yourselves? ^{145} The hypocrites will be in the bottommost pit of Hell, and you will never find a helper for them; ^{146} except *that is* for those who repent, reform themselves, hold firmly to *the religion of* Allah, and become genuine in their worship of Allah; such people will be with the believers. Allah will give the believers a great reward.[a] ^{147} Why should Allah punish you, if you believe and are grateful? Allah is Appreciative, the Knower.

The victim may speak publicly against the offender

^{148} Allah dislikes *anyone* talking openly about a wrongdoing, except the person who has been wronged. Allah is Hearer, Knower. ^{149} Whether you do good *work* openly or you conceal it or you pardon a wrong, Allah is Pardoning, the Powerful.

Believers do not cherry pick from Allah's commandments

^{150} Those who deny Allah and His messengers, and who wish to separate Allah and His messengers, claim: "We believe in some *aspects* and reject others"; and they wish to steer a middle course; ^{151} these people are disbelievers. We have prepared for the disbelievers a humiliating punishment. ^{152} Those who believe in Allah and His messengers and make no distinction between any of them, will be rewarded. Allah is Forgiving, Most Kind.

---

[a]   While a disbeliever must declare his faith to be forgiven, a hypocrite must: repent, reform, practise religion and show sincerity.

أَحَدٍ مِّنْهُمْ أُولٰٓئِكَ سَوْفَ يُؤْتِيْهِمْ أُجُوْرَهُمْ ۗ وَكَانَ اللّٰهُ غَفُوْرًا رَّحِيْمًا ۞ يَسْـَٔلُكَ أَهْلُ الْكِتٰبِ أَنْ تُنَزِّلَ عَلَيْهِمْ كِتٰبًا مِّنَ السَّمَآءِ فَقَدْ سَأَلُوْا مُوْسٰٓى أَكْبَرَ مِنْ ذٰلِكَ فَقَالُوْۤا أَرِنَا اللّٰهَ جَهْرَةً فَأَخَذَتْهُمُ الصّٰعِقَةُ بِظُلْمِهِمْ ۚ ثُمَّ اتَّخَذُوا الْعِجْلَ مِنْ بَعْدِ مَا جَآءَتْهُمُ الْبَيِّنٰتُ فَعَفَوْنَا عَنْ ذٰلِكَ ۚ وَاٰتَيْنَا مُوْسٰى سُلْطٰنًا مُّبِيْنًا ۞ وَرَفَعْنَا فَوْقَهُمُ الطُّوْرَ بِمِيْثَاقِهِمْ وَقُلْنَا لَهُمُ ادْخُلُوا الْبَابَ سُجَّدًا وَّ قُلْنَا لَهُمْ لَا تَعْدُوْا فِى السَّبْتِ وَأَخَذْنَا مِنْهُمْ مِّيْثَاقًا غَلِيْظًا ۞ فَبِمَا نَقْضِهِمْ مِّيْثَاقَهُمْ وَكُفْرِهِمْ بِاٰيٰتِ اللّٰهِ وَقَتْلِهِمُ الْأَنْبِيَآءَ بِغَيْرِ حَقٍّ وَّقَوْلِهِمْ قُلُوْبُنَا غُلْفٌ ۗ بَلْ طَبَعَ اللّٰهُ عَلَيْهَا بِكُفْرِهِمْ فَلَا يُؤْمِنُوْنَ إِلَّا قَلِيْلًا ۞ وَّ بِكُفْرِهِمْ وَقَوْلِهِمْ عَلٰى مَرْيَمَ بُهْتَانًا عَظِيْمًا ۞ وَّ قَوْلِهِمْ إِنَّا قَتَلْنَا الْمَسِيْحَ عِيْسَى ابْنَ مَرْيَمَ رَسُوْلَ اللّٰهِ ۚ وَمَا قَتَلُوْهُ وَمَا صَلَبُوْهُ وَلٰكِنْ شُبِّهَ لَهُمْ ۗ وَإِنَّ الَّذِيْنَ اخْتَلَفُوْا فِيْهِ لَفِىْ شَكٍّ مِّنْهُ ۚ مَا لَهُمْ بِهٖ مِنْ عِلْمٍ إِلَّا اتِّبَاعَ الظَّنِّ ۚ وَمَا قَتَلُوْهُ يَقِيْنًا ۞ بَلْ رَّفَعَهُ اللّٰهُ إِلَيْهِ ۗ وَكَانَ اللّٰهُ عَزِيْزًا حَكِيْمًا ۞ وَإِنْ مِّنْ أَهْلِ الْكِتٰبِ إِلَّا لَيُؤْمِنَنَّ بِهٖ قَبْلَ مَوْتِهٖ ۚ وَيَوْمَ الْقِيٰمَةِ

Isa was raised to Heaven, and will return before the Final Day.

191

The Jews experience Allah's willingness to pardon

153 The People of The Book ask you for a book to be sent down to them from Heaven. They asked Musa for something even more outrageous than that: "Show us Allah with the naked eye," so a thunderbolt struck them for their rudeness. Then they adopted the *golden* calf *as an idol*, after clear signs had come to them; nevertheless, We pardoned them for that. We gave Musa clear authority; 154 *whilst taking* their contract with the mountain towering above them, We said, "Prostrate as you enter the gate," and We told them not to violate *the sanctity of* the Sabbath, taking a solemn pledge from them.

Jews made false allegations against Maryam and Isa

155 What about their breaking the contract, their denial of Allah's signs, their unlawful killing of the prophets, and their saying, "Our minds are locked"?ᵃ Indeed! Allah has sealed their hearts and minds because of their disbelief, so that none but a few of them believe 156 and because of their denial, and their spreading a terrible slander against Maryam.

Allah raised Isa to the Heavens before crucifixion

157 They *mockingly* say: "We have killed the Messiah, Isa son of Maryam, the Messenger of Allah," though they didn't kill him nor crucify him, but it appeared like that to them. Those who differed over *the matter* are *still* in doubt about him. They have no knowledge of it except speculation, and they certainly didn't kill Isa. 158 In fact, Allah raised him to Himself. Allah is Almighty, Wise. 159 There is no one from the People of The Book who will not believe in *the Messiah* before his death,ᵇ and on the Day of Judgement he will be a witness against them.

ᵃ The arrogant Israelites were prepared to use any excuse to evade responsibility for their sinful behaviour.
ᵇ This refers to the second coming of Isa the Messiah, when all will believe in him.

يَكُوْنُ عَلَيْهِمْ شَهِيْدًا ۰۵۹۝ فَبِظُلْمٍ مِّنَ الَّذِيْنَ هَادُوْا

حَرَّمْنَا عَلَيْهِمْ طَيِّبٰتٍ أُحِلَّتْ لَهُمْ وَبِصَدِّهِمْ عَنْ

سَبِيْلِ اللّٰهِ كَثِيْرًا ۰۶۰۝ وَّأَخْذِهِمُ الرِّبٰوا وَقَدْ نُهُوْا

عَنْهُ وَأَكْلِهِمْ أَمْوَالَ النَّاسِ بِالْبَاطِلِ ط وَأَعْتَدْنَا

لِلْكٰفِرِيْنَ مِنْهُمْ عَذَابًا أَلِيْمًا ۰۶۱۝ لٰكِنِ الرّٰسِخُوْنَ فِى

الْعِلْمِ مِنْهُمْ وَالْمُؤْمِنُوْنَ يُؤْمِنُوْنَ بِمَآ أُنْزِلَ

إِلَيْكَ وَمَآ أُنْزِلَ مِنْ قَبْلِكَ وَالْمُقِيْمِيْنَ الصَّلٰوةَ وَ

الْمُؤْتُوْنَ الزَّكٰوةَ وَالْمُؤْمِنُوْنَ بِاللّٰهِ وَالْيَوْمِ الْاٰخِرِ ط

أُولٰٓئِكَ سَنُؤْتِيْهِمْ أَجْرًا عَظِيْمًا ۰۶۲۝ عٍ إِنَّآ أَوْحَيْنَآ

The global nature of Prophethood: All from the same source, with the same programme. ٢٢ ع ٢

إِلَيْكَ كَمَآ أَوْحَيْنَآ إِلٰى نُوْحٍ وَّالنَّبِيّٖنَ مِنْ بَعْدِهٖ ج

وَأَوْحَيْنَآ إِلٰٓى إِبْرٰهِيْمَ وَإِسْمٰعِيْلَ وَإِسْحٰقَ وَيَعْقُوْبَ

وَالْاَسْبَاطِ وَعِيْسٰى وَأَيُّوْبَ وَيُوْنُسَ وَهٰرُوْنَ

وَسُلَيْمٰنَ ج وَأٰتَيْنَا دَاوٗدَ زَبُوْرًا ۰۶۳۝ وَرُسُلًا قَدْ

قَصَصْنٰهُمْ عَلَيْكَ مِنْ قَبْلُ وَرُسُلًا لَّمْ نَقْصُصْهُمْ

عَلَيْكَ ط وَكَلَّمَ اللّٰهُ مُوْسٰى تَكْلِيْمًا ۰۶۴۝ رُّسُلًا مُّبَشِّرِيْنَ

وَمُنْذِرِيْنَ لِئَلَّا يَكُوْنَ لِلنَّاسِ عَلَى اللّٰهِ حُجَّةٌ

بَعْدَ الرُّسُلِ ط وَكَانَ اللّٰهُ عَزِيْزًا حَكِيْمًا ۰۶۵۝ لٰكِنِ

اللّٰهُ يَشْهَدُ بِمَآ أَنْزَلَ إِلَيْكَ أَنْزَلَهٗ بِعِلْمِهٖ ج وَ

الْمَلٰٓئِكَةُ يَشْهَدُوْنَ ط وَكَفٰى بِاللّٰهِ شَهِيْدًا ۰۶۶۝ إِنَّ

الَّذِيْنَ كَفَرُوْا وَصَدُّوْا عَنْ سَبِيْلِ اللّٰهِ قَدْ ضَلُّوْا

The Jews will be punished or rewarded, based on their belief

¹⁶⁰Because of the wrongdoing of the Jews, We prohibited some of the wholesome things that were lawful for them, and they stopped many *people* from following the way of Allah, ¹⁶¹and adopted usury despite it being forbidden, and they squandered people's wealth. For the disbelievers among them, We have prepared a painful punishment. ¹⁶²But some of them are firmly grounded in knowledge and are believers in what is revealed to you and what was revealed before you; *likewise,* those who perform the prayer, pay Zakat and believe in Allah and the Last Day will be given a great reward.

The process of revelation was the same for all Prophets

¹⁶³We revealed to you as We revealed to Nuh and the prophets after him; and We revealed to Ibrahim, Ismael, Ishaq, Yaqub, the Tribes, Isa, Ayyub, Yunus, Harun and Sulayman; and We gave Dawud the Psalms. ¹⁶⁴*There were* messengers that We told you about, and *there are other* messengers that We haven't told you about. Allah spoke directly to Musa. ¹⁶⁵*There have been* messengers bearing good news and warnings so that, after the messengers, people would have no defence against Allah. Allah is the Almighty, Wise. ¹⁶⁶Allah bears witness of what He has sent down to you – He has sent it down with His knowledge – and the Angels are witnesses *too.* Allah is a sufficient Witness.

No forgiveness for him who obstructs Allah's path

¹⁶⁷Those who deny *the truth* and stop others from the path of Allah have wandered far, far astray, they deny *the truth* and do wrong,

ضَلَالًا بَعِيدًا ۝ اِنَّ الَّذِيْنَ كَفَرُوْا وَ ظَلَمُوْا لَمْ

يَكُنِ اللهُ لِيَغْفِرَ لَهُمْ وَلَا لِيَهْدِيَهُمْ طَرِيْقًا ۙ ۝

اِلَّا طَرِيْقَ جَهَنَّمَ خٰلِدِيْنَ فِيْهَآ اَبَدًا ط وَ كَانَ

ذٰلِكَ عَلَى اللهِ يَسِيْرًا ۝ يٰٓاَيُّهَا النَّاسُ قَدْ جَآءَكُمُ

الرَّسُوْلُ بِالْحَقِّ مِنْ رَّبِّكُمْ فَاٰمِنُوْا خَيْرًا لَّكُمْ ط

وَاِنْ تَكْفُرُوْا فَاِنَّ لِلّٰهِ مَا فِى السَّمٰوٰتِ وَالْاَرْضِ ط

وَكَانَ اللهُ عَلِيْمًا حَكِيْمًا ۝ يٰٓاَهْلَ الْكِتٰبِ لَا تَغْلُوْا

في دِيْنِكُمْ وَلَا تَقُوْلُوْا عَلَى اللهِ اِلَّا الْحَقَّ ط اِنَّمَا

الْمَسِيْحُ عِيْسَى ابْنُ مَرْيَمَ رَسُوْلُ اللهِ وَكَلِمَتُهٗ ج

اَلْقٰهَآ اِلٰى مَرْيَمَ وَرُوْحٌ مِّنْهُ ز فَاٰمِنُوْا بِاللهِ

وَرُسُلِهٖ ۚ وَلَا تَقُوْلُوْا ثَلٰثَةٌ ط اِنْتَهُوْا خَيْرًا لَّكُمْ ط

اِنَّمَا اللهُ اِلٰهٌ وَّاحِدٌ ط سُبْحٰنَهٗ اَنْ يَّكُوْنَ لَهٗ وَلَدٌ ۘ

لَهٗ مَا فِى السَّمٰوٰتِ وَمَا فِى الْاَرْضِ ط وَكَفٰى بِاللهِ

وَكِيْلًا ۝ لَنْ يَّسْتَنْكِفَ الْمَسِيْحُ اَنْ يَّكُوْنَ عَبْدًا

لِّلّٰهِ وَلَا الْمَلٰٓئِكَةُ الْمُقَرَّبُوْنَ ط وَمَنْ يَّسْتَنْكِفْ عَنْ

عِبَادَتِهٖ وَيَسْتَكْبِرْ فَسَيَحْشُرُهُمْ اِلَيْهِ جَمِيْعًا ۝

فَاَمَّا الَّذِيْنَ اٰمَنُوْا وَعَمِلُوا الصّٰلِحٰتِ فَيُوَفِّيْهِمْ

اُجُوْرَهُمْ وَيَزِيْدُهُمْ مِّنْ فَضْلِهٖ ۚ وَاَمَّا الَّذِيْنَ

اسْتَنْكَفُوْا وَاسْتَكْبَرُوْا فَيُعَذِّبُهُمْ عَذَابًا اَلِيْمًا ۙ وَّلَا

يَجِدُوْنَ لَهُمْ مِّنْ دُوْنِ اللهِ وَلِيًّا وَّلَا نَصِيْرًا ۝

Extremism is forbidden: it closes the mind and leads to injustice towards others.

[168]Allah will not forgive nor guide them along a path, [169]except the path to Hell, remaining there forever and to do so is easy for Allah.

Christians are warned against offensive beliefs
[170]People, the Messenger has come to you with the truth from Your Lord, so it is better that you believe than to reject *the message*, whatever is in the Heavens and the Earth belongs to Allah. Allah is All-Knowing, Wise. [171]People of The Book, do not go to extremes in your religion; always speak the truth about Allah. The Messiah, Isa son of Maryam, was a *noble* messenger of Allah, His word, which He blew into Maryam, and a spirit from Him. So believe in Allah and His messengers and talk no more of "three"; it is better that you stop *believing this*. Allah is the only one God. He is free from such defects, so how can He have a son! Whatever is in the Heavens and the Earth belongs to Him; and Allah is a sufficient Guardian.

Isa is not embarrassed to be called the servant of Allah
[172]The Messiah would never be ashamed of being *called* a servant of Allah, nor would the angels near *His Throne*. Whoever is ashamed of worshipping Him is arrogant, Allah will gather them all. [173]Those who believe and do righteous deeds will be repaid in full, and He will grant them an increase from His grace. However, those who are ashamed and arrogant, He will give them a painful punishment and they will find no helper or protector other than Allah.

يَآ اَيُّهَا النَّاسُ قَدْ جَآءَكُمْ بُرْهَانٌ مِّنْ رَّبِّكُمْ وَ

اَنْزَلْنَآ اِلَيْكُمْ نُوْرًا مُّبِيْنًا ۝ فَاَمَّا الَّذِيْنَ اٰمَنُوْا بِاللهِ

وَاعْتَصَمُوْا بِهِ فَسَيُدْخِلُهُمْ فِيْ رَحْمَةٍ مِّنْهُ وَفَضْلٍ ۙ

Beloved Muhammad ﷺ is the proof, the light and the chosen one.

وَّيَهْدِيْهِمْ اِلَيْهِ صِرَاطًا مُّسْتَقِيْمًا ۝ يَسْتَفْتُوْنَكَ ؕ

قُلِ اللهُ يُفْتِيْكُمْ فِي الْكَلٰلَةِ ؕ اِنِ امْرُؤٌا هَلَكَ لَيْسَ

لَهٗ وَلَدٌ وَّلَهٗٓ اُخْتٌ فَلَهَا نِصْفُ مَا تَرَكَ ۚ وَهُوَ

يَرِثُهَآ اِنْ لَّمْ يَكُنْ لَّهَا وَلَدٌ ؕ فَاِنْ كَانَتَا اثْنَتَيْنِ

فَلَهُمَا الثُّلُثٰنِ مِمَّا تَرَكَ ؕ وَاِنْ كَانُوْٓا اِخْوَةً رِّجَالًا وَّ

نِسَآءً فَلِلذَّكَرِ مِثْلُ حَظِّ الْاُنْثَيَيْنِ ؕ يُبَيِّنُ اللهُ لَكُمْ

اَنْ تَضِلُّوْا ؕ وَاللهُ بِكُلِّ شَيْءٍ عَلِيْمٌ ۝

197

The Messenger ﷺ is a clear proof of Allah's majesty

[174] People, a clear proof has come to you from your Lord and We have sent down to you a shining light. [175] So, those who believe in Allah and hold firmly to *their belief in* Him, will be kindly treated with His grace, and He will guide them towards Himself along a straight path.

Rule of inheritance for those who die childless

[176] They ask you for a ruling, say: "Allah instructs about the one who dies without descendants. If a man dies childless, but had a sister, she would inherit half of what he has left and he would be her only heir, if she were *to die* childless. If *the deceased* had two sisters, they would inherit *between them* two-thirds of what he left. *However,* if the siblings were both male and female, then each male would receive the share of two females." Allah explains this so that you do not make mistakes. Allah is the Knower of everything.

5. Surat Al-Ma'idah

The Feast

This surat was revealed in Madinah in 6 AH/628 CE, after the Treaty of Hudaibiyah. The period after the Treaty of Hudaibiyah marked a new era in the history of Muslims; now they were free to propagate Islam in the Arabian Peninsula, as agreed in the treaty. By now the economic prowess of the Jewish tribes had faded, while the Muslims were confident and upbeat.

This surat lays out the basis of Allah's contract with Muslims as the final law to be revealed. It puts it in the context of the contracts the Jews and Christians had made with God, but who unfortunately broke the law, invented false beliefs, and changed some laws of the Torah and Gospel. Consequently, they lost the privilege of being the favourite people of Allah. Cautioning Muslims: if you don't abide by the Shariah, then you too will fall out of favour, Allah has no special preference for any people except those who obey and submit to Him.

The new Muslim state needed laws to function as a well-ordered civil society, that is mindful of Allah. In this surat, eighteen new laws are announced on: contracts; testimony and the importance of honest witnesses; respecting sacred months; slaughtering animals; the lawfulness of seafood; rules of entering into a state of *ihram* for pilgrimage; intermarriage with Jewish and Christian women; apostasy; rules for cleanliness; the penalty for stealing; the penalty for sedition; prohibition of intoxicants and gambling; atonement for breaking an oath; hunting whilst in a state of *ihram*; making a will at the time of death; and the penalty for those who violate divine laws.

These laws are set in the context of various historical events. An example of this is the story of the Israelites' refusal to obey Musa when told to enter the Holy Land. The moral is: disobeying Allah's messengers merits severe punishment. The second story describes the murder by Cain of his brother Abel, showing that murder is an abominable crime. The relationships of various groups in the Arabian Peninsula are surveyed, and the Christian-Muslim relationship is highlighted in particular:

You will find the nearest and most affectionate to the believers are those who say, 'We are Christians', because among them are priests and monks who are not arrogant (82).

The surat's central theme is the fulfilment of contracts. It explains how the Jews and

Christians failed to fulfil their contracts, and gives examples of how they violated the divine laws, so they were rejected by Allah. The Christians are further condemned for violating their contract with Allah by tampering with the teachings of Prophet Isa; their adoption of the doctrine of the Trinity in 325 CE, which gave rise to a misunderstanding of the oneness of Allah. "Those who say: 'The Messiah, the son of Maryam, is God' are denying the truth" (17). Furthermore, "Those who said: 'Allah is the third of three,' have committed an act of disbelief" (73). Since the glorious Quran is a final contract of Allah, both the Jews and the Christians are invited to follow the Messenger ﷺ.

There is an emphasis on honouring pledges and contracts, which should be taken seriously. However, the contract that humanity has with Allah is the most serious and solemn, especially belief in His oneness. These laws appear harsh and difficult to apply because they require a high level of self-discipline, and a sense of justice, impartiality and courage. Hence, a stress on their benefits and why they shouldn't be violated. By pointing out weaknesses of the Jews and the Christians, Muslims are in a way being alerted. It is in the best interest of humanity to live by Allah's laws:

> So beware that they do not tempt you away from what Allah has revealed to you ... Is it the customary law of the Age of Ignorance that they want? For those who have firm belief, whose rule can possibly be better than Allah's (49–50).

The key lesson is: the only way of drawing near to Allah and forging a special relationship with Him is to have a sincere belief in His oneness, love Him and follow His commandments. The surat ends by describing a scene of Judgement Day:

> Allah will say: "Isa, son of Maryam, did you say to the people: 'Take me and my mother as two gods besides Allah'?", and he will say, "Glory be to You! How could I say something I had no right to say ... I only said what You commanded me to say: 'Worship Allah, my Lord and your Lord'" (116–117).

۞ (٥) ۞ سُورَةُ الْمَآئِدَةِ مَدَنِيَّةٌ (١١٢) ۞ رُكُوعَاتُهَا ١٦
أَيَاتُهَا ١٢٠

بِسْمِ اللّٰهِ الرَّحْمٰنِ الرَّحِيمِ

يَآأَيُّهَا الَّذِينَ آمَنُوٓا أَوْفُوا بِالْعُقُودِ ۚ أُحِلَّتْ لَكُمْ

بَهِيمَةُ الْأَنْعَامِ إِلَّا مَا يُتْلٰى عَلَيْكُمْ غَيْرَ مُحِلِّي

الصَّيْدِ وَأَنْتُمْ حُرُمٌ ۗ إِنَّ اللّٰهَ يَحْكُمُ مَا يُرِيدُ ①

يَآأَيُّهَا الَّذِينَ آمَنُوا لَا تُحِلُّوا شَعَآئِرَ اللّٰهِ وَلَا

الشَّهْرَ الْحَرَامَ وَلَا الْهَدْيَ وَلَا الْقَلَآئِدَ وَلَآ

آمِّينَ الْبَيْتَ الْحَرَامَ يَبْتَغُونَ فَضْلًا مِّنْ رَّبِّهِمْ وَ

رِضْوَانًا ۚ وَإِذَا حَلَلْتُمْ فَاصْطَادُوا ۚ وَلَا يَجْرِمَنَّكُمْ

شَنَآنُ قَوْمٍ أَنْ صَدُّوكُمْ عَنِ الْمَسْجِدِ الْحَرَامِ أَنْ

تَعْتَدُوا ۘ وَتَعَاوَنُوا عَلَى الْبِرِّ وَالتَّقْوٰى ۖ وَلَا تَعَاوَنُوا

عَلَى الْإِثْمِ وَالْعُدْوَانِ ۚ وَاتَّقُوا اللّٰهَ ۖ إِنَّ اللّٰهَ شَدِيدُ

الْعِقَابِ ② حُرِّمَتْ عَلَيْكُمُ الْمَيْتَةُ وَالدَّمُ وَلَحْمُ

الْخِنْزِيرِ وَمَآ أُهِلَّ لِغَيْرِ اللّٰهِ بِهِ وَالْمُنْخَنِقَةُ وَ

الْمَوْقُوذَةُ وَالْمُتَرَدِّيَةُ وَالنَّطِيحَةُ وَمَآ أَكَلَ السَّبُعُ

إِلَّا مَا ذَكَّيْتُمْ ۗ وَمَا ذُبِحَ عَلَى النُّصُبِ وَأَنْ

تَسْتَقْسِمُوا بِالْأَزْلَامِ ۚ ذٰلِكُمْ فِسْقٌ ۗ الْيَوْمَ يَئِسَ الَّذِينَ

كَفَرُوا مِنْ دِينِكُمْ فَلَا تَخْشَوْهُمْ وَاخْشَوْنِ ۚ الْيَوْمَ

أَكْمَلْتُ لَكُمْ دِينَكُمْ وَأَتْمَمْتُ عَلَيْكُمْ نِعْمَتِي وَ

رَضِيتُ لَكُمُ الْإِسْلَامَ دِينًا ۚ فَمَنِ اضْطُرَّ فِي مَخْمَصَةٍ

Cooperation and teamwork is the best way to accomplish major works of goodness.

In the name of Allah, the Kind, the Caring

Honour contracts and keep promises

¹Believers, fulfil all your contracts and responsibilities. Livestock animals are lawful to eat except what will be mentioned to you in the coming verses, and you are not allowed to hunt while you wear the pilgrim's garb. Allah commands what He wills. ²Believers, don't violate Allah's symbols: the sacred months; the sacrificial animals, and animals with garlands around their necks; and those on their way to the Sacred House, seeking grace and pleasure of their Lord. Once you have removed the pilgrim's garb then you may hunt. Don't let the hatred of people who once blocked your way to the Sacred Mosque lead you to break the rules. Cooperate in matters of goodness and piety, and don't cooperate in matters of sin and hostility. Fear Allah, He's severe in punishing.

Which kind of meat is forbidden?

³You are forbidden to eat: carrion;[a] blood; pork; whatever is slaughtered in a name other than Allah's; animals killed by strangulation, a blow to the body, fallen from a height, gored; eaten by beasts of prey – unless you are able to slaughter it before it dies – and anything slaughtered on the altars of idols. Nor are you allowed to divide meat by drawing lots using marked arrows; this is clearly sinful. Today, the disbelievers have lost hope of you *abandoning* your religion; so don't fear them, fear Me. Today, I have completed your religion for you; I gave My favour in full, and I am pleased that Islam is your religion. So, anyone forced by famine to eat these forbidden meats, without the desire to sin, will find Allah Forgiving, Kind[b].

[a] "Carrion" refers to the meat of animals that are found already dead, like road kill.
[b] Commentators believe this verse was revealed on the 9th Dhul Hijjah during the Messenger's ﷺ farewell pilgrimage in the year 10AH (631 CE).

غَيْرَ مُتَجَانِفٍ لِّإِثْمٍ ۙ فَإِنَّ اللهَ غَفُورٌ رَّحِيمٌ ۞

يَسْـَٔلُونَكَ مَاذَآ أُحِلَّ لَهُمْ ۖ قُلْ أُحِلَّ لَكُمُ الطَّيِّبٰتُ ۙ

وَمَا عَلَّمْتُمْ مِّنَ الْجَوَارِحِ مُكَلِّبِينَ تُعَلِّمُونَهُنَّ مِمَّا

عَلَّمَكُمُ اللهُ ۖ فَكُلُوا مِمَّآ أَمْسَكْنَ عَلَيْكُمْ وَاذْكُرُوا اسْمَ

اللهِ عَلَيْهِ ۖ وَاتَّقُوا اللهَ ۚ إِنَّ اللهَ سَرِيعُ الْحِسَابِ ۞

الْيَوْمَ أُحِلَّ لَكُمُ الطَّيِّبٰتُ ۖ وَطَعَامُ الَّذِينَ أُوتُوا

الْكِتٰبَ حِلٌّ لَّكُمْ ۖ وَطَعَامُكُمْ حِلٌّ لَّهُمْ ۖ وَالْمُحْصَنٰتُ

مِنَ الْمُؤْمِنٰتِ وَالْمُحْصَنٰتُ مِنَ الَّذِينَ أُوتُوا الْكِتٰبَ

مِنْ قَبْلِكُمْ إِذَآ ءَاتَيْتُمُوهُنَّ أُجُورَهُنَّ مُحْصِنِينَ

غَيْرَ مُسٰفِحِينَ وَلَا مُتَّخِذِىٓ أَخْدَانٍ ۗ وَمَنْ يَكْفُرْ

بِالْإِيمٰانِ فَقَدْ حَبِطَ عَمَلُهُ ۖ وَهُوَ فِي الْأَخِرَةِ مِنَ

الْخٰسِرِينَ ۞ يٰٓأَيُّهَا الَّذِينَ ءَامَنُوٓا إِذَا قُمْتُمْ إِلَى

الصَّلٰوةِ فَاغْسِلُوا وُجُوهَكُمْ وَأَيْدِيَكُمْ إِلَى الْمَرَافِقِ

وَامْسَحُوا بِرُءُوسِكُمْ وَأَرْجُلَكُمْ إِلَى الْكَعْبَيْنِ ۚ وَإِنْ

كُنْتُمْ جُنُبًا فَاطَّهَّرُوا ۚ وَإِنْ كُنْتُمْ مَّرْضٰىٓ أَوْ عَلَىٰ

سَفَرٍ أَوْ جَآءَ أَحَدٌ مِّنْكُمْ مِّنَ الْغَآئِطِ أَوْ لٰمَسْتُمُ

النِّسَآءَ فَلَمْ تَجِدُوا مَآءً فَتَيَمَّمُوا صَعِيدًا طَيِّبًا

فَامْسَحُوا بِوُجُوهِكُمْ وَأَيْدِيكُمْ مِّنْهُ ۚ مَا يُرِيدُ اللهُ

لِيَجْعَلَ عَلَيْكُمْ مِّنْ حَرَجٍ وَّلٰكِنْ يُرِيدُ لِيُطَهِّرَكُمْ

وَلِيُتِمَّ نِعْمَتَهُ عَلَيْكُمْ لَعَلَّكُمْ تَشْكُرُونَ ۞ وَاذْكُرُوا

Only through marriage men and women can have intimacy and love.

[4] They ask you, Messenger, what is lawful for them. Say: "All healthy foods are made lawful for you, including what you have trained birds and beasts of prey to hunt, teaching them as Allah has taught you; so, eat what they catch for you, as long as you declare Allah's name over it, be mindful of Allah. Allah is swift in settling the account of your deeds. [5] Today, all healthy foods are made lawful for you; the food[a] of People of The Book is lawful for you, and your food is lawful for them.

Extramarital affairs are forbidden, be pure and marry

Chaste women from the believers and the People of The Book are lawful to marry after you have given the bridal gift. Live honourably with them, don't engage in sex outside of marriage, or take them as lovers. Anyone who rejects faith, their deeds will be worthless, and in the Hereafter, they will be the losers.

Instructions on ritual cleanliness for prayer

[6] Believers, when you intend to perform the prayer, wash your face and arms up to the elbow; wipe your head and then wash your feet up to the ankles. If you are in a state of ritual impurity[b] purify yourselves by taking a bath; however, if you are ill, or on a journey, or you have relieved yourselves, or you have touched your wives in a sexual way, and are unable to find water, then take clean Earth and wipe your face and arms with it. Allah doesn't want to impose hardship on you, but wants to purify and complete His favours on you so you thank Him.

---

[a]   This refers to the meat of animals slaughtered by the Jews and the Christians, though Muslim scholars disagree, since Christians don't practise biblical laws, but the Jewish Kosher meat is considered *Halal*.

[b]   *"Junub"* is the ritual impurity due to sexual intercourse, a discharge of semen, menstruation, or after childbirth.

نِعْمَةَ اللهِ عَلَيْكُمْ وَمِيْثَاقَهُ الَّذِىْ وَاثَقَكُمْ بِهٖ

اِذْ قُلْتُمْ سَمِعْنَا وَاَطَعْنَا ۖ وَاتَّقُوا اللهَ ؕ اِنَّ اللهَ

عَلِيْمٌۢ بِذَاتِ الصُّدُوْرِ ۞ يٰۤاَيُّهَا الَّذِيْنَ اٰمَنُوْا كُوْنُوْا

قَوّٰمِيْنَ لِلّٰهِ شُهَدَآءَ بِالْقِسْطِ ۖ وَلَا يَجْرِمَنَّكُمْ

شَنَاٰنُ قَوْمٍ عَلٰۤى اَلَّا تَعْدِلُوْا ؕ اِعْدِلُوْا ۟ هُوَ اَقْرَبُ

لِلتَّقْوٰى ۖ وَاتَّقُوا اللهَ ؕ اِنَّ اللهَ خَبِيْرٌۢ بِمَا تَعْمَلُوْنَ ۞

وَعَدَ اللهُ الَّذِيْنَ اٰمَنُوْا وَعَمِلُوا الصّٰلِحٰتِ ۙ لَهُمْ

مَّغْفِرَةٌ وَّ اَجْرٌ عَظِيْمٌ ۞ وَالَّذِيْنَ كَفَرُوْا وَكَذَّبُوْا

بِاٰيٰتِنَاۤ اُولٰٓئِكَ اَصْحٰبُ الْجَحِيْمِ ۞ يٰۤاَيُّهَا الَّذِيْنَ

اٰمَنُوا اذْكُرُوْا نِعْمَتَ اللهِ عَلَيْكُمْ اِذْ هَمَّ قَوْمٌ اَنْ

يَّبْسُطُوْۤا اِلَيْكُمْ اَيْدِيَهُمْ فَكَفَّ اَيْدِيَهُمْ عَنْكُمْ ۚ

وَاتَّقُوا اللهَ ؕ وَعَلَى اللهِ فَلْيَتَوَكَّلِ الْمُؤْمِنُوْنَ ۞

وَلَقَدْ اَخَذَ اللهُ مِيْثَاقَ بَنِيْۤ اِسْرَآءِيْلَ ۚ وَبَعَثْنَا

مِنْهُمُ اثْنَيْ عَشَرَ نَقِيْبًا ؕ وَقَالَ اللهُ اِنِّيْ مَعَكُمْ ؕ

لَئِنْ اَقَمْتُمُ الصَّلٰوةَ وَاٰتَيْتُمُ الزَّكٰوةَ وَاٰمَنْتُمْ

بِرُسُلِيْ وَعَزَّرْتُمُوْهُمْ وَاَقْرَضْتُمُ اللهَ قَرْضًا حَسَنًا

لَّاُكَفِّرَنَّ عَنْكُمْ سَيِّاٰتِكُمْ وَلَاُدْخِلَنَّكُمْ جَنّٰتٍ

تَجْرِيْ مِنْ تَحْتِهَا الْاَنْهٰرُ ۚ فَمَنْ كَفَرَ بَعْدَ ذٰلِكَ

مِنْكُمْ فَقَدْ ضَلَّ سَوَآءَ السَّبِيْلِ ۞ فَبِمَا نَقْضِهِمْ

مِّيْثَاقَهُمْ لَعَنّٰهُمْ وَجَعَلْنَا قُلُوْبَهُمْ قٰسِيَةً ۚ

Develop your sense of fairness, it will stop you from being racist, prejudiced and judgemental about others.

[7] Remember Allah's favour and the contract He solemnly took from you when you said, "We hear and obey." Be mindful of Allah, He knows well what is in your hearts and minds.

Always behave justly, give up discrimination

[8] Believers, be committed to Allah as witnesses for justice, and don't let hatred of a community stop you being just. Be just, that is closest to piety. Be mindful of Allah. Allah is aware of what you do. [9] Allah has promised forgiveness and a great reward to believers who do righteous deeds, [10] and disbelievers who deny Our signs will be the companions of Hell. [11] Believers, remember Allah's favour when certain people intended to attack you, but He held them back. So, fear Allah, and let the believers put their trust in Him.

The Israelites who kept the contract were rewarded

[12] Allah took a contract from the Israelites when We appointed twelve chieftains for them. Then said, "I am with you so long you perform the prayer, pay the Zakat, believe in My messengers and support them, and give Allah a beautiful loan, I will erase your sins and admit you to gardens beneath which rivers flow. Anyone who breaks the contract after that will stray from the right path."

يُحَرِّفُوْنَ الْكَلِمَ عَنْ مَّوَاضِعِهٖ لا وَنَسُوْا حَظًّا مِّمَّا
ذُكِّرُوْا بِهٖ ۚ وَلَا تَزَالُ تَطَّلِعُ عَلٰى خَآئِنَةٍ مِّنْهُمْ
اِلَّا قَلِيْلًا مِّنْهُمْ فَاعْفُ عَنْهُمْ وَاصْفَحْ ط اِنَّ اللَّهَ
يُحِبُّ الْمُحْسِنِيْنَ ۝ وَمِنَ الَّذِيْنَ قَالُوْٓا اِنَّا نَصٰرٰٓى
اَخَذْنَا مِيْثَاقَهُمْ فَنَسُوْا حَظًّا مِّمَّا ذُكِّرُوْا بِهٖ ۫
فَاَغْرَيْنَا بَيْنَهُمُ الْعَدَاوَةَ وَالْبَغْضَآءَ اِلٰى يَوْمِ الْقِيٰمَةِ ط
وَسَوْفَ يُنَبِّئُهُمُ اللَّهُ بِمَا كَانُوْا يَصْنَعُوْنَ ۝ يٰٓاَهْلَ
الْكِتٰبِ قَدْ جَآءَكُمْ رَسُوْلُنَا يُبَيِّنُ لَكُمْ كَثِيْرًا مِّمَّا
كُنْتُمْ تُخْفُوْنَ مِنَ الْكِتٰبِ وَيَعْفُوْا عَنْ كَثِيْرٍ ط قَدْ
جَآءَكُمْ مِّنَ اللَّهِ نُوْرٌ وَّكِتٰبٌ مُّبِيْنٌ ۝ يَّهْدِىْ
بِهِ اللَّهُ مَنِ اتَّبَعَ رِضْوَانَهٗ سُبُلَ السَّلٰمِ وَ
يُخْرِجُهُمْ مِّنَ الظُّلُمٰتِ اِلَى النُّوْرِ بِاِذْنِهٖ وَ
يَهْدِيْهِمْ اِلٰى صِرَاطٍ مُّسْتَقِيْمٍ ۝ لَقَدْ كَفَرَ الَّذِيْنَ
قَالُوْٓا اِنَّ اللَّهَ هُوَ الْمَسِيْحُ ابْنُ مَرْيَمَ ط قُلْ فَمَنْ
يَّمْلِكُ مِنَ اللَّهِ شَيْئًا اِنْ اَرَادَ اَنْ يُّهْلِكَ الْمَسِيْحَ
ابْنَ مَرْيَمَ وَاُمَّهٗ وَمَنْ فِى الْاَرْضِ جَمِيْعًا ط وَلِلَّهِ
مُلْكُ السَّمٰوٰتِ وَالْاَرْضِ وَمَا بَيْنَهُمَا ط يَخْلُقُ
مَا يَشَآءُ ط وَاللَّهُ عَلٰى كُلِّ شَيْءٍ قَدِيْرٌ ۝ وَقَالَتِ
الْيَهُوْدُ وَالنَّصٰرٰى نَحْنُ اَبْنٰٓؤُا اللَّهِ وَاَحِبَّآؤُهٗ ط
قُلْ فَلِمَ يُعَذِّبُكُمْ بِذُنُوْبِكُمْ ط بَلْ اَنْتُمْ بَشَرٌ

The Messenger ﷺ is a light for guidance and a lighthouse that warns us of the rocks of life.

207

The Prophet ﷺ is advised to overlook the faults of the Jews

¹³ When the Jews broke their contract, We cursed them, and hardened their hearts. They misquote verses from the Book and neglect parts of what they were taught. Even today you can see treachery in most, except for a few of them. Despite that you should pardon them and overlook their faults. Allah loves those who benefit others.

Breaking the contract leads to conflict

¹⁴ We took a contract from those who said "We are Christians." When they neglected parts of the teachings, We whipped up enmity and resentment among them, which will continue till Judgement Day. Allah will inform them of what they invented.^a

Invitation to follow the paths of peace

¹⁵ People of The Book, Our Messenger has come to clarify a lot of things in the Book that you used to cover up and to pardon your disobedience. A light from Allah has come to you, and a clear Book, ¹⁶by this Allah guides anyone who follows the path of peace in search of Divine pleasure. The Quran by His authority takes them out of darkness into the light, and guides them on the straight path.

It is irrational to believe Jesus is God

¹⁷ Those who say: "The Messiah, the son of Maryam, is God" are denying the truth. Say: "Who has the power to stop Allah, if He so wished, to finish off the Messiah, son of Maryam, his mother and life from the face of the Earth?" Allah has control of the Heavens, the Earth and whatever exists between them; He creates what He wills. Allah has the power over everything.

---

^a There are thousands of Christian sects or denominations in the world, and they continue to grow.

مِّمَّنْ خَلَقَ ط يَغْفِرُ لِمَنْ يَّشَآءُ وَ يُعَذِّبُ مَنْ

يَّشَآءُ ط وَ لِلّٰهِ مُلْكُ السَّمٰوٰتِ وَالْاَرْضِ وَمَا بَيْنَهُمَا ز

وَ اِلَيْهِ الْمَصِيْرُ ۞ يٰاَهْلَ الْكِتٰبِ قَدْ جَآءَكُمْ رَسُوْلُنَا

يُبَيِّنُ لَكُمْ عَلٰى فَتْرَةٍ مِّنَ الرُّسُلِ اَنْ تَقُوْلُوْا

مَا جَآءَنَا مِنْ بَشِيْرٍ وَّ لَا نَذِيْرٍ ز فَقَدْ جَآءَكُمْ

بَشِيْرٌ وَّ نَذِيْرٌ ط وَاللهُ عَلٰى كُلِّ شَيْءٍ قَدِيْرٌ ۞ وَ اِذْ

قَالَ مُوْسٰى لِقَوْمِهٖ يٰقَوْمِ اذْكُرُوْا نِعْمَةَ اللهِ

عَلَيْكُمْ اِذْ جَعَلَ فِيْكُمْ اَنْبِيَآءَ وَجَعَلَكُمْ مُّلُوْكًا ص

وَّاٰتٰىكُمْ مَّا لَمْ يُؤْتِ اَحَدًا مِّنَ الْعٰلَمِيْنَ ۞ يٰقَوْمِ

ادْخُلُوا الْاَرْضَ الْمُقَدَّسَةَ الَّتِيْ كَتَبَ اللهُ لَكُمْ وَلَا

تَرْتَدُّوْا عَلٰى اَدْبَارِكُمْ فَتَنْقَلِبُوْا خٰسِرِيْنَ ۞ قَالُوْا

يٰمُوْسٰى اِنَّ فِيْهَا قَوْمًا جَبَّارِيْنَ ۖص وَ اِنَّا لَنْ نَّدْخُلَهَا

حَتّٰى يَخْرُجُوْا مِنْهَا ۚ فَاِنْ يَّخْرُجُوْا مِنْهَا فَاِنَّا

دٰخِلُوْنَ ۞ قَالَ رَجُلٰنِ مِنَ الَّذِيْنَ يَخَافُوْنَ اَنْعَمَ

اللهُ عَلَيْهِمَا ادْخُلُوْا عَلَيْهِمُ الْبَابَ ۚ فَاِذَا دَخَلْتُمُوْهُ

فَاِنَّكُمْ غٰلِبُوْنَ ۚ وَ عَلَى اللهِ فَتَوَكَّلُوْا اِنْ كُنْتُمْ

مُّؤْمِنِيْنَ ۞ قَالُوْا يٰمُوْسٰى اِنَّا لَنْ نَّدْخُلَهَا اَبَدًا

مَّا دَامُوْا فِيْهَا فَاذْهَبْ اَنْتَ وَ رَبُّكَ فَقَاتِلَا اِنَّا

هٰهُنَا قٰعِدُوْنَ ۞ قَالَ رَبِّ اِنِّيْ لَا اَمْلِكُ اِلَّا نَفْسِيْ

وَ اَخِيْ فَافْرُقْ بَيْنَنَا وَ بَيْنَ الْقَوْمِ الْفٰسِقِيْنَ ۞

Be courageous and fearless when serving community and country. Allah is the Helper.

The Jews and Christians cannot deny having been warned

[18] The Jews and Christians say, "We are the children of Allah and His beloved." Say: "So why does He then punish you for your sins? The reality is you are ordinary human beings from His creation. He forgives anyone He wants, and He punishes anyone He wants." Allah has control of the Heavens, the Earth and whatever exists between, and finally they will return to Him. [19] People of The Book, Our Messenger came to explain the truth after an interval – when no messengers appeared – so that you can't say: "No herald of good news or warner ever came to us." But now, a herald of good news and a warner has come to you. Allah has control over everything.

The results of fear

[20] So, when Musa said, "My people, remember Allah's favour on you, He appointed prophets and kings among you, and gave you what no one else was given in the world. [21] My people, enter the Holy Land Allah has promised you, and don't turn your backs, or you will become losers." [22] They said, "Musa, fearsome people live there. We won't enter until they leave, once they have left, we'll go in." [23] Two of their Allah-fearing men said, "March against them and enter through the gate, if you enter through it, you will conquer. Put your trust in Allah if you are believers." [24] They said, "Musa, we will never enter the land as long as they remain there. Go and fight, you and your Lord, we'll stay here."

قَالَ فَاِنَّهَا مُحَرَّمَةٌ عَلَيْهِمْ اَرْبَعِيْنَ سَنَةً ۚ

يَتِيْهُوْنَ فِي الْاَرْضِ ط فَلَا تَاْسَ عَلَى الْقَوْمِ

الْفٰسِقِيْنَ ۞ وَاتْلُ عَلَيْهِمْ نَبَاَ ابْنَيْ اٰدَمَ بِالْحَقِّ ۚ

اِذْ قَرَّبَا قُرْبَانًا فَتُقُبِّلَ مِنْ اَحَدِهِمَا وَلَمْ يُتَقَبَّلْ

مِنَ الْاٰخَرِ ط قَالَ لَاَقْتُلَنَّكَ ط قَالَ اِنَّمَا يَتَقَبَّلُ

اللّٰهُ مِنَ الْمُتَّقِيْنَ ۞ لَئِنْ بَسَطْتَّ اِلَيَّ يَدَكَ

لِتَقْتُلَنِيْ مَآ اَنَا بِبَاسِطٍ يَّدِيَ اِلَيْكَ لِاَقْتُلَكَ ۚ

اِنِّيْ اَخَافُ اللّٰهَ رَبَّ الْعٰلَمِيْنَ ۞ اِنِّيْ اُرِيْدُ اَنْ

تَبُوْٓاَ بِاِثْمِيْ وَاِثْمِكَ فَتَكُوْنَ مِنْ اَصْحٰبِ النَّارِ ۚ

وَ ذٰلِكَ جَزٰٓؤُا الظّٰلِمِيْنَ ۞ فَطَوَّعَتْ لَهُ نَفْسُهُ

قَتْلَ اَخِيْهِ فَقَتَلَهُ فَاَصْبَحَ مِنَ الْخٰسِرِيْنَ ۞

فَبَعَثَ اللّٰهُ غُرَابًا يَّبْحَثُ فِي الْاَرْضِ لِيُرِيَهُ

كَيْفَ يُوَارِيْ سَوْءَةَ اَخِيْهِ ط قَالَ يٰوَيْلَتٰٓى اَعَجَزْتُ

اَنْ اَكُوْنَ مِثْلَ هٰذَا الْغُرَابِ فَاُوَارِيَ سَوْءَةَ

اَخِيْ ۚ فَاَصْبَحَ مِنَ النّٰدِمِيْنَ ۞ مِنْ اَجْلِ ذٰلِكَ ۚ

كَتَبْنَا عَلٰى بَنِيْ اِسْرَآءِيْلَ اَنَّهُ مَنْ قَتَلَ نَفْسًا

بِغَيْرِ نَفْسٍ اَوْ فَسَادٍ فِي الْاَرْضِ فَكَاَنَّمَا قَتَلَ

النَّاسَ جَمِيْعًا ط وَمَنْ اَحْيَاهَا فَكَاَنَّمَآ اَحْيَا

النَّاسَ جَمِيْعًا ط وَلَقَدْ جَآءَتْهُمْ رُسُلُنَا بِالْبَيِّنٰتِ ۙ

ثُمَّ اِنَّ كَثِيْرًا مِّنْهُمْ بَعْدَ ذٰلِكَ فِي الْاَرْضِ

Human life is sacred, killing one person is tantamount to killing all of humanity!

211

²⁵ Musa said, "My Lord, I only have control over myself and my brother, so separate the two of us and these sinful people." ²⁶ Allah said, "The Holy Land is now forbidden for them. They shall roam the wilderness for forty years, so don't worry about these sinners."

Jealousy led a man to kill his brother

²⁷ Give them an exact account of two sons of Adam.ᵃ When both offered a sacrifice, and it was accepted from one but not from the other, *Cain* angrily said, "I'm going to kill you." Abel replied, "Allah only accepts from the pious. ²⁸ If you raise your hand to kill me, I will not raise my hand to kill you. I fear Allah, Lord of the universe. ²⁹ I hope you'll be burdened with mine and your sins and become one of the companions of the Fire; that is a fitting reward for wrongdoers." ³⁰ Yet *Cain* was tempted by his passion to kill his brother Abel, so he killed him and became a loser in this world and the next. ³¹ Allah sent a crow, it dug the ground to show him how to bury his brother's corpse. He said, "How pathetic am I! I am no better than this crow, I can't even hide my brother's corpse?" So he was regretful.

Every human life is momentous

³² Because of that murder, We decreed for the Israelites that whoever kills another person – unless it is in lawful retaliation for taking a life or for creating terror in the countryᵇ – it is as though he has killed the whole of humanity, and anyone who saves a life, it is as though he has saved the whole of humanity. Our messengers came to them with clear signs, but many of them became extremists in their country.

ᵃ A reference to the biblical story of Adam's two sons, Abel and Cain, in the book of Genesis.
ᵇ *"Fasad"* means a heinous act; violence and conflict that undermines the peace and order of a country.

لَمُسْرِفُوْنَ ۝ اِنَّمَا جَزٰٓؤُا الَّذِيْنَ يُحَارِبُوْنَ اللّٰهَ

وَرَسُوْلَهٗ وَيَسْعَوْنَ فِى الْاَرْضِ فَسَادًا اَنْ يُّقَتَّلُوْٓا

اَوْ يُصَلَّبُوْٓا اَوْ تُقَطَّعَ اَيْدِيْهِمْ وَاَرْجُلُهُمْ مِّنْ

خِلَافٍ اَوْ يُنْفَوْا مِنَ الْاَرْضِ ۚ ذٰلِكَ لَهُمْ خِزْيٌ

فِى الدُّنْيَا وَلَهُمْ فِى الْاٰخِرَةِ عَذَابٌ عَظِيْمٌ ۝

اِلَّا الَّذِيْنَ تَابُوْا مِنْ قَبْلِ اَنْ تَقْدِرُوْا عَلَيْهِمْ ۚ

فَاعْلَمُوْٓا اَنَّ اللّٰهَ غَفُوْرٌ رَّحِيْمٌ ۝ يٰٓاَيُّهَا

الَّذِيْنَ اٰمَنُوا اتَّقُوا اللّٰهَ وَابْتَغُوْٓا اِلَيْهِ الْوَسِيْلَةَ

وَجَاهِدُوْا فِىْ سَبِيْلِهٖ لَعَلَّكُمْ تُفْلِحُوْنَ ۝ اِنَّ

الَّذِيْنَ كَفَرُوْا لَوْ اَنَّ لَهُمْ مَّا فِى الْاَرْضِ جَمِيْعًا وَّ

مِثْلَهٗ مَعَهٗ لِيَفْتَدُوْا بِهٖ مِنْ عَذَابِ يَوْمِ الْقِيٰمَةِ

مَا تُقُبِّلَ مِنْهُمْ ۚ وَلَهُمْ عَذَابٌ اَلِيْمٌ ۝ يُرِيْدُوْنَ

اَنْ يَّخْرُجُوْا مِنَ النَّارِ وَمَا هُمْ بِخٰرِجِيْنَ مِنْهَا ۚ

وَلَهُمْ عَذَابٌ مُّقِيْمٌ ۝ وَالسَّارِقُ وَالسَّارِقَةُ

فَاقْطَعُوْٓا اَيْدِيَهُمَا جَزَآءً بِمَا كَسَبَا نَكَالًا مِّنَ

اللّٰهِ ۚ وَاللّٰهُ عَزِيْزٌ حَكِيْمٌ ۝ فَمَنْ تَابَ مِنْ بَعْدِ

ظُلْمِهٖ وَاَصْلَحَ فَاِنَّ اللّٰهَ يَتُوْبُ عَلَيْهِ ۚ اِنَّ اللّٰهَ

غَفُوْرٌ رَّحِيْمٌ ۝ اَلَمْ تَعْلَمْ اَنَّ اللّٰهَ لَهٗ مُلْكُ

السَّمٰوٰتِ وَالْاَرْضِ ۚ يُعَذِّبُ مَنْ يَّشَآءُ وَيَغْفِرُ

لِمَنْ يَّشَآءُ ۚ وَاللّٰهُ عَلٰى كُلِّ شَىْءٍ قَدِيْرٌ ۝ يٰٓاَيُّهَا

Seek means and opportunities to get close to Allah.

213

The punishments for unrepentant terrorists

³³The fitting punishment for those who start war to destroy the people of Allah and His Messenger is: the death penalty, or crucifixion, or amputation of their hands and feet on opposite sides, or be exiled from the city. That's how they will be disgraced in this world, and in the Hereafter they will be severely punished, ³⁴except for those who repent before you arrest them. Know, Allah is Forgiving, Kind.

Draw close to Allah, wealth will not save you

³⁵Believers, be mindful of Allah and search for ways to draw close to Him[a] and strive in His way, so you may be successful. ³⁶Even if the disbelievers owned everything on Earth twice over and tried to ransom themselves with it from the punishment of Judgement Day, it would not be accepted from them; theirs will be a painful punishment. ³⁷They will long to come out of the Fire but won't be able to do so; theirs will be a lasting punishment.

Reformed thieves are forgiven

³⁸The penalty for thieves, male and female, is to cut off their hands to the wrist, a deterrent from Allah. Allah is Almighty, Wise. ³⁹Allah relents towards him who repents after wrongdoings and reforms himself, He is Forgiving, Kind. ⁴⁰Don't you know Allah controls everything in the Heavens and Earth? He punishes anyone He pleases, and He forgives anyone He pleases. Allah has power over everything.

---

[a] *"Wasila"* is a means of getting to one's destination, or getting nearer to it (Lisan al-Arab). Faith, good works, charity, good character and worship are all examples of *Wasila*. Similarly having a teacher who guides one to Allah is a *Wasila*.

الرَّسُوۡلُ لَا يَحۡزُنۡكَ الَّذِيۡنَ يُسَارِعُوۡنَ فِى الۡكُفۡرِ مِنَ الَّذِيۡنَ قَالُوۡۤا اٰمَنَّا بِاَفۡوَاهِهِمۡ وَلَمۡ تُؤۡمِنۡ قُلُوۡبُهُمۡ ۛ وَمِنَ الَّذِيۡنَ هَادُوۡا ۛ سَمّٰعُوۡنَ لِلۡكَذِبِ سَمّٰعُوۡنَ لِقَوۡمٍ اٰخَرِيۡنَ ۙ لَمۡ يَاۡتُوۡكَ ؕ يُحَرِّفُوۡنَ الۡكَلِمَ مِنۡۢ بَعۡدِ مَوَاضِعِهٖ ۚ يَقُوۡلُوۡنَ اِنۡ اُوۡتِيۡتُمۡ هٰذَا فَخُذُوۡهُ وَاِنۡ لَّمۡ تُؤۡتَوۡهُ فَاحۡذَرُوۡا ؕ وَمَنۡ يُّرِدِ اللهُ فِتۡنَتَهٗ فَلَنۡ تَمۡلِكَ لَهٗ مِنَ اللهِ شَيۡئًا ؕ اُولٰٓئِكَ الَّذِيۡنَ لَمۡ يُرِدِ اللهُ اَنۡ يُّطَهِّرَ قُلُوۡبَهُمۡ ؕ لَهُمۡ فِى الدُّنۡيَا خِزۡىٌ ۖ وَّ لَهُمۡ فِى الۡاٰخِرَةِ عَذَابٌ عَظِيۡمٌ ۞ سَمّٰعُوۡنَ لِلۡكَذِبِ اَكّٰلُوۡنَ لِلسُّحۡتِ ؕ فَاِنۡ جَآءُوۡكَ فَاحۡكُمۡ بَيۡنَهُمۡ اَوۡ اَعۡرِضۡ عَنۡهُمۡ ۚ وَاِنۡ تُعۡرِضۡ عَنۡهُمۡ فَلَنۡ يَّضُرُّوۡكَ شَيۡئًا ؕ وَاِنۡ حَكَمۡتَ فَاحۡكُمۡ بَيۡنَهُمۡ بِالۡقِسۡطِ ؕ اِنَّ اللهَ يُحِبُّ الۡمُقۡسِطِيۡنَ ۞ وَكَيۡفَ يُحَكِّمُوۡنَكَ وَعِنۡدَهُمُ التَّوۡرٰىةُ فِيۡهَا حُكۡمُ اللهِ ثُمَّ يَتَوَلَّوۡنَ مِنۡۢ بَعۡدِ ذٰلِكَ ؕ وَمَاۤ اُولٰٓئِكَ بِالۡمُؤۡمِنِيۡنَ ۞ اِنَّاۤ اَنۡزَلۡنَا التَّوۡرٰىةَ فِيۡهَا هُدًى وَّ نُوۡرٌ ۚ يَحۡكُمُ بِهَا النَّبِيُّوۡنَ الَّذِيۡنَ اَسۡلَمُوۡا لِلَّذِيۡنَ هَادُوۡا وَالرَّبّٰنِيُّوۡنَ وَالۡاَحۡبَارُ بِمَا اسۡتُحۡفِظُوۡا مِنۡ كِتٰبِ اللهِ وَكَانُوۡا عَلَيۡهِ شُهَدَآءَ ۚ فَلَا

The Jews and Christians didn't take the Bible seriously, Muslims are warned: be careful with the Quran.

215

Beware of hypocrites misquoting the Quran

⁴¹ Messenger, don't be saddened by those rushing headlong into disbelief, they say: "We believe," while there is no belief in their hearts, and likewise some who call themselves Jews. They are listening eagerly to lies and other people who have yet to come to you; they deliberately misquote the verses after the revelation has been laid down, saying, "If you are given this ruling, accept it, but if not, then beware." If Allah wishes to test anyone, you will have no means to save him from Allah. Allah doesn't wish to clean their hearts since they don't want that. They will suffer disgrace in this world, and they will be severely punished in the Hereafter.

A caution: don't follow those who deviated from the Torah

⁴² They listen eagerly to lies and live on deceitfully-earned wealth. If they come, you may either judge them or turn them away. If you decide to turn them away they will not harm you in the least; however, if you judge between them, be just. Allah loves the just. ⁴³ How is it they ask you to judge when they have the Torah containing Allah's laws; and after asking you, they still turn away. Those aren't believers. ⁴⁴ He revealed the Torah, which has guidance and light. The prophets who submitted themselves to Allah's will used to judge the Jews according to it, as did the rabbis and the scholars according to what they had preserved of the Book of Allah, and they were witnesses. So, don't fear people but fear Me, and don't sell My verses for a small price. Whoever doesn't judge by Allah's revelation are the disbelievers.

تَخْشَوُا النَّاسَ وَاخْشَوْنِ وَلَا تَشْتَرُوْا بِاٰيٰتِيْ ثَمَنًا

قَلِيْلًا ط وَمَنْ لَّمْ يَحْكُمْ بِمَآ اَنْزَلَ اللّٰهُ فَاُولٰٓئِكَ

هُمُ الْكٰفِرُوْنَ ۝ وَكَتَبْنَا عَلَيْهِمْ فِيْهَآ اَنَّ النَّفْسَ

بِالنَّفْسِ وَالْعَيْنَ بِالْعَيْنِ وَالْاَنْفَ بِالْاَنْفِ

وَالْاُذُنَ بِالْاُذُنِ وَالسِّنَّ بِالسِّنِّ وَالْجُرُوْحَ

قِصَاصٌ ط فَمَنْ تَصَدَّقَ بِهٖ فَهُوَ كَفَّارَةٌ لَّهٗ ط

وَمَنْ لَّمْ يَحْكُمْ بِمَآ اَنْزَلَ اللّٰهُ فَاُولٰٓئِكَ هُمُ

الظّٰلِمُوْنَ ۝ وَقَفَّيْنَا عَلٰٓى اٰثَارِهِمْ بِعِيْسَى ابْنِ

مَرْيَمَ مُصَدِّقًا لِّمَا بَيْنَ يَدَيْهِ مِنَ التَّوْرٰىةِ ۫

وَاٰتَيْنٰهُ الْاِنْجِيْلَ فِيْهِ هُدًى وَّنُوْرٌ ۙ وَّمُصَدِّقًا

لِّمَا بَيْنَ يَدَيْهِ مِنَ التَّوْرٰىةِ وَهُدًى وَّمَوْعِظَةً

لِّلْمُتَّقِيْنَ ۝ وَلْيَحْكُمْ اَهْلُ الْاِنْجِيْلِ بِمَآ اَنْزَلَ

اللّٰهُ فِيْهِ ط وَمَنْ لَّمْ يَحْكُمْ بِمَآ اَنْزَلَ اللّٰهُ فَاُولٰٓئِكَ

هُمُ الْفٰسِقُوْنَ ۝ وَاَنْزَلْنَآ اِلَيْكَ الْكِتٰبَ بِالْحَقِّ

مُصَدِّقًا لِّمَا بَيْنَ يَدَيْهِ مِنَ الْكِتٰبِ وَمُهَيْمِنًا

عَلَيْهِ فَاحْكُمْ بَيْنَهُمْ بِمَآ اَنْزَلَ اللّٰهُ وَلَا

تَتَّبِعْ اَهْوَآءَهُمْ عَمَّا جَآءَكَ مِنَ الْحَقِّ ط لِكُلٍّ

جَعَلْنَا مِنْكُمْ شِرْعَةً وَّمِنْهَاجًا ط وَلَوْ شَآءَ اللّٰهُ

لَجَعَلَكُمْ اُمَّةً وَّاحِدَةً وَّلٰكِنْ لِّيَبْلُوَكُمْ فِيْ مَآ

اٰتٰىكُمْ فَاسْتَبِقُوا الْخَيْرٰتِ ط اِلَى اللّٰهِ مَرْجِعُكُمْ جَمِيْعًا

The Quran is the final testament; humanity is invited to embrace it.

An eye for an eye is just, but to pardon is charity[a]

⁴⁵ In the Torah We commanded: a life for a life; an eye for an eye; a nose for a nose; an ear for an ear; a tooth for a tooth; all injuries like for like. Whoever gives up his right out of charity, that will serve as an atonement for him on Judgement Day, but whoever does not judge by what Allah has revealed will be the wrongdoers.

Sin is the violation of the law of the scripture

⁴⁶ Afterwards, We sent Isa, son of Maryam, to follow in their footsteps. He confirmed what was revealed in the Torah before him, and We gave him the Gospel, in which there is guidance and light, and it confirmed what was in the Torah, as a guidance and clear warning for the mindful. ⁴⁷ So let the people of the Gospel judge with what Allah has revealed in it, and whoever doesn't judge by what Allah has revealed are sinners.

Religious differences are by Allah's will

⁴⁸ We revealed to you the Quran, full of truth, confirming what was revealed before from the Book, and superseding all earlier revelation. So, judge between them according to what Allah has revealed, and don't follow their whims that contradict the truth that has come to you. To every community in the past, We gave a specific law and a way of life. Had Allah wanted, He would have made you one nation, but He chose to test you regarding what He gave you; so compete with each other in doing good works. In the end you will all return to Allah, and He will clarify your differences.

ᵃ   The law can be ignored by: not paying attention to it, making up rulings, being excessively harsh or lenient. Setting rates of compensation for certain injuries is not ignoring the law, as is mentioned in the Quran (e.g. *Surat Al-Nisa'*: 92). See Exodus 12:23 for penalties according to Jewish law.

فَيُنَبِّئُكُمْ بِمَا كُنْتُمْ فِيهِ تَخْتَلِفُوْنَ ۞ وَاَنِ احْكُمْ

بَيْنَهُمْ بِمَا اَنْزَلَ اللّٰهُ وَلَا تَتَّبِعْ اَهْوَآءَهُمْ

وَاحْذَرْهُمْ اَنْ يَّفْتِنُوْكَ عَنْ بَعْضِ مَا اَنْزَلَ

اللّٰهُ اِلَيْكَ ۗ فَاِنْ تَوَلَّوْا فَاعْلَمْ اَنَّمَا يُرِيْدُ اللّٰهُ

اَنْ يُّصِيْبَهُمْ بِبَعْضِ ذُنُوْبِهِمْ ۗ وَاِنَّ كَثِيْرًا مِّنَ

النَّاسِ لَفٰسِقُوْنَ ۞ اَفَحُكْمَ الْجَاهِلِيَّةِ يَبْغُوْنَ ۗ

وَمَنْ اَحْسَنُ مِنَ اللّٰهِ حُكْمًا لِّقَوْمٍ يُّوْقِنُوْنَ ۞

يٰٓاَيُّهَا الَّذِيْنَ اٰمَنُوْا لَا تَتَّخِذُوا الْيَهُوْدَ وَ

النَّصٰرٰى اَوْلِيَآءَ ۘ بَعْضُهُمْ اَوْلِيَآءُ بَعْضٍ ۗ وَمَنْ

يَّتَوَلَّهُمْ مِّنْكُمْ فَاِنَّهٗ مِنْهُمْ ۗ اِنَّ اللّٰهَ لَا يَهْدِى

الْقَوْمَ الظّٰلِمِيْنَ ۞ فَتَرَى الَّذِيْنَ فِيْ قُلُوْبِهِمْ مَّرَضٌ

يُّسَارِعُوْنَ فِيْهِمْ يَقُوْلُوْنَ نَخْشٰٓى اَنْ تُصِيْبَنَا

دَآئِرَةٌ ۗ فَعَسَى اللّٰهُ اَنْ يَّأْتِيَ بِالْفَتْحِ اَوْ اَمْرٍ

مِّنْ عِنْدِهٖ فَيُصْبِحُوْا عَلٰى مَآ اَسَرُّوْا فِيْٓ اَنْفُسِهِمْ

نٰدِمِيْنَ ۞ وَيَقُوْلُ الَّذِيْنَ اٰمَنُوْٓا اَهٰٓؤُلَآءِ الَّذِيْنَ

اَقْسَمُوْا بِاللّٰهِ جَهْدَ اَيْمَانِهِمْ ۙ اِنَّهُمْ لَمَعَكُمْ ۗ

حَبِطَتْ اَعْمَالُهُمْ فَاَصْبَحُوْا خٰسِرِيْنَ ۞ يٰٓاَيُّهَا

الَّذِيْنَ اٰمَنُوْا مَنْ يَّرْتَدَّ مِنْكُمْ عَنْ دِيْنِهٖ

فَسَوْفَ يَأْتِى اللّٰهُ بِقَوْمٍ يُّحِبُّهُمْ وَيُحِبُّوْنَهٗٓ ۙ

اَذِلَّةٍ عَلَى الْمُؤْمِنِيْنَ اَعِزَّةٍ عَلَى الْكٰفِرِيْنَ

Be firm in faith, proud to be a Muslim, don't be afraid of critics.

219

The Prophet ﷺ is commanded to judge justly

⁴⁹ Judge between them according to what Allah has revealed, and do not follow their whims. So beware they don't tempt you away from what Allah has revealed to you. If they choose to turn away, then you should know that Allah intends to punish them because of their sins, many are sinners. ⁵⁰ Do they want the old law of the Age of Ignorance?^a There is no better rule than Allah's, for firm believers.

A warning against choosing sides out of fear

⁵¹ Believers, don't take the Jews and the Christians as protectors;^b they're only each other's protectors. Anyone who takes them as his protector might as well join them. Allah doesn't guide people who do wrong. ⁵² You will see people with sickness in their hearts rushing to join them, saying, "We fear tragedy may strike us." It may be that Allah will grant us victory or bring about some other positive outcome, causing them to regret what they kept secret in their hearts. ⁵³ The believers will say, "Didn't they swear a solemn oath; by Allah they were with you?" Their deeds have proved to be worthless, and they are the losers.

Victory is for the lovers of Allah

⁵⁴ Believers, if anyone leaves his religion then Allah will bring forward people He loves and who love Him, who are gentle towards the believers and unflinching against the disbelievers, who strive in the path of Allah and aren't afraid of the critics' comments. That positive attitude is a favour of Allah; He gives it to whomever He pleases. Allah is Vast, All-Knowing.

---

^a The Age of Ignorance refers to the time before the coming of the Messenger ﷺ in 610 CE, when power and wealth ruled in Arabia and customs were based on superstition not the law, and there was a lack of moral, social and spiritual values.

^b *"Awliya"* is plural of *Wali;* a friend but it can also mean allies, supporters and protectors. The context here suggests it is protectors not friends at the time of war.

يُجَاهِدُوْنَ فِىْ سَبِيْلِ اللّٰهِ وَلَا يَخَافُوْنَ لَوْمَةَ
لَآئِمٍ ۚ ذٰلِكَ فَضْلُ اللّٰهِ يُؤْتِيْهِ مَنْ يَّشَآءُ ۚ
وَاللّٰهُ وَاسِعٌ عَلِيْمٌ ۵۴ اِنَّمَا وَلِيُّكُمُ اللّٰهُ وَرَسُوْلُهٗ
وَالَّذِيْنَ اٰمَنُوا الَّذِيْنَ يُقِيْمُوْنَ الصَّلٰوةَ وَ
يُؤْتُوْنَ الزَّكٰوةَ وَهُمْ رٰكِعُوْنَ ۵۵ وَمَنْ يَّتَوَلَّ
اللّٰهَ وَرَسُوْلَهٗ وَالَّذِيْنَ اٰمَنُوْا فَاِنَّ حِزْبَ
اللّٰهِ هُمُ الْغٰلِبُوْنَ ۵۶ يٰۤاَيُّهَا الَّذِيْنَ اٰمَنُوْا
لَا تَتَّخِذُوا الَّذِيْنَ اتَّخَذُوْا دِيْنَكُمْ هُزُوًا وَّلَعِبًا
مِّنَ الَّذِيْنَ اُوْتُوا الْكِتٰبَ مِنْ قَبْلِكُمْ وَالْكُفَّارَ
اَوْلِيَآءَ ۚ وَاتَّقُوا اللّٰهَ اِنْ كُنْتُمْ مُّؤْمِنِيْنَ ۵۷
وَاِذَا نَادَيْتُمْ اِلَى الصَّلٰوةِ اتَّخَذُوْهَا هُزُوًا وَّ
لَعِبًا ۚ ذٰلِكَ بِاَنَّهُمْ قَوْمٌ لَّا يَعْقِلُوْنَ ۵۸ قُلْ
يٰۤاَهْلَ الْكِتٰبِ هَلْ تَنْقِمُوْنَ مِنَّاۤ اِلَّاۤ اَنْ اٰمَنَّا
بِاللّٰهِ وَمَاۤ اُنْزِلَ اِلَيْنَا وَمَاۤ اُنْزِلَ مِنْ قَبْلُ
وَاَنَّ اَكْثَرَكُمْ فٰسِقُوْنَ ۵۹ قُلْ هَلْ اُنَبِّئُكُمْ
بِشَرٍّ مِّنْ ذٰلِكَ مَثُوْبَةً عِنْدَ اللّٰهِ ۚ مَنْ لَّعَنَهُ
اللّٰهُ وَغَضِبَ عَلَيْهِ وَجَعَلَ مِنْهُمُ الْقِرَدَةَ
وَالْخَنَازِيْرَ وَعَبَدَ الطَّاغُوْتَ ۚ اُولٰٓئِكَ شَرٌّ
مَّكَانًا وَّاَضَلُّ عَنْ سَوَآءِ السَّبِيْلِ ۶۰ وَاِذَا
جَآءُوْكُمْ قَالُوْۤا اٰمَنَّا وَقَدْ دَّخَلُوْا بِالْكُفْرِ

Be brave and face the challenges of evil, don't succumb to the weaknesses of society.

[55] Allah is your only true protector, along with His Messenger and the believers who perform the prayer, pay Zakat and bow down to Allah. [56] Anyone who turns to Allah for protection, His Messenger and the believers, should know Allah's party will be victorious.

A warning to those who poke fun at religious practices

[57] Believers, do not take as allies those who treat your religion as a joke and a game, whether they are from the people who were given the Book before you or the disbelievers. Be mindful of Allah, if you are true believers. [58] When you are called to the prayer, they poke fun at it since they don't understand. [59] Say: "People of The Book, what do you have against us, other than we believe in Allah and in what was revealed to us and to those before us? Most of you are sinners." [60] Say: "Shall I tell you of an even worse kind of reward from Allah? Anyone incurring the curse and anger of Allah will become like monkeys, pigs[a] and the worshippers of false gods. They are in a far worse position, and have wandered far from the right path."

---

[a] The phrase "monkeys and pigs", which appears elsewhere in the Quran, is a figure of speech that refers to disobedient people with no sense of morality, becoming like monkeys and pigs in selfish pursuit of their lust.

وَهُمْ قَدْ خَرَجُوْا بِهٖ ط وَاللهُ اَعْلَمُ بِمَا كَانُوْا

يَكْتُمُوْنَ ۞ وَتَرٰى كَثِيْرًا مِّنْهُمْ يُسَارِعُوْنَ فِى

الْاِثْمِ وَالْعُدْوَانِ وَاَكْلِهِمُ السُّحْتَ ط لَبِئْسَ مَا كَانُوْا

يَعْمَلُوْنَ ۞ لَوْلَا يَنْهٰىهُمُ الرَّبّٰنِيُّوْنَ وَالْاَحْبَارُ عَنْ

قَوْلِهِمُ الْاِثْمَ وَاَكْلِهِمُ السُّحْتَ ط لَبِئْسَ مَا كَانُوْا

يَصْنَعُوْنَ ۞ وَقَالَتِ الْيَهُوْدُ يَدُ اللهِ مَغْلُوْلَةٌ ط غُلَّتْ

اَيْدِيْهِمْ وَلُعِنُوْا بِمَا قَالُوْا م بَلْ يَدٰهُ مَبْسُوْطَتٰنِ ۙ

يُنْفِقُ كَيْفَ يَشَآءُ ط وَلَيَزِيْدَنَّ كَثِيْرًا مِّنْهُمْ مَّاۤ

اُنْزِلَ اِلَيْكَ مِنْ رَّبِّكَ طُغْيَانًا وَّكُفْرًا ط وَاَلْقَيْنَا

بَيْنَهُمُ الْعَدَاوَةَ وَالْبَغْضَآءَ اِلٰى يَوْمِ الْقِيٰمَةِ ط كُلَّمَاۤ

اَوْقَدُوْا نَارًا لِّلْحَرْبِ اَطْفَاَهَا اللهُ ۙ وَيَسْعَوْنَ

فِى الْاَرْضِ فَسَادًا ط وَاللهُ لَا يُحِبُّ الْمُفْسِدِيْنَ ۞

وَلَوْ اَنَّ اَهْلَ الْكِتٰبِ اٰمَنُوْا وَاتَّقَوْا لَكَفَّرْنَا عَنْهُمْ

سَيِّاٰتِهِمْ وَلَاَدْخَلْنٰهُمْ جَنّٰتِ النَّعِيْمِ ۞ وَلَوْ اَنَّهُمْ

اَقَامُوا التَّوْرٰةَ وَالْاِنْجِيْلَ وَمَاۤ اُنْزِلَ اِلَيْهِمْ مِّنْ

رَّبِّهِمْ لَاَكَلُوْا مِنْ فَوْقِهِمْ وَمِنْ تَحْتِ اَرْجُلِهِمْ ط

مِنْهُمْ اُمَّةٌ مُّقْتَصِدَةٌ ط وَكَثِيْرٌ مِّنْهُمْ سَآءَ مَا

يَعْمَلُوْنَ ۞ يٰۤاَيُّهَا الرَّسُوْلُ بَلِّغْ مَاۤ اُنْزِلَ اِلَيْكَ

مِنْ رَّبِّكَ ط وَاِنْ لَّمْ تَفْعَلْ فَمَا بَلَّغْتَ رِسَالَتَهٗ ط

وَاللهُ يَعْصِمُكَ مِنَ النَّاسِ ط اِنَّ اللهَ لَا يَهْدِى

The Quran criticises the people of the Book, because it wants to save them from Hell.

ع
٩
١٠
١٣

223

Belief requires conviction, not mere words

⁶¹ If they come to you saying, "We believe," they have entered the same state of denial that they were in previously. Allah knows well what they conceal. ⁶² You will see many of them rushing towards sinfulness, enmity and consuming unlawful gains. How foul is what they are in the habit of doing! ⁶³ If only the rabbis and scholars would have stopped them from their sinful speech and consuming unlawful gains. How foul is what they do!

Arrogance leads to disunity and conflict

⁶⁴ The Jews said, "Allah is tight-fisted."ᵃ May their hands be tied, and may they be cursed for what they have said. Allah's hands are wide openᵇ, He gives generously as He pleases. What's revealed to you increases their rebelliousness and disbelief. We have cast enmity and hatred between them until Judgement Day. Every time they kindle the fire of war, Allah extinguishes it; so they move about the country creating terror, and Allah dislikes those who create terror. ⁶⁵ Had the People of The Book believed and become mindful, then We would erase their sins and admit them into the gardens of bliss. ⁶⁶ And if only they were to apply the Torah, the Gospel and what has been revealed to them from their Lord, they would be given plenty to eat from the sky above and from beneath their feet. Some of them are moderate in their behaviour, but many behave wickedly.

The Messenger ﷺ preaches without fear or favour

⁶⁷ Messenger, communicate all that's revealed to you by your Lord, if you don't, you won't have delivered His message. Allah will protect you from the people who wish to harm you. Allah does not guide the disbelievers.

ᵃ This blasphemous phrase literally means "Allah's hand is tied", i.e. He isn't generous.

ᵇ "Allah's hands" is a melonym for the power of Allah.

الْقَوْمَ الْكَفِرِيْنَ ۝ قُلْ يٰٓاَهْلَ الْكِتٰبِ لَسْتُمْ عَلٰى

شَىْءٍ حَتّٰى تُقِيْمُوا التَّوْرٰىةَ وَالْاِنْجِيْلَ وَمَآ اُنْزِلَ

اِلَيْكُمْ مِّنْ رَّبِّكُمْ ط وَلَيَزِيْدَنَّ كَثِيْرًا مِّنْهُمْ مَّآ

اُنْزِلَ اِلَيْكَ مِنْ رَّبِّكَ طُغْيَانًا وَّكُفْرًا ۚ فَلَا

تَأْسَ عَلَى الْقَوْمِ الْكَفِرِيْنَ ۝ اِنَّ الَّذِيْنَ اٰمَنُوْا

وَالَّذِيْنَ هَادُوْا وَالصّٰبِـُٔوْنَ وَالنَّصٰرٰى مَنْ اٰمَنَ

بِاللّٰهِ وَالْيَوْمِ الْاٰخِرِ وَعَمِلَ صَالِحًا فَلَا خَوْفٌ

عَلَيْهِمْ وَلَا هُمْ يَحْزَنُوْنَ ۝ لَقَدْ اَخَذْنَا مِيْثَاقَ

بَنِىْٓ اِسْرَآءِيْلَ وَاَرْسَلْنَآ اِلَيْهِمْ رُسُلًا ط كُلَّمَا

جَآءَهُمْ رَسُوْلٌۢ بِمَا لَا تَهْوٰىٓ اَنْفُسُهُمْ ۙ فَرِيْقًا

كَذَّبُوْا وَفَرِيْقًا يَّقْتُلُوْنَ ۝ وَحَسِبُوْٓا اَلَّا تَكُوْنَ

فِتْنَةٌ فَعَمُوْا وَصَمُّوْا ثُمَّ تَابَ اللّٰهُ عَلَيْهِمْ

ثُمَّ عَمُوْا وَصَمُّوْا كَثِيْرٌ مِّنْهُمْ ط وَاللّٰهُ بَصِيْرٌۢ

بِمَا يَعْمَلُوْنَ ۝ لَقَدْ كَفَرَ الَّذِيْنَ قَالُوْٓا اِنَّ

اللّٰهَ هُوَ الْمَسِيْحُ ابْنُ مَرْيَمَ ط وَقَالَ الْمَسِيْحُ

يٰبَنِىْٓ اِسْرَآءِيْلَ اعْبُدُوا اللّٰهَ رَبِّىْ وَرَبَّكُمْ ط اِنَّهُ

مَنْ يُّشْرِكْ بِاللّٰهِ فَقَدْ حَرَّمَ اللّٰهُ عَلَيْهِ الْجَنَّةَ

وَمَأْوٰىهُ النَّارُ ط وَمَا لِلظّٰلِمِيْنَ مِنْ اَنْصَارٍ ۝

لَقَدْ كَفَرَ الَّذِيْنَ قَالُوْٓا اِنَّ اللّٰهَ ثَالِثُ

ثَلٰثَةٍ ۘ وَمَا مِنْ اِلٰهٍ اِلَّآ اِلٰهٌ وَّاحِدٌ ط وَاِنْ لَّمْ

The condition for entering Paradise is: have faith in Allah and live by His commands.

Allah will reward the faithful

⁶⁸ Say: "People of the Book, you will have no excuse on Judgment Day unless you implement the Torah and the Gospels and what has been revealed to you from Your Lord." What has been revealed to you causes many of them to increase in their rebelliousness and disbelief, so don't feel pity for the disbelievers. ⁶⁹ The believers, the Jews, the Sabians and the Christians, and anyone who believes in Allah and the Last Day and performs honourable deeds, they shouldn't fear, they shouldn't grieve.

A warning to those who turn a blind eye and a deaf ear

⁷⁰ We made a contract with the Israelites and sent many messengers to them. However, every time a messenger came to them with a revelation that didn't suit their wishes, they denied some and killed others, ⁷¹ and they didn't think it was a test, so they chose to turn a blind eye and a deaf ear. Then Allah relented towards them, but once again many of them chose to turn a blind eye and a deaf ear. Allah clearly sees what they are doing.

Christians invited to give up Trinity so they may achieve salvation

⁷² Those who say, "Allah is the Messiah son of Maryam," have committed an act of disbelief. The Messiah said: "Jews, worship Allah, my Lord and your Lord. Whoever associates anything with Allah, Allah will forbid his entry into Paradise, and his home will be the Fire, and there shall be no helpers for the wrongdoers."

يَنْتَهُوْا عَمَّا يَقُوْلُوْنَ لَيَمَسَّنَّ الَّذِيْنَ كَفَرُوْا

مِنْهُمْ عَذَابٌ اَلِيْمٌ ۝ اَفَلَا يَتُوْبُوْنَ اِلَى

اللّٰهِ وَ يَسْتَغْفِرُوْنَهٗ ط وَ اللّٰهُ غَفُوْرٌ رَّحِيْمٌ ۝

مَا الْمَسِيْحُ ابْنُ مَرْيَمَ اِلَّا رَسُوْلٌ ۚ قَدْ خَلَتْ

مِنْ قَبْلِهِ الرُّسُلُ ط وَ اُمُّهٗ صِدِّيْقَةٌ ط كَانَا

يَاْكُلٰنِ الطَّعَامَ ط اُنْظُرْ كَيْفَ نُبَيِّنُ لَهُمُ الْاٰيٰتِ

ثُمَّ انْظُرْ اَنّٰى يُؤْفَكُوْنَ ۝ قُلْ اَتَعْبُدُوْنَ مِنْ

دُوْنِ اللّٰهِ مَا لَا يَمْلِكُ لَكُمْ ضَرًّا وَّلَا نَفْعًا ط

وَ اللّٰهُ هُوَ السَّمِيْعُ الْعَلِيْمُ ۝ قُلْ يٰاَهْلَ

الْكِتٰبِ لَا تَغْلُوْا فِيْ دِيْنِكُمْ غَيْرَ الْحَقِّ وَلَا

تَتَّبِعُوْا اَهْوَآءَ قَوْمٍ قَدْ ضَلُّوْا مِنْ قَبْلُ وَ

اَضَلُّوْا كَثِيْرًا وَّ ضَلُّوْا عَنْ سَوَآءِ السَّبِيْلِ ۝

لُعِنَ الَّذِيْنَ كَفَرُوْا مِنْۢ بَنِيْۤ اِسْرَآءِيْلَ عَلٰى لِسَانِ

دَاوٗدَ وَ عِيْسَى ابْنِ مَرْيَمَ ط ذٰلِكَ بِمَا عَصَوْا وَّ

كَانُوْا يَعْتَدُوْنَ ۝ كَانُوْا لَا يَتَنَاهَوْنَ عَنْ مُّنْكَرٍ

فَعَلُوْهُ ط لَبِئْسَ مَا كَانُوْا يَفْعَلُوْنَ ۝ تَرٰى كَثِيْرًا

مِّنْهُمْ يَتَوَلَّوْنَ الَّذِيْنَ كَفَرُوْا ط لَبِئْسَ مَا قَدَّمَتْ

لَهُمْ اَنْفُسُهُمْ اَنْ سَخِطَ اللّٰهُ عَلَيْهِمْ وَ فِى

الْعَذَابِ هُمْ خٰلِدُوْنَ ۝ وَلَوْ كَانُوْا يُؤْمِنُوْنَ بِاللّٰهِ

وَالنَّبِيِّ وَمَاۤ اُنْزِلَ اِلَيْهِ مَا اتَّخَذُوْهُمْ اَوْلِيَآءَ

Religious extremism is condemned: using religion for personal prejudices is evil.

227

⁷³ *Likewise those who say,* "Allah is one of three," have committed an act of disbelief. There is no god apart from the One God. If they don't stop saying what they say, the disbelievers among them will be severely punished. ⁷⁴ Why don't they repent before Allah and seek His forgiveness? Allah is Forgiving, Most Kind.

Isa was a Messenger

⁷⁵ The Messiah son of Maryam was a messenger, like the many messengers who went before him, and his mother was a truthful woman; both ate like other humans. See how We explain Our signs to them, and look how they ignore the truth? ⁷⁶ Say: "Why, instead of worshipping Allah, do you worship what can neither help nor harm you?" Allah is the Hearer, the Knower. ⁷⁷ Say: "People of The Book, don't go beyond the bounds of truth in your religion, and don't follow the whims of people who went astray before you, misleading many others, themselves wandering far off the straight path."

Not challenging evil turned some Jews into disbelievers

⁷⁸ The disbelievers among the Israelites were cursed by Dawud and Isa, son of Maryam, because they were disobedient and went beyond the limits of the Torah: ⁷⁹ they didn't condemn wrong in their society. They were wretched! ⁸⁰ You will see many of them seeking the protection of disbelievers. How wretched is what they've stored for themselves, inviting Allah's wrath and punishment forever!

وَلٰكِنَّ كَثِيْرًا مِّنْهُمْ فٰسِقُوْنَ ۞ لَتَجِدَنَّ اَشَدَّ

النَّاسِ عَدَاوَةً لِّلَّذِيْنَ اٰمَنُوا الْيَهُوْدَ وَالَّذِيْنَ

اَشْرَكُوْا ۚ وَلَتَجِدَنَّ اَقْرَبَهُمْ مَّوَدَّةً لِّلَّذِيْنَ اٰمَنُوا

الَّذِيْنَ قَالُوْۤا اِنَّا نَصٰرٰى ؕ ذٰلِكَ بِاَنَّ مِنْهُمْ

قِسِّيْسِيْنَ وَ رُهْبَانًا وَّ اَنَّهُمْ لَا يَسْتَكْبِرُوْنَ ۞

وَ اِذَا سَمِعُوْا مَاۤ اُنْزِلَ اِلَى الرَّسُوْلِ تَرٰى اَعْيُنَهُمْ

تَفِيْضُ مِنَ الدَّمْعِ مِمَّا عَرَفُوْا مِنَ الْحَقِّ ۚ يَقُوْلُوْنَ

رَبَّنَاۤ اٰمَنَّا فَاكْتُبْنَا مَعَ الشّٰهِدِيْنَ ۞ وَمَا لَنَا

لَا نُؤْمِنُ بِاللّٰهِ وَمَا جَآءَنَا مِنَ الْحَقِّ ۙ وَنَطْمَعُ اَنْ

يُّدْخِلَنَا رَبُّنَا مَعَ الْقَوْمِ الصّٰلِحِيْنَ ۞ فَاَثَابَهُمُ اللّٰهُ

بِمَا قَالُوْا جَنّٰتٍ تَجْرِيْ مِنْ تَحْتِهَا الْاَنْهٰرُ خٰلِدِيْنَ

فِيْهَا ؕ وَ ذٰلِكَ جَزَآءُ الْمُحْسِنِيْنَ ۞ وَالَّذِيْنَ كَفَرُوْا

وَكَذَّبُوْا بِاٰيٰتِنَاۤ اُولٰٓئِكَ اَصْحٰبُ الْجَحِيْمِ ۞ يٰۤاَيُّهَا

الَّذِيْنَ اٰمَنُوْا لَا تُحَرِّمُوْا طَيِّبٰتِ مَاۤ اَحَلَّ اللّٰهُ

لَكُمْ وَلَا تَعْتَدُوْا ؕ اِنَّ اللّٰهَ لَا يُحِبُّ الْمُعْتَدِيْنَ ۞

وَ كُلُوْا مِمَّا رَزَقَكُمُ اللّٰهُ حَلٰلًا طَيِّبًا ۪ وَّ اتَّقُوا

اللّٰهَ الَّذِيْۤ اَنْتُمْ بِه مُؤْمِنُوْنَ ۞ لَا يُؤَاخِذُكُمُ

اللّٰهُ بِاللَّغْوِ فِيْۤ اَيْمَانِكُمْ وَلٰكِنْ يُّؤَاخِذُكُمْ بِمَا

عَقَّدْتُّمُ الْاَيْمَانَ ۚ فَكَفَّارَتُه اِطْعَامُ عَشَرَةِ

مَسٰكِيْنَ مِنْ اَوْسَطِ مَا تُطْعِمُوْنَ اَهْلِيْكُمْ اَوْ

Don't rattle off pointless oaths; take oaths seriously and fulfil them.

229

81 If they had believed in Allah, the Prophet and what was revealed to him, and hadn't taken the disbelievers as allies! Alas most of them are shameless sinners.

The Christians are most friendly to Muslims

82 Of all the people, you will find the most hostile to the believers are some Jews and idolaters,ᵃ and you will find the nearest and most affectionate to the believers are those who say, "We are Christians" because among them are priests and monks who are not arrogant. 83 When they hear what's revealed to the Messenger, you'll see their eyes well up with tears as they recognise its truth, saying, "Our Lord, we believe, so count us among the witnesses. 84 Why shouldn't we believe in Allah and what came to us of the truth, and why shouldn't we long for our Lord to join us with the righteous?" 85 So may Allah reward them for what they have said, with gardens under which rivers flow, to live there forever: that is the reward of the righteous! 86 Those who disbelieve and deny Our signs are the prisoners of Hell.

Do not make life difficult for yourselves

87 Believers, don't declare unlawful healthy foods made lawful by Allah, and don't go beyond the limits set by Him; Allah dislikes those who go beyond the limits. 88 Eat the lawful and healthy food that He has provided you, and be mindful of Allah who you believe.

Penalty for breaking an oath

89 Allah won't take you to task over oaths you make thoughtlessly, however, He will take you to task over any contracts that you seal with solemn oaths. The atonement for the breaking of oaths is: feed ten needy people the same food as you would typically feed your family; clothe them, or free a slave. Whoever hasn't the means to do this should fast for three days. That is the atonement for breaking oaths that you have sworn, so keep your oaths. This is how Allah explains His verses so that you might be grateful.

ᵃ The "al" definite article of "al-Yahood" is not "al" of *Jinssiya*, inclusive of all Jews but can also refer to a specific group mentioned here, the Jews of Madinah.

كِسْوَتُهُمْ اَوْ تَحْرِيْرُ رَقَبَةٍ ۚ فَمَنْ لَّمْ يَجِدْ فَصِيَامُ

ثَلٰثَةِ اَيَّامٍ ۗ ذٰلِكَ كَفَّارَةُ اَيْمَانِكُمْ اِذَا حَلَفْتُمْ ۗ وَ

احْفَظُوْۤا اَيْمَانَكُمْ ۗ كَذٰلِكَ يُبَيِّنُ اللّٰهُ لَكُمْ اٰيٰتِهٖ

لَعَلَّكُمْ تَشْكُرُوْنَ ۝ يٰۤاَيُّهَا الَّذِيْنَ اٰمَنُوْۤا اِنَّمَا

الْخَمْرُ وَالْمَيْسِرُ وَالْاَنْصَابُ وَالْاَزْلَامُ رِجْسٌ مِّنْ

عَمَلِ الشَّيْطٰنِ فَاجْتَنِبُوْهُ لَعَلَّكُمْ تُفْلِحُوْنَ ۝ اِنَّمَا

يُرِيْدُ الشَّيْطٰنُ اَنْ يُّوْقِعَ بَيْنَكُمُ الْعَدَاوَةَ وَالْبَغْضَآءَ

فِى الْخَمْرِ وَالْمَيْسِرِ وَيَصُدَّكُمْ عَنْ ذِكْرِ اللّٰهِ وَ

عَنِ الصَّلٰوةِ ۚ فَهَلْ اَنْتُمْ مُّنْتَهُوْنَ ۝ وَاَطِيْعُوا

اللّٰهَ وَاَطِيْعُوا الرَّسُوْلَ وَاحْذَرُوْا ۚ فَاِنْ تَوَلَّيْتُمْ

فَاعْلَمُوْۤا اَنَّمَا عَلٰى رَسُوْلِنَا الْبَلٰغُ الْمُبِيْنُ ۝ لَيْسَ

عَلَى الَّذِيْنَ اٰمَنُوْا وَعَمِلُوا الصّٰلِحٰتِ جُنَاحٌ فِيْمَا

طَعِمُوْۤا اِذَا مَا اتَّقَوْا وَّاٰمَنُوْا وَعَمِلُوا الصّٰلِحٰتِ ثُمَّ

اتَّقَوْا وَّاٰمَنُوْا ثُمَّ اتَّقَوْا وَّاَحْسَنُوْا ۗ وَاللّٰهُ يُحِبُّ

الْمُحْسِنِيْنَ ۝ يٰۤاَيُّهَا الَّذِيْنَ اٰمَنُوْا لَيَبْلُوَنَّكُمُ اللّٰهُ

بِشَىْءٍ مِّنَ الصَّيْدِ تَنَالُهٗۤ اَيْدِيْكُمْ وَرِمَاحُكُمْ لِيَعْلَمَ

اللّٰهُ مَنْ يَّخَافُهٗ بِالْغَيْبِ ۚ فَمَنِ اعْتَدٰى بَعْدَ ذٰلِكَ

فَلَهٗ عَذَابٌ اَلِيْمٌ ۝ يٰۤاَيُّهَا الَّذِيْنَ اٰمَنُوْا لَا تَقْتُلُوا

الصَّيْدَ وَاَنْتُمْ حُرُمٌ ۗ وَمَنْ قَتَلَهٗ مِنْكُمْ مُّتَعَمِّدًا

فَجَزَآءٌ مِّثْلُ مَا قَتَلَ مِنَ النَّعَمِ يَحْكُمُ بِهٖ ذَوَا عَدْلٍ

Satan uses alcohol and gambling to spread evil and immorality.

ع
۱۲
۲

231

Intoxicants and gambling are unlawful

⁹⁰ Believers, wine,ᵃ gambling by drawing lots, the use of pagan sacrificial altars, or foretelling the future with arrows are filthy works of Satan; reject them so that you may succeed in life. ⁹¹ Satan wishes to sow enmity and hatred between you using wine and gambling, and to divert you from the remembrance of Allah and performance of the prayer. So, won't you stop? ⁹² Obey Allah and the Messenger, and beware. If you turn away that will be bad, you know Our Messenger's duty is to deliver the message clearly. ⁹³ The believers who do righteous deeds shouldn't be blamed for what they consumed in the past, so long as they are mindful believers, doing righteous deeds, and thereafter they continue to be mindful and to believe in Allah, and now they are still mindful and striving for perfection. Allah loves the righteous.

Pilgrims should not hunt

⁹⁴ Believers, Allah will test you by bringing the animals you hunt within reach of your hands and spears, so Allah marks out whoever fears Him without ever having seen Him; so whoever after this warning goes beyond the limits set by Allah will suffer a painful punishment.

ᵃ Wine is specifically mentioned, but the Sunnah mentions anything that intoxicates is haram to consume – or trade in – including narcotics, drugs and alcoholic drinks. The sad fact that these vices are now rampant in our society demands that we must practise these teachings.

مِنْكُمْ هَدْيًا بَالِغَ الْكَعْبَةِ اَوْ كَفَّارَةٌ طَعَامُ مَسٰكِيْنَ

اَوْ عَدْلُ ذٰلِكَ صِيَامًا لِّيَذُوْقَ وَبَالَ اَمْرِهٖ ؕ عَفَا

اللّٰهُ عَمَّا سَلَفَ ؕ وَمَنْ عَادَ فَيَنْتَقِمُ اللّٰهُ مِنْهُ ؕ

وَاللّٰهُ عَزِيْزٌ ذُو انْتِقَامٍ ۝ اُحِلَّ لَكُمْ صَيْدُ الْبَحْرِ

وَطَعَامُهٗ مَتَاعًا لَّكُمْ وَلِلسَّيَّارَةِ ۚ وَحُرِّمَ عَلَيْكُمْ

صَيْدُ الْبَرِّ مَا دُمْتُمْ حُرُمًا ؕ وَاتَّقُوا اللّٰهَ الَّذِيْٓ

اِلَيْهِ تُحْشَرُوْنَ ۝ جَعَلَ اللّٰهُ الْكَعْبَةَ الْبَيْتَ

الْحَرَامَ قِيٰمًا لِّلنَّاسِ وَالشَّهْرَ الْحَرَامَ وَالْهَدْيَ

وَالْقَلَآئِدَ ؕ ذٰلِكَ لِتَعْلَمُوْٓا اَنَّ اللّٰهَ يَعْلَمُ مَا فِي

السَّمٰوٰتِ وَمَا فِي الْاَرْضِ وَاَنَّ اللّٰهَ بِكُلِّ شَيْءٍ

عَلِيْمٌ ۝ اِعْلَمُوْٓا اَنَّ اللّٰهَ شَدِيْدُ الْعِقَابِ وَاَنَّ اللّٰهَ

غَفُوْرٌ رَّحِيْمٌ ۝ مَا عَلَى الرَّسُوْلِ اِلَّا الْبَلٰغُ ؕ وَاللّٰهُ

يَعْلَمُ مَا تُبْدُوْنَ وَمَا تَكْتُمُوْنَ ۝ قُلْ لَّا يَسْتَوِي

الْخَبِيْثُ وَالطَّيِّبُ وَلَوْ اَعْجَبَكَ كَثْرَةُ الْخَبِيْثِ ۚ فَاتَّقُوا

اللّٰهَ يٰٓاُولِي الْاَلْبَابِ لَعَلَّكُمْ تُفْلِحُوْنَ ۝ يٰٓاَيُّهَا

الَّذِيْنَ اٰمَنُوْا لَا تَسْئَلُوْا عَنْ اَشْيَآءَ اِنْ تُبْدَ لَكُمْ

تَسُؤْكُمْ ۚ وَاِنْ تَسْئَلُوْا عَنْهَا حِيْنَ يُنَزَّلُ الْقُرْاٰنُ

تُبْدَ لَكُمْ ؕ عَفَا اللّٰهُ عَنْهَا ؕ وَاللّٰهُ غَفُوْرٌ حَلِيْمٌ ۝ قَدْ

سَاَلَهَا قَوْمٌ مِّنْ قَبْلِكُمْ ثُمَّ اَصْبَحُوْا بِهَا كٰفِرِيْنَ ۝

مَا جَعَلَ اللّٰهُ مِنْ بَحِيْرَةٍ وَّلَا سَآئِبَةٍ وَّلَا وَصِيْلَةٍ

Religion is taught with reasoning, religion is spread gently and not forced on people.

۱۳
ع
۳

⁹⁵ Believers, don't hunt and kill animals while you are in the sanctified state of pilgrims.^a The penalty for killing an animal intentionally is: sacrifice a livestock animal near the Kaaba that is judged to be equivalent by two just men; atone by feeding the needy or fast an equivalent number of days to realise the seriousness of his action. Allah has pardoned what happened in the past, but whoever transgresses from now on, Allah will punish him. Allah is the Almighty, the Avenger. ⁹⁶ Catching fish from the sea and eating it are made lawful for your benefit and for the traveller. However, you are forbidden to hunt on land while you are in the sanctified state of the pilgrim; so be mindful of Allah, before Whom you will be gathered. ⁹⁷ Allah has made the Kaaba a sacred house,^b built for the benefit of humanity, along with the sacred months, and the sacrificial and garlanded animals. This is so you know Allah has knowledge of all that is in the Heavens and on Earth. Allah knows everything.

The Messenger ﷺ delivers the message but doesn't force it on others

⁹⁸ You must realise that Allah is severe in His punishment, nevertheless Forgiving, Kind. ⁹⁹ The Messenger's duty is to convey the message, Allah knows well what you reveal and what you conceal. ¹⁰⁰ Say: "The good and bad are not the same, though the abundance of the bad will surprise you. So be mindful of Allah, you who are understanding, so you may succeed."

Don't ask too many questions

¹⁰¹ Believers, don't ask too many questions, if they were answered they would cause you difficulty, and if you ask while the Quran is being revealed they will be made clear to you. Allah has kept silence^c about them. Allah is Forgiving, Gentle. ¹⁰² People before you asked such questions *and when they were answered*, then they denied it.

---

^a The sanctified state (*ihram*) of a Muslim pilgrim is two pieces of unsewn white cloth. When a pilgrim enters that state, it becomes unlawful to do certain things like hunting. See also *Surat Al-Baqarah*: 196–203.

^b The Kaaba is the cube-shaped building in Makkah, and is mentioned in *Surat Al 'Imran*: 96 as the oldest sanctuary on Earth, a holy place.

^c Literally, "Allah has passed over them." The story of the cow in *Surat Al-Baqarah*: 67–71 is an example of what can happen when people ask too many questions.

وَّلَا حَامٍ ۙ وَّلٰكِنَّ الَّذِيْنَ كَفَرُوْا يَفْتَرُوْنَ عَلَى اللّٰهِ الْكَذِبَ ؕ وَاَكْثَرُهُمْ لَا يَعْقِلُوْنَ ۝ وَاِذَا قِيْلَ لَهُمْ تَعَالَوْا اِلٰى مَاۤ اَنْزَلَ اللّٰهُ وَاِلَى الرَّسُوْلِ قَالُوْا حَسْبُنَا مَا وَجَدْنَا عَلَيْهِ اٰبَآءَنَا ؕ اَوَلَوْ كَانَ اٰبَآؤُهُمْ لَا يَعْلَمُوْنَ شَيْئًا وَّلَا يَهْتَدُوْنَ ۝ يٰۤاَيُّهَا الَّذِيْنَ اٰمَنُوْا عَلَيْكُمْ اَنْفُسَكُمْ ۚ لَا يَضُرُّكُمْ مَّنْ ضَلَّ اِذَا اهْتَدَيْتُمْ ؕ اِلَى اللّٰهِ مَرْجِعُكُمْ جَمِيْعًا فَيُنَبِّئُكُمْ بِمَا كُنْتُمْ تَعْمَلُوْنَ ۝ يٰۤاَيُّهَا الَّذِيْنَ اٰمَنُوْا شَهَادَةُ بَيْنِكُمْ اِذَا حَضَرَ اَحَدَكُمُ الْمَوْتُ حِيْنَ الْوَصِيَّةِ اثْنٰنِ ذَوَا عَدْلٍ مِّنْكُمْ اَوْ اٰخَرٰنِ مِنْ غَيْرِكُمْ اِنْ اَنْتُمْ ضَرَبْتُمْ فِى الْاَرْضِ فَاَصَابَتْكُمْ مُّصِيْبَةُ الْمَوْتِ ؕ تَحْبِسُوْنَهُمَا مِنْۢ بَعْدِ الصَّلٰوةِ فَيُقْسِمٰنِ بِاللّٰهِ اِنِ ارْتَبْتُمْ لَا نَشْتَرِيْ بِهٖ ثَمَنًا وَّلَوْ كَانَ ذَا قُرْبٰى ۙ وَلَا نَكْتُمُ شَهَادَةَ اللّٰهِ اِنَّاۤ اِذًا لَّمِنَ الْاٰثِمِيْنَ ۝ فَاِنْ عُثِرَ عَلٰۤى اَنَّهُمَا اسْتَحَقَّاۤ اِثْمًا فَاٰخَرٰنِ يَقُوْمٰنِ مَقَامَهُمَا مِنَ الَّذِيْنَ اسْتَحَقَّ عَلَيْهِمُ الْاَوْلَيٰنِ فَيُقْسِمٰنِ بِاللّٰهِ لَشَهَادَتُنَاۤ اَحَقُّ مِنْ شَهَادَتِهِمَا وَمَا اعْتَدَيْنَا ۖؗ اِنَّاۤ اِذًا لَّمِنَ الظّٰلِمِيْنَ ۝ ذٰلِكَ اَدْنٰۤى اَنْ يَّاْتُوْا بِالشَّهَادَةِ عَلٰى وَجْهِهَاۤ اَوْ يَخَافُوْۤا اَنْ تُرَدَّ اَيْمَانٌۢ بَعْدَ اَيْمَانِهِمْ ؕ وَاتَّقُوا اللّٰهَ وَاسْمَعُوْا ؕ وَاللّٰهُ لَا يَهْدِى الْقَوْمَ

You are personally responsible for your lives, others can't do much about you! An empowering message.

235

Rid yourselves of the superstitions of past generations

[103] Allah didn't order the veneration of: camels whose ears are split before being turned loose; she-camels which roam free; camels dedicated to idols that can't be slaughtered; and camels which mustn't be mounted;[a] rather it was the disbelievers who invented lies about Allah, and most of them lack the power of reason. [104] When they are told: "Come closer to what Allah has revealed and to His Messenger," they say, "What we found our forefathers practising is enough," yet their forefathers knew nothing and had no guidance. [105] Believers, you are responsible for yourselves. Those who are misguided can't harm you if you stay on the right path. You will all return to Allah, and He will tell you what you did.

The appointing of witnesses for one's last will

[106] Believers, when death approaches you, get two just persons to be witnesses to your last will and testament. If you are on a journey when the pangs of death strike, take any two witnesses from another tribe. Keep the two witnesses back after the prayer and, should you have any doubts, let them both swear by Allah: "We will not sell the testimony for any price, even if a close relative is involved, nor will we hide Allah's testimony, in that case, we would be sinful." [107] If it turns out that the two witnesses are judged guilty of a sin of perjury, then let two other witnesses take their place from amongst those whose right has been taken away, then let them both swear by Allah: "Our testimony is more truthful then theirs, and we haven't transgressed, in that case, we would be wrongdoers." [108] It's more fitting they produce their testimony in this way or stand in fear that the previous oaths be upheld after they had pronounced their oaths. Be mindful of Allah and listen carefully. Allah does not guide the disobedient.

---

[a] Names of four types of animals that pagans dedicated to their idols: *bahira*, a she-camel with a cleft ear; *sa'iba*, an animal left to roam; *wasila*, an animal which must not be slaughtered; and *hami*, a camel forbidden for riding. These superstitious practises are condemned.

الْفَسِقِينَ ۝ يَوْمَ يَجْمَعُ اللهُ الرُّسُلَ فَيَقُولُ مَاذَآ

اُجِبْتُمْ ۖ قَالُوا لَا عِلْمَ لَنَا ۖ اِنَّكَ اَنْتَ عَلَّامُ الْغُيُوبِ ۝

اِذْ قَالَ اللهُ يَعِيسَى ابْنَ مَرْيَمَ اذْكُرْ نِعْمَتِي

عَلَيْكَ وَعَلَى وَالِدَتِكَ ۘ اِذْ اَيَّدْتُّكَ بِرُوحِ الْقُدُسِ ۙ

تُكَلِّمُ النَّاسَ فِي الْمَهْدِ وَكَهْلًا ۚ وَاِذْ عَلَّمْتُكَ

الْكِتَابَ وَالْحِكْمَةَ وَالتَّوْرَاةَ وَالْاِنْجِيلَ ۚ وَاِذْ تَخْلُقُ

مِنَ الطِّينِ كَهَيْئَةِ الطَّيْرِ بِاِذْنِي فَتَنْفُخُ فِيهَا

فَتَكُونُ طَيْرًا بِاِذْنِي وَتُبْرِئُ الْاَكْمَهَ وَالْاَبْرَصَ

بِاِذْنِي ۚ وَاِذْ تُخْرِجُ الْمَوْتَى بِاِذْنِي ۚ وَاِذْ كَفَفْتُ

بَنِي اِسْرَآءِيلَ عَنْكَ اِذْ جِئْتَهُمْ بِالْبَيِّنَاتِ فَقَالَ

الَّذِينَ كَفَرُوا مِنْهُمْ اِنْ هٰذَآ اِلَّا سِحْرٌ مُبِينٌ ۝ وَاِذْ

اَوْحَيْتُ اِلَى الْحَوَارِيِّنَ اَنْ اٰمِنُوا بِي وَبِرَسُولِي ۚ قَالُوا

اٰمَنَّا وَاشْهَدْ بِاَنَّنَا مُسْلِمُونَ ۝ اِذْ قَالَ الْحَوَارِيُّونَ

يَعِيسَى ابْنَ مَرْيَمَ هَلْ يَسْتَطِيعُ رَبُّكَ اَنْ يُنَزِّلَ

عَلَيْنَا مَآئِدَةً مِّنَ السَّمَآءِ ۖ قَالَ اتَّقُوا اللهَ اِنْ كُنْتُمْ

مُؤْمِنِينَ ۝ قَالُوا نُرِيدُ اَنْ نَّاكُلَ مِنْهَا وَتَطْمَئِنَّ

قُلُوبُنَا وَنَعْلَمَ اَنْ قَدْ صَدَقْتَنَا وَنَكُونَ عَلَيْهَا مِنَ

الشَّاهِدِينَ ۝ قَالَ عِيسَى ابْنُ مَرْيَمَ اللّٰهُمَّ رَبَّنَآ

اَنْزِلْ عَلَيْنَا مَآئِدَةً مِّنَ السَّمَآءِ تَكُونُ لَنَا عِيدًا

لِّاَوَّلِنَا وَاٰخِرِنَا وَاٰيَةً مِّنْكَ ۖ وَارْزُقْنَا وَاَنْتَ خَيْرُ

The Prophet Isa is praised for his marvellous miracles and spiritual teachings.

237

The miracles of Prophet Isa

¹⁰⁹On the day when Allah will gather His messengers and ask, "What response did you get?"ᵃ They will say, "We have no knowledge. You are the Knower of the unseen realms." ¹¹⁰Then Allah will ask, "Isa, son of Maryam, do you remember My favours on you and your mother: I helped you with the Holy Spiritᵇ, so you could speak to people when you were in the cradle and preach when you were a young man. I taught you the Book, wisdom, Torah and the Gospel, and gave you miracles: you made clay birds and blew into them so they flew like live birds; you healed the blind and the lepers, and with My permission, you raised the dead from their graves. And remember I protected you from the attacks of Israelites when you preached to them with clear signs, and their disbelievers said, "This is magic!"

The miracle of Isa; feeding of a large crowd

¹¹¹Once I inspired the disciples "Believe in Me and My Messenger," they said, "We believe, and bear witness we have submitted ourselves to the will of Allah." ¹¹²The disciples said: "Isa, son of Maryam, can Your Lord send down from Heaven a table laden with food?" Isa said: "Fear Allah, if you are believers." ¹¹³They said, "We want to eat from it for reassurance, to know for certain that you have told us the truth, and we will be the witnesses of this miracle." ¹¹⁴Isa, son of Maryam, prayed: "God, Our Lord, send down from Heaven a table laden with food, which becomes a festival for the believers of past and future,ᶜ and a sign from You, and provide for us, for You are the Best Provider."ᵈ

ᵃ Meaning, "What response did you get to your preaching?"
ᵇ "Ruh al-Quds" refers to the Angel Jibreel.
ᶜ Literally: 'for the first and last of us.'
ᵈ This could be the story mentioned in Mark 6:31, dubbed as 'The miracle of feeding the five thousand.'

الرّزِقِيْنَ ۝ قَالَ اللّٰهُ اِنِّىْ مُنَزِّلُهَا عَلَيْكُمْ ۚ فَمَنْ

يَّكْفُرْ بَعْدُ مِنْكُمْ فَاِنِّىْۤ اُعَذِّبُهُ عَذَابًا لَّاۤ اُعَذِّبُهٗۤ

اَحَدًا مِّنَ الْعٰلَمِيْنَ ۝ وَاِذْ قَالَ اللّٰهُ يٰعِيْسَى

ابْنَ مَرْيَمَ ءَاَنْتَ قُلْتَ لِلنَّاسِ اتَّخِذُوْنِىْ وَاُمِّىَ

اِلٰهَيْنِ مِنْ دُوْنِ اللّٰهِ ۚ قَالَ سُبْحٰنَكَ مَا يَكُوْنُ لِىْۤ

اَنْ اَقُوْلَ مَا لَيْسَ لِىْ ۛ بِحَقٍّ ۛ اِنْ كُنْتُ قُلْتُهٗ فَقَدْ

عَلِمْتَهٗ ۚ تَعْلَمُ مَا فِىْ نَفْسِىْ وَلَاۤ اَعْلَمُ مَا فِىْ نَفْسِكَ ۚ

اِنَّكَ اَنْتَ عَلَّامُ الْغُيُوْبِ ۝ مَا قُلْتُ لَهُمْ اِلَّا مَاۤ

Isa denies he ever claimed to be God.

اَمَرْتَنِىْ بِهٖۤ اَنِ اعْبُدُوا اللّٰهَ رَبِّىْ وَرَبَّكُمْ ۚ وَكُنْتُ

عَلَيْهِمْ شَهِيْدًا مَّا دُمْتُ فِيْهِمْ ۚ فَلَمَّا تَوَفَّيْتَنِىْ كُنْتَ

اَنْتَ الرَّقِيْبَ عَلَيْهِمْ ۚ وَاَنْتَ عَلٰى كُلِّ شَىْءٍ شَهِيْدٌ ۝

اِنْ تُعَذِّبْهُمْ فَاِنَّهُمْ عِبَادُكَ ۚ وَاِنْ تَغْفِرْ لَهُمْ فَاِنَّكَ

اَنْتَ الْعَزِيْزُ الْحَكِيْمُ ۝ قَالَ اللّٰهُ هٰذَا يَوْمُ يَنْفَعُ

الصّٰدِقِيْنَ صِدْقُهُمْ ۚ لَهُمْ جَنّٰتٌ تَجْرِىْ مِنْ تَحْتِهَا

الْاَنْهٰرُ خٰلِدِيْنَ فِيْهَاۤ اَبَدًا ۚ رَضِىَ اللّٰهُ عَنْهُمْ وَرَضُوْا

عَنْهُ ۚ ذٰلِكَ الْفَوْزُ الْعَظِيْمُ ۝ لِلّٰهِ مُلْكُ السَّمٰوٰتِ وَ

الْاَرْضِ وَمَا فِيْهِنَّ ۚ وَهُوَ عَلٰى كُلِّ شَىْءٍ قَدِيْرٌ ۝

239

[115] Allah said, "I will send it down for you. Whoever denies My favour after this miracle, I will punish him with a punishment that no creature has ever been punished with."

Prophet Isa a witness against disbelievers

[116] On the Day of Judgement, Allah will say: "Isa son of Maryam, did you tell people, 'Take me and my mother as two gods besides Allah'?" He will say: "Glory be to you! How could I say something that I had no right to say, had I said it, You would know. You know what's in my innermost being, and I don't know what is in Yours. You are the Knower of the unseen realms. [117] I only told them what You commanded me to say: 'Worship Allah, my Lord and Your Lord,' I was a witness all the time I live amidst them. Then, when You took me to Yourself, it was You Who were the Guardian over them. You Witness everything. [118] If You punish them, they're Your servants, and if You forgive them, You are the Almighty, Wise." [119] Allah said, "This day the truth of the truthful will benefit them; they will be in gardens under which rivers flow, living there forever. Allah is well pleased with them, and they are pleased with Him." That is the glorious victory. [120] Control of the Heavens, the Earth, and whatever lies within them belongs to Allah, and He has power over all things.

6. Surat Al-An'am

The Cattle

A late Makkan surat revealed in its entirety on a single occasion, at a time of severe tension between the Muslims and the idolaters. Ibn Abbas said that some Makkans told the Prophet ﷺ: "We shall not believe until you bring us a book which we can touch and accompanied by the angels." (Al-Qurtubi). The surat presents powerful arguments supporting beliefs in *Tawhid, Risalah,* and *Akhirah;* typical subject matter of Makkan surats, unlike the Madinan surats that deal with law, worship and the organization of the community. The title, *Al-An'am,* "the Cattle", is derived from several references to the idolaters' superstitious practises of dedicating animals to their idols.

The Quran adopts five methods of reasoning to prove the creative power of Allah; a way of putting forward propositions about the existence of Allah, and His dominance:

1. Self-evident truths: these maxims are pithy statements of truth: "This worldly life is a sport and an amusement, the home in the Hereafter is far better for mindful people" (32). Is there a doubt about the fleeting and temporary nature of this life?

2. The Nature: "Allah cleaves the seed and the fruit-stone; He brings the living from the dead and the dead from the living" (95). Ibrahim uses the example of celestial bodies, that they aren't gods but Allah's creation. How can one fail to see the hand of Allah in the vast universe?

3. Human history: the stories of the prophets are frequent lines of evidence that the Quran presents to support its teachings (74–110). Prophet Ibrahim is instructed: "Worship Allah, there is no God beside Him." Steering stubborn and materialistic people to Allah by drawing their attention to the helplessness and mechanical nature of their gods. He concludes: "I turn my face to Him Who created the Heavens and the Earth; I am dedicated to Him alone and I am not one of the idolaters" (79).

4. Human conscience: The Quran appeals to human goodness and kindness to awaken the conscience, and frequently condemns human vices of greed, arrogance, and anger.

5. Human interest: people are naturally inclined to knowing what benefits or harms them. The Quran repeatedly demonstrates how idols are incapable of inflicting harm or benefit. So, why would anyone worship idols? Shouldn't they worship their genuine benefactor and creator?

The surat opened with a powerful verse praising the creative power of Allah and criticising the idolaters for equating their idols with Him. It reminds the idolaters that its denial will land them into Hell, and that no matter how many miracles they see, they will not be convinced. The only remedy for stubbornness is submission. The Quran is a book of guidance; it reminds the idolaters that on Judgement Day they will regret their idolatry and will want to return to the world to do good.

The blessed Messenger ﷺ is reassured that the arrogance of the idolaters is disastrous. The safest policy is to be humble: knowing who you are, your strengths, weaknesses and purpose in life. Several tips are given to be humble: patience, keeping the company of righteous, reliance on Allah and having a deep knowledge of the greatness of Allah (74–90). The next section, until verse 104, provides powerful evidence for the resurrection.

Possible Reasons for Idolatry

The Quran explains the underlying cause of the idolaters' disbelief: they are close-minded. The Quran criticises them: stubborn and deaf, refusing to listen to the Prophet ﷺ, unwilling to pay attention to human reason. When the Prophet ﷺ pointed out their superstitious and illogical ways, they reacted by mocking him, and employed bully tactics to intimidate him. No miracle could convince them, since their hearts were inclined towards evil. Satan motivates them and makes their works look attractive to them (105–24). The next verse contrasts them with the believers, who are described as open-minded: "The person Allah wishes to guide, He opens his mind *to Islam*; and whomever He wishes to go astray, He closes his mind, as if he were struggling to climb skywards: by such means Allah *disgraces the disbelievers*" (125).

The purpose of this criticism is to prick the conscience of the disbelievers, to encourage them towards awareness of reality and bring them out of their delusion. So, the Quran in its guidance provided the following ten new Commandments: don't commit idolatry; care for parents; stop infanticide; avoid sinning openly and secretly; don't murder; look after orphans' wealth; weigh and measure things accurately; be just; fulfil the contract of Allah; and follow the straight path. The final advice: "He made you representatives on Earth... to test you with what He has given you" (165). The message is that human life is both precious and purposeful, so take it seriously!

The Makkah of seventh century is steeped in paganism; a human society that relishes in pride, power and pleasure. Set in opposition to Allah, He is pushed to the margins. In that sense Makkah wasn't too different from London, New York or Paris of today.

بِسْمِ اللهِ الرَّحْمٰنِ الرَّحِيْمِ

اَلْحَمْدُ لِلّٰهِ الَّذِىْ خَلَقَ السَّمٰوٰتِ وَالْأَرْضَ وَجَعَلَ الظُّلُمٰتِ وَالنُّوْرَ ۬ ثُمَّ الَّذِيْنَ كَفَرُوْا بِرَبِّهِمْ يَعْدِلُوْنَ ۝

هُوَ الَّذِىْ خَلَقَكُمْ مِّنْ طِيْنٍ ثُمَّ قَضٰى اَجَلًا ط وَ اَجَلٌ مُّسَمًّى عِنْدَهٗ ثُمَّ اَنْتُمْ تَمْتَرُوْنَ ۝

وَهُوَ اللهُ فِى السَّمٰوٰتِ وَفِى الْأَرْضِ ط يَعْلَمُ سِرَّكُمْ وَ جَهْرَكُمْ وَيَعْلَمُ مَا تَكْسِبُوْنَ ۝ وَمَا تَأْتِيْهِمْ مِّنْ اٰيَةٍ مِّنْ اٰيٰتِ رَبِّهِمْ اِلَّا كَانُوْا عَنْهَا مُعْرِضِيْنَ ۝

فَقَدْ كَذَّبُوْا بِالْحَقِّ لَمَّا جَآءَهُمْ ط فَسَوْفَ يَأْتِيْهِمْ اَنْۢبٰٓؤُا مَا كَانُوْا بِهٖ يَسْتَهْزِءُوْنَ ۝ اَلَمْ يَرَوْا كَمْ اَهْلَكْنَا مِنْ قَبْلِهِمْ مِّنْ قَرْنٍ مَّكَّنّٰهُمْ فِى الْأَرْضِ مَا لَمْ نُمَكِّنْ لَّكُمْ وَاَرْسَلْنَا السَّمَآءَ عَلَيْهِمْ مِّدْرَارًا ۪ وَّجَعَلْنَا الْأَنْهٰرَ تَجْرِىْ مِنْ تَحْتِهِمْ فَاَهْلَكْنٰهُمْ بِذُنُوْبِهِمْ وَاَنْشَأْنَا مِنْۢ بَعْدِهِمْ قَرْنًا اٰخَرِيْنَ ۝

وَلَوْ نَزَّلْنَا عَلَيْكَ كِتٰبًا فِىْ قِرْطَاسٍ فَلَمَسُوْهُ بِاَيْدِيْهِمْ لَقَالَ الَّذِيْنَ كَفَرُوْۤا اِنْ هٰذَاۤ اِلَّا سِحْرٌ مُّبِيْنٌ ۝ وَقَالُوْا لَوْلَاۤ اُنْزِلَ عَلَيْهِ مَلَكٌ ط وَلَوْ اَنْزَلْنَا مَلَكًا لَّقُضِىَ الْأَمْرُ ثُمَّ لَا يُنْظَرُوْنَ ۝ وَلَوْ جَعَلْنٰهُ مَلَكًا لَّجَعَلْنٰهُ رَجُلًا وَّلَلَبَسْنَا عَلَيْهِمْ مَّا

Have faith, praise and glorify the Lord of the universe. He is so near!

243

In the name of Allah, the Kind, the Caring

Evidence for the Power and might of Allah

¹ Praise be to Allah, Who created the Heavens and the Earth and made darkness and light; though the disbelievers hold up *others* as equal to their Lord. ² He created you from clay and fixed your lifespan, a lifespan *firmly* fixed by Him;ª but you still doubt. ³ He is Allah in the Heavens and on Earth. He knows your secrets and all that you reveal, and He knows all that you do.

Every civilisation that denied Allah perished

⁴ When a sign from their Lord comes they turn their backs on it, ⁵ denying the truth when it comes to them, *but* news of what they joked aboutᵇ will soon come to them. ⁶ Don't they realise We destroyed many previous generations, We gave them far more power in the land than We gave you, and how We sent abundant rain from the sky, making rivers flow. *Eventually,* We destroyed them for their sins, and raised up other people after them.

Miracles fail to convince the sceptics

⁷ Even if We sent down a book written on paperᶜ which they could touch with their hands, the disbelievers would say, "This is nothing but magic." ⁸ They said, "If only an angel would come down to him," if We were to send an angel, that would *only be to* decide *their fate* and they would have no more time after that. ⁹ Just as We could have made *the Messenger* an angel, We could equally have made *the angel appear* as a man, thus confusing them with their own attempt to create confusion.ᵈ

ª   "Fixed time" in the first instance refers to death, and the second time it refers to the Day of Judgement.
ᵇ   Irrefutable proof of the existence of the Resurrection, Judgement Day, and Hell.
ᶜ   Literally, "parchment" of leather.
ᵈ   This is because angels are ordinarily only visible at the time of our death.

يَلْبِسُونَ ۹ وَلَقَدِ اسْتُهْزِئَ بِرُسُلٍ مِّنْ قَبْلِكَ فَحَاقَ

بِالَّذِينَ سَخِرُوا مِنْهُم مَّا كَانُوا بِهِ يَسْتَهْزِءُونَ ۞

قُلْ سِيرُوا فِي الْأَرْضِ ثُمَّ انْظُرُوا كَيْفَ كَانَ عَاقِبَةُ

الْمُكَذِّبِينَ ۞ قُل لِّمَن مَّا فِي السَّمٰوٰتِ وَالْأَرْضِ ط

قُل لِلّٰهِ ط كَتَبَ عَلَىٰ نَفْسِهِ الرَّحْمَةَ ط لَيَجْمَعَنَّكُمْ اِلَىٰ

يَوْمِ الْقِيٰمَةِ لَا رَيْبَ فِيهِ ط اَلَّذِينَ خَسِرُوا اَنْفُسَهُمْ

فَهُمْ لَا يُؤْمِنُونَ ۞ وَلَهُ مَا سَكَنَ فِي الَّيْلِ وَالنَّهَارِ ط

وَهُوَ السَّمِيعُ الْعَلِيمُ ۞ قُلْ اَغَيْرَ اللّٰهِ اَتَّخِذُ وَلِيًّا

فَاطِرِ السَّمٰوٰتِ وَالْأَرْضِ وَهُوَ يُطْعِمُ وَلَا يُطْعَمُ ط

قُلْ اِنِّي اُمِرْتُ اَنْ اَكُونَ اَوَّلَ مَنْ اَسْلَمَ وَلَا

تَكُونَنَّ مِنَ الْمُشْرِكِينَ ۞ قُلْ اِنِّي اَخَافُ اِنْ

عَصَيْتُ رَبِّي عَذَابَ يَوْمٍ عَظِيمٍ ۞ مَن يُصْرَفْ

عَنْهُ يَوْمَئِذٍ فَقَدْ رَحِمَهُ ط وَذٰلِكَ الْفَوْزُ الْمُبِينُ ۞

وَاِنْ يَّمْسَسْكَ اللّٰهُ بِضُرٍّ فَلَا كَاشِفَ لَهُ اِلَّا هُوَ ط

وَاِنْ يَّمْسَسْكَ بِخَيْرٍ فَهُوَ عَلَىٰ كُلِّ شَيْءٍ قَدِيرٌ ۞

وَهُوَ الْقَاهِرُ فَوْقَ عِبَادِهِ ط وَهُوَ الْحَكِيمُ الْخَبِيرُ ۞

قُلْ اَيُّ شَيْءٍ اَكْبَرُ شَهَادَةً ط قُلِ اللّٰهُ شَهِيدٌ

بَيْنِي وَبَيْنَكُمْ ط وَاُوحِيَ اِلَيَّ هٰذَا الْقُرْآنُ لِاُنْذِرَكُمْ

بِهِ وَمَنْ بَلَغَ ط اَئِنَّكُمْ لَتَشْهَدُونَ اَنَّ مَعَ اللّٰهِ اٰلِهَةً

اُخْرَىٰ ط قُل لَّا اَشْهَدُ ط قُلْ اِنَّمَا هُوَ اِلٰهٌ وَّاحِدٌ

Allah is kind to everyone, al-Rahman: gave life, intelligence, guidance and ability.

¹⁰Messengers were mocked before you, and the very punishment they once mocked swept away those who poked fun. ¹¹Say: "Travel about the land and see what happened to the deniers." ¹²Say: "Who owns what's in the Heavens and Earth?" Say: *"Is it not* Allah? He has decreed that He will be kind.ᵃ Then He will gather you all on Judgement Day; in that, there is no doubt. Those who, *through wrong life choices*, have failed themselves will not believe. ¹³Anything that is living – be it during the night or the day – belongs to Him. He is the Hearer, the Knower.

Allah ultimately decides what He wills, so submit

¹⁴Say: "Should I take a protector beside Allah, the Creator of the Heavens and the Earth, Who feeds and is not fed?" Say: "I am commanded to be the first who submits and not to be among idolators." ¹⁵Say: "I fear the punishment of a mighty day if I disobeyed My Lord." ¹⁶Whoever escapes the *punishment* of that day, and is treated kindly; will have a clear victory. ¹⁷If Allah decides to punish you, no one can remove it except Him, and if He decides to benefit you, He has power over all things. ¹⁸He is the controller of His creatures, the Wise, the Aware.

The Oneness of Allah is self-evident

¹⁹Say: "Who could be the biggest witness?" Say: *"It is* Allah, a witness for you and me. This Quran has been revealed to me so I should warn you and anyone *else its message* reaches. Do you believe there are other gods beside Allah?" Say: "I won't bear witness *to that."* Say: "There's only One God, and I am not involved in what you associate *with Him."*

ᵃ Literally means, "He decreed kindness *as obligatory* on Himself." My translation expresses the idea that nothing can be imposed on Allah, other than by Himself. He is independent.

وَاِنَّنِيْ بَرِيْٓءٌ مِّمَّا تُشْرِكُوْنَ ۞ اَلَّذِيْنَ اٰتَيْنٰهُمُ الْكِتٰبَ يَعْرِفُوْنَهٗ كَمَا يَعْرِفُوْنَ اَبْنَآءَهُمْ ۚ اَلَّذِيْنَ خَسِرُوْٓا اَنْفُسَهُمْ فَهُمْ لَا يُؤْمِنُوْنَ ۞ وَمَنْ اَظْلَمُ مِمَّنِ افْتَرٰى عَلَى اللّٰهِ كَذِبًا اَوْ كَذَّبَ بِاٰيٰتِهٖ ؕ اِنَّهٗ لَا يُفْلِحُ الظّٰلِمُوْنَ ۞ وَيَوْمَ نَحْشُرُهُمْ جَمِيْعًا ثُمَّ نَقُوْلُ لِلَّذِيْنَ اَشْرَكُوْٓا اَيْنَ شُرَكَآؤُكُمُ الَّذِيْنَ كُنْتُمْ تَزْعُمُوْنَ ۞ ثُمَّ لَمْ تَكُنْ فِتْنَتُهُمْ اِلَّآ اَنْ قَالُوْا وَاللّٰهِ رَبِّنَا مَا كُنَّا مُشْرِكِيْنَ ۞ اُنْظُرْ كَيْفَ كَذَبُوْا عَلٰٓى اَنْفُسِهِمْ وَضَلَّ عَنْهُمْ مَّا كَانُوْا يَفْتَرُوْنَ ۞ وَمِنْهُمْ مَّنْ يَّسْتَمِعُ اِلَيْكَ ۚ وَجَعَلْنَا عَلٰى قُلُوْبِهِمْ اَكِنَّةً اَنْ يَّفْقَهُوْهُ وَفِيْٓ اٰذَانِهِمْ وَقْرًا ؕ وَاِنْ يَّرَوْا كُلَّ اٰيَةٍ لَّا يُؤْمِنُوْا بِهَا ؕ حَتّٰٓى اِذَا جَآءُوْكَ يُجَادِلُوْنَكَ يَقُوْلُ الَّذِيْنَ كَفَرُوْٓا اِنْ هٰذَآ اِلَّآ اَسَاطِيْرُ الْاَوَّلِيْنَ ۞ وَهُمْ يَنْهَوْنَ عَنْهُ وَيَنْـَٔوْنَ عَنْهُ ۚ وَاِنْ يُّهْلِكُوْنَ اِلَّآ اَنْفُسَهُمْ وَمَا يَشْعُرُوْنَ ۞ وَلَوْ تَرٰٓى اِذْ وُقِفُوْا عَلَى النَّارِ فَقَالُوْا يٰلَيْتَنَا نُرَدُّ وَلَا نُكَذِّبَ بِاٰيٰتِ رَبِّنَا وَنَكُوْنَ مِنَ الْمُؤْمِنِيْنَ ۞ بَلْ بَدَا لَهُمْ مَّا كَانُوْا يُخْفُوْنَ مِنْ قَبْلُ ؕ وَلَوْ رُدُّوْا لَعَادُوْا لِمَا نُهُوْا عَنْهُ وَاِنَّهُمْ لَكٰذِبُوْنَ ۞ وَقَالُوْٓا اِنْ هِيَ اِلَّا حَيَاتُنَا الدُّنْيَا وَمَا نَحْنُ بِمَبْعُوْثِيْنَ ۞ وَلَوْ تَرٰٓى اِذْ وُقِفُوْا عَلٰى رَبِّهِمْ ؕ

Disbelievers will regret they wasted their lives.

²⁰Those *previously* given the Book know this is true just as they know their own children. As for those who, *through their choices in life*, have failed, they will not believe. ²¹Who is a worst wrongdoer than the one who invents lies about Allah and denies His signs? Those who have failed themselves will not believe.

The idolaters' excuses will fail them on Judgement Day

²²The day We gather them all, We shall say to idolaters, "Where are the partners you claimed? ²³In their confused state they will say, "By Allah, Our Lord, we never worshipped false gods." ²⁴Look how they proved themselves liars, and how they deserted those they invented. ²⁵Some hear you, but We have placed a veil over their hearts so they fail to understand *the Quran*, and there is deafness in their ears.ᵃ Were they to see all the signs, they still would not believe. When they come to argue with you, the disbelievers say, "These are only the myths of the ancients," ²⁶they prevent others from *listening to* it and themselves, walk away. They are unwittingly destroying themselves.

Admission of wasted life

²⁷If you could see them *on Judgement Day* when they stand *staring at* the Fire; they will say, "If only we could be returned and, instead of denying Our Lord's signs, become believers." ²⁸No way! What they once used to hide will appear before them. Suppose they were returned, they would *simply* go back to doing what they had been forbidden; they are liars. ²⁹They say, "Only our worldly life exists. We won't be brought back to life."

ᵃ This spiritual blindness and deafness is a result of their attitude and stubbornness. They have chosen to shut-off the faculty of believing, the Lord leaves them in their state of delusion.

قَالَ أَلَيْسَ هٰذَا بِالْحَقِّ ۚ قَالُوا بَلٰى وَرَبِّنَا ۚ قَالَ فَذُوقُوا الْعَذَابَ بِمَا كُنْتُمْ تَكْفُرُونَ ۞ قَدْ خَسِرَ الَّذِينَ كَذَّبُوا بِلِقَآءِ اللهِ ۖ حَتّٰى إِذَا جَآءَتْهُمُ السَّاعَةُ بَغْتَةً قَالُوا يٰحَسْرَتَنَا عَلٰى مَا فَرَّطْنَا فِيْهَا ۙ وَهُمْ يَحْمِلُونَ أَوْزَارَهُمْ عَلٰى ظُهُورِهِمْ ۚ أَلَا سَآءَ مَا يَزِرُونَ ۞ وَمَا الْحَيٰوةُ الدُّنْيَآ إِلَّا لَعِبٌ وَّلَهْوٌ ۗ وَلَلدَّارُ الْأٰخِرَةُ خَيْرٌ لِّلَّذِينَ يَتَّقُونَ ۗ أَفَلَا تَعْقِلُونَ ۞ قَدْ نَعْلَمُ إِنَّهُ لَيَحْزُنُكَ الَّذِي يَقُولُونَ فَإِنَّهُمْ لَا يُكَذِّبُونَكَ وَلٰكِنَّ الظّٰلِمِينَ بِاٰيٰتِ اللهِ يَجْحَدُونَ ۞ وَلَقَدْ كُذِّبَتْ رُسُلٌ مِّنْ قَبْلِكَ فَصَبَرُوا عَلٰى مَا كُذِّبُوا وَأُوذُوا حَتّٰى أَتٰىهُمْ نَصْرُنَا ۚ وَلَا مُبَدِّلَ لِكَلِمٰتِ اللهِ ۚ وَلَقَدْ جَآءَكَ مِنْ نَّبَإِ الْمُرْسَلِينَ ۞ وَإِنْ كَانَ كَبُرَ عَلَيْكَ إِعْرَاضُهُمْ فَإِنِ اسْتَطَعْتَ أَنْ تَبْتَغِيَ نَفَقًا فِي الْأَرْضِ أَوْ سُلَّمًا فِي السَّمَآءِ فَتَأْتِيَهُمْ بِاٰيَةٍ ۚ وَلَوْ شَآءَ اللهُ لَجَمَعَهُمْ عَلَى الْهُدٰى فَلَا تَكُونَنَّ مِنَ الْجٰهِلِينَ ۞ إِنَّمَا يَسْتَجِيبُ الَّذِينَ يَسْمَعُونَ ۚ وَالْمَوْتٰى يَبْعَثُهُمُ اللهُ ثُمَّ إِلَيْهِ يُرْجَعُونَ ۞ وَقَالُوا لَوْلَا نُزِّلَ عَلَيْهِ أٰيَةٌ مِّنْ رَّبِّهِ ۚ قُلْ إِنَّ اللهَ قَادِرٌ عَلٰى أَنْ يُّنَزِّلَ أٰيَةً وَّلٰكِنَّ أَكْثَرَهُمْ لَا يَعْلَمُونَ ۞ وَمَا مِنْ دَآبَّةٍ فِي الْأَرْضِ وَلَا طٰٓئِرٍ يَّطِيرُ بِجَنَاحَيْهِ إِلَّا أُمَمٌ أَمْثَالُكُمْ ۚ مَا فَرَّطْنَا فِي

Be prepared: divine judgement, punishment or pleasure may come at any moment.

[30] If you could see them as they stand before their Lord. He will ask them, "Isn't this real?" They will say, "By Our Lord, it is." It will be said, "Taste the torment of what you denied." [31] Those who deny meeting Allah shall be losers when the Final Hour suddenly overtakes them, and they will be carrying a burden on their backs, and say, "Alas for us, we wasted this *life*!" Isn't evil what weighs them down? [32] This worldly life is a sport and an amusement, the home of the Hereafter is far better for mindful people. Don't you understand?

The Messenger ﷺ is consoled and urged to be humble:
[33] We know, *Muhammad*, you are saddened by what they say. They can't turn you into a liar, but the wrongdoers are disputing Allah's signs. [34] Messengers before you were also called liars, they were patient in the face of the lies and insults they suffered, until Our help came to them. No one can change Allah's words, and reports of the messengers have already come to you *confirming this*. [35] If you find it difficult to bear their rejection then, if you can, look for a tunnel in the ground or a ladder to climb to the sky to bring them a miracle. If Allah wanted, He could have united them all on *the path of* guidance. Followers of the Prophet[a], you mustn't be like the ignorant. [36] Only those who listen will answer. Allah will resurrect the dead, and they will return to Him. [37] They say, "If a sign were to come down to him from his Lord?" Say: "Allah has the power to send down a sign," but most of them do not know.

Humility: animals live in communities
[38] There is no creature on land or a bird flying in the sky that does not belong to a community just like yours. We haven't left anything out of the Book. They will be gathered before their Lord.

---

[a]   This change of address from the Prophet ﷺ to the followers is hinted to in Zia ul Quran.

الْكِتٰبِ مِنْ شَيْءٍ ثُمَّ اِلٰى رَبِّهِمْ يُحْشَرُوْنَ ۞ وَالَّذِيْنَ

كَذَّبُوْا بِاٰيٰتِنَا صُمٌّ وَّبُكْمٌ فِي الظُّلُمٰتِ ؕ مَنْ يَّشَاِ اللّٰهُ

يُضْلِلْهُ ؕ وَمَنْ يَّشَأْ يَجْعَلْهُ عَلٰى صِرَاطٍ مُّسْتَقِيْمٍ ۞

قُلْ اَرَءَيْتَكُمْ اِنْ اَتٰىكُمْ عَذَابُ اللّٰهِ اَوْ اَتَتْكُمُ السَّاعَةُ

اَغَيْرَ اللّٰهِ تَدْعُوْنَ ۚ اِنْ كُنْتُمْ صٰدِقِيْنَ ۞ بَلْ اِيَّاهُ

تَدْعُوْنَ فَيَكْشِفُ مَا تَدْعُوْنَ اِلَيْهِ اِنْ شَاءَ وَ

تَنْسَوْنَ مَا تُشْرِكُوْنَ ۞ وَلَقَدْ اَرْسَلْنَا اِلٰى اُمَمٍ

مِّنْ قَبْلِكَ فَاَخَذْنٰهُمْ بِالْبَأْسَاءِ وَالضَّرَّاءِ لَعَلَّهُمْ

يَتَضَرَّعُوْنَ ۞ فَلَوْ لَاۤ اِذْ جَاءَهُمْ بَأْسُنَا تَضَرَّعُوْا

وَلٰكِنْ قَسَتْ قُلُوْبُهُمْ وَزَيَّنَ لَهُمُ الشَّيْطٰنُ مَا كَانُوْا

يَعْمَلُوْنَ ۞ فَلَمَّا نَسُوْا مَا ذُكِّرُوْا بِهٖ فَتَحْنَا عَلَيْهِمْ

اَبْوَابَ كُلِّ شَيْءٍ ؕ حَتّٰۤى اِذَا فَرِحُوْا بِمَاۤ اُوْتُوْۤا اَخَذْنٰهُمْ

بَغْتَةً فَاِذَا هُمْ مُّبْلِسُوْنَ ۞ فَقُطِعَ دَابِرُ الْقَوْمِ

الَّذِيْنَ ظَلَمُوْا ؕ وَالْحَمْدُ لِلّٰهِ رَبِّ الْعٰلَمِيْنَ ۞ قُلْ

اَرَءَيْتُمْ اِنْ اَخَذَ اللّٰهُ سَمْعَكُمْ وَاَبْصَارَكُمْ وَخَتَمَ

عَلٰى قُلُوْبِكُمْ مَّنْ اِلٰهٌ غَيْرُ اللّٰهِ يَأْتِيْكُمْ بِهٖ ؕ اُنْظُرْ

كَيْفَ نُصَرِّفُ الْاٰيٰتِ ثُمَّ هُمْ يَصْدِفُوْنَ ۞ قُلْ

اَرَءَيْتَكُمْ اِنْ اَتٰىكُمْ عَذَابُ اللّٰهِ بَغْتَةً اَوْ جَهْرَةً

هَلْ يُهْلَكُ اِلَّا الْقَوْمُ الظّٰلِمُوْنَ ۞ وَمَا نُرْسِلُ

الْمُرْسَلِيْنَ اِلَّا مُبَشِّرِيْنَ وَمُنْذِرِيْنَ ۚ فَمَنْ اٰمَنَ

Beware of worldly pleasures and delights, they will deceive!

251

³⁹Those who deny Our signs *might as well be* deaf and dumb, and *groping about* in the dark. Anyone Allah wills, He lets him go astray, and anyone He wills, He puts on a straight path. ⁴⁰Say: "Suppose Allah's punishment, or the Final Hour, was to come; now would you call anyone other than Allah? ⁴¹No! You would call Him alone, and if He so willed, He would sweep away whatever made you do so, and you would forget what you associated *with Him*."

Humility comes through suffering

⁴²We sent *messengers* to *many* communities before you, and put those communities through sufferings and hardships so that they might submit *to Allah*. ⁴³They should have submitted when the sufferings came but instead their hearts hardened, and Satan made their works appear attractive to them. ⁴⁴Once they forgot what they should remember, We opened up the floodgates of worldly provisions for them and, just as they were revelling in what they had, We suddenly seized them, and they were left in utter despair. ⁴⁵The last traces of the evildoers were razed to the ground. Praise Allah, Lord of *all* the realms. ⁴⁶Say: "Suppose Allah were to take away your hearing and sight, and seal your hearts,ᵃ which god beside Allah would make them work for you?" See how We explain the signs, but they turn away. ⁴⁷Say: "Suppose Allah's punishment was to catch you unaware or fully aware *the fact is* only the wrongdoers would be destroyed."

ᵃ This means if Allah made you deaf, blind or mentally disabled no one could heal you except Allah.

وَاَصْلَحَ فَلَا خَوْفٌ عَلَيْهِمْ وَلَا هُمْ يَحْزَنُوْنَ ۞ وَ

الَّذِيْنَ كَذَّبُوْا بِاٰيٰتِنَا يَمَسُّهُمُ الْعَذَابُ بِمَا كَانُوْا

يَفْسُقُوْنَ ۞ قُلْ لَّاۤ اَقُوْلُ لَكُمْ عِنْدِيْ خَزَآئِنُ اللّٰهِ

وَلَاۤ اَعْلَمُ الْغَيْبَ وَلَاۤ اَقُوْلُ لَكُمْ اِنِّيْ مَلَكٌ ۚ اِنْ

اَتَّبِعُ اِلَّا مَا يُوْحٰۤى اِلَيَّ ۚ قُلْ هَلْ يَسْتَوِى الْاَعْمٰى

وَالْبَصِيْرُ ۚ اَفَلَا تَتَفَكَّرُوْنَ ۞ وَ اَنْذِرْ بِهِ الَّذِيْنَ

يَخَافُوْنَ اَنْ يُّحْشَرُوْاۤ اِلٰى رَبِّهِمْ لَيْسَ لَهُمْ مِّنْ

دُوْنِهٖ وَلِيٌّ وَّلَا شَفِيْعٌ لَّعَلَّهُمْ يَتَّقُوْنَ ۞ وَلَا

تَطْرُدِ الَّذِيْنَ يَدْعُوْنَ رَبَّهُمْ بِالْغَدٰوةِ وَ الْعَشِيِّ

يُرِيْدُوْنَ وَجْهَهٗ ۚ مَا عَلَيْكَ مِنْ حِسَابِهِمْ مِّنْ شَيْءٍ

وَّ مَا مِنْ حِسَابِكَ عَلَيْهِمْ مِّنْ شَيْءٍ فَتَطْرُدَهُمْ

فَتَكُوْنَ مِنَ الظّٰلِمِيْنَ ۞ وَكَذٰلِكَ فَتَنَّا بَعْضَهُمْ

بِبَعْضٍ لِّيَقُوْلُوْاۤ اَهٰۤؤُلَآءِ مَنَّ اللّٰهُ عَلَيْهِمْ مِّنْ

بَيْنِنَا ۚ اَلَيْسَ اللّٰهُ بِاَعْلَمَ بِالشّٰكِرِيْنَ ۞ وَاِذَا جَآءَكَ

الَّذِيْنَ يُؤْمِنُوْنَ بِاٰيٰتِنَا فَقُلْ سَلٰمٌ عَلَيْكُمْ كَتَبَ

رَبُّكُمْ عَلٰى نَفْسِهِ الرَّحْمَةَ ۙ اَنَّهٗ مَنْ عَمِلَ مِنْكُمْ

سُوْٓءًا بِجَهَالَةٍ ثُمَّ تَابَ مِنْ بَعْدِهٖ وَ اَصْلَحَ فَاَنَّهٗ

غَفُوْرٌ رَّحِيْمٌ ۞ وَكَذٰلِكَ نُفَصِّلُ الْاٰيٰتِ وَلِتَسْتَبِيْنَ

سَبِيْلُ الْمُجْرِمِيْنَ ۞ قُلْ اِنِّيْ نُهِيْتُ اَنْ اَعْبُدَ الَّذِيْنَ

تَدْعُوْنَ مِنْ دُوْنِ اللّٰهِ ۚ قُلْ لَّاۤ اَتَّبِعُ اَهْوَآءَكُمْ ۙ

Righteous fellowship: keep the company of good people.

The humility of the Messenger ﷺ; no extravagant claims for himself

[48] We only sent messengers as bearers of good news and as warners. So, whoever believes and puts his life in order will neither fear nor grieve; [49] whereas those who reject Our signs will taste the punishment for their sins. [50] Say: "I don't say, 'I own the stores of Allah's riches,' or 'I know the unseen'; nor do I say, 'I am an angel.' I only follow what is revealed to me." Say: "Are the blind and the seeing equal? Why don't you think?"

Humility in practice; keep the company of devout people

[51] Warn, by means of *the Quran*, those who fear being gathered before their Lord. Beside Him they have no protector or intercessor, so they may be mindful, [52] and don't drive away those who worship their Lord morning and evening, seeking His pleasure. It isn't for you to judge them, nor for them to judge you. Were you to drive them away, you would be a wrongdoer. [53] That is how We test some of them by means of others, so they say, "Are these the ones that Allah has favoured over us?"[a] Doesn't Allah know best who is grateful? [54] When believers in Our revelation come to you, say, "Peace be on you." Your Lord has decreed that He will be kind. Whoever unwittingly[b] does evil and then repents and reforms himself, *will find Allah Forgiving, Kind.* [55] This is how We explain the signs, so that the way of the sinful may be clearly distinguished.

---

[a] The rich and powerful in society often find it hard to accept that Allah loves the poor and weak.

[b] Literally, "out of ignorance." Some Companions said that includes any major sin since, if we were in our right minds, we wouldn't do it.

قَدْ ضَلَلْتُ اِذًا وَّمَآ اَنَا مِنَ الْمُهْتَدِيْنَ ۵۷ قُلْ

اِنِّيْ عَلٰى بَيِّنَةٍ مِّنْ رَّبِّيْ وَكَذَّبْتُمْ بِهٖ ط مَا عِنْدِيْ

مَا تَسْتَعْجِلُوْنَ بِهٖ ط اِنِ الْحُكْمُ اِلَّا لِلّٰهِ ط يَقُصُّ

الْحَقَّ وَهُوَ خَيْرُ الْفٰصِلِيْنَ ۵۵ قُلْ لَّوْ اَنَّ عِنْدِيْ

مَا تَسْتَعْجِلُوْنَ بِهٖ لَقُضِيَ الْاَمْرُ بَيْنِيْ وَ بَيْنَكُمْ ط

وَاللّٰهُ اَعْلَمُ بِالظّٰلِمِيْنَ ۵۸ وَعِنْدَهٗ مَفَاتِحُ الْغَيْبِ

لَا يَعْلَمُهَآ اِلَّا هُوَ ط وَيَعْلَمُ مَا فِى الْبَرِّ وَ الْبَحْرِ ط

وَمَا تَسْقُطُ مِنْ وَّرَقَةٍ اِلَّا يَعْلَمُهَا وَلَا حَبَّةٍ

Don't join corrupt people,
they'll drag you down.

فِيْ ظُلُمٰتِ الْاَرْضِ وَلَا رَطْبٍ وَّلَا يَابِسٍ اِلَّا

فِيْ كِتٰبٍ مُّبِيْنٍ ۵۹ وَهُوَ الَّذِيْ يَتَوَفّٰىكُمْ بِالَّيْلِ

وَ يَعْلَمُ مَا جَرَحْتُمْ بِالنَّهَارِ ثُمَّ يَبْعَثُكُمْ فِيْهِ

لِيُقْضٰى اَجَلٌ مُّسَمًّى ج ثُمَّ اِلَيْهِ مَرْجِعُكُمْ ثُمَّ

يُنَبِّئُكُمْ بِمَا كُنْتُمْ تَعْمَلُوْنَ ۶۰ وَهُوَ الْقَاهِرُ فَوْقَ

عِبَادِهٖ وَيُرْسِلُ عَلَيْكُمْ حَفَظَةً ط حَتّٰى اِذَا جَآءَ

اَحَدَكُمُ الْمَوْتُ تَوَفَّتْهُ رُسُلُنَا وَهُمْ لَا يُفَرِّطُوْنَ ۶۱

ثُمَّ رُدُّوْا اِلَى اللّٰهِ مَوْلٰىهُمُ الْحَقِّ ط اَلَا لَهُ الْحُكْمُ ۥ

وَهُوَ اَسْرَعُ الْحٰسِبِيْنَ ۶۲ قُلْ مَنْ يُّنَجِّيْكُمْ مِّنْ

ظُلُمٰتِ الْبَرِّ وَالْبَحْرِ تَدْعُوْنَهٗ تَضَرُّعًا وَّ خُفْيَةً ج

لَئِنْ اَنْجٰىنَا مِنْ هٰذِهٖ لَنَكُوْنَنَّ مِنَ الشّٰكِرِيْنَ ۶۳

قُلِ اللّٰهُ يُنَجِّيْكُمْ مِّنْهَا وَمِنْ كُلِّ كَرْبٍ ثُمَّ اَنْتُمْ

The Prophet ﷺ is equipped to respond to the disbelievers

⁵⁶ Say: "I am forbidden to worship those you serve beside Allah." Say: "I will not follow your desires because, if I did so, I would go astray and fail to be guided." ⁵⁷ Say: "I have clear proof from My Lord, the one you have rejected. What you want to hasten is not in my *control*; the decision is Allah's, Who tells the truth and is the best Judge *of truth and falsehood*." ⁵⁸ Say: "If what you seek to hasten were in my *control*, then the matter that divides us would have been settled by now." Allah knows well the wrongdoers.

Evidence of Allah's control; natural occurrences

⁵⁹ He has the keys of the unseen realm, only He knows them. He knows all that is in the land and sea. Not a single leaf falls without His knowledge, no seed *buried* in the darkness of the Earth, nor any fresh or withered plant is left unrecorded in a clear Book.[a] ⁶⁰ He receives your soul at night[b] and knows what *good or evil* you have done during the day, and He raises you up *every morning* so that your fixed term[c] may reach its conclusion. After that you shall return to Him, and it is then that He will inform you of what you did. ⁶¹ He is Dominant[d] over His servants, and He sends forth *angel* guards so that whenever death overtakes one of you Our angels bring back his soul, never failing in their duty. ⁶² Then they will be returned to Allah, their True Master. Doesn't the final decision rest with Him? He is the swiftest of reckoners.

Even surviving a storm does not make them humble

⁶³ Ask *them*: "Who rescues you from the dark forces of land and sea when you call Him humbly in secret for help, *all the while saying*, 'If He rescues us from this we will, indeed, be thankful'?"

---

a   This "clear Book" refers to *al-Lawh al-Mahfuz*, Allah's official record of our deeds, in which everything that has ever happened or will happen is kept.

b   Literally, "He causes you to die," or, "He takes you in His custody," or, "He puts you to sleep."

c   The "fixed time" here means the time of death.

d   *Al-Qahir* is a name of Allah, it refers to His overwhelming power, complete authority, and control.

تُشْرِكُوْنَ ۞ قُلْ هُوَ الْقَادِرُ عَلٰٓى اَنْ يَّبْعَثَ
عَلَيْكُمْ عَذَابًا مِّنْ فَوْقِكُمْ اَوْ مِنْ تَحْتِ اَرْجُلِكُمْ
اَوْ يَلْبِسَكُمْ شِيَعًا وَّيُذِيْقَ بَعْضَكُمْ بَأْسَ بَعْضٍ ط
اُنْظُرْ كَيْفَ نُصَرِّفُ الْاٰيٰتِ لَعَلَّهُمْ يَفْقَهُوْنَ ۞ وَ
كَذَّبَ بِهٖ قَوْمُكَ وَهُوَ الْحَقُّ ط قُلْ لَّسْتُ عَلَيْكُمْ
بِوَكِيْلٍ ۞ لِكُلِّ نَبَإٍ مُّسْتَقَرٌّ وَّسَوْفَ تَعْلَمُوْنَ ۞ وَ
اِذَا رَاَيْتَ الَّذِيْنَ يَخُوْضُوْنَ فِيْٓ اٰيٰتِنَا فَاَعْرِضْ عَنْهُمْ
حَتّٰى يَخُوْضُوْا فِيْ حَدِيْثٍ غَيْرِهٖ ط وَاِمَّا يُنْسِيَنَّكَ
الشَّيْطٰنُ فَلَا تَقْعُدْ بَعْدَ الذِّكْرٰى مَعَ الْقَوْمِ الظّٰلِمِيْنَ ۞
وَمَا عَلَى الَّذِيْنَ يَتَّقُوْنَ مِنْ حِسَابِهِمْ مِّنْ شَيْءٍ وَّ
لٰكِنْ ذِكْرٰى لَعَلَّهُمْ يَتَّقُوْنَ ۞ وَذَرِ الَّذِيْنَ اتَّخَذُوْا
دِيْنَهُمْ لَعِبًا وَّلَهْوًا وَّغَرَّتْهُمُ الْحَيٰوةُ الدُّنْيَا وَ
ذَكِّرْ بِهٖٓ اَنْ تُبْسَلَ نَفْسٌۢ بِمَا كَسَبَتْ لَيْسَ لَهَا
مِنْ دُوْنِ اللهِ وَلِيٌّ وَّلَا شَفِيْعٌ وَاِنْ تَعْدِلْ كُلَّ
عَدْلٍ لَّا يُؤْخَذْ مِنْهَا ط اُولٰٓئِكَ الَّذِيْنَ اُبْسِلُوْا بِمَا
كَسَبُوْا لَهُمْ شَرَابٌ مِّنْ حَمِيْمٍ وَّعَذَابٌ اَلِيْمٌۢ
بِمَا كَانُوْا يَكْفُرُوْنَ ۞ قُلْ اَنَدْعُوْا مِنْ دُوْنِ اللهِ
مَا لَا يَنْفَعُنَا وَلَا يَضُرُّنَا وَنُرَدُّ عَلٰٓى اَعْقَابِنَا
بَعْدَ اِذْ هَدٰىنَا اللهُ كَالَّذِى اسْتَهْوَتْهُ الشَّيٰطِيْنُ
فِى الْاَرْضِ حَيْرَانَ لَهٗٓ اَصْحٰبٌ يَّدْعُوْنَهٗٓ اِلَى

The deceptive nature of the world sucks us in. Beware of its traps.

⁶⁴Say: "It is Allah Who rescues you from that and every other danger, but then you go back to associating *false gods*."ᵃ ⁶⁵Say: "*Only* He is able to punish you from above or from beneath your feet, or create conflict and factions; so some may taste the violence of the other." Consider, how We explain the signs so they might understand.

Avoid gatherings where Islam is maligned
⁶⁶Your people, *Muhammad*, deny *all* this, even though it is the truth. Say: "I will not be your guardian *on Judgement Day*. ⁶⁷Fulfilment comes to every prophecy, as you will discover *in due course*." ⁶⁸Whenever you see anyone mocking Our verses, turn away from them until they change the topic of conversation, and if Satan made you forget, as soon as you remember leave the gathering of the wrongdoers. ⁶⁹Those that are *already* mindful *of Allah* are in no way accountable for the *wrongdoers; their role is to* remind so they might become mindful. ⁷⁰Stay away from those who regard their religion as a sport, amusement, and are deceived by *the attractions of* this worldly life.ᵇ *To prevent* any person being *needlessly* lost to Hell because of the fruits of their actions, mention the fact that they will have no protector or intercessor beside Allah, nor will any ransom be accepted. They will be in Hell as a result of their actions; they denied so they shall have boiling water and painful punishment.

Example of getting lost in worldly attractions
⁷¹Say: "Shall we worship beside Allah things that can neither benefit nor harm us, and turn back on our heels once Allah has guided us, like someone who is distracted and tempted by Earthly demons, *even though* he has friends calling him to the truth, saying, 'Come to us'?" Say: "Allah's guidance is the only guidance; and we have been ordered to submit to the Lord of *all* the realms,

---

ᵃ This example helps to explain why Allah refuses the deniers a second chance at life on Earth. Even after staring in the face of death, such people always revert to their old ways.
ᵇ This includes people who call themselves Muslims but lack sincerity in their belief and practise of the faith.

الْهُدٰى ائْتِنَا ۭ قُلْ اِنَّ هُدَى اللهِ هُوَ الْهُدٰى ۭ وَ اُمِرْنَا لِنُسْلِمَ لِرَبِّ الْعٰلَمِيْنَ ۙ وَ اَنْ اَقِيْمُوا الصَّلٰوةَ وَاتَّقُوْهُ ۭ وَهُوَ الَّذِيْٓ اِلَيْهِ تُحْشَرُوْنَ ۝ وَ هُوَ الَّذِيْ خَلَقَ السَّمٰوٰتِ وَالْاَرْضَ بِالْحَقِّ ۭ وَيَوْمَ يَقُوْلُ كُنْ فَيَكُوْنُ ۬ ۥ قَوْلُهُ الْحَقُّ ۭ وَ لَهُ الْمُلْكُ يَوْمَ يُنْفَخُ فِى الصُّوْرِ ۭ عٰلِمُ الْغَيْبِ وَ الشَّهَادَةِ ۭ وَهُوَ الْحَكِيْمُ الْخَبِيْرُ ۝ وَ اِذْ قَالَ اِبْرٰهِيْمُ لِاَبِيْهِ اٰزَرَ اَتَتَّخِذُ اَصْنَامًا اٰلِهَةً ۚ اِنِّيْٓ اَرٰىكَ وَ قَوْمَكَ فِيْ ضَلٰلٍ مُّبِيْنٍ ۝ وَ كَذٰلِكَ نُرِيْٓ اِبْرٰهِيْمَ مَلَكُوْتَ السَّمٰوٰتِ وَ الْاَرْضِ وَ لِيَكُوْنَ مِنَ الْمُوْقِنِيْنَ ۝ فَلَمَّا جَنَّ عَلَيْهِ الَّيْلُ رَاٰ كَوْكَبًا ۚ قَالَ هٰذَا رَبِّيْ ۚ فَلَمَّآ اَفَلَ قَالَ لَآ اُحِبُّ الْاٰفِلِيْنَ ۝ فَلَمَّا رَاَ الْقَمَرَ بَازِغًا قَالَ هٰذَا رَبِّيْ ۚ فَلَمَّآ اَفَلَ قَالَ لَىِٕنْ لَّمْ يَهْدِنِيْ رَبِّيْ لَاَكُوْنَنَّ مِنَ الْقَوْمِ الضَّآلِّيْنَ ۝ فَلَمَّا رَاَ الشَّمْسَ بَازِغَةً قَالَ هٰذَا رَبِّيْ هٰذَآ اَكْبَرُ ۚ فَلَمَّآ اَفَلَتْ قَالَ يٰقَوْمِ اِنِّيْ بَرِيْٓءٌ مِّمَّا تُشْرِكُوْنَ ۝ اِنِّيْ وَجَّهْتُ وَجْهِيَ لِلَّذِيْ فَطَرَ السَّمٰوٰتِ وَ الْاَرْضَ حَنِيْفًا وَّمَآ اَنَا مِنَ الْمُشْرِكِيْنَ ۝ وَحَآجَّهُ قَوْمُهُ ۭ قَالَ اَتُحَآجُّوْٓنِّيْ فِى اللهِ وَ قَدْ هَدٰىنِ ۭ وَ لَآ اَخَافُ

Ibrahim saw the fleeting, transient and pesky nature of the world, so he committed himself to Allah.

⁷² and to perform the prayer and to be mindful of Him; before Him you will *all* be gathered." ⁷³ He created the Heavens and the Earth for a purpose. A day *will come* when He says, "Be!" And it will be; His word is the *absolute* truth, all things will *return* to Him on the day when the *last* trumpet sounds. He is the Knower of the seen and unseen realms, the Wise, the Aware.

Ibrahim exposes the folly of idolatry

⁷⁴ *Remember* when Ibrahim said to his father, Azar,[a] "Have you taken idols as gods? I see you and your people are misguided." ⁷⁵ That's how We showed Ibrahim the splendour[b] of the Heavens and the Earth, so he became a firm believer. ⁷⁶ As the night grew dark around him, he saw a star, he thought, "*Could* this be My Lord?" After it set, he said, "I don't like *things* that set." ⁷⁷ *Similarly*, after seeing the moon rising, he said, "*Could* this be My Lord?" But, after it set, he said, "If My Lord doesn't guide me, I will stray." ⁷⁸ When he saw the sun rising, he *again* said, "*Could* this be My Lord? This is big." After it set, he said, "My people, I am free from what you associate *with Allah*. ⁷⁹ I naturally turn my face to Him Who created the Heavens and the Earth; I won't associate *partners with Him*."

---

[a] Some commentators translate *Abeehay* as his uncle. They contend that the lineage of the blessed Prophet ﷺ has been free of idolaters from the time of Adam, a pure breed of the Noble Messenger.

[b] The word *malakut* refers to Allah's control, authority and power over the operation of the universe.

مَا تُشْرِكُوْنَ بِهٖۤ اِلَّاۤ اَنْ يَّشَآءَ رَبِّيْ شَيْئًا ط وَسِعَ

رَبِّيْ كُلَّ شَيْءٍ عِلْمًا ط اَفَلَا تَتَذَكَّرُوْنَ ۸۰ وَكَيْفَ

اَخَافُ مَاۤ اَشْرَكْتُمْ وَلَا تَخَافُوْنَ اَنَّكُمْ اَشْرَكْتُمْ

بِاللّٰهِ مَا لَمْ يُنَزِّلْ بِهٖ عَلَيْكُمْ سُلْطٰنًا ط فَاَيُّ

الْفَرِيْقَيْنِ اَحَقُّ بِالْاَمْنِ ۚ اِنْ كُنْتُمْ تَعْلَمُوْنَ ۸۱

اَلَّذِيْنَ اٰمَنُوْا وَلَمْ يَلْبِسُوْۤا اِيْمَانَهُمْ بِظُلْمٍ اُولٰٓئِكَ

لَهُمُ الْاَمْنُ وَهُمْ مُّهْتَدُوْنَ ۸۲ وَتِلْكَ حُجَّتُنَاۤ

اٰتَيْنٰهَاۤ اِبْرٰهِيْمَ عَلٰى قَوْمِهٖ ط نَرْفَعُ دَرَجٰتٍ مَّنْ نَّشَآءُ ط

اِنَّ رَبَّكَ حَكِيْمٌ عَلِيْمٌ ۸۳ وَوَهَبْنَا لَهٗۤ اِسْحٰقَ وَيَعْقُوْبَ ط

كُلًّا هَدَيْنَا ۚ وَنُوْحًا هَدَيْنَا مِنْ قَبْلُ وَمِنْ ذُرِّيَّتِهٖ دَاوٗدَ

وَسُلَيْمٰنَ وَاَيُّوْبَ وَيُوْسُفَ وَمُوْسٰى وَهٰرُوْنَ ط وَكَذٰلِكَ

نَجْزِي الْمُحْسِنِيْنَ ۸۴ وَزَكَرِيَّا وَيَحْيٰى وَعِيْسٰى وَالْيَاسَ ۚ

كُلٌّ مِّنَ الصّٰلِحِيْنَ ۸۵ وَاِسْمٰعِيْلَ وَالْيَسَعَ وَيُوْنُسَ وَ

لُوْطًا ط وَكُلًّا فَضَّلْنَا عَلَى الْعٰلَمِيْنَ ۸۶ وَمِنْ اٰبَآئِهِمْ وَ

ذُرِّيّٰتِهِمْ وَاِخْوَانِهِمْ ۚ وَاجْتَبَيْنٰهُمْ وَهَدَيْنٰهُمْ اِلٰى

صِرَاطٍ مُّسْتَقِيْمٍ ۸۷ ذٰلِكَ هُدَى اللّٰهِ يَهْدِيْ بِهٖ مَنْ

يَّشَآءُ مِنْ عِبَادِهٖ ط وَلَوْ اَشْرَكُوْا لَحَبِطَ عَنْهُمْ مَّا كَانُوْا

يَعْمَلُوْنَ ۸۸ اُولٰٓئِكَ الَّذِيْنَ اٰتَيْنٰهُمُ الْكِتٰبَ وَالْحُكْمَ وَالنُّبُوَّةَ ۚ

فَاِنْ يَّكْفُرْ بِهَا هٰٓؤُلَآءِ فَقَدْ وَكَّلْنَا بِهَا قَوْمًا لَّيْسُوْا

بِهَا بِكٰفِرِيْنَ ۸۹ اُولٰٓئِكَ الَّذِيْنَ هَدَى اللّٰهُ فَبِهُدٰىهُمُ

Ibrahim debates, discusses and has discourse about Allah's existence with his people.

261

Ibrahim used logic to disprove the idolaters' arguments

⁸⁰ *On hearing this*, his people *began to* argue with him, *so* he said, "Are you arguing with me about Allah, Who guided me? I am not afraid of those you associate with Him, unless My Lord wants something else. My Lord has knowledge of all things. Will you not listen? ⁸¹ Why should I be afraid of things you associate *with Him*, when you are not afraid to associate others with Allah about which He sent you no authority? Which of *our* two parties, *you or me*, deserves *to enjoy* security, if you have knowledge?" ⁸² Those who believe without confusing their faith with idolatry^a who shall enjoy security, and it is they who are guided. ⁸³ Such was the evidence that We gave to Ibrahim *to use* against his people; We raised him high as We wanted. Your Lord is Wise, Knowing.

Ibrahim was the father and the leader of many prophets

⁸⁴ We gave him Ishaq and Yaqub and guided both as We had previously guided Nuh – and among Ibrahim's offspring were: Dawud, Sulayman, Ayyub, Yusuf, Musa, Harun – that is how We reward the righteous. ⁸⁵ Zakariyya, Yahya, Isa, Ilyas – each one was upright – ⁸⁶ Ismail, al-Yasa, Yunus and Lut^b – every one of them, We favoured over all the people – ⁸⁷ and *some* among their fathers – offspring and brothers – We chose them and guided them along a straight path. ⁸⁸ Such is Allah's guidance, by which He guides His servants as He pleases. If *any of* them had associated *partners with Allah*, then *the reward of* whatever *good* deeds they had done would be worthless. ⁸⁹ We gave the Book, the law and the prophethood to them. Even if these *people* reject it, We *nevertheless* entrusted it to people who accepted it.^c

---

^a *Zulm* is generally wrongdoing, because of the context, it refers to idolatry, as explained in *Surat Luqman* 31: 13.

^b The Biblical names of the prophets mentioned in verses 83–86 are, in order: Abraham, Isaac, Jacob, Noah, David, Solomon, Job, Joseph, Moses, Aaron, Zachariah, John, Jesus, Elias, Ishmael, Elisha, Jonah and Lot.

^c In other words, Muslims who will believe them.

اقْتِدِهْ ۚ قُلْ لَّا اَسْئَلُكُمْ عَلَيْهِ اَجْرًا ۚ اِنْ هُوَ اِلَّا ذِكْرٰى

لِلْعٰلَمِيْنَ ۞ وَمَا قَدَرُوا اللّٰهَ حَقَّ قَدْرِهٖۤ اِذْ قَالُوْا مَاۤ

اَنْزَلَ اللّٰهُ عَلٰى بَشَرٍ مِّنْ شَىْءٍ ۚ قُلْ مَنْ اَنْزَلَ الْكِتٰبَ

الَّذِىْ جَآءَ بِهٖ مُوْسٰى نُوْرًا وَّهُدًى لِّلنَّاسِ تَجْعَلُوْنَهٗ

قَرَاطِيْسَ تُبْدُوْنَهَا وَتُخْفُوْنَ كَثِيْرًا ۚ وَعُلِّمْتُمْ مَّا لَمْ

تَعْلَمُوْۤا اَنْتُمْ وَلَاۤ اٰبَآؤُكُمْ ۚ قُلِ اللّٰهُ ۙ ثُمَّ ذَرْهُمْ فِىْ

خَوْضِهِمْ يَلْعَبُوْنَ ۞ وَهٰذَا كِتٰبٌ اَنْزَلْنٰهُ مُبٰرَكٌ مُّصَدِّقُ

الَّذِىْ بَيْنَ يَدَيْهِ وَلِتُنْذِرَ اُمَّ الْقُرٰى وَمَنْ حَوْلَهَا ۚ وَ

الَّذِيْنَ يُؤْمِنُوْنَ بِالْاٰخِرَةِ يُؤْمِنُوْنَ بِهٖ وَهُمْ عَلٰى صَلَاتِهِمْ

يُحَافِظُوْنَ ۞ وَمَنْ اَظْلَمُ مِمَّنِ افْتَرٰى عَلَى اللّٰهِ كَذِبًا اَوْ

قَالَ اُوْحِىَ اِلَىَّ وَلَمْ يُوْحَ اِلَيْهِ شَىْءٌ وَّمَنْ قَالَ سَاُنْزِلُ

مِثْلَ مَاۤ اَنْزَلَ اللّٰهُ ۚ وَلَوْ تَرٰۤى اِذِ الظّٰلِمُوْنَ فِىْ غَمَرٰتِ

الْمَوْتِ وَالْمَلٰٓئِكَةُ بَاسِطُوْۤا اَيْدِيْهِمْ ۚ اَخْرِجُوْۤا اَنْفُسَكُمْ ۚ

اَلْيَوْمَ تُجْزَوْنَ عَذَابَ الْهُوْنِ بِمَا كُنْتُمْ تَقُوْلُوْنَ عَلَى

اللّٰهِ غَيْرَ الْحَقِّ وَكُنْتُمْ عَنْ اٰيٰتِهٖ تَسْتَكْبِرُوْنَ ۞ وَلَقَدْ

جِئْتُمُوْنَا فُرَادٰى كَمَا خَلَقْنٰكُمْ اَوَّلَ مَرَّةٍ وَّتَرَكْتُمْ مَّا

خَوَّلْنٰكُمْ وَرَآءَ ظُهُوْرِكُمْ ۚ وَمَا نَرٰى مَعَكُمْ شُفَعَآءَكُمُ الَّذِيْنَ

زَعَمْتُمْ اَنَّهُمْ فِيْكُمْ شُرَكٰٓؤُا ۚ لَقَدْ تَّقَطَّعَ بَيْنَكُمْ وَ

ضَلَّ عَنْكُمْ مَّا كُنْتُمْ تَزْعُمُوْنَ ۞ اِنَّ اللّٰهَ فَالِقُ الْحَبِّ

وَالنَّوٰى ۚ يُخْرِجُ الْحَىَّ مِنَ الْمَيِّتِ وَمُخْرِجُ الْمَيِّتِ مِنَ

The return to Allah will be solitary, lonely and difficult. Are you ready for it?

⁹⁰ Allah guided them, so imitate *them in* their guidance. Say: "I don't ask you for any reward for this; it's a reminder for all people."

People believed in some parts of scripture and rejected others

⁹¹ When they said, "Allah has never revealed anything to a human being," they failed to recognise *the true greatness* of Allah which is His due. Ask: "Who revealed the Book Musa brought as a light to guide people which you keep in scrolls. You openly declare *some of* it and hide a lot *of it*; and you were taught what neither you nor your ancestors knew?" Say: "It is Allah," then leave them to amuse themselves with their *foolish* chatter. ⁹² This is a blessed Book that We have sent down, confirming what came before it, so you might warn *the people of* the Mother of Cities[a] and of its surroundings. Those who believe in the Hereafter, they believe in *this Book*,[b] taking care to observe their *daily* prayers.

The disbelievers in death throes

⁹³ Who is more wrong than the one who invents lies about Allah, or says, "It has been revealed to me," when *in fact* nothing has been revealed to him, or says, "I will send down the same as what Allah has sent down"? Were you to see the wrongdoers in death throes, when the angels stretch out their hands, *saying*, "Let out your souls, today you will be rewarded with the punishment of contempt because of what you falsely said about Allah, arrogantly rejecting His signs. ⁹⁴ You will come to Us all alone like the first time We created you. You have left behind the favours We gave you; nor do We see your intercessors with you, those whom you claimed were Allah's partners. The ties between you *and them* have been severed, and whatever you used to *claim as a partner* has deserted you."

---

[a] The "Mother of Cities" is Makkah.
[b] The pronoun 'it' in the Arabic refers to the glorious Quran.

الْحَيِّ ۙ ذٰلِكُمُ اللهُ فَاَنّٰى تُؤْفَكُوْنَ ۝ فَالِقُ الْاِصْبَاحِ ۚ وَ
جَعَلَ الَّيْلَ سَكَنًا وَّالشَّمْسَ وَالْقَمَرَ حُسْبَانًا ؕ ذٰلِكَ
تَقْدِيْرُ الْعَزِيْزِ الْعَلِيْمِ ۝ وَهُوَ الَّذِيْ جَعَلَ لَكُمُ النُّجُوْمَ
لِتَهْتَدُوْا بِهَا فِيْ ظُلُمٰتِ الْبَرِّ وَالْبَحْرِ ؕ قَدْ فَصَّلْنَا الْاٰيٰتِ
لِقَوْمٍ يَّعْلَمُوْنَ ۝ وَهُوَ الَّذِيْ اَنْشَاَكُمْ مِّنْ نَّفْسٍ
وَّاحِدَةٍ فَمُسْتَقَرٌّ وَّمُسْتَوْدَعٌ ؕ قَدْ فَصَّلْنَا الْاٰيٰتِ لِقَوْمٍ
يَّفْقَهُوْنَ ۝ وَهُوَ الَّذِيْ اَنْزَلَ مِنَ السَّمَآءِ مَآءً ۚ فَاَخْرَجْنَا

The beauty of flora, the diversity of fauna and vastness of space reveals the Creator's inventiveness.

بِهٖ نَبَاتَ كُلِّ شَيْءٍ فَاَخْرَجْنَا مِنْهُ خَضِرًا نُّخْرِجُ مِنْهُ
حَبًّا مُّتَرَاكِبًا ۚ وَمِنَ النَّخْلِ مِنْ طَلْعِهَا قِنْوَانٌ دَانِيَةٌ وَّ
جَنّٰتٍ مِّنْ اَعْنَابٍ وَّالزَّيْتُوْنَ وَالرُّمَّانَ مُشْتَبِهًا وَّغَيْرَ
مُتَشَابِهٍ ؕ اُنْظُرُوْا اِلٰى ثَمَرِهٖ اِذَآ اَثْمَرَ وَيَنْعِهٖ ؕ اِنَّ فِيْ
ذٰلِكُمْ لَاٰيٰتٍ لِّقَوْمٍ يُّؤْمِنُوْنَ ۝ وَجَعَلُوْا لِلهِ شُرَكَآءَ
الْجِنَّ وَخَلَقَهُمْ وَخَرَقُوْا لَهٗ بَنِيْنَ وَبَنٰتٍ بِغَيْرِ عِلْمٍ ؕ
سُبْحٰنَهٗ وَتَعٰلٰى عَمَّا يَصِفُوْنَ ۞ بَدِيْعُ السَّمٰوٰتِ وَالْاَرْضِ ؕ
اَنّٰى يَكُوْنُ لَهٗ وَلَدٌ وَّلَمْ تَكُنْ لَّهٗ صَاحِبَةٌ ؕ وَخَلَقَ
كُلَّ شَيْءٍ ۚ وَهُوَ بِكُلِّ شَيْءٍ عَلِيْمٌ ۝ ذٰلِكُمُ اللهُ رَبُّكُمْ ۚ
لَآ اِلٰهَ اِلَّا هُوَ ۚ خَالِقُ كُلِّ شَيْءٍ فَاعْبُدُوْهُ ۚ وَهُوَ عَلٰى
كُلِّ شَيْءٍ وَّكِيْلٌ ۝ لَا تُدْرِكُهُ الْاَبْصَارُ ؗ وَهُوَ يُدْرِكُ
الْاَبْصَارَ ۚ وَهُوَ اللَّطِيْفُ الْخَبِيْرُ ۝ قَدْ جَآءَكُمْ بَصَآئِرُ مِنْ
رَّبِّكُمْ ۚ فَمَنْ اَبْصَرَ فَلِنَفْسِهٖ ۚ وَمَنْ عَمِيَ فَعَلَيْهَا ؕ وَمَآ

265

Evidence of Allah's ingenious creativity: Seeds, buds, flowers

[95] Allah is the one who splits open the seed and the fruit-stone; He brings the living from the dead and the dead from the living. Such is Allah, so how were you misled *from the truth*? [96] *He* splits *the darkness with* the dawn, and made the night for resting, and the sun and moon for accurately measuring *time*. Such is the precision with which He reassures, the Almighty, the Knowing. [97] He made the stars for your guidance through the darkness of land and sea. We explained the signs to *a group of* people who know. [98] He created you from a single soul, with a place of settlement *in life* and *another* where you will be buried.[a] We have explained the signs to *a group of* people who understand. [99] He sent down water from the sky, by which We produce blossoms of every kind, and lush greenery. Furthermore, We produce *pods* with seeds packed together and from the flowering part of palm trees, low-hanging clusters of dates, and orchards of vines, olives and pomegranates, some look-alike and others different. Look at their fruits as they grow and ripen; there are signs in that for people who believe.

Allah, the Originator of the universe

[100] *Some people* have taken jinn[b] as partners of Allah, yet He created them, and falsely ascribed sons and daughters to Him without any knowledge. Glory be to Him! He is Exalted far above what they describe. [101] He's the Originator of the Heavens and the Earth. How could He have a son when He has no mate? He created everything, and He knows everything. [102] Such is Allah, your Lord; there is no god but Him, the Creator of everything, so worship Him. He governs everything. [103] *Our* eyes cannot perceive Him, but He perceives *what* our eyes see. He is the Subtle, the Aware. [104] *Say, Muhammad*: "Visible proofs have come to you from your Lord; anyone who looks at them, it is for his own benefit, and whoever remains blind *to them*, on *his head* be it. I am not *sent* to watch over you."

---

[a]   The word *mustaqarr* means a fixed term (*Surat Al-Baqarah* 2: 36). Al-Qurtubi translates it as "depositing" in the grave, where one awaits the Day of Judgement.

[b]   The Jinn are an invisible species created from fire. Like humans, they possess intellect and are accountable for their actions, and among them are both believers and disbelievers.

اَنَا عَلَيْكُمْ بِحَفِيظٍ ۞ وَكَذٰلِكَ نُصَرِّفُ الْاٰيٰتِ وَلِيَقُوْلُوْا

دَرَسْتَ وَلِنُبَيِّنَهُ لِقَوْمٍ يَّعْلَمُوْنَ ۞ اِتَّبِعْ مَا اُوْحِيَ اِلَيْكَ

مِنْ رَّبِّكَ ۚ لَا اِلٰهَ اِلَّا هُوَ ۚ وَاَعْرِضْ عَنِ الْمُشْرِكِيْنَ ۞

وَلَوْ شَاءَ اللّٰهُ مَا اَشْرَكُوْا ۗ وَمَا جَعَلْنٰكَ عَلَيْهِمْ حَفِيْظًا ۚ

وَمَا اَنْتَ عَلَيْهِمْ بِوَكِيْلٍ ۞ وَلَا تَسُبُّوا الَّذِيْنَ يَدْعُوْنَ

مِنْ دُوْنِ اللّٰهِ فَيَسُبُّوا اللّٰهَ عَدْوًۢا بِغَيْرِ عِلْمٍ ۗ كَذٰلِكَ

زَيَّنَّا لِكُلِّ اُمَّةٍ عَمَلَهُمْ ۠ ثُمَّ اِلٰى رَبِّهِمْ مَّرْجِعُهُمْ

فَيُنَبِّئُهُمْ بِمَا كَانُوْا يَعْمَلُوْنَ ۞ وَاَقْسَمُوْا بِاللّٰهِ جَهْدَ

اَيْمَانِهِمْ لَئِنْ جَاءَتْهُمْ اٰيَةٌ لَّيُؤْمِنُنَّ بِهَا ۚ قُلْ اِنَّمَا

الْاٰيٰتُ عِنْدَ اللّٰهِ وَمَا يُشْعِرُكُمْ ۙ اَنَّهَا اِذَا جَاءَتْ لَا

يُؤْمِنُوْنَ ۞ وَنُقَلِّبُ اَفْئِدَتَهُمْ وَاَبْصَارَهُمْ كَمَا لَمْ يُؤْمِنُوْا

بِهٖ اَوَّلَ مَرَّةٍ وَّنَذَرُهُمْ فِيْ طُغْيَانِهِمْ يَعْمَهُوْنَ ۞

وَلَوْ اَنَّنَا نَزَّلْنَا اِلَيْهِمُ الْمَلٰئِكَةَ وَكَلَّمَهُمُ الْمَوْتٰى

وَحَشَرْنَا عَلَيْهِمْ كُلَّ شَيْءٍ قُبُلًا مَّا كَانُوْا لِيُؤْمِنُوْا

اِلَّا اَنْ يَّشَاءَ اللّٰهُ وَلٰكِنَّ اَكْثَرَهُمْ يَجْهَلُوْنَ ۞

وَكَذٰلِكَ جَعَلْنَا لِكُلِّ نَبِيٍّ عَدُوًّا شَيٰطِيْنَ الْاِنْسِ

وَالْجِنِّ يُوْحِيْ بَعْضُهُمْ اِلٰى بَعْضٍ زُخْرُفَ الْقَوْلِ

غُرُوْرًا ۗ وَلَوْ شَاءَ رَبُّكَ مَا فَعَلُوْهُ فَذَرْهُمْ وَمَا

يَفْتَرُوْنَ ۞ وَلِتَصْغٰى اِلَيْهِ اَفْئِدَةُ الَّذِيْنَ لَا

يُؤْمِنُوْنَ بِالْاٰخِرَةِ وَلِيَرْضَوْهُ وَلِيَقْتَرِفُوْا مَا هُمْ

Satan could be the entertainment industry that spreads evil notions in mass media. Beware what you watch and hear.

۱۳
ع
۱۰
۱۹

[105] This is how We explain the signs, but *the disbelievers* say, "You have learnt it[a]." So, We *wish to* make them clear for people who know *the truth*.

Muslims forbidden to insult the beliefs of non-Muslims

[106] *Messenger,* follow what is revealed to you from your Lord – there is no god but Him – and turn away from the idolaters. [107] Had Allah willed, they would not have associated *anything with Him.* We've not put you *there* to watch over them, nor are you responsible for them. [108] *Believers,* don't insult anything[b] they worship beside Allah, then they will insult Allah out of hostility and ignorance. That is how We made every community's actions appear attractive to them, they will return to their Lord, and He will inform them about what they did.

Even miracles fail to convince sceptics

[109] *The idolaters* swear solemn oaths by Allah that if a miracle came to them they would believe. Say: "Miracles come only from Allah." What would make you realise that even if a *miracle* came, they still wouldn't believe; [110] and that We would turn their faculties of intellect and sight upside down because they failed to believe in it the first time, leaving them to wander blindly about in their wickedness? [111] Even if We sent down angels, or the dead spoke, or We gathered everything before them, they wouldn't believe unless Allah so willed. Most of them are ignorant.

How demons mislead?

[112] For every prophet We assigned an enemy, demons from humans and jinn, who inspired one another with flowery speech to deceive. If Your Lord wanted, they wouldn't have done this; so, leave them and what they invent. [113] *They do so that* the intellects of disbelievers of the Hereafter might turn towards *their flowery speech,* and be pleased with it, and so that they might get what is coming to them *because of their wicked ways.*

---

[a] From the People of The Book, it's not from Allah.

[b] The classical commentaries talk specifically of idols, which were relevant to the context of Makkah, but the Quran is general, so it also includes non-religious belief systems: atheism and secularism.

مُّقْتَرِفُوْنَ ۝ اَفَغَيْرَ اللّٰهِ اَبْتَغِيْ حَكَمًا وَّهُوَ الَّذِيْ

اَنْزَلَ اِلَيْكُمُ الْكِتٰبَ مُفَصَّلًا ۛ وَالَّذِيْنَ اٰتَيْنٰهُمُ

الْكِتٰبَ يَعْلَمُوْنَ اَنَّهٗ مُنَزَّلٌ مِّنْ رَّبِّكَ بِالْحَقِّ

فَلَا تَكُوْنَنَّ مِنَ الْمُمْتَرِيْنَ ۝ وَتَمَّتْ كَلِمَتُ رَبِّكَ

صِدْقًا وَّعَدْلًا ۛ لَا مُبَدِّلَ لِكَلِمٰتِهٖ ۚ وَهُوَ السَّمِيْعُ

الْعَلِيْمُ ۝ وَاِنْ تُطِعْ اَكْثَرَ مَنْ فِي الْاَرْضِ

يُضِلُّوْكَ عَنْ سَبِيْلِ اللّٰهِ ۚ اِنْ يَّتَّبِعُوْنَ اِلَّا الظَّنَّ

وَاِنْ هُمْ اِلَّا يَخْرُصُوْنَ ۝ اِنَّ رَبَّكَ هُوَ اَعْلَمُ

مَنْ يَّضِلُّ عَنْ سَبِيْلِهٖ ۚ وَهُوَ اَعْلَمُ بِالْمُهْتَدِيْنَ ۝

فَكُلُوْا مِمَّا ذُكِرَ اسْمُ اللّٰهِ عَلَيْهِ اِنْ كُنْتُمْ بِاٰيٰتِهٖ

مُؤْمِنِيْنَ ۝ وَمَا لَكُمْ اَلَّا تَاْكُلُوْا مِمَّا ذُكِرَ اسْمُ

اللّٰهِ عَلَيْهِ وَقَدْ فَصَّلَ لَكُمْ مَّا حَرَّمَ عَلَيْكُمْ اِلَّا

مَا اضْطُرِرْتُمْ اِلَيْهِ ۚ وَاِنَّ كَثِيْرًا لَّيُضِلُّوْنَ بِاَهْوَآئِهِمْ

بِغَيْرِ عِلْمٍ ۚ اِنَّ رَبَّكَ هُوَ اَعْلَمُ بِالْمُعْتَدِيْنَ ۝

وَذَرُوْا ظَاهِرَ الْاِثْمِ وَبَاطِنَهٗ ۚ اِنَّ الَّذِيْنَ يَكْسِبُوْنَ

الْاِثْمَ سَيُجْزَوْنَ بِمَا كَانُوْا يَقْتَرِفُوْنَ ۝ وَلَا تَاْكُلُوْا

مِمَّا لَمْ يُذْكَرِ اسْمُ اللّٰهِ عَلَيْهِ وَاِنَّهٗ لَفِسْقٌ ۗ وَاِنَّ

الشَّيٰطِيْنَ لَيُوْحُوْنَ اِلٰى اَوْلِيٰٓئِهِمْ لِيُجَادِلُوْكُمْ ۚ وَاِنْ

اَطَعْتُمُوْهُمْ اِنَّكُمْ لَمُشْرِكُوْنَ ۝ اَوَمَنْ كَانَ مَيْتًا

فَاَحْيَيْنٰهُ وَجَعَلْنَا لَهٗ نُوْرًا يَّمْشِيْ بِهٖ فِي النَّاسِ

Avoid sins of all kind; secret or open; intentional or unintentional; big or small.

١١ ع ١٤

269

¹¹⁴ *Say*: "Should I seek a judge beside Allah, when He has sent down the Book to you, clearly explained?" Those given the Book know it has been sent by Your Lord with truth so, listener don't be among the doubters. ¹¹⁵ Truly and justly has your Lord's promise been fulfilled;ᵃ no power can change His promise. He is the Hearer, the Knower. ¹¹⁶ If you were to obey *the whims of* most of those in the city, they would mislead you from Allah's way. They do nothing but follow speculation and tell lies. ¹¹⁷ Your Lord knows best those straying from His way, and those guided.

A warning for those fussy about food

¹¹⁸ So eat of the *meat* on which Allah's name has been invoked,ᵇ if you believe in His signs. ¹¹⁹ Why wouldn't you eat that on which Allah's name has been invoked, after He has explained in detail what He has forbidden you *to eat* except out of necessity? Many of them are misled because of their desires and lack of knowledge. Your Lord knows best the sinners. ¹²⁰ Stay away from open and hidden sins; those who commit sins will be punished for what they gained from it. ¹²¹ Do not eat that *meat* on which the name of Allah has not been invoked; to do so is sinful. *Believers*, the *human* demons inspire their followers to dispute with you; and if you were to obey them, you would be *guilty of* associating *partners with Allah*.

ᵃ   *Kalima*, literally "word", here refers to Allah's promise of judgement in the Hereafter. It could also refer to the Quran.

ᵇ   The verses 118–121 contain a challenge for our times, with so many halal certifiers competing against each other for business. Al-Qurtubi says Allah revealed them in relation to Muslims who only ate what they slaughtered themselves, refusing any other meat.

كَمَنْ مَّثَلُهُ فِى الظُّلُمَاتِ لَيْسَ بِخَارِجٍ مِّنْهَا ط كَذٰلِكَ زُيِّنَ لِلْكٰفِرِيْنَ مَا كَانُوْا يَعْمَلُوْنَ ۞ وَ كَذٰلِكَ جَعَلْنَا فِىْ كُلِّ قَرْيَةٍ أَكٰبِرَ مُجْرِمِيْهَا لِيَمْكُرُوْا فِيْهَا ط وَمَا يَمْكُرُوْنَ إِلَّا بِأَنْفُسِهِمْ وَمَا يَشْعُرُوْنَ ۞ وَإِذَا جَاءَتْهُمْ اٰيَةٌ قَالُوْا لَنْ نُّؤْمِنَ حَتّٰى نُؤْتٰى مِثْلَ مَا أُوْتِىَ رُسُلُ اللّٰهِ ط اَللّٰهُ أَعْلَمُ حَيْثُ يَجْعَلُ رِسَالَتَهُ ط سَيُصِيْبُ الَّذِيْنَ أَجْرَمُوْا صَغَارٌ عِنْدَ اللّٰهِ وَعَذَابٌ شَدِيْدٌۢ بِمَا كَانُوْا يَمْكُرُوْنَ ۞ فَمَنْ يُّرِدِ اللّٰهُ أَنْ يَّهْدِيَهُ يَشْرَحْ صَدْرَهُ لِلْإِسْلَامِ ۚ وَمَنْ يُّرِدْ أَنْ يُّضِلَّهُ يَجْعَلْ صَدْرَهُ ضَيِّقًا حَرَجًا كَأَنَّمَا يَصَّعَّدُ فِى السَّمَاءِ ط كَذٰلِكَ يَجْعَلُ اللّٰهُ الرِّجْسَ عَلَى الَّذِيْنَ لَا يُؤْمِنُوْنَ ۞ وَهٰذَا صِرَاطُ رَبِّكَ مُسْتَقِيْمًا ط قَدْ فَصَّلْنَا الْاٰيٰتِ لِقَوْمٍ يَّذَّكَّرُوْنَ ۞ لَهُمْ دَارُ السَّلٰمِ عِنْدَ رَبِّهِمْ وَهُوَ وَلِيُّهُمْ بِمَا كَانُوْا يَعْمَلُوْنَ ۞ وَيَوْمَ يَحْشُرُهُمْ جَمِيْعًا ۚ يٰمَعْشَرَ الْجِنِّ قَدِ اسْتَكْثَرْتُمْ مِّنَ الْإِنْسِ ۚ وَقَالَ أَوْلِيَاؤُهُمْ مِّنَ الْإِنْسِ رَبَّنَا اسْتَمْتَعَ بَعْضُنَا بِبَعْضٍ وَّبَلَغْنَا أَجَلَنَا الَّذِىْ أَجَّلْتَ لَنَا ط قَالَ النَّارُ مَثْوٰىكُمْ خٰلِدِيْنَ فِيْهَا إِلَّا مَا شَاءَ اللّٰهُ ط إِنَّ رَبَّكَ حَكِيْمٌ عَلِيْمٌ ۞ وَكَذٰلِكَ نُوَلِّىْ بَعْضَ الظّٰلِمِيْنَ بَعْضًۢا بِمَا كَانُوْا يَكْسِبُوْنَ ۞

The opening of the heart and mind to divine message is a special favour from Allah.

Evil works look attractive

¹²² *Take for example a* person spiritually dead who We gave a life and a light to walk among people, is he like someone who lives in utter darkness which he never leaves? That is why what disbelievers did appeared attractive to them. ¹²³ In the same way, We have placed sinners in every town who go about plotting *evil*, but *they* are only unwittingly deceiving themselves. ¹²⁴ When a revelation came to them, they said, "We shall not believe until we are given what Allah's *earlier* messengers were given." Allah knows best where to place His Message. Those who break the law will face humiliation in front of Allah, and severe punishment for their former plotting.

Submission to Allah is a sign of open-mindedness

¹²⁵ The person Allah wishes to guide, He opens his mind[a] to surrender *to Allah*; and anyone He allows to go astray, He closes his mind, as if he were struggling to climb skywards: by such means Allah allows evil to come about on those who do not believe. ¹²⁶ This is the straight path of your Lord, and We have explained the verses in detail for people who are open to reminders. ¹²⁷ They shall enjoy a house of peace with their Lord, and He shall be their Protector for what they did.

How the sinners can influence others?

¹²⁸ On the day when He gathers them all, *He will say*, "Company of jinn, you derived much pleasure from *misleading* humans," and their allies among the humans will say, "Our Lord, we benefitted from each other, but now we have reached the end of the span of life that you appointed for us." He will say, "The Fire is your eternal abode, unless Allah wishes otherwise." Indeed, *messenger*, your Lord is Wise, Knowing. ¹²⁹ This is how We give some sinners influence over others because of the deeds they earned.

---

[a] *Sadr* means the "chest"; it can be a metaphor for the intellect and emotions, but can also be quite literal when followed by a simile: 'the narrowing of the chest'.

يٰمَعْشَرَ الْجِنِّ وَالْاِنْسِ اَلَمْ يَاْتِكُمْ رُسُلٌ مِّنْكُمْ
يَقُصُّوْنَ عَلَيْكُمْ اٰيٰتِيْ وَيُنْذِرُوْنَكُمْ لِقَآءَ يَوْمِكُمْ
هٰذَا ؕ قَالُوْا شَهِدْنَا عَلٰى اَنْفُسِنَا وَغَرَّتْهُمُ
الْحَيٰوةُ الدُّنْيَا وَشَهِدُوْا عَلٰى اَنْفُسِهِمْ اَنَّهُمْ كَانُوْا
كٰفِرِيْنَ ۝ ذٰلِكَ اَنْ لَّمْ يَكُنْ رَّبُّكَ مُهْلِكَ الْقُرٰى
بِظُلْمٍ وَّ اَهْلُهَا غٰفِلُوْنَ ۝ وَلِكُلٍّ دَرَجٰتٌ مِّمَّا
عَمِلُوْا ؕ وَمَا رَبُّكَ بِغَافِلٍ عَمَّا يَعْمَلُوْنَ ۝ وَرَبُّكَ
الْغَنِيُّ ذُو الرَّحْمَةِ ؕ اِنْ يَّشَاْ يُذْهِبْكُمْ وَيَسْتَخْلِفْ
مِنْ بَعْدِكُمْ مَّا يَشَآءُ كَمَاۤ اَنْشَاَكُمْ مِّنْ ذُرِّيَّةِ
قَوْمٍ اٰخَرِيْنَ ۝ اِنَّ مَا تُوْعَدُوْنَ لَاٰتٍ ۙ وَّمَاۤ اَنْتُمْ
بِمُعْجِزِيْنَ ۝ قُلْ يٰقَوْمِ اعْمَلُوْا عَلٰى مَكَانَتِكُمْ اِنِّيْ
عَامِلٌ ۚ فَسَوْفَ تَعْلَمُوْنَ ۙ مَنْ تَكُوْنُ لَهٗ عَاقِبَةُ
الدَّارِ ؕ اِنَّهٗ لَا يُفْلِحُ الظّٰلِمُوْنَ ۝ وَجَعَلُوْا لِلّٰهِ مِمَّا
ذَرَاَ مِنَ الْحَرْثِ وَالْاَنْعَامِ نَصِيْبًا فَقَالُوْا هٰذَا لِلّٰهِ
بِزَعْمِهِمْ وَهٰذَا لِشُرَكَآئِنَا ۚ فَمَا كَانَ لِشُرَكَآئِهِمْ
فَلَا يَصِلُ اِلَى اللّٰهِ ۚ وَمَا كَانَ لِلّٰهِ فَهُوَ يَصِلُ اِلٰى
شُرَكَآئِهِمْ ؕ سَآءَ مَا يَحْكُمُوْنَ ۝ وَكَذٰلِكَ زَيَّنَ لِكَثِيْرٍ
مِّنَ الْمُشْرِكِيْنَ قَتْلَ اَوْلَادِهِمْ شُرَكَآؤُهُمْ لِيُرْدُوْهُمْ
وَلِيَلْبِسُوْا عَلَيْهِمْ دِيْنَهُمْ ؕ وَلَوْ شَآءَ اللّٰهُ مَا فَعَلُوْهُ
فَذَرْهُمْ وَمَا يَفْتَرُوْنَ ۝ وَقَالُوْا هٰذِهٖۤ اَنْعَامٌ

Jinn are invisible creations that influence humans. How, when and who?

¹³⁰ *Allah will ask*: "Company of jinn and humans, did messengers not come to you from among your own kind, telling you of My signs and warning you that you would meet *Me* on this day?" They will say, "We testify against ourselves," but the worldly life deceived them, and they testified against themselves that they were disbelievers. ¹³¹ Your Lord was never unjust, He would not destroy towns whose inhabitants had no knowledge *of the truth.*

Different ranks in the Hereafter based on righteous deeds
¹³² Everyone's rank *in the Hereafter* will be based on what they did *in this life*, and Your Lord is not ignorant of what they do. ¹³³ Your Lord is Self-Sufficient, Most Kind. If He wanted, He could get rid of you altogether and replace you with whomever He pleases, just as He raised you from the offspring of other people. ¹³⁴ What you have been promised is coming, and you will not be able to stop *it*. ¹³⁵ Say: "My people, do it your way, and I'll do it my way. Soon you will know who will gain the happy home in the Hereafter." Evildoers don't succeed.

Pagan customs and superstitions about livestock
¹³⁶ They set aside for Allah a share of the crops and cattle that He has produced, saying, "This is for Allah," as they claim, "and this is for our partner *gods*." *Whatever* is for their partners doesn't reach Allah, and whatever is for Allah reaches their partners. How badly they judge!

They commit infanticide
¹³⁷ In this way their partners *in falsehood* have made it appear attractive to many of the idolaters to kill their children.^a *Their false gods do this* to destroy them and to dress up their religion. Of course, if Allah had so wished, they wouldn't have done it; so leave them and whatever they have invented.

---

^a   These pagan Arab superstitions were to justify infanticide, especially of females, by claiming that it was forbidden to feed this baby girl from the milk of this ewe, for example, but her twin brother can be fed from it. A few verses later, the comparison is made between what the Arabs before Islam used to forbid with what was forbidden for the Jews. In Mark 7: 11, Isa the Messiah criticised the Jews for refusing to help their parents, claiming that his time was *qurban*: in other words, dedicated to God as a kind of sacrifice.

وَّحَرْثٌ حِجْرٌ لَّا يَطْعَمُهَاۤ اِلَّا مَنْ نَّشَاۤءُ بِزَعْمِهِمْ وَاَنْعَامٌ حُرِّمَتْ ظُهُوْرُهَا وَاَنْعَامٌ لَّا يَذْكُرُوْنَ اسْمَ اللّٰهِ عَلَيْهَا افْتِرَآءً عَلَيْهِؕ سَيَجْزِيْهِمْ بِمَا كَانُوْا يَفْتَرُوْنَ ۝ وَقَالُوْا مَا فِيْ بُطُوْنِ هٰذِهِ الْاَنْعَامِ خَالِصَةٌ لِّذُكُوْرِنَا وَمُحَرَّمٌ عَلٰۤى اَزْوَاجِنَاۚ وَاِنْ يَّكُنْ مَّيْتَةً فَهُمْ فِيْهِ شُرَكَآءُؕ سَيَجْزِيْهِمْ وَصْفَهُمْؕ اِنَّهٗ حَكِيْمٌ عَلِيْمٌ ۝ قَدْ خَسِرَ الَّذِيْنَ قَتَلُوْۤا اَوْلَادَهُمْ سَفَهًۢا بِغَيْرِ عِلْمٍ وَّحَرَّمُوْا مَا رَزَقَهُمُ اللّٰهُ افْتِرَآءً عَلَى اللّٰهِؕ قَدْ ضَلُّوْا وَمَا كَانُوْا مُهْتَدِيْنَ ۝ وَهُوَ الَّذِيْۤ اَنْشَاَ جَنّٰتٍ مَّعْرُوْشٰتٍ وَّغَيْرَ مَعْرُوْشٰتٍ وَّالنَّخْلَ وَالزَّرْعَ مُخْتَلِفًا اُكُلُهٗ وَالزَّيْتُوْنَ وَالرُّمَّانَ مُتَشَابِهًا وَّغَيْرَ مُتَشَابِهٍؕ كُلُوْا مِنْ ثَمَرِهٖۤ اِذَاۤ اَثْمَرَ وَاٰتُوْا حَقَّهٗ يَوْمَ حَصَادِهٖ ۖ وَلَا تُسْرِفُوْاؕ اِنَّهٗ لَا يُحِبُّ الْمُسْرِفِيْنَ ۝ وَمِنَ الْاَنْعَامِ حَمُوْلَةً وَّفَرْشًاؕ كُلُوْا مِمَّا رَزَقَكُمُ اللّٰهُ وَلَا تَتَّبِعُوْا خُطُوٰتِ الشَّيْطٰنِؕ اِنَّهٗ لَكُمْ عَدُوٌّ مُّبِيْنٌ ۝ ثَمٰنِيَةَ اَزْوَاجٍۚ مِنَ الضَّاْنِ اثْنَيْنِ وَمِنَ الْمَعْزِ اثْنَيْنِؕ قُلْ ءٰٓالذَّكَرَيْنِ حَرَّمَ اَمِ الْاُنْثَيَيْنِ اَمَّا اشْتَمَلَتْ عَلَيْهِ اَرْحَامُ الْاُنْثَيَيْنِؕ نَبِّئُوْنِيْ بِعِلْمٍ اِنْ كُنْتُمْ صٰدِقِيْنَ ۝ وَمِنَ الْاِبِلِ اثْنَيْنِ وَمِنَ

The strange and weird practices of the materialist: the modern pagan.

The prohibition to ride some animals

[138] They say, "These cattle and crops are set aside. No one may eat them without our authorisation." *Some* cattle are forbidden to ride; and on other cattle they do not invoke Allah's name *when slaughtering*, falsely attributing these rules to Him. He will deal *appropriately* with whatever *lies* they invented.

Superstition about the stillborn

[139] They say, "What is in the wombs of these cattle are exclusively for our men and forbidden for our wives. But, if it is stillborn, then they all share in it." He will reward them *appropriately* for their *false* description *of Him*. He is Wise, Knowing. [140] Those who kill their children foolishly without knowledge, and who forbid what Allah has provided them, falsely attributing it to Allah, they have *already* lost: they have gone astray; they aren't guided. [141] He grows gardens, both with and without trellises,[a] date palms, plants of different flavours, olives and pomegranates, some alike and others different. Eat of their fruits when they are ripe, give *the needy* their due on harvest day, and do not squander; He dislikes spendthrifts.

Four pairs of animals

[142] Some cattle are for carrying loads and some are for food; so eat what Allah has provided you and don't follow in Satan's footsteps, *for* he is your open enemy. [143] There are eight *animals in* pairs: two sheep and two goats. Say: "Is it the two males that He has forbidden, or the two females; or is it perhaps what lies within the wombs of the two females? Tell me based on some sound knowledge, which is it if you are telling the truth."

---

[a]   A trellis is a wooden or metal lattice used to support fruit trees or vines.

الْبَقَرِ اثْنَيْنِ ؕ قُلْ ءٰٓاۤلذَّكَرَيْنِ حَرَّمَ اَمِ الْاُنْثَيَيْنِ

اَمَّا اشْتَمَلَتْ عَلَيْهِ اَرْحَامُ الْاُنْثَيَيْنِ ؕ اَمْ كُنْتُمْ

شُهَدَاۤءَ اِذْ وَصّٰكُمُ اللّٰهُ بِهٰذَا ۚ فَمَنْ اَظْلَمُ مِمَّنِ

افْتَرٰى عَلَى اللّٰهِ كَذِبًا لِّيُضِلَّ النَّاسَ بِغَيْرِ عِلْمٍ ؕ اِنَّ

اللّٰهَ لَا يَهْدِى الْقَوْمَ الظّٰلِمِيْنَ ۧ قُلْ لَّاۤ اَجِدُ فِيْ

مَاۤ اُوْحِيَ اِلَيَّ مُحَرَّمًا عَلٰى طَاعِمٍ يَّطْعَمُهٗۤ اِلَّاۤ اَنْ

يَّكُوْنَ مَيْتَةً اَوْ دَمًا مَّسْفُوْحًا اَوْ لَحْمَ خِنْزِيْرٍ فَاِنَّهٗ

رِجْسٌ اَوْ فِسْقًا اُهِلَّ لِغَيْرِ اللّٰهِ بِهٖ ۚ فَمَنِ اضْطُرَّ غَيْرَ

بَاغٍ وَّلَا عَادٍ فَاِنَّ رَبَّكَ غَفُوْرٌ رَّحِيْمٌ ۝ وَعَلَى الَّذِيْنَ

هَادُوْا حَرَّمْنَا كُلَّ ذِيْ ظُفُرٍ ۚ وَمِنَ الْبَقَرِ وَالْغَنَمِ

حَرَّمْنَا عَلَيْهِمْ شُحُوْمَهُمَاۤ اِلَّا مَا حَمَلَتْ ظُهُوْرُهُمَاۤ اَوِ

الْحَوَايَاۤ اَوْ مَا اخْتَلَطَ بِعَظْمٍ ؕ ذٰلِكَ جَزَيْنٰهُمْ بِبَغْيِهِمْ ۖ

وَاِنَّا لَصٰدِقُوْنَ ۝ فَاِنْ كَذَّبُوْكَ فَقُلْ رَّبُّكُمْ ذُوْ

رَحْمَةٍ وَّاسِعَةٍ ۚ وَلَا يُرَدُّ بَاْسُهٗ عَنِ الْقَوْمِ

الْمُجْرِمِيْنَ ۝ سَيَقُوْلُ الَّذِيْنَ اَشْرَكُوْا لَوْ شَاۤءَ اللّٰهُ

مَاۤ اَشْرَكْنَا وَلَاۤ اٰبَاۤؤُنَا وَلَا حَرَّمْنَا مِنْ شَيْءٍ ؕ

كَذٰلِكَ كَذَّبَ الَّذِيْنَ مِنْ قَبْلِهِمْ حَتّٰى ذَاقُوْا بَاْسَنَا ؕ

قُلْ هَلْ عِنْدَكُمْ مِّنْ عِلْمٍ فَتُخْرِجُوْهُ لَنَا ؕ اِنْ

تَتَّبِعُوْنَ اِلَّا الظَّنَّ وَاِنْ اَنْتُمْ اِلَّا تَخْرُصُوْنَ ۝

قُلْ فَلِلّٰهِ الْحُجَّةُ الْبَالِغَةُ ۚ فَلَوْ شَاۤءَ لَهَدٰىكُمْ

Respect Allah's laws, don't violate them.

¹⁴⁴*Likewise, there are* two camels and two oxen. Say: "Is it the two males that He has forbidden, or the two females; or is it perhaps what lies within the wombs of the two females? Or were you *even* present when Allah ordered you to do this? Who is more wrong than the one who ignorantly invents lies about Allah to mislead people? Allah does not guide the wrongdoers." ¹⁴⁵Say: "I find nothing in what has been revealed to me that people are forbidden to eat except carrion, blood products, pork, which is impure, or else meat *from animals* slaughtered in the name of anything other than Allah." However, if anyone is compelled, not because he desires it or wishes to disobey *Allah*, then your Lord is Forgiving, Kind. ¹⁴⁶We forbade the Jews *from eating* animals with claws; and the fat of oxen and sheep, except whatever *fat* clings to their backs or to the offal, or is stuck to bones. That penalty was imposed because of their rebelliousness. We are Most Truthful. ¹⁴⁷If they accuse you of lying, say: "Your Lord is gracious, and yet His punishment will not be deflected from the sinful people."

The idolaters' practices have no sound basis

¹⁴⁸The idolaters will say, "If Allah wanted, neither we nor our ancestors would have associated *anything with Allah*, nor would we have forbidden *the eating of* anything." In the same way, people before them used to lie outrageously, until they tasted Our punishment. Say: "Have you got any knowledge? If so, produce it for us. You only follow speculation and tell lies." ¹⁴⁹Say: "Allah has conclusive proof, If He so wished, He would have guided you all."ᵃ

ᵃ This clarifies the belief about predestination; the relationship between Allah's knowledge of the future and human free-will. Seemingly, the two are contradictory. That's not so, We believe Allah's knowledge is infinite and humans have been given a responsibility; the moral choice to be either good or bad. If Allah wanted He could have made us all righteous, without a free-will. The Day of Judgement would then be meaningless and worldly life no longer a test. From here to the end of the surat is clarification of this moral choice.

اَجۡمَعِیۡنَ ۩ قُلۡ هَلُمَّ شُهَدَآءَكُمُ الَّذِیۡنَ یَشۡهَدُوۡنَ اَنَّ اللّٰهَ حَرَّمَ هٰذَا ۚ فَاِنۡ شَهِدُوۡا فَلَا تَشۡهَدۡ مَعَهُمۡ ۚ وَلَا تَتَّبِعۡ اَهۡوَآءَ الَّذِیۡنَ كَذَّبُوۡا بِاٰیٰتِنَا وَالَّذِیۡنَ لَا یُؤۡمِنُوۡنَ بِالۡاٰخِرَةِ وَهُمۡ بِرَبِّهِمۡ یَعۡدِلُوۡنَ ۩ قُلۡ تَعَالَوۡا اَتۡلُ مَا حَرَّمَ رَبُّكُمۡ عَلَیۡكُمۡ اَلَّا تُشۡرِكُوۡا بِهٖ شَیۡئًا وَّبِالۡوَالِدَیۡنِ اِحۡسَانًا ۚ وَلَا تَقۡتُلُوۡٓا اَوۡلَادَكُمۡ مِّنۡ اِمۡلَاقٍ ؕ نَحۡنُ نَرۡزُقُكُمۡ وَاِیَّاهُمۡ ۚ وَلَا تَقۡرَبُوا الۡفَوَاحِشَ مَا ظَهَرَ مِنۡهَا وَمَا بَطَنَ ۚ وَلَا تَقۡتُلُوا النَّفۡسَ الَّتِیۡ حَرَّمَ اللّٰهُ اِلَّا بِالۡحَقِّ ؕ ذٰلِكُمۡ وَصّٰكُمۡ بِهٖ لَعَلَّكُمۡ تَعۡقِلُوۡنَ ۩ وَلَا تَقۡرَبُوۡا مَالَ الۡیَتِیۡمِ اِلَّا بِالَّتِیۡ هِیَ اَحۡسَنُ حَتّٰی یَبۡلُغَ اَشُدَّهٗ ۚ وَاَوۡفُوا الۡكَیۡلَ وَالۡمِیۡزَانَ بِالۡقِسۡطِ ۚ لَا نُكَلِّفُ نَفۡسًا اِلَّا وُسۡعَهَا ۚ وَاِذَا قُلۡتُمۡ فَاعۡدِلُوۡا وَلَوۡ كَانَ ذَا قُرۡبٰی ۚ وَبِعَهۡدِ اللّٰهِ اَوۡفُوۡا ؕ ذٰلِكُمۡ وَصّٰكُمۡ بِهٖ لَعَلَّكُمۡ تَذَكَّرُوۡنَ ۩ وَاَنَّ هٰذَا صِرَاطِیۡ مُسۡتَقِیۡمًا فَاتَّبِعُوۡهُ ۚ وَلَا تَتَّبِعُوا السُّبُلَ فَتَفَرَّقَ بِكُمۡ عَنۡ سَبِیۡلِهٖ ؕ ذٰلِكُمۡ وَصّٰكُمۡ بِهٖ لَعَلَّكُمۡ تَتَّقُوۡنَ ۩ ثُمَّ اٰتَیۡنَا مُوۡسَی الۡكِتٰبَ تَمَامًا عَلَی الَّذِیۡٓ اَحۡسَنَ وَتَفۡصِیۡلًا لِّكُلِّ شَیۡءٍ وَّهُدًی وَّرَحۡمَةً لَّعَلَّهُمۡ بِلِقَآءِ رَبِّهِمۡ یُؤۡمِنُوۡنَ ۩ وَهٰذَا كِتٰبٌ اَنۡزَلۡنٰهُ مُبٰرَكٌ

Do you know and understand the ten commandments?

279

¹⁵⁰ Say: "Bring your witnesses who will testify that Allah forbade this." Even if they testify, you do not testify with them. Do not follow the desires of deniers of our signs and those who don't believe in the Hereafter, and hold *others* up as equals to their Lord.

Commandments for Muslims; the new contract

¹⁵¹ Say: "Step forward *and* I will tell you what your Lord has forbidden for you: Associate nothing with Him, treat parents well, don't kill your children due to poverty, We provide for both you and them. Stay well clear of gross indecency, whether openly or in secret. Don't kill anyone, Allah has made *life* sacred, unless by some lawful right. This is what He has commanded you, so that you might reflect. ¹⁵² Stay well clear of the property of orphans, except if it be to do good *by investing it wisely*, until they come of age. Be honest in *your* weights and measures, *because* We do not task any person beyond its capacity. Whenever you speak, be just even regarding your own relatives. Be true to the contract of Allah. This is what He has commanded you, so that you might pay attention. ¹⁵³ This path of Mine is straight, so follow it and do not follow other paths, as they will cause you to deviate from His path. This is what He has commanded you, so that you might be mindful."

Allah's revelation removes doubts

¹⁵⁴ After that, We gave Musa the Book as a comprehensive *manual* for the one who strives for righteousness, explaining everything in detail, and as a guidance and kindness so that people might believe in meeting their Lord. ¹⁵⁵ And this *too* is a blessed book that We have sent down, so follow it and be mindful, so that you might be treated kindly *by Allah*.

فَاتَّبِعُوْهُ وَاتَّقُوْا لَعَلَّكُمْ تُرْحَمُوْنَ ۝ اَنْ تَقُوْلُوْا

اِنَّمَاۤ اُنْزِلَ الْكِتٰبُ عَلٰى طَآئِفَتَيْنِ مِنْ قَبْلِنَا ۪

وَاِنْ كُنَّا عَنْ دِرَاسَتِهِمْ لَغٰفِلِيْنَ ۝ اَوْ تَقُوْلُوْا لَوْ

اَنَّاۤ اُنْزِلَ عَلَيْنَا الْكِتٰبُ لَكُنَّاۤ اَهْدٰى مِنْهُمْ ۚ فَقَدْ

جَآءَكُمْ بَيِّنَةٌ مِّنْ رَّبِّكُمْ وَهُدًى وَّرَحْمَةٌ ۚ فَمَنْ

اَظْلَمُ مِمَّنْ كَذَّبَ بِاٰيٰتِ اللّٰهِ وَصَدَفَ عَنْهَا ۗ

سَنَجْزِي الَّذِيْنَ يَصْدِفُوْنَ عَنْ اٰيٰتِنَا سُوْٓءَ

الْعَذَابِ بِمَا كَانُوْا يَصْدِفُوْنَ ۝ هَلْ يَنْظُرُوْنَ اِلَّاۤ

اَنْ تَاْتِيَهُمُ الْمَلٰٓئِكَةُ اَوْ يَاْتِيَ رَبُّكَ اَوْ يَاْتِيَ بَعْضُ

اٰيٰتِ رَبِّكَ ۗ يَوْمَ يَاْتِيْ بَعْضُ اٰيٰتِ رَبِّكَ لَا يَنْفَعُ نَفْسًا

اِيْمَانُهَا لَمْ تَكُنْ اٰمَنَتْ مِنْ قَبْلُ اَوْ كَسَبَتْ فِيْ

اِيْمَانِهَا خَيْرًا ۗ قُلِ انْتَظِرُوْۤا اِنَّا مُنْتَظِرُوْنَ ۝

اِنَّ الَّذِيْنَ فَرَّقُوْا دِيْنَهُمْ وَكَانُوْا شِيَعًا لَّسْتَ

مِنْهُمْ فِيْ شَيْءٍ ۗ اِنَّمَاۤ اَمْرُهُمْ اِلَى اللّٰهِ ثُمَّ

يُنَبِّئُهُمْ بِمَا كَانُوْا يَفْعَلُوْنَ ۝ مَنْ جَآءَ بِالْحَسَنَةِ

فَلَهٗ عَشْرُ اَمْثَالِهَا ۚ وَمَنْ جَآءَ بِالسَّيِّئَةِ فَلَا

يُجْزٰۤى اِلَّا مِثْلَهَا وَهُمْ لَا يُظْلَمُوْنَ ۝ قُلْ اِنَّنِيْ

هَدٰىنِيْ رَبِّيْۤ اِلٰى صِرَاطٍ مُّسْتَقِيْمٍ ۚ دِيْنًا قِيَمًا

مِّلَّةَ اِبْرٰهِيْمَ حَنِيْفًا ۚ وَمَا كَانَ مِنَ الْمُشْرِكِيْنَ ۝

قُلْ اِنَّ صَلَاتِيْ وَنُسُكِيْ وَمَحْيَايَ وَمَمَاتِيْ لِلّٰهِ

Help to keep families, communities and friends united. Stay away from sectarianism.

¹⁵⁶ *This is* just in case you should say, "The Book was only sent to two groups before us, and we were unaware of what they had been taught," ¹⁵⁷ or you say, "If only the Book had been revealed to us, then we would have been better guided than them." Now clear evidence has come to you from your Lord, along with guidance and kindness. Who then does greater wrong than the one who denies Allah's signs and turns away from them? We will award those who turn away from Our signs the worst of punishments because of what they used to do. ¹⁵⁸ Is this what they are waiting for: that angels should come to them, or your Lord, or some signs of your Lord? On the day when some of your Lord's signs come, *there* a person's faith will be of no benefit unless it already believed, or had earned some good because of faith. Say: "Wait *and see*, for we too are waiting."

Sectarianism is condemned

¹⁵⁹ You have nothing to do with those who divided their religion and made sects; their case rests with Allah, and He will inform them about what they did. ¹⁶⁰ Whoever *on Judgement Day* produces a good deed will have *the reward of* ten like it, and whoever produces an evil deed will be awarded just one like it; and they will not be wronged *in the least.*

Faith in Allah calls for complete commitment

¹⁶¹ Say: "My Lord has guided me on a straight path, an upright religion, tending naturally towards Ibrahim's way of worship, he wasn't an idolater." ¹⁶² Say: "My prayers, my sacrifices, my life, my death; are for Allah, Lord of *all* the realms;

رَبِّ الْعَلَمِينَ ۞ لَا شَرِيكَ لَهُ ۚ وَبِذَٰلِكَ أُمِرْتُ

وَأَنَا أَوَّلُ الْمُسْلِمِينَ ۞ قُلْ أَغَيْرَ اللّٰهِ أَبْغِى رَبًّا

وَهُوَ رَبُّ كُلِّ شَىْءٍ ۚ وَلَا تَكْسِبُ كُلُّ نَفْسٍ إِلَّا

عَلَيْهَا ۚ وَلَا تَزِرُ وَازِرَةٌ وِّزْرَ أُخْرَىٰ ۚ ثُمَّ إِلَىٰ رَبِّكُمْ

مَّرْجِعُكُمْ فَيُنَبِّئُكُمْ بِمَا كُنْتُمْ فِيهِ تَخْتَلِفُونَ ۞

وَهُوَ الَّذِى جَعَلَكُمْ خَلَٰئِفَ الْأَرْضِ وَرَفَعَ بَعْضَكُمْ

فَوْقَ بَعْضٍ دَرَجَٰتٍ لِّيَبْلُوَكُمْ فِى مَآ أَتَكُمْ ۚ إِنَّ

رَبَّكَ سَرِيعُ الْعِقَابِ ۖ وَإِنَّهُ لَغَفُورٌ رَّحِيمٌ ۞

٢٠
ع
١١
ٱلْمَفْصِل

Seek the mighty Lord;
you will have all.

283

¹⁶³ He has no partners. That's what I have been ordered to do, and I am the first to surrender *to Him.*" ¹⁶⁴ Say: "How can I long for a lord other than Allah, when He is Lord of everything? No person earns anything except towards its own account, and no one will bear the burden of another; then to your Lord shall you return, and He will inform you about whatever you differed over." ¹⁶⁵ He made you representatives on Earth, raising some of you over others in rank in order to test you with what He has given you. Your Lord is swift to punish but always Forgiving, Kind.

7. Surat Al-Aʿraf

The Heights

A late Makkan surat, revealed possibly a year before the Hijrah and after *Surat Al-Anʿam*. It deals with the three basic beliefs of Islam, presenting proofs from nature, stories from human history, and evidence from the human condition and experience. Simultaneously, it rejects false beliefs and provides an authoritative critique of idolatry and erroneous behaviour. Concepts, images, stories and powerful metaphors are presented to make the meaning clear, such that it touches the heart and mind.

The Quranic sentence is not the same as sentences in our writings that have clearly defined subject, verb and object sequences. Instead, it is diverse and complex, reflecting the complexity of nature and the world around us. It does not talk in past, present and future sequences either, often flips from past to future, from the present to the past, and vice versa, sometimes with one foot in the present and the other in the future; reflecting the timeless nature of the Almighty Creator.

The stories of the prophets Nuh, Saleh, Hud, Lut, Shuʾayb and Musa are a reassurance for the Messenger ﷺ and the Muslims and warning for the Idolaters. In all these cases the prophets were rejected, condemned, and even killed. However, they continued their mission: teaching, preaching and mentoring rebellious people. Finally, the divine punishment destroyed them.

The surat opens with a powerful description of the Quran as the guidance, and a reminder that should be heeded. Otherwise, the consequences would be devastating. By relating the story of Adam and Satan, the Quran is alluding to the causes of human failure to follow the path of religion. The Satan is the arch enemy, and we are warned to remain alert to his temptations. On the other hand, the weakness of humankind is that it readily falls into temptations that appeal to psychological hungers: lust, food, senses of belonging and honour. This is precisely what Satan did with Adam and Eve. He tempted them and they fell in his trap, but quickly repented.

The surat flips to the Hereafter, presents a detailed conversation between the people of Heaven and Hell, and introduces a third group of people, "The people of the heights," after whom the surat takes its name. Most commentators define them as "people whose good and evil deeds are equal." They are in limbo, an undefined state, anxiously awaiting the judgement. Another explanation of Aʿraf is the following:

The term Al-A'raf is the plural of 'Urf meaning acknowledgement ... and discernment. This interpretation has been adopted by some of the early commentators and cited by Razi ... People thus described were those who in their lifetime could discern between right and wrong but didn't incline to either way; they were indifferent. Their luke-warm attitude prevented them from doing either much good or much wrong – with the result that as the next sentence shows they deserve neither Paradise nor Hell. A third explanation of people of A'raf is: people who were most pious, the martyrs and the scholars who worked for the glory of Allah and strengthening Islam and serving humanity. Since A'raf refers to the heights and raised decks, it points to their elevated position from where they can see the delights of Paradise and the horrific punishment of Hell-fire and can comment on it. (Shaikh Muhammad al-Ghazali)

The Divine Laws

The next section of the surat (59–102) describes the work and lives of six great prophets. The story of Musa is presented at length, giving details of his encounter with Pharaoh, the magicians and the Israelites. Allah has always guided humanity by sending the prophets, their beautiful character was a model to be followed. Their clean and God-filled lives were attractive role models, their love of humanity – the weak and vulnerable – was heart-warming. Yet as we read these stories we notice human stubbornness, unwillingness to listen, and obey them.

The Key Concepts

The surat teaches us to dress smartly when worshipping Allah, see verse 26 but insisting that inner smartness is as important, as it is a way of defending oneself against both inde-cency and arrogance. By linking clothing with piety, the Quran teaches the relationship of the outer to the inner, the physical to the spiritual, and the connection between words and behaviour.

In verse 172 another important notion mentioned in this surat is the nature of human-kind; it is Divine nature, made by Allah with the potential of recognising and believing its creator.

However, as mentioned earlier in the surat, people often fail to resist temptations, and fall into them. This is demonstrated in the story of Bal'am ibn Ba'ura, a follower of Musa who became arrogant and contested his master. The Quran comments: "If We wanted, We could have raised his status because of those signs, but he chose to pursue Earthly matters and follow his whims" (176).

بِسۡمِ اللهِ الرَّحۡمٰنِ الرَّحِيۡمِ

الٓمّٓصٓ ۞ كِتٰبٌ اُنۡزِلَ اِلَيۡكَ فَلَا يَكُنۡ فِىۡ صَدۡرِكَ حَرَجٌ مِّنۡهُ لِتُنۡذِرَ بِهٖ وَذِكۡرٰى لِلۡمُؤۡمِنِيۡنَ ۞ اِتَّبِعُوۡا مَاۤ اُنۡزِلَ اِلَيۡكُمۡ مِّنۡ رَّبِّكُمۡ وَلَا تَتَّبِعُوۡا مِنۡ دُوۡنِهٖۤ اَوۡلِيَآءَ ؕ قَلِيۡلًا مَّا تَذَكَّرُوۡنَ ۞ وَكَمۡ مِّنۡ قَرۡيَةٍ اَهۡلَكۡنٰهَا فَجَآءَهَا بَاۡسُنَا بَيَاتًا اَوۡ هُمۡ قَآئِلُوۡنَ ۞ فَمَا كَانَ دَعۡوٰىهُمۡ اِذۡ جَآءَهُمۡ بَاۡسُنَاۤ اِلَّاۤ اَنۡ قَالُوۡۤا

What is success? Heavy scales on the Day of Judgement.

اِنَّا كُنَّا ظٰلِمِيۡنَ ۞ فَلَنَسۡـَٔلَنَّ الَّذِيۡنَ اُرۡسِلَ اِلَيۡهِمۡ وَلَنَسۡـَٔلَنَّ الۡمُرۡسَلِيۡنَ ۞ فَلَنَقُصَّنَّ عَلَيۡهِمۡ بِعِلۡمٍ وَّمَا كُنَّا غَآئِبِيۡنَ ۞ وَالۡوَزۡنُ يَوۡمَئِذِۨ الۡحَقُّ ۚ فَمَنۡ ثَقُلَتۡ مَوَازِيۡنُهٗ فَاُولٰٓئِكَ هُمُ الۡمُفۡلِحُوۡنَ ۞ وَمَنۡ خَفَّتۡ مَوَازِيۡنُهٗ فَاُولٰٓئِكَ الَّذِيۡنَ خَسِرُوۡۤا اَنۡفُسَهُمۡ بِمَا كَانُوۡا بِاٰيٰتِنَا يَظۡلِمُوۡنَ ۞ وَلَقَدۡ مَكَّنّٰكُمۡ فِى الۡاَرۡضِ وَ جَعَلۡنَا لَكُمۡ فِيۡهَا مَعَايِشَ ؕ قَلِيۡلًا مَّا تَشۡكُرُوۡنَ ۞ وَلَقَدۡ خَلَقۡنٰكُمۡ ثُمَّ صَوَّرۡنٰكُمۡ ثُمَّ قُلۡنَا لِلۡمَلٰٓئِكَةِ اسۡجُدُوۡا لِاٰدَمَ ۖ فَسَجَدُوۡۤا اِلَّاۤ اِبۡلِيۡسَ ؕ لَمۡ يَكُنۡ مِّنَ السّٰجِدِيۡنَ ۞ قَالَ مَا مَنَعَكَ اَلَّا تَسۡجُدَ اِذۡ اَمَرۡتُكَ ؕ قَالَ اَنَا خَيۡرٌ مِّنۡهُ ۚ خَلَقۡتَنِىۡ مِنۡ نَّارٍ وَّ خَلَقۡتَهٗ مِنۡ طِيۡنٍ ۞ قَالَ فَاهۡبِطۡ مِنۡهَا فَمَا يَكُوۡنُ

In the name of Allah, the Kind, the Caring.

[1] *Alif Lam Meem Sad.*

The Quran is a warning and a reminder

[2] A book has been sent down to you, *Messenger*, so have no worries about it; through it you warn, it's a reminder for the believers. [3] Follow what's sent down to you by Your Lord, and follow no other masters beside Him. *People*, you pay too little attention.

In the Hereafter, all deeds will be weighed

[4] How many towns did We destroy? Our scourge struck them at night, or during their afternoon nap, [5] and when Our scourge struck, they pleaded, "We were wrongdoers." [6] We'll question both the messengers and their people to whom they were sent. [7] Let Us tell them our side of the story based on *irrefutable* knowledge, for We were not absent. [8] The weighing up *of deeds* on that day is a certainty. Anyone with heavy scales *of good deeds* will be successful, [9] and anyone with light scales will lose out because they used to go against Our scripture. [10] We established you on Earth, and gave you the means to live. *People*, you give little thanks.

Satan vows to mislead people

[11] *Humanity*, We created you and gave you the present form; then We told the angels, "Prostrate before Adam," they all prostrated, except Satan who didn't prostrate. [12] "What stopped you from prostrating when I commanded you?" *Allah*, Satan replied, "I am better than him *since* You created me from fire, and him from clay."

لَكَ أَن تَتَكَبَّرَ فِيهَا فَٱخْرُجْ إِنَّكَ مِنَ ٱلصَّٰغِرِينَ ۝

قَالَ أَنظِرْنِىٓ إِلَىٰ يَوْمِ يُبْعَثُونَ ۝ قَالَ إِنَّكَ

مِنَ ٱلْمُنظَرِينَ ۝ قَالَ فَبِمَآ أَغْوَيْتَنِى لَأَقْعُدَنَّ

لَهُمْ صِرَٰطَكَ ٱلْمُسْتَقِيمَ ۝ ثُمَّ لَأَتِيَنَّهُم مِّنۢ

بَيْنِ أَيْدِيهِمْ وَمِنْ خَلْفِهِمْ وَعَنْ أَيْمَٰنِهِمْ وَعَن

شَمَآئِلِهِمْ ۖ وَلَا تَجِدُ أَكْثَرَهُمْ شَٰكِرِينَ ۝ قَالَ

ٱخْرُجْ مِنْهَا مَذْءُومًا مَّدْحُورًا ۖ لَّمَن تَبِعَكَ

مِنْهُمْ لَأَمْلَأَنَّ جَهَنَّمَ مِنكُمْ أَجْمَعِينَ ۝ وَيَٰٓـَٔادَمُ

ٱسْكُنْ أَنتَ وَزَوْجُكَ ٱلْجَنَّةَ فَكُلَا مِنْ حَيْثُ شِئْتُمَا

وَلَا تَقْرَبَا هَٰذِهِ ٱلشَّجَرَةَ فَتَكُونَا مِنَ ٱلظَّٰلِمِينَ ۝

فَوَسْوَسَ لَهُمَا ٱلشَّيْطَٰنُ لِيُبْدِىَ لَهُمَا مَا وُۥرِىَ

عَنْهُمَا مِن سَوْءَٰتِهِمَا وَقَالَ مَا نَهَىٰكُمَا رَبُّكُمَا

عَنْ هَٰذِهِ ٱلشَّجَرَةِ إِلَّآ أَن تَكُونَا مَلَكَيْنِ أَوْ

تَكُونَا مِنَ ٱلْخَٰلِدِينَ ۝ وَقَاسَمَهُمَآ إِنِّى لَكُمَا لَمِنَ

ٱلنَّٰصِحِينَ ۝ فَدَلَّىٰهُمَا بِغُرُورٍ ۚ فَلَمَّا ذَاقَا ٱلشَّجَرَةَ

بَدَتْ لَهُمَا سَوْءَٰتُهُمَا وَطَفِقَا يَخْصِفَانِ عَلَيْهِمَا مِن

وَرَقِ ٱلْجَنَّةِ ۖ وَنَادَىٰهُمَا رَبُّهُمَآ أَلَمْ أَنْهَكُمَا عَن

تِلْكُمَا ٱلشَّجَرَةِ وَأَقُل لَّكُمَآ إِنَّ ٱلشَّيْطَٰنَ لَكُمَا عَدُوٌّ

مُّبِينٌ ۝ قَالَا رَبَّنَا ظَلَمْنَآ أَنفُسَنَا سكتة وَإِن لَّمْ

تَغْفِرْ لَنَا وَتَرْحَمْنَا لَنَكُونَنَّ مِنَ ٱلْخَٰسِرِينَ ۝ قَالَ

Satan vowed to mislead humans: therefore, beware of his traps, temptations and tests.

¹³ *Allah* said to him, "Get down from here, how dare you be arrogant, so get out, you are despised." ¹⁴ *Satan* said, "Give me time until the Day of Resurrection." ¹⁵ *Allah* said, "You shall have your time." ¹⁶ *Satan* said, "Since You let me go astray, I shall sit near Your straight path for *a chance to lure* them; ¹⁷ then I will pounce on them from the front, behind, and from their right and left, You will find most of them are ungrateful *to You*." ¹⁸ *Allah* said, "Get out of here, despised and an outcast. Anyone who follows you, I will fill Hell with the lot of you."

How Satan misled Adam and Eve

¹⁹ "Adam, live with your wife in Paradise and eat from wherever you wish, but don't come near this tree otherwise you will be wrongdoers," *Allah said.* ²⁰ So Satan whispered to the two of them, in order to reveal their nakedness, of which they had until then been unaware, and said, "Your Lord has only forbidden you from eating *fruit* of this tree to stop you becoming angels or eternal." ²¹ Then he swore an oath, "I am a sincere adviser for you both." ²² So, by deception, he brought about their fall. On tasting *the fruit of* the tree, they became aware of their nakedness and began to cover themselves with the leaves of *the trees of* Paradise. Their Lord called out to them, "Didn't I forbid you from *going near* that tree and warned you Satan is your open enemy?"

Adam and Eve pray for Allah's forgiveness

²³ Both said, "Our Lord, we've wronged ourselves. If You don't forgive us and treat us kindly we will be the losers."

اهْبِطُوْا بَعْضُكُمْ لِبَعْضٍ عَدُوٌّ ۚ وَلَكُمْ فِى الْاَرْضِ

مُسْتَقَرٌّ وَّ مَتَاعٌ اِلٰى حِيْنٍ ۞ قَالَ فِيْهَا تَحْيَوْنَ

وَفِيْهَا تَمُوْتُوْنَ وَمِنْهَا تُخْرَجُوْنَ ۞ يٰبَنِىْٓ اٰدَمَ

قَدْ اَنْزَلْنَا عَلَيْكُمْ لِبَاسًا يُّوَارِىْ سَوْاٰتِكُمْ وَرِيْشًا ۗ

وَلِبَاسُ التَّقْوٰى ۙ ذٰلِكَ خَيْرٌ ۗ ذٰلِكَ مِنْ اٰيٰتِ اللّٰهِ

لَعَلَّهُمْ يَذَّكَّرُوْنَ ۞ يٰبَنِىْٓ اٰدَمَ لَا يَفْتِنَنَّكُمُ الشَّيْطٰنُ

كَمَآ اَخْرَجَ اَبَوَيْكُمْ مِّنَ الْجَنَّةِ يَنْزِعُ عَنْهُمَا لِبَاسَهُمَا

لِيُرِيَهُمَا سَوْاٰتِهِمَا ۗ اِنَّهٗ يَرٰىكُمْ هُوَ وَقَبِيْلُهٗ مِنْ

حَيْثُ لَا تَرَوْنَهُمْ ۗ اِنَّا جَعَلْنَا الشَّيٰطِيْنَ اَوْلِيَآءَ

لِلَّذِيْنَ لَا يُؤْمِنُوْنَ ۞ وَاِذَا فَعَلُوْا فَاحِشَةً قَالُوْا

وَجَدْنَا عَلَيْهَآ اٰبَآءَنَا وَاللّٰهُ اَمَرَنَا بِهَا ۗ قُلْ

اِنَّ اللّٰهَ لَا يَأْمُرُ بِالْفَحْشَآءِ ۗ اَتَقُوْلُوْنَ عَلَى اللّٰهِ

مَا لَا تَعْلَمُوْنَ ۞ قُلْ اَمَرَ رَبِّىْ بِالْقِسْطِ ۫ وَاَقِيْمُوْا

وُجُوْهَكُمْ عِنْدَ كُلِّ مَسْجِدٍ وَّ ادْعُوْهُ مُخْلِصِيْنَ

لَهُ الدِّيْنَ ۗ كَمَا بَدَاَكُمْ تَعُوْدُوْنَ ۞ فَرِيْقًا هَدٰى

وَفَرِيْقًا حَقَّ عَلَيْهِمُ الضَّلٰلَةُ ۗ اِنَّهُمُ اتَّخَذُوا

الشَّيٰطِيْنَ اَوْلِيَآءَ مِنْ دُوْنِ اللّٰهِ وَيَحْسَبُوْنَ

اَنَّهُمْ مُّهْتَدُوْنَ ۞ يٰبَنِىْٓ اٰدَمَ خُذُوْا زِيْنَتَكُمْ عِنْدَ

كُلِّ مَسْجِدٍ وَّ كُلُوْا وَاشْرَبُوْا وَلَا تُسْرِفُوْا ۚ اِنَّهٗ

لَا يُحِبُّ الْمُسْرِفِيْنَ ۞ قُلْ مَنْ حَرَّمَ زِيْنَةَ اللّٰهِ

Satan's common trap is sexual misconduct. Modesty is prevention against it.

²⁴*Allah* said, "Get down *from here*, each of you the enemy of the other.ᵃ On Earth you shall have a home for a while and a means of livelihood, ²⁵there you will live and die, and *eventually* be raised from it."

Clothing is for modesty and looking beautiful

²⁶Children of Adam, We've inspired you to wear clothing to look beautiful and to cover your nakedness,ᵇ and the clothing of piety is the best. That is one of Allah's signs *to humans*, so they may pay attention. ²⁷Children of Adam, don't let Satan tempt you as *he tempted* your parents and had them expelled from Paradise, stripping them of their clothes, exposing their nakedness. He and his type watch you from a place where you can't see them. We made *those* demons the friends of disbelievers. ²⁸Whenever they perform an act of indecency, they say, "We found our forefathers doing it; Allah has ordered us to do it." Say: "Allah does not order acts of indecency. You are saying things about Allah that you don't know?"ᶜ

Show your love of Allah by dressing smartly for worship

²⁹*Messenger*, say: "My Lord orders *you* to be just; turn your faces *towards Him* at all *time in* places of worship,ᵈ and call upon Him, reserving your worship for Him alone. As He created you, so you shall return *to Him*." ³⁰*Allah* guided one group, whilst He let the other group go astray *because* they took devils as protectors instead of Allah, thinking they were rightly guided. ³¹Children of Adam, dress beautifully when attending the place of worship, and eat and drink, but don't squander; He dislikes the squanderers.

ᵃ   Here the story switches from addressing just Adam and Eve to the plural form, meaning that He is now referring to Satan on the one side, and the two humans on the other, being enemies of each other.

ᵇ   *Reesh* refers to a bird's plumage, the beautifully coloured and patterned feathers.

ᶜ   This verse condemns the unlawful sexual acts and also the idolaters' practice of performing the Hajj in the nude.

ᵈ   The Arabic word *masjid* literally means place of prostration, and an "act of worship".

اَلَّتِيْٓ اَخْرَجَ لِعِبَادِهٖ وَالطَّيِّبٰتِ مِنَ الرِّزْقِ ۚ قُلْ هِيَ لِلَّذِيْنَ اٰمَنُوْا فِى الْحَيٰوةِ الدُّنْيَا خَالِصَةً يَّوْمَ الْقِيٰمَةِ ۚ كَذٰلِكَ نُفَصِّلُ الْاٰيٰتِ لِقَوْمٍ يَّعْلَمُوْنَ ۝

قُلْ اِنَّمَا حَرَّمَ رَبِّيَ الْفَوَاحِشَ مَا ظَهَرَ مِنْهَا وَمَا بَطَنَ وَالْاِثْمَ وَالْبَغْيَ بِغَيْرِ الْحَقِّ وَاَنْ تُشْرِكُوْا بِاللّٰهِ مَا لَمْ يُنَزِّلْ بِهٖ سُلْطٰنًا وَّاَنْ تَقُوْلُوْا عَلَى اللّٰهِ مَا لَا تَعْلَمُوْنَ ۝ وَلِكُلِّ اُمَّةٍ اَجَلٌ ۚ فَاِذَا جَاۤءَ اَجَلُهُمْ لَا يَسْتَاْخِرُوْنَ سَاعَةً وَّلَا يَسْتَقْدِمُوْنَ ۝

يٰبَنِيْٓ اٰدَمَ اِمَّا يَاْتِيَنَّكُمْ رُسُلٌ مِّنْكُمْ يَقُصُّوْنَ عَلَيْكُمْ اٰيٰتِيْ ۙ فَمَنِ اتَّقٰى وَاَصْلَحَ فَلَا خَوْفٌ عَلَيْهِمْ وَلَا هُمْ يَحْزَنُوْنَ ۝ وَالَّذِيْنَ كَذَّبُوْا بِاٰيٰتِنَا وَاسْتَكْبَرُوْا عَنْهَآ اُولٰۤئِكَ اَصْحٰبُ النَّارِ ۚ هُمْ فِيْهَا خٰلِدُوْنَ ۝ فَمَنْ اَظْلَمُ مِمَّنِ افْتَرٰى عَلَى اللّٰهِ كَذِبًا اَوْ كَذَّبَ بِاٰيٰتِهٖ ۚ اُولٰۤئِكَ يَنَالُهُمْ نَصِيْبُهُمْ مِّنَ الْكِتٰبِ ۚ حَتّٰٓى اِذَا جَاۤءَتْهُمْ رُسُلُنَا يَتَوَفَّوْنَهُمْ ۙ قَالُوْٓا اَيْنَ مَا كُنْتُمْ تَدْعُوْنَ مِنْ دُوْنِ اللّٰهِ ۭ قَالُوْا ضَلُّوْا عَنَّا وَشَهِدُوْا عَلٰٓى اَنْفُسِهِمْ اَنَّهُمْ كَانُوْا كٰفِرِيْنَ ۝ قَالَ ادْخُلُوْا فِيْٓ اُمَمٍ قَدْ خَلَتْ مِنْ قَبْلِكُمْ مِّنَ الْجِنِّ وَالْاِنْسِ فِى النَّارِ ۭ كُلَّمَا دَخَلَتْ اُمَّةٌ لَّعَنَتْ اُخْتَهَا ۭ حَتّٰٓى اِذَا ادَّارَكُوْا فِيْهَا

³²Say: "Who has forbidden the adornment which Allah has produced for His servants, along with the provision of healthy foods?" Say: "It is for those who believed *in Allah and the Last Day* during this worldly life, reserved for them alone *to wear* on Judgement Day." This is how We explain Our signs for people who know.

Sins harm us and lead to Hell

³³Say: "My Lord has forbidden acts of indecency, whether openly or in secret; *likewise any* sin; unlawful rebellion; associating with Allah anything for which He has revealed no authority;ᵃ and saying things that you have no knowledge about Allah." ³⁴Every community has an allotted term, and when their allotted term comes *to an end*, they can neither delay it by a *single* hour, nor can they hasten it. ³⁵Children of Adam, whenever messengers from among yourselves come to teach you My scripture; whoever is mindful and reforms himself will have nothing to fear nor grieve. ³⁶*However*, those who deny Our signs and consider *those signs* to be beneath them, such people shall be the companions of the Fire, living there forever.

Each successive generation of disbelievers will blame the other

³⁷Who can be more wicked than the one who invents lies about Allah, or denies His signs? Such people will receive their portion of *enjoyment decreed in* the Book, up until Our *angelic* messengers come to take their souls, saying to them, "Where are those you worshipped beside Allah?" They will say, "They have deserted us and testified against themselves that they were disbelievers."

ᵃ It is perfectly acceptable to associate knowledge, for example, or speech with Allah, since authority for calling these divine attributes exists in the Quran and Sunnah.

جَمِيعًا ۚ قَالَتْ أُخْرَاهُمْ لِأُولَاهُمْ رَبَّنَا هَٰؤُلَآءِ
أَضَلُّونَا فَأْتِهِمْ عَذَابًا ضِعْفًا مِّنَ النَّارِ ۚ قَالَ
لِكُلٍّ ضِعْفٌ وَّلَٰكِن لَّا تَعْلَمُونَ ۝ وَقَالَتْ أُولَاهُمْ
لِأُخْرَاهُمْ فَمَا كَانَ لَكُمْ عَلَيْنَا مِن فَضْلٍ فَذُوقُوا
الْعَذَابَ بِمَا كُنتُمْ تَكْسِبُونَ ۝ إِنَّ الَّذِينَ كَذَّبُوا
بِـَٔايَٰتِنَا وَاسْتَكْبَرُوا عَنْهَا لَا تُفَتَّحُ لَهُمْ أَبْوَابُ
السَّمَآءِ وَلَا يَدْخُلُونَ الْجَنَّةَ حَتَّىٰ يَلِجَ الْجَمَلُ
فِى سَمِّ الْخِيَاطِ ۚ وَكَذَٰلِكَ نَجْزِى الْمُجْرِمِينَ ۝
لَهُم مِّن جَهَنَّمَ مِهَادٌ وَّمِن فَوْقِهِمْ غَوَاشٍ ۚ
وَكَذَٰلِكَ نَجْزِى الظَّالِمِينَ ۝ وَالَّذِينَ ءَامَنُوا
وَعَمِلُوا الصَّالِحَاتِ لَا نُكَلِّفُ نَفْسًا إِلَّا وُسْعَهَآ
أُولَٰٓئِكَ أَصْحَابُ الْجَنَّةِ ۖ هُمْ فِيهَا خَالِدُونَ ۝
وَنَزَعْنَا مَا فِى صُدُورِهِم مِّنْ غِلٍّ تَجْرِى مِن
تَحْتِهِمُ الْأَنْهَارُ ۖ وَقَالُوا الْحَمْدُ لِلَّهِ الَّذِى هَدَانَا
لِهَٰذَا وَمَا كُنَّا لِنَهْتَدِىَ لَوْلَآ أَنْ هَدَانَا اللَّهُ ۖ
لَقَدْ جَآءَتْ رُسُلُ رَبِّنَا بِالْحَقِّ ۖ وَنُودُوٓا أَن
تِلْكُمُ الْجَنَّةُ أُورِثْتُمُوهَا بِمَا كُنتُمْ تَعْمَلُونَ ۝
وَنَادَىٰٓ أَصْحَابُ الْجَنَّةِ أَصْحَابَ النَّارِ أَن قَدْ
وَجَدْنَا مَا وَعَدَنَا رَبُّنَا حَقًّا فَهَلْ وَجَدتُّم مَّا
وَعَدَ رَبُّكُمْ حَقًّا ۖ قَالُوا نَعَمْ ۚ فَأَذَّنَ مُؤَذِّنٌۢ

The delights, comforts and beautiful scenes of Paradise are an incentive for the faithful.

295

38 He will say, "Enter the Fire along with the communities of jinn and humans who've passed away." Whenever a community *enters the Fire*, it will curse its fellow *community*, up until each of them has followed all the others into it, and the last of them will say about the first of them, "Our Lord, here are those who misled us, so double their punishment in the Fire." He will say, "Each *of you* will have double *the punishment*, though you don't know *it*." 39 Then the first *to enter* will say to the last, "You were no better than us, so taste the punishment for what you earned."

The arrogant will be thrown in Hell
40 Those who deny Our signs and consider *them* beneath their dignity, the gates of Heaven will not open for them, nor will they enter Paradise until a camel can pass through the eye of a needle;ᵃ that is how We punish sinners. 41 They shall have a bed of Hell *fire*, and there will be a covering *of fire* above them; that is how We punish wrongdoers.

The righteous recognise that it was Allah Who guided them
42 The believers who did righteous deeds – We don't task any soul beyond its capacity – will be the inhabitants of Paradise, living there forever. 43 We shall remove malice from their hearts, *and let them enjoy*: rivers flowing beneath them in Paradise, they shall say, "Praise be to Allah, Who guided us to this, and *we* wouldn't be guided had Allah not guided us. The messengers of Our Lord came with the truth." They will hear the call: "This is Paradise, you've inherited it because of what you did." 44 The people in Paradise will call out the people of the Fire: "We've found what our Lord promised to be true, have you found what your Lord promised you to be true?" They will say, "Yes!" So, an announcement will be made: "The curse of Allah is on the wrongdoers 45 who block Allah's path, wishing to distort it, and who deny the Hereafter."

ᵃ Some commentators translate *jamal* not as camel but as "thick twisted rope" (*Razi*), meaning it will be impossible for an arrogant person to enter Paradise.

بَيْنَهُمْ اَنْ لَّعْنَةُ اللّٰهِ عَلَى الظّٰلِمِيْنَ ۞ الَّذِيْنَ
يَصُدُّوْنَ عَنْ سَبِيْلِ اللّٰهِ وَيَبْغُوْنَهَا عِوَجًا ۚ
وَهُمْ بِالْاٰخِرَةِ كٰفِرُوْنَ ۞ وَبَيْنَهُمَا حِجَابٌ ۚ
وَعَلَى الْاَعْرَافِ رِجَالٌ يَّعْرِفُوْنَ كُلًّا بِسِيْمٰهُمْ ۚ
وَنَادَوْا اَصْحٰبَ الْجَنَّةِ اَنْ سَلٰمٌ عَلَيْكُمْ ۚ لَمْ
يَدْخُلُوْهَا وَهُمْ يَطْمَعُوْنَ ۞ وَاِذَا صُرِفَتْ اَبْصَارُهُمْ
تِلْقَآءَ اَصْحٰبِ النَّارِ ۙ قَالُوْا رَبَّنَا لَا تَجْعَلْنَا مَعَ
الْقَوْمِ الظّٰلِمِيْنَ ۞ وَنَادٰى اَصْحٰبُ الْاَعْرَافِ
رِجَالًا يَّعْرِفُوْنَهُمْ بِسِيْمٰهُمْ قَالُوْا مَآ اَغْنٰى
عَنْكُمْ جَمْعُكُمْ وَمَا كُنْتُمْ تَسْتَكْبِرُوْنَ ۞ اَهٰٓؤُلَآءِ
الَّذِيْنَ اَقْسَمْتُمْ لَا يَنَالُهُمُ اللّٰهُ بِرَحْمَةٍ ؕ اُدْخُلُوا
الْجَنَّةَ لَا خَوْفٌ عَلَيْكُمْ وَلَآ اَنْتُمْ تَحْزَنُوْنَ ۞
وَنَادٰٓى اَصْحٰبُ النَّارِ اَصْحٰبَ الْجَنَّةِ اَنْ اَفِيْضُوْا
عَلَيْنَا مِنَ الْمَآءِ اَوْ مِمَّا رَزَقَكُمُ اللّٰهُ ؕ قَالُوْٓا اِنَّ
اللّٰهَ حَرَّمَهُمَا عَلَى الْكٰفِرِيْنَ ۞ الَّذِيْنَ اتَّخَذُوْا
دِيْنَهُمْ لَهْوًا وَّلَعِبًا وَّغَرَّتْهُمُ الْحَيٰوةُ الدُّنْيَا ۚ
فَالْيَوْمَ نَنْسٰهُمْ كَمَا نَسُوْا لِقَآءَ يَوْمِهِمْ هٰذَا ۙ وَمَا
كَانُوْا بِاٰيٰتِنَا يَجْحَدُوْنَ ۞ وَلَقَدْ جِئْنٰهُمْ بِكِتٰبٍ
فَصَّلْنٰهُ عَلٰى عِلْمٍ هُدًى وَّرَحْمَةً لِّقَوْمٍ يُّؤْمِنُوْنَ ۞
هَلْ يَنْظُرُوْنَ اِلَّا تَأْوِيْلَهٗ ؕ يَوْمَ يَأْتِيْ تَأْوِيْلُهٗ

The desperate, demeaning and devastating conduct of the people of Hell. Work to avoid it.

The people on the heights

⁴⁶ A wall *will appear* between both *groups*, and on the high places there will be men[a] who recognise each *other* from their features, and they will call out to the people of Paradise, "Peace be on you." They won't have entered it, but they will be longing to do so. ⁴⁷ When their eyes turn toward the companions of Hell, they will say, "Our Lord, don't put us with the evildoers." ⁴⁸ The companions of the high places will call out to *other* men whom they recognise by their features, and they will say to them, "Your large group and pride hasn't benefitted you. ⁴⁹ Are these the ones about whom you swore Allah's kindness would never reach?" *The angels will say*, "Enter Paradise. You shall neither fear nor grieve."

The people of Hell ask for water

⁵⁰ The companions of Hell will ask the companions of Paradise: "Give us some water or anything else Allah has provided you." They will say, "Allah has forbidden both for the disbelievers, ⁵¹ who made their religion a fanfare, a sport and were deceived by worldly life. Today We shall abandon them just as they neglected their meeting *with Us* on this day, they disputed Our signs."

Disbelievers will find themselves without any support

⁵² We brought them a book, which explained *things* intelligently, a guidance and source of kindness for the believers.

---

[a]   The phrase A'raf' is "companions of the high places" for more see the introduction to the surat.

يَقُوْلُ الَّذِيْنَ نَسُوْهُ مِنْ قَبْلُ قَدْ جَآءَتْ رُسُلُ

رَبِّنَا بِالْحَقِّ ۚ فَهَلْ لَّنَا مِنْ شُفَعَآءَ فَيَشْفَعُوْا لَنَآ

اَوْ نُرَدُّ فَنَعْمَلَ غَيْرَ الَّذِيْ كُنَّا نَعْمَلُ ۗ قَدْ خَسِرُوْٓا

اَنْفُسَهُمْ وَضَلَّ عَنْهُمْ مَّا كَانُوْا يَفْتَرُوْنَ ۵۳

اِنَّ رَبَّكُمُ اللّٰهُ الَّذِيْ خَلَقَ السَّمٰوٰتِ وَالْاَرْضَ

فِيْ سِتَّةِ اَيَّامٍ ثُمَّ اسْتَوٰى عَلَى الْعَرْشِ ۚ يُغْشِى

الَّيْلَ النَّهَارَ يَطْلُبُهٗ حَثِيْثًا ۙ وَّالشَّمْسَ وَالْقَمَرَ

وَالنُّجُوْمَ مُسَخَّرٰتٍ بِاَمْرِهٖ ۗ اَلَا لَهُ الْخَلْقُ وَالْاَمْرُ ۗ

تَبٰرَكَ اللّٰهُ رَبُّ الْعٰلَمِيْنَ ۵۴ اُدْعُوْا رَبَّكُمْ

تَضَرُّعًا وَّخُفْيَةً ۗ اِنَّهٗ لَا يُحِبُّ الْمُعْتَدِيْنَ ۵۵

وَلَا تُفْسِدُوْا فِى الْاَرْضِ بَعْدَ اِصْلَاحِهَا وَادْعُوْهُ خَوْفًا

وَّطَمَعًا ۗ اِنَّ رَحْمَتَ اللّٰهِ قَرِيْبٌ مِّنَ الْمُحْسِنِيْنَ ۵۶

وَهُوَ الَّذِيْ يُرْسِلُ الرِّيٰحَ بُشْرًا بَيْنَ يَدَيْ

رَحْمَتِهٖ ۗ حَتّٰى اِذَآ اَقَلَّتْ سَحَابًا ثِقَالًا سُقْنٰهُ

لِبَلَدٍ مَّيِّتٍ فَاَنْزَلْنَا بِهِ الْمَآءَ فَاَخْرَجْنَا بِهٖ

مِنْ كُلِّ الثَّمَرٰتِ ۗ كَذٰلِكَ نُخْرِجُ الْمَوْتٰى لَعَلَّكُمْ

تَذَكَّرُوْنَ ۵۷ وَالْبَلَدُ الطَّيِّبُ يَخْرُجُ نَبَاتُهٗ

بِاِذْنِ رَبِّهٖ ۚ وَالَّذِيْ خَبُثَ لَا يَخْرُجُ اِلَّا نَكِدًا ۗ

كَذٰلِكَ نُصَرِّفُ الْاٰيٰتِ لِقَوْمٍ يَّشْكُرُوْنَ ۵۸ لَقَدْ

اَرْسَلْنَا نُوْحًا اِلٰى قَوْمِهٖ فَقَالَ يٰقَوْمِ اعْبُدُوا

To receive Allah's kindness just ask, He will give.

299

⁵³ Are they waiting for its fulfilment? On the day when it is fulfilled, those who had neglected it will say, "Our Lord's messengers came with the truth. Are there any intercessors to plead on our behalf, or *is there a possibility that* we will be returned *to our former life* so we can act differently from how we used to?" They've failed themselves, and things they invented have deserted them.

Pray humbly to the Lord Who created the universe
⁵⁴ Allah is your Lord, Who created the Heavens and the Earth in six days[a] and then established Himself as befits Him on the throne[b]. He causes the night to cover the day, which follows it swiftly. The sun, moon and stars all obey His command. Doesn't *all the* creation and the command *to control it* belong to Him? Blessed be Allah, Lord of *all* the Universe. ⁵⁵ Call on your Lord, humbly and in secret. He dislikes transgressors. ⁵⁶ Do not make conflict in the land after it has been made peaceful but call on Him with fear and longing. Allah's Kindness is close to the righteous.

A comparison of rain to raising the dead
⁵⁷ He sends winds – bearing glad tidings, a sign of His kindness – that carry along heavy clouds driving them towards arid lands, and We send rain, producing fruits of all kind. This is how We will bring the dead *to life*; perhaps you will reflect. ⁵⁸ Good soil brings forth its crops by its Lord's permission, whereas poor *soil* produces only a little bit. This is how We explain the signs for people who are grateful.

---

[a] This period of "six days" is not six lots of twenty-four hours. In the Quran (*Surat Al-Hajj* 22: 47), a day is equated with a thousand years, this isn't literal either, a thousand represented the largest numerical concept then known to the Arabs, unlike in India at that time where they already had words for 100,000 (*lakh*) and 10,000,000 (*crore*). So this refers to six relatively distinct eras and doesn't conflict with the scientific theory that the universe was created 14 billion years ago, with the Big Bang.
[b] This is interpreted as the completion of the creation of the universe and Allah has control of it.

اللهُ مَا لَكُم مِّنْ إِلَهٍ غَيْرُهُ ۖ إِنِّى أَخَافُ
عَلَيْكُمْ عَذَابَ يَوْمٍ عَظِيمٍ ۞ قَالَ الْمَلَأُ
مِن قَوْمِهِ إِنَّا لَنَرَىٰكَ فِى ضَلَٰلٍ مُّبِينٍ ۞
قَالَ يَٰقَوْمِ لَيْسَ بِى ضَلَٰلَةٌ وَّلَٰكِنِّى رَسُولٌ مِّن
رَّبِّ الْعَٰلَمِينَ ۞ أُبَلِّغُكُمْ رِسَٰلَٰتِ رَبِّى وَأَنصَحُ
لَكُمْ وَأَعْلَمُ مِنَ اللهِ مَا لَا تَعْلَمُونَ ۞
أَوَعَجِبْتُمْ أَن جَاءَكُمْ ذِكْرٌ مِّن رَّبِّكُمْ عَلَىٰ
رَجُلٍ مِّنكُمْ لِيُنذِرَكُمْ وَلِتَتَّقُوا وَلَعَلَّكُمْ
تُرْحَمُونَ ۞ فَكَذَّبُوهُ فَأَنجَيْنَٰهُ وَالَّذِينَ مَعَهُ
فِى الْفُلْكِ وَأَغْرَقْنَا الَّذِينَ كَذَّبُوا بِـَٔايَٰتِنَا ۚ
إِنَّهُمْ كَانُوا قَوْمًا عَمِينَ ۞ وَإِلَىٰ عَادٍ
أَخَاهُمْ هُودًا ۗ قَالَ يَٰقَوْمِ اعْبُدُوا اللهَ مَا لَكُم
مِّنْ إِلَهٍ غَيْرُهُ ۚ أَفَلَا تَتَّقُونَ ۞ قَالَ الْمَلَأُ
الَّذِينَ كَفَرُوا مِن قَوْمِهِ إِنَّا لَنَرَىٰكَ فِى
سَفَاهَةٍ وَّإِنَّا لَنَظُنُّكَ مِنَ الْكَٰذِبِينَ ۞ قَالَ
يَٰقَوْمِ لَيْسَ بِى سَفَاهَةٌ وَّلَٰكِنِّى رَسُولٌ مِّن
رَّبِّ الْعَٰلَمِينَ ۞ أُبَلِّغُكُمْ رِسَٰلَٰتِ رَبِّى وَأَنَا
لَكُمْ نَاصِحٌ أَمِينٌ ۞ أَوَعَجِبْتُمْ أَن جَاءَكُمْ
ذِكْرٌ مِّن رَّبِّكُمْ عَلَىٰ رَجُلٍ مِّنكُمْ لِيُنذِرَكُمْ ۚ
وَاذْكُرُوا إِذْ جَعَلَكُمْ خُلَفَاءَ مِن بَعْدِ قَوْمِ

Do you have inner conversations? Are they positive?

301

The people of Nuh ignored his sincere advice

[59] *When* We sent Nuh to his people, he said, "My people, worship Allah; you have no other god but Him. I fear the torment of a dreadful day." [60] The leaders of his community said, "We believe you're mistaken." [61] He said, "My people, I am not mistaken; rather I am a messenger of *the* Lord of the Universe, [62] conveying to you, as a sincere advisor, the messages of My Lord, and I have knowledge from Allah that you don't have. [63] Are you surprised that a reminder has come from your Lord through one of your men, *who* teaches you to be mindful *of Allah* and wants you to be treated kindly" [64] They called him a liar, but We saved him and his followers aboard the ship, and those who denied Our signs We drowned; they were blind people.

The people of Hud rebelled

[65] And to *the* tribe of Ad, We sent their brother Hud, who said, "My people, worship Allah; you have no god but Him. Will you not be mindful *of Allah*?" [66] The disbelieving leaders of his community said, "We think you have gone crazy, and you're a liar." [67] He replied, "My people, there is nothing crazy about me; rather I am a messenger from the Lord of the Universe, [68] conveying to you, as a sincere advisor His messages." [69] Are you surprised that a reminder should come to you to warn you from your Lord through one of your men? *Remember what happened to* the people of Nuh, He made you *their* successors and made your body strong. So remember Allah's gifts, and you will be successful."

نُوحٍ وَّزَادَكُمْ فِي الْخَلْقِ بَصْۜطَةً ۚ فَاذْكُرُوٓا

اٰلَآءَ اللّٰهِ لَعَلَّكُمْ تُفْلِحُوْنَ ۞ قَالُوٓا اَجِئْتَنَا

لِنَعْبُدَ اللّٰهَ وَحْدَهٗ وَنَذَرَ مَا كَانَ يَعْبُدُ

اٰبَآؤُنَا ۚ فَأْتِنَا بِمَا تَعِدُنَآ اِنْ كُنْتَ مِنَ

الصّٰدِقِيْنَ ۞ قَالَ قَدْ وَقَعَ عَلَيْكُمْ مِّنْ رَّبِّكُمْ

رِجْسٌ وَّغَضَبٌ ۗ اَتُجَادِلُوْنَنِيْ فِيْٓ اَسْمَآءٍ

سَمَّيْتُمُوْهَآ اَنْتُمْ وَاٰبَآؤُكُمْ مَّا نَزَّلَ اللّٰهُ

بِهَا مِنْ سُلْطٰنٍ ۗ فَانْتَظِرُوٓا اِنِّيْ مَعَكُمْ مِّنَ

الْمُنْتَظِرِيْنَ ۞ فَاَنْجَيْنٰهُ وَالَّذِيْنَ مَعَهٗ بِرَحْمَةٍ

مِّنَّا وَقَطَعْنَا دَابِرَ الَّذِيْنَ كَذَّبُوْا بِاٰيٰتِنَا وَمَا

كَانُوْا مُؤْمِنِيْنَ ۞ وَاِلٰى ثَمُوْدَ اَخَاهُمْ صٰلِحًا ۘ

قَالَ يٰقَوْمِ اعْبُدُوا اللّٰهَ مَا لَكُمْ مِّنْ اِلٰهٍ غَيْرُهٗ ۗ

قَدْ جَآءَتْكُمْ بَيِّنَةٌ مِّنْ رَّبِّكُمْ ۗ هٰذِهٖ نَاقَةُ اللّٰهِ

لَكُمْ اٰيَةً فَذَرُوْهَا تَأْكُلْ فِيْٓ اَرْضِ اللّٰهِ وَلَا

تَمَسُّوْهَا بِسُوْٓءٍ فَيَأْخُذَكُمْ عَذَابٌ اَلِيْمٌ ۞ وَاذْكُرُوٓا

اِذْ جَعَلَكُمْ خُلَفَآءَ مِنْ بَعْدِ عَادٍ وَّبَوَّاَكُمْ

فِي الْاَرْضِ تَتَّخِذُوْنَ مِنْ سُهُوْلِهَا قُصُوْرًا

وَّتَنْحِتُوْنَ الْجِبَالَ بُيُوْتًا ۚ فَاذْكُرُوٓا اٰلَآءَ

اللّٰهِ وَلَا تَعْثَوْا فِي الْاَرْضِ مُفْسِدِيْنَ ۞ قَالَ

الْمَلَاُ الَّذِيْنَ اسْتَكْبَرُوْا مِنْ قَوْمِهٖ لِلَّذِيْنَ

What's the reality of things you love? Colourful, tasty, pleasurable? They fade quickly.

[70] They said, "Have you come to us *to make us* worship Allah alone and to abandon what our forefathers worshipped? If so, bring on what you are threatening us with, if you are telling the truth." [71] *Hud* said, "May punishment and wrath befall you from your Lord! Are you arguing with me about simple names that you and your forefathers have made up, and for which Allah has sent no authority? Wait *for Allah's decree*, and I shall wait with you." [72] We were kind so We rescued him and his followers, but destroyed the deniers of Our signs; they weren't believers.

Arrogance led the Prophet Salih's people to disobey Allah

[73] And to *the tribe of* Thamud, We sent their brother Salih who said, "My people, worship Allah; you have no god but Him. Clear proof has come to you from your Lord; this is the she-camel of Allah, a sign for you. Let her graze *wherever she wants* in Allah's Earth, but do not harm her, or else you'll be severely punished. [74] And remember how He made you successors after *what had happened to* Ad, establishing you in the land, where on its plains you *now* build mansions and carved homes in the mountainsides. So, remember Allah's gifts, and don't spread violence in the land."

اسْتُضْعِفُوْا لِمَنْ اٰمَنَ مِنْهُمْ اَتَعْلَمُوْنَ اَنَّ

صٰلِحًا مُّرْسَلٌ مِّنْ رَّبِّهٖ ۖ قَالُوْا اِنَّا بِمَآ اُرْسِلَ

بِهٖ مُؤْمِنُوْنَ ۝ قَالَ الَّذِيْنَ اسْتَكْبَرُوْا اِنَّا بِالَّذِيْٓ

اٰمَنْتُمْ بِهٖ كٰفِرُوْنَ ۝ فَعَقَرُوا النَّاقَةَ وَعَتَوْا عَنْ

اَمْرِ رَبِّهِمْ وَقَالُوْا يٰصٰلِحُ ائْتِنَا بِمَا تَعِدُنَآ اِنْ كُنْتَ

مِنَ الْمُرْسَلِيْنَ ۝ فَاَخَذَتْهُمُ الرَّجْفَةُ فَاَصْبَحُوْا

فِيْ دَارِهِمْ جٰثِمِيْنَ ۝ فَتَوَلّٰى عَنْهُمْ وَقَالَ يٰقَوْمِ

لَقَدْ اَبْلَغْتُكُمْ رِسَالَةَ رَبِّيْ وَنَصَحْتُ لَكُمْ وَلٰكِنْ

لَّا تُحِبُّوْنَ النّٰصِحِيْنَ ۝ وَلُوْطًا اِذْ قَالَ لِقَوْمِهٖٓ

اَتَأْتُوْنَ الْفَاحِشَةَ مَا سَبَقَكُمْ بِهَا مِنْ اَحَدٍ

مِّنَ الْعٰلَمِيْنَ ۝ اِنَّكُمْ لَتَأْتُوْنَ الرِّجَالَ شَهْوَةً

مِّنْ دُوْنِ النِّسَآءِ ۚ بَلْ اَنْتُمْ قَوْمٌ مُّسْرِفُوْنَ ۝

وَمَا كَانَ جَوَابَ قَوْمِهٖٓ اِلَّآ اَنْ قَالُوْٓا اَخْرِجُوْهُمْ

مِّنْ قَرْيَتِكُمْ ۚ اِنَّهُمْ اُنَاسٌ يَّتَطَهَّرُوْنَ ۝ فَاَنْجَيْنٰهُ

وَاَهْلَهٗٓ اِلَّا امْرَاَتَهٗ ۖ كَانَتْ مِنَ الْغٰبِرِيْنَ ۝

وَاَمْطَرْنَا عَلَيْهِمْ مَّطَرًا ۗ فَانْظُرْ كَيْفَ كَانَ

عَاقِبَةُ الْمُجْرِمِيْنَ ۞ وَاِلٰى مَدْيَنَ اَخَاهُمْ شُعَيْبًا ۗ

قَالَ يٰقَوْمِ اعْبُدُوا اللّٰهَ مَا لَكُمْ مِّنْ اِلٰهٍ غَيْرُهٗ ۗ

قَدْ جَآءَتْكُمْ بَيِّنَةٌ مِّنْ رَّبِّكُمْ فَاَوْفُوا الْكَيْلَ

وَالْمِيْزَانَ وَلَا تَبْخَسُوا النَّاسَ اَشْيَآءَهُمْ وَلَا

Sexual purity and decency is key to lasting happiness and social relations.

⁷⁵ *Some* arrogant leaders from his community said to the believers from the weak *people*, "Do you know *for certain* that Salih is a messenger from his Lord?" They said, "We believe in the message he's been sent with." ⁷⁶ But the arrogant leaders said, "We reject what you believe in." ⁷⁷ So they hamstrung the she-camel, disobeying their Lord's command, saying, "Salih, bring on what you have threatened us with, if you are a messenger." ⁷⁸ An Earthquake seized them so violently that they ended up lying face down in their homes. ⁷⁹ *Salih* turned away from them, saying, "My people, I delivered My Lord's message sincerely to you, but you don't like the one who gives you sincere advice."ᵃ

The people of the Prophet Lut reject him as too puritanical

⁸⁰ And *remember* Lut, when he said to his people, "Why do you commit indecent acts that have no precedence anywhere in the whole world? ⁸¹ You approach men with lust rather than women. You've gone to excess *in satisfying your sexual appetites*." ⁸² His people said, "Expel them from your town. They are puritanical." ⁸³ So We saved him and his family, except his wife, who stayed behind, ⁸⁴ and We pelted them with hailstones. Look at the outcome of the sinners!

Prophet Shu'ayb stops his people cheating

⁸⁵ And to Madyan, We sent their brother Shu'ayb,ᵇ who said, "My people, worship Allah; you have no god but Him. Clear proof has come from your Lord, so be honest in *your* weights and measures, and don't deprive people of their rights, and don't create conflict in the land after it has been made peaceful. That's *the* best *advice* for you, if you are believers.

ᵃ   It may be that dim memories of this story, preserved incorrectly in their folk-tales, form the basis of the pagan Arab superstitions detailed in *Surat Al-Anʿam* (6: 136–150).

ᵇ   Shu'ayb is the biblical Jethro, father-in-law of Musa.

تُفْسِدُوا فِي الْأَرْضِ بَعْدَ إِصْلَاحِهَا ۚ ذٰلِكُمْ خَيْرٌ

لَّكُمْ إِنْ كُنْتُمْ مُّؤْمِنِيْنَ ۞ وَلَا تَقْعُدُوْا بِكُلِّ

صِرَاطٍ تُوْعِدُوْنَ وَتَصُدُّوْنَ عَنْ سَبِيْلِ اللّٰهِ مَنْ

اٰمَنَ بِهٖ وَتَبْغُوْنَهَا عِوَجًا ۚ وَاذْكُرُوْا إِذْ كُنْتُمْ

قَلِيْلًا فَكَثَّرَكُمْ ۖ وَانْظُرُوْا كَيْفَ كَانَ عَاقِبَةُ

الْمُفْسِدِيْنَ ۞ وَإِنْ كَانَ طَآئِفَةٌ مِّنْكُمْ اٰمَنُوْا

بِالَّذِيْٓ أُرْسِلْتُ بِهٖ وَطَآئِفَةٌ لَّمْ يُؤْمِنُوْا فَاصْبِرُوْا

حَتّٰى يَحْكُمَ اللّٰهُ بَيْنَنَا ۚ وَهُوَ خَيْرُ الْحٰكِمِيْنَ ۞

People's arrogance and stubbornness prevented them from seeing the truth. Lesson: be open to good ideas.

قَالَ الْمَلَأُ الَّذِيْنَ اسْتَكْبَرُوْا مِنْ قَوْمِهٖ لَنُخْرِجَنَّكَ

يٰشُعَيْبُ وَالَّذِيْنَ اٰمَنُوْا مَعَكَ مِنْ قَرْيَتِنَآ أَوْ

لَتَعُوْدُنَّ فِيْ مِلَّتِنَا ۚ قَالَ أَوَلَوْ كُنَّا كٰرِهِيْنَ ۞ قَدِ

افْتَرَيْنَا عَلَى اللّٰهِ كَذِبًا إِنْ عُدْنَا فِيْ مِلَّتِكُمْ بَعْدَ

إِذْ نَجّٰنَا اللّٰهُ مِنْهَا ۚ وَمَا يَكُوْنُ لَنَآ أَنْ نَّعُوْدَ فِيْهَآ

إِلَّآ أَنْ يَّشَآءَ اللّٰهُ رَبُّنَا ۚ وَسِعَ رَبُّنَا كُلَّ شَيْءٍ

عِلْمًا ۚ عَلَى اللّٰهِ تَوَكَّلْنَا ۚ رَبَّنَا افْتَحْ بَيْنَنَا وَبَيْنَ

قَوْمِنَا بِالْحَقِّ وَأَنْتَ خَيْرُ الْفٰتِحِيْنَ ۞ وَقَالَ الْمَلَأُ

الَّذِيْنَ كَفَرُوْا مِنْ قَوْمِهٖ لَئِنِ اتَّبَعْتُمْ شُعَيْبًا إِنَّكُمْ

إِذًا لَّخٰسِرُوْنَ ۞ فَأَخَذَتْهُمُ الرَّجْفَةُ فَأَصْبَحُوْا

فِيْ دَارِهِمْ جٰثِمِيْنَ ۞ الَّذِيْنَ كَذَّبُوْا شُعَيْبًا

كَأَنْ لَّمْ يَغْنَوْا فِيْهَا ۚ الَّذِيْنَ كَذَّبُوْا شُعَيْبًا كَانُوْا

⁸⁶ Don't sit at the roadside, threatening *people* and preventing believers from *following* the path of Allah, wishing to distort it. Remember how few you were in number, and how He increased you. Look at the fate of trouble-makers. ⁸⁷ A group of you believes in what I was sent with while the other group doesn't, so let us wait until Allah decides between us: He is the best judge."

Shuʿayb and his followers face rejection and persecution

⁸⁸ The arrogant leaders of his community said, "We will expel you from our town, Shuʿayb, *you* and *all* those who believe in you, unless you return to our way of worship." He said, "Even if we don't want to? ⁸⁹ We would be inventing lies about Allah if we returned to your way of worship after Allah had saved us. There is no way that we would return unless Allah, Our Lord, should wish it. Our Lord has the knowledge of everything. We place our trust in Him. Our Lord! Decide justly between us and our people, for You are the best judge." ⁹⁰ The disbelieving leaders of his community said, "If you follow Shuʿayb, you will be losers." ⁹¹ After that they were seized by an Earthquake so violent that they ended up lying face down in their homes. ⁹² As though those who treated Shuʿayb as a liar never lived there; the *ultimate* losers were those who called Shuʿayb a liar.

هُمُ الْخٰسِرِيْنَ ۹۲ فَتَوَلّٰى عَنْهُمْ وَقَالَ يٰقَوْمِ لَقَدْ

اَبْلَغْتُكُمْ رِسٰلٰتِ رَبِّيْ وَنَصَحْتُ لَكُمْ فَكَيْفَ اٰسٰى

عَلٰى قَوْمٍ كٰفِرِيْنَ ۹۳ وَمَاۤ اَرْسَلْنَا فِيْ قَرْيَةٍ مِّنْ

نَّبِيٍّ اِلَّاۤ اَخَذْنَاۤ اَهْلَهَا بِالْبَاْسَاۤءِ وَالضَّرَّاۤءِ لَعَلَّهُمْ

يَضَّرَّعُوْنَ ۹۴ ثُمَّ بَدَّلْنَا مَكَانَ السَّيِّئَةِ الْحَسَنَةَ حَتّٰى

عَفَوْا وَّقَالُوْا قَدْ مَسَّ اٰبَاۤءَنَا الضَّرَّاۤءُ وَالسَّرَّاۤءُ

فَاَخَذْنٰهُمْ بَغْتَةً وَّهُمْ لَا يَشْعُرُوْنَ ۹۵ وَلَوْ اَنَّ اَهْلَ

الْقُرٰۤى اٰمَنُوْا وَاتَّقَوْا لَفَتَحْنَا عَلَيْهِمْ بَرَكٰتٍ مِّنَ

السَّمَاۤءِ وَالْاَرْضِ وَلٰكِنْ كَذَّبُوْا فَاَخَذْنٰهُمْ بِمَا كَانُوْا

يَكْسِبُوْنَ ۹۶ اَفَاَمِنَ اَهْلُ الْقُرٰۤى اَنْ يَّاْتِيَهُمْ بَاْسُنَا

بَيَاتًا وَّهُمْ نَاۤئِمُوْنَ ۹۷ اَوَ اَمِنَ اَهْلُ الْقُرٰۤى اَنْ

يَّاْتِيَهُمْ بَاْسُنَا ضُحًى وَّهُمْ يَلْعَبُوْنَ ۹۸ اَفَاَمِنُوْا مَكْرَ

اللّٰهِ فَلَا يَاْمَنُ مَكْرَ اللّٰهِ اِلَّا الْقَوْمُ الْخٰسِرُوْنَ ۹۹

اَوَلَمْ يَهْدِ لِلَّذِيْنَ يَرِثُوْنَ الْاَرْضَ مِنْۢ بَعْدِ

اَهْلِهَاۤ اَنْ لَّوْ نَشَاۤءُ اَصَبْنٰهُمْ بِذُنُوْبِهِمْ ۚ وَنَطْبَعُ

عَلٰى قُلُوْبِهِمْ فَهُمْ لَا يَسْمَعُوْنَ ۱۰۰ تِلْكَ الْقُرٰى

نَقُصُّ عَلَيْكَ مِنْ اَنْۢبَاۤئِهَا ۚ وَلَقَدْ جَاۤءَتْهُمْ

رُسُلُهُمْ بِالْبَيِّنٰتِ ۚ فَمَا كَانُوْا لِيُؤْمِنُوْا بِمَا كَذَّبُوْا مِنْ

قَبْلُ ۚ كَذٰلِكَ يَطْبَعُ اللّٰهُ عَلٰى قُلُوْبِ الْكٰفِرِيْنَ ۱۰۱ وَمَا

وَجَدْنَا لِاَكْثَرِهِمْ مِّنْ عَهْدٍ ۚ وَاِنْ وَّجَدْنَاۤ اَكْثَرَهُمْ

The best way to get Allah's caring attention is to obey Him!

⁹³ So he withdrew from them saying, "My people, I delivered to you the messages of my Lord, and I was sincere towards you. So why should I mourn people who *choose to* disbelieve?"

Allah always sends a warning before punishing
⁹⁴ We haven't sent a single prophet to any community without initially putting its inhabitants through suffering and hardship to humble them. ⁹⁵ Then We would replace the evil with good until they overtook *their predecessors* and, *without a thought for Allah*, said, "Hardship and prosperity affected our forefathers too." Suddenly, We would take them unaware. ⁹⁶ If the people of the communities had believed and been mindful, We would have opened up for them blessings of the Heavens and Earth, but they rejected *Our signs*, so We seized them for what they did. ⁹⁷ Were the people of the communities confident that Our punishment wouldn't come when they were asleep at night? ⁹⁸ Or were they confident that Our punishment wouldn't come as they played at mid-morning? ⁹⁹ Or did they feel secure from Allah's plan? It is only the losers who are not afraid of Allah's plan.

The more one rejects guidance, the harder it becomes to believe
¹⁰⁰ Didn't any guidance come to those who inherited the land from previous inhab- itants, if We wished, We could afflict them *too* because of their sins, and We could seal their minds so they would no longer hear? ¹⁰¹ Such communities, We have told you some of what happened to them. Their messengers came to them with clear proofs but, because they had already denied them, they were not *prepared* to believe; that is how Allah seals the hearts of disbelievers. ¹⁰² We found most of them uncommitted to the contract, they were mostly disobedient.

لَفْسِقِينَ ۝ ثُمَّ بَعَثْنَا مِنْ بَعْدِهِمْ مُّوْسَى بِاٰيٰتِنَا اِلٰى

فِرْعَوْنَ وَمَلَإِ هٖ فَظَلَمُوْا بِهَا ۚ فَانْظُرْ كَيْفَ كَانَ

عَاقِبَةُ الْمُفْسِدِيْنَ ۝ وَقَالَ مُوْسَى يٰفِرْعَوْنُ اِنِّيْ

رَسُوْلٌ مِّنْ رَّبِّ الْعٰلَمِيْنَ ۝ حَقِيْقٌ عَلٰى اَنْ لَّا اَقُوْلَ

عَلَى اللّٰهِ اِلَّا الْحَقَّ ؕ قَدْ جِئْتُكُمْ بِبَيِّنَةٍ مِّنْ رَّبِّكُمْ

فَاَرْسِلْ مَعِيَ بَنِيْ اِسْرَآءِيْلَ ۝ قَالَ اِنْ كُنْتَ جِئْتَ

بِاٰيَةٍ فَاْتِ بِهَآ اِنْ كُنْتَ مِنَ الصّٰدِقِيْنَ ۝ فَاَلْقٰى

عَصَاهُ فَاِذَا هِيَ ثُعْبَانٌ مُّبِيْنٌ ۚ وَّنَزَعَ يَدَهٗ فَاِذَا

هِيَ بَيْضَآءُ لِلنّٰظِرِيْنَ ۝ قَالَ الْمَلَأُ مِنْ قَوْمِ

فِرْعَوْنَ اِنَّ هٰذَا لَسٰحِرٌ عَلِيْمٌ ۙ يُّرِيْدُ اَنْ يُّخْرِجَكُمْ

مِّنْ اَرْضِكُمْ ۚ فَمَاذَا تَأْمُرُوْنَ ۝ قَالُوْٓا اَرْجِهْ وَاَخَاهُ

وَاَرْسِلْ فِي الْمَدَآئِنِ حٰشِرِيْنَ ۝ يَأْتُوْكَ بِكُلِّ سٰحِرٍ

عَلِيْمٍ ۝ وَجَآءَ السَّحَرَةُ فِرْعَوْنَ قَالُوْٓا اِنَّ لَنَا لَاَجْرًا

اِنْ كُنَّا نَحْنُ الْغٰلِبِيْنَ ۝ قَالَ نَعَمْ وَاِنَّكُمْ لَمِنَ

الْمُقَرَّبِيْنَ ۝ قَالُوْا يٰمُوْسٰٓى اِمَّآ اَنْ تُلْقِيَ وَاِمَّآ اَنْ

نَّكُوْنَ نَحْنُ الْمُلْقِيْنَ ۝ قَالَ اَلْقُوْا ۚ فَلَمَّآ اَلْقَوْا

سَحَرُوْٓا اَعْيُنَ النَّاسِ وَاسْتَرْهَبُوْهُمْ وَجَآءُوْ بِسِحْرٍ

عَظِيْمٍ ۝ وَاَوْحَيْنَآ اِلٰى مُوْسٰٓى اَنْ اَلْقِ عَصَاكَ ۚ

فَاِذَا هِيَ تَلْقَفُ مَا يَأْفِكُوْنَ ۝ فَوَقَعَ الْحَقُّ وَبَطَلَ

مَا كَانُوْا يَعْمَلُوْنَ ۝ فَغُلِبُوْا هُنَالِكَ وَانْقَلَبُوْا

What stopped Pharaoh from listening to Musa? Arrogance, stubbornness and prejudice.

١٣
ع
٣

In the face of Musa's miracles, Pharaoh plays for time

¹⁰³ After them, We sent Musa with our miracles to Pharaoh and his leaders, but they rejected them. Look what happened to the trouble makers. ¹⁰⁴ Musa said, "Pharaoh, I am a messenger from the Lord of the universe. ¹⁰⁵ I am duty-bound to speak the truth about Allah. I have come to you with clear proof from your Lord, so let the Israelites go with me." ¹⁰⁶ He replied, "If you have come with a sign, then show it, if you are telling the truth." ¹⁰⁷ So he threw his staff, and straightaway it turned into a snake, everyone saw that; ¹⁰⁸ next he pulled his hand out *from his cloak*, and it looked white to the onlookers. ¹⁰⁹ The leaders of Pharaoh's people said, "He's an expert magician, ¹¹⁰ he wants to expel you from your land, so what do you command?" ¹¹¹ They said, "Delay him and his brother and, *in the meantime*, send messengers to the cities ¹¹² to bring every experienced magician *here*."

The magicians, confronted with the truth, accept it

¹¹³ The magicians came to the Pharaoh, they asked, "Will we be rewarded if we win?" ¹¹⁴ He said, "Yes! You will join people who are in my inner circle." ¹¹⁵ They said, "Musa, either you go *first*, or let us go first?" ¹¹⁶ He said, "You start." So they went first, with trickery charmed people's eyes to frighten them, and made an impressive magical spectacle. ¹¹⁷ Then We urged Musa, "Throw down your staff," and at once it began to swallow up their fake devices. ¹¹⁸ So the truth came out, and what they had done was shown to be fake. ¹¹⁹ They were defeated there, and humiliated.

صٰغِرِيْنَ ۱۱۹ وَاُلْقِيَ السَّحَرَةُ سٰجِدِيْنَ ۱۲۰ قَالُوْٓا

اٰمَنَّا بِرَبِّ الْعٰلَمِيْنَ ۱۲۱ رَبِّ مُوْسٰى وَهٰرُوْنَ ۱۲۲

قَالَ فِرْعَوْنُ اٰمَنْتُمْ بِهٖ قَبْلَ اَنْ اٰذَنَ لَكُمْ ۚ اِنَّ

هٰذَا لَمَكْرٌ مَّكَرْتُمُوْهُ فِى الْمَدِيْنَةِ لِتُخْرِجُوْا مِنْهَا

اَهْلَهَا ۚ فَسَوْفَ تَعْلَمُوْنَ ۱۲۳ لَاُقَطِّعَنَّ اَيْدِيَكُمْ

وَاَرْجُلَكُمْ مِّنْ خِلَافٍ ثُمَّ لَاُصَلِّبَنَّكُمْ اَجْمَعِيْنَ ۱۲۴

قَالُوْٓا اِنَّآ اِلٰى رَبِّنَا مُنْقَلِبُوْنَ ۱۲۵ وَمَا تَنْقِمُ مِنَّآ

اِلَّآ اَنْ اٰمَنَّا بِاٰيٰتِ رَبِّنَا لَمَّا جَآءَتْنَا ۚ رَبَّنَآ اَفْرِغْ

When the magicians saw the light of truth, they changed and gave up their trickery.

عَلَيْنَا صَبْرًا وَّتَوَفَّنَا مُسْلِمِيْنَ ۱۲۶ وَقَالَ الْمَلَأُ مِنْ

قَوْمِ فِرْعَوْنَ اَتَذَرُ مُوْسٰى وَقَوْمَهٗ لِيُفْسِدُوْا فِى

الْاَرْضِ وَيَذَرَكَ وَاٰلِهَتَكَ ۚ قَالَ سَنُقَتِّلُ اَبْنَآءَهُمْ

وَنَسْتَحْيٖ نِسَآءَهُمْ ۚ وَاِنَّا فَوْقَهُمْ قٰهِرُوْنَ ۱۲۷ قَالَ

مُوْسٰى لِقَوْمِهِ اسْتَعِيْنُوْا بِاللّٰهِ وَاصْبِرُوْا ۚ اِنَّ

الْاَرْضَ لِلّٰهِ ۚ يُوْرِثُهَا مَنْ يَّشَآءُ مِنْ عِبَادِهٖ ۚ وَ

الْعَاقِبَةُ لِلْمُتَّقِيْنَ ۱۲۸ قَالُوْٓا اُوْذِيْنَا مِنْ قَبْلِ اَنْ

تَأْتِيَنَا وَمِنْ بَعْدِ مَا جِئْتَنَا ۚ قَالَ عَسٰى رَبُّكُمْ اَنْ

يُّهْلِكَ عَدُوَّكُمْ وَيَسْتَخْلِفَكُمْ فِى الْاَرْضِ فَيَنْظُرَ

كَيْفَ تَعْمَلُوْنَ ۱۲۹ وَلَقَدْ اَخَذْنَآ اٰلَ فِرْعَوْنَ

بِالسِّنِيْنَ وَنَقْصٍ مِّنَ الثَّمَرٰتِ لَعَلَّهُمْ يَذَّكَّرُوْنَ ۱۳۰

فَاِذَا جَآءَتْهُمُ الْحَسَنَةُ قَالُوْا لَنَا هٰذِهٖ ۚ وَاِنْ

¹²⁰ The magicians threw themselves *to the ground* in prostration, ¹²¹ saying: "We believe in the Lord of the universe, ¹²² the Lord of Musa and Harun."

The Pharaoh orders killing of magicians

¹²³ Pharaoh said, "How dare you believe before I give you permission! This is some cunning plot that you have *all* devised in this city to expel its people. You will soon know *where true power lies*. ¹²⁴ I will have your hands and feet cut off on the opposite sides and crucify you all." ¹²⁵ They said, "We hand ourselves over to our Lord. ¹²⁶ What reason do you have to take revenge on us except that we believed in signs of our Lord when they came? Our Lord, give us patience, and let us die in submission *to You*."

Pharaoh threatens to punish the Israelites

¹²⁷ The leaders of Pharaoh's community said, "Are you going to leave Musa and his people to wreak havoc in the land, disregarding you and your gods?" He said, "We will slay their sons and let their women live *to show* that we are dominant over them." ¹²⁸ Musa told his people, "Seek Allah's help and be patient. The Earth belongs to Allah, and He gives it to any of His servants to inherit it, and *only* the mindful *of Allah* shall have *success in* the end. ¹²⁹ They said, "We suffered before you came and continue to suffer." He said, "It may be that your Lord will destroy your enemy and make you successors in the land, so that He may see how you will behave."

The plagues that befell the people of Pharaoh

¹³⁰ For years there was a drought, We caused crop failure for Pharaoh's people, *hopeful* they might reflect. ¹³¹ In good times they would say, "We deserve this," but in hard times they would take it as an *evil* omenᵃ brought on by Musa and those with him. Is it not the case that their omen comes from Allah? Most of them are ignorant.

ᵃ   The Arabic word *ta'ir* means "bird". The pagans had lots of superstitious practices: before embarking on a journey they would release a bird into the air, and if it flew towards the right it would signal success.

تُصِبْهُمْ سَيِّئَةٌ يَطَّيَّرُوا بِمُوسَى وَمَن مَّعَهُ ۚ أَلَا إِنَّمَا طَٰٓئِرُهُمْ عِندَ اللَّهِ وَلَٰكِنَّ أَكْثَرَهُمْ لَا يَعْلَمُونَ ۝ وَقَالُوا مَهْمَا تَأْتِنَا بِهِ مِنْ ءَايَةٍ لِّتَسْحَرَنَا بِهَا فَمَا نَحْنُ لَكَ بِمُؤْمِنِينَ ۝ فَأَرْسَلْنَا عَلَيْهِمُ الطُّوفَانَ وَالْجَرَادَ وَالْقُمَّلَ وَالضَّفَادِعَ وَالدَّمَ ءَايَٰتٍ مُّفَصَّلَٰتٍ فَاسْتَكْبَرُوا وَكَانُوا قَوْمًا مُّجْرِمِينَ ۝ وَلَمَّا وَقَعَ عَلَيْهِمُ الرِّجْزُ قَالُوا يَٰمُوسَى ادْعُ لَنَا رَبَّكَ بِمَا عَهِدَ عِندَكَ ۖ لَئِن كَشَفْتَ عَنَّا الرِّجْزَ لَنُؤْمِنَنَّ لَكَ وَلَنُرْسِلَنَّ مَعَكَ بَنِىٓ إِسْرَآءِيلَ ۝ فَلَمَّا كَشَفْنَا عَنْهُمُ الرِّجْزَ إِلَىٰٓ أَجَلٍ هُم بَٰلِغُوهُ إِذَا هُمْ يَنكُثُونَ ۝ فَانتَقَمْنَا مِنْهُمْ فَأَغْرَقْنَٰهُمْ فِى الْيَمِّ بِأَنَّهُمْ كَذَّبُوا بِـَٔايَٰتِنَا وَكَانُوا عَنْهَا غَٰفِلِينَ ۝ وَأَوْرَثْنَا الْقَوْمَ الَّذِينَ كَانُوا يُسْتَضْعَفُونَ مَشَٰرِقَ الْأَرْضِ وَمَغَٰرِبَهَا الَّتِى بَٰرَكْنَا فِيهَا ۖ وَتَمَّتْ كَلِمَتُ رَبِّكَ الْحُسْنَىٰ عَلَىٰ بَنِىٓ إِسْرَآءِيلَ بِمَا صَبَرُوا ۖ وَدَمَّرْنَا مَا كَانَ يَصْنَعُ فِرْعَوْنُ وَقَوْمُهُ وَمَا كَانُوا يَعْرِشُونَ ۝ وَجَٰوَزْنَا بِبَنِىٓ إِسْرَآءِيلَ الْبَحْرَ فَأَتَوْا عَلَىٰ قَوْمٍ يَعْكُفُونَ عَلَىٰٓ أَصْنَامٍ لَّهُمْ ۚ قَالُوا يَٰمُوسَى اجْعَل لَّنَآ إِلَٰهًا كَمَا لَهُمْ ءَالِهَةٌ ۚ قَالَ إِنَّكُمْ قَوْمٌ تَجْهَلُونَ ۝ إِنَّ

Pharaoh was given nine chances, nine signs, nine plagues. Look how patient Allah was.

¹³² They said, "Any signs you come up with to captivate us, we will not believe." ¹³³ So We sent down clear signs to them: floods, locusts, lice, frogs and blood, but they were arrogant and sinful people. ¹³⁴ When caught in a plague, they would say: "Musa, pray to your Lord for us through the contract you have. If you can relieve us of the plague, we will believe you and send the Israelites with you." ¹³⁵ However, when We relieved them of the plague and gave them a respite, after a while they'd go back on their word. ¹³⁶ So We took revenge, drowning them in the sea since they denied Our signs and paid no attention to them.

The Israelites forget Allah's favours soon after the exodus!
¹³⁷ Those who were once helpless We made them inherit the lands We had blessed from the east to west, and so it was that the gracious word of your Lord to the Israelites came to be fulfilled, because of what they had suffered: and We destroyed what Pharaoh and his people had built. ¹³⁸ After We had led the Israelites across the sea, they came across people who worshipped idols. *The Israelites* requested, "Musa, let us have a god like their gods." He said, "You are ignorant people.

هٰٓؤُلَاءِ مُتَبَّرٌ مَّا هُمْ فِيْهِ وَبٰطِلٌ مَّا كَانُوْا

يَعْمَلُوْنَ ۝ قَالَ اَغَيْرَ اللّٰهِ اَبْغِيْكُمْ اِلٰهًا وَّهُوَ

فَضَّلَكُمْ عَلَى الْعٰلَمِيْنَ ۝ وَاِذْ اَنْجَيْنٰكُمْ مِّنْ اٰلِ

فِرْعَوْنَ يَسُوْمُوْنَكُمْ سُوْٓءَ الْعَذَابِ ۚ يُقَتِّلُوْنَ

اَبْنَآءَكُمْ وَيَسْتَحْيُوْنَ نِسَآءَكُمْ ۗ وَفِيْ ذٰلِكُمْ بَلَآءٌ

مِّنْ رَّبِّكُمْ عَظِيْمٌ ۝ وَوٰعَدْنَا مُوْسٰى ثَلٰثِيْنَ

لَيْلَةً وَّاَتْمَمْنٰهَا بِعَشْرٍ فَتَمَّ مِيْقَاتُ رَبِّهٖۤ اَرْبَعِيْنَ

لَيْلَةً ۚ وَقَالَ مُوْسٰى لِاَخِيْهِ هٰرُوْنَ اخْلُفْنِيْ فِيْ

قَوْمِيْ وَاَصْلِحْ وَلَا تَتَّبِعْ سَبِيْلَ الْمُفْسِدِيْنَ ۝

وَلَمَّا جَآءَ مُوْسٰى لِمِيْقَاتِنَا وَكَلَّمَهٗ رَبُّهٗ ۙ قَالَ

رَبِّ اَرِنِيْۤ اَنْظُرْ اِلَيْكَ ۚ قَالَ لَنْ تَرٰنِيْ وَلٰكِنِ

انْظُرْ اِلَى الْجَبَلِ فَاِنِ اسْتَقَرَّ مَكَانَهٗ فَسَوْفَ

تَرٰنِيْ ۚ فَلَمَّا تَجَلّٰى رَبُّهٗ لِلْجَبَلِ جَعَلَهٗ دَكًّا وَّخَرَّ

مُوْسٰى صَعِقًا ۚ فَلَمَّاۤ اَفَاقَ قَالَ سُبْحٰنَكَ تُبْتُ

اِلَيْكَ وَاَنَا اَوَّلُ الْمُؤْمِنِيْنَ ۝ قَالَ يٰمُوْسٰۤى اِنِّى

اصْطَفَيْتُكَ عَلَى النَّاسِ بِرِسٰلٰتِيْ وَبِكَلَامِيْ ۖ فَخُذْ

مَاۤ اٰتَيْتُكَ وَكُنْ مِّنَ الشّٰكِرِيْنَ ۝ وَكَتَبْنَا لَهٗ فِى

الْاَلْوَاحِ مِنْ كُلِّ شَيْءٍ مَّوْعِظَةً وَّتَفْصِيْلًا لِّكُلِّ

شَيْءٍ ۚ فَخُذْهَا بِقُوَّةٍ وَّأْمُرْ قَوْمَكَ يَأْخُذُوْا بِاَحْسَنِهَا ۗ

سَاُورِيْكُمْ دَارَ الْفٰسِقِيْنَ ۝ سَاَصْرِفُ عَنْ اٰيٰتِيَ

Musa longed to see His Lord, but Divine manifestation was too much to bear.

¹³⁹These *people*, whatever *state* they are in is beyond repair,ᵃ and whatever they have been doing is null and void." ¹⁴⁰He said, "How can I seek a god other than Allah for you, it is He Who has favoured you over the rest of humanity?" ¹⁴¹*Remember* when We saved you from Pharaoh's people, who inflicted the worst punishment *imaginable on you*: slaying your sons and leaving your women to live; that was a big test from Your Lord.

Musa goes to Mount Sinai to receive the tablets

¹⁴²We kept Musa *on mount Sinai* for thirty nights, to which We added ten, so he stayed a total of forty nights with his Lord. *When* Musa was *leaving, he* said to his brother, Harun, "Be deputy over my people, do what is right, and do not follow the path of those who are mischievous." ¹⁴³After Musa came to Us according to his appointment, and his Lord spoke to him, he said: "My Lord, let me see You." *Allah* said, "You will not *be able to* see Me, but look towards the mountain; if it stays in its place, then you will *be able to* see Me." When His Lord appeared in His glory on the mountain, it crumbled, and Musa fell unconscious as though struck by lightning. When *Musa* regained consciousness, he said, "Glory be to You! I seek Your repentance, and I am the first believer." ¹⁴⁴*Allah* said, "Musa, in *giving you* My messages and My words, I have chosen you above all people, so take what I have given you and be grateful." ¹⁴⁵We wrote everything on the tablets for him as a warning, explaining things in detail: "So hold *the tablets* firmly, and order your people to take hold of the best of *what is in* them.ᵇ I'll show you the houses of the sinners.

ᵃ *Mutabbar* means "broken", like broken pottery or glass that can't be repaired.

ᵇ "The best of *what is in* them," means follow what Allah commanded and avoid what He forbids or, if two lawful alternatives existed, as with pardoning and retaliation, adopt pardon (Al-Qurtubi).

الَّذِيْنَ يَتَكَبَّرُوْنَ فِى الْاَرْضِ بِغَيْرِ الْحَقِّ ۚ وَاِنْ يَّرَوْا

كُلَّ اٰيَةٍ لَّا يُؤْمِنُوْا بِهَا ۚ وَاِنْ يَّرَوْا سَبِيْلَ الرُّشْدِ

لَا يَتَّخِذُوْهُ سَبِيْلًا ۚ وَاِنْ يَّرَوْا سَبِيْلَ الْغَيِّ يَتَّخِذُوْهُ

سَبِيْلًا ۚ ذٰلِكَ بِاَنَّهُمْ كَذَّبُوْا بِاٰيٰتِنَا وَكَانُوْا

عَنْهَا غٰفِلِيْنَ ۝ وَالَّذِيْنَ كَذَّبُوْا بِاٰيٰتِنَا وَلِقَآءِ

الْاٰخِرَةِ حَبِطَتْ اَعْمَالُهُمْ ۗ هَلْ يُجْزَوْنَ اِلَّا مَا

كَانُوْا يَعْمَلُوْنَ ۝ وَاتَّخَذَ قَوْمُ مُوْسٰى مِنْ بَعْدِهٖ

مِنْ حُلِيِّهِمْ عِجْلًا جَسَدًا لَّهٗ خُوَارٌ ۗ اَلَمْ يَرَوْا

اَنَّهٗ لَا يُكَلِّمُهُمْ وَلَا يَهْدِيْهِمْ سَبِيْلًا ۘ اِتَّخَذُوْهُ

وَكَانُوْا ظٰلِمِيْنَ ۝ وَلَمَّا سُقِطَ فِيْ اَيْدِيْهِمْ وَرَاَوْا

اَنَّهُمْ قَدْ ضَلُّوْا ۙ قَالُوْا لَئِنْ لَّمْ يَرْحَمْنَا رَبُّنَا

وَيَغْفِرْ لَنَا لَنَكُوْنَنَّ مِنَ الْخٰسِرِيْنَ ۝ وَلَمَّا رَجَعَ

مُوْسٰى اِلٰى قَوْمِهٖ غَضْبَانَ اَسِفًا ۙ قَالَ بِئْسَمَا

خَلَفْتُمُوْنِيْ مِنْ بَعْدِيْ ۚ اَعَجِلْتُمْ اَمْرَ رَبِّكُمْ ۚ وَاَلْقَى

الْاَلْوَاحَ وَاَخَذَ بِرَأْسِ اَخِيْهِ يَجُرُّهٗ اِلَيْهِ ۗ قَالَ ابْنَ

اُمَّ اِنَّ الْقَوْمَ اسْتَضْعَفُوْنِيْ وَكَادُوْا يَقْتُلُوْنَنِيْ ۖ

فَلَا تُشْمِتْ بِيَ الْاَعْدَآءَ وَلَا تَجْعَلْنِيْ مَعَ الْقَوْمِ

الظّٰلِمِيْنَ ۝ قَالَ رَبِّ اغْفِرْ لِيْ وَلِاَخِيْ وَاَدْخِلْنَا

فِيْ رَحْمَتِكَ ۖ وَاَنْتَ اَرْحَمُ الرّٰحِمِيْنَ ۝ اِنَّ الَّذِيْنَ

اتَّخَذُوا الْعِجْلَ سَيَنَالُهُمْ غَضَبٌ مِّنْ رَّبِّهِمْ وَذِلَّةٌ

Bad habits don't die easily; the Israelites after seeing so many miracles still had an idol. Do you have an idol?

319

Arrogance blinds people to the blessings of Allah's guidance

¹⁴⁶ Those who behave arrogantly unjustifiably in the land shall be deprived of seeing My signs, even if they saw every single sign, they still wouldn't believe, if they were to see the path of guidance, they wouldn't take it; but if they see the path of error, they follow it. That's because they denied Our signs and paid no attention to them. ¹⁴⁷ Those who denied Our signs and meeting in the Hereafter, their deeds will prove worthless. Wouldn't they be rewarded for their deeds?

The Israelites make a golden calf

¹⁴⁸ Meanwhile Musa's people took a calf *as god,* with a mooing sound and a body *moulded* from their jewellery. Wasn't it obvious to them it neither spoke to them nor guided them along any path? *Nevertheless,* they adopted it *as a god* and so became wrongdoers. ¹⁴⁹ When the enormity of what they had done struck them[a] they realised they were misled, so they said, "If our Lord isn't kind and forgives us, we will be losers." ¹⁵⁰ Musa returned to his people, and *saw what they had done;* he was angry and sad and said, "How foul is what you did after me! Were you so keen to hasten your Lord's judgement?" He lay down the tablets and grabbed hold of his brother's head *by the hair,* pulling him towards himself. *Harun* said, "Son of my mother, they thought I was weak and almost killed me. So do not give *our* enemies any reason to ridicule me, and don't put me *in the same category* with the wrongdoers." ¹⁵¹ *Musa* said, "My Lord, forgive me and my brother, embrace us with Your Kindness, for you are the most Kind." ¹⁵² Those who accepted the calf *as a god* will have their Lord's wrath and disgrace in this worldly life. That is how We reward those who invent *lies.*

---

[a] *Suqita fi aydihim,* is an idiom meaning, "it fell into their hands," referring to the moment of bewilderment when it is no longer possible to deny the truth, the evidence is in one's hands, "staring one in the face."

فِى الْحَيٰوةِ الدُّنْيَا ۚ وَكَذٰلِكَ نَجْزِى الْمُفْتَرِيْنَ ۝

وَالَّذِيْنَ عَمِلُوا السَّيِّاٰتِ ثُمَّ تَابُوْا مِنْۢ بَعْدِهَا وَاٰمَنُوْا ۙ اِنَّ رَبَّكَ مِنْۢ بَعْدِهَا لَغَفُوْرٌ رَّحِيْمٌ ۝ وَلَمَّا سَكَتَ عَنْ مُّوْسَى الْغَضَبُ اَخَذَ الْاَلْوَاحَ ۖ وَفِىْ نُسْخَتِهَا هُدًى وَّرَحْمَةٌ لِّلَّذِيْنَ هُمْ لِرَبِّهِمْ يَرْهَبُوْنَ ۝

وَاخْتَارَ مُوْسٰى قَوْمَهٗ سَبْعِيْنَ رَجُلًا لِّمِيْقَاتِنَا ۚ فَلَمَّآ اَخَذَتْهُمُ الرَّجْفَةُ قَالَ رَبِّ لَوْ شِئْتَ

اَهْلَكْتَهُمْ مِّنْ قَبْلُ وَاِيَّايَ ۚ اَتُهْلِكُنَا بِمَا فَعَلَ السُّفَهَآءُ مِنَّا ۚ اِنْ هِىَ اِلَّا فِتْنَتُكَ ۚ تُضِلُّ بِهَا مَنْ تَشَآءُ وَتَهْدِىْ مَنْ تَشَآءُ ۚ اَنْتَ وَلِيُّنَا فَاغْفِرْ لَنَا وَارْحَمْنَا وَاَنْتَ خَيْرُ الْغٰفِرِيْنَ ۝ وَاكْتُبْ لَنَا فِىْ هٰذِهِ الدُّنْيَا حَسَنَةً وَّفِى الْاٰخِرَةِ اِنَّا هُدْنَآ اِلَيْكَ ۚ قَالَ عَذَابِىْٓ اُصِيْبُ بِهٖ مَنْ اَشَآءُ ۚ وَرَحْمَتِىْ وَسِعَتْ كُلَّ شَىْءٍ ۚ فَسَاَكْتُبُهَا لِلَّذِيْنَ يَتَّقُوْنَ وَيُؤْتُوْنَ الزَّكٰوةَ وَالَّذِيْنَ هُمْ بِاٰيٰتِنَا يُؤْمِنُوْنَ ۝ اَلَّذِيْنَ يَتَّبِعُوْنَ الرَّسُوْلَ النَّبِىَّ الْاُمِّىَّ الَّذِىْ يَجِدُوْنَهٗ مَكْتُوْبًا عِنْدَهُمْ فِى التَّوْرٰىةِ وَالْاِنْجِيْلِ ۖ يَاْمُرُهُمْ بِالْمَعْرُوْفِ وَيَنْهٰهُمْ عَنِ الْمُنْكَرِ وَيُحِلُّ لَهُمُ الطَّيِّبٰتِ وَيُحَرِّمُ عَلَيْهِمُ الْخَبٰٓئِثَ وَيَضَعُ عَنْهُمْ اِصْرَهُمْ وَالْاَغْلٰلَ الَّتِىْ كَانَتْ

¹⁵³Those who were evil then repented and believed, your Lord will forgive and be Kind."

Musa returns to Mount Sinai, where he talks once more to Allah

¹⁵⁴Once Musa's anger had subsided, he picked up the tablets. They contained guidance and *teachings of* kindness for anyone who fears their Lord. ¹⁵⁵*Then* Musa chose seventy men from his people to meet with Us. After a blast had taken them, *Musa* said, "My Lord, if this is what You wanted, You could have killed them and me long before. Will You now kill us *all* because of what the fools among us did? This was Your way of testing to let anyone you wish to go astray and anyone You wish to guide; You are our Protector, so forgive us and be kind to us; You are the best Forgiver. ¹⁵⁶Decree for us in this world what is good and in the Hereafter; we return *in humility* to serve you." *Allah* said, "I afflict My punishment whomever I please, while My kindness embraces everything. I shall decree *what is good* for those who are mindful *of Me*, pay Zakat and believe in Our signs."

A portrait of Allah's obedient servants

¹⁵⁷Those who follow the Messenger, the untutored Prophet, they will find him mentioned in the Torah and the Gospel. He who instructs them to do good and forbids evil, declares lawful all that is pure and healthy, and prohibits whatever is unclean, and relieves them of their burden and the shackles that once bound them. So, they believe in him, honour him, support him, and obey the light that was sent with him, they shall be successful.^a

---

^a   "*Ummi*" is from *Umm* meaning the mother, the Quran calls Makkah '*Umm al-Qura*', mother of cities. Since the Prophet 🕌 was born there he is referred to as *Ummi*. A person who is not tutored is also called *Ummi*; here it means that Allah 🕌 taught him directly without a human teacher.

عَلَيْهِمْ ۚ فَالَّذِيْنَ اٰمَنُوْا بِهٖ وَعَزَّرُوْهُ وَنَصَرُوْهُ

وَاتَّبَعُوا النُّوْرَ الَّذِيْٓ اُنْزِلَ مَعَهٗٓ ۙ اُولٰٓئِكَ هُمُ

الْمُفْلِحُوْنَ ۝ قُلْ يٰٓاَيُّهَا النَّاسُ اِنِّيْ رَسُوْلُ اللّٰهِ

اِلَيْكُمْ جَمِيْعَا ۨ الَّذِيْ لَهٗ مُلْكُ السَّمٰوٰتِ وَالْاَرْضِ ۚ

لَآ اِلٰهَ اِلَّا هُوَ يُحْيٖ وَيُمِيْتُ ۖ فَاٰمِنُوْا بِاللّٰهِ وَ

رَسُوْلِهِ النَّبِيِّ الْاُمِّيِّ الَّذِيْ يُؤْمِنُ بِاللّٰهِ وَكَلِمٰتِهٖ

وَاتَّبِعُوْهُ لَعَلَّكُمْ تَهْتَدُوْنَ ۝ وَمِنْ قَوْمِ مُوْسٰىٓ

اُمَّةٌ يَّهْدُوْنَ بِالْحَقِّ وَبِهٖ يَعْدِلُوْنَ ۝ وَقَطَّعْنٰهُمُ

اثْنَتَيْ عَشْرَةَ اَسْبَاطًا اُمَمًا ۚ وَاَوْحَيْنَآ اِلٰى مُوْسٰىٓ

اِذِ اسْتَسْقٰهُ قَوْمُهٗٓ اَنِ اضْرِبْ بِّعَصَاكَ الْحَجَرَ ۚ

فَانْۢبَجَسَتْ مِنْهُ اثْنَتَا عَشْرَةَ عَيْنًا ۗ قَدْ عَلِمَ كُلُّ

اُنَاسٍ مَّشْرَبَهُمْ ۚ وَظَلَّلْنَا عَلَيْهِمُ الْغَمَامَ وَاَنْزَلْنَا

عَلَيْهِمُ الْمَنَّ وَالسَّلْوٰى ۗ كُلُوْا مِنْ طَيِّبٰتِ مَا رَزَقْنٰكُمْ ۚ

وَمَا ظَلَمُوْنَا وَلٰكِنْ كَانُوْٓا اَنْفُسَهُمْ يَظْلِمُوْنَ ۝

وَاِذْ قِيْلَ لَهُمُ اسْكُنُوْا هٰذِهِ الْقَرْيَةَ وَكُلُوْا مِنْهَا

حَيْثُ شِئْتُمْ وَقُوْلُوْا حِطَّةٌ وَّادْخُلُوا الْبَابَ

سُجَّدًا نَّغْفِرْ لَكُمْ خَطِيْٓئٰتِكُمْ ۚ سَنَزِيْدُ الْمُحْسِنِيْنَ ۝

فَبَدَّلَ الَّذِيْنَ ظَلَمُوْا مِنْهُمْ قَوْلًا غَيْرَ الَّذِيْ قِيْلَ

لَهُمْ فَاَرْسَلْنَا عَلَيْهِمْ رِجْزًا مِّنَ السَّمَآءِ بِمَا

كَانُوْا يَظْلِمُوْنَ ۝ وَسْـَٔلْهُمْ عَنِ الْقَرْيَةِ الَّتِيْ

Four duties towards the Messenger ﷺ: have faith, respect, help and obey him.

The beloved Messenger ﷺ is sent to all people

¹⁵⁸ Say: "People, I am the Messenger to you all from Allah, sovereignty of the Heavens and the Earth belongs to Him; He is the only God, He gives life and death. So, believe in Allah and His Messenger, the untutored Prophet, who believes in Allah and His words, and follow him so that you might be guided."

The twelve tribes of Israel are offered a chance to repent

¹⁵⁹ Among Musa's people is a community that guides *others* with the truth and practises justice. ¹⁶⁰ We divided *the Israelites* into twelve tribes, each a community, *and* when his people asked Musa for water We told him: "Strike the rock with your *shepherd's* staff." Twelve springs gushed out, and the people of each *tribe* knew their drinking place. We made the clouds shade them and sent them manna and quails, saying, "Eat of the wholesome things We provided you." *The Israelites* never harmed Us, but they harmed themselves. ¹⁶¹ *For example*, when they were told: "Settle down in this town and eat *of its fruits* from wherever you please, and when you enter the gates, prostrate yourselves and say: '*Forgive us our sins,*' so that We forgive your wrongs, and We will increase the reward of the righteous *ones*." ¹⁶² The wrongdoers among them altered the phrase to something else than what they were told *to say*, so We sent punishment from Heaven because of the wrong they did.

كَانَتْ حَاضِرَةَ الْبَحْرِ اِذْ يَعْدُوْنَ فِي السَّبْتِ
اِذْ تَأْتِيْهِمْ حِيْتَانُهُمْ يَوْمَ سَبْتِهِمْ شُرَّعًا وَّ يَوْمَ
لَا يَسْبِتُوْنَ لَا تَأْتِيْهِمْ ۚ كَذٰلِكَ ۛ نَبْلُوْهُمْ بِمَا
كَانُوْا يَفْسُقُوْنَ ۝ وَ اِذْ قَالَتْ اُمَّةٌ مِّنْهُمْ لِمَ
تَعِظُوْنَ قَوْمًا ۙ اللّٰهُ مُهْلِكُهُمْ اَوْ مُعَذِّبُهُمْ عَذَابًا
شَدِيْدًا ؕ قَالُوْا مَعْذِرَةً اِلٰى رَبِّكُمْ وَ لَعَلَّهُمْ
يَتَّقُوْنَ ۝ فَلَمَّا نَسُوْا مَا ذُكِّرُوْا بِهٖٓ اَنْجَيْنَا
الَّذِيْنَ يَنْهَوْنَ عَنِ السُّوْٓءِ وَ اَخَذْنَا الَّذِيْنَ ظَلَمُوْا
بِعَذَابٍ بَئِيْسٍ بِمَا كَانُوْا يَفْسُقُوْنَ ۝ فَلَمَّا
عَتَوْا عَنْ مَّا نُهُوْا عَنْهُ قُلْنَا لَهُمْ كُوْنُوْا قِرَدَةً
خٰسِئِيْنَ ۝ وَ اِذْ تَاَذَّنَ رَبُّكَ لَيَبْعَثَنَّ عَلَيْهِمْ اِلٰى
يَوْمِ الْقِيٰمَةِ مَنْ يَّسُوْمُهُمْ سُوْٓءَ الْعَذَابِ ؕ اِنَّ
رَبَّكَ لَسَرِيْعُ الْعِقَابِ ۚ وَ اِنَّهٗ لَغَفُوْرٌ رَّحِيْمٌ ۝
وَ قَطَّعْنٰهُمْ فِي الْاَرْضِ اُمَمًا ۚ مِنْهُمُ الصّٰلِحُوْنَ وَ
مِنْهُمْ دُوْنَ ذٰلِكَ ۫ وَ بَلَوْنٰهُمْ بِالْحَسَنٰتِ وَ السَّيِّاٰتِ
لَعَلَّهُمْ يَرْجِعُوْنَ ۝ فَخَلَفَ مِنْ بَعْدِهِمْ خَلْفٌ
وَرِثُوا الْكِتٰبَ يَأْخُذُوْنَ عَرَضَ هٰذَا الْاَدْنٰى وَ
يَقُوْلُوْنَ سَيُغْفَرُ لَنَا ۚ وَ اِنْ يَّأْتِهِمْ عَرَضٌ مِّثْلُهٗ
يَأْخُذُوْهُ ؕ اَلَمْ يُؤْخَذْ عَلَيْهِمْ مِّيْثَاقُ الْكِتٰبِ
اَنْ لَّا يَقُوْلُوْا عَلَى اللّٰهِ اِلَّا الْحَقَّ وَ دَرَسُوْا مَا فِيْهِ ؕ

What should you do when you see an evil? Ignore it? Stay silent? Or stop it?

Those who broke the law of Sabbath were punished

[163] Ask them, *messenger*, about the town by the sea; they broke the *law of* Sabbath. On the Sabbath, the fish would appear on the surface *of the sea*, but not on any other days when they were *fishing*. We tested them because they sinned. [164] Another group from the *Israelites* said, "Why are you preaching to people, who Allah will destroy or punish?" They said, "It is a plea for clemency from your Lord,[a] and in the hope that they might be mindful *of Allah*." [165] Once they forgot all they had been reminded of, We punished them severely because of their sinfulness and saved those who warned them against doing evil. [166] When they disrespectfully continued doing what they were forbidden, We said, "Become like apes, despised!"[b]

The Israelites will be scattered around the world

[167] *Remember* when your Lord declared: "Let there arise against *the wrongdoers, people* who will inflict the terrible torment on them *from now* until Judgement Day." Your Lord is quick to punish, but He is *also* Forgiving, Kind. [168] And so it was that We dispersed *the Israelites* across *the face of* the Earth as *separate* communities – some are righteous and others not at all like them – and We tested them through good and bad times hoping they may return to Us. [169] After them came a successor *nation*, who inherited the Book but practised only the easy parts of the *Book's teachings*, saying, "We'll be forgiven," and if the like of it comes their way *from a source other than the Book*, they *willingly* take that too. Will they not be taken *to task* over the pledge in the Book to say nothing but the truth about Allah, given that they have studied whatever is in *the Book*? The home of the Hereafter is better for the mindful. Do you not understand?

---

[a] It is a collective obligation on the community to "enjoin the common good and forbid evil" (*Surat Al 'Imran* 3: 110). In this example, there were two groups: obedient, those who advised the wrongdoers to obey the law; and those who saw no point in advising the wrongdoers (Al-Qurtubi).

[b] Did they literally turn into apes or is this a metaphor? The most likely meaning is they became objects of ridicule like monkeys often are. However, it is totally wrong to call Jews monkeys.

وَالدَّارُ الْاٰخِرَةُ خَيْرٌ لِّلَّذِيْنَ يَتَّقُوْنَ ط اَفَلَا تَعْقِلُوْنَ ۝ وَالَّذِيْنَ يُمَسِّكُوْنَ بِالْكِتٰبِ وَاَقَامُوا الصَّلٰوةَ ط اِنَّا لَا نُضِيْعُ اَجْرَ الْمُصْلِحِيْنَ ۝ وَاِذْ نَتَقْنَا الْجَبَلَ فَوْقَهُمْ كَاَنَّهٗ ظُلَّةٌ وَّ ظَنُّوْا اَنَّهٗ وَاقِعٌۢ بِهِمْ ۚ خُذُوْا مَاۤ اٰتَيْنٰكُمْ بِقُوَّةٍ وَّاذْكُرُوْا مَا فِيْهِ لَعَلَّكُمْ تَتَّقُوْنَ ۝ وَاِذْ اَخَذَ رَبُّكَ مِنْۢ بَنِيْۤ اٰدَمَ مِنْ ظُهُوْرِهِمْ ذُرِّيَّتَهُمْ وَاَشْهَدَهُمْ عَلٰۤى اَنْفُسِهِمْ ۚ اَلَسْتُ بِرَبِّكُمْ ط قَالُوْا بَلٰى ۚۛ شَهِدْنَا ۚۛ اَنْ تَقُوْلُوْا يَوْمَ الْقِيٰمَةِ اِنَّا كُنَّا عَنْ هٰذَا غٰفِلِيْنَ ۝

اَوْ تَقُوْلُوْۤا اِنَّمَاۤ اَشْرَكَ اٰبَآؤُنَا مِنْ قَبْلُ وَكُنَّا ذُرِّيَّةً مِّنْۢ بَعْدِهِمْ ۚ اَفَتُهْلِكُنَا بِمَا فَعَلَ الْمُبْطِلُوْنَ ۝ وَكَذٰلِكَ نُفَصِّلُ الْاٰيٰتِ وَلَعَلَّهُمْ يَرْجِعُوْنَ ۝ وَاتْلُ عَلَيْهِمْ نَبَاَ الَّذِيْۤ اٰتَيْنٰهُ اٰيٰتِنَا فَانْسَلَخَ مِنْهَا فَاَتْبَعَهُ الشَّيْطٰنُ فَكَانَ مِنَ الْغٰوِيْنَ ۝ وَلَوْ شِئْنَا لَرَفَعْنٰهُ بِهَا وَلٰكِنَّهٗۤ اَخْلَدَ اِلَى الْاَرْضِ وَاتَّبَعَ هَوٰىهُ ۚ فَمَثَلُهٗ كَمَثَلِ الْكَلْبِ ۚ اِنْ تَحْمِلْ عَلَيْهِ يَلْهَثْ اَوْ تَتْرُكْهُ يَلْهَثْ ط ذٰلِكَ مَثَلُ الْقَوْمِ الَّذِيْنَ كَذَّبُوْا بِاٰيٰتِنَا ۚ فَاقْصُصِ الْقَصَصَ لَعَلَّهُمْ يَتَفَكَّرُوْنَ ۝ سَآءَ مَثَلَا ۨالْقَوْمُ الَّذِيْنَ كَذَّبُوْا بِاٰيٰتِنَا وَاَنْفُسَهُمْ

[170] Those who hold fast to the Book and perform the prayer, We do not allow the reward to go to waste for people who strive for improvement *in society*. [171] *Remember,* We shook the mountain *that loomed* over them like a shadow, and they thought it would fall over them; *and We said,* "Hold firmly what We gave you and remember what's in it so that you become mindful."

The first assembly of human souls; pledge of loyalty

[172] *Remember* when Your Lord took *all* the offspring from the loins of the children of Adam to be witnesses, *saying,* "Am I not Your Lord?" They replied, "Yes, we bear witness." This was so that, on Judgement Day, you would not say, "We were unaware of this *contract*"[a] [173] or say, "It was our forefathers who first associated *partners with Allah,* and we are *merely* descendants who came afterwards. Will You kill us because of the actions of the falsifiers?" [174] This is how We explain *Our* signs, perhaps they will return *to the right path.*

The deniers of Allah's signs are like panting dogs

[175] Tell them about the one who We gave knowledge of Scriptures, but he shed them *as a snake sheds its skin;* then Satan made him follow him so that he became disobedient.[b] [176] If We wanted, We could have raised his *status* because of those *signs,* but he chose to pursue Earthly matters and follow his whims. His type is like a dog: if you attack it pants, and if you leave it alone it pants, and the people who deny Our signs are like that. So, repeat these stories to them, perhaps they might reflect. [177] How wretched is that type of person who denies Our Scripture and, in the process, wrongs himself.

---

[a] The Day of *Alast,* was the first assembly of human souls. While memory of this momentous assembly in the divine presence may have faded from human consciousness, it remains etched in human nature. That's why whenever a person is properly guided, the seed of faith in Allah sprouts and grows.

[b] Al-Qurtubi refers to a traditional Jewish story of a scholar called Balʿam ibn Baʿuraʾ, when he spoke thousands of students wrote down his words until, one day, he chose to write that the world had no maker, and became a disbeliever.

كَانُوْا يَظْلِمُوْنَ ۝ مَنْ يَّهْدِ اللّٰهُ فَهُوَ الْمُهْتَدِيْ ۚ

وَمَنْ يُّضْلِلْ فَأُولٰٓئِكَ هُمُ الْخٰسِرُوْنَ ۝ وَلَقَدْ

ذَرَأْنَا لِجَهَنَّمَ كَثِيْرًا مِّنَ الْجِنِّ وَالْإِنْسِ ۖ

لَهُمْ قُلُوْبٌ لَّا يَفْقَهُوْنَ بِهَا ۫ وَلَهُمْ أَعْيُنٌ لَّا

يُبْصِرُوْنَ بِهَا ۫ وَلَهُمْ اٰذَانٌ لَّا يَسْمَعُوْنَ بِهَا ۗ

أُولٰٓئِكَ كَالْأَنْعَامِ بَلْ هُمْ أَضَلُّ ۚ أُولٰٓئِكَ هُمُ

الْغٰفِلُوْنَ ۝ وَلِلّٰهِ الْأَسْمَآءُ الْحُسْنٰى فَادْعُوْهُ

بِهَا ۖ وَذَرُوا الَّذِيْنَ يُلْحِدُوْنَ فِيْ أَسْمَآئِهٖ ۗ

سَيُجْزَوْنَ مَا كَانُوْا يَعْمَلُوْنَ ۝ وَمِمَّنْ خَلَقْنَا

أُمَّةٌ يَّهْدُوْنَ بِالْحَقِّ وَبِهٖ يَعْدِلُوْنَ ۝ وَالَّذِيْنَ

كَذَّبُوْا بِاٰيٰتِنَا سَنَسْتَدْرِجُهُمْ مِّنْ حَيْثُ لَا

يَعْلَمُوْنَ ۝ وَأُمْلِيْ لَهُمْ ۚ إِنَّ كَيْدِيْ مَتِيْنٌ ۝

أَوَلَمْ يَتَفَكَّرُوْا مَا بِصَاحِبِهِمْ مِّنْ جِنَّةٍ ۗ إِنْ

هُوَ إِلَّا نَذِيْرٌ مُّبِيْنٌ ۝ أَوَلَمْ يَنْظُرُوْا فِيْ مَلَكُوْتِ

السَّمٰوٰتِ وَالْأَرْضِ وَمَا خَلَقَ اللّٰهُ مِنْ شَيْءٍ ۙ

وَّأَنْ عَسٰٓى أَنْ يَّكُوْنَ قَدِ اقْتَرَبَ أَجَلُهُمْ ۚ فَبِأَيِّ

حَدِيْثٍ بَعْدَهٗ يُؤْمِنُوْنَ ۝ مَنْ يُّضْلِلِ اللّٰهُ فَلَا

هَادِيَ لَهٗ ۚ وَيَذَرُهُمْ فِيْ طُغْيَانِهِمْ يَعْمَهُوْنَ ۝

يَسْئَلُوْنَكَ عَنِ السَّاعَةِ أَيَّانَ مُرْسٰهَا ۗ قُلْ

إِنَّمَا عِلْمُهَا عِنْدَ رَبِّيْ ۚ لَا يُجَلِّيْهَا لِوَقْتِهَا إِلَّا

Who are the biggest losers? People who fail to listen, fail to see and fail to be moved.

¹⁷⁸ Anyone Allah guides is truly guided, but anyone He allows to go astray; such people are the losers. ¹⁷⁹ *And so it is that* many of the jinn and humans that We've created *are intended* for Hell. They have brains which don't think, eyes that don't see, and ears that don't hear, such people are like cattle, even more dumb, worse than them; they are unaware *of reality.*

The beautiful names of Allah prompt us to reflect

¹⁸⁰ Allah has the most beautiful names, so call Him by those *names,* and avoid those who take His names in vain, they will be *appropriately* rewarded for what they earned. ¹⁸¹ Among Our created beings there is a community that lives according to the guidance, and practises justice in agreement with the truth. ¹⁸² But others who deny Our signs, We will let them edge their way little by little *towards destruction* from where they least expect it. ¹⁸³ I will give them some respite, but My decision is made. ¹⁸⁴ Have they not thought it through? There is no madness in their companion;^a he is a clear warner. ¹⁸⁵ Haven't they seen the realm of the Heavens and the Earth and in all that Allah has created a single thing *to suggest* that perhaps their end is near? *If not,* then what message will they *ever* believe in after this? ¹⁸⁶ Anyone Allah allows to go astray will have no guide, and *Allah* will leave them to stumble blindly into wickedness.

---

^a Meaning the Prophet Muhammad ﷺ.

هُوَطْ ثَقُلَتْ فِى السَّمٰوٰتِ وَالْاَرْضِ ط لَا تَاْتِيْكُمْ

اِلَّا بَغْتَةً ط يَسْئَلُوْنَكَ كَاَنَّكَ حَفِىٌّ عَنْهَا ط

قُلْ اِنَّمَا عِلْمُهَا عِنْدَ اللّٰهِ وَلٰكِنَّ اَكْثَرَ النَّاسِ لَا

يَعْلَمُوْنَ ۱۸۶ قُلْ لَّا اَمْلِكُ لِنَفْسِىْ نَفْعًا وَّلَا ضَرًّا اِلَّا

مَا شَاءَ اللّٰهُ ط وَلَوْ كُنْتُ اَعْلَمُ الْغَيْبَ لَاسْتَكْثَرْتُ

مِنَ الْخَيْرِ ۚ وَمَا مَسَّنِىَ السُّوْٓءُ ۚ اِنْ اَنَا اِلَّا نَذِيْرٌ

وَّبَشِيْرٌ لِّقَوْمٍ يُّؤْمِنُوْنَ ۱۸۸ هُوَ الَّذِىْ خَلَقَكُمْ مِّنْ

نَّفْسٍ وَّاحِدَةٍ وَّجَعَلَ مِنْهَا زَوْجَهَا لِيَسْكُنَ

اِلَيْهَا ۚ فَلَمَّا تَغَشّٰهَا حَمَلَتْ حَمْلًا خَفِيْفًا فَمَرَّتْ

بِهٖ ۚ فَلَمَّآ اَثْقَلَتْ دَّعَوَا اللّٰهَ رَبَّهُمَا لَئِنْ اٰتَيْتَنَا

صَالِحًا لَّنَكُوْنَنَّ مِنَ الشّٰكِرِيْنَ ۱۸۹ فَلَمَّآ اٰتٰىهُمَا

صَالِحًا جَعَلَا لَهٗ شُرَكَاءَ فِيْمَآ اٰتٰىهُمَا ۚ فَتَعٰلَى

اللّٰهُ عَمَّا يُشْرِكُوْنَ ۱۹۰ اَيُشْرِكُوْنَ مَا لَا يَخْلُقُ شَيْئًا

وَّهُمْ يُخْلَقُوْنَ ۱۹۱ وَلَا يَسْتَطِيْعُوْنَ لَهُمْ نَصْرًا

وَّلَآ اَنْفُسَهُمْ يَنْصُرُوْنَ ۱۹۲ وَاِنْ تَدْعُوْهُمْ اِلَى

الْهُدٰى لَا يَتَّبِعُوْكُمْ ط سَوَاءٌ عَلَيْكُمْ اَدَعَوْتُمُوْهُمْ

اَمْ اَنْتُمْ صَامِتُوْنَ ۱۹۳ اِنَّ الَّذِيْنَ تَدْعُوْنَ مِنْ

دُوْنِ اللّٰهِ عِبَادٌ اَمْثَالُكُمْ فَادْعُوْهُمْ فَلْيَسْتَجِيْبُوْا

لَكُمْ اِنْ كُنْتُمْ صٰدِقِيْنَ ۱۹۴ اَلَهُمْ اَرْجُلٌ يَّمْشُوْنَ

بِهَآ اَمْ لَهُمْ اَيْدٍ يَّبْطِشُوْنَ بِهَآ اَمْ لَهُمْ اَعْيُنٌ

The miracle of childbirth; notice the modesty and restraint in describing the intimacy of spouses.

People's continuous questioning about the Final Hour

[187] They ask you about the Final Hour, "When will it come?" Tell them: "My Lord alone knows it; except for Him, no one can reveal its timing. However, it hangs heavy in the Heavens and Earth and will come to you suddenly." They ask you as though you were thoroughly acquainted with it. Say: "Knowledge of it rests with my Lord alone," but most people are ignorant *of that fact*. [188] Say: "I have no control to bring benefit or harm *even* for myself, except *to the extent* that Allah wills. If I had full knowledge of the unseen, then I would have amassed a lot of wealth, and no harm to come my way. *As it is*, I am a warner and bearer of good news for people who believe."

Parents' promise gratitude, if blessed with a healthy child

[189] He created you from a single soul, and from that made its spouse to live together. When he slept with her, she became pregnant, *the pregnancy was* a light burden at first, allowing her to go about *her daily life*, but as *the foetus* grew heavier they both prayed to Allah, their Lord: "If You bless us with a healthy *child*, we will be grateful." [190] When He delivered them a healthy *child*, both set about attributing partners to Him regarding what He gave them. Allah is exalted above whatever *people* associate *with Him*.

The reality of idolatry is exposed

[191] Do *people* associate *partners with Allah* that create nothing, but are created; [192] they can't help them, or even help themselves; [193] if you call them towards guidance, they will not follow you? It is all the same for *those partners* whether you pray to them or stay silent. [194] Those you worship beside Allah are *His* servants just like yourselves, so pray to them and let them respond to you, if you are telling the truth.

يُبْصِرُوْنَ بِهَا ۚ اَمْ لَهُمْ اٰذَانٌ يَّسْمَعُوْنَ بِهَا ؕ قُلِ ادْعُوْا شُرَكَآءَكُمْ ثُمَّ كِيْدُوْنِ فَلَا تُنْظِرُوْنِ ۞

اِنَّ وَلِيِّ اللّٰهُ الَّذِيْ نَزَّلَ الْكِتٰبَ ۖ وَهُوَ يَتَوَلَّى الصّٰلِحِيْنَ ۞ وَالَّذِيْنَ تَدْعُوْنَ مِنْ دُوْنِهٖ لَا يَسْتَطِيْعُوْنَ نَصْرَكُمْ وَلَا اَنْفُسَهُمْ يَنْصُرُوْنَ ۞

وَاِنْ تَدْعُوْهُمْ اِلَى الْهُدٰى لَا يَسْمَعُوْا ؕ وَتَرٰىهُمْ يَنْظُرُوْنَ اِلَيْكَ وَهُمْ لَا يُبْصِرُوْنَ ۞ خُذِ الْعَفْوَ

*Three virtues to follow:
forgive those who
mistreat you; enjoin the
good; stay away from the
ignorant.*

وَأْمُرْ بِالْعُرْفِ وَاَعْرِضْ عَنِ الْجٰهِلِيْنَ ۞ وَاِمَّا يَنْزَغَنَّكَ مِنَ الشَّيْطٰنِ نَزْغٌ فَاسْتَعِذْ بِاللّٰهِ ؕ اِنَّهٗ سَمِيْعٌ عَلِيْمٌ ۞ اِنَّ الَّذِيْنَ اتَّقَوْا اِذَا مَسَّهُمْ طٰٓئِفٌ مِّنَ الشَّيْطٰنِ تَذَكَّرُوْا فَاِذَا هُمْ مُّبْصِرُوْنَ ۞ وَاِخْوَانُهُمْ يَمُدُّوْنَهُمْ فِي الْغَيِّ ثُمَّ لَا يُقْصِرُوْنَ ۞ وَاِذَا لَمْ تَأْتِهِمْ بِاٰيَةٍ قَالُوْا لَوْلَا اجْتَبَيْتَهَا ؕ قُلْ اِنَّمَا اَتَّبِعُ مَا يُوْحٰٓى اِلَيَّ مِنْ رَّبِّيْ ۚ هٰذَا بَصَآئِرُ مِنْ رَّبِّكُمْ وَهُدًى وَّرَحْمَةٌ لِّقَوْمٍ يُّؤْمِنُوْنَ ۞ وَاِذَا قُرِئَ الْقُرْاٰنُ فَاسْتَمِعُوْا لَهٗ وَاَنْصِتُوْا لَعَلَّكُمْ تُرْحَمُوْنَ ۞ وَاذْكُرْ رَّبَّكَ فِيْ نَفْسِكَ تَضَرُّعًا وَّخِيْفَةً وَّدُوْنَ الْجَهْرِ مِنَ الْقَوْلِ بِالْغُدُوِّ وَالْاٰصَالِ وَلَا تَكُنْ مِّنَ الْغٰفِلِيْنَ ۞ اِنَّ الَّذِيْنَ عِنْدَ رَبِّكَ لَا يَسْتَكْبِرُوْنَ

[195] Do they have legs to walk? Do they have hands to hold? Do they have eyes to see? Do they have ears to hear? Tell *them*: "Pray *to* your idols, plot against me, be quick about it. [196] My protector is Allah, Who revealed the Book, and He protects the righteous. [197] Those you worship beside Him cannot help you, nor help themselves: [198] if you call them towards guidance, they won't hear. You may think they are seeing you, but they can't see." [199] *Messenger* pardon *them*, enjoin the common good, and avoid the ignorant people.

How the pious avoid being trapped by Satan

[200] When Satan tempts you, seek Allah's refuge. He is Hearing, Knowing. [201] Whenever Satan tries to run rings around those who are mindful *of Allah,* they remind each other and at once they see straight *again.* [202] As for their *unmindful brothers, the* demons draw them further and further into error, sparing no effort *in doing so.* [203] If you don't bring *a fresh* sign, *such unmindful people* say, "If only you could choose one yourself!" Say: "I follow only what's revealed to me by My Lord. These are *deep* insights from your Lord and guidance and kindness for the believers."

The correct way to listen to the Quran

[204] Whenever the Quran is recited, listen carefully to it, and be silent so that you may benefit from it. [205] Humbly remind yourself morning and evening of Your Lord and be in awe of Him, without speaking loud, and don't be one of the neglectful. [206] The *angels* in the Divine Presence do not turn away from His worship arrogantly; *rather* they glorify Him and prostrate before Him.[a]

---

[a] This is one of the verses of prostration.

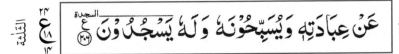

8. Surat Al-Anfal
The Spoils of War

Background to the Battle of Badr

This surat was revealed after the Battle of Badr, which took place in Ramadan in the second year of Hijra (624 CE). The new Muslim community in Madinah was growing rapidly, both in numbers and economic strength, under the brilliant leadership of the Messenger ﷺ. This growing prowess in the new community made the hypocrites and also the Jews feel threatened. The Makkans too were uncomfortable, for they knew that their trade route to Syria might be blocked. For this reason, the Makkans repeatedly dispatched small armed bands to attack cattle grazing in pastures outside Madinah, resulting in "low-intensity conflict". Hence in 2 AH, when the Prophet ﷺ learnt of the Makkan caravan returning from Syria, he openly told his companions of his intention to attack it. This would be retaliation for the repeated raids and the property confiscated from the Muslims who left Makkah. A clear message: give up hostility.

When Abu Sufyan heard of the plan to attack his caravan, he sent a fast rider to Makkah with an urgent request for help. On receiving this unpleasant news, the Makkans instantly assembled a large army of a thousand fighters to defend their caravan. In the meantime, Abu Sufyan changed his route and veered towards the coastal lowlands, to be further away from Madinah. The Muslim army left Madinah, hoping to catch up with the caravan. They hadn't gone too far when they learnt that Abu Sufyan had safely escaped, and the Makkans were coming with a huge army. After a consultation with the companions, the Prophet ﷺ decided to meet the army at Badr, 150 km southwest of Madinah.

The Outcomes of the Battle of Badr

This surat effectively draws out the important lessons to be learnt from this first military encounter between Muslims and Makkans. Interestingly, the Quran spiritualises war as a brutal and materialistic activity. It begins by describing the virtues of believers: trust, steadfastness and honesty. Then demonstrates that victory can be achieved against the odds, including the odds of victory against an enemy army many times larger, as well as teaching that believers should be willing to make peace. The question of the spoils of war is raised, and it instructs that spoils should not be the prime purpose of war, as they tended to be during the Jahiliya, or Age of Ignorance. Instead, there must be a higher objective: justice and peace for all.

The Battle of Badr marked a turning point in the life of the Muslims, who had been persecuted till that point. So aptly the surat calls the event *yawm al-furqan*, "The day of separation", truth is now clearly separate from falsehood. The victory was not just in worldly terms, but also in a spiritual and moral sense. So it marked the beginning of a new era for Muslims, the result delivered a shattering blow to the pride of the Makkans. It boosted the Muslims' morale and credibility in the sight of the Arabs, offering conclusive proof of the words: "Power and might belong to Allah." This functioned as an indicator of the truthfulness of the message of Islam, and the Muslims began to understand more clearly the socio-political dimension of the religious order that the Messenger ﷺ was proclaiming. As Asad put it:

> The spirit of passive sacrifice, so characteristic of their earlier days, received its complement in the idea of sacrifice through action. The doctrine of action as the most fundamental, creative element of life was, perhaps for the first time in the history of man, consciously realized not only by a few select individuals but by a whole community; and the intense activism which was to distinguish Muslim history in the coming decades and centuries was a direct, immediate consequence of the Battle of Badr.

بِسْمِ اللهِ الرَّحْمٰنِ الرَّحِيْمِ

يَسْـَٔلُوْنَكَ عَنِ الْاَنْفَالِۚ قُلِ الْاَنْفَالُ لِلّٰهِ وَالرَّسُوْلِۚ

فَاتَّقُوا اللهَ وَاَصْلِحُوْا ذَاتَ بَيْنِكُمْۖ وَاَطِيْعُوا اللهَ

وَرَسُوْلَهٗٓ اِنْ كُنْتُمْ مُّؤْمِنِيْنَ ۞ اِنَّمَا الْمُؤْمِنُوْنَ

الَّذِيْنَ اِذَا ذُكِرَ اللهُ وَجِلَتْ قُلُوْبُهُمْ وَاِذَا تُلِيَتْ

عَلَيْهِمْ اٰيٰتُهٗ زَادَتْهُمْ اِيْمَانًا وَّعَلٰى رَبِّهِمْ

يَتَوَكَّلُوْنَ ۞ الَّذِيْنَ يُقِيْمُوْنَ الصَّلٰوةَ وَمِمَّا

رَزَقْنٰهُمْ يُنْفِقُوْنَ ۞ اُولٰٓئِكَ هُمُ الْمُؤْمِنُوْنَ حَقًّا ۚ

لَهُمْ دَرَجٰتٌ عِنْدَ رَبِّهِمْ وَمَغْفِرَةٌ وَّرِزْقٌ كَرِيْمٌ ۞

كَمَآ اَخْرَجَكَ رَبُّكَ مِنْۢ بَيْتِكَ بِالْحَقِّ ۖ وَاِنَّ

فَرِيْقًا مِّنَ الْمُؤْمِنِيْنَ لَكٰرِهُوْنَ ۞ يُجَادِلُوْنَكَ فِى

الْحَقِّ بَعْدَ مَا تَبَيَّنَ كَاَنَّمَا يُسَاقُوْنَ اِلَى الْمَوْتِ

وَهُمْ يَنْظُرُوْنَ ۞ وَاِذْ يَعِدُكُمُ اللهُ اِحْدَى

الطَّآئِفَتَيْنِ اَنَّهَا لَكُمْ وَتَوَدُّوْنَ اَنَّ غَيْرَ ذَاتِ

الشَّوْكَةِ تَكُوْنُ لَكُمْ وَيُرِيْدُ اللهُ اَنْ يُّحِقَّ

الْحَقَّ بِكَلِمٰتِهٖ وَيَقْطَعَ دَابِرَ الْكٰفِرِيْنَ ۞ لِيُحِقَّ

الْحَقَّ وَيُبْطِلَ الْبَاطِلَ وَلَوْ كَرِهَ الْمُجْرِمُوْنَ ۞

اِذْ تَسْتَغِيْثُوْنَ رَبَّكُمْ فَاسْتَجَابَ لَكُمْ اَنِّيْ

مُمِدُّكُمْ بِاَلْفٍ مِّنَ الْمَلٰٓئِكَةِ مُرْدِفِيْنَ ۞ وَمَا

Soft-hearted believers' faith grows day by day, and they rely on Allah.

337

In the name of Allah, the Kind, the Caring.

Mobilisation for the Battle of Badr

¹They ask you about the spoils *of war,* say: "The spoils belong to Allah and the Messenger. So, fear Allah and make peace among yourselves, and obey Allah and His Messenger, if you are true believers." ²The believers' hearts tremble *with fear* at the mention of Allah, their faith grows stronger whenever His verses are recited, and they put trust in their Lord. ³They perform the prayer and spend from what We have provided, ⁴they're true believers; *reserved* for them are lofty ranks near their Lord, and forgiveness and a generous provision.

The preparations for the Battle of Badr

⁵*It was* your Lord Who led you out of your home *for* a purpose, though a group of the believers disliked it, ⁶they argue with you about its purpose that has become apparent, as though they were being led to their deaths as they looked on. ⁷*Remember* when Allah promised that one of the two parties[a] would be yours, while you were longing for the weaker target. Allah wanted *by the power of* His words, to establish the truth and to break the back of the disbelievers' *might,* ⁸to establish the truth and to overturn falsehood, though the sinful hate it.

The Believers are promised a victory

⁹*Remember* when you prayed to your Lord for help, and He answered: "I will help you with a thousand angels in rows upon rows."

---

[a] Either the Makkans' army or their trade caravan.

جَعَلَهُ اللّٰهُ اِلَّا بُشْرٰى وَلِتَطْمَئِنَّ بِهٖ قُلُوْبُكُمْ ج

وَمَا النَّصْرُ اِلَّا مِنْ عِنْدِ اللّٰهِ ط اِنَّ اللّٰهَ عَزِيْزٌ

حَكِيْمٌ ۞ اِذْ يُغَشِّيْكُمُ النُّعَاسَ اَمَنَةً مِّنْهُ

وَيُنَزِّلُ عَلَيْكُمْ مِّنَ السَّمَاءِ مَاءً لِّيُطَهِّرَكُمْ بِهٖ

وَيُذْهِبَ عَنْكُمْ رِجْزَ الشَّيْطٰنِ وَلِيَرْبِطَ عَلٰى

قُلُوْبِكُمْ وَيُثَبِّتَ بِهِ الْاَقْدَامَ ۞ اِذْ يُوْحِىْ

رَبُّكَ اِلَى الْمَلٰئِكَةِ اَنِّىْ مَعَكُمْ فَثَبِّتُوا الَّذِيْنَ

اٰمَنُوْا ط سَاُلْقِىْ فِىْ قُلُوْبِ الَّذِيْنَ كَفَرُوا

الرُّعْبَ فَاضْرِبُوْا فَوْقَ الْاَعْنَاقِ وَاضْرِبُوْا

مِنْهُمْ كُلَّ بَنَانٍ ۞ ذٰلِكَ بِاَنَّهُمْ شَآقُّوا اللّٰهَ

وَرَسُوْلَهٗ ج وَمَنْ يُّشَاقِقِ اللّٰهَ وَرَسُوْلَهٗ فَاِنَّ

اللّٰهَ شَدِيْدُ الْعِقَابِ ۞ ذٰلِكُمْ فَذُوْقُوْهُ وَاَنَّ

لِلْكٰفِرِيْنَ عَذَابَ النَّارِ ۞ يٰٓاَيُّهَا الَّذِيْنَ اٰمَنُوْٓا

اِذَا لَقِيْتُمُ الَّذِيْنَ كَفَرُوْا زَحْفًا فَلَا تُوَلُّوْهُمُ

الْاَدْبَارَ ۞ وَمَنْ يُّوَلِّهِمْ يَوْمَئِذٍ دُبُرَهٗٓ اِلَّا

مُتَحَرِّفًا لِّقِتَالٍ اَوْ مُتَحَيِّزًا اِلٰى فِئَةٍ فَقَدْ

بَآءَ بِغَضَبٍ مِّنَ اللّٰهِ وَمَاْوٰهُ جَهَنَّمُ ط وَبِئْسَ

الْمَصِيْرُ ۞ فَلَمْ تَقْتُلُوْهُمْ وَلٰكِنَّ اللّٰهَ

قَتَلَهُمْ ص وَمَا رَمَيْتَ اِذْ رَمَيْتَ وَلٰكِنَّ اللّٰهَ

رَمٰى ج وَلِيُبْلِىَ الْمُؤْمِنِيْنَ مِنْهُ بَلَاءً حَسَنًا اِنَّ

Allah helps his servants in mysterious ways.

[10]Allah made it glad tidings and to boost your morale. Victory is from Allah alone. Allah is Almighty, Wise. [11]*Remember* when He caused drowsiness to overtake you, *granting you* of His reassurance, and He sent rain from the sky for you so you could clean yourselves, remove Satan's filth from you, strengthen your hearts, and help you to stand firm. [12]*Remember* when Your Lord revealed to the angels: "I am with you, so make the believers stand their ground, while I strike terror into the disbelievers' hearts. So, beat *your wings* above their necks and beat each of their limbs." [13]Since they opposed Allah and His Messenger, and anyone who opposes Allah and His Messenger will have severe punishment, [14]a taste for you *of what is to come* for the disbelievers, the torment of the Fire *is waiting*.

The days of running away from the battle are over

[15]Believers, whenever you meet disbelievers *in battle* advancing towards you, don't turn your backs to them *to flee*. [16]On that day, whoever turns his back except in tactical retreat to attack again, or else to rejoin *another* fighting party, will suffer the fury of Allah, and Hell will be his home. What an evil destination! [17]You didn't kill them, but Allah killed them nor did you throw *the pebbles* when you threw, *Messenger*, but it was Allah Who threw *it*.[a] *This was* as a positive test of the believers from Him. Allah is the Hearer, the Knower.

---

[a] At the start of the Battle, the Messenger ﷺ picked up a handful of sand and threw it in the direction of the Makkan army and prayed for their defeat. The lessons for believers is not to be proud of winning, victory comes from Allah.

اللهُ سَمِيعٌ عَلِيمٌ ۝ ذٰلِكُمْ وَاَنَّ اللهَ مُوهِنُ

كَيْدِ الْكٰفِرِيْنَ ۝ اِنْ تَسْتَفْتِحُوْا فَقَدْ جَاءَكُمُ

الْفَتْحُ ۚ وَاِنْ تَنْتَهُوْا فَهُوَ خَيْرٌ لَّكُمْ ۚ وَاِنْ

تَعُوْدُوْا نَعُدْ ۚ وَلَنْ تُغْنِيَ عَنْكُمْ فِئَتُكُمْ شَيْئًا

وَّلَوْ كَثُرَتْ ۙ وَاَنَّ اللهَ مَعَ الْمُؤْمِنِيْنَ ۝ يٰٓاَيُّهَا

الَّذِيْنَ اٰمَنُوْٓا اَطِيْعُوا اللهَ وَرَسُوْلَهُ وَلَا تَوَلَّوْا

عَنْهُ وَاَنْتُمْ تَسْمَعُوْنَ ۝ وَلَا تَكُوْنُوْا كَالَّذِيْنَ

قَالُوْا سَمِعْنَا وَهُمْ لَا يَسْمَعُوْنَ ۝ اِنَّ شَرَّ الدَّوَآبِّ

عِنْدَ اللهِ الصُّمُّ الْبُكْمُ الَّذِيْنَ لَا يَعْقِلُوْنَ ۝

وَلَوْ عَلِمَ اللهُ فِيْهِمْ خَيْرًا لَّاَسْمَعَهُمْ ۙ وَلَوْ

اَسْمَعَهُمْ لَتَوَلَّوْا وَّهُمْ مُّعْرِضُوْنَ ۝ يٰٓاَيُّهَا

الَّذِيْنَ اٰمَنُوا اسْتَجِيْبُوْا لِلّٰهِ وَلِلرَّسُوْلِ اِذَا دَعَاكُمْ

لِمَا يُحْيِيْكُمْ ۚ وَاعْلَمُوْٓا اَنَّ اللهَ يَحُوْلُ بَيْنَ الْمَرْءِ

وَقَلْبِهِ وَاَنَّهُ اِلَيْهِ تُحْشَرُوْنَ ۝ وَاتَّقُوْا فِتْنَةً

لَّا تُصِيْبَنَّ الَّذِيْنَ ظَلَمُوْا مِنْكُمْ خَاصَّةً ۚ وَاعْلَمُوْٓا

اَنَّ اللهَ شَدِيْدُ الْعِقَابِ ۝ وَاذْكُرُوْٓا اِذْ اَنْتُمْ

قَلِيْلٌ مُّسْتَضْعَفُوْنَ فِي الْاَرْضِ تَخَافُوْنَ اَنْ

يَّتَخَطَّفَكُمُ النَّاسُ فَاٰوٰىكُمْ وَاَيَّدَكُمْ بِنَصْرِهِ

وَرَزَقَكُمْ مِّنَ الطَّيِّبٰتِ لَعَلَّكُمْ تَشْكُرُوْنَ ۝

يٰٓاَيُّهَا الَّذِيْنَ اٰمَنُوْا لَا تَخُوْنُوا اللهَ وَالرَّسُوْلَ

Do you want a happy life? Then respond to Allah's teachings.

¹⁸That was *a sign* for you, that Allah will weaken the disbelievers' plot. ¹⁹If you are seeking a clear outcome, *disbelievers*, then that was an outcome clearly against you. Were you to put an end *to your harassment*, that would be better for you; *but if* you return *to it*, then so shall We. Your army will not benefit you at all, no matter how large it is. Allah is with the believers.

A warning to those who don't listen

²⁰Believers, obey Allah and His Messenger and don't turn away from him while you can hear him calling you; ²¹and don't be like those who said, "We have heard," while they were not listening at all. ²²The worst of creatures in the sight of Allah are the wilfully deaf and dumb who refuse to think. ²³If Allah saw any good in them, He would have made them hear; but even if He had made them hear, they would still have turned away, rejecting the message. ²⁴Believers, answer Allah and His Messenger when they call to that which will give you life; and beware Allah intervenes between a man and his heart,ᵃ and that you'll be gathered before Him. ²⁵Be mindful of a *future* test that wouldn't just affect the wrongdoers amongst you, and know that Allah's punishment is severe.

Believers are reminded of future trials

²⁶Remember when you were an oppressed few in the land, afraid of being wiped out; Allah gave you protection and strengthened you with His help and provided you with wholesome things so you might be thankful. ²⁷Believers, don't betray Allah and the Messenger knowingly, nor be disloyal to your trusts;

ᵃ Allah comes between a person's desires, attitude and behaviour; this shows Allah can turn people away from what their desires urge them to do. It is Allah-consciousness that can stop them from being misled by evil desires. The Messenger ﷺ prayed "O turner of hearts, keep me steadfast on your religion."

وَتَخُونُوۤا اَمٰنٰتِكُمْ وَاَنۡتُمۡ تَعۡلَمُوۡنَ ۝ وَاعۡلَمُوۤا اَنَّمَاۤ

اَمۡوَالُكُمۡ وَاَوۡلَادُكُمۡ فِتۡنَةٌ ۙ وَّاَنَّ اللّٰهَ عِنۡدَهٗۤ

اَجۡرٌ عَظِيۡمٌ ۝ يٰۤاَيُّهَا الَّذِيۡنَ اٰمَنُوۤا اِنۡ تَتَّقُوا

اللّٰهَ يَجۡعَلۡ لَّكُمۡ فُرۡقَانًا وَّيُكَفِّرۡ عَنۡكُمۡ سَيِّاٰتِكُمۡ

وَيَغۡفِرۡ لَكُمۡ ۙ وَاللّٰهُ ذُو الۡفَضۡلِ الۡعَظِيۡمِ ۝ وَاِذۡ

يَمۡكُرُ بِكَ الَّذِيۡنَ كَفَرُوۡا لِيُثۡبِتُوۡكَ اَوۡ يَقۡتُلُوۡكَ اَوۡ

يُخۡرِجُوۡكَ ۚ وَيَمۡكُرُوۡنَ وَيَمۡكُرُ اللّٰهُ ۙ وَاللّٰهُ خَيۡرُ

الۡمٰكِرِيۡنَ ۝ وَاِذَا تُتۡلٰى عَلَيۡهِمۡ اٰيٰتُنَا قَالُوۡا قَدۡ

سَمِعۡنَا لَوۡ نَشَآءُ لَقُلۡنَا مِثۡلَ هٰذَاۤ ۙ اِنۡ هٰذَاۤ اِلَّاۤ

اَسَاطِيۡرُ الۡاَوَّلِيۡنَ ۝ وَاِذۡ قَالُوا اللّٰهُمَّ اِنۡ كَانَ

هٰذَا هُوَ الۡحَقَّ مِنۡ عِنۡدِكَ فَاَمۡطِرۡ عَلَيۡنَا

حِجَارَةً مِّنَ السَّمَآءِ اَوِ ائۡتِنَا بِعَذَابٍ اَلِيۡمٍ ۝

وَمَا كَانَ اللّٰهُ لِيُعَذِّبَهُمۡ وَاَنۡتَ فِيۡهِمۡ ۚ وَمَا

كَانَ اللّٰهُ مُعَذِّبَهُمۡ وَهُمۡ يَسۡتَغۡفِرُوۡنَ ۝ وَمَا لَهُمۡ

اَلَّا يُعَذِّبَهُمُ اللّٰهُ وَهُمۡ يَصُدُّوۡنَ عَنِ الۡمَسۡجِدِ

الۡحَرَامِ وَمَا كَانُوۤا اَوۡلِيَآءَهٗ ۚ اِنۡ اَوۡلِيَآؤُهٗۤ اِلَّا

الۡمُتَّقُوۡنَ وَلٰكِنَّ اَكۡثَرَهُمۡ لَا يَعۡلَمُوۡنَ ۝ وَمَا كَانَ

صَلَاتُهُمۡ عِنۡدَ الۡبَيۡتِ اِلَّا مُكَآءً وَّتَصۡدِيَةً ۚ

فَذُوۡقُوا الۡعَذَابَ بِمَا كُنۡتُمۡ تَكۡفُرُوۡنَ ۝ اِنَّ

الَّذِيۡنَ كَفَرُوۡا يُنۡفِقُوۡنَ اَمۡوَالَهُمۡ لِيَصُدُّوۡا عَنۡ

Being Allah-conscious attracts special divine favours and forgiveness.

343

[28] and know that your wealth and children are a test,[a] and that Allah has a great reward *in store for you.* [29] Believers, if you are mindful of Allah He will give you the standard to judge *between right and wrong,*[b] and He will cover up your wrongdoings and forgive you. Allah is Gracious in *His* favour.

Disbelievers can't deceive Allah

[30] *Remember* when the disbelievers plotted to imprison, kill or expel you. They plotted, and Allah planned something else, and Allah is the best of planners. [31] When Our verses are recited to them, they say, "We've heard *it all before.* If we wanted, we could have said something similar. These are just legends of old." [32] They said, "Allah, if this is, indeed, the truth from You then pelt us with hailstones from *the sky,* or fetch us *some other* painful punishment." [33] But Allah will not punish them as long as you, *Messenger,* are among them; nor will Allah punish them if they *repent and* ask forgiveness. [34] However, Allah will punish them for stopping *people* from the Sacred Mosque even though they are not its *real* keepers. Its *real* keepers are those who are mindful *of Allah,* but most of the disbelievers don't know. [35] Their worship at the *Sacred* House is merely whistling and clapping. So, taste the punishment for your disbelief.

The wickedness of disbelievers will not go unpunished

[36] The disbelievers spend their wealth to stop *people* from the path of Allah, they'll continue doing so until it becomes a source of regret, and they are defeated. The disbelievers will be banished to Hell,

---

[a] *Fitnah* can mean: a temptation, seduction, trial, test, confusion, dissension, persecution, oppression, sedition, or civil war.

[b] *Furqan* means, "criterion" the ability to differentiate between truth and falsehood.

سَبِيْلِ اللهِ ۫ فَسَيُنْفِقُوْنَهَا ثُمَّ تَكُوْنُ عَلَيْهِمْ

حَسْرَةً ثُمَّ يُغْلَبُوْنَ ۬ؕ وَالَّذِيْنَ كَفَرُوْاۤ اِلٰى

جَهَنَّمَ يُحْشَرُوْنَ ۙ۳۶ لِيَمِيْزَ اللهُ الْخَبِيْثَ مِنَ

الطَّيِّبِ وَيَجْعَلَ الْخَبِيْثَ بَعْضَهٗ عَلٰى بَعْضٍ

فَيَرْكُمَهٗ جَمِيْعًا فَيَجْعَلَهٗ فِيْ جَهَنَّمَ ؕ اُولٰٓئِكَ هُمُ

الْخٰسِرُوْنَ ۳۷ قُلْ لِّلَّذِيْنَ كَفَرُوْۤا اِنْ يَّنْتَهُوْا يُغْفَرْ

لَهُمْ مَّا قَدْ سَلَفَ ۚ وَاِنْ يَّعُوْدُوْا فَقَدْ مَضَتْ

سُنَّتُ الْاَوَّلِيْنَ ۳۸ وَقَاتِلُوْهُمْ حَتّٰى لَا تَكُوْنَ

فِتْنَةٌ وَّيَكُوْنَ الدِّيْنُ كُلُّهٗ لِلّٰهِ ۚ فَاِنِ انْتَهَوْا فَاِنَّ

اللهَ بِمَا يَعْمَلُوْنَ بَصِيْرٌ ۳۹ وَاِنْ تَوَلَّوْا فَاعْلَمُوْۤا

اَنَّ اللهَ مَوْلٰىكُمْ ؕ نِعْمَ الْمَوْلٰى وَنِعْمَ النَّصِيْرُ ۴۰

وَاعْلَمُوْۤا اَنَّمَا غَنِمْتُمْ مِّنْ شَيْءٍ فَاَنَّ لِلّٰهِ خُمُسَهٗ

وَلِلرَّسُوْلِ وَلِذِى الْقُرْبٰى وَالْيَتٰمٰى وَالْمَسٰكِيْنِ وَابْنِ

السَّبِيْلِ ۙ اِنْ كُنْتُمْ اٰمَنْتُمْ بِاللهِ وَمَاۤ اَنْزَلْنَا عَلٰى

عَبْدِنَا يَوْمَ الْفُرْقَانِ يَوْمَ الْتَقَى الْجَمْعٰنِ ؕ وَاللهُ

عَلٰى كُلِّ شَيْءٍ قَدِيْرٌ ۴۱ اِذْ اَنْتُمْ بِالْعُدْوَةِ الدُّنْيَا

وَهُمْ بِالْعُدْوَةِ الْقُصْوٰى وَالرَّكْبُ اَسْفَلَ مِنْكُمْ ؕ

وَلَوْ تَوَاعَدْتُّمْ لَاخْتَلَفْتُمْ فِى الْمِيْعٰدِ ۙ وَلٰكِنْ

لِّيَقْضِيَ اللهُ اَمْرًا كَانَ مَفْعُوْلًا ۙ لِّيَهْلِكَ مَنْ

هَلَكَ عَنْ بَيِّنَةٍ وَّيَحْيٰى مَنْ حَيَّ عَنْ بَيِّنَةٍ ؕ

Allah tests people in various ways, to prepare them for bigger things.

345

[37] so that Allah may sort out the wicked from the good; and He will pile up the wicked, layer on layer, in a heap and bulldoze them into Hell. Those are the losers.

Fight to bring an end to maltreatment

[38] Tell the disbelievers to stop *their wrongdoings* so they may be forgiven *sins of the past*. If they go back *to their evil ways*, the example of the people of old is there *for them*. [39] Fight them so there is no more persecution, and people are free to worship Allah.[a] But if they stop, then Allah sees what they do, [40] but if they turn away then, know that Allah is your Protector. What a wonderful Protector, and what a wonderful Helper!

The distribution of the spoils of war

[41] Whatever *spoils of war* you seize, know that a fifth of it belongs to Allah and to the Messenger and *his* relatives, to orphans, the needy and the traveller. That's if you believe in Allah and in what We revealed to Our servant on the day of separation of *truth from falsehood*,[b] the day the two armies met. Allah has power over all things.[c]

The arrangement of the armies in the battlefield

[42] *Remember* when you were *grouped* on the near side of the valley, and *Makkans* on the far side, and the caravan below you. If you had *tried to reach* a formal agreement to meet *there*, you would certainly have differed over the time and place; but *that occurred* so that Allah could accomplish what was preordained, so that whoever perished should do so on the basis of clear proof and whoever survived should do so on the same basis. Allah is the Hearer, the Knower.

---

[a] As in *Surat al-Baqarah* (2: 193), the words of this verse do not incite Muslims to impose their religion on others, but urges them to fight to bring an end to all persecution, including forced conversions.

[b] The phrase, *yawm al-furqan*, is an apt description for the Battle of Badr; the sincerity of those who called themselves Muslims was put to the test, and truth and falsehood were clearly distinguished.

[c] This verse provides an answer to the question at the very start of the surat.

وَاِنَّ اللهَ لَسَمِيعٌ عَلِيمٌ ۞ اِذْ يُرِيكَهُمُ اللهُ

فِىْ مَنَامِكَ قَلِيْلًا ط وَلَوْ اَرٰكَهُمْ كَثِيْرًا لَّفَشِلْتُمْ

وَلَتَنَازَعْتُمْ فِى الْاَمْرِ وَلٰكِنَّ اللهَ سَلَّمَ ط اِنَّهٗ

عَلِيمٌ بِذَاتِ الصُّدُوْرِ ۞ وَاِذْ يُرِيكَهُمُوْهُمْ اِذِ

الْتَقَيْتُمْ فِىْ اَعْيُنِكُمْ قَلِيْلًا وَّيُقَلِّلُكُمْ فِىْ اَعْيُنِهِمْ

لِيَقْضِىَ اللهُ اَمْرًا كَانَ مَفْعُوْلًا ط وَاِلَى اللهِ تُرْجَعُ

الْاُمُوْرُ ۞ يٰٓاَيُّهَا الَّذِيْنَ اٰمَنُوْٓا اِذَا لَقِيْتُمْ فِئَةً

فَاثْبُتُوْا وَاذْكُرُوا اللهَ كَثِيْرًا لَّعَلَّكُمْ تُفْلِحُوْنَ ۞

وَاَطِيْعُوا اللهَ وَرَسُوْلَهٗ وَلَا تَنَازَعُوْا فَتَفْشَلُوْا

وَتَذْهَبَ رِيْحُكُمْ وَاصْبِرُوْا ط اِنَّ اللهَ مَعَ

الصّٰبِرِيْنَ ۞ وَلَا تَكُوْنُوْا كَالَّذِيْنَ خَرَجُوْا مِنْ

دِيَارِهِمْ بَطَرًا وَّرِئَآءَ النَّاسِ وَيَصُدُّوْنَ عَنْ

سَبِيْلِ اللهِ ط وَاللهُ بِمَا يَعْمَلُوْنَ مُحِيْطٌ ۞ وَاِذْ

زَيَّنَ لَهُمُ الشَّيْطٰنُ اَعْمَالَهُمْ وَقَالَ لَا غَالِبَ لَكُمُ

الْيَوْمَ مِنَ النَّاسِ وَاِنِّىْ جَارٌ لَّكُمْ ۚ فَلَمَّا تَرَآءَتِ

الْفِئَتٰنِ نَكَصَ عَلٰى عَقِبَيْهِ وَقَالَ اِنِّىْ بَرِىْٓءٌ

مِّنْكُمْ اِنِّىْٓ اَرٰى مَا لَا تَرَوْنَ اِنِّىْٓ اَخَافُ اللهَ ط

وَاللهُ شَدِيْدُ الْعِقَابِ ۞ اِذْ يَقُوْلُ الْمُنٰفِقُوْنَ

وَالَّذِيْنَ فِىْ قُلُوْبِهِمْ مَّرَضٌ غَرَّ هٰٓؤُلَآءِ دِيْنُهُمْ ط

وَمَنْ يَّتَوَكَّلْ عَلَى اللهِ فَاِنَّ اللهَ عَزِيْزٌ حَكِيْمٌ ۞

⁴³*Remember* when Allah showed them to you to be small in number as you dozed. If He had shown them to you as large in number, you would have lost heart and quarrelled over the matter amongst yourselves, but Allah saved you *from disagreements*. He knows well *people's* innermost thoughts. ⁴⁴And when you faced each other, He made them appear to be few in your eyes, and He made you seem even fewer in number in their eyes, so that He could accomplish what had been preordained. *Eventually* all matters return to Allah.

Be steadfastness in the battlefield

⁴⁵Believers, whenever you face an army *in battle*, stand firm and remember Allah a lot so you may triumph. ⁴⁶Obey Allah and His Messenger; don't quarrel among yourselves nor lose heart and become demoralised, but persevere. Allah is with those who persevere. ⁴⁷And don't be like those who set out from their homes pompously, showing off to people and stopping *people* from coming to Allah's way. Allah has complete control of what they do. ⁴⁸*Remember* when Satan made their action appear attractive to them and said, "No one will be able to defeat you today, with me close beside you." However, when the two armies caught sight of each other, *Satan* turned on his heels, saying, "I have nothing to do with you, I see what you can't see, *and* I fear Allah. Allah's punishment is severe."

Angels fought alongside the believers

⁴⁹*Remember* when the hypocrites and those with sickness in their hearts said, "Their religion has deceived these people." Whoever puts his trust in Allah *shall find* Allah is Almighty, Wise.

وَلَوْ تَرَىٰٓ إِذْ يَتَوَفَّى الَّذِينَ كَفَرُوا الْمَلَٰٓئِكَةُ يَضْرِبُونَ وُجُوهَهُمْ وَأَدْبَارَهُمْ ۚ وَ ذُوقُوا عَذَابَ الْحَرِيقِ ۝ ذَٰلِكَ بِمَا قَدَّمَتْ أَيْدِيكُمْ وَأَنَّ اللَّهَ لَيْسَ بِظَلَّٰمٍ لِّلْعَبِيدِ ۝ كَدَأْبِ آلِ فِرْعَوْنَ ۙ وَالَّذِينَ مِن قَبْلِهِمْ ۚ كَفَرُوا بِـَٔايَٰتِ اللَّهِ فَأَخَذَهُمُ اللَّهُ بِذُنُوبِهِمْ ۗ إِنَّ اللَّهَ قَوِيٌّ شَدِيدُ الْعِقَابِ ۝ ذَٰلِكَ بِأَنَّ اللَّهَ لَمْ يَكُ مُغَيِّرًا نِّعْمَةً أَنْعَمَهَا عَلَىٰ قَوْمٍ حَتَّىٰ يُغَيِّرُوا مَا بِأَنفُسِهِمْ ۙ وَأَنَّ اللَّهَ سَمِيعٌ عَلِيمٌ ۝ كَدَأْبِ آلِ فِرْعَوْنَ ۙ وَالَّذِينَ مِن قَبْلِهِمْ ۚ كَذَّبُوا بِـَٔايَٰتِ رَبِّهِمْ فَأَهْلَكْنَٰهُم بِذُنُوبِهِمْ وَأَغْرَقْنَآ آلَ فِرْعَوْنَ ۚ وَكُلٌّ كَانُوا ظَٰلِمِينَ ۝ إِنَّ شَرَّ الدَّوَآبِّ عِندَ اللَّهِ الَّذِينَ كَفَرُوا فَهُمْ لَا يُؤْمِنُونَ ۝ الَّذِينَ عَٰهَدتَّ مِنْهُمْ ثُمَّ يَنقُضُونَ عَهْدَهُمْ فِي كُلِّ مَرَّةٍ وَهُمْ لَا يَتَّقُونَ ۝ فَإِمَّا تَثْقَفَنَّهُمْ فِي الْحَرْبِ فَشَرِّدْ بِهِم مَّنْ خَلْفَهُمْ لَعَلَّهُمْ يَذَّكَّرُونَ ۝ وَإِمَّا تَخَافَنَّ مِن قَوْمٍ خِيَانَةً فَانبِذْ إِلَيْهِمْ عَلَىٰ سَوَآءٍ ۚ إِنَّ اللَّهَ لَا يُحِبُّ الْخَآئِنِينَ ۝ وَلَا يَحْسَبَنَّ الَّذِينَ كَفَرُوا سَبَقُوا ۚ إِنَّهُمْ لَا يُعْجِزُونَ ۝ وَأَعِدُّوا لَهُم مَّا اسْتَطَعْتُم مِّن قُوَّةٍ وَّمِن

Allah withdraws his blessing when you become undeserving.

٣٤٩

⁵⁰ If you could see, as the disbelievers' souls were taken from them, the angels striking their faces and backs, *saying,* "Taste the punishment of the Blaze. ⁵¹ This is *in return* for what your hands produced. Allah never wrongs *His* servants." ⁵² The same happened to Pharaoh's people and those before them: they rejected Allah's signs, so Allah punished them for their sins. Allah is Strong, Severe in *His* punishment. ⁵³ That is because Allah does not change a favour that He bestowed on a people until they change what is within themselves; and Allah is Hearing, Knowing. ⁵⁴ Similar to Pharaoh's people and those before them: they denied their Lord's signs, so We destroyed them for their sins, and We caused Pharaoh's people to be drowned. They were all wrongdoers.

Lessons from the Battle of Badr
⁵⁵ The worst of creatures in the sight of Allah are the deniers, they don't believe; ⁵⁶ *and* those you made a treaty with, and each time they broke their treaty they weren't mindful *of Allah.* ⁵⁷ Whenever you come across them in battle crush them so that those who come after them may learn a lesson. ⁵⁸ If you fear treachery from *someone,* then tackle them in the same way. Allah dislikes traitors.

Be prepared for war, but work for peace
⁵⁹ Don't let the disbelievers think they have won, they can't undo *Allah's decree.*

رِّبَاطِ الْخَيْلِ تُرْهِبُوْنَ بِهٖ عَدُوَّ اللّٰهِ وَعَدُوَّكُمْ

وَاٰخَرِيْنَ مِنْ دُوْنِهِمْ ۚ لَا تَعْلَمُوْنَهُمْ ۚ اَللّٰهُ

يَعْلَمُهُمْ ط وَمَا تُنْفِقُوْا مِنْ شَيْءٍ فِيْ سَبِيْلِ اللّٰهِ

يُوَفَّ اِلَيْكُمْ وَاَنْتُمْ لَا تُظْلَمُوْنَ ۝ وَاِنْ جَنَحُوْا

لِلسَّلْمِ فَاجْنَحْ لَهَا وَتَوَكَّلْ عَلَى اللّٰهِ ط اِنَّهٗ هُوَ

السَّمِيْعُ الْعَلِيْمُ ۝ وَاِنْ يُّرِيْدُوْۤا اَنْ يَّخْدَعُوْكَ

فَاِنَّ حَسْبَكَ اللّٰهُ ط هُوَ الَّذِيْۤ اَيَّدَكَ بِنَصْرِهٖ

وَبِالْمُؤْمِنِيْنَ ۝ وَاَلَّفَ بَيْنَ قُلُوْبِهِمْ ط لَوْ اَنْفَقْتَ

مَا فِي الْاَرْضِ جَمِيْعًا مَّاۤ اَلَّفْتَ بَيْنَ قُلُوْبِهِمْ

وَلٰكِنَّ اللّٰهَ اَلَّفَ بَيْنَهُمْ ط اِنَّهٗ عَزِيْزٌ حَكِيْمٌ ۝

يٰۤاَيُّهَا النَّبِيُّ حَسْبُكَ اللّٰهُ وَمَنِ اتَّبَعَكَ مِنَ

الْمُؤْمِنِيْنَ ۝ يٰۤاَيُّهَا النَّبِيُّ حَرِّضِ الْمُؤْمِنِيْنَ

عَلَى الْقِتَالِ ط اِنْ يَّكُنْ مِّنْكُمْ عِشْرُوْنَ صٰبِرُوْنَ

يَغْلِبُوْا مِائَتَيْنِ ۚ وَاِنْ يَّكُنْ مِّنْكُمْ مِّائَةٌ

يَّغْلِبُوْۤا اَلْفًا مِّنَ الَّذِيْنَ كَفَرُوْا بِاَنَّهُمْ قَوْمٌ

لَّا يَفْقَهُوْنَ ۝ اَلْـٰٔنَ خَفَّفَ اللّٰهُ عَنْكُمْ وَعَلِمَ

اَنَّ فِيْكُمْ ضَعْفًا ط فَاِنْ يَّكُنْ مِّنْكُمْ مِّائَةٌ صَابِرَةٌ

يَّغْلِبُوْا مِائَتَيْنِ ۚ وَاِنْ يَّكُنْ مِّنْكُمْ اَلْفٌ يَّغْلِبُوْۤا

اَلْفَيْنِ بِاِذْنِ اللّٰهِ ط وَاللّٰهُ مَعَ الصّٰبِرِيْنَ ۝ مَا

كَانَ لِنَبِيٍّ اَنْ يَّكُوْنَ لَهٗۤ اَسْرٰى حَتّٰى يُثْخِنَ فِي

Be prepared, ever ready to defend your country – never start a war.

351

⁶⁰ *So* prepare whatever force you can against them, and cavalry, to deter Allah's and your enemies, and others beside them whom you don't know, but Allah knows them. Whatever you spend in Allah's way will be reimbursed to you, and you will not be deprived. ⁶¹ However, if they incline towards peace you incline towards it, and put your trust in Allah. He is the Hearer, the Knower. ⁶² Should they wish to trick you, *Messenger,* then Allah is sufficient for you, He strengthened you with His support and with the believers. ⁶³ He united their hearts together. Even if you spent all that there is on Earth, you couldn't unite their hearts together, but Allah united them. He is Almighty, the Wise.

True faith can give the believers the strength of ten men

⁶⁴ Prophet, Allah is sufficient for you and who follow you *into battle* from among the believers. ⁶⁵ Prophet, urge the believers to fight *in His way*. It may be that your twenty steadfast men can defeat *a force of* two hundred, and a hundred of you can defeat a thousand of the disbelievers, because they are people who don't understand. ⁶⁶ *But for* now Allah has lightened your load, knowing that there is some weakness in you. So it may be that a hundred steadfast men amongst you can defeat two hundred, and that a thousand of you can defeat two thousand with Allah's help; and *rest assured*, Allah is with the steadfast.

Fighting in Allah's way shouldn't be for worldly gains

⁶⁷ It is not fitting for a prophet to take captives until he has won on the *battle* field. *Believers,* you want what this world offers,^a but Allah desires the Hereafter *for you.* Allah is Almighty, Wise.

---

^a The purpose of inter-tribal fighting before Islam was mostly to take hostages for ransom rather than to kill the enemy.

ٱلْأَرْضِ ۗ تُرِيدُوْنَ عَرَضَ الدُّنْيَا ۖ وَاللّٰهُ يُرِيْدُ
الْأَخِرَةَ ۗ وَاللّٰهُ عَزِيْزٌ حَكِيْمٌ ۝ لَوْلَا كِتٰبٌ مِّنَ
اللّٰهِ سَبَقَ لَمَسَّكُمْ فِيْمَاۤ أَخَذْتُمْ عَذَابٌ عَظِيْمٌ ۝
فَكُلُوْا مِمَّا غَنِمْتُمْ حَلٰلًا طَيِّبًا ۚ وَّاتَّقُوا اللّٰهَ ۗ إِنَّ
اللّٰهَ غَفُوْرٌ رَّحِيْمٌ ۝ يٰٓأَيُّهَا النَّبِيُّ قُلْ لِّمَنْ فِيْٓ
أَيْدِيْكُمْ مِّنَ الْأَسْرٰىٓ إِنْ يَّعْلَمِ اللّٰهُ فِيْ قُلُوْبِكُمْ
خَيْرًا يُّؤْتِكُمْ خَيْرًا مِّمَّاۤ أُخِذَ مِنْكُمْ وَيَغْفِرْ لَكُمْ ۗ
وَاللّٰهُ غَفُوْرٌ رَّحِيْمٌ ۝ وَإِنْ يُّرِيْدُوْا خِيَانَتَكَ
فَقَدْ خَانُوا اللّٰهَ مِنْ قَبْلُ فَأَمْكَنَ مِنْهُمْ ۗ
وَاللّٰهُ عَلِيْمٌ حَكِيْمٌ ۝ إِنَّ الَّذِيْنَ اٰمَنُوْا وَهَاجَرُوْا
وَجَاهَدُوْا بِأَمْوَالِهِمْ وَأَنْفُسِهِمْ فِيْ سَبِيْلِ
اللّٰهِ وَالَّذِيْنَ اٰوَوْا وَّنَصَرُوْٓا أُولٰٓئِكَ بَعْضُهُمْ
أَوْلِيَآءُ بَعْضٍ ۗ وَالَّذِيْنَ اٰمَنُوْا وَلَمْ يُهَاجِرُوْا
مَا لَكُمْ مِّنْ وَّلَايَتِهِمْ مِّنْ شَيْءٍ حَتّٰى
يُهَاجِرُوْا ۚ وَإِنِ اسْتَنْصَرُوْكُمْ فِي الدِّيْنِ
فَعَلَيْكُمُ النَّصْرُ إِلَّا عَلٰى قَوْمٍ بَيْنَكُمْ وَبَيْنَهُمْ
مِّيْثَاقٌ ۗ وَاللّٰهُ بِمَا تَعْمَلُوْنَ بَصِيْرٌ ۝ وَالَّذِيْنَ
كَفَرُوْا بَعْضُهُمْ أَوْلِيَآءُ بَعْضٍ ۚ إِلَّا تَفْعَلُوْهُ
تَكُنْ فِتْنَةٌ فِي الْأَرْضِ وَفَسَادٌ كَبِيْرٌ ۝
وَالَّذِيْنَ اٰمَنُوْا وَهَاجَرُوْا وَجَاهَدُوْا فِيْ سَبِيْلِ

Islam is a religion of truth. How committed are you?

⁶⁸ Had it not been for a decree issued in advance from Allah, you would have been mightily punished for *the action* that you took. ⁶⁹ So enjoy of your spoils of war, the lawful and healthy, and be *ever* mindful of Allah. Allah is Forgiving, Kind. ⁷⁰ Prophet, tell the captives you are holding: "If Allah finds any good in your hearts, He will give you better than what has been taken from you and will forgive you. Allah is Forgiving, Kind." ⁷¹ If they act treacherously towards you, they have done so previously with Allah, yet He has *given you* control over them. Allah is the Knower, the Wise.

The companions of the Prophet ﷺ are praised

⁷² The believers who emigrated and struggled with their wealth and lives in Allah's way, and those who offered *them* refuge and support, they are each other's protectors. Those who believed but didn't emigrate, you are not responsible for them until they emigrate. If they should seek your help on religious grounds, then you must help them except against a people with whom you have a treaty. Allah sees what you do. ⁷³ The disbelievers protect each other. If you don't do likewise, there will be a lot of persecution and violence in the land. ⁷⁴ The believers who emigrated and struggled in Allah's way, and those who offered *them* refuge and support *in Madinah* are the true believers; they shall have forgiveness and a generous provision. ⁷⁵ And those later believers who emigrated and struggled with you *in Allah's way*, they are one with you. *However,* blood relationships give them *even* greater rights over each other in Allah's Book. Allah knows everything.

9. Surat At-Tawbah

Repentance

Surat At-Tawbah was revealed during the second half of 9 AH (630–631 CE) following the successful campaign of Tabuk in the month of Rajab. Tabuk is 560 kilometres Northwest of Madinah. The cancellation of treaties with idolaters was announced five months later during Hajj in the same year. This surat is set against the background of a looming battle, and therefore harsh. This explains why it doesn't begin with the Basmala in the usual way, "In the name of Allah, the Kind, the Caring". The blessed Messenger ﷺ didn't instruct the writing of Basmala either, and some commentators take this to mean that this is a continuation of the previous *Surat Al-Anfal*, the two together constituting a single surat, since the Basmala is considered as the divider between surats.

Historical Background

After the Conquest of Makkah in 8 AH (629 CE), the influence of Islam in the Arabian Peninsula spread rapidly and many Arab tribes embraced Islam. The Messenger ﷺ sent letters to the rulers of neighbouring countries, inviting them to Islam. They began to take notice of this religious and geopolitical change. Until now, foreign powers had shown little interest in the Arabs. The Romans were nervous and planned to attack Madinah, so the planning for the Tabuk campaign started. The Messenger ﷺ, after consultation, decided to meet the enemy on the border. Muslims gave generously, and eventually a 30,000 strong army was mobilised northwards to deter the Romans, who decided to remain in their forts rather than come out. The Messenger ﷺ stayed there for twenty days. He made excursions along the Roman Empire's south-eastern border to win allies and sign treaties with local rulers, including the King of Aila, near Aqaba in Jordan. This increased Muslim influence in that area considerably.

The Themes of the Surat

The important event with which this surat begins (1–29) is the immediate cancellation of treaties with those Arab idolaters who had repeatedly breached them, whilst continuing to honour the treaties with the tribes that remained loyal. For the second Hajj after the Conquest of Makkah, the Messenger ﷺ dispatched a delegation under the leadership of Abu Bakr, who made this announcement: "From now on the Kaaba will be in the custody of Muslims; idolaters are no longer its keepers," hinting that the Muslims were now the rulers of the Arabian Peninsula.

A short passage (29–35) follows, it criticises their religious leaders for not being sincere and faithful in a way that's not dissimilar to Christian reformers who criticised Christian priests in the fifteenth century CE such as Martin Luther.

The Viciousness of the Hypocrites

Allah is Kind and Loving, but this surat clearly shows His anger towards the idolaters and the hypocrites. The wretched character of the hypocrites is vividly described in verses 38–83: they make excuses, have evil motives, and criticise and insult the Messenger ﷺ and the Muslims; they spread rumours, blaspheme and are miserly; they are a lazy bunch, who love only the worldly life; and they constantly lie and break promises. Human beings who have such characteristics cannot be trusted and pose a real threat to the welfare and security of society. They were the enemy within, and their presence in Madinah was so damaging that the Prophet ﷺ was told to take a very harsh position against them; they were no longer to be tolerated. The Prophet ﷺ denounced them as a group, and expelled them from his Mosque. When the hypocrites built a mosque of their own, he was told to demolish it because they wanted to divide Muslims and to build an outpost to fight Allah and His Messenger (107). When the call came to march to Tabuk, the hypocrites stayed behind in Madinah and didn't take part in the campaign. This partly explains the anger against them. However, as well as the hypocrites who made excuses, there were three sincere Muslims who put off their preparations until it was too late to join the campaign. They were forgiven because of their truthfulness and honest admission, but only after their sincerity had been severely tested over fifty days. The surat takes its name, *Al-Tawbah*, from Allah's acceptance of their repentance.

The Beauty of the Faithful

Whilst the surat exposes the wicked nature of hypocrites, it honours the true believers as Allah's property (111); people who "repent, worship, praise Allah, fast, bow, prostrate, enjoin good, forbid evil, and stay within the boundaries of Allah" (112). The loyal and dedicated companions are further admired and congratulated with the news that "Allah is well pleased with *them, and* they are pleased with Him," (100). After congratulating the true Muslims on what they have achieved, verse 122 urges them to take the learning of religion seriously.

One cannot fail to notice a striking contrast between the opening passage of the surat and its end. The beginning shows divine anger towards the disbelievers who breached treaties, while the ending shows kindness and the loving nature of the beloved Messenger ﷺ. In some ways explaining the paradox of war and peace, the harshness of the battlefield is a reality of life as long as its purpose is to establish justice and remove human suffering.

﴿ ٩ ﴾ سُوْرَةُ التَّوْبَةِ مَدَنِيَّةٌ (١١٣) اٰیَاتُهَا ١٢٩ رُكُوْعَاتُهَا ١٦

بَرَآءَةٌ مِّنَ اللّٰهِ وَرَسُوْلِهٖٓ اِلَى الَّذِيْنَ عَاهَدتُّمْ مِّنَ الْمُشْرِكِيْنَ ۙ۝ فَسِيْحُوْا فِى الْاَرْضِ اَرْبَعَةَ اَشْهُرٍ وَّاعْلَمُوْٓا اَنَّكُمْ غَيْرُ مُعْجِزِى اللّٰهِ ۙ وَاَنَّ اللّٰهَ مُخْزِى الْكٰفِرِيْنَ۝ وَاَذَانٌ مِّنَ اللّٰهِ وَرَسُوْلِهٖٓ اِلَى النَّاسِ يَوْمَ الْحَجِّ الْاَكْبَرِ اَنَّ اللّٰهَ بَرِىْٓءٌ مِّنَ الْمُشْرِكِيْنَ ۙ۬ وَرَسُوْلُهٗ ؕ فَاِنْ تُبْتُمْ فَهُوَ خَيْرٌ لَّكُمْ ۚ وَاِنْ تَوَلَّيْتُمْ فَاعْلَمُوْٓا اَنَّكُمْ غَيْرُ مُعْجِزِى اللّٰهِ ؕ وَبَشِّرِ الَّذِيْنَ كَفَرُوْا بِعَذَابٍ اَلِيْمٍ ۙ۝ اِلَّا الَّذِيْنَ عَاهَدتُّمْ مِّنَ الْمُشْرِكِيْنَ ثُمَّ لَمْ يَنْقُصُوْكُمْ شَيْئًا وَّلَمْ يُظَاهِرُوْا عَلَيْكُمْ اَحَدًا فَاَتِمُّوْٓا اِلَيْهِمْ عَهْدَهُمْ اِلٰى مُدَّتِهِمْ ؕ اِنَّ اللّٰهَ يُحِبُّ الْمُتَّقِيْنَ۝ فَاِذَا انْسَلَخَ الْاَشْهُرُ الْحُرُمُ فَاقْتُلُوا الْمُشْرِكِيْنَ حَيْثُ وَجَدتُّمُوْهُمْ وَخُذُوْهُمْ وَاحْصُرُوْهُمْ وَاقْعُدُوْا لَهُمْ كُلَّ مَرْصَدٍ ۚ فَاِنْ تَابُوْا وَاَقَامُوا الصَّلٰوةَ وَاٰتَوُا الزَّكٰوةَ فَخَلُّوْا سَبِيْلَهُمْ ؕ اِنَّ اللّٰهَ غَفُوْرٌ رَّحِيْمٌ۝ وَاِنْ اَحَدٌ مِّنَ الْمُشْرِكِيْنَ اسْتَجَارَكَ فَاَجِرْهُ حَتّٰى يَسْمَعَ كَلٰمَ اللّٰهِ ثُمَّ اَبْلِغْهُ مَاْمَنَهٗ ؕ ذٰلِكَ بِاَنَّهُمْ قَوْمٌ لَّا يَعْلَمُوْنَ۠۝ كَيْفَ يَكُوْنُ لِلْمُشْرِكِيْنَ عَهْدٌ

Unfortunately, war is sometimes a necessity, but not a licence to randomly kill other humans.

All treaties with treacherous disbelievers are cancelled

¹ Allah and His Messenger have cancelled any treaty you made with the idolaters. ²So, you *idolaters* have four months to travel freely in the land; you cannot escape Allah's grip,ᵃ Allah will disgrace the disbelievers. ³An announcement *of this will be made* by Allah and His Messenger on the day of the great pilgrimage to all the people: "Allah and His Messenger are free of *any previous obligation towards* the idolaters. So, if you *idolaters* repent that will be best for you, but if you turn away, then beware you can't escape Allah's grip." Give the disbelievers glad tidings of a painful punishment. ⁴But the idolaters who haven't broken their treaty, nor have they supported anyone against you, continue to fulfil your treaty with them for the fixed term. Allah loves the mindful.

A second chance is given to those who repent

⁵When the sacred months are over, fight the idolaters wherever you find them, lie in ambush for them, arrest and besiege them.ᵇ However, if they repent, perform the prayer and pay Zakat, then let them go. Allah is Most Forgiving and Kind. ⁶If an idolater seeks your protection give him protection, he may hear Allah's Word, then take him to his place of safety; this is because they are people who don't know.

ᵃ Alternative meaning: "Allah's purpose cannot be thwarted."

ᵇ Critics of Islam call this the "Sword Verse", due to an order to kill the idolaters. It is clear from the verses before and after it, that this doesn't refer to all the idolaters, but only to those who had no regard for family ties (8, 10), repeatedly broke the treaties they had with the Messenger ﷺ, and plotted to undermine the stability that followed the Conquest of Makkah. Allah specifically orders the Muslims to continue to respect their treaties with the idolaters who had not been hostile towards them (4, 7). What is also clear is that anyone who chose to enter Islam should be allowed to go about their lives free of any threat of attack (5). In fact, they should be treated as brothers in faith (11), and anyone who chose to remain idolaters but asked for safe passage must be granted it (6). Some extremist Muslims also use this Sword Verse as a general licence to kill anybody whom they considered to not be a Muslim, young or old, whether a combatant or not. This indiscriminate approach clearly goes against the teachings of the Quran.

عِندَ اللهِ وَعِندَ رَسُولِهِ اِلَّا الَّذِينَ عٰهَدْتُّمْ
عِندَ الْمَسْجِدِ الْحَرَامِ ۚ فَمَا اسْتَقَامُوا لَكُمْ
فَاسْتَقِيمُوا لَهُمْ ۚ اِنَّ اللهَ يُحِبُّ الْمُتَّقِينَ ۞
كَيْفَ وَاِنْ يَّظْهَرُوْا عَلَيْكُمْ لَا يَرْقُبُوْا فِيكُمْ
اِلًّا وَّلَا ذِمَّةً ۚ يُرْضُوْنَكُمْ بِاَفْوَاهِهِمْ وَتَأْبٰى
قُلُوْبُهُمْ ۚ وَاَكْثَرُهُمْ فٰسِقُوْنَ ۞ اشْتَرَوْا بِاٰيٰتِ
اللهِ ثَمَنًا قَلِيْلًا فَصَدُّوْا عَنْ سَبِيْلِهِ ۚ اِنَّهُمْ
سَآءَ مَا كَانُوْا يَعْمَلُوْنَ ۞ لَا يَرْقُبُوْنَ فِيْ مُؤْمِنٍ
اِلًّا وَّلَا ذِمَّةً ۚ وَاُولٰٓئِكَ هُمُ الْمُعْتَدُوْنَ ۞
فَاِنْ تَابُوْا وَاَقَامُوا الصَّلٰوةَ وَاٰتَوُا الزَّكٰوةَ
فَاِخْوَانُكُمْ فِى الدِّيْنِ ۚ وَنُفَصِّلُ الْاٰيٰتِ لِقَوْمٍ
يَّعْلَمُوْنَ ۞ وَاِنْ نَّكَثُوْٓا اَيْمَانَهُمْ مِّنْ بَعْدِ
عَهْدِهِمْ وَطَعَنُوْا فِيْ دِيْنِكُمْ فَقَاتِلُوْٓا اَئِمَّةَ
الْكُفْرِ ۙ اِنَّهُمْ لَآ اَيْمَانَ لَهُمْ لَعَلَّهُمْ يَنْتَهُوْنَ ۞
اَلَا تُقَاتِلُوْنَ قَوْمًا نَّكَثُوْٓا اَيْمَانَهُمْ وَهَمُّوْا
بِاِخْرَاجِ الرَّسُوْلِ وَهُمْ بَدَءُوْكُمْ اَوَّلَ مَرَّةٍ ۚ
اَتَخْشَوْنَهُمْ ۚ فَاللهُ اَحَقُّ اَنْ تَخْشَوْهُ اِنْ كُنْتُمْ
مُّؤْمِنِيْنَ ۞ قَاتِلُوْهُمْ يُعَذِّبْهُمُ اللهُ بِاَيْدِيْكُمْ
وَيُخْزِهِمْ وَيَنْصُرْكُمْ عَلَيْهِمْ وَيَشْفِ صُدُوْرَ قَوْمٍ
مُّؤْمِنِيْنَ ۞ وَيُذْهِبْ غَيْظَ قُلُوْبِهِمْ ۚ وَيَتُوْبُ

Betrayal is a serious crime that is punishable, always be loyal to your country.

The disbelievers have relationship problems

[7] How could Allah and his Messenger have a treaty with the idolaters, except for those whom you *previously* made a treaty with at the Sacred Mosque? So long as they remain true, you must remain true to them. Allah loves the pious. [8] Were they to have the upper hand over you then they wouldn't show respect for either family relationship or the treaty. They try to please you with their speech, but their hearts reject you, and most of them are criminals. [9] They sell Allah's words for a small price and stop people from His path. Evil is what they do. [10] When it comes to the believers; they show no respect for family relationship or the treaty. They are transgressors. [11] However, if they repent, perform the prayer and pay Zakat they're your brothers in religion. We explain the verses for people who understand.

Treachery will not go unpunished

[12] If they break their oaths once they have made a treaty *with you*, and they criticise your religion, then fight the chiefs of the disbelievers. Their oaths mean nothing to them, so *this* might stop *them*. [13] Will you not fight those who have broken their oaths and plotted to expel the Messenger, they were the ones who started the hostilities in the first place? Are you afraid of them? Allah is far more deserving to be feared if you are *true* believers. [14] Fight them so that Allah may punish and disgrace them at your hands; Allah wants to soothe the *aching* breasts of the believers, [15] and remove the fury from their hearts. Allah forgives whomever He pleases. Allah is the Knower, Wise.

اللهُ عَلٰى مَنْ يَّشَاءُ ط وَاللهُ عَلِيْمٌ حَكِيْمٌ ۝

اَمْ حَسِبْتُمْ اَنْ تُتْرَكُوْا وَلَمَّا يَعْلَمِ اللهُ الَّذِيْنَ

جَهَدُوْا مِنْكُمْ وَلَمْ يَتَّخِذُوْا مِنْ دُوْنِ اللهِ وَلَا

رَسُوْلِهٖ وَلَا الْمُؤْمِنِيْنَ وَلِيْجَةً ط وَاللهُ خَبِيْرٌ

بِمَا تَعْمَلُوْنَ ۝ مَا كَانَ لِلْمُشْرِكِيْنَ اَنْ يَّعْمُرُوْا

مَسٰجِدَ اللهِ شٰهِدِيْنَ عَلٰۤى اَنْفُسِهِمْ بِالْكُفْرِ ط

اُولٰٓئِكَ حَبِطَتْ اَعْمَالُهُمْ ۚ وَفِى النَّارِ هُمْ

خٰلِدُوْنَ ۝ اِنَّمَا يَعْمُرُ مَسٰجِدَ اللهِ مَنْ اٰمَنَ

بِاللهِ وَالْيَوْمِ الْاٰخِرِ وَاَقَامَ الصَّلٰوةَ وَاٰتَى الزَّكٰوةَ

وَلَمْ يَخْشَ اِلَّا اللهَ فَعَسٰٓى اُولٰٓئِكَ اَنْ يَّكُوْنُوْا

مِنَ الْمُهْتَدِيْنَ ۝ اَجَعَلْتُمْ سِقَايَةَ الْحَآجِّ

وَعِمَارَةَ الْمَسْجِدِ الْحَرَامِ كَمَنْ اٰمَنَ بِاللهِ

وَالْيَوْمِ الْاٰخِرِ وَجٰهَدَ فِىْ سَبِيْلِ اللهِ ط لَا يَسْتَوٗنَ

عِنْدَ اللهِ ط وَاللهُ لَا يَهْدِى الْقَوْمَ الظّٰلِمِيْنَ ۝

اَلَّذِيْنَ اٰمَنُوْا وَهَاجَرُوْا وَجٰهَدُوْا فِىْ سَبِيْلِ

اللهِ بِاَمْوَالِهِمْ وَاَنْفُسِهِمْ اَعْظَمُ دَرَجَةً عِنْدَ

اللهِ ط وَاُولٰٓئِكَ هُمُ الْفَآئِزُوْنَ ۝ يُبَشِّرُهُمْ رَبُّهُمْ

بِرَحْمَةٍ مِّنْهُ وَرِضْوَانٍ وَّجَنّٰتٍ لَّهُمْ فِيْهَا نَعِيْمٌ

مُّقِيْمٌ ۝ خٰلِدِيْنَ فِيْهَآ اَبَدًا ط اِنَّ اللهَ عِنْدَهٗۤ

اَجْرٌ عَظِيْمٌ ۝ يٰۤاَيُّهَا الَّذِيْنَ اٰمَنُوْا لَا تَتَّخِذُوْٓا

The caretakers of the Mosque are described as true believers.

361

Believers are challenged to prove their faith

¹⁶ Or did you think you would be left *untested*? Allah has not *yet* marked out those amongst you who are willing to struggle on His path, and those who will keep secrets safe from anyone besides Allah, His Messenger and the believers. Allah is well aware of what you do.

Who is fit to be the caretaker of the Mosque?

¹⁷ It isn't right for the idolaters to be caretakers of Allah's Mosques while they are witnesses of their disbelief. Their deeds are worthless, and they will live in the Fire forever. ¹⁸ The Mosques of Allah are looked after by people who believe in Allah and the Last Day, perform prayer, pay Zakat and fear none but Allah; these are the rightly guided. ¹⁹ Do you consider providing water to the pilgrims and the maintenance of the Sacred Mosque equal *to piety* of those who believe in Allah and the Last Day and do Jihad in Allah's way? In Allah's sight the two things are not equal;[a] and Allah does not guide the wrongdoers. ²⁰ Those who believed, migrated and struggled in Allah's way with their wealth and lives have *a* special place near Allah; those are the *real* winners. ²¹ Your Lord gives them glad tidings of kindness, pleasure and gardens in which they will enjoy everlasting delights, ²² living there forever. Surely, Allah will give them a mighty reward.

[a] In the battle of Badr, Abbas the Prophet's ﷺ uncle was taken prisoner, someone condemned him for not embracing Islam. He replied "If you're so proud of becoming a Muslim and doing Jihad, we are no less than you, we take care of Allah's house, and take care of the pilgrims." This verse was revealed to emphasise the superiority of faith and Jihad over isolated good works.

اٰبَآؤُكُمْ وَ اِخْوَانُكُمْ اَوْلِيَآءَ اِنِ اسْتَحَبُّوا الْكُفْرَ

عَلَى الْاِيْمَانِ ط وَمَنْ يَّتَوَلَّهُمْ مِّنْكُمْ فَاُولٰٓئِكَ

هُمُ الظّٰلِمُوْنَ ۞ قُلْ اِنْ كَانَ اٰبَآؤُكُمْ وَ اَبْنَآؤُكُمْ

وَ اِخْوَانُكُمْ وَ اَزْوَاجُكُمْ وَعَشِيْرَتُكُمْ وَ اَمْوَالُّ

اقْتَرَفْتُمُوْهَا وَ تِجَارَةٌ تَخْشَوْنَ كَسَادَهَا وَمَسٰكِنُ

تَرْضَوْنَهَآ اَحَبَّ اِلَيْكُمْ مِّنَ اللهِ وَ رَسُوْلِهٖ

وَجِهَادٍ فِيْ سَبِيْلِهٖ فَتَرَبَّصُوْا حَتّٰى يَاْتِيَ اللهُ

بِاَمْرِهٖ ط وَاللهُ لَا يَهْدِى الْقَوْمَ الْفٰسِقِيْنَ ۞

لَقَدْ نَصَرَكُمُ اللهُ فِيْ مَوَاطِنَ كَثِيْرَةٍ لا وَّيَوْمَ

حُنَيْنٍ لا اِذْ اَعْجَبَتْكُمْ كَثْرَتُكُمْ فَلَمْ تُغْنِ

عَنْكُمْ شَيْئًا وَّضَاقَتْ عَلَيْكُمُ الْاَرْضُ بِمَا رَحُبَتْ

ثُمَّ وَلَّيْتُمْ مُّدْبِرِيْنَ ۞ ثُمَّ اَنْزَلَ اللهُ سَكِيْنَتَهٗ

عَلٰى رَسُوْلِهٖ وَ عَلَى الْمُؤْمِنِيْنَ وَاَنْزَلَ جُنُوْدًا لَّمْ

تَرَوْهَا وَعَذَّبَ الَّذِيْنَ كَفَرُوْا ط وَ ذٰلِكَ جَزَآءُ

الْكٰفِرِيْنَ ۞ ثُمَّ يَتُوْبُ اللهُ مِنْ بَعْدِ ذٰلِكَ عَلٰى

مَنْ يَّشَآءُ ط وَاللهُ غَفُوْرٌ رَّحِيْمٌ ۞ يٰٓاَيُّهَا الَّذِيْنَ

اٰمَنُوْٓا اِنَّمَا الْمُشْرِكُوْنَ نَجَسٌ فَلَا يَقْرَبُوا الْمَسْجِدَ

الْحَرَامَ بَعْدَ عَامِهِمْ هٰذَا ج وَاِنْ خِفْتُمْ عَيْلَةً

فَسَوْفَ يُغْنِيْكُمُ اللهُ مِنْ فَضْلِهٖٓ اِنْ شَآءَ ط اِنَّ

اللهَ عَلِيْمٌ حَكِيْمٌ ۞ قَاتِلُوا الَّذِيْنَ لَا يُؤْمِنُوْنَ

What is dearest to you, Allah or worldly things?

Allah is dearest to believers than anything else

²³ Believers, don't take your fathers and brothers as supporters if they prefer disbelief over faith; anyone who does so is a wrongdoer. ²⁴ Say: "If your fathers, children, brothers, spouses, relatives and the wealth you have gathered, the business whose downturn you fear and the houses that delight you, if *these things* are dearer to you than Allah, His Messenger and struggling in His path, then you should wait until Allah's Judgement comes to pass. Allah doesn't guide the disobedient."

The dreadful outcome of the Battle of Hunain

²⁵ Allah helped you in many battlefields, including on the day of Hunain[a] when you were proud of your large numbers, but that wasn't any use to you. The Earth, for all its vastness, seemed to close in on you, and you turned back and fled. ²⁶ Then Allah sent down His stillness[b] on his Messenger and the believers; and He sent down troops that you couldn't see, and He punished the disbelievers; that was the reward of their disbelief. ²⁷ Afterwards, Allah forgave whom He pleased; Allah is Most Forgiving and Kind. ²⁸ Believers, the idolaters are *spiritually* unclean; so don't let them enter the Sacred Mosque after this year.[c] If you are afraid of poverty, soon Allah will enrich you with His gifts as He wills. Allah is the Knower, Wise.

---

[a] Hunain is a valley twenty-two kilometres east of Makkah. A battle took place there in the eighth year of Hijrah, after the conquest of Makkah. The Muslim army numbered 12,000 and the idolaters were only 4,000.

[b] *Sakinah* means tranquillity and calmness, a mental state of placing one's trust in Allah and being content with Allah.

[c] Although it seems to indicate the opposite, this verse shows the tolerance of Islam: even after the Conquest of Makkah, idolaters were not told to convert or be put to the sword, but allowed to practise their religion. It was only when many of them chose to abuse that tolerance and to act with treachery that steps had to be taken to banish them from the sacred sites.

The people of scripture ignored and invented beliefs and practices.

بِاللّٰهِ وَلَا بِالْيَوْمِ الْاٰخِرِ وَلَا يُحَرِّمُوْنَ مَا حَرَّمَ

اللّٰهُ وَرَسُوْلُهٗ وَلَا يَدِيْنُوْنَ دِيْنَ الْحَقِّ مِنَ

الَّذِيْنَ اُوْتُوا الْكِتٰبَ حَتّٰى يُعْطُوا الْجِزْيَةَ عَنْ

يَّدٍ وَّهُمْ صٰغِرُوْنَ ۲۹ وَقَالَتِ الْيَهُوْدُ عُزَيْرُ ابْنُ

اللّٰهِ وَقَالَتِ النَّصٰرَى الْمَسِيْحُ ابْنُ اللّٰهِ ذٰلِكَ

قَوْلُهُمْ بِاَفْوَاهِهِمْ يُضَاهِـُٔوْنَ قَوْلَ الَّذِيْنَ كَفَرُوْا

مِنْ قَبْلُ قٰتَلَهُمُ اللّٰهُ اَنّٰى يُؤْفَكُوْنَ ۳۰ اِتَّخَذُوْٓا

اَحْبَارَهُمْ وَرُهْبَانَهُمْ اَرْبَابًا مِّنْ دُوْنِ اللّٰهِ

وَالْمَسِيْحَ ابْنَ مَرْيَمَ وَمَآ اُمِرُوْٓا اِلَّا لِيَعْبُدُوْٓا اِلٰهًا

وَّاحِدًا لَآ اِلٰهَ اِلَّا هُوَ سُبْحٰنَهٗ عَمَّا يُشْرِكُوْنَ ۳۱

يُرِيْدُوْنَ اَنْ يُّطْفِـُٔوْا نُوْرَ اللّٰهِ بِاَفْوَاهِهِمْ وَيَأْبَى

اللّٰهُ اِلَّآ اَنْ يُّتِمَّ نُوْرَهٗ وَلَوْ كَرِهَ الْكٰفِرُوْنَ ۳۲ هُوَ

الَّذِيْٓ اَرْسَلَ رَسُوْلَهٗ بِالْهُدٰى وَدِيْنِ الْحَقِّ

لِيُظْهِرَهٗ عَلَى الدِّيْنِ كُلِّهٖ وَلَوْ كَرِهَ الْمُشْرِكُوْنَ ۳۳

يٰٓاَيُّهَا الَّذِيْنَ اٰمَنُوْٓا اِنَّ كَثِيْرًا مِّنَ الْاَحْبَارِ

وَالرُّهْبَانِ لَيَأْكُلُوْنَ اَمْوَالَ النَّاسِ بِالْبَاطِلِ

وَيَصُدُّوْنَ عَنْ سَبِيْلِ اللّٰهِ وَالَّذِيْنَ يَكْنِزُوْنَ

الذَّهَبَ وَالْفِضَّةَ وَلَا يُنْفِقُوْنَهَا فِيْ سَبِيْلِ اللّٰهِ

فَبَشِّرْهُمْ بِعَذَابٍ اَلِيْمٍ ۳۴ يَوْمَ يُحْمٰى عَلَيْهَا فِيْ

نَارِ جَهَنَّمَ فَتُكْوٰى بِهَا جِبَاهُهُمْ وَجُنُوْبُهُمْ

365

The Jews and Christians rejected the original teachings

²⁹ Fight those among the people who were given the Book; they don't believe in Allah or the Last Day, don't regard unlawful what Allah and His Messenger have made unlawful, nor do they accept the rule of justice. Fight them until they agree to pay the tax promptlyᵃ and submit themselves. ³⁰ The Jews say that Uzairᵇ was the son of Allah, and the Christians say the Messiah was the son of Allah; these are false claims, they just imitate what the disbelievers said before them, may Allah destroy them! How misguided they are!

The corrupt practices of their religious leaders

³¹ They made lords beside Allah; their rabbis, monks, and Messiah son of Maryam, even though they were commanded to worship only one God, other than Whom there is no God. Glory to Him *Who is far removed* from what they associate with Him. ³² They would love to put out Allah's light with *the words of* their mouths but Allah rejects *the thought* that His light should not be perfected, no matter how much the disbelievers hate it. ³³ It is He who sent His Messenger with guidance and the true religion to prevail all other religions, no matter how much the idolaters hate it.

Those who hoard wealth will be punished

³⁴ Believers, many rabbis and monks take people's wealth dishonestly and stop people from Allah's way. So, *those* who hoard gold and silver and don't spend in Allah's way, give them glad tidings of a painful punishment ³⁵ on the day when it will be heated up in the fire of Hell and their foreheads, sides and backs will be branded with it. *It will be said,* "This is what you use to hoard, so taste the treasures you hoarded."

ᵃ *Jizya* is a tax that non-Muslim citizens living in an Islamic state pay in return for the protection of their lives, property, civic rights and religious freedom. It is a compensation paid to the Muslim community for providing these services to the non-Muslim citizens.

ᵇ Uzair refers to biblical Prophet Ezra. It has to be recognised that, unlike the Christian doctrine about Jesus, few if any Jews today hold this belief, which may have been restricted to relatively small and remote Jewish communities like those of Madinah.

وَظُهُورُهُمْ ۚ هٰذَا مَا كَنَزْتُمْ لِاَنْفُسِكُمْ فَذُوْقُوْا

مَا كُنْتُمْ تَكْنِزُوْنَ ۞ اِنَّ عِدَّةَ الشُّهُوْرِ عِنْدَ

اللّٰهِ اثْنَا عَشَرَ شَهْرًا فِيْ كِتٰبِ اللّٰهِ يَوْمَ خَلَقَ

السَّمٰوٰتِ وَالْاَرْضَ مِنْهَاۤ اَرْبَعَةٌ حُرُمٌ ۚ ذٰلِكَ

الدِّيْنُ الْقَيِّمُ ۙ فَلَا تَظْلِمُوْا فِيْهِنَّ اَنْفُسَكُمْ

وَقَاتِلُوا الْمُشْرِكِيْنَ كَآفَّةً كَمَا يُقَاتِلُوْنَكُمْ كَآفَّةً ۚ

وَاعْلَمُوْآ اَنَّ اللّٰهَ مَعَ الْمُتَّقِيْنَ ۞ اِنَّمَا النَّسِيْٓءُ

زِيَادَةٌ فِى الْكُفْرِ يُضَلُّ بِهِ الَّذِيْنَ كَفَرُوْا يُحِلُّوْنَهٗ

عَامًا وَّيُحَرِّمُوْنَهٗ عَامًا لِّيُوَاطِئُوْا عِدَّةَ مَا حَرَّمَ

اللّٰهُ فَيُحِلُّوْا مَا حَرَّمَ اللّٰهُ ۚ زُيِّنَ لَهُمْ سُوْٓءُ

اَعْمَالِهِمْ ۗ وَاللّٰهُ لَا يَهْدِى الْقَوْمَ الْكٰفِرِيْنَ ۞

يٰٓاَيُّهَا الَّذِيْنَ اٰمَنُوْا مَا لَكُمْ اِذَا قِيْلَ لَكُمُ انْفِرُوْا

فِيْ سَبِيْلِ اللّٰهِ اثَّاقَلْتُمْ اِلَى الْاَرْضِ ۗ اَرَضِيْتُمْ

بِالْحَيٰوةِ الدُّنْيَا مِنَ الْاٰخِرَةِ ۚ فَمَا مَتَاعُ

الْحَيٰوةِ الدُّنْيَا فِى الْاٰخِرَةِ اِلَّا قَلِيْلٌ ۞ اِلَّا

تَنْفِرُوْا يُعَذِّبْكُمْ عَذَابًا اَلِيْمًا ۙ وَّيَسْتَبْدِلْ قَوْمًا

غَيْرَكُمْ وَلَا تَضُرُّوْهُ شَيْئًا ۗ وَاللّٰهُ عَلٰى كُلِّ شَيْءٍ

قَدِيْرٌ ۞ اِلَّا تَنْصُرُوْهُ فَقَدْ نَصَرَهُ اللّٰهُ اِذْ اَخْرَجَهُ

الَّذِيْنَ كَفَرُوْا ثَانِيَ اثْنَيْنِ اِذْ هُمَا فِى الْغَارِ اِذْ

يَقُوْلُ لِصَاحِبِهٖ لَا تَحْزَنْ اِنَّ اللّٰهَ مَعَنَا ۚ فَاَنْزَلَ

The lack of energy to stand up for truth is a sign of weak faith. How do you fair on this scale?

Bending Allah's rules to suit one's ego

[36] The number of months *recorded* in Allah's book since the day He created *the* Heavens and the Earth is twelve, four of them are sacred; this is the established law of nature, so don't be mistaken regarding them.[a] You may fight the idolaters all out just as they fight you all out, and know Allah is with those who are mindful of Him. [37] The postponing *of sacred months* is an extreme disbelief, by which the disbelievers cause *others* to be misled, making it lawful one year and unlawful the next. They do it to match the number of months that Allah has made sacred; but, in doing so, they make permissible what Allah has forbidden. Their foul deeds seem attractive to them, but Allah doesn't guide the disbelievers.

The Tabuk campaign and obeying the order to march

[38] Believers, what is the matter with you? When you are told: "Mobilise[b] yourself in Allah's way!" Why do you feel weighed down to the ground? Are you happy with this life instead of the Hereafter? The pleasures of this life are nothing compared to the Hereafter. [39] If you don't mobilise, He will punish you severely and replace *you* with other people, and you won't harm Him in any way. Allah has power over all things.

---

[a] The four sacred months mentioned in verse 5 provided a time when the Arabs could travel freely without fear of attack. Even the idolaters respected them on the whole, except that they would sometimes cheat by swapping the sacred month of Rajab around if they thought it would give them an advantage in fighting other tribes.

[b] *Infirou* means to mobilise men, the marching off to war and all the preparations for it.

اللهُ سَكِيْنَتَهٗ عَلَيْهِ وَ اَيَّدَهٗ بِجُنُوْدٍ لَّمْ تَرَوْهَا وَ جَعَلَ كَلِمَةَ الَّذِيْنَ كَفَرُوا السُّفْلٰىؕ وَ كَلِمَةُ اللهِ هِىَ الْعُلْيَاؕ وَ اللهُ عَزِيْزٌ حَكِيْمٌ ۞ اِنْفِرُوْا خِفَافًا وَّ ثِقَالًا وَّ جَاهِدُوْا بِاَمْوَالِكُمْ وَ اَنْفُسِكُمْ فِىْ سَبِيْلِ اللهِؕ ذٰلِكُمْ خَيْرٌ لَّكُمْ اِنْ كُنْتُمْ تَعْلَمُوْنَ ۞ لَوْ كَانَ عَرَضًا قَرِيْبًا وَّسَفَرًا قَاصِدًا لَّاتَّبَعُوْكَ وَ لٰكِنْ بَعُدَتْ عَلَيْهِمُ الشُّقَّةُؕ وَسَيَحْلِفُوْنَ بِاللهِ لَوِ اسْتَطَعْنَا لَخَرَجْنَا مَعَكُمْۚ يُهْلِكُوْنَ اَنْفُسَهُمْۚ وَ اللهُ يَعْلَمُ اِنَّهُمْ لَكٰذِبُوْنَ ۞ عَفَا اللهُ عَنْكَۚ لِمَ اَذِنْتَ لَهُمْ حَتّٰى يَتَبَيَّنَ لَكَ الَّذِيْنَ صَدَقُوْا وَ تَعْلَمَ الْكٰذِبِيْنَ ۞ لَا يَسْتَاْذِنُكَ الَّذِيْنَ يُؤْمِنُوْنَ بِاللهِ وَ الْيَوْمِ الْاٰخِرِ اَنْ يُّجَاهِدُوْا بِاَمْوَالِهِمْ وَ اَنْفُسِهِمْؕ وَ اللهُ عَلِيْمٌۢ بِالْمُتَّقِيْنَ ۞ اِنَّمَا يَسْتَاْذِنُكَ الَّذِيْنَ لَا يُؤْمِنُوْنَ بِاللهِ وَ الْيَوْمِ الْاٰخِرِ وَ ارْتَابَتْ قُلُوْبُهُمْ فَهُمْ فِىْ رَيْبِهِمْ يَتَرَدَّدُوْنَ ۞ وَ لَوْ اَرَادُوا الْخُرُوْجَ لَاَعَدُّوْا لَهٗ عُدَّةً وَّ لٰكِنْ كَرِهَ اللهُ انْۢبِعَاثَهُمْ فَثَبَّطَهُمْ وَ قِيْلَ اقْعُدُوْا مَعَ الْقٰعِدِيْنَ ۞ لَوْ خَرَجُوْا فِيْكُمْ مَّا زَادُوْكُمْ اِلَّا خَبَالًا وَّ لَا اَوْضَعُوْا خِلٰلَكُمْ يَبْغُوْنَكُمُ الْفِتْنَةَۚ وَ فِيْكُمْ سَمّٰعُوْنَ

The people who dodge the duty of defending their country are weak and hypocritical.

A lesson from the Messenger's ﷺ migration from Makkah

40 If you won't help him, Allah has already helped when the disbelievers expelled him *from Makkah*. They were two in the cave when he said to his companion,[a] "Do not worry. Allah is with us." So, Allah comforted him and helped him with armies that you didn't see, and He foiled their plan, Allah's plan is supreme. Allah is Almighty, Wise.

The hypocrite's response to the order to march on Tabuk

41 Mobilise whether you are lightly or heavily armed, and struggle with your wealth and your lives in Allah's way, that's better for you, if you knew. 42 Had there been an instant gain and an easy journey they would have followed you; however, *Tabuk* was too far away and the journey difficult. They will swear by Allah, "If we were capable we certainly would have come out with you." They have ruined themselves. Allah knows they are liars.

The attitudes and behaviours of Hypocrites: Making excuses

43 Allah pardons you! Why did you allow them *to remain behind* before it became clear who was telling the truth, and you had identified the liars. 44 Those who believe in Allah and the Last Day won't seek your permission *to stay behind* so as not to strive with their wealth and lives. Allah knows the righteous people. 45 Only those who don't believe in Allah and the Last Day will seek your permission to remain behind because their hearts are full of doubts which makes them hesitant. 46 Had they wished to go forth *for Jihad* they would have prepared properly for it. However, because Allah disliked their going forth, He let them hold back *until* it was said: "Remain with those who are staying behind." 47 Had they gone out with you they would have made trouble for you, scurrying among you to wreak havoc, and some would have listened to them. Allah knows well the wrongdoers.

---

a The companion mentioned here was Abu Bakr, who accompanied him in the cave of Thaur, south of Makkah. He became the first Caliph after the Prophet ﷺ passed away in 632 CE.

لَهُمْ ط وَاللهُ عَلِيْمٌ بِالظّٰلِمِيْنَ ۞ لَقَدِ ابْتَغَوُا

الْفِتْنَةَ مِنْ قَبْلُ وَ قَلَّبُوْا لَكَ الْاُمُوْرَ حَتّٰى جَآءَ

الْحَقُّ وَ ظَهَرَ اَمْرُ اللهِ وَ هُمْ كٰرِهُوْنَ ۞ وَمِنْهُمْ

مَّنْ يَّقُوْلُ ائْذَنْ لِّيْ وَ لَا تَفْتِنِّيْ ط اَلَا فِي الْفِتْنَةِ

سَقَطُوْا ط وَاِنَّ جَهَنَّمَ لَمُحِيْطَةٌ بِالْكٰفِرِيْنَ ۞ اِنْ

تُصِبْكَ حَسَنَةٌ تَسُؤْهُمْ ۚ وَاِنْ تُصِبْكَ مُصِيْبَةٌ

يَّقُوْلُوْا قَدْ اَخَذْنَا اَمْرَنَا مِنْ قَبْلُ وَ يَتَوَلَّوْا

وَ هُمْ فَرِحُوْنَ ۞ قُلْ لَّنْ يُّصِيْبَنَا اِلَّا مَا كَتَبَ

Never be happy at the misfortune of others.

اللهُ لَنَا ۚ هُوَ مَوْلٰىنَا ۚ وَعَلَى اللهِ فَلْيَتَوَكَّلِ

الْمُؤْمِنُوْنَ ۞ قُلْ هَلْ تَرَبَّصُوْنَ بِنَا اِلَّا اِحْدَى

الْحُسْنَيَيْنِ ط وَنَحْنُ نَتَرَبَّصُ بِكُمْ اَنْ يُّصِيْبَكُمُ

اللهُ بِعَذَابٍ مِّنْ عِنْدِهٖ اَوْ بِاَيْدِيْنَا ۙ فَتَرَبَّصُوْا

اِنَّا مَعَكُمْ مُّتَرَبِّصُوْنَ ۞ قُلْ اَنْفِقُوْا طَوْعًا اَوْ

كَرْهًا لَّنْ يُّتَقَبَّلَ مِنْكُمْ ط اِنَّكُمْ كُنْتُمْ قَوْمًا

فٰسِقِيْنَ ۞ وَمَا مَنَعَهُمْ اَنْ تُقْبَلَ مِنْهُمْ نَفَقٰتُهُمْ

اِلَّا اَنَّهُمْ كَفَرُوْا بِاللهِ وَبِرَسُوْلِهٖ وَلَا يَاْتُوْنَ

الصَّلٰوةَ اِلَّا وَهُمْ كُسَالٰى وَلَا يُنْفِقُوْنَ اِلَّا وَهُمْ

كٰرِهُوْنَ ۞ فَلَا تُعْجِبْكَ اَمْوَالُهُمْ وَلَا اَوْلَادُهُمْ ط

اِنَّمَا يُرِيْدُ اللهُ لِيُعَذِّبَهُمْ بِهَا فِي الْحَيٰوةِ الدُّنْيَا

وَ تَزْهَقَ اَنْفُسُهُمْ وَهُمْ كٰفِرُوْنَ ۞ وَيَحْلِفُوْنَ

[48] They tried to stir up conflict among you in the past and turn everything upside down for you until the truth *finally* came out, and Allah's decree was made clear, even though they detested *being exposed*. [49] Some of them say, "Permit me *to stay* and do not put me to the test." Haven't they already failed the test? Hell will encircle the disbelievers.

Hypocrites gloat at the misfortune of others

[50] When times are good for you, they grieve, but when some tragedy strikes you, they say, "We took proper precautions beforehand," and they go away rejoicing. [51] Say: "We are only affected by what Allah decreed for us, He is Our Protector, and the believers put their trust in Allah." [52] Say: "Are you waiting for anything besides two good things to happen to us?[a] We are *also* waiting with you for Allah to inflict on you some punishment, either by Himself or at our hands. So, carry on waiting, we'll wait as well." [53] Say: "Whether you give willingly or unwillingly, your *charity* will not be accepted, because you are disobedient people." [54] Since they do not believe in Allah and His Messenger their charity will not be accepted, furthermore, they come lazily to the prayer and give *charity* grudgingly. [55] Don't be impressed by their wealth and children: Allah wishes to torment them with these in their worldly life, and allow their souls to perish as disbelievers.

---

[a]   Either in victory in the battle, or martyrdom and Paradise in the Hereafter.

بِاللّٰهِ اِنَّهُمْ لَمِنْكُمْ ط وَمَا هُمْ مِّنْكُمْ وَلٰكِنَّهُمْ

قَوْمٌ يَّفْرَقُوْنَ ۵۷ لَوْ يَجِدُوْنَ مَلْجَاً اَوْ مَغٰرٰتٍ اَوْ

مُدَّخَلًا لَّوَلَّوْا اِلَيْهِ وَهُمْ يَجْمَحُوْنَ ۵۷ وَمِنْهُمْ

مَّنْ يَّلْمِزُكَ فِى الصَّدَقٰتِ ۚ فَاِنْ اُعْطُوْا مِنْهَا

رَضُوْا وَاِنْ لَّمْ يُعْطَوْا مِنْهَآ اِذَا هُمْ يَسْخَطُوْنَ ۵۸

وَلَوْ اَنَّهُمْ رَضُوْا مَآ اٰتٰهُمُ اللّٰهُ وَرَسُوْلُهٗ ۙ

وَقَالُوْا حَسْبُنَا اللّٰهُ سَيُؤْتِيْنَا اللّٰهُ مِنْ فَضْلِهٖ

وَرَسُوْلُهٗٓ ۙ اِنَّآ اِلَى اللّٰهِ رٰغِبُوْنَ ۵۹ اِنَّمَا

Criticism of the Messenger ﷺ is bad and a sign of weak faith.

الصَّدَقٰتُ لِلْفُقَرَآءِ وَالْمَسٰكِيْنِ وَالْعٰمِلِيْنَ عَلَيْهَا

وَالْمُؤَلَّفَةِ قُلُوْبُهُمْ وَفِى الرِّقَابِ وَالْغٰرِمِيْنَ

وَفِىْ سَبِيْلِ اللّٰهِ وَابْنِ السَّبِيْلِ ط فَرِيْضَةً مِّنَ

اللّٰهِ ط وَاللّٰهُ عَلِيْمٌ حَكِيْمٌ ۶۰ وَمِنْهُمُ الَّذِيْنَ

يُؤْذُوْنَ النَّبِيَّ وَيَقُوْلُوْنَ هُوَ اُذُنٌ ط قُلْ اُذُنُ خَيْرٍ

لَّكُمْ يُؤْمِنُ بِاللّٰهِ وَيُؤْمِنُ لِلْمُؤْمِنِيْنَ وَرَحْمَةٌ

لِّلَّذِيْنَ اٰمَنُوْا مِنْكُمْ ط وَالَّذِيْنَ يُؤْذُوْنَ

رَسُوْلَ اللّٰهِ لَهُمْ عَذَابٌ اَلِيْمٌ ۶۱ يَحْلِفُوْنَ

بِاللّٰهِ لَكُمْ لِيُرْضُوْكُمْ ۚ وَاللّٰهُ وَرَسُوْلُهٗٓ

اَحَقُّ اَنْ يُّرْضُوْهُ اِنْ كَانُوْا مُؤْمِنِيْنَ ۶۲ اَلَمْ

يَعْلَمُوْٓا اَنَّهٗ مَنْ يُّحَادِدِ اللّٰهَ وَرَسُوْلَهٗ فَاَنَّ

لَهٗ نَارَ جَهَنَّمَ خَالِدًا فِيْهَا ط ذٰلِكَ الْخِزْىُ

Hypocrites are only in it for themselves

[56] They swear by Allah: they are with you *all the way*, but they aren't with you; they are cowardly people. [57] Were they to find a place to flee to, a cave or any opening, they would turn to it as they run away *from the truth*. [58] Some of them criticise you over *the redistribution of* charitable donations; if they are given some, they are pleased, but if not, they become angry. [59] They should be content with what Allah and His Messenger gave them and say: "Allah is enough for us, and soon Allah and His Messenger will give us from His bounty. *So,* we place our hopes in Allah."

The eight recipients of Zakat

[60] Zakat[a] is for the poor, the needy, *its* administrators, people whose hearts and minds are to be won, freeing the slaves, *helping* people in debt, to *advance* Allah's cause, and for the *needy* traveller. This is a duty instructed by Allah, and Allah is the Knower, Wise.

Hypocrites sow conflict among Muslims

[61] Some people insulted the Messenger saying, "He is all ears."[b] Say: "He has an ear for what is good for you. He believes in Allah and looks out for the safety of the believers, and he is kind[c] to those of you who believe. However, those who insult Allah's Messenger will have painful punishment." [62] They swear by Allah to please you, yet it is Allah and his Messenger who they should try to please, if they are *true* believers. [63] Don't they know that anyone who opposes Allah and His Messenger will live in the Fire, forever? What a terrible disgrace!

---

[a] The commentators are agreed that *Sadaqah* here refers to Zakat, a pillar of Islam.
[b] "He is all ears" means that he believes everything he hears.
[c] Literally "kindness".

الْعَظِيمُ ۞ يَحْذَرُ الْمُنٰفِقُوْنَ اَنْ تُنَزَّلَ عَلَيْهِمْ

سُوْرَةٌ تُنَبِّئُهُمْ بِمَا فِيْ قُلُوْبِهِمْ ؕ قُلِ اسْتَهْزِءُوْا ۚ

اِنَّ اللّٰهَ مُخْرِجٌ مَّا تَحْذَرُوْنَ ۞ وَلَئِنْ سَاَلْتَهُمْ

لَيَقُوْلُنَّ اِنَّمَا كُنَّا نَخُوْضُ وَنَلْعَبُ ؕ قُلْ اَبِاللّٰهِ

وَاٰيٰتِهٖ وَرَسُوْلِهٖ كُنْتُمْ تَسْتَهْزِءُوْنَ ۞ لَا تَعْتَذِرُوْا

قَدْ كَفَرْتُمْ بَعْدَ اِيْمَانِكُمْ ؕ اِنْ نَّعْفُ عَنْ

طَآئِفَةٍ مِّنْكُمْ نُعَذِّبْ طَآئِفَةًۢ بِاَنَّهُمْ كَانُوْا

مُجْرِمِيْنَ ۞ اَلْمُنٰفِقُوْنَ وَالْمُنٰفِقٰتُ بَعْضُهُمْ

مِّنْۢ بَعْضٍ ۘ يَاْمُرُوْنَ بِالْمُنْكَرِ وَيَنْهَوْنَ

عَنِ الْمَعْرُوْفِ وَيَقْبِضُوْنَ اَيْدِيَهُمْ ؕ نَسُوا اللّٰهَ

فَنَسِيَهُمْ ؕ اِنَّ الْمُنٰفِقِيْنَ هُمُ الْفٰسِقُوْنَ ۞ وَعَدَ

اللّٰهُ الْمُنٰفِقِيْنَ وَالْمُنٰفِقٰتِ وَالْكُفَّارَ نَارَ

جَهَنَّمَ خٰلِدِيْنَ فِيْهَا ؕ هِيَ حَسْبُهُمْ ۚ وَلَعَنَهُمُ

اللّٰهُ ۚ وَلَهُمْ عَذَابٌ مُّقِيْمٌ ۞ كَالَّذِيْنَ مِنْ

قَبْلِكُمْ كَانُوْٓا اَشَدَّ مِنْكُمْ قُوَّةً وَّاَكْثَرَ اَمْوَالًا

وَّاَوْلَادًا ؕ فَاسْتَمْتَعُوْا بِخَلَاقِهِمْ فَاسْتَمْتَعْتُمْ

بِخَلَاقِكُمْ كَمَا اسْتَمْتَعَ الَّذِيْنَ مِنْ قَبْلِكُمْ

بِخَلَاقِهِمْ وَخُضْتُمْ كَالَّذِيْ خَاضُوْا ؕ اُولٰٓئِكَ

حَبِطَتْ اَعْمَالُهُمْ فِي الدُّنْيَا وَالْاٰخِرَةِ ۚ وَاُولٰٓئِكَ

هُمُ الْخٰسِرُوْنَ ۞ اَلَمْ يَاْتِهِمْ نَبَاُ الَّذِيْنَ مِنْ

The disloyalty and mistrust of the hypocrites makes them despicable citizens.

The hypocrites are an anxious bunch

⁶⁴ The hypocrites are afraid that a surat may be revealed about them informing them *and the rest of the Muslims* of what is in their hearts. Say: "Keep mocking. Allah will produce what you most fear." ⁶⁵ If you ask them *about some incident,* they will say, "We were just discussing and having fun." Say: "Are you mocking Allah, His verses and His Messenger? ⁶⁶ Don't make excuses, you have *clearly* disbelieved after *declaring* belief." Even if We choose to forgive few of you, We will punish the rest because they are sinners.

Hypocrites don't walk the talk

⁶⁷ Hypocrite, men and women, stand by each other; they enjoin evil and forbid good and are tight-fisted. They ignore Allah, so He will ignore them *in the Hereafter.* The hypocrites are disobedient. ⁶⁸ Allah has promised the hypocrites, men and women, and the disbelievers the fire of Hell to be there forever; that's good enough for them. Allah has cursed them, and they will suffer endless torment.

The hypocrites talk but don't live the values

⁶⁹ *Hypocrites! You are* like those before you, but they were more powerful than you, and had greater wealth and children; they enjoyed their share *of the worldly comforts,* so you too enjoy your share just as they did before you; and go on indulging in idle talk just as they did. Their deeds are worthless in this world and the Hereafter; they were losers.

قَبْلِهِمْ قَوْمِ نُوْحٍ وَّعَادٍ وَّثَمُوْدَهْ وَقَوْمِ اِبْرٰهِيْمَ

وَاَصْحٰبِ مَدْيَنَ وَالْمُؤْتَفِكٰتِ ۚ اَتَتْهُمْ رُسُلُهُمْ

بِالْبَيِّنٰتِ ۚ فَمَا كَانَ اللّٰهُ لِيَظْلِمَهُمْ وَلٰكِنْ كَانُوْٓا

اَنْفُسَهُمْ يَظْلِمُوْنَ ۞ وَالْمُؤْمِنُوْنَ وَالْمُؤْمِنٰتُ

بَعْضُهُمْ اَوْلِيَآءُ بَعْضٍ ۘ يَاْمُرُوْنَ بِالْمَعْرُوْفِ

وَيَنْهَوْنَ عَنِ الْمُنْكَرِ وَيُقِيْمُوْنَ الصَّلٰوةَ وَيُؤْتُوْنَ

الزَّكٰوةَ وَيُطِيْعُوْنَ اللّٰهَ وَرَسُوْلَهٗ ۚ اُولٰٓئِكَ

سَيَرْحَمُهُمُ اللّٰهُ ۚ اِنَّ اللّٰهَ عَزِيْزٌ حَكِيْمٌ ۞

Believers are friends who stand united.

وَعَدَ اللّٰهُ الْمُؤْمِنِيْنَ وَالْمُؤْمِنٰتِ جَنّٰتٍ

تَجْرِىْ مِنْ تَحْتِهَا الْاَنْهٰرُ خٰلِدِيْنَ فِيْهَا

وَمَسٰكِنَ طَيِّبَةً فِيْ جَنّٰتِ عَدْنٍ ۚ وَرِضْوَانٌ

مِّنَ اللّٰهِ اَكْبَرُ ۚ ذٰلِكَ هُوَ الْفَوْزُ الْعَظِيْمُ ۞

يٰٓاَيُّهَا النَّبِيُّ جَاهِدِ الْكُفَّارَ وَالْمُنٰفِقِيْنَ

وَاغْلُظْ عَلَيْهِمْ ۚ وَمَاْوٰىهُمْ جَهَنَّمُ ۚ وَبِئْسَ

الْمَصِيْرُ ۞ يَحْلِفُوْنَ بِاللّٰهِ مَا قَالُوْا ۚ وَلَقَدْ قَالُوْا

كَلِمَةَ الْكُفْرِ وَكَفَرُوْا بَعْدَ اِسْلَامِهِمْ وَهَمُّوْا

بِمَا لَمْ يَنَالُوْا ۚ وَمَا نَقَمُوْٓا اِلَّآ اَنْ اَغْنٰىهُمُ اللّٰهُ

وَرَسُوْلُهٗ مِنْ فَضْلِهٖ ۚ فَاِنْ يَّتُوْبُوْا يَكُ

خَيْرًا لَّهُمْ ۚ وَاِنْ يَّتَوَلَّوْا يُعَذِّبْهُمُ اللّٰهُ

عَذَابًا اَلِيْمًا ۙ فِى الدُّنْيَا وَالْاٰخِرَةِ ۚ وَمَا

⁷⁰ Haven't stories of previous people come down to them, like the people of Nuh, Ad, Thamud; of Ibrahim, of Madyan and the overturned cities? Messengers came with clear signs; Allah wasn't unfair to them, but they wronged themselves.

The reward for believers is Paradise

⁷¹ Believing men and women, are one another's friends; they enjoin what is good and forbid what is evil; they perform the prayer, pay Zakat, they obey Allah and His Messenger, so Allah will take care of them. Allah is Almighty, Wise. ⁷² Allah has prepared for the believing men and women, gardens under which rivers flow, where they shall live forever, and comfortable homes *enclosed by* gardens of everlasting bliss, and the Divine pleasure is the greatest *reward* of all,[a] the supreme achievement.

Hypocrites make promises that they don't keep

⁷³ Blessed Prophet, struggle against the disbelievers and hypocrites and be strict with them. Hell is their *lasting* home. What an evil destination! ⁷⁴ They swear by Allah they didn't say *what they are accused of,* but they blasphemed and disbelieved after embracing Islam. They worry about what they failed to achieve. They were angry because Allah and His Messenger enriched them with His bounty. It would be better for them, if they repented. But, if they turn away Allah will punish them severely in this life and the Hereafter, and no one on Earth would protect or help them.

---

[a] The Divine pleasure means that Allah ﷻ is happy with them, He has approved their worldly achievements and taken them as friends.

لَهُمْ فِى الْاَرْضِ مِنْ وَّلِيٍّ وَّلَا نَصِيْرٍ ۞ وَ
مِنْهُمْ مَّنْ عَاهَدَ اللّٰهَ لَئِنْ اٰتٰىنَا مِنْ فَضْلِهٖ
لَنَصَّدَّقَنَّ وَلَنَكُوْنَنَّ مِنَ الصّٰلِحِيْنَ ۞ فَلَمَّاۤ
اٰتٰىهُمْ مِّنْ فَضْلِهٖ بَخِلُوْا بِهٖ وَتَوَلَّوْا وَّهُمْ
مُّعْرِضُوْنَ ۞ فَاَعْقَبَهُمْ نِفَاقًا فِىْ قُلُوْبِهِمْ اِلٰى
يَوْمِ يَلْقَوْنَهٗ بِمَاۤ اَخْلَفُوا اللّٰهَ مَا وَعَدُوْهُ
وَبِمَا كَانُوْا يَكْذِبُوْنَ ۞ اَلَمْ يَعْلَمُوٓا اَنَّ اللّٰهَ
يَعْلَمُ سِرَّهُمْ وَنَجْوٰىهُمْ وَاَنَّ اللّٰهَ عَلَّامُ
الْغُيُوْبِ ۞ اَلَّذِيْنَ يَلْمِزُوْنَ الْمُطَّوِّعِيْنَ مِنَ
الْمُؤْمِنِيْنَ فِى الصَّدَقٰتِ وَالَّذِيْنَ لَا يَجِدُوْنَ
اِلَّا جُهْدَهُمْ فَيَسْخَرُوْنَ مِنْهُمْ سَخِرَ اللّٰهُ
مِنْهُمْ وَلَهُمْ عَذَابٌ اَلِيْمٌ ۞ اِسْتَغْفِرْ لَهُمْ اَوْ
لَا تَسْتَغْفِرْ لَهُمْ اِنْ تَسْتَغْفِرْ لَهُمْ سَبْعِيْنَ مَرَّةً
فَلَنْ يَّغْفِرَ اللّٰهُ لَهُمْ ذٰلِكَ بِاَنَّهُمْ كَفَرُوْا بِاللّٰهِ
وَرَسُوْلِهٖ وَاللّٰهُ لَا يَهْدِى الْقَوْمَ الْفٰسِقِيْنَ ۞
فَرِحَ الْمُخَلَّفُوْنَ بِمَقْعَدِهِمْ خِلٰفَ رَسُوْلِ اللّٰهِ
وَكَرِهُوٓا اَنْ يُّجَاهِدُوْا بِاَمْوَالِهِمْ وَاَنْفُسِهِمْ
فِىْ سَبِيْلِ اللّٰهِ وَقَالُوْا لَا تَنْفِرُوْا فِى الْحَرِّ قُلْ
نَارُ جَهَنَّمَ اَشَدُّ حَرًّا لَّوْ كَانُوْا يَفْقَهُوْنَ ۞
فَلْيَضْحَكُوْا قَلِيْلًا وَّلْيَبْكُوْا كَثِيْرًا جَزَآءً بِمَا

The wretchedness and the sheer evil of hypocrites makes them sheer failures.

379

⁷⁵ Some of them vowed to Allah: "If He gives us of His bounty, we will donate generously and be righteous." ⁷⁶ However, when He blessed them with His bounty, they became miserly and turned away, unwilling to give.ᵃ ⁷⁷ Since they broke their promise to Allah and lied repeatedly, Allah has put hypocrisy in their hearts until the day they meet Him.

Hypocrites mock generous Muslims

⁷⁸ Aren't they aware Allah knows their secrets and private conversations. Allah is the Knower of the unseen. ⁷⁹ Those who criticise the believers – who make voluntary donations, and who have nothing *to give* but their *time and* talent – and they poke fun at them, Allah will make a laughing stock of them; and they shall have a painful punishment. ⁸⁰ Whether you ask for their forgiveness or not, even if you ask seventy times for their forgiveness,ᵇ Allah will never forgive them because they rejected Allah and His Messenger, and Allah does not guide the sinners.

Hypocrites aren't trustworthy

⁸¹ Those who stayed at home were delighted after Allah's Messenger had left. They hated *the thought of* struggling with their wealth and lives in Allah's way, saying *to others*, "Don't march in this heat." Say: "The fire of Hell is far hotter." If only they understood. ⁸² So, let them laugh a little, *soon* they will cry a lot, a reward for what they did.

ᵃ This refers to Saliba Ibn Hatib, who came to the Messenger ﷺ and said "pray to Allah to give me wealth". The Messenger ﷺ cautioned him "O Saliba, a small amount for which you are thankful is better than a lot which you can't appreciate." However Saliba kept insisting that He ﷺ pray for him, and he will give the needy their due. So, the Messenger ﷺ prayed and his wealth grew enormously. Unfortunately, he was miserly and refused to give in charity. (Al Sabuni)

ᵇ The number seventy here is like "umpteen" in English.

كَانُوْا يَكْسِبُوْنَ ۞ فَاِنْ رَّجَعَكَ اللّٰهُ اِلٰى طَآئِفَةٍ

مِّنْهُمْ فَاسْتَاْذَنُوْكَ لِلْخُرُوْجِ فَقُلْ لَّنْ تَخْرُجُوْا

مَعِيَ اَبَدًا وَّلَنْ تُقَاتِلُوْا مَعِيَ عَدُوًّا ۖ اِنَّكُمْ

رَضِيْتُمْ بِالْقُعُوْدِ اَوَّلَ مَرَّةٍ فَاقْعُدُوْا مَعَ

الْخٰلِفِيْنَ ۞ وَلَا تُصَلِّ عَلٰٓى اَحَدٍ مِّنْهُمْ مَّاتَ اَبَدًا

وَّلَا تَقُمْ عَلٰى قَبْرِهٖ ۖ اِنَّهُمْ كَفَرُوْا بِاللّٰهِ وَرَسُوْلِهٖ

وَمَاتُوْا وَهُمْ فٰسِقُوْنَ ۞ وَلَا تُعْجِبْكَ اَمْوَالُهُمْ

وَاَوْلَادُهُمْ ۖ اِنَّمَا يُرِيْدُ اللّٰهُ اَنْ يُّعَذِّبَهُمْ بِهَا

فِى الدُّنْيَا وَتَزْهَقَ اَنْفُسُهُمْ وَهُمْ كٰفِرُوْنَ ۞

وَاِذَآ اُنْزِلَتْ سُوْرَةٌ اَنْ اٰمِنُوْا بِاللّٰهِ وَجَاهِدُوْا مَعَ

رَسُوْلِهِ اسْتَاْذَنَكَ اُولُوا الطَّوْلِ مِنْهُمْ وَقَالُوْا

ذَرْنَا نَكُنْ مَّعَ الْقٰعِدِيْنَ ۞ رَضُوْا بِاَنْ يَّكُوْنُوْا مَعَ

الْخَوَالِفِ وَطُبِعَ عَلٰى قُلُوْبِهِمْ فَهُمْ لَا يَفْقَهُوْنَ ۞

لٰكِنِ الرَّسُوْلُ وَالَّذِيْنَ اٰمَنُوْا مَعَهٗ جٰهَدُوْا

بِاَمْوَالِهِمْ وَاَنْفُسِهِمْ ۖ وَاُولٰٓئِكَ لَهُمُ الْخَيْرٰتُ

وَاُولٰٓئِكَ هُمُ الْمُفْلِحُوْنَ ۞ اَعَدَّ اللّٰهُ لَهُمْ جَنّٰتٍ

تَجْرِيْ مِنْ تَحْتِهَا الْاَنْهٰرُ خٰلِدِيْنَ فِيْهَا ۖ

ذٰلِكَ الْفَوْزُ الْعَظِيْمُ ۞ وَجَآءَ الْمُعَذِّرُوْنَ مِنَ

الْاَعْرَابِ لِيُؤْذَنَ لَهُمْ وَقَعَدَ الَّذِيْنَ كَذَبُوا اللّٰهَ

وَرَسُوْلَهٗ ۖ سَيُصِيْبُ الَّذِيْنَ كَفَرُوْا مِنْهُمْ عَذَابٌ

The hypocrites are lethargic and lack the energy to stand up and defend their city.

⁸³ When Allah brings you back *to Madinah*, a group of them will ask permission to march out with you *next time*. Say *to them*: "You will never march out with me, nor will you fight with me against an enemy. You were happy to stay *at home* the first time, so stay with those who were left behind."

Hypocrisy deprives you of the Messenger's ﷺ prayers

⁸⁴ *Blessed Prophet*, never pray for any of their dead nor stand by their grave. They disbelieved in Allah and His Messenger and died as sinners. ⁸⁵ Don't be impressed by their wealth or children, Allah wishes to torment them with these in this world, and their souls will perish while they are still disbelievers. ⁸⁶ Whenever a surat is revealed *saying*: "Believe in Allah and strive along with His Messenger," the wealthy among them seek an exemption from you, saying, "Leave us with those who stay behind." ⁸⁷ They are pleased to stay with those who remain behind, and their hearts have been sealed so they do not understand. ⁸⁸ However, the Messenger and believers strive with their wealth and lives. They shall have all the best things, and they're successful. ⁸⁹ Allah has prepared for them gardens beneath which rivers flow, here they shall live forever; that is the supreme achievement.

Those who long to defend the community but lack the means are not to blame

⁹⁰ Some Bedouins who stayed behind at home came with excuses, sought exemption, and some lied about Allah and His Messenger. The disbelievers shall soon be afflicted by a painful punishment.

اَلِيْمٌ ۞ لَيْسَ عَلَى الضُّعَفَاءِ وَلَا عَلَى الْمَرْضَى وَلَا

عَلَى الَّذِيْنَ لَا يَجِدُوْنَ مَا يُنْفِقُوْنَ حَرَجٌ اِذَا

نَصَحُوْا لِلّٰهِ وَرَسُوْلِهٖ ط مَا عَلَى الْمُحْسِنِيْنَ مِنْ

سَبِيْلٍ ط وَاللّٰهُ غَفُوْرٌ رَّحِيْمٌ ۞ وَّلَا عَلَى الَّذِيْنَ

اِذَا مَا اَتَوْكَ لِتَحْمِلَهُمْ قُلْتَ لَا اَجِدُ مَا

اَحْمِلُكُمْ عَلَيْهِ ۬ تَوَلَّوْا وَّاَعْيُنُهُمْ تَفِيْضُ مِنَ

الدَّمْعِ حَزَنًا اَلَّا يَجِدُوْا مَا يُنْفِقُوْنَ ۞ اِنَّمَا

السَّبِيْلُ عَلَى الَّذِيْنَ يَسْتَأْذِنُوْنَكَ وَهُمْ

اَغْنِيَآءُ ۚ رَضُوْا بِاَنْ يَّكُوْنُوْا مَعَ الْخَوَالِفِ لَا

وَطَبَعَ اللّٰهُ عَلَى قُلُوْبِهِمْ فَهُمْ لَا يَعْلَمُوْنَ ۞

Those who have a good excuse: sick or too poor, to remain behind shouldn't be blamed.

يَعْتَذِرُوْنَ اِلَيْكُمْ اِذَا رَجَعْتُمْ اِلَيْهِمْ ط قُلْ لَّا

تَعْتَذِرُوْا لَنْ نُّؤْمِنَ لَكُمْ قَدْ نَبَّاَنَا اللّٰهُ مِنْ اَخْبَارِكُمْ ط

وَسَيَرَى اللّٰهُ عَمَلَكُمْ وَرَسُوْلُهٗ ثُمَّ تُرَدُّوْنَ اِلٰى عٰلِمِ

الْغَيْبِ وَالشَّهَادَةِ فَيُنَبِّئُكُمْ بِمَا كُنْتُمْ تَعْمَلُوْنَ ۞

سَيَحْلِفُوْنَ بِاللّٰهِ لَكُمْ اِذَا انْقَلَبْتُمْ اِلَيْهِمْ لِتُعْرِضُوْا

عَنْهُمْ ط فَاَعْرِضُوْا عَنْهُمْ ط اِنَّهُمْ رِجْسٌ وَّمَأْوٰىهُمْ

جَهَنَّمُ ۚ جَزَآءً بِمَا كَانُوْا يَكْسِبُوْنَ ۞ يَحْلِفُوْنَ

لَكُمْ لِتَرْضَوْا عَنْهُمْ ۚ فَاِنْ تَرْضَوْا عَنْهُمْ فَاِنَّ اللّٰهَ

لَا يَرْضٰى عَنِ الْقَوْمِ الْفٰسِقِيْنَ ۞ اَلْاَعْرَابُ اَشَدُّ

كُفْرًا وَّنِفَاقًا وَّاَجْدَرُ اَلَّا يَعْلَمُوْا حُدُوْدَ مَا اَنْزَلَ

⁹¹ No blame shall rest on the weak, the sick and those who lack the financial means, so long as they remain sincere towards Allah and His Messenger; the righteous shouldn't be blamed, Allah is Forgiving, Caring. ⁹² Nor *does any blame rest* on those who came to you expecting to find mounts,^a and you said, "I can't find a mount for you," so they turned away, their eyes overflowing with tears of grief since they had no money to equip themselves.

The wealthy are to blame for not contributing

⁹³ Blame is on those who seek an exemption, yet they are wealthy. They are happy to stay with those who remain behind, so Allah has sealed their hearts, they don't know. ⁹⁴ They will make *all sorts of* excuses when you return to them *in Madinah.* Say: "Don't make excuses. We won't believe you. Allah has already informed us about you. Allah and His Messenger will soon see your actions, then you will be turned over to the Knower of all that is seen and unseen, and He will inform you of what you used to do." ⁹⁵ When you return to them they will swear by Allah to be left alone, so leave them alone; they're wicked people. Their home is Hell, a reward for what they did. ⁹⁶ They will swear an oath to please you, but even if you are pleased with them, Allah will not be pleased with disobedient people.

---

^a A mount here refers to an animal for transportation.

اللهُ عَلَى رَسُولِهِ ط وَاللهُ عَلِيمٌ حَكِيمٌ ۝ وَمِنَ

الْأَعْرَابِ مَنْ يَّتَّخِذُ مَا يُنْفِقُ مَغْرَمًا وَّيَتَرَبَّصُ

بِكُمُ الدَّوَآئِرَ ط عَلَيْهِمْ دَآئِرَةُ السَّوْءِ ط وَاللهُ سَمِيعٌ

عَلِيمٌ ۝ وَمِنَ الْأَعْرَابِ مَنْ يُّؤْمِنُ بِاللهِ وَالْيَوْمِ

الْأَخِرِ وَيَتَّخِذُ مَا يُنْفِقُ قُرُبٰتٍ عِنْدَ اللهِ وَصَلَوٰتِ

الرَّسُولِ ط أَلَا إِنَّهَا قُرْبَةٌ لَّهُمْ ط سَيُدْخِلُهُمُ اللهُ

فِي رَحْمَتِهِ ط إِنَّ اللهَ غَفُورٌ رَّحِيمٌ ۝ وَالسّٰبِقُونَ

الْأَوَّلُونَ مِنَ الْمُهٰجِرِينَ وَالْأَنْصَارِ وَالَّذِينَ

اتَّبَعُوهُمْ بِإِحْسَانٍ لَّا رَّضِيَ اللهُ عَنْهُمْ وَرَضُوا عَنْهُ

وَأَعَدَّ لَهُمْ جَنّٰتٍ تَجْرِي تَحْتَهَا الْأَنْهٰرُ خٰلِدِينَ

فِيهَا أَبَدًا ط ذٰلِكَ الْفَوْزُ الْعَظِيمُ ۝ وَمِمَّنْ حَوْلَكُمْ

مِّنَ الْأَعْرَابِ مُنٰفِقُونَ ط وَمِنْ أَهْلِ الْمَدِينَةِ قف

مَرَدُوا عَلَى النِّفَاقِ قف لَا تَعْلَمُهُمْ ط نَحْنُ نَعْلَمُهُمْ ط

سَنُعَذِّبُهُمْ مَّرَّتَيْنِ ثُمَّ يُرَدُّونَ إِلَى عَذَابٍ عَظِيمٍ ۝

وَّاخَرُونَ اعْتَرَفُوا بِذُنُوبِهِمْ خَلَطُوا عَمَلًا صَالِحًا

وَّاخَرَ سَيِّئًا ط عَسَى اللهُ أَنْ يَّتُوبَ عَلَيْهِمْ ط إِنَّ اللهَ

غَفُورٌ رَّحِيمٌ ۝ خُذْ مِنْ أَمْوَالِهِمْ صَدَقَةً تُطَهِّرُهُمْ

وَتُزَكِّيهِمْ بِهَا وَصَلِّ عَلَيْهِمْ ط إِنَّ صَلَوٰتَكَ سَكَنٌ

لَّهُمْ ط وَاللهُ سَمِيعٌ عَلِيمٌ ۝ أَلَمْ يَعْلَمُوا أَنَّ اللهَ

هُوَ يَقْبَلُ التَّوْبَةَ عَنْ عِبَادِهِ وَيَأْخُذُ الصَّدَقٰتِ

The Prophets' ﷺ *prayer is a source of consolation but pay charity for the privilege.*

385

Many Bedouins remain uncommitted, but others are sincere

[97] Some Bedouins are the worst in terms of disbelief and hypocrisy and are least likely to understand the limits sent by Allah to His Messenger. Allah is Knowing, Wise. [98] Some Bedouins regard charity as a fine, and are waiting for your luck to turn. An evil turn of fortune awaits them. Allah is the Hearer, the Knower. [99] There are other Bedouins who believe in Allah and the Last Day, and regard charity as a means of drawing closer to Allah and gaining the Messenger's blessings.[a] No doubt it is a means of drawing closer. Allah will treat them kindly.[b] Allah is Forgiving, Caring.

Praise of the companions of the Prophet ﷺ

[100] Allah is pleased with those who were the first Migrants and Helpers, and those who followed them in righteousness, they are pleased with Him. He has prepared for them gardens under which rivers flow where they will live forever; that is the greatest victory.

No ethnic group should be stereotyped

[101] Among the Bedouins *who live* around you there are *some* hypocrites, and some people of Madinah are inflexible; you don't know them, but We know them. We will punish them twice and then turn them over to horrendous torment *in the Hereafter.* [102] *Yet* there are others who have confessed their sins, and have mixed good deeds with the bad, *hoping that* Allah may forgive them. Surely, Allah is Forgiving, Kind. [103] Accept charity from their wealth to purify them and to develop them *spiritually*, and pray for them; your prayers are a comfort for them. Allah is the Hearer, the Knower.

Allah forgives those who strive to please Him

[104] Don't they know Allah accepts repentance and charitable donations from His servants? He is the Relenting, the Kind.

---

a   Messengers blessing means His prayers and seeking forgiveness for you.

b   Literally translated as: "enter you in his kindness."

وَاَنَّ اللّٰهَ هُوَ التَّوَّابُ الرَّحِيْمُ ۝ وَقُلِ اعْمَلُوْا

فَسَيَرَى اللّٰهُ عَمَلَكُمْ وَرَسُوْلُهُ وَالْمُؤْمِنُوْنَ ط

وَسَتُرَدُّوْنَ اِلٰى عٰلِمِ الْغَيْبِ وَالشَّهَادَةِ فَيُنَبِّئُكُمْ

بِمَا كُنْتُمْ تَعْمَلُوْنَ ۝ وَاٰخَرُوْنَ مُرْجَوْنَ لِاَمْرِ اللّٰهِ

اِمَّا يُعَذِّبُهُمْ وَاِمَّا يَتُوْبُ عَلَيْهِمْ ط وَاللّٰهُ عَلِيْمٌ

حَكِيْمٌ ۝ وَالَّذِيْنَ اتَّخَذُوْا مَسْجِدًا ضِرَارًا وَّكُفْرًا

وَّتَفْرِيْقًا بَيْنَ الْمُؤْمِنِيْنَ وَاِرْصَادًا لِّمَنْ حَارَبَ

اللّٰهَ وَرَسُوْلَهُ مِنْ قَبْلُ ط وَلَيَحْلِفُنَّ اِنْ اَرَدْنَآ اِلَّا

الْحُسْنٰى ط وَاللّٰهُ يَشْهَدُ اِنَّهُمْ لَكٰذِبُوْنَ ۝ لَا تَقُمْ

Any project that divides the community is condemnable. Work to create unity.

فِيْهِ اَبَدًا ط لَمَسْجِدٌ اُسِّسَ عَلَى التَّقْوٰى مِنْ اَوَّلِ

يَوْمٍ اَحَقُّ اَنْ تَقُوْمَ فِيْهِ ط فِيْهِ رِجَالٌ يُّحِبُّوْنَ اَنْ

يَّتَطَهَّرُوْا ط وَاللّٰهُ يُحِبُّ الْمُطَّهِّرِيْنَ ۝ اَفَمَنْ اَسَّسَ

بُنْيَانَهُ عَلٰى تَقْوٰى مِنَ اللّٰهِ وَرِضْوَانٍ خَيْرٌ اَمْ مَّنْ

اَسَّسَ بُنْيَانَهُ عَلٰى شَفَا جُرُفٍ هَارٍ فَانْهَارَ بِهٖ فِيْ

نَارِ جَهَنَّمَ ط وَاللّٰهُ لَا يَهْدِى الْقَوْمَ الظّٰلِمِيْنَ ۝

لَا يَزَالُ بُنْيَانُهُمُ الَّذِيْ بَنَوْا رِيْبَةً فِيْ قُلُوْبِهِمْ اِلَّآ

اَنْ تَقَطَّعَ قُلُوْبُهُمْ ط وَاللّٰهُ عَلِيْمٌ حَكِيْمٌ ۝ اِنَّ اللّٰهَ

اشْتَرٰى مِنَ الْمُؤْمِنِيْنَ اَنْفُسَهُمْ وَاَمْوَالَهُمْ بِاَنَّ

لَهُمُ الْجَنَّةَ ط يُقَاتِلُوْنَ فِيْ سَبِيْلِ اللّٰهِ فَيَقْتُلُوْنَ وَ

يُقْتَلُوْنَ وَعْدًا عَلَيْهِ حَقًّا فِى التَّوْرٰىةِ وَالْاِنْجِيْلِ

[105] Say: "Keep doing *good deeds*! Allah and His Messenger sees what you do, *so do* the believers. Then you will be returned to the Knower of all that is seen and unseen, and He will inform you of what you used to do." [106] And there are others who are full of hope for Allah's decree, as to whether He will punish or pardon them. Allah is All-Knowing, Wise.

Pray in a Masjid founded on piety

[107] The *hypocrites* who built a Mosque – to incite violence, disbelief and disunity amongst the believers, and as an outpost for those who had previously waged war on Allah and His Messenger – will swear: "We intended good only." Allah bears witness, "They are liars." [108] *So never pray in it. Without a doubt*, it is more fitting by far that you pray in a Mosque founded on piety from the first day *that* deserves to be prayed in. In that *Mosque*, there are men who like to be pure, and Allah loves the pure. [109] Which *of the two* is better: the person who laid his foundations on fear of Allah and *Divine* pleasure; or the one who lays his foundations on the very edge of a crumbling cliff edge, so it tumbles into the fire of Hell, taking him with it? Allah doesn't guide the wicked people. [110] The building they have built will always create doubt in their hearts, unless *they feel* their hearts torn apart *with remorse*.[a] Allah is the Knower, Wise.

What is the price of a believer?

[111] Allah has purchased from the believers their lives and their wealth in exchange for Paradise. They fight in Allah's way, slaying and being slain. This is a valid pledge from Him *recorded* in the Torah, the Gospel and the Quran. And who is more true to his word than Allah? So rejoice at your bargain. This is a mighty victory for

---

[a] Literally, "until their hearts are cut to shreds," a metaphor for regret and repentance.

وَالْقُرْاٰنِ ط وَمَنْ اَوْفٰى بِعَهْدِهٖ مِنَ اللّٰهِ فَاسْتَبْشِرُوْا
بِبَيْعِكُمُ الَّذِىْ بَايَعْتُمْ بِهٖ ط وَذٰلِكَ هُوَ الْفَوْزُ
الْعَظِيْمُ ۝ اَلتَّآئِبُوْنَ الْعٰبِدُوْنَ الْحٰمِدُوْنَ
السَّآئِحُوْنَ الرّٰكِعُوْنَ السّٰجِدُوْنَ الْاٰمِرُوْنَ
بِالْمَعْرُوْفِ وَ النَّاهُوْنَ عَنِ الْمُنْكَرِ وَ الْحٰفِظُوْنَ
لِحُدُوْدِ اللّٰهِ ط وَبَشِّرِ الْمُؤْمِنِيْنَ ۝ مَا كَانَ لِلنَّبِيِّ
وَ الَّذِيْنَ اٰمَنُوْۤا اَنْ يَّسْتَغْفِرُوْا لِلْمُشْرِكِيْنَ وَلَوْ كَانُوْۤا
اُولِىْ قُرْبٰى مِنْ بَعْدِ مَا تَبَيَّنَ لَهُمْ اَنَّهُمْ اَصْحٰبُ
الْجَحِيْمِ ۝ وَمَا كَانَ اسْتِغْفَارُ اِبْرٰهِيْمَ لِاَبِيْهِ اِلَّا
عَنْ مَّوْعِدَةٍ وَّعَدَهَاۤ اِيَّاهُ ۚ فَلَمَّا تَبَيَّنَ لَهٗۤ اَنَّهٗ
عَدُوٌّ لِّلّٰهِ تَبَرَّاَ مِنْهُ ط اِنَّ اِبْرٰهِيْمَ لَاَوَّاهٌ حَلِيْمٌ ۝
وَمَا كَانَ اللّٰهُ لِيُضِلَّ قَوْمًا بَعْدَ اِذْ هَدٰىهُمْ حَتّٰى
يُبَيِّنَ لَهُمْ مَّا يَتَّقُوْنَ ط اِنَّ اللّٰهَ بِكُلِّ شَىْءٍ عَلِيْمٌ ۝
اِنَّ اللّٰهَ لَهٗ مُلْكُ السَّمٰوٰتِ وَالْاَرْضِ ط يُحْىٖ وَيُمِيْتُ ط
وَمَا لَكُمْ مِّنْ دُوْنِ اللّٰهِ مِنْ وَّلِىٍّ وَّلَا نَصِيْرٍ ۝ لَقَدْ
تَّابَ اللّٰهُ عَلَى النَّبِيِّ وَالْمُهٰجِرِيْنَ وَالْاَنْصَارِ الَّذِيْنَ
اتَّبَعُوْهُ فِىْ سَاعَةِ الْعُسْرَةِ مِنْ بَعْدِ مَا كَادَ يَزِيْغُ
قُلُوْبُ فَرِيْقٍ مِّنْهُمْ ثُمَّ تَابَ عَلَيْهِمْ ط اِنَّهٗ بِهِمْ
رَءُوْفٌ رَّحِيْمٌ ۝ وَّعَلَى الثَّلٰثَةِ الَّذِيْنَ خُلِّفُوْا ط
حَتّٰۤى اِذَا ضَاقَتْ عَلَيْهِمُ الْاَرْضُ بِمَا رَحُبَتْ وَضَاقَتْ

Prayer of forgiveness for disbelievers is forbidden. But you can pray for their guidance, well-being and health.

[112] those who repent, worship, praise Allah, fast, bow, prostrate, enjoin good, forbid evil, and stay within the boundaries set by Allah:[a] give glad tidings to *such* believers.

Why Ibrahim sought forgiveness for his father

[113] It is not fitting for the Prophet and the believers to seek forgiveness for idolaters, even if they are close relatives, after it has been made clear to them that they are people of the Blazing Fire. [114] Ibrahim sought forgiveness for his father[b] because of a promise he made to him. However, after it became clear to Ibrahim he was Allah's enemy, he immediately dissociated himself from his father. Ibrahim was soft-hearted and gentle. [115] Allah would not let people go astray after having guided them, not until He has made it absolutely clear to them what they should be mindful of. Allah knows all things. [116] Control of the Heavens and Earth belongs to Allah. He gives life, and He takes it away. You have no protector or helper other than Allah.

Allah accepted the repentance of the three believers

[117] Allah has turned in kindness to the Prophet, the Migrants and the Helpers who stood by him at that time of extreme hardship,[c] after the hearts of a group of them had wavered. Then He forgave them. He was Compassionate and Kind to them. [118] *As for* the three who stayed behind,[d] the Earth seemed to close in on them, despite its vastness, their own souls strangled them, and they realised that the only refuge from Allah lay in *turning to* Him, it was then Allah forgave them because they repented. Allah is acceptor of repentance, the Kind.

---

[a]   Guardians of Allah's boundaries.

[b]   According to some commentators, "his father" refers here metaphorically to Ibrahim's uncle, Azar, and not his biological father. "His father's name was Tharah, and the Prophet ﷺ once said, 'I have been raised among the best in the children of Adam;' it's therefore impossible that any of the ancestors of the Prophet were disbelievers." (Mazhari)

[c]   Literally, "hour of distress or difficulty."

[d]   The phrase "the three who delayed," refers to companions who admitted their mistake of staying behind: Ka'b ibn Malik, Marrah ibn al-Rabi, Hilal ibn Umayyah.

عَلَيْهِمْ اَنْفُسُهُمْ وَظَنُّوٓا اَنْ لَّا مَلْجَاَ مِنَ اللّٰهِ اِلَّآ

اِلَيْهِ ط ثُمَّ تَابَ عَلَيْهِمْ لِيَتُوْبُوْا ط اِنَّ اللّٰهَ هُوَ التَّوَّابُ

الرَّحِيْمُ ۱۱۸ؕ يٰۤاَيُّهَا الَّذِيْنَ اٰمَنُوا اتَّقُوا اللّٰهَ وَكُوْنُوْا

مَعَ الصّٰدِقِيْنَ ۱۱۹ مَا كَانَ لِاَهْلِ الْمَدِيْنَةِ وَمَنْ

حَوْلَهُمْ مِّنَ الْاَعْرَابِ اَنْ يَّتَخَلَّفُوْا عَنْ رَّسُوْلِ اللّٰهِ

وَلَا يَرْغَبُوْا بِاَنْفُسِهِمْ عَنْ نَّفْسِهٖ ط ذٰلِكَ بِاَنَّهُمْ لَا

يُصِيْبُهُمْ ظَمَاٌ وَّلَا نَصَبٌ وَّلَا مَخْمَصَةٌ فِيْ سَبِيْلِ

اللّٰهِ وَلَا يَطَـٔوْنَ مَوْطِئًا يَّغِيْظُ الْكُفَّارَ وَلَا يَنَالُوْنَ

مِنْ عَدُوٍّ نَّيْلًا اِلَّا كُتِبَ لَهُمْ بِهٖ عَمَلٌ صَالِحٌ ط اِنَّ

اللّٰهَ لَا يُضِيْعُ اَجْرَ الْمُحْسِنِيْنَ ۱۲۰ وَلَا يُنْفِقُوْنَ نَفَقَةً

صَغِيْرَةً وَّلَا كَبِيْرَةً وَّلَا يَقْطَعُوْنَ وَادِيًا اِلَّا كُتِبَ

لَهُمْ لِيَجْزِيَهُمُ اللّٰهُ اَحْسَنَ مَا كَانُوْا يَعْمَلُوْنَ ۱۲۱ وَمَا

كَانَ الْمُؤْمِنُوْنَ لِيَنْفِرُوْا كَآفَّةً ط فَلَوْ لَا نَفَرَ مِنْ كُلِّ

فِرْقَةٍ مِّنْهُمْ طَآئِفَةٌ لِّيَتَفَقَّهُوْا فِي الدِّيْنِ وَلِيُنْذِرُوْا

قَوْمَهُمْ اِذَا رَجَعُوٓا اِلَيْهِمْ لَعَلَّهُمْ يَحْذَرُوْنَ ۱۲۲

يٰۤاَيُّهَا الَّذِيْنَ اٰمَنُوْا قَاتِلُوا الَّذِيْنَ يَلُوْنَكُمْ مِّنَ

الْكُفَّارِ وَلْيَجِدُوْا فِيْكُمْ غِلْظَةً ط وَاعْلَمُوٓا اَنَّ اللّٰهَ

مَعَ الْمُتَّقِيْنَ ۱۲۳ وَاِذَا مَآ اُنْزِلَتْ سُوْرَةٌ فَمِنْهُمْ مَّنْ

يَّقُوْلُ اَيُّكُمْ زَادَتْهُ هٰذِهٖٓ اِيْمَانًا ۚ فَاَمَّا الَّذِيْنَ

اٰمَنُوْا فَزَادَتْهُمْ اِيْمَانًا وَّهُمْ يَسْتَبْشِرُوْنَ ۱۲۴ وَاَمَّا

A group of dedicated people for learning and teaching is a mark of religious community.

None of our good deeds shall ever go to waste

[119] Believers, fear Allah and stand firmly with the truthful. [120] It was not fitting for the people of Madinah and the surrounding Bedouins to stay behind *instead of marching with* Allah's Messenger, nor *was it fitting* to prefer their lives over his; that is because whatever thirst, suffering or hunger they endure in Allah's way, whatever path they tread to the fury of the disbelievers, and whatever advantage they gain over an enemy, it is recorded for them as a good deed. Allah doesn't waste the reward of the righteous. [121] Whatever amount they spend, large or small, and whatever valley they cross, it's all written down for them, Allah will reward them for the finest things they did.

The community should invest in religious learning

[122] It isn't right all the believers mobilise for *fighting*; rather a group from each community should stay behind and apply themselves to thorough understanding of the religion to warn their people on their return to them, so that they *too* might be mindful.

Disbelievers would rather mock others than reflect

[123] Believers, fight the disbelievers who are nearest to you.[a] Let them find you tough. Know Allah is with the pious. [124] Whenever a surat is revealed, some ask: "Whose faith has been increased by this?" Those who believe, their faith has certainly increased, and they rejoice.

---

[a] Those who fight you, since the Quran only allows war in self-defence

الَّذِيْنَ فِيْ قُلُوْبِهِمْ مَّرَضٌ فَزَادَتْهُمْ رِجْسًا اِلٰى

رِجْسِهِمْ وَمَاتُوْا وَهُمْ كٰفِرُوْنَ ۝ اَوَلَا يَرَوْنَ

اَنَّهُمْ يُفْتَنُوْنَ فِيْ كُلِّ عَامٍ مَّرَّةً اَوْ مَرَّتَيْنِ ثُمَّ لَا

يَتُوْبُوْنَ وَلَا هُمْ يَذَّكَّرُوْنَ ۝ وَاِذَا مَاۤ اُنْزِلَتْ سُوْرَةٌ

نَّظَرَ بَعْضُهُمْ اِلٰى بَعْضٍ ۚ هَلْ يَرٰىكُمْ مِّنْ اَحَدٍ

ثُمَّ انْصَرَفُوْا ۚ صَرَفَ اللّٰهُ قُلُوْبَهُمْ بِاَنَّهُمْ قَوْمٌ لَّا

يَفْقَهُوْنَ ۝ لَقَدْ جَآءَكُمْ رَسُوْلٌ مِّنْ اَنْفُسِكُمْ عَزِيْزٌ

عَلَيْهِ مَا عَنِتُّمْ حَرِيْصٌ عَلَيْكُمْ بِالْمُؤْمِنِيْنَ رَءُوْفٌ

رَّحِيْمٌ ۝ فَاِنْ تَوَلَّوْا فَقُلْ حَسْبِيَ اللّٰهُ ۖ لَاۤ اِلٰهَ اِلَّا

هُوَ ۖ عَلَيْهِ تَوَكَّلْتُ وَهُوَ رَبُّ الْعَرْشِ الْعَظِيْمِ ۝

The Messenger ﷺ cares for our welfare and well-being. What do we do for his mission?

[125] But those whose hearts are diseased become more and more sick, and will die disbelievers. [126] Don't they realise once or twice a year they are tested, but they don't repent or pay attention. [127] Whenever a surat is revealed, they look at each other, saying, "Is anyone watching you?" Then they slip away. Allah has turned their hearts away *from truth* because they are people who *simply* do not understand.

The blessing of a Messenger ﷺ who understands and cares for the believers

[128] A *noble* Messenger has come to you from among yourselves. He's grieved by your hardships and cares about your well-being, for the believers he is compassionate and kind. [129] So if they *choose to* turn away, tell them: "Allah is sufficient for me, there is no god but Him. I have put my trust in Him, the Lord of the mighty throne."

10. Surat Yunus

The Prophet Yunus

This is a late Makkan surat, revealed possibly a year before the Hijrah in 622 CE. This is the first of the six surats named after a prophet; the others are: Hud, Yusuf, Ibrahim, Muhammad and Nuh. The surat opens by asking why people are surprised that Allah sent the revelation to a human being. This is followed by verses in which Allah is introduced as the Creator of the universe: the sun and the moon, that establish daily cycles of night and day on Earth, all for a purpose.

The central theme of the surat is the truthfulness of the Majestic Quran. The Makkans demanded that the Quran be changed because it criticised their false beliefs and bogus religious practices, the reply was: "Who ... is a greater wrongdoer than the one who makes up lies about Allah or who denies His verses? Certainly, evildoers will not succeed" (17). When they accused the Messenger ﷺ of making it up, the Prophet ﷺ was told to ask them: "Produce a single chapter like it, then call on whomever you can besides Allah to act as a witness, if you are telling the truth" (38). The significance of the Quran lies in its life-changing teachings and its solution to human misery caused by lack of morality: "People, your Lord's teachings have come to you; they're a healing balm for the diseases of the heart, and guidance and goodwill for the believers" (57). When the Prophet ﷺ is accused of writing the Quran himself, the answer is they are being deaf, dumb and blind (42–43). The past generations of disbelievers were severely punished, the Quran warns, so beware that you could be next.

The human habit of turning to Allah in time of hardship is cited as a proof of "the inbuilt faith in Allah." At times of need humans, believers or disbelievers, instinctively tend to turn to Allah, but as soon as the hardship is removed they return to their old ways. The Quran warns against this ungrateful attitude: "People, your disrespect weighs against you" (23). What is the reality of idols? They are "imagined gods," (30) and they are totally helpless and powerless of doing anything: "Say: Can any of your idols begin the Creation and then restore it?" (34). If they can't then why don't they turn to Allah? The stories of prophets Nuh, Musa and Yunus are given as examples of past nations that refused to listen to their prophets. Each of them perished, so "listen or else" the Makkans are warned. Even the most arrogant and stubborn disbeliever, like the Pharaoh, eventually submitted when drowning. However, his repentance was not accepted as it was too late (90). The story of the titular character; Yunus is given as an example of people who repented.

The short passage from 61 to 63 vividly describes the qualities of Allah's friends: people with unshakable faith, righteous deeds, and mindful of their duties towards Allah. The surat ends with a persuasive instruction: religion is a serious commitment to Allah: "I was ordered to be a believer and told, 'Keep your face *directed* towards the *true* religion, in tune with your nature, and don't be an idolater'" (104–105).

Nature is an open book, full of signs like the scripture. Can you read them both?

بِسْمِ اللهِ الرَّحْمٰنِ الرَّحِيْمِ

الٓرٰ ۚ تِلْكَ اٰيٰتُ الْكِتٰبِ الْحَكِيْمِ ۞ اَكَانَ لِلنَّاسِ عَجَبًا اَنْ اَوْحَيْنَا اِلٰى رَجُلٍ مِّنْهُمْ اَنْ اَنْذِرِ النَّاسَ وَبَشِّرِ الَّذِيْنَ اٰمَنُوْۤا اَنَّ لَهُمْ قَدَمَ صِدْقٍ عِنْدَ رَبِّهِمْ ۗ قَالَ الْكٰفِرُوْنَ اِنَّ هٰذَا لَسٰحِرٌ مُّبِيْنٌ ۞ اِنَّ رَبَّكُمُ اللهُ الَّذِيْ خَلَقَ السَّمٰوٰتِ وَالْاَرْضَ فِيْ سِتَّةِ اَيَّامٍ ثُمَّ اسْتَوٰى عَلَى الْعَرْشِ يُدَبِّرُ الْاَمْرَ ۗ مَا مِنْ شَفِيْعٍ اِلَّا مِنْۢ بَعْدِ اِذْنِهٖ ۗ ذٰلِكُمُ اللهُ رَبُّكُمْ فَاعْبُدُوْهُ اَفَلَا تَذَكَّرُوْنَ ۞ اِلَيْهِ مَرْجِعُكُمْ جَمِيْعًا ۗ وَعْدَ اللهِ حَقًّا ۗ اِنَّهٗ يَبْدَؤُا الْخَلْقَ ثُمَّ يُعِيْدُهٗ لِيَجْزِىَ الَّذِيْنَ اٰمَنُوْا وَعَمِلُوا الصّٰلِحٰتِ بِالْقِسْطِ ۗ وَالَّذِيْنَ كَفَرُوْا لَهُمْ شَرَابٌ مِّنْ حَمِيْمٍ وَّعَذَابٌ اَلِيْمٌۢ بِمَا كَانُوْا يَكْفُرُوْنَ ۞ هُوَ الَّذِيْ جَعَلَ الشَّمْسَ ضِيَآءً وَّالْقَمَرَ نُوْرًا وَّقَدَّرَهٗ مَنَازِلَ لِتَعْلَمُوْا عَدَدَ السِّنِيْنَ وَ الْحِسَابَ ۗ مَا خَلَقَ اللهُ ذٰلِكَ اِلَّا بِالْحَقِّ ۚ يُفَصِّلُ الْاٰيٰتِ لِقَوْمٍ يَّعْلَمُوْنَ ۞ اِنَّ فِى اخْتِلَافِ الَّيْلِ وَالنَّهَارِ وَمَا خَلَقَ اللهُ فِى السَّمٰوٰتِ وَالْاَرْضِ لَاٰيٰتٍ لِّقَوْمٍ يَّتَّقُوْنَ ۞ اِنَّ الَّذِيْنَ لَا يَرْجُوْنَ لِقَآءَنَا وَرَضُوْا بِالْحَيٰوةِ الدُّنْيَا وَاطْمَاَنُّوْا بِهَا وَالَّذِيْنَ هُمْ عَنْ اٰيٰتِنَا

397

In the name of Allah, the Kind, the Caring.

[1] *Alif Lam Ra'.*

The Quran holds wisdom
These are the verses of the Book full of wisdom. [2] Are people surprised We revealed to one of their men: "Warn the people, and give good news to the believers that they are on sure footing with their Lord"? The disbelievers say, "He's clearly a magician."

Allah has created everything for a purpose
[3] Allah is Your Lord, He created *the* Heavens and the Earth in six days then established Himself on the throne *as befits Him*, overseeing the running *of the entire universe*. No one can intercede without His permission: such is Allah, your Lord, so worship Him. Won't you pay attention? [4] You will return to Him. Allah's promise is true. He initiates *the process of* creation and *after its death will* restore it, to reward fairly the believers and those who performed righteous deeds. But the disbelievers will have scalding water to drink and a painful punishment because of what they denied. [5] He gave the sun *its* radiant glow and the moon *its* light, He determined their phases precisely, so you might calculate the *passing* years and keep time. Allah created *this* for a purpose; so people of knowledge can understand the signs *of creation*. [6] In the rotation of day and night, and in the creation of the Heavens and the Earth, there are signs for people who are mindful.

The value of faith
[7] Those who don't expect to meet Us, are pleased with worldly life, feel at ease and have chosen to ignore Our signs,

غٰفِلُوْنَ ۞ اُولٰٓئِكَ مَاْوٰىهُمُ النَّارُ بِمَا كَانُوْا يَكْسِبُوْنَ ۞

اِنَّ الَّذِيْنَ اٰمَنُوْا وَعَمِلُوا الصّٰلِحٰتِ يَهْدِيْهِمْ رَبُّهُمْ بِاِيْمَانِهِمْ ۚ تَجْرِيْ مِنْ تَحْتِهِمُ الْاَنْهٰرُ فِيْ جَنّٰتِ النَّعِيْمِ ۞ دَعْوٰىهُمْ فِيْهَا سُبْحٰنَكَ اللّٰهُمَّ وَتَحِيَّتُهُمْ فِيْهَا سَلٰمٌ ۚ وَاٰخِرُ دَعْوٰىهُمْ اَنِ الْحَمْدُ لِلّٰهِ رَبِّ الْعٰلَمِيْنَ ۞ وَلَوْ يُعَجِّلُ اللّٰهُ لِلنَّاسِ الشَّرَّ اسْتِعْجَالَهُمْ بِالْخَيْرِ لَقُضِيَ اِلَيْهِمْ اَجَلُهُمْ ۗ فَنَذَرُ الَّذِيْنَ لَا يَرْجُوْنَ لِقَآءَنَا فِيْ طُغْيَانِهِمْ يَعْمَهُوْنَ ۞ وَاِذَا مَسَّ الْاِنْسَانَ الضُّرُّ دَعَانَا لِجَنْبِهٖٓ اَوْ قَاعِدًا اَوْ قَآئِمًا ۚ فَلَمَّا كَشَفْنَا عَنْهُ ضُرَّهٗ مَرَّ كَاَنْ لَّمْ يَدْعُنَآ اِلٰى ضُرٍّ مَّسَّهٗ ۗ كَذٰلِكَ زُيِّنَ لِلْمُسْرِفِيْنَ مَا كَانُوْا يَعْمَلُوْنَ ۞ وَلَقَدْ اَهْلَكْنَا الْقُرُوْنَ مِنْ قَبْلِكُمْ لَمَّا ظَلَمُوْا ۙ وَجَآءَتْهُمْ رُسُلُهُمْ بِالْبَيِّنٰتِ وَمَا كَانُوْا لِيُؤْمِنُوْا ۗ كَذٰلِكَ نَجْزِى الْقَوْمَ الْمُجْرِمِيْنَ ۞ ثُمَّ جَعَلْنٰكُمْ خَلٰٓئِفَ فِي الْاَرْضِ مِنْ بَعْدِهِمْ لِنَنْظُرَ كَيْفَ تَعْمَلُوْنَ ۞ وَاِذَا تُتْلٰى عَلَيْهِمْ اٰيَاتُنَا بَيِّنٰتٍ ۙ قَالَ الَّذِيْنَ لَا يَرْجُوْنَ لِقَآءَنَا ائْتِ بِقُرْاٰنٍ غَيْرِ هٰذَآ اَوْ بَدِّلْهُ ۗ قُلْ مَا يَكُوْنُ لِيْٓ اَنْ اُبَدِّلَهٗ مِنْ تِلْقَآئِ نَفْسِيْ ۚ اِنْ اَتَّبِعُ اِلَّا مَا يُوْحٰٓى اِلَيَّ ۚ اِنِّيْٓ اَخَافُ اِنْ عَصَيْتُ رَبِّيْ عَذَابَ يَوْمٍ عَظِيْمٍ ۞ قُلْ لَّوْ شَآءَ

When in trouble, everyone turns to the Almighty Creator. Do you recall when you called on him?

399

[8]their final home shall be the Fire, a consequence of their activities. [9]Those who believed and did righteous deeds, their Lord will guide them by strengthening their faith, *and lead them* to the gardens of delight beneath *which* rivers flow. [10]Here their prayer will be, "Glory to you, Allah!" And their greeting will be, "Peace," and the closing prayer will be, "Praise be to Allah, Lord of *all* realms."

Allah delays passing judgement; He gives people time

[11]If Allah were hasty in punishing people as they would hasten their reward, their fate would have been sealed, so We leave those who do not expect to meet Us to wander aimlessly in their disobedience. [12]Whenever troubles distress a person, he prays to Us sitting, standing or *lying down* on his side; *but* as soon as We remove *the cause of* his hardship, he carries on as though he had never prayed to Us to *ease* his hardship. That is how their activities appear attractive to the extravagant. [13]We destroyed *many* generations before you when they did wrong, and messengers came with clear signs to them, but *still* they didn't believe. That's how We deal with sinful people. [14]Then afterwards, We made you successors in the land, so We could see how you would behave.

The Prophet ﷺ can't change the Quran

[15]Whenever Our verses are recited, those who don't expect to meet Us say, "Bring us a Quran other than this one, or else alter it." Say: "It is not for me to change it by myself. I follow what is revealed to me; *and* I fear the torment of an overwhelming day, if I disobey My Lord."

اللهُ مَا تَلَوْتُهٗ عَلَيْكُمْ وَلَاۤ اَدْرٰىكُمْ بِهٖ ۫ فَقَدْ

لَبِثْتُ فِيْكُمْ عُمُرًا مِّنْ قَبْلِهٖ ؕ اَفَلَا تَعْقِلُوْنَ ۝ فَمَنْ

اَظْلَمُ مِمَّنِ افْتَرٰى عَلَى اللهِ كَذِبًا اَوْ كَذَّبَ بِاٰيٰتِهٖ ؕ

اِنَّهٗ لَا يُفْلِحُ الْمُجْرِمُوْنَ ۝ وَيَعْبُدُوْنَ مِنْ دُوْنِ

اللهِ مَا لَا يَضُرُّهُمْ وَلَا يَنْفَعُهُمْ وَيَقُوْلُوْنَ هٰۤؤُلَاءِ

شُفَعَاؤُنَا عِنْدَ اللهِ ؕ قُلْ اَتُنَبِّئُوْنَ اللهَ بِمَا لَا

يَعْلَمُ فِي السَّمٰوٰتِ وَلَا فِي الْاَرْضِ ؕ سُبْحٰنَهٗ وَتَعٰلٰى

عَمَّا يُشْرِكُوْنَ ۝ وَمَا كَانَ النَّاسُ اِلَّاۤ اُمَّةً وَّاحِدَةً

فَاخْتَلَفُوْا ؕ وَلَوْلَا كَلِمَةٌ سَبَقَتْ مِنْ رَّبِّكَ لَقُضِيَ

بَيْنَهُمْ فِيْمَا فِيْهِ يَخْتَلِفُوْنَ ۝ وَيَقُوْلُوْنَ لَوْلَاۤ

اُنْزِلَ عَلَيْهِ اٰيَةٌ مِّنْ رَّبِّهٖ ۚ فَقُلْ اِنَّمَا الْغَيْبُ

لِلّٰهِ فَانْتَظِرُوْا ۚ اِنِّيْ مَعَكُمْ مِّنَ الْمُنْتَظِرِيْنَ ۝

وَاِذَاۤ اَذَقْنَا النَّاسَ رَحْمَةً مِّنْ بَعْدِ ضَرَّاءَ مَسَّتْهُمْ

اِذَا لَهُمْ مَّكْرٌ فِيْۤ اٰيَاتِنَا ؕ قُلِ اللهُ اَسْرَعُ مَكْرًا ؕ

اِنَّ رُسُلَنَا يَكْتُبُوْنَ مَا تَمْكُرُوْنَ ۝ هُوَ الَّذِيْ

يُسَيِّرُكُمْ فِي الْبَرِّ وَالْبَحْرِ ؕ حَتّٰۤى اِذَا كُنْتُمْ فِي

الْفُلْكِ ۚ وَجَرَيْنَ بِهِمْ بِرِيْحٍ طَيِّبَةٍ وَّفَرِحُوْا بِهَا

جَاءَتْهَا رِيْحٌ عَاصِفٌ وَّجَاءَهُمُ الْمَوْجُ مِنْ كُلِّ

مَكَانٍ وَّظَنُّوْۤا اَنَّهُمْ اُحِيْطَ بِهِمْ ۙ دَعَوُا اللهَ مُخْلِصِيْنَ

لَهُ الدِّيْنَ ۚ۬ لَئِنْ اَنْجَيْتَنَا مِنْ هٰذِهٖ لَنَكُوْنَنَّ مِنَ

Even the sceptics, the doubters when in trouble turn to Allah.

401

¹⁶ Say: "If Allah wanted, I would not have recited it to you, nor would He have informed you of it. I spent my entire life among you before it *was revealed*. Can you not think *it through*?" ¹⁷ Who then is a greater wrongdoer than the one who makes up lies about Allah or who denies His verses? Certainly, evildoers will not succeed. ¹⁸ Yet they worship besides Allah *idols* which can't harm or benefit them, and they say, "These are our intercessors with Allah." Say: "Are you informing Allah of what He doesn't know in *the* Heavens and the Earth?" Glory be to Him! He is exalted above *all* they associate *with Him*.

People's differences are part of Allah's plan

¹⁹ At one time *all* people were a single community, then they started to disagree, and if it had not been for an earlier decree of Your Lord, the differences between them would have been settled long ago. ²⁰ They say, "If only a sign would come down to him from his Lord," Say: "The unseen belongs to Allah alone. So, wait *for that sign*, and I shall be waiting with you."

Faith is deep-rooted in humans

²¹ When We let people enjoy Our kindness following a hard time they plot to cover up Our goodness. Say: "Allah is the swiftest planner." Our messenger *angels* record all you're plotting. ²² He lets you travel by land and sea, and when you are on board a ship, sailing happily along with a favourable wind, *then* suddenly a gale wind blows with waves from every direction and they realise they are trapped; *at that moment* they pray to Allah, sincerely and faithfully: "If You save us from this, we will be *forever* grateful."

الشَّاكِرِينَ ۞ فَلَمَّا اَنْجهُمْ اِذَا هُمْ يَبْغُونَ فِى الْاَرْضِ

بِغَيْرِ الْحَقِّ ۚ يٰٓاَيُّهَا النَّاسُ اِنَّمَا بَغْيُكُمْ عَلٰٓى اَنْفُسِكُمْ

مَّتَاعَ الْحَيٰوةِ الدُّنْيَا ۖ ثُمَّ اِلَيْنَا مَرْجِعُكُمْ فَنُنَبِّئُكُمْ

بِمَا كُنْتُمْ تَعْمَلُونَ ۞ اِنَّمَا مَثَلُ الْحَيٰوةِ الدُّنْيَا

كَمَآءٍ اَنْزَلْنٰهُ مِنَ السَّمَآءِ فَاخْتَلَطَ بِهٖ نَبَاتُ

الْاَرْضِ مِمَّا يَاْكُلُ النَّاسُ وَالْاَنْعَامُ ۖ حَتّٰى اِذَآ

اَخَذَتِ الْاَرْضُ زُخْرُفَهَا وَازَّيَّنَتْ وَظَنَّ اَهْلُهَآ

اَنَّهُمْ قٰدِرُونَ عَلَيْهَآ ۙ اَتٰىهَآ اَمْرُنَا لَيْلًا اَوْ نَهَارًا

فَجَعَلْنٰهَا حَصِيْدًا كَاَنْ لَّمْ تَغْنَ بِالْاَمْسِ ۚ كَذٰلِكَ

نُفَصِّلُ الْاٰيٰتِ لِقَوْمٍ يَّتَفَكَّرُونَ ۞ وَاللّٰهُ يَدْعُوٓا

اِلٰى دَارِ السَّلٰمِ ۚ وَيَهْدِىْ مَنْ يَّشَآءُ اِلٰى صِرَاطٍ

مُّسْتَقِيْمٍ ۞ لِلَّذِيْنَ اَحْسَنُوا الْحُسْنٰى وَزِيَادَةٌ ۖ وَلَا

يَرْهَقُ وُجُوْهَهُمْ قَتَرٌ وَّلَا ذِلَّةٌ ۚ اُولٰٓئِكَ اَصْحٰبُ

الْجَنَّةِ ۚ هُمْ فِيْهَا خٰلِدُونَ ۞ وَالَّذِيْنَ كَسَبُوا السَّيِّاٰتِ

جَزَآءُ سَيِّئَةٍ بِمِثْلِهَا ۙ وَتَرْهَقُهُمْ ذِلَّةٌ ۚ مَا لَهُمْ

مِّنَ اللّٰهِ مِنْ عَاصِمٍ ۚ كَاَنَّمَآ اُغْشِيَتْ وُجُوْهُهُمْ قِطَعًا

مِّنَ الَّيْلِ مُظْلِمًا ۚ اُولٰٓئِكَ اَصْحٰبُ النَّارِ ۚ هُمْ فِيْهَا

خٰلِدُونَ ۞ وَيَوْمَ نَحْشُرُهُمْ جَمِيْعًا ثُمَّ نَقُوْلُ لِلَّذِيْنَ

اَشْرَكُوْا مَكَانَكُمْ اَنْتُمْ وَشُرَكَآؤُكُمْ ۚ فَزَيَّلْنَا بَيْنَهُمْ

وَقَالَ شُرَكَآؤُهُمْ مَّا كُنْتُمْ اِيَّانَا تَعْبُدُونَ ۞ فَكَفٰى

The fleeting, facile, and superficial nature of worldly life, yet we indulge in it as though it is permanent.

403

²³ However, no sooner does He rescue them then, unashamedly, they are disrespectful throughout the land. People, your disrespect will only count against you – *How brief is* the enjoyment of this worldly life! – You will return to Us, and We shall inform you what you did.

The parable of withered crops represents Earthly life

²⁴ This worldly life is like the water We send down from the sky, it soaks the soil and the plants, which are eaten by the people and livestock. *They grow* until the land takes on beautiful colours and appears attractive, and its owners think they have control over it, *then* Our command comes, at night or by day, and We leave it looking like stubble *after the harvest*, as though it never existed a day earlier. This is how We explain the signs for people who reflect. ²⁵ Allah calls *people* to the home of *Heavenly* peace, and He guides the one who pleases Him along a straight path. ²⁶ For those who are righteous, there will be an excellent reward and more beside; neither dust nor disgrace will stain their faces, such people will be the companions of Paradise, living there forever.

The idols are nonentities

²⁷ The wrongdoers will get a matching reward; disgrace will stain them, and they will have no one to protect them from Allah's *punishment*. As though their faces are masked bit by bit with the *pitch* darkness of night. Such people will be the companions of the Fire, living there forever. ²⁸ The day We gather them together, We will say to idolaters, "*This* place is for you and your partners." Then We shall separate them, and their partners will say, "You didn't worship us,

بِاللّٰهِ شَهِيْدًا بَيْنَنَا وَبَيْنَكُمْ اِنْ كُنَّا عَنْ عِبَادَتِكُمْ

لَغٰفِلِيْنَ ۲۹ هُنَالِكَ تَبْلُوْا كُلُّ نَفْسٍ مَّا اَسْلَفَتْ وَ

رُدُّوْا اِلَى اللّٰهِ مَوْلٰىهُمُ الْحَقِّ وَضَلَّ عَنْهُمْ مَّا

كَانُوْا يَفْتَرُوْنَ ۳۰ قُلْ مَنْ يَّرْزُقُكُمْ مِّنَ السَّمَآءِ

وَالْاَرْضِ اَمَّنْ يَّمْلِكُ السَّمْعَ وَالْاَبْصَارَ وَمَنْ

يُّخْرِجُ الْحَيَّ مِنَ الْمَيِّتِ وَيُخْرِجُ الْمَيِّتَ مِنَ

الْحَيِّ وَمَنْ يُّدَبِّرُ الْاَمْرَ فَسَيَقُوْلُوْنَ اللّٰهُ فَقُلْ اَفَلَا

تَتَّقُوْنَ ۳۱ فَذٰلِكُمُ اللّٰهُ رَبُّكُمُ الْحَقُّ فَمَا ذَا بَعْدَ

الْحَقِّ اِلَّا الضَّلٰلُ فَاَنّٰى تُصْرَفُوْنَ ۳۲ كَذٰلِكَ حَقَّتْ

كَلِمَتُ رَبِّكَ عَلَى الَّذِيْنَ فَسَقُوْا اَنَّهُمْ لَا يُؤْمِنُوْنَ ۳۳

قُلْ هَلْ مِنْ شُرَكَآئِكُمْ مَّنْ يَّبْدَؤُا الْخَلْقَ ثُمَّ

يُعِيْدُهٗ قُلِ اللّٰهُ يَبْدَؤُا الْخَلْقَ ثُمَّ يُعِيْدُهٗ فَاَنّٰى

تُؤْفَكُوْنَ ۳۴ قُلْ هَلْ مِنْ شُرَكَآئِكُمْ مَّنْ يَّهْدِيْ اِلَى

الْحَقِّ قُلِ اللّٰهُ يَهْدِيْ لِلْحَقِّ اَفَمَنْ يَّهْدِيْ اِلَى

الْحَقِّ اَحَقُّ اَنْ يُّتَّبَعَ اَمَّنْ لَّا يَهِدِّيْ اِلَّا اَنْ يُّهْدٰى

فَمَا لَكُمْ كَيْفَ تَحْكُمُوْنَ ۳۵ وَمَا يَتَّبِعُ اَكْثَرُهُمْ اِلَّا

ظَنًّا اِنَّ الظَّنَّ لَا يُغْنِيْ مِنَ الْحَقِّ شَيْئًا اِنَّ اللّٰهَ

عَلِيْمٌ بِمَا يَفْعَلُوْنَ ۳۶ وَمَا كَانَ هٰذَا الْقُرْاٰنُ اَنْ

يُّفْتَرٰى مِنْ دُوْنِ اللّٰهِ وَلٰكِنْ تَصْدِيْقَ الَّذِيْ بَيْنَ

يَدَيْهِ وَتَفْصِيْلَ الْكِتٰبِ لَا رَيْبَ فِيْهِ مِنْ رَّبِّ

The Quran presents absolute truth. The rest, including scientific knowledge, are guesswork.

²⁹ Allah is sufficient as a witness between us and you, we were unaware of your worship." ³⁰ There, every soul will *be forced to* confront what it did in the past as they are returned to Allah, their true Master, all *the idols* they devised will desert them.

The ineffectiveness of idols

³¹ Say: "Who provides for you from the Heavens and Earth, and Who has the power of *granting* hearing and sight? And Who brings forth the living from the dead and the dead from the living? And Who oversees the running *of the entire universe?*" "Allah!" They will say. So, say: "Won't you be mindful *of Him?* ³² Such is Allah, your true Lord. And, beyond truth, what is there except falsehood? So where else can you turn?" ³³ This is how your Lord's statement against the evildoers has been justified, that they don't believe. ³⁴ Say: "Has any of your partners initiated *the process of* creation and will then restore it *to its original state?*" Tell them: "It is Allah Who initiates creation and then restores it. Why then are you telling lies?" ³⁵ Say: "Does any of your partners guide to the truth?" Say: "Only Allah guides to the truth. So isn't He deserving to be followed or is it the one who can't act as a guide unless he is guided? So, what's the matter with you, that you make *such* decisions?"

The sceptics are challenged to produce a book like the Quran

³⁶ Most of them are simply speculating, but speculation is no substitute for the truth. Allah knows well what they do. ³⁷ This Quran could not have been invented independently of Allah; rather it confirms what came before it and is an explanation of *that* Book in which there is no doubt, which is from the Lord of the universe.

الْعٰلَمِيْنَ ۞ اَمْ يَقُوْلُوْنَ افْتَرٰىهُ ۗ قُلْ فَاْتُوْا بِسُوْرَةٍ

مِّثْلِهٖ وَادْعُوْا مَنِ اسْتَطَعْتُمْ مِّنْ دُوْنِ اللّٰهِ اِنْ

كُنْتُمْ صٰدِقِيْنَ ۞ بَلْ كَذَّبُوْا بِمَا لَمْ يُحِيْطُوْا بِعِلْمِهٖ

وَلَمَّا يَاْتِهِمْ تَاْوِيْلُهٗ ۗ كَذٰلِكَ كَذَّبَ الَّذِيْنَ مِنْ

قَبْلِهِمْ فَانْظُرْ كَيْفَ كَانَ عَاقِبَةُ الظّٰلِمِيْنَ ۞

وَمِنْهُمْ مَّنْ يُّؤْمِنُ بِهٖ وَمِنْهُمْ مَّنْ لَّا يُؤْمِنُ بِهٖ ۗ

وَرَبُّكَ اَعْلَمُ بِالْمُفْسِدِيْنَ ۞ وَاِنْ كَذَّبُوْكَ فَقُلْ لِّيْ

عَمَلِيْ وَلَكُمْ عَمَلُكُمْ ۚ اَنْتُمْ بَرِيْـُٔوْنَ مِمَّآ اَعْمَلُ

وَاَنَا بَرِيْٓءٌ مِّمَّا تَعْمَلُوْنَ ۞ وَمِنْهُمْ مَّنْ يَّسْتَمِعُوْنَ

اِلَيْكَ ۗ اَفَاَنْتَ تُسْمِعُ الصُّمَّ وَلَوْ كَانُوْا لَا

يَعْقِلُوْنَ ۞ وَمِنْهُمْ مَّنْ يَّنْظُرُ اِلَيْكَ ۗ اَفَاَنْتَ تَهْدِى

الْعُمْىَ وَلَوْ كَانُوْا لَا يُبْصِرُوْنَ ۞ اِنَّ اللّٰهَ لَا يَظْلِمُ

النَّاسَ شَيْـًٔا وَّلٰكِنَّ النَّاسَ اَنْفُسَهُمْ يَظْلِمُوْنَ ۞

وَيَوْمَ يَحْشُرُهُمْ كَاَنْ لَّمْ يَلْبَثُوْٓا اِلَّا سَاعَةً مِّنَ

النَّهَارِ يَتَعَارَفُوْنَ بَيْنَهُمْ ۗ قَدْ خَسِرَ الَّذِيْنَ كَذَّبُوْا

بِلِقَآءِ اللّٰهِ وَمَا كَانُوْا مُهْتَدِيْنَ ۞ وَاِمَّا نُرِيَنَّكَ

بَعْضَ الَّذِيْ نَعِدُهُمْ اَوْ نَتَوَفَّيَنَّكَ فَاِلَيْنَا مَرْجِعُهُمْ

ثُمَّ اللّٰهُ شَهِيْدٌ عَلٰى مَا يَفْعَلُوْنَ ۞ وَلِكُلِّ اُمَّةٍ

رَّسُوْلٌ ۚ فَاِذَا جَآءَ رَسُوْلُهُمْ قُضِيَ بَيْنَهُمْ بِالْقِسْطِ

وَهُمْ لَا يُظْلَمُوْنَ ۞ وَيَقُوْلُوْنَ مَتٰى هٰذَا الْوَعْدُ

The Messenger delivers the message. You must read, understand and act on it.

407

[38] Or do they say, "He has invented it"? *If so*, say: "Produce a *single* chapter like it, then call on anyone you can besides Allah *to act as a witness*, if you are telling the truth." [39] Rather they deny that which they lack the knowledge to understand, and whose interpretation has yet to reach them. That is exactly how those before them used to *falsely* deny, so wait and see what the outcome will be for the wrongdoers. [40] Some believe in it, but others don't; Your Lord is aware of the immoral crooks.

Human free will: everyone is responsible for their actions

[41] If they deny you, say: "For me, my deeds and for you yours! You are innocent of what I do, *just as* I am innocent of what you do." [42] Some of them pretend to listen to you. Can you make the deaf hear? Especially those who don't think? [43] Some of them look at you but how can you guide the blind, since they can't see? [44] Allah doesn't wrong people in any way; rather it is they who wrong themselves. [45] On the day when He gathers them, and as they recognise each other, it will be as though they had lingered *no more than* a daylight hour. Those who denied they would meet Allah will *find out they* have lost *everything* and were not *at all* guided. [46] Whether We show you *in advance* something of what We have threatened them with, or whether We cause you to die *first*, they will return to Us; Allah is a witness of all they do.

Lifespan is unchangeable

[47] Every community had a messenger; and when their messenger came, justice was done *and no one* was wronged. [48] And they say, "When is this promise *to be fulfilled*, if you are truthful?"

اِنْ كُنْتُمْ صٰدِقِيْنَ ۝ قُلْ لَّاۤ اَمْلِكُ لِنَفْسِيْ ضَرًّا

وَّلَا نَفْعًا اِلَّا مَا شَآءَ اللّٰهُ ط لِكُلِّ اُمَّةٍ اَجَلٌ ط

اِذَا جَآءَ اَجَلُهُمْ فَلَا يَسْتَأْخِرُوْنَ سَاعَةً وَّلَا

يَسْتَقْدِمُوْنَ ۝ قُلْ اَرَءَيْتُمْ اِنْ اَتٰىكُمْ عَذَابُهٗ

بَيَاتًا اَوْ نَهَارًا مَّا ذَا يَسْتَعْجِلُ مِنْهُ الْمُجْرِمُوْنَ ۝

اَثُمَّ اِذَا مَا وَقَعَ اٰمَنْتُمْ بِهٖ ط آلْئٰنَ وَقَدْ كُنْتُمْ بِهٖ

تَسْتَعْجِلُوْنَ ۝ ثُمَّ قِيْلَ لِلَّذِيْنَ ظَلَمُوْا ذُوْقُوْا عَذَابَ

الْخُلْدِ ۚ هَلْ تُجْزَوْنَ اِلَّا بِمَا كُنْتُمْ تَكْسِبُوْنَ ۝

وَيَسْتَنْبِئُوْنَكَ اَحَقٌّ هُوَ ط قُلْ اِيْ وَرَبِّيْ اِنَّهٗ لَحَقٌّ ط

وَمَاۤ اَنْتُمْ بِمُعْجِزِيْنَ ۞ وَلَوْ اَنَّ لِكُلِّ نَفْسٍ ظَلَمَتْ

مَا فِى الْاَرْضِ لَافْتَدَتْ بِهٖ ط وَاَسَرُّوا النَّدَامَةَ

لَمَّا رَاَوُا الْعَذَابَ ۚ وَقُضِيَ بَيْنَهُمْ بِالْقِسْطِ

وَهُمْ لَا يُظْلَمُوْنَ ۝ اَلَاۤ اِنَّ لِلّٰهِ مَا فِى السَّمٰوٰتِ

وَالْاَرْضِ ط اَلَاۤ اِنَّ وَعْدَ اللّٰهِ حَقٌّ وَّلٰكِنَّ اَكْثَرَهُمْ لَا

يَعْلَمُوْنَ ۝ هُوَ يُحْىٖ وَيُمِيْتُ وَاِلَيْهِ تُرْجَعُوْنَ ۝

يٰۤاَيُّهَا النَّاسُ قَدْ جَآءَتْكُمْ مَّوْعِظَةٌ مِّنْ رَّبِّكُمْ

وَشِفَآءٌ لِّمَا فِى الصُّدُوْرِ ۙ وَهُدًى وَّرَحْمَةٌ

لِّلْمُؤْمِنِيْنَ ۝ قُلْ بِفَضْلِ اللّٰهِ وَبِرَحْمَتِهٖ فَبِذٰلِكَ

فَلْيَفْرَحُوْا ط هُوَ خَيْرٌ مِّمَّا يَجْمَعُوْنَ ۝ قُلْ

اَرَءَيْتُمْ مَّاۤ اَنْزَلَ اللّٰهُ لَكُمْ مِّنْ رِّزْقٍ فَجَعَلْتُمْ

The Quran is a healing, that presents solutions for human psychological and social diseases. It's a medicine for the heart and mind.

⁴⁹ Say: "Even for myself, I have no control over what brings benefit or harm, except *to the extent* that Allah wills. Every community has a *certain* span of life; and, when their lifespan comes *to an end*, they can neither postpone nor advance *it* by a *single* hour." ⁵⁰ Say: "Have you considered, if His torment were to come to you, at night or day, what part of it the sinners would want to hasten? ⁵¹ Is it then you would believe in it once it has happened, *only to be told*, 'What? Now', when *before* you wanted to hasten it?" ⁵² The wrongdoers will be told, "Taste the everlasting torment. This is the only fitting reward for what you did."

The sinners' vain wishes on Judgement Day

⁵³ They question you, "Is it really true?" Say: "Yes, by My Lord, it is true, and you are unable to stop *it*." ⁵⁴ If every soul that sinned possessed all that is on Earth, it would offer it as a ransom. They will *scarcely* conceal their regret when they see the punishment, and justice will be done *so that* none of them is wronged. ⁵⁵ Doesn't everything in the Heavens and the Earth belong to Allah? Isn't Allah's promise true? Most don't know. ⁵⁶ He gives life and death, *finally* you will return to Him.

The Quran is a soothing balm

⁵⁷ People, your Lord's teachings have come to you; they're a healing balm for *the diseases* of the heart, guidance and beneficial teachings for the believers. ⁵⁸ Say: "It's Allah's grace and kindness, so celebrate, it's better than all *the wealth* they accumulate." ⁵⁹ Say: "Have you *ever* thought about the provision that Allah has sent down for you, and which you declare either lawful or unlawful?" Say: "Has Allah given you permission *to do so*, or are you inventing lies about Allah?"

مِنْهُ حَرَامًا وَّحَلَالًا ط قُلْ آٰللّٰهُ اَذِنَ لَكُمْ اَمْ عَلَى

اللّٰهِ تَفْتَرُوْنَ ۵۹ وَمَا ظَنُّ الَّذِيْنَ يَفْتَرُوْنَ عَلَى

اللّٰهِ الْكَذِبَ يَوْمَ الْقِيٰمَةِ ط اِنَّ اللّٰهَ لَذُوْ فَضْلٍ

عَلَى النَّاسِ وَلٰكِنَّ اَكْثَرَهُمْ لَا يَشْكُرُوْنَ ۶۰ ع

وَمَا تَكُوْنُ فِيْ شَاْنٍ وَّمَا تَتْلُوْا مِنْهُ مِنْ

قُرْاٰنٍ وَّلَا تَعْمَلُوْنَ مِنْ عَمَلٍ اِلَّا كُنَّا عَلَيْكُمْ

شُهُوْدًا اِذْ تُفِيْضُوْنَ فِيْهِ ط وَمَا يَعْزُبُ عَنْ

رَّبِّكَ مِنْ مِّثْقَالِ ذَرَّةٍ فِي الْاَرْضِ وَلَا فِي

السَّمَآءِ وَلَاۤ اَصْغَرَ مِنْ ذٰلِكَ وَلَاۤ اَكْبَرَ اِلَّا فِيْ

كِتٰبٍ مُّبِيْنٍ ۶۱ اَلَاۤ اِنَّ اَوْلِيَآءَ اللّٰهِ لَا خَوْفٌ

عَلَيْهِمْ وَلَا هُمْ يَحْزَنُوْنَ ۶۲ الَّذِيْنَ اٰمَنُوْا وَكَانُوْا

يَتَّقُوْنَ ۶۳ لَهُمُ الْبُشْرٰى فِي الْحَيٰوةِ الدُّنْيَا

وَفِي الْاٰخِرَةِ ط لَا تَبْدِيْلَ لِكَلِمٰتِ اللّٰهِ ط ذٰلِكَ

هُوَ الْفَوْزُ الْعَظِيْمُ ۶۴ وَلَا يَحْزُنْكَ قَوْلُهُمْ ؞

اِنَّ الْعِزَّةَ لِلّٰهِ جَمِيْعًا ط هُوَ السَّمِيْعُ الْعَلِيْمُ ۶۵

اَلَاۤ اِنَّ لِلّٰهِ مَنْ فِي السَّمٰوٰتِ وَمَنْ فِي الْاَرْضِ ط

وَمَا يَتَّبِعُ الَّذِيْنَ يَدْعُوْنَ مِنْ دُوْنِ اللّٰهِ

شُرَكَآءَ ط اِنْ يَّتَّبِعُوْنَ اِلَّا الظَّنَّ وَاِنْ هُمْ اِلَّا

يَخْرُصُوْنَ ۶۶ هُوَ الَّذِيْ جَعَلَ لَكُمُ الَّيْلَ لِتَسْكُنُوْا

فِيْهِ وَالنَّهَارَ مُبْصِرًا ط اِنَّ فِيْ ذٰلِكَ لَاٰيٰتٍ

Good news for friends of Allah, what are their qualities? Do you qualify for this honourable title?

60 What do those who invent lies about Allah think *will happen* on Judgement Day? Allah is Gracious towards people, yet most of them are ungrateful.

A picture of the friends of Allah

61 Whatever matter you are dealing with, *Messenger*, and whatever part of the Quran you are reciting; and whatever you are doing, We are witnessing what you are doing. Not an atom's weight on Earth or in the Heavens is hidden from your Lord; nothing bigger or smaller exists that isn't *recorded* in a clear Book. 62 Beware, Allah's friends have no fear, nor do they grieve. 63 They believe and are mindful *of Allah*, 64 for them are glad tidings in this worldly life and in the Hereafter. There is no change to Allah's rulings; that's a great victory. 65 So don't be saddened by what they say. All the power is Allah's. He is the Hearer, the Knower.

Allah's creation cannot be His partner

66 Beware, everything in the Heavens and Earth belongs to Allah! Whatever they follow and who they call on as partners beside Allah are merely speculations and lies. 67 He made the night for you to rest and the day to earn *a livelihood*. In this there are signs for people who listen.

لِّقَوْمٍ يَّسْمَعُوْنَ ﴿٦٧﴾ قَالُوا اتَّخَذَ اللّٰهُ وَلَدًا سُبْحٰنَهٗ ط
هُوَ الْغَنِيُّ ط لَهٗ مَا فِي السَّمٰوٰتِ وَمَا فِي الْاَرْضِ ط
اِنْ عِنْدَكُمْ مِّنْ سُلْطٰنٍۭ بِهٰذَا ط اَتَقُوْلُوْنَ عَلَى اللّٰهِ
مَا لَا تَعْلَمُوْنَ ﴿٦٨﴾ قُلْ اِنَّ الَّذِيْنَ يَفْتَرُوْنَ عَلَى
اللّٰهِ الْكَذِبَ لَا يُفْلِحُوْنَ ﴿٦٩﴾ ط مَتَاعٌ فِي الدُّنْيَا ثُمَّ
اِلَيْنَا مَرْجِعُهُمْ ثُمَّ نُذِيْقُهُمُ الْعَذَابَ الشَّدِيْدَ
ع ٧ ١٢ الثلثة بِمَا كَانُوْا يَكْفُرُوْنَ ﴿٧٠﴾ ع وَاتْلُ عَلَيْهِمْ نَبَاَ نُوْحٍ م اِذْ
قَالَ لِقَوْمِهٖ يٰقَوْمِ اِنْ كَانَ كَبُرَ عَلَيْكُمْ مَّقَامِيْ
وَتَذْكِيْرِيْ بِاٰيٰتِ اللّٰهِ فَعَلَى اللّٰهِ تَوَكَّلْتُ فَاَجْمِعُوْٓا
اَمْرَكُمْ وَشُرَكَآءَكُمْ ثُمَّ لَا يَكُنْ اَمْرُكُمْ عَلَيْكُمْ
غُمَّةً ثُمَّ اقْضُوْٓا اِلَيَّ وَلَا تُنْظِرُوْنِ ﴿٧١﴾ فَاِنْ تَوَلَّيْتُمْ
فَمَا سَاَلْتُكُمْ مِّنْ اَجْرٍ ط اِنْ اَجْرِيَ اِلَّا عَلَى اللّٰهِ لا
وَاُمِرْتُ اَنْ اَكُوْنَ مِنَ الْمُسْلِمِيْنَ ﴿٧٢﴾ فَكَذَّبُوْهُ
فَنَجَّيْنٰهُ وَمَنْ مَّعَهٗ فِي الْفُلْكِ وَجَعَلْنٰهُمْ خَلٰٓئِفَ
وَاَغْرَقْنَا الَّذِيْنَ كَذَّبُوْا بِاٰيٰتِنَا ج فَانْظُرْ كَيْفَ كَانَ
عَاقِبَةُ الْمُنْذَرِيْنَ ﴿٧٣﴾ ثُمَّ بَعَثْنَا مِنْۢ بَعْدِهٖ رُسُلًا
اِلٰى قَوْمِهِمْ فَجَآءُوْهُمْ بِالْبَيِّنٰتِ فَمَا كَانُوْا لِيُؤْمِنُوْا
بِمَا كَذَّبُوْا بِهٖ مِنْ قَبْلُ ط كَذٰلِكَ نَطْبَعُ عَلٰى قُلُوْبِ
الْمُعْتَدِيْنَ ﴿٧٤﴾ ثُمَّ بَعَثْنَا مِنْۢ بَعْدِهِمْ مُّوْسٰى
وَهٰرُوْنَ اِلٰى فِرْعَوْنَ وَمَلَا۟ئِهٖ بِاٰيٰتِنَا فَاسْتَكْبَرُوْا

The disbelievers of the twenty-first century are materialists: they consider wealth and luxuries as the be all and end all. They ignore spiritual and social values.

⁶⁸They said, "Allah has adopted a son." Glory to Him! He is the Self-Sufficient. Whatever is in the Heavens and on Earth belongs to Him. Do you have any proof for this *claim*? How can you say what you don't know about Allah? ⁶⁹Say: "Those who fabricate lies about Allah never succeed." ⁷⁰*Let them experience* enjoyment in this world; then they will return to Us, *and* We shall make them taste severe punishment because of their disbelief.

The story of Nuh

⁷¹Tell them about Nuh, when he said to his people, "My people, if you find my presence and my reminder of Allah's signs offensive, I put my trust in Allah. Agree together with your partners a plan *of action*, then do not be hesitant to carry it out, and grant me no respite. ⁷²If you *choose to* turn your backs, then *know that* I have not asked you for any reward; my reward is with Allah, and I have been told to be with those who submit *to His will.*" ⁷³They rejected him, so We rescued him and his followers in a ship and made them successors *in the land*, and We drowned those who denied Our signs. So, take note of the fate of those who were warned. ⁷⁴After *Nuh*, We sent messengers, *each* to their *own* people. *They* came to them with clear signs, but *they* weren't willing to believe in what they had previously denied. That is how We seal the hearts of offenders.

وَكَانُوْا قَوْمًا مُّجْرِمِيْنَ ۴۵ فَلَمَّا جَآءَهُمُ الْحَقُّ

مِنْ عِنْدِنَا قَالُوْٓا اِنَّ هٰذَا لَسِحْرٌ مُّبِيْنٌ ۴۶ قَالَ

مُوْسٰٓى اَتَقُوْلُوْنَ لِلْحَقِّ لَمَّا جَآءَكُمْ ؕ اَسِحْرٌ هٰذَا ؕ وَلَا

يُفْلِحُ السّٰحِرُوْنَ ۴۷ قَالُوْٓا اَجِئْتَنَا لِتَلْفِتَنَا عَمَّا وَجَدْنَا

عَلَيْهِ اٰبَآءَنَا وَتَكُوْنَ لَكُمَا الْكِبْرِيَآءُ فِى الْاَرْضِ ؕ

وَمَا نَحْنُ لَكُمَا بِمُؤْمِنِيْنَ ۴۸ وَقَالَ فِرْعَوْنُ ائْتُوْنِىْ

بِكُلِّ سٰحِرٍ عَلِيْمٍ ۴۹ فَلَمَّا جَآءَ السَّحَرَةُ قَالَ لَهُمْ

مُّوْسٰٓى اَلْقُوْا مَآ اَنْتُمْ مُّلْقُوْنَ ۸۰ فَلَمَّآ اَلْقَوْا قَالَ

مُوْسٰى مَا جِئْتُمْ بِهِ ۙ السِّحْرُ ؕ اِنَّ اللّٰهَ سَيُبْطِلُهٗ ؕ

اِنَّ اللّٰهَ لَا يُصْلِحُ عَمَلَ الْمُفْسِدِيْنَ ۸۱ وَيُحِقُّ

اللّٰهُ الْحَقَّ بِكَلِمٰتِهٖ وَلَوْ كَرِهَ الْمُجْرِمُوْنَ ۸۲ فَمَآ

اٰمَنَ لِمُوْسٰٓى اِلَّا ذُرِّيَّةٌ مِّنْ قَوْمِهٖ عَلٰى خَوْفٍ مِّنْ

فِرْعَوْنَ وَمَلَا۟ئِهِمْ اَنْ يَّفْتِنَهُمْ ؕ وَاِنَّ فِرْعَوْنَ

لَعَالٍ فِى الْاَرْضِ ۚ وَاِنَّهٗ لَمِنَ الْمُسْرِفِيْنَ ۸۳ وَقَالَ

مُوْسٰى يٰقَوْمِ اِنْ كُنْتُمْ اٰمَنْتُمْ بِاللّٰهِ فَعَلَيْهِ تَوَكَّلُوْٓا

اِنْ كُنْتُمْ مُّسْلِمِيْنَ ۸۴ فَقَالُوْا عَلَى اللّٰهِ تَوَكَّلْنَا ۚ

رَبَّنَا لَا تَجْعَلْنَا فِتْنَةً لِّلْقَوْمِ الظّٰلِمِيْنَ ۸۵ وَنَجِّنَا

بِرَحْمَتِكَ مِنَ الْقَوْمِ الْكٰفِرِيْنَ ۸۶ وَاَوْحَيْنَآ

اِلٰى مُوْسٰى وَاَخِيْهِ اَنْ تَبَوَّاٰ لِقَوْمِكُمَا بِمِصْرَ

بُيُوْتًا وَّاجْعَلُوْا بُيُوْتَكُمْ قِبْلَةً وَّاَقِيْمُوا الصَّلٰوةَ ؕ

Worldly wealth enchants like magic, are you enchanted?

The story of Musa, magicians and the Pharaoh

75 After them, We sent Musa and Harun with Our signs to Pharaoh and his courtiers, but they responded arrogantly, they were wicked people. 76 When the truth came to them from Us, they said, "This is clearly magic." 77 Musa said, "Is this how you speak about truth when it comes to you? *Do you call* this magic, when *you know that* magicians never achieve anything?" 78 They said, "Have you come to turn us away from what we found our forefathers doing, so you two may rule over us? We don't believe you." 79 Pharaoh said, "Bring me every expert magician." 80 So, when the magicians came, Musa said to them, "Cast your *spells*." 81 When they had cast *their spells*, Musa said, "You've performed magic. Allah will prove it to be fake; Allah will not allow the actions of those bent on corruption to succeed; 82 *rather* Allah will uphold the truth of His words, though the sinners hate that."

Musa motivates his people to be prayerful

83 No one believed in Musa – fearing that Pharaoh and his courtiers will persecute them – except some young people. Pharaoh behaved high-handedly throughout the land, and he was one of those who went beyond the bounds. 84 Musa said, "My people, since you chose to believe in Allah then put your trust in Him, if you have really submitted *to His will*." 85 They replied, "We have put our trust in Allah, Our Lord, do not leave us at the mercy of the wicked people 86 and, by Your kindness, rescue us from the disbelieving people." 87 We revealed to Musa and his brother: "Let your people take up residence in Egypt; and, *Israelites*, turn your homes into places of worship, and perform the prayer; and *Musa*, give glad tidings to the believers."

وَبَشِّرِ الْمُؤْمِنِينَ ۝ وَقَالَ مُوسَى رَبَّنَا إِنَّكَ

اٰتَيْتَ فِرْعَوْنَ وَمَلَأَهٗ زِينَةً وَّأَمْوَالًا فِي الْحَيٰوةِ

الدُّنْيَا ۙ رَبَّنَا لِيُضِلُّوا عَنْ سَبِيلِكَ ۚ رَبَّنَا

اطْمِسْ عَلَىٰ أَمْوَالِهِمْ وَاشْدُدْ عَلَىٰ قُلُوبِهِمْ

فَلَا يُؤْمِنُوا حَتَّىٰ يَرَوُا الْعَذَابَ الْأَلِيمَ ۝

قَالَ قَدْ أُجِيبَتْ دَّعْوَتُكُمَا فَاسْتَقِيمَا وَلَا

تَتَّبِعَانِّ سَبِيلَ الَّذِينَ لَا يَعْلَمُونَ ۝ وَجَاوَزْنَا

بِبَنِي إِسْرَآءِيلَ الْبَحْرَ فَأَتْبَعَهُمْ فِرْعَوْنُ وَجُنُودُهٗ

بَغْيًا وَّعَدْوًا ۗ حَتَّىٰ إِذَآ أَدْرَكَهُ الْغَرَقُ ۙ قَالَ

آمَنْتُ أَنَّهٗ لَآ إِلٰهَ إِلَّا الَّذِيٓ آمَنَتْ بِهٖ

بَنُوٓا إِسْرَآءِيلَ وَأَنَا مِنَ الْمُسْلِمِينَ ۝ آلْآنَ

وَقَدْ عَصَيْتَ قَبْلُ وَكُنْتَ مِنَ الْمُفْسِدِينَ ۝

فَالْيَوْمَ نُنَجِّيكَ بِبَدَنِكَ لِتَكُونَ لِمَنْ خَلْفَكَ

آيَةً ۗ وَإِنَّ كَثِيرًا مِّنَ النَّاسِ عَنْ آيَاتِنَا

لَغَافِلُونَ ۝ وَلَقَدْ بَوَّأْنَا بَنِي إِسْرَآءِيلَ مُبَوَّأَ

صِدْقٍ وَّرَزَقْنٰهُمْ مِّنَ الطَّيِّبٰتِ ۚ فَمَا اخْتَلَفُوا

حَتَّىٰ جَآءَهُمُ الْعِلْمُ ۗ إِنَّ رَبَّكَ يَقْضِي بَيْنَهُمْ

يَوْمَ الْقِيٰمَةِ فِيمَا كَانُوا فِيهِ يَخْتَلِفُونَ ۝ فَإِنْ

كُنْتَ فِي شَكٍّ مِّمَّآ أَنْزَلْنَآ إِلَيْكَ فَسْـَٔلِ الَّذِينَ

يَقْرَءُونَ الْكِتٰبَ مِنْ قَبْلِكَ ۚ لَقَدْ جَآءَكَ الْحَقُّ

Pharaoh's mummy is displayed in Cairo Museum. The word of Allah is true.

Musa's prayer for the destruction of Pharaoh

⁸⁸ Musa said, "Our Lord, You have given Pharaoh and his courtiers splendour and wealth in this worldly life so they are leading *others* astray from Your path. Our Lord, destroy their wealth and harden their hearts so that they do not believe until they see the painful punishment *with their eyes.*" ⁸⁹ *Allah* said, "Your prayer has been accepted, remain steadfast, both of you, and do not follow the path of those who have no knowledge."

Pharaoh's body is preserved as a sign

⁹⁰ *Eventually,* We led the Israelites across the sea, with Pharaoh and his army following them, full of aggression and hatred, until he drowned,^a *Pharaoh* said, "I believe there is no god except Him Who the Israelites believe, and I am one who submits *to His will.*" ⁹¹ "What, now?" *Pharaoh was asked,* "After all your disobedience as one of those bent on corruption? ⁹² Today We shall preserve your body, as a *warning* sign for whoever comes after you." *Unfortunately,* many people are unaware of Our signs.^b ⁹³ We settled the Israelites in comfortable houses and provided them wholesome food, and they did not disagree amongst themselves until after knowledge had come to them. Your Lord will judge between them on Judgement Day regarding their differences.

Doubting will not drive away the punishment

⁹⁴ So, if you are in doubt about what We have revealed, then ask those who read the Book before you, *the Jews.* The truth has come to you from your Lord, so *listener* don't be one of those who have doubts.

---

^a *Idrakahu algharaq*, literally means 'overwhelmed by the sea'.
^b Commentators think this Pharaoh was the famous Ramesses II (1303-1213 BC), whilst others say it was his predecessor Tutankhamun (1341-1323 BC), (Asad). His body embalmed now is in the Egyptian Museum.

مِنْ رَّبِّكَ فَلَا تَكُوْنَنَّ مِنَ الْمُمْتَرِيْنَ ۙ﴿٩٤﴾ وَلَا

تَكُوْنَنَّ مِنَ الَّذِيْنَ كَذَّبُوْا بِاٰيٰتِ اللّٰهِ فَتَكُوْنَ

مِنَ الْخٰسِرِيْنَ ﴿٩٥﴾ اِنَّ الَّذِيْنَ حَقَّتْ عَلَيْهِمْ

كَلِمَتُ رَبِّكَ لَا يُؤْمِنُوْنَ ۙ﴿٩٦﴾ وَلَوْ جَآءَتْهُمْ كُلُّ

اٰيَةٍ حَتّٰى يَرَوُا الْعَذَابَ الْاَلِيْمَ ﴿٩٧﴾ فَلَوْلَا

كَانَتْ قَرْيَةٌ اٰمَنَتْ فَنَفَعَهَآ اِيْمَانُهَآ اِلَّا قَوْمَ

يُوْنُسَ ؕ لَمَّآ اٰمَنُوْا كَشَفْنَا عَنْهُمْ عَذَابَ الْخِزْيِ

فِى الْحَيٰوةِ الدُّنْيَا وَمَتَّعْنٰهُمْ اِلٰى حِيْنٍ ﴿٩٨﴾ وَلَوْ

شَآءَ رَبُّكَ لَاٰمَنَ مَنْ فِى الْاَرْضِ كُلُّهُمْ جَمِيْعًا ؕ

اَفَاَنْتَ تُكْرِهُ النَّاسَ حَتّٰى يَكُوْنُوْا مُؤْمِنِيْنَ ﴿٩٩﴾ وَمَا

كَانَ لِنَفْسٍ اَنْ تُؤْمِنَ اِلَّا بِاِذْنِ اللّٰهِ ؕ وَيَجْعَلُ

الرِّجْسَ عَلَى الَّذِيْنَ لَا يَعْقِلُوْنَ ﴿١٠٠﴾ قُلِ انْظُرُوْا

مَاذَا فِى السَّمٰوٰتِ وَالْاَرْضِ ؕ وَمَا تُغْنِى الْاٰيٰتُ

وَالنُّذُرُ عَنْ قَوْمٍ لَّا يُؤْمِنُوْنَ ﴿١٠١﴾ فَهَلْ يَنْتَظِرُوْنَ

اِلَّا مِثْلَ اَيَّامِ الَّذِيْنَ خَلَوْا مِنْ قَبْلِهِمْ ؕ قُلْ

فَانْتَظِرُوْآ اِنِّيْ مَعَكُمْ مِّنَ الْمُنْتَظِرِيْنَ ﴿١٠٢﴾ ثُمَّ

نُنَجِّيْ رُسُلَنَا وَالَّذِيْنَ اٰمَنُوْا كَذٰلِكَ ۚ حَقًّا

عَلَيْنَا نُنْجِ الْمُؤْمِنِيْنَ ﴿١٠٣﴾ قُلْ يٰٓاَيُّهَا النَّاسُ اِنْ

كُنْتُمْ فِيْ شَكٍّ مِّنْ دِيْنِيْ فَلَا اَعْبُدُ الَّذِيْنَ

تَعْبُدُوْنَ مِنْ دُوْنِ اللّٰهِ وَلٰكِنْ اَعْبُدُ اللّٰهَ الَّذِيْ

Faith is a matter of choice; but once a believer, you must be convinced, humble and fall in love with Allah.

⁹⁵ and do not be one of those who deny Allah's signs, *ultimately* becoming the losers. ⁹⁶ Those against whom your Lord's statement is justified, they will not believe, ⁹⁷ even if all the signs were to come to them *at once*, until – *like Pharaoh* – they see the painful punishment.

All the people of Yunus believed

⁹⁸ What a pity not a single town believed and benefitted from its faith, except the people of Yunus. When they believed, We removed the *looming* punishment of disgrace from them in this life, and We granted them respite for a while. ⁹⁹ If Your Lord wanted, everyone on Earth would have believed. Will you force people to believe? ¹⁰⁰ No one can believe without Allah's approval, and He casts doubt in *the minds of* those who do not think.ᵃ ¹⁰¹ Say: "Look at what's in the Heavens and the Earth." Yet signs and warnings are of no benefit to people who choose not to believe. ¹⁰² Do they expect *an outcome* other than what happened to those who passed before them? Say: "So wait *for a sign*, and I shall be with you waiting." ¹⁰³ We always rescued Our messengers and the believers. That is how it is: the believers rightly expect Us to save them.

Do not change to please others, but stick to what Allah has revealed

¹⁰⁴ Say: "People, if you have doubts about my religion, I won't worship those you worship beside Allah; I shall worship Allah, Who will *ultimately* take your souls. I was ordered to be a believer,

---

ᵃ The reason Allah let's them go astray is because they "do not think", were they to use reason they would get Allah's approval and win His grace.

يَتَوَفّٰكُمْ ۚ وَ أُمِرْتُ اَنْ اَكُوْنَ مِنَ الْمُؤْمِنِيْنَ ۞

وَاَنْ اَقِمْ وَجْهَكَ لِلدِّيْنِ حَنِيْفًا ۚ وَلَا تَكُوْنَنَّ

مِنَ الْمُشْرِكِيْنَ ۞ وَلَا تَدْعُ مِنْ دُوْنِ اللّٰهِ مَا لَا

يَنْفَعُكَ وَلَا يَضُرُّكَ ۚ فَاِنْ فَعَلْتَ فَاِنَّكَ اِذًا

مِّنَ الظّٰلِمِيْنَ ۞ وَاِنْ يَّمْسَسْكَ اللّٰهُ بِضُرٍّ فَلَا

كَاشِفَ لَهٗٓ اِلَّا هُوَ ۚ وَاِنْ يُّرِدْكَ بِخَيْرٍ فَلَا رَآدَّ

لِفَضْلِهٖ ۚ يُصِيْبُ بِهٖ مَنْ يَّشَآءُ مِنْ عِبَادِهٖ ۚ

وَهُوَ الْغَفُوْرُ الرَّحِيْمُ ۞ قُلْ يٰٓاَيُّهَا النَّاسُ قَدْ

جَآءَكُمُ الْحَقُّ مِنْ رَّبِّكُمْ ۚ فَمَنِ اهْتَدٰى فَاِنَّمَا

يَهْتَدِيْ لِنَفْسِهٖ ۚ وَمَنْ ضَلَّ فَاِنَّمَا يَضِلُّ عَلَيْهَا ۚ

وَمَآ اَنَا عَلَيْكُمْ بِوَكِيْلٍ ۞ وَاتَّبِعْ مَا يُوْحٰى اِلَيْكَ

وَاصْبِرْ حَتّٰى يَحْكُمَ اللّٰهُ ۚ وَهُوَ خَيْرُ الْحٰكِمِيْنَ ۞

The divine function: provide gifts of all kind, energy and intelligence to do good.

¹⁰⁵ and *told*: 'Keep your face *directed* towards the *true* religion, in tune with your nature, and do not become an idolator. ¹⁰⁶ Do not pray to something beside Allah that can neither benefit nor harm you; if you were to do so, you'll be a wrongdoer."' ¹⁰⁷ If Allah allows harm to distress you, no one can remove it but Him, if He wishes good for you, then no one can turn aside His grace, which He grants to any one of His servants He pleases. He is the Forgiving, the Kind. ¹⁰⁸ Say: "People, the truth from your Lord came. So, whoever accepts the guidance will benefit himself, and whoever goes astray will be harmed by doing so; I am not guardian over you." ¹⁰⁹ *Messenger*, follow what is revealed to you, and be patient until Allah makes judgement, He is the best judge.

11. Surat Hud

The Prophet Hud

The central theme of this late Makkan surat is the history of human disobedience. The Messenger ﷺ and the Muslims are reassured by a narrative based on the experiences of seven prophets. The prophets are told: say, "Worship no one besides Allah, I am a warner to you from Him and a giver of good news" (2). The response from the pagans was mockery and denial. They were warned of the dire consequences of their belligerent attitude and challenged: "fetch ten surats like it that *you have* invented, and call *as witnesses* whomever you can besides Allah, if you are telling the truth" (13).

The story of Prophet Nuh ﷺ is the first of the seven stories, and it outlines his bold preaching. His people were particularly prejudiced against the poor: "It's clear to us that you are a mortal like us, and only the dregs of our society follow you. You have no special quality that we lack." (27). Eventually Nuh ﷺ and his followers are saved from the flood. The story of Prophet Hud ﷺ follows in the same manner. His people rejected him by saying, "You haven't brought us any proof" (53), re-enacting the same old story of unwilling disbelievers, so finally they are destroyed. The people of Makkah were familiar with the ruins of the People of Thamud, who lived near Sana in Yemen. Their messenger was Salih ﷺ, who invited them to Allah. Their moral disease seems to be the caste system, discriminating against people from poor backgrounds. They rejected their prophet and were punished by a blast that killed them all.

The next story is of Prophet Ibrahim ﷺ pleading on behalf of his nephew Lut ﷺ. Lut was sent to the infamous people of Sodom and Gomorrah, plagued by homosexuality. This is followed by the story of Prophet Shu'ayb ﷺ in Madyan, a prosperous community that refused to listen to him. He warned them:

My people, don't let your hostility to me lead you to suffer the same *fate* as the people of Nuh, Hud, Salih; and *remember* the people of Lut *didn't live* far away from you. *So* seek your Lord's forgiveness and then turn to Him in repentance. Indeed, My Lord is Most Kind, Loving (89–90).

They were morally corrupt and cheated when doing business. The seventh story in this series is Musa ﷺ and Pharaoh. Pharaoh, like his predecessors, rejected the teachings of Musa ﷺ, and was drowned for his injustice and his oppression of the Israelites. The surat concludes by dividing humanity into two groups: the blessed heirs of Paradise, and the wretched inhabitants of Hellfire. After narrating the stories of the prophets, peacemakers and pious men's struggle against wicked people, the surat repeats the original instruction: "worship Allah." The common thread that weaves through these seven stories is the rejection of the prophets, the punishment of the disbelievers, and the final victory of the righteous. The Quran in its matchless way is reassuring the beloved Messenger ﷺ of a victory, but is also instructing him ﷺ to be patient in the meanwhile, to perform the prayer and to accept this unfortunate human condition. In these stories, the Quran keeps reminding the reader that the reason for human rebellion and denial is the love of wealth, arrogance and mindlessness. The antidote: reflect, believe in resurrection and reform yourselves; overcome prejudice against the poor, show thankfulness to Allah and accept the Prophet.

Abu Bakr ؓ once pointed out the grey hair in the Prophet's ﷺ beard, he replied, "*Surat Hud* and its sister surats are the cause of my greying hair" (Tirmidhi). This surat, like most other Makkan surats, displays the majestic mode, *Jalali*, which conveys Allah's avenging will and unwavering justice. Hinting that like the previous prophets you too will have to abandon your home city, and see its demise. On the other hand, it also includes the *Jamali* mode: Allah the Gentle, Compassionate and Generous, but the majestic mode is dominant in this surat.

سُوْرَةُ هُوْدٍ مَكِّيَّةٌ (٥٢)   (١١)   اٰیَاتُهَا ١٢٣   رُكُوْعَاتُهَا ١٠

بِسْمِ اللّٰهِ الرَّحْمٰنِ الرَّحِيْمِ

الٓرٰ ۚ كِتٰبٌ اُحْكِمَتْ اٰیٰتُهٗ ثُمَّ فُصِّلَتْ مِنْ لَّدُنْ حَكِيْمٍ خَبِيْرٍ ۙ ۞ اَلَّا تَعْبُدُوْۤا اِلَّا اللّٰهَ ؕ اِنَّنِیْ لَكُمْ مِّنْهُ نَذِيْرٌ وَّبَشِيْرٌ ۙ ۞ وَّاَنِ اسْتَغْفِرُوْا رَبَّكُمْ ثُمَّ تُوْبُوْۤا اِلَيْهِ يُمَتِّعْكُمْ مَّتَاعًا حَسَنًا اِلٰۤی اَجَلٍ مُّسَمًّی وَّيُؤْتِ كُلَّ ذِیْ فَضْلٍ فَضْلَهٗ ؕ وَاِنْ تَوَلَّوْا فَاِنِّیْۤ اَخَافُ عَلَيْكُمْ عَذَابَ يَوْمٍ كَبِيْرٍ ۞ اِلَی اللّٰهِ مَرْجِعُكُمْ ۚ وَهُوَ عَلٰی كُلِّ شَیْءٍ قَدِيْرٌ ۞ اَلَاۤ اِنَّهُمْ يَثْنُوْنَ صُدُوْرَهُمْ لِيَسْتَخْفُوْا مِنْهُ ؕ اَلَا حِيْنَ يَسْتَغْشُوْنَ ثِيَابَهُمْ ۙ يَعْلَمُ مَا يُسِرُّوْنَ وَمَا يُعْلِنُوْنَ ۚ اِنَّهٗ عَلِيْمٌۢ بِذَاتِ الصُّدُوْرِ ۞ وَمَا مِنْ دَآبَّةٍ فِی الْاَرْضِ اِلَّا عَلَی اللّٰهِ رِزْقُهَا وَيَعْلَمُ مُسْتَقَرَّهَا وَمُسْتَوْدَعَهَا ؕ كُلٌّ فِیْ كِتٰبٍ مُّبِيْنٍ ۞ وَهُوَ الَّذِیْ خَلَقَ السَّمٰوٰتِ وَالْاَرْضَ فِیْ سِتَّةِ اَيَّامٍ وَّكَانَ عَرْشُهٗ عَلَی الْمَآءِ لِيَبْلُوَكُمْ اَيُّكُمْ اَحْسَنُ عَمَلًا ؕ وَلَئِنْ قُلْتَ اِنَّكُمْ مَّبْعُوْثُوْنَ مِنْۢ بَعْدِ الْمَوْتِ لَيَقُوْلَنَّ الَّذِيْنَ كَفَرُوْۤا اِنْ هٰذَاۤ اِلَّا سِحْرٌ مُّبِيْنٌ ۞ وَلَئِنْ اَخَّرْنَا عَنْهُمُ الْعَذَابَ اِلٰۤی اُمَّةٍ مَّعْدُوْدَةٍ لَّيَقُوْلُنَّ مَا يَحْبِسُهٗ ؕ اَلَا يَوْمَ

Allah has taken responsibility to provide for every creature. So why worry so much about sustenance?

425

In the name of Allah, the Kind, the Caring.

¹ *Alif Lam Ra'*.

Divine guidance: gentle reminders, warnings and promises

This is a Book whose verses give *clear* instructions, explained by a Wise, Knowledgeable *Lord*: ² "Worship no one besides Allah, I am a warner to you from Him and a giver of good news. ³ Seek your Lord's forgiveness and turn to Him in repentance, so He grants you good provision for a fixed term and gives His grace to whoever is worthy of it. If you turn away, I fear for you the torment of a terrible day. ⁴ You shall return to Allah. He has control over all things". ⁵ Isn't it *true* that they try to cover their breasts in order to hide *their innermost thoughts* from Him? Isn't it *true* that when they cover themselvesᵃ with their clothes He knows what they conceal or reveal? He knows *people's* innermost thoughts.

The fickleness of those with little or no faith

⁶ The sustenance of every animal comes from Allah, He knows where it lives and where it will die. Everything is *recorded* in a clear Book. ⁷ He created the Heavens and the Earth in six days, His throne is over the water, to test who among you lives morally. *Messenger*, suppose you were to say, "You will be resurrected after death," the disbelievers would say, "This is magic." ⁸ And suppose We were to delay their punishment for a short while, they would say, "What is holding it back?" Isn't it *true* on the day that it does come upon them, it won't be deflected from them, and the very thing they used to mock will engulf them?

ᵃ *Sanun Sudurahum* means to sit with knees folded in front of the chest, to hide ones face, a metaphor for 'hide feelings'.

يَاْتِيْهِمْ لَيْسَ مَصْرُوْفًا عَنْهُمْ وَحَاقَ بِهِمْ مَّا كَانُوْا

بِهٖ يَسْتَهْزِءُوْنَ ۞ وَلَئِنْ اَذَقْنَا الْاِنْسَانَ مِنَّا

رَحْمَةً ثُمَّ نَزَعْنٰهَا مِنْهُ ۚ اِنَّهٗ لَيَـُٔوْسٌ كَفُوْرٌ ۞ وَلَئِنْ

اَذَقْنٰهُ نَعْمَآءَ بَعْدَ ضَرَّآءَ مَسَّتْهُ لَيَقُوْلَنَّ ذَهَبَ

السَّيِّاٰتُ عَنِّىْ ؕ اِنَّهٗ لَفَرِحٌ فَخُوْرٌ ۞ اِلَّا الَّذِيْنَ

صَبَرُوْا وَعَمِلُوا الصّٰلِحٰتِ ؕ اُولٰٓئِكَ لَهُمْ مَّغْفِرَةٌ

وَّ اَجْرٌ كَبِيْرٌ ۞ فَلَعَلَّكَ تَارِكٌ بَعْضَ مَا يُوْحٰٓى

اِلَيْكَ وَضَآئِقٌ بِهٖ صَدْرُكَ اَنْ يَّقُوْلُوْا لَوْ لَآ اُنْزِلَ

عَلَيْهِ كَنْزٌ اَوْ جَآءَ مَعَهٗ مَلَكٌ ؕ اِنَّمَآ اَنْتَ نَذِيْرٌ ؕ

وَاللّٰهُ عَلٰى كُلِّ شَيْءٍ وَّكِيْلٌ ۞ اَمْ يَقُوْلُوْنَ افْتَرٰىهُ ؕ

قُلْ فَاْتُوْا بِعَشْرِ سُوَرٍ مِّثْلِهٖ مُفْتَرَيٰتٍ وَّادْعُوْا مَنِ

اسْتَطَعْتُمْ مِّنْ دُوْنِ اللّٰهِ اِنْ كُنْتُمْ صٰدِقِيْنَ ۞

فَاِلَّمْ يَسْتَجِيْبُوْا لَكُمْ فَاعْلَمُوْۤا اَنَّمَآ اُنْزِلَ بِعِلْمِ

اللّٰهِ وَاَنْ لَّاۤ اِلٰهَ اِلَّا هُوَ ۚ فَهَلْ اَنْتُمْ مُّسْلِمُوْنَ ۞

مَنْ كَانَ يُرِيْدُ الْحَيٰوةَ الدُّنْيَا وَ زِيْنَتَهَا نُوَفِّ

اِلَيْهِمْ اَعْمَالَهُمْ فِيْهَا وَهُمْ فِيْهَا لَا يُبْخَسُوْنَ ۞

اُولٰٓئِكَ الَّذِيْنَ لَيْسَ لَهُمْ فِى الْاٰخِرَةِ اِلَّا

النَّارُ ۖ وَحَبِطَ مَا صَنَعُوْا فِيْهَا وَ بٰطِلٌ مَّا كَانُوْا

يَعْمَلُوْنَ ۞ اَفَمَنْ كَانَ عَلٰى بَيِّنَةٍ مِّنْ رَّبِّهٖ

وَيَتْلُوْهُ شَاهِدٌ مِّنْهُ وَمِنْ قَبْلِهٖ كِتٰبُ مُوْسٰٓى

Are you overly concerned with worldly life and neglecting the Hereafter?

How quickly people's mood swings from sadness to joy

⁹ If We give people a taste of Our compassion then withdraw it abruptly from them, they become broken-hearted and ungrateful. ¹⁰ And if We gave someone a taste of *Our* favours after hardship they say, "Misfortune has left me," and become thrilled and proud, ¹¹ *all* except the patient and those who perform good works; they'll have forgiveness and a great reward.

Disbelievers challenged to produce ten surats

¹² So is it possible that you may *think of* leaving out part of what is revealed to you, since you are troubled because they say: "Why didn't a treasure come down to him, or an angel accompany him." You are a warner. Allah oversees everything. ¹³ And they say, "He has invented it"? Say: "Then fetch ten surats like it *that you have* invented, and call *as helpers* whomever you can besides Allah, if you are telling the truth. ¹⁴ And if *your witnesses* fail to respond to you, *doubters*, then be *certain* what is sent down *comes* with Allah's knowledge, and there is no god but Him. So will you submit *to Allah's will*?" ¹⁵ Whoever desires the worldly life and its attraction, We shall pay them back in full for their deeds during this life, and they won't be short-changed; ¹⁶ but, they will have nothing in the Hereafter except the Fire; their works will be worthless, and whatever they used to do will be null and void.

اِمَامًا وَّرَحْمَةً ؕ اُولٰٓئِكَ يُؤْمِنُوْنَ بِهٖ ؕ وَمَنْ يَّكْفُرْ
بِهٖ مِنَ الْاَحْزَابِ فَالنَّارُ مَوْعِدُهٗ ۚ فَلَا تَكُ فِيْ
مِرْيَةٍ مِّنْهُ ۗ اِنَّهُ الْحَقُّ مِنْ رَّبِّكَ وَلٰكِنَّ اَكْثَرَ
النَّاسِ لَا يُؤْمِنُوْنَ ﴿١٧﴾ وَمَنْ اَظْلَمُ مِمَّنِ افْتَرٰى
عَلَى اللّٰهِ كَذِبًا ؕ اُولٰٓئِكَ يُعْرَضُوْنَ عَلٰى رَبِّهِمْ وَيَقُوْلُ
الْاَشْهَادُ هٰٓؤُلَآءِ الَّذِيْنَ كَذَبُوْا عَلٰى رَبِّهِمْ ۚ اَلَا
لَعْنَةُ اللّٰهِ عَلَى الظّٰلِمِيْنَ ۙ ﴿١٨﴾ الَّذِيْنَ يَصُدُّوْنَ عَنْ
سَبِيْلِ اللّٰهِ وَيَبْغُوْنَهَا عِوَجًا ؕ وَهُمْ بِالْاٰخِرَةِ هُمْ
كٰفِرُوْنَ ﴿١٩﴾ اُولٰٓئِكَ لَمْ يَكُوْنُوْا مُعْجِزِيْنَ فِي الْاَرْضِ
وَمَا كَانَ لَهُمْ مِّنْ دُوْنِ اللّٰهِ مِنْ اَوْلِيَآءَ ۘ يُضٰعَفُ
لَهُمُ الْعَذَابُ ؕ مَا كَانُوْا يَسْتَطِيْعُوْنَ السَّمْعَ وَمَا
كَانُوْا يُبْصِرُوْنَ ﴿٢٠﴾ اُولٰٓئِكَ الَّذِيْنَ خَسِرُوْٓا اَنْفُسَهُمْ
وَضَلَّ عَنْهُمْ مَّا كَانُوْا يَفْتَرُوْنَ ﴿٢١﴾ لَا جَرَمَ اَنَّهُمْ
فِي الْاٰخِرَةِ هُمُ الْاَخْسَرُوْنَ ﴿٢٢﴾ اِنَّ الَّذِيْنَ اٰمَنُوْا
وَعَمِلُوا الصّٰلِحٰتِ وَاَخْبَتُوْٓا اِلٰى رَبِّهِمْ ۙ اُولٰٓئِكَ
اَصْحٰبُ الْجَنَّةِ ۚ هُمْ فِيْهَا خٰلِدُوْنَ ﴿٢٣﴾ مَثَلُ الْفَرِيْقَيْنِ
كَالْاَعْمٰى وَالْاَصَمِّ وَالْبَصِيْرِ وَالسَّمِيْعِ ؕ هَلْ يَسْتَوِيٰنِ
مَثَلًا ؕ اَفَلَا تَذَكَّرُوْنَ ﴿٢٤﴾ ع وَلَقَدْ اَرْسَلْنَا نُوْحًا اِلٰى ع ٢ ١٦ ٢
قَوْمِهٖٓ ۫ اِنِّيْ لَكُمْ نَذِيْرٌ مُّبِيْنٌ ﴿٢٥﴾ ۙ اَنْ لَّا تَعْبُدُوْٓا اِلَّا
اللّٰهَ ؕ اِنِّيْٓ اَخَافُ عَلَيْكُمْ عَذَابَ يَوْمٍ اَلِيْمٍ ﴿٢٦﴾ فَقَالَ

The biggest losers will be those who wanted this life.

Believers and disbelievers; contrasting beliefs and practices

[17] Can they *be compared with* someone who has clear proof from His Lord which he reads, bears witness to it and what came before it, *namely* the Book of Musa, as a guide and *Divine* kindness? These *people* believe in it. Anyone who denies from the groups allied *against you*, the Fire will be his promised destination, be in no doubt about it; it is the truth from your Lord, but most people don't believe.

The disbelievers failed to use the inner eye

[18] Who is more sinful than the one who invents lies about Allah? Such people will be brought before their Lord, and the witnesses will say, "These are the people who lied about their Lord." Beware, Allah's curse is on the wrongdoers [19] who block Allah's path, wishing to make it crooked, and who deny the Hereafter. [20] They couldn't thwart *Allah's plan* on Earth, and they had no *real* protector besides Allah. Their punishment will be multiplied. They were unwilling to listen, and they did not *try to* see. [21] Such people have lost themselves, and all that they used to invent has deserted them. [22] Without doubt, they will be the biggest losers in the Hereafter. [23] Those who believed, did noble deeds and were humble before their Lord, they will be the companions of Paradise, and live there forever. [24] The two types are like a deaf, blind person compared to a seeing and hearing person. Can they ever be alike? Won't you pay attention?

Stories of seven prophets: Nuh tries to reason with his people

[25] We sent Nuh to his people, *saying*, "I am a clear warner to you. [26] Worship Allah alone. I fear for you the torment of an agonizing day."

الْمَلَأُ الَّذِيْنَ كَفَرُوْا مِنْ قَوْمِهٖ مَا نَرٰىكَ اِلَّا

بَشَرًا مِّثْلَنَا وَمَا نَرٰىكَ اتَّبَعَكَ اِلَّا الَّذِيْنَ هُمْ

اَرَاذِلُنَا بَادِيَ الرَّأْيِ ۚ وَمَا نَرٰى لَكُمْ عَلَيْنَا مِنْ

فَضْلٍۭ بَلْ نَظُنُّكُمْ كٰذِبِيْنَ ۝ قَالَ يٰقَوْمِ اَرَءَيْتُمْ

اِنْ كُنْتُ عَلٰى بَيِّنَةٍ مِّنْ رَّبِّيْ وَاٰتٰىنِيْ رَحْمَةً مِّنْ

عِنْدِهٖ فَعُمِّيَتْ عَلَيْكُمْ ؕ اَنُلْزِمُكُمُوْهَا وَاَنْتُمْ لَهَا

كٰرِهُوْنَ ۝ وَيٰقَوْمِ لَاۤ اَسْـَٔلُكُمْ عَلَيْهِ مَالًا ؕ اِنْ

اَجْرِيَ اِلَّا عَلَى اللّٰهِ وَمَاۤ اَنَا بِطَارِدِ الَّذِيْنَ اٰمَنُوْا ؕ

اِنَّهُمْ مُّلٰقُوْا رَبِّهِمْ وَلٰكِنِّيْ اَرٰىكُمْ قَوْمًا تَجْهَلُوْنَ ۝

وَيٰقَوْمِ مَنْ يَّنْصُرُنِيْ مِنَ اللّٰهِ اِنْ طَرَدْتُّهُمْ ؕ

اَفَلَا تَذَكَّرُوْنَ ۝ وَلَاۤ اَقُوْلُ لَكُمْ عِنْدِيْ خَزَآئِنُ

اللّٰهِ وَلَاۤ اَعْلَمُ الْغَيْبَ وَلَاۤ اَقُوْلُ اِنِّيْ مَلَكٌ وَّلَاۤ

اَقُوْلُ لِلَّذِيْنَ تَزْدَرِيْۤ اَعْيُنُكُمْ لَنْ يُّؤْتِيَهُمُ

اللّٰهُ خَيْرًا ؕ اَللّٰهُ اَعْلَمُ بِمَا فِيْۤ اَنْفُسِهِمْ ۖ اِنِّيْۤ

اِذًا لَّمِنَ الظّٰلِمِيْنَ ۝ قَالُوْا يٰنُوْحُ قَدْ جٰدَلْتَنَا

فَاَكْثَرْتَ جِدَالَنَا فَاْتِنَا بِمَا تَعِدُنَاۤ اِنْ كُنْتَ

مِنَ الصّٰدِقِيْنَ ۝ قَالَ اِنَّمَا يَاْتِيْكُمْ بِهِ اللّٰهُ اِنْ

شَآءَ وَمَاۤ اَنْتُمْ بِمُعْجِزِيْنَ ۝ وَلَا يَنْفَعُكُمْ

نُصْحِيْۤ اِنْ اَرَدْتُّ اَنْ اَنْصَحَ لَكُمْ اِنْ كَانَ

اللّٰهُ يُرِيْدُ اَنْ يُّغْوِيَكُمْ ؕ هُوَ رَبُّكُمْ ۚ وَاِلَيْهِ

Allah doesn't compel people to believe, He gives free choice.

431

²⁷So, the leaders of the disbelievers said, "It's clear to us that you are human like us, and only the lowest of our society follow you, and we don't see you have any special quality that we lack. On the contrary, we think you are liars." ²⁸*Nuh* said, "My people, haven't you considered what if I have the clear proof from My Lord, and that He's blessed me with kindness? If you are blind *to the truth*, could we force it on you against your will? ²⁹My people, I am not asking you for wealth in return. My reward comes from Allah alone. I am not driving away the believers. They will meet their Lord, but it's clear to me that you are ignorant people. ³⁰My people, suppose I drove them away, who would help me against Allah? Why do you not pay attention? ³¹I am not telling you I have *access to* Allah's treasures, or knowledge of the unseen, or I am an angel; and I *will* not tell those you look down on that they will be deprived of Allah's goodness – Allah knows best what is in their hearts – *if I said these things*, I would be a wrongdoer."

Nuh's people ask for punishment

³²They said, "Nuh, you argued with us, and have gone on arguing with us *for a long time*, so now bring us what you promised if you are telling the truth." ³³He said, "Only Allah can bring it on you if He wishes, and you won't be able to stop it.

تُرْجَعُوْنَ ۝ اَمْ يَقُوْلُوْنَ افْتَرٰىهُ ؕ قُلْ اِنِ افْتَرَيْتُهٗ

فَعَلَيَّ اِجْرَامِيْ وَاَنَا بَرِيْٓءٌ مِّمَّا تُجْرِمُوْنَ ۝ وَ

اُوْحِيَ اِلٰى نُوْحٍ اَنَّهٗ لَنْ يُّؤْمِنَ مِنْ قَوْمِكَ اِلَّا

مَنْ قَدْ اٰمَنَ فَلَا تَبْتَئِسْ بِمَا كَانُوْا يَفْعَلُوْنَ ۝

وَاصْنَعِ الْفُلْكَ بِاَعْيُنِنَا وَوَحْيِنَا وَلَا تُخَاطِبْنِيْ

فِى الَّذِيْنَ ظَلَمُوْا ۚ اِنَّهُمْ مُّغْرَقُوْنَ ۝ وَ يَصْنَعُ

الْفُلْكَ ۟ وَكُلَّمَا مَرَّ عَلَيْهِ مَلَاٌ مِّنْ قَوْمِهٖ سَخِرُوْا

مِنْهُ ؕ قَالَ اِنْ تَسْخَرُوْا مِنَّا فَاِنَّا نَسْخَرُ مِنْكُمْ كَمَا

تَسْخَرُوْنَ ۝ فَسَوْفَ تَعْلَمُوْنَ ۙ مَنْ يَّاْتِيْهِ عَذَابٌ

يُّخْزِيْهِ وَيَحِلُّ عَلَيْهِ عَذَابٌ مُّقِيْمٌ ۝ حَتّٰٓى اِذَا

جَآءَ اَمْرُنَا وَفَارَ التَّنُّوْرُ ۙ قُلْنَا احْمِلْ فِيْهَا مِنْ كُلٍّ

زَوْجَيْنِ اثْنَيْنِ وَاَهْلَكَ اِلَّا مَنْ سَبَقَ عَلَيْهِ الْقَوْلُ

وَمَنْ اٰمَنَ ؕ وَمَاۤ اٰمَنَ مَعَهٗٓ اِلَّا قَلِيْلٌ ۝ وَقَالَ

ارْكَبُوْا فِيْهَا بِسْمِ اللّٰهِ مَجْرٰىهَا وَمُرْسٰىهَا ؕ اِنَّ رَبِّيْ

لَغَفُوْرٌ رَّحِيْمٌ ۝ وَهِيَ تَجْرِيْ بِهِمْ فِيْ مَوْجٍ كَالْجِبَالِ ۟

وَنَادٰى نُوْحُ ابْنَهٗ وَكَانَ فِيْ مَعْزِلٍ يّٰبُنَيَّ ارْكَبْ

مَّعَنَا وَلَا تَكُنْ مَّعَ الْكٰفِرِيْنَ ۝ قَالَ سَاٰوِيْٓ اِلٰى

جَبَلٍ يَّعْصِمُنِيْ مِنَ الْمَآءِ ؕ قَالَ لَا عَاصِمَ الْيَوْمَ

مِنْ اَمْرِ اللّٰهِ اِلَّا مَنْ رَّحِمَ ۚ وَحَالَ بَيْنَهُمَا الْمَوْجُ

فَكَانَ مِنَ الْمُغْرَقِيْنَ ۝ وَقِيْلَ يٰٓاَرْضُ ابْلَعِيْ

Building the ship, can it symbolise the good deeds we do for the Hereafter?

433

³⁴Nor will my advice benefit you no matter how much I advise you, if Allah wants you to go astray.ᵃ He is your Lord, and to Him you will return." ³⁵Sometimes they say, "He has invented it"? Say: "If I invented it, then my sins will fall on me, but I am innocent of the sins that you commit."

Nuh is instructed to build a ship

³⁶It was revealed to Nuh: "No one else from your people will believe except those who have already done so, so don't be saddened by what they have done. ³⁷Build a ship under Our supervision and guidance, and don't ask Me to *sympathize for* evildoers: they are *as good as* drowned." ³⁸Whenever the leaders of his people passed by him building the ship, they mocked him, and he would say: "If you mock us, we too shall be mocking you in the same way. ³⁹You will *come to* learn *soon enough* who will be humiliated, and deserves an everlasting punishment."

The flood comes!

⁴⁰*Finally*, by Our order, the baked Earth started flooding *with water*.ᵇ We said *to Nuh*: "Load the ship with a pair of each *animal*, as well as your family – except those against whom Our sentence has been passed – and whoever believes." Those who believed in him were few. ⁴¹"Board her," he said, "In the name of Allah, she will sail and weigh anchor *to rest*. My Lord is Forgiving, Kind." ⁴²As she set sail with them, amid waves as high as mountains, Nuh called out to his son, who was standing apart from the rest: "My dear son, come on board with us. Don't stay with the disbelievers." ⁴³He said, "I will take refuge on a mountain, which will protect me from the *rising* waters." Nuh said, "There is no protection from Allah's order today, except the one who He treats kindly." Then a wave came between them, and *his son* drowned.

ᵃ Literally "He will lead you astray", has been interpreted as "He will punish you for your sins". Here I have expressed this as human choice, Allah doesn't compel people to believe.

ᵇ *Tannur* literally means a clay oven or kiln, but here it is the sun-baked river bank or the shore of the lake around which they lived.

مَآءَكِ وَيَسَمَآءُ اَقْلِعِيْ وَغِيْضَ الْمَآءُ وَقُضِيَ
الْاَمْرُ وَاسْتَوَتْ عَلَى الْجُوْدِيِّ وَقِيْلَ بُعْدًا لِّلْقَوْمِ
الظّٰلِمِيْنَ ۴۴ وَنَادٰى نُوْحُ رَّبَّهٗ فَقَالَ رَبِّ اِنَّ ابْنِيْ
مِنْ اَهْلِيْ وَاِنَّ وَعْدَكَ الْحَقُّ وَاَنْتَ اَحْكَمُ
الْحٰكِمِيْنَ ۴۵ قَالَ يٰنُوْحُ اِنَّهٗ لَيْسَ مِنْ اَهْلِكَ
اِنَّهٗ عَمَلٌ غَيْرُ صَالِحٍ ۣ فَلَا تَسْـَٔلْنِ مَا لَيْسَ لَكَ
بِهٖ عِلْمٌ ؕ اِنِّيْۤ اَعِظُكَ اَنْ تَكُوْنَ مِنَ الْجٰهِلِيْنَ ۴۶
قَالَ رَبِّ اِنِّيْۤ اَعُوْذُ بِكَ اَنْ اَسْـَٔلَكَ مَا لَيْسَ لِيْ
بِهٖ عِلْمٌ ؕ وَاِلَّا تَغْفِرْ لِيْ وَتَرْحَمْنِيْۤ اَكُنْ مِّنَ
الْخٰسِرِيْنَ ۴۷ قِيْلَ يٰنُوْحُ اهْبِطْ بِسَلٰمٍ مِّنَّا وَبَرَكٰتٍ
عَلَيْكَ وَعَلٰۤى اُمَمٍ مِّمَّنْ مَّعَكَ ؕ وَاُمَمٌ سَنُمَتِّعُهُمْ
ثُمَّ يَمَسُّهُمْ مِّنَّا عَذَابٌ اَلِيْمٌ ۴۸ تِلْكَ مِنْ اَنْۢبَآءِ
الْغَيْبِ نُوْحِيْهَآ اِلَيْكَ ۚ مَا كُنْتَ تَعْلَمُهَآ اَنْتَ وَلَا
قَوْمُكَ مِنْ قَبْلِ هٰذَا ۛ فَاصْبِرْ ؕ اِنَّ الْعَاقِبَةَ
لِلْمُتَّقِيْنَ ۴۹ وَاِلٰى عَادٍ اَخَاهُمْ هُوْدًا ؕ قَالَ يٰقَوْمِ
اعْبُدُوا اللّٰهَ مَا لَكُمْ مِّنْ اِلٰهٍ غَيْرُهٗ ؕ اِنْ اَنْتُمْ اِلَّا
مُفْتَرُوْنَ ۵۰ يٰقَوْمِ لَاۤ اَسْـَٔلُكُمْ عَلَيْهِ اَجْرًا ؕ اِنْ اَجْرِيَ
اِلَّا عَلَى الَّذِيْ فَطَرَنِيْ ؕ اَفَلَا تَعْقِلُوْنَ ۵۱ وَيٰقَوْمِ
اسْتَغْفِرُوْا رَبَّكُمْ ثُمَّ تُوْبُوْۤا اِلَيْهِ يُرْسِلِ السَّمَآءَ
عَلَيْكُمْ مِّدْرَارًا وَّيَزِدْكُمْ قُوَّةً اِلٰى قُوَّتِكُمْ وَلَا

Why does the Quran exclude Nuh's son from his family? What does this tell us about our relationship with Allah?

⁴⁴ *A voice* called out: "Earth, swallow your water!" And "Sky, clear away *the clouds* and the water receded!" *Allah's* order was carried out, and *the ship* came to rest on Mount Judi.ᵃ A *voice* said: "Away with the wrongdoers!"

Nuh is told not to mourn his son's death

⁴⁵ Nuh called out to His Lord, "My Lord, my son was a member of my family; Your promise is true, and You are the best judge." ⁴⁶ *Allah* said, "Nuh, he wasn't *a member* of your family his deeds were evil; so don't ask Me about things which you don't know. I am warning you, in case you become ignorant people." ⁴⁷ He said, "My Lord, I seek your refuge from asking You about things I don't know. If you don't forgive me and show compassion to me, I will be a loser." ⁴⁸ A *voice* said, "Nuh, disembark with peace and blessings from Us and on the nations *who will be the descendants* of those who are with you. There will be *other* nations We shall grant enjoyment *for a while*, but then afflict them with a painful punishment." ⁴⁹ This is an account from the unseen that We revealed to you, *Messenger,* neither you nor your people knew it before this. So be patient, the future shall be good for those mindful *of Allah.*

Prophet Hud promises prosperity if they repent

⁵⁰ *We sent* Hud, their brother, to *the people of* Ad, he told them: "My people, worship Allah. You have no other god but Him. You have invented idols. ⁵¹ My people, I am not asking you for any reward, my reward comes from Him Who created me, don't you understand? ⁵² My people, seek your Lord's forgiveness and turn to Him in repentance, and He will give you plentiful rain and make you stronger. Don't turn away as sinners."

ᵃ The precise location of Mount Judi is not clear. Some say it's near Lake Van in Eastern Turkey.

تَتَوَلَّوْا مُجْرِمِيْنَ ۵۲ قَالُوْا يٰهُوْدُ مَا جِئْتَنَا بِبَيِّنَةٍ

وَّمَا نَحْنُ بِتَارِكِيْ اٰلِهَتِنَا عَنْ قَوْلِكَ وَمَا نَحْنُ لَكَ

بِمُؤْمِنِيْنَ ۵۳ اِنْ نَّقُوْلُ اِلَّا اعْتَرٰىكَ بَعْضُ اٰلِهَتِنَا

بِسُوْۤءٍ ؕ قَالَ اِنِّىْٓ اُشْهِدُ اللّٰهَ وَاشْهَدُوْۤا اَنِّىْ بَرِيْۤءٌ

مِّمَّا تُشْرِكُوْنَ ۵۴ مِنْ دُوْنِهٖ فَكِيْدُوْنِىْ جَمِيْعًا ثُمَّ

لَا تُنْظِرُوْنِ ۵۵ اِنِّىْ تَوَكَّلْتُ عَلَى اللّٰهِ رَبِّىْ وَرَبِّكُمْ ؕ مَا

مِنْ دَآبَّةٍ اِلَّا هُوَ اٰخِذٌۢ بِنَاصِيَتِهَا ؕ اِنَّ رَبِّىْ عَلٰى

صِرَاطٍ مُّسْتَقِيْمٍ ۵۶ فَاِنْ تَوَلَّوْا فَقَدْ اَبْلَغْتُكُمْ مَّاۤ

What an amazing strength Prophet Hud had, how he stood up to the tyrants.

اُرْسِلْتُ بِهٖۤ اِلَيْكُمْ ؕ وَيَسْتَخْلِفُ رَبِّىْ قَوْمًا غَيْرَكُمْ ۚ

وَلَا تَضُرُّوْنَهٗ شَيْئًا ؕ اِنَّ رَبِّىْ عَلٰى كُلِّ شَىْءٍ

حَفِيْظٌ ۵۷ وَلَمَّا جَآءَ اَمْرُنَا نَجَّيْنَا هُوْدًا وَّالَّذِيْنَ

اٰمَنُوْا مَعَهٗ بِرَحْمَةٍ مِّنَّا ۚ وَنَجَّيْنٰهُمْ مِّنْ عَذَابٍ

غَلِيْظٍ ۵۸ وَتِلْكَ عَادٌ ۙ جَحَدُوْا بِاٰيٰتِ رَبِّهِمْ وَعَصَوْا

رُسُلَهٗ وَاتَّبَعُوْۤا اَمْرَ كُلِّ جَبَّارٍ عَنِيْدٍ ۵۹ وَاُتْبِعُوْا

فِىْ هٰذِهِ الدُّنْيَا لَعْنَةً وَّيَوْمَ الْقِيٰمَةِ ؕ اَلَاۤ اِنَّ

عَادًا كَفَرُوْا رَبَّهُمْ ؕ اَلَا بُعْدًا لِّعَادٍ قَوْمِ هُوْدٍ ۶۰

وَاِلٰى ثَمُوْدَ اَخَاهُمْ صٰلِحًا ۘ قَالَ يٰقَوْمِ اعْبُدُوا

اللّٰهَ مَا لَكُمْ مِّنْ اِلٰهٍ غَيْرُهٗ ؕ هُوَ اَنْشَاَكُمْ مِّنَ

الْاَرْضِ وَاسْتَعْمَرَكُمْ فِيْهَا فَاسْتَغْفِرُوْهُ ثُمَّ تُوْبُوْۤا

اِلَيْهِ ؕ اِنَّ رَبِّىْ قَرِيْبٌ مُّجِيْبٌ ۶۱ قَالُوْا يٰصٰلِحُ قَدْ

The people refused to listen

⁵³They said, "Hud, you haven't brought us any proof. We won't give up our gods because of your words. We don't believe you. ⁵⁴We think some of our gods have made you mad." He said, "I call Allah as my witness – and you be witnesses – I am free from those you associate with Him. ⁵⁵So plot against me, all of you, and grant me no respite. ⁵⁶I have put my trust in Allah, my Lord and yours. There isn't a single creature whose destiny He doesn't control.^a My Lord *guides me* along a straight path. ⁵⁷If you turn away, *so be it*. I have conveyed what I was sent with to you. My Lord will get other people to succeed you, and you can't harm Him in the least. My Lord oversees everything."

Allah's curse tracks the evildoers

⁵⁸When Our verdict came to pass, We rescued Hud and the believers with him, We were kind and saved them from a severe punishment. ⁵⁹Such was *the story* of Ad. They rejected their Lord's signs, disobeyed His messengers, and adopted the way of every stubborn tyrant. ⁶⁰They were tracked in this *world* by *Allah's* curse and *again* on Judgement Day. Didn't Ad reject their Lord? Away with Ad, the people of Hud.

---

^a Literally means "He has hold of them by their forelocks", which is an idiom for Allah's control over the destiny of His creation.

كُنْتَ فِيْنَا مَرْجُوًّا قَبْلَ هٰذَآ اَتَنْهٰنَآ اَنْ نَّعْبُدَ
مَا يَعْبُدُ اٰبَآؤُنَا وَ اِنَّنَا لَفِيْ شَكٍّ مِّمَّا تَدْعُوْنَآ
اِلَيْهِ مُرِيْبٍ ۝ قَالَ يٰقَوْمِ اَرَءَيْتُمْ اِنْ كُنْتُ
عَلٰى بَيِّنَةٍ مِّنْ رَّبِّيْ وَ اٰتٰنِيْ مِنْهُ رَحْمَةً فَمَنْ
يَّنْصُرُنِيْ مِنَ اللّٰهِ اِنْ عَصَيْتُهُ ۙ فَمَا تَزِيْدُوْنَنِيْ
غَيْرَ تَخْسِيْرٍ ۝ وَيٰقَوْمِ هٰذِهٖ نَاقَةُ اللّٰهِ لَكُمْ
اٰيَةً فَذَرُوْهَا تَأْكُلْ فِيْٓ اَرْضِ اللّٰهِ وَلَا تَمَسُّوْهَا
بِسُوْٓءٍ فَيَأْخُذَكُمْ عَذَابٌ قَرِيْبٌ ۝ فَعَقَرُوْهَا
فَقَالَ تَمَتَّعُوْا فِيْ دَارِكُمْ ثَلٰثَةَ اَيَّامٍ ۭ ذٰلِكَ
وَعْدٌ غَيْرُ مَكْذُوْبٍ ۝ فَلَمَّا جَآءَ اَمْرُنَا نَجَّيْنَا
صٰلِحًا وَّ الَّذِيْنَ اٰمَنُوْا مَعَهٗ بِرَحْمَةٍ مِّنَّا وَمِنْ
خِزْيِ يَوْمِئِذٍ ۭ اِنَّ رَبَّكَ هُوَ الْقَوِيُّ الْعَزِيْزُ ۝
وَ اَخَذَ الَّذِيْنَ ظَلَمُوا الصَّيْحَةُ فَاَصْبَحُوْا فِيْ
دِيَارِهِمْ جٰثِمِيْنَ ۝ كَاَنْ لَّمْ يَغْنَوْا فِيْهَا ۭ اَلَآ
اِنَّ ثَمُوْدَا۟ كَفَرُوْا رَبَّهُمْ ۭ اَلَا بُعْدًا لِّثَمُوْدَ ۝
وَلَقَدْ جَآءَتْ رُسُلُنَآ اِبْرٰهِيْمَ بِالْبُشْرٰى قَالُوْا
سَلٰمًا ۭ قَالَ سَلٰمٌ فَمَا لَبِثَ اَنْ جَآءَ بِعِجْلٍ
حَنِيْذٍ ۝ فَلَمَّا رَآٰ اَيْدِيَهُمْ لَا تَصِلُ اِلَيْهِ نَكِرَهُمْ
وَاَوْجَسَ مِنْهُمْ خِيْفَةً ۭ قَالُوْا لَا تَخَفْ اِنَّآ اُرْسِلْنَآ
اِلٰى قَوْمِ لُوْطٍ ۝ وَامْرَاَتُهٗ قَآئِمَةٌ فَضَحِكَتْ

Why do people ignore the big signs? They saw the she-camel's miraculous appearance, but denied it?

439

People defy Salih's call not to harm the she-camel

⁶¹ *We sent* their brother Salih *to people of* Thamud, he told *them*: "My people, worship Allah. You have no other god but Him. It is He Who raised you up in *this* land and helped you to settle in it, so seek His forgiveness and turn to Him in repentance. My Lord is near, and answers the *prayers*." ⁶² They said, "Salih, before this *preaching* we had pinned our hopes on you, are you forbidding us to worship what our forefathers worshipped? We have grave doubts about what you are calling us to."

The miracle of the she-camel

⁶³ He said, "My people don't you realise I have clear proof from My Lord, He's been kind to me. If I disobeyed Him, Who would help me against Him? *In that case*, you would only add to my loss. ⁶⁴ My people, this is the she-camel of Allah, a sign for you. Let her graze *wherever she wants* in Allah's Earth, and don't harm her, or else you'll be quickly punished." ⁶⁵ They hamstrung her, so *Salih* said, "For three days, enjoy yourselves in your homes: that's no idle threat." ⁶⁶ When Our decree came to pass, We rescued Salih and the believers with him from that day's humiliation, an act of Our kindness. Your Lord is the Powerful, the Almighty. ⁶⁷ A single blast devastated the wrongdoers and, when morning came, there they lay, dead in their homes, ⁶⁸ as though they never existed. Listen, Thamud rejected their Lord. So away with Thamud!

The angels visit Ibrahim with good and bad news

⁶⁹ Our Angel messengers came to Ibrahim with good news, greeting him; "Peace!" He *greeted them* with peace too, and he quickly brought them a roasted calf. ⁷⁰ However, when he saw their hands were not reaching for it, he felt uneasy about them, which gradually turned to fright. "Fear not," they said, "We've been sent to the people of Lut."

فَبَشَّرْنٰهَا بِاِسْحٰقَ ۙ وَمِنْ وَّرَآءِ اِسْحٰقَ يَعْقُوْبَ ۝

قَالَتْ يٰوَيْلَتٰٓى ءَاَلِدُ وَاَنَا عَجُوْزٌ وَّهٰذَا بَعْلِيْ

شَيْخًا ۗ اِنَّ هٰذَا لَشَىْءٌ عَجِيْبٌ ۝ قَالُوْٓا اَتَعْجَبِيْنَ

مِنْ اَمْرِ اللّٰهِ رَحْمَتُ اللّٰهِ وَبَرَكٰتُهٗ عَلَيْكُمْ اَهْلَ

الْبَيْتِ ۗ اِنَّهٗ حَمِيْدٌ مَّجِيْدٌ ۝ فَلَمَّا ذَهَبَ عَنْ

اِبْرٰهِيْمَ الرَّوْعُ وَجَآءَتْهُ الْبُشْرٰى يُجَادِلُنَا فِيْ

قَوْمِ لُوْطٍ ۝ اِنَّ اِبْرٰهِيْمَ لَحَلِيْمٌ اَوَّاهٌ مُّنِيْبٌ ۝

يٰٓاِبْرٰهِيْمُ اَعْرِضْ عَنْ هٰذَا ۚ اِنَّهٗ قَدْ جَآءَ اَمْرُ

رَبِّكَ ۚ وَاِنَّهُمْ اٰتِيْهِمْ عَذَابٌ غَيْرُ مَرْدُوْدٍ ۝

وَلَمَّا جَآءَتْ رُسُلُنَا لُوْطًا سِيْٓءَ بِهِمْ وَضَاقَ

بِهِمْ ذَرْعًا وَّقَالَ هٰذَا يَوْمٌ عَصِيْبٌ ۝ وَجَآءَهٗ

قَوْمُهٗ يُهْرَعُوْنَ اِلَيْهِ ۗ وَمِنْ قَبْلُ كَانُوْا يَعْمَلُوْنَ

السَّيِّاٰتِ ۗ قَالَ يٰقَوْمِ هٰٓؤُلَآءِ بَنَاتِيْ هُنَّ اَطْهَرُ

لَكُمْ فَاتَّقُوا اللّٰهَ وَلَا تُخْزُوْنِ فِيْ ضَيْفِيْ ۗ اَلَيْسَ

مِنْكُمْ رَجُلٌ رَّشِيْدٌ ۝ قَالُوْا لَقَدْ عَلِمْتَ مَا لَنَا فِيْ

بَنٰتِكَ مِنْ حَقٍّ ۚ وَاِنَّكَ لَتَعْلَمُ مَا نُرِيْدُ ۝ قَالَ

لَوْ اَنَّ لِيْ بِكُمْ قُوَّةً اَوْ اٰوِيْٓ اِلٰى رُكْنٍ شَدِيْدٍ ۝

قَالُوْا يٰلُوْطُ اِنَّا رُسُلُ رَبِّكَ لَنْ يَّصِلُوْٓا اِلَيْكَ

فَاَسْرِ بِاَهْلِكَ بِقِطْعٍ مِّنَ الَّيْلِ وَلَا يَلْتَفِتْ

مِنْكُمْ اَحَدٌ اِلَّا امْرَاَتَكَ ۗ اِنَّهٗ مُصِيْبُهَا مَآ

How sincerely Lut warned his community against their vile and wicked habit.

⁷¹ His wife, who was standing *nearby*, laughed, so We gave her good news of Ishaq and, after Ishaq, of Yaqub. ⁷² "How come!" She said, "How will I have a child, when I am an old woman and my husband is an old man? This will be an odd thing." ⁷³ "Are you surprised at Allah's command?" They said, "May Allah's compassion and blessings be on you, people of *this* household. He is Praiseworthy, Glorious." ⁷⁴ Once Ibrahim's fear lessened, and the good news had sunk in, he began to plead with Us about the people of Lut: ⁷⁵ Ibrahim was gentle, soft-hearted and devout. ⁷⁶ "Ibrahim," We told him, "put this aside. *The time for* Your Lord's command has come, and the punishment can't be turned back, it will come to them."

The angels visit Lut to warn him of his people's fate

⁷⁷ When Our *angel* messengers came to Lut, he was sad and anxious about them, saying, "What a dreadful day this is!" ⁷⁸ His people, who committed evil deeds came hurriedly to him; he said, "My people, my daughters and *the tribe's women* are far purer for you^a. So fear Allah, and don't shame me in front of my guests. Isn't there a single sensible man among you?" ⁷⁹ They said, "You know we have no right to your tribes daughters, *just as* you know what we want." ⁸⁰ "If only I had power against you," he said, "or I had a strong supporting group to protect me." ⁸¹ "Lut, we are your Lord's messengers," *the angels* said, "They will not get you, so leave with your family in the dark of the night, and let none of you turn back to look. Only your wife will suffer the fate of the others. Their appointed time is the morning. Won't it be morning soon?"

---

^a Prophet Lut is telling them to behave themselves and satisfy their desires with their wives.

أَصَابَهُمْ ۭ إِنَّ مَوْعِدَهُمُ الصُّبْحُ ۭ أَلَيْسَ الصُّبْحُ

بِقَرِيبٍ ۞ فَلَمَّا جَآءَ أَمْرُنَا جَعَلْنَا عَالِيَهَا سَافِلَهَا

وَأَمْطَرْنَا عَلَيْهَا حِجَارَةً مِّن سِجِّيلٍ ۙ مَّنضُودٍ ۞

مُّسَوَّمَةً عِنْدَ رَبِّكَ ۭ وَمَا هِيَ مِنَ الظّٰلِمِيْنَ

بِبَعِيدٍ ۞ وَإِلٰى مَدْيَنَ أَخَاهُمْ شُعَيْبًا ۭ قَالَ

يٰقَوْمِ اعْبُدُوا اللّٰهَ مَا لَكُمْ مِّنْ إِلٰهٍ غَيْرُهُ ۭ وَلَا

تَنقُصُوا الْمِكْيَالَ وَالْمِيزَانَ إِنِّيْ أَرٰىكُمْ بِخَيْرٍ وَّإِنِّيْ

أَخَافُ عَلَيْكُمْ عَذَابَ يَوْمٍ مُّحِيطٍ ۞ وَيٰقَوْمِ أَوْفُوا

الْمِكْيَالَ وَالْمِيزَانَ بِالْقِسْطِ وَلَا تَبْخَسُوا النَّاسَ

أَشْيَآءَهُمْ وَلَا تَعْثَوْا فِي الْأَرْضِ مُفْسِدِيْنَ ۞ بَقِيَّتُ

اللّٰهِ خَيْرٌ لَّكُمْ إِنْ كُنتُمْ مُّؤْمِنِيْنَ ۚ وَمَآ أَنَا

عَلَيْكُمْ بِحَفِيظٍ ۞ قَالُوا يٰشُعَيْبُ أَصَلٰوتُكَ تَأْمُرُكَ

أَنْ نَّتْرُكَ مَا يَعْبُدُ اٰبَآؤُنَا أَوْ أَنْ نَّفْعَلَ فِيْ

أَمْوَالِنَا مَا نَشٰٓؤُا ۭ إِنَّكَ لَأَنتَ الْحَلِيْمُ الرَّشِيْدُ ۞

قَالَ يٰقَوْمِ أَرَءَيْتُمْ إِنْ كُنتُ عَلٰى بَيِّنَةٍ مِّن رَّبِّيْ

وَرَزَقَنِيْ مِنْهُ رِزْقًا حَسَنًا ۭ وَمَآ أُرِيْدُ أَنْ أُخَالِفَكُمْ

إِلٰى مَآ أَنْهٰكُمْ عَنْهُ ۭ إِنْ أُرِيْدُ إِلَّا الْإِصْلَاحَ مَا

اسْتَطَعْتُ ۭ وَمَا تَوْفِيْقِيْٓ إِلَّا بِاللّٰهِ ۭ عَلَيْهِ تَوَكَّلْتُ

وَإِلَيْهِ أُنِيْبُ ۞ وَيٰقَوْمِ لَا يَجْرِمَنَّكُمْ شِقَاقِيْٓ أَنْ

يُّصِيْبَكُمْ مِّثْلُ مَآ أَصَابَ قَوْمَ نُوْحٍ أَوْ قَوْمَ هُوْدٍ أَوْ

The community of Shu'ayb was dishonest in business.

⁸² When *at last the time* came for Our command *to be fulfilled*, We turned their town upside down, and We continuously pelted it with stones of baked clay. ⁸³ *The site* has been clearly marked out by Your Lord, and it is by no means far from the wrongdoers *of Makkah*.^a

Shu'ayb warns his people against fraudulent practises

⁸⁴ *We sent* their brother Shu'ayb to Madyan, he told *them*: "My people worship Allah. You have no god but Him. Don't *cheat by giving* in short measure or weights; you are well off, but I fear for you the punishment of an overwhelming day. ⁸⁵ My people, be scrupulously honest in your weights and measures, and don't defraud people out of what is theirs or wander around making trouble in the land. ⁸⁶ The profit margin *permitted* by Allah should be sufficient earnings for you, if you were believers, and I am not *your guardian*." ⁸⁷ They said, "Shu'ayb, does your prayer teach you to stop us from worshipping what our forefathers worshipped and doing as we please with our wealth? You are too civil and sensible!"

Shu'ayb warns his people

⁸⁸ He said, "My people, don't you realise that I have clear proof from My Lord, Who has generously provided for me. I don't want to do anything that I forbid you to do; I wish to reform *society* to the best of my ability. My success depends entirely on Allah, I have put my trust in Him and I turn in repentance to Him. ⁸⁹ My people, don't let your hostility to me lead you to the same *fate* as the people of Nuh, Hud, Salih; and *remember* the people of Lut *didn't live* far away from you.^b

---

^a   Lut's town was on the trading route north from Makkah to Syria, and was a terrifying reminder to the passers-by of what happens to those who rebel against Allah.

^b   The reference here to the people of Lut is significant. Many commentators interpret the distance as one of time. However, it's possible to see in this verse a sort of moral equivalence is being drawn between the evils of all these peoples: a society that practises wholesale cheating and fraud is every bit as deserving of Allah's wrath as another that mocks His signs, or one that has given itself over to sexual lewdness.

قَوْمُ صٰلِحٍ ط وَمَا قَوْمُ لُوْطٍ مِّنْكُمْ بِبَعِيْدٍ ۸۹ وَاسْتَغْفِرُوْا

رَبَّكُمْ ثُمَّ تُوْبُوْۤا اِلَيْهِ ط اِنَّ رَبِّيْ رَحِيْمٌ وَّدُوْدٌ ۹۰ قَالُوْا

يٰشُعَيْبُ مَا نَفْقَهُ كَثِيْرًا مِّمَّا تَقُوْلُ وَاِنَّا لَنَرٰىكَ

فِيْنَا ضَعِيْفًا ۚ وَلَوْلَا رَهْطُكَ لَرَجَمْنٰكَ ۫ وَمَاۤ اَنْتَ

عَلَيْنَا بِعَزِيْزٍ ۹۱ قَالَ يٰقَوْمِ اَرَهْطِيْۤ اَعَزُّ عَلَيْكُمْ مِّنَ

اللّٰهِ ط وَاتَّخَذْتُمُوْهُ وَرَآءَكُمْ ظِهْرِيًّا ط اِنَّ رَبِّيْ بِمَا

تَعْمَلُوْنَ مُحِيْطٌ ۹۲ وَيٰقَوْمِ اعْمَلُوْا عَلٰى مَكَانَتِكُمْ

اِنِّيْ عَامِلٌ ط سَوْفَ تَعْلَمُوْنَ ۙ مَنْ يَّأْتِيْهِ عَذَابٌ

يُّخْزِيْهِ وَمَنْ هُوَ كَاذِبٌ ط وَارْتَقِبُوْۤا اِنِّيْ مَعَكُمْ

رَقِيْبٌ ۹۳ وَلَمَّا جَآءَ اَمْرُنَا نَجَّيْنَا شُعَيْبًا وَّالَّذِيْنَ

اٰمَنُوْا مَعَهٗ بِرَحْمَةٍ مِّنَّا ۚ وَاَخَذَتِ الَّذِيْنَ ظَلَمُوا

الصَّيْحَةُ فَاَصْبَحُوْا فِيْ دِيَارِهِمْ جٰثِمِيْنَ ۙ ۹۴ كَاَنْ لَّمْ

يَغْنَوْا فِيْهَا ط اَلَا بُعْدًا لِّمَدْيَنَ كَمَا بَعِدَتْ ثَمُوْدُ ۹۵

وَلَقَدْ اَرْسَلْنَا مُوْسٰى بِاٰيٰتِنَا وَسُلْطٰنٍ مُّبِيْنٍ ۙ ۹۶

اِلٰى فِرْعَوْنَ وَمَلَا۟ئِهٖ فَاتَّبَعُوْۤا اَمْرَ فِرْعَوْنَ ۚ وَمَاۤ

اَمْرُ فِرْعَوْنَ بِرَشِيْدٍ ۹۷ يَقْدُمُ قَوْمَهٗ يَوْمَ الْقِيٰمَةِ

فَاَوْرَدَهُمُ النَّارَ ط وَبِئْسَ الْوِرْدُ الْمَوْرُوْدُ ۹۸ وَاُتْبِعُوْا

فِيْ هٰذِهٖ لَعْنَةً وَّيَوْمَ الْقِيٰمَةِ ط بِئْسَ الرِّفْدُ

الْمَرْفُوْدُ ۹۹ ذٰلِكَ مِنْ اَنْبَآءِ الْقُرٰى نَقُصُّهٗ عَلَيْكَ

مِنْهَا قَآئِمٌ وَّحَصِيْدٌ ۱۰۰ وَمَا ظَلَمْنٰهُمْ وَلٰكِنْ

Musa preached valiantly in Pharaoh's court. Are you brave enough to challenge the wrongs in your family, friends and society?

⁹⁰ *So* seek your Lord's forgiveness and then turn to Him in repentance. Indeed, My Lord is Most Kind, Loving."

Empty threats from Shu'ayb's people
⁹¹ "Shu'ayb," they said, "We don't understand most of your preaching, and consider you to be the weak one among us, were it not for your clan, we would have stoned you, we have no respect for you." ⁹² "My people," he said, "is my clan dearer to you than Allah, that you should *ignore Him and* put Him behind you? My Lord is aware of what you do. ⁹³ My people, do as you see fit, and I will do *likewise*. You will come to know *soon* who will suffer a humiliating punishment and who is a liar. *So* watch carefully, and I will watch with you!" ⁹⁴ When Our decree came to pass, We rescued Shu'ayb with dignity and those who believed in him. A single blast devastated the wrongdoers, and when morning came, there they laid in their homes, dead. ⁹⁵ As though they had never existed. Away with Madyan, just as Thamud were done away with!

Musa is sent to Pharaoh
⁹⁶ We sent Musa with Our signs and clear authority ⁹⁷ to Pharaoh and his courtiers, who *chose* to follow Pharaoh's plan, although Pharaoh's plan was not well thought out. ⁹⁸ On Judgement Day, he will walk ahead of his people and take them to the Fire. What a dreadful pit to be taken to! ⁹⁹ *Allah's* curse tracked them in this *world* and *again* on Judgement Day. What a dreadful gift to be given!

Allah wrongs no one, people wrong themselves
¹⁰⁰ We told you these stories about some of the towns; some are still standing and *others* have been razed to the ground.

ظَلَمُوْٓا اَنْفُسَهُمْ فَمَآ اَغْنَتْ عَنْهُمْ اٰلِهَتُهُمُ الَّتِيْ
يَدْعُوْنَ مِنْ دُوْنِ اللّٰهِ مِنْ شَيْءٍ لَّمَّا جَآءَ اَمْرُ
رَبِّكَ ط وَمَا زَادُوْهُمْ غَيْرَ تَتْبِيْبٍ ۝ وَكَذٰلِكَ اَخْذُ
رَبِّكَ اِذَآ اَخَذَ الْقُرٰى وَهِيَ ظَالِمَةٌ ط اِنَّ اَخْذَهٗٓ
اَلِيْمٌ شَدِيْدٌ ۝ اِنَّ فِيْ ذٰلِكَ لَاٰيَةً لِّمَنْ خَافَ
عَذَابَ الْاٰخِرَةِ ط ذٰلِكَ يَوْمٌ مَّجْمُوْعٌ لَّهُ النَّاسُ
وَذٰلِكَ يَوْمٌ مَّشْهُوْدٌ ۝ وَمَا نُؤَخِّرُهٗٓ اِلَّا لِاَجَلٍ

What makes a person blessed – Saeed, or wretched – Shaqee?

مَّعْدُوْدٍ ۝ يَوْمَ يَاْتِ لَا تَكَلَّمُ نَفْسٌ اِلَّا بِاِذْنِهٖ ۚ
فَمِنْهُمْ شَقِيٌّ وَّسَعِيْدٌ ۝ فَاَمَّا الَّذِيْنَ شَقُوْا فَفِى
النَّارِ لَهُمْ فِيْهَا زَفِيْرٌ وَّشَهِيْقٌ ۝ خٰلِدِيْنَ فِيْهَا مَا
دَامَتِ السَّمٰوٰتُ وَالْاَرْضُ اِلَّا مَا شَآءَ رَبُّكَ ط اِنَّ
رَبَّكَ فَعَّالٌ لِّمَا يُرِيْدُ ۝ وَاَمَّا الَّذِيْنَ سُعِدُوْا
فَفِى الْجَنَّةِ خٰلِدِيْنَ فِيْهَا مَا دَامَتِ السَّمٰوٰتُ
وَالْاَرْضُ اِلَّا مَا شَآءَ رَبُّكَ ط عَطَآءً غَيْرَ مَجْذُوْذٍ ۝
فَلَا تَكُ فِيْ مِرْيَةٍ مِّمَّا يَعْبُدُ هٰٓؤُلَآءِ ط مَا يَعْبُدُوْنَ
اِلَّا كَمَا يَعْبُدُ اٰبَآؤُهُمْ مِّنْ قَبْلُ ط وَاِنَّا لَمُوَفُّوْهُمْ
نَصِيْبَهُمْ غَيْرَ مَنْقُوْصٍ ع ۝ وَلَقَدْ اٰتَيْنَا مُوْسَى
الْكِتٰبَ فَاخْتُلِفَ فِيْهِ ط وَلَوْلَا كَلِمَةٌ سَبَقَتْ
مِنْ رَّبِّكَ لَقُضِيَ بَيْنَهُمْ ط وَاِنَّهُمْ لَفِيْ شَكٍّ
مِّنْهُ مُرِيْبٍ ۝ وَاِنَّ كُلًّا لَّمَّا لَيُوَفِّيَنَّهُمْ رَبُّكَ

447

¹⁰¹ We didn't wrong them, they wronged themselves. The gods they used to call on beside Allah didn't benefit them at all when Your Lord's verdict came to pass; they only increased their devastation. ¹⁰² That is how your Lord snatches away towns that are steeped in evil: His punishment is severely painful. ¹⁰³ In this are signs for anyone who fears the punishment of the Hereafter, a day when humanity will be gathered, a day to be witnessed.

People will be divided into two groups

¹⁰⁴ We will delay it only for a limited time. ¹⁰⁵ *That* day, when it comes, not a soul will speak without His permission, and some of them will be miserably sad whilst others will be happy. ¹⁰⁶ The sad ones will be tossed in the Fire, where *they will* scream and groan, ¹⁰⁷ staying there until the Heavens and Earth remain, unless it pleases your Lord *to do* otherwise. Your Lord does what He pleases. ¹⁰⁸ The happy ones will be in Paradise, staying there if the Heavens and Earth remain, unless it pleases your Lord *to do* otherwise, an infinite gift. ¹⁰⁹ So don't be doubtful about what these people worship; they worship what their forefathers worshipped before *them*, and We will give them their share *in full*, without reduction.

Muslims are reminded to avoid sectarianism

¹¹⁰ We gave Musa the Book, but *his followers* disagreed about it, and if it had not been for an earlier decree issued by Your Lord, *the matter* would have been settled between them; *meanwhile* they remain in grave doubt about it. ¹¹¹ Every one *of them* will be repaid in full by your Lord *according to* their deeds. He is aware of what they do.

اَعْمَالَهُمْ ط اِنَّهٗ بِمَا يَعْمَلُوْنَ خَبِيْرٌ ۱۱۱ فَاسْتَقِمْ

كَمَآ اُمِرْتَ وَمَنْ تَابَ مَعَكَ وَلَا تَطْغَوْا ط اِنَّهٗ

بِمَا تَعْمَلُوْنَ بَصِيْرٌ ۱۱۲ وَلَا تَرْكَنُوْا اِلَى الَّذِيْنَ

ظَلَمُوْا فَتَمَسَّكُمُ النَّارُ لا وَمَا لَكُمْ مِّنْ دُوْنِ اللّٰهِ

مِنْ اَوْلِيَآءَ ثُمَّ لَا تُنْصَرُوْنَ ۱۱۳ وَاَقِمِ الصَّلٰوةَ طَرَفَيِ

النَّهَارِ وَزُلَفًا مِّنَ الَّيْلِ ط اِنَّ الْحَسَنٰتِ يُذْهِبْنَ

السَّيِّاٰتِ ط ذٰلِكَ ذِكْرٰى لِلذّٰكِرِيْنَ ۱۱۴ وَاصْبِرْ فَاِنَّ

اللّٰهَ لَا يُضِيْعُ اَجْرَ الْمُحْسِنِيْنَ ۱۱۵ فَلَوْلَا كَانَ مِنَ

الْقُرُوْنِ مِنْ قَبْلِكُمْ اُولُوْا بَقِيَّةٍ يَّنْهَوْنَ عَنِ

الْفَسَادِ فِى الْاَرْضِ اِلَّا قَلِيْلًا مِّمَّنْ اَنْجَيْنَا مِنْهُمْ ۚ

وَاتَّبَعَ الَّذِيْنَ ظَلَمُوْا مَآ اُتْرِفُوْا فِيْهِ وَكَانُوْا

مُجْرِمِيْنَ ۱۱۶ وَمَا كَانَ رَبُّكَ لِيُهْلِكَ الْقُرٰى بِظُلْمٍ

وَّاَهْلُهَا مُصْلِحُوْنَ ۱۱۷ وَلَوْ شَآءَ رَبُّكَ لَجَعَلَ

النَّاسَ اُمَّةً وَّاحِدَةً وَّلَا يَزَالُوْنَ مُخْتَلِفِيْنَ ۱۱۸ لا

اِلَّا مَنْ رَّحِمَ رَبُّكَ ط وَلِذٰلِكَ خَلَقَهُمْ ط وَتَمَّتْ

كَلِمَةُ رَبِّكَ لَاَمْلَأَنَّ جَهَنَّمَ مِنَ الْجِنَّةِ وَالنَّاسِ

اَجْمَعِيْنَ ۱۱۹ وَكُلًّا نَّقُصُّ عَلَيْكَ مِنْ اَنْبَآءِ

الرُّسُلِ مَا نُثَبِّتُ بِهٖ فُؤَادَكَ ۚ وَجَآءَكَ فِيْ هٰذِهِ

الْحَقُّ وَمَوْعِظَةٌ وَّذِكْرٰى لِلْمُؤْمِنِيْنَ ۱۲۰ وَقُلْ

لِّلَّذِيْنَ لَا يُؤْمِنُوْنَ اعْمَلُوْا عَلٰى مَكَانَتِكُمْ ط اِنَّا

What is the moral lesson from the stories of these seven Prophets?

¹¹² So remain firm, just as you have been told, *you* and those who have repented with you, and don't exceed the limits. *Allah* sees whatever you do.

Avoid wrongdoing, pray regularly and be patient

¹¹³ Don't be persuaded by those who do wrong, then you'll be punished with fire; and, as you have no protectors besides Allah, you won't be helped *in any way*. ¹¹⁴ Perform the prayer at both ends of the day and in some part of the night. Good deeds shall erase evil deeds. That is a *powerful* reminder for the mindful people. ¹¹⁵ Be patient, for Allah doesn't waste the reward of the righteous. ¹¹⁶ If only there had been *more* righteous people in the previous generations who prevented corruption in the land! We saved few of them whilst the wrongdoers enjoyed the luxuries of life and continued sinning. ¹¹⁷ Your Lord would never destroy a town unjustly whilst its citizens were acting righteously.

Religious differences are part of the Divine plan

¹¹⁸ If your Lord wanted, He could have made people a single nation, but *that's not the case* so they continue to differ; ¹¹⁹ except anyone who is treated kindly by Allah: that's why He created them. Your Lord's decree: "I shall fill up Hell with jinn and humans," is fulfilled. ¹²⁰ We tell you the stories of the messengers to make your heart strong, and what has come to you in this *account* is the truth, teachings and a reminder for the believers. ¹²¹ Tell those who don't believe: "Do as you see fit, and we will do *likewise*. ¹²² Wait *and see*, for we too are waiting." ¹²³ Allah knows the secrets of the Heaven and the Earth, and all that exists will be returned to Him; so worship Him and put your trust in Him. Your Lord isn't unaware of what you do.

عَمِلُوْنَ ۝ وَانتَظِرُوٓا إِنَّا مُنتَظِرُوْنَ ۝ وَلِلّٰهِ غَيْبُ
السَّمٰوٰتِ وَالْأَرْضِ وَإِلَيْهِ يُرْجَعُ الْأَمْرُ كُلُّهُ فَاعْبُدْهُ
وَتَوَكَّلْ عَلَيْهِ ۗ وَمَا رَبُّكَ بِغَافِلٍ عَمَّا تَعْمَلُوْنَ ۝

12. Surat Yusuf
The Prophet Yusuf

This is a late Makkan surat revealed some time after *Surat Hud*. It tells the story of Prophet Yusuf ﷺ, and is called "the most beautiful story" (3). It employs a commanding narrative that is lyrical at times, with an outstanding drama woven around moral and spiritual values. Deeply embedded in Quranic guidance, values such as truthfulness, patience, modesty, justice, forgiveness, kindness and courage are presented in a variety of contexts in this story, to show that in the end they will prevail over tyranny and immorality. Yusuf ﷺ was the great grandson of the Prophet Ibrahim ﷺ, this would be approximately 1600 BC.

The Bible also tells the story of Yusuf ﷺ, in Genesis 37 and 39. The Biblical story contrasts in tone and tenor with the Quranic narration; it appears as an account of the envy between brothers, the youthful naiveté of Yusuf ﷺ, romance and his triumph over his brothers. It stresses the cleverness of a young bureaucrat against the Egyptians; he takes advantage of the famine and buys the cattle of the Egyptians cheaply for the King. However, the Quranic story is free from such charges against a prophet of Allah. Through its twenty-seven scenes, Surat Yusuf effectively plots the complexity of human life, and sudden and unexpected changes in fortunes: one moment living at home, the next languishing in a dark, dank well; one moment enjoying life in a palace, the next in prison; one moment a prisoner, the next a Prince. The story of Yusuf ﷺ provides a real-life illustration of a Quranic principle: "Sometimes you may dislike something that is good for you, and sometimes you may like something that is bad for you. Only Allah knows *the whole truth*, not you" (*Al-Baqarah* 2: 216). The surat teaches that life on Earth is an extraordinary gift, full of trials and tribulations, and with endless opportunities. The message is patience and perseverance give plentiful fruit; on the other hand, short-term instant gratification can be damaging.

The eloquence and the stylistic features of the surat consists of series of scenes, one after the other, carrying on with the main narrative which then leads to next. Each scene has a rich dialogue and detail that produce a well-knit passage. Throughout the story, the faith of Prophet Yusuf ﷺ helps him maintain integrity. When he was thrown into a well, Allah reassured him: "*One day* you will tell them about their conspiracy, at a time when they least expect it" (15). Similarly, when the governor's wife tries to seduce him the Quran demonstrates the delicacy and propriety required for the discussion of sexual matters, and at the same time it reveals the modesty and loyalty of Yusuf ﷺ: "She tried to seduce," yet he said, "Allah forbid!" (23).

This is a model of self-control, loyalty and restraint. What a difficult test for someone in the prime of his youth! Yet Yusuf ﷺ was no ordinary young man. He feared Allah, with a religious identity and a sense of personal honour. Young people today can learn a great deal from the modesty of Yusuf ﷺ.

Four Dreams; four Different Endings

Four dreams are mentioned in this surat: Yusuf's ﷺ, the butler's and the baker's dream, and the king's dream. His interpretations are spot on, perhaps hinting to the idea that life itself is a dream, interpretable by stories. What is a dream? A sequence of images that appear in the mind of a sleeping person, a juxtaposition of real and imaginary people, places, and events. Dreams can be the expectation of achieving one's wishes and hopes in the future. We all entertain dreams, but the bold and brave invest in them. Yusuf ﷺ believed in his dream, but knew that he had to undergo tests before Allah would make it happen. He knew well his dream would not come to fruition before its fixed time. Where the dream carries you is not known at the outset; one has to place trust in Allah. Throughout this story we see the faithfulness, loyalty and kindness of Yusuf ﷺ, ingredients that led to the actualization of his dream. Although Yusuf ﷺ is the central character of this story, his father Yaqub ﷺ is important as well, for he too suffered the loss of a beloved son for so many years. The Quran presents his exemplary patience; a model of perseverance in the face of sorrow and distress.

In conclusion, the surat highlights the moral virtue of forgiveness as practised by various people in the story: the governor, Yaqub, and especially the forgiveness of Yusuf ﷺ in the face of the cruelty of his brothers. All he says to them is: "There is no blame on you today. Allah will forgive you, for He is the most Kind" (92). The surat was quietly foretelling the victory of the Prophet Muhammad ﷺ. Just as Yusuf ﷺ succeeded against his brothers, the Prophet ﷺ would soon succeed against the Quraysh.

Lessons from the Story of Yusuf ﷺ

- We may have great dreams, but Allah fulfils them in different ways. The boyhood dream of Yusuf ﷺ was about becoming a king, but Allah had a far greater plan for him: to be his Prophet, who would teach *Tawhid* and who would save Egypt.
- When life gets tough; and you suffer trials, and unfair treatment at the hands of those from whom you least expect it, don't complain! Be patient; remember the patience of Yaqub ﷺ, and of Yusuf ﷺ.

بِسْمِ اللهِ الرَّحْمٰنِ الرَّحِيْمِ

الٓرٰ ۚ تِلْكَ اٰيٰتُ الْكِتٰبِ الْمُبِيْنِ ۞ اِنَّآ اَنْزَلْنٰهُ

قُرْءٰنًا عَرَبِيًّا لَّعَلَّكُمْ تَعْقِلُوْنَ ۞ نَحْنُ نَقُصُّ

عَلَيْكَ اَحْسَنَ الْقَصَصِ بِمَآ اَوْحَيْنَآ اِلَيْكَ هٰذَا

الْقُرْاٰنَ ۖ وَاِنْ كُنْتَ مِنْ قَبْلِهٖ لَمِنَ الْغٰفِلِيْنَ ۞

اِذْ قَالَ يُوْسُفُ لِاَبِيْهِ يٰۤاَبَتِ اِنِّيْ رَاَيْتُ اَحَدَ عَشَرَ

كَوْكَبًا وَّالشَّمْسَ وَالْقَمَرَ رَاَيْتُهُمْ لِيْ سٰجِدِيْنَ ۞

قَالَ يٰبُنَيَّ لَا تَقْصُصْ رُءْيَاكَ عَلٰۤى اِخْوَتِكَ

فَيَكِيْدُوْا لَكَ كَيْدًا ۗ اِنَّ الشَّيْطٰنَ لِلْاِنْسَانِ عَدُوٌّ

مُّبِيْنٌ ۞ وَكَذٰلِكَ يَجْتَبِيْكَ رَبُّكَ وَيُعَلِّمُكَ مِنْ

تَاْوِيْلِ الْاَحَادِيْثِ وَيُتِمُّ نِعْمَتَهٗ عَلَيْكَ وَعَلٰۤى

اٰلِ يَعْقُوْبَ كَمَآ اَتَمَّهَا عَلٰۤى اَبَوَيْكَ مِنْ قَبْلُ

اِبْرٰهِيْمَ وَاِسْحٰقَ ۗ اِنَّ رَبَّكَ عَلِيْمٌ حَكِيْمٌ ۞ لَقَدْ

كَانَ فِيْ يُوْسُفَ وَاِخْوَتِهٖ اٰيٰتٌ لِّلسَّآئِلِيْنَ ۞ اِذْ

قَالُوْا لَيُوْسُفُ وَاَخُوْهُ اَحَبُّ اِلٰۤى اَبِيْنَا مِنَّا وَنَحْنُ

عُصْبَةٌ ۗ اِنَّ اَبَانَا لَفِيْ ضَلٰلٍ مُّبِيْنٍ ۞ اِقْتُلُوْا

يُوْسُفَ اَوِ اطْرَحُوْهُ اَرْضًا يَّخْلُ لَكُمْ وَجْهُ اَبِيْكُمْ

وَتَكُوْنُوْا مِنْۢ بَعْدِهٖ قَوْمًا صٰلِحِيْنَ ۞ قَالَ قَآئِلٌ

مِّنْهُمْ لَا تَقْتُلُوْا يُوْسُفَ وَاَلْقُوْهُ فِيْ غَيٰبَتِ الْجُبِّ

Yusuf's optimistic dream kick-started his adventurous and perilous life journey, what's your dream?

In the name of Allah, the Kind, the Caring.

¹ *Alif Lam Ra'.*

The most beautiful story

These are the verses of a clear Book. ² We revealed it as an Arabic Quran so you may understand. ³ We will tell you the most beautiful story by revealing to you this Quran, *a story of which* you were unaware before.

Young Yusuf dreams

⁴ *Consider* when Yusuf said to his father, "My dear father, I saw eleven stars, the sun and the moon, all prostrating before me." ⁵ *Yaqub* said, "My dear son, don't tell your brothers your dream, they will hatch a plot against you, Satan is a sworn enemy of humanity. ⁶ This *dream shows* your Lord has chosen you, will teach you interpretations of dreams,ᵃ and fulfil His favour on you and the family of Yaqub just as He fulfilled it on your forefathers, Ibrahim and Ishaq. Your Lord is Knowing, Wise.

The brothers hatch a nasty plot

⁷ In the story of Yusuf and his brothers there are signs for the questioners. ⁸ When *the step-brothers* whined, "Our father loves Yusuf and his brother more than us, even though we are a large group; our father is obviously mistaken."ᵇ ⁹ "Kill Yusuf," *said one of them*, "or get rid of him in a *far-off* land, so you will have your father's full attention; afterwards you can be good. ¹⁰ Another spoke out, "Don't kill Yusuf, if you are determined to do something, throw him into the bottom of a well. Perhaps a *passing* caravan will pick him up."

ᵃ 'Interpretation of dreams' also implies 'problem-solving'. As we will see Yusuf solved the problems of other people.

ᵇ Yusuf and his brother Benyamin were the son's of Yaqub's wife Rachel and the other 10 children were his half-brothers.

يَلْتَقِطْهُ بَعْضُ السَّيَّارَةِ اِنْ كُنْتُمْ فٰعِلِيْنَ ۞

قَالُوْا يٰٓاَبَانَا مَا لَكَ لَا تَأْمَنَّا عَلٰى يُوْسُفَ وَاِنَّا

لَهٗ لَنٰصِحُوْنَ ۞ اَرْسِلْهُ مَعَنَا غَدًا يَّرْتَعْ وَيَلْعَبْ وَاِنَّا

لَهٗ لَحٰفِظُوْنَ ۞ قَالَ اِنِّيْ لَيَحْزُنُنِيْٓ اَنْ تَذْهَبُوْا بِهٖ

وَاَخَافُ اَنْ يَّأْكُلَهُ الذِّئْبُ وَاَنْتُمْ عَنْهُ غٰفِلُوْنَ ۞

قَالُوْا لَئِنْ اَكَلَهُ الذِّئْبُ وَنَحْنُ عُصْبَةٌ اِنَّآ اِذًا

لَّخٰسِرُوْنَ ۞ فَلَمَّا ذَهَبُوْا بِهٖ وَاَجْمَعُوْٓا اَنْ يَّجْعَلُوْهُ فِيْ

غَيٰبَتِ الْجُبِّ ۚ وَاَوْحَيْنَآ اِلَيْهِ لَتُنَبِّئَنَّهُمْ بِاَمْرِهِمْ هٰذَا

وَهُمْ لَا يَشْعُرُوْنَ ۞ وَجَآءُوْ اَبَاهُمْ عِشَآءً يَّبْكُوْنَ ۞

قَالُوْا يٰٓاَبَانَآ اِنَّا ذَهَبْنَا نَسْتَبِقُ وَتَرَكْنَا يُوْسُفَ

عِنْدَ مَتَاعِنَا فَاَكَلَهُ الذِّئْبُ ۚ وَمَآ اَنْتَ بِمُؤْمِنٍ

لَّنَا وَلَوْ كُنَّا صٰدِقِيْنَ ۞ وَجَآءُوْ عَلٰى قَمِيْصِهٖ بِدَمٍ

كَذِبٍ ۚ قَالَ بَلْ سَوَّلَتْ لَكُمْ اَنْفُسُكُمْ اَمْرًا ۚ فَصَبْرٌ

جَمِيْلٌ ۚ وَاللّٰهُ الْمُسْتَعَانُ عَلٰى مَا تَصِفُوْنَ ۞ وَجَآءَتْ

سَيَّارَةٌ فَاَرْسَلُوْا وَارِدَهُمْ فَاَدْلٰى دَلْوَهٗ ۚ قَالَ يٰبُشْرٰى

هٰذَا غُلٰمٌ ۚ وَاَسَرُّوْهُ بِضَاعَةً ۚ وَاللّٰهُ عَلِيْمٌ بِمَا

يَعْمَلُوْنَ ۞ وَشَرَوْهُ بِثَمَنٍ بَخْسٍ دَرَاهِمَ مَعْدُوْدَةٍ ۚ

وَكَانُوْا فِيْهِ مِنَ الزَّاهِدِيْنَ ۞ وَقَالَ الَّذِي اشْتَرٰىهُ

مِنْ مِّصْرَ لِامْرَاَتِهٖٓ اَكْرِمِيْ مَثْوٰىهُ عَسٰٓى اَنْ يَّنْفَعَنَآ

اَوْ نَتَّخِذَهٗ وَلَدًا ۚ وَكَذٰلِكَ مَكَّنَّا لِيُوْسُفَ فِي الْاَرْضِ

Notice the callousness and cruelty of human barbarity. We must nurture compassion.

¹¹ *So* they said, "Our father, why don't you trust us with Yusuf, though we are sincere *about* him. ¹² Tomorrow, send him with us so he may enjoy himself and play, and we'll take good care of him." ¹³ *Yaqub* said, "The *mere* thought of you taking him worries me, and I am afraid that a wolf might *snatch and* eat him whilst you are not paying attention to him." ¹⁴ They said, "How could a wolf eat him when we are a large group, then we would be losers."

Yusuf accompanies his brothers

¹⁵ So, having taken him, they agreed to leave him at the bottom of a well. We inspired him: "*One day* you will tell them about this conspiracy of theirs, at a time when they least expect it." ¹⁶ That late evening they came to their father crying, ¹⁷ saying: "Our father, we went off to race one another, leaving Yusuf with our belongings, and the wolf *came and* ate him. Though we're telling the truth, you won't believe us." ¹⁸ *Then* they brought his shirt, *stained* with false blood. *Yaqub* said, "You've made *all* this up. *I will bear patiently*, patience is a beautiful quality. Allah is *My only* supporter against what you describe."

Yusuf sold as a slave

¹⁹ Along came a caravan, sending their water-bearer *on ahead*; as he lowered his bucket, he shouted, "Great news! There's a boy here." *Then* they hid him with their goods, but Allah was aware what they did. ²⁰ They sold him for a paltry price, a few silver coins, because they weren't interested in him.^a ²¹ The Egyptian^b who bought him said to his wife, "Look after him well. He could be useful to us, or else we could adopt him as a son." That's how We settled Yusuf in the land of Egypt, and taught him to interpret dreams; Allah had complete control of *Yusuf's* situation, but most people are ignorant.

---

^a 'Zuhd' is to be indifferent; refuse to have anything to do with someone or something. The people of the caravan weren't at all interested in Yusuf, they didn't value him,

^b In the Bible (Genesis 39: 1), the Egyptian was called Potiphar, the captain of the Pharaoh's guard. Notice the difference Potiphar valued Yusuf highly.

وَنُعَلِّمَهُ مِنْ تَأْوِيْلِ الْأَحَادِيْثِ ط وَاللّٰهُ غَالِبٌ عَلٰى أَمْرِهٖ

وَلٰكِنَّ أَكْثَرَ النَّاسِ لَا يَعْلَمُوْنَ ۝ وَلَمَّا بَلَغَ أَشُدَّهٗ

اٰتَيْنٰهُ حُكْمًا وَّعِلْمًا ط وَكَذٰلِكَ نَجْزِى الْمُحْسِنِيْنَ ۝

وَرَاوَدَتْهُ الَّتِيْ هُوَ فِيْ بَيْتِهَا عَنْ نَّفْسِهٖ وَغَلَّقَتِ

الْأَبْوَابَ وَقَالَتْ هَيْتَ لَكَ ط قَالَ مَعَاذَ اللّٰهِ اِنَّهٗ

رَبِّيْ أَحْسَنَ مَثْوَاىَ ط اِنَّهٗ لَا يُفْلِحُ الظّٰلِمُوْنَ ۝ وَلَقَدْ

هَمَّتْ بِهٖ ج وَهَمَّ بِهَا لَوْلَا أَنْ رَّاٰ بُرْهَانَ رَبِّهٖ ط

كَذٰلِكَ لِنَصْرِفَ عَنْهُ السُّوْٓءَ وَالْفَحْشَآءَ ط اِنَّهٗ مِنْ

عِبَادِنَا الْمُخْلَصِيْنَ ۝ وَاسْتَبَقَا الْبَابَ وَقَدَّتْ قَمِيْصَهٗ

مِنْ دُبُرٍ وَّأَلْفَيَا سَيِّدَهَا لَدَا الْبَابِ ط قَالَتْ مَا جَزَآءُ

مَنْ أَرَادَ بِأَهْلِكَ سُوْٓءًا اِلَّا أَنْ يُّسْجَنَ أَوْ عَذَابٌ

أَلِيْمٌ ۝ قَالَ هِيَ رَاوَدَتْنِيْ عَنْ نَّفْسِيْ وَشَهِدَ شَاهِدٌ

مِّنْ أَهْلِهَا ج اِنْ كَانَ قَمِيْصُهٗ قُدَّ مِنْ قُبُلٍ فَصَدَقَتْ

وَهُوَ مِنَ الْكٰذِبِيْنَ ۝ وَاِنْ كَانَ قَمِيْصُهٗ قُدَّ مِنْ

دُبُرٍ فَكَذَبَتْ وَهُوَ مِنَ الصّٰدِقِيْنَ ۝ فَلَمَّا رَاٰ قَمِيْصَهٗ

قُدَّ مِنْ دُبُرٍ قَالَ اِنَّهٗ مِنْ كَيْدِكُنَّ ط اِنَّ كَيْدَكُنَّ

عَظِيْمٌ ۝ يُوْسُفُ أَعْرِضْ عَنْ هٰذَا ۚ وَاسْتَغْفِرِيْ

لِذَنْۢبِكِ ۘ اِنَّكِ كُنْتِ مِنَ الْخَاطِئِيْنَ ۝ وَقَالَ نِسْوَةٌ

فِي الْمَدِيْنَةِ امْرَاَتُ الْعَزِيْزِ تُرَاوِدُ فَتٰىهَا عَنْ نَّفْسِهٖ ج

قَدْ شَغَفَهَا حُبًّا ط اِنَّا لَنَرٰىهَا فِيْ ضَلٰلٍ مُّبِيْنٍ ۝

Yusuf's ordeal is rewarded, he is blessed with intelligence, good communication and problem-solving skills.

٣
ع
١٣

457

²²When he reached maturity, We gave him wisdom and knowledge; that is how We reward the righteous.

The captain's wife tries to seduce Yusuf

²³The lady in whose house he was *living* tried to seduce him, bolting the doors and saying, "Come here!" "Allah forbid!" He said, "My master has given me a good home, and, *in any case*, wrongdoers never succeed." ²⁴She lusted for him, and he would have desired her *too* if he hadn't seen *overwhelming* proof from his Lord; that was how We deflected the evil and indecency away from him. He was one of Our devoted servants. ²⁵They raced to the door, and she tore his shirt from behind; there, at the door, they bumped into her husband. "What should be the punishment for someone who wishes to harm your family," she cried, "except imprisonment or torture?" ²⁶*Yusuf* cried out, "She's the one who tried to seduce me!" A member of her household recommended, "If his shirt is torn from the front then she's telling the truth, and he's lying; ²⁷but if his shirt is torn from behind then she's lying, and he's telling the truth." ²⁸When *her husband* saw the shirt was torn from behind, he said, "This *cunning* scheme of yours; is a big trick, ²⁹Yusuf overlook this," *and told his wife*, "Seek forgiveness for your sin, you are wrong."

Rumours of seduction soon spread

³⁰Some *prominent* women of the city *began* to say, "The captain's wife was in love with her servant; she has fallen in love. We believe she is wrong."

فَلَمَّا سَمِعَتْ بِمَكْرِهِنَّ أَرْسَلَتْ إِلَيْهِنَّ وَ أَعْتَدَتْ لَهُنَّ مُتَّكَأً وَّ اٰتَتْ كُلَّ وَاحِدَةٍ مِّنْهُنَّ سِكِّيْنًا وَّ قَالَتِ اخْرُجْ عَلَيْهِنَّ فَلَمَّا رَأَيْنَهٗٓ أَكْبَرْنَهٗ وَقَطَّعْنَ أَيْدِيَهُنَّ وَقُلْنَ حَاشَ لِلّٰهِ مَا هٰذَا بَشَرًا اِنْ هٰذَا إِلَّا مَلَكٌ كَرِيْمٌ ۝ قَالَتْ فَذٰلِكُنَّ الَّذِيْ لُمْتُنَّنِيْ فِيْهِ ط وَلَقَدْ رَاوَدْتُّهٗ عَنْ نَّفْسِهٖ فَاسْتَعْصَمَ ط وَلَئِنْ لَّمْ يَفْعَلْ مَا اٰمُرُهٗ لَيُسْجَنَنَّ وَلَيَكُوْنًا مِّنَ الصّٰغِرِيْنَ ۝ قَالَ رَبِّ السِّجْنُ أَحَبُّ إِلَيَّ مِمَّا يَدْعُوْنَنِيْٓ إِلَيْهِ ۚ وَإِلَّا تَصْرِفْ عَنِّيْ كَيْدَهُنَّ أَصْبُ إِلَيْهِنَّ وَأَكُنْ مِّنَ الْجٰهِلِيْنَ ۝ فَاسْتَجَابَ لَهٗ رَبُّهٗ فَصَرَفَ عَنْهُ كَيْدَهُنَّ ط إِنَّهٗ هُوَ السَّمِيْعُ الْعَلِيْمُ ۝ ثُمَّ بَدَا لَهُمْ مِّنْ بَعْدِ مَا رَأَوُا الْاٰيٰتِ لَيَسْجُنُنَّهٗ حَتّٰى حِيْنٍ ۝ وَدَخَلَ مَعَهُ السِّجْنَ فَتَيٰنِ ط قَالَ أَحَدُهُمَآ إِنِّيْٓ أَرٰنِيْٓ أَعْصِرُ خَمْرًا ۚ وَ قَالَ الْاٰخَرُ إِنِّيْٓ أَرٰنِيْٓ أَحْمِلُ فَوْقَ رَأْسِيْ خُبْزًا تَأْكُلُ الطَّيْرُ مِنْهُ ط نَبِّئْنَا بِتَأْوِيْلِهٖ ۚ إِنَّا نَرٰكَ مِنَ الْمُحْسِنِيْنَ ۝ قَالَ لَا يَأْتِيْكُمَا طَعَامٌ تُرْزَقٰنِهٖٓ إِلَّا نَبَّأْتُكُمَا بِتَأْوِيْلِهٖ قَبْلَ أَنْ يَّأْتِيَكُمَا ط ذٰلِكُمَا مِمَّا عَلَّمَنِيْ رَبِّيْ ط إِنِّيْ تَرَكْتُ مِلَّةَ قَوْمٍ لَّا يُؤْمِنُوْنَ بِاللّٰهِ وَهُمْ بِالْاٰخِرَةِ هُمْ كٰفِرُوْنَ ۝ وَاتَّبَعْتُ مِلَّةَ اٰبَآءِيْٓ إِبْرٰهِيْمَ وَإِسْحٰقَ وَيَعْقُوْبَ ط مَا كَانَ لَنَآ أَنْ نُّشْرِكَ بِاللّٰهِ مِنْ شَيْءٍ ط

Yusuf is jailed for no reason. How would Yusuf react? Have you ever been mistreated?

459

³¹ After hearing their gossip, she sent for them, and prepared sofas for them *at a banquet*, giving each of them a knife *before telling Yusuf*, "Go out to *present yourself before* them." When they saw him, they were captivated by *his beauty*, and cut their hands and said, "Allah the Great! This is no mortal. This can only be a splendid great angel." ³² Then she said, "That's the one you blamed me for. I tried to seduce him, but he held back. However, if he doesn't do as I tell him now, he will go to prison and be disgraced."

Yusuf prays to Allah for help

³³ "My Lord," said Yusuf, "I prefer prison to what they tell me to do. If You hadn't deflected their *cunning* scheme from me, I would have yielded to them and acted unwisely." ³⁴ His Lord accepted his prayer and deflected their scheme away from him. He is the Listener, the Knower. ³⁵ And so, even after seeing the evidence, of his innocence they thought it is right to imprison him for a short term.

Yusuf preaches *Tawhid* in the prison

³⁶ Two young men entered the prison with him, one asked him, "I had a dream, I was pressing grapes," the other said, "I had a dream, I was carrying bread on my head and birds were eating from it. Tell us their meaning, we see you're a righteous person." ³⁷ He said, "I will tell you their meaning before your *next* meal arrives, it's one of the things My Lord has taught me. I have kept away from the religion of people who don't believe in Allah and who deny the Hereafter, ³⁸ I follow *instead* the religion of my forefathers Ibrahim, Ishaq and Yaqub. The associating of anything with Allah is not for us; that is one of Allah's favours to us and to people *generally*, but most people are ungrateful.

ذٰلِكَ مِنْ فَضْلِ اللّٰهِ عَلَيْنَا وَعَلَى النَّاسِ وَلٰكِنَّ اَكْثَرَ

النَّاسِ لَا يَشْكُرُوْنَ ۝ يٰصَاحِبَيِ السِّجْنِ ءَاَرْبَابٌ

مُّتَفَرِّقُوْنَ خَيْرٌ اَمِ اللّٰهُ الْوَاحِدُ الْقَهَّارُ ۝ مَا تَعْبُدُوْنَ

مِنْ دُوْنِهٖ اِلَّآ اَسْمَآءً سَمَّيْتُمُوْهَآ اَنْتُمْ وَاٰبَآؤُكُمْ مَّآ

اَنْزَلَ اللّٰهُ بِهَا مِنْ سُلْطٰنٍ ط اِنِ الْحُكْمُ اِلَّا لِلّٰهِ ط اَمَرَ

اَلَّا تَعْبُدُوْٓا اِلَّآ اِيَّاهُ ط ذٰلِكَ الدِّيْنُ الْقَيِّمُ وَلٰكِنَّ اَكْثَرَ

النَّاسِ لَا يَعْلَمُوْنَ ۝ يٰصَاحِبَيِ السِّجْنِ اَمَّآ اَحَدُكُمَا

How true are dreams?
Have your dreams ever
come true?

فَيَسْقِيْ رَبَّهٗ خَمْرًا ج وَاَمَّا الْاٰخَرُ فَيُصْلَبُ فَتَأْكُلُ

الطَّيْرُ مِنْ رَّأْسِهٖ ط قُضِيَ الْاَمْرُ الَّذِيْ فِيْهِ تَسْتَفْتِيٰنِ ۝

وَقَالَ لِلَّذِيْ ظَنَّ اَنَّهٗ نَاجٍ مِّنْهُمَا اذْكُرْنِيْ عِنْدَ رَبِّكَ

فَاَنْسٰهُ الشَّيْطٰنُ ذِكْرَ رَبِّهٖ فَلَبِثَ فِي السِّجْنِ بِضْعَ

سِنِيْنَ ط ۝ وَقَالَ الْمَلِكُ اِنِّيْٓ اَرٰى سَبْعَ بَقَرٰتٍ سِمَانٍ

يَّأْكُلُهُنَّ سَبْعٌ عِجَافٌ وَّسَبْعَ سُنْبُلٰتٍ خُضْرٍ وَّاُخَرَ

يٰبِسٰتٍ ط يٰٓاَيُّهَا الْمَلَاُ اَفْتُوْنِيْ فِيْ رُءْيَايَ اِنْ كُنْتُمْ

لِلرُّءْيَا تَعْبُرُوْنَ ۝ قَالُوْٓا اَضْغَاثُ اَحْلَامٍ ج وَمَا

نَحْنُ بِتَأْوِيْلِ الْاَحْلَامِ بِعٰلِمِيْنَ ۝ وَقَالَ الَّذِيْ

نَجَا مِنْهُمَا وَادَّكَرَ بَعْدَ اُمَّةٍ اَنَا اُنَبِّئُكُمْ بِتَأْوِيْلِهٖ

فَاَرْسِلُوْنِ ۝ يُوْسُفُ اَيُّهَا الصِّدِّيْقُ اَفْتِنَا فِيْ

سَبْعِ بَقَرٰتٍ سِمَانٍ يَّأْكُلُهُنَّ سَبْعٌ عِجَافٌ وَّسَبْعِ

سُنْبُلٰتٍ خُضْرٍ وَّاُخَرَ يٰبِسٰتٍ لَّعَلِّيْٓ اَرْجِعُ اِلَى النَّاسِ

³⁹ My fellow prisoners, tell me, are many gods better or the one, Allah, the Supreme? ⁴⁰ Whatever you worship besides Him are only names you and your forefathers coined, Allah hasn't revealed any authority for them. *Ultimate* authority belongs to Allah alone; He has commanded you to worship Him alone. That's the true religion, unfortunately, most people are ignorant.

Yusuf interprets the baker and the butler's dreams

⁴¹ My fellow inmates, one of you will serve wine to his master *once more*; *sadly*, the other will be crucified, and the birds will peck his head. The matter on which you sought my opinion has *already* been decided." ⁴² Then *Yusuf* asked the one who he knew would be spared, "Mention me to your master." However, Satan made him forget to mention him to his master, and so Yusuf lingered in the prison for several years.

Yusuf explains the king's baffling dream

⁴³ The King said, "I had a dream of seven fat cows eating seven lean ones, and of seven green ears *of grain* and *seven* others all dried up. Counsellors, advise me concerning my dream, if you can interpret dreams." ⁴⁴ They replied, "What baffling dreams! We have no expertise in interpreting dreams." ⁴⁵ Then the one who had been spared of the two *in prison finally* remembered *Yusuf* after a long time, said, "I can tell you how to interpret it, so send me." ⁴⁶ *Returning to the prison, he said,* "Yusuf, you who tells the truth, advise us concerning seven fat cows eating seven lean, and seven green ears *of grain* and *seven* others all dried up, so that I may go back to the people, so they may know."

لَعَلَّهُمۡ يَعۡلَمُوۡنَ ۝ قَالَ تَزۡرَعُوۡنَ سَبۡعَ سِنِيۡنَ دَاَبًا ۚ

فَمَا حَصَدۡتُّمۡ فَذَرُوۡهُ فِىۡ سُنۢبُلِهٖۤ اِلَّا قَلِيۡلًا مِّمَّا

تَاۡكُلُوۡنَ ۝ ثُمَّ يَاۡتِىۡ مِنۡۢ بَعۡدِ ذٰلِكَ سَبۡعٌ شِدَادٌ

يَّاۡكُلۡنَ مَا قَدَّمۡتُمۡ لَهُنَّ اِلَّا قَلِيۡلًا مِّمَّا تُحۡصِنُوۡنَ ۝

ثُمَّ يَاۡتِىۡ مِنۡۢ بَعۡدِ ذٰلِكَ عَامٌ فِيۡهِ يُغَاثُ النَّاسُ

وَفِيۡهِ يَعۡصِرُوۡنَ ۝ وَقَالَ الۡمَلِكُ ائۡتُوۡنِىۡ بِهٖ ۚ فَلَمَّا

جَآءَهُ الرَّسُوۡلُ قَالَ ارۡجِعۡ اِلٰى رَبِّكَ فَسۡـَٔلۡهُ مَا بَالُ

النِّسۡوَةِ الّٰتِىۡ قَطَّعۡنَ اَيۡدِيَهُنَّ ؕ اِنَّ رَبِّىۡ بِكَيۡدِهِنَّ

عَلِيۡمٌ ۝ قَالَ مَا خَطۡبُكُنَّ اِذۡ رَاوَدتُّنَّ يُوۡسُفَ عَنۡ

نَّفۡسِهٖ ؕ قُلۡنَ حَاشَ لِلّٰهِ مَا عَلِمۡنَا عَلَيۡهِ مِنۡ سُوۡٓءٍ ؕ قَالَتِ

امۡرَاَتُ الۡعَزِيۡزِ الۡـٰٔنَ حَصۡحَصَ الۡحَقُّ ۫ اَنَا رَاوَدتُّهٗ عَنۡ

نَّفۡسِهٖ وَاِنَّهٗ لَمِنَ الصّٰدِقِيۡنَ ۝ ذٰلِكَ لِيَعۡلَمَ اَنِّىۡ لَمۡ

اَخُنۡهُ بِالۡغَيۡبِ وَاَنَّ اللّٰهَ لَا يَهۡدِىۡ كَيۡدَ الۡخَآئِنِيۡنَ ۝

وَمَآ اُبَرِّئُ نَفۡسِىۡ ۚ اِنَّ النَّفۡسَ لَاَمَّارَةٌۢ بِالسُّوۡٓءِ

اِلَّا مَا رَحِمَ رَبِّىۡ ؕ اِنَّ رَبِّىۡ غَفُوۡرٌ رَّحِيۡمٌ ۝ وَقَالَ

الۡمَلِكُ ائۡتُوۡنِىۡ بِهٖۤ اَسۡتَخۡلِصۡهُ لِنَفۡسِىۡ ۚ فَلَمَّا كَلَّمَهٗ

قَالَ اِنَّكَ الۡيَوۡمَ لَدَيۡنَا مَكِيۡنٌ اَمِيۡنٌ ۝ قَالَ

اجۡعَلۡنِىۡ عَلٰى خَزَآئِنِ الۡاَرۡضِ ۚ اِنِّىۡ حَفِيۡظٌ عَلِيۡمٌ ۝

وَكَذٰلِكَ مَكَّنَّا لِيُوۡسُفَ فِى الۡاَرۡضِ ۚ يَتَبَوَّاُ مِنۡهَا

حَيۡثُ يَشَآءُ ؕ نُصِيۡبُ بِرَحۡمَتِنَا مَنۡ نَّشَآءُ وَلَا نُضِيۡعُ

Yusuf is appointed as the Keeper of King's treasures.

463

[47] *Yusuf* said, "For seven years you will plant *crops* as normal, but you will leave what you harvest in the ears, except for a small amount that you will eat. [48] This will be followed by seven years of hardship, during which you will consume all but a little of what you have stored. [49] After that will come a year of rain aplenty, in which people will press *grapes for wine.*"

Yusuf demands his name be cleared

[50] "Bring him to me," said the King, when the King's envoy came to him, *Yusuf* told him, "Go back to your master and let him inquire about the women who cut their hands. My Lord knows all about their *cunning* scheme." [51] So *the King* asked *the women*, "What happened when you tried to seduce Yusuf?" They said, "Allah the Great! We know nothing bad about him." Then the captain's wife said, "Now the truth is out. It was me who tried to seduce him, and he told the truth." [52] *Yusuf said,* "*All* this was so that my master would know I didn't betray him in his absence," and Allah does not guide the schemers of cunning plots. [53] "I don't claim to be blameless *since* human ego continually incites one to do evil, except when My Lord is kind to me. My Lord is Forgiving, Kind."

Yusuf is appointed the treasurer of Egypt

[54] "Bring him to me," the King said, "I will select him for my personal service." Once he had interviewed him, he said, "From this day *on,* you will hold a position of trust with us." [55] "Put me in charge of the country's stores," *Yusuf* said, "*for* I am prudent and knowledgeable." [56] And that is how We gave Yusuf power to exercise in the land *of Egypt,* and to live wherever he wished. We treat anyone kindly, and never allow the reward of the righteous to be lost.

اَجْرَ الْمُحْسِنِيْنَ ۵۶ وَلَاَجْرُ الْاٰخِرَةِ خَيْرٌ لِّلَّذِيْنَ
اٰمَنُوْا وَ كَانُوْا يَتَّقُوْنَ ۵۷ وَ جَآءَ اِخْوَةُ يُوْسُفَ
فَدَخَلُوْا عَلَيْهِ فَعَرَفَهُمْ وَهُمْ لَهُ مُنْكِرُوْنَ ۵۸
وَلَمَّا جَهَّزَهُمْ بِجَهَازِهِمْ قَالَ ائْتُوْنِىْ بِاَخٍ لَّكُمْ
مِّنْ اَبِيْكُمْ ۚ اَلَا تَرَوْنَ اَنِّىْ اُوْفِى الْكَيْلَ وَاَنَا خَيْرُ
الْمُنْزِلِيْنَ ۵۹ فَاِنْ لَّمْ تَاْتُوْنِىْ بِهٖ فَلَا كَيْلَ لَكُمْ
عِنْدِىْ وَلَا تَقْرَبُوْنِ ۶۰ قَالُوْا سَنُرَاوِدُ عَنْهُ اَبَاهُ
وَاِنَّا لَفٰعِلُوْنَ ۶۱ وَقَالَ لِفِتْيٰنِهِ اجْعَلُوْا بِضَاعَتَهُمْ
فِىْ رِحَالِهِمْ لَعَلَّهُمْ يَعْرِفُوْنَهَآ اِذَا انْقَلَبُوْٓا اِلٰٓى
اَهْلِهِمْ لَعَلَّهُمْ يَرْجِعُوْنَ ۶۲ فَلَمَّا رَجَعُوْٓا اِلٰٓى
اَبِيْهِمْ قَالُوْا يٰٓاَبَانَا مُنِعَ مِنَّا الْكَيْلُ فَاَرْسِلْ مَعَنَآ
اَخَانَا نَكْتَلْ وَاِنَّا لَهٗ لَحٰفِظُوْنَ ۶۳ قَالَ هَلْ اٰمَنُكُمْ
عَلَيْهِ اِلَّا كَمَآ اَمِنْتُكُمْ عَلٰٓى اَخِيْهِ مِنْ قَبْلُ ؕ فَاللّٰهُ
خَيْرٌ حٰفِظًا ۫ وَّهُوَ اَرْحَمُ الرّٰحِمِيْنَ ۶۴ وَلَمَّا فَتَحُوْا
مَتَاعَهُمْ وَجَدُوْا بِضَاعَتَهُمْ رُدَّتْ اِلَيْهِمْ ؕ قَالُوْا
يٰٓاَبَانَا مَا نَبْغِىْ ؕ هٰذِهٖ بِضَاعَتُنَا رُدَّتْ اِلَيْنَا ۚ
وَنَمِيْرُ اَهْلَنَا وَ نَحْفَظُ اَخَانَا وَ نَزْدَادُ كَيْلَ بَعِيْرٍ ؕ
ذٰلِكَ كَيْلٌ يَّسِيْرٌ ۶۵ قَالَ لَنْ اُرْسِلَهٗ مَعَكُمْ حَتّٰى
تُؤْتُوْنِ مَوْثِقًا مِّنَ اللّٰهِ لَتَاْتُنَّنِىْ بِهٖٓ اِلَّآ اَنْ
يُّحَاطَ بِكُمْ ۚ فَلَمَّآ اٰتَوْهُ مَوْثِقَهُمْ قَالَ اللّٰهُ عَلٰى مَا

Yusuf treated his brothers generously, would you have done so?

⁵⁷ And the reward of the Hereafter is even better for those who believe and are mindful *of Allah.*

Yusuf's brothers visit Egypt

⁵⁸ *Years later,* Yusuf's brothers came and entered his office, and he recognised them *at once,* but they didn't recognise him. ⁵⁹ After he had supplied them with their provisions, he said, "Bring me a *half-*brother of yours from your father's side. Don't you see that I am honest in my measures, and that I am the best host? ⁶⁰ If you fail to bring him to me then you won't get a single measure from me, nor should you approach me *ever again.*" ⁶¹ "We will try to persuade his father," they said, "We will certainly do that." ⁶² And *so Yusuf* told his servants, "Put the goods they exchanged with us back in their saddlebags so they recognise them when they return to their family and, hopefully, they will come back."

Yusuf's brothers are overjoyed

⁶³ When they returned to their father, they said, "Father, we will be stopped from taking *a single* measure next time so send our brother along with us so that we may get more. We will take care of him." ⁶⁴ He said, "If I entrust you with him, won't it be the same as before, when I entrusted you with his brother? Allah is the best guardian, and He is the most kind." ⁶⁵ When they opened their saddlebags, they found their goods were returned to them, *so* they said, "Our father, what *more* do we want? These goods of ours have been returned to us. We can provide for our family, take care of our brother, and we'll get an extra camel-load. That would be an easy load!"

Yaqub reluctantly sends Benyamin

⁶⁶ "I will not send him with you," said *Yaqub,* "until you give me *a* solemn pledge by Allah to bring him back safely to me unless it happens that if you are ambushed." When they had given their pledge to him, he said, "Allah is the Guardian over what we have pledged *here.*"

نَقُوْلُ وَكِيْلٌ ۝ وَقَالَ يٰبَنِيَّ لَا تَدْخُلُوْا مِنْۢ بَابٍ

وَّاحِدٍ وَّادْخُلُوْا مِنْ اَبْوَابٍ مُّتَفَرِّقَةٍ ؕ وَمَاۤ اُغْنِيْ

عَنْكُمْ مِّنَ اللّٰهِ مِنْ شَيْءٍ ؕ اِنِ الْحُكْمُ اِلَّا لِلّٰهِ ؕ

عَلَيْهِ تَوَكَّلْتُ ۚ وَعَلَيْهِ فَلْيَتَوَكَّلِ الْمُتَوَكِّلُوْنَ ۝

وَلَمَّا دَخَلُوْا مِنْ حَيْثُ اَمَرَهُمْ اَبُوْهُمْ ؕ مَا كَانَ

يُغْنِيْ عَنْهُمْ مِّنَ اللّٰهِ مِنْ شَيْءٍ اِلَّا حَاجَةً فِيْ

نَفْسِ يَعْقُوْبَ قَضٰهَا ؕ وَاِنَّهٗ لَذُوْ عِلْمٍ لِّمَا

عَلَّمْنٰهُ وَلٰكِنَّ اَكْثَرَ النَّاسِ لَا يَعْلَمُوْنَ ۝ وَلَمَّا

دَخَلُوْا عَلٰى يُوْسُفَ اٰوٰۤى اِلَيْهِ اَخَاهُ قَالَ اِنِّيْۤ اَنَا

اَخُوْكَ فَلَا تَبْتَئِسْ بِمَا كَانُوْا يَعْمَلُوْنَ ۝ فَلَمَّا

جَهَّزَهُمْ بِجَهَازِهِمْ جَعَلَ السِّقَايَةَ فِيْ رَحْلِ

اَخِيْهِ ثُمَّ اَذَّنَ مُؤَذِّنٌ اَيَّتُهَا الْعِيْرُ اِنَّكُمْ

لَسٰرِقُوْنَ ۝ قَالُوْا وَاَقْبَلُوْا عَلَيْهِمْ مَّاذَا تَفْقِدُوْنَ ۝

قَالُوْا نَفْقِدُ صُوَاعَ الْمَلِكِ وَلِمَنْ جَآءَ بِهٖ حِمْلُ

بَعِيْرٍ وَّاَنَا بِهٖ زَعِيْمٌ ۝ قَالُوْا تَاللّٰهِ لَقَدْ عَلِمْتُمْ

مَّا جِئْنَا لِنُفْسِدَ فِى الْاَرْضِ وَمَا كُنَّا سٰرِقِيْنَ ۝

قَالُوْا فَمَا جَزَآؤُهٗۤ اِنْ كُنْتُمْ كٰذِبِيْنَ ۝ قَالُوْا

جَزَآؤُهٗ مَنْ وُّجِدَ فِيْ رَحْلِهٖ فَهُوَ جَزَآؤُهٗ ؕ كَذٰلِكَ

نَجْزِى الظّٰلِمِيْنَ ۝ فَبَدَاَ بِاَوْعِيَتِهِمْ قَبْلَ وِعَآءِ

اَخِيْهِ ثُمَّ اسْتَخْرَجَهَا مِنْ وِّعَآءِ اَخِيْهِ ؕ كَذٰلِكَ

ع
١١
٢

Was this a practical joke or was Yusuf teaching his brothers a valuable lesson?

Advice on how to avoid the evil eye

⁶⁷He said, "My sons, don't enter together through one gate, but enter from different gates. I can't shield you against anything from Allah, as *ultimate* authority belongs to Him alone.ª I have put my trust in Him, so let everyone put his trust in Him." ⁶⁸When they entered the way their father had told them, it couldn't shield them against anything from Allah; but, it satisfied Yaqub's wish. He had knowledge that We had taught him, unfortunately most people are ignorant.

How Yusuf gets to keep his brother

⁶⁹When they entered Yusuf's office again, he took his brother aside, saying, "I'm your brother. Don't be saddened by what they did." ⁷⁰After giving their provisions, he placed a drinking cup in his brother's saddlebag, then a herald called out: "*people of the* caravan, you are thieves." ⁷¹"What have you lost?" *The brothers* said, as they turned to face them. ⁷²"We have lost the King's measuring bowl," they said, "and whoever brings it back will get an *extra* camel-load; I guarantee it." ⁷³"By Allah," they said, "you know that we didn't come to make trouble in the land, nor are we thieves." ⁷⁴*They* said, "What is the penalty, if you are lying?" ⁷⁵"In whoever's saddlebag *the measuring bowl* is found will have to give himself up and *become a slave*," *the brothers* said, "that is how we punish wrongdoers." ᵇ

ª Imam Razi gives two explanations of this order of Yaqub: If a band of strong men entered from one gate of the city, it could arouse suspicion and they could be arrested, secondly (the one Imam Razi prefers), to avoid the evil eye. The Messenger 鐥 said "An evil eye can drive a person into a grave and a Camel into a cooking pot".

ᵇ Yusuf gives a gift of a precious drinking cup to his brother. The King's measuring bowl was misplaced by the guards and they suspected it was stolen by the brothers.

كِدْنَا لِيُوسُفَ ۚ مَا كَانَ لِيَأْخُذَ اَخَاهُ فِيْ دِيْنِ

الْمَلِكِ اِلَّا اَنْ يَّشَاۤءَ اللّٰهُ ۚ نَرْفَعُ دَرَجٰتٍ مَّنْ نَّشَاۤءُ ۚ

وَفَوْقَ كُلِّ ذِيْ عِلْمٍ عَلِيْمٌ ۝ قَالُوْۤا اِنْ يَّسْرِقْ

فَقَدْ سَرَقَ اَخٌ لَّهٗ مِنْ قَبْلُ ۚ فَاَسَرَّهَا يُوْسُفُ

فِيْ نَفْسِهٖ وَلَمْ يُبْدِهَا لَهُمْ ۚ قَالَ اَنْتُمْ شَرٌّ

مَّكَانًا ۚ وَاللّٰهُ اَعْلَمُ بِمَا تَصِفُوْنَ ۝ قَالُوْا يٰۤاَيُّهَا

الْعَزِيْزُ اِنَّ لَهٗۤ اَبًا شَيْخًا كَبِيْرًا فَخُذْ اَحَدَنَا

مَكَانَهٗ ۚ اِنَّا نَرٰىكَ مِنَ الْمُحْسِنِيْنَ ۝ قَالَ مَعَاذَ

اللّٰهِ اَنْ نَّأْخُذَ اِلَّا مَنْ وَّجَدْنَا مَتَاعَنَا عِنْدَهٗۤ ۙ

اِنَّاۤ اِذًا لَّظٰلِمُوْنَ ۝ فَلَمَّا اسْتَيْـَٔسُوْا مِنْهُ خَلَصُوْا

نَجِيًّا ۚ قَالَ كَبِيْرُهُمْ اَلَمْ تَعْلَمُوْۤا اَنَّ اَبَاكُمْ

قَدْ اَخَذَ عَلَيْكُمْ مَّوْثِقًا مِّنَ اللّٰهِ وَمِنْ قَبْلُ

مَا فَرَّطْتُمْ فِيْ يُوْسُفَ ۚ فَلَنْ اَبْرَحَ الْاَرْضَ

حَتّٰى يَأْذَنَ لِيْۤ اَبِيْۤ اَوْ يَحْكُمَ اللّٰهُ لِيْ ۚ وَهُوَ خَيْرُ

الْحٰكِمِيْنَ ۝ اِرْجِعُوْۤا اِلٰۤى اَبِيْكُمْ فَقُوْلُوْا يٰۤاَبَانَاۤ

اِنَّ ابْنَكَ سَرَقَ ۚ وَمَا شَهِدْنَاۤ اِلَّا بِمَا عَلِمْنَا

وَمَا كُنَّا لِلْغَيْبِ حٰفِظِيْنَ ۝ وَسْـَٔلِ الْقَرْيَةَ الَّتِيْ

كُنَّا فِيْهَا وَالْعِيْرَ الَّتِيْۤ اَقْبَلْنَا فِيْهَا ۚ وَاِنَّا

لَصٰدِقُوْنَ ۝ قَالَ بَلْ سَوَّلَتْ لَكُمْ اَنْفُسُكُمْ اَمْرًا ۚ

فَصَبْرٌ جَمِيْلٌ ۖ عَسَى اللّٰهُ اَنْ يَّأْتِيَنِيْ بِهِمْ جَمِيْعًا ۚ

What do you do when you get stuck? Consult, plan and stick together.

⁷⁶ So *Yusuf* began by searching their bags before his brother's bag, then he produced *the goblet* from his brothers. That is how We devised a plan for Yusuf to succeed. It would not have been proper for him to arrest his brother under the king's law, unless Allah had so willed. We elevate in rank anyone We please; and above every knowledgeable person is the One who knows all.

The brothers plead in vain for Benyamin's freedom

⁷⁷ "If he has stolen," the brothers said, "then his full-brother before him also stole." Yusuf kept *his feelings* to himself and didn't reveal anything to them. *Instead* he said, "You are *all* in far worse position. Allah is well aware of what you describe." ⁷⁸ "Your Lordship," they said, "his father is an old man, so arrest one of us instead. We consider you to be a gracious person." ⁷⁹ "Allah forbid! We should arrest anyone other than him in whose possession we found our belongings," he said, "Then we would be *blatant* wrongdoers." ⁸⁰ When they were hopeless about him *changing his mind*, they went off into a huddle *to talk privately*, and the eldest of them said, "Don't you know that your father took *your* solemn pledge by Allah because you had previously been negligent with Yusuf? I won't leave this land until either my father gives me permission or else Allah decides for me, He is the best Judge."

The brothers return home bearing sad news

⁸¹ Go back to your father and say, "Our father, your son has stolen." *They told him,* "We are only testifying to what we know, and we could not *be expected to protect* against the unforeseen. ⁸² Ask the townsfolk where we have been and the caravan with whom we travelled. We're telling the truth." ⁸³ "On the contrary," *Yaqub* said, "you have made *all* this up. It's better to be patient! It may be that Allah brings them all back to me, for it is He Who is Knowing, Wise."

اِنَّهٗ هُوَ الْعَلِيْمُ الْحَكِيْمُ ۝ وَتَوَلّٰى عَنْهُمْ وَقَالَ
يٰٓاَسَفٰى عَلٰى يُوْسُفَ وَابْيَضَّتْ عَيْنٰهُ مِنَ الْحُزْنِ
فَهُوَ كَظِيْمٌ ۝ قَالُوْا تَاللّٰهِ تَفْتَؤُا تَذْكُرُ يُوْسُفَ
حَتّٰى تَكُوْنَ حَرَضًا اَوْ تَكُوْنَ مِنَ الْهٰلِكِيْنَ ۝ قَالَ
اِنَّمَآ اَشْكُوْا بَثِّيْ وَحُزْنِيْ اِلَى اللّٰهِ وَاَعْلَمُ مِنَ اللّٰهِ
مَا لَا تَعْلَمُوْنَ ۝ يٰبَنِيَّ اذْهَبُوْا فَتَحَسَّسُوْا مِنْ
يُّوْسُفَ وَاَخِيْهِ وَلَا تَايْئَسُوْا مِنْ رَّوْحِ اللّٰهِ اِنَّهٗ لَا
يَايْئَسُ مِنْ رَّوْحِ اللّٰهِ اِلَّا الْقَوْمُ الْكٰفِرُوْنَ ۝ فَلَمَّا
دَخَلُوْا عَلَيْهِ قَالُوْا يٰٓاَيُّهَا الْعَزِيْزُ مَسَّنَا وَاَهْلَنَا
الضُّرُّ وَجِئْنَا بِبِضَاعَةٍ مُّزْجٰةٍ فَاَوْفِ لَنَا الْكَيْلَ
وَتَصَدَّقْ عَلَيْنَا ۚ اِنَّ اللّٰهَ يَجْزِى الْمُتَصَدِّقِيْنَ ۝
قَالَ هَلْ عَلِمْتُمْ مَّا فَعَلْتُمْ بِيُوْسُفَ وَاَخِيْهِ اِذْ
اَنْتُمْ جٰهِلُوْنَ ۝ قَالُوْٓا ءَاِنَّكَ لَاَنْتَ يُوْسُفُ ۚ قَالَ
اَنَا يُوْسُفُ وَهٰذَآ اَخِيْ ۫ قَدْ مَنَّ اللّٰهُ عَلَيْنَا ۚ
اِنَّهٗ مَنْ يَّتَّقِ وَيَصْبِرْ فَاِنَّ اللّٰهَ لَا يُضِيْعُ اَجْرَ
الْمُحْسِنِيْنَ ۝ قَالُوْا تَاللّٰهِ لَقَدْ اٰثَرَكَ اللّٰهُ عَلَيْنَا
وَاِنْ كُنَّا لَخٰطِئِيْنَ ۝ قَالَ لَا تَثْرِيْبَ عَلَيْكُمُ الْيَوْمَ ۗ
يَغْفِرُ اللّٰهُ لَكُمْ ۫ وَهُوَ اَرْحَمُ الرّٰحِمِيْنَ ۝ اِذْهَبُوْا
بِقَمِيْصِيْ هٰذَا فَاَلْقُوْهُ عَلٰى وَجْهِ اَبِيْ يَاْتِ بَصِيْرًا ۚ
وَاْتُوْنِيْ بِاَهْلِكُمْ اَجْمَعِيْنَ ۝ وَلَمَّا فَصَلَتِ الْعِيْرُ

Yaqub trusted Allah. Years after losing Yusuf, he believed Yusuf was safe.

Yaqub cries for the loss of his sons

⁸⁴ *Yaqub* turned away from them, saying, "Oh, how I grieve for Yusuf!" His eyes *clouded over*, turning white, such was his sadness; yet he controlled his emotions. ⁸⁵ "By Allah," they said, "Will you never stop mentioning Yusuf until you become ill or die?" ⁸⁶ "I am complaining to Allah of My deep sorrow and sadness," Yaqub said, "I have knowledge from Allah that you don't. ⁸⁷ My sons, go and search for Yusuf and his brother; don't despair of Allah's kindness, it is only the disbelievers who despair of Allah's kindness."

The great forgiveness

⁸⁸ When they entered *again* into *Yusuf's* office, they said, "Your Lordship, severe hardship has struck us and our family. We have brought but a few goods, so give in full measure and be charitable to us; the reward of the charitable rests with Allah." ⁸⁹ He said, "Do you *now* know what you did to Yusuf and his brother when you were ignorant?" ⁹⁰ They said, "Yusuf, is that really you?" "I am Yusuf," he said, "and this is my brother. Allah has favoured us. Whoever is mindful *of Allah* and is patient, Allah will not waste the reward of the righteous." ⁹¹ "By Allah," they said, "Allah has preferred you over us, and we are the sinners." ⁹² Yusuf said, "There is no blame on you today. Allah will forgive you, for He is the most Kind."

The miracle of Yusuf's shirt

⁹³ *Then Yusuf said*, "Take this shirt of mine, and place it over my father's face, and his sight will return; then bring your whole family *here* to me."

قَالَ أَبُوهُمْ إِنِّي لَأَجِدُ رِيحَ يُوسُفَ لَوْلَا أَنْ

تُفَنِّدُونِ ۝ قَالُوا تَاللّٰهِ إِنَّكَ لَفِي ضَلٰلِكَ الْقَدِيمِ ۝

فَلَمَّا أَنْ جَاءَ الْبَشِيرُ أَلْقَاهُ عَلٰى وَجْهِهٖ فَارْتَدَّ

بَصِيرًا ۚ قَالَ أَلَمْ أَقُلْ لَّكُمْ إِنِّي أَعْلَمُ مِنَ اللّٰهِ مَا لَا

تَعْلَمُونَ ۝ قَالُوا يَٰٓأَبَانَا اسْتَغْفِرْ لَنَا ذُنُوبَنَا إِنَّا

كُنَّا خٰطِئِينَ ۝ قَالَ سَوْفَ أَسْتَغْفِرُ لَكُمْ رَبِّيۤ إِنَّهُ

هُوَ الْغَفُورُ الرَّحِيمُ ۝ فَلَمَّا دَخَلُوا عَلٰى يُوسُفَ

أَوٰۤى إِلَيْهِ أَبَوَيْهِ وَقَالَ ادْخُلُوا مِصْرَ إِنْ شَاءَ

اللّٰهُ ءَامِنِينَ ۝ وَرَفَعَ أَبَوَيْهِ عَلَى الْعَرْشِ وَخَرُّوا

لَهُ سُجَّدًا ۚ وَقَالَ يَٰٓأَبَتِ هٰذَا تَأْوِيلُ رُءْيَايَ مِنْ

قَبْلُ قَدْ جَعَلَهَا رَبِّي حَقًّا ۖ وَقَدْ أَحْسَنَ بِيۤ إِذْ

أَخْرَجَنِي مِنَ السِّجْنِ وَجَاءَ بِكُمْ مِّنَ الْبَدْوِ مِنۢ

بَعْدِ أَنْ نَّزَغَ الشَّيْطٰنُ بَيْنِي وَبَيْنَ إِخْوَتِي ۚ إِنَّ

رَبِّي لَطِيفٌ لِّمَا يَشَاءُ ۚ إِنَّهُ هُوَ الْعَلِيمُ الْحَكِيمُ ۝

رَبِّ قَدْ ءَاتَيْتَنِي مِنَ الْمُلْكِ وَعَلَّمْتَنِي مِنْ

تَأْوِيلِ الْأَحَادِيثِ ۚ فَاطِرَ السَّمٰوٰتِ وَالْأَرْضِ

أَنْتَ وَلِيِّي فِي الدُّنْيَا وَالْءَاخِرَةِ ۖ تَوَفَّنِي مُسْلِمًا

وَأَلْحِقْنِي بِالصّٰلِحِينَ ۝ ذٰلِكَ مِنْ أَنۢبَاءِ الْغَيْبِ

نُوحِيهِ إِلَيْكَ ۖ وَمَا كُنْتَ لَدَيْهِمْ إِذْ أَجْمَعُوۤا أَمْرَهُمْ

وَهُمْ يَمْكُرُونَ ۝ وَمَا أَكْثَرُ النَّاسِ وَلَوْ حَرَصْتَ

Yusuf's dream is fulfilled, a reward for his trust in Allah.

^{94} Once the caravan had set off *from Egypt*, their father said, "I smell Yusuf's breath *in the air*, even though you might think I am senile." ^{95} *Those around him* said, "By Allah, you are back to your old love again." ^{96} But when the bearer of good news came and placed *the shirt* over his face, his eyesight returned, he said, "Did I not tell you that I have knowledge from Allah that you don't have?" ^{97} "Our father," *the brothers* said, "seek forgiveness for our sins, we have been sinners." ^{98} He said, "I will seek my Lord's forgiveness for you," Yaqub said, " He is the Forgiver, the Kind."

Yusuf thanks Allah for the fulfilment of his dream

^{99} When they entered Yusuf's office, he received his parents as honoured guests, saying, "Enter Egypt, Allah willing, in safety." ^{100} As he invited his parents to sit on the throne, they fell before him in prostration. *Yusuf* said, "My dear father, this is the meaning of my long ago dream, which My Lord has made come true. *Allah* has been gracious to me, getting me out of the prison and bringing you from the desert after Satan had sown enmity between me and my brothers. My Lord has made it come true as He pleases. He is the Knower, the Wise.

Yusuf's Prayer

^{101} My Lord, you have given me power and authority and taught me how to interpret dreams,[a] Creator of the Heavens and Earth, You are my Protector in this world and the Hereafter; let me die submitting *to Your will*, and include me among the righteous."

The Prophet ﷺ is reminded

^{102} This is one of the accounts of the unseen that We have revealed to you; and you were not there with them, *Messenger*, when they conspired to hatch a plot *against Yusuf*. ^{103} Most people will never believe, no matter how keen you are *to guide them*,

---

[a] It also means "taught me to solve problems, to find solutions." Yusuf solved the problems of the Butler and the King.

بِمُؤْمِنِيْنَ ۝ وَمَا تَسْئَلُهُمْ عَلَيْهِ مِنْ أَجْرٍ ۚ إِنْ

هُوَ إِلَّا ذِكْرٌ لِّلْعَالَمِيْنَ ۝ وَكَأَيِّنْ مِّنْ اٰيَةٍ فِى

السَّمٰوٰتِ وَالْأَرْضِ يَمُرُّوْنَ عَلَيْهَا وَهُمْ عَنْهَا

مُعْرِضُوْنَ ۝ وَمَا يُؤْمِنُ أَكْثَرُهُمْ بِاللّٰهِ إِلَّا وَهُمْ

مُّشْرِكُوْنَ ۝ أَفَأَمِنُوْا أَنْ تَأْتِيَهُمْ غَاشِيَةٌ مِّنْ

عَذَابِ اللّٰهِ أَوْ تَأْتِيَهُمُ السَّاعَةُ بَغْتَةً وَّهُمْ

لَا يَشْعُرُوْنَ ۝ قُلْ هٰذِهٖ سَبِيْلِىْ أَدْعُوْا إِلَى اللّٰهِ ۚ

عَلٰى بَصِيْرَةٍ أَنَا وَمَنِ اتَّبَعَنِىْ ۚ وَسُبْحٰنَ اللّٰهِ وَمَا

أَنَا مِنَ الْمُشْرِكِيْنَ ۝ وَمَا أَرْسَلْنَا مِنْ قَبْلِكَ إِلَّا

رِجَالًا نُّوْحِىْ إِلَيْهِمْ مِّنْ أَهْلِ الْقُرٰى ۗ أَفَلَمْ يَسِيْرُوْا

فِى الْأَرْضِ فَيَنْظُرُوْا كَيْفَ كَانَ عَاقِبَةُ الَّذِيْنَ

مِنْ قَبْلِهِمْ ۗ وَلَدَارُ الْأٰخِرَةِ خَيْرٌ لِّلَّذِيْنَ اتَّقَوْا ۗ

أَفَلَا تَعْقِلُوْنَ ۝ حَتّٰى إِذَا اسْتَيْئَسَ الرُّسُلُ وَظَنُّوْا

أَنَّهُمْ قَدْ كُذِبُوْا جَاءَهُمْ نَصْرُنَا ۙ فَنُجِّىَ مَنْ

نَّشَاءُ ۗ وَلَا يُرَدُّ بَأْسُنَا عَنِ الْقَوْمِ الْمُجْرِمِيْنَ ۝

لَقَدْ كَانَ فِىْ قَصَصِهِمْ عِبْرَةٌ لِّأُولِى الْأَلْبَابِ ۗ

مَا كَانَ حَدِيْثًا يُّفْتَرٰى وَلٰكِنْ تَصْدِيْقَ الَّذِىْ

بَيْنَ يَدَيْهِ وَتَفْصِيْلَ كُلِّ شَىْءٍ وَّهُدًى

وَّرَحْمَةً لِّقَوْمٍ يُّؤْمِنُوْنَ ۝

What is the moral lesson of Yusuf's beautiful story? Always be confident and hopeful of Allah's kindness.

[104] you don't seek reward for it from them. This *Quran* is a reminder for humanity.

Signs of Allah's Creative power

[105] How many signs in the Heaven and Earth do they pass by and they turn their backs to. [106] Most of them will believe in Allah whilst also associating partners with Him. [107] Are they insured against being overwhelmed by Allah's punishment, or being taken all of a sudden and unaware by the Final Hour? [108] Say: "This is the path that I am on: I call others to Allah. I and those who follow me base our beliefs on clear evidence. Glory be to Allah! I am no associator of partners with Allah." [109] Even before you, Messenger, the men who We sent, and to who We revealed Our signs to, were townsfolk. Have the disbelievers not travelled about the land and seen how the end came to those who rejected Allah's signs before them? The home in the Hereafter is much better for the mindful. Doesn't any one of you understand? [110] When the messengers lost hope in outward signs of success, and the disbelievers believed they were lied to, then Our help came to them.[a] Whoever We wanted was saved, but nothing can turn away Our punishment from the guilty. [111] In the story of Yusuf and his brothers, there is a lesson for those who understand. It isn't a made-up account, but confirmation of what happened in the past, it explains all things, a guidance that is useful for those who believe.

---

[a]   Abdullah ibn Abbas used to recite the verse "...even the Messenger *of that time* and those who believed him cried out: 'When will Allah's help come?' The help of Allah is near" (2: 214). Meaning they were frustrated with their people and lost hope in them but they were never hopeless of Allah's kindness.

13. Surat Ar-Raʿd

The Thunder

The central theme of this late Makkan surat is to grasp the Greatness of Allah, as stated in scripture and nature. Nature, like the scripture, is an open book, where Allah's creativity can be seen, felt and experienced. On the other hand, the divine revelation brought by the prophets ﷺ is a set of general teachings: moral values influencing a person's character and behaviour, and spiritual ideals that fill life with meaning and answer big questions: Who are we? Where do we come from? And where are we going?

Reason, Not Wizardry

The Makkans employed many hostile tactics to oppose the Prophet ﷺ: ran a smear campaign, mocked, ridiculed, and made physical threats. Some Muslims wished that Allah would send a miracle so that their fellow citizens would see and believe. However, "Even if such a Quran was revealed that could move the mountains or destroy the Earth or make dead speak *they still wouldn't believe*" (31). Miracles are not performed on request, and Allah doesn't want to persuade people with miraculous wizardry. Instead, the Quran offers logical reasons to believe, as well as evidence from nature, physical phenomena, and human history. These appeals to human intellect and emotions, can stir faith in Allah and motivate people. In other words, the Quran wants people to decide for themselves: to accept Allah or reject faith. It's their moral choice. The Quran states that change only comes from within: "Allah doesn't change the condition *of people* until they change what's in themselves" (11).

The Awesome Creation and the Infinite Knowledge of Allah

The surat opens with a list of amazing natural phenomena: the sky without pillars, the rising and setting of the sun and the moon, massive mountains, running rivers, gorgeous groves of palm trees, vast vineyards, and fields of maize and wheat. Verse 4 draws our attention to an extraordinary fact:

> There are neighbouring plots ... all are fed by the same water, yet some are better to eat than others. Surely, in this are signs for people who understand.

The Quran disapproves of the disbelievers' stubbornness and rejection of truth: all of this is the creation of a supreme, powerful Lord. What are their idols in comparison? However, the "intelligent people", believe the Messenger ﷺ. Verses 20–23 highlight eight of their qualities, including how they fulfil their promise with Allah, and develop good human relationships. The Messenger ﷺ is reassured: continue preaching confidently, already signs of victory are appearing. "Haven't they realised how We are moving forward in the land, shrinking the boundaries *of their territory*" (41). A possible reference to the group from Madinah – who had embraced Islam and were now inviting the Prophet ﷺ to come to their city – a lead up to the Hijrah and the final departure of the Prophet ﷺ from Makkah.

۞ (١٣) سُوْرَةُ الرَّعْدِ مَدَنِيَّةٌ (٩٢) ۞ رُكُوْعُهَا ٦ ۞ اٰيَاتُهَا ٤٣ ۞

بِسْمِ اللّٰهِ الرَّحْمٰنِ الرَّحِيْمِ

الٓمٓرٰ ۚ تِلْكَ اٰيٰتُ الْكِتٰبِ ۗ وَالَّذِىْٓ اُنْزِلَ اِلَيْكَ مِنْ رَّبِّكَ الْحَقُّ وَلٰكِنَّ اَكْثَرَ النَّاسِ لَا يُؤْمِنُوْنَ ۞

اَللّٰهُ الَّذِىْ رَفَعَ السَّمٰوٰتِ بِغَيْرِ عَمَدٍ تَرَوْنَهَا ثُمَّ اسْتَوٰى عَلَى الْعَرْشِ وَسَخَّرَ الشَّمْسَ وَالْقَمَرَ ۗ كُلٌّ يَّجْرِىْ لِاَجَلٍ مُّسَمًّى ۗ يُدَبِّرُ الْاَمْرَ يُفَصِّلُ الْاٰيٰتِ لَعَلَّكُمْ بِلِقَآءِ رَبِّكُمْ تُوْقِنُوْنَ ۞ وَهُوَ الَّذِىْ مَدَّ الْاَرْضَ وَجَعَلَ فِيْهَا رَوَاسِىَ وَاَنْهٰرًا ۗ وَمِنْ كُلِّ الثَّمَرٰتِ جَعَلَ فِيْهَا زَوْجَيْنِ اثْنَيْنِ يُغْشِى الَّيْلَ النَّهَارَ ۗ اِنَّ فِىْ ذٰلِكَ لَاٰيٰتٍ لِّقَوْمٍ يَّتَفَكَّرُوْنَ ۞

وَفِى الْاَرْضِ قِطَعٌ مُّتَجٰوِرٰتٌ وَّجَنّٰتٌ مِّنْ اَعْنَابٍ وَّزَرْعٌ وَّنَخِيْلٌ صِنْوَانٌ وَّغَيْرُ صِنْوَانٍ يُّسْقٰى بِمَآءٍ وَّاحِدٍ ۗ وَنُفَضِّلُ بَعْضَهَا عَلٰى بَعْضٍ فِى الْاُكُلِ ۗ اِنَّ فِىْ ذٰلِكَ لَاٰيٰتٍ لِّقَوْمٍ يَّعْقِلُوْنَ ۞ وَاِنْ تَعْجَبْ فَعَجَبٌ قَوْلُهُمْ ءَاِذَا كُنَّا تُرٰبًا ءَاِنَّا لَفِىْ خَلْقٍ جَدِيْدٍ ۗ اُولٰٓئِكَ الَّذِيْنَ كَفَرُوْا بِرَبِّهِمْ ۚ وَاُولٰٓئِكَ الْاَغْلٰلُ فِىْٓ اَعْنَاقِهِمْ ۚ وَاُولٰٓئِكَ اَصْحٰبُ النَّارِ ۚ هُمْ فِيْهَا خٰلِدُوْنَ ۞ وَيَسْتَعْجِلُوْنَكَ بِالسَّيِّئَةِ قَبْلَ الْحَسَنَةِ وَقَدْ خَلَتْ مِنْ قَبْلِهِمُ الْمَثُلٰتُ ۗ

The vastness of the universe, the countless stars, the beauty of the landscape is truly amazing.

479

In the name of Allah, the Kind, the Caring.

¹ *Alif Lam Meem Ra'.*

The amazing, diverse creation of Allah

These are the verses of the Book that's come down to you from your Lord; it is the truth, but many people don't believe. ²It is Allah Who raised the sky without any pillars *that you can see*; He established His throne *of authority*, and made the sun and the moon subject *to His will*, each one orbiting *until it sets* at an appointed time.ª He manages the running *of the universe*, and explains the signs *of creation* so you are convinced of meeting Him. ³He laid out the land *with mountains* and *running* rivers, produced fruits in pairs, and covered the day by *the darkness of* the night. Surely, in this are signs for insightful people. ⁴There are neighbouring plots, vineyards, fields and palms, *growing* either in clusters or standing alone; all are fed by the same water, yet some are better to eat than others. Surely, in this are signs for people who understand.

The disbelievers remain unconvinced

⁵If you are amazed *at anything*, then what is more amazing than their slogan: "How can we be created anew once we have turned to dust?" They disbelieve their Lord. Such people *shall* have iron collars around their necks, and they'll be the companions of the Fire, remaining there forever. ⁶They challenge you to hasten what is bad *for them* instead asking for what is good, even though *many* exemplary punishments have happened before them. Without doubt, your Lord is ever willing to forgive people their evil. But your Lord is *also* severe in *His* punishment. ⁷The disbelievers say, "If only a *miraculous* sign were to come down to him from His Lord." You are a warner, and there was a guide for every nation.

ª *Jara* in Arabic means "running" or "coursing" through the sky, however, metaphorically it means "orbiting".

وَاِنَّ رَبَّكَ لَذُوْ مَغْفِرَةٍ لِّلنَّاسِ عَلٰى ظُلْمِهِمْ

وَاِنَّ رَبَّكَ لَشَدِيْدُ الْعِقَابِ ۶ وَيَقُوْلُ الَّذِيْنَ

كَفَرُوْا لَوْلَاۤ اُنْزِلَ عَلَيْهِ اٰيَةٌ مِّنْ رَّبِّهٖ ۗ اِنَّمَاۤ اَنْتَ

مُنْذِرٌ وَّلِكُلِّ قَوْمٍ هَادٍ ۷ اَللّٰهُ يَعْلَمُ مَا تَحْمِلُ

كُلُّ اُنْثٰى وَمَا تَغِيْضُ الْاَرْحَامُ وَمَا تَزْدَادُ ۗ وَكُلُّ

شَىْءٍ عِنْدَهٗ بِمِقْدَارٍ ۸ عٰلِمُ الْغَيْبِ وَالشَّهَادَةِ

الْكَبِيْرُ الْمُتَعَالِ ۹ سَوَآءٌ مِّنْكُمْ مَّنْ اَسَرَّ الْقَوْلَ

وَمَنْ جَهَرَ بِهٖ وَمَنْ هُوَ مُسْتَخْفٍ بِالَّيْلِ وَسَارِبٌ

بِالنَّهَارِ ۱۰ لَهٗ مُعَقِّبٰتٌ مِّنْۢ بَيْنِ يَدَيْهِ وَمِنْ

خَلْفِهٖ يَحْفَظُوْنَهٗ مِنْ اَمْرِ اللّٰهِ ۗ اِنَّ اللّٰهَ

لَا يُغَيِّرُ مَا بِقَوْمٍ حَتّٰى يُغَيِّرُوْا مَا بِاَنْفُسِهِمْ ۗ وَاِذَاۤ

اَرَادَ اللّٰهُ بِقَوْمٍ سُوْٓءًا فَلَا مَرَدَّ لَهٗ ۚ وَمَا لَهُمْ مِّنْ

دُوْنِهٖ مِنْ وَّالٍ ۱۱ هُوَ الَّذِيْ يُرِيْكُمُ الْبَرْقَ خَوْفًا

وَّطَمَعًا وَّيُنْشِئُ السَّحَابَ الثِّقَالَ ۱۲ وَيُسَبِّحُ الرَّعْدُ

بِحَمْدِهٖ وَالْمَلٰٓئِكَةُ مِنْ خِيْفَتِهٖ ۚ وَيُرْسِلُ الصَّوَاعِقَ

فَيُصِيْبُ بِهَا مَنْ يَّشَآءُ وَهُمْ يُجَادِلُوْنَ فِى اللّٰهِ ۚ

وَهُوَ شَدِيْدُ الْمِحَالِ ۱۳ لَهٗ دَعْوَةُ الْحَقِّ ۗ وَالَّذِيْنَ

يَدْعُوْنَ مِنْ دُوْنِهٖ لَا يَسْتَجِيْبُوْنَ لَهُمْ بِشَىْءٍ

اِلَّا كَبَاسِطِ كَفَّيْهِ اِلَى الْمَآءِ لِيَبْلُغَ فَاهُ وَمَا هُوَ

بِبَالِغِهٖ ۗ وَمَا دُعَآءُ الْكٰفِرِيْنَ اِلَّا فِىْ ضَلٰلٍ ۱۴ وَلِلّٰهِ

Become a change maker; change begins with yourself – Be an agent of change.

481

Change only comes from within

⁸Allah knows what every female carries, *even* the shrinking and the swelling of the wombs. Everything is *calculated* with precision for Him, ⁹the Knower of the seen and unseen realms, the Great, the Highest. ¹⁰Whether you call out quietly or loudly, or whether one tries to hide *in the darkness of* the night or walk in the broad daylight its all the same for *Him*. ¹¹A chain of angels in front and behind him is assigned by Allah to watch over him. Allah never changes the *condition of* a nation until they change what is in themselves, and if Allah wanted to destroy people, no one could stop Him, and they would have no protector besides Him. ¹²He displays the lightning which stirs fear and hope in you as He causes the heavy clouds to build up. ¹³*Likewise* the *roaring* thunder glorifies His praise, and the angels *too glorify Him* out of awe of Him, and He sends thunderbolts, striking anyone He wants, as they continue to argue about Allah, He is Mighty in power.

It is pointless to resist worshipping Allah

¹⁴A true prayer is for Him *alone*. Those they pray to besides Him never answer, they're like a person who stretches out his hands to *catch* water to put into his mouth, but it doesn't reach it. The disbelievers' prayer is ineffective.

يَسْجُدُ مَنْ فِى السَّمٰوٰتِ وَالْاَرْضِ طَوْعًا وَّكَرْهًا

وَّظِلٰلُهُمْ بِالْغُدُوِّ وَالْاٰصَالِ ۩ ﴿١٥﴾ قُلْ مَنْ رَّبُّ

السَّمٰوٰتِ وَالْاَرْضِ ۗ قُلِ اللّٰهُ ۗ قُلْ اَفَاتَّخَذْتُمْ مِّنْ

دُوْنِهٖٓ اَوْلِيَآءَ لَا يَمْلِكُوْنَ لِاَنْفُسِهِمْ نَفْعًا وَّلَا ضَرًّا ۗ

قُلْ هَلْ يَسْتَوِى الْاَعْمٰى وَالْبَصِيْرُ ۙ اَمْ هَلْ تَسْتَوِى

الظُّلُمٰتُ وَالنُّوْرُ ۚ اَمْ جَعَلُوْا لِلّٰهِ شُرَكَآءَ خَلَقُوْا

كَخَلْقِهٖ فَتَشَابَهَ الْخَلْقُ عَلَيْهِمْ ۗ قُلِ اللّٰهُ خَالِقُ

كُلِّ شَىْءٍ وَّهُوَ الْوَاحِدُ الْقَهَّارُ ﴿١٦﴾ اَنْزَلَ مِنَ السَّمَآءِ

مَآءً فَسَالَتْ اَوْدِيَةٌۢ بِقَدَرِهَا فَاحْتَمَلَ السَّيْلُ زَبَدًا

رَّابِيًا ۗ وَمِمَّا يُوْقِدُوْنَ عَلَيْهِ فِى النَّارِ ابْتِغَآءَ

حِلْيَةٍ اَوْ مَتَاعٍ زَبَدٌ مِّثْلُهٗ ۗ كَذٰلِكَ يَضْرِبُ اللّٰهُ

الْحَقَّ وَالْبَاطِلَ ڛ فَاَمَّا الزَّبَدُ فَيَذْهَبُ جُفَآءً ۚ

وَاَمَّا مَا يَنْفَعُ النَّاسَ فَيَمْكُثُ فِى الْاَرْضِ ۗ كَذٰلِكَ

يَضْرِبُ اللّٰهُ الْاَمْثَالَ ﴿١٧﴾ لِلَّذِيْنَ اسْتَجَابُوْا لِرَبِّهِمُ

الْحُسْنٰى ۗ وَالَّذِيْنَ لَمْ يَسْتَجِيْبُوْا لَهٗ لَوْ اَنَّ لَهُمْ مَّا

فِى الْاَرْضِ جَمِيْعًا وَّمِثْلَهٗ مَعَهٗ لَافْتَدَوْا بِهٖ ۗ

اُولٰٓئِكَ لَهُمْ سُوْٓءُ الْحِسَابِ ۙ وَمَأْوٰىهُمْ جَهَنَّمُ ۗ

وَبِئْسَ الْمِهَادُ ﴿١٨﴾ اَفَمَنْ يَّعْلَمُ اَنَّمَآ اُنْزِلَ اِلَيْكَ

مِنْ رَّبِّكَ الْحَقُّ كَمَنْ هُوَ اَعْمٰى ۗ اِنَّمَا يَتَذَكَّرُ اُولُوا

الْاَلْبَابِ ۙ ﴿١٩﴾ الَّذِيْنَ يُوْفُوْنَ بِعَهْدِ اللّٰهِ وَلَا يَنْقُضُوْنَ

Only beneficial things remain. Useless things are forgotten. What will you leave behind?

[15] All things in the Heavens and the Earth worship Allah willingly or unwillingly, just as their shadows in the morning and the late afternoon do.[a] [16] Say: "Who is Lord of the Heavens and the Earth?" Say: "It's Allah." Say: "Have you adopted protectors besides Him that lack the power either to benefit or harm *even* themselves?" Say *to them*: "Are the blind and the sighted equal, or is darkness and light the same?" Or have they assigned partners to Allah who have created *something* so like His creation, so *this* creation *of theirs* appears indistinguishable to them? Say: "Allah is the Creator of everything, and He is the One, the Compelling."

Only the valuable things remain

[17] He brings rain from the sky that flood the valleys, as the flash flood flows carrying away the surface froth, and from *the ores* that *blacksmiths* smelt in the fire to make jewellery and tools, a similar froth appears. This is how Allah illustrates truth and falsehood. The froth is carried away like garbage, but *the* useful *minerals* remain in the Earth for people. This is how Allah gives examples. [18] An excellent reward *awaits* those who have responded to their Lord, but those who ignored Him, even if they owned everything on Earth twice over, they would *try to* ransom themselves with it. They'll have an evil reckoning, and remain in Hell, a dreadful resting place!

The People of understanding obey the Lord

[19] Can the one who knows the truthfulness of what's revealed to you by Your Lord be compared to the blind? Only the understanding will note the warning. [20] *They fulfil their contract with Allah and don't break their pledge,*

---

[a] This is one of the verses of prostration in the Quran.

الْمِيثَاقَ ۞ وَالَّذِينَ يَصِلُونَ مَآ أَمَرَ اللهُ بِهِ أَن

يُّوصَلَ وَيَخْشَوْنَ رَبَّهُمْ وَيَخَافُونَ سُوٓءَ الْحِسَابِ ۞

وَالَّذِينَ صَبَرُوا ابْتِغَآءَ وَجْهِ رَبِّهِمْ وَأَقَامُوا الصَّلٰوةَ

وَأَنْفَقُوا مِمَّا رَزَقْنٰهُمْ سِرًّا وَّعَلَانِيَةً وَّيَدْرَءُونَ

بِالْحَسَنَةِ السَّيِّئَةَ أُولٰٓئِكَ لَهُمْ عُقْبَى الدَّارِ ۞

جَنّٰتُ عَدْنٍ يَّدْخُلُونَهَا وَمَنْ صَلَحَ مِنْ أَبَآئِهِمْ

وَأَزْوَاجِهِمْ وَذُرِّيّٰتِهِمْ وَالْمَلٰٓئِكَةُ يَدْخُلُونَ عَلَيْهِمْ

مِّنْ كُلِّ بَابٍ ۞ سَلٰمٌ عَلَيْكُمْ بِمَا صَبَرْتُمْ فَنِعْمَ

عُقْبَى الدَّارِ ۞ وَالَّذِينَ يَنْقُضُونَ عَهْدَ اللهِ مِنْ بَعْدِ

مِيثَاقِهِ وَيَقْطَعُونَ مَآ أَمَرَ اللهُ بِهِ أَن يُّوصَلَ

وَيُفْسِدُونَ فِي الْأَرْضِ أُولٰٓئِكَ لَهُمُ اللَّعْنَةُ وَلَهُمْ

سُوٓءُ الدَّارِ ۞ اللهُ يَبْسُطُ الرِّزْقَ لِمَنْ يَّشَآءُ

وَيَقْدِرُ وَفَرِحُوا بِالْحَيٰوةِ الدُّنْيَا وَمَا الْحَيٰوةُ

الدُّنْيَا فِي الْأٰخِرَةِ إِلَّا مَتَاعٌ ۞ وَيَقُولُ الَّذِينَ كَفَرُوا

لَوْلَآ أُنْزِلَ عَلَيْهِ أٰيَةٌ مِّنْ رَّبِّهِ قُلْ إِنَّ اللهَ يُضِلُّ

مَنْ يَّشَآءُ وَيَهْدِيٓ إِلَيْهِ مَنْ أَنَابَ ۞ الَّذِينَ

أٰمَنُوا وَتَطْمَئِنُّ قُلُوبُهُمْ بِذِكْرِ اللهِ أَلَا بِذِكْرِ

اللهِ تَطْمَئِنُّ الْقُلُوبُ ۞ الَّذِينَ أٰمَنُوا وَعَمِلُوا

الصّٰلِحٰتِ طُوبٰى لَهُمْ وَحُسْنُ مَأٰبٍ ۞ كَذٰلِكَ أَرْسَلْنٰكَ

فِيٓ أُمَّةٍ قَدْ خَلَتْ مِنْ قَبْلِهَا أُمَمٌ لِّتَتْلُوَا۟ عَلَيْهِمُ

The remembrance of Allah is a source of solace, serenity and steadfastness.

²¹ they maintain the ties *of kinship* as instructed by Allah, fear their Lord, afraid of an evil reckoning, ²²and are steadfast in seeking their Lord's pleasure, performing the prayer, spending in charity openly and secretly from what We have provided them, and warding off evil with good – their reward is a home *in Paradise.* ²³ They'll walk into the gardens of Paradise accompanied by their righteous forefathers, spouses and children. The angels will greet and welcome them from every gate, ²⁴saying, "Peace be on you for your steadfastness." How excellent is the reward of a home *in Paradise*? ²⁵ *However*, those who break their contract with Allah after making a solemn pledge, and sever the ties *of kinship* Allah has ordered to be maintained, and spread corruption in the land are cursed, and theirs is a miserable home.

What is the source of lasting happiness?

²⁶ Allah allocates sustenance to *all* as He pleases, measuring *it* with care. They are delighted with worldly life, yet it is only a passing pleasure compared to the Hereafter. ²⁷ The disbelievers say, "Why doesn't a *miraculous* sign come down to him from his Lord." Say: "Allah allows some to go astray, but He guides to Himself anyone who repents: ²⁸those who believe, their hearts will find peace in Allah's remembrance." The fact is, hearts find peace in the remembrance of Allah! ²⁹ Blessed are those who believe and perform righteous deeds, *for* them is the best place of return.

الَّذِىٓ اَوْحَيْنَآ اِلَيْكَ وَهُمْ يَكْفُرُوْنَ بِالرَّحْمٰنِ ۚ قُلْ

هُوَ رَبِّىْ لَآ اِلٰهَ اِلَّا هُوَ ۚ عَلَيْهِ تَوَكَّلْتُ وَاِلَيْهِ

مَتَابِ ۝ وَلَوْ اَنَّ قُرْاٰنًا سُيِّرَتْ بِهِ الْجِبَالُ اَوْ

قُطِّعَتْ بِهِ الْاَرْضُ اَوْ كُلِّمَ بِهِ الْمَوْتٰى ۚ بَلْ لِّلّٰهِ

الْاَمْرُ جَمِيْعًا ۗ اَفَلَمْ يَايْـَٔسِ الَّذِيْنَ اٰمَنُوٓا اَنْ لَّوْ

يَشَآءُ اللّٰهُ لَهَدَى النَّاسَ جَمِيْعًا ۗ وَلَا يَزَالُ

الَّذِيْنَ كَفَرُوْا تُصِيْبُهُمْ بِمَا صَنَعُوْا قَارِعَةٌ اَوْ تَحُلُّ

قَرِيْبًا مِّنْ دَارِهِمْ حَتّٰى يَاْتِىَ وَعْدُ اللّٰهِ ۗ اِنَّ اللّٰهَ

لَا يُخْلِفُ الْمِيْعَادَ ۝ وَلَقَدِ اسْتُهْزِئَ بِرُسُلٍ مِّنْ

قَبْلِكَ فَاَمْلَيْتُ لِلَّذِيْنَ كَفَرُوْا ثُمَّ اَخَذْتُهُمْ ۫

فَكَيْفَ كَانَ عِقَابِ ۝ اَفَمَنْ هُوَ قَآئِمٌ عَلٰى كُلِّ نَفْسٍ

بِمَا كَسَبَتْ ۚ وَجَعَلُوْا لِلّٰهِ شُرَكَآءَ ۗ قُلْ سَمُّوْهُمْ ۗ اَمْ

تُنَبِّـُٔوْنَهٗ بِمَا لَا يَعْلَمُ فِى الْاَرْضِ اَمْ بِظَاهِرٍ مِّنَ

الْقَوْلِ ۗ بَلْ زُيِّنَ لِلَّذِيْنَ كَفَرُوْا مَكْرُهُمْ وَصُدُّوْا

عَنِ السَّبِيْلِ ۗ وَمَنْ يُّضْلِلِ اللّٰهُ فَمَا لَهٗ مِنْ هَادٍ ۝

لَهُمْ عَذَابٌ فِى الْحَيٰوةِ الدُّنْيَا وَلَعَذَابُ الْاٰخِرَةِ

اَشَقُّ ۚ وَمَا لَهُمْ مِّنَ اللّٰهِ مِنْ وَّاقٍ ۝ مَثَلُ الْجَنَّةِ

الَّتِىْ وُعِدَ الْمُتَّقُوْنَ ۗ تَجْرِىْ مِنْ تَحْتِهَا الْاَنْهٰرُ ۗ

اُكُلُهَا دَآئِمٌ وَّظِلُّهَا ۗ تِلْكَ عُقْبَى الَّذِيْنَ اتَّقَوْا ۖ

وَّعُقْبَى الْكٰفِرِيْنَ النَّارُ ۝ وَالَّذِيْنَ اٰتَيْنٰهُمُ الْكِتٰبَ

Believe and be convinced of the words of Allah – this is the greatest miracle.

This Quran is the miracle that the disbelievers seek

³⁰ This is why We've sent you *to be* among a community like many that have passed away, to recite what We have revealed to you, while they continue denying the Kind *Lord*. Say: "He is my Lord; there is no god but Him. I place my trust in Him, and I turn in repentance to Him." ³¹ If ever there was a Quran to move the mountains, or to tear down the Earth, or to make dead speak, *it would be this one*. Indeed, Allah has complete control *of the universe*. Haven't the believers realised, if Allah wanted, He could guide the whole of humanity? The disbelievers will continue to be afflicted by tragedy because of what they've done, or else it will strike near their homes until Allah's promise is fulfilled. Allah does not break *His* promise.

The disbelievers' mockery and lies are short-lived

³² Messengers before you were mocked, the disbelievers were given a brief respite and then I would seize them. How *terrible* was My punishment! ³³ Is He Who oversees every person and what it does *comparable to anything*? And they attribute partners to Allah. Say: "Name them. Do you *pretend to* inform Him of something on *this* Earth that He doesn't know, or is this just play with words?" Their plots appear attractive to the disbelievers, as they block the path *of Allah*, but those Allah lets to go stray will have no guide. ³⁴ They'll be punished in this life, but the punishment of the Hereafter will be more severe, and they will have no one to protect them from Allah. ³⁵ What has been promised to those who are wakeful *of Allah* is like a garden under which rivers flow, and whose *supply of* food and shade is endless. This is the reward of those who are mindful *of Allah*, whereas the reward for disbelievers will be the Fire.

يَفْرَحُوْنَ بِمَآ اُنْزِلَ اِلَيْكَ وَمِنَ الْاَحْزَابِ مَنْ يُّنْكِرُ

بَعْضَهٗ ط قُلْ اِنَّمَآ اُمِرْتُ اَنْ اَعْبُدَ اللهَ وَلَآ اُشْرِكَ

بِهٖ ط اِلَيْهِ اَدْعُوْا وَاِلَيْهِ مَاٰبِ ۳۶ وَكَذٰلِكَ اَنْزَلْنٰهُ

حُكْمًا عَرَبِيًّا ط وَلَئِنِ اتَّبَعْتَ اَهْوَآءَهُمْ بَعْدَ مَا

جَآءَكَ مِنَ الْعِلْمِ ۙ مَا لَكَ مِنَ اللهِ مِنْ وَّلِيٍّ وَّلَا

وَاقٍ ۳۷ وَلَقَدْ اَرْسَلْنَا رُسُلًا مِّنْ قَبْلِكَ وَجَعَلْنَا

لَهُمْ اَزْوَاجًا وَّذُرِّيَّةً ط وَمَا كَانَ لِرَسُوْلٍ اَنْ

يَّاْتِيَ بِاٰيَةٍ اِلَّا بِاِذْنِ اللهِ ط لِكُلِّ اَجَلٍ كِتَابٌ ۳۸

يَمْحُوا اللهُ مَا يَشَآءُ وَيُثْبِتُ ۚ وَعِنْدَهٗ

اُمُّ الْكِتٰبِ ۳۹ وَاِنْ مَّا نُرِيَنَّكَ بَعْضَ الَّذِيْ

نَعِدُهُمْ اَوْ نَتَوَفَّيَنَّكَ فَاِنَّمَا عَلَيْكَ الْبَلٰغُ وَعَلَيْنَا

الْحِسَابُ ۴۰ اَوَلَمْ يَرَوْا اَنَّا نَاْتِي الْاَرْضَ نَنْقُصُهَا

مِنْ اَطْرَافِهَا ط وَاللهُ يَحْكُمُ لَا مُعَقِّبَ لِحُكْمِهٖ ط

وَهُوَ سَرِيْعُ الْحِسَابِ ۴۱ وَقَدْ مَكَرَ الَّذِيْنَ مِنْ

قَبْلِهِمْ فَلِلّٰهِ الْمَكْرُ جَمِيْعًا ط يَعْلَمُ مَا تَكْسِبُ كُلُّ

نَفْسٍ ط وَسَيَعْلَمُ الْكُفّٰرُ لِمَنْ عُقْبَى الدَّارِ ۴۲ وَيَقُوْلُ

الَّذِيْنَ كَفَرُوْا لَسْتَ مُرْسَلًا ط قُلْ كَفٰى بِاللهِ شَهِيْدًا

بَيْنِيْ وَبَيْنَكُمْ ۙ وَمَنْ عِنْدَهٗ عِلْمُ الْكِتٰبِ ۴۳

Following selfish thoughts and lusts is a recipe for disaster – instead follow the Quran.

People's different reactions to the Quran

36 Those to whom We gave the Book, *the Jews and Christians*, are delighted at what is revealed to you, though among *their* groups are those who deny some of it. Say: "I've been ordered to worship Allah and not associate *anyone* with Him. I call to Him, and I'll return to Him." 37 This is how We revealed *the Quran* with laws in Arabic. If after *receiving* such knowledge you follow their desires, then you will have no helper or protector against Allah.

Reassurance for the beloved Messenger ﷺ

38 We sent messengers before you, and gave them wives and children, *they were humans*. No messenger produced a *miraculous* sign without Allah's approval, and *Allah's* decree *determines* the right time for everything. 39 Allah either gets rid of *things* or keeps them as He pleases, and the Original Decree remains with Him.[a] 40 Whether We show you *in advance* something of what We have threatened them with, or whether We cause you to die *first*, your duty is to communicate *the message*, the *final* reckoning is Ours. 41 Haven't they realised how We are moving forward in the land, shrinking the boundaries *of their territory?* When Allah decides, no one can reverse it, and He is swift in reckoning. 42 Those who lived before them used to plot, but Allah *controls* every plot, Who knows what every person will earn. The disbelievers will learn who will have a home in *Paradise*. 43 The disbelievers say, "You aren't a messenger." Say: "Allah and those who have knowledge of the Book are a sufficient witness for me and you."

---

[a]   *Umm al-Kitab* literally means "the Mother of the Decree" or Book, which refers to the *Lawh Mahfuz* (*Al-Buruj* 85: 22), "the Preserved Tablet", containing a complete record of everything that has and will ever happen or exist.

14. Surat Ibrahim

The Prophet Ibrahim

This surat was revealed in the late Makkan period, after the Prophet's ﷺ journey to Taif, two years before the Hijrah. He planned to call the Banu Thaqif to Islam, only to be shockingly thrown out of the town and pelted with stones.

The surat begins and ends with a simple statement of the purpose of revelation: to affirm the Oneness of Allah, and to bring people out of the darkness of idolatry into the light of *Tawhid*. Why is true belief equated with gratitude, and so deserving of reward (7), while idolatry is associated with ingratitude (*kufr*)? It is because everything upon which we rely for our existence ultimately comes from Allah. To pretend that it belongs to a carved statue or idol is frankly insulting to human dignity. Those who worship idols, including the modern materialist, are reminded (9–14) of the stories they knew about the disbelievers of Nuh, Ad and Thamud. A graphic account of Hell (15–17) should remind them that punishment in this world will not be the end of it.

Followed by two parables: first, the ashes scattered by the wind (18–20) to give ungrateful disbelievers pause to question the lasting value, if any, of the worldly wealth and power of which they're so proud. The second is the parable of two trees (24–27), one firmly rooted and bearing fruit, and the other uprooted and slowly rotting. The surat ends with an account of the anguished prayer of Ibrahim (35– 41), seeking forgiveness for himself, his parents, and his family. The impact of these words on the pagan Arabs, who took pride in their forefather, Ibrahim عليه السلام, could have been considerable.

بِسْمِ اللهِ الرَّحْمٰنِ الرَّحِيمِ

الٓرٰ كِتٰبٌ اَنْزَلْنٰهُ اِلَيْكَ لِتُخْرِجَ النَّاسَ مِنَ الظُّلُمٰتِ اِلَى النُّوْرِ ۙ بِاِذْنِ رَبِّهِمْ اِلٰى صِرَاطِ الْعَزِيْزِ الْحَمِيْدِ ۙ اللهِ الَّذِيْ لَهٗ مَا فِى السَّمٰوٰتِ وَمَا فِى الْاَرْضِ ۗ وَوَيْلٌ لِّلْكٰفِرِيْنَ مِنْ عَذَابٍ شَدِيْدِۨ ۙ الَّذِيْنَ يَسْتَحِبُّوْنَ الْحَيٰوةَ الدُّنْيَا عَلَى الْاٰخِرَةِ وَيَصُدُّوْنَ عَنْ سَبِيْلِ اللهِ وَيَبْغُوْنَهَا عِوَجًا ۗ اُولٰٓئِكَ فِيْ ضَلٰلٍۭ بَعِيْدٍ ۙ وَمَآ اَرْسَلْنَا مِنْ رَّسُوْلٍ اِلَّا بِلِسَانِ قَوْمِهٖ لِيُبَيِّنَ لَهُمْ ۗ فَيُضِلُّ اللهُ مَنْ يَّشَآءُ وَيَهْدِيْ مَنْ يَّشَآءُ ۗ وَهُوَ الْعَزِيْزُ الْحَكِيْمُ ۙ وَلَقَدْ اَرْسَلْنَا مُوْسٰى بِاٰيٰتِنَآ اَنْ اَخْرِجْ قَوْمَكَ مِنَ الظُّلُمٰتِ اِلَى النُّوْرِ ۙ وَذَكِّرْهُمْ بِاَيّٰمِ اللهِ ۗ اِنَّ فِيْ ذٰلِكَ لَاٰيٰتٍ لِّكُلِّ صَبَّارٍ شَكُوْرٍ ۙ وَاِذْ قَالَ مُوْسٰى لِقَوْمِهِ اذْكُرُوْا نِعْمَةَ اللهِ عَلَيْكُمْ اِذْ اَنْجٰكُمْ مِّنْ اٰلِ فِرْعَوْنَ يَسُوْمُوْنَكُمْ سُوْٓءَ الْعَذَابِ وَيُذَبِّحُوْنَ اَبْنَآءَكُمْ وَيَسْتَحْيُوْنَ نِسَآءَكُمْ ۗ وَفِيْ ذٰلِكُمْ بَلَآءٌ مِّنْ رَّبِّكُمْ عَظِيْمٌ ۙ وَاِذْ تَاَذَّنَ رَبُّكُمْ لَئِنْ شَكَرْتُمْ لَاَزِيْدَنَّكُمْ وَلَئِنْ كَفَرْتُمْ اِنَّ عَذَابِيْ لَشَدِيْدٌ ۙ وَقَالَ مُوْسٰٓى اِنْ تَكْفُرُوْا اَنْتُمْ وَمَنْ فِى الْاَرْضِ

What is the Lord's demand? Simple, be thankful, appreciate and acknowledge His gifts.

In the name of Allah, the Kind, the Caring

¹ *Alif Lam Ra'.*

The path of light

This is a Book which We revealed so that you may lead humanity out of darkness into light, and on the road *to* the Almighty, *as* you have been authorised by Your Lord, the Praiseworthy, ² Allah; everything in the Heavens and on Earth belongs to Him. And the misery of a severe punishment *awaits* the disbelievers, ³ who prefer the worldly life to the Hereafter, they block Allah's path, wishing to obstruct others from it and to twist *its meanings*; such people are misled. ⁴ We never sent a messenger unless *he spoke* the language of his people, so he could explain *the message* to them; Allah lets anyone He wills to go off track and guides anyone who pleases Him. He is Almighty, the Wise.ᵃ

Gratitude is generously rewarded

⁵ We sent Musa with Our signs, *telling him*: "Take your people out of the darkness into the light and remind them of the days of Allah."ᵇ There are signs in that for every grateful, patient person. ⁶ Musa said to his people, "Remember how Allah blessed you when He saved you from Pharaoh's people; they gave you the worst punishment *imaginable*, slaughtering your sons and leaving your women to live; that was surely a most difficult test from your Lord." ⁷ *Remember* when Your Lord declared, "If you are grateful, I will surely increase *My favours* to you, but if you are ungrateful, then My punishment is severe." ⁸ Musa said, "Even if you and everyone on Earth were to be ungrateful, Allah is the Self-Sufficient, the Praiseworthy."

ᵃ   This is a clear statement about 'free-choice'. The 'moral choice' humans have been given. Those who want to be guided, the Lord supports, encourages and energises them to achieve (Tawfeeq). Anyone who refuses to take the opportunity is left to wonder aimlessly.

ᵇ   "The days of Allah" means the time when Allah freed the Israelites from the Pharaoh.

جَمِيْعًا ۚ فَاِنَّ اللّٰهَ لَغَنِيٌّ حَمِيْدٌ ۞ اَلَمْ يَاْتِكُمْ نَبَؤُا

الَّذِيْنَ مِنْ قَبْلِكُمْ قَوْمِ نُوْحٍ وَّعَادٍ وَّثَمُوْدَ ۚ

وَالَّذِيْنَ مِنْ بَعْدِهِمْ ۚ لَا يَعْلَمُهُمْ اِلَّا اللّٰهُ ۚ

جَآءَتْهُمْ رُسُلُهُمْ بِالْبَيِّنٰتِ فَرَدُّوْۤا اَيْدِيَهُمْ فِيْ

اَفْوَاهِهِمْ وَقَالُوْۤا اِنَّا كَفَرْنَا بِمَآ اُرْسِلْتُمْ بِهٖ وَاِنَّا

لَفِيْ شَكٍّ مِّمَّا تَدْعُوْنَنَاۤ اِلَيْهِ مُرِيْبٍ ۞ قَالَتْ

رُسُلُهُمْ اَفِى اللّٰهِ شَكٌّ فَاطِرِ السَّمٰوٰتِ وَالْاَرْضِ ۚ

يَدْعُوْكُمْ لِيَغْفِرَ لَكُمْ مِّنْ ذُنُوْبِكُمْ وَيُؤَخِّرَكُمْ اِلٰۤى

اَجَلٍ مُّسَمًّى ۚ قَالُوْۤا اِنْ اَنْتُمْ اِلَّا بَشَرٌ مِّثْلُنَا ۚ

تُرِيْدُوْنَ اَنْ تَصُدُّوْنَا عَمَّا كَانَ يَعْبُدُ اٰبَآؤُنَا

فَاْتُوْنَا بِسُلْطٰنٍ مُّبِيْنٍ ۞ قَالَتْ لَهُمْ رُسُلُهُمْ اِنْ

نَّحْنُ اِلَّا بَشَرٌ مِّثْلُكُمْ وَلٰكِنَّ اللّٰهَ يَمُنُّ عَلٰى مَنْ

يَّشَآءُ مِنْ عِبَادِهٖ ۚ وَمَا كَانَ لَنَاۤ اَنْ نَّاْتِيَكُمْ بِسُلْطٰنٍ

اِلَّا بِاِذْنِ اللّٰهِ ۚ وَعَلَى اللّٰهِ فَلْيَتَوَكَّلِ الْمُؤْمِنُوْنَ ۞

وَمَا لَنَاۤ اَلَّا نَتَوَكَّلَ عَلَى اللّٰهِ وَقَدْ هَدٰىنَا سُبُلَنَا ۚ

وَلَنَصْبِرَنَّ عَلٰى مَاۤ اٰذَيْتُمُوْنَا ۚ وَعَلَى اللّٰهِ فَلْيَتَوَكَّلِ

الْمُتَوَكِّلُوْنَ ۞ وَقَالَ الَّذِيْنَ كَفَرُوْا لِرُسُلِهِمْ

لَنُخْرِجَنَّكُمْ مِّنْ اَرْضِنَاۤ اَوْ لَتَعُوْدُنَّ فِيْ مِلَّتِنَا ۚ فَاَوْحٰۤى

اِلَيْهِمْ رَبُّهُمْ لَنُهْلِكَنَّ الظّٰلِمِيْنَ ۞ وَلَنُسْكِنَنَّكُمُ

الْاَرْضَ مِنْ بَعْدِهِمْ ۚ ذٰلِكَ لِمَنْ خَافَ مَقَامِيْ

What three practices Prophets adopted to face persecution? Reliance, guidance and patience.

Disbelievers react angrily when told about their faults

⁹ Hasn't the story of past generations reached you: the people of Nuh, Ad, Thamud, and of those after them whom only Allah knows? When their messengers came with clear proofs, they put their hands on their mouths *to silence them*ᵃ and said, "We reject what you have been sent with, and we seriously doubt what you are calling us to." ¹⁰ Their messengers replied, "Is there any doubt about *the existence of* Allah, Creator of the Heavens and the Earth? He invites you, so He can forgive your sins and give you time *to think* till the appointed term." *They* said, "You are a mortal like us, who wants to stop us from *worshipping* what our forefathers worshipped; so bring us a miracle." ¹¹ The messengers said to them, "We may be humans like you, but Allah favours anyone of His servants He pleases. It's not for us to bring you a miracle except with Allah's approval, and believers *always* put their trust in Allah. ¹² So why would we not put our trust in Allah when He has guided us on our paths *to His kindness*. We shall patiently endure your persecution; so let all who trust *in Him* put their trust in Allah."

Allah tells the messengers not to fear the disbelievers' threats

¹³ The disbelievers said to their messengers, "We will expel you from our town unless you revert to our religion." Then their Lord revealed to them: "We will destroy the evildoers, ¹⁴ and We will settle you in this town after them. This *reward* is for anyone who's afraid of My punishment and of standing before Me *on Judgement Day*."

ᵃ According to Al-Qurtubi, this Arabic idiom refers to a gesture expressing shock or anger, as in *Al 'Imran* 3: 119 ("they bite on their fingertips out of rage").

وَخَافَ وَعِيْدِ ۝ وَاسْتَفْتَحُوْا وَخَابَ كُلُّ جَبَّارٍ

عَنِيْدٍ ۝ مِّنْ وَّرَآئِهٖ جَهَنَّمُ وَيُسْقٰى مِنْ مَّآءٍ

صَدِيْدٍ ۝ يَّتَجَرَّعُهٗ وَلَا يَكَادُ يُسِيْغُهٗ وَيَأْتِيْهِ

الْمَوْتُ مِنْ كُلِّ مَكَانٍ وَّمَا هُوَ بِمَيِّتٍ ط وَمِنْ

وَّرَآئِهٖ عَذَابٌ غَلِيْظٌ ۝ مَثَلُ الَّذِيْنَ كَفَرُوْا

بِرَبِّهِمْ اَعْمَالُهُمْ كَرَمَادٍ اشْتَدَّتْ بِهِ الرِّيْحُ فِيْ

يَوْمٍ عَاصِفٍ ط لَا يَقْدِرُوْنَ مِمَّا كَسَبُوْا عَلٰى شَيْءٍ ط

ذٰلِكَ هُوَ الضَّلٰلُ الْبَعِيْدُ ۝ اَلَمْ تَرَ اَنَّ اللهَ خَلَقَ

السَّمٰوٰتِ وَالْاَرْضَ بِالْحَقِّ ط اِنْ يَّشَأْ يُذْهِبْكُمْ وَيَأْتِ

بِخَلْقٍ جَدِيْدٍ ۝ وَّمَا ذٰلِكَ عَلَى اللهِ بِعَزِيْزٍ ۝

وَبَرَزُوْا لِلّٰهِ جَمِيْعًا فَقَالَ الضُّعَفٰٓؤُا لِلَّذِيْنَ اسْتَكْبَرُوْٓا

اِنَّا كُنَّا لَكُمْ تَبَعًا فَهَلْ اَنْتُمْ مُّغْنُوْنَ عَنَّا

مِنْ عَذَابِ اللهِ مِنْ شَيْءٍ ط قَالُوْا لَوْ هَدٰىنَا اللهُ

لَهَدَيْنٰكُمْ ط سَوَآءٌ عَلَيْنَآ اَجَزِعْنَآ اَمْ صَبَرْنَا مَا

لَنَا مِنْ مَّحِيْصٍ ۝ وَقَالَ الشَّيْطٰنُ لَمَّا قُضِيَ

الْاَمْرُ اِنَّ اللهَ وَعَدَكُمْ وَعْدَ الْحَقِّ وَوَعَدْتُّكُمْ

فَاَخْلَفْتُكُمْ ط وَمَا كَانَ لِيَ عَلَيْكُمْ مِّنْ سُلْطٰنٍ اِلَّآ

اَنْ دَعَوْتُكُمْ فَاسْتَجَبْتُمْ لِيْ ۚ فَلَا تَلُوْمُوْنِيْ وَلُوْمُوْٓا

اَنْفُسَكُمْ ط مَآ اَنَا بِمُصْرِخِكُمْ وَمَآ اَنْتُمْ بِمُصْرِخِيَّ ط

اِنِّيْ كَفَرْتُ بِمَآ اَشْرَكْتُمُوْنِ مِنْ قَبْلُ ط اِنَّ الظّٰلِمِيْنَ

The life-long works of the deniers will be worthless on Judgement Day, since they were deprived of Allah's kindness.

٣
ع
١٥

497

Sipping scalding water in Hell

¹⁵ *They* prayed to win *over their people*, and *the scheming of* every stubborn tyrant failed. ¹⁶ Hell awaits them, where *only* scalding water will be served, ¹⁷ they will sip it but can't swallow it, and death will loom all around them, but they will not die, and beyond that *experience* will be an *even more* severe punishment.

Disbelievers deeds are worthless, like the ashes swept up by the wind

¹⁸ An *apt* example of the disbeliever's deeds *is*: ashes scattered by the winds on a stormy day. They will have no control over anything that they owned. That is *the meaning of* going far astray. ¹⁹ Have you not considered that in truth Allah is the One Who created the Heavens and the Earth? If He so willed, He could remove you all and produce a new creation *to replace you*; ²⁰ nor would that be too difficult *a challenge* for Allah.

Satan admits he has no control over people

²¹ They will all appear before Allah *on Judgement Day*, and the oppressed will say to their arrogant *leaders*, "We followed you, so will you rescue us from Allah's punishment?" They will say, "If Allah had guided us, then we would have guided you. It's all the same to us now whether we are anxious or patient; there's no escape for us." ²² Once the sentence has been passed, Satan will say, "Allah's promise to you was true, whereas I made you a promise and broke it. I had no control over you, I called you and you accepted my call. So, don't blame me blame yourselves. I can't help you and you can't help me. I have rejected whatever you previously associated with me. For evildoers, is a painful punishment."

لَهُمْ عَذَابٌ اَلِيْمٌ ۞ وَاُدْخِلَ الَّذِيْنَ اٰمَنُوْا وَعَمِلُوا

الصّٰلِحٰتِ جَنّٰتٍ تَجْرِيْ مِنْ تَحْتِهَا الْاَنْهٰرُ خٰلِدِيْنَ

فِيْهَا بِاِذْنِ رَبِّهِمْ ۚ تَحِيَّتُهُمْ فِيْهَا سَلٰمٌ ۞ اَلَمْ تَرَ

كَيْفَ ضَرَبَ اللهُ مَثَلًا كَلِمَةً طَيِّبَةً كَشَجَرَةٍ

طَيِّبَةٍ اَصْلُهَا ثَابِتٌ وَّفَرْعُهَا فِى السَّمَآءِ ۞ تُؤْتِيْ

اُكُلَهَا كُلَّ حِيْنٍ بِاِذْنِ رَبِّهَا ۚ وَيَضْرِبُ اللهُ

الْاَمْثَالَ لِلنَّاسِ لَعَلَّهُمْ يَتَذَكَّرُوْنَ ۞ وَمَثَلُ

كَلِمَةٍ خَبِيْثَةٍ كَشَجَرَةٍ خَبِيْثَةِ ۨاجْتُثَّتْ مِنْ

فَوْقِ الْاَرْضِ مَا لَهَا مِنْ قَرَارٍ ۞ يُثَبِّتُ اللهُ

الَّذِيْنَ اٰمَنُوْا بِالْقَوْلِ الثَّابِتِ فِى الْحَيٰوةِ الدُّنْيَا

وَفِى الْاٰخِرَةِ ۚ وَيُضِلُّ اللهُ الظّٰلِمِيْنَ ۙ وَيَفْعَلُ

اللهُ مَا يَشَآءُ ۞ اَلَمْ تَرَ اِلَى الَّذِيْنَ بَدَّلُوْا نِعْمَتَ اللهِ كُفْرًا

وَّاَحَلُّوْا قَوْمَهُمْ دَارَ الْبَوَارِ ۞ جَهَنَّمَ ۚ يَصْلَوْنَهَا ۚ

وَبِئْسَ الْقَرَارُ ۞ وَجَعَلُوْا لِلّٰهِ اَنْدَادًا لِّيُضِلُّوْا عَنْ

سَبِيْلِهٖ ۚ قُلْ تَمَتَّعُوْا فَاِنَّ مَصِيْرَكُمْ اِلَى النَّارِ ۞

قُلْ لِّعِبَادِيَ الَّذِيْنَ اٰمَنُوْا يُقِيْمُوا الصَّلٰوةَ وَيُنْفِقُوْا

مِمَّا رَزَقْنٰهُمْ سِرًّا وَّعَلَانِيَةً مِّنْ قَبْلِ اَنْ يَّأْتِيَ

يَوْمٌ لَّا بَيْعٌ فِيْهِ وَلَا خِلٰلٌ ۞ اَللهُ الَّذِيْ خَلَقَ

السَّمٰوٰتِ وَالْاَرْضَ وَاَنْزَلَ مِنَ السَّمَآءِ مَآءً فَاَخْرَجَ

بِهٖ مِنَ الثَّمَرٰتِ رِزْقًا لَّكُمْ ۚ وَسَخَّرَ لَكُمُ الْفُلْكَ

The symbol for the teachings of Islam is a mighty, healthy tree that gives fruit in all seasons.

²³ *Meanwhile* those who believed and performed righteous deeds will enter gardens beneath which rivers flow, living there by their Lord's approval forever, in it their greeting will be: "Peace!"

The parable of the fruit tree

²⁴ Have you not considered how Allah likened a good word[a] to a good tree, whose roots are fixed and whose branches *reach* to the sky; ²⁵ every season, it bears fruit by the Lord's favour. Allah gives people parables so they may reflect. ²⁶ *Similarly*, He likened an evil word to a rotting tree, whose roots have been pulled out lying on the ground. ²⁷ Allah will firmly ground the believers to stand firm in this worldly life and in the Hereafter by means of well-founded words, whereas *He* allows disbelievers to go astray. Allah does what He wills.

Disbelievers have short-changed themselves

²⁸ Haven't you seen those who exchanged Allah's gift *of belief* for disbelief, and who push their people on towards the house of destruction: ²⁹ Hell is where they'll burn, what a bleak place to stay! ³⁰ They made idols equal to Allah to mislead *people* from His path. Say *to them*: "Enjoy yourselves *while you can*, for the Fire shall be your journey's end."

The things that people take for granted

³¹ Tell My faithful servants; perform the prayer *regularly,* spend in charity openly and secretly from what We have provided, before *that* day comes when bargaining and friendship will serve no purpose. ³² Allah created the Heavens and the Earth and sent down rain from the sky, by which He produces fruits to provide for you, and made possible for you to sail by ship across the sea by His command, made rivers for your benefit,

---

[a] "Good word" according to Ibn Abbas is *La ilah illa Allah* ("There is no god but Allah"), and by Mujahid either, a believer's faith, or the believer (Al-Qurtubi).

لِتَجْرِيَ فِى الْبَحْرِ بِاَمْرِهٖ ۚ وَسَخَّرَ لَكُمُ الْاَنْهٰرَ ۞

وَسَخَّرَ لَكُمُ الشَّمْسَ وَالْقَمَرَ دَآئِبَيْنِ ۚ وَسَخَّرَ لَكُمُ

الَّيْلَ وَالنَّهَارَ ۞ وَاٰتٰىكُمْ مِّنْ كُلِّ مَا سَاَلْتُمُوْهُ ؕ

وَاِنْ تَعُدُّوْا نِعْمَتَ اللّٰهِ لَا تُحْصُوْهَا ؕ اِنَّ الْاِنْسَانَ

لَظَلُوْمٌ كَفَّارٌ ۞ وَاِذْ قَالَ اِبْرٰهِيْمُ رَبِّ اجْعَلْ هٰذَا

الْبَلَدَ اٰمِنًا وَّاجْنُبْنِىْ وَبَنِىَّ اَنْ نَّعْبُدَ الْاَصْنَامَ ۞

رَبِّ اِنَّهُنَّ اَضْلَلْنَ كَثِيْرًا مِّنَ النَّاسِ ۚ فَمَنْ تَبِعَنِىْ

فَاِنَّهٗ مِنِّىْ ۚ وَمَنْ عَصَانِىْ فَاِنَّكَ غَفُوْرٌ رَّحِيْمٌ ۞

رَبَّنَآ اِنِّىْ اَسْكَنْتُ مِنْ ذُرِّيَّتِىْ بِوَادٍ غَيْرِ ذِىْ زَرْعٍ

عِنْدَ بَيْتِكَ الْمُحَرَّمِ ۙ رَبَّنَا لِيُقِيْمُوا الصَّلٰوةَ فَاجْعَلْ

اَفْئِدَةً مِّنَ النَّاسِ تَهْوِىْٓ اِلَيْهِمْ وَارْزُقْهُمْ مِّنَ

الثَّمَرٰتِ لَعَلَّهُمْ يَشْكُرُوْنَ ۞ رَبَّنَآ اِنَّكَ تَعْلَمُ مَا

نُخْفِىْ وَمَا نُعْلِنُ ؕ وَمَا يَخْفٰى عَلَى اللّٰهِ مِنْ شَىْءٍ

فِى الْاَرْضِ وَلَا فِى السَّمَآءِ ۞ اَلْحَمْدُ لِلّٰهِ الَّذِىْ

وَهَبَ لِىْ عَلَى الْكِبَرِ اِسْمٰعِيْلَ وَاِسْحٰقَ ؕ اِنَّ رَبِّىْ

لَسَمِيْعُ الدُّعَآءِ ۞ رَبِّ اجْعَلْنِىْ مُقِيْمَ الصَّلٰوةِ

وَمِنْ ذُرِّيَّتِىْ ۖ رَبَّنَا وَتَقَبَّلْ دُعَآءِ ۞ رَبَّنَا اغْفِرْ لِىْ

وَلِوَالِدَىَّ وَلِلْمُؤْمِنِيْنَ يَوْمَ يَقُوْمُ الْحِسَابُ ۞ وَلَا

تَحْسَبَنَّ اللّٰهَ غَافِلًا عَمَّا يَعْمَلُ الظّٰلِمُوْنَ ؕ اِنَّمَا

يُؤَخِّرُهُمْ لِيَوْمٍ تَشْخَصُ فِيْهِ الْاَبْصَارُ ۞ مُهْطِعِيْنَ

Ibrahim prays for ten things, what are they? Which one is your favourite?

501

³³ made the sun and the moon orbit, for your benefit, He made night and day. ³⁴ He has given you a portion of whatever you have asked Him for. If you were to count Allah's gifts, you would not be able to count them. Humans are most ungrateful, unjust!

Ibrahim's prayer for the security of his children

³⁵ *Remember* when Ibrahim prayed: "My Lord, make this town safe *and secure*, and keep me and my children away from idol worship. ³⁶ My Lord, *idols* have misled many people. So, whoever follows me is one with me, and the one who disobeys me, well, You are Forgiving, Kind. ³⁷ Our Lord, I have settled my children in a barren valley near Your Sacred House so they may perform the prayer, soften people's hearts towards them and provide them with the fruits *of the Earth* so they may be grateful. ³⁸ Our Lord, You know what we conceal and what we reveal. Nothing on Earth or in the sky is hidden from Allah. ³⁹ Praise be to Allah Who granted Ismail and Ishaq to me in my old age. My Lord is the Hearer of prayers. ⁴⁰ My Lord, make me and my children steadfast in prayer. Our Lord accept my prayer. ⁴¹ Our Lord, forgive me, my parents and *all* the believers on Judgement Day."

The disbelievers' bewilderment on Judgement Day

⁴² Don't think Allah is unaware of what the wrongdoers do. He is giving them time *to think* till a day when eyes will stare in horror,

مُقْنِعِىْ رُءُوْسِهِمْ لَا يَرْتَدُّ اِلَيْهِمْ طَرْفُهُمْ ۚ

وَاَفْئِدَتُهُمْ هَوَآءٌ ۞ وَاَنْذِرِ النَّاسَ يَوْمَ يَاْتِيْهِمُ

الْعَذَابُ فَيَقُوْلُ الَّذِيْنَ ظَلَمُوْا رَبَّنَآ اَخِّرْنَآ اِلَى اَجَلٍ

قَرِيْبٍ ۙ نُّجِبْ دَعْوَتَكَ وَنَتَّبِعِ الرُّسُلَ ؕ اَوَلَمْ تَكُوْنُوْٓا

اَقْسَمْتُمْ مِّنْ قَبْلُ مَا لَكُمْ مِّنْ زَوَالٍ ۙ ۞ وَّسَكَنْتُمْ فِيْ

مَسٰكِنِ الَّذِيْنَ ظَلَمُوْٓا اَنْفُسَهُمْ وَتَبَيَّنَ لَكُمْ كَيْفَ

فَعَلْنَا بِهِمْ وَضَرَبْنَا لَكُمُ الْاَمْثَالَ ۞ وَقَدْ مَكَرُوْا

Divine punishment will be severe, accept the Lord now!

مَكْرَهُمْ وَعِنْدَ اللّٰهِ مَكْرُهُمْ ؕ وَاِنْ كَانَ مَكْرُهُمْ

لِتَزُوْلَ مِنْهُ الْجِبَالُ ۞ فَلَا تَحْسَبَنَّ اللّٰهَ مُخْلِفَ

وَعْدِهٖ رُسُلَهٗ ؕ اِنَّ اللّٰهَ عَزِيْزٌ ذُو انْتِقَامٍ ۙ ۞ يَوْمَ

تُبَدَّلُ الْاَرْضُ غَيْرَ الْاَرْضِ وَالسَّمٰوٰتُ وَبَرَزُوْا

لِلّٰهِ الْوَاحِدِ الْقَهَّارِ ۞ وَتَرَى الْمُجْرِمِيْنَ يَوْمَئِذٍ

مُّقَرَّنِيْنَ فِي الْاَصْفَادِ ۞ سَرَابِيْلُهُمْ مِّنْ قَطِرَانٍ

وَّتَغْشٰى وُجُوْهَهُمُ النَّارُ ۞ لِيَجْزِيَ اللّٰهُ كُلَّ

نَفْسٍ مَّا كَسَبَتْ ؕ اِنَّ اللّٰهَ سَرِيْعُ الْحِسَابِ ۞

هٰذَا بَلٰغٌ لِّلنَّاسِ وَلِيُنْذَرُوْا بِهٖ وَلِيَعْلَمُوْٓا اَنَّمَا

هُوَ اِلٰهٌ وَّاحِدٌ وَّلِيَذَّكَّرَ اُولُوا الْاَلْبَابِ ۞

⁴³ rushing to and fro, craning their necks, no one returning their gaze, and their hearts empty. ⁴⁴ *So* warn people of a day when the punishment will come to them, and the evildoers will say, "Our Lord, give us more time so we may answer Your call and follow the messengers." *The reply*, "Didn't you swear an oath that your *power* would never diminish? ⁴⁵ You lived in the homes of those who had wronged themselves, so you clearly knew what We had done with them, and We had made *them* examples for you."

The Earth will be modified for Judgement Day

⁴⁶ They hatched a plot and Allah *knew* their plots, their plots could move the mountains, *they couldn't thwart Allah's plan.* ⁴⁷ So don't think Allah will break His promise with His messengers. Allah is Almighty, the Avenger. ⁴⁸ One day the Earth will be exchanged for another Earth, and the Heavens *likewise*, and they will *all* appear before Allah, the One, the Supreme, ⁴⁹ and on that day you will see the sinners bound together in chains, ⁵⁰ their coats made of tar, and their faces ablaze. ⁵¹ *This is* so that Allah may repay every soul according to their labour. Allah is swift in accounting.

The Quran's purpose is simple: to declare Allah's oneness

⁵² This is to convey *a message* to people, to warn them so they realise He is the One God Who *exists*, and *people of* understanding may pay attention.

15. Surat Al-Hijr

The Rock City

This Makkan surat was revealed in the final years of the Prophetic mission. The central theme is to expose the Makkans' attitude towards the Prophet ﷺ. They are not serious about spiritual matters, and love worldly life: "*Leave them to eat and enjoy themselves, preoccupied with self-indulging* long hopes" (3). They were stubborn, and unwilling to listen to reasonable arguments. The Quran's diagnosis of the Makkans was they needed moral and spiritual guidance, since their economic success had made them materialistic individuals, selfish and greedy; the solution was a dose of moral and spiritual values.

The Quran presents the fates of past communities who opposed their prophets, so the Makkans are warned of a similar fate if they continue their rebellion.[a] The story of Ibrahim ﷺ is a case in point, he was informed that the people of Lut ﷺ would be punished. At the same time, it describes the angels bringing him the good news of a son; Allah's kindness to his servants and His punishment of the disobedient.

Further illustrations of the disastrous fate of the people of the Madyan woodlands and the cave dwellers of Thamud, after whom the surat gets its name (*Al-Hijr*) are given. The Makkans were familiar with these ancient communities since their ruins were on the trade route to Syria.

The final section offers consolation to the beloved Messenger ﷺ and his harassed followers: you are blessed with the Glorious Quran; this is more valuable than anything the others possess and will help to bring balance to your materialistic lives. The Gracious Lord consoles the Prophet ﷺ with heartening words: "We are sufficient for you against those who mock … We know what they say distresses you" (95–97). The surat opened, "*They will regret ...*" but the closing verse instructs: "Continue to worship your Lord until you die."

---

[a] This use of references to disobedient communities in the past is a recurrent device in the Quran.

بِسْمِ اللهِ الرَّحْمٰنِ الرَّحِیْمِ

الٓرٰ ۚ تِلْكَ اٰیٰتُ الْكِتٰبِ وَ قُرْاٰنٍ مُّبِیْنٍ ۝

رُبَمَا یَوَدُّ الَّذِیْنَ كَفَرُوْا لَوْ كَانُوْا مُسْلِمِیْنَ ۝

ذَرْهُمْ یَاْكُلُوْا وَیَتَمَتَّعُوْا وَ یُلْهِهِمُ الْاَمَلُ فَسَوْفَ یَعْلَمُوْنَ ۝ وَمَاۤ اَهْلَكْنَا مِنْ قَرْیَةٍ اِلَّا وَلَهَا كِتَابٌ مَّعْلُوْمٌ ۝ مَا تَسْبِقُ مِنْ اُمَّةٍ اَجَلَهَا وَمَا یَسْتَاْخِرُوْنَ ۝ وَقَالُوْا یٰۤاَیُّهَا الَّذِیْ نُزِّلَ عَلَیْهِ الذِّكْرُ اِنَّكَ لَمَجْنُوْنٌ ۝ لَوْمَا تَاْتِیْنَا بِالْمَلٰٓئِكَةِ اِنْ كُنْتَ مِنَ الصّٰدِقِیْنَ ۝ مَا نُنَزِّلُ الْمَلٰٓئِكَةَ اِلَّا بِالْحَقِّ وَمَا كَانُوْۤا اِذًا مُّنْظَرِیْنَ ۝ اِنَّا نَحْنُ نَزَّلْنَا الذِّكْرَ وَاِنَّا لَهٗ لَحٰفِظُوْنَ ۝ وَلَقَدْ اَرْسَلْنَا مِنْ قَبْلِكَ فِیْ شِیَعِ الْاَوَّلِیْنَ ۝ وَمَا یَاْتِیْهِمْ مِّنْ رَّسُوْلٍ اِلَّا كَانُوْا بِهٖ یَسْتَهْزِءُوْنَ ۝ كَذٰلِكَ نَسْلُكُهٗ فِیْ قُلُوْبِ الْمُجْرِمِیْنَ ۝ لَا یُؤْمِنُوْنَ بِهٖ وَقَدْ خَلَتْ سُنَّةُ الْاَوَّلِیْنَ ۝ وَلَوْ فَتَحْنَا عَلَیْهِمْ بَابًا مِّنَ السَّمَاۤءِ فَظَلُّوْا فِیْهِ یَعْرُجُوْنَ ۝ لَقَالُوْۤا اِنَّمَا سُكِّرَتْ اَبْصَارُنَا بَلْ نَحْنُ قَوْمٌ مَّسْحُوْرُوْنَ ۝ وَلَقَدْ جَعَلْنَا فِی السَّمَاۤءِ بُرُوْجًا وَّ زَیَّنّٰهَا لِلنّٰظِرِیْنَ ۝ وَحَفِظْنٰهَا مِنْ كُلِّ شَیْطٰنٍ رَّجِیْمٍ ۝ اِلَّا مَنِ

Being regretful on Judgement Day will be pointless; now is the time to believe and love Allah.

507

In the name of Allah, the Kind, the Caring.

¹ *Alif Lam Ra'.*

The disbelievers' regret on Judgement Day

These are the verses of a *Majestic* Book, the clear Quran. ²*One day the* disbelievers *will* wish they had submitted *to Allah's will.* ³Now they can eat and enjoy themselves *with long* hopes distracting them; soon they will come to know *the truth.* ⁴We have never destroyed a town until its appointed time; ⁵no town can go beyond its appointed time, nor can they delay it. ⁶They said, "Messenger,ᵃ you are certainly mad. ⁷If you are telling the truth, why don't you bring angels?" ⁸We only send angels with the task *to destroy them,* in which case they would not be spared.

Disbelievers have always mocked the truth

⁹We revealed the Reminder, and We are its Protectors. ¹⁰We sent messengers to the ancient communities before you, ¹¹and they mocked every messenger who came to them. ¹²That is how We ease the way of *disbelief* into the hearts of the sinners. ¹³They will not believe in *the truth* despite *knowing* the example of what happened to previous generations. ¹⁴Even if We opened a gate for them in the sky, through which they could climb up, ¹⁵they would say, "Our eyes are deceived, we've been bewitched."

The starry skies and cross-pollinating winds

¹⁶We positioned constellations *of stars* in the sky, making it beautiful for the onlookers,ᵇ ¹⁷and protected it from every doomed demon,

---

ᵃ   Literally, "You to whom the Reminder has been revealed."
ᵇ   Constellations are groups of stars that form recognisable patterns in the night sky.

اسْتَرَقَ السَّمْعَ فَاَتْبَعَهُ شِهَابٌ مُّبِيْنٌ ۞ وَالْاَرْضَ

مَدَدْنٰهَا وَاَلْقَيْنَا فِيْهَا رَوَاسِىَ وَاَنْبَتْنَا فِيْهَا مِنْ

كُلِّ شَىْءٍ مَّوْزُوْنٍ ۞ وَجَعَلْنَا لَكُمْ فِيْهَا مَعَايِشَ

وَمَنْ لَّسْتُمْ لَهُ بِرٰزِقِيْنَ ۞ وَاِنْ مِّنْ شَىْءٍ اِلَّا

عِنْدَنَا خَزَائِنُهُ ۟ وَمَا نُنَزِّلُهُ اِلَّا بِقَدَرٍ مَّعْلُوْمٍ ۞

وَاَرْسَلْنَا الرِّيٰحَ لَوَاقِحَ فَاَنْزَلْنَا مِنَ السَّمَاءِ مَاءً

فَاَسْقَيْنٰكُمُوْهُ وَمَاۤ اَنْتُمْ لَهُ بِخٰزِنِيْنَ ۞ وَاِنَّا لَنَحْنُ

نُحْى وَنُمِيْتُ وَنَحْنُ الْوٰرِثُوْنَ ۞ وَلَقَدْ عَلِمْنَا

الْمُسْتَقْدِمِيْنَ مِنْكُمْ وَلَقَدْ عَلِمْنَا الْمُسْتَاْخِرِيْنَ ۞

وَاِنَّ رَبَّكَ هُوَ يَحْشُرُهُمْ ط اِنَّهُ حَكِيْمٌ عَلِيْمٌ ۞

وَلَقَدْ خَلَقْنَا الْاِنْسَانَ مِنْ صَلْصَالٍ مِّنْ حَمَاٍ

مَّسْنُوْنٍ ۞ وَالْجَاۤنَّ خَلَقْنٰهُ مِنْ قَبْلُ مِنْ نَّارِ

السَّمُوْمِ ۞ وَاِذْ قَالَ رَبُّكَ لِلْمَلٰٓئِكَةِ اِنِّىْ خَالِقٌ بَشَرًا

مِّنْ صَلْصَالٍ مِّنْ حَمَاٍ مَّسْنُوْنٍ ۞ فَاِذَا سَوَّيْتُهُ

وَنَفَخْتُ فِيْهِ مِنْ رُّوْحِىْ فَقَعُوْا لَهُ سٰجِدِيْنَ ۞ فَسَجَدَ

الْمَلٰٓئِكَةُ كُلُّهُمْ اَجْمَعُوْنَ ۞ اِلَّاۤ اِبْلِيْسَ ط اَبٰٓى اَنْ

يَّكُوْنَ مَعَ السّٰجِدِيْنَ ۞ قَالَ يٰٓاِبْلِيْسُ مَا لَكَ اَلَّا

تَكُوْنَ مَعَ السّٰجِدِيْنَ ۞ قَالَ لَمْ اَكُنْ لِّاَسْجُدَ لِبَشَرٍ

خَلَقْتَهُ مِنْ صَلْصَالٍ مِّنْ حَمَاٍ مَّسْنُوْنٍ ۞ قَالَ

فَاخْرُجْ مِنْهَا فَاِنَّكَ رَجِيْمٌ ۞ وَّاِنَّ عَلَيْكَ اللَّعْنَةَ اِلٰى

Allah created the vast universe, its ecosystems and humanity all for a purpose: worship of Allah.

ع
١٠
٢

¹⁸ except those who try to eavesdrop and are chased away by the fiery flame *of a shooting star.* ¹⁹ We have spread out the Earth, set mountains on it, and grew all kinds of plants and animals in a balanced *ecosystem,* ²⁰ and We made livelihood on *Earth* for you and others you don't provide for. ²¹ There is no *living* thing for which We don't have storehouses, which We release in known quantities. ²² We send winds to cross-pollinate *the flowers,*ᵃ rain from the sky which you drink; you have no control over the water wells. ²³ We give life and death, and We are the heirs *of all things.*ᵇ ²⁴ We know those who went before you; We know those who will come after you; ²⁵ and He's Your Lord, Who will gather all, the Wise, the Knower.

Satan vows to mislead humanity

²⁶ We created the *first* human from dried clay out of dark mud, ²⁷ before which We created the jinn from smokeless fire. ²⁸ *Remember* when Your Lord said to the angels, "I am creating a human with dried clay out of dark mud. ²⁹ Once I have shaped and blown My spirit into him, then prostrate before him." ³⁰ So all the angels prostrated, ³¹ except Iblis,ᶜ who refused to prostrate. ³² Allah said, "Iblis, why didn't you prostrate?" ³³ He replied, "I'm not prepared to prostrate before a human You created with dried clay out of dark mud." ³⁴ *Allah* said, "Then leave, you shall be pelted *with stones.* ³⁵ *My* curse will be on you until Judgement Day."

ᵃ   The word *lawaqih* meant "pregnant with rainwater" and the fertilisation of plants by the process of pollination, adding a new layer of meaning and appreciation to the text for modern readers.

ᵇ   In other words, everything returns to Allah in the end, as it says in verse 25.

ᶜ   Iblis is one of the names of Satan.

٣
ع
۱۹
٣

Satan doesn't have control over us, he just hints, suggests and lures us. His web of deception is weak. Seek Allah's protection.

يَوْمِ الدِّيْنِ ۞ قَالَ رَبِّ فَاَنْظِرْنِيْ اِلٰى يَوْمِ يُبْعَثُوْنَ ۞

قَالَ فَاِنَّكَ مِنَ الْمُنْظَرِيْنَ ۞ اِلٰى يَوْمِ الْوَقْتِ

الْمَعْلُوْمِ ۞ قَالَ رَبِّ بِمَآ اَغْوَيْتَنِيْ لَاُزَيِّنَنَّ لَهُمْ فِي

الْاَرْضِ وَلَاُغْوِيَنَّهُمْ اَجْمَعِيْنَ ۞ اِلَّا عِبَادَكَ مِنْهُمُ

الْمُخْلَصِيْنَ ۞ قَالَ هٰذَا صِرَاطٌ عَلَيَّ مُسْتَقِيْمٌ ۞ اِنَّ

عِبَادِيْ لَيْسَ لَكَ عَلَيْهِمْ سُلْطٰنٌ اِلَّا مَنِ اتَّبَعَكَ

مِنَ الْغٰوِيْنَ ۞ وَاِنَّ جَهَنَّمَ لَمَوْعِدُهُمْ اَجْمَعِيْنَ ۞

لَهَا سَبْعَةُ اَبْوَابٍ ۖ لِكُلِّ بَابٍ مِّنْهُمْ جُزْءٌ

مَّقْسُوْمٌ ۞ اِنَّ الْمُتَّقِيْنَ فِيْ جَنّٰتٍ وَّعُيُوْنٍ ۞

اُدْخُلُوْهَا بِسَلٰمٍ اٰمِنِيْنَ ۞ وَنَزَعْنَا مَا فِيْ صُدُوْرِهِمْ

مِّنْ غِلٍّ اِخْوَانًا عَلٰى سُرُرٍ مُّتَقٰبِلِيْنَ ۞ لَا يَمَسُّهُمْ

فِيْهَا نَصَبٌ وَّمَا هُمْ مِّنْهَا بِمُخْرَجِيْنَ ۞ نَبِّئْ عِبَادِيْ

اَنِّيْ اَنَا الْغَفُوْرُ الرَّحِيْمُ ۞ وَاَنَّ عَذَابِيْ هُوَ الْعَذَابُ

الْاَلِيْمُ ۞ وَنَبِّئْهُمْ عَنْ ضَيْفِ اِبْرٰهِيْمَ ۞ اِذْ دَخَلُوْا

عَلَيْهِ فَقَالُوْا سَلٰمًا ۖ قَالَ اِنَّا مِنْكُمْ وَجِلُوْنَ ۞ قَالُوْا

لَا تَوْجَلْ اِنَّا نُبَشِّرُكَ بِغُلٰمٍ عَلِيْمٍ ۞ قَالَ اَبَشَّرْتُمُوْنِيْ

عَلٰۤى اَنْ مَّسَّنِيَ الْكِبَرُ فَبِمَ تُبَشِّرُوْنَ ۞ قَالُوْا

بَشَّرْنٰكَ بِالْحَقِّ فَلَا تَكُنْ مِّنَ الْقٰنِطِيْنَ ۞ قَالَ

وَمَنْ يَّقْنَطُ مِنْ رَّحْمَةِ رَبِّهٖۤ اِلَّا الضَّآلُّوْنَ ۞ قَالَ

فَمَا خَطْبُكُمْ اَيُّهَا الْمُرْسَلُوْنَ ۞ قَالُوْٓا اِنَّآ اُرْسِلْنَآ

³⁶ *Satan* asked, "My Lord, grant me respite until the day they are resurrected." ³⁷ *Allah* said, "You are granted respite ³⁸ until the date of appointed time." ³⁹ *Satan* said, "My Lord, since You have left me to go astray, I will make *life* on Earth attractive to them and lead them astray, ⁴⁰ except some of Your chosen servants."

Hell, compared with Paradise

⁴¹ *Allah* said, "This is a straight path *that leads* to Me. ⁴² You shall have no control over My servants, except the misled ones who *chose to* follow you. ⁴³ The promised destiny for all of them is Hell ⁴⁴ with its seven gates, each *gate receiving* its allotted share." ⁴⁵ The mindful will be in gardens with fountains. ⁴⁶ *They will be invited*: "Enter *Paradise* in peace and safety." ⁴⁷ We shall remove any grudges *they had* in their hearts *towards others,* making them brothers, *relaxing* on sofas face-to-face. ⁴⁸ They will never feel tired nor be expelled from it. ⁴⁹ Tell My servants I am the Forgiver, the Kind, ⁵⁰ but My punishment is painful.

Ibrahim receives good and bad news

⁵¹ Tell them about Ibrahim's guests, ⁵² when they came to him, saying, "Peace!" He answered, "We're afraid of you." ⁵³ *The angels* said, "Don't be afraid. We bring you good news of a scholarly son." ⁵⁴ He said, "You've brought me good news when old age has caught up with me? What good news have you brought me?" ⁵⁵ They said, "Don't despair, we bring you good news." ⁵⁶ He said, "Only the misguided despair of the Lord's kindness." ⁵⁷ He *then* asked, "Messengers, what's your mission?" ⁵⁸ They told him, "We've been sent to *destroy* the sinners' community,

اِلٰى قَوْمٍ مُّجْرِمِيْنَ ۟ۙ ۵۸ اِلَّآ اٰلَ لُوْطٍ ؕ اِنَّا لَمُنَجُّوْهُمْ

اَجْمَعِيْنَ ۟ۙ ۵۹ اِلَّا امْرَاَتَهٗ قَدَّرْنَاۤ اِنَّهَا لَمِنَ

الْغٰبِرِيْنَ ۟ ۶۰ فَلَمَّا جَآءَ اٰلَ لُوْطِ الْمُرْسَلُوْنَ ۟ۙ ۶۱ قَالَ

اِنَّكُمْ قَوْمٌ مُّنْكَرُوْنَ ۟ ۶۲ قَالُوْا بَلْ جِئْنٰكَ بِمَا كَانُوْا

فِيْهِ يَمْتَرُوْنَ ۟ ۶۳ وَاَتَيْنٰكَ بِالْحَقِّ وَاِنَّا لَصٰدِقُوْنَ ۟ ۶۴

فَاَسْرِ بِاَهْلِكَ بِقِطْعٍ مِّنَ الَّيْلِ وَاتَّبِعْ اَدْبَارَهُمْ وَلَا

يَلْتَفِتْ مِنْكُمْ اَحَدٌ وَّامْضُوْا حَيْثُ تُؤْمَرُوْنَ ۟ ۶۵

وَقَضَيْنَاۤ اِلَيْهِ ذٰلِكَ الْاَمْرَ اَنَّ دَابِرَ هٰٓؤُلَآءِ

مَقْطُوْعٌ مُّصْبِحِيْنَ ۟ ۶۶ وَجَآءَ اَهْلُ الْمَدِيْنَةِ

يَسْتَبْشِرُوْنَ ۟ ۶۷ قَالَ اِنَّ هٰٓؤُلَآءِ ضَيْفِيْ فَلَا

تَفْضَحُوْنِ ۟ۙ ۶۸ وَاتَّقُوا اللّٰهَ وَلَا تُخْزُوْنِ ۟ ۶۹ قَالُوْۤا اَوَلَمْ

نَنْهَكَ عَنِ الْعٰلَمِيْنَ ۟ ۷۰ قَالَ هٰٓؤُلَآءِ بَنٰتِيْۤ اِنْ كُنْتُمْ

فٰعِلِيْنَ ۟ؕ ۷۱ لَعَمْرُكَ اِنَّهُمْ لَفِيْ سَكْرَتِهِمْ يَعْمَهُوْنَ ۟ ۷۲

فَاَخَذَتْهُمُ الصَّيْحَةُ مُشْرِقِيْنَ ۟ۙ ۷۳ فَجَعَلْنَا عَالِيَهَا

سَافِلَهَا وَاَمْطَرْنَا عَلَيْهِمْ حِجَارَةً مِّنْ سِجِّيْلٍ ۟ؕ ۷۴

اِنَّ فِيْ ذٰلِكَ لَاٰيٰتٍ لِّلْمُتَوَسِّمِيْنَ ۟ ۷۵ وَاِنَّهَا

لَبِسَبِيْلٍ مُّقِيْمٍ ۟ ۷۶ اِنَّ فِيْ ذٰلِكَ لَاٰيَةً لِّلْمُؤْمِنِيْنَ ۟ؕ ۷۷

وَاِنْ كَانَ اَصْحٰبُ الْاَيْكَةِ لَظٰلِمِيْنَ ۟ۙ ۷۸ فَانْتَقَمْنَا

مِنْهُمْ ۘ وَاِنَّهُمَا لَبِاِمَامٍ مُّبِيْنٍ ۟ؕ ۷۹ وَلَقَدْ كَذَّبَ

اَصْحٰبُ الْحِجْرِ الْمُرْسَلِيْنَ ۟ۙ ۸۰ وَاٰتَيْنٰهُمْ اٰيٰتِنَا

People of Lut are an example of disobedient people, whose perverted sexual habits were condemned.

⁵⁹ but we'll save Lut's family ⁶⁰ except his wife, who'll remain behind."

The angels tell Lut to leave
⁶¹ When the angels came to Lut's home, ⁶² he said, "You're strangers *for me*." ⁶³ They said, "We've brought you what they doubt. ⁶⁴ We've brought the truth, and we are the truthful. ⁶⁵ Tonight set off with your family, following behind them. Let no one look back, but continue as you are told." ⁶⁶ We decided this for him; all traces of the *sinners* will be smashed when they wake up at dawn.

The shameless people of Lut destroyed
⁶⁷ The people of the town came excitedly *to Lut's home*. ⁶⁸ Lut told *them*, "These are my guests, so don't shame me. ⁶⁹ Fear Allah and don't disgrace me." ⁷⁰ They said, "Haven't we told you not to interfere *in our affairs*" ⁷¹ Lut said, "Here are my daughters *of my community*[a], if you must do something." ⁷² *Allah swears* by your life, *Muhammad*,[b] that they were reeling about in their drunkenness[c] ⁷³ when the Blast overtook them at sunrise; ⁷⁴ and We turned *their town* upside down and pelted them with stones of baked clay. ⁷⁵ In this are signs for the intelligent people. ⁷⁶ It is still *visible* along one of the established *trade* routes. ⁷⁷ Here are signs for the believers.

Punishment of the people of Madyan and Thamud
⁷⁸ The people of the woodland[d] were evil, ⁷⁹ so We took vengeance on them, and both *towns remain* easily visible off an open highway. ⁸⁰ The people of the Hijr *region* called the messengers liars.

---

a   "Here are my daughters" means the women of my community are your wives, so satisfy yourselves with them.

b   According to Ibn Abbas, The Messenger ﷺ is the only human by whose life Allah has sworn.

c   This refers to their over-excited state of lust.

d   This refers to people of Thamud, from whom the Prophet Salih ﷺ was chosen by Allah to preach. Thamud lies in North West Arabia, in southern Syria.

فَكَانُوْا عَنْهَا مُعْرِضِيْنَ ۝ وَكَانُوْا يَنْحِتُوْنَ

مِنَ الْجِبَالِ بُيُوْتًا اٰمِنِيْنَ ۝ فَاَخَذَتْهُمُ الصَّيْحَةُ

مُصْبِحِيْنَ ۝ فَمَآ اَغْنٰى عَنْهُمْ مَّا كَانُوْا يَكْسِبُوْنَ ۝

وَمَا خَلَقْنَا السَّمٰوٰتِ وَالْاَرْضَ وَمَا بَيْنَهُمَآ اِلَّا

بِالْحَقِّ ط وَاِنَّ السَّاعَةَ لَاٰتِيَةٌ فَاصْفَحِ الصَّفْحَ

الْجَمِيْلَ ۝ اِنَّ رَبَّكَ هُوَ الْخَلّٰقُ الْعَلِيْمُ ۝ وَلَقَدْ

اٰتَيْنٰكَ سَبْعًا مِّنَ الْمَثَانِيْ وَالْقُرْاٰنَ الْعَظِيْمَ ۝

لَا تَمُدَّنَّ عَيْنَيْكَ اِلٰى مَا مَتَّعْنَا بِهٖٓ اَزْوَاجًا

Are you impressed by the glamour, glitter and gorgeous displays of the wealthy? Remember it is fleeting.

مِنْهُمْ وَلَا تَحْزَنْ عَلَيْهِمْ وَاخْفِضْ جَنَاحَكَ

لِلْمُؤْمِنِيْنَ ۝ وَقُلْ اِنِّيْٓ اَنَا النَّذِيْرُ الْمُبِيْنُ ۝ كَمَآ

اَنْزَلْنَا عَلَى الْمُقْتَسِمِيْنَ ۝ الَّذِيْنَ جَعَلُوا الْقُرْاٰنَ

عِضِيْنَ ۝ فَوَرَبِّكَ لَنَسْـَٔلَنَّهُمْ اَجْمَعِيْنَ ۝ عَمَّا

كَانُوْا يَعْمَلُوْنَ ۝ فَاصْدَعْ بِمَا تُؤْمَرُ وَاَعْرِضْ

عَنِ الْمُشْرِكِيْنَ ۝ اِنَّا كَفَيْنٰكَ الْمُسْتَهْزِءِيْنَ ۝

الَّذِيْنَ يَجْعَلُوْنَ مَعَ اللّٰهِ اِلٰهًا اٰخَرَ ج فَسَوْفَ

يَعْلَمُوْنَ ۝ وَلَقَدْ نَعْلَمُ اَنَّكَ يَضِيْقُ صَدْرُكَ بِمَا

يَقُوْلُوْنَ ۝ فَسَبِّحْ بِحَمْدِ رَبِّكَ وَكُنْ مِّنَ السّٰجِدِيْنَ ۝

وَاعْبُدْ رَبَّكَ حَتّٰى يَأْتِيَكَ الْيَقِيْنُ ۝

⁸¹We brought them Our signs, but they turned away from them. ⁸²They carved houses in the mountains, living safely ⁸³*until* the Blast overtook them at dawn; ⁸⁴and their wealth didn't benefit them in any way.

The Quran is the most valuable gift

⁸⁵We created the Heavens, the Earth and what lies between them for a *true* purpose. *Messenger,* the Final Hour is coming, pardon them graciously.ᵃ ⁸⁶Your Lord *alone* is the Creator, the Knower. ⁸⁷We've given you seven oft-recited versesᵇ and the *Majestic* Quran. ⁸⁸Don't look longingly at *worldly pleasures* We gave *some* of their groups to enjoy, and don't be unhappy about them; *instead* take the believers under your wing, ⁸⁹and say: "I'm, a clear warner."

The Messenger ﷺ told to stand tall

⁹⁰We have already spoken regarding those who divided the scripture ⁹¹and those who abused the Quran; ⁹²by your Lord, *Messenger,* We'll question them ⁹³about what they did. ⁹⁴So openly announce what you are commanded, and turn away from the idolaters. ⁹⁵We are sufficient for you against those who mock, ⁹⁶who set up another god besides Allah, they will surely come to know. ⁹⁷We know what they say distresses you. ⁹⁸So glorify your Lord with praises, and prostrate, ⁹⁹and *continue to* worship your Lord until you die.ᶜ

ᵃ   Here Allah is addressing the Prophet ﷺ directly, making clear that the purpose of the references to the people of Lut, and to the inhabitants of Madyan and Thamud, is to serve as a warning to the people of Makkah to mend their godless ways.

ᵇ   The Arabic phrase *al-Sab' al-Mathani* could also mean: the first seven surats of the Quran; *Surat Al-Fatiha*; or the whole Quran (*Islahi*).

ᶜ   *Al-yaqin* refers to death, literally it means certainty, since it's the only aspect of our lives which is certain.

16. Surat An-Nahl

The Bee

This Makkan surat was revealed in the last months of 622 CE, before the Prophet's ﷺ migration to Madinah. The tension between Makkans and Muslims had reached its peak, the Muslims were disheartened, while the disbelievers felt confident since Islam was no longer gaining new followers. However, the surat is optimistic and encourages Muslims to keep faith in the promise of a victory. It tells them: "Be patient, your patience *is a gift* from Allah. Don't grieve over them nor distress yourself because of their plotting" (127).

The Quran often mentions two kinds of books: the revealed Scripture that presents divine instructions, explanations and a set of beliefs, and an open book: the universe, the sun and stars, the moon, the flight of birds, the seas, pearls and rubies, ships ploughing through mighty waves, the rivers, mountains, cattle, riding animals, rain, plants, fruit and crops. Two nourishing and healing foods are mentioned: milk and honey. It draws our attention to the mystery of their production from the udders of the cow and the stomach of bees. Allah's wonders and marvels, which He made "for your benefit ..." (14). Despite these clear signs, when the pagans are asked: "What has your Lord revealed?" They say, "Stories of the ancient people" (24). A rejection of the truth expressing their narrow-mindedness. On the other hand, when the believers are asked the same question, they respond, "He has revealed the best" (30).

Surat Al-Nahl is also called *Al-Nia'mah*, meaning, "the gift", since it lists some of Allah's gifts to humanity. Thankfulness is the only way to appreciate these gifts; this is the very essence of Islam. Its opposite is un-thankfulness, the meaning of *kufr*; the kafir fails to acknowledge Allah's gift.

The following verse accurately captures the essence of Divine Message: "Allah commands justice, generosity and giving to relatives. He forbids indecency, all *kinds of* evil and cruelty" (90). The Prophet Ibrahim ﷺ is mentioned as a model of a thankful person. The Quran tells the Messenger ﷺ: "Invite to the way of your Lord with wisdom and courtesy" (125).

بِسْمِ اللهِ الرَّحْمٰنِ الرَّحِيْمِ

اَتٰۤى اَمْرُ اللهِ فَلَا تَسْتَعْجِلُوْهُ ؕ سُبْحٰنَهٗ وَتَعٰلٰى عَمَّا يُشْرِكُوْنَ ۞ يُنَزِّلُ الْمَلٰٓئِكَةَ بِالرُّوْحِ مِنْ اَمْرِهٖ عَلٰى مَنْ يَّشَآءُ مِنْ عِبَادِهٖۤ اَنْ اَنْذِرُوْۤا اَنَّهٗ لَاۤ اِلٰهَ اِلَّاۤ اَنَا فَاتَّقُوْنِ ۞ خَلَقَ السَّمٰوٰتِ وَالْاَرْضَ بِالْحَقِّ ؕ تَعٰلٰى عَمَّا يُشْرِكُوْنَ ۞ خَلَقَ الْاِنْسَانَ مِنْ نُّطْفَةٍ فَاِذَا هُوَ خَصِيْمٌ مُّبِيْنٌ ۞ وَالْاَنْعَامَ خَلَقَهَا ۚ لَكُمْ فِيْهَا دِفْءٌ وَّمَنَافِعُ وَمِنْهَا تَاْكُلُوْنَ ۞ وَلَكُمْ فِيْهَا جَمَالٌ حِيْنَ تُرِيْحُوْنَ وَحِيْنَ تَسْرَحُوْنَ ۞ وَتَحْمِلُ اَثْقَالَكُمْ اِلٰى بَلَدٍ لَّمْ تَكُوْنُوْا بٰلِغِيْهِ اِلَّا بِشِقِّ الْاَنْفُسِ ؕ اِنَّ رَبَّكُمْ لَرَءُوْفٌ رَّحِيْمٌ ۞ وَّالْخَيْلَ وَالْبِغَالَ وَالْحَمِيْرَ لِتَرْكَبُوْهَا وَزِيْنَةً ؕ وَيَخْلُقُ مَا لَا تَعْلَمُوْنَ ۞ وَعَلَى اللهِ قَصْدُ السَّبِيْلِ وَمِنْهَا جَآئِرٌ ؕ وَلَوْ شَآءَ لَهَدٰىكُمْ اَجْمَعِيْنَ ۞ هُوَ الَّذِيْۤ اَنْزَلَ مِنَ السَّمَآءِ مَآءً لَّكُمْ مِّنْهُ شَرَابٌ وَّمِنْهُ شَجَرٌ فِيْهِ تُسِيْمُوْنَ ۞ يُنْۢبِتُ لَكُمْ بِهِ الزَّرْعَ وَالزَّيْتُوْنَ وَالنَّخِيْلَ وَالْاَعْنَابَ وَمِنْ كُلِّ الثَّمَرٰتِ ؕ اِنَّ فِيْ ذٰلِكَ لَاٰيَةً لِّقَوْمٍ يَّتَفَكَّرُوْنَ ۞ وَسَخَّرَ لَكُمُ الَّيْلَ وَالنَّهَارَ

Life has a purpose: acknowledging Allah and preparing for the Hereafter.

In the name of Allah, the Kind the Caring

Creation has a purpose

[1] Allah's inevitable judgement is coming, so don't wish for it to come sooner. Glory be to Him; He is far above anything they associate with Him. [2] He sends the angels with the Revelation[a] to his chosen servants to give warning, *telling them*: "There is no God but I, so fear Me." [3] He created the Heavens and the Earth for a purpose; He is far above what they associate with Him. [4] He created Humans from a drop of semen, so is that why humans are quarrelsome?

Domestic animals are Divine gifts

[5] He created the livestock to provide you *wool for* warmth, meat for you to eat, and much more. [6] How beautiful they look when you bring them home in the evening and take them to the pastures in the morning. [7] They carry your loads from one city to another, *without them* you would travel with great difficulty. Your Lord is Compassionate and Kind. [8] He created the horse, the mule and the donkey for you to ride and they make you proud, and He created what you don't yet know. [9] Allah has signposted the straight path, thus making it distinct from the wrong paths; had He wished He could have guided all.[b]

Allah's gifts on Earth

[10] He sent water from the sky for you to drink and to grow the grasses on which cattle graze. [11] With rainwater He grows crops: olives, dates, grapes and every kind of fruit. In that are signs for those who reflect deeply.

[a] *Al Ruh* literally means "the spirit" here; it is used for revelation, pointing to the essence of revelation as giving life, reviving individuals and people (cf. *Surat Al-Shura*, verse 52).
[b] Allah doesn't impose his guidance on people, He lets them choose to become believers or reject it. This is freedom of choice that is the foundation of morality.

وَالشَّمْسَ وَالْقَمَرَ ط وَالنُّجُومُ مُسَخَّرَاتٌ بِأَمْرِهِ ط إِنَّ

فِىْ ذٰلِكَ لَاٰيٰتٍ لِّقَوْمٍ يَّعْقِلُوْنَ ۝ وَمَا ذَرَأَ لَكُمْ

فِى الْاَرْضِ مُخْتَلِفًا اَلْوَانُهٗ ط إِنَّ فِىْ ذٰلِكَ لَاٰيَةً

لِّقَوْمٍ يَّذَّكَّرُوْنَ ۝ وَهُوَ الَّذِىْ سَخَّرَ الْبَحْرَ لِتَأْكُلُوْا

مِنْهُ لَحْمًا طَرِيًّا وَّتَسْتَخْرِجُوْا مِنْهُ حِلْيَةً

تَلْبَسُوْنَهَا ۚ وَتَرَى الْفُلْكَ مَوَاخِرَ فِيْهِ وَلِتَبْتَغُوْا

مِنْ فَضْلِهٖ وَلَعَلَّكُمْ تَشْكُرُوْنَ ۝ وَاَلْقٰى فِى

الْاَرْضِ رَوَاسِىَ اَنْ تَمِيْدَ بِكُمْ وَاَنْهٰرًا وَّسُبُلًا

لَّعَلَّكُمْ تَهْتَدُوْنَ ۝ وَعَلٰمٰتٍ ط وَبِالنَّجْمِ هُمْ

يَهْتَدُوْنَ ۝ اَفَمَنْ يَّخْلُقُ كَمَنْ لَّا يَخْلُقُ ط اَفَلَا

تَذَكَّرُوْنَ ۝ وَاِنْ تَعُدُّوْا نِعْمَةَ اللّٰهِ لَا تُحْصُوْهَا ط

اِنَّ اللّٰهَ لَغَفُوْرٌ رَّحِيْمٌ ۝ وَاللّٰهُ يَعْلَمُ مَا تُسِرُّوْنَ

وَمَا تُعْلِنُوْنَ ۝ وَالَّذِيْنَ يَدْعُوْنَ مِنْ دُوْنِ

اللّٰهِ لَا يَخْلُقُوْنَ شَيْئًا وَّهُمْ يُخْلَقُوْنَ ۝ اَمْوَاتٌ

غَيْرُ اَحْيَآءٍ ۚ وَمَا يَشْعُرُوْنَ ۙ اَيَّانَ يُبْعَثُوْنَ ۝

اِلٰهُكُمْ اِلٰهٌ وَّاحِدٌ ۚ فَالَّذِيْنَ لَا يُؤْمِنُوْنَ بِالْاٰخِرَةِ

قُلُوْبُهُمْ مُّنْكِرَةٌ وَّهُمْ مُّسْتَكْبِرُوْنَ ۝ لَا جَرَمَ اَنَّ

اللّٰهَ يَعْلَمُ مَا يُسِرُّوْنَ وَمَا يُعْلِنُوْنَ ط اِنَّهٗ لَا يُحِبُّ

الْمُسْتَكْبِرِيْنَ ۝ وَاِذَا قِيْلَ لَهُمْ مَّا ذَا اَنْزَلَ

رَبُّكُمْ ۙ قَالُوْا اَسَاطِيْرُ الْاَوَّلِيْنَ ۝ لِيَحْمِلُوْا اَوْزَارَهُمْ

How often do you think about Allah's gifts? Thank Him.

¹² He created the night and the day for your benefit; the sun, the moon and the stars *all* follow His command. In that are signs for those who understand. ¹³ He produced objects of many colours on the Earth for you; In that are signs for those who accept advice. ¹⁴ For your benefit He created the sea; from it you get fresh meat to eat, and extract jewellery that you wear. You see the ships sailing over the waves to seek His gifts, so you may be thankful. ¹⁵ He placed the mountains firmly on the Earth, so it doesn't shake beneath you, made the rivers and the tracks so you can find your way, ¹⁶ and many other signposts, including the stars for guiding the travellers.

Allah's gifts are countless

¹⁷ So how can the One who creates be like the one who can't create; why don't you listen? ¹⁸ If you were to count the gifts of Allah; you would not be able to count them; Allah is the Forgiver, the Kind. ¹⁹ Allah knows what you hide and what you expose. ²⁰ The idols they worship besides Allah didn't create anything; in fact, they are created; ²¹ they are dead, lifeless and unaware of when they will be resurrected. ²² Your God is one God; those who don't believe in the Hereafter have a heart that refuses to accept the truth, because they are arrogant.

The fate of those who denied Allah's gifts

²³ Allah knows what they hide and what they reveal. He doesn't like the arrogant. ²⁴ When it is said to them, "What has your Lord revealed?" They say, "Stories of the ancient people."

كَامِلَةً يَّوْمَ الْقِيَمَةِ ۙ وَمِنْ اَوْزَارِ الَّذِيْنَ يُضِلُّوْنَهُمْ بِغَيْرِ عِلْمٍ ؕ اَلَا سَآءَ مَا يَزِرُوْنَ ۝

قَدْ مَكَرَ الَّذِيْنَ مِنْ قَبْلِهِمْ فَاَتَى اللّٰهُ بُنْيَانَهُمْ مِّنَ الْقَوَاعِدِ فَخَرَّ عَلَيْهِمُ السَّقْفُ مِنْ فَوْقِهِمْ وَاَتٰىهُمُ الْعَذَابُ مِنْ حَيْثُ لَا يَشْعُرُوْنَ ۝ ثُمَّ يَوْمَ الْقِيٰمَةِ يُخْزِيْهِمْ وَيَقُوْلُ اَيْنَ شُرَكَآءِيَ الَّذِيْنَ كُنْتُمْ تُشَآقُّوْنَ فِيْهِمْ ؕ قَالَ الَّذِيْنَ اُوْتُوا الْعِلْمَ اِنَّ الْخِزْيَ الْيَوْمَ وَالسُّوْٓءَ عَلَى الْكٰفِرِيْنَ ۝

الَّذِيْنَ تَتَوَفّٰىهُمُ الْمَلٰٓئِكَةُ ظَالِمِيْٓ اَنْفُسِهِمْ ۪ فَاَلْقَوُا السَّلَمَ مَا كُنَّا نَعْمَلُ مِنْ سُوْٓءٍ ؕ بَلٰٓى اِنَّ اللّٰهَ عَلِيْمٌۢ بِمَا كُنْتُمْ تَعْمَلُوْنَ ۝ فَادْخُلُوْٓا اَبْوَابَ جَهَنَّمَ خٰلِدِيْنَ فِيْهَا ؕ فَلَبِئْسَ مَثْوَى الْمُتَكَبِّرِيْنَ ۝ وَقِيْلَ لِلَّذِيْنَ اتَّقَوْا مَا ذَآ اَنْزَلَ رَبُّكُمْ ؕ قَالُوْا خَيْرًا ؕ لِلَّذِيْنَ اَحْسَنُوْا فِيْ هٰذِهِ الدُّنْيَا حَسَنَةٌ ؕ وَلَدَارُ الْاٰخِرَةِ خَيْرٌ ؕ وَلَنِعْمَ دَارُ الْمُتَّقِيْنَ ۝ جَنّٰتُ عَدْنٍ يَّدْخُلُوْنَهَا تَجْرِيْ مِنْ تَحْتِهَا الْاَنْهٰرُ لَهُمْ فِيْهَا مَا يَشَآءُوْنَ ؕ كَذٰلِكَ يَجْزِى اللّٰهُ الْمُتَّقِيْنَ ۝ الَّذِيْنَ تَتَوَفّٰىهُمُ الْمَلٰٓئِكَةُ طَيِّبِيْنَ ۙ يَقُوْلُوْنَ سَلٰمٌ عَلَيْكُمُ ۙ ادْخُلُوا الْجَنَّةَ بِمَا كُنْتُمْ تَعْمَلُوْنَ ۝ هَلْ يَنْظُرُوْنَ اِلَّآ اَنْ

Those who appreciated Allah's gifts will enjoy Paradise.

523

25 On Judgement Day they will carry the full burden, as well as the burden of those they misled naively. What a wretched burden they bear. 26 Previously people had plotted, so Allah's punishment came and uprooted them from their foundations, and the roof fell from above them and the punishment came from where they least expected. 27 On Judgement Day they will be disgraced and it will be asked: "Where are my associates that you used to disagree about?" The people given knowledge will say, "The evil and shame of this Day is on the disbelievers." 28 Those whose souls were taken by the angels when they were wronging themselves will fall into submission, saying: "We did no evil." Indeed, Allah knows well what you did. 29 So go through the gates of Hell to live there forever, a wretched place for the arrogant.

The fate of those who valued Allah's gifts

30 When the devoutly pious are asked: "What did your Lord send down?" They answer, "He has revealed the best". Those who do good in this world will get the reward; *their* home in the Hereafter will be even better. And how excellent is the home of the pious. 31 They will enter gardens of eternity with rivers flowing beneath them; they will have whatever they desire; that is how Allah rewards the pious. 32 The ones whose souls were taken by the angels while they were in the state of purity; they will be greeted with: "Peace be on you; enter Paradise for what you use to do in the world."

تَأْتِيَهُمُ الْمَلَئِكَةُ اَوْ يَأْتِيَ اَمْرُ رَبِّكَ ط كَذٰلِكَ فَعَلَ
الَّذِيْنَ مِنْ قَبْلِهِمْ ط وَمَا ظَلَمَهُمُ اللّٰهُ وَلٰكِنْ كَانُوْٓا
اَنْفُسَهُمْ يَظْلِمُوْنَ ۝ فَاَصَابَهُمْ سَيِّاٰتُ مَا عَمِلُوْا
وَحَاقَ بِهِمْ مَّا كَانُوْا بِهٖ يَسْتَهْزِءُوْنَ ۝ وَقَالَ
الَّذِيْنَ اَشْرَكُوْا لَوْ شَآءَ اللّٰهُ مَا عَبَدْنَا مِنْ دُوْنِهٖ
مِنْ شَيْءٍ نَّحْنُ وَلَآ اٰبَآؤُنَا وَلَا حَرَّمْنَا مِنْ دُوْنِهٖ
مِنْ شَيْءٍ ط كَذٰلِكَ فَعَلَ الَّذِيْنَ مِنْ قَبْلِهِمْ ۚ فَهَلْ
عَلَى الرُّسُلِ اِلَّا الْبَلٰغُ الْمُبِيْنُ ۝ وَلَقَدْ بَعَثْنَا
فِيْ كُلِّ اُمَّةٍ رَّسُوْلًا اَنِ اعْبُدُوا اللّٰهَ وَاجْتَنِبُوا
الطَّاغُوْتَ ۚ فَمِنْهُمْ مَّنْ هَدَى اللّٰهُ وَمِنْهُمْ مَّنْ
حَقَّتْ عَلَيْهِ الضَّلٰلَةُ ط فَسِيْرُوْا فِي الْاَرْضِ فَانْظُرُوْا
كَيْفَ كَانَ عَاقِبَةُ الْمُكَذِّبِيْنَ ۝ اِنْ تَحْرِصْ
عَلٰى هُدٰىهُمْ فَاِنَّ اللّٰهَ لَا يَهْدِيْ مَنْ يُّضِلُّ
وَمَا لَهُمْ مِّنْ نّٰصِرِيْنَ ۝ وَاَقْسَمُوْا بِاللّٰهِ جَهْدَ
اَيْمَانِهِمْ لَا يَبْعَثُ اللّٰهُ مَنْ يَّمُوْتُ ط بَلٰى وَعْدًا
عَلَيْهِ حَقًّا وَّلٰكِنَّ اَكْثَرَ النَّاسِ لَا يَعْلَمُوْنَ ۝
لِيُبَيِّنَ لَهُمُ الَّذِيْ يَخْتَلِفُوْنَ فِيْهِ وَلِيَعْلَمَ
الَّذِيْنَ كَفَرُوْٓا اَنَّهُمْ كَانُوْا كٰذِبِيْنَ ۝ اِنَّمَا قَوْلُنَا
لِشَيْءٍ اِذَآ اَرَدْنٰهُ اَنْ نَّقُوْلَ لَهٗ كُنْ فَيَكُوْنُ ۝
وَالَّذِيْنَ هَاجَرُوْا فِي اللّٰهِ مِنْ بَعْدِ مَا ظُلِمُوْا

The greatest gift of the gracious Lord is faith, so cherish it.

۴ ۹ ۱۰ ع

۵ ۶ ۱۱ ع

The Messenger ﷺ is eager to guide

³³ Are you waiting for the angels or Your Lord's command to come down? Those before them did the same. Allah didn't wrong them, but they wronged themselves. ³⁴ The evil they had done caught up with them, and all they used to mock will engulf them as punishment. ³⁵ The idolaters will say, "If Allah wished we wouldn't have worshipped anyone beside Him; neither our forefathers nor we would have made anything unlawful without *His permission.*" That's how those gone before them behaved; what else can the messengers do except give clear warning? ³⁶ Indeed to every community We sent messengers who taught: "Worship Allah and turn away from idols."ᵃ Some Allah guided, whilst others remained misguided. Travel around the Earth and see the punishment of the deniers. ³⁷ Though you are keen to guide them, Allah will not guide the one He's *allowed to* stray, and they will have no Helpers.

The power of Allah's words

³⁸ They swear their strongest oath that Allah will not raise them from the dead, but it is a true promise, He shall fulfil it – but most people don't realise. ³⁹ *It is* to explain to them *the truth of* what they differed in, and to show the disbelievers they were the liars. ⁴⁰ Whenever We wish something to happen We say, "Be", and it becomes.

ᵃ   "Taghut" according to the Jalalain means idols they worship.

لَنُبَوِّئَنَّهُمْ فِى الدُّنْيَا حَسَنَةً ط وَلَأَجْرُ الْاٰخِرَةِ اَكْبَرُ ۖ

لَوْ كَانُوْا يَعْلَمُوْنَ ۞ الَّذِيْنَ صَبَرُوْا وَعَلٰى رَبِّهِمْ

يَتَوَكَّلُوْنَ ۞ وَمَآ اَرْسَلْنَا مِنْ قَبْلِكَ اِلَّا رِجَالًا

نُّوْحِىْ اِلَيْهِمْ فَسْـَٔلُوْٓا اَهْلَ الذِّكْرِ اِنْ كُنْتُمْ لَا

تَعْلَمُوْنَ ۙ بِالْبَيِّنٰتِ وَالزُّبُرِ ط وَاَنْزَلْنَآ اِلَيْكَ الذِّكْرَ

لِتُبَيِّنَ لِلنَّاسِ مَا نُزِّلَ اِلَيْهِمْ وَلَعَلَّهُمْ يَتَفَكَّرُوْنَ ۞

اَفَاَمِنَ الَّذِيْنَ مَكَرُوا السَّيِّاٰتِ اَنْ يَّخْسِفَ اللّٰهُ

بِهِمُ الْاَرْضَ اَوْ يَأْتِيَهُمُ الْعَذَابُ مِنْ حَيْثُ لَا

يَشْعُرُوْنَ ۙ ۞ اَوْ يَأْخُذَهُمْ فِىْ تَقَلُّبِهِمْ فَمَا هُمْ

بِمُعْجِزِيْنَ ۙ ۞ اَوْ يَأْخُذَهُمْ عَلٰى تَخَوُّفٍ ط فَاِنَّ رَبَّكُمْ

لَرَءُوْفٌ رَّحِيْمٌ ۞ اَوَلَمْ يَرَوْا اِلٰى مَا خَلَقَ اللّٰهُ مِنْ شَىْءٍ

يَّتَفَيَّؤُا ظِلٰلُهٗ عَنِ الْيَمِيْنِ وَالشَّمَآئِلِ سُجَّدًا لِّلّٰهِ

وَهُمْ دٰخِرُوْنَ ۞ وَلِلّٰهِ يَسْجُدُ مَا فِى السَّمٰوٰتِ وَمَا فِى

الْاَرْضِ مِنْ دَآبَّةٍ وَّالْمَلٰٓئِكَةُ وَهُمْ لَا يَسْتَكْبِرُوْنَ ۞

يَخَافُوْنَ رَبَّهُمْ مِّنْ فَوْقِهِمْ وَيَفْعَلُوْنَ مَا يُؤْمَرُوْنَ ۞

وَقَالَ اللّٰهُ لَا تَتَّخِذُوْٓا اِلٰهَيْنِ اثْنَيْنِ ۚ اِنَّمَا هُوَ اِلٰهٌ

وَّاحِدٌ ۚ فَاِيَّايَ فَارْهَبُوْنِ ۞ وَلَهٗ مَا فِى السَّمٰوٰتِ

وَالْاَرْضِ وَلَهُ الدِّيْنُ وَاصِبًا ط اَفَغَيْرَ اللّٰهِ تَتَّقُوْنَ ۞

وَمَا بِكُمْ مِّنْ نِّعْمَةٍ فَمِنَ اللّٰهِ ثُمَّ اِذَا مَسَّكُمُ الضُّرُّ

فَاِلَيْهِ تَجْـَٔرُوْنَ ۞ ثُمَّ اِذَا كَشَفَ الضُّرَّ عَنْكُمْ اِذَا

Everything we possess is a gift from Allah. So why not turn to him in obedience.

527

[41] Those who migrated for Allah's sake after facing persecution will soon settle in a pleasant place. But the reward of the Hereafter will be greatest, if they knew. [42] These are patient people who trust their Lord.

All prophets were men

[43] We sent revelations to men before you, ask those who have received the message if you don't know. [44] *They came* with miracles and Scriptures, and We sent down to you the Majestic Message so that you can explain to people what is revealed for them, so they may reflect.

Why are people fearless of Allah's punishment?

[45] Are those who planned to do evil feeling safe from Allah's *punishment*? He may *order* the Earth to swallow them up or send unexpected punishment, [46] or He may punish them whilst they are busy in their everyday jobs; they can't escape Him. [47] Then again, He may punish them gradually through fear. Indeed, your Lord is the Compassionate, the Kind.

All things in the universe submit to Allah

[48] Haven't they seen what Allah has created? How the shadows turn from right to left and left to right as though they are prostrating before Allah in complete submission? [49] Everything in the Heavens and the Earth, the animals and the Angels, prostrate before Allah; they aren't arrogant, [50] *but* frightened of their Lord above, and they do as they are told. [51] Allah said, "Don't serve two gods; He is one God so fear me alone." [52] All that is in the Heavens and the Earth belongs to Him, and so obedience[a] to Him is obligatory. So, will you fear anyone other than Allah?

People don't appreciate Allah's gifts

[53] All your property is a gift from Allah. In hardship you turn to Him, moaning and groaning. [54] He removes it, but some of you *still* associate others with Your Lord,

---

[a]   *Al-Din* literally means religion, I have taken its functional meaning.

فَرِيْقٌ مِّنْكُمْ بِرَبِّهِمْ يُشْرِكُوْنَ ۞ لِيَكْفُرُوْا بِمَآ

اٰتَيْنٰهُمْ ط فَتَمَتَّعُوْا ڡ فَسَوْفَ تَعْلَمُوْنَ ۞ وَيَجْعَلُوْنَ

لِمَا لَا يَعْلَمُوْنَ نَصِيْبًا مِّمَّا رَزَقْنٰهُمْ ط تَاللّٰهِ

لَتُسْـَٔلُنَّ عَمَّا كُنْتُمْ تَفْتَرُوْنَ ۞ وَيَجْعَلُوْنَ لِلّٰهِ

الْبَنٰتِ سُبْحٰنَهٗ لا وَلَهُمْ مَّا يَشْتَهُوْنَ ۞ وَاِذَا

بُشِّرَ اَحَدُهُمْ بِالْاُنْثٰى ظَلَّ وَجْهُهٗ مُسْوَدًّا وَّهُوَ

كَظِيْمٌ ۞ يَتَوَارٰى مِنَ الْقَوْمِ مِنْ سُوْٓءِ مَا بُشِّرَ

بِهٖ ط اَيُمْسِكُهٗ عَلٰى هُوْنٍ اَمْ يَدُسُّهٗ فِى التُّرَابِ ط

اَلَا سَآءَ مَا يَحْكُمُوْنَ ۞ لِلَّذِيْنَ لَا يُؤْمِنُوْنَ

بِالْاٰخِرَةِ مَثَلُ السَّوْءِ ج وَلِلّٰهِ الْمَثَلُ الْاَعْلٰى ط

وَهُوَ الْعَزِيْزُ الْحَكِيْمُ ۞ وَلَوْ يُؤَاخِذُ اللّٰهُ النَّاسَ

بِظُلْمِهِمْ مَّا تَرَكَ عَلَيْهَا مِنْ دَآبَّةٍ وَّلٰكِنْ

يُّؤَخِّرُهُمْ اِلٰٓى اَجَلٍ مُّسَمًّى ۚ فَاِذَا جَآءَ اَجَلُهُمْ لَا

يَسْتَأْخِرُوْنَ سَاعَةً وَّلَا يَسْتَقْدِمُوْنَ ۞ وَيَجْعَلُوْنَ

لِلّٰهِ مَا يَكْرَهُوْنَ وَتَصِفُ اَلْسِنَتُهُمُ الْكَذِبَ اَنَّ

لَهُمُ الْحُسْنٰى ط لَاجَرَمَ اَنَّ لَهُمُ النَّارَ وَ اَنَّهُمْ

مُّفْرَطُوْنَ ۞ تَاللّٰهِ لَقَدْ اَرْسَلْنَآ اِلٰٓى اُمَمٍ

مِّنْ قَبْلِكَ فَزَيَّنَ لَهُمُ الشَّيْطٰنُ اَعْمَالَهُمْ

فَهُوَ وَلِيُّهُمُ الْيَوْمَ وَلَهُمْ عَذَابٌ اَلِيْمٌ ۞

وَمَآ اَنْزَلْنَا عَلَيْكَ الْكِتٰبَ اِلَّا لِتُبَيِّنَ لَهُمُ

Baby daughters are a wonderful gift of Allah. Cherish and nurture them faithfully.

⁵⁵ showing how ungrateful they are for the gifts We gave them, so enjoy for a while, but soon you will know.

How the pagans hate the gift of a baby girl

⁵⁶ They assign a share of sustenance, We gave them to their idols, out of ignorance! By Allah, you will be questioned about what you concocted . ⁵⁷ They assign daughters for Allah, glory to Him, for themselves they want sons! ⁵⁸ When one of them is given the news of the birth of a girl, his face darkens, full of fuming anger; ⁵⁹ he hides from the community because of the bad news he received, *feeling* undecided – will he keep her with shame or bury her in the dust? How immorally they judge! ⁶⁰ Those who don't believe in the Hereafter set a bad example, and Allah the exalted sets a good example. He is Almighty, Wise.

Allah does not rush to punish

⁶¹ If Allah were to punish people *right away* for their wrongs, then there wouldn't be *a single* creature left. But He delays it until the fixed term which can't be delayed nor brought forward. ⁶² They allocate to Allah what they dislike themselves. Yet they falsely claim that for themselves is all good, but let there be no doubt the Hellfire awaits them; *they will be* the first to be sent there. ⁶³ By Allah, We sent messengers to communities before you, but Satan made their deeds look attractive to them, so today he is their Guardian, and for them will be painful punishment. ⁶⁴ We revealed the Book so you can explain to them what they differed about; it's a guide that is beneficial for believers.

الَّذِى اخْتَلَفُوا فِيْهِ ۙ وَهُدًى وَّرَحْمَةً لِّقَوْمٍ

يُّؤْمِنُوْنَ ۝ وَاللّٰهُ اَنْزَلَ مِنَ السَّمَاءِ مَآءً فَاَحْيَا

بِهِ الْاَرْضَ بَعْدَ مَوْتِهَا ؕ اِنَّ فِيْ ذٰلِكَ لَاٰيَةً

لِّقَوْمٍ يَّسْمَعُوْنَ ۝ وَاِنَّ لَكُمْ فِي الْاَنْعَامِ لَعِبْرَةً ؕ

نُّسْقِيْكُمْ مِّمَّا فِيْ بُطُوْنِهٖ مِنْۢ بَيْنِ فَرْثٍ وَّدَمٍ

لَّبَنًا خَالِصًا سَآئِغًا لِّلشّٰرِبِيْنَ ۝ وَمِنْ ثَمَرٰتِ

النَّخِيْلِ وَالْاَعْنَابِ تَتَّخِذُوْنَ مِنْهُ سَكَرًا وَّرِزْقًا

حَسَنًا ؕ اِنَّ فِيْ ذٰلِكَ لَاٰيَةً لِّقَوْمٍ يَّعْقِلُوْنَ ۝

وَاَوْحٰى رَبُّكَ اِلَى النَّحْلِ اَنِ اتَّخِذِيْ مِنَ الْجِبَالِ

بُيُوْتًا وَّمِنَ الشَّجَرِ وَمِمَّا يَعْرِشُوْنَ ۝ ثُمَّ كُلِيْ

مِنْ كُلِّ الثَّمَرٰتِ فَاسْلُكِيْ سُبُلَ رَبِّكِ ذُلُلًا ؕ

يَخْرُجُ مِنْۢ بُطُوْنِهَا شَرَابٌ مُّخْتَلِفٌ اَلْوَانُهٗ

فِيْهِ شِفَآءٌ لِّلنَّاسِ ؕ اِنَّ فِيْ ذٰلِكَ لَاٰيَةً لِّقَوْمٍ

يَّتَفَكَّرُوْنَ ۝ وَاللّٰهُ خَلَقَكُمْ ثُمَّ يَتَوَفّٰىكُمْ ۙ

وَمِنْكُمْ مَّنْ يُّرَدُّ اِلٰۤى اَرْذَلِ الْعُمُرِ لِكَيْ لَا يَعْلَمَ

بَعْدَ عِلْمٍ شَيْئًا ؕ اِنَّ اللّٰهَ عَلِيْمٌ قَدِيْرٌ ۝ وَاللّٰهُ

فَضَّلَ بَعْضَكُمْ عَلٰى بَعْضٍ فِي الرِّزْقِ ۚ فَمَا

الَّذِيْنَ فُضِّلُوْا بِرَآدِّيْ رِزْقِهِمْ عَلٰى مَا مَلَكَتْ

اَيْمَانُهُمْ فَهُمْ فِيْهِ سَوَآءٌ ؕ اَفَبِنِعْمَةِ اللّٰهِ

يَجْحَدُوْنَ ۝ وَاللّٰهُ جَعَلَ لَكُمْ مِّنْ اَنْفُسِكُمْ

The bee gives delicious sweet honey, and pollinates the farmers' crops. Without these the harvest would be very poor.

⁶⁵ Allah sends rain from the sky to revive the Earth after its death; in that is a sign for those who listen.

Milk and honey: Two amazing gifts

⁶⁶ You have a lesson in livestock, We gave you a drink from inside their bellies – it is from between the bowels and blood – pure milk, healthy nourishment for its drinkers. ⁶⁷ And you make juice from the fruits of dates and grapes, delicious and nourishing; in this is a sign for those who understand. ⁶⁸ Your Lord gave the bee an instinct to build hives in the mountains, the trees and buildings, inspiring her: ⁶⁹ "Eat *the nectar* from different fruits and follow the ways of your Lord humbly." *Then* from its belly comes a syrup of different colours in which there is a healing for people, it is a sign for those who think.[a]

The gift of children and grandchildren

⁷⁰ Allah created you and will let you die; some of you will turn back to frail old age, when all they once knew they won't know it anymore. Allah is the Knower and Powerful. ⁷¹ He gave some more provisions than others, those given more are unwilling to share their provisions with their slaves, in case they become their equals. How can they deny the gifts of Allah?

---

[a]   Scientists estimate that in Britain if there were no bees it would cost farmers £4 billion to pollinate the crops (2017).

اَزْوَاجًا وَّجَعَلَ لَكُمْ مِّنْ اَزْوَاجِكُمْ بَنِيْنَ وَحَفَدَةً

وَّرَزَقَكُمْ مِّنَ الطَّيِّبٰتِ ؕ اَفَبِالْبَاطِلِ يُؤْمِنُوْنَ

وَبِنِعْمَتِ اللّٰهِ هُمْ يَكْفُرُوْنَ ۙ۴۲ وَيَعْبُدُوْنَ

مِنْ دُوْنِ اللّٰهِ مَا لَا يَمْلِكُ لَهُمْ رِزْقًا مِّنَ

السَّمٰوٰتِ وَالْاَرْضِ شَيْئًا وَّلَا يَسْتَطِيْعُوْنَ ۪۴۳ فَلَا

تَضْرِبُوْا لِلّٰهِ الْاَمْثَالَ ؕ اِنَّ اللّٰهَ يَعْلَمُ وَاَنْتُمْ

لَا تَعْلَمُوْنَ ۴۴ ضَرَبَ اللّٰهُ مَثَلًا عَبْدًا مَّمْلُوْكًا

لَّا يَقْدِرُ عَلٰى شَيْءٍ وَّمَنْ رَّزَقْنٰهُ مِنَّا رِزْقًا

حَسَنًا فَهُوَ يُنْفِقُ مِنْهُ سِرًّا وَّجَهْرًا ؕ هَلْ

يَسْتَوٗنَ ؕ اَلْحَمْدُ لِلّٰهِ ؕ بَلْ اَكْثَرُهُمْ لَا يَعْلَمُوْنَ ۴۵

وَضَرَبَ اللّٰهُ مَثَلًا رَّجُلَيْنِ اَحَدُهُمَآ اَبْكَمُ لَا

يَقْدِرُ عَلٰى شَيْءٍ وَّهُوَ كَلٌّ عَلٰى مَوْلٰىهُ ۙ اَيْنَمَا

يُوَجِّهْهُّ لَا يَاْتِ بِخَيْرٍ ؕ هَلْ يَسْتَوِيْ هُوَ ۙ وَمَنْ

يَّاْمُرُ بِالْعَدْلِ ۙ وَهُوَ عَلٰى صِرَاطٍ مُّسْتَقِيْمٍ ۴۶ وَلِلّٰهِ

غَيْبُ السَّمٰوٰتِ وَالْاَرْضِ ؕ وَمَآ اَمْرُ السَّاعَةِ اِلَّا

كَلَمْحِ الْبَصَرِ اَوْ هُوَ اَقْرَبُ ؕ اِنَّ اللّٰهَ عَلٰى كُلِّ شَيْءٍ

قَدِيْرٌ ۴۷ وَاللّٰهُ اَخْرَجَكُمْ مِّنْ بُطُوْنِ اُمَّهٰتِكُمْ لَا

تَعْلَمُوْنَ شَيْئًا ۙ وَّجَعَلَ لَكُمُ السَّمْعَ وَالْاَبْصَارَ

وَالْاَفْئِدَةَ ۙ لَعَلَّكُمْ تَشْكُرُوْنَ ۴۸ اَلَمْ يَرَوْا اِلَى

الطَّيْرِ مُسَخَّرٰتٍ فِيْ جَوِّ السَّمَآءِ ؕ مَا يُمْسِكُهُنَّ

How active, concerned and caring are you for others? Are you using Allah's gifts?

⁷² Allah made for you spouses from your own kind, and from them gave you sons and grandchildren and provided you nourishing sustenance. How can they accept falsehood and deny Allah's gifts?

Who are thankful and the unthankful for the gifts

⁷³ They worship helpless idols instead of Allah that can't provide them *with* any provisions from Heaven or the Earth. ⁷⁴ So don't make images of Allah; Allah knows but you don't know. ⁷⁵ Allah gives you an example: a slave who is the helpless property of his master, and on the other hand a man blessed with gifts from which he gives in charity secretly and openly. Are they equal? All praise is for Allah, but most don't recognise. ⁷⁶ Allah gives you another example *of* two men; one of them is dumb, helpless and a burden to his master. Whatever task he sets him, he fails miserably; can he be equal to the man who commands justice and is on the straight path? ⁷⁷ Allah *knows* the secret of the Heavens and the Earth. The coming of the Hour of Judgement will be as quick as the glance of an eye^a or quicker, and Allah is in command of all things. ⁷⁸ Allah brought you out from your mothers' wombs not knowing anything, and then gave you hearing, sight and a mind so you may be thankful.

Allah's gifts of shelter, shields, and clothes

⁷⁹ Haven't they seen birds flying in the sky? It is Allah Who keeps them *afloat*; in this are signs for true believers.

---

^a   I have translated this literally, English idiom, 'twinkling of an eye' would be equally good.

اِلَّا اللّٰهُ ط اِنَّ فِیْ ذٰلِكَ لَاٰیٰتٍ لِّقَوْمٍ یُّؤْمِنُوْنَ ۴۹

وَاللّٰهُ جَعَلَ لَكُمْ مِّنْ بُیُوْتِكُمْ سَكَنًا وَّجَعَلَ لَكُمْ مِّنْ جُلُوْدِ الْاَنْعَامِ بُیُوْتًا تَسْتَخِفُّوْنَهَا یَوْمَ ظَعْنِكُمْ وَیَوْمَ اِقَامَتِكُمْ ۙ وَمِنْ اَصْوَافِهَا وَاَوْبَارِهَا وَاَشْعَارِهَا اَثَاثًا وَّمَتَاعًا اِلٰی حِیْنٍ ۸۰

وَاللّٰهُ جَعَلَ لَكُمْ مِّمَّا خَلَقَ ظِلٰلًا وَّجَعَلَ لَكُمْ مِّنَ الْجِبَالِ اَكْنَانًا وَّجَعَلَ لَكُمْ سَرَابِیْلَ تَقِیْكُمُ الْحَرَّ وَسَرَابِیْلَ تَقِیْكُمْ بَأْسَكُمْ ط كَذٰلِكَ یُتِمُّ

Look at the gifts, from leather to lace, fur to furniture. How thankful are we?

نِعْمَتَهٗ عَلَیْكُمْ لَعَلَّكُمْ تُسْلِمُوْنَ ۸۱ فَاِنْ تَوَلَّوْا فَاِنَّمَا عَلَیْكَ الْبَلٰغُ الْمُبِیْنُ ۸۲ یَعْرِفُوْنَ نِعْمَتَ اللّٰهِ ثُمَّ یُنْكِرُوْنَهَا وَاَكْثَرُهُمُ الْكٰفِرُوْنَ ۸۳ وَیَوْمَ نَبْعَثُ مِنْ كُلِّ اُمَّةٍ شَهِیْدًا ثُمَّ لَا یُؤْذَنُ لِلَّذِیْنَ كَفَرُوْا وَلَا هُمْ یُسْتَعْتَبُوْنَ ۸۴ وَاِذَا رَاَ الَّذِیْنَ ظَلَمُوا الْعَذَابَ فَلَا یُخَفَّفُ عَنْهُمْ وَلَا هُمْ یُنْظَرُوْنَ ۸۵ وَاِذَا رَاَ الَّذِیْنَ اَشْرَكُوْا شُرَكَآءَهُمْ قَالُوْا رَبَّنَا هٰۤؤُلَآءِ شُرَكَآؤُنَا الَّذِیْنَ كُنَّا نَدْعُوْا مِنْ دُوْنِكَ ۚ فَاَلْقَوْا اِلَیْهِمُ الْقَوْلَ اِنَّكُمْ لَكٰذِبُوْنَ ۸۶ وَاَلْقَوْا اِلَی اللّٰهِ یَوْمَئِذِنِ السَّلَمَ وَضَلَّ عَنْهُمْ مَّا كَانُوْا یَفْتَرُوْنَ ۸۷ اَلَّذِیْنَ كَفَرُوْا وَصَدُّوْا عَنْ سَبِیْلِ اللّٰهِ زِدْنٰهُمْ عَذَابًا فَوْقَ الْعَذَابِ بِمَا كَانُوْا

⁸⁰ Allah made for you homes to live in, and from the skins of animals you make tents that are light for you to carry *about* when travelling and camping, and from their wool, fur and hair *you make* furnishings that last for years. ⁸¹ Allah made shade to protect you from what He has created, like the places of shelter in the hillsides, and made for you clothes that protect you from heat, and armour that protects you in battle. Allah gave you His gifts so that you might submit to Him. ⁸² But if they turn away, your job is only to deliver the clear message. ⁸³ They know Allah's blessings but fail to recognise them, most of them are ungrateful.

On Judgement Day they will abandon idols

⁸⁴ We will pick a witness from each community that Day; the disbelievers won't be allowed to plead *ignorance* nor to repent. ⁸⁵ When the wrongdoers see the punishment, *they will realise that* it will not be lightened, nor will they be given respite. ⁸⁶ When the idolaters see their idols they will say, "Our Lord, these are our idols we worshipped besides you," but they will reply angrily, "Indeed you are liars." ⁸⁷ That day, they will submit before Allah and abandon what they had invented as gods. ⁸⁸ Those people who disbelieved and stopped others from Allah's path, their punishment will be increased many times over because they were rebellious.

يُفْسِدُوْنَ ۸۸ وَيَوْمَ نَبْعَثُ فِىْ كُلِّ اُمَّةٍ شَهِيْدًا

عَلَيْهِمْ مِّنْ اَنْفُسِهِمْ وَجِئْنَا بِكَ شَهِيْدًا عَلٰى

هٰؤُلَآءِ ط وَنَزَّلْنَا عَلَيْكَ الْكِتٰبَ تِبْيَانًا لِّكُلِّ

شَىْءٍ وَّهُدًى وَّرَحْمَةً وَّبُشْرٰى لِلْمُسْلِمِيْنَ ۸۹

اِنَّ اللّٰهَ يَأْمُرُ بِالْعَدْلِ وَالْاِحْسَانِ وَاِيْتَآئِ ذِى

الْقُرْبٰى وَيَنْهٰى عَنِ الْفَحْشَآءِ وَالْمُنْكَرِ وَالْبَغْىِ ج

يَعِظُكُمْ لَعَلَّكُمْ تَذَكَّرُوْنَ ۹۰ وَاَوْفُوْا بِعَهْدِ اللّٰهِ

اِذَا عَاهَدْتُّمْ وَلَا تَنْقُضُوا الْاَيْمَانَ بَعْدَ تَوْكِيْدِهَا

وَقَدْ جَعَلْتُمُ اللّٰهَ عَلَيْكُمْ كَفِيْلًا ط اِنَّ اللّٰهَ يَعْلَمُ

مَا تَفْعَلُوْنَ ۹۱ وَلَا تَكُوْنُوْا كَالَّتِىْ نَقَضَتْ غَزْلَهَا

مِنْۢ بَعْدِ قُوَّةٍ اَنْكَاثًا ط تَتَّخِذُوْنَ اَيْمَانَكُمْ دَخَلًا

بَيْنَكُمْ اَنْ تَكُوْنَ اُمَّةٌ هِىَ اَرْبٰى مِنْ اُمَّةٍ ط اِنَّمَا

يَبْلُوْكُمُ اللّٰهُ بِهٖ ط وَلَيُبَيِّنَنَّ لَكُمْ يَوْمَ الْقِيٰمَةِ مَا

كُنْتُمْ فِيْهِ تَخْتَلِفُوْنَ ۹۲ وَلَوْ شَآءَ اللّٰهُ لَجَعَلَكُمْ

اُمَّةً وَّاحِدَةً وَّلٰكِنْ يُّضِلُّ مَنْ يَّشَآءُ وَيَهْدِىْ

مَنْ يَّشَآءُ ط وَلَتُسْـَٔلُنَّ عَمَّا كُنْتُمْ تَعْمَلُوْنَ ۹۳ وَلَا

تَتَّخِذُوْٓا اَيْمَانَكُمْ دَخَلًۢا بَيْنَكُمْ فَتَزِلَّ قَدَمٌۢ

بَعْدَ ثُبُوْتِهَا وَتَذُوْقُوا السُّوْٓءَ بِمَا صَدَدْتُّمْ عَنْ

سَبِيْلِ اللّٰهِ ج وَلَكُمْ عَذَابٌ عَظِيْمٌ ۹۴ وَلَا تَشْتَرُوْا

بِعَهْدِ اللّٰهِ ثَمَنًا قَلِيْلًا ط اِنَّمَا عِنْدَ اللّٰهِ هُوَ خَيْرٌ

Allah gives teachings that instruct us to do good, bless us and will save us.

⁸⁹ On that Day, We will pick a witness from each community against them. We will bring you as a witness against them all. We revealed to you a glorious Book that explains *the truth* about all things; it is guidance, a kindness and good news for the Muslims.

Law of fulfilling a pledge

⁹⁰ Allah commands justice, generosity and giving to relatives. He forbids indecency, all *kinds of* evil and cruelty. He teaches you, perhaps you will accept advice. ⁹¹ Fulfil Allah's pledge, and once you made Allah a witness of your promise, don't break it after confirming it; Allah knows what you do. ⁹² *Sometimes* you make promises to deceive others – don't be like the woman who tears to pieces the cloth she spun – so you might make more profit than others. Surely Allah will test you by this, and on Judgement Day He will make clear what you were disagreeing about. ⁹³ If Allah wanted He could have made you *all* one community *of believers*, but he lets go astray anyone who wants to do so, and guides anyone who wants to be guided. You will be questioned about your deeds. ⁹⁴ Don't take oaths to deceive others; this will shake you after being steadfast, and you must taste *the* evil consequences of stopping people from Allah's path, and there will be grievous punishment for you.

The works of men and women are of equal value

⁹⁵ Don't sell Allah's pledge for a small price; what Allah has for you is good, if you knew.

لَكُمْ اِنْ كُنْتُمْ تَعْلَمُوْنَ ۝ مَا عِنْدَكُمْ يَنْفَدُ وَمَا

عِنْدَ اللّٰهِ بَاقٍ ط وَلَنَجْزِيَنَّ الَّذِيْنَ صَبَرُوْۤا

اَجْرَهُمْ بِاَحْسَنِ مَا كَانُوْا يَعْمَلُوْنَ ۝ مَنْ عَمِلَ

صَالِحًا مِّنْ ذَكَرٍ اَوْ اُنْثٰى وَهُوَ مُؤْمِنٌ فَلَنُحْيِيَنَّهٗ

حَيٰوةً طَيِّبَةً ج وَلَنَجْزِيَنَّهُمْ اَجْرَهُمْ بِاَحْسَنِ مَا

كَانُوْا يَعْمَلُوْنَ ۝ فَاِذَا قَرَأْتَ الْقُرْاٰنَ فَاسْتَعِذْ

بِاللّٰهِ مِنَ الشَّيْطٰنِ الرَّجِيْمِ ۝ اِنَّهٗ لَيْسَ لَهٗ

سُلْطٰنٌ عَلَى الَّذِيْنَ اٰمَنُوْا وَعَلٰى رَبِّهِمْ يَتَوَكَّلُوْنَ ۝

اِنَّمَا سُلْطٰنُهٗ عَلَى الَّذِيْنَ يَتَوَلَّوْنَهٗ وَالَّذِيْنَ هُمْ

بِهٖ مُشْرِكُوْنَ ع ۝ وَاِذَا بَدَّلْنَاۤ اٰيَةً مَّكَانَ اٰيَةٍ لا

وَاللّٰهُ اَعْلَمُ بِمَا يُنَزِّلُ قَالُوْۤا اِنَّمَاۤ اَنْتَ مُفْتَرٍ ط بَلْ

اَكْثَرُهُمْ لَا يَعْلَمُوْنَ ۝ قُلْ نَزَّلَهٗ رُوْحُ الْقُدُسِ

مِنْ رَّبِّكَ بِالْحَقِّ لِيُثَبِّتَ الَّذِيْنَ اٰمَنُوْا وَهُدًى

وَّبُشْرٰى لِلْمُسْلِمِيْنَ ۝ وَلَقَدْ نَعْلَمُ اَنَّهُمْ

يَقُوْلُوْنَ اِنَّمَا يُعَلِّمُهٗ بَشَرٌ ط لِسَانُ الَّذِيْ

يُلْحِدُوْنَ اِلَيْهِ اَعْجَمِيٌّ وَّهٰذَا لِسَانٌ عَرَبِيٌّ

مُّبِيْنٌ ۝ اِنَّ الَّذِيْنَ لَا يُؤْمِنُوْنَ بِاٰيٰتِ اللّٰهِ لا

لَا يَهْدِيْهِمُ اللّٰهُ وَلَهُمْ عَذَابٌ اَلِيْمٌ ۝ اِنَّمَا

يَفْتَرِى الْكَذِبَ الَّذِيْنَ لَا يُؤْمِنُوْنَ بِاٰيٰتِ اللّٰهِ ج

وَاُولٰٓئِكَ هُمُ الْكٰذِبُوْنَ ۝ مَنْ كَفَرَ بِاللّٰهِ مِنْ

Pure life promised for those who regard the Quran as the greatest gift of Allah.

⁹⁶ Whatever you have will perish, but what is with Allah will continue, and We will certainly give the patient people *their* reward for what they did. ⁹⁷ Whoever – whether male or female – does good deeds, while being a true believer, We shall bless them with a happy life, and give them reward equal to their beautiful deeds.

The Quran is Allah's greatest gift

⁹⁸ When you *start* reading the Majestic Quran, seek Allah's protection from the rejected Satan. ⁹⁹ He has no influence over believers who trust in their Lord. ¹⁰⁰ But he does have influence on those who befriend him and the idolaters. ¹⁰¹ When We change a verse in place of another – *of course* Allah knows well what He reveals – they say, "You have made it up." No, most of them don't know. ¹⁰² Say: "The Holy One, *angel Jibreel*, has gradually brought it down from your Lord truthfully, to strengthen the morale of the believers; it is guidance and good news for the Muslims." ¹⁰³ We know they will say, "A certain man teaches it to him." Yet the language of the one who they point to is foreign, whilst this Quran is in plain Arabic. ¹⁰⁴ If people don't believe in Allah's revelation, Allah will not guide them; for them will be painful punishment.

Faith lies deep in the heart

¹⁰⁵ Those who don't believe in Allah's verses invented lies; they are liars.

بَعْدِ اِيْمَانِهٖٓ اِلَّا مَنْ اُكْرِهَ وَقَلْبُهٗ مُطْمَئِنٌّ

بِالْاِيْمَانِ وَلٰكِنْ مَّنْ شَرَحَ بِالْكُفْرِ صَدْرًا

فَعَلَيْهِمْ غَضَبٌ مِّنَ اللّٰهِ ۚ وَلَهُمْ عَذَابٌ عَظِيْمٌ ﴿١٠٦﴾

ذٰلِكَ بِاَنَّهُمُ اسْتَحَبُّوا الْحَيٰوةَ الدُّنْيَا عَلَى الْاٰخِرَةِ ۙ

وَاَنَّ اللّٰهَ لَا يَهْدِى الْقَوْمَ الْكٰفِرِيْنَ ﴿١٠٧﴾ اُولٰٓئِكَ

الَّذِيْنَ طَبَعَ اللّٰهُ عَلٰى قُلُوْبِهِمْ وَسَمْعِهِمْ

وَاَبْصَارِهِمْ ۚ وَاُولٰٓئِكَ هُمُ الْغٰفِلُوْنَ ﴿١٠٨﴾

لَا جَرَمَ اَنَّهُمْ فِى الْاٰخِرَةِ هُمُ الْخٰسِرُوْنَ ﴿١٠٩﴾

ثُمَّ اِنَّ رَبَّكَ لِلَّذِيْنَ هَاجَرُوْا مِنْ بَعْدِ مَا

فُتِنُوْا ثُمَّ جٰهَدُوْا وَصَبَرُوْا ۙ اِنَّ رَبَّكَ مِنْ

بَعْدِهَا لَغَفُوْرٌ رَّحِيْمٌ ﴿١١٠﴾ ۞ يَوْمَ تَاْتِىْ كُلُّ نَفْسٍ

تُجَادِلُ عَنْ نَّفْسِهَا وَتُوَفّٰى كُلُّ نَفْسٍ مَّا عَمِلَتْ

وَهُمْ لَا يُظْلَمُوْنَ ﴿١١١﴾ وَضَرَبَ اللّٰهُ مَثَلًا قَرْيَةً

كَانَتْ اٰمِنَةً مُّطْمَئِنَّةً يَّاْتِيْهَا رِزْقُهَا رَغَدًا

مِّنْ كُلِّ مَكَانٍ فَكَفَرَتْ بِاَنْعُمِ اللّٰهِ فَاَذَاقَهَا

اللّٰهُ لِبَاسَ الْجُوْعِ وَالْخَوْفِ بِمَا كَانُوْا يَصْنَعُوْنَ ﴿١١٢﴾

وَلَقَدْ جَآءَهُمْ رَسُوْلٌ مِّنْهُمْ فَكَذَّبُوْهُ فَاَخَذَهُمُ

الْعَذَابُ وَهُمْ ظٰلِمُوْنَ ﴿١١٣﴾ فَكُلُوْا مِمَّا رَزَقَكُمُ

اللّٰهُ حَلٰلًا طَيِّبًا ۖ وَّاشْكُرُوْا نِعْمَتَ اللّٰهِ اِنْ

كُنْتُمْ اِيَّاهُ تَعْبُدُوْنَ ﴿١١٤﴾ اِنَّمَا حَرَّمَ عَلَيْكُمُ

Too much of the worldly luxuries can deaden the heart, numb the mind and lead to unthankfulness.

541

¹⁰⁶ The one who disbelieves Allah after believing him – except the one who is forced and his heart remains secure in faith – their hearts accept disbelief. For them is Allah's fury and a grievous punishment, ¹⁰⁷ because they prefer worldly life over the Hereafter and Allah doesn't guide the disbelievers. ¹⁰⁸ He has sealed their hearts, hearing, and seeing, and they are neglectful. ¹⁰⁹ No doubt in the Hereafter they will be the losers. ¹¹⁰ Your Lord is Forgiving and was Kind towards those who migrated after persecution and kept struggling and remained patient. ¹¹¹ That day everyone will plead for himself, and everyone will be fully rewarded for what they did, and no one will be wronged.

Riches made them forget Allah's gifts
¹¹² Allah gives an example of a city *where people* believed they were safe and comfortable, *as* plenty of goods came from all directions, but they were unthankful for Allah's gifts. Therefore, Allah punished them with famine and fear for what they did. ¹¹³ A messenger from them came, but they denied him, so punishment came to them whilst they were doing wrong.

Observing the lawful and unlawful
¹¹⁴ So eat from lawful pure sustenance, and be thankful for Allah's gifts if you worship Him alone.

عربي

الْمَيْتَةَ وَالدَّمَ وَلَحْمَ الْخِنْزِيرِ وَمَا أُهِلَّ

لِغَيْرِ اللهِ بِهِ ۚ فَمَنِ اضْطُرَّ غَيْرَ بَاغٍ وَّلَا

عَادٍ فَإِنَّ اللهَ غَفُورٌ رَّحِيمٌ ۞ وَلَا تَقُولُوا

لِمَا تَصِفُ أَلْسِنَتُكُمُ الْكَذِبَ هٰذَا حَلَالٌ وَّهٰذَا

حَرَامٌ لِّتَفْتَرُوا عَلَى اللهِ الْكَذِبَ ۗ إِنَّ الَّذِينَ

يَفْتَرُونَ عَلَى اللهِ الْكَذِبَ لَا يُفْلِحُونَ ۞

مَتَاعٌ قَلِيلٌ ۖ وَّلَهُمْ عَذَابٌ أَلِيمٌ ۞ وَعَلَى

الَّذِينَ هَادُوا حَرَّمْنَا مَا قَصَصْنَا عَلَيْكَ

مِنْ قَبْلُ ۖ وَمَا ظَلَمْنٰهُمْ وَلٰكِنْ كَانُوا أَنْفُسَهُمْ

يَظْلِمُونَ ۞ ثُمَّ إِنَّ رَبَّكَ لِلَّذِينَ عَمِلُوا

السُّوٓءَ بِجَهَالَةٍ ثُمَّ تَابُوا مِنْ بَعْدِ ذٰلِكَ

وَأَصْلَحُوٓا ۙ إِنَّ رَبَّكَ مِنْ بَعْدِهَا لَغَفُورٌ

رَّحِيمٌ ۞ إِنَّ إِبْرٰهِيمَ كَانَ أُمَّةً قَانِتًا لِّلّٰهِ

حَنِيفًا ۖ وَلَمْ يَكُ مِنَ الْمُشْرِكِينَ ۞ شَاكِرًا

لِّأَنْعُمِهِ ۚ اجْتَبٰهُ وَهَدٰهُ إِلَى صِرَاطٍ مُّسْتَقِيمٍ ۞

وَآتَيْنٰهُ فِي الدُّنْيَا حَسَنَةً ۗ وَإِنَّهُ فِي الْآخِرَةِ

لَمِنَ الصّٰلِحِينَ ۞ ثُمَّ أَوْحَيْنَآ إِلَيْكَ أَنِ

اتَّبِعْ مِلَّةَ إِبْرٰهِيمَ حَنِيفًا ۖ وَمَا كَانَ مِنَ

الْمُشْرِكِينَ ۞ إِنَّمَا جُعِلَ السَّبْتُ عَلَى الَّذِينَ

اخْتَلَفُوا فِيهِ ۗ وَإِنَّ رَبَّكَ لَيَحْكُمُ بَيْنَهُمْ يَوْمَ

Ibrahim's greatness was due to being thankful for the gifts he received.

[115] He has forbidden for you carrion, blood, pork, and anything slaughtered without invoking Allah's name. However, the one in dire need is exempt from this, if he eats without the intention of disobeying and transgressing; Allah is Forgiving and Kind. [116] Don't make things up to say, "This is lawful and this is unlawful," thereby inventing a lie about Allah. Those who invent lies about Allah will not succeed. [117] This is unfair; for them is a painful punishment. [118] What is forbidden for the Jews has been narrated previously to you; We didn't wrong them, but they wronged themselves. [119] Those who ignorantly committed evil then repented and afterwards reformed themselves will *find* Your Lord to be Forgiving and Kind.

Ibrahim, a role model of thankfulness

[120] Ibrahim was an exemplary leader, obedient to Allah, pure in faith and didn't associate anything with Allah. [121] He was thankful for His gifts, so Allah selected him and guided him on the straight path. [122] We gave him the best in the world, and in the Hereafter he will be among the righteous. [123] We revealed to you: "Follow Ibrahim's religion, the pure in faith, who wasn't an idolater." [124] The *rules of* Sabbath were made obligatory only on those who differed about it; your Lord will decide between them on Judgement Day concerning their disagreements.

الْقِيٰمَةِ فِيْمَا كَانُوْا فِيْهِ يَخْتَلِفُوْنَ ۞ اُدْعُ اِلٰى

سَبِيْلِ رَبِّكَ بِالْحِكْمَةِ وَالْمَوْعِظَةِ الْحَسَنَةِ

وَجَادِلْهُمْ بِالَّتِيْ هِيَ اَحْسَنُ ۗ اِنَّ رَبَّكَ هُوَ اَعْلَمُ

بِمَنْ ضَلَّ عَنْ سَبِيْلِهٖ وَهُوَ اَعْلَمُ بِالْمُهْتَدِيْنَ ۞

وَاِنْ عَاقَبْتُمْ فَعَاقِبُوْا بِمِثْلِ مَا عُوْقِبْتُمْ بِهٖ ۗ

وَلَئِنْ صَبَرْتُمْ لَهُوَ خَيْرٌ لِّلصّٰبِرِيْنَ ۞ وَاصْبِرْ

وَمَا صَبْرُكَ اِلَّا بِاللّٰهِ وَلَا تَحْزَنْ عَلَيْهِمْ وَلَا

تَكُ فِيْ ضَيْقٍ مِّمَّا يَمْكُرُوْنَ ۞ اِنَّ اللّٰهَ مَعَ

الَّذِيْنَ اتَّقَوْا وَّالَّذِيْنَ هُمْ مُّحْسِنُوْنَ ۞

Patience is to resist knee-jerk reactions so you see the bigger picture. It helps to see your inner gifts.

Invite to Allah in a courteous manner

¹²⁵ Invite to your Lord's way wisely: teaching in a pleasant manner, and debating with courtesy; Your Lord knows the one who strayed from His way and the one guided. ¹²⁶ If you retaliate, then do so to the same extent, but if you are patient that would be better, being patient is good. ¹²⁷ Be patient; your patience *is* Allah's *gift*. Don't grieve over them, nor distress yourself because of their plotting. ¹²⁸ Allah is with the mindful and the righteous.

17. Surat Al-Isra'

The Ascension

This late Makkan surat opens with the miracle of the Ascension: the Prophet's ﷺ night journey from Makkah to Jerusalem, and from there to celestial heights, finishing in the Divine Presence. The journey is an unspoken announcement of the aptness of the message of the Prophet ﷺ for the entire world, and hints to the coming glory of Islam. The Ascension took place on 27 Rajab, seventeen months before the Hijrah in the year of sorrow. The purpose of this two-phased journey was, "To show him Our signs". The hadith literature gives graphic details of this momentous journey. The verse begins with the Divine attribute, "Subhan", 'the one who is flawless without defect or weakness, the Glorified.' The Quran states the One who took His servant on this miraculous journey is the One who is free from every kind of weakness. Whose mere command *'kun'* (be) and *'fa-yakun'* (it becomes), is enough.

Imam Bukhari has a chapter devoted to Miraj, whilst Imam Muslim has a chapter called "Isra". Therefore, we see an agreement among Muslim scholars, "The Prophet's ascension was a bodily journey in a wakeful state to the Heavens and then to the heights where Allah wished him to go." (Aqaid-an-Nasafi)[a] For the vertical phase of the Ascension see Surat Al Najm.

The Quran is mentioned eleven times in the surat, describing its various aspects: a guide to the straightest path; an explanation of divine proofs; why disbelievers cannot understand it so they turn away from it; a test of faith; a recitation at dawn with special effects; a healing and Divine Kindness; an inimitable masterpiece; full of powerful arguments for Allah's existence; the truth; and revealed in comprehensible bites.

Man's nature is described 'hasty' and why he craves for instant gratification and immediate results. Is that why people love the fleeting world, instead of the everlasting Hereafter? To help humanity overcome this weakness the surat presents a new, just and peaceful way of living – an outline for a new world order: here people are kind, patient and forgiving. It's summarised in the ten commandments announced in this surat: worship Allah; care for parents; give to the needy; give up the Seven Deadly Sins (wastefulness, miserliness, murder, adultery, dishonesty, blind imitation and arrogance).

The Messenger ﷺ of Islam was devout and spiritual, so a special night vigil is recommended for him: "At night, wake up to offer voluntary prayer that is only for you. Soon

---

[a]   See *Introduction to Islam* (Bibliography).

your Lord will raise you to a glorious station of praise" (79). The Quran warns that Satan will exert maximum effort to misguide, so be on guard. But, the true servants will be protected from his insinuations (64– 65).

بِسْمِ اللّٰهِ الرَّحْمٰنِ الرَّحِيْمِ

سُبْحٰنَ الَّذِىْۤ اَسْرٰى بِعَبْدِهٖ لَيْلًا مِّنَ الْمَسْجِدِ الْحَرَامِ اِلَى الْمَسْجِدِ الْاَقْصَا الَّذِىْ بٰرَكْنَا حَوْلَهٗ لِنُرِيَهٗ مِنْ اٰيٰتِنَا ؕ اِنَّهٗ هُوَ السَّمِيْعُ الْبَصِيْرُ ۝ وَاٰتَيْنَا مُوْسَى الْكِتٰبَ وَجَعَلْنٰهُ هُدًى لِّبَنِىْۤ اِسْرَآءِيْلَ اَلَّا تَتَّخِذُوْا مِنْ دُوْنِىْ وَكِيْلًا ؕ ۝ ذُرِّيَّةَ مَنْ حَمَلْنَا مَعَ نُوْحٍ ؕ اِنَّهٗ كَانَ عَبْدًا شَكُوْرًا ۝ وَقَضَيْنَاۤ اِلٰى بَنِىْۤ اِسْرَآءِيْلَ فِى الْكِتٰبِ لَتُفْسِدُنَّ فِى الْاَرْضِ مَرَّتَيْنِ وَلَتَعْلُنَّ عُلُوًّا كَبِيْرًا ۝ فَاِذَا جَآءَ وَعْدُ اُوْلٰىهُمَا بَعَثْنَا عَلَيْكُمْ عِبَادًا لَّنَاۤ اُولِىْ بَاْسٍ شَدِيْدٍ فَجَاسُوْا خِلٰلَ الدِّيَارِ ؕ وَكَانَ وَعْدًا مَّفْعُوْلًا ۝ ثُمَّ رَدَدْنَا لَكُمُ الْكَرَّةَ عَلَيْهِمْ وَ اَمْدَدْنٰكُمْ بِاَمْوَالٍ وَّبَنِيْنَ وَجَعَلْنٰكُمْ اَكْثَرَ نَفِيْرًا ۝ اِنْ اَحْسَنْتُمْ اَحْسَنْتُمْ لِاَنْفُسِكُمْ ؕ وَاِنْ اَسَاْتُمْ فَلَهَا ؕ فَاِذَا جَآءَ وَعْدُ الْاٰخِرَةِ لِيَسُوْٓءُوْا وُجُوْهَكُمْ وَلِيَدْخُلُوا الْمَسْجِدَ كَمَا دَخَلُوْهُ اَوَّلَ مَرَّةٍ وَّلِيُتَبِّرُوْا مَا عَلَوْا تَتْبِيْرًا ۝ عَسٰى رَبُّكُمْ اَنْ يَّرْحَمَكُمْ ۚ وَاِنْ عُدْتُّمْ عُدْنَا ؕ وَجَعَلْنَا جَهَنَّمَ لِلْكٰفِرِيْنَ حَصِيْرًا ۝ اِنَّ هٰذَا الْقُرْاٰنَ يَهْدِىْ لِلَّتِىْ هِىَ اَقْوَمُ وَيُبَشِّرُ الْمُؤْمِنِيْنَ الَّذِيْنَ يَعْمَلُوْنَ الصّٰلِحٰتِ اَنَّ لَهُمْ اَجْرًا كَبِيْرًا ۝

The Ascension of the messenger ﷺ was a great honour for him and a reassurance that the Lord was supporting him.

In the name of Allah, the Kind, the Caring.

The Ascension of the Messenger ﷺ

¹ Glory to Him Who took His *noble* servant on a night journey[a] from the Sacred Mosque to the farthest Mosque – whose surroundings we made holy – to show him Our signs. He is the Hearer, the Seeing. ² We gave Musa the Book of guidance for the Israelites saying: "Don't take a Guardian besides Me." ³ *You are the* descendants of the people We carried in Nuh's ship; he was a thankful servant.

The Israelites will face troubled times twice

⁴ We stated in the Scripture: twice you would create mischief on the land and become arrogant.[b] ⁵ So We sent against them Our servants who were severely brutal, they demolished their homes; hence the first prediction was fulfilled. ⁶ Later on We gave you victory over them and helped you with wealth and children and increased your numbers – ⁷ if you do good it will be for your good, and if you do evil it's against yourselves – when the second promise came, you were again disgraced; they entered the masjid *in Jerusalem* as they entered the first time and destroyed what they could get hold of. ⁸ It is still possible that your Lord may be kind to you. However, if you turn back to evil We will again punish you; We made Hell a prison for the disbelievers.

The Majestic Quran is good news

⁹ This Majestic Quran guides to the straightest *path*[c] it brings good news for the believers who perform excellent deeds; they'll have a great reward.

---

[a] This was not all night but for a part of the night.

[b] The two punishments were; 586 BC, the Babylonians under Nebuchadnezzar destroyed the Temple of Solomon and took the Israelites into captivity. The second punishment occurred in 70 CE, at the hands of Roman emperor Titus, who scattered the Jews all over the world.

[c] *Aqwam* means "straightest"; without bends, curves or deviations, it is candid, rather than soft or deceptive.

ع
١

وَاَنَّ الَّذِيْنَ لَا يُؤْمِنُوْنَ بِالْاٰخِرَةِ اَعْتَدْنَا لَهُمْ عَذَابًا اَلِيْمًا ۩ وَيَدْعُ الْاِنْسَانُ بِالشَّرِّ دُعَآءَهٗ بِالْخَيْرِ ط وَكَانَ الْاِنْسَانُ عَجُوْلًا ۩ وَجَعَلْنَا الَّيْلَ وَالنَّهَارَ اٰيَتَيْنِ فَمَحَوْنَآ اٰيَةَ الَّيْلِ وَجَعَلْنَآ اٰيَةَ النَّهَارِ مُبْصِرَةً لِّتَبْتَغُوْا فَضْلًا مِّنْ رَّبِّكُمْ وَلِتَعْلَمُوْا عَدَدَ السِّنِيْنَ وَالْحِسَابَ ط وَكُلَّ شَيْءٍ فَصَّلْنٰهُ تَفْصِيْلًا ۩ وَكُلَّ اِنْسَانٍ اَلْزَمْنٰهُ طٰٓئِرَهٗ فِيْ عُنُقِهٖ ط وَنُخْرِجُ لَهٗ يَوْمَ الْقِيٰمَةِ كِتٰبًا يَّلْقٰهُ مَنْشُوْرًا ۩ اِقْرَأْ كِتٰبَكَ ط كَفٰى بِنَفْسِكَ الْيَوْمَ عَلَيْكَ حَسِيْبًا ۩ مَنِ اهْتَدٰى فَاِنَّمَا يَهْتَدِيْ لِنَفْسِهٖ ۚ وَمَنْ ضَلَّ فَاِنَّمَا يَضِلُّ عَلَيْهَا ط وَلَا تَزِرُ وَازِرَةٌ وِّزْرَ اُخْرٰى ط وَمَا كُنَّا مُعَذِّبِيْنَ حَتّٰى نَبْعَثَ رَسُوْلًا ۩ وَاِذَآ اَرَدْنَآ اَنْ نُّهْلِكَ قَرْيَةً اَمَرْنَا مُتْرَفِيْهَا فَفَسَقُوْا فِيْهَا فَحَقَّ عَلَيْهَا الْقَوْلُ فَدَمَّرْنٰهَا تَدْمِيْرًا ۩ وَكَمْ اَهْلَكْنَا مِنَ الْقُرُوْنِ مِنْۢ بَعْدِ نُوْحٍ ط وَكَفٰى بِرَبِّكَ بِذُنُوْبِ عِبَادِهٖ خَبِيْرًۢا بَصِيْرًا ۩ مَنْ كَانَ يُرِيْدُ الْعَاجِلَةَ عَجَّلْنَا لَهٗ فِيْهَا مَا نَشَآءُ لِمَنْ نُّرِيْدُ ثُمَّ جَعَلْنَا لَهٗ جَهَنَّمَ ۚ يَصْلٰىهَا مَذْمُوْمًا مَّدْحُوْرًا ۩ وَمَنْ اَرَادَ الْاٰخِرَةَ وَسَعٰى لَهَا سَعْيَهَا وَهُوَ مُؤْمِنٌ فَاُولٰٓئِكَ كَانَ سَعْيُهُمْ مَّشْكُوْرًا ۩ كُلًّا نُّمِدُّ هٰٓؤُلَآءِ وَهٰٓؤُلَآءِ مِنْ عَطَآءِ رَبِّكَ ط

Your destiny, fate, luck and fortune are in your hands. Allah created them, but you are responsible for realising them.

[10] Those who don't believe in the Hereafter, for them We've prepared a painful punishment. [11] *Sometimes* people pray for evil as keenly as they pray for good; people are hasty.

Man's hasty nature

[12] We made the night and the day two signs; We darkened the night and made the day bright, so you can seek sustenance from your Lord and for calculating the number *of years*. We have explained all things. [13] We tied the destiny of every person around their neck;[a] on Judgement Day, We shall bring out the document and spread it wide open before them; [14] read your own document! You should be able to calculate your *own* account today. [15] Whoever accepts the guidance does for his own good, and whoever strays is in loss; no one will bear the burden of another person. We don't punish people until We have sent a messenger.

The fate of those who love the world

[16] When We plan to destroy a town, first We teach its well-off people *to change*, if they continue to disobey, the judgement comes to pass and We destroy them. [17] How many generations did we destroy after Nuh? Your Lord is sufficiently aware and sees the sins of His servants. [18] Whoever wants the fleeting world, We readily give whatever We will to whom We please. We have made Hell for him that will burn him, he will be disgraced and rejected. [19] Whoever wants the Hereafter and works hard for it as a true believer; their works will be fully appreciated. [20] On all – these and those – We give the gifts of Your Lord. Your Lord's gifts are not restricted to one group alone.

---

[a] This refers to human destiny, fate and the outcome of one's life achievements. Outcome of life is determined by one's beliefs, attitudes and behaviour, since Allah has ordered man to behave responsibly. This could also allude to the human genome, the code that determines a person's make up and structure.

وَمَا كَانَ عَطَآءُ رَبِّكَ مَحْظُوْرًا ۞ اُنْظُرْ كَيْفَ فَضَّلْنَا

بَعْضَهُمْ عَلٰى بَعْضٍ ط وَ لَلْاٰخِرَةُ اَكْبَرُ دَرَجٰتٍ وَّ اَكْبَرُ

تَفْضِيْلًا ۞ لَا تَجْعَلْ مَعَ اللهِ اِلٰهًا اٰخَرَ فَتَقْعُدَ مَذْمُوْمًا

مَّخْذُوْلًا ۞ وَ قَضٰى رَبُّكَ اَلَّا تَعْبُدُوْۤا اِلَّاۤ اِيَّاهُ وَ بِالْوَالِدَيْنِ

اِحْسَانًا ط اِمَّا يَبْلُغَنَّ عِنْدَكَ الْكِبَرَ اَحَدُهُمَاۤ اَوْ كِلٰهُمَا

فَلَا تَقُلْ لَّهُمَاۤ اُفٍّ وَّ لَا تَنْهَرْهُمَا وَ قُلْ لَّهُمَا قَوْلًا

كَرِيْمًا ۞ وَ اخْفِضْ لَهُمَا جَنَاحَ الذُّلِّ مِنَ الرَّحْمَةِ

وَ قُلْ رَّبِّ ارْحَمْهُمَا كَمَا رَبَّيٰنِيْ صَغِيْرًا ۞ رَبُّكُمْ اَعْلَمُ

بِمَا فِيْ نُفُوْسِكُمْ ط اِنْ تَكُوْنُوْا صٰلِحِيْنَ فَاِنَّهٗ كَانَ

لِلْاَوَّابِيْنَ غَفُوْرًا ۞ وَ اٰتِ ذَا الْقُرْبٰى حَقَّهٗ وَ الْمِسْكِيْنَ

وَ ابْنَ السَّبِيْلِ وَ لَا تُبَذِّرْ تَبْذِيْرًا ۞ اِنَّ الْمُبَذِّرِيْنَ

كَانُوْۤا اِخْوَانَ الشَّيٰطِيْنِ ط وَ كَانَ الشَّيْطٰنُ لِرَبِّهٖ كَفُوْرًا ۞

وَ اِمَّا تُعْرِضَنَّ عَنْهُمُ ابْتِغَآءَ رَحْمَةٍ مِّنْ رَّبِّكَ تَرْجُوْهَا

فَقُلْ لَّهُمْ قَوْلًا مَّيْسُوْرًا ۞ وَ لَا تَجْعَلْ يَدَكَ مَغْلُوْلَةً

اِلٰى عُنُقِكَ وَ لَا تَبْسُطْهَا كُلَّ الْبَسْطِ فَتَقْعُدَ مَلُوْمًا

مَّحْسُوْرًا ۞ اِنَّ رَبَّكَ يَبْسُطُ الرِّزْقَ لِمَنْ يَّشَآءُ وَ يَقْدِرُ ط

اِنَّهٗ كَانَ بِعِبَادِهٖ خَبِيْرًۢا بَصِيْرًا ۞ وَ لَا تَقْتُلُوْۤا اَوْلَادَكُمْ

خَشْيَةَ اِمْلَاقٍ ط نَحْنُ نَرْزُقُهُمْ وَ اِيَّاكُمْ ط اِنَّ قَتْلَهُمْ

كَانَ خِطْأً كَبِيْرًا ۞ وَ لَا تَقْرَبُوا الزِّنٰۤى اِنَّهٗ كَانَ فَاحِشَةً ط

وَ سَآءَ سَبِيْلًا ۞ وَ لَا تَقْتُلُوا النَّفْسَ الَّتِيْ حَرَّمَ اللهُ

²¹ Notice how We give more to some than others; the Hereafter has far greater status in rank and excellence *than worldly life.* ²² Don't take any other god besides Allah, as you will end up condemned and rejected.

The Ten Commandments:ᵃ Worshipping Allah and caring for parents

²³ Your Lord has commanded that you shouldn't worship anyone except Him, and you must care for parents; if one or both of them become old do not say "Uffᵇ to them, nor snap at them; instead, speak to them with respect ²⁴ and be kind; lower your wings with humility for them and pray: "My Lord, be kind to them, as they cared for me in childhood." ²⁵ Your Lord knows well what is in your minds; if you are righteous, He forgives those who repent.

Keep away from the Seven Deadly Sins: Neither be a waster nor a miser

²⁶ Give a relative his due, the poor and the traveller – don't spend your wealth wastefully. ²⁷ Those who waste are the brothers of Satan, and Satan is most unthankful to His Lord. ²⁸ If you must turn them away empty-handed, *due to your poverty,* speak gently with them, since you are full of expectation of kindness from your Lord. ²⁹ Neither be tight-fisted nor wasteful, as you will be blamed and regretful.ᶜ ³⁰ Your Lord gives plentiful sustenance or limited amounts to whom he pleases. He sees and is fully aware of his servants' *needs.*

Neither kill nor commit adultery

³¹ You shall not kill your children out of fear of poverty. We shall feed them and you; to kill them is a major sin *and a crime.* ³² You must not go near adultery; it is indecency and an evil way of life.

ᵃ The Ten Commandments are: worship Allah, care for parents, give to the needy, don't waste wealth or be a miser, kill, engage in adultery, dishonesty, blind imitation and arrogance.

ᵇ "Uff" is a sound that indicates dislike and annoyance towards parents.

ᶜ Literally: "do not be tight fisted, nor so open handed."

اِلَّا بِالْحَقِّ ؕ وَمَنْ قُتِلَ مَظْلُوْمًا فَقَدْ جَعَلْنَا لِوَلِیِّهٖ

سُلْطٰنًا فَلَا یُسْرِفْ فِّی الْقَتْلِ ؕ اِنَّهٗ کَانَ مَنْصُوْرًا ۝

وَلَا تَقْرَبُوْا مَالَ الْیَتِیْمِ اِلَّا بِالَّتِیْ هِیَ اَحْسَنُ حَتّٰی

یَبْلُغَ اَشُدَّهٗ ۪ وَاَوْفُوْا بِالْعَهْدِ ۚ اِنَّ الْعَهْدَ کَانَ

مَسْئُوْلًا ۝ وَاَوْفُوا الْکَیْلَ اِذَا کِلْتُمْ وَزِنُوْا بِالْقِسْطَاسِ

الْمُسْتَقِیْمِ ؕ ذٰلِکَ خَیْرٌ وَّاَحْسَنُ تَاْوِیْلًا ۝ وَلَا تَقْفُ

مَا لَیْسَ لَکَ بِهٖ عِلْمٌ ؕ اِنَّ السَّمْعَ وَالْبَصَرَ وَالْفُؤَادَ

کُلُّ اُولٰٓئِکَ کَانَ عَنْهُ مَسْئُوْلًا ۝ وَلَا تَمْشِ فِی

الْاَرْضِ مَرَحًا ۚ اِنَّکَ لَنْ تَخْرِقَ الْاَرْضَ وَلَنْ تَبْلُغَ

الْجِبَالَ طُوْلًا ۝ کُلُّ ذٰلِکَ کَانَ سَیِّئُهٗ عِنْدَ رَبِّکَ

مَکْرُوْهًا ۝ ذٰلِکَ مِمَّا اَوْحٰٓی اِلَیْکَ رَبُّکَ مِنَ الْحِکْمَةِ ؕ

وَلَا تَجْعَلْ مَعَ اللّٰهِ اِلٰهًا اٰخَرَ فَتُلْقٰی فِیْ جَهَنَّمَ مَلُوْمًا

مَّدْحُوْرًا ۝ اَفَاَصْفٰکُمْ رَبُّکُمْ بِالْبَنِیْنَ وَاتَّخَذَ مِنَ

الْمَلٰٓئِکَةِ اِنَاثًا ؕ اِنَّکُمْ لَتَقُوْلُوْنَ قَوْلًا عَظِیْمًا ۝

وَلَقَدْ صَرَّفْنَا فِیْ هٰذَا الْقُرْاٰنِ لِیَذَّکَّرُوْا ؕ وَمَا یَزِیْدُهُمْ

اِلَّا نُفُوْرًا ۝ قُلْ لَّوْ کَانَ مَعَهٗٓ اٰلِهَةٌ کَمَا یَقُوْلُوْنَ اِذًا

لَّابْتَغَوْا اِلٰی ذِی الْعَرْشِ سَبِیْلًا ۝ سُبْحٰنَهٗ وَتَعٰلٰی

عَمَّا یَقُوْلُوْنَ عُلُوًّا کَبِیْرًا ۝ تُسَبِّحُ لَهُ السَّمٰوٰتُ

السَّبْعُ وَالْاَرْضُ وَمَنْ فِیْهِنَّ ؕ وَاِنْ مِّنْ شَیْءٍ اِلَّا

یُسَبِّحُ بِحَمْدِهٖ وَلٰکِنْ لَّا تَفْقَهُوْنَ تَسْبِیْحَهُمْ ؕ اِنَّهٗ

What's worrying you? Most likely you're ignorant of it, think and stop worrying.

³³ You shall not kill anyone *since* Allah has made *life* sacred, except for a just cause. However, if someone is wrongly killed, then We give his heirs authority *to take revenge*, but shouldn't exceed in taking life. He shall be supported *by the authorities*.

Do not cheat anyone

³⁴ You shall not go near the wealth of the orphans, except with good intentions, until they are mature. And fulfil pledges; you will be questioned about pledges. ³⁵ When measuring, give in full measure, and weigh with correctly calibrated scales; that is fair, and will produce good outcomes.

Don't follow blindly or walk arrogantly

³⁶ Do not follow blindly without knowledge, *use your senses:* hearing, seeing and thinking, you will be questioned about *them.* ³⁷ You shouldn't walk about on Earth arrogantly, since you cannot tear it up nor can you reach mountains in tallness. ³⁸ These are evil activities, most disliked by your Lord. ³⁹ These are some of *the pearls of* wisdom revealed by your Lord; do not take gods besides Allah. Be fearful, you may end up in Hell, condemned and rejected. ⁴⁰ How come Your Lord preferred sons for you, and angelic daughters for Himself? You've said a terrible thing.

If there were gods, they would have defeated Allah

⁴¹ We have variously explained *proofs of Allah* in this Quran for their reminder, but it has only added to their bitterness. ⁴² Say: "If there were other gods beside Allah as they say, then these gods would have found a way to defeat the owner of the *Mighty* Throne." ⁴³ Glory to Him, He is far above what they say, Exalted and Great. ⁴⁴ The Seven Heavens and the Earth and what is in them all glorify Him; there isn't a single thing that doesn't glorify and praise Him, but you don't understand their *way of* celebrating His glory. He is the Gentle and the Forgiving.

كَانَ حَلِيْمًا غَفُوْرًا ۞ وَاِذَا قَرَاْتَ الْقُرْاٰنَ جَعَلْنَا بَيْنَكَ

وَبَيْنَ الَّذِيْنَ لَا يُؤْمِنُوْنَ بِالْاٰخِرَةِ حِجَابًا مَّسْتُوْرًا ۞

وَّجَعَلْنَا عَلٰى قُلُوْبِهِمْ اَكِنَّةً اَنْ يَّفْقَهُوْهُ وَفِىْ اٰذَانِهِمْ

وَقْرًا ۭ وَاِذَا ذَكَرْتَ رَبَّكَ فِى الْقُرْاٰنِ وَحْدَهٗ وَلَّوْا عَلٰى

اَدْبَارِهِمْ نُفُوْرًا ۞ نَحْنُ اَعْلَمُ بِمَا يَسْتَمِعُوْنَ بِهٖٓ اِذْ

يَسْتَمِعُوْنَ اِلَيْكَ وَاِذْ هُمْ نَجْوٰٓى اِذْ يَقُوْلُ الظّٰلِمُوْنَ

اِنْ تَتَّبِعُوْنَ اِلَّا رَجُلًا مَّسْحُوْرًا ۞ اُنْظُرْ كَيْفَ ضَرَبُوْا

لَكَ الْاَمْثَالَ فَضَلُّوْا فَلَا يَسْتَطِيْعُوْنَ سَبِيْلًا ۞ وَقَالُوْٓا

ءَاِذَا كُنَّا عِظَامًا وَّرُفَاتًا ءَاِنَّا لَمَبْعُوْثُوْنَ خَلْقًا

جَدِيْدًا ۞ قُلْ كُوْنُوْا حِجَارَةً اَوْ حَدِيْدًا ۞ اَوْ خَلْقًا

مِّمَّا يَكْبُرُ فِىْ صُدُوْرِكُمْ ۚ فَسَيَقُوْلُوْنَ مَنْ يُّعِيْدُنَاط

قُلِ الَّذِىْ فَطَرَكُمْ اَوَّلَ مَرَّةٍ ۚ فَسَيُنْغِضُوْنَ اِلَيْكَ

رُءُوْسَهُمْ وَيَقُوْلُوْنَ مَتٰى هُوَط قُلْ عَسٰٓى اَنْ يَّكُوْنَ

قَرِيْبًا ۞ يَوْمَ يَدْعُوْكُمْ فَتَسْتَجِيْبُوْنَ بِحَمْدِهٖ وَتَظُنُّوْنَ

اِنْ لَّبِثْتُمْ اِلَّا قَلِيْلًا ۞ وَقُلْ لِّعِبَادِىْ يَقُوْلُوا الَّتِىْ

هِىَ اَحْسَنُ ۭ اِنَّ الشَّيْطٰنَ يَنْزَغُ بَيْنَهُمْ ۭ اِنَّ الشَّيْطٰنَ

كَانَ لِلْاِنْسَانِ عَدُوًّا مُّبِيْنًا ۞ رَبُّكُمْ اَعْلَمُ بِكُمْ ۭ

اِنْ يَّشَاْ يَرْحَمْكُمْ اَوْ اِنْ يَّشَاْ يُعَذِّبْكُمْ ۭ وَمَآ اَرْسَلْنٰكَ

عَلَيْهِمْ وَكِيْلًا ۞ وَرَبُّكَ اَعْلَمُ بِمَنْ فِى السَّمٰوٰتِ

وَالْاَرْضِ ۭ وَلَقَدْ فَضَّلْنَا بَعْضَ النَّبِيّٖنَ عَلٰى بَعْضٍ

What are the invisible screens that prevent disbelievers from understanding the Quran?

An invisible screen stops them from seeing the Truth

⁴⁵ *Messenger,* when you recite the Quran We place an invisible screen between you and the disbelievers of the Hereafter.ᵃ ⁴⁶ We placed coverings over their minds so they can't understand, and made them hard of hearing. Whenever you mention Your Lord's Oneness in the Quran, they turn their backs hatefully. ⁴⁷ We know well what they wish to hear when they listen to you and when they meet secretly; these wrongdoers say, "The man you follow is bewitched." ⁴⁸ Notice how they portray you; they are mistaken and will not be able to find a way.

Allah is capable of giving life to inanimate things

⁴⁹ They say, "When we have become white washed bones and dust, will we be raised up again, a brand-new creation?" ⁵⁰ Say *yes:* "*Even* if you turned into stones or iron ⁵¹ or any substance you may think unlikely to be given life." They ask, "Who will bring us back?" Say: "The One who created you the first time." They will shake their heads saying, "When will that be?" Say: "It's perhaps near." ⁵² The day Allah will call you, and all will answer by praising Him, then you'll realise you only stayed a short while *in the world.*

Politeness can prevent quarrels

⁵³ Tell My servants: "Always be courteous *when speaking",* or else Satan will stir disagreement among you; surely Satan is the sworn enemy of humanity. ⁵⁴ Your Lord knows you best; He will be kind to you or punish you if He wants. *Anyway,* We haven't sent you as a guardian over them. ⁵⁵ Your Lord knows who is in the Heavens and the Earth. We favoured some prophets over others, and We gave blessed Dawud the book *of Psalms.*

ᵃ This 'screen' is a consequence of a person's persistence not to listen, be stubborn and break the natural bond with the Creator. For further explanation see; 2:7, 2:27, 6:25, and 14:4.

وَّاٰتَيۡنَا دَاوٗدَ زَبُوۡرًا ۟ قُلِ ادۡعُوا الَّذِيۡنَ زَعَمۡتُمۡ مِّنۡ
دُوۡنِهٖ فَلَا يَمۡلِكُوۡنَ كَشۡفَ الضُّرِّ عَنۡكُمۡ وَلَا تَحۡوِيۡلًا ۞
اُولٰٓئِكَ الَّذِيۡنَ يَدۡعُوۡنَ يَبۡتَغُوۡنَ اِلٰى رَبِّهِمُ
الۡوَسِيۡلَةَ اَيُّهُمۡ اَقۡرَبُ وَيَرۡجُوۡنَ رَحۡمَتَهٗ وَيَخَافُوۡنَ
عَذَابَهٗ ؕ اِنَّ عَذَابَ رَبِّكَ كَانَ مَحۡذُوۡرًا ۞ وَاِنۡ مِّنۡ
قَرۡيَةٍ اِلَّا نَحۡنُ مُهۡلِكُوۡهَا قَبۡلَ يَوۡمِ الۡقِيٰمَةِ اَوۡ مُعَذِّبُوۡهَا
عَذَابًا شَدِيۡدًا ؕ كَانَ ذٰلِكَ فِى الۡكِتٰبِ مَسۡطُوۡرًا ۞ وَمَا
مَنَعَنَاۤ اَنۡ نُّرۡسِلَ بِالۡاٰيٰتِ اِلَّاۤ اَنۡ كَذَّبَ بِهَا الۡاَوَّلُوۡنَ ؕ
وَاٰتَيۡنَا ثَمُوۡدَ النَّاقَةَ مُبۡصِرَةً فَظَلَمُوۡا بِهَا ؕ وَمَا نُرۡسِلُ
بِالۡاٰيٰتِ اِلَّا تَخۡوِيۡفًا ۞ وَاِذۡ قُلۡنَا لَكَ اِنَّ رَبَّكَ اَحَاطَ
بِالنَّاسِ ؕ وَمَا جَعَلۡنَا الرُّءۡيَا الَّتِىۡۤ اَرَيۡنٰكَ اِلَّا فِتۡنَةً
لِّلنَّاسِ وَالشَّجَرَةَ الۡمَلۡعُوۡنَةَ فِى الۡقُرۡاٰنِ ؕ وَنُخَوِّفُهُمۡ ۙ
فَمَا يَزِيۡدُهُمۡ اِلَّا طُغۡيَانًا كَبِيۡرًا ۞ وَاِذۡ قُلۡنَا لِلۡمَلٰٓئِكَةِ
اسۡجُدُوۡا لِاٰدَمَ فَسَجَدُوۡۤا اِلَّاۤ اِبۡلِيۡسَ ؕ قَالَ ءَاَسۡجُدُ
لِمَنۡ خَلَقۡتَ طِيۡنًا ۟ قَالَ اَرَءَيۡتَكَ هٰذَا الَّذِىۡ كَرَّمۡتَ
عَلَيَّ ۫ لَئِنۡ اَخَّرۡتَنِ اِلٰى يَوۡمِ الۡقِيٰمَةِ لَاَحۡتَنِكَنَّ
ذُرِّيَّتَهٗۤ اِلَّا قَلِيۡلًا ۞ قَالَ اذۡهَبۡ فَمَنۡ تَبِعَكَ مِنۡهُمۡ
فَاِنَّ جَهَنَّمَ جَزَآؤُكُمۡ جَزَآءً مَّوۡفُوۡرًا ۞ وَاسۡتَفۡزِزۡ مَنِ
اسۡتَطَعۡتَ مِنۡهُمۡ بِصَوۡتِكَ وَاَجۡلِبۡ عَلَيۡهِمۡ بِخَيۡلِكَ وَ
رَجِلِكَ وَشَارِكۡهُمۡ فِى الۡاَمۡوَالِ وَالۡاَوۡلَادِ وَعِدۡهُمۡ ؕ وَمَا

What are Satan's tactics to mislead people? He uses pleasures to lure.

ع
٨

Miracles may come as warnings

⁵⁶ Say: "Call those you think are your gods besides Him; they cannot remove harm from you or turn it away." ⁵⁷ Those who they call are themselves looking for the means to be nearer to Him; they long for His kindness and dread His punishment. Your Lord's punishment is dreadful. ⁵⁸ Any town We destroy before Judgement Day or punish sternly is recorded in the *eternal* document. ⁵⁹ What stopped Us from sending miracles is people's denial in the past, *for example,* We gave Thamud *the miracle* of the she-camel; it was self-evident but they hamstrung her. So, We now send miracles only as a warning. ⁶⁰ And remember when We said to you, "Your Lord knows all about the people."ᵃ The dream We showed you and the cursed tree mentioned in the Quran were for testing people.ᵇ We warned them, but that made them bolder in their disobedience.

Satan's tactics to mislead humanity

⁶¹ Remember, We told the angels, "Prostrate before Adam!" They all prostrated, except Satan. He said, "Why should I prostrate to one You created from clay?" ⁶² He continued, "Do you see this *human* being who You have honoured over me, if You give me time till Judgement Day then I will have *all* his children under my control, except a few. ⁶³ Allah said, "Go away! Anyone who follows you will be punished in Hell, a fitting reward." ⁶⁴ Persuade them with your *enchanting* voice; try winning them over with all the might you can musterᶜ; be a shareholder in their wealth and children and make promises to them; Satan's promises are mere deceptions.

ᵃ "Encompasses all people" means surrounds, and knows them well to protect you from their harm.

ᵇ The 'dream' here according to commentators refers to the Messenger's ﷺ Ascension mentioned in the opening verse of the Surat. This miracle became a test of their faith; would they believe that he travelled through space and beyond to be in Divine presence.

ᶜ Literally "your soldiers on horseback and on foot".

يَعِدُهُمُ الشَّيْطٰنُ اِلَّا غُرُوْرًا ۞ اِنَّ عِبَادِیْ لَيْسَ لَكَ

عَلَيْهِمْ سُلْطٰنٌ ط وَكَفٰى بِرَبِّكَ وَكِيْلًا ۞ رَبُّكُمُ الَّذِیْ یُزْجِیْ

لَكُمُ الْفُلْكَ فِی الْبَحْرِ لِتَبْتَغُوْا مِنْ فَضْلِهٖ ط اِنَّهٗ كَانَ

بِكُمْ رَحِيْمًا ۞ وَاِذَا مَسَّكُمُ الضُّرُّ فِی الْبَحْرِ ضَلَّ مَنْ

تَدْعُوْنَ اِلَّآ اِيَّاهُ ۚ فَلَمَّا نَجّٰكُمْ اِلَى الْبَرِّ اَعْرَضْتُمْ ط

وَكَانَ الْاِنْسَانُ كَفُوْرًا ۞ اَفَاَمِنْتُمْ اَنْ يَّخْسِفَ بِكُمْ

جَانِبَ الْبَرِّ اَوْ يُرْسِلَ عَلَيْكُمْ حَاصِبًا ثُمَّ لَا تَجِدُوْا لَكُمْ

وَكِيْلًا ۞ اَمْ اَمِنْتُمْ اَنْ یُّعِيْدَكُمْ فِيْهِ تَارَةً اُخْرٰی

فَيُرْسِلَ عَلَيْكُمْ قَاصِفًا مِّنَ الرِّيْحِ فَيُغْرِقَكُمْ بِمَا كَفَرْتُمْ

ثُمَّ لَا تَجِدُوْا لَكُمْ عَلَيْنَا بِهٖ تَبِيْعًا ۞ وَلَقَدْ كَرَّمْنَا

بَنِیْٓ اٰدَمَ وَحَمَلْنٰهُمْ فِی الْبَرِّ وَالْبَحْرِ وَرَزَقْنٰهُمْ مِّنَ

الطَّيِّبٰتِ وَفَضَّلْنٰهُمْ عَلٰى كَثِيْرٍ مِّمَّنْ خَلَقْنَا تَفْضِيْلًا ۞

یَوْمَ نَدْعُوْا كُلَّ اُنَاسٍ بِاِمَامِهِمْ ۚ فَمَنْ اُوْتِیَ كِتٰبَهٗ

بِيَمِيْنِهٖ فَاُولٰٓئِكَ یَقْرَءُوْنَ كِتٰبَهُمْ وَلَا یُظْلَمُوْنَ

فَتِيْلًا ۞ وَمَنْ كَانَ فِیْ هٰذِهٖٓ اَعْمٰی فَهُوَ فِی الْاٰخِرَةِ

اَعْمٰی وَاَضَلُّ سَبِيْلًا ۞ وَاِنْ كَادُوْا لَيَفْتِنُوْنَكَ عَنِ

الَّذِیْٓ اَوْحَيْنَآ اِلَيْكَ لِتَفْتَرِیَ عَلَيْنَا غَيْرَهٗ ۟ وَاِذًا

لَّاتَّخَذُوْكَ خَلِيْلًا ۞ وَلَوْلَآ اَنْ ثَبَّتْنٰكَ لَقَدْ كِدْتَّ

تَرْكَنُ اِلَيْهِمْ شَيْئًا قَلِيْلًا ۞ اِذًا لَّاَذَقْنٰكَ ضِعْفَ

الْحَيٰوةِ وَضِعْفَ الْمَمَاتِ ثُمَّ لَا تَجِدُ لَكَ عَلَيْنَا نَصِيْرًا ۞

Why did Allah confer an honour on humanity? Do we appreciate it? Do we fulfil its conditions?

ع

⁶⁵*But* you will have no power and influence over My servants; Your Lord is their Guardian.

A false sense of security

⁶⁶Your Lord makes the ships sail across the sea for you to seek His bounty; He is most Kind to you. ⁶⁷When you are distressed at sea, those you worship besides Allah desert you, but He brings you safely to the land yet you turn away. Man, is unthankful. ⁶⁸Are you sure that He won't sink you in the ground or send a sandstorm? You won't find any protector. ⁶⁹Are you sure when you return to the sea He will not send a violent storm to drown you for your unthankfulness? You will not find any helper in opposition to Us.

The dignity of humanity

⁷⁰We honoured the children of Adam and enabled them to travel across land and sea, to seek healthy sustenance and favoured them above all Our creation. ⁷¹The Day We call the communities along with their leaders, some will be given their book in the right hand, and will *happily* read it; they will not be treated unjustly in the least.[a] ⁷²The blind in this world will also be blind in the Hereafter, and far away from the path.

Tempting the Prophet ﷺ unsuccessfully

⁷³ *Messenger,* they tempt you away from Our revelation so you might produce something different, then they would befriend you. ⁷⁴Had We not made you steadfast then you might have inclined a little bit towards them. ⁷⁵In that case We would have made you taste double *punishment in* this life and after death; moreover, you will not find a helper against Us. [b]

---

[a] *Fatelan* is a cord-like fibre in the groove of a date stone, a metaphor for a tiny amount.
[b] It would be impossible for the Messenger of Allah ﷺ to disobey. But the verse is making a bigger point; rejection of a fundamental truth is unforgivable. (Asad)

وَ اِنْ كَادُوْا لَيَسْتَفِزُّوْنَكَ مِنَ الْاَرْضِ لِيُخْرِجُوْكَ

مِنْهَا وَ اِذًا لَّا يَلْبَثُوْنَ خِلٰفَكَ اِلَّا قَلِيْلًا ۞ سُنَّةَ

مَنْ قَدْ اَرْسَلْنَا قَبْلَكَ مِنْ رُّسُلِنَا وَ لَا تَجِدُ لِسُنَّتِنَا

تَحْوِيْلًا ۞ اَقِمِ الصَّلٰوةَ لِدُلُوْكِ الشَّمْسِ اِلٰى غَسَقِ

الَّيْلِ وَ قُرْاٰنَ الْفَجْرِ اِنَّ قُرْاٰنَ الْفَجْرِ كَانَ مَشْهُوْدًا ۞

وَ مِنَ الَّيْلِ فَتَهَجَّدْ بِهٖ نَافِلَةً لَّكَ عَسٰى اَنْ يَّبْعَثَكَ

رَبُّكَ مَقَامًا مَّحْمُوْدًا ۞ وَ قُلْ رَّبِّ اَدْخِلْنِيْ مُدْخَلَ

صِدْقٍ وَّ اَخْرِجْنِيْ مُخْرَجَ صِدْقٍ وَّ اجْعَلْ لِّيْ مِنْ

لَّدُنْكَ سُلْطٰنًا نَّصِيْرًا ۞ وَ قُلْ جَآءَ الْحَقُّ وَ زَهَقَ

The Quran distinguishes between Truth and falsehood. How well do you recognise Truth?

الْبَاطِلُ اِنَّ الْبَاطِلَ كَانَ زَهُوْقًا ۞ وَ نُنَزِّلُ مِنَ

الْقُرْاٰنِ مَا هُوَ شِفَآءٌ وَّ رَحْمَةٌ لِّلْمُؤْمِنِيْنَ وَ لَا يَزِيْدُ

الظّٰلِمِيْنَ اِلَّا خَسَارًا ۞ وَ اِذَآ اَنْعَمْنَا عَلَى الْاِنْسَانِ

اَعْرَضَ وَ نَاٰ بِجَانِبِهٖ وَ اِذَا مَسَّهُ الشَّرُّ كَانَ يَـُٔوْسًا ۞

قُلْ كُلٌّ يَّعْمَلُ عَلٰى شَاكِلَتِهٖ فَرَبُّكُمْ اَعْلَمُ بِمَنْ هُوَ

اَهْدٰى سَبِيْلًا ۞ وَ يَسْـَٔلُوْنَكَ عَنِ الرُّوْحِ قُلِ الرُّوْحُ

مِنْ اَمْرِ رَبِّيْ وَ مَآ اُوْتِيْتُمْ مِّنَ الْعِلْمِ اِلَّا قَلِيْلًا ۞

وَ لَئِنْ شِئْنَا لَنَذْهَبَنَّ بِالَّذِيْ اَوْحَيْنَا اِلَيْكَ ثُمَّ

لَا تَجِدُ لَكَ بِهٖ عَلَيْنَا وَكِيْلًا ۞ اِلَّا رَحْمَةً مِّنْ

رَبِّكَ اِنَّ فَضْلَهٗ كَانَ عَلَيْكَ كَبِيْرًا ۞ قُلْ لَّئِنِ

اجْتَمَعَتِ الْاِنْسُ وَ الْجِنُّ عَلٰى اَنْ يَّاْتُوْا بِمِثْلِ هٰذَا

ع
۹

⁷⁶ They tried hard to scare you, so you would leave the city, they too wouldn't have stayed there for long either. ⁷⁷ Such was our practice with messengers We sent before you. You will find no change in our practice.

Prayers during day and night

⁷⁸ Pray regularly from midday ᵃ until the darkness of the night, and the Morning Prayer, since the recitation of the Quran in the Morning Prayer is witnessed *by the Angels.* ⁷⁹ At night, wake up to offer a voluntary prayer that is *compulsory* only for you.ᵇ Soon your Lord will raise you to a glorious station of praise.ᶜ ⁸⁰ Say: "My Lord, wherever you take me, let me enter truthfully and let me leave truthfully, and give me power and authority from Yourself."

The Majestic Quran: truth, healing and kindness

⁸¹ Say: "The truth has come and falsehood vanished; falsehood is bound to vanish." ⁸² We revealed the Quran it is a healing and benefits the believers, but for the disbelievers it adds to their loss. ⁸³ Often, when We give gifts to people, they turn away unthankfully, remain indifferent, and despair in hard times. ⁸⁴ Say: "Everyone behaves according to their character,"ᵈ Your Lord knows best who follows the best-guided path.

The mystery of the human soul

⁸⁵ They ask you about the soul; say: "The soul is my Lord's command, and you have been given little knowledge about it." ⁸⁶ If We wanted, We could have withdrawn what We have revealed to you. Then you would not find an advocate against Us, ⁸⁷ except for your Lord's kindness; He has indeed been very gracious to you. ⁸⁸ Say: "If all humanity and jinn got together to bring a book like this Quran, they wouldn't be able to bring it, no matter how much they helped each other."

ᵃ *Daluq ashams* also means sunset. Here it means midday, so from midday to darkness of night includes Zuhr, Asr, Maghrib and Isha prayers.

ᵇ *Tahajjud,* or night prayer, is a voluntary prayer, but compulsory for the Messenger ﷺ.

ᶜ *Maqaman Mahmoodan* literally means a glorious station of praise. The Prophet ﷺ explained it to be "the place from where I will intercede for my people."

ᵈ *Shakilat* means disposition, temperament and character.

القُرْاٰنَ لَا يَأْتُوْنَ بِمِثْلِهٖ وَلَوْ كَانَ بَعْضُهُمْ لِبَعْضٍ

ظَهِيْرًا ۸۸ وَلَقَدْ صَرَّفْنَا لِلنَّاسِ فِىْ هٰذَا الْقُرْاٰنِ

مِنْ كُلِّ مَثَلٍ ۙ فَأَبٰٓى اَكْثَرُ النَّاسِ اِلَّا كُفُوْرًا ۸۹

وَقَالُوْا لَنْ نُّؤْمِنَ لَكَ حَتّٰى تَفْجُرَ لَنَا مِنَ الْاَرْضِ

يَنْبُوْعًا ۹۰ اَوْ تَكُوْنَ لَكَ جَنَّةٌ مِّنْ نَّخِيْلٍ وَّعِنَبٍ

فَتُفَجِّرَ الْاَنْهٰرَ خِلٰلَهَا تَفْجِيْرًا ۹۱ اَوْ تُسْقِطَ السَّمَآءَ

كَمَا زَعَمْتَ عَلَيْنَا كِسَفًا اَوْ تَأْتِىَ بِاللّٰهِ وَالْمَلٰٓئِكَةِ

قَبِيْلًا ۹۲ اَوْ يَكُوْنَ لَكَ بَيْتٌ مِّنْ زُخْرُفٍ اَوْ تَرْقٰى

فِى السَّمَآءِ ؕ وَلَنْ نُّؤْمِنَ لِرُقِيِّكَ حَتّٰى تُنَزِّلَ عَلَيْنَا

كِتٰبًا نَّقْرَؤُهٗ ؕ قُلْ سُبْحَانَ رَبِّىْ هَلْ كُنْتُ اِلَّا بَشَرًا

رَّسُوْلًا ۹۳ وَمَا مَنَعَ النَّاسَ اَنْ يُّؤْمِنُوْٓا اِذْ جَآءَهُمُ

الْهُدٰٓى اِلَّآ اَنْ قَالُوْٓا اَبَعَثَ اللّٰهُ بَشَرًا رَّسُوْلًا ۹۴ قُلْ

لَّوْ كَانَ فِى الْاَرْضِ مَلٰٓئِكَةٌ يَّمْشُوْنَ مُطْمَئِنِّيْنَ لَنَزَّلْنَا

عَلَيْهِمْ مِّنَ السَّمَآءِ مَلَكًا رَّسُوْلًا ۹۵ قُلْ كَفٰى بِاللّٰهِ

شَهِيْدًۢا بَيْنِىْ وَبَيْنَكُمْ ؕ اِنَّهٗ كَانَ بِعِبَادِهٖ خَبِيْرًۢا

بَصِيْرًا ۹۶ وَمَنْ يَّهْدِ اللّٰهُ فَهُوَ الْمُهْتَدِ ۚ وَمَنْ يُّضْلِلْ

فَلَنْ تَجِدَ لَهُمْ اَوْلِيَآءَ مِنْ دُوْنِهٖ ؕ وَنَحْشُرُهُمْ يَوْمَ

الْقِيٰمَةِ عَلٰى وُجُوْهِهِمْ عُمْيًا وَّبُكْمًا وَّصُمًّا ؕ مَأْوٰىهُمْ

جَهَنَّمُ ؕ كُلَّمَا خَبَتْ زِدْنٰهُمْ سَعِيْرًا ۹۷ ذٰلِكَ جَزَآؤُهُمْ

بِاَنَّهُمْ كَفَرُوْا بِاٰيٰتِنَا وَقَالُوْٓا ءَاِذَا كُنَّا عِظَامًا وَّرُفَاتًا

⁸⁹ In this Quran We explained every kind of example for people's *benefit,* but most refuse to acknowledge *the truth.*

Disbelievers' unreasonable demands

⁹⁰ They said, "We won't believe you until you bring for us a gushing spring from the Earth. ⁹¹ Or until you have a garden of date trees and grapes with a river flowing through it, ⁹² or *you* cause a piece of the sky to fall on us as you claim, or bring Allah and the angels before us, ⁹³ or have a house decorated with gold, or bring a ladder that goes up to the sky. No, we will not believe your *miracle of* Ascension; *we will believe* if you can bring a book we can read." Say: "Glory to My Lord, I am only a human being, a messenger."

Humanity needs human messengers

⁹⁴ An argument that stops some people from accepting the guidance is, "How could Allah have sent a messenger who is a mortal?" ⁹⁵ Say: "If angels walked and lived on Earth then *naturally* We would have sent from the Heavens a messenger who was an angel."ᵃ ⁹⁶ Say: "Allah is sufficient witness for me and you." He is aware and sees His servants. ⁹⁷ The one who Allah guides is guided, and the one who He lets go astray, you won't find a protector for him beside Allah. We will gather them on Judgement Day with their faces down, blind, dumb and deaf. Hell, will be their dwelling; when the flames die down We will intensify the blazing flames once again. ⁹⁸ That will be *their* reward, they rejected Our signs and said, "When we become bones and dust will we be resurrected as a brand-new creation?"

Allah's generosity and human miserliness

⁹⁹ Do they not realise Allah created the Heavens and the Earth, can't he produce the likes of them *again*? He has fixed their lifespan. The wrongdoers refuse everything except disbelief. ¹⁰⁰ Say: "If you controlled the treasures of My Lord's kindness, you would hold them tightly for fear of spending them. People are tight-fisted, miserly."

ᵃ   For their guidance. Since humans live on Earth, We sent human messengers.

The effectiveness, eloquence and energy of the Majestic Quran will only be experienced by those who believe its Lord.

ءَاِنَّا لَمَبْعُوْثُوْنَ خَلْقًا جَدِيْدًا ۹۸ اَوَلَمْ يَرَوْا اَنَّ اللهَ الَّذِیْ خَلَقَ السَّمٰوٰتِ وَالْاَرْضَ قَادِرٌ عَلٰۤى اَنْ يَّخْلُقَ مِثْلَهُمْ وَجَعَلَ لَهُمْ اَجَلًا لَّا رَيْبَ فِيْهِ ۚ فَاَبَى الظّٰلِمُوْنَ اِلَّا كُفُوْرًا ۹۹ قُلْ لَّوْ اَنْتُمْ تَمْلِكُوْنَ خَزَآئِنَ رَحْمَةِ رَبِّیْۤ اِذًا لَّاَمْسَكْتُمْ خَشْيَةَ الْاِنْفَاقِ ۚ وَكَانَ الْاِنْسَانُ قَتُوْرًا ۱۰۰ وَلَقَدْ اٰتَيْنَا مُوْسٰى تِسْعَ اٰيٰتٍۭ بَيِّنٰتٍ فَسْئَلْ بَنِیْۤ اِسْرَآئِیْلَ اِذْ جَآءَهُمْ فَقَالَ لَهٗ فِرْعَوْنُ اِنِّیْ لَاَظُنُّكَ يٰمُوْسٰى مَسْحُوْرًا ۱۰۱ قَالَ لَقَدْ عَلِمْتَ مَاۤ اَنْزَلَ هٰؤُلَآءِ اِلَّا رَبُّ السَّمٰوٰتِ وَالْاَرْضِ بَصَآئِرَ ۚ وَاِنِّیْ لَاَظُنُّكَ يٰفِرْعَوْنُ مَثْبُوْرًا ۱۰۲ فَاَرَادَ اَنْ يَّسْتَفِزَّهُمْ مِّنَ الْاَرْضِ فَاَغْرَقْنٰهُ وَمَنْ مَّعَهٗ جَمِيْعًا ۱۰۳ وَّقُلْنَا مِنْۢ بَعْدِهٖ لِبَنِیْۤ اِسْرَآئِیْلَ اسْكُنُوا الْاَرْضَ فَاِذَا جَآءَ وَعْدُ الْاٰخِرَةِ جِئْنَا بِكُمْ لَفِيْفًا ۱۰۴ وَبِالْحَقِّ اَنْزَلْنٰهُ وَبِالْحَقِّ نَزَلَ ۚ وَمَاۤ اَرْسَلْنٰكَ اِلَّا مُبَشِّرًا وَّنَذِيْرًا ۱۰۵ وَقُرْاٰنًا فَرَقْنٰهُ لِتَقْرَاَهٗ عَلَى النَّاسِ عَلٰى مُكْثٍ وَّنَزَّلْنٰهُ تَنْزِيْلًا ۱۰۶ قُلْ اٰمِنُوْا بِهٖۤ اَوْ لَا تُؤْمِنُوْا ۗ اِنَّ الَّذِيْنَ اُوْتُوا الْعِلْمَ مِنْ قَبْلِهٖۤ اِذَا يُتْلٰى عَلَيْهِمْ يَخِرُّوْنَ لِلْاَذْقَانِ سُجَّدًا ۱۰۷ وَّيَقُوْلُوْنَ سُبْحٰنَ رَبِّنَاۤ اِنْ كَانَ وَعْدُ رَبِّنَا لَمَفْعُوْلًا ۱۰۸ وَيَخِرُّوْنَ لِلْاَذْقَانِ يَبْكُوْنَ وَيَزِيْدُهُمْ خُشُوْعًا ۱۰۹ قُلِ ادْعُوا اللهَ اَوِ ادْعُوا الرَّحْمٰنَ ۗ اَيًّا مَّا تَدْعُوْا فَلَهُ الْاَسْمَآءُ الْحُسْنٰى ۚ

Musa's nine miracles

[101] We gave Musa nine miracles; ask the Israelites, when he came to them, the Pharaoh said, "Musa, I believe you're under a spell." [102] Musa said, "You know, no one except the Lord of the Heavens and the Earth could have sent these clear signs. Pharaoh! I believe you're doomed." [103] The Pharaoh wanted to wipe them off from the land *of* Egypt, so We drowned him and those with him. [104] Afterwards, We told the Israelites: "Live in the land, and when the promise of the Hereafter comes to pass, We will bring you all together as a mixed crowd."[a]

The mystical nature of Quranic revelation

[105] We revealed the Quran with truth, so it came down with truth. We sent you to proclaim good news and to warn. [106] *This is* a reading, revealed in separate sections so that you may slowly read it to the people; We revealed it gradually *over a period.* [107] Say: "*It is up to you* to believe it or not. Those who were given knowledge before this *certainly acknowledge it* when it is read to them; they fall on their faces in prostration." [108] Say: "Glory to Our Lord; Our Lord's promise is fulfilled." [109] They fall on their faces in prostration, weeping as their humility grows.

Allah's Beautiful Names

[110] Say: "Call Allah or Rahman by whichever names you call, He has most beautiful names." So, when you pray don't call *Him* too loudly or too quietly; instead seek a middle way. [111] Say: "All Praises are for Allah. He has no son and no partner in His Kingdom; He needs no such petty protectors – to proclaim His absolute greatness."

---

a   *Lafeefan* refers to a human crowd that is made up of all kinds of people from different races, groups, cultures and civilisations, and economic backgrounds: a reflection of human diversity. The Quran is making it clear that the Israelites will be part of this mixed crowd; they will have no special privilege on Judgement Day.

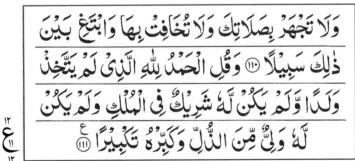

18. Surat Al-Kahf

The Cave

This late Makkan surat was revealed between the eighth and tenth year of the Prophet's ﷺ mission. Its central theme is the contrasting nature of the spiritual and the material world: One permanent, the other temporary, one mysterious the other manifest. Humanity is tempted by the attractions of the material world, but fails to realise the importance of spiritual life. In this surat, these contrasts are illustrated by five moving stories, each one representing a feature of spiritual and material life. Each story is followed by a terse and helpful commentary, which instils the love, majesty and grandeur of Allah. The five stories are:

- The story of the sleepers in the cave is about young men of faith, serious believers, unwilling to compromise their faith. They confronted society's evil, and abandoned their families to save their faith from an oppressive ruler. The story illustrates Allah's power of resurrection, bringing the dead to life.
- The story of the poor and the rich man reveals the nature of a greedy, self-centred and insensitive rich man who is ready to pick a fight.
- The Story of Adam ﷺ and Satan provides a clue to understanding the cause of spiritual sickness.
- The story of Musa ﷺ and Khidr, the sage who explains serendipity, "always making discoveries, by accidents and sagacity, of things which they were not in quest of". The paradox of outward actions and inner meanings. What appears to be harmful turns out to be beneficial, and a loss becomes a gain. The lesson is that we should accept Allah's will, since His plan is mysterious and full of wisdom.
- The story of Zulqarnayn, the mighty ruler who challenges the view that the world must be abandoned for spiritual growth. It shows that's not necessary to gain Paradise. What is needed is Allah-consciousness.

The Connection Between the Five Stories

The underlying theme in these stories, is the temptations individual's face:
- Faith: the young men feared the Emperor would forcefully convert them. Our faith is always being challenged by society. How well we face this determines its strength. The company of righteous people can help to develop a strong faith that will resist the wrongs of society.

- Wealth: we are tempted by wealth, we love it and when wealth opposes religious duties we often prefer wealth, we are unable to sacrifice it and unable to spend it for others good. The solution; avoid attachment to the world.
- Temptations of Satan: He tempted Adam and Eve. He tempts us all the time. How can we protect ourselves against these temptations?
- Knowledge, competence and skills, often lead to arrogant behaviour. Resistance against this is found in humility: in recognising one's weaknesses and frailties. The example of the humility of Musa 🕊 is an excellent model for us.
- Power can corrupt and lead people to commit atrocities and injustices. Protection against corruptive power can be found in being sincere and genuine in one's desire to serve others.

In each story, the conflict between good and evil is clear. The five types of trials are like a thread binding these stories together. The surat also features much movement, plodding from place to place: the sleepers of the Cave climb a mountain; the rich man and poor man walk to an orchard; Musa travels by foot and boat, and the adventures of Zulqarnayn wandering from East to West with his army. Hint: goodness is promised in movement and searching for Allah's gifts.

بِسْمِ اللّٰهِ الرَّحْمٰنِ الرَّحِيْمِ

اَلْحَمْدُ لِلّٰهِ الَّذِىٓ اَنْزَلَ عَلٰى عَبْدِهِ الْكِتٰبَ وَلَمْ يَجْعَلْ لَّهٗ عِوَجًا ۟ؕ قَيِّمًا لِّيُنْذِرَ بَأْسًا شَدِيْدًا مِّنْ لَّدُنْهُ وَيُبَشِّرَ الْمُؤْمِنِيْنَ الَّذِيْنَ يَعْمَلُوْنَ الصّٰلِحٰتِ اَنَّ لَهُمْ اَجْرًا حَسَنًا ۟ۙ مَّاكِثِيْنَ فِيْهِ اَبَدًا ۟ۙ وَّ يُنْذِرَ الَّذِيْنَ قَالُوا اتَّخَذَ اللّٰهُ وَلَدًا ۟ۗ مَا لَهُمْ بِهٖ مِنْ عِلْمٍ وَّلَا لِاٰبَآئِهِمْ ؕ كَبُرَتْ كَلِمَةً تَخْرُجُ مِنْ اَفْوَاهِهِمْ ؕ اِنْ يَّقُوْلُوْنَ اِلَّا كَذِبًا ۟ فَلَعَلَّكَ بَاخِعٌ نَّفْسَكَ عَلٰٓى اٰثَارِهِمْ اِنْ لَّمْ يُؤْمِنُوْا بِهٰذَا الْحَدِيْثِ اَسَفًا ۟ اِنَّا جَعَلْنَا مَا عَلَى الْاَرْضِ زِيْنَةً لَّهَا لِنَبْلُوَهُمْ اَيُّهُمْ اَحْسَنُ عَمَلًا ۟ وَاِنَّا لَجٰعِلُوْنَ مَا عَلَيْهَا صَعِيْدًا جُرُزًا ۟ؕ اَمْ حَسِبْتَ اَنَّ اَصْحٰبَ الْكَهْفِ وَالرَّقِيْمِ ۟ۙ كَانُوْا مِنْ اٰيٰتِنَا عَجَبًا ۟ اِذْ اَوَى الْفِتْيَةُ اِلَى الْكَهْفِ فَقَالُوْا رَبَّنَآ اٰتِنَا مِنْ لَّدُنْكَ رَحْمَةً وَّهَيِّئْ لَنَا مِنْ اَمْرِنَا رَشَدًا ۟ فَضَرَبْنَا عَلٰٓى اٰذَانِهِمْ فِى الْكَهْفِ سِنِيْنَ عَدَدًا ۟ۙ ثُمَّ بَعَثْنٰهُمْ لِنَعْلَمَ اَىُّ الْحِزْبَيْنِ اَحْصٰى لِمَا لَبِثُوْٓا اَمَدًا ۟ نَحْنُ نَقُصُّ عَلَيْكَ نَبَاَهُمْ بِالْحَقِّ ؕ اِنَّهُمْ فِتْيَةٌ اٰمَنُوْا بِرَبِّهِمْ وَزِدْنٰهُمْ هُدًى ۟ۖ وَّرَبَطْنَا

The Quran lays out the reality. So, keep spreading the guidance of the Majestic Quran.

In the name of Allah, the Kind, the Caring.

The Majestic Quran is a guidance

¹All praises are for Allah, He who sent down the Book to his servant. It does not bend the truth, ²but is factual,ᵃ so He gives warning of severe punishment and good news to the believers who do righteous deeds, they will have Paradise, ³where they will stay forever. ⁴You must warn those who said Allah has taken a child;ᵇ ⁵neither they nor their forefathers had any knowledge. It is an outrageous insult they spout with their mouths; they are lying. ⁶So will you worry yourself to death over their actions, if they don't believe in this message? ⁷We've made attractive what is on Earth, to test who is best in deeds. ⁸Eventually, We will turn the Earth into a barren land.

The story of the Sleepers of the Cave

⁹*Messenger*, did you know the People of the Cave and Al-Raqimᶜ were our amazing signs? ¹⁰The young men took refuge in the cave and prayed: "Our Lord be kind to us and guide us during our test." ¹¹While they were inside the cave for many years We blocked their ears, ¹²then awakened them, to see which of the two groups was better in assessing the length of their stay.

The Sleepers of the Cave were men of strong faith

¹³We will tell you their story exactly as it happened: they were young men who had faith in their Lord; We increased them in guidance,

---

ᵃ *Qayyiman* literally means "straight", and implies the Quran is factual, as it presents reality.

ᵇ Literally a son, since the people of Makkah believed in angels as daughters of Allah. Therefore, I have adopted this context-sensitive meaning.

ᶜ Al-Raqim refers to either the name of the town, or the valley where the cave was located. Others think it means "the written", referring to the brass tablet with the names inscribed (Zia-ul-Quran).

عَلٰى قُلُوْبِهِمْ اِذْ قَامُوْا فَقَالُوْا رَبُّنَا رَبُّ السَّمٰوٰتِ

وَالْاَرْضِ لَنْ نَّدْعُوَا۟ مِنْ دُوْنِهٖۤ اِلٰهًا لَّقَدْ قُلْنَاۤ اِذًا

شَطَطًا ۝ هٰۤؤُلَآءِ قَوْمُنَا اتَّخَذُوْا مِنْ دُوْنِهٖۤ اٰلِهَةً ؕ

لَوْلَا يَاْتُوْنَ عَلَيْهِمْ بِسُلْطٰنٍۭ بَيِّنٍ ؕ فَمَنْ اَظْلَمُ

مِمَّنِ افْتَرٰى عَلَى اللّٰهِ كَذِبًا ۝ وَاِذِ اعْتَزَلْتُمُوْهُمْ

وَمَا يَعْبُدُوْنَ اِلَّا اللّٰهَ فَاْوٗۤا اِلَى الْكَهْفِ يَنْشُرْ

لَكُمْ رَبُّكُمْ مِّنْ رَّحْمَتِهٖ وَيُهَيِّئْ لَكُمْ مِّنْ اَمْرِكُمْ

مِّرْفَقًا ۝ وَتَرَى الشَّمْسَ اِذَا طَلَعَتْ تَّزٰوَرُ عَنْ

كَهْفِهِمْ ذَاتَ الْيَمِيْنِ وَاِذَا غَرَبَتْ تَّقْرِضُهُمْ

ذَاتَ الشِّمَالِ وَهُمْ فِىْ فَجْوَةٍ مِّنْهُ ؕ ذٰلِكَ مِنْ

اٰيٰتِ اللّٰهِ ؕ مَنْ يَّهْدِ اللّٰهُ فَهُوَ الْمُهْتَدِ ۚ وَمَنْ يُّضْلِلْ

فَلَنْ تَجِدَ لَهٗ وَلِيًّا مُّرْشِدًا ۝ وَتَحْسَبُهُمْ اَيْقَاظًا

وَّهُمْ رُقُوْدٌ ۖ وَّنُقَلِّبُهُمْ ذَاتَ الْيَمِيْنِ وَ ذَاتَ

الشِّمَالِ ۖ وَكَلْبُهُمْ بَاسِطٌ ذِرَاعَيْهِ بِالْوَصِيْدِ ؕ لَوِ

اطَّلَعْتَ عَلَيْهِمْ لَوَلَّيْتَ مِنْهُمْ فِرَارًا وَّلَمُلِئْتَ مِنْهُمْ

رُعْبًا ۝ وَكَذٰلِكَ بَعَثْنٰهُمْ لِيَتَسَآءَلُوْا بَيْنَهُمْ ؕ قَالَ

قَآئِلٌ مِّنْهُمْ كَمْ لَبِثْتُمْ ؕ قَالُوْا لَبِثْنَا يَوْمًا اَوْ بَعْضَ

يَوْمٍ ؕ قَالُوْا رَبُّكُمْ اَعْلَمُ بِمَا لَبِثْتُمْ ؕ فَابْعَثُوْۤا اَحَدَكُمْ

بِوَرِقِكُمْ هٰذِهٖۤ اِلَى الْمَدِيْنَةِ فَلْيَنْظُرْ اَيُّهَاۤ اَزْكٰى

طَعَامًا فَلْيَاْتِكُمْ بِرِزْقٍ مِّنْهُ وَلْيَتَلَطَّفْ وَلَا

For spiritual growth,
physical separation from
evil people becomes a
necessity.

¹⁴ and improved self-confidence. They stood up boldly *before their people* and proclaimed: "Our Lord is the Lord of the Heavens and the Earth. Never will we worship gods beside Him; that would be an outrageous lie. ¹⁵ Our people have taken gods beside Him, without any clear evidence. Can anyone be more wrong than the one who makes up lies about Allah?" ¹⁶ It was said, "You have now separated yourselves from those people and what they worship beside Allah, so take refuge in the cave and your Lord will be kind to you, He will prepare suitable arrangements for you."

The miraculous deep sleep

¹⁷ *Messenger*, while they laid in the clear opening of the cave, you could see the sun rise then move away from them, and turned to their left as it set. This was from the signs of Allah. Anyone guided by Allah is truly guided, and anyone gone astray won't find a guide or a protector. ¹⁸ You thought they were awake, but they were asleep. We kept turning them from right to left. At the entrance *of the cave* lay their dog with its forelegs stretched out. Were you to stumble across them, you would be filled with fear, turn your back on them, and flee.

Their awakening

¹⁹ *Eventually* We awakened them, and they questioned each other. One of them asked, "How long did we stay here?" They said, "We stayed a day or a part of a day." Others said, "Your Lord knows best how long you stayed, now send someone with the silver coin to town to buy pure food so he may bring it for you. *They told him,* "Be polite and courteous,ᵃ and don't let anyone know who you are,

---

ᵃ *Walyathalatuf* means to be subtle, hidden, yet exert an influence. The middle letter 'Ta' of this word is exactly the middle letter of the Quran.

يُشْعِرَنَّ بِكُمْ اَحَدًا ۞ اِنَّهُمْ اِنْ يَّظْهَرُوْا عَلَيْكُمْ

يَرْجُمُوْكُمْ اَوْ يُعِيْدُوْكُمْ فِىْ مِلَّتِهِمْ وَلَنْ تُفْلِحُوْۤا اِذًا

اَبَدًا ۞ وَكَذٰلِكَ اَعْثَرْنَا عَلَيْهِمْ لِيَعْلَمُوْۤا اَنَّ وَعْدَ

اللهِ حَقٌّ وَّاَنَّ السَّاعَةَ لَا رَيْبَ فِيْهَا ۚ اِذْ يَتَنَازَعُوْنَ

بَيْنَهُمْ اَمْرَهُمْ فَقَالُوا ابْنُوْا عَلَيْهِمْ بُنْيَانًا ۗ رَبُّهُمْ

اَعْلَمُ بِهِمْ ط قَالَ الَّذِيْنَ غَلَبُوْا عَلٰٓى اَمْرِهِمْ لَنَتَّخِذَنَّ

عَلَيْهِمْ مَّسْجِدًا ۞ سَيَقُوْلُوْنَ ثَلٰثَةٌ رَّابِعُهُمْ

كَلْبُهُمْ ۚ وَيَقُوْلُوْنَ خَمْسَةٌ سَادِسُهُمْ كَلْبُهُمْ رَجْمًۢا

بِالْغَيْبِ ۚ وَيَقُوْلُوْنَ سَبْعَةٌ وَّثَامِنُهُمْ كَلْبُهُمْ ط قُلْ

We plan, but only what Allah plans happens, our plans can fail.

رَّبِّىْۤ اَعْلَمُ بِعِدَّتِهِمْ مَّا يَعْلَمُهُمْ اِلَّا قَلِيْلٌ ۥ فَلَا

تُمَارِ فِيْهِمْ اِلَّا مِرَآءً ظَاهِرًا ۪ وَّلَا تَسْتَفْتِ فِيْهِمْ

مِّنْهُمْ اَحَدًا ۞ وَلَا تَقُوْلَنَّ لِشَائٍ اِنِّىْ فَاعِلٌ

ذٰلِكَ غَدًا ۙ ۞ اِلَّاۤ اَنْ يَّشَآءَ اللهُ ز وَاذْكُرْ رَّبَّكَ

اِذَا نَسِيْتَ وَقُلْ عَسٰٓى اَنْ يَّهْدِيَنِ رَبِّىْ لِاَقْرَبَ

مِنْ هٰذَا رَشَدًا ۞ وَلَبِثُوْا فِىْ كَهْفِهِمْ ثَلٰثَ مِائَةٍ

سِنِيْنَ وَازْدَادُوْا تِسْعًا ۞ قُلِ اللهُ اَعْلَمُ بِمَا

لَبِثُوْا ۚ لَهٗ غَيْبُ السَّمٰوٰتِ وَالْاَرْضِ ط اَبْصِرْ بِهٖ وَ

اَسْمِعْ ط مَا لَهُمْ مِّنْ دُوْنِهٖ مِنْ وَّلِىٍّ ز وَّلَا يُشْرِكُ فِىْ

حُكْمِهٖۤ اَحَدًا ۞ وَاتْلُ مَاۤ اُوْحِىَ اِلَيْكَ مِنْ كِتَابِ

رَبِّكَ ط لَا مُبَدِّلَ لِكَلِمٰتِهٖ ۚ وَلَنْ تَجِدَ مِنْ دُوْنِهٖ

²⁰if they find out who you are, they will torture you, or force you to revert to their religion. Then you will never be successful." ²¹In this way We brought them to people's attention, so they may know that Allah's promise is true, and there is no doubt about the Final Hour. The townspeople disputed about *what to do with* them. Some said, "Erect a building over the cave; their Lord knows best about them." However, those who had an upperhand concerning their matter said, "We'll build a Mosque over the cave."

How many were they?

²²Some will say the People of the Cave were three, and their dog was the fourth; others will say they were five and the sixth their dog; these are mere guesses; some will say they were seven and the eighth their dog. Say: "My Lord knows best their number." Only a few have real knowledge of them. So, don't argue or ask anyone else about them, say what's known clearly.

When making a plan say, "Allah willing"

²³When you intend to do something don't say, "I will do it tomorrow." ²⁴*Instead* say, "Allah willing *I will do it*." Remember your Lord whenever you forget Him, and say, "I hope my Lord will guide me to the right path closer, and closer."ᵃ

How long did they stay in the cave?

²⁵"People say they stayed in the cave for three hundred years, plus nine." ²⁶Say: "only Allah knows exactly how long they stayed. He has the knowledge of the unseen in the Heavens and the Earth. How wonderful is His Seeing and Hearing. They have no helper beside Him, and He does not allow anyone to share His rule." ²⁷And recite what is revealed to you from your Lord's book; none can change His words, nor can you find beside Him a place of refuge.

ᵃ The digression from the story is an explanation of the reason for the revelation of this story. When Makkans asked the Messenger ﷺ about the People of the Cave, he said, "I will tell you tomorrow," but forgot to say, "Allah Willing."

مُلْتَحَدًا ۞ وَاصْبِرْ نَفْسَكَ مَعَ الَّذِيْنَ يَدْعُوْنَ
رَبَّهُمْ بِالْغَدٰوةِ وَالْعَشِيِّ يُرِيْدُوْنَ وَجْهَهٗ وَلَا
تَعْدُ عَيْنٰكَ عَنْهُمْ ۚ تُرِيْدُ زِيْنَةَ الْحَيٰوةِ الدُّنْيَا ۚ
وَلَا تُطِعْ مَنْ اَغْفَلْنَا قَلْبَهٗ عَنْ ذِكْرِنَا وَاتَّبَعَ
هَوٰىهُ وَكَانَ اَمْرُهٗ فُرُطًا ۞ وَقُلِ الْحَقُّ مِنْ رَّبِّكُمْ ۖ
فَمَنْ شَاءَ فَلْيُؤْمِنْ وَّمَنْ شَاءَ فَلْيَكْفُرْ ۙ اِنَّا
اَعْتَدْنَا لِلظّٰلِمِيْنَ نَارًا ۙ اَحَاطَ بِهِمْ سُرَادِقُهَا ۚ وَاِنْ
يَّسْتَغِيْثُوْا يُغَاثُوْا بِمَاءٍ كَالْمُهْلِ يَشْوِى الْوُجُوْهَ ۗ
بِئْسَ الشَّرَابُ ۗ وَسَاءَتْ مُرْتَفَقًا ۞ اِنَّ الَّذِيْنَ
اٰمَنُوْا وَعَمِلُوا الصّٰلِحٰتِ اِنَّا لَا نُضِيْعُ اَجْرَ مَنْ اَحْسَنَ
عَمَلًا ۞ اُولٰئِكَ لَهُمْ جَنّٰتُ عَدْنٍ تَجْرِيْ مِنْ
تَحْتِهِمُ الْاَنْهٰرُ يُحَلَّوْنَ فِيْهَا مِنْ اَسَاوِرَ مِنْ ذَهَبٍ
وَّيَلْبَسُوْنَ ثِيَابًا خُضْرًا مِّنْ سُنْدُسٍ وَّاِسْتَبْرَقٍ
مُّتَّكِئِيْنَ فِيْهَا عَلَى الْاَرَائِكِ ۗ نِعْمَ الثَّوَابُ ۗ وَحَسُنَتْ
مُرْتَفَقًا ۞ وَاضْرِبْ لَهُمْ مَّثَلًا رَّجُلَيْنِ جَعَلْنَا
لِاَحَدِهِمَا جَنَّتَيْنِ مِنْ اَعْنَابٍ وَّحَفَفْنٰهُمَا بِنَخْلٍ وَّ
جَعَلْنَا بَيْنَهُمَا زَرْعًا ۞ كِلْتَا الْجَنَّتَيْنِ اٰتَتْ اُكُلَهَا
وَلَمْ تَظْلِمْ مِّنْهُ شَيْئًا ۙ وَّفَجَّرْنَا خِلٰلَهُمَا نَهَرًا ۞
وَّكَانَ لَهٗ ثَمَرٌ ۚ فَقَالَ لِصَاحِبِهٖ وَهُوَ يُحَاوِرُهٗ اَنَا
اَكْثَرُ مِنْكَ مَالًا وَّاَعَزُّ نَفَرًا ۞ وَدَخَلَ جَنَّتَهٗ وَهُوَ

Mind who you befriend; good friends will stop you doing wrong.

Lesson 1: Keep company of good people

²⁸ Keep yourself with those who worship their Lord morning and evening, longing for His pleasure. Don't turn your eyes away from them to seek the delights of worldly life. Neither follow him whose mind is forgetful of Our remembrance, and follows his whims; his case is beyond limits.ᵃ

Lesson 2: The contrasting fate of the Sleepers of the cave and the Tyrant disbelievers

²⁹ Say: "The truth is from Your Lord; so, whoever wants to believe, let him do so, and whoever wishes to deny, let him." We have prepared for the evil doers a fire; its walls will surround them. When they plead for water, they will be relieved with boiling water *hotter than* molten brass that will burn their faces – a dreadful drink, and an unbearable place of rest. ³⁰ *On the other hand*, those who believed and did righteous deeds, We will not waste the reward of those who did good *work;* ³¹ they will have everlasting gardens with streams running beneath them. Here, they will be wearing golden bracelets, green dresses with silk embroidery, and rich patterns. They will be sitting on couches. What a wonderful reward, an amazing resting place.

Parable of the rich man

³² Tell them the parable of two men; to one We gave two vineyards, hedged by palm trees, with a cornfield lying in the middle. ³³ Both vineyards had a stream running between them, so they produced an abundant crop throughout the year,

---

ᵃ   The wealthy Makkans told the Messenger 🏵 that they were embarrassed to sit with him, alongside the slaves and poor Muslim. This section was revealed to reject their reservations.

ظَالِمٌ لِّنَفْسِهٖ ۚ قَالَ مَآ اَظُنُّ اَنْ تَبِيْدَ هٰذِهٖٓ

اَبَدًا ۙ٣٥ وَّمَآ اَظُنُّ السَّاعَةَ قَآئِمَةً ۙ وَّلَئِنْ رُّدِدْتُّ

اِلٰى رَبِّيْ لَاَجِدَنَّ خَيْرًا مِّنْهَا مُنْقَلَبًا ٣٦ قَالَ لَهٗ

صَاحِبُهٗ وَهُوَ يُحَاوِرُهٗٓ اَكَفَرْتَ بِالَّذِيْ خَلَقَكَ

مِنْ تُرَابٍ ثُمَّ مِنْ نُّطْفَةٍ ثُمَّ سَوّٰىكَ رَجُلًا ٣٧

لٰكِنَّا۠ هُوَ اللّٰهُ رَبِّيْ وَلَآ اُشْرِكُ بِرَبِّيْٓ اَحَدًا ٣٨

وَلَوْلَآ اِذْ دَخَلْتَ جَنَّتَكَ قُلْتَ مَا شَآءَ اللّٰهُ ۙ

لَا قُوَّةَ اِلَّا بِاللّٰهِ ۚ اِنْ تَرَنِ اَنَا اَقَلَّ مِنْكَ مَالًا

وَّوَلَدًا ۚ٣٩ فَعَسٰى رَبِّيْٓ اَنْ يُّؤْتِيَنِ خَيْرًا مِّنْ

جَنَّتِكَ وَيُرْسِلَ عَلَيْهَا حُسْبَانًا مِّنَ السَّمَآءِ

فَتُصْبِحَ صَعِيْدًا زَلَقًا ۙ٤٠ اَوْ يُصْبِحَ مَآؤُهَا غَوْرًا

فَلَنْ تَسْتَطِيْعَ لَهٗ طَلَبًا ٤١ وَاُحِيْطَ بِثَمَرِهٖ فَاَصْبَحَ

يُقَلِّبُ كَفَّيْهِ عَلٰى مَآ اَنْفَقَ فِيْهَا وَهِيَ خَاوِيَةٌ

عَلٰى عُرُوْشِهَا وَيَقُوْلُ يٰلَيْتَنِيْ لَمْ اُشْرِكْ

بِرَبِّيْٓ اَحَدًا ٤٢ وَلَمْ تَكُنْ لَّهٗ فِئَةٌ يَّنْصُرُوْنَهٗ

مِنْ دُوْنِ اللّٰهِ وَمَا كَانَ مُنْتَصِرًا ۭ٤٣ هُنَالِكَ

الْوَلَايَةُ لِلّٰهِ الْحَقِّ ۭ هُوَ خَيْرٌ ثَوَابًا وَّخَيْرٌ عُقْبًا ٤٤

وَاضْرِبْ لَهُمْ مَّثَلَ الْحَيٰوةِ الدُّنْيَا كَمَآءٍ اَنْزَلْنٰهُ

مِنَ السَّمَآءِ فَاخْتَلَطَ بِهٖ نَبَاتُ الْاَرْضِ فَاَصْبَحَ

هَشِيْمًا تَذْرُوْهُ الرِّيٰحُ ۭ وَكَانَ اللّٰهُ عَلٰى كُلِّ شَيْءٍ

See, how the love of wealth can make a person arrogant, so be on your guard.

ع
٦٣
١٢

579

³⁴ he had plenty of *agricultural* produce. One day he said to his friend, as they were talking *among themselves,* "I have more wealth and a larger family than you." ³⁵ He walked into his garden with these wrong thoughts and said, "I don't think that these vineyards will ever perish, ³⁶ nor do I think that Judgement Day will come. Even if I was returned to My Lord, I will certainly go to somewhere better than this."

The wisdom of the humble man

³⁷ His friend said to him as they argued, "How can you deny the One who created you from dust and then from a drop of sperm? ³⁸ For me, He is Allah, my Lord, and I do not associate anyone with my Lord. ³⁹ When you entered your vineyard why didn't you say, "There is no power except that of Allah. Even if you saw that I was less than you in wealth and number of children, ⁴⁰ I am hopeful that my Lord will give me better than your vineyards; He could send a thunderbolt from the sky on them and turn the land barren, ⁴¹ or make its water sink deep into the ground so that you wouldn't be able to reach it."

The vineyards are destroyed

⁴² So his fruits were destroyed. There he was, wringing his hands, regretting what he had spent on it. The trellises had fallen; he sobbed, "I wish I had never associated anyone with my Lord." ⁴³ There was no army that could help him against Allah, nor could he defend himself. ⁴⁴ This shows, *all* power belongs to Allah, the Truth. *The belief in Him* produces the best reward and the best outcome.

Lesson 1: The parable of life and death

⁴⁵ Tell them a parable of worldly life; it's like the rain We send down from the sky, the soil soaks it, plants grow, then turn into dry straw that is scattered by the winds. Allah has power over all things.

مُّقْتَدِرًا ۝ اَلْمَالُ وَالْبَنُوْنَ زِيْنَةُ الْحَيٰوةِ الدُّنْيَا ۚ

وَالْبٰقِيٰتُ الصّٰلِحٰتُ خَيْرٌ عِنْدَ رَبِّكَ ثَوَابًا وَّخَيْرٌ

اَمَلًا ۝ وَيَوْمَ نُسَيِّرُ الْجِبَالَ وَتَرَى الْاَرْضَ بَارِزَةً ۙ

وَّحَشَرْنٰهُمْ فَلَمْ نُغَادِرْ مِنْهُمْ اَحَدًا ۝ وَعُرِضُوْا

عَلٰى رَبِّكَ صَفًّا ۭ لَقَدْ جِئْتُمُوْنَا كَمَا خَلَقْنٰكُمْ اَوَّلَ

مَرَّةٍ ۫ بَلْ زَعَمْتُمْ اَلَّنْ نَّجْعَلَ لَكُمْ مَّوْعِدًا ۝

وَوُضِعَ الْكِتٰبُ فَتَرَى الْمُجْرِمِيْنَ مُشْفِقِيْنَ

مِمَّا فِيْهِ وَيَقُوْلُوْنَ يٰوَيْلَتَنَا مَالِ هٰذَا الْكِتٰبِ

Imagine standing in front of the Lord, holding your book of deeds. Are you ready to face Him?

لَا يُغَادِرُ صَغِيْرَةً وَّلَا كَبِيْرَةً اِلَّآ اَحْصٰىهَا ۚ

وَوَجَدُوْا مَا عَمِلُوْا حَاضِرًا ۭ وَلَا يَظْلِمُ رَبُّكَ

اَحَدًا ۝ وَاِذْ قُلْنَا لِلْمَلٰٓئِكَةِ اسْجُدُوْا لِاٰدَمَ

فَسَجَدُوْٓا اِلَّآ اِبْلِيْسَ ۭ كَانَ مِنَ الْجِنِّ فَفَسَقَ

عَنْ اَمْرِ رَبِّهٖ ۭ اَفَتَتَّخِذُوْنَهٗ وَذُرِّيَّتَهٗٓ اَوْلِيَآءَ

مِنْ دُوْنِيْ وَهُمْ لَكُمْ عَدُوٌّ ۭ بِئْسَ لِلظّٰلِمِيْنَ

بَدَلًا ۝ مَآ اَشْهَدْتُّهُمْ خَلْقَ السَّمٰوٰتِ وَالْاَرْضِ

وَلَا خَلْقَ اَنْفُسِهِمْ ۠ وَمَا كُنْتُ مُتَّخِذَ الْمُضِلِّيْنَ

عَضُدًا ۝ وَيَوْمَ يَقُوْلُ نَادُوْا شُرَكَآءِيَ الَّذِيْنَ

زَعَمْتُمْ فَدَعَوْهُمْ فَلَمْ يَسْتَجِيْبُوْا لَهُمْ وَجَعَلْنَا

بَيْنَهُمْ مَّوْبِقًا ۝ وَرَاَ الْمُجْرِمُوْنَ النَّارَ فَظَنُّوْٓا

اَنَّهُمْ مُّوَاقِعُوْهَا وَلَمْ يَجِدُوْا عَنْهَا مَصْرِفًا ۝

⁴⁶ Wealth and children are beautiful decorations of this life. However, the fruit of good deeds will remain with your Lord, an excellent reward and hope.

Lesson 2: Opening of personal records on Judgement Day

⁴⁷ The day when We clear away the mountains, you will see the Earth spread out as a *vast* plain, and We shall gather *the dead*; no one will be left out. ⁴⁸ They will be presented before your Lord in rows, *it will be said,* "You have come to Us as We created you the first time; you thought We wouldn't fulfil Our promise." ⁴⁹ When the record^a will be laid out before them, the sinners will be frightened of what they see in it, and they will say, "Woe to us, what kind of record is this that doesn't leave out anything small or big, it records everything." They will find everything they had ever done in front of them. And your Lord is not unjust to anyone.

Satan misleads

⁵⁰ And remember when We said to the Angels, "Prostrate to Adam," they prostrated, though Satan, who was from the Jinns, did not. He disobeyed his Lord's order. So, are you going to take him and his followers as your friends beside Me, yet they are your enemies? What a wretched alternative have the wrongdoers chosen! ⁵¹ I didn't make them witnesses at the time of creation of the Heavens and Earth, nor in their own creation. I don't take as helpers those who misguide others. ⁵² On the Day He will say, "Call upon those who you thought were My partners," they will not answer them. We will place between them an unbridgeable gulf.^b ⁵³ When the sinners see the Fire they will be convinced they are falling into it, and they will find no other place to turn to.

---

a   Personal record in the Book of Deeds.

b   *Muabiqan*, according to Ibn Abbas, is a valley in Hell.

وَلَقَدْ صَرَّفْنَا فِىْ هٰذَا الْقُرْاٰنِ لِلنَّاسِ
مِنْ كُلِّ مَثَلٍ ط وَكَانَ الْاِنْسَانُ اَكْثَرَ شَىْءٍ
جَدَلًا ۵۴ وَمَا مَنَعَ النَّاسَ اَنْ يُّؤْمِنُوْٓا اِذْ جَآءَهُمُ
الْهُدٰى وَيَسْتَغْفِرُوْا رَبَّهُمْ اِلَّآ اَنْ تَاْتِيَهُمْ
سُنَّةُ الْاَوَّلِيْنَ اَوْ يَاْتِيَهُمُ الْعَذَابُ قُبُلًا ۵۵
وَمَا نُرْسِلُ الْمُرْسَلِيْنَ اِلَّا مُبَشِّرِيْنَ وَمُنْذِرِيْنَ ۚ
وَيُجَادِلُ الَّذِيْنَ كَفَرُوْا بِالْبَاطِلِ لِيُدْحِضُوْا بِهِ
الْحَقَّ وَاتَّخَذُوْٓا اٰيٰتِىْ وَمَآ اُنْذِرُوْا هُزُوًا ۵۶ وَمَنْ
اَظْلَمُ مِمَّنْ ذُكِّرَ بِاٰيٰتِ رَبِّهٖ فَاَعْرَضَ عَنْهَا وَ
نَسِىَ مَا قَدَّمَتْ يَدٰهُ ط اِنَّا جَعَلْنَا عَلٰى قُلُوْبِهِمْ
اَكِنَّةً اَنْ يَّفْقَهُوْهُ وَفِىْٓ اٰذَانِهِمْ وَقْرًا ط وَاِنْ
تَدْعُهُمْ اِلَى الْهُدٰى فَلَنْ يَّهْتَدُوْٓا اِذًا اَبَدًا ۵۷
وَرَبُّكَ الْغَفُوْرُ ذُو الرَّحْمَةِ ط لَوْ يُؤَاخِذُهُمْ بِمَا
كَسَبُوْا لَعَجَّلَ لَهُمُ الْعَذَابَ ط بَلْ لَّهُمْ مَّوْعِدٌ
لَّنْ يَّجِدُوْا مِنْ دُوْنِهٖ مَوْئِلًا ۵۸ وَتِلْكَ الْقُرٰٓى
اَهْلَكْنٰهُمْ لَمَّا ظَلَمُوْا وَجَعَلْنَا لِمَهْلِكِهِمْ مَّوْعِدًا ۵۹
وَاِذْ قَالَ مُوْسٰى لِفَتٰهُ لَآ اَبْرَحُ حَتّٰىٓ اَبْلُغَ
مَجْمَعَ الْبَحْرَيْنِ اَوْ اَمْضِىَ حُقُبًا ۶۰ فَلَمَّا بَلَغَا
مَجْمَعَ بَيْنِهِمَا نَسِيَا حُوْتَهُمَا فَاتَّخَذَ سَبِيْلَهٗ
فِى الْبَحْرِ سَرَبًا ۶۱ فَلَمَّا جَاوَزَا قَالَ لِفَتٰهُ اٰتِنَا

Denial of the Lord's favours leads to a mind that fails to understand.

ع
٢٠

Humanity is quarrelsome

[54] We have *explained* all sorts of lessons for people's benefit in this Quran, *but* humans are quarrelsome *creatures*. [55] What stops people from believing and seeking the forgiveness of their Lord when the guidance has come to them? Are they waiting *for the same fate* as the earlier generations? Or for the punishment to be brought right in front of them? [56] The messengers were sent to give good news and a warning; the disbelievers disputed using false arguments to weaken the truth, and they mocked My verses and warnings.

The locked minds of disbelievers

[57] Who is more unjust than the one who is reminded of his Lord's verses and turns away from them? Forgetting what he is sending ahead of him. We have locked their minds: they cannot understand. We made them hard of hearing, so when you call them to the guidance, they will never be guided. [58] Your Lord is Forgiving, Kind. Had He punished them for what they did, then it would have come sooner, but there is a fixed time from which they will find no escape. [59] We destroyed these towns because they did wrong; We fixed the time of their destruction.

The story of Musa and Khidr, the green man

[60] Remember when Musa said to his young servant, "I will travel on until I reach the place where the two seas meet, no matter how long it takes."[a] [61] When they reached it, they forgot the fish, which quietly made its way into the sea and swam away.

---

[a] The background to this story is given in Bukhari: Musa was asked a question; who is the most knowledgeable person? Musa replied 'I am'. Allah rebuked him of Khidr being wiser than him.

غَدَآءَنَا ۚ لَقَدْ لَقِیْنَا مِنْ سَفَرِنَا هٰذَا نَصَبًا ۝

قَالَ اَرَءَیْتَ اِذْ اَوَیْنَآ اِلَى الصَّخْرَةِ فَاِنِّیْ نَسِیْتُ

الْحُوْتَ ۚ وَمَآ اَنْسٰنِیْهُ اِلَّا الشَّیْطٰنُ اَنْ اَذْكُرَهٗ ۚ

وَاتَّخَذَ سَبِیْلَهٗ فِی الْبَحْرِ ۙ عَجَبًا ۝ قَالَ ذٰلِكَ

مَا كُنَّا نَبْغِ ۚ فَارْتَدَّا عَلٰۤى اٰثَارِهِمَا قَصَصًا ۝

فَوَجَدَا عَبْدًا مِّنْ عِبَادِنَآ اٰتَیْنٰهُ رَحْمَةً مِّنْ

عِنْدِنَا وَعَلَّمْنٰهُ مِنْ لَّدُنَّا عِلْمًا ۝ قَالَ لَهٗ

مُوْسٰى هَلْ اَتَّبِعُكَ عَلٰۤى اَنْ تُعَلِّمَنِ مِمَّا عُلِّمْتَ

Patience is the key quality in coping with sufferings.

رُشْدًا ۝ قَالَ اِنَّكَ لَنْ تَسْتَطِیْعَ مَعِیَ صَبْرًا ۝

وَكَیْفَ تَصْبِرُ عَلٰى مَا لَمْ تُحِطْ بِهٖ خُبْرًا ۝

قَالَ سَتَجِدُنِیْۤ اِنْ شَآءَ اللّٰهُ صَابِرًا وَّلَاۤ اَعْصِیْ

لَكَ اَمْرًا ۝ قَالَ فَاِنِ اتَّبَعْتَنِیْ فَلَا تَسْـَٔلْنِیْ

عَنْ شَیْءٍ حَتّٰۤى اُحْدِثَ لَكَ مِنْهُ ذِكْرًا ۝

فَانْطَلَقَا ۥ حَتّٰۤى اِذَا رَكِبَا فِی السَّفِیْنَةِ خَرَقَهَا ۗ

قَالَ اَخَرَقْتَهَا لِتُغْرِقَ اَهْلَهَا ۚ لَقَدْ جِئْتَ

شَیْـًٔا اِمْرًا ۝ قَالَ اَلَمْ اَقُلْ اِنَّكَ لَنْ تَسْتَطِیْعَ

مَعِیَ صَبْرًا ۝ قَالَ لَا تُؤَاخِذْنِیْ بِمَا نَسِیْتُ

وَلَا تُرْهِقْنِیْ مِنْ اَمْرِیْ عُسْرًا ۝ فَانْطَلَقَا ۥ

حَتّٰۤى اِذَا لَقِیَا غُلٰمًا فَقَتَلَهٗ ۙ قَالَ اَقَتَلْتَ نَفْسًا

زَكِیَّةًۢ بِغَیْرِ نَفْسٍ ؕ لَقَدْ جِئْتَ شَیْـًٔا نُّكْرًا ۝

585

^{62} After travelling for some time, Musa asked his young servant, "Bring our meal, the journey has worn us out!" ^{63} He replied, "Did you notice, when we rested at the rock I forgot the fish – none but Satan made me forget it – amazingly it made its way into the sea." ^{64} Musa said, "That's *the place* we were looking for." So they turned back, carefully retracing their footsteps. ^{65} They found a servant of Ours there, *Khidr, to whom* We were especially kind – We taught him Our special knowledge.

Musa asks Khidr for permission to accompany him

^{66} Musa asked him, "Can I follow you, so you may teach me something of higher guidance which you have been taught?" ^{67} He replied, "You will not be able to have patience with me; ^{68} how could you have patience about things that you don't fully know?" ^{69} Musa said, "Allah willing, you will find me patient and I will not disobey your orders." ^{70} The man said, "If you *must* follow me then don't ask questions until I speak about it to you."

Three bizarre events

^{71} So both *set off walking along the beach* until they got a boat, *but when they got off* Khidr damaged it. Musa said, "Did you damage it to drown those on board? You've done an awful thing." ^{72} Khidr said, "Didn't I say you will never have patience with me?" ^{73} Musa replied, "Don't be harsh with me for forgetting; please don't make my task any more difficult." ^{74} So they travelled on until they met a boy; Khidr killed him, and Musa *angrily* said, "You've killed an innocent person who hasn't done anything wrong; you've done a dreadful thing."

قَالَ اَلَمْ اَقُلْ لَّكَ اِنَّكَ لَنْ تَسْتَطِيعَ مَعِىَ

صَبْرًا ۝ قَالَ اِنْ سَاَلْتُكَ عَنْ شَىْءٍ بَعْدَهَا فَلَا

تُصٰحِبْنِى ۚ قَدْ بَلَغْتَ مِنْ لَّدُنِّىْ عُذْرًا ۝ فَانْطَلَقَا ۫

حَتّٰى اِذَآ اَتَيَآ اَهْلَ قَرْيَةِ ِۨاسْتَطْعَمَآ اَهْلَهَا فَاَبَوْا

اَنْ يُّضَيِّفُوْهُمَا فَوَجَدَا فِيْهَا جِدَارًا يُّرِيْدُ اَنْ

يَّنْقَضَّ فَاَقَامَهٗ ؕ قَالَ لَوْ شِئْتَ لَتَّخَذْتَ عَلَيْهِ

اَجْرًا ۝ قَالَ هٰذَا فِرَاقُ بَيْنِى وَبَيْنِكَ ۚ سَاُنَبِّئُكَ

بِتَاْوِيْلِ مَا لَمْ تَسْتَطِعْ عَّلَيْهِ صَبْرًا ۝ اَمَّا السَّفِيْنَةُ

فَكَانَتْ لِمَسٰكِيْنَ يَعْمَلُوْنَ فِى الْبَحْرِ فَاَرَدْتُّ اَنْ

اَعِيْبَهَا وَكَانَ وَرَآءَهُمْ مَّلِكٌ يَّاْخُذُ كُلَّ سَفِيْنَةٍ

غَصْبًا ۝ وَاَمَّا الْغُلٰمُ فَكَانَ اَبَوٰهُ مُؤْمِنَيْنِ

فَخَشِيْنَآ اَنْ يُّرْهِقَهُمَا طُغْيَانًا وَّكُفْرًا ۝ فَاَرَدْنَآ اَنْ

يُّبْدِلَهُمَا رَبُّهُمَا خَيْرًا مِّنْهُ زَكٰوةً وَّاَقْرَبَ رُحْمًا ۝

وَاَمَّا الْجِدَارُ فَكَانَ لِغُلٰمَيْنِ يَتِيْمَيْنِ فِى الْمَدِيْنَةِ

وَكَانَ تَحْتَهٗ كَنْزٌ لَّهُمَا وَكَانَ اَبُوْهُمَا صَالِحًا ۚ فَاَرَادَ

رَبُّكَ اَنْ يَّبْلُغَآ اَشُدَّهُمَا وَيَسْتَخْرِجَا كَنْزَهُمَا ۖ رَحْمَةً

مِّنْ رَّبِّكَ ۚ وَمَا فَعَلْتُهٗ عَنْ اَمْرِىْ ؕ ذٰلِكَ تَاْوِيْلُ مَا

لَمْ تَسْطِعْ عَّلَيْهِ صَبْرًا ۝ وَيَسْـَٔلُوْنَكَ عَنْ ذِى الْقَرْنَيْنِ ؕ

قُلْ سَاَتْلُوْا عَلَيْكُمْ مِّنْهُ ذِكْرًا ۝ اِنَّا مَكَّنَّا لَهٗ فِى

الْاَرْضِ وَاٰتَيْنٰهُ مِنْ كُلِّ شَىْءٍ سَبَبًا ۝ فَاَتْبَعَ

Life is mysteries, we can't understand the reality without the divine guidance.

[75] He said, "Didn't I tell you, you will never have patience with me?" [76] Musa said, "If I ask anything after this then tell me to leave you. You will have a valid excuse from me." [77] So, they set off till they reached a village, here they asked the villagers for food, but they refused to take them as guests. They found a wall about to fall down, so *Khidr* rebuilt it. Musa complained, "You could have asked for a payment, if you wanted."

Khidr explains the three bizarre events

[78] *He* replied, "We must go our separate ways now! I shall give you an explanation for what you were unable to bear patiently. [79] The boat belonged to poor fishermen, I damaged it because a king was coming after them to forcefully seize all seaworthy boats. [80] The boy, his parents were believers, but we feared he would distress them by being disobedient and unthankful. [81] We hope their Lord will give them a righteous child in exchange, one who will be more caring. [82] The falling wall belonged to two orphan boys in the town; buried beneath it was their treasure, their father was a righteous man. Your Lord wanted them to reach maturity, so they could dig up their treasure; *this was* your Lord's kindness. What I did wasn't done by my will; that's an explanation of those events you couldn't bear patiently."

The story of Zul Qarnayn

[83] They ask you about Zul Qarnayn. Say: "I will tell you part of his story." [84] We established and gave him power on Earth, and gave him the resources to achieve great things.[a] [85] So he set off on an expedition,

---

[a] *Sabab* here means to achieve something i.e. a resource.

سَبَبًا ۸۵ حَتّٰى اِذَا بَلَغَ مَغْرِبَ الشَّمْسِ وَجَدَهَا

تَغْرُبُ فِيْ عَيْنٍ حَمِئَةٍ وَّوَجَدَ عِنْدَهَا قَوْمًا ۛ قُلْنَا

يٰذَا الْقَرْنَيْنِ اِمَّآ اَنْ تُعَذِّبَ وَاِمَّآ اَنْ تَتَّخِذَ فِيْهِمْ

حُسْنًا ۸٦ قَالَ اَمَّا مَنْ ظَلَمَ فَسَوْفَ نُعَذِّبُهُ ثُمَّ يُرَدُّ

اِلٰى رَبِّهٖ فَيُعَذِّبُهُ عَذَابًا نُّكْرًا ۸۸ وَاَمَّا مَنْ اٰمَنَ وَ

عَمِلَ صَالِحًا فَلَهُ جَزَآءَ ۨ الْحُسْنٰى ۚ وَسَنَقُوْلُ لَهُ مِنْ

اَمْرِنَا يُسْرًا ۚ ثُمَّ اَتْبَعَ سَبَبًا ۸۹ حَتّٰى اِذَا بَلَغَ مَطْلِعَ

الشَّمْسِ وَجَدَهَا تَطْلُعُ عَلٰى قَوْمٍ لَّمْ نَجْعَلْ لَّهُمْ مِّنْ

دُوْنِهَا سِتْرًا ۹۰ كَذٰلِكَ ۚ وَقَدْ اَحَطْنَا بِمَا لَدَيْهِ خُبْرًا ۹۱

ثُمَّ اَتْبَعَ سَبَبًا ۹۲ حَتّٰى اِذَا بَلَغَ بَيْنَ السَّدَّيْنِ وَجَدَ

مِنْ دُوْنِهِمَا قَوْمًا ۙ لَّا يَكَادُوْنَ يَفْقَهُوْنَ قَوْلًا ۹۳ قَالُوْا

يٰذَا الْقَرْنَيْنِ اِنَّ يَاْجُوْجَ وَمَاْجُوْجَ مُفْسِدُوْنَ فِى الْاَرْضِ

فَهَلْ نَجْعَلُ لَكَ خَرْجًا عَلٰى اَنْ تَجْعَلَ بَيْنَنَا وَبَيْنَهُمْ

سَدًّا ۹٤ قَالَ مَا مَكَّنِّيْ فِيْهِ رَبِّيْ خَيْرٌ فَاَعِيْنُوْنِيْ بِقُوَّةٍ

اَجْعَلْ بَيْنَكُمْ وَبَيْنَهُمْ رَدْمًا ۹۵ اٰتُوْنِيْ زُبَرَ الْحَدِيْدِ ۚ

حَتّٰى اِذَا سَاوٰى بَيْنَ الصَّدَفَيْنِ قَالَ انْفُخُوْا ۚ حَتّٰى

اِذَا جَعَلَهُ نَارًا ۙ قَالَ اٰتُوْنِيْ اُفْرِغْ عَلَيْهِ قِطْرًا ۹٦ فَمَا

اسْطَاعُوْۤا اَنْ يَّظْهَرُوْهُ وَمَا اسْتَطَاعُوْا لَهُ نَقْبًا ۹۷ قَالَ

هٰذَا رَحْمَةٌ مِّنْ رَّبِّيْ ۚ فَاِذَا جَآءَ وَعْدُ رَبِّيْ جَعَلَهُ

دَكَّآءَ ۚ وَكَانَ وَعْدُ رَبِّيْ حَقًّا ۹۸ وَتَرَكْنَا بَعْضَهُمْ

Who are the Gog Magog? A powerful but evil people who plunder other people's lands.

⁸⁶until he reached the place where the sun sets; he found it setting in a spring of murky water.^a He found some people there, We said: "Zul Qarnayn, you can reprimand or be kind to them." ⁸⁷He said, "Whoever does wrong, we will punish him, but when he returns to his Lord, the punishment will be dreadful. ⁸⁸However, whoever believes and does good deeds will have a beautiful reward, and We will only ask him to do easy tasks."

His journey to the East

⁸⁹So he *again* set off on another expedition, ⁹⁰until he reached the place of sunrise *in the east*. He found people there who lived in the open, without any shelter. ⁹¹So it was; We knew all about him.

Delivering protection from Gog and Magog^b

⁹²Then he set off on another expedition, ⁹³till he reached an area lying between two mountains; here he found people who didn't fully understand him. ⁹⁴They said, "Zul Qarnayn, Gog and Magog are making trouble in the land; we shall pay you money if you can build a solid wall between us and them. ⁹⁵He replied, "The power given by My Lord is enough, but you give me manpower so I can make a rampart between them and you. ⁹⁶Bring me pieces of iron" – when he had filled the gap between the two mountainsides, he said, "Blow the bellows!" And he made it glow like fire; he then said, "Bring me molten brass to pour over it. ⁹⁷Now they will not be able to cross over it, nor will they be able to pierce it." ⁹⁸He told *them,* "This is my Lord's kindness, so when My Lord's promise comes *the wall* will crumble to dust, and my Lord's promise is true."

---

^a This is a figurative phrase, illustrating how the sun appears to the observer. It is not a scientific fact that the sun sets in murky water.

^b These are names of the enemies of God's people, as mentioned in the Bible (Ezkel: 38). Or two nations that plunder other people's lands.

يَوْمَئِذٍ يَّمُوجُ فِيْ بَعْضٍ وَّنُفِخَ فِي الصُّوْرِ فَجَمَعْنٰهُمْ

جَمْعًا ۹۹ وَّعَرَضْنَا جَهَنَّمَ يَوْمَئِذٍ لِّلْكٰفِرِيْنَ عَرْضَا ۞

الَّذِيْنَ كَانَتْ اَعْيُنُهُمْ فِيْ غِطَاءٍ عَنْ ذِكْرِيْ وَكَانُوْا

لَا يَسْتَطِيْعُوْنَ سَمْعًا ۞ اَفَحَسِبَ الَّذِيْنَ كَفَرُوْٓا اَنْ

يَّتَّخِذُوْا عِبَادِيْ مِنْ دُوْنِيْٓ اَوْلِيَآءَ ؕ اِنَّآ اَعْتَدْنَا جَهَنَّمَ

لِلْكٰفِرِيْنَ نُزُلًا ۞ قُلْ هَلْ نُنَبِّئُكُمْ بِالْاَخْسَرِيْنَ

اَعْمَالًا ؕ الَّذِيْنَ ضَلَّ سَعْيُهُمْ فِي الْحَيٰوةِ الدُّنْيَا وَهُمْ

يَحْسَبُوْنَ اَنَّهُمْ يُحْسِنُوْنَ صُنْعًا ۞ اُولٰٓئِكَ الَّذِيْنَ

كَفَرُوْا بِاٰيٰتِ رَبِّهِمْ وَلِقَآئِهٖ فَحَبِطَتْ اَعْمَالُهُمْ فَلَا

نُقِيْمُ لَهُمْ يَوْمَ الْقِيٰمَةِ وَزْنًا ۞ ذٰلِكَ جَزَآؤُهُمْ

جَهَنَّمُ بِمَا كَفَرُوْا وَاتَّخَذُوْٓا اٰيٰتِيْ وَرُسُلِيْ هُزُوًا ۞

اِنَّ الَّذِيْنَ اٰمَنُوْا وَعَمِلُوا الصّٰلِحٰتِ كَانَتْ لَهُمْ جَنّٰتُ

الْفِرْدَوْسِ نُزُلًا ۞ خٰلِدِيْنَ فِيْهَا لَا يَبْغُوْنَ عَنْهَا

حِوَلًا ۞ قُلْ لَّوْ كَانَ الْبَحْرُ مِدَادًا لِّكَلِمٰتِ رَبِّيْ لَنَفِدَ

الْبَحْرُ قَبْلَ اَنْ تَنْفَدَ كَلِمٰتُ رَبِّيْ وَلَوْ جِئْنَا بِمِثْلِهٖ

مَدَدًا ۞ قُلْ اِنَّمَآ اَنَا بَشَرٌ مِّثْلُكُمْ يُوْحٰٓى اِلَيَّ اَنَّمَآ

اِلٰهُكُمْ اِلٰهٌ وَّاحِدٌ ۚ فَمَنْ كَانَ يَرْجُوْا لِقَآءَ رَبِّهٖ فَلْيَعْمَلْ

عَمَلًا صَالِحًا وَّلَا يُشْرِكْ بِعِبَادَةِ رَبِّهٖٓ اَحَدًا ۞

How useful are your works? Or are you just imagining that you are doing good.

The terrible scenario of the Final Hour

[99] That Day, the Trumpet will be blown. We'll let them surge like waves against each other, and We shall gather them together. [100] That Day, We shall introduce Hell to the disbelievers – [101] whose eyes were veiled from Our remembrance and they were not able to hear. [102] Do the disbelievers think they can take My servants as protectors beside Me? We have prepared Hell as hospitality for the disbelievers. [103] Say: "Shall We tell you who are the biggest losers with respect to works? [104] Whose efforts were misguided, yet they thought they were doing good work: [105] people who disbelieved *in* the signs and *in their* meeting with their Lord, so their deeds are worthless. Nor would We give them on the Day of Judgement any weight. [106] Hell is their reward, because they mocked My signs and My messengers." [107] Those who believed and did righteous deeds will have *the* hospitality of *the* Gardens of Paradise. [108] They will stay there forever, never wanting a change.

Allah's commands, creation and care are Infinite

[109] Say: "If the seas became ink for writing down the words of My Lord, the seas would quickly run dry before My Lord's words were finished, even if We added sea upon sea to it." [110] Say: "I am a human being like you. It has been revealed to me: your God is one God. Anyone expecting to meet his Lord, let him do good deeds and not associate anyone with Him from His creation."

19. Surat Maryam

The Mother of Prophet Isa

This early Makkan surat was revealed before the first wave of migration to Abyssinia, in the fifth year of the Prophet's 🕌 mission. The surat is lyrical, most verses ending with a long vowel "aa"– a generous peppering of *Yaa* and *Daa* beautifies a familiar subject. This is complemented with the repetition of the divine name *al-Rahman* ("the Most Kind") sixteen times.

It opens with the solemn prayer of Prophet Zakariyya, 🕌 for a successor. He was old, childless, and worried about who would be his heir. This prayer reflects his deep faith and reliance on Allah: "My prayer has never gone unanswered by My Lord" (4). Allah blessed him with Yahya 🕌, "The soft-hearted, pure and pious" (13). The story of the miraculous conception and birth of Isa 🕌 emphasises the Power, Majesty and Independent nature of the Divine, who is beyond the law of cause and effect. The first words Isa 🕌 said: "I am a servant of Allah; He has given me the Book and made me a prophet, and made me blessed wherever I go" (31). The Quran rejects the Christian belief of Trinity, and states how objectionable and unacceptable this is to Allah: "What a monstrous thing you have said! Even the skies would crack, the Earth would rip apart and the mountains crumble" (89–91). This outrageous claim shows the extent of Allah's anger, a powerful condemnation of idolatry.

A highly-charged conversation then follows between a nephew and an uncle: Ibrahim 🕌 very gently tries to persuade and win over Azar, his uncle, from idolatry. The courtesy and logic he employs are persuasive enough to prompt even a stone heart to move. However, idolatry makes one deaf, locks the mind and seals the heart. Ibrahim 🕌 sets a wonderful example for preachers and obedient sons on how to differ politely. There are four stories mentioned here: Zakariyya 🕌 and Yahya 🕌, Maryam 🕌 and Isa 🕌, Ibrahim 🕌 and Azar, Musa 🕌 and Harun 🕌. They reflect a father and son relationship, a mother and son relationship, and two brotherly relationships. The relationships between prophets and their communities also reveal the great importance of human relationships.

Faith forms an important element of relationships. The Quran condemns those generations who were the children of prophets yet: "After them came generations who neglected the prayer and followed their lusts. Soon they will face the consequences of their evil" (59). Salah is a powerful expression of a person's relationship with Allah, the Lord. Neglecting it demonstrates a lack of commitment to the relationship. Yet Allah's love for believers is remarkable: "The Kind Lord will make for them love *in people's hearts*" (96). This could also be taken to mean: "The Kind Lord loves them dearly."

بِسْمِ اللّٰهِ الرَّحْمٰنِ الرَّحِيْمِ

كٓهٰيٓعٓصٓ ۚ۰ ذِكْرُ رَحْمَتِ رَبِّكَ عَبْدَهٗ زَكَرِيَّا ۞

اِذْ نَادٰى رَبَّهٗ نِدَآءً خَفِيًّا ۞ قَالَ رَبِّ اِنِّيْ وَهَنَ

الْعَظْمُ مِنِّيْ وَاشْتَعَلَ الرَّاْسُ شَيْبًا وَّلَمْ اَكُنْ

بِدُعَآئِكَ رَبِّ شَقِيًّا ۞ وَاِنِّيْ خِفْتُ الْمَوَالِيَ مِنْ

وَّرَآءِىْ وَكَانَتِ امْرَاَتِيْ عَاقِرًا فَهَبْ لِيْ مِنْ لَّدُنْكَ

وَلِيًّا ۙ يَّرِثُنِيْ وَيَرِثُ مِنْ اٰلِ يَعْقُوْبَ ۖ وَاجْعَلْهُ رَبِّ

رَضِيًّا ۞ يٰزَكَرِيَّآ اِنَّا نُبَشِّرُكَ بِغُلٰمِ ِۨاسْمُهٗ يَحْيٰى ۙ لَمْ

نَجْعَلْ لَّهٗ مِنْ قَبْلُ سَمِيًّا ۞ قَالَ رَبِّ اَنّٰى يَكُوْنُ لِيْ

غُلٰمٌ وَّكَانَتِ امْرَاَتِيْ عَاقِرًا وَّقَدْ بَلَغْتُ مِنَ الْكِبَرِ

عِتِيًّا ۞ قَالَ كَذٰلِكَ ۚ قَالَ رَبُّكَ هُوَ عَلَيَّ هَيِّنٌ وَّقَدْ

خَلَقْتُكَ مِنْ قَبْلُ وَلَمْ تَكُ شَيْئًا ۞ قَالَ رَبِّ اجْعَلْ

لِّيْٓ اٰيَةً ؕ قَالَ اٰيَتُكَ اَلَّا تُكَلِّمَ النَّاسَ ثَلٰثَ لَيَالٍ

سَوِيًّا ۞ فَخَرَجَ عَلٰى قَوْمِهٖ مِنَ الْمِحْرَابِ فَاَوْحٰٓى اِلَيْهِمْ

اَنْ سَبِّحُوْا بُكْرَةً وَّعَشِيًّا ۞ يٰيَحْيٰى خُذِ الْكِتٰبَ بِقُوَّةٍ ؕ

وَاٰتَيْنٰهُ الْحُكْمَ صَبِيًّا ۙ وَّحَنَانًا مِّنْ لَّدُنَّا وَزَكٰوةً ؕ

وَّكَانَ تَقِيًّا ۙ وَّبَرًّا بِوَالِدَيْهِ وَلَمْ يَكُنْ جَبَّارًا

عَصِيًّا ۞ وَسَلٰمٌ عَلَيْهِ يَوْمَ وُلِدَ وَيَوْمَ يَمُوْتُ وَيَوْمَ

يُبْعَثُ حَيًّا ۞ وَاذْكُرْ فِى الْكِتٰبِ مَرْيَمَ ۚ اِذِ انْتَبَذَتْ

Allah is the Responder, the Listener; so pray, He will never disappoint you.

In the name of Allah, the Kind, the Caring.

¹ *Kaf Ha Ya Ain Sad.*

The story of Zakariyya

² This is an account of your Lord's compassion for Zakariyya, His servant, ³ when he quietly prayed to His Lord ⁴ saying, "My Lord, my bones are weak because of old age, my hair has turned grey, but My prayer has never gone unanswered by My Lord. ⁵ I am afraid of what my relatives might do after me. My wife is childless, give me a gift, a successor, ⁶ who will be my successor and the successor of Yaqub's family. My Lord, make him pleasing *to all.*"

Zakariyya is given good news of a son

⁷ Zakariyya, We give you good news of a son! He shall be called Yahya, no one has been named like him before. ⁸ He said, "Lord, will I have a son when my wife is barren and I'm old? ⁹ *An angel* said, "It will be so; your Lord said, 'That is easy for me, I created you before this when you were nothing.'" ¹⁰ Zakariyya said, "Lord, make for me a sign." He said, "Your sign is: you won't be able to speak to people for three days and nights." ¹¹ So, he came out of his prayer room and signalled to *the congregation* to glorify Allah morning and evening. ¹² "Yahya, hold the Book firmly," and We gave him wisdom in his childhood, ¹³ soft-hearted, pure and pious. ¹⁴ He was kind to his parents, never a tormentor or disobedient. ¹⁵ So Allah's peace be on him the day he was born, the day he will die and the day he will be resurrected.

مِنْ اَهْلِهَا مَكَانًا شَرْقِيًّا ۞ فَاتَّخَذَتْ مِنْ دُوْنِهِمْ

حِجَابًا ۚ فَاَرْسَلْنَا اِلَيْهَا رُوْحَنَا فَتَمَثَّلَ لَهَا بَشَرًا

سَوِيًّا ۞ قَالَتْ اِنِّىْٓ اَعُوْذُ بِالرَّحْمٰنِ مِنْكَ اِنْ كُنْتَ

تَقِيًّا ۞ قَالَ اِنَّمَآ اَنَا رَسُوْلُ رَبِّكِ ۖ لِاَهَبَ لَكِ غُلٰمًا

زَكِيًّا ۞ قَالَتْ اَنّٰى يَكُوْنُ لِىْ غُلٰمٌ وَّلَمْ يَمْسَسْنِىْ بَشَرٌ

وَّلَمْ اَكُ بَغِيًّا ۞ قَالَ كَذٰلِكِ ۚ قَالَ رَبُّكِ هُوَ عَلَىَّ هَيِّنٌ ۚ

وَّلِنَجْعَلَهٗٓ اٰيَةً لِّلنَّاسِ وَرَحْمَةً مِّنَّا ۚ وَكَانَ اَمْرًا

مَّقْضِيًّا ۞ فَحَمَلَتْهُ فَانْتَبَذَتْ بِهٖ مَكَانًا قَصِيًّا ۞

فَاَجَآءَهَا الْمَخَاضُ اِلٰى جِذْعِ النَّخْلَةِ ۚ قَالَتْ يٰلَيْتَنِىْ

مِتُّ قَبْلَ هٰذَا وَكُنْتُ نَسْيًا مَّنْسِيًّا ۞ فَنَادٰىهَا مِنْ

تَحْتِهَآ اَلَّا تَحْزَنِىْ قَدْ جَعَلَ رَبُّكِ تَحْتَكِ سَرِيًّا ۞

وَهُزِّىْٓ اِلَيْكِ بِجِذْعِ النَّخْلَةِ تُسٰقِطْ عَلَيْكِ رُطَبًا

جَنِيًّا ۞ فَكُلِىْ وَاشْرَبِىْ وَقَرِّىْ عَيْنًا ۚ فَاِمَّا تَرَيِنَّ مِنَ

الْبَشَرِ اَحَدًا ۙ فَقُوْلِىْٓ اِنِّىْ نَذَرْتُ لِلرَّحْمٰنِ صَوْمًا فَلَنْ

اُكَلِّمَ الْيَوْمَ اِنْسِيًّا ۞ فَاَتَتْ بِهٖ قَوْمَهَا تَحْمِلُهٗ ۚ قَالُوْا

يٰمَرْيَمُ لَقَدْ جِئْتِ شَيْئًا فَرِيًّا ۞ يٰٓاُخْتَ هٰرُوْنَ مَا كَانَ

اَبُوْكِ امْرَاَ سَوْءٍ وَّمَا كَانَتْ اُمُّكِ بَغِيًّا ۞ فَاَشَارَتْ

اِلَيْهِ ۚ قَالُوْا كَيْفَ نُكَلِّمُ مَنْ كَانَ فِى الْمَهْدِ صَبِيًّا ۞

قَالَ اِنِّىْ عَبْدُ اللّٰهِ ۖ۫ اٰتٰىنِىَ الْكِتٰبَ وَجَعَلَنِىْ نَبِيًّا ۞

وَّجَعَلَنِىْ مُبٰرَكًا اَيْنَ مَا كُنْتُ ۖ وَاَوْصٰنِىْ بِالصَّلٰوةِ

The miraculous birth of Isa is amazing evidence of Divine power and creativity. With Allah the impossible can happen.

597

The story of Maryam

¹⁶ Mention Maryam, when she left her family to go to a place in the East. ¹⁷ She separated herself from them *to stay* in an isolated place; We sent the Angel of Revelation to her and he appeared in human form. ¹⁸ She said, "I seek the protection of the Kind *Lord* from you if you fear Allah." ¹⁹ He said, "I am a messenger from Your Lord, and I have come to give you a pure son." ²⁰ She replied, "How can I have a son when no man has touched me and I am not loose woman?"^a ²¹ He told her, "That is how it will be; your Lord said, 'This is easy for me, and We shall make him a sign of Our Kindness for people, a command, done!'"

Mary gives birth to Isa

²² And so it was she conceived him and moved to a far-off place. ²³ When the pains of childbirth drove her to the trunk of a date tree, she cried: "I wish I were dead and forgotten long before all this." ²⁴ A voice from below cried out to her: "Do not worry; your Lord has provided flowing water at your feet; ²⁵ shake the trunk of the date Palm and fresh ripe dates will fall. ²⁶ Eat and drink, be happy. When you see someone say, 'I vowed to the Kind *Lord* a fast, so today I shall not speak to anyone.'

Isa speaks to defend his mother

²⁷ She came to her family, carrying him. They said, "Maryam, you have brought something unheard of; ²⁸ sister of Harun, your father was not evil, nor was your mother loose woman." ²⁹ She pointed to him. They replied, "How can we speak to an infant in a cradle?" ³⁰ *Isa* spoke: "I am a servant of Allah; He has given me the Book, made me a prophet, ³¹ made me blessed wherever I go, commanded me to pray and to give charity. *I shall do so* as long as I live,

---

^a But a virgin.

وَالزَّكٰوةِ مَا دُمۡتُ حَيًّا ۖ وَّبَرًّۢا بِوَالِدَتِیۡ وَلَمۡ یَجۡعَلۡنِیۡ جَبَّارًا شَقِیًّا ۝ وَالسَّلٰمُ عَلَیَّ یَوۡمَ وُلِدۡتُّ وَیَوۡمَ اَمُوۡتُ وَیَوۡمَ اُبۡعَثُ حَیًّا ۝ ذٰلِكَ عِیۡسَی ابۡنُ مَرۡیَمَ ۚ قَوۡلَ الۡحَقِّ الَّذِیۡ فِیۡهِ یَمۡتَرُوۡنَ ۝ مَا كَانَ لِلّٰهِ اَنۡ یَّتَّخِذَ مِنۡ وَّلَدٍ ۙ سُبۡحٰنَهٗ ؕ اِذَا قَضٰۤی اَمۡرًا فَاِنَّمَا یَقُوۡلُ لَهٗ كُنۡ فَیَكُوۡنُ ۝ وَاِنَّ اللّٰهَ رَبِّیۡ وَرَبُّكُمۡ فَاعۡبُدُوۡهُ ؕ هٰذَا صِرَاطٌ مُّسۡتَقِیۡمٌ ۝ فَاخۡتَلَفَ الۡاَحۡزَابُ مِنۡۢ بَیۡنِهِمۡ ۚ فَوَیۡلٌ لِّلَّذِیۡنَ كَفَرُوۡا مِنۡ مَّشۡهَدِ یَوۡمٍ عَظِیۡمٍ ۝ اَسۡمِعۡ بِهِمۡ وَاَبۡصِرۡ ۙ یَوۡمَ یَاۡتُوۡنَنَا لٰكِنِ الظّٰلِمُوۡنَ الۡیَوۡمَ فِیۡ ضَلٰلٍ مُّبِیۡنٍ ۝ وَاَنۡذِرۡهُمۡ یَوۡمَ الۡحَسۡرَةِ اِذۡ قُضِیَ الۡاَمۡرُ ۘ وَهُمۡ فِیۡ غَفۡلَةٍ وَّهُمۡ لَا یُؤۡمِنُوۡنَ ۝ اِنَّا نَحۡنُ نَرِثُ الۡاَرۡضَ وَمَنۡ عَلَیۡهَا وَاِلَیۡنَا یُرۡجَعُوۡنَ ۝ وَاذۡكُرۡ فِی الۡكِتٰبِ اِبۡرٰهِیۡمَ ؕ اِنَّهٗ كَانَ صِدِّیۡقًا نَّبِیًّا ۝ اِذۡ قَالَ لِاَبِیۡهِ یٰۤاَبَتِ لِمَ تَعۡبُدُ مَا لَا یَسۡمَعُ وَلَا یُبۡصِرُ وَلَا یُغۡنِیۡ عَنۡكَ شَیۡئًا ۝ یٰۤاَبَتِ اِنِّیۡ قَدۡ جَآءَنِیۡ مِنَ الۡعِلۡمِ مَا لَمۡ یَاۡتِكَ فَاتَّبِعۡنِیۡۤ اَهۡدِكَ صِرَاطًا سَوِیًّا ۝ یٰۤاَبَتِ لَا تَعۡبُدِ الشَّیۡطٰنَ ؕ اِنَّ الشَّیۡطٰنَ كَانَ لِلرَّحۡمٰنِ عَصِیًّا ۝ یٰۤاَبَتِ اِنِّیۡۤ اَخَافُ اَنۡ یَّمَسَّكَ عَذَابٌ مِّنَ الرَّحۡمٰنِ فَتَكُوۡنَ لِلشَّیۡطٰنِ وَلِیًّا ۝ قَالَ اَرَاغِبٌ اَنۡتَ عَنۡ اٰلِهَتِیۡ یٰۤاِبۡرٰهِیۡمُ ۚ لَئِنۡ لَّمۡ تَنۡتَهِ لَاَرۡجُمَنَّكَ

Baby Isa spoke from his cradle to defend the honour of his mother. Have you spoken up for someone?

599

³²and I will take care of my mother. He has not made me overbearing or disobedient. ³³So Allah's peace be on me the day I was born, the day I die and the day that I am resurrected."

Isa is the servant of Allah
³⁴That was Isa, son of Maryam; that's the truth they have doubt about. ³⁵Allah has not taken a son, glory to Him. When he gives an order, He says to it, "Be," and it becomes. ³⁶Surely Allah is My Lord and Your Lord, so worship Him; this is the straight path. ³⁷The sects differed among themselves; anguish awaits the disbelievers when the terrible Day comes. ³⁸How well they will hear and see the day they come to Us, yet today the evildoers are totally lost. ³⁹Warn them of a fateful Day when the decree shall be fulfilled; they were neglectful and didn't believe. ⁴⁰We shall inherit the Earth and all that's in it, and to Us they will all be returned.

Ibrahim challenges idol worship
⁴¹Mention Ibrahim in the Book; he was a truthful man and a prophet. ⁴²When he said to his father,ᵃ "My father, why do you worship idols that cannot hear nor see nor benefit you in the least? ⁴³My father, the knowledge that didn't reach you has come to me. Therefore, follow me; I shall guide you on the straight path. ⁴⁴My father, do not worship Satan, he has disobeyed the Kind Lord. ⁴⁵My father, I fear that you shall be punished by the most Kind, and become a friend of Satan." ⁴⁶His father replied, "Ibrahim, are you turning away from my gods? If you do not stop this, I will torture you; off you go and leave me alone."

ᵃ Here, classical commentators take "father" to mean "uncle".

وَاهۡجُرۡنِیۡ مَلِیًّا ۞ قَالَ سَلٰمٌ عَلَیۡكَ ۚ سَاَسۡتَغۡفِرُ لَكَ

رَبِّیۡ ؕ اِنَّهٗ كَانَ بِیۡ حَفِیًّا ۞ وَاَعۡتَزِلُكُمۡ وَمَا تَدۡعُوۡنَ

مِنۡ دُوۡنِ اللّٰهِ وَاَدۡعُوۡا رَبِّیۡ ۖ عَسٰۤی اَلَّاۤ اَكُوۡنَ بِدُعَآءِ

رَبِّیۡ شَقِیًّا ۞ فَلَمَّا اعۡتَزَلَهُمۡ وَمَا یَعۡبُدُوۡنَ مِنۡ دُوۡنِ

اللّٰهِ ۙ وَهَبۡنَا لَهٗۤ اِسۡحٰقَ وَیَعۡقُوۡبَ ؕ وَكُلًّا جَعَلۡنَا نَبِیًّا ۞

وَوَهَبۡنَا لَهُمۡ مِّنۡ رَّحۡمَتِنَا وَجَعَلۡنَا لَهُمۡ لِسَانَ صِدۡقٍ

عَلِیًّا ۞ وَاذۡكُرۡ فِی الۡكِتٰبِ مُوۡسٰۤی ۫ اِنَّهٗ كَانَ مُخۡلَصًا

وَّكَانَ رَسُوۡلًا نَّبِیًّا ۞ وَنَادَیۡنٰهُ مِنۡ جَانِبِ الطُّوۡرِ

الۡاَیۡمَنِ وَقَرَّبۡنٰهُ نَجِیًّا ۞ وَوَهَبۡنَا لَهٗ مِنۡ رَّحۡمَتِنَاۤ

اَخَاهُ هٰرُوۡنَ نَبِیًّا ۞ وَاذۡكُرۡ فِی الۡكِتٰبِ اِسۡمٰعِیۡلَ ۫ اِنَّهٗ

كَانَ صَادِقَ الۡوَعۡدِ وَكَانَ رَسُوۡلًا نَّبِیًّا ۞ وَكَانَ

یَاۡمُرُ اَهۡلَهٗ بِالصَّلٰوةِ وَالزَّكٰوةِ ۖ وَكَانَ عِنۡدَ رَبِّهٖ

مَرۡضِیًّا ۞ وَاذۡكُرۡ فِی الۡكِتٰبِ اِدۡرِیۡسَ ۫ اِنَّهٗ كَانَ صِدِّیۡقًا

نَّبِیًّا ۞ وَّرَفَعۡنٰهُ مَكَانًا عَلِیًّا ۞ اُولٰٓئِكَ الَّذِیۡنَ اَنۡعَمَ

اللّٰهُ عَلَیۡهِمۡ مِّنَ النَّبِیّٖنَ مِنۡ ذُرِّیَّةِ اٰدَمَ ۖ وَمِمَّنۡ

حَمَلۡنَا مَعَ نُوۡحٍ ۖ وَّمِنۡ ذُرِّیَّةِ اِبۡرٰهِیۡمَ وَاِسۡرَآئِیۡلَ ۖ

وَمِمَّنۡ هَدَیۡنَا وَاجۡتَبَیۡنَا ؕ اِذَا تُتۡلٰی عَلَیۡهِمۡ اٰیٰتُ

الرَّحۡمٰنِ خَرُّوۡا سُجَّدًا وَّبُكِیًّا ۩ ۞ فَخَلَفَ مِنۡ بَعۡدِهِمۡ

خَلۡفٌ اَضَاعُوا الصَّلٰوةَ وَاتَّبَعُوا الشَّهَوٰتِ فَسَوۡفَ

یَلۡقَوۡنَ غَیًّا ۞ اِلَّا مَنۡ تَابَ وَاٰمَنَ وَعَمِلَ صَالِحًا

Ibrahim trusted Allah: "My prayer will not go unheard by My Lord." How passionately do you pray?

601

⁴⁷ He said, "Peace be on you. I shall seek My Lord's forgiveness for you, since He is Most Kind to me. ⁴⁸ In the meantime, I shall leave you and those you call upon beside Allah. I shall pray to My Lord and believe that my prayer will not go unanswered." ⁴⁹ When he detached himself from them and what they worshipped beside Allah, We gave him Ishaq and Yaqub, and We made them all prophets. ⁵⁰ We gave them Our gifts and We gave them fame and honour.

Prophets Musa, Ismail, Idris and Nuh

⁵¹ Mention Musa in the Book; he was a chosen messenger and a prophet. ⁵² We called out to him from the right-hand side of the mount *Sinai* and brought him closer to speak to him in secret. ⁵³ We treated him kindly and gave him as a *support* Harun, his brother, a prophet. ⁵⁴ Mention Ismail in the Book; he was a man of his word, a messenger and a prophet. ⁵⁵ He used to tell his family to pray and to give Zakat, and his Lord liked him. ⁵⁶ Mention Idris in the Book; he was a man of truth, and a prophet. ⁵⁷ And We raised him to a high rank. ⁵⁸ Allah favoured these *wonderful* men; the prophets from the children of Adam, and they came from those We carried with Nuh, and they were from the children of Ibrahim and Yaqub. We guided and selected them. When the verses of the Kind Lord were recited to them, they fell in prostration tearfully.

The importance of regular prayers

⁵⁹ After them came generations who neglected the prayer and followed their lusts. Soon they will face the consequences of their evil. ⁶⁰ Except those who repent, believe and do righteous deeds – they shall enter Paradise, and they will not be wronged in the slightest.

فَاُولٰٓئِكَ يَدْخُلُوْنَ الْجَنَّةَ وَلَا يُظْلَمُوْنَ شَيْئًا ۟ ۝

جَنّٰتِ عَدْنِۣ الَّتِیْ وَعَدَ الرَّحْمٰنُ عِبَادَهٗ بِالْغَیْبِ ؕ

اِنَّهٗ كَانَ وَعْدُهٗ مَاْتِیًّا ۝ لَا یَسْمَعُوْنَ فِیْهَا لَغْوًا اِلَّا

سَلٰمًا ؕ وَلَهُمْ رِزْقُهُمْ فِیْهَا بُكْرَةً وَّعَشِیًّا ۝ تِلْكَ

الْجَنَّةُ الَّتِیْ نُوْرِثُ مِنْ عِبَادِنَا مَنْ كَانَ تَقِیًّا ۝

وَمَا نَتَنَزَّلُ اِلَّا بِاَمْرِ رَبِّكَ ۚ لَهٗ مَا بَیْنَ اَیْدِیْنَا وَمَا

خَلْفَنَا وَمَا بَیْنَ ذٰلِكَ ۚ وَمَا كَانَ رَبُّكَ نَسِیًّا ۝ رَبُّ

السَّمٰوٰتِ وَالْاَرْضِ وَمَا بَیْنَهُمَا فَاعْبُدْهُ وَاصْطَبِرْ

ع ٥ ٣

لِعِبَادَتِهٖ ؕ هَلْ تَعْلَمُ لَهٗ سَمِیًّا ۝ وَیَقُوْلُ الْاِنْسَانُ

ءَاِذَا مَا مِتُّ لَسَوْفَ اُخْرَجُ حَیًّا ۝ اَوَلَا یَذْكُرُ الْاِنْسَانُ

اَنَّا خَلَقْنٰهُ مِنْ قَبْلُ وَلَمْ یَكُ شَیْئًا ۝ فَوَرَبِّكَ

لَنَحْشُرَنَّهُمْ وَالشَّیٰطِیْنَ ثُمَّ لَنُحْضِرَنَّهُمْ حَوْلَ جَهَنَّمَ

جِثِیًّا ۝ ثُمَّ لَنَنْزِعَنَّ مِنْ كُلِّ شِیْعَةٍ اَیُّهُمْ اَشَدُّ

عَلَی الرَّحْمٰنِ عِتِیًّا ۝ ثُمَّ لَنَحْنُ اَعْلَمُ بِالَّذِیْنَ هُمْ

اَوْلٰی بِهَا صِلِیًّا ۝ وَاِنْ مِّنْكُمْ اِلَّا وَارِدُهَا ۚ كَانَ عَلٰی

رَبِّكَ حَتْمًا مَّقْضِیًّا ۝ ثُمَّ نُنَجِّی الَّذِیْنَ اتَّقَوْا وَّنَذَرُ

الظّٰلِمِیْنَ فِیْهَا جِثِیًّا ۝ وَاِذَا تُتْلٰی عَلَیْهِمْ اٰیٰتُنَا بَیِّنٰتٍ

قَالَ الَّذِیْنَ كَفَرُوْا لِلَّذِیْنَ اٰمَنُوْۤا ۙ اَیُّ الْفَرِیْقَیْنِ خَیْرٌ

مَّقَامًا وَّاَحْسَنُ نَدِیًّا ۝ وَكَمْ اَهْلَكْنَا قَبْلَهُمْ مِّنْ قَرْنٍ

هُمْ اَحْسَنُ اَثَاثًا وَّرِءْیًا ۝ قُلْ مَنْ كَانَ فِی الضَّلٰلَةِ

The punishment of Hell will be painful, a sign of Divine displeasure, distance and remoteness.

[61] The Kind Lord's Promise to his servants are Gardens of Eternity, the unseen. His Promise will certainly be fulfilled. [62] They will not hear any useless chatter but peace, there will be plentiful provisions for them morning and evening. [63] Such *a marvellous* Paradise We shall bless Our pious servants to inherit.

Jibreel speaks

[64] "We don't come down except by the command of your Lord.[a] To Him belongs what is in front and behind us, and that which is in between. Your Lord never forgets – [65] Lord of the Heavens and the Earth and what is between them. So, worship Him and be committed to His worship. Is there anyone who is equal to Him?"

Disbelievers kneeling around Hell

[66] A person queries: "Once I am dead will I be raised up again?" [67] Don't people remember We created them before when they were non-existent? [68] So your Lord will gather them all and the Satan; We will make them kneel around Hell, [69] and from every group We will drag out the bitterest enemy of the Kind Lord. [70] We know who deserves to burn in it. [71] However, every one of you will come near it – a decree of your Lord that will be fulfilled. [72] Then We shall save the pious whilst leaving the wrongdoers on their knees in Hell.

The boasting of disbelievers

[73] When Our clear verses are recited to them, the disbelievers say to the believers, "Which of the two groups has better dwellings and who has luxurious clubs?"[b] [74] How many generations did We destroy before them who were more affluent and looked smart?

---

[a] This is Angel Jibreel speaking.
[b] Affluent disbelievers boasting about their wealth and material prowess.

فَلْيَمْدُدْ لَهُ الرَّحْمٰنُ مَدًّا ۚ حَتّٰى إِذَا رَاَوْا مَا يُوعَدُونَ
إِمَّا الْعَذَابَ وَإِمَّا السَّاعَةَ ۚ فَسَيَعْلَمُونَ مَنْ هُوَ
شَرٌّ مَّكَانًا وَّأَضْعَفُ جُنْدًا ۝ وَيَزِيدُ اللّٰهُ الَّذِينَ
اهْتَدَوْا هُدًى ۚ وَالْبٰقِيٰتُ الصّٰلِحٰتُ خَيْرٌ عِنْدَ
رَبِّكَ ثَوَابًا وَّخَيْرٌ مَّرَدًّا ۝ اَفَرَءَيْتَ الَّذِى كَفَرَ
بِاٰيٰتِنَا وَقَالَ لَاُوتَيَنَّ مَالًا وَّوَلَدًا ۝ اَطَّلَعَ الْغَيْبَ
اَمِ اتَّخَذَ عِنْدَ الرَّحْمٰنِ عَهْدًا ۝ كَلَّا ۚ سَنَكْتُبُ مَا
يَقُولُ وَنَمُدُّ لَهُ مِنَ الْعَذَابِ مَدًّا ۝ وَّنَرِثُهُ مَا
يَقُولُ وَيَأْتِينَا فَرْدًا ۝ وَاتَّخَذُوا مِنْ دُونِ اللّٰهِ اٰلِهَةً
لِّيَكُونُوا لَهُمْ عِزًّا ۝ كَلَّا ۚ سَيَكْفُرُونَ بِعِبَادَتِهِمْ
وَيَكُونُونَ عَلَيْهِمْ ضِدًّا ۝ اَلَمْ تَرَ اَنَّا اَرْسَلْنَا
الشَّيٰطِينَ عَلَى الْكٰفِرِينَ تَؤُزُّهُمْ اَزًّا ۝ فَلَا تَعْجَلْ
عَلَيْهِمْ ۚ اِنَّمَا نَعُدُّ لَهُمْ عَدًّا ۝ يَوْمَ نَحْشُرُ الْمُتَّقِينَ اِلَى
الرَّحْمٰنِ وَفْدًا ۝ وَّنَسُوقُ الْمُجْرِمِينَ اِلٰى جَهَنَّمَ وِرْدًا ۝
لَا يَمْلِكُونَ الشَّفَاعَةَ اِلَّا مَنِ اتَّخَذَ عِنْدَ الرَّحْمٰنِ
عَهْدًا ۝ وَقَالُوا اتَّخَذَ الرَّحْمٰنُ وَلَدًا ۝ لَقَدْ جِئْتُمْ
شَيْئًا اِدًّا ۝ تَكَادُ السَّمٰوٰتُ يَتَفَطَّرْنَ مِنْهُ وَتَنْشَقُّ
الْاَرْضُ وَتَخِرُّ الْجِبَالُ هَدًّا ۝ اَنْ دَعَوْا لِلرَّحْمٰنِ وَلَدًا ۝
وَمَا يَنْبَغِي لِلرَّحْمٰنِ اَنْ يَّتَّخِذَ وَلَدًا ۝ اِنْ كُلُّ مَنْ فِي
السَّمٰوٰتِ وَالْاَرْضِ اِلَّا اٰتِي الرَّحْمٰنِ عَبْدًا ۝ لَقَدْ اَحْصٰهُمْ

Why is Allah angry with idolaters? Idolatry is false, it limits the power, the love and greatness of the Lord to a material thing.

⁷⁵Say: "Whoever is misguided, the Kind Lord gives him time until he sees what has been promised – either the punishment or the Final Hour. Then they will know who was in a bad place and who had the weakest forces." ⁷⁶Allah keeps developing the guided in *their* guidance, and the lasting deeds of goodness are best with your Lord as a reward and the best outcome.

Disbelievers' confusion

⁷⁷Have you seen him, who denies Our signs and boasts: "I will certainly be given wealth and children." ⁷⁸Has he got knowledge of the unseen? Or has he taken a pledge from the Kind? ⁷⁹No, We shall write down what he speaks and We shall prolong his punishment. ⁸⁰We shall divest himᵃ of what he spoke when he comes to us alone. ⁸¹They took Gods beside Allah to gain strength; ⁸²but it will not be so, their idols will reject their worship and become their enemies. ⁸³Haven't you realised We sent devils to the disbelievers, who constantly rouse them?

Contrasting the assembly of believers and disbelievers

⁸⁴Don't be hasty about them, since We are counting their days. ⁸⁵On the Day We shall ceremoniously gather the pious before the Kind Lord, ⁸⁶and the sinful will be driven to Hell like thirsty cattle driven to a waterhole, ⁸⁷no one will be able to make intercession except the one given permission by the Kind Lord.

When is Allah most angry?

⁸⁸They said, "The Kind Lord has taken a child." ⁸⁹What a monstrous thing you have said! ⁹⁰The skies would crack, the Earth shudder, and the mountains crumble to dust ⁹¹when they attribute a child to the Kind *Lord*. ⁹²It is not befitting for the Kind Lord to have children. ⁹³Everyone in the Heavens and on Earth must come to the Kind Lord as an obedient servant.

ᵃ Literally: "inherit from him". This is "a metaphor based on the concept of one person's taking over what once belonged to another" (Asad).

وَعَدَّهُمْ عَدًّا ۝ وَكُلُّهُمْ اٰتِيْهِ يَوْمَ الْقِيٰمَةِ فَرْدًا ۝ اِنَّ
الَّذِيْنَ اٰمَنُوْا وَعَمِلُوا الصّٰلِحٰتِ سَيَجْعَلُ لَهُمُ الرَّحْمٰنُ
وُدًّا ۝ فَاِنَّمَا يَسَّرْنٰهُ بِلِسَانِكَ لِتُبَشِّرَ بِهِ الْمُتَّقِيْنَ وَ
تُنْذِرَ بِهٖ قَوْمًا لُّدًّا ۝ وَكَمْ اَهْلَكْنَا قَبْلَهُمْ مِّنْ قَرْنٍ ۚ
هَلْ تُحِسُّ مِنْهُمْ مِّنْ اَحَدٍ اَوْ تَسْمَعُ لَهُمْ رِكْزًا ۝

Receiving public acclaim and love is a favour from Allah for his special friends.

٦
١٦ ع
٩

النُّصْف

⁹⁴He has accurately counted[a] them and numbered them exactly. ⁹⁵So on the Day of Judgement, each one of them will come to Him alone.

Love for good people

⁹⁶The Kind Lord will put love for those who believe and do righteous deeds *in people's hearts*.[b] ⁹⁷We made the Quran easy in your language so you can give good news to the pious, and warn the opponents with it.[c] ⁹⁸How many generations have We destroyed before them? Do you find any one of them alive or hear as much as *their* whisper?

---

[a] *Ahsa* is literally "bookkeeping"

[b] In the hadith, the Messenger ﷺ said: "When Allah loves his servant, He tells Jibreel to love him, so Jibreel loves him, and makes the announcement in Heaven that so and so is Allah's beloved, therefore you should all love him" (Bukhari).

[c] *Qauman Luddan:* obstinate, stubborn and contentious people. Luddites were people who disliked and rebelled against new forms of technology, a parallel with disbelievers who disliked the new message of the Prophet ﷺ.

20. Surat Ta Ha

Ta Ha

This is an early Makkan surat, its central theme is how Allah guides humanity through messengers, exemplified by featuring the life story of Musa ﷺ. The story begins when Musa ﷺ is returning from Madyan to Egypt. He is appointed as a messenger and given miracles. The surat flips back to the time of his birth, recalling how as a baby he was rescued from Pharaoh's murderous plan: "I wrapped you up in My Divine Love so that you may grow up under My Eyes" (39). How loving is Allah! Musa ﷺ heads straight for Pharaoh's court. A heated conversation follows and the Pharaoh gets angry, but Musa boldly – yet gently – continues to invite him to Allah. Despite witnessing the two miracles of Musa ﷺ, the Pharaoh remains stubbornly unwilling to listen to him. He mistakenly believes Musa ﷺ is a magician so challenges him to duel his magicians.

A vivid description of the duel offers insights into the working of magic, and why magic failed. These expert magicians realised that Musa ﷺ was not a magician, so they accepted his victory and his prophethood. The Pharaoh was enraged and had them martyred.

Even after this defeat and witnessing nine miracles, the Pharaoh refused to accept Musa ﷺ. Finally, Musa ﷺ led the Israelites out of Egypt. The Pharaoh chased them, but was drowned. Once in the Sinai Peninsula, the Israelites enjoyed freedom and were blessed with the Heavenly gifts of quail and Manna. However, when Musa ﷺ left them for a short while – he visited Mount Sinai to meet Allah – the Israelites made an idol to worship. Musa ﷺ was angry with his brother Harun for not stopping them. Samiri the Goldsmith, the mastermind of this ordeal, forged a golden calf and Musa ﷺ cursed him for his blasphemy and evil action.

As a commentary on the story of Musa ﷺ, the Quran tells the Makkans to learn a lesson: the Quran is a reminder, and warns of the dire consequences of rejecting the Prophet ﷺ.

The surat opened by telling the beloved Prophet Mustafa ﷺ not to be stressed by sarcasm and scornful attitude of Makkans, at the end he's told: be patient, be calm, and seek help through constant prayer.

بِسْمِ اللّٰهِ الرَّحْمٰنِ الرَّحِیْمِ

طٰهٰ ۚ ۞ مَاۤ اَنْزَلْنَا عَلَیْكَ الْقُرْاٰنَ لِتَشْقٰۤی ۞ اِلَّا تَذْكِرَۃً لِّمَنْ یَّخْشٰی ۞ تَنْزِیْلًا مِّمَّنْ خَلَقَ الْاَرْضَ وَالسَّمٰوٰتِ الْعُلٰی ۞ اَلرَّحْمٰنُ عَلَی الْعَرْشِ اسْتَوٰی ۞ لَهٗ مَا فِی السَّمٰوٰتِ وَمَا فِی الْاَرْضِ وَمَا بَیْنَهُمَا وَمَا تَحْتَ الثَّرٰی ۞ وَاِنْ تَجْهَرْ بِالْقَوْلِ فَاِنَّهٗ یَعْلَمُ السِّرَّ وَاَخْفٰی ۞ اَللّٰهُ لَاۤ اِلٰهَ اِلَّا هُوَ ۚ لَهُ الْاَسْمَآءُ الْحُسْنٰی ۞ وَهَلْ اَتٰىكَ حَدِیْثُ مُوْسٰی ۞ اِذْ رَاٰ نَارًا فَقَالَ لِاَهْلِهِ امْكُثُوْۤا اِنِّیْۤ اٰنَسْتُ نَارًا لَّعَلِّیْۤ اٰتِیْكُمْ مِّنْهَا بِقَبَسٍ اَوْ اَجِدُ عَلَی النَّارِ هُدًی ۞ فَلَمَّاۤ اَتٰىهَا نُوْدِیَ یٰمُوْسٰی ۞ اِنِّیْۤ اَنَا رَبُّكَ فَاخْلَعْ نَعْلَیْكَ ۚ اِنَّكَ بِالْوَادِ الْمُقَدَّسِ طُوًی ۞ وَاَنَا اخْتَرْتُكَ فَاسْتَمِعْ لِمَا یُوْحٰی ۞ اِنَّنِیْۤ اَنَا اللّٰهُ لَاۤ اِلٰهَ اِلَّاۤ اَنَا فَاعْبُدْنِیْ ۙ وَاَقِمِ الصَّلٰوۃَ لِذِكْرِیْ ۞ اِنَّ السَّاعَۃَ اٰتِیَۃٌ اَكَادُ اُخْفِیْهَا لِتُجْزٰی كُلُّ نَفْسٍۭ بِمَا تَسْعٰی ۞ فَلَا یَصُدَّنَّكَ عَنْهَا مَنْ لَّا یُؤْمِنُ بِهَا وَاتَّبَعَ هَوٰىهُ فَتَرْدٰی ۞ وَمَا تِلْكَ بِیَمِیْنِكَ یٰمُوْسٰی ۞ قَالَ هِیَ عَصَایَ ۚ اَتَوَكَّؤُا عَلَیْهَا وَاَهُشُّ بِهَا عَلٰی غَنَمِیْ وَلِیَ فِیْهَا مَاٰرِبُ اُخْرٰی ۞ قَالَ اَلْقِهَا یٰمُوْسٰی ۞ فَاَلْقٰىهَا فَاِذَا هِیَ حَیَّۃٌ تَسْعٰی ۞ قَالَ خُذْهَا وَلَا تَخَفْ ۟ سَنُعِیْدُهَا سِیْرَتَهَا

Musa is brave and undeterred by the disbelievers. Do you ever challenge your society?

In the name of Allah, the Kind, the Caring.

¹ *Ta Ha.*ᵃ

Allah, the Knower of all secrets

²We did not send the *Majestic* Quran to distress you; ³but a reminder to anyone who fears Allah, ⁴a revelation from the one who created the Earth and the soaring skies. ⁵The Most Kind established on the throne *as befits Him.* ⁶The owner of what lies in the Heavens, the Earth and between them, and all that's buried deep in the soil. ⁷Whether you speak aloud or quietly; He knows all the secrets and all that is hidden. ⁸Allah – there is no god but He. His names are the most beautiful.

Musa goes to fetch fire

⁹Have you heard the story of Musa? ¹⁰When he saw the fire he said to his wife, "Stay here, I've noticed a fire; perhaps I can bring a live coal for you or find a guide *nearby.*ᵇ ¹¹When he came near *the bush* a voice called: "Musa, ¹²I am your Lord; take off your sandals you're in the Sacred Valley of Tuwa.ᶜ ¹³I've chosen you, so listen to the Revelation. ¹⁴I am Allah. There is no god but Me, so worship Me. Perform the prayer to remember Me. ¹⁵The Hour shall come, but I will keep it secret, to ensure paying everyone for what they did. ¹⁶So don't let the disbelievers who follow their whims stop you from it, otherwise you will be ruined too."

Musa is blessed with miracles

¹⁷*Allah asked*, "What's in your right-hand Musa?" ¹⁸He replied, "This is my walking stick; I lean on it *sometimes*, I gather leaves for my sheep, and I use it for other things." ¹⁹Allah said, "Throw it down, Musa!" ²⁰So he threw it down, and it turned into a snake scurrying about. ²¹Allah ordered: "Pick it up and don't be afraid; We will return it to its original state.

ᵃ Most commentators agree this means, "O man", however, Al-Qurtubi said it is also the name of the blessed Messenger ﷺ.
ᵇ As he was returning from Madyan.
ᶜ The valley of Tuwa is located near Mount Sinai (Egypt) and it is a sacred valley.

الْاُولٰى ۝ وَاضْمُمْ يَدَكَ اِلٰى جَنَاحِكَ تَخْرُجْ بَيْضَآءَ مِنْ

غَيْرِ سُوْٓءٍ اٰيَةً اُخْرٰى ۝ لِنُرِيَكَ مِنْ اٰيٰتِنَا الْكُبْرٰى ۝

اِذْهَبْ اِلٰى فِرْعَوْنَ اِنَّهٗ طَغٰى ۝ قَالَ رَبِّ اشْرَحْ لِيْ

صَدْرِيْ ۝ وَيَسِّرْ لِيْٓ اَمْرِيْ ۝ وَاحْلُلْ عُقْدَةً مِّنْ

لِّسَانِيْ ۝ يَفْقَهُوْا قَوْلِيْ ۝ وَاجْعَلْ لِّيْ وَزِيْرًا مِّنْ اَهْلِيْ ۝

هٰرُوْنَ اَخِي ۝ اشْدُدْ بِهٖٓ اَزْرِيْ ۝ وَاَشْرِكْهُ فِيْٓ

اَمْرِيْ ۝ كَيْ نُسَبِّحَكَ كَثِيْرًا ۝ وَّنَذْكُرَكَ كَثِيْرًا ۝

اِنَّكَ كُنْتَ بِنَا بَصِيْرًا ۝ قَالَ قَدْ اُوْتِيْتَ سُؤْلَكَ

Musa's Prayer is an invitation to change; from silence to speaking out, compliance to complaining. Are you ready?

يٰمُوْسٰى ۝ وَلَقَدْ مَنَنَّا عَلَيْكَ مَرَّةً اُخْرٰى ۝ اِذْ اَوْحَيْنَآ

اِلٰٓى اُمِّكَ مَا يُوْحٰٓى ۝ اَنِ اقْذِفِيْهِ فِي التَّابُوْتِ فَاقْذِفِيْهِ

فِي الْيَمِّ فَلْيُلْقِهِ الْيَمُّ بِالسَّاحِلِ يَأْخُذْهُ عَدُوٌّ لِّيْ

وَعَدُوٌّ لَّهٗ ط وَاَلْقَيْتُ عَلَيْكَ مَحَبَّةً مِّنِّيْ ۚ وَلِتُصْنَعَ

عَلٰى عَيْنِيْ ۝ اِذْ تَمْشِيْٓ اُخْتُكَ فَتَقُوْلُ هَلْ اَدُلُّكُمْ عَلٰى

مَنْ يَّكْفُلُهٗ ط فَرَجَعْنٰكَ اِلٰٓى اُمِّكَ كَيْ تَقَرَّ عَيْنُهَا وَلَا

تَحْزَنَ ط وَقَتَلْتَ نَفْسًا فَنَجَّيْنٰكَ مِنَ الْغَمِّ وَفَتَنّٰكَ

فُتُوْنًا ۚ فَلَبِثْتَ سِنِيْنَ فِيْٓ اَهْلِ مَدْيَنَ ۙ ثُمَّ جِئْتَ

عَلٰى قَدَرٍ يّٰمُوْسٰى ۝ وَاصْطَنَعْتُكَ لِنَفْسِيْ ۝ اِذْهَبْ

اَنْتَ وَاَخُوْكَ بِاٰيٰتِيْ وَلَا تَنِيَا فِيْ ذِكْرِيْ ۝ اِذْهَبَآ

اِلٰى فِرْعَوْنَ اِنَّهٗ طَغٰى ۝ فَقُوْلَا لَهٗ قَوْلًا لَّيِّنًا لَّعَلَّهٗ

يَتَذَكَّرُ اَوْ يَخْشٰى ۝ قَالَا رَبَّنَآ اِنَّنَا نَخَافُ اَنْ يَّفْرُطَ

²²Now put your hand under your armpit; it will come out white and unharmed – here is another sign, ²³to show you some of Our great signs. ²⁴Go to Pharaoh, he's overstepped the limits."ᵃ

Musa's prayer for greater understanding

²⁵He prayed: "My Lord, expand my chest, ²⁶make my work easy, ²⁷and untie my tongue ²⁸so *people* may understand my speech, ²⁹and from my family give me a helper, ³⁰my brother Harun, ³¹to strengthen my back ³²and to help me in my task, ³³so that we may always glorify ³⁴and remember you. ³⁵Surely you are Ever-Watching." ³⁶Allah answered, "I grant you what you asked for, Musa. ³⁷We have already done you a favour in the past.

Musa is wrapped up in Divine Love

³⁸Remember, We inspired your mother to ³⁹place you in a basket and let it float in the river. *We told her*: 'The river will take him to the bank from where Mine and your enemy will pick him up.' I wrapped you up in my Divine Love so you may grow up under My watchful eye. ⁴⁰Remember, your sister came and told them:ᵇ 'Shall I tell you who can look after him?' So We returned you to your mother, so that she may be happy and not worry. *Later in your youth* you killed someone, and We saved you *again* from trouble and tested you in various ways; you lived among the People of Madyan *for some time*, then you came here, Musa, as decreed. ⁴¹I have chosen you for Myself.

Musa in Pharaoh's court

⁴²Go with your brother and take My miracles; don't lapse in My remembrance. ⁴³Go to Pharaoh both of you, he has overstepped the limits, ⁴⁴speak gently with him, so he might pay attention or fear Allah." ⁴⁵They said, "Our Lord, we dread he will torture us and transgress bounds."

ᵃ Pharaoh overstepped the limits of being Allah's servant, claiming to be god.

ᵇ Pharaoh's wife had just rescued Musa 🕊 from the river.

عَلَيْنَآ اَوْ اَنْ يَّطْغٰى ۞ قَالَ لَا تَخَافَآ اِنَّنِىْ مَعَكُمَآ اَسْمَعُ

وَاَرٰى ۞ فَاْتِيٰهُ فَقُوْلَآ اِنَّا رَسُوْلَا رَبِّكَ فَاَرْسِلْ مَعَنَا

بَنِىْٓ اِسْرَآءِيْلَ ۙ وَلَا تُعَذِّبْهُمْ ط قَدْ جِئْنٰكَ بِاٰيَةٍ مِّنْ

رَّبِّكَ ط وَالسَّلٰمُ عَلٰى مَنِ اتَّبَعَ الْهُدٰى ۞ اِنَّا قَدْ اُوْحِىَ

اِلَيْنَآ اَنَّ الْعَذَابَ عَلٰى مَنْ كَذَّبَ وَتَوَلّٰى ۞ قَالَ فَمَنْ

رَّبُّكُمَا يٰمُوْسٰى ۞ قَالَ رَبُّنَا الَّذِىْٓ اَعْطٰى كُلَّ شَىْءٍ خَلْقَهٗ

ثُمَّ هَدٰى ۞ قَالَ فَمَا بَالُ الْقُرُوْنِ الْاُوْلٰى ۞ قَالَ

عِلْمُهَا عِنْدَ رَبِّىْ فِىْ كِتٰبٍ ۚ لَا يَضِلُّ رَبِّىْ وَلَا يَنْسَى ۞

الَّذِىْ جَعَلَ لَكُمُ الْاَرْضَ مَهْدًا وَّسَلَكَ لَكُمْ فِيْهَا

سُبُلًا وَّاَنْزَلَ مِنَ السَّمَآءِ مَآءً ط فَاَخْرَجْنَا بِهٖٓ اَزْوَاجًا

مِّنْ نَّبَاتٍ شَتّٰى ۞ كُلُوْا وَارْعَوْا اَنْعَامَكُمْ ط اِنَّ فِىْ

ذٰلِكَ لَاٰيٰتٍ لِّاُولِى النُّهٰى ۞ مِنْهَا خَلَقْنٰكُمْ وَ

فِيْهَا نُعِيْدُكُمْ وَمِنْهَا نُخْرِجُكُمْ تَارَةً اُخْرٰى ۞

وَلَقَدْ اَرَيْنٰهُ اٰيٰتِنَا كُلَّهَا فَكَذَّبَ وَاَبٰى ۞ قَالَ

اَجِئْتَنَا لِتُخْرِجَنَا مِنْ اَرْضِنَا بِسِحْرِكَ يٰمُوْسٰى ۞

فَلَنَاْتِيَنَّكَ بِسِحْرٍ مِّثْلِهٖ فَاجْعَلْ بَيْنَنَا وَ بَيْنَكَ

مَوْعِدًا لَّا نُخْلِفُهٗ نَحْنُ وَلَآ اَنْتَ مَكَانًا سُوًى ۞

قَالَ مَوْعِدُكُمْ يَوْمُ الزِّيْنَةِ وَاَنْ يُّحْشَرَ النَّاسُ

ضُحًى ۞ فَتَوَلّٰى فِرْعَوْنُ فَجَمَعَ كَيْدَهٗ ثُمَّ اَتٰى ۞

قَالَ لَهُمْ مُّوْسٰى وَيْلَكُمْ لَا تَفْتَرُوْا عَلَى اللّٰهِ كَذِبًا

٢
ع
٣٠
١١

Musa's encounter with the Pharaoh was challenging, but Musa invited him to believe in Allah.

615

[46] Allah replied, "Don't worry, I am with you, listening to and observing everything. [47] Now go to him and say: 'We are messengers of your Lord, so send the Israelites with us and do not oppress them; we have come to you with miracles from your Lord. Peace on the one who follows the guidance. [48] It has been revealed to us that the punishment will come on those who reject and turn away.'"

Musa and Pharaoh in heated conversation

[49] *Pharaoh* said, "Who is your Lord, Musa?" [50] He answered, "Our Lord is the One Who gave everything that exists, a body and guidance." [51] He asked, "What about the previous generation?" [52] *Musa* said, "My Lord has full knowledge of them, and *their works* are properly recorded. My Lord never makes a mistake nor forgets." [53] It is He who made the Earth a cradle and made for you means and ways of *livelihood,* and sent down from the sky the rain, so *He* produces with it various pairs of plants, [54] *which you* eat and graze your cattle on; such are Our signs for the understanding. [55] From the Earth We created you; We shall return you there and *finally* We shall bring you back to life once more. [56] We showed him[a] all Our signs, but he denied and refused.

Pharaoh threatens Musa

[57] He said, "Have you come to drive us out of our country with your magic, Musa? [58] We will bring magic to match it, so *let us* set a time for a contest at an agreed place; neither of us shall break the promise." [59] Musa said, "Meet me on the day of the festival when people gather at mid-morning." [60] Pharaoh withdrew and formalised his plans, and came back. [61] Musa said to him, "Woe to you, do not make up lies about Allah, in case He destroys you with punishment; the one who makes up lies will lose."

---

[a] Pharaoh.

فَيُسْحِتَكُمْ بِعَذَابٍ ۚ وَقَدْ خَابَ مَنِ افْتَرٰى ۝

فَتَنَازَعُوٓا اَمْرَهُمْ بَيْنَهُمْ وَاَسَرُّوا النَّجْوٰى ۝

قَالُوٓا اِنْ هٰذٰنِ لَسٰحِرٰنِ يُرِيدٰنِ اَنْ يُّخْرِجٰكُمْ مِّنْ اَرْضِكُمْ بِسِحْرِهِمَا وَيَذْهَبَا بِطَرِيقَتِكُمُ الْمُثْلٰى ۝ فَاَجْمِعُوا كَيْدَكُمْ ثُمَّ ائْتُوا صَفًّا ۚ وَقَدْ اَفْلَحَ الْيَوْمَ مَنِ اسْتَعْلٰى ۝ قَالُوا يٰمُوسٰٓى اِمَّآ اَنْ تُلْقِيَ وَاِمَّآ اَنْ نَّكُوْنَ اَوَّلَ مَنْ اَلْقٰى ۝ قَالَ بَلْ اَلْقُوا ۚ فَاِذَا حِبَالُهُمْ وَعِصِيُّهُمْ يُخَيَّلُ اِلَيْهِ مِنْ سِحْرِهِمْ اَنَّهَا تَسْعٰى ۝ فَاَوْجَسَ فِيْ نَفْسِهٖ خِيْفَةً مُّوسٰى ۝ قُلْنَا لَا تَخَفْ اِنَّكَ اَنْتَ الْاَعْلٰى ۝ وَاَلْقِ مَا فِيْ يَمِيْنِكَ تَلْقَفْ مَا صَنَعُوا ۗ اِنَّمَا صَنَعُوا كَيْدُ سٰحِرٍ ۗ وَلَا يُفْلِحُ السَّاحِرُ حَيْثُ اَتٰى ۝ فَاُلْقِيَ السَّحَرَةُ سُجَّدًا قَالُوٓا اٰمَنَّا بِرَبِّ هٰرُوْنَ وَمُوسٰى ۝ قَالَ اٰمَنْتُمْ لَهٗ قَبْلَ اَنْ اٰذَنَ لَكُمْ ۚ اِنَّهٗ لَكَبِيْرُكُمُ الَّذِيْ عَلَّمَكُمُ السِّحْرَ ۚ فَلَاُقَطِّعَنَّ اَيْدِيَكُمْ وَاَرْجُلَكُمْ مِّنْ خِلَافٍ وَّلَاُصَلِّبَنَّكُمْ فِيْ جُذُوْعِ النَّخْلِ ۚ وَلَتَعْلَمُنَّ اَيُّنَآ اَشَدُّ عَذَابًا وَّاَبْقٰى ۝ قَالُوا لَنْ نُّؤْثِرَكَ عَلٰى مَا جَآءَنَا مِنَ الْبَيِّنٰتِ وَالَّذِيْ فَطَرَنَا فَاقْضِ مَآ اَنْتَ قَاضٍ ۗ اِنَّمَا تَقْضِيْ هٰذِهِ الْحَيٰوةَ الدُّنْيَا ۝ اِنَّآ اٰمَنَّا بِرَبِّنَا لِيَغْفِرَ لَنَا

In the magic duel, the Pharoah's magicians recognised the miracle of Musa and believed it.

[62] So they secretly discussed their plans among themselves. [63] They said, "These two magicians want to drive you out of your country with their magic, and put an end to your cherished lifestyle." [64] Therefore, put together your plans and then come organised in rows. Whoever triumphs today will succeed.

Musa's contest with the magicians

[65] The magicians said, "Musa, either you throw or we'll throw first." [66] Musa replied, "You throw first!" So by their magic, their ropes and sticks appeared to him to be moving around. [67] Musa was alarmed. [68] We told him, "Don't worry, you will have the upper hand. [69] Throw down what is in your right hand, it will swallow up what they have made. They performed magicians' tricks, and the magicians are never successful in what they do." [70] So the magicians fell in prostration saying, "We believe in the Lord of Harun and Musa."

Pharaoh opposes freedom of faith

[71] The Pharaoh said, "You have believed him before I gave you permission, so he must be your mentor who taught you magic. I'll cut off your hands and your feet from the opposite sides, and hang you on the trunks of palm trees, so you will know whose punishment is more severe and everlasting." [72] They replied, "We will never prefer you, we saw the clear proofs of the One who created us, so decide what you will, and the most you can do is end our worldly life. [a]

---

[a]   *Taqdi* means 'he decided' but also 'he ended something'.

خَطِيْنَا وَمَاۤ اَكْرَهْتَنَا عَلَيْهِ مِنَ السِّحْرِ ؕ وَاللّٰهُ

خَيْرٌ وَّ اَبْقٰى ۝ اِنَّهٗ مَنْ يَّاْتِ رَبَّهٗ مُجْرِمًا فَاِنَّ

لَهٗ جَهَنَّمَ ؕ لَا يَمُوْتُ فِيْهَا وَلَا يَحْيٰى ۝ وَمَنْ

يَّاْتِهٖ مُؤْمِنًا قَدْ عَمِلَ الصّٰلِحٰتِ فَاُولٰٓئِكَ لَهُمُ

الدَّرَجٰتُ الْعُلٰى ۝ جَنّٰتُ عَدْنٍ تَجْرِيْ مِنْ تَحْتِهَا

الْاَنْهٰرُ خٰلِدِيْنَ فِيْهَا ؕ وَذٰلِكَ جَزٰٓؤُا مَنْ تَزَكّٰى ۝

وَلَقَدْ اَوْحَيْنَاۤ اِلٰى مُوْسٰٓى ۙ اَنْ اَسْرِ بِعِبَادِيْ

فَاضْرِبْ لَهُمْ طَرِيْقًا فِى الْبَحْرِ يَبَسًا ۙ لَّا تَخٰفُ

دَرَكًا وَّلَا تَخْشٰى ۝ فَاَتْبَعَهُمْ فِرْعَوْنُ بِجُنُوْدِهٖ

فَغَشِيَهُمْ مِّنَ الْيَمِّ مَا غَشِيَهُمْ ؕ وَاَضَلَّ فِرْعَوْنُ

قَوْمَهٗ وَمَا هَدٰى ۝ يٰبَنِيْۤ اِسْرَآئِيْلَ قَدْ اَنْجَيْنٰكُمْ

مِّنْ عَدُوِّكُمْ وَوٰعَدْنٰكُمْ جَانِبَ الطُّوْرِ الْاَيْمَنَ

وَنَزَّلْنَا عَلَيْكُمُ الْمَنَّ وَ السَّلْوٰى ۝ كُلُوْا مِنْ

طَيِّبٰتِ مَا رَزَقْنٰكُمْ وَلَا تَطْغَوْا فِيْهِ فَيَحِلَّ

عَلَيْكُمْ غَضَبِيْ ۚ وَمَنْ يَّحْلِلْ عَلَيْهِ غَضَبِيْ فَقَدْ

هَوٰى ۝ وَاِنِّيْ لَغَفَّارٌ لِّمَنْ تَابَ وَاٰمَنَ وَعَمِلَ

صَالِحًا ثُمَّ اهْتَدٰى ۝ وَمَاۤ اَعْجَلَكَ عَنْ قَوْمِكَ

يٰمُوْسٰى ۝ قَالَ هُمْ اُولَآءِ عَلٰٓى اَثَرِيْ وَعَجِلْتُ

اِلَيْكَ رَبِّ لِتَرْضٰى ۝ قَالَ فَاِنَّا قَدْ فَتَنَّا قَوْمَكَ

مِنْۢ بَعْدِكَ وَاَضَلَّهُمُ السَّامِرِيُّ ۝ فَرَجَعَ

Musa hurriedly climbed Mount Sinai, displaying his eagerness to be with the Lord. Do you rush on the path to the Lord?

⁷³ We have believed in Our Lord, may He forgive us our mistakes and the magic that you have forced us to practice. Allah is the Best and the Everlasting." ⁷⁴ Whoever comes to His Lord sinning, for him is Hell where he will neither die nor live. ⁷⁵ *On the other hand,* whoever comes to Him believing and doing righteous deeds, they shall have a lofty place. ⁷⁶ They will live in Gardens of Eternity, with streams flowing beneath them. Such is the reward of those who purify themselves.

Musa leads the Israelites out of Egypt

⁷⁷ We revealed to Musa: "Take our servants by night and make a dry way for them across the sea, and don't fear being caught, nor be worried." ⁷⁸ The Pharaoh and his army followed them, and they were besieged and covered up by the sea. ⁷⁹ The Pharaoh misled his people, and he didn't guide them. ⁸⁰ Israelites! We saved you from your enemy and We made a contract with you on the right-hand side of the mountain, and We sent down to you Manna and quails.^a ⁸¹ Eat from the wholesome food We gave you, but don't overstep the limits. Otherwise, I shall be angry with you, and anyone who suffers my anger, will fail. ⁸² *However,* I am Forgiving for anyone who repents, believes, does righteous deeds and remains on the straight path.

Israelites make an idol to worship

⁸³ "Musa, why have you come hastily ahead of your followers?"^b ⁸⁴ He said, "They are coming behind me, I rushed to please you My Lord." ⁸⁵ Allah said, "After you left, We tested your people, when Samiri misled them."^c

---

^a Manna is a special type of food like honey that was graciously provided to them; quail is a small game bird.

^b When you climbed Mount Sinai.

^c Samiri, or the Samirian, was from one of the tribes of the Israelites.

مُوْسٰۤى اِلٰى قَوْمِهٖ غَضْبَانَ اَسِفًا ۬ قَالَ يٰقَوْمِ
اَلَمْ يَعِدْكُمْ رَبُّكُمْ وَعْدًا حَسَنًا ۬ اَفَطَالَ
عَلَيْكُمُ الْعَهْدُ اَمْ اَرَدْتُّمْ اَنْ يَّحِلَّ عَلَيْكُمْ
غَضَبٌ مِّنْ رَّبِّكُمْ فَاَخْلَفْتُمْ مَّوْعِدِيْ ۝ قَالُوْا مَاۤ
اَخْلَفْنَا مَوْعِدَكَ بِمَلْكِنَا وَلٰكِنَّا حُمِّلْنَاۤ اَوْزَارًا
مِّنْ زِيْنَةِ الْقَوْمِ فَقَذَفْنٰهَا فَكَذٰلِكَ اَلْقَى
السَّامِرِيُّ ۝ فَاَخْرَجَ لَهُمْ عِجْلًا جَسَدًا لَّهٗ خُوَارٌ
فَقَالُوْا هٰذَاۤ اِلٰهُكُمْ وَاِلٰهُ مُوْسٰى ۬ فَنَسِيَ ۝ اَفَلَا
يَرَوْنَ اَلَّا يَرْجِعُ اِلَيْهِمْ قَوْلًا ۬ وَّلَا يَمْلِكُ لَهُمْ
ضَرًّا وَّلَا نَفْعًا ۝ وَلَقَدْ قَالَ لَهُمْ هٰرُوْنُ مِنْ
قَبْلُ يٰقَوْمِ اِنَّمَا فُتِنْتُمْ بِهٖ ۬ وَاِنَّ رَبَّكُمُ الرَّحْمٰنُ
فَاتَّبِعُوْنِيْ وَاَطِيْعُوْۤا اَمْرِيْ ۝ قَالُوْا لَنْ نَّبْرَحَ عَلَيْهِ
عٰكِفِيْنَ حَتّٰى يَرْجِعَ اِلَيْنَا مُوْسٰى ۝ قَالَ يٰهٰرُوْنُ مَا
مَنَعَكَ اِذْ رَاَيْتَهُمْ ضَلُّوْۤا ۝ اَلَّا تَتَّبِعَنِ ۬ اَفَعَصَيْتَ
اَمْرِيْ ۝ قَالَ يَبْنَؤُمَّ لَا تَاْخُذْ بِلِحْيَتِيْ وَلَا بِرَاْسِيْ ۬
اِنِّيْ خَشِيْتُ اَنْ تَقُوْلَ فَرَّقْتَ بَيْنَ بَنِيْۤ اِسْرَآءِيْلَ
وَلَمْ تَرْقُبْ قَوْلِيْ ۝ قَالَ فَمَا خَطْبُكَ يٰسَامِرِيُّ ۝
قَالَ بَصُرْتُ بِمَا لَمْ يَبْصُرُوْا بِهٖ فَقَبَضْتُ قَبْضَةً
مِّنْ اَثَرِ الرَّسُوْلِ فَنَبَذْتُهَا وَكَذٰلِكَ سَوَّلَتْ لِيْ
نَفْسِيْ ۝ قَالَ فَاذْهَبْ فَاِنَّ لَكَ فِي الْحَيٰوةِ اَنْ تَقُوْلَ

The golden calf symbolised the materialistic mentality of the Israelites. Are you influenced by crass capitalism?

[86] Musa *quickly* returned to his people; angry and saddened. He said, "My people, didn't your Lord make a contract with you? Or have you forgotten it? Or you wanted to invite your Lord's anger on yourself by breaking the contract with me?" [87] They said, "We didn't deliberately break the promise; we were carrying too much weight from people's jewellery, so we threw it *in the fire* and the Samiri threw likewise." [88] Samiri shaped for them a statue of a calf that made a mooing sound, so they said, "This is god and the god of Musa, but he deceived them." [89] Why didn't they realise the calf couldn't answer them, and neither harm nor benefit them? [90] Harun had already told them: "My people, you have been tested with this; your Lord is Kind, so follow me and obey my orders. [91] They replied, "We'll carry on worshipping it until Musa comes back."

Musa is angry with Harun and the Israelites

[92] *Musa* said, "Harun, when you saw them being misled what stopped you [93] from *leaving them and* following me? Why did you disobey my orders?" [94] Harun replied, "My mother's son, don't grab my beard or my hair, I was afraid you would say: 'You divided the Israelites and you didn't wait for my decision.'" [95] Musa said, "Samiri, why did you do this?" [96] He said, "I saw what they didn't see, I picked up a handful of dust from the trail of the Messenger[a] and threw it *at the statue of the calf*; unfortunately that's what seemed pleasing to me."

---

[a] Angel Jibreel.

لَا مِسَاسَ ۫ وَاِنَّ لَكَ مَوْعِدًا لَّنْ تُخْلَفَهٗ ۚ وَانْظُرْ
اِلٰٓى اِلٰهِكَ الَّذِىْ ظَلْتَ عَلَيْهِ عَاكِفًا ۗ لَّنُحَرِّقَنَّهٗ
ثُمَّ لَنَنْسِفَنَّهٗ فِى الْيَمِّ نَسْفًا ۞ اِنَّمَآ اِلٰهُكُمُ اللّٰهُ
الَّذِىْ لَاۤ اِلٰهَ اِلَّا هُوَ ؕ وَسِعَ كُلَّ شَىْءٍ عِلْمًا ۞
كَذٰلِكَ نَقُصُّ عَلَيْكَ مِنْ اَنْۢبَآءِ مَا قَدْ سَبَقَ ۚ وَقَدْ
اٰتَيْنٰكَ مِنْ لَّدُنَّا ذِكْرًا ۞ مَنْ اَعْرَضَ عَنْهُ فَاِنَّهٗ
يَحْمِلُ يَوْمَ الْقِيٰمَةِ وِزْرًا ۞ خٰلِدِيْنَ فِيْهِ ؕ وَسَآءَ لَهُمْ
يَوْمَ الْقِيٰمَةِ حِمْلًا ۞ يَوْمَ يُنْفَخُ فِى الصُّوْرِ وَنَحْشُرُ
الْمُجْرِمِيْنَ يَوْمَئِذٍ زُرْقًا ۞ يَّتَخَافَتُوْنَ بَيْنَهُمْ اِنْ
لَّبِثْتُمْ اِلَّا عَشْرًا ۞ نَحْنُ اَعْلَمُ بِمَا يَقُوْلُوْنَ اِذْ يَقُوْلُ
اَمْثَلُهُمْ طَرِيْقَةً اِنْ لَّبِثْتُمْ اِلَّا يَوْمًا ۞ وَيَسْئَلُوْنَكَ
عَنِ الْجِبَالِ فَقُلْ يَنْسِفُهَا رَبِّيْ نَسْفًا ۞ فَيَذَرُهَا
قَاعًا صَفْصَفًا ۞ لَّا تَرٰى فِيْهَا عِوَجًا وَّلَاۤ اَمْتًا ۞
يَوْمَئِذٍ يَّتَّبِعُوْنَ الدَّاعِىَ لَا عِوَجَ لَهٗ ۚ وَخَشَعَتِ
الْاَصْوَاتُ لِلرَّحْمٰنِ فَلَا تَسْمَعُ اِلَّا هَمْسًا ۞ يَوْمَئِذٍ
لَّا تَنْفَعُ الشَّفَاعَةُ اِلَّا مَنْ اَذِنَ لَهُ الرَّحْمٰنُ وَرَضِىَ
لَهٗ قَوْلًا ۞ يَعْلَمُ مَا بَيْنَ اَيْدِيْهِمْ وَمَا خَلْفَهُمْ
وَلَا يُحِيْطُوْنَ بِهٖ عِلْمًا ۞ وَعَنَتِ الْوُجُوْهُ لِلْحَىِّ
الْقَيُّوْمِ ؕ وَقَدْ خَابَ مَنْ حَمَلَ ظُلْمًا ۞ وَمَنْ يَّعْمَلْ
مِنَ الصّٰلِحٰتِ وَهُوَ مُؤْمِنٌ فَلَا يَخٰفُ ظُلْمًا

How often do you remember the Day of Judgement? Shouldn't it be always in our hearts and minds?

⁹⁷Musa told him, "Go away; your life will be such that you will cry: 'Don't touch me'. There is also a promise *of punishment* for you that will not be broken. Look at your god that you worshipped. We'll burn it! Then scatter it in the sea. ⁹⁸Indeed your Lord is Allah; there is no god but He; His knowledge embraces all things."

The Quran is a reminder

⁹⁹In this way We tell you stories of what happened in the past. We gave you a reminder, *the Quran.* ¹⁰⁰Whoever turns away from it will be carrying a heavy burden on Judgement Day. ¹⁰¹They will remain in that state forever, a dreadful burden to be carrying on that Day.

Cataclysmic events when the world ends

¹⁰²The Day the Trumpet is blown, We shall gather the sinners, blind.ᵃ ¹⁰³They will be whispering among themselves: "You stayed no more than ten days *in the world*" ¹⁰⁴We know best what they are saying when their most intelligent one will say, "You were *there* for no longer than a day." ¹⁰⁵They ask you about the mountains. Tell them: "My Lord will grind them into dust, ¹⁰⁶creating a vast area of flatland ¹⁰⁷ where you won't see a valley or hill.

What will happen on the Day of Judgement?

¹⁰⁸That Day they will follow a caller, who no one will ignore. Their voices will be hushed for the Kind Lord; you will not hear but a whisper. ¹⁰⁹On the Day intercession will not benefit anyone except by the permission of the Kind Lord and whoever He approves. ¹¹⁰He knows what they achieved and what they failed to achieve, but they don't know that.ᵇ ¹¹¹With long, sad faces they will stand before the Ever-Living, the Everlasting Lord. Whoever carries *an* evil burden will be feeling hopeless. ¹¹²*In contrast,* whoever did righteous deeds and was a believer will have nothing to fear of being wronged or unjustly treated."

ᵃ *Zurqan* means blue eyed, dim-sighted and blind.
ᵇ This translation is according to Ibn Abbas, literally it means "He knows what is in front and what is behind him".

وَّلَا هَضْمًا ۝ وَكَذٰلِكَ اَنْزَلْنٰهُ قُرْاٰنًا عَرَبِيًّا

وَّصَرَّفْنَا فِيْهِ مِنَ الْوَعِيْدِ لَعَلَّهُمْ يَتَّقُوْنَ

اَوْ يُحْدِثُ لَهُمْ ذِكْرًا ۝ فَتَعٰلَى اللّٰهُ الْمَلِكُ الْحَقُّ ۚ

وَلَا تَعْجَلْ بِالْقُرْاٰنِ مِنْ قَبْلِ اَنْ يُّقْضٰى اِلَيْكَ

وَحْيُهٗ ۖ وَقُلْ رَّبِّ زِدْنِيْ عِلْمًا ۝ وَلَقَدْ عَهِدْنَا اِلٰى

اٰدَمَ مِنْ قَبْلُ فَنَسِيَ وَلَمْ نَجِدْ لَهٗ عَزْمًا ۝ وَ

اِذْ قُلْنَا لِلْمَلٰئِكَةِ اسْجُدُوْا لِاٰدَمَ فَسَجَدُوْا اِلَّا

اِبْلِيْسَ ۗ اَبٰى ۝ فَقُلْنَا يٰاٰدَمُ اِنَّ هٰذَا عَدُوٌّ لَّكَ

وَلِزَوْجِكَ فَلَا يُخْرِجَنَّكُمَا مِنَ الْجَنَّةِ فَتَشْقٰى ۝

اِنَّ لَكَ اَلَّا تَجُوْعَ فِيْهَا وَلَا تَعْرٰى ۝ وَ اَنَّكَ

لَا تَظْمَؤُا فِيْهَا وَلَا تَضْحٰى ۝ فَوَسْوَسَ اِلَيْهِ

الشَّيْطٰنُ قَالَ يٰاٰدَمُ هَلْ اَدُلُّكَ عَلٰى شَجَرَةِ

الْخُلْدِ وَمُلْكٍ لَّا يَبْلٰى ۝ فَاَكَلَا مِنْهَا فَبَدَتْ

لَهُمَا سَوْاٰتُهُمَا وَطَفِقَا يَخْصِفٰنِ عَلَيْهِمَا مِنْ

وَّرَقِ الْجَنَّةِ ۚ وَعَصٰى اٰدَمُ رَبَّهٗ فَغَوٰى ۝ ثُمَّ

اجْتَبٰهُ رَبُّهٗ فَتَابَ عَلَيْهِ وَهَدٰى ۝ قَالَ اهْبِطَا

مِنْهَا جَمِيْعًا بَعْضُكُمْ لِبَعْضٍ عَدُوٌّ ۚ فَاِمَّا يَاْتِيَنَّكُمْ

مِّنِّيْ هُدًى ۙ فَمَنِ اتَّبَعَ هُدَايَ فَلَا يَضِلُّ وَلَا

يَشْقٰى ۝ وَمَنْ اَعْرَضَ عَنْ ذِكْرِيْ فَاِنَّ لَهٗ

مَعِيْشَةً ضَنْكًا وَّنَحْشُرُهٗ يَوْمَ الْقِيٰمَةِ اَعْمٰى ۝ قَالَ

How do you read the Quran? Slowly? Thoughtfully? Or with eagerness.

Prayer for boosting knowledge

¹¹³ This is how We revealed an Arabic Quran, and in it We explained warnings so *people* might fear and pay attention. ¹¹⁴ Allah is the Highest, the Absolute Controller and the Truth. Do not be hasty with the Majestic Quran before it is completely revealed to you, *Prophet,* and pray: "My Lord, increase my knowledge."

How Satan tricked Adam

¹¹⁵ Previously We taught Adam, but he forgot; We didn't find him determined *to sin.* ¹¹⁶ When We told the Angels, "Prostrate before Adam," they prostrated, except Satan who refused. ¹¹⁷ So We said, "Adam, this is your and your wife's enemy, so don't let him drive you out of Paradise – in that case you will be in trouble. ¹¹⁸ There is enough provision *in Paradise,* so you won't be hungry or unclothed; ¹¹⁹ here you won't suffer pangs of thirst or the *scorching* heat of the sun." ¹²⁰ Satan whispered to him and said, "Adam, shall I show you the tree of eternity and power that will never diminish?" ¹²¹ So both ate from it, and instantly became aware of their nakedness, so they began covering themselves with the leaves of Paradise. Adam forgot his Lord's command and failed.^a ¹²² Then your Lord forgave him, chose him and guided him. ¹²³ Allah said, "Get down from here, all of you as enemies of one another. If guidance comes to you from Me, whoever follows My guidance will not be misguided nor be miserable."

Remembering Allah and being ever conscious of Him

¹²⁴ Anyone who turns away from My remembrance will live a difficult life and We shall raise him up blind on Judgement Day.

---

^a *Ghawa* also means "go astray" and "fail to achieve one's purpose and ruin the comforts of one's life".

رَبِّ لِمَ حَشَرْتَنِىْ اَعْمٰى وَقَدْ كُنْتُ بَصِيْرًا ۞ قَالَ

كَذٰلِكَ اَتَتْكَ اٰيٰتُنَا فَنَسِيْتَهَا ۚ وَكَذٰلِكَ الْيَوْمَ

تُنْسٰى ۞ وَكَذٰلِكَ نَجْزِىْ مَنْ اَسْرَفَ وَلَمْ يُؤْمِنْ

بِاٰيٰتِ رَبِّهٖ ۭ وَلَعَذَابُ الْاٰخِرَةِ اَشَدُّ وَاَبْقٰى ۞ اَفَلَمْ

يَهْدِ لَهُمْ كَمْ اَهْلَكْنَا قَبْلَهُمْ مِّنَ الْقُرُوْنِ يَمْشُوْنَ

فِىْ مَسٰكِنِهِمْ ۭ اِنَّ فِىْ ذٰلِكَ لَاٰيٰتٍ لِّاُولِى النُّهٰى ۞

وَلَوْلَا كَلِمَةٌ سَبَقَتْ مِنْ رَّبِّكَ لَكَانَ لِزَامًا وَّ

اَجَلٌ مُّسَمًّى ۞ فَاصْبِرْ عَلٰى مَا يَقُوْلُوْنَ وَسَبِّحْ

بِحَمْدِ رَبِّكَ قَبْلَ طُلُوْعِ الشَّمْسِ وَقَبْلَ غُرُوْبِهَا ۚ

وَمِنْ اٰنَآئِ الَّيْلِ فَسَبِّحْ وَاَطْرَافَ النَّهَارِ لَعَلَّكَ

تَرْضٰى ۞ وَلَا تَمُدَّنَّ عَيْنَيْكَ اِلٰى مَا مَتَّعْنَا بِهٖٓ

اَزْوَاجًا مِّنْهُمْ زَهْرَةَ الْحَيٰوةِ الدُّنْيَا ۙ لِنَفْتِنَهُمْ

فِيْهِ ۭ وَرِزْقُ رَبِّكَ خَيْرٌ وَّاَبْقٰى ۞ وَاْمُرْ اَهْلَكَ

بِالصَّلٰوةِ وَاصْطَبِرْ عَلَيْهَا ۭ لَا نَسْـَٔلُكَ رِزْقًا ۭ

نَحْنُ نَرْزُقُكَ ۭ وَالْعَاقِبَةُ لِلتَّقْوٰى ۞ وَقَالُوْا لَوْلَا

يَاْتِيْنَا بِاٰيَةٍ مِّنْ رَّبِّهٖ ۭ اَوَلَمْ تَاْتِهِمْ بَيِّنَةُ مَا

فِى الصُّحُفِ الْاُوْلٰى ۞ وَلَوْ اَنَّا اَهْلَكْنٰهُمْ بِعَذَابٍ

مِّنْ قَبْلِهٖ لَقَالُوْا رَبَّنَا لَوْلَآ اَرْسَلْتَ اِلَيْنَا رَسُوْلًا

فَنَتَّبِعَ اٰيٰتِكَ مِنْ قَبْلِ اَنْ نَّذِلَّ وَنَخْزٰى ۞ قُلْ

كُلٌّ مُّتَرَبِّصٌ فَتَرَبَّصُوْا ۚ فَسَتَعْلَمُوْنَ مَنْ اَصْحٰبُ

Do you envy those who are better off than you? Such comparisons will always make you miserable. Look at those who are worse off than you.

627

¹²⁵ He will say, "My Lord, why did you raise me up blind, I was sighted *in the world?*" ¹²⁶ He will say, "That's because Our signs came to you and you forgot them; likewise, you are forgotten today." ¹²⁷ This is how We deal with those who wasted the *opportunity*, and didn't believe in their Lord's signs. The punishment of the Hereafter is more severe and everlasting. ¹²⁸ The fact that We destroyed many generations before them, whose houses they used to walk around, *should be* a source of guidance for them; in this are signs for the understanding. ¹²⁹ If it wasn't for the previous verdict from your Lord, the inevitable would have happened. But there is a fixed time *for it.*

The importance of prayer throughout the day

¹³⁰ So be patient with what they say, and glorify your Lord with praise before sunrise and sunset, and during the night, and at the ends of the day, so you may be happy. ¹³¹ Don't look with envy at what We gave them to enjoy from life's worldly luxuries; it's Our way of testing them, and your Lord's sustenance is better and everlasting. ¹³² Teach your family to pray and perform it yourself as well. We don't ask you for provision, actually, We provide for you, and a good outcome is a result of righteousness.

The Quran is a final reminder, so wait

¹³³ They said, "Why didn't he bring a book from His Lord? Hasn't a clear sign already come to them in former books of revelation?" ¹³⁴ Had We destroyed them with a punishment before this they would say, "Our Lord, why did you not send a messenger to us? We would have followed your revelation, so we wouldn't be disgraced and put to shame." ¹³⁵ Say: "Each one of us is waiting, so you wait as well; soon you will know those who were on the straight path and rightly guided."

21. Surat Al-Anbiya'

The Prophets

This is a late Makkan surat. The central theme is an explanation of the three basic beliefs of Islam: monotheism, prophethood and the Hereafter, with focus on prophethood. It opens by criticising the Makkans and their drunkenness with worldly life. Divine judgement is presented through the effects of historical disobedience: how past nations who denied prophets were destroyed. The next section is about the creation of the universe, and how all living things were created from water – clear evidence that Allah can recreate humanity after death.

A frequent theme in the Quran is Allah's care for his creatures. This is illustrated by constant repetition of His Beautiful Names (the Kind, the Caring, the Loving, the Generous and the Responder). Allah is Al-Hadi, the Guide, evidence of this is Him sending prophets. The Quran presents an historical record of how Allah intervened in human history by sending the prophets, and established a clear framework for human salvation. The Quran mentions only twenty-five prophets by name, yet there were more than 124,000 prophets according to one prophetic saying. Five of them are recognised in Islamic theology as commanding a special status: the Prophet Muhammad ﷺ, Isa ﷺ, Ibrahim ﷺ, Musa ﷺ and Nuh ﷺ. The prophets Ibrahim ﷺ, Yusuf ﷺ, Yunus ﷺ, Hud ﷺ, and Nuh ﷺ have full surats dedicated to their life and mission. Many others, like David ﷺ and Sulayman ﷺ, are mentioned several times in the Quran. They are a symbol of Allah's care for humanity, as is their distinct role in guiding people. Seventeen prophets are mentioned briefly, their struggles, sufferings and steadfastness, followed by their pleas to the Lord for help. In each case, the eventual Divine wrath destroyed their detractors. For example, the prayer of Prophet Yunus ﷺ from inside the whale: "There is no god except You; glory be to You, I was wrong. We saved him and rescued him from distress, and that is how We rescue the believers" (87–88). The conclusion: "This is your community, a single *united* community. I am your Lord, so worship Me. *Unfortunately,* people tore the unity of their religion; all will be returning to Us" (92–93).

The surat ends with a delightful description of Paradise, and the happiness of believers. Perhaps the crowning verse of the surat is: "We sent you as Kindness for all the worlds" (107). What a tribute for the blessed Messenger ﷺ! How wonderfully Allah boosted the morale of beloved Muhammad ﷺ.

بِسْمِ اللهِ الرَّحْمٰنِ الرَّحِیْمِ

اِقْتَرَبَ لِلنَّاسِ حِسَابُهُمْ وَهُمْ فِیْ غَفْلَةٍ

مُّعْرِضُوْنَ ۞ مَا یَاْتِیْهِمْ مِّنْ ذِکْرٍ مِّنْ رَّبِّهِمْ مُّحْدَثٍ

اِلَّا اسْتَمَعُوْهُ وَهُمْ یَلْعَبُوْنَ ۞ لَاهِیَةً قُلُوْبُهُمْ ؕ

وَاَسَرُّوا النَّجْوَی الَّذِیْنَ ظَلَمُوْا هَلْ هٰذَآ اِلَّا بَشَرٌ

مِّثْلُکُمْ ۚ اَفَتَاْتُوْنَ السِّحْرَ وَاَنْتُمْ تُبْصِرُوْنَ ۞ قٰلَ

رَبِّیْ یَعْلَمُ الْقَوْلَ فِی السَّمَآءِ وَالْاَرْضِ وَهُوَ السَّمِیْعُ

الْعَلِیْمُ ۞ بَلْ قَالُوْۤا اَضْغَاثُ اَحْلَامٍ بَلِ افْتَرٰىهُ بَلْ

هُوَ شَاعِرٌ ۚ فَلْیَاْتِنَا بِاٰیَةٍ کَمَاۤ اُرْسِلَ الْاَوَّلُوْنَ ۞

مَاۤ اٰمَنَتْ قَبْلَهُمْ مِّنْ قَرْیَةٍ اَهْلَکْنٰهَا ۚ اَفَهُمْ

یُؤْمِنُوْنَ ۞ وَمَاۤ اَرْسَلْنَا قَبْلَکَ اِلَّا رِجَالًا نُّوْحِیْۤ

اِلَیْهِمْ فَسْئَلُوْۤا اَهْلَ الذِّکْرِ اِنْ کُنْتُمْ لَا تَعْلَمُوْنَ ۞

وَمَا جَعَلْنٰهُمْ جَسَدًا لَّا یَاْکُلُوْنَ الطَّعَامَ وَمَا

کَانُوْا خٰلِدِیْنَ ۞ ثُمَّ صَدَقْنٰهُمُ الْوَعْدَ فَاَنْجَیْنٰهُمْ

وَمَنْ نَّشَآءُ وَاَهْلَکْنَا الْمُسْرِفِیْنَ ۞ لَقَدْ اَنْزَلْنَاۤ

اِلَیْکُمْ کِتٰبًا فِیْهِ ذِکْرُکُمْ ؕ اَفَلَا تَعْقِلُوْنَ ۞ وَکَمْ

قَصَمْنَا مِنْ قَرْیَةٍ کَانَتْ ظَالِمَةً وَّاَنْشَاْنَا

بَعْدَهَا قَوْمًا اٰخَرِیْنَ ۞ فَلَمَّاۤ اَحَسُّوْا بَاْسَنَاۤ اِذَا

هُمْ مِّنْهَا یَرْکُضُوْنَ ۞ لَا تَرْکُضُوْا وَارْجِعُوْۤا اِلٰی مَا

In the name of Allah, the Kind, the Caring.

Distracted minds forget the Hereafter

¹The time of reckoning for humanity is drawing closer, yet they turn away thoughtlessly. ²Whenever a new revelation from your Lord comes to them they listen to it playfully, ³their hearts distracted *by worldly activities*. In private the evildoers say, "Isn't he just a man like you? Are you going to follow the magic *of Muhammad* with your eyes open?" ⁴*The Prophet* said, "My Lord knows every word spoken in the Heavens and the Earth; He is the Listener, the Knower." ⁵They replied, "These are just confused dreams; he's made them up. In fact, he's a poet, so let him bring us a miracle like the prophets of the past brought."

Disbelievers criticise the Prophet ﷺ

⁶The communities We destroyed before them didn't believe either, so will they now believe? ⁷We sent Revelation to communities in the past; if you don't know this ask the people of the Scripture. ⁸We didn't make their bodies to live *on Earth* forever, nor could they survive without food. ⁹We fulfilled Our promise and saved those who We wanted, and destroyed those who wasted *the opportunity of life*. ¹⁰Indeed We revealed a Book to you that mentions you too!ᵃ Why do you not understand?

The Divine reckoning

¹¹We destroyed many towns of the sinners, and afterwards raised up other people in their place. ¹²When they sensed our punishment coming they fled, ¹³*and We said*: "Do not run away; come back to the places of your enjoyment and homes so you may be questioned."

ᵃ *Zikra* also means: fame, honour, and reminder, as well as being a name of the Quran.

اُتْرِفْتُمْ فِيْهِ وَمَسٰكِنِكُمْ لَعَلَّكُمْ تُسْـَٔلُوْنَ ۞ قَالُوْا

يٰوَيْلَنَآ اِنَّا كُنَّا ظٰلِمِيْنَ ۞ فَمَا زَالَتْ تِّلْكَ

دَعْوٰىهُمْ حَتّٰى جَعَلْنٰهُمْ حَصِيْدًا خٰمِدِيْنَ ۞ وَمَا

خَلَقْنَا السَّمَآءَ وَالْاَرْضَ وَمَا بَيْنَهُمَا لٰعِبِيْنَ ۞ لَوْ

اَرَدْنَآ اَنْ نَّتَّخِذَ لَهْوًا لَّاتَّخَذْنٰهُ مِنْ لَّدُنَّآ ۚ

اِنْ كُنَّا فٰعِلِيْنَ ۞ بَلْ نَقْذِفُ بِالْحَقِّ عَلَى

الْبَاطِلِ فَيَدْمَغُهُ فَاِذَا هُوَ زَاهِقٌ ؕ وَلَكُمُ الْوَيْلُ

مِمَّا تَصِفُوْنَ ۞ وَلَهُ مَنْ فِى السَّمٰوٰتِ وَالْاَرْضِ ؕ

وَمَنْ عِنْدَهُ لَا يَسْتَكْبِرُوْنَ عَنْ عِبَادَتِهٖ وَلَا

يَسْتَحْسِرُوْنَ ۞ يُسَبِّحُوْنَ الَّيْلَ وَالنَّهَارَ لَا

يَفْتُرُوْنَ ۞ اَمِ اتَّخَذُوْٓا اٰلِهَةً مِّنَ الْاَرْضِ هُمْ

يُنْشِرُوْنَ ۞ لَوْ كَانَ فِيْهِمَآ اٰلِهَةٌ اِلَّا اللّٰهُ لَفَسَدَتَا ۚ

فَسُبْحٰنَ اللّٰهِ رَبِّ الْعَرْشِ عَمَّا يَصِفُوْنَ ۞ لَا

يُسْـَٔلُ عَمَّا يَفْعَلُ وَهُمْ يُسْـَٔلُوْنَ ۞ اَمِ اتَّخَذُوْا

مِنْ دُوْنِهٖٓ اٰلِهَةً ؕ قُلْ هَاتُوْا بُرْهَانَكُمْ ۚ هٰذَا

ذِكْرُ مَنْ مَّعِيَ وَذِكْرُ مَنْ قَبْلِيْ ؕ بَلْ اَكْثَرُهُمْ لَا

يَعْلَمُوْنَ ۙ الْحَقَّ فَهُمْ مُّعْرِضُوْنَ ۞ وَمَآ اَرْسَلْنَا

مِنْ قَبْلِكَ مِنْ رَّسُوْلٍ اِلَّا نُوْحِيْٓ اِلَيْهِ اَنَّهٗ لَا

اِلٰهَ اِلَّآ اَنَا فَاعْبُدُوْنِ ۞ وَقَالُوا اتَّخَذَ الرَّحْمٰنُ

وَلَدًا سُبْحٰنَهٗ ؕ بَلْ عِبَادٌ مُّكْرَمُوْنَ ۞ لَا يَسْبِقُوْنَهٗ

The Surat draws our attention to the transcendence of Allah. How can He have a son?

¹⁴ They said, "Suffering has come upon us; we were evildoers." ¹⁵ They screamed till We made them like dried up stubble.

Life is not casual, like sport

¹⁶ We didn't create the Heavens and the Earth and what is between the two as a sport. ¹⁷ If We wanted a pastime then We would have found it within Us, were We to do such a *frivolous* thing. ¹⁸ No, We pitched the truth against falsehood, so it wiped it out; falsehood is weak. For you is Hell[a] for the things you attributed to Allah. ¹⁹ Everything in the Heavens and the Earth belongs to Him; those near Him are not arrogant about worshipping Him, nor do they get tired. ²⁰ *They are* always glorifying Him, night and day, never growing weary. ²¹ Or have they taken gods from the Earth who can resurrect?

The orderliness in the universe is proof of one Creator

²² If there were gods other than Allah, then there would be devastation in *the Heavens and the Earth*. Glory to Allah, Lord of the Throne, *He isn't the way* they describe Him. ²³ He won't be questioned about what He does, but they'll be questioned! ²⁴ Or have they taken gods besides Him? Say: "Bring your proof; this is a reminder for those who are with me and a reminder for those before me," but most of them don't know the truth, they have turned away. ²⁵ Every messenger before you was inspired to say: "There is no god but Me, so worship Me." ²⁶ They said, "The Kind Lord has a child." Glory to Him, they are honourable servants,[b]

---

[a] *Wail* is the name of one of the seven Hells and also means woe, suffering.
[b] The idolaters of Makkah believed that angels were God's daughters.

بِالْقَوْلِ وَهُمْ بِاَمْرِهٖ يَعْمَلُوْنَ ۲۷ يَعْلَمُ مَا بَيْنَ اَيْدِيْهِمْ وَمَا خَلْفَهُمْ وَلَا يَشْفَعُوْنَ ۙ اِلَّا لِمَنِ ارْتَضٰى وَهُمْ مِّنْ خَشْيَتِهٖ مُشْفِقُوْنَ ۲۸ وَمَنْ يَّقُلْ مِنْهُمْ اِنِّيْۤ اِلٰهٌ مِّنْ دُوْنِهٖ فَذٰلِكَ نَجْزِيْهِ جَهَنَّمَ ۭ كَذٰلِكَ نَجْزِى الظّٰلِمِيْنَ ۲۹ اَوَلَمْ يَرَ الَّذِيْنَ كَفَرُوْۤا اَنَّ السَّمٰوٰتِ وَالْاَرْضَ كَانَتَا رَتْقًا فَفَتَقْنٰهُمَا ۭ وَجَعَلْنَا مِنَ الْمَآءِ كُلَّ شَيْءٍ حَيٍّ ۭ

Scientists believe 14 billion years ago there was a big bang, and the universe was born.

اَفَلَا يُؤْمِنُوْنَ ۳۰ وَجَعَلْنَا فِى الْاَرْضِ رَوَاسِيَ اَنْ تَمِيْدَ بِهِمْ ۙ وَجَعَلْنَا فِيْهَا فِجَاجًا سُبُلًا لَّعَلَّهُمْ يَهْتَدُوْنَ ۳۱ وَجَعَلْنَا السَّمَآءَ سَقْفًا مَّحْفُوْظًا ۚ وَهُمْ عَنْ اٰيٰتِهَا مُعْرِضُوْنَ ۳۲ وَهُوَ الَّذِيْ خَلَقَ الَّيْلَ وَالنَّهَارَ وَالشَّمْسَ وَالْقَمَرَ ۭ كُلٌّ فِيْ فَلَكٍ يَّسْبَحُوْنَ ۳۳ وَمَا جَعَلْنَا لِبَشَرٍ مِّنْ قَبْلِكَ الْخُلْدَ ۭ اَفَاۡئِنْ مِّتَّ فَهُمُ الْخٰلِدُوْنَ ۳۴ كُلُّ نَفْسٍ ذَآئِقَةُ الْمَوْتِ ۭ وَنَبْلُوْكُمْ بِالشَّرِّ وَالْخَيْرِ فِتْنَةً ۭ وَاِلَيْنَا تُرْجَعُوْنَ ۳۵ وَاِذَا رَاٰكَ الَّذِيْنَ كَفَرُوْۤا اِنْ يَّتَّخِذُوْنَكَ اِلَّا هُزُوًا ۭ اَهٰذَا الَّذِيْ يَذْكُرُ اٰلِهَتَكُمْ ۚ وَهُمْ بِذِكْرِ الرَّحْمٰنِ هُمْ كٰفِرُوْنَ ۳۶ خُلِقَ الْاِنْسَانُ مِنْ عَجَلٍ ۭ سَاُرِيْكُمْ اٰيٰتِيْ فَلَا تَسْتَعْجِلُوْنِ ۳۷ وَيَقُوْلُوْنَ مَتٰى هٰذَا

²⁷ who don't speak before He speaks and obey His command. ²⁸ Allah knows what is in front and behind them, and they will not intercede except for him who He is pleased with, since they are in fear of Him. ²⁹ If any among them claimed, "I am god beside Him," then We shall punish him in Hell; that's how We treat the evildoers.

The beginning of the universe
³⁰ Don't the disbelievers know the Heavens and the Earth were joined *at one time?* We split them apart and made every living thing from water; won't they believe? ³¹ We made mountains on Earth *for stability*, so it does not shake *beneath* them, and We made wide, open pathways so they can find their way. ³² And We made the sky a roof that gives protection, they *still* turn away from these marvellous signs. ³³ He created night and day, sun and moon, each one moving in its orbit. ³⁴ In the past We didn't make any human being who lived forever, so if you should die, will they live forever? ³⁵ Everyone will taste death; We shall test you all with something good and something bad, and *finally* you will be returned to Us.

Mocking others is the habit of disbelievers
³⁶ The disbelievers mock when they see you and say, "Is this the one who talks about your gods?" They fail to acknowledge the name of the most Kind Lord.^a ³⁷ Man was made hasty *and impatient*; I will show you My signs, so don't ask Me to hasten them. ³⁸ They ask, "When will this promise be fulfilled if you are truthful?"

---

^a Failure to acknowledge Allah, they ignore and give the cold shoulder.

الْوَعْدُ اِنْ كُنْتُمْ صٰدِقِيْنَ ۝ لَوْ يَعْلَمُ الَّذِيْنَ

كَفَرُوْا حِيْنَ لَا يَكُفُّوْنَ عَنْ وُّجُوْهِهِمُ النَّارَ

وَلَا عَنْ ظُهُوْرِهِمْ وَلَا هُمْ يُنْصَرُوْنَ ۝ بَلْ

تَاْتِيْهِمْ بَغْتَةً فَتَبْهَتُهُمْ فَلَا يَسْتَطِيْعُوْنَ رَدَّهَا

وَلَا هُمْ يُنْظَرُوْنَ ۝ وَلَقَدِ اسْتُهْزِئَ بِرُسُلٍ مِّنْ

قَبْلِكَ فَحَاقَ بِالَّذِيْنَ سَخِرُوْا مِنْهُمْ مَّا كَانُوْا بِهٖ

يَسْتَهْزِءُوْنَ ۝ قُلْ مَنْ يَّكْلَؤُكُمْ بِالَّيْلِ وَالنَّهَارِ

مِنَ الرَّحْمٰنِ ۚ بَلْ هُمْ عَنْ ذِكْرِ رَبِّهِمْ مُّعْرِضُوْنَ ۝

اَمْ لَهُمْ اٰلِهَةٌ تَمْنَعُهُمْ مِّنْ دُوْنِنَا ۭ لَا يَسْتَطِيْعُوْنَ

نَصْرَ اَنْفُسِهِمْ وَلَا هُمْ مِّنَّا يُصْحَبُوْنَ ۝ بَلْ مَتَّعْنَا

هٰٓؤُلَاۤءِ وَاٰبَاۤءَهُمْ حَتّٰى طَالَ عَلَيْهِمُ الْعُمُرُ ۭ اَفَلَا

يَرَوْنَ اَنَّا نَاْتِى الْاَرْضَ نَنْقُصُهَا مِنْ اَطْرَافِهَا ۭ

اَفَهُمُ الْغٰلِبُوْنَ ۝ قُلْ اِنَّمَآ اُنْذِرُكُمْ بِالْوَحْيِ ۤ

وَلَا يَسْمَعُ الصُّمُّ الدُّعَاۤءَ اِذَا مَا يُنْذَرُوْنَ ۝

وَلَئِنْ مَّسَّتْهُمْ نَفْحَةٌ مِّنْ عَذَابِ رَبِّكَ لَيَقُوْلُنَّ

يٰوَيْلَنَآ اِنَّا كُنَّا ظٰلِمِيْنَ ۝ وَنَضَعُ الْمَوَازِيْنَ الْقِسْطَ

لِيَوْمِ الْقِيٰمَةِ فَلَا تُظْلَمُ نَفْسٌ شَيْـًٔا ۭ وَاِنْ كَانَ

مِثْقَالَ حَبَّةٍ مِّنْ خَرْدَلٍ اَتَيْنَا بِهَا ۭ وَكَفٰى

بِنَا حٰسِبِيْنَ ۝ وَلَقَدْ اٰتَيْنَا مُوْسٰى وَهٰرُوْنَ

الْفُرْقَانَ وَضِيَاۤءً وَّذِكْرًا لِّلْمُتَّقِيْنَ ۝ الَّذِيْنَ

In the Hereafter you will get reward for your good deed, so be honest about your expectations!

³⁹ If only the disbelievers knew, a time will come when they won't be able to stop the Fire burning their faces and backs, and they will be helpless. ⁴⁰ It will come unexpectedly, taking them by surprise, they won't be able to get away, nor get any relief. ⁴¹ Messengers were mocked before you, and the jokers were punished by *the punishment* they use to mock.

Allah is the only protector

⁴² Say: "Who can protect you at night and during the day from the Most Kind Lord?" They turn away from their Lord's remembrance. ⁴³ Or do they have gods that can protect them beside Us? They're incapable of helping themselves, or being safe from Us. ⁴⁴ For a long time, We allowed them and their fathers to enjoy the good things of life. Haven't they noticed how We are gradually reducing the borders of their city? So, are they dominant? ⁴⁵ Say: "I am warning you with the revelation." Unfortunately, the deaf will not hear the warning call when it's given. ⁴⁶ If a mere puff of your Lord's punishment strikes them they say, "It's too bad for us; we were wrong." ⁴⁷ On Judgement Day, We shall set up the scales of justice so that no one is misjudged. Even if there is something as little as the weight of a mustard seed, We shall bring it out; We are good in weighing.

The message of Musa and Harun

⁴⁸ We gave Musa and Harun the standard to distinguish between right and wrong, a light and a message for the mindful people –

يَخۡشَوۡنَ رَبَّهُم بِالۡغَيۡبِ وَهُم مِّنَ السَّاعَةِ

مُشۡفِقُوۡنَ ۴۹ وَهٰذَا ذِكۡرٌ مُّبَارَكٌ اَنۡزَلۡنٰهُ ط اَفَاَنۡتُمۡ

لَهٗ مُنۡكِرُوۡنَ ۵۰ وَلَقَدۡ اٰتَيۡنَآ اِبۡرٰهِيۡمَ رُشۡدَهٗ مِنۡ

قَبۡلُ وَكُنَّا بِهٖ عٰلِمِيۡنَ ۵۱ اِذۡ قَالَ لِاَبِيۡهِ وَقَوۡمِهٖ

مَا هٰذِهِ التَّمَاثِيۡلُ الَّتِيۡۤ اَنۡتُمۡ لَهَا عٰكِفُوۡنَ ۵۲ قَالُوۡا

وَجَدۡنَآ اٰبَآءَنَا لَهَا عٰبِدِيۡنَ ۵۳ قَالَ لَقَدۡ كُنۡتُمۡ

اَنۡتُمۡ وَاٰبَآؤُكُمۡ فِيۡ ضَلٰلٍ مُّبِيۡنٍ ۵۴ قَالُوۡۤا اَجِئۡتَنَا

بِالۡحَقِّ اَمۡ اَنۡتَ مِنَ اللّٰعِبِيۡنَ ۵۵ قَالَ بَلۡ رَّبُّكُمۡ

رَبُّ السَّمٰوٰتِ وَالۡاَرۡضِ الَّذِيۡ فَطَرَهُنَّ وَاَنَا

عَلٰى ذٰلِكُمۡ مِّنَ الشّٰهِدِيۡنَ ۵۶ وَتَاللّٰهِ لَاَكِيۡدَنَّ

اَصۡنَامَكُمۡ بَعۡدَ اَنۡ تُوَلُّوۡا مُدۡبِرِيۡنَ ۵۷ فَجَعَلَهُمۡ

جُذٰذًا اِلَّا كَبِيۡرًا لَّهُمۡ لَعَلَّهُمۡ اِلَيۡهِ يَرۡجِعُوۡنَ ۵۸

قَالُوۡا مَنۡ فَعَلَ هٰذَا بِاٰلِهَتِنَآ اِنَّهٗ لَمِنَ

الظّٰلِمِيۡنَ ۵۹ قَالُوۡا سَمِعۡنَا فَتًى يَّذۡكُرُهُمۡ يُقَالُ لَهٗۤ

اِبۡرٰهِيۡمُ ۶۰ قَالُوۡا فَاۡتُوۡا بِهٖ عَلٰٓى اَعۡيُنِ النَّاسِ لَعَلَّهُمۡ

يَشۡهَدُوۡنَ ۶۱ قَالُوۡۤا ءَاَنۡتَ فَعَلۡتَ هٰذَا بِاٰلِهَتِنَا

يٰۤاِبۡرٰهِيۡمُ ۶۲ قَالَ بَلۡ فَعَلَهٗ كَبِيۡرُهُمۡ هٰذَا

فَسۡئَلُوۡهُمۡ اِنۡ كَانُوۡا يَنۡطِقُوۡنَ ۶۳ فَرَجَعُوۡۤا اِلٰٓى اَنۡفُسِهِمۡ

فَقَالُوۡۤا اِنَّكُمۡ اَنۡتُمُ الظّٰلِمُوۡنَ ۶۴ ثُمَّ نُكِسُوۡا عَلٰى

رُءُوۡسِهِمۡ لَقَدۡ عَلِمۡتَ مَا هٰٓؤُلَآءِ يَنۡطِقُوۡنَ ۶۵ قَالَ

The idolaters will hang their heads in shame, admitting the helplessness of idols, so why don't you admit the worthlessness of your idols?

639

⁴⁹ those who fear their Lord without seeing Him, and they are fearful of the Final Hour. ⁵⁰ This is a sacred message We have sent down, so will you reject it?

Ibrahim confronts his people

⁵¹ Long before *that* We gave Ibrahim guidance;ᵃ We knew him well. ⁵² Remember when He said to his father and the community: "What are these idols you worship?" ⁵³ They said, "Our forefathers were their worshippers." ⁵⁴ He said, "You and your forefathers are obviously wrong." ⁵⁵ They replied, "Have you come with the truth or are you joking?" ⁵⁶ He said, "Your Lord is the Lord of the Heavens and the Earth Who created them, and I am one of the witnesses to this. ⁵⁷ By Allah, I will plan something for your idols after you have turned your backs and *gone away*."

Ibrahim smashes the idols

⁵⁸ He smashed them to pieces except the biggest, which He left *intact* so they would return to it. ⁵⁹ They said, "Who has done this to our gods? He must be evil!" ⁶⁰ Some said, "We heard a young man called Ibrahim speak *disapprovingly* about them. ⁶¹ So they demanded: "Bring him in front of the people, so they will see *him*." ⁶² They asked, "Ibrahim, did you do this to our gods? ⁶³ He replied, "It was the big one who did this; ask them if they can speak." ⁶⁴ So they turned to themselves saying *secretly*,ᵇ "You are the ones who are wrong." ⁶⁵ They shook their heads in disbelief and said, "You know they can't speak."

ᵃ *Rushd* means being straight in faith and actions, good conduct, maturity of mind, and reason.
ᵇ An idiom for introspection, to do self-appraisal (Suyuti).

اَفَتَعْبُدُوْنَ مِنْ دُوْنِ اللّٰهِ مَا لَا يَنْفَعُكُمْ شَيْـًٔا
وَّلَا يَضُرُّكُمْ ﴿٦٦﴾ اُفٍّ لَّكُمْ وَلِمَا تَعْبُدُوْنَ مِنْ دُوْنِ
اللّٰهِ ﴿ اَفَلَا تَعْقِلُوْنَ ﴿٦٧﴾ قَالُوْا حَرِّقُوْهُ وَانْصُرُوْۤا
اٰلِهَتَكُمْ اِنْ كُنْتُمْ فٰعِلِيْنَ ﴿٦٨﴾ قُلْنَا يٰنَارُ كُوْنِيْ بَرْدًا
وَّسَلٰمًا عَلٰۤى اِبْرٰهِيْمَ ﴿٦٩﴾ وَاَرَادُوْا بِهٖ كَيْدًا فَجَعَلْنٰهُمُ
الْاَخْسَرِيْنَ ﴿٧٠﴾ وَنَجَّيْنٰهُ وَلُوْطًا اِلَى الْاَرْضِ الَّتِيْ
بٰرَكْنَا فِيْهَا لِلْعٰلَمِيْنَ ﴿٧١﴾ وَوَهَبْنَا لَهٗۤ اِسْحٰقَ ﴿
وَيَعْقُوْبَ نَافِلَةً ﴿ وَكُلًّا جَعَلْنَا صٰلِحِيْنَ ﴿٧٢﴾

Prophets preach: We persist in pestilence! Moral degradation! Harmful pursuits!

وَجَعَلْنٰهُمْ اَئِمَّةً يَّهْدُوْنَ بِاَمْرِنَا وَاَوْحَيْنَاۤ
اِلَيْهِمْ فِعْلَ الْخَيْرٰتِ وَاِقَامَ الصَّلٰوةِ وَاِيْتَاۤءَ
الزَّكٰوةِ ﴿ وَكَانُوْا لَنَا عٰبِدِيْنَ ﴿٧٣﴾ وَلُوْطًا اٰتَيْنٰهُ
حُكْمًا وَّعِلْمًا وَّنَجَّيْنٰهُ مِنَ الْقَرْيَةِ الَّتِيْ كَانَتْ
تَّعْمَلُ الْخَبٰٓئِثَ ﴿ اِنَّهُمْ كَانُوْا قَوْمَ سَوْءٍ فٰسِقِيْنَ ﴿٧٤﴾
وَاَدْخَلْنٰهُ فِيْ رَحْمَتِنَا ﴿ اِنَّهٗ مِنَ الصّٰلِحِيْنَ ﴿٧٥﴾
وَنُوْحًا اِذْ نَادٰى مِنْ قَبْلُ فَاسْتَجَبْنَا لَهٗ فَنَجَّيْنٰهُ
وَاَهْلَهٗ مِنَ الْكَرْبِ الْعَظِيْمِ ﴿٧٦﴾ وَنَصَرْنٰهُ مِنَ
الْقَوْمِ الَّذِيْنَ كَذَّبُوْا بِاٰيٰتِنَا ﴿ اِنَّهُمْ كَانُوْا
قَوْمَ سَوْءٍ فَاَغْرَقْنٰهُمْ اَجْمَعِيْنَ ﴿٧٧﴾ وَدَاوٗدَ وَ
سُلَيْمٰنَ اِذْ يَحْكُمٰنِ فِي الْحَرْثِ اِذْ نَفَشَتْ
فِيْهِ غَنَمُ الْقَوْمِ ﴿ وَكُنَّا لِحُكْمِهِمْ شٰهِدِيْنَ ﴿٧٨﴾

⁶⁶Ibrahim quipped, "So, why do you worship beside Allah something unable to benefit or harm you? ⁶⁷A disgrace for you and what you worship beside Allah; why don't you understand?" ⁶⁸They shouted *angrily*: "Burn him and help your gods if you are going to do something." ⁶⁹We ordered: "Fire, be cool and comforting for Ibrahim." ⁷⁰They wished to harm him, so We made them the biggest losers.

Lut, Ishaq and Yaqub

⁷¹We rescued Ibrahim and Lut, and took them to the land We blessed for all humanity. ⁷²So We gave Ibrahim, Ishaq, and Yaqub as a grandson, and We made them righteous ⁷³and *great* leaders, guiding *others* with Our commandments, and inspired *many* virtues: the performance of the prayer, and the giving of Zakat. They were Our true worshippers. ⁷⁴We gave Lut authority and knowledge, and rescued him from a town which practised filthy acts of indecency; they were sinful people. ⁷⁵We were kind to *Lut* since he was righteous.

Nuh, Dawud and Sulayman

⁷⁶Remember the bygone days when Nuh called for help. We answered, and rescued him and his followers from a terrible torment. ⁷⁷We helped him against people who denied Our revelations. They were evil; so We drowned them. ⁷⁸Remember when Dawud and Sulayman were making judgement regarding the cornfield where some people's sheep had wandered off to graze. We were Witness of their judgement.

فَفَهَّمْنٰهَا سُلَيْمٰنَ ۚ وَكُلًّا اٰتَيْنَا حُكْمًا وَّعِلْمًا ۖ

وَّسَخَّرْنَا مَعَ دَاوٗدَ الْجِبَالَ يُسَبِّحْنَ وَالطَّيْرَ ۚ وَكُنَّا

فٰعِلِيْنَ ۷۹ وَعَلَّمْنٰهُ صَنْعَةَ لَبُوْسٍ لَّكُمْ لِتُحْصِنَكُمْ

مِّنْۢ بَأْسِكُمْ ۚ فَهَلْ أَنْتُمْ شٰكِرُوْنَ ۸۰ وَلِسُلَيْمٰنَ

الرِّيْحَ عَاصِفَةً تَجْرِيْ بِأَمْرِهٖ إِلَى الْأَرْضِ الَّتِيْ

بٰرَكْنَا فِيْهَا ۖ وَكُنَّا بِكُلِّ شَيْءٍ عٰلِمِيْنَ ۸۱ وَمِنَ

الشَّيٰطِيْنِ مَنْ يَّغُوْصُوْنَ لَهٗ وَيَعْمَلُوْنَ عَمَلًا

دُوْنَ ذٰلِكَ ۚ وَكُنَّا لَهُمْ حٰفِظِيْنَ ۸۲ وَأَيُّوْبَ

إِذْ نَادٰى رَبَّهٗ أَنِّيْ مَسَّنِيَ الضُّرُّ وَأَنْتَ أَرْحَمُ

الرّٰحِمِيْنَ ۸۳ فَاسْتَجَبْنَا لَهٗ فَكَشَفْنَا مَا بِهٖ مِنْ

ضُرٍّ وَّاٰتَيْنٰهُ أَهْلَهٗ وَمِثْلَهُمْ مَّعَهُمْ رَحْمَةً

مِّنْ عِنْدِنَا وَذِكْرٰى لِلْعٰبِدِيْنَ ۸۴ وَإِسْمٰعِيْلَ

وَإِدْرِيْسَ وَذَا الْكِفْلِ ۚ كُلٌّ مِّنَ الصّٰبِرِيْنَ ۸۵

وَأَدْخَلْنٰهُمْ فِيْ رَحْمَتِنَا ۖ إِنَّهُمْ مِّنَ الصّٰلِحِيْنَ ۸۶

وَذَا النُّوْنِ إِذْ ذَّهَبَ مُغَاضِبًا فَظَنَّ أَنْ لَّنْ

نَّقْدِرَ عَلَيْهِ فَنَادٰى فِي الظُّلُمٰتِ أَنْ لَّا إِلٰهَ

إِلَّا أَنْتَ سُبْحٰنَكَ ۖ إِنِّيْ كُنْتُ مِنَ الظّٰلِمِيْنَ ۸۷

فَاسْتَجَبْنَا لَهٗ ۙ وَنَجَّيْنٰهُ مِنَ الْغَمِّ ۚ وَكَذٰلِكَ

نُنْجِى الْمُؤْمِنِيْنَ ۸۸ وَزَكَرِيَّا إِذْ نَادٰى رَبَّهٗ

رَبِّ لَا تَذَرْنِيْ فَرْدًا وَّأَنْتَ خَيْرُ الْوٰرِثِيْنَ ۸۹

⁷⁹ We helped Sulayman understand *the problem*. Each one We blessed with judgment and knowledge. We made mountains echo and the birds sing our praises together with Dawud; We did all these things. ⁸⁰ We taught him how to make coats of armour, so that you can protect yourself from others. Will you be thankful for this? ⁸¹ Sulayman could command the stormy winds *blowing* to the land which We had blessed. We know all things. ⁸² He also controlled the jinn that dived deep in the sea for him, and would do other work *for him* too. We were their keepers.

Ayyub, Ismael, Idrees and Zul-Kifl

⁸³ And remember Ayyub when He called his Lord: "I am suffering. You are the Kindest of all." ⁸⁴ We answered and relieved him of the sufferings, gave back his family, even bigger *than before*. For the worshippers, this was a special kindness from Us and a reminder. ⁸⁵ Ismael, Idrees and Zul-Kifl – each one was patient and steadfast. ⁸⁶ We blessed them with prophethood. They were righteous.

The prayers of Yunus, Zakariyya and Yahya

⁸⁷ Remember Dhan-Nun,^a when he left *Nineveh* angrily thinking We wouldn't restrain *or question* him. He prayed in the depths of darkness: "There is no god except You. Glory be to You; I was wrong." ⁸⁸ We saved and rescued him from distress, and that's how We save the believers. ⁸⁹ And remember Zakariyya, when He called to His Lord: "My Lord, do not leave me childless, you are the best of inheritors."

---

^a *Dha-Nun* means "man of fish", and refers to Prophet Yunus.

فَاسْتَجَبْنَا لَهٗ ۚ وَوَهَبْنَا لَهٗ يَحْيٰى وَاَصْلَحْنَا

لَهٗ زَوْجَهٗ ؕ اِنَّهُمْ كَانُوْا يُسَارِعُوْنَ فِي الْخَيْرٰتِ وَ

يَدْعُوْنَنَا رَغَبًا وَّرَهَبًا ؕ وَكَانُوْا لَنَا خٰشِعِيْنَ ۝

وَالَّتِيْۤ اَحْصَنَتْ فَرْجَهَا فَنَفَخْنَا فِيْهَا مِنْ رُّوْحِنَا

وَجَعَلْنٰهَا وَابْنَهَاۤ اٰيَةً لِّلْعٰلَمِيْنَ ۝ اِنَّ هٰذِهٖۤ

اُمَّتُكُمْ اُمَّةً وَّاحِدَةً ۖ وَّاَنَا رَبُّكُمْ فَاعْبُدُوْنِ ۝

وَتَقَطَّعُوْۤا اَمْرَهُمْ بَيْنَهُمْ ؕ كُلٌّ اِلَيْنَا رٰجِعُوْنَ ۝

فَمَنْ يَّعْمَلْ مِنَ الصّٰلِحٰتِ وَهُوَ مُؤْمِنٌ فَلَا كُفْرَانَ

لِسَعْيِهٖ ۚ وَاِنَّا لَهٗ كٰتِبُوْنَ ۝ وَحَرٰمٌ عَلٰى قَرْيَةٍ

اَهْلَكْنٰهَاۤ اَنَّهُمْ لَا يَرْجِعُوْنَ ۝ حَتّٰۤى اِذَا فُتِحَتْ

يَاْجُوْجُ وَمَاْجُوْجُ وَهُمْ مِّنْ كُلِّ حَدَبٍ يَّنْسِلُوْنَ ۝

وَاقْتَرَبَ الْوَعْدُ الْحَقُّ فَاِذَا هِيَ شَاخِصَةٌ اَبْصَارُ

الَّذِيْنَ كَفَرُوْا ؕ يٰوَيْلَنَا قَدْ كُنَّا فِيْ غَفْلَةٍ مِّنْ

هٰذَا بَلْ كُنَّا ظٰلِمِيْنَ ۝ اِنَّكُمْ وَمَا تَعْبُدُوْنَ

مِنْ دُوْنِ اللّٰهِ حَصَبُ جَهَنَّمَ ؕ اَنْتُمْ لَهَا

وٰرِدُوْنَ ۝ لَوْ كَانَ هٰۤؤُلَاءِ اٰلِهَةً مَّا وَرَدُوْهَا ؕ

وَكُلٌّ فِيْهَا خٰلِدُوْنَ ۝ لَهُمْ فِيْهَا زَفِيْرٌ وَّهُمْ فِيْهَا

لَا يَسْمَعُوْنَ ۝ اِنَّ الَّذِيْنَ سَبَقَتْ لَهُمْ مِّنَّا الْحُسْنٰۤى

اُولٰٓئِكَ عَنْهَا مُبْعَدُوْنَ ۝ لَا يَسْمَعُوْنَ حَسِيْسَهَا ۚ

وَهُمْ فِيْ مَا اشْتَهَتْ اَنْفُسُهُمْ خٰلِدُوْنَ ۝ لَا

The enormity of Judgement Day is indescribable: the blazing Fire, people filled with apprehension, and the long wait.

⁹⁰We answered him, gave him Yahya and healed his wife. They were always quick to do good works, pray to Us with *profound* longing and fear, they were humble before Us.

All the Prophets had the same religion

⁹¹Mention the *lady* who protected her chastity; We breathed in her Our Spirit, and made her and her son a miraculous sign for all people. ⁹²This is your community, a single *united* community. I am your Lord, so worship Me. ⁹³*Unfortunately,* people tore the unity of their religion; all will be returning to Us. ⁹⁴Whoever does righteous deeds as a believer, the reward of their good efforts will not be denied to them, We record it for them. ⁹⁵The communities We destroyed just couldn't turn away from their evil ways.ᵃ

When will Gog and Magog come?

⁹⁶When Gog and Magog are let loose – rushing down swiftly from every direction – ⁹⁷the true promise will draw near, then the disbelievers will watch in horror and say, "Woe to us, we were not aware of this; in fact, we were wrong." ⁹⁸*It will be said*: "You and those you worshipped beside Allah are the fuel of Hell; that is where you will go." ⁹⁹If these were really your gods then they wouldn't be here. They will stay there forever, ¹⁰⁰hearing nothing but sobbing.

The delights of Paradise

¹⁰¹*The people* We promised Heaven will be *kept* far away from *Hell*. ¹⁰²They won't hear the slightest noise of Hell; they will have whatever they want forever.

ᵃ Another interpretation is, "it is impossible for communities We destroyed to ever rise again."

يَحْزُنُهُمُ الْفَزَعُ الْأَكْبَرُ وَتَتَلَقّٰهُمُ الْمَلٰٓئِكَةُ ۚ

هٰذَا يَوْمُكُمُ الَّذِيْ كُنْتُمْ تُوْعَدُوْنَ ۞ يَوْمَ نَطْوِى

السَّمَآءَ كَطَيِّ السِّجِلِّ لِلْكُتُبِ ۚ كَمَا بَدَأْنَا أَوَّلَ

خَلْقٍ نُّعِيْدُهٗ ۚ وَعْدًا عَلَيْنَا ۚ إِنَّا كُنَّا فٰعِلِيْنَ ۞

وَلَقَدْ كَتَبْنَا فِى الزَّبُوْرِ مِنْ بَعْدِ الذِّكْرِ أَنَّ

الْأَرْضَ يَرِثُهَا عِبَادِيَ الصّٰلِحُوْنَ ۞ إِنَّ فِىْ

هٰذَا لَبَلٰغًا لِّقَوْمٍ عٰبِدِيْنَ ۞ وَمَا أَرْسَلْنٰكَ إِلَّا

رَحْمَةً لِّلْعٰلَمِيْنَ ۞ قُلْ إِنَّمَا يُوْحٰى إِلَيَّ أَنَّمَا

إِلٰهُكُمْ إِلٰهٌ وَّاحِدٌ ۚ فَهَلْ أَنْتُمْ مُّسْلِمُوْنَ ۞

فَإِنْ تَوَلَّوْا فَقُلْ اٰذَنْتُكُمْ عَلٰى سَوَآءٍ ۚ وَإِنْ

أَدْرِيٓ أَقَرِيْبٌ أَمْ بَعِيْدٌ مَّا تُوْعَدُوْنَ ۞ إِنَّهٗ

يَعْلَمُ الْجَهْرَ مِنَ الْقَوْلِ وَيَعْلَمُ مَا تَكْتُمُوْنَ ۞

وَإِنْ أَدْرِيْ لَعَلَّهٗ فِتْنَةٌ لَّكُمْ وَمَتَاعٌ إِلٰى

حِيْنٍ ۞ قٰلَ رَبِّ احْكُمْ بِالْحَقِّ ۚ وَرَبُّنَا الرَّحْمٰنُ

الْمُسْتَعَانُ عَلٰى مَا تَصِفُوْنَ ۞

Consider the caring, kind nature of the beloved Messenger ﷺ, kind to all.

¹⁰³ They won't be distressed by the great terror of Judgement Day. The angels will greet them saying, "This is your Day, which you were promised." ¹⁰⁴ That Day We will roll up the sky like the writer rolls up the scroll. We will recreate as We created the first time; it's a promise We've undertaken and will fulfil it.

Allah's Kindness for all the worlds

¹⁰⁵ In the Psalms and the previous Scriptures, We wrote: "My righteous servants will inherit the Earth." ¹⁰⁶ In this *Quran* is a message for the worshippers. ¹⁰⁷ We sent you, *Messenger,* as a kindness for all the worlds. ¹⁰⁸ Say: "It is revealed to me, Your Lord is one, so won't you submit?" ¹⁰⁹ If they turn away, say: "I have declared what you've been promised; I am not sure whether it is near or far. ¹¹⁰ He knows what you say openly and what you hide. ¹¹¹ What do I know? This may be a test for you or *a respite in the form* of enjoyment for a short while." ¹¹² The messenger prayed: "My Lord, make fair judgement. Our Lord the Kind is the One Whose Help is sought against what you say."

22. Surat Al-Hajj
The Pilgrimage

This is a late Makkan surat (621 CE) that includes some verses revealed in Madinah. The central theme is the spiritual progress of humanity, connecting with Allah. The opening verses paint a terrifying image of Judgement Day, striking fear in the heart of the reader, to urge belief in resurrection. The Quran doesn't use fear but employs reason to support its claim for resurrection. The seven stages of human life are one such line of rational evidence that reveals divine creative power. Secondly: "You see the dry lifeless Earth, and when We send down rain it stirs and swells, producing colourful pairs of plants" (5). The surat points out that, "The creation of life is not an unusual accident, brought about by blind chance or by some unintelligible laws of probability."[a] The doubters are warned: disbelief is shrugging off one's responsibility.

The perennial question: "Why are there so many different religions?" Is tackled in the next section: "We prescribed rituals for every community to practise. So let them not argue with you over *such* matters. *Instead* invite them to your Lord" (67). Allah will pass His judgement on them. The Quran teaches that diversity in religions is part of a Divine plan.

Hajj is the fifth pillar of Islam. It consists of several rites which were familiar to the Makkans since its establishment 4,000 years ago by their forefather Ibrahim 🕌. However, the Quran clarifies the spiritual significance of these rites; circling the Kaaba and slaughtering animals. These rites are not merely mechanical rituals, but purposeful; impacting health, mindset and welfare. "Those who respect Allah's symbols[b] show true piety of the heart" (32).

Muslims were persecuted in Makkah for thirteen years, and continued to be oppressed even after their migration to Madinah. Here they were attacked several times, and in the second year of Hijra Muslims were given permission to take up arms against their oppressors: "Permission *to fight* is given to those who were attacked *and oppressed*" (39). The consensus among Muslim scholars about war is: it's permissible in defence – offensive invasions are not permitted.

The next part of the surat reassures the beloved Prophet 🕌 of the success he is to achieve in the near future, and reassures him not to be distressed by the current hardships.

---

[a] Muhammad al-Ghazali, *Thematic Commentary on the Quran.*
[b] *Sha'irallah* symbols of Allah means all sacred things: the Quran, Kaaba, Mosque, etc.

Examples of past prophets are given as an assertion of the eternal triumph of truth. The surat concludes by outlining what needs to be done to achieve salvation, and how to escape the terror of Judgement Day, which is described graphically in the opening of the surat:

> Believers, bow down and prostrate in worship of your Lord, and do good so you may succeed. Strive for the sake of Allah *to do what is right*, as much as He deserves. (77–78).

اٰيَاتُهَا ٤٨ (٢٢) سُوْرَةُ الْحَجّ مَدَنِيَّةٌ (١٠٣) رُكُوْعَاتُهَا ١٠

بِسْمِ اللهِ الرَّحْمٰنِ الرَّحِيْمِ

يٰٓاَيُّهَا النَّاسُ اتَّقُوْا رَبَّكُمْ ۚ اِنَّ زَلْزَلَةَ السَّاعَةِ شَيْءٌ عَظِيْمٌ ۞ يَوْمَ تَرَوْنَهَا تَذْهَلُ كُلُّ مُرْضِعَةٍ عَمَّآ اَرْضَعَتْ وَ تَضَعُ كُلُّ ذَاتِ حَمْلٍ حَمْلَهَا وَ تَرَى النَّاسَ سُكٰرٰى وَ مَا هُمْ بِسُكٰرٰى وَ لٰكِنَّ عَذَابَ اللهِ شَدِيْدٌ ۞ وَ مِنَ النَّاسِ مَنْ يُّجَادِلُ فِى اللهِ بِغَيْرِ عِلْمٍ وَّ يَتَّبِعُ كُلَّ شَيْطٰنٍ مَّرِيْدٍ ۞ كُتِبَ عَلَيْهِ اَنَّهٗ مَنْ تَوَلَّاهُ فَاَنَّهٗ يُضِلُّهٗ وَ يَهْدِيْهِ اِلٰى عَذَابِ السَّعِيْرِ ۞ يٰٓاَيُّهَا النَّاسُ اِنْ كُنْتُمْ فِيْ رَيْبٍ مِّنَ الْبَعْثِ فَاِنَّا خَلَقْنٰكُمْ مِّنْ تُرَابٍ ثُمَّ مِنْ نُّطْفَةٍ ثُمَّ مِنْ عَلَقَةٍ ثُمَّ مِنْ مُّضْغَةٍ مُّخَلَّقَةٍ وَّ غَيْرِ مُخَلَّقَةٍ لِّنُبَيِّنَ لَكُمْ ۚ وَ نُقِرُّ فِى الْاَرْحَامِ مَا نَشَآءُ اِلٰٓى اَجَلٍ مُّسَمًّى ثُمَّ نُخْرِجُكُمْ طِفْلًا ثُمَّ لِتَبْلُغُوْٓا اَشُدَّكُمْ ۚ وَ مِنْكُمْ مَّنْ يُّتَوَفّٰى وَ مِنْكُمْ مَّنْ يُّرَدُّ اِلٰٓى اَرْذَلِ الْعُمُرِ لِكَيْلَا يَعْلَمَ مِنْ بَعْدِ عِلْمٍ شَيْئًا ۚ وَ تَرَى الْاَرْضَ هَامِدَةً فَاِذَآ اَنْزَلْنَا عَلَيْهَا الْمَآءَ اهْتَزَّتْ وَ رَبَتْ وَ اَنْبَتَتْ مِنْ كُلِّ زَوْجٍ بَهِيْجٍ ۞ ذٰلِكَ بِاَنَّ اللهَ هُوَ الْحَقُّ وَ اَنَّهٗ يُحْيِ

Spiritual awakening comes from mindfulness and the awareness of the Hereafter.

In the name of Allah, the Kind, the Caring.

The horrors of Judgement Day

¹People, fear Your Lord. The Earthquake of the Final Hour will be a significant event: ²you will see every breastfeeding mother forget her suckling baby, every pregnant woman will miscarry, and every person will appear drunk that day, though they won't be drunk, but such will be the severity of Allah's punishment. ³There are some people who argue about Allah without any knowledge, and follow every rebellious demon. ⁴It is decreed: Whoever befriends *Satan*, he will misguide him and lead him towards the punishment of the blazing Fire.

The seven stages of human life

⁵People, if you are in *any* doubt about the resurrection, We *originally* created you from clay, then from a drop of semen, *this became* a clot of blood, *then* a lump of flesh – some parts recognisable others unrecognisable – then *a foetus. We revealed this* to make *the Resurrection* clear for you. We plant in wombs whatever We choose for a fixed term, then We bring you out as a baby; then you reach maturity, *after which* some of you die *young* while others proceed to feeble old age, to the extent that they know nothing after having known *so much. Likewise,* you see the Earth *appear* lifeless; then, when We send down rain, it stirs and swells, producing beautiful pairs of plants. ᵃ

ᵃ   The seven stages of human life are: The semen and the egg; a clot; lump of flesh; foetus; birth of baby; childhood and adulthood; and old age.

الْمَوْتٰى وَاَنَّهٗ عَلٰى كُلِّ شَيْءٍ قَدِيْرٌ ۚ۶ وَاَنَّ

السَّاعَةَ اٰتِيَةٌ لَّا رَيْبَ فِيْهَا ۙ وَاَنَّ اللّٰهَ يَبْعَثُ

مَنْ فِي الْقُبُوْرِ ۶ وَمِنَ النَّاسِ مَنْ يُّجَادِلُ فِي

اللّٰهِ بِغَيْرِ عِلْمٍ وَّلَا هُدًى وَّلَا كِتٰبٍ مُّنِيْرٍ ۙ۸

ثَانِيَ عِطْفِهٖ لِيُضِلَّ عَنْ سَبِيْلِ اللّٰهِ ۙ لَهٗ فِي

الدُّنْيَا خِزْيٌ وَّنُذِيْقُهٗ يَوْمَ الْقِيٰمَةِ عَذَابَ

الْحَرِيْقِ ۹ ذٰلِكَ بِمَا قَدَّمَتْ يَدٰكَ وَاَنَّ اللّٰهَ لَيْسَ

بِظَلَّامٍ لِّلْعَبِيْدِ ۟۱۰ وَمِنَ النَّاسِ مَنْ يَّعْبُدُ اللّٰهَ

عَلٰى حَرْفٍ ۚ فَاِنْ اَصَابَهٗ خَيْرٌ ۨ اطْمَاَنَّ بِهٖ ۚ وَاِنْ

اَصَابَتْهُ فِتْنَةُ ۨ انْقَلَبَ عَلٰى وَجْهِهٖ ۟ۚ خَسِرَ الدُّنْيَا

وَالْاٰخِرَةَ ۟ ذٰلِكَ هُوَ الْخُسْرَانُ الْمُبِيْنُ ۱۱ يَدْعُوْا

مِنْ دُوْنِ اللّٰهِ مَا لَا يَضُرُّهٗ وَمَا لَا يَنْفَعُهٗ ۟ ذٰلِكَ

هُوَ الضَّلٰلُ الْبَعِيْدُ ۚ۱۲ يَدْعُوْا لَمَنْ ضَرُّهٗٓ اَقْرَبُ

مِنْ نَّفْعِهٖ ۟ لَبِئْسَ الْمَوْلٰى وَلَبِئْسَ الْعَشِيْرُ ۱۳ اِنَّ

اللّٰهَ يُدْخِلُ الَّذِيْنَ اٰمَنُوْا وَعَمِلُوا الصّٰلِحٰتِ جَنّٰتٍ

تَجْرِيْ مِنْ تَحْتِهَا الْاَنْهٰرُ ۟ اِنَّ اللّٰهَ يَفْعَلُ مَا

يُرِيْدُ ۱۴ مَنْ كَانَ يَظُنُّ اَنْ لَّنْ يَّنْصُرَهُ اللّٰهُ فِي

الدُّنْيَا وَالْاٰخِرَةِ فَلْيَمْدُدْ بِسَبَبٍ اِلَى السَّمَآءِ ثُمَّ

لِيَقْطَعْ فَلْيَنْظُرْ هَلْ يُذْهِبَنَّ كَيْدُهٗ مَا يَغِيْظُ ۱۵

وَكَذٰلِكَ اَنْزَلْنٰهُ اٰيٰتٍۭ بَيِّنٰتٍ ۙ وَّاَنَّ اللّٰهَ يَهْدِيْ

The Quran is a serious book of guidance, like a lighthouse. So take it seriously.

⁶ *This shows* Allah is the Truth. He brings the dead back to life, and has power over all things. ⁷ The Final Hour is coming without a doubt – *when* Allah will resurrect *all* who are in *their* graves.

Only the thoughtless can reject Allah and His creation

⁸ People argue about Allah without knowledge or guidance, or any enlightening book, ⁹ turning aside *disapprovingly* to cause *others* to stray from Allah's way. *Such a person* will be disgraced in this world, and on Judgement Day We will make him taste the punishment of the blazing inferno. ¹⁰ *He will be told*: "That's what your hands produced. Allah isn't at all unjust to *His* servants."

Half-hearted believers are the biggest losers

¹¹ People who worship Allah doubting Him, are satisfied at the best of times, but at the worst of times they go back to their old ways, losing in both, this world and the next; that is a big loss. ¹² Instead of Allah they call on what cannot harm or benefit them. That's straying far away. ¹³ *In fact*, they call on that which is more likely to harm than benefit them. What wretched allies, and what wretched company! ¹⁴ *However*, Allah will admit into gardens beneath which rivers flow those who believe and do righteous deeds. Allah does what He wishes. ¹⁵ Whoever imagines that Allah will not help *Muhammad* either in this world or the next, let him hang himself from a rope tied to the ceiling then cut it off and see if his cunning plan has made his anger go away. ¹⁶ That is how We have sent *the Quran* down as clear verses; and Allah guides whomever He wishes.

مَنْ يُّرِيْدُ ۞ اِنَّ الَّذِيْنَ اٰمَنُوْا وَالَّذِيْنَ هَادُوْا

وَالصّٰبِئِيْنَ وَالنَّصٰرٰى وَالْمَجُوْسَ وَالَّذِيْنَ اَشْرَكُوْٓا

اِنَّ اللّٰهَ يَفْصِلُ بَيْنَهُمْ يَوْمَ الْقِيٰمَةِ ط اِنَّ اللّٰهَ عَلٰى

كُلِّ شَيْءٍ شَهِيْدٌ ۞ اَلَمْ تَرَ اَنَّ اللّٰهَ يَسْجُدُ لَهٗ

مَنْ فِى السَّمٰوٰتِ وَمَنْ فِى الْاَرْضِ وَالشَّمْسُ وَالْقَمَرُ

وَالْقَمَرُ وَالنُّجُوْمُ وَالْجِبَالُ وَالشَّجَرُ وَالدَّوَآبُّ

وَكَثِيْرٌ مِّنَ النَّاسِ ط وَكَثِيْرٌ حَقَّ عَلَيْهِ الْعَذَابُ ط

وَمَنْ يُّهِنِ اللّٰهُ فَمَا لَهٗ مِنْ مُّكْرِمٍ ط اِنَّ اللّٰهَ يَفْعَلُ

مَا يَشَآءُ ۞ هٰذٰنِ خَصْمٰنِ اخْتَصَمُوْا فِىْ رَبِّهِمْ ز

فَالَّذِيْنَ كَفَرُوْا قُطِّعَتْ لَهُمْ ثِيَابٌ مِّنْ نَّارٍ ط

يُصَبُّ مِنْ فَوْقِ رُءُوْسِهِمُ الْحَمِيْمُ ۞ يُصْهَرُ

بِهٖ مَا فِىْ بُطُوْنِهِمْ وَالْجُلُوْدُ ۞ وَلَهُمْ مَّقَامِعُ

مِنْ حَدِيْدٍ ۞ كُلَّمَآ اَرَادُوْٓا اَنْ يَّخْرُجُوْا مِنْهَا مِنْ

غَمٍّ اُعِيْدُوْا فِيْهَا ز وَذُوْقُوْا عَذَابَ الْحَرِيْقِ ۞

اِنَّ اللّٰهَ يُدْخِلُ الَّذِيْنَ اٰمَنُوْا وَعَمِلُوا الصّٰلِحٰتِ

جَنّٰتٍ تَجْرِيْ مِنْ تَحْتِهَا الْاَنْهٰرُ يُحَلَّوْنَ فِيْهَا

مِنْ اَسَاوِرَ مِنْ ذَهَبٍ وَّلُؤْلُؤًا ط وَلِبَاسُهُمْ

فِيْهَا حَرِيْرٌ ۞ وَهُدُوْٓا اِلَى الطَّيِّبِ مِنَ الْقَوْلِ ۚ

وَهُدُوْٓا اِلٰى صِرَاطِ الْحَمِيْدِ ۞ اِنَّ الَّذِيْنَ كَفَرُوْا

وَيَصُدُّوْنَ عَنْ سَبِيْلِ اللّٰهِ وَالْمَسْجِدِ الْحَرَامِ

Everything in the universe complies with the Divine will and carries out Allah's orders. Why don't you?

Religious differences shall be settled on Judgement Day

17The Muslims, the Jews, the Sabians, the Christians, the Zoroastrians, and the idolaters, We shall decide between them on Judgement Day. Allah witnesses everything. 18Don't you see whatever is in the Heavens and on Earth prostrates before Allah: the sun, the moon, the stars, the mountains, the trees, the animals, and many people; *but* there are many who justly deserve punishment. Anyone Allah disgraces will have no one to honour him. Allah does whatever He pleases.[a]

Contrasting fates of the people of Hell and Heaven

19These are two opposite groups who argue about their Lord, those who disbelieve will have suits cut out of fire, *and* scalding water poured over their heads, 20causing their insides and their skins to dissolve; 21and they will be restrained with iron rods. 22Whenever, out of agony, they try to escape *their torment*, they will be returned into it and *told*: "Taste the punishment of the blazing inferno." 23However, Allah will admit those who believe and do righteous deeds into gardens with rivers flowing beneath them; they will be decorated with bracelets of gold and pearls, and their clothes will be of silk – 24*those who* were guided *in this world* to the very best of speech,[b] and were guided to the path of the Praiseworthy,

---

[a] This is another of the Verses of Prostration.

[b] "The very best of speech" is the *Shahada*: "There is no god but Allah" (Ibn Abbas). Others suggest it's the Quran.

اَلَّذِى جَعَلْنٰهُ لِلنَّاسِ سَوَآءَ ۨ الْعَاكِفُ فِيهِ

وَالْبَادِ ط وَمَنْ يُّرِدْ فِيهِ بِإِلْحَادٍ بِظُلْمٍ نُّذِقْهُ

مِنْ عَذَابٍ اَلِيمٍ ۞ وَاِذْ بَوَّأْنَا لِاِبْرٰهِيمَ

مَكَانَ الْبَيْتِ اَنْ لَّا تُشْرِكْ بِى شَيْئًا وَّطَهِّرْ

بَيْتِىَ لِلطَّآئِفِينَ وَالْقَآئِمِينَ وَالرُّكَّعِ السُّجُودِ ۞

وَاَذِّنْ فِى النَّاسِ بِالْحَجِّ يَأْتُوكَ رِجَالًا وَّعَلٰى

كُلِّ ضَامِرٍ يَّأْتِينَ مِنْ كُلِّ فَجٍّ عَمِيقٍ ۞

لِّيَشْهَدُوا مَنَافِعَ لَهُمْ وَيَذْكُرُوا اسْمَ اللهِ فِىْ

أَيَّامٍ مَّعْلُومٰتٍ عَلٰى مَا رَزَقَهُمْ مِّنْ بَهِيمَةِ

الْاَنْعَامِ ۚ فَكُلُوا مِنْهَا وَاَطْعِمُوا الْبَآئِسَ الْفَقِيرَ ۞

ثُمَّ لْيَقْضُوا تَفَثَهُمْ وَلْيُوفُوا نُذُورَهُمْ وَلْيَطَّوَّفُوا

بِالْبَيْتِ الْعَتِيقِ ۞ ذٰلِكَ ۬ وَمَنْ يُّعَظِّمْ حُرُمٰتِ

اللهِ فَهُوَ خَيْرٌ لَّهُ عِنْدَ رَبِّهِ ط وَاُحِلَّتْ لَكُمُ

الْاَنْعَامُ اِلَّا مَا يُتْلٰى عَلَيْكُمْ فَاجْتَنِبُوا الرِّجْسَ

مِنَ الْاَوْثَانِ وَاجْتَنِبُوا قَوْلَ الزُّورِ ۞ حُنَفَآءَ لِلهِ

غَيْرَ مُشْرِكِينَ بِهِ ط وَمَنْ يُّشْرِكْ بِاللهِ فَكَاَنَّمَا

خَرَّ مِنَ السَّمَآءِ فَتَخْطَفُهُ الطَّيْرُ اَوْ تَهْوِى بِهِ

الرِّيحُ فِى مَكَانٍ سَحِيقٍ ۞ ذٰلِكَ ۬ وَمَنْ يُّعَظِّمْ

شَعَآئِرَ اللهِ فَاِنَّهَا مِنْ تَقْوَى الْقُلُوبِ ۞ لَكُمْ

فِيهَا مَنَافِعُ اِلٰى اَجَلٍ مُّسَمًّى ثُمَّ مَحِلُّهَآ اِلَى

Respecting the Divine commands: Halal and Haram is proof of one's faith.

657

²⁵ *but not* those who disbelieve and block *others* from Allah's way and from the Sacred Mosque, which We established for *all* the people, whether resident or traveller. Anyone who seeks to violate its *sanctity* by wrongdoing, We shall make him taste a painful punishment.

Allah instructs Ibrahim about the Kaaba and the Hajj

²⁶ *Remember* when We marked out for Ibrahim the place of the *Ancient* House,ᵃ *saying*: "Don't associate anything with Me; keep My House clean for those who circle it, *worship there*, standing, bowing and prostrating. ²⁷ Announce the pilgrimage to people. They will come to you on foot and mounted on all kinds of lean camels, through every deep mountain pass, ²⁸ to take part in *rites* that benefit them and to invoke the name of Allah on specific days over such livestock as He has provided for them *to sacrifice*. Eat the *cattle*, and feed the needy and poor. ²⁹ Then complete the rites *of cleansing*,ᵇ fulfil the vows, and circle the Ancient House."

The rights of Hajj: Allah's symbols visited

³⁰ Anyone who respects the sacred rites of Allah shall fare better in the Lord's sight. Livestock is lawful for you except ones already mentioned.ᶜ Stay away from the impurity of idols, and words of falsehood. ³¹ Incline towards Allah without associating *partners* with Him. The one who associates *partners* with Allah, is like the one fallen from the sky, and birds snatch at him, or like the wind that carries him off to a faraway place. ³² Anyone who respects Allah's symbols,ᵈ displays true piety of the heart. ³³ There are benefits for you in those *symbols* for a designated period, *the rites conclude* at the place of sacrificeᵉ near the Ancient House.

ᵃ The "Ancient House" is the Kaaba.
ᵇ Such as shaving one's head and throwing stones at the three pillars.
ᶜ "The only things He has made unlawful for you are carcasses, blood, pork, and animals slaughtered in any name other than Allah's" (*Al-Baqarah* 2: 173 and *Al-An'am* 6: 145).
ᵈ The sacred symbols of Allah in the Hajj are the Kaaba, the Sacred Months, staying at Arafa, walking between the hills of Safa and Marwa, and the sacrifice of livestock.
ᵉ Or, as mentioned by Al-Qurtubi, the place where one symbolically emerges from the sanctified state (*ihram*) of a pilgrim with the final circling of the Kaaba.

الْبَيْتِ الْعَتِيقِ ﴿٣٣﴾ وَلِكُلِّ اُمَّةٍ جَعَلْنَا مَنْسَكًا

لِّيَذْكُرُوا اسْمَ اللّٰهِ عَلٰى مَا رَزَقَهُمْ مِّنْ بَهِيْمَةِ

الْاَنْعَامِ ۗ فَاِلٰهُكُمْ اِلٰهٌ وَّاحِدٌ فَلَهٗٓ اَسْلِمُوْا ۗ

وَبَشِّرِ الْمُخْبِتِيْنَ ﴿٣٤﴾ الَّذِيْنَ اِذَا ذُكِرَ اللّٰهُ

وَجِلَتْ قُلُوْبُهُمْ وَالصّٰبِرِيْنَ عَلٰى مَآ اَصَابَهُمْ

وَالْمُقِيْمِى الصَّلٰوةِ ۙ وَمِمَّا رَزَقْنٰهُمْ يُنْفِقُوْنَ ﴿٣٥﴾

وَالْبُدْنَ جَعَلْنٰهَا لَكُمْ مِّنْ شَعَآئِرِ اللّٰهِ لَكُمْ

Humble people are characterised by worship. How revering are you?

فِيْهَا خَيْرٌ ۖ فَاذْكُرُوا اسْمَ اللّٰهِ عَلَيْهَا صَوَآفَّ ۚ

فَاِذَا وَجَبَتْ جُنُوْبُهَا فَكُلُوْا مِنْهَا وَاَطْعِمُوا

الْقَانِعَ وَالْمُعْتَرَّ ۗ كَذٰلِكَ سَخَّرْنٰهَا لَكُمْ

لَعَلَّكُمْ تَشْكُرُوْنَ ﴿٣٦﴾ لَنْ يَّنَالَ اللّٰهَ لُحُوْمُهَا

وَلَا دِمَآؤُهَا وَلٰكِنْ يَّنَالُهُ التَّقْوٰى مِنْكُمْ ۗ

كَذٰلِكَ سَخَّرَهَا لَكُمْ لِتُكَبِّرُوا اللّٰهَ عَلٰى مَا

هَدٰىكُمْ ۗ وَبَشِّرِ الْمُحْسِنِيْنَ ﴿٣٧﴾ اِنَّ اللّٰهَ يُدٰفِعُ

عَنِ الَّذِيْنَ اٰمَنُوْا ۗ اِنَّ اللّٰهَ لَا يُحِبُّ كُلَّ خَوَّانٍ

كَفُوْرٍ ﴿٣٨﴾ اُذِنَ لِلَّذِيْنَ يُقَاتَلُوْنَ بِاَنَّهُمْ ظُلِمُوْا ۗ

وَاِنَّ اللّٰهَ عَلٰى نَصْرِهِمْ لَقَدِيْرٌ ﴿٣٩﴾ الَّذِيْنَ

اُخْرِجُوْا مِنْ دِيَارِهِمْ بِغَيْرِ حَقٍّ اِلَّآ اَنْ يَّقُوْلُوْا

رَبُّنَا اللّٰهُ ۗ وَلَوْلَا دَفْعُ اللّٰهِ النَّاسَ بَعْضَهُمْ

بِبَعْضٍ لَّهُدِّمَتْ صَوَامِعُ وَبِيَعٌ وَّصَلَوٰتٌ

Those who show reverence to Allah's symbols

³⁴We prescribed a rite *of sacrifice* for every community, so they may invoke the name of Allah over such livestock as provided for them. Your God is One God, so submit to Him. And, *Messenger*, give glad tidings to humble *servants* ³⁵whose hearts tremble at the mention of Allah, respond patiently to any affliction, perform the prayer and spend in charity from what We provided them.

How to sacrifice camels, and why

³⁶The sacrificial camels you find valuable are included among Allah's symbols; so invoke Allah's name on them as they stand ready *for slaughter*; and, once they have fallen *dead* on their side, eat from them and feed the needy, whether they ask or not. That is how We tamed them for you, so you may be thankful. ³⁷Neither their meat nor their blood reaches Allah, but it is your piety that reaches Allah. That's how We made them obedient for you, so praise Allah for guiding you. Give glad tidings to the righteous.

War in self-defence is allowed

³⁸Allah will defend the believers, Allah dislikes ungrateful traitors. ³⁹Permission *to fight* is given to those who were attacked because they have been wronged; and Allah has the power to help those[a] ⁴⁰who were unfairly driven out of their homes for saying, "Our Lord is Allah." If Allah didn't defend some people by means of others, then monasteries, churches, synagogues and mosques where Allah's name is regularly praised would have been destroyed. Allah will support whoever supports His *cause*. Allah is Strong, Almighty. [b]

---

[a] This was revealed in Madinah just after the migration. It is the first time that the Quran gives permission for physical fighting. It was further elaborated in verses 190-192 of Al-Baqarah.

[b] "Military Jihad is prescribed only for self-defence and defence of the oppressed" (M.A.Haleem: Exploring the Quran).

وَّ مَسْجِدٌ يُّذْكَرُ فِيهَا اسْمُ اللّٰهِ كَثِيْرًا ط

وَلَيَنْصُرَنَّ اللّٰهُ مَنْ يَّنْصُرُهٗ ط اِنَّ اللّٰهَ لَقَوِيٌّ

عَزِيْزٌ ۞ اَلَّذِيْنَ اِنْ مَّكَّنّٰهُمْ فِى الْاَرْضِ

اَقَامُوا الصَّلٰوةَ وَاٰتَوُا الزَّكٰوةَ وَاَمَرُوْا بِالْمَعْرُوْفِ

وَنَهَوْا عَنِ الْمُنْكَرِ ط وَلِلّٰهِ عَاقِبَةُ الْاُمُوْرِ ۞

وَاِنْ يُّكَذِّبُوْكَ فَقَدْ كَذَّبَتْ قَبْلَهُمْ قَوْمُ

نُوْحٍ وَّ عَادٌ وَّ ثَمُوْدُ ۞ وَ قَوْمُ اِبْرٰهِيْمَ

وَ قَوْمُ لُوْطٍ ۞ وَّ اَصْحٰبُ مَدْيَنَ ج وَكُذِّبَ

مُوْسٰى فَاَمْلَيْتُ لِلْكٰفِرِيْنَ ثُمَّ اَخَذْتُهُمْ ج

فَكَيْفَ كَانَ نَكِيْرِ ۞ فَكَاَيِّنْ مِّنْ قَرْيَةٍ

اَهْلَكْنٰهَا وَهِيَ ظَالِمَةٌ فَهِيَ خَاوِيَةٌ عَلٰى

عُرُوْشِهَا ز وَبِئْرٍ مُّعَطَّلَةٍ وَّ قَصْرٍ مَّشِيْدٍ ۞

اَفَلَمْ يَسِيْرُوْا فِى الْاَرْضِ فَتَكُوْنَ لَهُمْ قُلُوْبٌ

يَّعْقِلُوْنَ بِهَآ اَوْ اٰذَانٌ يَّسْمَعُوْنَ بِهَا ج فَاِنَّهَا

لَا تَعْمَى الْاَبْصَارُ وَلٰكِنْ تَعْمَى الْقُلُوْبُ الَّتِيْ

فِى الصُّدُوْرِ ۞ وَيَسْتَعْجِلُوْنَكَ بِالْعَذَابِ وَلَنْ

يُّخْلِفَ اللّٰهُ وَعْدَهٗ ط وَاِنَّ يَوْمًا عِنْدَ رَبِّكَ

كَاَلْفِ سَنَةٍ مِّمَّا تَعُدُّوْنَ ۞ وَكَاَيِّنْ مِّنْ

قَرْيَةٍ اَمْلَيْتُ لَهَا وَهِيَ ظَالِمَةٌ ثُمَّ اَخَذْتُهَا ج

وَ اِلَيَّ الْمَصِيْرُ ۞ قُلْ يٰٓاَيُّهَا النَّاسُ اِنَّمَآ

Travelling around the world opens the heart and mind to the greatness of the Creator and leads to true awakening.

⁴¹*If* We granted some people authority on Earth, they would establish the prayer, collect Zakat, enjoin the common good and forbid evil. The outcome in *all* matters is determined by Allah.

The Messenger ﷺ is reassured

⁴²If *today* they are denying you, then *long* before them the people of Nuh, Ad and Thamud denied *their prophets* too; ⁴³*likewise* the people of Ibrahim and of Lut, ⁴⁴and the inhabitants of Madyan. *Even* Musa was denied. So I gave the disbelievers time to think, then I seized them. How *great* was My rejection *of their actions*! ⁴⁵How many towns have We destroyed whilst they were doing wrong, so *today* their buildings are razed to the ground, and wells *are* abandoned; and *how many* lofty palaces? ⁴⁶Have they not travelled the Earth, so *you would think* they had either minds with which to reflect or ears with which to hear? *In truth*, it's not the *lack of* sight that causes blindness but *lack of* insight, which is *found in people's* chests.ᵃ

Waiting a millennium or a day are the same to Allah

⁴⁷They ask you to bring forward the punishment, but Allah will never break His promise. Your Lord's *single* day is like a thousand years by your calculations. ⁴⁸I granted respite to many towns whilst they were doing wrong, then I seized them; and to Me is the final return. ⁴⁹Say: "People, I'm only a clear warner to you."

ᵃ The idea that the mind resides in the brain, not the heart, is relatively modern. However, recent research in neuroscience shows a close link between the heart and the brain. Possibly the mind also resides in the heart.

اَنَا لَكُمْ نَذِيْرٌ مُّبِيْنٌ ۴۹ فَالَّذِيْنَ اٰمَنُوْا

وَعَمِلُوا الصّٰلِحٰتِ لَهُمْ مَّغْفِرَةٌ وَّ رِزْقٌ

كَرِيْمٌ ۵۰ وَ الَّذِيْنَ سَعَوْا فِيْ اٰيٰتِنَا مُعٰجِزِيْنَ

اُولٰٓئِكَ اَصْحٰبُ الْجَحِيْمِ ۵۱ وَمَآ اَرْسَلْنَا مِنْ

قَبْلِكَ مِنْ رَّسُوْلٍ وَّلَا نَبِيٍّ اِلَّآ اِذَا تَمَنّٰى

اَلْقَى الشَّيْطٰنُ فِيْٓ اُمْنِيَّتِهٖ ۚ فَيَنْسَخُ اللّٰهُ مَا

يُلْقِي الشَّيْطٰنُ ثُمَّ يُحْكِمُ اللّٰهُ اٰيٰتِهٖ ط وَ اللّٰهُ

عَلِيْمٌ حَكِيْمٌ ۵۲ لِّيَجْعَلَ مَا يُلْقِي الشَّيْطٰنُ

فِتْنَةً لِّلَّذِيْنَ فِيْ قُلُوْبِهِمْ مَّرَضٌ وَّ الْقَاسِيَةِ

Satan tried to deceive the messengers, but Allah protected them. Are you an easy target for Satan?

قُلُوْبُهُمْ ط وَاِنَّ الظّٰلِمِيْنَ لَفِيْ شِقَاقٍۭ بَعِيْدٍ ۵۳

وَلِيَعْلَمَ الَّذِيْنَ اُوْتُوا الْعِلْمَ اَنَّهُ الْحَقُّ مِنْ

رَّبِّكَ فَيُؤْمِنُوْا بِهٖ فَتُخْبِتَ لَهٗ قُلُوْبُهُمْ ط وَاِنَّ

اللّٰهَ لَهَادِ الَّذِيْنَ اٰمَنُوْٓا اِلٰى صِرَاطٍ مُّسْتَقِيْمٍ ۵۴

وَلَا يَزَالُ الَّذِيْنَ كَفَرُوْا فِيْ مِرْيَةٍ مِّنْهُ حَتّٰى

تَاْتِيَهُمُ السَّاعَةُ بَغْتَةً اَوْ يَاْتِيَهُمْ عَذَابُ

يَوْمٍ عَقِيْمٍ ۵۵ اَلْمُلْكُ يَوْمَئِذٍ لِّلّٰهِ ط يَحْكُمُ

بَيْنَهُمْ ط فَالَّذِيْنَ اٰمَنُوْا وَعَمِلُوا الصّٰلِحٰتِ فِيْ

جَنّٰتِ النَّعِيْمِ ۵۶ وَالَّذِيْنَ كَفَرُوْا وَكَذَّبُوْا بِاٰيٰتِنَا

فَاُولٰٓئِكَ لَهُمْ عَذَابٌ مُّهِيْنٌ ۵۷ وَ الَّذِيْنَ

هَاجَرُوْا فِيْ سَبِيْلِ اللّٰهِ ثُمَّ قُتِلُوْٓا اَوْ مَاتُوْا

⁵⁰ As for those who believe and do righteous deeds, they will have forgiveness and generous provision; ⁵¹ but those who strive against Our signs will be the companions of Hell, in vain.

Allah thwarts all attempts to lead prophets astray
⁵² We haven't sent a *single* messenger or prophet before you who recited *Our revelation*, but Satan suggested *errors* in his recitation. Allah removes whatever Satan suggests, then Allah makes clear His verses – Allah is Knowing, Wise – ⁵³ thereby turning whatever Satanᵃ suggests into a test for those in whose hearts is sickness and for the hard of heart. The wrongdoers are far removed *from the truth.* ⁵⁴ And *Allah does this* so those given knowledge should know that it is the truth from your Lord and believe in it, their hearts turning to Him in humility. Allah guides the believers towards a straight path. ⁵⁵ The disbelievers will continue to be in doubt about *the truth* until the Final Hour comes abruptly, or the punishment of a barren day.ᵇ

Allah's promise to victims of persecution
⁵⁶ On that Day, Allah will have the authority to judge between them. Those who believed and did righteous deeds will be in the gardens of delight, ⁵⁷ but those who disbelieved and rejected Our signs will have a humiliating punishment. ⁵⁸ Those who migrated for the sake of Allah, or were killed or died *on the way*, Allah will provide for them handsomely – and Allah is the best Provider –

ᵃ According to some commentators, "Satan" here refers not to the Devil himself, but to those humans who try, like Satan, to tempt others away from Allah's path. One example is when the leaders of Makkah offered the Prophet ﷺ power and wealth, in return for giving up the teaching of Islam.

ᵇ Judgement Day is described as "barren" because there will be no further opportunities to add to the fruit of one's actions.

لِيَرْزُقَنَّهُمُ اللهُ رِزْقًا حَسَنًا ط وَاِنَّ اللهَ لَهُوَ

خَيْرُ الرّٰزِقِيْنَ ۵۸ لَيُدْخِلَنَّهُمْ مُّدْخَلًا يَّرْضَوْنَهٗ ط

وَاِنَّ اللهَ لَعَلِيْمٌ حَلِيْمٌ ۵۹ ذٰلِكَ ج وَمَنْ عَاقَبَ

بِمِثْلِ مَا عُوْقِبَ بِهٖ ثُمَّ بُغِيَ عَلَيْهِ لَيَنْصُرَنَّهُ

اللهُ ط اِنَّ اللهَ لَعَفُوٌّ غَفُوْرٌ ۶۰ ذٰلِكَ بِاَنَّ اللهَ

يُوْلِجُ الَّيْلَ فِي النَّهَارِ وَيُوْلِجُ النَّهَارَ فِي

الَّيْلِ وَاَنَّ اللهَ سَمِيْعٌۢ بَصِيْرٌ ۶۱ ذٰلِكَ بِاَنَّ اللهَ

هُوَ الْحَقُّ وَاَنَّ مَا يَدْعُوْنَ مِنْ دُوْنِهٖ هُوَ

الْبَاطِلُ وَاَنَّ اللهَ هُوَ الْعَلِيُّ الْكَبِيْرُ ۶۲ اَلَمْ

تَرَ اَنَّ اللهَ اَنْزَلَ مِنَ السَّمَاءِ مَاءً ز فَتُصْبِحُ

الْاَرْضُ مُخْضَرَّةً ط اِنَّ اللهَ لَطِيْفٌ خَبِيْرٌ ۶۳ لَهٗ

مَا فِي السَّمٰوٰتِ وَمَا فِي الْاَرْضِ ط وَاِنَّ اللهَ لَهُوَ

الْغَنِيُّ الْحَمِيْدُ ۶۴ اَلَمْ تَرَ اَنَّ اللهَ سَخَّرَ لَكُمْ

مَّا فِي الْاَرْضِ وَالْفُلْكَ تَجْرِيْ فِي الْبَحْرِ بِاَمْرِهٖ ط

وَيُمْسِكُ السَّمَاءَ اَنْ تَقَعَ عَلَى الْاَرْضِ اِلَّا

بِاِذْنِهٖ ط اِنَّ اللهَ بِالنَّاسِ لَرَءُوْفٌ رَّحِيْمٌ ۶۵ وَ

هُوَ الَّذِيْ اَحْيَاكُمْ ز ثُمَّ يُمِيْتُكُمْ ثُمَّ يُحْيِيْكُمْ ط

اِنَّ الْاِنْسَانَ لَكَفُوْرٌ ۶۶ لِكُلِّ اُمَّةٍ جَعَلْنَا مَنْسَكًا

هُمْ نَاسِكُوْهُ فَلَا يُنَازِعُنَّكَ فِي الْاَمْرِ وَ ادْعُ

اِلٰى رَبِّكَ ط اِنَّكَ لَعَلٰى هُدًى مُّسْتَقِيْمٍ ۶۷ وَاِنْ

Allah runs the solar system, the cycles of day and night, the winds and the tides. These are the marvels of Allah.

ع
٨
١۵

⁵⁹admitting them *to a place* that pleases them. Allah is Knowing, Gentle.

Allah urges believers to stand up against oppression

⁶⁰That *is Allah's command*, and whoever retaliates in equal measure to any injury received, and is then wronged again, Allah will support him *to regain his right*. Allah is Pardoning, Forgiving. ⁶¹Allah merges night into day and day into night, and Allah is Hearing, Seeing. ⁶²That is *also* because Allah *alone* is Real, and anything else they call on besides Him is false. It is Allah who is the Exalted, the Great.

The Creation is for the service of humanity

⁶³Have you not considered how Allah sends rain from the sky, turning the Earth green? Allah is Subtle, Aware. ⁶⁴Everything in the Heavens and the Earth belongs to Him. Allah is the Self-Sufficient, the Praiseworthy. ⁶⁵Have you not considered how Allah made everything on Earth to serve you?ᵃ Ships sail on the sea by His command, and He holds the sky *in place* so that it does not fall on to the Earth; everything happens with His permission. Allah is Compassionate, Kind to people. ⁶⁶It is He who brought you to life, then causes you to die, and will then bring you back to life. How ungrateful are humans!

Encouragement for interfaith harmony

⁶⁷We prescribed rituals for every community to practise. So let them not argue with you over *such* matters. *Instead* invite them to your Lord, *for* you are guided on a straight path.

ᵃ The verb means Allah causing His creation "to submit to the will or power" of human beings, who will then be judged according to how they made use of them, either for good or ill, be it carefully or wastefully.

جَدَلُوْكَ فَقُلِ اللّٰهُ اَعْلَمُ بِمَا تَعْمَلُوْنَ ۞ اَللّٰهُ

يَحْكُمُ بَيْنَكُمْ يَوْمَ الْقِيٰمَةِ فِيْمَا كُنْتُمْ فِيْهِ

تَخْتَلِفُوْنَ ۞ اَلَمْ تَعْلَمْ اَنَّ اللّٰهَ يَعْلَمُ مَا فِى

السَّمَآءِ وَالْاَرْضِ ط اِنَّ ذٰلِكَ فِىْ كِتٰبٍ ط اِنَّ

ذٰلِكَ عَلَى اللّٰهِ يَسِيْرٌ ۞ وَيَعْبُدُوْنَ مِنْ دُوْنِ

اللّٰهِ مَا لَمْ يُنَزِّلْ بِهٖ سُلْطٰنًا وَّمَا لَيْسَ لَهُمْ

بِهٖ عِلْمٌ ط وَمَا لِلظّٰلِمِيْنَ مِنْ نَّصِيْرٍ ۞ وَاِذَا

تُتْلٰى عَلَيْهِمْ اٰيٰتُنَا بَيِّنٰتٍ تَعْرِفُ فِىْ وُجُوْهِ

الَّذِيْنَ كَفَرُوا الْمُنْكَرَ ط يَكَادُوْنَ يَسْطُوْنَ بِالَّذِيْنَ

يَتْلُوْنَ عَلَيْهِمْ اٰيٰتِنَا ط قُلْ اَفَاُنَبِّئُكُمْ بِشَرٍّ

مِّنْ ذٰلِكُمْ ط اَلنَّارُ ط وَعَدَهَا اللّٰهُ الَّذِيْنَ كَفَرُوْا ط

وَبِئْسَ الْمَصِيْرُ ۞ يٰٓاَيُّهَا النَّاسُ ضُرِبَ مَثَلٌ

فَاسْتَمِعُوْا لَهٗ ط اِنَّ الَّذِيْنَ تَدْعُوْنَ مِنْ دُوْنِ

اللّٰهِ لَنْ يَّخْلُقُوْا ذُبَابًا وَّلَوِ اجْتَمَعُوْا لَهٗ ط وَ

اِنْ يَّسْلُبْهُمُ الذُّبَابُ شَيْئًا لَّا يَسْتَنْقِذُوْهُ

مِنْهُ ط ضَعُفَ الطَّالِبُ وَالْمَطْلُوْبُ ۞ مَا قَدَرُوا

اللّٰهَ حَقَّ قَدْرِهٖ ط اِنَّ اللّٰهَ لَقَوِيٌّ عَزِيْزٌ ۞ اَللّٰهُ

يَصْطَفِىْ مِنَ الْمَلٰٓئِكَةِ رُسُلًا وَّمِنَ النَّاسِ ط اِنَّ

اللّٰهَ سَمِيْعٌۢ بَصِيْرٌ ۞ يَعْلَمُ مَا بَيْنَ اَيْدِيْهِمْ

وَمَا خَلْفَهُمْ ط وَاِلَى اللّٰهِ تُرْجَعُ الْاُمُوْرُ ۞ يٰٓاَيُّهَا

Can you really comprehend the Divine grandeur? Impossible! So, let's commit to Him.

⁶⁸ If they argue with you, say: "Allah knows best what you are doing. ⁶⁹ Allah will decide between you on Judgement Day regarding your differences." ⁷⁰ Do you not accept[a] that Allah knows *whatever exists* in the sky and on Earth? *All* is *recorded* in a Book, that's easy for Allah.

The pent-up violence of those who go astray

⁷¹ They worship beside Allah things for which no authority has been revealed, nor do they have knowledge. *Consequently, such* wrongdoers shall have no helper. ⁷² Whenever you recite Our clear verses to them, you *can* recognise disapproval on the disbelievers' faces, *to the extent that* they are almost violent towards those who recite Our verses to them. Say: "Shall I inform you of something even worse? The Fire which Allah has promised those who disbelieve. A wretched destination!"

A single fly is all it takes to disprove idolatry

⁷³ People, here is an example, so listen to it *carefully*: the *idols* you worship beside Allah can't create a fly, even if they all got together to do so. In fact, if a fly were to snatch something from *them*, they would be unable to take it back. How weak are both the devotee and the object of devotion![b] ⁷⁴ They fail to accord Allah the power that He deserves. Allah is Strong, Mighty. ⁷⁵ Allah chooses messengers from among the angels and humans; Allah is Hearing, Seeing. ⁷⁶ He knows their past, and future *deeds*, and *eventually* all affairs return to Allah.

---

[a] Literally "know".

[b] The commentators note how the pagan Arabs would put offerings of food out for their gods, only to watch the flies come and spoil it.

الَّذِيْنَ اٰمَنُوا ارْكَعُوْا وَاسْجُدُوْا وَاعْبُدُوْا رَبَّكُمْ

وَافْعَلُوا الْخَيْرَ لَعَلَّكُمْ تُفْلِحُوْنَ ۩ وَجَاهِدُوْا

فِى اللّٰهِ حَقَّ جِهَادِهٖ ؕ هُوَ اجْتَبٰىكُمْ وَمَا جَعَلَ

عَلَيْكُمْ فِى الدِّيْنِ مِنْ حَرَجٍ ؕ مِلَّةَ اَبِيْكُمْ

اِبْرٰهِيْمَ ؕ هُوَ سَمّٰىكُمُ الْمُسْلِمِيْنَ ۙ مِنْ قَبْلُ

وَفِىْ هٰذَا لِيَكُوْنَ الرَّسُوْلُ شَهِيْدًا عَلَيْكُمْ

وَتَكُوْنُوْا شُهَدَآءَ عَلَى النَّاسِ ۚ فَاَقِيْمُوا الصَّلٰوةَ

وَاٰتُوا الزَّكٰوةَ وَاعْتَصِمُوْا بِاللّٰهِ ؕ هُوَ مَوْلٰىكُمْ ۚ

فَنِعْمَ الْمَوْلٰى وَنِعْمَ النَّصِيْرُ ۞

Jihad: struggling, striving and serving Allah for the good of others.

Striving and struggling for the sake of Allah

[77] Believers, bow down and prostrate in worship of your Lord, and do good so you may succeed. [78] Strive for the sake of Allah *to do what is right*, as much as He deserves. He chose you and placed no hardship in the religion.[a] *It is* the way of worship of your father Ibrahim. Long ago he named you "Muslims", as in this *Quran*, so that the Messenger might stand witness against you *if you strayed*, and that you might stand witness against humanity's *vices*. So perform the prayer, give Zakat and hold firmly to *faith in* Allah your Protector. How excellent a Protector, and how excellent a Helper!

---

[a]   There is no hardship in Islam, the Lord knows human weaknesses. What makes Islam easy to believe and practise is, it's free from myths and superstitions, it's rational and appeals to common sense; has no ritualism but simple practises of worship and social habits; allows it's followers to benefit from worldly wealth in moderation but condemns excessive consumerism.

23. Surat Al-Mu'minun

The Believers

This surat was revealed in the late Makkan period. The central theme is the resurrection, arguing that faith in Allah and the Hereafter are knotted into the purpose of life: the two are inseparable. This may explain why the believer is ideally contemplative and socially active, rather than an "armchair" faithful. It opens with a description of successful believers: faith, humility, avoiding useless pursuits, generosity, sexual purity, a sense of responsibility, taking care of contracts, and yearning for closeness to the Divine. Seven beautiful traits of the believers that reflect; firm faith, generous spirit, lively conscience: a restless soul ready to produce good works. The Quran gives a glowing tribute to such lucky souls for their truthfulness, boldness and self-sacrifice: the reward is Paradise.

This is followed by proof of Allah's creative power in the creation of humanity, the universe, and human history, particularly the ancient prophets. It presents a history of disobedience – humanity rejected the prophets, and killed some. The life stories of some prophets inform the blessed Messenger ﷺ that the Makkans are behaving like the ancient people. The Quran also points out the unity of the prophets' message; a universal message. However, Allah dealt severely with those who rejected it by destroying them. The disbeliever's criticisms of the prophets are rejected as baseless, due to arrogance. They are confused; they hate the truth and doggedly follow their whims.

The disbelievers frequently demanded the Prophet ﷺ to bring about the punishment. However, these demands were rejected; Allah gave them time to reform, those who persisted in asking for miracles were similarly refused, and are told they should use their Allah-given faculties of hearing, seeing and feeling. They are warned about the severe punishment of Hell, and how regretful they will be in the Hereafter, then it will be too late.

Three questions are asked: "Who owns the Earth?"; "Who is the Lord of the Seven Heavens?"; And "In whose hands lies the control of all things?" Their natural response is "Allah", so they're asked why not accept resurrection. The surat concludes by emphasising the purpose of human life; a time of preparation for the Hereafter.

بِسْمِ اللهِ الرَّحْمٰنِ الرَّحِيْمِ

قَدْ اَفْلَحَ الْمُؤْمِنُوْنَ ۙ١ الَّذِيْنَ هُمْ فِيْ صَلَاتِهِمْ خٰشِعُوْنَ ۙ٢ وَالَّذِيْنَ هُمْ عَنِ اللَّغْوِ مُعْرِضُوْنَ ۙ٣ وَالَّذِيْنَ هُمْ لِلزَّكٰوةِ فٰعِلُوْنَ ۙ٤ وَالَّذِيْنَ هُمْ لِفُرُوْجِهِمْ حٰفِظُوْنَ ۙ٥ اِلَّا عَلٰۤى اَزْوَاجِهِمْ اَوْ مَا مَلَكَتْ اَيْمَانُهُمْ فَاِنَّهُمْ غَيْرُ مَلُوْمِيْنَ ۚ٦ فَمَنِ ابْتَغٰى وَرَآءَ ذٰلِكَ فَاُولٰٓئِكَ هُمُ الْعٰدُوْنَ ۚ٧ وَالَّذِيْنَ هُمْ لِاَمٰنٰتِهِمْ وَعَهْدِهِمْ رٰعُوْنَ ۙ٨ وَالَّذِيْنَ هُمْ عَلٰى صَلَوٰتِهِمْ يُحَافِظُوْنَ ۘ٩ اُولٰٓئِكَ هُمُ الْوٰرِثُوْنَ ۙ١٠ الَّذِيْنَ يَرِثُوْنَ الْفِرْدَوْسَ ؕ هُمْ فِيْهَا خٰلِدُوْنَ ١١ وَلَقَدْ خَلَقْنَا الْاِنْسَانَ مِنْ سُلٰلَةٍ مِّنْ طِيْنٍ ۚ١٢ ثُمَّ جَعَلْنٰهُ نُطْفَةً فِيْ قَرَارٍ مَّكِيْنٍ ۪١٣ ثُمَّ خَلَقْنَا النُّطْفَةَ عَلَقَةً فَخَلَقْنَا الْعَلَقَةَ مُضْغَةً فَخَلَقْنَا الْمُضْغَةَ عِظٰمًا فَكَسَوْنَا الْعِظٰمَ لَحْمًا ۗ ثُمَّ اَنْشَاْنٰهُ خَلْقًا اٰخَرَ ؕ فَتَبٰرَكَ اللهُ اَحْسَنُ الْخٰلِقِيْنَ ؕ١٤ ثُمَّ اِنَّكُمْ بَعْدَ ذٰلِكَ لَمَيِّتُوْنَ ؕ١٥ ثُمَّ اِنَّكُمْ يَوْمَ الْقِيٰمَةِ تُبْعَثُوْنَ ١٦ وَلَقَدْ خَلَقْنَا فَوْقَكُمْ سَبْعَ طَرَآئِقَ ۖٞ وَمَا كُنَّا عَنِ الْخَلْقِ غٰفِلِيْنَ ١٧ وَاَنْزَلْنَا مِنَ السَّمَآءِ مَآءً بِقَدَرٍ فَاَسْكَنّٰهُ فِي الْاَرْضِ ۖٞ وَاِنَّا عَلٰى ذَهَابٍ بِهٖ لَقٰدِرُوْنَ ۚ١٨ فَاَنْشَاْنَا لَكُمْ بِهٖ جَنّٰتٍ مِّنْ

The seven qualities of true believers distilled into worship and commitment to the common good.

In the name of Allah, the Kind, the Caring.

The seven habits of successful believers; they're goal oriented
¹The believers have succeeded: ²those who are humbly focused in their prayer; ³who turn away from meaningless activities; ⁴who give Zakat; ⁵who guard their modesty and *sexual purity,* ⁶except from their spouses or their slaves, in which case they are free from blame – ⁷but whoever desires *sexual gratification* beyond that are transgressors – ⁸*who* honour trusts placed in them and their contract; ⁹and regularly perform their prayers. ¹⁰Such people are the *true* heirs, ¹¹they will inherit Paradise, living in it forever.[a]

The seven stages of human life[b]
¹²We *first* created humanity from an extract of clay. ¹³Thereafter *born,* We placed him as a drop of semen in the stable environment *of the womb.* ¹⁴The drop of semen turned to a blood-like clot; and, from the blood-like clot, We made the fleshy lump into bones and covered them with flesh; then We produce from it another created being. Blessed is Allah, the best Creator. ¹⁵After all that, you will die, ¹⁶and on Judgement Day you will be resurrected.

The seven types of food
¹⁷We created seven orbits of *the Heavens* above you; and We never neglected *Our* creation. ¹⁸We send rain from the sky in *exact* measure, and We hold it in the Earth; and We are *equally* capable of taking it away.

---

[a] These seven habits are: faith, humility, avoiding useless pursuits, generosity, sexual purity, having a sense of responsibility, taking care of contracts, and are prayerful.
[b] See Surat Al Hajj: 5.

نَخِيلٍ وَّاَعْنَابٍ ۚ لَّكُمْ فِيْهَا فَوَاكِهُ كَثِيْرَةٌ وَّمِنْهَا
تَأْكُلُوْنَ ۞ وَشَجَرَةً تَخْرُجُ مِنْ طُوْرِ سَيْنَآءَ تَنْبُتُ
بِالدُّهْنِ وَصِبْغٍ لِّلْاٰكِلِيْنَ ۞ وَاِنَّ لَكُمْ فِى الْاَنْعَامِ لَعِبْرَةً ۚ
نُّسْقِيْكُمْ مِّمَّا فِيْ بُطُوْنِهَا وَلَكُمْ فِيْهَا مَنَافِعُ كَثِيْرَةٌ وَّ
مِنْهَا تَأْكُلُوْنَ ۞ وَعَلَيْهَا وَعَلَى الْفُلْكِ تُحْمَلُوْنَ ۞ وَلَقَدْ
اَرْسَلْنَا نُوْحًا اِلٰى قَوْمِهٖ فَقَالَ يٰقَوْمِ اعْبُدُوا اللّٰهَ مَا
لَكُمْ مِّنْ اِلٰهٍ غَيْرُهٗ ۗ اَفَلَا تَتَّقُوْنَ ۞ فَقَالَ الْمَلَؤُا الَّذِيْنَ
كَفَرُوْا مِنْ قَوْمِهٖ مَا هٰذَآ اِلَّا بَشَرٌ مِّثْلُكُمْ ۙ يُرِيْدُ اَنْ
يَّتَفَضَّلَ عَلَيْكُمْ ۗ وَلَوْ شَآءَ اللّٰهُ لَاَنْزَلَ مَلٰٓئِكَةً ۖ مَّا
سَمِعْنَا بِهٰذَا فِيْٓ اٰبَآئِنَا الْاَوَّلِيْنَ ۞ اِنْ هُوَ اِلَّا رَجُلٌۢ
بِهٖ جِنَّةٌ فَتَرَبَّصُوْا بِهٖ حَتّٰى حِيْنٍ ۞ قَالَ رَبِّ انْصُرْنِيْ
بِمَا كَذَّبُوْنِ ۞ فَاَوْحَيْنَآ اِلَيْهِ اَنِ اصْنَعِ الْفُلْكَ
بِاَعْيُنِنَا وَوَحْيِنَا فَاِذَا جَآءَ اَمْرُنَا وَفَارَ التَّنُّوْرُ ۙ فَاسْلُكْ
فِيْهَا مِنْ كُلٍّ زَوْجَيْنِ اثْنَيْنِ وَاَهْلَكَ اِلَّا مَنْ سَبَقَ
عَلَيْهِ الْقَوْلُ مِنْهُمْ ۚ وَلَا تُخَاطِبْنِيْ فِى الَّذِيْنَ ظَلَمُوْا ۚ
اِنَّهُمْ مُّغْرَقُوْنَ ۞ فَاِذَا اسْتَوَيْتَ اَنْتَ وَمَنْ مَّعَكَ
عَلَى الْفُلْكِ فَقُلِ الْحَمْدُ لِلّٰهِ الَّذِيْ نَجّٰنَا مِنَ
الْقَوْمِ الظّٰلِمِيْنَ ۞ وَقُلْ رَّبِّ اَنْزِلْنِيْ مُنْزَلًا مُّبٰرَكًا وَّ
اَنْتَ خَيْرُ الْمُنْزِلِيْنَ ۞ اِنَّ فِيْ ذٰلِكَ لَاٰيٰتٍ وَّاِنْ كُنَّا
لَمُبْتَلِيْنَ ۞ ثُمَّ اَنْشَأْنَا مِنْ بَعْدِهِمْ قَرْنًا اٰخَرِيْنَ ۞

What do we learn from the story of Nuh? The truthful are saved.

¹⁹ With *water*, We produce gardens of date palms and grape vines. There is plenty of fruit for you to eat. ²⁰ *We produced a* tree that grows on *the side of* Mount Sinai, it produces *olive* oil, a seasoning for people to eat. ²¹ The livestock offer you a lesson; We give you to drink from what is in their bellies, *not to mention* the many other benefits in them, and you eat their meat, ²² and they carry you *across the land*. And you're transported by the ships.

The seven habits of the disbelievers

²³ We sent Nuh to his people, he preached: "My people, worship Allah; you have no other god beside Him. Won't you be mindful *of Him*?" ²⁴ The leaders of disbelievers of his community said, "He is only a mortal like yourselves, who wants dominance over you. If Allah so wished, He would have sent angels. Never have we heard *the like of* this from our forefathers. ²⁵ He's just a man who's mad, so bear with him a while *till he recovers*." ²⁶ *Nuh* said, "My Lord, help me, they've denied me."

Nuh onboard the ship and his prayer

²⁷ *Eventually* We inspired him: "Build a ship under Our supervision and according to Our instructions; then, when Our command comes, and the geysers *begin to* flood, then take aboard two of every kind *of creature* and your family, except those who've already been condemned. And do not speak to me about the evildoers. They are *as good as* drowned. ²⁸ Then, once you and your followers are onboard the ship, say: 'Praise be to Allah, Who has rescued us from the wrongdoers,' ²⁹ and say: 'My Lord, settle me in a blessed place, for You are the best provider of a home.'" ³⁰ In this are signs. We have always put *people* to the test.

Criticisms made against the messengers: "They are only human"

³¹ We raised another generation after them,[a]

---

[a] From verse 31-80, seven habits of disbelievers are mentioned, they are; critical, deny resurrection, contempt of Prophets, confused, hate the truth, whimsical and stubborn.

فَاَرْسَلْنَا فِيْهِمْ رَسُوْلًا مِّنْهُمْ اَنِ اعْبُدُوا اللّٰهَ مَا لَكُمْ مِنْ اِلٰهٍ غَيْرُهُ ط اَفَلَا تَتَّقُوْنَ ۞ وَقَالَ الْمَلَأُ مِنْ قَوْمِهِ الَّذِيْنَ كَفَرُوْا وَكَذَّبُوْا بِلِقَآءِ الْاٰخِرَةِ وَاَتْرَفْنٰهُمْ فِي الْحَيٰوةِ الدُّنْيَا ۙ مَا هٰذَآ اِلَّا بَشَرٌ مِّثْلُكُمْ ۙ يَاْكُلُ مِمَّا تَاْكُلُوْنَ مِنْهُ وَيَشْرَبُ مِمَّا تَشْرَبُوْنَ ۞ وَلَئِنْ اَطَعْتُمْ بَشَرًا مِّثْلَكُمْ اِنَّكُمْ اِذًا لَّخٰسِرُوْنَ ۞ اَيَعِدُكُمْ اَنَّكُمْ اِذَا مِتُّمْ وَكُنْتُمْ تُرَابًا وَّعِظَامًا اَنَّكُمْ مُّخْرَجُوْنَ ۞ هَيْهَاتَ هَيْهَاتَ لِمَا تُوْعَدُوْنَ ۞ اِنْ هِيَ اِلَّا حَيَاتُنَا الدُّنْيَا نَمُوْتُ وَنَحْيَا وَمَا نَحْنُ بِمَبْعُوْثِيْنَ ۞ اِنْ هُوَ اِلَّا رَجُلُ نِ افْتَرٰى عَلَى اللّٰهِ كَذِبًا وَّمَا نَحْنُ لَهُ بِمُؤْمِنِيْنَ ۞ قَالَ رَبِّ انْصُرْنِيْ بِمَا كَذَّبُوْنِ ۞ قَالَ عَمَّا قَلِيْلٍ لَّيُصْبِحُنَّ نٰدِمِيْنَ ۞ فَاَخَذَتْهُمُ الصَّيْحَةُ بِالْحَقِّ فَجَعَلْنٰهُمْ غُثَآءً ۚ فَبُعْدًا لِّلْقَوْمِ الظّٰلِمِيْنَ ۞ ثُمَّ اَنْشَاْنَا مِنْ بَعْدِهِمْ قُرُوْنًا اٰخَرِيْنَ ۞ مَا تَسْبِقُ مِنْ اُمَّةٍ اَجَلَهَا وَمَا يَسْتَاْخِرُوْنَ ۞ ثُمَّ اَرْسَلْنَا رُسُلَنَا تَتْرَا ط كُلَّمَا جَآءَ اُمَّةً رَّسُوْلُهَا كَذَّبُوْهُ فَاَتْبَعْنَا بَعْضَهُمْ بَعْضًا وَّجَعَلْنٰهُمْ اَحَادِيْثَ ۚ فَبُعْدًا لِّقَوْمٍ لَّا يُؤْمِنُوْنَ ۞ ثُمَّ اَرْسَلْنَا مُوْسٰى وَاَخَاهُ هٰرُوْنَ ۙ بِاٰيٰتِنَا وَسُلْطٰنٍ مُّبِيْنٍ ۞ اِلٰى فِرْعَوْنَ وَمَلَئِهِ فَاسْتَكْبَرُوْا وَكَانُوْا قَوْمًا عَالِيْنَ ۞ فَقَالُوْا اَنُؤْمِنُ لِبَشَرَيْنِ مِثْلِنَا وَقَوْمُهُمَا

Human history is one of disobedience, but Allah continues to take care of His people.

[32] and sent a messenger from themselves, *who said*: "Worship Allah; you have no other god beside Him. Will you not be mindful *of Him*?" [33] The leaders of disbelievers from his community who denied meeting *Allah* in the Hereafter, and those We lavished *with luxuries* in this worldly life, *said*, "He's only a human like yourselves; he eats what you eat and drinks what you drink. [34] If you were to obey a human like yourselves, you would be losers."

Denial of life after death

[35] "Does he promise that, when you die and turn to dust and bones, you will be brought out *of your graves*? [36] What you are promised is utter nonsense! [37] This worldly life of ours is it! We will live, die, and we will not be resurrected. [38] He is only a man who has made up lies about Allah, *so* we won't believe him." [39] *The messenger* said, "My Lord, help me because they've denied me." [40] *Allah* said, "They will regret, soon." [41] The Blast took them *by surprise*; and We turned them into dust. So away with the evildoers! [42] We raised other generations after them. [43] No community can bring forward or delay its fixed lifespan.

Contempt for Prophets

[44] We continued sending Our messengers, one after another. Each time their messenger came to a community, they denied him. So, We made one community succeed another, and We made of them tales *to be told*. So away with people who do not believe! [45] After that We sent Musa and his brother, Harun, with Our signs and a clear proof [46] to Pharaoh and his court, but they were arrogant and too proud. [47] They said, "Should we believe two men like ourselves, whose people are our slaves?"

لَنَا عٰبِدُوْنَ ۞ فَكَذَّبُوْهُمَا فَكَانُوْا مِنَ الْمُهْلَكِيْنَ ۞

وَلَقَدْ اٰتَيْنَا مُوْسَى الْكِتٰبَ لَعَلَّهُمْ يَهْتَدُوْنَ ۞ وَ

جَعَلْنَا ابْنَ مَرْيَمَ وَاُمَّهٗٓ اٰيَةً وَّ اٰوَيْنٰهُمَآ اِلٰى رَبْوَةٍ

ذَاتِ قَرَارٍ وَّمَعِيْنٍ ۞ يٰٓاَيُّهَا الرُّسُلُ كُلُوْا مِنَ

الطَّيِّبٰتِ وَاعْمَلُوْا صَالِحًا ؕ اِنِّيْ بِمَا تَعْمَلُوْنَ عَلِيْمٌ ۞

وَاِنَّ هٰذِهٖٓ اُمَّتُكُمْ اُمَّةً وَّاحِدَةً وَّاَنَا رَبُّكُمْ فَاتَّقُوْنِ ۞

فَتَقَطَّعُوْٓا اَمْرَهُمْ بَيْنَهُمْ زُبُرًا ؕ كُلُّ حِزْبٍۭ بِمَا لَدَيْهِمْ

فَرِحُوْنَ ۞ فَذَرْهُمْ فِيْ غَمْرَتِهِمْ حَتّٰى حِيْنٍ ۞ اَيَحْسَبُوْنَ

اَنَّمَا نُمِدُّهُمْ بِهٖ مِنْ مَّالٍ وَّبَنِيْنَ ۞ نُسَارِعُ لَهُمْ فِي

الْخَيْرٰتِ ؕ بَلْ لَّا يَشْعُرُوْنَ ۞ اِنَّ الَّذِيْنَ هُمْ مِّنْ خَشْيَةِ

رَبِّهِمْ مُّشْفِقُوْنَ ۞ وَالَّذِيْنَ هُمْ بِاٰيٰتِ رَبِّهِمْ يُؤْمِنُوْنَ ۞

وَالَّذِيْنَ هُمْ بِرَبِّهِمْ لَا يُشْرِكُوْنَ ۞ وَالَّذِيْنَ يُؤْتُوْنَ

مَآ اٰتَوْا وَّ قُلُوْبُهُمْ وَجِلَةٌ اَنَّهُمْ اِلٰى رَبِّهِمْ رٰجِعُوْنَ ۞

اُولٰٓئِكَ يُسٰرِعُوْنَ فِي الْخَيْرٰتِ وَهُمْ لَهَا سٰبِقُوْنَ ۞ وَلَا

نُكَلِّفُ نَفْسًا اِلَّا وُسْعَهَا وَلَدَيْنَا كِتٰبٌ يَّنْطِقُ بِالْحَقِّ

وَهُمْ لَا يُظْلَمُوْنَ ۞ بَلْ قُلُوْبُهُمْ فِيْ غَمْرَةٍ مِّنْ هٰذَا

وَلَهُمْ اَعْمَالٌ مِّنْ دُوْنِ ذٰلِكَ هُمْ لَهَا عٰمِلُوْنَ ۞ حَتّٰى

اِذَآ اَخَذْنَا مُتْرَفِيْهِمْ بِالْعَذَابِ اِذَا هُمْ يَجْـَٔرُوْنَ ۞

لَا تَجْـَٔرُوا الْيَوْمَ ؕ اِنَّكُمْ مِّنَّا لَا تُنْصَرُوْنَ ۞ قَدْ كَانَتْ

اٰيٰتِيْ تُتْلٰى عَلَيْكُمْ فَكُنْتُمْ عَلٰٓى اَعْقَابِكُمْ تَنْكِصُوْنَ ۞

Unity among the believers is important. How are you trying to build that unity?

⁴⁸ So they denied them and were destroyed. ⁴⁹ We gave Musa the Book so they may be guided.

Isa, son of Maryam

⁵⁰ We made the son of Maryam and his mother a sign; We gave them refuge on a hilltop, a peaceful place with *a natural* spring. ⁵¹ Messengers, eat of what is pure wholesome and do good deeds; I know well what you do. ⁵² This community of yours is a single community, and I am your Lord, so be mindful of Me.

The disbelievers are confused, the believers know their goal

⁵³ *Their successors* split up into sects, each sect pleased with itself. ⁵⁴ So leave them *wallowing* in their confusion for a while. ⁵⁵ Do they reckon We granted them wealth and children because ⁵⁶ We are in a rush to do whatever is good for them? On the contrary, they have no sense *of what is coming.* ⁵⁷ *However,* those who fear their Lord; ⁵⁸ believe in the signs of their Lord; ⁵⁹ don't associate *partners* with their Lord; ⁶⁰ give charity from what they have been given, while their hearts tremble *at the thought* that they will be returning to their Lord; ⁶¹ they rush to do whatever is good, they are the high fliers.

The disbelievers hate the truth

⁶² We don't task anyone beyond their capacity, and *We keep* a Book with Us that speaks the truth; *so* they shall not be wronged. ⁶³ However, there's confusion in their minds about this; and *the wrongdoers* have even worse deeds than this, which they continue to do ⁶⁴ until We seize their well-off for punishment; then they will cry out. ⁶⁵ "Don't cry today," *they will be told,* "You will find no help against Us. ⁶⁶ When My verses were recited, you turned on your heels *and walked away,*

مُسْتَكْبِرِيْنَ ۤ بِهٖ سٰمِرًا تَهْجُرُوْنَ ۝ اَفَلَمْ يَدَّبَّرُوا

الْقَوْلَ اَمْ جَآءَهُمْ مَّا لَمْ يَأْتِ اٰبَآءَهُمُ الْاَوَّلِيْنَ ۝

اَمْ لَمْ يَعْرِفُوْا رَسُوْلَهُمْ فَهُمْ لَهٗ مُنْكِرُوْنَ ۝ اَمْ

يَقُوْلُوْنَ بِهٖ جِنَّةٌ ؕ بَلْ جَآءَهُمْ بِالْحَقِّ وَاَكْثَرُهُمْ

لِلْحَقِّ كٰرِهُوْنَ ۝ وَلَوِ اتَّبَعَ الْحَقُّ اَهْوَآءَهُمْ لَفَسَدَتِ

السَّمٰوٰتُ وَالْاَرْضُ وَمَنْ فِيْهِنَّ ؕ بَلْ اَتَيْنٰهُمْ بِذِكْرِهِمْ

فَهُمْ عَنْ ذِكْرِهِمْ مُّعْرِضُوْنَ ۝ اَمْ تَسْـَٔلُهُمْ خَرْجًا

فَخَرَاجُ رَبِّكَ خَيْرٌ ۤ وَّهُوَ خَيْرُ الرّٰزِقِيْنَ ۝ وَاِنَّكَ

لَتَدْعُوْهُمْ اِلٰى صِرَاطٍ مُّسْتَقِيْمٍ ۝ وَاِنَّ الَّذِيْنَ

لَا يُؤْمِنُوْنَ بِالْاٰخِرَةِ عَنِ الصِّرَاطِ لَنٰكِبُوْنَ ۝ وَلَوْ

رَحِمْنٰهُمْ وَكَشَفْنَا مَا بِهِمْ مِّنْ ضُرٍّ لَّلَجُّوْا فِيْ طُغْيَانِهِمْ

يَعْمَهُوْنَ ۝ وَلَقَدْ اَخَذْنٰهُمْ بِالْعَذَابِ فَمَا اسْتَكَانُوْا

لِرَبِّهِمْ وَمَا يَتَضَرَّعُوْنَ ۝ حَتّٰى اِذَا فَتَحْنَا عَلَيْهِمْ بَابًا

ذَا عَذَابٍ شَدِيْدٍ اِذَا هُمْ فِيْهِ مُبْلِسُوْنَ ۝ وَهُوَ

الَّذِيْٓ اَنْشَاَ لَكُمُ السَّمْعَ وَالْاَبْصَارَ وَالْاَفْئِدَةَ ؕ قَلِيْلًا

مَّا تَشْكُرُوْنَ ۝ وَهُوَ الَّذِيْ ذَرَاَكُمْ فِى الْاَرْضِ وَاِلَيْهِ

تُحْشَرُوْنَ ۝ وَهُوَ الَّذِيْ يُحْيٖ وَيُمِيْتُ وَلَهُ اخْتِلَافُ

الَّيْلِ وَالنَّهَارِ ؕ اَفَلَا تَعْقِلُوْنَ ۝ بَلْ قَالُوْا مِثْلَ مَا

قَالَ الْاَوَّلُوْنَ ۝ قَالُوْٓا ءَاِذَا مِتْنَا وَكُنَّا تُرَابًا وَّعِظَامًا

ءَاِنَّا لَمَبْعُوْثُوْنَ ۝ لَقَدْ وُعِدْنَا نَحْنُ وَاٰبَآؤُنَا هٰذَا

Our problem is we fail to use our senses! If we used our eyes and ears we would see the greatness of Allah all around us.

681

[67] arrogantly talking nonsense late into the night." [68] Haven't they reflected on what is said *in the Quran*? Or has something come to them that never came to their forefathers? [69] Or is it that they don't recognise their messenger, and so they reject him? [70] Or do they say that he's possessed? On the contrary, he has come to them with the truth, but most of them hate it.

They follow their whims

[71] If *Allah, the truth*[a] was to follow their whims, then the Heavens and the Earth and whatever exists in them would have fallen into ruin. We brought them a reminder, but they turned away from their reminder. [72] Or did you ask them to pay you something? The payment of your Lord is better by far; and He is the best Provider. [73] *At the same time as* you are calling them to the straight path, [74] those who deny the Hereafter have turned away from the path.

They are stubborn

[75] If We were kind to them and removed *all* hardship from them, they would still wander about disobediently. [76] We punished them *once before*, and they didn't surrender to their Lord, nor showed humility [77] until We opened the gate of punishment on them, and they fell into despair. [78] He gave you hearing, sight and mind. How little did you thank Him! [79] He scattered you all over the Earth, and eventually you will be gathered before Him. [80] He grants life and death, and His is the cycle of night and day. Don't you understand?

Hard-hitting questions for disbelievers

[81] On the contrary, *the Makkans* say the same as *their* ancestors. [82] They said: "When we are dead and turned to dust and bones, will we be resurrected?

---

[a]   According to some commentaries, "the truth" here refers to Allah.

مِنْ قَبْلُ اِنْ هٰذَاۤ اِلَّاۤ اَسَاطِيْرُ الْاَوَّلِيْنَ ۝ قُلْ لِّمَنِ

الْاَرْضُ وَمَنْ فِيْهَاۤ اِنْ كُنْتُمْ تَعْلَمُوْنَ ۝ سَيَقُوْلُوْنَ لِلّٰهِ ط

قُلْ اَفَلَا تَذَكَّرُوْنَ ۝ قُلْ مَنْ رَّبُّ السَّمٰوٰتِ السَّبْعِ

وَرَبُّ الْعَرْشِ الْعَظِيْمِ ۝ سَيَقُوْلُوْنَ لِلّٰهِ ط قُلْ اَفَلَا

تَتَّقُوْنَ ۝ قُلْ مَنْ بِيَدِهٖ مَلَكُوْتُ كُلِّ شَىْءٍ وَّهُوَ يُجِيْرُ

وَلَا يُجَارُ عَلَيْهِ اِنْ كُنْتُمْ تَعْلَمُوْنَ ۝ سَيَقُوْلُوْنَ لِلّٰهِ ط

قُلْ فَاَنّٰى تُسْحَرُوْنَ ۝ بَلْ اَتَيْنٰهُمْ بِالْحَقِّ وَاِنَّهُمْ

لَكٰذِبُوْنَ ۝ مَا اتَّخَذَ اللّٰهُ مِنْ وَّلَدٍ وَّمَا كَانَ مَعَهٗ

مِنْ اِلٰهٍ اِذًا لَّذَهَبَ كُلُّ اِلٰهٍ بِمَا خَلَقَ وَلَعَلَا بَعْضُهُمْ

عَلٰى بَعْضٍ ط سُبْحٰنَ اللّٰهِ عَمَّا يَصِفُوْنَ ۝ عٰلِمِ الْغَيْبِ وَ

الشَّهَادَةِ فَتَعٰلٰى عَمَّا يُشْرِكُوْنَ ۝ قُلْ رَّبِّ اِمَّا تُرِيَنِّىْ

مَا يُوْعَدُوْنَ ۝ رَبِّ فَلَا تَجْعَلْنِىْ فِى الْقَوْمِ الظّٰلِمِيْنَ ۝

وَاِنَّا عَلٰى اَنْ نُّرِيَكَ مَا نَعِدُهُمْ لَقٰدِرُوْنَ ۝ اِدْفَعْ بِالَّتِىْ

هِىَ اَحْسَنُ السَّيِّئَةَ ط نَحْنُ اَعْلَمُ بِمَا يَصِفُوْنَ ۝ وَقُلْ

رَّبِّ اَعُوْذُ بِكَ مِنْ هَمَزٰتِ الشَّيٰطِيْنِ ۝ وَاَعُوْذُ بِكَ

رَبِّ اَنْ يَّحْضُرُوْنِ ۝ حَتّٰى اِذَا جَاۤءَ اَحَدَهُمُ الْمَوْتُ

قَالَ رَبِّ ارْجِعُوْنِ ۝ لَعَلِّىْ اَعْمَلُ صَالِحًا فِيْمَا تَرَكْتُ

كَلَّا ط اِنَّهَا كَلِمَةٌ هُوَ قَاۤئِلُهَا ط وَمِنْ وَّرَاۤئِهِمْ بَرْزَخٌ

اِلٰى يَوْمِ يُبْعَثُوْنَ ۝ فَاِذَا نُفِخَ فِى الصُّوْرِ فَلَاۤ اَنْسَابَ

بَيْنَهُمْ يَوْمَئِذٍ وَّلَا يَتَسَاۤءَلُوْنَ ۝ فَمَنْ ثَقُلَتْ

An effective way to defeat evil is to return it by doing good. Look! How many times has Allah forgiven you?

۵
۱۵
ع

⁸³ We and our forefathers were promised this before. These are mere tales of the past." ⁸⁴ Say, *Muhammad*: "To Whom does the Earth and whoever *lives* on it belong, if you have knowledge?" ⁸⁵ They will say, "To Allah!" Say: "Why then don't you pay attention?" ⁸⁶ Say: "Who is the Lord of the Seven Heavens and the Lord of the Mighty Throne?" ⁸⁷ *Again* they will say, "Allah!" Say: "Why aren't you mindful *of Him*?" ⁸⁸ Say: "In Whose hand lies the control over everything, He protects, but against Him there is no protection, if you have knowledge?" ⁸⁹ They will say, "Allah!" Say: "So why are you bewitched?" ⁹⁰ On the other hand, We brought them the truth, but they deny it.

Allah has neither son nor partner

⁹¹ Allah has not taken a son, nor is there any other god with Him. If it had been so, each god would have gone off with what it had created, and some of them would be superior to others. Glory to Allah, *Who is far removed* from what they ascribe *to Him*! ⁹² The Knower of all that is seen and unseen, Sublimely exalted above whatever they associate *with Him*!

Prayer for protection from Satan

⁹³ Say: "My Lord, if You must show me what they've been promised ⁹⁴ then, My Lord, don't include me among the wrongdoers." ⁹⁵ We are quite capable of showing you what We promised them. ⁹⁶ Repel evil with good. We know well what they ascribe *to Us*. ⁹⁷ And say: "My Lord, I seek refuge in You from the murmurings of devils; ⁹⁸ and I seek Your refuge from harm they may cause me." ⁹⁹ Only when death comes to one of them will he say, "My Lord, let me return *to my life on Earth* ¹⁰⁰ so that I may act righteously in whatever I *previously* omitted." Never! What he is saying are *empty* words; and before them lies a vast barrier, *uncrossable* till the day they are resurrected.

Those sent to Hell will plead to return to life

¹⁰¹ When the *mighty* Trumpet is blown, that Day there will be no kinship *left* between them, nor will they ask about each other.

مَوَازِيْنُهُ فَاُولٰٓئِكَ هُمُ الْمُفْلِحُوْنَ ۞ وَمَنْ خَفَّتْ

مَوَازِيْنُهُ فَاُولٰٓئِكَ الَّذِيْنَ خَسِرُوْۤا اَنْفُسَهُمْ فِيْ

جَهَنَّمَ خٰلِدُوْنَ ۞ تَلْفَحُ وُجُوْهَهُمُ النَّارُ وَهُمْ فِيْهَا

كٰلِحُوْنَ ۞ اَلَمْ تَكُنْ اٰيٰتِيْ تُتْلٰى عَلَيْكُمْ فَكُنْتُمْ

بِهَا تُكَذِّبُوْنَ ۞ قَالُوْا رَبَّنَا غَلَبَتْ عَلَيْنَا شِقْوَتُنَا

وَكُنَّا قَوْمًا ضَآلِّيْنَ ۞ رَبَّنَاۤ اَخْرِجْنَا مِنْهَا فَاِنْ

عُدْنَا فَاِنَّا ظٰلِمُوْنَ ۞ قَالَ اخْسَـُٔوْا فِيْهَا وَلَا

تُكَلِّمُوْنِ ۞ اِنَّهٗ كَانَ فَرِيْقٌ مِّنْ عِبَادِيْ يَقُوْلُوْنَ

رَبَّنَاۤ اٰمَنَّا فَاغْفِرْ لَنَا وَارْحَمْنَا وَاَنْتَ خَيْرُ

الرّٰحِمِيْنَ ۞ فَاتَّخَذْتُمُوْهُمْ سِخْرِيًّا حَتّٰۤى اَنْسَوْكُمْ

ذِكْرِيْ وَكُنْتُمْ مِّنْهُمْ تَضْحَكُوْنَ ۞ اِنِّيْ جَزَيْتُهُمُ

الْيَوْمَ بِمَا صَبَرُوْۤا اَنَّهُمْ هُمُ الْفَآئِزُوْنَ ۞ قٰلَ

كَمْ لَبِثْتُمْ فِى الْاَرْضِ عَدَدَ سِنِيْنَ ۞ قَالُوْا لَبِثْنَا

يَوْمًا اَوْ بَعْضَ يَوْمٍ فَسْـَٔلِ الْعَآدِّيْنَ ۞ قٰلَ اِنْ لَّبِثْتُمْ

اِلَّا قَلِيْلًا لَّوْ اَنَّكُمْ كُنْتُمْ تَعْلَمُوْنَ ۞ اَفَحَسِبْتُمْ اَنَّمَا

خَلَقْنٰكُمْ عَبَثًا وَّاَنَّكُمْ اِلَيْنَا لَا تُرْجَعُوْنَ ۞ فَتَعٰلَى اللّٰهُ

الْمَلِكُ الْحَقُّ لَاۤ اِلٰهَ اِلَّا هُوَ رَبُّ الْعَرْشِ الْكَرِيْمِ ۞

وَمَنْ يَّدْعُ مَعَ اللّٰهِ اِلٰهًا اٰخَرَ لَا بُرْهَانَ لَهٗ بِهٖ

فَاِنَّمَا حِسَابُهٗ عِنْدَ رَبِّهٖ اِنَّهٗ لَا يُفْلِحُ الْكٰفِرُوْنَ ۞

وَقُلْ رَّبِّ اغْفِرْ وَارْحَمْ وَاَنْتَ خَيْرُ الرّٰحِمِيْنَ ۞

Allah created us for a purpose: faith and worship. That's humanity.

¹⁰² Anyone whose scales weigh heavy, will be successful; ¹⁰³ but anyone whose scales are light will be the loser, staying in Hell forever. ¹⁰⁴ The Fire will scorch their faces, leaving them grinning *like skulls*. ¹⁰⁵ "Were My verses not recited to you," *they will be asked*, "and you rejected them." ¹⁰⁶ They will say, "Our Lord, misfortune overwhelmed us, and *so* we went astray. ¹⁰⁷ Our Lord, get us out of here; if we return *to acting sinfully*, we shall *only* be wronging *ourselves*." ¹⁰⁸ *Allah* will say, "May you be driven *ever deeper* into *the Fire*. Don't speak to Me."

The patient are rewarded
¹⁰⁹ There was *once* a group of My servants who used to say, 'Our Lord, we believe; forgive us and be kind to us, for You are the most Kind.' ¹¹⁰ However, you took them as a laughing stock, your laughing at them made you forget My remembrance. ¹¹¹ This day I shall reward them for their patience. They are the victors." ¹¹² *Allah* will ask, "How long did you live on Earth?" ¹¹³ They will say, "We spent a day or so. Ask those who keep count." ¹¹⁴ *Allah* will say, "You spent but a short while, if only you knew."

Conclusion: Human life has a purpose
¹¹⁵ Did you reckon We created you without a purpose and you wouldn't be returned to Us? ¹¹⁶ Allah is the exalted, the True King! There is no god beside Him, Lord of the Honoured Throne. ¹¹⁷ Anyone who worships another god for which he has no proof, His Lord will bring him to account. The disbelievers shall never succeed. ¹¹⁸ And, *Messenger,* say: "My Lord, forgive and be kind, for You are the Most Kind."

24. Surat An-Nur

The Light

This surat was revealed in Madinah after the campaign of Banu Mustalaq in the fifth year of Hijrah. The central theme is social manners: modesty, and the penalty for adultery and slandering innocent people. The aim is to lay down firm foundations for building relationships between men and women based on modesty and respect. It opens with declaring a severe penalty for adultery, and continues by recommending rules for the mixing of men and women, the Hijab, and personal privacy inside and outside the home. The purpose of these rules is to develop a decent environment, free of sexual exploitation. If sexuality is not properly controlled, it can cause disorder in family life and chaos in wider society. These simple rules are powerful preventative measures that restrict shameful behaviour. Ignoring these rules leads to the spread of all kinds of sexual exploitation, indecency, pornography and prostitution.

The story of the false accusation against Aisha (Allah be pleased with Her), the Mother of the Believers, highlights the importance of these social regulations. The story concludes by declaring the innocence of the Mother of the Believers, and recommends six effective social rules: we are warned against spreading rumours; penalty for those who spread indecency; develop the value of forgiveness; permission should be sought to enter houses; women covering themselves in public; and assistance for single people to marry.

The parable of 'light' in verse 35 points to Allah's creative power; making living matter from the darkness of nothing. Evidence of the existence of God. The 'light' can be Allah's guidance – how he gives humanity the ability to discern right from wrong. As we witness marvellous phenomena in the physical world, such as rain, rainbows, and Earthquakes, we are filled with awe that leads to belief in Him, and we search for guidance. However, the disbelievers are told, "Anyone Allah deprives of light, shall have no light" (40). This spiritual passage comes in the middle of a legal discussion, and the point being made is that religious laws are only meaningful and effective if Allah is at the centre of it. This is followed by a passage that stresses the power of the Almighty, and why we need to observe His rules. Devout believers are promised: "*He will* make the believers and the righteous *His* deputies on Earth as He made those before you *His* deputies" (55).

Four more social manners are pronounced: visiting others; concessions in wearing the Hijab for mature women; eating together; and the company of the Messenger ﷺ.

The Quran's Position on Slavery

Since slavery was deep-rooted in the seventh century, the Quran didn't attempt banning it in one big swoop, it would have been impossible to give it up, instead it adopted a gradual tactic: first ensuring slaves have rights; owners were obliged to feed, clothe and allow them freedom to worship like themselves. Secondly, the Quran repeatedly praised those who freed slaves or took good care of them. It also prohibited making Muslims slaves. Thirdly, certain atonements could be achieved by freeing slaves, all of which encouraged and improved the status of slaves. Moreover, the Quranic subtext of kindness, generosity and justice required its followers to see slavery as incompatible with Quranic justice, since it violated the concept of Human brotherhood and sisterhood: "If any of your slaves asks for an *emancipation* contract, and you see some good in them, draft it for them; and give them of the wealth that Allah has given you." (33)

The surat concludes with a stern warning: "Let those who oppose His orders be aware, lest they are afflicted by suffering or receive painful punishment" (63).

بِسْمِ اللّٰهِ الرَّحْمٰنِ الرَّحِيْمِ

سُوْرَةٌ اَنْزَلْنٰهَا وَفَرَضْنٰهَا وَاَنْزَلْنَا فِيْهَاۤ اٰيٰتٍۢ بَيِّنٰتٍ

لَّعَلَّكُمْ تَذَكَّرُوْنَ ۱ اَلزَّانِيَةُ وَالزَّانِيْ فَاجْلِدُوْا كُلَّ

وَاحِدٍ مِّنْهُمَا مِائَةَ جَلْدَةٍ ۪ وَّلَا تَاْخُذْكُمْ بِهِمَا رَاْفَةٌ

فِيْ دِيْنِ اللّٰهِ اِنْ كُنْتُمْ تُؤْمِنُوْنَ بِاللّٰهِ وَالْيَوْمِ الْاٰخِرِ ۚ

وَلْيَشْهَدْ عَذَابَهُمَا طَآئِفَةٌ مِّنَ الْمُؤْمِنِيْنَ ۲ اَلزَّانِيْ

لَا يَنْكِحُ اِلَّا زَانِيَةً اَوْ مُشْرِكَةً ۫ وَّالزَّانِيَةُ لَا يَنْكِحُهَاۤ

اِلَّا زَانٍ اَوْ مُشْرِكٌ ۚ وَحُرِّمَ ذٰلِكَ عَلَى الْمُؤْمِنِيْنَ ۳

وَالَّذِيْنَ يَرْمُوْنَ الْمُحْصَنٰتِ ثُمَّ لَمْ يَاْتُوْا بِاَرْبَعَةِ

شُهَدَآءَ فَاجْلِدُوْهُمْ ثَمٰنِيْنَ جَلْدَةً وَّلَا تَقْبَلُوْا لَهُمْ

شَهَادَةً اَبَدًا ۚ وَاُولٰٓئِكَ هُمُ الْفٰسِقُوْنَ ۴ اِلَّا الَّذِيْنَ

تَابُوْا مِنْۢ بَعْدِ ذٰلِكَ وَاَصْلَحُوْا ۚ فَاِنَّ اللّٰهَ غَفُوْرٌ

رَّحِيْمٌ ۵ وَالَّذِيْنَ يَرْمُوْنَ اَزْوَاجَهُمْ وَلَمْ يَكُنْ لَّهُمْ

شُهَدَآءُ اِلَّاۤ اَنْفُسُهُمْ فَشَهَادَةُ اَحَدِهِمْ اَرْبَعُ شَهٰدٰتٍۢ

بِاللّٰهِ ۙ اِنَّهٗ لَمِنَ الصّٰدِقِيْنَ ۶ وَالْخَامِسَةُ اَنَّ لَعْنَتَ

اللّٰهِ عَلَيْهِ اِنْ كَانَ مِنَ الْكٰذِبِيْنَ ۷ وَيَدْرَؤُا عَنْهَا

الْعَذَابَ اَنْ تَشْهَدَ اَرْبَعَ شَهٰدٰتٍۢ بِاللّٰهِ ۙ اِنَّهٗ لَمِنَ

الْكٰذِبِيْنَ ۸ وَالْخَامِسَةَ اَنَّ غَضَبَ اللّٰهِ عَلَيْهَاۤ اِنْ

كَانَ مِنَ الصّٰدِقِيْنَ ۹ وَلَوْلَا فَضْلُ اللّٰهِ عَلَيْكُمْ وَ

Sexual purity is the key to spiritual enlightenment. Is that why the penalties for sexual impropriety are so harsh?

In the name of Allah, the Kind, the Caring.

The punishment for fornication

[1] *This is* a surat that We sent down with laws to be obeyed, and We revealed clear verses so you will pay attention. [2] Flog the fornicators,[a] male and female, each of them one-hundred lashes, and don't let sympathy for them hold you back from *fulfilling* Allah's orders, if you believe in Allah and the Last Day; and let a group of believers witness their punishment. [3] A male fornicator only marries a female fornicator or an idolatress; a female fornicator only marries a male fornicator or an idolater; and fornication is forbidden for the believers.[b]

The procedure in accusations of fornication

[4] *Those* who accuse chaste women *of fornication*,[c] but fail to produce four witnesses, should be flogged eighty lashes; and never accept their witness statement again. They are major sinners,[d] [5] except those who later repent and reform themselves. Allah is Forgiving, Kind. [6] Anyone who accuses his wife but has no witnesses other than himself, let him swear four times by Allah: he is telling the truth, [7] and the fifth time he says, Allah's curse be upon him if he is lying. [8] Punishment will be averted from her if she *also* swears by Allah four times that he is lying, [9] and the fifth time that Allah's wrath be upon her if he is telling the truth.

---

[a] *Zina*, like 'fornication', is general and refers to all unlawful penetrative sexual intercourse between men and women, regardless of their marital status. 'Adultery' is specifically fornication by a married person.

[b] This underlines the heinous crime of fornication, a Muslim convicted of it can't marry a believer of good character.

[c] The word *muhsanat* literally means "protected" or "fortified", be it by a bond of marriage or their own good name.

[d] The strict requirement of four independent witnesses of honourable reputation who happen to observe the act of penetration clearly with their eyes. In other words, it is insufficient merely to see two people naked together, or to make assumptions about what may or may not be going on under a sheet. Since it is almost impossible to imagine such a situation, the verse should be interpreted as emphasising the importance of truthfulness, the harmful effect on society of spreading unsubstantiated rumours – even if the rumours are true but do not meet the required level of proof – and the seriousness of making false or unprovable statements before a court of law.

رَحْمَتُهٗ ۖ وَاَنَّ اللّٰهَ تَوَّابٌ حَكِيْمٌ ۩ اِنَّ الَّذِيْنَ جَآءُوْ
بِالْاِفْكِ عُصْبَةٌ مِّنْكُمْ ۚ لَا تَحْسَبُوْهُ شَرًّا لَّكُمْ ۚ بَلْ هُوَ
خَيْرٌ لَّكُمْ ۚ لِكُلِّ امْرِئٍ مِّنْهُمْ مَّا اكْتَسَبَ مِنَ الْاِثْمِ ۚ
وَالَّذِيْ تَوَلّٰى كِبْرَهٗ مِنْهُمْ لَهٗ عَذَابٌ عَظِيْمٌ ۝ لَوْلَآ
اِذْ سَمِعْتُمُوْهُ ظَنَّ الْمُؤْمِنُوْنَ وَالْمُؤْمِنٰتُ بِاَنْفُسِهِمْ
خَيْرًا ۙ وَّقَالُوْا هٰذَآ اِفْكٌ مُّبِيْنٌ ۝ لَوْلَا جَآءُوْ
عَلَيْهِ بِاَرْبَعَةِ شُهَدَآءَ ۚ فَاِذْ لَمْ يَاْتُوْا بِالشُّهَدَآءِ
فَاُولٰٓئِكَ عِنْدَ اللّٰهِ هُمُ الْكٰذِبُوْنَ ۝ وَلَوْلَا فَضْلُ اللّٰهِ
عَلَيْكُمْ وَرَحْمَتُهٗ فِى الدُّنْيَا وَالْاٰخِرَةِ لَمَسَّكُمْ فِيْ مَآ
اَفَضْتُمْ فِيْهِ عَذَابٌ عَظِيْمٌ ۝ اِذْ تَلَقَّوْنَهٗ بِاَلْسِنَتِكُمْ وَ
تَقُوْلُوْنَ بِاَفْوَاهِكُمْ مَّا لَيْسَ لَكُمْ بِهٖ عِلْمٌ وَّتَحْسَبُوْنَهٗ
هَيِّنًا ۖ وَّهُوَ عِنْدَ اللّٰهِ عَظِيْمٌ ۝ وَلَوْلَآ اِذْ سَمِعْتُمُوْهُ
قُلْتُمْ مَّا يَكُوْنُ لَنَآ اَنْ نَّتَكَلَّمَ بِهٰذَا ۖ سُبْحٰنَكَ هٰذَا
بُهْتَانٌ عَظِيْمٌ ۝ يَعِظُكُمُ اللّٰهُ اَنْ تَعُوْدُوْا لِمِثْلِهٖ اَبَدًا
اِنْ كُنْتُمْ مُّؤْمِنِيْنَ ۝ وَيُبَيِّنُ اللّٰهُ لَكُمُ الْاٰيٰتِ ۚ وَاللّٰهُ
عَلِيْمٌ حَكِيْمٌ ۝ اِنَّ الَّذِيْنَ يُحِبُّوْنَ اَنْ تَشِيْعَ الْفَاحِشَةُ
فِى الَّذِيْنَ اٰمَنُوْا لَهُمْ عَذَابٌ اَلِيْمٌ ۙ فِى الدُّنْيَا وَالْاٰخِرَةِ ۚ
وَاللّٰهُ يَعْلَمُ وَاَنْتُمْ لَا تَعْلَمُوْنَ ۝ وَلَوْلَا فَضْلُ اللّٰهِ
عَلَيْكُمْ وَرَحْمَتُهٗ وَاَنَّ اللّٰهَ رَءُوْفٌ رَّحِيْمٌ ۝ يٰٓاَيُّهَا
الَّذِيْنَ اٰمَنُوْا لَا تَتَّبِعُوْا خُطُوٰتِ الشَّيْطٰنِ ۚ وَمَنْ يَّتَّبِعْ

Spreading promiscuity, pornography and indecency is a major sin because it harms the individual and the society.

691

¹⁰*Imagine the consequences*, if it were not for Allah's grace towards you and His kindness. Allah is Relenting, Wise.

The slander against Aisha, Mother of the Believers

¹¹Those who planned the slander were a handful of you, don't consider it bad for you; in fact, it's good for you.ᵃ Each person among them will bear the consequence of *his part in* the sin; and the one who played the leading role will receive a mighty punishment. ¹²If once they heard it – the believers, male and female – of their own accord should have thought the best *of Aisha* and said, "This is clearly a slander." ¹³If they had produced four witnesses, *it would be different*; but they failed to produce the witnesses, in Allah's sight they are liars.

The story of Aisha, Mother of the Believers; Never spread rumours

¹⁴Were it not for Allah's grace towards you and His kind treatment in this world and the Hereafter, then a mighty punishment would have affected you *all* because of the rumour you rushed *to spread*. ¹⁵You gave it *publicity* with your chatter and said things with your mouths you had no knowledge of, thinking it was a trivial, but in the sight of Allah it was serious. ¹⁶If only, when you heard it, you had said: "It is not *fitting* for us to talk about this. Glory be to Him! This is a terrible slander." ¹⁷Allah warns you: never repeat such *behaviour* again if you are believers. ¹⁸Allah is explaining the verses for you. Allah is Knowing, Wise.

Punishment for people who spread indecency

¹⁹Those who like to spread indecency among the believers *will suffer* a painful punishment in this worldly life and the Hereafter. Allah knows what you don't know. ²⁰*Imagine the consequences*, if it were not for Allah's grace towards you and His kindness. Allah is Compassionate, Kind.

ᵃ   Since this was a test for the believers, to see who would remain steadfast. Furthermore, for every hardship a person suffers they get a reward. "When a person suffers pain or anxiety, even if it is a prick of a thorn, Allah forgives their sins" (Bukhari)

خُطُوٰتِ الشَّيْطٰنِ فَاِنَّهٗ يَامُرُ بِالْفَحْشَآءِ وَالْمُنْكَرِ ط وَلَوْ

لَا فَضْلُ اللهِ عَلَيْكُمْ وَرَحْمَتُهٗ مَا زَكٰى مِنْكُمْ مِّنْ

اَحَدٍ اَبَدًا لَّا وَّلٰكِنَّ اللهَ يُزَكِّيْ مَنْ يَّشَآءُ ط وَاللهُ سَمِيْعٌ

عَلِيْمٌ ۲۱ وَلَا يَاْتَلِ اُولُوا الْفَضْلِ مِنْكُمْ وَالسَّعَةِ اَنْ

يُّؤْتُوْٓا اُولِى الْقُرْبٰى وَالْمَسٰكِيْنَ وَالْمُهٰجِرِيْنَ فِيْ سَبِيْلِ

اللهِ ۖ وَلْيَعْفُوْا وَلْيَصْفَحُوْا ط اَلَا تُحِبُّوْنَ اَنْ يَّغْفِرَ اللهُ

لَكُمْ ط وَاللهُ غَفُوْرٌ رَّحِيْمٌ ۲۲ اِنَّ الَّذِيْنَ يَرْمُوْنَ

الْمُحْصَنٰتِ الْغٰفِلٰتِ الْمُؤْمِنٰتِ لُعِنُوْا فِى الدُّنْيَا وَالْاٰخِرَةِ ۖ

وَلَهُمْ عَذَابٌ عَظِيْمٌ ۲۳ يَّوْمَ تَشْهَدُ عَلَيْهِمْ اَلْسِنَتُهُمْ

وَاَيْدِيْهِمْ وَاَرْجُلُهُمْ بِمَا كَانُوْا يَعْمَلُوْنَ ۲۴ يَوْمَئِذٍ

يُّوَفِّيْهِمُ اللهُ دِيْنَهُمُ الْحَقَّ وَيَعْلَمُوْنَ اَنَّ اللهَ هُوَ

الْحَقُّ الْمُبِيْنُ ۲۵ اَلْخَبِيْثٰتُ لِلْخَبِيْثِيْنَ وَالْخَبِيْثُوْنَ

لِلْخَبِيْثٰتِ ۚ وَالطَّيِّبٰتُ لِلطَّيِّبِيْنَ وَالطَّيِّبُوْنَ لِلطَّيِّبٰتِ ۚ

اُولٰٓئِكَ مُبَرَّءُوْنَ مِمَّا يَقُوْلُوْنَ ط لَهُمْ مَّغْفِرَةٌ وَّرِزْقٌ

كَرِيْمٌ ۲۶ يٰٓاَيُّهَا الَّذِيْنَ اٰمَنُوْا لَا تَدْخُلُوْا بُيُوْتًا غَيْرَ

بُيُوْتِكُمْ حَتّٰى تَسْتَاْنِسُوْا وَتُسَلِّمُوْا عَلٰٓى اَهْلِهَا ط ذٰلِكُمْ

خَيْرٌ لَّكُمْ لَعَلَّكُمْ تَذَكَّرُوْنَ ۲۷ فَاِنْ لَّمْ تَجِدُوْا

فِيْهَآ اَحَدًا فَلَا تَدْخُلُوْهَا حَتّٰى يُؤْذَنَ لَكُمْ ۚ وَاِنْ

قِيْلَ لَكُمُ ارْجِعُوْا فَارْجِعُوْا هُوَ اَزْكٰى لَكُمْ ط وَاللهُ بِمَا

تَعْمَلُوْنَ عَلِيْمٌ ۲۸ لَيْسَ عَلَيْكُمْ جُنَاحٌ اَنْ تَدْخُلُوْا

Forgive those who do wrong to you.

²¹ Believers, don't follow in Satan's footsteps. Whoever follows Satan's footsteps *will find* that he urges indecency and shameful acts. If it weren't for Allah's grace on you and His kindness, none of you would be pure, Allah purifies anyone He pleases. Allah is the Hearer, the Knower.

Muslims urged to forgive one another

²² Those of you who possess status and means shouldn't vow to stop giving to relatives, the needy and those who emigrated for the sake of Allah. Let them pardon and overlook *their shortcomings*. Wouldn't you like Allah to forgive you? Allah is Forgiving, Kind.ᵃ

Warning against false accusations

²³ Those who falsely accuse careless *but nonetheless* chaste believing women shall be cursed here and the Hereafter, and will be severely punished,ᵇ ²⁴ on the Day tongues, hands and feet will testify against them for what they did. ²⁵ That Day, Allah will settle their account for them in full, and they will know Allah alone is the Truth, the Clarifier. ²⁶ Vile women are *fit* for vile men, and vile men are *fit* for vile women; and *likewise*, moral women are for moral men, and moral men are for moral women. Such people are innocent of what *others* say about them; they will be forgiven and have generous provision.

Seeking permission to enter a house

²⁷ Believers, don't enter any houses other than your own homes until you have made yourselves known and greeted the occupants; that's best for you, so you may pay heed. ²⁸ If there is no one in, then don't enter until permission is given; and if you are told, "Go back!" Then go back: that is the best *course of action* for you. Allah knows well what you do.

ᵃ   This verse was revealed after Aisha's father, Abu Bakr, vowed never to support his cousin, Mistah ibn Uthatha, because he spread the slander against his daughter.

ᵇ   A shocking crime where a Muslim woman or girl has been seen in the company of non-mahram men is enough for her to become the victim of a horrific attack, or even the so-called "honour killing", at the hands of her closest relatives.

بُيُوْتًا غَيْرَ مَسْكُوْنَةٍ فِيْهَا مَتَاعٌ لَّكُمْ ۚ وَاللّٰهُ يَعْلَمُ

مَا تُبْدُوْنَ وَمَا تَكْتُمُوْنَ ۝ قُلْ لِّلْمُؤْمِنِيْنَ يَغُضُّوْا

مِنْ اَبْصَارِهِمْ وَيَحْفَظُوْا فُرُوْجَهُمْ ۚ ذٰلِكَ اَزْكٰى لَهُمْ ۗ

اِنَّ اللّٰهَ خَبِيْرٌۢ بِمَا يَصْنَعُوْنَ ۝ وَقُلْ لِّلْمُؤْمِنٰتِ

يَغْضُضْنَ مِنْ اَبْصَارِهِنَّ وَيَحْفَظْنَ فُرُوْجَهُنَّ وَلَا

يُبْدِيْنَ زِيْنَتَهُنَّ اِلَّا مَا ظَهَرَ مِنْهَا وَلْيَضْرِبْنَ

بِخُمُرِهِنَّ عَلٰى جُيُوْبِهِنَّ ۖ وَلَا يُبْدِيْنَ زِيْنَتَهُنَّ

اِلَّا لِبُعُوْلَتِهِنَّ اَوْ اٰبَائِهِنَّ اَوْ اٰبَاءِ بُعُوْلَتِهِنَّ اَوْ

اَبْنَائِهِنَّ اَوْ اَبْنَاءِ بُعُوْلَتِهِنَّ اَوْ اِخْوَانِهِنَّ اَوْ بَنِيْٓ

اِخْوَانِهِنَّ اَوْ بَنِيْٓ اَخَوَاتِهِنَّ اَوْ نِسَائِهِنَّ اَوْ مَا مَلَكَتْ

اَيْمَانُهُنَّ اَوِ التّٰبِعِيْنَ غَيْرِ اُولِى الْاِرْبَةِ مِنَ الرِّجَالِ

اَوِ الطِّفْلِ الَّذِيْنَ لَمْ يَظْهَرُوْا عَلٰى عَوْرٰتِ النِّسَاءِ ۖ وَلَا

يَضْرِبْنَ بِاَرْجُلِهِنَّ لِيُعْلَمَ مَا يُخْفِيْنَ مِنْ زِيْنَتِهِنَّ ۗ

وَتُوْبُوْٓا اِلَى اللّٰهِ جَمِيْعًا اَيُّهَ الْمُؤْمِنُوْنَ لَعَلَّكُمْ

تُفْلِحُوْنَ ۝ وَاَنْكِحُوا الْاَيَامٰى مِنْكُمْ وَالصّٰلِحِيْنَ مِنْ

عِبَادِكُمْ وَاِمَائِكُمْ ۗ اِنْ يَّكُوْنُوْا فُقَرَاءَ يُغْنِهِمُ اللّٰهُ

مِنْ فَضْلِهٖ ۗ وَاللّٰهُ وَاسِعٌ عَلِيْمٌ ۝ وَلْيَسْتَعْفِفِ الَّذِيْنَ

لَا يَجِدُوْنَ نِكَاحًا حَتّٰى يُغْنِيَهُمُ اللّٰهُ مِنْ فَضْلِهٖ ۗ

وَالَّذِيْنَ يَبْتَغُوْنَ الْكِتٰبَ مِمَّا مَلَكَتْ اَيْمَانُكُمْ

فَكَاتِبُوْهُمْ اِنْ عَلِمْتُمْ فِيْهِمْ خَيْرًا ۖ وَّاٰتُوْهُمْ مِّنْ

Modesty is the best behaviour to tackle sexual desire, it leads to purity of heart and mind.

²⁹You can enter without permission a non-residential place[a] that provides you amenities, Allah knows well what you reveal and what you conceal.

Men and women must behave modestly

³⁰Tell believing men to lower their gaze and be modest;[b] that is the best for them. Allah is aware of what they do. ³¹And tell believing women to lower their gaze and be modest; they shouldn't expose their beauty *in public*, except what is normally showing; and cover their bosoms with headscarves;[c] they should only display beauty to their husbands, fathers, fathers-in-law, sons, stepsons, brothers, brothers' sons, sisters' sons, female servants, slaves, *any* male attendants who are free of sexual desire, and children who are indifferent to *the sight of* women's private parts; and they shouldn't stamp their feet to draw attention to the beauty which they hide *beneath their clothes*. Believers, turn to Allah, all of you, so you may be successful *here and the Hereafter*.

Encouraging unmarried persons to marry

³²Help the unmarried people amongst you to marry, and your righteous male servants and maids. Even if they are poor, Allah will make them self-sufficient through His grace. Allah is Vast, All-Knowing. ³³And let those who lack the means to marry keep themselves chaste until Allah makes them self-sufficient through His grace. If any of your slaves asks for an *emancipation* contract, and you see some good in them, draft it for them; and give them of the wealth that Allah has given you. For your cravings to make worldly gains do not force your maidservants into promiscuity, if they wish to remain chaste, merely because you desire what this worldly life has to offer. Whoever forces them *into it*, then Allah will be Forgiving, Kind *to those maidservants* after being coerced *to perform sexual intercourse*.

[a] This refers to a public place like a hotel (Ibn Abbas).
[b] Literally 'safeguard their private parts.'
[c] Women's fashion at the time of revelation was to have the ends of their headscarves trailing down their backs, leaving their breasts partially visible through the opening of their dress at the front (Al-Qurtubi).

مَالُ اللّٰهِ الَّذِىٓ اٰتٰىكُمْ ۚ وَلَا تُكْرِهُوْا فَتَيٰتِكُمْ

عَلَى الْبِغَآءِ اِنْ اَرَدْنَ تَحَصُّنًا لِّتَبْتَغُوْا عَرَضَ الْحَيٰوةِ

الدُّنْيَا ۚ وَمَنْ يُّكْرِهْهُّنَّ فَاِنَّ اللّٰهَ مِنْۢ بَعْدِ اِكْرَاهِهِنَّ

غَفُوْرٌ رَّحِيْمٌ ۞ وَلَقَدْ اَنْزَلْنَآ اِلَيْكُمْ اٰيٰتٍ مُّبَيِّنٰتٍ وَّمَثَلًا

مِّنَ الَّذِيْنَ خَلَوْا مِنْ قَبْلِكُمْ وَمَوْعِظَةً لِّلْمُتَّقِيْنَ ۞

اَللّٰهُ نُوْرُ السَّمٰوٰتِ وَالْاَرْضِ ۚ مَثَلُ نُوْرِهٖ كَمِشْكٰوةٍ

فِيْهَا مِصْبَاحٌ ۚ اَلْمِصْبَاحُ فِيْ زُجَاجَةٍ ۚ اَلزُّجَاجَةُ كَاَنَّهَا

كَوْكَبٌ دُرِّيٌّ يُّوْقَدُ مِنْ شَجَرَةٍ مُّبٰرَكَةٍ زَيْتُوْنَةٍ لَّا

شَرْقِيَّةٍ وَّلَا غَرْبِيَّةٍ ۙ يَّكَادُ زَيْتُهَا يُضِيْٓءُ وَلَوْ لَمْ

تَمْسَسْهُ نَارٌ ۚ نُوْرٌ عَلٰى نُوْرٍ ۗ يَهْدِى اللّٰهُ لِنُوْرِهٖ مَنْ

يَّشَآءُ ۚ وَيَضْرِبُ اللّٰهُ الْاَمْثَالَ لِلنَّاسِ ۗ وَاللّٰهُ بِكُلِّ

شَىْءٍ عَلِيْمٌ ۞ فِىْ بُيُوْتٍ اَذِنَ اللّٰهُ اَنْ تُرْفَعَ وَيُذْكَرَ

فِيْهَا اسْمُهٗ ۙ يُسَبِّحُ لَهٗ فِيْهَا بِالْغُدُوِّ وَالْاٰصَالِ ۞

رِجَالٌ ۙ لَّا تُلْهِيْهِمْ تِجَارَةٌ وَّلَا بَيْعٌ عَنْ ذِكْرِ اللّٰهِ وَ

اِقَامِ الصَّلٰوةِ وَاِيْتَآءِ الزَّكٰوةِ ۙ يَخَافُوْنَ يَوْمًا تَتَقَلَّبُ

فِيْهِ الْقُلُوْبُ وَالْاَبْصَارُ ۞ لِيَجْزِيَهُمُ اللّٰهُ اَحْسَنَ مَا

عَمِلُوْا وَيَزِيْدَهُمْ مِّنْ فَضْلِهٖ ۗ وَاللّٰهُ يَرْزُقُ مَنْ يَّشَآءُ

بِغَيْرِ حِسَابٍ ۞ وَالَّذِيْنَ كَفَرُوْٓا اَعْمَالُهُمْ كَسَرَابٍۢ

بِقِيْعَةٍ يَّحْسَبُهُ الظَّمْاٰنُ مَآءً ۗ حَتّٰٓى اِذَا جَآءَهٗ لَمْ

يَجِدْهُ شَيْئًا وَّوَجَدَ اللّٰهَ عِنْدَهٗ فَوَفّٰىهُ حِسَابَهٗ ۗ

The light of Allah Almighty: the laws of the Quran shine a light on a great lifestyle and obligations to be good to others.

³⁴We sent down to you clarifying verses and an example of those who passed away before you, as well as teachings for those who are mindful *of Allah.*

Allah's light shines in the hearts of believers

³⁵Allah is the Light of the Heavens and the Earth. An example of His Light is a niche in which there is a lamp; the lamp *glowing* in a glass; the glass *bright* like a brilliant shining star, fuelled from a blessed olive tree, neither of the East nor of the West; its oil shines even though untouched by any flame; light upon light. Allah guides whomever He pleases towards His Light. Allah gives people examples and has full knowledge of all things.ᵃ ³⁶*Such lamps are to be found* in houses that Allah has permitted to be erected, and in which His name is mentioned; *and* where, glorifying Him morning and evening, ³⁷are men who are not distracted by buying and selling from Allah's remembrance, performing the prayer, and paying Zakat. They dread a day when hearts and eyes will be wandering, ³⁸*hoping* Allah will reward them according to the best they did and give them more from His grace. Allah provides without limit for whomever He pleases.

Disbelievers' hearts are drowning in a sea of darkness

³⁹However, the disbelievers deeds are like a mirage in a desert: the thirsty *traveller* imagines it to be water until he reaches it, only to find nothing there; but finds Allah before him, settling *his account* in full. Allah is swift in calculating *accounts.*ᵇ

ᵃ In this example the niche is the human heart; the lamp is the guidance of the Quran; the glass is reason and intellect and the olive oil is the emotions. The example shows that every person has God-given potential and the desire to see and accept the truth. This is a powerful desire in search of the truth, like petrol, a spark can set it aflame. So, whenever the Divine guidance (the light) is presented they accept it.

ᵇ There are two types of disbelievers; one who thinks and behaves well, has morals and manners that are pleasing. He believes he would reap full reward for his deeds. What he fails to realise is that in a state of disbelief his deeds are worthless they have no spiritual value. So, like the lonely, thirsty traveller he sees a broadsheet of water in the distance, so he runs towards it. There he finds nothing, it was an illusion. *The second type of disbeliever is mentioned in the next verse.*

وَاللّٰهُ سَرِيْعُ الْحِسَابِ ۝ اَوْ كَظُلُمٰتٍ فِيْ بَحْرٍ لُّجِّيٍّ

يَّغْشٰهُ مَوْجٌ مِّنْ فَوْقِهٖ مَوْجٌ مِّنْ فَوْقِهٖ سَحَابٌ ط

ظُلُمٰتٌۢ بَعْضُهَا فَوْقَ بَعْضٍ ط اِذَآ اَخْرَجَ يَدَهٗ لَمْ

يَكَدْ يَرٰىهَا ط وَمَنْ لَّمْ يَجْعَلِ اللّٰهُ لَهٗ نُوْرًا فَمَا لَهٗ

مِنْ نُّوْرٍ ۝ اَلَمْ تَرَ اَنَّ اللّٰهَ يُسَبِّحُ لَهٗ مَنْ فِي السَّمٰوٰتِ

وَالْاَرْضِ وَالطَّيْرُ صٰٓفّٰتٍ ط كُلٌّ قَدْ عَلِمَ صَلَاتَهٗ وَ

تَسْبِيْحَهٗ ط وَاللّٰهُ عَلِيْمٌۢ بِمَا يَفْعَلُوْنَ ۝ وَلِلّٰهِ مُلْكُ

السَّمٰوٰتِ وَالْاَرْضِ ج وَاِلَى اللّٰهِ الْمَصِيْرُ ۝ اَلَمْ تَرَ اَنَّ

اللّٰهَ يُزْجِيْ سَحَابًا ثُمَّ يُؤَلِّفُ بَيْنَهٗ ثُمَّ يَجْعَلُهٗ

رُكَامًا فَتَرَى الْوَدْقَ يَخْرُجُ مِنْ خِلٰلِهٖ ج وَيُنَزِّلُ

مِنَ السَّمَآءِ مِنْ جِبَالٍ فِيْهَا مِنْۢ بَرَدٍ فَيُصِيْبُ بِهٖ

مَنْ يَّشَآءُ وَيَصْرِفُهٗ عَنْ مَّنْ يَّشَآءُ ط يَكَادُ سَنَا بَرْقِهٖ

يَذْهَبُ بِالْاَبْصَارِ ۝ يُقَلِّبُ اللّٰهُ الَّيْلَ وَالنَّهَارَ ط

اِنَّ فِيْ ذٰلِكَ لَعِبْرَةً لِّاُولِي الْاَبْصَارِ ۝ وَاللّٰهُ خَلَقَ

كُلَّ دَآبَّةٍ مِّنْ مَّآءٍ ج فَمِنْهُمْ مَّنْ يَّمْشِيْ عَلٰى بَطْنِهٖ ج

وَمِنْهُمْ مَّنْ يَّمْشِيْ عَلٰى رِجْلَيْنِ ج وَمِنْهُمْ مَّنْ

يَّمْشِيْ عَلٰٓى اَرْبَعٍ ط يَخْلُقُ اللّٰهُ مَا يَشَآءُ ط اِنَّ اللّٰهَ عَلٰى

كُلِّ شَيْءٍ قَدِيْرٌ ۝ لَقَدْ اَنْزَلْنَآ اٰيٰتٍ مُّبَيِّنٰتٍ ط وَاللّٰهُ

يَهْدِيْ مَنْ يَّشَآءُ اِلٰى صِرَاطٍ مُّسْتَقِيْمٍ ۝ وَيَقُوْلُوْنَ

اٰمَنَّا بِاللّٰهِ وَبِالرَّسُوْلِ وَاَطَعْنَا ثُمَّ يَتَوَلّٰى فَرِيْقٌ

The proof of Allah's power and creativity.

٦ ع
١١

⁴⁰ Or *their deeds are* like veils of darkness in the deep sea covered by wave upon wave, over which clouds *loom*. The layers of darkness *lie so densely* over one another that, if one takes one's hand out *of the water*, one can barely see it. Anyone Allah deprives of light will have no light *at all*.ᵃ

All creatures come from water

⁴¹ Haven't you considered, everything in the Heavens and the Earth glorifies Allah? The birds flying in flocks, each one knows how it should pray and glorify Him; and Allah knows what they do. ⁴² Allah controls the Heavens and the Earth, and to Him is the final return. ⁴³ Haven't you considered how Allah moves the clouds along, joins them together, then piles them up *until* you see rain pouring from them. On mountains, He sends down from the sky hailstones that strike whomever He wills and spare whomever He wills; and the flash of its lightning nearly takes away one's sight. ⁴⁴ Allah causes the succession of night and day; in that are lessons for people of insight. ⁴⁵ *Moreover,* Allah created every creature from water; some crawl on their bellies, others walk on two feet or on four. Allah creates whatever He wills. Allah has power over all things.

The two-faced are not believers

⁴⁶ We revealed verses that clearly explain, and *by them* Allah guides anyone who wants to be guided towards a straight path.ᵇ ⁴⁷ *People* will say: "We believe in Allah and in the Messenger, and we obey," but afterwards a group of them turns away: such people are not believers.

ᵃ The second type of disbeliever is engrossed in the world; drowned in lust, in pursuit of wealth and health. He's sunk in hedonistic pleasures; in darkness. He can't receive the light since he is in pitch darkness. The example describes the four layers of darkness; the pitch dark night, the clouds, the depth of the sea and stormy tides upon tides.

ᵇ Alternatively Allah guides anyone He wills towards a straight path. My translation shows that a person witnesses so many persuasive proofs in nature as mentioned in the preceding verses, will want to be guided. This is empowering and reflects the idea of moral choice.

مِّنْهُمْ مِّنْ بَعْدِ ذٰلِكَ ۗ وَمَاۤ اُولٰٓئِكَ بِالْمُؤْمِنِيْنَ ۞

وَاِذَا دُعُوْۤا اِلَى اللهِ وَرَسُوْلِهٖ لِيَحْكُمَ بَيْنَهُمْ اِذَا

فَرِيْقٌ مِّنْهُمْ مُّعْرِضُوْنَ ۞ وَاِنْ يَّكُنْ لَّهُمُ الْحَقُّ يَاْتُوْۤا

اِلَيْهِ مُذْعِنِيْنَ ۞ اَفِيْ قُلُوْبِهِمْ مَّرَضٌ اَمِ ارْتَابُوْۤا

اَمْ يَخَافُوْنَ اَنْ يَّحِيْفَ اللهُ عَلَيْهِمْ وَرَسُوْلُهٗ ۗ بَلْ

اُولٰٓئِكَ هُمُ الظّٰلِمُوْنَ ۞ اِنَّمَا كَانَ قَوْلَ الْمُؤْمِنِيْنَ

اِذَا دُعُوْۤا اِلَى اللهِ وَرَسُوْلِهٖ لِيَحْكُمَ بَيْنَهُمْ اَنْ

يَّقُوْلُوْا سَمِعْنَا وَاَطَعْنَا ۗ وَاُولٰٓئِكَ هُمُ الْمُفْلِحُوْنَ ۞

وَمَنْ يُّطِعِ اللهَ وَرَسُوْلَهٗ وَيَخْشَ اللهَ وَيَتَّقْهِ

فَاُولٰٓئِكَ هُمُ الْفَآئِزُوْنَ ۞ وَاَقْسَمُوْا بِاللهِ جَهْدَ

اَيْمَانِهِمْ لَئِنْ اَمَرْتَهُمْ لَيَخْرُجُنَّ ۗ قُلْ لَّا تُقْسِمُوْا ۚ

طَاعَةٌ مَّعْرُوْفَةٌ ۗ اِنَّ اللهَ خَبِيْرٌ بِمَا تَعْمَلُوْنَ ۞ قُلْ

اَطِيْعُوا اللهَ وَاَطِيْعُوا الرَّسُوْلَ ۚ فَاِنْ تَوَلَّوْا فَاِنَّمَا

عَلَيْهِ مَا حُمِّلَ وَعَلَيْكُمْ مَّا حُمِّلْتُمْ ۗ وَاِنْ تُطِيْعُوْهُ

تَهْتَدُوْا ۗ وَمَا عَلَى الرَّسُوْلِ اِلَّا الْبَلٰغُ الْمُبِيْنُ ۞

وَعَدَ اللهُ الَّذِيْنَ اٰمَنُوْا مِنْكُمْ وَعَمِلُوا الصّٰلِحٰتِ

لَيَسْتَخْلِفَنَّهُمْ فِي الْاَرْضِ كَمَا اسْتَخْلَفَ الَّذِيْنَ مِنْ

قَبْلِهِمْ ۗ وَلَيُمَكِّنَنَّ لَهُمْ دِيْنَهُمُ الَّذِي ارْتَضٰى لَهُمْ

وَلَيُبَدِّلَنَّهُمْ مِّنْ بَعْدِ خَوْفِهِمْ اَمْنًا ۗ يَعْبُدُوْنَنِيْ لَا

يُشْرِكُوْنَ بِيْ شَيْئًا ۗ وَمَنْ كَفَرَ بَعْدَ ذٰلِكَ فَاُولٰٓئِكَ هُمُ

The materialist is satisfied with this worldly life. What an impoverishment!

⁴⁸ When they are summoned to Allah and his Messenger for judgement, a group of them objects. ⁴⁹ Had the decision been in their favour they would have submitted willingly. ⁵⁰ Is there sickness in their hearts? Or do they have doubts? Or are they afraid that Allah and His Messenger will deal with them unjustly? Such people are sinners.

The different responses of believers and hypocrites

⁵¹ The believers' response, when they are summoned to Allah and His Messenger for judgement, is: "We hear and obey." These are the successful. ⁵² Whoever obeys Allah and His Messenger, and fears Allah and is mindful of Him, these are the victorious. ⁵³ *Hypocrites* swear by Allah, using their strongest oaths, that if you were to command them, they would march out *to battle*. Say: "Don't swear. Obedience is recognisable!"ᵃ Allah is aware of your works. ⁵⁴ Say: "Obey Allah, and obey the Messenger. Then, if you *choose to* turn away, he *will answer* only for what he has taken on, and you *will answer* for what you have taken on.ᵇ If you obey him, you will be guided. The responsibility of the Messenger is to convey *the message* clearly."

Muslims promised a victory

⁵⁵ Allah has promised to make the believers and the righteous *His* deputies on Earth, as He made those before you *His* deputies; and He will make their religion strong, which pleases Him; and He will remove their fear and make them feel safe, since they worship Me alone, and don't associate *any partners* with Me. The disbelievers are the evildoers.

ᵃ In other words: "Actions speak louder than words."
ᵇ Meaning conveying Allah's message and obeying His Messenger 鬃, respectively.

الْفٰسِقُوْنَ ۵۵ وَاَقِيْمُوا الصَّلٰوةَ وَاٰتُوا الزَّكٰوةَ وَاَطِيْعُوا
الرَّسُوْلَ لَعَلَّكُمْ تُرْحَمُوْنَ ۵۶ لَا تَحْسَبَنَّ الَّذِيْنَ كَفَرُوْا
مُعْجِزِيْنَ فِي الْاَرْضِ ۚ وَمَاْوٰىهُمُ النَّارُ ۚ وَلَبِئْسَ
الْمَصِيْرُ ۵۷ يٰٓاَيُّهَا الَّذِيْنَ اٰمَنُوْا لِيَسْتَاْذِنْكُمُ الَّذِيْنَ
مَلَكَتْ اَيْمَانُكُمْ وَالَّذِيْنَ لَمْ يَبْلُغُوا الْحُلُمَ مِنْكُمْ
ثَلٰثَ مَرّٰتٍ ؕ مِنْ قَبْلِ صَلٰوةِ الْفَجْرِ وَحِيْنَ تَضَعُوْنَ
ثِيَابَكُمْ مِّنَ الظَّهِيْرَةِ وَمِنْ بَعْدِ صَلٰوةِ الْعِشَآءِ ۚ
ثَلٰثُ عَوْرٰتٍ لَّكُمْ ؕ لَيْسَ عَلَيْكُمْ وَلَا عَلَيْهِمْ جُنَاحٌ
بَعْدَهُنَّ ؕ طَوّٰفُوْنَ عَلَيْكُمْ بَعْضُكُمْ عَلٰى بَعْضٍ ؕ
كَذٰلِكَ يُبَيِّنُ اللّٰهُ لَكُمُ الْاٰيٰتِ ؕ وَاللّٰهُ عَلِيْمٌ حَكِيْمٌ ۵۸
وَاِذَا بَلَغَ الْاَطْفَالُ مِنْكُمُ الْحُلُمَ فَلْيَسْتَاْذِنُوْا كَمَا
اسْتَاْذَنَ الَّذِيْنَ مِنْ قَبْلِهِمْ ؕ كَذٰلِكَ يُبَيِّنُ اللّٰهُ
لَكُمْ اٰيٰتِهٖ ؕ وَاللّٰهُ عَلِيْمٌ حَكِيْمٌ ۵۹ وَالْقَوَاعِدُ مِنَ
النِّسَآءِ الّٰتِيْ لَا يَرْجُوْنَ نِكَاحًا فَلَيْسَ عَلَيْهِنَّ
جُنَاحٌ اَنْ يَّضَعْنَ ثِيَابَهُنَّ غَيْرَ مُتَبَرِّجٰتٍ
بِزِيْنَةٍ ؕ وَاَنْ يَّسْتَعْفِفْنَ خَيْرٌ لَّهُنَّ ؕ وَاللّٰهُ سَمِيْعٌ
عَلِيْمٌ ۶۰ لَيْسَ عَلَى الْاَعْمٰى حَرَجٌ وَّلَا عَلَى الْاَعْرَجِ
حَرَجٌ وَّلَا عَلَى الْمَرِيْضِ حَرَجٌ وَّلَا عَلٰٓى اَنْفُسِكُمْ
اَنْ تَاْكُلُوْا مِنْ بُيُوْتِكُمْ اَوْ بُيُوْتِ اٰبَآئِكُمْ اَوْ بُيُوْتِ
اُمَّهٰتِكُمْ اَوْ بُيُوْتِ اِخْوَانِكُمْ اَوْ بُيُوْتِ اَخَوٰتِكُمْ

Manners and encouragement to visit people in their homes.

703

⁵⁶ *So*, perform the prayer, pay Zakat, and obey the Messenger in order to be treated kindly. ⁵⁷ Never think the disbelievers can defeat *Allah's plan* on Earth. The Fire is their place of refuge. What a wretched home!

Some instructions on manners:

Respecting privacy when living together
⁵⁸ Believers, your slaves and *children* who haven't yet reached puberty should ask permission *before entering your room* three times *of the day*: before the dawn prayer, at midday when you get undressed, and after the evening prayer – three *times* of your privacy, outside these *times* there is no blame on you or them to wander in and out of each other's *rooms*. That is how Allah makes *His* verses clear for you. Allah is Knowing, Wise. ⁵⁹ When your children reach puberty, they must ask permission like those *mentioned* before. That is how Allah makes His verses clear for you. Allah is Knowing, Wise.

Concessions on dress for older women
⁶⁰ Older women who have no desire to marry may remove their *outer* garments as long as they don't display *any* beauty, there's no blame on them. However, even for them it's better to remain modest. Allah is Hearing, Knowing.

Permission to eat together
⁶¹ There is no restriction on the blind, the disabled, the sick, or yourselves eating in your own homes, or your fathers' homes, your mothers' homes, your brothers', sisters', paternal or maternal uncles' and aunts' homes, or homes whose keys you hold, or at your friends' *homes*. It isn't blameworthy whether you eat together or separately. Whenever you enter houses, greet each other with a sincere blessing from Allah. That is how Allah makes *His* verses clear for you, so you may reflect.

اَوْ بُيُوْتِ اَعْمَامِكُمْ اَوْ بُيُوْتِ عَمّٰتِكُمْ اَوْ بُيُوْتِ

اَخْوَالِكُمْ اَوْ بُيُوْتِ خٰلٰتِكُمْ اَوْ مَا مَلَكْتُمْ مَّفَاتِحَهٗٓ اَوْ

صَدِيْقِكُمْ ؕ لَيْسَ عَلَيْكُمْ جُنَاحٌ اَنْ تَاْكُلُوْا جَمِيْعًا

اَوْ اَشْتَاتًا ؕ فَاِذَا دَخَلْتُمْ بُيُوْتًا فَسَلِّمُوْا عَلٰٓى

اَنْفُسِكُمْ تَحِيَّةً مِّنْ عِنْدِ اللّٰهِ مُبٰرَكَةً طَيِّبَةً ؕ

كَذٰلِكَ يُبَيِّنُ اللّٰهُ لَكُمُ الْاٰيٰتِ لَعَلَّكُمْ تَعْقِلُوْنَ ۝۶۱

اِنَّمَا الْمُؤْمِنُوْنَ الَّذِيْنَ اٰمَنُوْا بِاللّٰهِ وَرَسُوْلِهٖ وَاِذَا

كَانُوْا مَعَهٗ عَلٰٓى اَمْرٍ جَامِعٍ لَّمْ يَذْهَبُوْا حَتّٰى

يَسْتَاْذِنُوْهُ ؕ اِنَّ الَّذِيْنَ يَسْتَاْذِنُوْنَكَ اُولٰٓئِكَ

الَّذِيْنَ يُؤْمِنُوْنَ بِاللّٰهِ وَرَسُوْلِهٖ ۚ فَاِذَا اسْتَاْذَنُوْكَ

لِبَعْضِ شَاْنِهِمْ فَاْذَنْ لِّمَنْ شِئْتَ مِنْهُمْ

وَاسْتَغْفِرْ لَهُمُ اللّٰهَ ؕ اِنَّ اللّٰهَ غَفُوْرٌ رَّحِيْمٌ ۝۶۲

لَا تَجْعَلُوْا دُعَآءَ الرَّسُوْلِ بَيْنَكُمْ كَدُعَآءِ بَعْضِكُمْ

بَعْضًا ؕ قَدْ يَعْلَمُ اللّٰهُ الَّذِيْنَ يَتَسَلَّلُوْنَ مِنْكُمْ

لِوَاذًا ۚ فَلْيَحْذَرِ الَّذِيْنَ يُخَالِفُوْنَ عَنْ اَمْرِهٖٓ اَنْ

تُصِيْبَهُمْ فِتْنَةٌ اَوْ يُصِيْبَهُمْ عَذَابٌ اَلِيْمٌ ۝۶۳

اَلَآ اِنَّ لِلّٰهِ مَا فِى السَّمٰوٰتِ وَالْاَرْضِ ؕ قَدْ يَعْلَمُ

مَآ اَنْتُمْ عَلَيْهِ ؕ وَيَوْمَ يُرْجَعُوْنَ اِلَيْهِ فَيُنَبِّئُهُمْ

بِمَا عَمِلُوْا ؕ وَاللّٰهُ بِكُلِّ شَىْءٍ عَلِيْمٌ ۝۶۴

The beloved Messenger ﷺ has a special status. So listen, and comply with his instructions.

How to behave in the Prophet's ﷺ presence

⁶²The believers firmly believe in Allah and His Messenger, and when they are with him *discussing* any matter of general concern, don't leave without seeking his permission. Those who seek your permission are true believers in Allah and His Messenger. If they ask your permission to attend to some private matter of theirs, give them permission as you wish, and seek Allah's forgiveness for them. Allah is Forgiving, Kind.

Don't treat the Messenger ﷺ like you treat others

⁶³Do not call out *in a loud voice* to the Messenger as you would call out to each other. Allah knows those of you who quietly slip away to avoid *being given a task*. Those who disagree with his commandment should beware in case they find themselves tested or are struck by a painful punishment. ⁶⁴Doesn't everything in the Heavens and the Earth belong to Allah? He knows *exactly* where you stand; and, on the Day *all* are returned to Him, He will inform them of what they did. Allah has full knowledge of all things.

25. Surat Al-Furqan
The Benchmark for Right and Wrong

This Makkan surat provides powerful arguments for the Oneness of God (*Tawhid*), the communication of His Message (*Risalah*), and life after death (*Akhirah*). These three fundamental beliefs were most at odds with the pagan beliefs. It opens by declaring the power and might of the exalted Lord, the Controller of the universe.

In Makkah, the Messenger ﷺ was constantly criticised. The Makkans accused him of lying, puzzled why the Quran was revealed gradually, rather than all at once, and emphasised that it was merely stories of the ancient people. Similarly, they targeted his person: why would a messenger of Allah be a mere mortal? The surat answers them, and warns them of the dire consequences of rejecting faith. The Messenger ﷺ is reassured: "Do you think you can be a guardian for the one who makes a god of his desires?" (43).

The surat then turns to the natural world, and points out the amazing creative power of Allah seen in nature: the shadow, the nightfall, the rain, fresh and seawater, blood and marriage relatives, the constellations, the sun and the moon: "a *sign* for anyone who wants to be reminded *of Allah's power* or wants to be thankful" (62). An excellent example of the Quran's two-pronged approach to answering the disbelievers' criticism: the first is an argumentative approach – an emotional appeal where disbelievers are threatened and warned of their rebellion and mischief. Stories of past communities are told and retold to stress the consequences of their disbelief. The second Quranic approach is a rational, scientific approach drawing attention to Allah's creative power. These awesome and marvellously created signs are all around us, and directly pointing to their creator; won't you believe?

The final passage catalogues the qualities of the pious: humility, peace loving, worshipful, prayerful, moderate, and penitent. They don't: squander wealth, murder, worship idols, commit adultery, give false testimony, engage in useless activities, nor follow blindly. The surat concludes with a powerful prayer of the pious servants: "Our Lord, grant us joy in our spouses and children, and make us an example for those who are mindful *of You*" (74). Effectively, recapping the opening statement that Allah is in control of the universe and His true servant submits and prays for divine intervention.

سُوْرَةُ الْفُرْقَانِ مَكِّيَّةٌ (٤٢)   (٢٥)   اٰيَاتُهَا ٧٧   رُكُوعَاتُهَا ٦

بِسْمِ اللّٰهِ الرَّحْمٰنِ الرَّحِيْمِ

تَبٰرَكَ الَّذِيْ نَزَّلَ الْفُرْقَانَ عَلٰى عَبْدِهٖ لِيَكُوْنَ لِلْعٰلَمِيْنَ نَذِيْرَا ۙ ١ الَّذِيْ لَهٗ مُلْكُ السَّمٰوٰتِ وَالْاَرْضِ وَلَمْ يَتَّخِذْ وَلَدًا وَّلَمْ يَكُنْ لَّهٗ شَرِيْكٌ فِى الْمُلْكِ وَخَلَقَ كُلَّ شَيْءٍ فَقَدَّرَهٗ تَقْدِيْرًا ٢ وَاتَّخَذُوْا مِنْ دُوْنِهٖ اٰلِهَةً لَّا يَخْلُقُوْنَ شَيْئًا وَّهُمْ يُخْلَقُوْنَ وَلَا يَمْلِكُوْنَ لِاَنْفُسِهِمْ ضَرًّا وَّلَا نَفْعًا وَّلَا يَمْلِكُوْنَ مَوْتًا وَّلَا حَيٰوةً وَّلَا نُشُوْرًا ٣ وَقَالَ الَّذِيْنَ كَفَرُوْا اِنْ هٰذَآ اِلَّآ اِفْكُ ﰳ افْتَرٰىهُ وَاَعَانَهٗ عَلَيْهِ قَوْمٌ اٰخَرُوْنَ ۛۚ فَقَدْ جَآءُوْ ظُلْمًا وَّزُوْرًا ۛ ٤ وَقَالُوْا اَسَاطِيْرُ الْاَوَّلِيْنَ اكْتَتَبَهَا فَهِيَ تُمْلٰى عَلَيْهِ بُكْرَةً وَّاَصِيْلًا ٥ قُلْ اَنْزَلَهُ الَّذِيْ يَعْلَمُ السِّرَّ فِى السَّمٰوٰتِ وَالْاَرْضِ ط اِنَّهٗ كَانَ غَفُوْرًا رَّحِيْمًا ٦ وَقَالُوْا مَالِ هٰذَا الرَّسُوْلِ يَأْكُلُ الطَّعَامَ وَيَمْشِيْ فِى الْاَسْوَاقِ ط لَوْلَآ اُنْزِلَ اِلَيْهِ مَلَكٌ فَيَكُوْنَ مَعَهٗ نَذِيْرًا ۙ اَوْ يُلْقٰى اِلَيْهِ كَنْزٌ اَوْ تَكُوْنُ لَهٗ جَنَّةٌ يَّأْكُلُ مِنْهَا ط وَقَالَ الظّٰلِمُوْنَ اِنْ تَتَّبِعُوْنَ اِلَّا رَجُلًا مَّسْحُوْرًا ٨

The Quran urges you to reflect on the future. Which future? The short term or the long-term?

In the name of Allah, the Kind, the Caring.

All regions of the universe belong to Allah

¹Blessed is the One Who sent down the benchmark to His *noble* servant: the warner for all communities;[a] ²Allah controls the Heavens and the Earth, has not adopted a child, nor taken a partner in *His* dominion, and has created everything carefully measured out. ³Yet *the disbelievers* have adopted beside Him gods that create nothing but were created, they have no power to harm or to benefit themselves, and don't control death, life or resurrection.

The disbelievers' excuses for denying the Messenger ﷺ

⁴The disbelievers said, "This is nothing but an outrageous lie that he has made up with the support of some people." *In truth*, it is they who have come to do wrong and bear false witness. ⁵And they said, "*These are* the tales of the ancients he has written down, that were dictated to him morning and evening." ⁶Say: "He sent it down, Who knows the secrets *concealed* in the Heavens and the Earth. He is Forgiving, Kind." ⁷They said, "What kind of messenger is this who eats food and walks about in the market? If an angel was sent with him as a warner, then *we would believe*; ⁸or *if* some treasure came down to him, or he had an orchard for his livelihood." The wrongdoers say, "You are following a bewitched man."

---

[a]   Al Alameen according to Jalalain is "humans, Jinns and excludes Angels".

اُنْظُرْ كَيْفَ ضَرَبُوا لَكَ الْاَمْثَالَ فَضَلُّوا فَلَا يَسْتَطِيعُونَ سَبِيلًا ۹ تَبَارَكَ الَّذِىٓ اِنْ شَآءَ جَعَلَ لَكَ خَيْرًا مِّنْ ذٰلِكَ جَنّٰتٍ تَجْرِىْ مِنْ تَحْتِهَا الْاَنْهٰرُ ۙ وَيَجْعَلْ لَّكَ قُصُورًا ۱۰ بَلْ كَذَّبُوْا بِالسَّاعَةِ ۟ وَاَعْتَدْنَا لِمَنْ كَذَّبَ بِالسَّاعَةِ سَعِيرًا ۱۱ اِذَا رَاَتْهُمْ مِّنْ مَّكَانٍ بَعِيْدٍ سَمِعُوْا لَهَا تَغَيُّظًا وَّ زَفِيْرًا ۱۲ وَاِذَآ اُلْقُوْا مِنْهَا مَكَانًا ضَيِّقًا مُّقَرَّنِيْنَ دَعَوْا هُنَالِكَ ثُبُوْرًا ۱۳ لَا تَدْعُوا الْيَوْمَ ثُبُوْرًا وَّاحِدًا وَّادْعُوْا ثُبُوْرًا كَثِيْرًا ۱۴ قُلْ اَذٰلِكَ خَيْرٌ اَمْ جَنَّةُ الْخُلْدِ الَّتِىْ وُعِدَ الْمُتَّقُوْنَ ؕ كَانَتْ لَهُمْ جَزَآءً وَّمَصِيْرًا ۱۵ لَهُمْ فِيْهَا مَا يَشَآءُوْنَ خٰلِدِيْنَ ؕ كَانَ عَلٰى رَبِّكَ وَعْدًا مَّسْـُٔوْلًا ۱۶ وَيَوْمَ يَحْشُرُهُمْ وَمَا يَعْبُدُوْنَ مِنْ دُوْنِ اللّٰهِ فَيَقُوْلُ ءَاَنْتُمْ اَضْلَلْتُمْ عِبَادِىْ هٰٓؤُلَآءِ اَمْ هُمْ ضَلُّوا السَّبِيْلَ ۱۷ قَالُوْا سُبْحٰنَكَ مَا كَانَ يَنْبَغِىْ لَنَآ اَنْ نَّتَّخِذَ مِنْ دُوْنِكَ مِنْ اَوْلِيَآءَ وَلٰكِنْ مَّتَّعْتَهُمْ وَاٰبَآءَهُمْ حَتّٰى نَسُوا الذِّكْرَ ۚ وَكَانُوْا قَوْمًا بُوْرًا ۱۸ فَقَدْ كَذَّبُوْكُمْ بِمَا تَقُوْلُوْنَ ۙ فَمَا تَسْتَطِيْعُوْنَ

The everlasting future: Hell or Heaven. You choose, and make it happen for you.

711

⁹Look what examples they make of you! They have gone astray, and they cannot find a *straight* path. ¹⁰Blessed is He Who will grant you better than that when He wants; gardens beneath which rivers flow and *luxurious* palaces.

The choice between unending punishment and bliss

¹¹They have denied *the coming of* the Final Hour, and We have prepared a fiery blaze for anyone who denies the Final Hour. ¹²When it sees them from afar, they will hear it raging and roaring; ¹³and they will be chained together and cast into a narrow pit in it; they will plead to perish. ¹⁴"Do not plead to perish once today," *they'll be told*, "but plead to perish many times over." ¹⁵Say: "Which is better, that or the garden of eternal life that those mindful *of Allah* have been promised?" That will be their reward and destination, ¹⁶they will have whatever they please forever: a promise which Your Lord will fulfil.

The idols are questioned on Judgement Day

¹⁷On the Day He gathers them and all they worship beside Allah, He will ask: "Was it you who led My servants astray, or did they stray by themselves from the path?"¹⁸*The idols* will say, "Glory be to You! It was not for us to take on protectors besides You. However, You let them and their forefathers enjoy themselves until they neglected the Reminder and were ruined people." ¹⁹"*Your idols* have denied what you said," *He will tell them*, "You can't avert *what's coming* or get help. So whoever continues doing wrong, then We'll let them taste a dreadful punishment."

صِرْفًا وَّلَا نَصْرًا ۚ وَمَنْ يَّظْلِمْ مِّنْكُمْ نُذِقْهُ

عَذَابًا كَبِيْرًا ۝ وَمَآ أَرْسَلْنَا قَبْلَكَ مِنَ

الْمُرْسَلِيْنَ إِلَّا إِنَّهُمْ لَيَأْكُلُوْنَ الطَّعَامَ وَ

يَمْشُوْنَ فِي الْأَسْوَاقِ ۗ وَجَعَلْنَا بَعْضَكُمْ لِبَعْضٍ

فِتْنَةً ۗ أَتَصْبِرُوْنَ ۚ وَكَانَ رَبُّكَ بَصِيْرًا ۝

وَقَالَ الَّذِيْنَ لَا يَرْجُوْنَ لِقَآءَنَا لَوْلَا أُنْزِلَ عَلَيْنَا

الْمَلَائِكَةُ أَوْ نَرَى رَبَّنَا ۗ لَقَدِ اسْتَكْبَرُوْا فِيْ أَنْفُسِهِمْ

وَعَتَوْا عُتُوًّا كَبِيْرًا ۝ يَوْمَ يَرَوْنَ الْمَلَائِكَةَ لَا بُشْرَى

يَوْمَئِذٍ لِّلْمُجْرِمِيْنَ وَيَقُوْلُوْنَ حِجْرًا مَّحْجُوْرًا ۝

وَقَدِمْنَا إِلَى مَا عَمِلُوْا مِنْ عَمَلٍ فَجَعَلْنَاهُ هَبَآءً

مَّنْثُوْرًا ۝ أَصْحَابُ الْجَنَّةِ يَوْمَئِذٍ خَيْرٌ مُّسْتَقَرًّا وَّأَحْسَنُ

مَقِيْلًا ۝ وَيَوْمَ تَشَقَّقُ السَّمَآءُ بِالْغَمَامِ وَنُزِّلَ الْمَلَائِكَةُ

تَنْزِيْلًا ۝ الْمُلْكُ يَوْمَئِذٍ الْحَقُّ لِلرَّحْمٰنِ ۗ وَكَانَ

يَوْمًا عَلَى الْكٰفِرِيْنَ عَسِيْرًا ۝ وَيَوْمَ يَعَضُّ الظَّالِمُ عَلَى

يَدَيْهِ يَقُوْلُ يٰلَيْتَنِي اتَّخَذْتُ مَعَ الرَّسُوْلِ سَبِيْلًا ۝

يٰوَيْلَتٰى لَيْتَنِي لَمْ أَتَّخِذْ فُلَانًا خَلِيْلًا ۝ لَقَدْ أَضَلَّنِيْ

عَنِ الذِّكْرِ بَعْدَ إِذْ جَآءَنِيْ ۗ وَكَانَ الشَّيْطٰنُ لِلْإِنْسَانِ

خَذُوْلًا ۝ وَقَالَ الرَّسُوْلُ يٰرَبِّ إِنَّ قَوْمِي اتَّخَذُوْا

هٰذَا الْقُرْآنَ مَهْجُوْرًا ۝ وَكَذٰلِكَ جَعَلْنَا لِكُلِّ نَبِيٍّ

عَدُوًّا مِّنَ الْمُجْرِمِيْنَ ۗ وَكَفٰى بِرَبِّكَ هَادِيًا وَّنَصِيْرًا ۝

Who we befriend can determine our future, so take friends carefully.

The disbelievers' excuses are addressed

²⁰ Never before you, *Muhammad*, have We sent any messenger who didn't eat food and walk about in the markets. We made some of you a test for others *to see* how patient you will be. Your Lord is Seeing. ²¹ Those who don't like to meet Us say: "If angels were sent down, or we could see our Lord *we would have believed*." They are proud of themselves and rude. ²² On the Day they see the angels, it won't be good news for the sinners; *the angels* will say, "*Paradise is* a forbidden place *for you*!" ²³ Whatever deeds they had done, We will turn them into scattered dust. ²⁴ That Day the companions of Paradise will *be living* in a *pleasant* home, a cool resting place.

The wrong type of friends

²⁵ That Day the sky and the clouds will be torn apart, and at last the angels will be sent down, ²⁶ that Day sovereignty will belong to the Most Kind; it will be a terrible Day for the disbelievers, ²⁷ a Day when the wrongdoer will bite his hands *regretfully*, saying, "If only I had followed the path of the Messenger. ²⁸ Woe to me! If only I hadn't taken so-and-so as a friend; ²⁹ he led me astray from the Reminder^a after it had come to me." The Satan deceived humanity. ³⁰ The Messenger will say, "My Lord, some of my people regard this Quran as something to be avoided."^b ³¹ This is how We have made the sinners an enemy for every prophet. Your Lord is sufficient as a Guide and Helper.

---

^a   Here "the Reminder" is a synonym for the Quran.

^b   "*Mahjuran*" can be interpreted as; to be shunned, out-of-date, to be discarded. So some nominal-followers regard it irrelevant to their lives.

وَقَالَ الَّذِينَ كَفَرُوا لَوْلَا نُزِّلَ عَلَيْهِ الْقُرْاٰنُ جُمْلَةً

وَّاحِدَةً ۚ كَذٰلِكَ ۚ لِنُثَبِّتَ بِهٖ فُؤَادَكَ وَرَتَّلْنٰهُ

تَرْتِيْلًا ۝ وَلَا يَاْتُوْنَكَ بِمَثَلٍ اِلَّا جِئْنٰكَ بِالْحَقِّ وَ

اَحْسَنَ تَفْسِيْرًا ۝ اَلَّذِيْنَ يُحْشَرُوْنَ عَلٰى وُجُوْهِهِمْ

اِلٰى جَهَنَّمَ ۙ اُولٰٓئِكَ شَرٌّ مَّكَانًا وَّاَضَلُّ سَبِيْلًا ۝ وَلَقَدْ

اٰتَيْنَا مُوْسَى الْكِتٰبَ وَجَعَلْنَا مَعَهٗٓ اَخَاهُ هٰرُوْنَ

وَزِيْرًا ۝ فَقُلْنَا اذْهَبَآ اِلَى الْقَوْمِ الَّذِيْنَ كَذَّبُوْا

بِاٰيٰتِنَا ؕ فَدَمَّرْنٰهُمْ تَدْمِيْرًا ۝ وَقَوْمَ نُوْحٍ لَّمَّا كَذَّبُوا

الرُّسُلَ اَغْرَقْنٰهُمْ وَجَعَلْنٰهُمْ لِلنَّاسِ اٰيَةً ؕ وَاَعْتَدْنَا

لِلظّٰلِمِيْنَ عَذَابًا اَلِيْمًا ۝ وَّعَادًا وَّثَمُوْدَا۠ وَاَصْحٰبَ

الرَّسِّ وَقُرُوْنًا بَيْنَ ذٰلِكَ كَثِيْرًا ۝ وَكُلًّا ضَرَبْنَا لَهُ

الْاَمْثَالَ ۖ وَكُلًّا تَبَّرْنَا تَتْبِيْرًا ۝ وَلَقَدْ اَتَوْا عَلَى الْقَرْيَةِ

الَّتِيْٓ اُمْطِرَتْ مَطَرَ السَّوْءِ ؕ اَفَلَمْ يَكُوْنُوْا يَرَوْنَهَا ۚ بَلْ

كَانُوْا لَا يَرْجُوْنَ نُشُوْرًا ۝ وَاِذَا رَاَوْكَ اِنْ يَّتَّخِذُوْنَكَ

اِلَّا هُزُوًا ؕ اَهٰذَا الَّذِيْ بَعَثَ اللّٰهُ رَسُوْلًا ۝ اِنْ كَادَ

لَيُضِلُّنَا عَنْ اٰلِهَتِنَا لَوْلَآ اَنْ صَبَرْنَا عَلَيْهَا ؕ وَسَوْفَ

يَعْلَمُوْنَ حِيْنَ يَرَوْنَ الْعَذَابَ مَنْ اَضَلُّ سَبِيْلًا ۝

اَرَءَيْتَ مَنِ اتَّخَذَ اِلٰهَهٗ هَوٰىهُ ؕ اَفَاَنْتَ تَكُوْنُ عَلَيْهِ

وَكِيْلًا ۝ اَمْ تَحْسَبُ اَنَّ اَكْثَرَهُمْ يَسْمَعُوْنَ اَوْ يَعْقِلُوْنَ ؕ

اِنْ هُمْ اِلَّا كَالْاَنْعَامِ بَلْ هُمْ اَضَلُّ سَبِيْلًا ۝ اَلَمْ تَرَ

A litmus test for self-control: do you follow your desires or Allah's orders?

715

[32] The disbelievers say, "Why wasn't the Quran sent down all at once to him?" *We revealed it* this way to build your confidence,[a] and arranged it as one book.[b] [33] Not a single example can they bring you of inconsistency in the book. However, We bring you the truth and the best explanation. [34] Those who will be dispatched face down to Hell will be in the worst place and furthest away from any path.

Generations who denied Allah's signs were wiped out

[35] We gave Musa the Book, and We made his brother Harun adviser. [36] We said, "Go, the two of you, to the people who have denied Our signs," then We destroyed them completely. [37] *Likewise* the people of Nuh, after they denied the messengers, We drowned them and made them a sign for people. We have prepared a painful torment for wrongdoers, [38] *such as* Ad, Thamud, the community of the well, and many generations in between. [39] We made examples of each of them; and We destroyed them. [40] They[c] have passed by the city that was struck by the terrible rain. Haven't they seen it? They hope not to be brought back to life.

Disbelievers made their whims gods

[41] When they see you, they mockingly *say*, "Is this the one who Allah sent as a messenger? [42] If we hadn't been committed *to our idols* he would have lead us away from our gods." They will know, who had gone astray from the path when they see the punishment. [43] Do you think you can be a guardian of someone who makes his desires, god? [44] Do you reckon they listen *to you, or* reflect? They are like cattle. No, *in fact* they are even further astray from the *straight* path.

---

[a] Literally means "to steady your heart with it."

[b] "*Rattalnahu tartilan*" means to put together parts of a thing consistently. (cf 39:23). The Quran is very consistent, free of contradictions. (4:82).

[c] This refers to Makkan traders who passed by the ruins of the people of Lut ﷵ on their way to Syria.

اِلٰى رَبِّكَ كَيْفَ مَدَّ الظِّلَّ ۚ وَلَوْ شَاءَ لَجَعَلَهٗ سَاكِنًا ۚ

ثُمَّ جَعَلْنَا الشَّمْسَ عَلَيْهِ دَلِيْلًا ۙ ۞ ثُمَّ قَبَضْنٰهُ اِلَيْنَا

قَبْضًا يَّسِيْرًا ۞ وَهُوَ الَّذِيْ جَعَلَ لَكُمُ الَّيْلَ لِبَاسًا

وَّالنَّوْمَ سُبَاتًا وَّجَعَلَ النَّهَارَ نُشُوْرًا ۞ وَهُوَ الَّذِيْ

اَرْسَلَ الرِّيٰحَ بُشْرًۢا بَيْنَ يَدَيْ رَحْمَتِهٖ ۚ وَاَنْزَلْنَا مِنَ

السَّمَاءِ مَاءً طَهُوْرًا ۙ لِّنُحْـِۦ بِهٖ بَلْدَةً مَّيْتًا وَّنُسْقِيَهٗ

مِمَّا خَلَقْنَا اَنْعَامًا وَّاَنَاسِيَّ كَثِيْرًا ۞ وَلَقَدْ صَرَّفْنٰهُ

بَيْنَهُمْ لِيَذَّكَّرُوْا ۖ فَاَبٰٓى اَكْثَرُ النَّاسِ اِلَّا كُفُوْرًا ۞ وَلَوْ

Are you actively involved
in spreading the message
of the Quran?

شِئْنَا لَبَعَثْنَا فِيْ كُلِّ قَرْيَةٍ نَّذِيْرًا ۞ فَلَا تُطِعِ الْكٰفِرِيْنَ

وَجَاهِدْهُمْ بِهٖ جِهَادًا كَبِيْرًا ۞ وَهُوَ الَّذِيْ مَرَجَ الْبَحْرَيْنِ

هٰذَا عَذْبٌ فُرَاتٌ وَّهٰذَا مِلْحٌ اُجَاجٌ ۚ وَجَعَلَ بَيْنَهُمَا

بَرْزَخًا وَّحِجْرًا مَّحْجُوْرًا ۞ وَهُوَ الَّذِيْ خَلَقَ مِنَ الْمَاءِ

بَشَرًا فَجَعَلَهٗ نَسَبًا وَّصِهْرًا ؕ وَكَانَ رَبُّكَ قَدِيْرًا ۞ وَ

يَعْبُدُوْنَ مِنْ دُوْنِ اللّٰهِ مَا لَا يَنْفَعُهُمْ وَلَا يَضُرُّهُمْ ؕ

وَكَانَ الْكَافِرُ عَلٰى رَبِّهٖ ظَهِيْرًا ۞ وَمَا اَرْسَلْنٰكَ اِلَّا مُبَشِّرًا

وَّنَذِيْرًا ۞ قُلْ مَا اَسْـَٔلُكُمْ عَلَيْهِ مِنْ اَجْرٍ اِلَّا مَنْ شَاءَ

اَنْ يَّتَّخِذَ اِلٰى رَبِّهٖ سَبِيْلًا ۞ وَتَوَكَّلْ عَلَى الْحَيِّ الَّذِيْ

لَا يَمُوْتُ وَسَبِّحْ بِحَمْدِهٖ ؕ وَكَفٰى بِهٖ بِذُنُوْبِ عِبَادِهٖ

خَبِيْرًا ۙ ۞ الَّذِيْ خَلَقَ السَّمٰوٰتِ وَالْاَرْضَ وَمَا بَيْنَهُمَا

فِيْ سِتَّةِ اَيَّامٍ ثُمَّ اسْتَوٰى عَلَى الْعَرْشِ ۚ الرَّحْمٰنُ فَسْـَٔلْ

Allah's creative power: the example of the shadow

⁴⁵ Don't you see how Your Lord makes the shadow get longer and longer, if He wanted He could have fixed *its size*. We made the sun a pointer to *His existence,* ⁴⁶ then We gradually shorten *the shadow.* ⁴⁷ He made the night a garment to *cover* you, the sleep for your rest, and the daytime for rising up again.

The rainwater gives creatures life

⁴⁸ He sends the winds as a herald before the rain;[a] and We send clean water from the sky ⁴⁹ to bring barren land back to life, and to provide drink to creatures, a great many cattle and people *alike.* ⁵⁰ We distribute *the rain* to remind them *of Our power,* but most people turn away ungratefully. ⁵¹ If We wanted, We could have sent a warner to every city. ⁵² So don't give in to the disbelievers, but struggle tirelessly *to convince* them with this *Quran.*[b] ⁵³ And He brings the two seas close together,[c] one sweet and fresh, the other salty and bitter; and He has set a non-breachable barrier between them. ⁵⁴ And He created humans from water,[d] and gave them blood relatives and in-laws. Your Lord is Powerful. ⁵⁵ Yet they worship beside Allah what can't benefit or harm them. The disbeliever[e] is openly opposed to His Lord. ⁵⁶ We sent you a bearer of glad tidings and a warner. ⁵⁷ Say: "I'm not asking you for payment for this *preaching,* all I ask of you is: let those who wish to take the path to their Lord *do so.*"

Constellations, the stars in the sky

⁵⁸ Put your trust in the Ever-Living, Who will never die, glorify Him with His praise. Sufficient is He in being, Aware of His servants' sins, ⁵⁹ Who created the Heavens and Earth and whatever lies between them in six days, then established according to His Majesty on the Throne. *He is* the Most Kind; the Best informed. ⁶⁰ If they are told: "Prostrate before the Most Kind," they say, "And what is the Most Kind? Should we prostrate to anything you tell us?" *This reminder* increases their hatred. ⁶¹ Blessed is He Who placed constellations in the sky, and made brilliant stars, a shining sun and a bright moon. ⁶² He made the night and day to follow

---

[a] Literally, His Kindness.

[b] The Prophet ﷺ is told to perform *jihad* with the pagans, not with the sword but the Quran. *Bihi* here, according to Ibn Abbas, is the Quran.

[c] This is the literal meaning, but in Arabic 'sea' can mean any large mass of water, including lakes and rivers.

[d] According to Al-Qurtubi, "water" here refers to seminal fluid by which the mother's egg is fertilised.

[e] According to Ibn Abbas, "the disbeliever" here refers to Abu Jahl, who would make a public show of worshipping idols. However, Ikrima interpreted this as meaning Satan.

بِهٖ خَبِيْرًا ۵۹ وَاِذَا قِيْلَ لَهُمُ اسْجُدُوْا لِلرَّحْمٰنِ قَالُوْا وَمَا

الرَّحْمٰنُ اَنَسْجُدُ لِمَا تَأْمُرُنَا وَزَادَهُمْ نُفُوْرًا ۶۰ تَبٰرَكَ

الَّذِيْ جَعَلَ فِي السَّمَآءِ بُرُوْجًا وَّجَعَلَ فِيْهَا سِرَاجًا وَّ

قَمَرًا مُّنِيْرًا ۶۱ وَهُوَ الَّذِيْ جَعَلَ الَّيْلَ وَالنَّهَارَ خِلْفَةً

لِّمَنْ اَرَادَ اَنْ يَّذَّكَّرَ اَوْ اَرَادَ شُكُوْرًا ۶۲ وَعِبَادُ الرَّحْمٰنِ

الَّذِيْنَ يَمْشُوْنَ عَلَى الْاَرْضِ هَوْنًا وَّاِذَا خَاطَبَهُمُ

الْجٰهِلُوْنَ قَالُوْا سَلٰمًا ۶۳ وَالَّذِيْنَ يَبِيْتُوْنَ لِرَبِّهِمْ

سُجَّدًا وَّقِيَامًا ۶۴ وَالَّذِيْنَ يَقُوْلُوْنَ رَبَّنَا اصْرِفْ عَنَّا

عَذَابَ جَهَنَّمَ اِنَّ عَذَابَهَا كَانَ غَرَامًا ۶۵ اِنَّهَا سَآءَتْ

مُسْتَقَرًّا وَّمُقَامًا ۶۶ وَالَّذِيْنَ اِذَآ اَنْفَقُوْا لَمْ يُسْرِفُوْا

وَلَمْ يَقْتُرُوْا وَكَانَ بَيْنَ ذٰلِكَ قَوَامًا ۶۷ وَالَّذِيْنَ لَا

يَدْعُوْنَ مَعَ اللّٰهِ اِلٰهًا اٰخَرَ وَلَا يَقْتُلُوْنَ النَّفْسَ الَّتِيْ

حَرَّمَ اللّٰهُ اِلَّا بِالْحَقِّ وَلَا يَزْنُوْنَ وَمَنْ يَّفْعَلْ ذٰلِكَ يَلْقَ

اَثَامًا ۶۸ يُّضٰعَفْ لَهُ الْعَذَابُ يَوْمَ الْقِيٰمَةِ وَيَخْلُدْ فِيْهِ

مُهَانًا ۶۹ اِلَّا مَنْ تَابَ وَاٰمَنَ وَعَمِلَ عَمَلًا صَالِحًا

فَاُولٰٓئِكَ يُبَدِّلُ اللّٰهُ سَيِّاٰتِهِمْ حَسَنٰتٍ طوَكَانَ اللّٰهُ

غَفُوْرًا رَّحِيْمًا ۷۰ وَمَنْ تَابَ وَعَمِلَ صَالِحًا فَاِنَّهٗ يَتُوْبُ

اِلَى اللّٰهِ مَتَابًا ۷۱ وَالَّذِيْنَ لَا يَشْهَدُوْنَ الزُّوْرَ وَاِذَا

مَرُّوْا بِاللَّغْوِ مَرُّوْا كِرَامًا ۷۲ وَالَّذِيْنَ اِذَا ذُكِّرُوْا بِاٰيٰتِ

رَبِّهِمْ لَمْ يَخِرُّوْا عَلَيْهَا صُمًّا وَّعُمْيَانًا ۷۳ وَالَّذِيْنَ

The servants of Allah are praised, what are three qualities that make them outstanding?

each other, *a sign* for anyone who wants to be reminded *of Allah's power* or wants to be thankful.

The qualities of the servants of the Most Kind

⁶³The servants of the Kind walk softly on the Earth, and when ignorant people speak with them, they say *words of* peace. ⁶⁴And *they* spend their nights *praying* to their Lord, standing and prostrating. ⁶⁵And pray: "Our Lord, turn away the torment of Hell from us; its torment is unending. ⁶⁶What a dreadful home and resting place!" ⁶⁷And they spend *in charity*, they are neither wasteful nor miserly, but moderate. ⁶⁸And *they* call on no other god beside Allah, and do not kill others that Allah has made sacred, unless by some lawful right, nor commit adultery – and whoever does that will face penalties; ⁶⁹his punishment will be multiplied on the Day of Judgement, forever disgraced and in *torment,* ⁷⁰except anyone who repents, believes and does righteous deeds. For them, Allah will turn their *past* sins into good deeds. Allah is Forgiving, Most Kind. ⁷¹Whoever repents and does righteous deeds, has indeed returned to Allah. ⁷²And *they* don't bear false testimony and, when they pass *people* gossiping, they *pass by* with dignity. ⁷³And when they are reminded of their Lord's signs, they don't fall for them, deaf and blind *to their true meaning.*

Prayer for the family

⁷⁴And they say, "Our Lord, grant us joy in our spouses and children, and make us an example for those who are mindful *of You.*" ⁷⁵They will be rewarded with the loftiest of apartments *in Paradise* for their patience; they shall be greeted with peace, ⁷⁶living forever in a lovely home and leisurely place! ⁷⁷Say: "What are you to My Lord without your prayer?" *Since* you have denied *My messenger,* the expected *punishment* will happen.

يَقُولُونَ رَبَّنَا هَبْ لَنَا مِنْ أَزْوَاجِنَا وَذُرِّيَّتِنَا قُرَّةَ أَعْيُنٍ وَّاجْعَلْنَا لِلْمُتَّقِينَ إِمَامًا ۞ أُولَٰئِكَ يُجْزَوْنَ الْغُرْفَةَ بِمَا صَبَرُوا وَيُلَقَّوْنَ فِيهَا تَحِيَّةً وَّسَلَامًا ۞ خَالِدِينَ فِيهَا ۚ حَسُنَتْ مُسْتَقَرًّا وَّمُقَامًا ۞ قُلْ مَا يَعْبَؤُا بِكُمْ رَبِّي لَوْلَا دُعَاؤُكُمْ ۖ فَقَدْ كَذَّبْتُمْ فَسَوْفَ يَكُونُ لِزَامًا ۞

26. Surat Ash-Shuʿara'

The Poets

This surat was revealed in the middle of the Makkan period, during the fifth or sixth year of the prophethood of the Messenger ﷺ. The beloved Messenger ﷺ was eagerly teaching and preaching Islam day and night, but only a handful of fortunate souls followed him. Opposition and hostility was growing and deepening. However, the Prophet ﷺ was constantly praying, and hoping the Makkans would accept Islam. Meanwhile, his night vigils, heartfelt prayers for his people, and crying to Allah for their guidance continued. The surat opens with these comforting words:

> Perhaps you are over-worried *your people* won't believe. If We wish, We can *easily* send down to them from the sky a sign to which their necks will bow humbly (3–4).

The central theme of the surat is relating the stories of seven prophets and how they were rejected by their people. This is the history of human disobedience: the unchanging character of man's weakness and his proneness to self-deception. This explains why people in all communities readily reject the truth.

> Consequently, they lose themselves in worship of power, wealth, and what is commonly described as 'glory', as well as in mindless acceptance of slogans and prevailing fashions of thought' (Asad).

The surat exposes humanity's weakness as well as its goodness. A dramatic story is mentioned: "Then Musa threw down his staff, and at once it swallowed up their trickery" (45). There were no arguments or debates; since the miracle was compelling, and the magicians could not fail to see Musa 🕊 was a man of God, a true prophet. However, the Pharaoh was arrogant and refused to believe. This succinct surat separates each prophetic story with the catchphrase: "In that is a sign; yet most will not believe, though Your Lord is the Almighty, the Caring" (8–9). Another compelling warning to the Makkans to reform themselves before meeting the same fate as these rebellious communities.

The stories make the point: all prophets had the same mission. "When their brother Nuh said to them, 'Will you not believe? I am an honest messenger for you, so believe in Allah and follow me. I don't ask you for a reward for this; my reward lies with Lord of the worlds, so believe and follow me" (106–110). Nearly all the prophets used this exhortation to invite their people to the truth.

The first story is the encounter between Musa ﷺ and Pharaoh: the debate between a prophet of God and a tyrant king, where Musa ﷺ convincingly talks about the power and the majesty of Allah. Similarly, Ibrahim ﷺ expresses Allah's generosity: "But My Lord is Lord of the worlds, Who created and guided me, the One who feeds and gives me to drink, and when I am ill heals me" (78–80). The story of Prophet Nuh ﷺ highlights the discrimination of the wealthy against the poor: "Why should we believe in you since only the poorest people are following you?" (111). Their prophets criticise them for their vanity: "You build monuments on every hilltop to please yourselves, and take castles *as homes* so you might live forever? And, when you seize *others' wealth and land*, you are utterly ruthless in doing so" (128–130). The story of Prophet Lut ﷺ describes the sexual perversion of his people. He pleads with them to give up their wretched way of life: "*Why*, of all the people of the world do you approach males lustfully, leaving your wives, whom your Lord has created for you? You are people who have crossed the bounds *of decency*" (165–166). The final story is of Prophet Shu'ayb ﷺ. His people were expert defrauders, Shu'ayb ﷺ kept warning them, but to no avail. The surat graphically depicts the destruction of each one of them, and warns us today that anyone who follows these evils is doomed.

The last part of the surat takes us back to the beginning: the people of Makkah accusing the Prophet ﷺ of being a poet, and the Quran proving their accusations false: "*Likewise* the poets, who are deceived, follow them *too*. Do you not see them wandering about in every valley" (224–225). The Prophet ﷺ is reassured; those who make such accusations are unreasonable. What comparison is there between the beauty, eloquence and life-changing message of the Quran and the works of the poets?

بِسْمِ اللّٰهِ الرَّحْمٰنِ الرَّحِيْمِ

طٰسٓمّٓ ۱ تِلْكَ اٰيٰتُ الْكِتٰبِ الْمُبِيْنِ ۲ لَعَلَّكَ بَاخِعٌ

نَّفْسَكَ اَلَّا يَكُوْنُوْا مُؤْمِنِيْنَ ۳ اِنْ نَّشَأْ نُنَزِّلْ عَلَيْهِمْ

مِّنَ السَّمَآءِ اٰيَةً فَظَلَّتْ اَعْنَاقُهُمْ لَهَا خٰضِعِيْنَ ۴ وَمَا

يَاْتِيْهِمْ مِّنْ ذِكْرٍ مِّنَ الرَّحْمٰنِ مُحْدَثٍ اِلَّا كَانُوْا عَنْهُ

مُعْرِضِيْنَ ۵ فَقَدْ كَذَّبُوْا فَسَيَاْتِيْهِمْ اَنْۢبٰٓؤُا مَا كَانُوْا

بِهٖ يَسْتَهْزِءُوْنَ ۶ اَوَلَمْ يَرَوْا اِلَى الْاَرْضِ كَمْ اَنْۢبَتْنَا

فِيْهَا مِنْ كُلِّ زَوْجٍ كَرِيْمٍ ۷ اِنَّ فِيْ ذٰلِكَ لَاٰيَةً ط وَمَا

كَانَ اَكْثَرُهُمْ مُّؤْمِنِيْنَ ۸ وَاِنَّ رَبَّكَ لَهُوَ الْعَزِيْزُ

الرَّحِيْمُ ۹ ع وَاِذْ نَادٰى رَبُّكَ مُوْسٰٓى اَنِ ائْتِ الْقَوْمَ

الظّٰلِمِيْنَ ۱۰ قَوْمَ فِرْعَوْنَ ط اَلَا يَتَّقُوْنَ ۱۱ قَالَ

رَبِّ اِنِّيْٓ اَخَافُ اَنْ يُّكَذِّبُوْنِ ۱۲ وَيَضِيْقُ صَدْرِيْ

وَلَا يَنْطَلِقُ لِسَانِيْ فَاَرْسِلْ اِلٰى هٰرُوْنَ ۱۳ وَلَهُمْ

عَلَيَّ ذَنْۢبٌ فَاَخَافُ اَنْ يَّقْتُلُوْنِ ۱۴ قَالَ كَلَّا ج

فَاذْهَبَا بِاٰيٰتِنَآ اِنَّا مَعَكُمْ مُّسْتَمِعُوْنَ ۱۵ فَاْتِيَا فِرْعَوْنَ

فَقُوْلَا اِنَّا رَسُوْلُ رَبِّ الْعٰلَمِيْنَ ۱۶ اَنْ اَرْسِلْ مَعَنَا

بَنِيْٓ اِسْرَآءِيْلَ ط قَالَ اَلَمْ نُرَبِّكَ فِيْنَا وَلِيْدًا وَّ

لَبِثْتَ فِيْنَا مِنْ عُمُرِكَ سِنِيْنَ ۱۸ وَفَعَلْتَ فَعْلَتَكَ

الَّتِيْ فَعَلْتَ وَاَنْتَ مِنَ الْكٰفِرِيْنَ ۱۹ قَالَ فَعَلْتُهَآ

Why did the Messenger ﷺ fear so much for the disbelievers? How concerned are you for the salvation of humanity?

١
ع
٥

723

In the name of Allah, the Kind, the Caring.

¹ *Ta Sin Meem.*

Have faith in Allah's plan

²These are the verses of the Book that clarifies *realities.* ³Perhaps you are over-worried *your people* won't believe. ⁴Had We wished, We could have sent down to them from the sky a sign to which their necks will bow humbly; ⁵and yet no fresh revelation has ever come to them from the Most Kind without them objecting to it. ⁶They are in denial, but soon news will come to them about their earlier mockery. ⁷Haven't they considered the Earth, and how We have grown abundantly every kind *of living thing*? ⁸In that is a sign; yet most will not believe, ⁹though Your Lord is the Almighty, the Caring.

Allah sends Musa to Pharaoh's court

¹⁰*Remember* when your Lord called Musa: "Go to the unjust people, ¹¹the people of Pharaoh. Will they not be mindful *of Me*?" ¹²*Musa* said, "My Lord, I fear they will deny me, ¹³and my chest feels tight, and my tongue is unable to speak without stammering; so, send Harun *with me*; ¹⁴*furthermore* they have a charge against me, so I fear they will kill me." ¹⁵*Allah* said, "Not at all! Go, both of you, with Our signs. We will be with you, listening in." ¹⁶So the two of them came to Pharaoh and said, "We are bearers of the message of the Lord of the worlds, ¹⁷so send the Israelites with us." ¹⁸*Pharaoh* said, "When you were a child didn't we bring you up? And didn't you live with us for many years? ¹⁹Only you could do what you did, and be ungrateful?"

اِذًا وَّاَنَا مِنَ الضَّآلِّيْنَ ۞ فَفَرَرْتُ مِنْكُمْ لَمَّا خِفْتُكُمْ

فَوَهَبَ لِيْ رَبِّيْ حُكْمًا وَّجَعَلَنِيْ مِنَ الْمُرْسَلِيْنَ ۞ وَ

تِلْكَ نِعْمَةٌ تَمُنُّهَا عَلَيَّ اَنْ عَبَّدْتَّ بَنِيْۤ اِسْرَآءِيْلَ ۞

قَالَ فِرْعَوْنُ وَمَا رَبُّ الْعٰلَمِيْنَ ۞ قَالَ رَبُّ السَّمٰوٰتِ

وَالْاَرْضِ وَمَا بَيْنَهُمَا اِنْ كُنْتُمْ مُّوْقِنِيْنَ ۞ قَالَ

لِمَنْ حَوْلَهٗۤ اَلَا تَسْتَمِعُوْنَ ۞ قَالَ رَبُّكُمْ وَرَبُّ اٰبَآئِكُمُ

الْاَوَّلِيْنَ ۞ قَالَ اِنَّ رَسُوْلَكُمُ الَّذِيْۤ اُرْسِلَ اِلَيْكُمْ

لَمَجْنُوْنٌ ۞ قَالَ رَبُّ الْمَشْرِقِ وَالْمَغْرِبِ وَمَا بَيْنَهُمَا

اِنْ كُنْتُمْ تَعْقِلُوْنَ ۞ قَالَ لَئِنِ اتَّخَذْتَ اِلٰهًا غَيْرِيْ

لَاَجْعَلَنَّكَ مِنَ الْمَسْجُوْنِيْنَ ۞ قَالَ اَوَلَوْ جِئْتُكَ بِشَيْءٍ

مُّبِيْنٍ ۞ قَالَ فَأْتِ بِهٖۤ اِنْ كُنْتَ مِنَ الصّٰدِقِيْنَ ۞

فَاَلْقٰى عَصَاهُ فَاِذَا هِيَ ثُعْبَانٌ مُّبِيْنٌ ۞ وَّنَزَعَ يَدَهٗ

فَاِذَا هِيَ بَيْضَآءُ لِلنّٰظِرِيْنَ ۞ قَالَ لِلْمَلَاِ حَوْلَهٗۤ اِنَّ

هٰذَا لَسٰحِرٌ عَلِيْمٌ ۞ يُّرِيْدُ اَنْ يُّخْرِجَكُمْ مِّنْ اَرْضِكُمْ

بِسِحْرِهٖ ۖ فَمَاذَا تَأْمُرُوْنَ ۞ قَالُوْۤا اَرْجِهْ وَاَخَاهُ وَابْعَثْ

فِي الْمَدَآئِنِ حٰشِرِيْنَ ۞ يَأْتُوْكَ بِكُلِّ سَحَّارٍ عَلِيْمٍ ۞

فَجُمِعَ السَّحَرَةُ لِمِيْقَاتِ يَوْمٍ مَّعْلُوْمٍ ۞ وَّقِيْلَ

لِلنَّاسِ هَلْ اَنْتُمْ مُّجْتَمِعُوْنَ ۞ لَعَلَّنَا نَتَّبِعُ السَّحَرَةَ

اِنْ كَانُوْا هُمُ الْغٰلِبِيْنَ ۞ فَلَمَّا جَآءَ السَّحَرَةُ قَالُوْا

لِفِرْعَوْنَ اَئِنَّ لَنَا لَاَجْرًا اِنْ كُنَّا نَحْنُ الْغٰلِبِيْنَ ۞

Here we notice the dark side of Pharaoh's individualism. Complete disconnect from reality.

٢
ع
٦

²⁰ *Musa* said, "I did that by mistake,ᵃ ²¹ and I fled from you because I feared you. Then my Lord granted me wisdom and made me a messenger. ²² What sort of favour do you remind me of? That you have enslaved *my people*, the Israelites?"

Pharaoh challenges Musa

²³ Pharaoh said, "Who is this 'Lord of the Worlds'?" ²⁴ *Musa* said, "The Lord of the Heavens and the Earth, and of whatever is between them, if you believe." ²⁵ *Pharaoh* said to those around him, "Are you listening? ²⁶ *Musa* said, "Your Lord and the Lord of your forefathers." ²⁷ *Pharaoh* said, "This messenger of yours, who has been sent to you, is clearly mad!" ²⁸ *Musa* said, "The Lord of the East and the West and whatever is in between, if only you would reflect." ²⁹ *Pharaoh* said, "If you take any god beside me, I will imprison you." ³⁰ *Musa* said, "Even if I bring you clear proof?" ³¹ *He* said, "Then fetch it, if you are telling the truth." ³² So *Musa* threw down his stick, and straightaway it turned into a wriggling snake; ³³ then he drew out his hand *from his cloak*, and it appeared to the onlookers *brilliant* white.

Pharaoh is frightened

³⁴ *Pharaoh* said to the nobles around him, "This *man* is an expert magician, ³⁵ who wants to expel you from your land with his magic. So, what do you suggest?" ³⁶ They said, "Put him and his brother off for a while, and send marshals to the cities ³⁷ to bring you every expert magician *of ours*." ³⁸ So the magicians gathered for a tournament on an appointed day; ³⁹ and people were asked: "Will you be gathering for the *tournament*?" ⁴⁰ *They replied*, "We'll follow the magicians, if they win." ⁴¹ When the magicians arrived, they asked Pharaoh: "Will we be rewarded, if we win?"

ᵃ   Musa never intended to kill the Coptic, but it was to save the Israelite.

قَالَ نَعَمْ وَإِنَّكُمْ إِذًا لَّمِنَ الْمُقَرَّبِينَ ۞ قَالَ لَهُم مُّوسَى

أَلْقُوا مَا أَنتُم مُّلْقُونَ ۞ فَأَلْقَوْا حِبَالَهُمْ وَعِصِيَّهُمْ

وَقَالُوا بِعِزَّةِ فِرْعَوْنَ إِنَّا لَنَحْنُ الْغَالِبُونَ ۞ فَأَلْقَى

مُوسَى عَصَاهُ فَإِذَا هِيَ تَلْقَفُ مَا يَأْفِكُونَ ۞ فَأُلْقِيَ

السَّحَرَةُ سَاجِدِينَ ۞ قَالُوٓا ءَامَنَّا بِرَبِّ الْعَالَمِينَ ۞

رَبِّ مُوسَى وَهَارُونَ ۞ قَالَ ءَامَنتُمْ لَهُ قَبْلَ أَنْ

أَذَنَ لَكُمْ إِنَّهُ لَكَبِيرُكُمُ الَّذِى عَلَّمَكُمُ السِّحْرَ

فَلَسَوْفَ تَعْلَمُونَ لَأُقَطِّعَنَّ أَيْدِيَكُمْ وَأَرْجُلَكُم مِّنْ

خِلَافٍ وَلَأُصَلِّبَنَّكُمْ أَجْمَعِينَ ۞ قَالُوا لَا ضَيْرَ

إِنَّا إِلَى رَبِّنَا مُنقَلِبُونَ ۞ إِنَّا نَطْمَعُ أَن يَغْفِرَ لَنَا

رَبُّنَا خَطَايَانَا أَن كُنَّا أَوَّلَ الْمُؤْمِنِينَ ۞ وَأَوْحَيْنَا

إِلَى مُوسَى أَنْ أَسْرِ بِعِبَادِيٓ إِنَّكُم مُّتَّبَعُونَ ۞

فَأَرْسَلَ فِرْعَوْنُ فِي الْمَدَائِنِ حَاشِرِينَ ۞ إِنَّ هَٰؤُلَاءِ

لَشِرْذِمَةٌ قَلِيلُونَ ۞ وَإِنَّهُمْ لَنَا لَغَائِظُونَ ۞

وَإِنَّا لَجَمِيعٌ حَاذِرُونَ ۞ فَأَخْرَجْنَاهُم مِّن جَنَّاتٍ وَ

عُيُونٍ ۞ وَكُنُوزٍ وَمَقَامٍ كَرِيمٍ ۞ كَذَٰلِكَ وَأَوْرَثْنَاهَا

بَنِيٓ إِسْرَائِيلَ ۞ فَأَتْبَعُوهُم مُّشْرِقِينَ ۞ فَلَمَّا تَرَاءَا

الْجَمْعَانِ قَالَ أَصْحَابُ مُوسَى إِنَّا لَمُدْرَكُونَ ۞ قَالَ

كَلَّا إِنَّ مَعِيَ رَبِّي سَيَهْدِينِ ۞ فَأَوْحَيْنَا إِلَى مُوسَى

أَنِ اضْرِب بِّعَصَاكَ الْبَحْرَ فَانفَلَقَ فَكَانَ كُلُّ

Pharaoh's hopes and dreams were tied to the magic. Musa's stick destroyed it all. Notice the spiritual power and the weakness of materialism.

⁴²"Yes," he said, "Then you'll be among my close ones."

The grand tournament of magicians

⁴³Musa said to *the magicians*, "Cast whatever *spells* you have." ⁴⁴So they threw down their ropes and sticks, saying, "By Pharaoh's might, we are surely the winners." ⁴⁵Then Musa threw down his staff, and at once it swallowed up their trickery. ⁴⁶The magicians fell in prostration, ⁴⁷saying, "We believe in the Lord of the worlds, ⁴⁸the Lord of Musa and Harun." ⁴⁹*Pharaoh* said, "You've believed him before I granted you permission? He must be your tutor, who taught you magic, but you will learn your lesson. I will cut off your hands and your feet from the opposite sides and crucify the lot of you." ⁵⁰They said, "it doesn't matter!^a We shall be returning to our Lord. ⁵¹We hope Our Lord will forgive our mistakes, since we were the first believers."

Musa leads the Israelites out of Egypt

⁵²We revealed to Musa: "Set off with My servants at night, no doubt you will be chased." ⁵³Pharaoh sent *word* to the cities *for his soldiers* to muster, ⁵⁴*saying*, "These *Israelites* are a tiny ragbag bunch ⁵⁵who have enraged us, ⁵⁶*while* we are a united force, well trained and equipped." ⁵⁷So *it was* We brought them out of gardens and springs, ⁵⁸and treasures and comfortable homes. ⁵⁹That is how it was, and *later* We caused the Israelites to inherit it.^b

The parting of the sea

⁶⁰At sunrise, *the Egyptians* set off in pursuit of *the Israelites*. ⁶¹When eventually the two groups spotted each other, Musa's companions said, "We've been caught." ⁶²But *Musa* said, "No way! My Lord is with me, *and* He will guide me." ⁶³We revealed to Musa: "Strike the sea with your staff." The sea parted, each side like a mighty mountain.

---

^a Literally "it won't harm us."

^b Al-Qurtubi mentions how, after the destruction of the Ancient Egyptians, some Israelites returned to Egypt well before the coming of Islam. Indeed, Jews continued to live there as a thriving community until the mid-twentieth century.

فِرْقٍ كَالطَّوْدِ الْعَظِيْمِ ۝ وَاَزْلَفْنَا ثَمَّ الْاٰخَرِيْنَ ۝

وَاَنْجَيْنَا مُوْسٰى وَمَنْ مَّعَهٗ اَجْمَعِيْنَ ۝ ثُمَّ اَغْرَقْنَا

الْاٰخَرِيْنَ ۝ اِنَّ فِيْ ذٰلِكَ لَاٰيَةً ؕ وَمَا كَانَ اَكْثَرُهُمْ

مُّؤْمِنِيْنَ ۝ وَاِنَّ رَبَّكَ لَهُوَ الْعَزِيْزُ الرَّحِيْمُ ۝ وَاتْلُ

عَلَيْهِمْ نَبَاَ اِبْرٰهِيْمَ ۝ اِذْ قَالَ لِاَبِيْهِ وَقَوْمِهٖ مَا

تَعْبُدُوْنَ ۝ قَالُوْا نَعْبُدُ اَصْنَامًا فَنَظَلُّ لَهَا عٰكِفِيْنَ ۝

قَالَ هَلْ يَسْمَعُوْنَكُمْ اِذْ تَدْعُوْنَ ۝ اَوْ يَنْفَعُوْنَكُمْ

اَوْ يَضُرُّوْنَ ۝ قَالُوْا بَلْ وَجَدْنَا اٰبَآءَنَا كَذٰلِكَ

يَفْعَلُوْنَ ۝ قَالَ اَفَرَءَيْتُمْ مَّا كُنْتُمْ تَعْبُدُوْنَ ۝

اَنْتُمْ وَاٰبَآؤُكُمُ الْاَقْدَمُوْنَ ۝ فَاِنَّهُمْ عَدُوٌّ لِّيْ اِلَّا رَبَّ

الْعٰلَمِيْنَ ۝ الَّذِيْ خَلَقَنِيْ فَهُوَ يَهْدِيْنِ ۝ وَالَّذِيْ

هُوَ يُطْعِمُنِيْ وَيَسْقِيْنِ ۝ وَاِذَا مَرِضْتُ فَهُوَ يَشْفِيْنِ ۝

وَالَّذِيْ يُمِيْتُنِيْ ثُمَّ يُحْيِيْنِ ۝ وَالَّذِيْ اَطْمَعُ اَنْ

يَّغْفِرَ لِيْ خَطِيْٓئَتِيْ يَوْمَ الدِّيْنِ ؕ رَبِّ هَبْ لِيْ حُكْمًا

وَّاَلْحِقْنِيْ بِالصّٰلِحِيْنَ ۝ وَاجْعَلْ لِّيْ لِسَانَ صِدْقٍ

فِي الْاٰخِرِيْنَ ۝ وَاجْعَلْنِيْ مِنْ وَّرَثَةِ جَنَّةِ النَّعِيْمِ ۝

وَاغْفِرْ لِاَبِيْٓ اِنَّهٗ كَانَ مِنَ الضَّآلِّيْنَ ۝ وَلَا تُخْزِنِيْ يَوْمَ

يُبْعَثُوْنَ ۝ يَوْمَ لَا يَنْفَعُ مَالٌ وَّلَا بَنُوْنَ ۝ اِلَّا مَنْ

اَتَى اللّٰهَ بِقَلْبٍ سَلِيْمٍ ؕ وَاُزْلِفَتِ الْجَنَّةُ لِلْمُتَّقِيْنَ ۝

وَبُرِّزَتِ الْجَحِيْمُ لِلْغٰوِيْنَ ۝ وَقِيْلَ لَهُمْ اَيْنَمَا كُنْتُمْ

Ibrahim challenged people for worshipping idols, helpless things. What about modern idols: fame, glory, pleasure.

⁶⁴We lured *Pharaoh* to approach that place. ⁶⁵We saved Musa and anyone was with him ⁶⁶and drowned the others. ⁶⁷There *was* a lesson in that, but most of them didn't believe. ⁶⁸Your Lord is the Almighty, the Caring.

Ibrahim quizzes his people

⁶⁹Tell them the story of Ibrahim, ⁷⁰when he asked his father and community: "What do you worship?" ⁷¹They said, "We worship idols and remain devoted to them." ⁷²He said, "Do they hear you when you pray, ⁷³or benefit or harm you in any way?" ⁷⁴They said, "We found our forefathers doing so." ⁷⁵*Ibrahim* said, "Have you thought about what you worship, ⁷⁶you and your ancestors? ⁷⁷*These gods* are my enemies, all apart from the Lord of the worlds ⁷⁸Who has created and now guides me, ⁷⁹and Who feeds me and gives me to drink. ⁸⁰And when I am ill He heals me, ⁸¹and will make me die and bring me back to life; ⁸²and I sincerely wish that He will forgive my sins on Judgement Day."

Ibrahim's prayer

⁸³"My Lord, grant me wisdom and unite me with the righteous, ⁸⁴and grant me a reputation for truthfulness among the later *generations*. ⁸⁵Make me one of the heirs of the Garden of Bliss; ⁸⁶and forgive my father[a] – he's gone astray. ⁸⁷Do not disgrace me on the Day when *humanity* will be resurrected, ⁸⁸the Day when neither wealth nor children will benefit. ⁸⁹*Success is* for the one who comes to Allah with a pure heart."

The disbelievers come face-to-face with Hell

⁹⁰Paradise will be brought close to the righteous; ⁹¹and Hell will be shown to the misguided,

---

[a] Cf 19:41. This refers to his paternal uncle.

تَعْبُدُوْنَ ۞ مِنْ دُوْنِ اللهِ ط هَلْ يَنْصُرُوْنَكُمْ اَوْ
يَنْتَصِرُوْنَ ۞ ط فَكُبْكِبُوْا فِيْهَا هُمْ وَالْغَاوٗنَ ۞ وَجُنُوْدُ
اِبْلِيْسَ اَجْمَعُوْنَ ۞ قَالُوْا وَهُمْ فِيْهَا يَخْتَصِمُوْنَ ۞
تَاللهِ اِنْ كُنَّا لَفِىْ ضَلٰلٍ مُّبِيْنٍ ۞ اِذْ نُسَوِّيْكُمْ بِرَبِّ
الْعٰلَمِيْنَ ۞ وَمَاۤ اَضَلَّنَاۤ اِلَّا الْمُجْرِمُوْنَ ۞ فَمَا لَنَا
مِنْ شَافِعِيْنَ ۞ وَلَا صَدِيْقٍ حَمِيْمٍ ۞ فَلَوْ اَنَّ لَنَا
كَرَّةً فَنَكُوْنَ مِنَ الْمُؤْمِنِيْنَ ۞ اِنَّ فِىْ ذٰلِكَ لَاٰيَةً ط
وَمَا كَانَ اَكْثَرُهُمْ مُّؤْمِنِيْنَ ۞ وَاِنَّ رَبَّكَ لَهُوَ الْعَزِيْزُ
الرَّحِيْمُ ۞ كَذَّبَتْ قَوْمُ نُوْحِۨ الْمُرْسَلِيْنَ ۞ اِذْ قَالَ
لَهُمْ اَخُوْهُمْ نُوْحٌ اَلَا تَتَّقُوْنَ ۞ اِنِّيْ لَكُمْ رَسُوْلٌ
اَمِيْنٌ ۞ فَاتَّقُوا اللهَ وَاَطِيْعُوْنِ ۞ وَمَاۤ اَسْـَٔلُكُمْ عَلَيْهِ
مِنْ اَجْرٍ ج اِنْ اَجْرِيَ اِلَّا عَلٰى رَبِّ الْعٰلَمِيْنَ ۞ فَاتَّقُوا
اللهَ وَاَطِيْعُوْنِ ۞ قَالُوْاۤ اَنُؤْمِنُ لَكَ وَاتَّبَعَكَ
الْاَرْذَلُوْنَ ۞ قَالَ وَمَا عِلْمِيْ بِمَا كَانُوْا يَعْمَلُوْنَ ۞
اِنْ حِسَابُهُمْ اِلَّا عَلٰى رَبِّيْ لَوْ تَشْعُرُوْنَ ۞ وَمَاۤ اَنَا
بِطَارِدِ الْمُؤْمِنِيْنَ ۞ اِنْ اَنَا اِلَّا نَذِيْرٌ مُّبِيْنٌ ۞ قَالُوْا
لَئِنْ لَّمْ تَنْتَهِ يٰنُوْحُ لَتَكُوْنَنَّ مِنَ الْمَرْجُوْمِيْنَ ۞
قَالَ رَبِّ اِنَّ قَوْمِيْ كَذَّبُوْنِ ۞ فَافْتَحْ بَيْنِيْ وَبَيْنَهُمْ
فَتْحًا وَّنَجِّنِيْ وَمَنْ مَّعِيَ مِنَ الْمُؤْمِنِيْنَ ۞ فَاَنْجَيْنٰهُ
وَمَنْ مَّعَهٗ فِى الْفُلْكِ الْمَشْحُوْنِ ۞ ثُمَّ اَغْرَقْنَا بَعْدُ

Do tall buildings make us feel grand and immortal? A worldly approach, to make us forget the reality.

⁹²who will be *asked*: "Where is what you used to worship ⁹³beside Allah? Are they helping you or even defending themselves?" ⁹⁴Then they will be hurled into *Hell*, they and the misguided ⁹⁵and the soldiers of Satan, all of them together. ⁹⁶They will say, as they argue among themselves in *Hell*, ⁹⁷"By Allah, we were mistaken ⁹⁸when we made you equal to the Lord of the worlds. ⁹⁹It was the *brazen* sinners who misguided us. ¹⁰⁰Now we have no one to plead for us, ¹⁰¹nor even a close friend. ¹⁰²If we could have a second chance we will be believers." ¹⁰³There is a sign in that, but most of them will not believe. ¹⁰⁴Your Lord is the Almighty, the Caring.

Nuh invites his people to Allah

¹⁰⁵The people of Nuh denied *Allah's* messengers ¹⁰⁶when their brother Nuh said to them, "Will you not be mindful *of Allah*? ¹⁰⁷You have in me a messenger to be trusted, ¹⁰⁸so be mindful of Allah and follow me. ¹⁰⁹I don't ask you for a reward for this. The Lord of the worlds will give me reward. ¹¹⁰So *again*, be mindful of Allah and follow me." ¹¹¹They said, "Shall we believe in you, when only the poorest follow you?" ¹¹²He said, "What knowledge have I of what they did. ¹¹³Their account rests with My Lord – if only you could sense *that*. ¹¹⁴I will not drive the believers away. ¹¹⁵I am a clear warner." ¹¹⁶They said, "Nuh, if you don't stop preaching, you will be tortured."

Nuh's prayer for deliverance

¹¹⁷*Nuh* said, "My Lord, my people have denied me, ¹¹⁸so judge between me and them, and save me and those who believe me." ¹¹⁹So We saved him and those with him in the fully-laden ship, ¹²⁰and We drowned anyone who remained behind.

الْبٰقِينَ ۝ اِنَّ فِىْ ذٰلِكَ لَاٰيَةً ؕ وَمَا كَانَ اَكْثَرُهُمْ

مُّؤْمِنِيْنَ ۝ وَاِنَّ رَبَّكَ لَهُوَ الْعَزِيْزُ الرَّحِيْمُ ۝ كَذَّبَتْ

عَادُ الْمُرْسَلِيْنَ ۣ ۝ اِذْ قَالَ لَهُمْ اَخُوْهُمْ هُوْدٌ اَلَا

تَتَّقُوْنَ ۝ اِنِّىْ لَكُمْ رَسُوْلٌ اَمِيْنٌ ۝ فَاتَّقُوا اللهَ وَ

اَطِيْعُوْنِ ۚ ۝ وَمَاۤ اَسْئَلُكُمْ عَلَيْهِ مِنْ اَجْرٍ ۚ اِنْ اَجْرِىَ

اِلَّا عَلٰى رَبِّ الْعٰلَمِيْنَ ؕ ۝ اَتَبْنُوْنَ بِكُلِّ رِيْعٍ اٰيَةً

تَعْبَثُوْنَ ۙ ۝ وَتَتَّخِذُوْنَ مَصَانِعَ لَعَلَّكُمْ تَخْلُدُوْنَ ۝

وَاِذَا بَطَشْتُمْ بَطَشْتُمْ جَبَّارِيْنَ ۚ ۝ فَاتَّقُوا اللهَ وَ

اَطِيْعُوْنِ ۚ ۝ وَاتَّقُوا الَّذِىْۤ اَمَدَّكُمْ بِمَا تَعْلَمُوْنَ ۝

اَمَدَّكُمْ بِاَنْعَامٍ وَّبَنِيْنَ ۙ ۝ وَجَنّٰتٍ وَّعُيُوْنٍ ۚ ۝ اِنِّىْۤ

اَخَافُ عَلَيْكُمْ عَذَابَ يَوْمٍ عَظِيْمٍ ؕ ۝ قَالُوْا سَوَآءٌ عَلَيْنَاۤ

اَوَعَظْتَ اَمْ لَمْ تَكُنْ مِّنَ الْوٰعِظِيْنَ ۝ اِنْ هٰذَاۤ اِلَّا

خُلُقُ الْاَوَّلِيْنَ ۙ ۝ وَمَا نَحْنُ بِمُعَذَّبِيْنَ ۚ ۝ فَكَذَّبُوْهُ

فَاَهْلَكْنٰهُمْ ؕ اِنَّ فِىْ ذٰلِكَ لَاٰيَةً ؕ وَمَا كَانَ اَكْثَرُهُمْ

مُّؤْمِنِيْنَ ۝ وَاِنَّ رَبَّكَ لَهُوَ الْعَزِيْزُ الرَّحِيْمُ ۝ كَذَّبَتْ

ثَمُوْدُ الْمُرْسَلِيْنَ ۣ ۝ اِذْ قَالَ لَهُمْ اَخُوْهُمْ صٰلِحٌ اَلَا

تَتَّقُوْنَ ۝ اِنِّىْ لَكُمْ رَسُوْلٌ اَمِيْنٌ ۝ فَاتَّقُوا اللهَ وَ

اَطِيْعُوْنِ ۚ ۝ وَمَاۤ اَسْئَلُكُمْ عَلَيْهِ مِنْ اَجْرٍ ۚ اِنْ اَجْرِىَ

اِلَّا عَلٰى رَبِّ الْعٰلَمِيْنَ ؕ ۝ اَتُتْرَكُوْنَ فِىْ مَا هٰهُنَاۤ

اٰمِنِيْنَ ۙ ۝ فِىْ جَنّٰتٍ وَّعُيُوْنٍ ۙ ۝ وَّزُرُوْعٍ وَّنَخْلٍ طَلْعُهَا

Do tall buildings make us feel grand and immortal? A worldly approach, to make us forget the reality.

733

¹²¹ There is a lesson in that, but many will not believe. ¹²² Your Lord is the Almighty, the Caring.

The story of Prophet Hud

¹²³ *The people of* Ad denied the messengers ¹²⁴ when their brother Hud said to them, "Won't you believe in Allah? ¹²⁵ I am a trustworthy messenger to you, ¹²⁶ so believe in Allah and follow me; ¹²⁷ I won't ask you for a fee; the Lord of the worlds will reward me. ¹²⁸ You build monuments on every hilltop to please yourselves, ¹²⁹ and take castles *as homes* so you might live forever? ¹³⁰ And, when you seize *others' wealth and land*, you are utterly ruthless in doing so. ¹³¹ So be mindful of Allah and follow me. ¹³² Be mindful of Him Who has given you abundantly: what you know, ¹³³ cattle and children, ¹³⁴ gardens and *freshwater* springs. ¹³⁵ I fear for you the torment of a dreadful Day." ¹³⁶ They said, "It is all the same to us, whether you preach or not; ¹³⁷ these are the customs of the past generations. ¹³⁸ We will not be punished." ¹³⁹ They refused to believe him, so We destroyed them. There is a sign in that, but most won't believe. ¹⁴⁰ Your Lord is the Almighty, the Caring.

The people of Thamud demand a sign from Salih

¹⁴¹ *The people of* Thamud also denied *Allah's* messengers. ¹⁴² When their brother, Salih, said to them, "Will you not be mindful *of Allah*? ¹⁴³ You have in me a trustworthy messenger, ¹⁴⁴ so be mindful of Allah and follow me. ¹⁴⁵ I don't ask you for a reward for this. The Lord of the worlds will reward me. ¹⁴⁶ Will you *really* be left safe and secure with all this, ¹⁴⁷ in gardens and springs, ¹⁴⁸ and fields and date palms with their ripe fruits,

هَضِيْمٌ ۝ وَتَنْحِتُوْنَ مِنَ الْجِبَالِ بُيُوْتًا فَرِهِيْنَ ۝

فَاتَّقُوا اللّٰهَ وَاَطِيْعُوْنِ ۝ وَلَا تُطِيْعُوْا اَمْرَ الْمُسْرِفِيْنَ ۝

الَّذِيْنَ يُفْسِدُوْنَ فِى الْاَرْضِ وَلَا يُصْلِحُوْنَ ۝

قَالُوْا اِنَّمَا اَنْتَ مِنَ الْمُسَحَّرِيْنَ ۝ مَا اَنْتَ اِلَّا بَشَرٌ

مِّثْلُنَا ۙ فَاْتِ بِاٰيَةٍ اِنْ كُنْتَ مِنَ الصّٰدِقِيْنَ ۝ قَالَ

هٰذِهٖ نَاقَةٌ لَّهَا شِرْبٌ وَّلَكُمْ شِرْبُ يَوْمٍ مَّعْلُوْمٍ ۝

وَلَا تَمَسُّوْهَا بِسُوْٓءٍ فَيَاْخُذَكُمْ عَذَابُ يَوْمٍ عَظِيْمٍ ۝

فَعَقَرُوْهَا فَاَصْبَحُوْا نٰدِمِيْنَ ۝ فَاَخَذَهُمُ الْعَذَابُ ط

إِنَّ فِيْ ذٰلِكَ لَاٰيَةً ط وَمَا كَانَ اَكْثَرُهُمْ مُّؤْمِنِيْنَ ۝ وَ

اِنَّ رَبَّكَ لَهُوَ الْعَزِيْزُ الرَّحِيْمُ ۝ كَذَّبَتْ قَوْمُ لُوْطِ

الْمُرْسَلِيْنَ ۝ اِذْ قَالَ لَهُمْ اَخُوْهُمْ لُوْطٌ اَلَا تَتَّقُوْنَ ۝

اِنِّيْ لَكُمْ رَسُوْلٌ اَمِيْنٌ ۝ فَاتَّقُوا اللّٰهَ وَاَطِيْعُوْنِ ۝

وَمَآ اَسْئَلُكُمْ عَلَيْهِ مِنْ اَجْرٍ ۚ اِنْ اَجْرِيَ اِلَّا عَلٰى رَبِّ

الْعٰلَمِيْنَ ط اَتَاْتُوْنَ الذُّكْرَانَ مِنَ الْعٰلَمِيْنَ ۝ وَ

تَذَرُوْنَ مَا خَلَقَ لَكُمْ رَبُّكُمْ مِّنْ اَزْوَاجِكُمْ ط بَلْ اَنْتُمْ

قَوْمٌ عٰدُوْنَ ۝ قَالُوْا لَئِنْ لَّمْ تَنْتَهِ يٰلُوْطُ لَتَكُوْنَنَّ مِنَ

الْمُخْرَجِيْنَ ۝ قَالَ اِنِّيْ لِعَمَلِكُمْ مِّنَ الْقَالِيْنَ ۝ رَبِّ

نَجِّنِيْ وَاَهْلِيْ مِمَّا يَعْمَلُوْنَ ۝ فَنَجَّيْنٰهُ وَاَهْلَهٗ اَجْمَعِيْنَ ۝

اِلَّا عَجُوْزًا فِى الْغٰبِرِيْنَ ۝ ثُمَّ دَمَّرْنَا الْاٰخَرِيْنَ ۝ وَ

اَمْطَرْنَا عَلَيْهِمْ مَّطَرًا ۚ فَسَآءَ مَطَرُ الْمُنْذَرِيْنَ ۝ اِنَّ

The people of Lut were obsessed with degenerate sexuality, so they lost common sense.

¹⁴⁹while you skilfully carve houses out of the mountains? ¹⁵⁰So be mindful of Allah and follow me, ¹⁵¹don't follow the way of the wasteful ¹⁵²who spread corruption in the land rather than acting righteously." ¹⁵³They said, "You've been bewitched. ¹⁵⁴You are a mortal like us; so bring a miracle, if you're telling the truth."

Salih produces the she-camel as a miracle

¹⁵⁵Salih said, "Here is a she-camel. She may drink and you may drink, *each* on fixed days. ¹⁵⁶Don't harm her in case the punishment of a terrible Day befalls you." ¹⁵⁷They hamstrung her, only to wake up *the next day* regretting it, ¹⁵⁸*when* the torment overtook them. There is a lesson in this, though most of them will not believe. ¹⁵⁹Your Lord is the Almighty, the Caring.

Lut confronts lustful men

¹⁶⁰The people of Lut denied their messengers. ¹⁶¹When their brother, Lut, said to them, "Won't you believe? ¹⁶²I am a trustworthy messenger, ¹⁶³so believe in Allah and follow me; ¹⁶⁴I won't ask you for a fee, the Lord of the worlds will reward me. ¹⁶⁵*Why*, of all the people of the world do you approach males lustfully, ¹⁶⁶leaving your wives whom your Lord has created for you? You are people who have crossed the bounds *of decency*." ¹⁶⁷They said, "If you don't stop *preaching* Lut, you will be exiled." ¹⁶⁸He said, "I am disgusted by your actions."

Lut's prayer

¹⁶⁹"My Lord, save me and my family from what they do." ¹⁷⁰So We saved him and all his family, ¹⁷¹except an old woman, who stayed behind. ¹⁷²Then We destroyed the others, ¹⁷³pelting them with a rain of *brimstone*. How dreadful was the rain on those who had been forewarned!

فِىْ ذٰلِكَ لَاٰيَةً ط وَمَا كَانَ اَكْثَرُهُمْ مُّؤْمِنِيْنَ ۞ وَاِنَّ

رَبَّكَ لَهُوَ الْعَزِيْزُ الرَّحِيْمُ ۞ كَذَّبَ اَصْحٰبُ لْئَيْكَةِ

الْمُرْسَلِيْنَ ۞ اِذْ قَالَ لَهُمْ شُعَيْبٌ اَلَا تَتَّقُوْنَ ۞

اِنِّىْ لَكُمْ رَسُوْلٌ اَمِيْنٌ ۞ فَاتَّقُوا اللّٰهَ وَاَطِيْعُوْنِ ۞

وَمَاۤ اَسْئَلُكُمْ عَلَيْهِ مِنْ اَجْرٍ اِنْ اَجْرِىَ اِلَّا عَلٰى رَبِّ

الْعٰلَمِيْنَ ط اَوْفُوا الْكَيْلَ وَلَا تَكُوْنُوْا مِنَ الْمُخْسِرِيْنَ ۞

وَزِنُوْا بِالْقِسْطَاسِ الْمُسْتَقِيْمِ ۞ وَلَا تَبْخَسُوا النَّاسَ

اَشْيَآءَهُمْ وَلَا تَعْثَوْا فِى الْاَرْضِ مُفْسِدِيْنَ ۞ وَاتَّقُوا

الَّذِىْ خَلَقَكُمْ وَالْجِبِلَّةَ الْاَوَّلِيْنَ ط قَالُوْۤا اِنَّمَاۤ

اَنْتَ مِنَ الْمُسَحَّرِيْنَ ۞ وَمَاۤ اَنْتَ اِلَّا بَشَرٌ مِّثْلُنَا

وَاِنْ نَّظُنُّكَ لَمِنَ الْكٰذِبِيْنَ ۞ فَاَسْقِطْ عَلَيْنَا كِسَفًا

مِّنَ السَّمَآءِ اِنْ كُنْتَ مِنَ الصّٰدِقِيْنَ ۞ قَالَ رَبِّىْۤ

اَعْلَمُ بِمَا تَعْمَلُوْنَ ۞ فَكَذَّبُوْهُ فَاَخَذَهُمْ عَذَابُ

يَوْمِ الظُّلَّةِ ط اِنَّهٗ كَانَ عَذَابَ يَوْمٍ عَظِيْمٍ ۞ اِنَّ

فِىْ ذٰلِكَ لَاٰيَةً ط وَمَا كَانَ اَكْثَرُهُمْ مُّؤْمِنِيْنَ ۞ وَاِنَّ

رَبَّكَ لَهُوَ الْعَزِيْزُ الرَّحِيْمُ ۞ وَاِنَّهٗ لَتَنْزِيْلُ رَبِّ

الْعٰلَمِيْنَ ط نَزَلَ بِهِ الرُّوْحُ الْاَمِيْنُ ۞ عَلٰى قَلْبِكَ

لِتَكُوْنَ مِنَ الْمُنْذِرِيْنَ ۞ بِلِسَانٍ عَرَبِىٍّ مُّبِيْنٍ ۞

وَاِنَّهٗ لَفِىْ زُبُرِ الْاَوَّلِيْنَ ۞ اَوَلَمْ يَكُنْ لَّهُمْ اٰيَةً

اَنْ يَّعْلَمَهٗ عُلَمٰٓؤُا بَنِىْۤ اِسْرَآءِيْلَ ۞ وَلَوْ نَزَّلْنٰهُ عَلٰى

The love of the world is dazzling and can make us blind to the Hereafter.

¹⁷⁴There is a sign in that, but most will not believe. ¹⁷⁵Your Lord is the Almighty, the Caring.

The story of Prophet Shuʿayb

¹⁷⁶The companions of the forest *also* denied *Allah's* messengers. ¹⁷⁷When their brother, Shuʿayb, said to them, "Will you not fear *Allah*? ¹⁷⁸I am a trustworthy messenger to you, ¹⁷⁹so be mindful of Allah and follow me. ¹⁸⁰I won't ask you for a fee for this. The Lord of the worlds will reward me. ¹⁸¹Be honest in *your* measures, and don't be cheats. ¹⁸²Weigh with accurate scales; ¹⁸³don't serve people short, and don't spread corruption in the land. ¹⁸⁴Be mindful of Him Who created you and many previous generations." ¹⁸⁵They said, "You are bewitched. ¹⁸⁶You are a mortal like us; and we think you're a liar. ¹⁸⁷Cause a chunk of sky to fall on us, if you are telling the truth." ¹⁸⁸He said, "My Lord knows well what you do." ¹⁸⁹They refused to believe him, so the torment of a Day of *impenetrable* shade^a overtook them. What a dreadful Day of torment that was! ¹⁹⁰There is a sign in that, but most will not believe. ¹⁹¹Your Lord is the Almighty, the Caring.

Revelation of the Quran through Jibreel

¹⁹²And this is the Revelation of the Lord of the worlds, ¹⁹³which that trustworthy spirit, *the Angel Jibreel*, brought down ¹⁹⁴straight into your heart so you become a warner ¹⁹⁵in a clear Arabic language; ¹⁹⁶and it is *found* in the scriptures of earlier *nations*. ¹⁹⁷Have they not *received* a sign that the scholars of the Israelites will recognise? ¹⁹⁸If We had revealed it to someone who wasn't an Arab,

---

^a This "*impenetrable* shade" conjures up images of the darkness that we are told occurred when a meteorite struck our planet and brought an end to the dinosaurs 65 million years ago. Or it may refer to the darkness that follows an Earthquake or a volcanic eruption.

بَعْضِ الْأَعْجَمِينَ ۝ فَقَرَأَهُ عَلَيْهِمْ مَّا كَانُوا بِهِ

مُؤْمِنِينَ ۝ كَذَٰلِكَ سَلَكْنَاهُ فِي قُلُوبِ الْمُجْرِمِينَ ۝

لَا يُؤْمِنُونَ بِهِ حَتَّىٰ يَرَوُا الْعَذَابَ الْأَلِيمَ ۝

فَيَأْتِيَهُمْ بَغْتَةً وَّهُمْ لَا يَشْعُرُونَ ۝ فَيَقُولُوا

هَلْ نَحْنُ مُنْظَرُونَ ۝ أَفَبِعَذَابِنَا يَسْتَعْجِلُونَ ۝

أَفَرَءَيْتَ إِن مَّتَّعْنَاهُمْ سِنِينَ ۝ ثُمَّ جَاءَهُم

مَّا كَانُوا يُوعَدُونَ ۝ مَا أَغْنَىٰ عَنْهُم مَّا كَانُوا

يَمْتَعُونَ ۝ وَمَا أَهْلَكْنَا مِن قَرْيَةٍ إِلَّا لَهَا مُنذِرُونَ ۝

ذِكْرَىٰ وَمَا كُنَّا ظَالِمِينَ ۝ وَمَا تَنَزَّلَتْ بِهِ الشَّيَاطِينُ ۝

وَمَا يَنۢبَغِي لَهُمْ وَمَا يَسْتَطِيعُونَ ۝ إِنَّهُمْ عَنِ السَّمْعِ

لَمَعْزُولُونَ ۝ فَلَا تَدْعُ مَعَ اللَّهِ إِلَٰهًا آخَرَ فَتَكُونَ

مِنَ الْمُعَذَّبِينَ ۝ وَأَنذِرْ عَشِيرَتَكَ الْأَقْرَبِينَ ۝

وَاخْفِضْ جَنَاحَكَ لِمَنِ اتَّبَعَكَ مِنَ الْمُؤْمِنِينَ ۝

فَإِنْ عَصَوْكَ فَقُلْ إِنِّي بَرِيءٌ مِّمَّا تَعْمَلُونَ ۝ وَتَوَكَّلْ

عَلَى الْعَزِيزِ الرَّحِيمِ ۝ الَّذِي يَرَاكَ حِينَ تَقُومُ ۝ وَ

تَقَلُّبَكَ فِي السَّاجِدِينَ ۝ إِنَّهُ هُوَ السَّمِيعُ الْعَلِيمُ ۝ هَلْ

أُنَبِّئُكُمْ عَلَىٰ مَن تَنَزَّلُ الشَّيَاطِينُ ۝ تَنَزَّلُ عَلَىٰ كُلِّ

أَفَّاكٍ أَثِيمٍ ۝ يُلْقُونَ السَّمْعَ وَأَكْثَرُهُمْ كَاذِبُونَ ۝

وَالشُّعَرَاءُ يَتَّبِعُهُمُ الْغَاوُونَ ۝ أَلَمْ تَرَ أَنَّهُمْ فِي كُلِّ

وَادٍ يَهِيمُونَ ۝ وَأَنَّهُمْ يَقُولُونَ مَا لَا يَفْعَلُونَ ۝

So what's your responsibility for society? Understand this, since it will help you tackle your individualism.

[199] and he had recited it to them, they still wouldn't have believed it.

Punishment for those who reject the Quran

[200] That's how We allow *rejection of the Quran* to find its way into the hearts of the sinful. [201] They will never believe in it until they see the painful punishment, [202] which will come upon them all of a sudden, when they are unaware. [203] They will say: "Can we be given some more time?" [204] But are they not currently trying to hasten Our punishment? [205] Suppose We granted them years of enjoyment, [206] then when what they had been promised befell them, [207] would what they had enjoyed benefit them? [208] We never destroyed a city which hadn't *received* warners [209] as a reminder. We are never unjust.

The Quran is uncorrupted by demons and jinns

[210] It is not demons who brought down this *Quran*; [211] nor would it be fitting for them, nor are they capable *of doing so.* [212] They are barred from *even* hearing *it.* [213] Therefore, don't call upon any other god alongside Allah so you *end up* among the tormented.

Instruction to invite relatives to Islam

[214] Warn your nearest relatives, [215] and take whoever follows you from among the believers under your wing. [216] Then, if they disobey you, say: "I am innocent of what you do," [217] and put your trust in the Almighty, the Caring, [218] Who sees you while you stand *in prayer* [219] and when you change *position to be* amongst those prostrating. [220] He is the Hearer, the Knower.

Some poets are misguided

[221] Shall I tell you who will be visited by demons? [222] They visit every sinful slanderer, [223] who listens readily, and who is a liar. [224] *Likewise* the poets, who are deceived, follow them *too.* [225] Do you not see them wandering about in every valley, [226] *boastfully* saying things they don't do? [227] Except the believing *poets* who are righteous, constantly remember Allah, and defend themselves against oppression. The oppressors will soon know the fate they will be returned to.

إِلَّا الَّذِينَ ءَامَنُوا وَعَمِلُوا الصَّٰلِحَٰتِ وَذَكَرُوا اللَّهَ كَثِيرًا وَٱنتَصَرُوا مِنۢ بَعْدِ مَا ظُلِمُوا ۗ وَسَيَعْلَمُ الَّذِينَ ظَلَمُوٓا أَىَّ مُنقَلَبٍ يَنقَلِبُونَ ﴿٢٢٧﴾

27. Surat An-Naml

The Ant

This surat was revealed in the middle-Makkan period, either in the fifth or sixth year of the mission of the Prophet ﷺ. It charts part of the history of human spirituality by reference to five prophets: Musa ﷺ, Sulayman ﷺ, Dawud ﷺ, Salih ﷺ, and Lut ﷺ. The opening verses describe the nature of divine revelation as being guidance and good news. The proof of this proposition: the story of Musa ﷺ and how he received divine revelation on Mount Sinai.

The story of Sulayman ﷺ – a prophet and king who successfully combined the two roles: worldly wealth and spiritual devotion – sets the scene for understanding divine mysteries. Allah gave him gifts, including the ability to communicate with various creatures – jinn, birds and even insects like the ant: see verses 17 to 19. The stories of King Sulayman and the Queen of Sheba abound with symbolism, and subtly weave together the realities of worldly life and spiritual realities. In some ways, it represents the story of the human soul's spiritual awakening and eventual realisation of moral and spiritual truths. The story of the Hoopoe bird, and the transportation of the mighty throne of the Queen of Sheba thousands of miles in the twinkling of an eye express great truths. There is a certain spiritual truth underlying each one of them:

> The many sided, many layered truths which the Quran invariably brings out, sometimes explicitly, sometimes elliptically, often allegorically, but always with a definite bearing on some of the hidden depths and conflicts within our own human psyche (Asad).

When the Hoopoe told Sulayman ﷺ about the Queen of Sheba, Sulayman ﷺ dispatched a letter inviting her to become a believer and give up her idolatry. The Queen, after consulting her advisers, decided to play it safe, and to pacify Sulayman ﷺ sent him precious gifts and waited for her envoys to bring news about him. Sulayman refused to accept her gifts, which convinced her that this was no king in pursuit of worldly gains. She wisely decided to meet him in person, and made a journey of 1,000 miles from Yemen to Jerusalem. Sulayman, in the meantime, decided to receive her: "Who can bring me her throne before they come to me in submission?" (38). One of his knowledgeable followers was able to bring it in the "blink of an eye." The transportation of the queen's throne from

Yemen to his palace in Jerusalem hints at the ephemeral, fleeting nature of material power. The throne is a metonym for power and sovereignty:

> It appears that Sulayman intends to confront his guest with an image of her worldly power, and thus to convince her that her throne is as nothing when compared with the awesome almightiness of God (Asad).

This is, of course, a miracle which cannot be explained by the science of particle physics. However, the law of thermodynamics may hold a clue to this miracle. This law states that neither mass nor energy are destroyed, but converted, so they can travel at the extraordinary speed of light.

In the story of the Hoopoe, the Quran teaches a powerful lesson: the lowliest being can sometimes have knowledge of things that even experts may lack. This is a clear reminder counteracting arrogance and self-deceit. Similarly, the story of the Queen of Sheba entering the hall of Sulayman is a symbol of a woman confronting something new. She is full of fear, and does not wish to abandon the realm of what she finds familiar, comforting and secure in favour of venturing into the unknown. Yet the Queen of Sheba takes the leap, and sees that the floor of the hall is not dangerous:

> It is a glass-clear light of truth: and with her perception of the ever[-]existing difference between appearance and reality … the Queen of Sheba comes to the end of her spiritual journey (Asad).

The surat quickly moves on to the stories of Prophet Salih ﷺ and Prophet Lut ﷺ, who faced serious opposition from their people. Their story contrasts with that of the Queen of Sheba, who eagerly accepted faith and realised the foolishness of idolatry. The severe opposition and the hostility faced by these two prophets is a commentary on the human condition. People are being warned against their thoughtless addiction to materialism and idolatry, and are invited to adopt the attitude of the Queen of Sheba. A subtle hope to the Prophet ﷺ and his small band of followers.

There is mention of a mysterious creature: "When the judgement against them comes to pass, We shall bring forth from the Earth a beast that will tell them *about* the people who didn't believe in Our signs" (82). The books of hadith hint that when this creature comes it will trigger the beginning of the end of the world.

بِسْمِ اللهِ الرَّحْمٰنِ الرَّحِيْمِ

طٰس ۚ تِلْكَ اٰيٰتُ الْقُرْاٰنِ وَكِتَابٍ مُّبِيْنٍ ۙ١ هُدًى

وَّبُشْرٰى لِلْمُؤْمِنِيْنَ ۙ٢ الَّذِيْنَ يُقِيْمُوْنَ الصَّلٰوةَ

وَيُؤْتُوْنَ الزَّكٰوةَ وَهُمْ بِالْاٰخِرَةِ هُمْ يُوْقِنُوْنَ ٣ اِنَّ

الَّذِيْنَ لَا يُؤْمِنُوْنَ بِالْاٰخِرَةِ زَيَّنَّا لَهُمْ اَعْمَالَهُمْ

فَهُمْ يَعْمَهُوْنَ ؕ٤ اُولٰٓئِكَ الَّذِيْنَ لَهُمْ سُوْٓءُ الْعَذَابِ

وَهُمْ فِي الْاٰخِرَةِ هُمُ الْاَخْسَرُوْنَ ٥ وَاِنَّكَ لَتُلَقَّى

الْقُرْاٰنَ مِنْ لَّدُنْ حَكِيْمٍ عَلِيْمٍ ٦ اِذْ قَالَ مُوْسٰى

Musa goes to get a flame to light a fire, but instead gets prophethood, miracles and a Book of guidance.

لِاَهْلِهٖٓ اِنِّيْٓ اٰنَسْتُ نَارًا ؕ سَاٰتِيْكُمْ مِّنْهَا بِخَبَرٍ اَوْ اٰتِيْكُمْ

بِشِهَابٍ قَبَسٍ لَّعَلَّكُمْ تَصْطَلُوْنَ ٧ فَلَمَّا جَاۤءَهَا

نُوْدِيَ اَنْ بُوْرِكَ مَنْ فِي النَّارِ وَمَنْ حَوْلَهَا ؕ وَ

سُبْحٰنَ اللهِ رَبِّ الْعٰلَمِيْنَ ٨ يٰمُوْسٰٓى اِنَّهٗٓ اَنَا اللهُ

الْعَزِيْزُ الْحَكِيْمُ ۙ٩ وَاَلْقِ عَصَاكَ ؕ فَلَمَّا رَاٰهَا تَهْتَزُّ

كَاَنَّهَا جَاۤنٌّ وَّلّٰى مُدْبِرًا وَّلَمْ يُعَقِّبْ ؕ يٰمُوْسٰى

لَا تَخَفْ ۪ اِنِّيْ لَا يَخَافُ لَدَيَّ الْمُرْسَلُوْنَ ۙ١٠ اِلَّا

مَنْ ظَلَمَ ثُمَّ بَدَّلَ حُسْنًا بَعْدَ سُوْٓءٍ فَاِنِّيْ غَفُوْرٌ

رَّحِيْمٌ ١١ وَاَدْخِلْ يَدَكَ فِيْ جَيْبِكَ تَخْرُجْ بَيْضَاۤءَ

مِنْ غَيْرِ سُوْٓءٍ ۪ فِيْ تِسْعِ اٰيٰتٍ اِلٰى فِرْعَوْنَ وَقَوْمِهٖ ؕ

اِنَّهُمْ كَانُوْا قَوْمًا فٰسِقِيْنَ ١٢ فَلَمَّا جَاۤءَتْهُمْ اٰيٰتُنَا

In the name of Allah, the Kind, the Caring.

¹ *Ta Sin.*

The glorious Quran, a source of guidance and good news

These are the verses of the Quran, a Clear Book, ²a guide and glad tidings for the believers, ³who perform the prayer, give Zakat and believe firmly in the Hereafter. ⁴As for those who don't believe in the Hereafter, We made their deeds appear attractive to them, so they wander about blindly. ⁵These *people* will have the worst punishment, and they shall be the biggest losers in the Hereafter. ⁶But you have received the Quran from the Wise, All-Knowing.

The story of Musa

⁷*Remember* when Musa said to his wife, "I've seen a fire. I will bring you some news from there, or fetch you a burning coal so you can warm yourself." ⁸When he reached there, a voice called out: "Blessed is Whoever is *veiled by* the fireᵃ and whoever is close to it. Glory be to Allah, the Lord of the worlds! ⁹Musa, it is I, Allah, the Almighty, the Wise, ¹⁰so throw down your *shepherd's* staff." When he saw it wriggling, he turned and fled, without looking back. "Musa," *the voice said,* "Don't be afraid. Messengers shouldn't be afraid in My presence, ¹¹even the one who has done wrong but then changes himself to do good; for I am Forgiving, Caring. ¹²Now put your hand inside your cloak *and* it will come out *brilliant* white but unharmed, *yet another of* nine signs *to show* Pharaoh and his people; they are brazen sinners." ¹³*However,* when Our self-evident signs came to them, they said, "This is magic,"

ᵃ The Arabic literally says, "is in the fire".

مُبْصِرَةً قَالُوا هٰذَا سِحْرٌ مُّبِيْنٌ ۞ وَجَحَدُوْا بِهَا

وَاسْتَيْقَنَتْهَا أَنْفُسُهُمْ ظُلْمًا وَّعُلُوًّا ۗ فَانْظُرْ كَيْفَ

كَانَ عَاقِبَةُ الْمُفْسِدِيْنَ ۞ وَلَقَدْ اٰتَيْنَا دَاوٗدَ

وَسُلَيْمٰنَ عِلْمًا ۚ وَقَالَا الْحَمْدُ لِلّٰهِ الَّذِيْ فَضَّلَنَا

عَلٰى كَثِيْرٍ مِّنْ عِبَادِهِ الْمُؤْمِنِيْنَ ۞ وَوَرِثَ

سُلَيْمٰنُ دَاوٗدَ وَقَالَ يٰٓاَيُّهَا النَّاسُ عُلِّمْنَا مَنْطِقَ

الطَّيْرِ وَأُوْتِيْنَا مِنْ كُلِّ شَيْءٍ ۗ إِنَّ هٰذَا لَهُوَ

الْفَضْلُ الْمُبِيْنُ ۞ وَحُشِرَ لِسُلَيْمٰنَ جُنُوْدُهٗ مِنَ

الْجِنِّ وَالْإِنْسِ وَالطَّيْرِ فَهُمْ يُوْزَعُوْنَ ۞ حَتّٰى إِذَآ

اَتَوْا عَلٰى وَادِ النَّمْلِ ۙ قَالَتْ نَمْلَةٌ يٰٓاَيُّهَا النَّمْلُ

ادْخُلُوْا مَسٰكِنَكُمْ ۚ لَا يَحْطِمَنَّكُمْ سُلَيْمٰنُ وَجُنُوْدُهٗ ۙ

وَهُمْ لَا يَشْعُرُوْنَ ۞ فَتَبَسَّمَ ضَاحِكًا مِّنْ قَوْلِهَا وَ

قَالَ رَبِّ اَوْزِعْنِيْٓ اَنْ اَشْكُرَ نِعْمَتَكَ الَّتِيْٓ اَنْعَمْتَ

عَلَيَّ وَعَلٰى وَالِدَيَّ وَاَنْ اَعْمَلَ صَالِحًا تَرْضٰهُ وَ

اَدْخِلْنِيْ بِرَحْمَتِكَ فِيْ عِبَادِكَ الصّٰلِحِيْنَ ۞ وَتَفَقَّدَ

الطَّيْرَ فَقَالَ مَا لِيَ لَآ اَرَى الْهُدْهُدَ ۖ اَمْ كَانَ

مِنَ الْغَآئِبِيْنَ ۞ لَاُعَذِّبَنَّهٗ عَذَابًا شَدِيْدًا اَوْ

لَاَاذْبَحَنَّهٗٓ اَوْ لَيَاْتِيَنِّيْ بِسُلْطٰنٍ مُّبِيْنٍ ۞ فَمَكَثَ غَيْرَ

بَعِيْدٍ فَقَالَ اَحَطتُّ بِمَا لَمْ تُحِطْ بِهٖ وَجِئْتُكَ مِنْ

سَبَإٍ بِنَبَإٍ يَّقِيْنٍ ۞ إِنِّيْ وَجَدْتُّ امْرَاَةً تَمْلِكُهُمْ وَ

Even the ants recognised Sulayman, so why don't humans recognise and acknowledge the prophets?

¹⁴and they rejected them, and yet they were certain of their truth; this was due to their wickedness and pride. So look what happened to those who spread corruption.

Sulayman's prayer of thanksgiving

¹⁵ We gave Dawud and Sulayman knowledge, and both prayed: "Praise be to Allah, Who favoured us over many of His believing servants." ¹⁶ *Then* Sulayman succeeded Dawud, and he said, "People, we have been taught the language of birds, and have been given all kinds of things, a clear *sign of* favour." ¹⁷ Sulayman's armies of jinn, men and birds gathered to parade before him; ¹⁸ *and they marched* until they came to the Valley of Ants, *where* one of the ants said: "Ants, get into your anthills so that Sulayman and his armies don't crush you unwittingly." ¹⁹ *Sulayman* smiled and laughed at her words and said, "Lord, make me grateful to You for the blessings that You have given me and my father; and grant me strength to do righteous deeds to please You; and kindly, include me with Your righteous servants."

The hoopoe tells his amazing story

²⁰ *One day,* whilst looking for *a missing* bird, *Sulayman* said: "Why can't I see the Hoopoe? He's absent? ²¹ Either he brings me a valid reason *for his absence,* or I will punish him severely, maybe even slaughter him!" ²² *The hoopoe* did not stay away for long; *he returned* and said, "I know of something that you don't, and I bring you an accurate report from Sheba. ²³ There I found a woman ruling over them; and, *like you,* she has been given everything and has a mighty throne.

أُوْتِيَتْ مِنْ كُلِّ شَىْءٍ وَّلَهَا عَرْشٌ عَظِيْمٌ ۝ وَجَدْتُّهَا

وَقَوْمَهَا يَسْجُدُوْنَ لِلشَّمْسِ مِنْ دُوْنِ اللّٰهِ وَزَيَّنَ لَهُمُ

الشَّيْطٰنُ اَعْمَالَهُمْ فَصَدَّهُمْ عَنِ السَّبِيْلِ فَهُمْ لَا

يَهْتَدُوْنَ ۝ اَلَّا يَسْجُدُوْا لِلّٰهِ الَّذِىْ يُخْرِجُ الْخَبْءَ فِى

السَّمٰوٰتِ وَالْاَرْضِ وَيَعْلَمُ مَا تُخْفُوْنَ وَمَا تُعْلِنُوْنَ ۝

اَللّٰهُ لَا اِلٰهَ اِلَّا هُوَ رَبُّ الْعَرْشِ الْعَظِيْمِ ۩ ۝ قَالَ سَنَنْظُرُ

اَصَدَقْتَ اَمْ كُنْتَ مِنَ الْكٰذِبِيْنَ ۝ اِذْهَبْ بِّكِتٰبِىْ

هٰذَا فَاَلْقِهْ اِلَيْهِمْ ثُمَّ تَوَلَّ عَنْهُمْ فَانْظُرْ مَاذَا

يَرْجِعُوْنَ ۝ قَالَتْ يٰاَيُّهَا الْمَلَؤُا اِنِّىْٓ اُلْقِىَ اِلَىَّ كِتٰبٌ

كَرِيْمٌ ۝ اِنَّهٗ مِنْ سُلَيْمٰنَ وَاِنَّهٗ بِسْمِ اللّٰهِ الرَّحْمٰنِ

الرَّحِيْمِ ۝ اَلَّا تَعْلُوْا عَلَىَّ وَاْتُوْنِىْ مُسْلِمِيْنَ ۝ قَالَتْ

يٰاَيُّهَا الْمَلَؤُا اَفْتُوْنِىْ فِىْٓ اَمْرِىْ مَا كُنْتُ قَاطِعَةً اَمْرًا

حَتّٰى تَشْهَدُوْنِ ۝ قَالُوْا نَحْنُ اُولُوْا قُوَّةٍ وَّاُولُوْا بَاْسٍ

شَدِيْدٍ ۙ وَّالْاَمْرُ اِلَيْكِ فَانْظُرِىْ مَاذَا تَاْمُرِيْنَ ۝

قَالَتْ اِنَّ الْمُلُوْكَ اِذَا دَخَلُوْا قَرْيَةً اَفْسَدُوْهَا وَ

جَعَلُوْٓا اَعِزَّةَ اَهْلِهَآ اَذِلَّةً ۚ وَكَذٰلِكَ يَفْعَلُوْنَ ۝

وَاِنِّىْ مُرْسِلَةٌ اِلَيْهِمْ بِهَدِيَّةٍ فَنٰظِرَةٌۢ بِمَ يَرْجِعُ

الْمُرْسَلُوْنَ ۝ فَلَمَّا جَآءَ سُلَيْمٰنَ قَالَ اَتُمِدُّوْنَنِ

بِمَالٍ ۫ فَمَآ اٰتٰىنِۦَ اللّٰهُ خَيْرٌ مِّمَّآ اٰتٰىكُمْ ۚ بَلْ اَنْتُمْ

بِهَدِيَّتِكُمْ تَفْرَحُوْنَ ۝ اِرْجِعْ اِلَيْهِمْ فَلَنَاْتِيَنَّهُمْ

The Queen of Sheba's consultation and reconciliatory position demonstrates her wisdom. How often do you behave wisely?

Their idolatry puzzled the hoopoe

²⁴I found her and her people worshipping the sun instead of Allah, and Satan had made their deeds attractive to them, and blocked them from the *true* way, so they were not guided. ²⁵Shouldn't they worship *only* Allah, Who discloses whatever is hidden in the Heavens and the Earth, and Who knows whatever you *choose either* to conceal or to reveal? ²⁶There is no god but Allah, the Lord of the mighty Throne."

Sulayman sends a letter to the Queen of Sheba

²⁷*Sulayman* said, "We shall see if you are telling the truth or lying. ²⁸Go with this letter of mine and make sure they receive it, then move a little way from them and see what *response* they come back with." ²⁹*The queen* said, "My lords, I have received a gracious letter. ³⁰It is from Sulayman and reads: 'In the name of Allah, the Kind, the Caring. ³¹Do not think yourselves above me, but come to me in submission.'" ³²So she asked, "My lords, advise me in this matter. I don't make any decision without your presence and advice." ³³They said, "We possess power and military might, but the *final* decision rests with you; so, tell *us* what to do."

The queen sends gifts to Sulayman

³⁴She said, "When kings enter a city, they lay waste to it and humiliate its nobility; that is their way. ³⁵So I will send them a gift and wait to see what the envoys come back with." ³⁶When they reached Sulayman, he said *to her envoys*, "Do you *think you can* increase my wealth? What Allah has given me is far better than what He has given you. Only the likes of you rejoice in such gifts. ³⁷Go back to *your people* and tell them We shall come with armies that they can't face, and we shall expel them from *their city*, humiliated and disgraced."

بِجُنُوْدٍ لَّا قِبَلَ لَهُمْ بِهَا وَلَنُخْرِجَنَّهُمْ مِّنْهَاۤ

اَذِلَّةً وَّهُمْ صٰغِرُوْنَ ۝ قَالَ يٰٓاَيُّهَا الْمَلَؤُا اَيُّكُمْ

يَاْتِيْنِيْ بِعَرْشِهَا قَبْلَ اَنْ يَّاْتُوْنِيْ مُسْلِمِيْنَ ۝ قَالَ

عِفْرِيْتٌ مِّنَ الْجِنِّ اَنَا اٰتِيْكَ بِهٖ قَبْلَ اَنْ تَقُوْمَ

مِنْ مَّقَامِكَ ۚ وَاِنِّيْ عَلَيْهِ لَقَوِيٌّ اَمِيْنٌ ۝ قَالَ

الَّذِيْ عِنْدَهٗ عِلْمٌ مِّنَ الْكِتٰبِ اَنَا اٰتِيْكَ بِهٖ قَبْلَ

اَنْ يَّرْتَدَّ اِلَيْكَ طَرْفُكَ ؕ فَلَمَّا رَاٰهُ مُسْتَقِرًّا عِنْدَهٗ

قَالَ هٰذَا مِنْ فَضْلِ رَبِّيْ ۖ لِيَبْلُوَنِيْٓ ءَاَشْكُرُ اَمْ

اَكْفُرُ ؕ وَمَنْ شَكَرَ فَاِنَّمَا يَشْكُرُ لِنَفْسِهٖ ۚ وَمَنْ كَفَرَ

فَاِنَّ رَبِّيْ غَنِيٌّ كَرِيْمٌ ۝ قَالَ نَكِّرُوْا لَهَا عَرْشَهَا نَنْظُرْ

اَتَهْتَدِيْٓ اَمْ تَكُوْنُ مِنَ الَّذِيْنَ لَا يَهْتَدُوْنَ ۝ فَلَمَّا

جَآءَتْ قِيْلَ اَهٰكَذَا عَرْشُكِ ؕ قَالَتْ كَاَنَّهٗ هُوَ ۚ وَ

اُوْتِيْنَا الْعِلْمَ مِنْ قَبْلِهَا وَكُنَّا مُسْلِمِيْنَ ۝ وَصَدَّهَا

مَا كَانَتْ تَّعْبُدُ مِنْ دُوْنِ اللّٰهِ ؕ اِنَّهَا كَانَتْ مِنْ

قَوْمٍ كٰفِرِيْنَ ۝ قِيْلَ لَهَا ادْخُلِي الصَّرْحَ ۚ فَلَمَّا رَاَتْهُ

حَسِبَتْهُ لُجَّةً وَّكَشَفَتْ عَنْ سَاقَيْهَا ؕ قَالَ اِنَّهٗ

صَرْحٌ مُّمَرَّدٌ مِّنْ قَوَارِيْرَ ؕ قَالَتْ رَبِّ اِنِّيْ ظَلَمْتُ

نَفْسِيْ وَاَسْلَمْتُ مَعَ سُلَيْمٰنَ لِلّٰهِ رَبِّ الْعٰلَمِيْنَ ۝

وَلَقَدْ اَرْسَلْنَاۤ اِلٰى ثَمُوْدَ اَخَاهُمْ صٰلِحًا اَنِ

اعْبُدُوا اللّٰهَ فَاِذَا هُمْ فَرِيْقٰنِ يَخْتَصِمُوْنَ ۝ قَالَ

The miracle of Sulayman's scholarly following shows the power of spiritual knowledge when guided by a prophet.

The queen's throne is brought to Sulayman

[38] *Sulayman* asked *his courtiers,* "Who can bring me her throne before they come to me in submission?" [39] An Efreet from the jinns said, "I can bring it to you before you get up from your place; I am strong *and* trustworthy." [40] *Another,* who had knowledge *of* the Book, said, "I can bring it to you in the blinking of an eye." When *Sulayman* saw it installed before him, he said, "This is by My Lord's favour, to test whether I am grateful or ungrateful. Whoever is grateful is grateful for his own benefit; but whoever is ungrateful *harms only himself,* as my Lord is Self-Sufficient, Generous." [41] He said, "Disguise her throne so that we can see if she is guided or not."

The queen comes to Sulayman

[42] After arriving, *the Queen* was asked, "Is your throne like this?" She said, "It looks just like it." *And Sulayman said,*[a] "We were given prior knowledge, and we submitted *to Allah.* [43] What had *previously* stopped her was what she used to worship beside Allah, as she came from a disbelieving community." [44] "Enter the *royal* chamber," she was told. When she saw it, she thought it was a pool and so bared her legs *to keep her robes dry. Sulayman* said, "The chamber is paved with glass." She said, "My Lord, I have wronged myself, but *now* I submit with Sulayman to Allah, the Lord of the worlds."

The story of the Prophet Salih

[45] We sent to *the people of* Thamud their brother Salih, *saying*: "Worship Allah," but they *split into* two groups and began to argue.

---

[a] Al-Qurtubi offers three alternatives for the speaker of these words: the Queen of Sheba, Sulayman ﷺ, or his followers.

يٰقَوْمِ لِمَ تَسْتَعْجِلُوْنَ بِالسَّيِّئَةِ قَبْلَ الْحَسَنَةِ ۚ

لَوْ لَا تَسْتَغْفِرُوْنَ اللهَ لَعَلَّكُمْ تُرْحَمُوْنَ ۞

قَالُوا اطَّيَّرْنَا بِكَ وَ بِمَنْ مَّعَكَ ؕ قَالَ طٰٓئِرُكُمْ

عِنْدَ اللهِ بَلْ اَنْتُمْ قَوْمٌ تُفْتَنُوْنَ ۞ وَ كَانَ فِى

الْمَدِيْنَةِ تِسْعَةُ رَهْطٍ يُّفْسِدُوْنَ فِى الْاَرْضِ

وَ لَا يُصْلِحُوْنَ ۞ قَالُوْا تَقَاسَمُوْا بِاللهِ لَنُبَيِّتَنَّهٗ

وَ اَهْلَهٗ ثُمَّ لَنَقُوْلَنَّ لِوَلِيِّهٖ مَا شَهِدْنَا مَهْلِكَ

اَهْلِهٖ وَ اِنَّا لَصٰدِقُوْنَ ۞ وَ مَكَرُوْا مَكْرًا وَّ مَكَرْنَا

مَكْرًا وَّ هُمْ لَا يَشْعُرُوْنَ ۞ فَانْظُرْ كَيْفَ كَانَ عَاقِبَةُ

مَكْرِهِمْ ۙ اَنَّا دَمَّرْنٰهُمْ وَ قَوْمَهُمْ اَجْمَعِيْنَ ۞

فَتِلْكَ بُيُوْتُهُمْ خَاوِيَةً ۢ بِمَا ظَلَمُوْا ؕ اِنَّ فِى ذٰلِكَ

لَاٰيَةً لِّقَوْمٍ يَّعْلَمُوْنَ ۞ وَ اَنْجَيْنَا الَّذِيْنَ اٰمَنُوْا

وَ كَانُوْا يَتَّقُوْنَ ۞ وَ لُوْطًا اِذْ قَالَ لِقَوْمِهٖٓ اَتَاْتُوْنَ

الْفَاحِشَةَ وَ اَنْتُمْ تُبْصِرُوْنَ ۞ اَئِنَّكُمْ لَتَاْتُوْنَ

الرِّجَالَ شَهْوَةً مِّنْ دُوْنِ النِّسَآءِ ؕ بَلْ اَنْتُمْ

قَوْمٌ تَجْهَلُوْنَ ۞ فَمَا كَانَ جَوَابَ قَوْمِهٖٓ اِلَّآ اَنْ

قَالُوْٓا اَخْرِجُوْٓا اٰلَ لُوْطٍ مِّنْ قَرْيَتِكُمْ ۚ اِنَّهُمْ اُنَاسٌ

يَّتَطَهَّرُوْنَ ۞ فَاَنْجَيْنٰهُ وَ اَهْلَهٗٓ اِلَّا امْرَاَتَهٗ ۫ قَدَّرْنٰهَا

مِنَ الْغٰبِرِيْنَ ۞ وَ اَمْطَرْنَا عَلَيْهِمْ مَّطَرًا ۚ فَسَآءَ

مَطَرُ الْمُنْذَرِيْنَ ۞ قُلِ الْحَمْدُ لِلهِ وَ سَلٰمٌ عَلٰى

The repetition of stories of human disobedience should teach us how destructive this path is, and we should follow the righteous.

⁴⁶ *Salih* said, "My people, why are you in a rush to do evil rather than good? If you would only seek Allah's forgiveness, you will be shown kindness." ⁴⁷ They said, "We feel uneasy about you and those with you." He said, "Your feeling of unease *rests* with Allah. The fact is that, as a people, you are being tested." ⁴⁸ There was a gang of nine *men* in the city who would not comply but went around wreaking havoc. ⁴⁹ They said, "Let us swear by Allah to attack him and his family by night, then tell his guardian that we were not witnesses to his family's demise and that we are telling the truth." ⁵⁰ They hatched a plot, and so We countered it; but they remained unaware. ⁵¹ Behold the outcome of their plot: We destroyed them all, and their community. ⁵² These are their houses, razed to the ground because of their wrongdoing. In that, there is a sign for people who know. ⁵³ And We saved those who believed and were mindful *of Us*.

The story of the Prophet Lut
⁵⁴ And remember Lut, when he said to his people: "How can you commit *acts of* indecency with your eyes wide open? ⁵⁵ Do you approach other men with lust rather than women? You people are utterly foolish." ⁵⁶ The only response they gave: "Expel Lut's household from your city, they are such puritans." ⁵⁷ So We saved him and his family except for his wife, whom We decreed would stay behind; ⁵⁸ and We pelted them with a rain *of brimstone.* How dreadful was the rain on those who had been forewarned!

Arguments about the creative power of Allah
⁵⁹ Say: "Praise be to Allah, and peace be upon His chosen servants! Is Allah better or whatever they associate *with Him*?"

عِبَادِهِ الَّذِيْنَ اصْطَفٰىؕ آللّٰهُ خَيْرٌ اَمَّا يُشْرِكُوْنَ ۝

اَمَّنْ خَلَقَ السَّمٰوٰتِ وَالْاَرْضَ وَاَنْزَلَ لَكُمْ مِّنَ

السَّمَآءِ مَآءً ۚ فَاَنْۢبَتْنَا بِهٖ حَدَآئِقَ ذَاتَ بَهْجَةٍ ۚ مَا كَانَ

لَكُمْ اَنْ تُنْۢبِتُوْا شَجَرَهَاؕ ءَاِلٰهٌ مَّعَ اللّٰهِؕ بَلْ هُمْ قَوْمٌ

يَّعْدِلُوْنَ ۝ اَمَّنْ جَعَلَ الْاَرْضَ قَرَارًا وَّجَعَلَ خِلٰلَهَآ

اَنْهٰرًا وَّجَعَلَ لَهَا رَوَاسِيَ وَجَعَلَ بَيْنَ الْبَحْرَيْنِ

حَاجِزًاؕ ءَاِلٰهٌ مَّعَ اللّٰهِؕ بَلْ اَكْثَرُهُمْ لَا يَعْلَمُوْنَ ۝

اَمَّنْ يُّجِيْبُ الْمُضْطَرَّ اِذَا دَعَاهُ وَيَكْشِفُ السُّوْٓءَ وَ

يَجْعَلُكُمْ خُلَفَآءَ الْاَرْضِؕ ءَاِلٰهٌ مَّعَ اللّٰهِؕ قَلِيْلًا مَّا

تَذَكَّرُوْنَ ۝ اَمَّنْ يَّهْدِيْكُمْ فِيْ ظُلُمٰتِ الْبَرِّ وَالْبَحْرِ

وَمَنْ يُّرْسِلُ الرِّيٰحَ بُشْرًۢا بَيْنَ يَدَيْ رَحْمَتِهٖؕ ءَاِلٰهٌ

مَّعَ اللّٰهِؕ تَعٰلَى اللّٰهُ عَمَّا يُشْرِكُوْنَ ۝ اَمَّنْ يَّبْدَؤُا الْخَلْقَ

ثُمَّ يُعِيْدُهٗ وَمَنْ يَّرْزُقُكُمْ مِّنَ السَّمَآءِ وَالْاَرْضِؕ ءَاِلٰهٌ

مَّعَ اللّٰهِؕ قُلْ هَاتُوْا بُرْهَانَكُمْ اِنْ كُنْتُمْ صٰدِقِيْنَ ۝

قُلْ لَّا يَعْلَمُ مَنْ فِي السَّمٰوٰتِ وَالْاَرْضِ الْغَيْبَ اِلَّا اللّٰهُؕ

وَمَا يَشْعُرُوْنَ اَيَّانَ يُبْعَثُوْنَ ۝ بَلِ ادّٰرَكَ عِلْمُهُمْ فِي

الْاٰخِرَةِ ۟ بَلْ هُمْ فِيْ شَكٍّ مِّنْهَا ۠ بَلْ هُمْ مِّنْهَا عَمُوْنَ ۝

وَقَالَ الَّذِيْنَ كَفَرُوْٓا ءَاِذَا كُنَّا تُرٰبًا وَّاٰبَآؤُنَآ اَئِنَّا

لَمُخْرَجُوْنَ ۝ لَقَدْ وُعِدْنَا هٰذَا نَحْنُ وَاٰبَآؤُنَا مِنْ قَبْلُ ۙ

اِنْ هٰذَآ اِلَّآ اَسَاطِيْرُ الْاَوَّلِيْنَ ۝ قُلْ سِيْرُوْا فِي الْاَرْضِ

True knowledge comes from reflection in nature and the realisation of Divine creative power.

⁶⁰ Who is it Who created the Heavens and the Earth and sends down rain for you from the sky with which We have produced delightful gardens. You cannot make its trees grow? Is there *another* god along with Allah? On the contrary, they are people who have turned away from truth. ⁶¹ Who is it Who made the Earth a place *for you* to live, made rivers to flow in it, made mountains, and set a barrier between the two seas? Is there *another* god along with Allah? No, most of them are ignorant.

Allah relieves human anxieties

⁶² Who answers the distressed when they cry out to Him, removes suffering, and causes you to inherit the land? Is there *another* god beside Allah? How little do you reflect! ⁶³ Who is it Who guides you through the darkness on land and sea; and Who is it Who sends winds heralding glad tidings of His kindness *in the form of rain*? Is there *another* god beside Allah? Allah is far exalted above anything they associate as partners *with Him*!

Allah is the absolute Creator

⁶⁴ Who sets in motion *the process of* creation, then returns it *to its former state*; and Who provides for you from the Earth and sky? Is there *another* god beside Allah? Say: "Fetch your proof, if you are telling the truth." ⁶⁵ Say: "No one in the Heavens or on Earth has knowledge of the unseen except Allah; nor do they have any knowledge of when they will be resurrected." ⁶⁶ Can their knowledge comprehend the Hereafter? On the contrary, they have doubts about it; in fact, they are blind to it.

The disbelievers deny the resurrection

⁶⁷ The disbelievers say, "How can it be that when we and our forefathers have turned to dust we will be brought back *to life*? ⁶⁸ We and our forefathers were promised this before. This is merely a tale of the ancient people." ⁶⁹ Say: "Travel on the Earth and see the fate of the sinners."

فَانْظُرُوْا كَيْفَ كَانَ عَاقِبَةُ الْمُجْرِمِيْنَ ۶۹ وَلَا تَحْزَنْ عَلَيْهِمْ

وَلَا تَكُنْ فِيْ ضَيْقٍ مِّمَّا يَمْكُرُوْنَ ۷۰ وَيَقُوْلُوْنَ مَتٰى هٰذَا

الْوَعْدُ اِنْ كُنْتُمْ صٰدِقِيْنَ ۷۱ قُلْ عَسٰى اَنْ يَّكُوْنَ رَدِفَ

لَكُمْ بَعْضُ الَّذِيْ تَسْتَعْجِلُوْنَ ۷۲ وَاِنَّ رَبَّكَ لَذُوْ فَضْلٍ

عَلَى النَّاسِ وَلٰكِنَّ اَكْثَرَهُمْ لَا يَشْكُرُوْنَ ۷۳ وَاِنَّ رَبَّكَ

لَيَعْلَمُ مَا تُكِنُّ صُدُوْرُهُمْ وَمَا يُعْلِنُوْنَ ۷۴ وَمَا مِنْ

غَآئِبَةٍ فِي السَّمَآءِ وَالْاَرْضِ اِلَّا فِيْ كِتٰبٍ مُّبِيْنٍ ۷۵ اِنَّ هٰذَا

الْقُرْاٰنَ يَقُصُّ عَلٰى بَنِيْ اِسْرَآءِيْلَ اَكْثَرَ الَّذِيْ هُمْ فِيْهِ

يَخْتَلِفُوْنَ ۷۶ وَاِنَّهٗ لَهُدًى وَّرَحْمَةٌ لِّلْمُؤْمِنِيْنَ ۷۷ اِنَّ

رَبَّكَ يَقْضِيْ بَيْنَهُمْ بِحُكْمِهٖ وَهُوَ الْعَزِيْزُ الْعَلِيْمُ ۷۸

فَتَوَكَّلْ عَلَى اللّٰهِ اِنَّكَ عَلَى الْحَقِّ الْمُبِيْنِ ۷۹ اِنَّكَ لَا تُسْمِعُ

الْمَوْتٰى وَلَا تُسْمِعُ الصُّمَّ الدُّعَآءَ اِذَا وَلَّوْا مُدْبِرِيْنَ ۸۰

وَمَآ اَنْتَ بِهٰدِى الْعُمْيِ عَنْ ضَلٰلَتِهِمْ اِنْ تُسْمِعُ اِلَّا

مَنْ يُّؤْمِنُ بِاٰيٰتِنَا فَهُمْ مُّسْلِمُوْنَ ۸۱ وَاِذَا وَقَعَ الْقَوْلُ

عَلَيْهِمْ اَخْرَجْنَا لَهُمْ دَآبَّةً مِّنَ الْاَرْضِ تُكَلِّمُهُمْ اَنَّ

النَّاسَ كَانُوْا بِاٰيٰتِنَا لَا يُوْقِنُوْنَ ۸۲ وَيَوْمَ نَحْشُرُ مِنْ كُلِّ

اُمَّةٍ فَوْجًا مِّمَّنْ يُّكَذِّبُ بِاٰيٰتِنَا فَهُمْ يُوْزَعُوْنَ ۸۳ حَتّٰى

اِذَا جَآءُوْ قَالَ اَكَذَّبْتُمْ بِاٰيٰتِيْ وَلَمْ تُحِيْطُوْا بِهَا عِلْمًا

اَمَّا ذَا كُنْتُمْ تَعْمَلُوْنَ ۸۴ وَوَقَعَ الْقَوْلُ عَلَيْهِمْ بِمَا

ظَلَمُوْا فَهُمْ لَا يَنْطِقُوْنَ ۸۵ اَلَمْ يَرَوْا اَنَّا جَعَلْنَا الَّيْلَ

The stubbornness of the Makkans deterred them from following the Messenger ﷺ. Are you stubborn?

⁷⁰ Do not grieve over them, *Messenger,* nor be anxious about what they are plotting. ⁷¹ They say, "When will this promise be fulfilled, if you are telling the truth?" ⁷² Say: "It may be, what you seek to hasten is already close behind you." ⁷³ Your Lord is most gracious towards people, but most are ungrateful.

Allah's infinite knowledge

⁷⁴ And your Lord knows whatever their hearts conceal, and what they reveal. ⁷⁵ There is nothing hidden in the Earth or sky which is not *found* in a Clear Book. ⁷⁶ This Quran narrates most of the disagreements of the Israelites. ⁷⁷ It is a guidance and kindness for the believers. ⁷⁸ Your Lord will decide wisely between them. He is the Almighty, the Knowing. ⁷⁹ So trust in Allah, *for* you are clearly in the right. ⁸⁰ You can no more make the deaf hear the call than you can the dead, if they turn their backs on you; ⁸¹ nor are you there to guide the blind away from their error. Only those will hear you who believe in Our signs and submit *to Our will.*

When Allah's promise against the disbelievers is fulfilled

⁸² When the judgement against them comes to pass, We shall bring forth from the Earth a beast that will tell them *about* the people who didn't believe in Our signs. ⁸³ And on the Day when We gather from every community an army of those who denied Our signs, they will march in ranks. ⁸⁴ And, when they arrive *before Him,* He will say, "Did you deny My signs *despite* not comprehending them? *If not,* what were you doing?" ⁸⁵ And, as the decree is passed against them because of their wrongdoing, they will say nothing.

لِيَسْكُنُوْا فِيْهِ وَالنَّهَارَ مُبْصِرًا ۖ اِنَّ فِيْ ذٰلِكَ لَاٰيٰتٍ
لِّقَوْمٍ يُّؤْمِنُوْنَ ۝ وَيَوْمَ يُنْفَخُ فِى الصُّوْرِ فَفَزِعَ مَنْ
فِى السَّمٰوٰتِ وَمَنْ فِى الْاَرْضِ اِلَّا مَنْ شَآءَ اللّٰهُ ؕ وَكُلٌّ
اَتَوْهُ دٰخِرِيْنَ ۝ وَتَرَى الْجِبَالَ تَحْسَبُهَا جَامِدَةً
وَّهِىَ تَمُرُّ مَرَّ السَّحَابِ ؕ صُنْعَ اللّٰهِ الَّذِىْٓ اَتْقَنَ كُلَّ
شَىْءٍ ؕ اِنَّهٗ خَبِيْرٌۢ بِمَا تَفْعَلُوْنَ ۝ مَنْ جَآءَ بِالْحَسَنَةِ
فَلَهٗ خَيْرٌ مِّنْهَا ۚ وَهُمْ مِّنْ فَزَعٍ يَّوْمَىِٕذٍ اٰمِنُوْنَ ۝
وَمَنْ جَآءَ بِالسَّيِّئَةِ فَكُبَّتْ وُجُوْهُهُمْ فِى النَّارِ ؕ هَلْ
تُجْزَوْنَ اِلَّا مَا كُنْتُمْ تَعْمَلُوْنَ ۝ اِنَّمَآ اُمِرْتُ اَنْ اَعْبُدَ
رَبَّ هٰذِهِ الْبَلْدَةِ الَّذِىْ حَرَّمَهَا وَلَهٗ كُلُّ شَىْءٍ ۫
وَاُمِرْتُ اَنْ اَكُوْنَ مِنَ الْمُسْلِمِيْنَ ۙ وَاَنْ اَتْلُوَا الْقُرْاٰنَ ۚ
فَمَنِ اهْتَدٰى فَاِنَّمَا يَهْتَدِىْ لِنَفْسِهٖ ۚ وَمَنْ ضَلَّ فَقُلْ
اِنَّمَآ اَنَا مِنَ الْمُنْذِرِيْنَ ۝ وَقُلِ الْحَمْدُ لِلّٰهِ سَيُرِيْكُمْ
اٰيٰتِهٖ فَتَعْرِفُوْنَهَا ؕ وَمَا رَبُّكَ بِغَافِلٍ عَمَّا تَعْمَلُوْنَ ۝

Science and technology are reproducing the miracles of nature in a way we can see, feel and use. Have you noticed Allah's power in modern gadgets?

The Trumpet sounds to mark the start of Judgement Day

⁸⁶ Haven't they seen We made the night for them to rest and the day to give them light? In that, there is a sign for people who believe. ⁸⁷ And on the Day that the Trumpet is blown, all those in the Heavens and the Earth will be terrified except those whom Allah pleases *to protect*; each of them shall come to Him, humbly. ⁸⁸ And you will see the mountains, which you thought were fixed, floating like clouds. This is the handiwork of Allah, Who has perfected everything. He is fully aware of what you do. ⁸⁹ Whoever brings good deeds with him, shall receive even better *in return*; and they will be safe from the terror of that Day; ⁹⁰ but anyone who comes with evil deeds will be hurled face-down into the Fire *and asked*: "Have you not been rewarded for what you did?"

The Prophet ﷺ is taught what to say to his community

⁹¹ "I have been ordered to worship the Lord of this city, Who made it sacred, and all things belong to Him; and I have been ordered to be among the committed, ⁹² who recite the Quran." *Thereafter,* whoever is guided it is for his own benefit; and anyone who goes astray tell them: "I am a warner." ⁹³ And say: "Praise be to Allah. He will show you His signs and you will recognise them. Your Lord is not unaware of what you do."

28. Surat Al-Qasas
The Story

This surat was revealed in the late Makkan period, just before the Ascension of the Prophet ﷺ in the tenth year of his mission. It relates several stories from the life of Musa ﷺ to show that history keeps repeating despite the passage of time. A convincing consolation for the Messenger ﷺ and his followers. It opens by describing the Pharaoh's oppression of the Israelites, and his policy of "divide and rule". This is the amazing story of the survival of baby Musa ﷺ at a time when Pharaoh's policy to kill all newborns was ruthlessly enforced. The Pharaoh is most likely Ramesses II, roughly from 1300 BC. Allah not only protected Musa ﷺ, but made him grow up like a prince in the opulent surroundings of Pharaoh's palace. The story highlights the weakness of a worldly king unable to distinguish between foe and friend, yet claiming to be "Almighty God", revealing the extent to which powerful men and women are deceived. The surat then relates the incident when Musa ﷺ killed an Egyptian in defence of an Israelite ... Musa was about to be arrested but managed to escape. He hurriedly left Egypt, and travelled to Madyan in the Arabian desert. Here he was given asylum by an elderly man, the Prophet Shuyab ﷺ. Musa ﷺ agreed to live and work for him in return for marriage to his daughter, so Musa ﷺ married a non-Israelite woman.

Musa ﷺ, who was raised as a prince in a palace, became a poor shepherd in the desert – a sharp contrast in lifestyle. The Divine Plan has its own way of unfolding reality. As a shepherd, Musa ﷺ was being trained for the role of leadership, looking after a flock of sheep. Not much different from caring for an uncouth and undisciplined community.

After ten years, Musa ﷺ returns to Egypt. On the way he passes Mount Sinai, where he is commissioned as a prophet to invite the Pharaoh to accept guidance. After relating the story of Musa ﷺ in detail, the Quran reminds the Prophet ﷺ: "You were not *present* on the west side *of the mountain* when We handed down *Our* commandments to Musa" (44). The Quran asks, isn't this proof the Prophet ﷺ receives revelation?

The Quran rejects the request of the Makkans for a written Quran; and reminds them Musa ﷺ had the Torah written on tablets, but still people denied it. However, the Quran goes on to praise those people who believed in it from the Arabs, the Jews and the Christians (53–54).

After a lengthy commentary that describes the fate of the idolaters in the Hereafter, the surat returns to the story of Musa ﷺ and picks up with the story of Qarun, the wealthiest

Israelite in Egypt. It vividly paints his pompous lifestyle, his miserly attitude and pride. Through the stories of Musa, Pharaoh, and Qarun, the surat explains human craving for worldly power and wealth. The cold-hearted way Pharaoh maintained a tight grip on people; the miserliness of Qarun, shows human greed. He ascribed his wealth to his knowledge and expertise in business and prudence in worldly affairs. The leaders of Makkah refused to believe, like Pharaoh, because they feared losing their hegemony and control of the Kaaba. Such reasoning continues today: as many of us fail to live by the Quran due to fear of worldly losses.

بِسْمِ اللهِ الرَّحْمٰنِ الرَّحِيْمِ

طٰسٓمّ ۞ تِلْكَ اٰيٰتُ الْكِتٰبِ الْمُبِيْنِ ۞ نَتْلُوْا عَلَيْكَ مِنْ نَّبَاِ مُوْسٰى وَفِرْعَوْنَ بِالْحَقِّ لِقَوْمٍ يُّؤْمِنُوْنَ ۞ اِنَّ فِرْعَوْنَ عَلَا فِى الْاَرْضِ وَجَعَلَ اَهْلَهَا شِيَعًا يَّسْتَضْعِفُ طَآئِفَةً مِّنْهُمْ يُذَبِّحُ اَبْنَآءَهُمْ وَيَسْتَحْىٖ نِسَآءَهُمْ ط اِنَّهٗ كَانَ مِنَ الْمُفْسِدِيْنَ ۞ وَنُرِيْدُ اَنْ نَّمُنَّ عَلَى الَّذِيْنَ اسْتُضْعِفُوْا فِى الْاَرْضِ وَنَجْعَلَهُمْ اَئِمَّةً وَّنَجْعَلَهُمُ الْوٰرِثِيْنَ ۞ وَنُمَكِّنَ لَهُمْ فِى الْاَرْضِ وَنُرِىَ فِرْعَوْنَ وَهَامٰنَ وَجُنُوْدَهُمَا مِنْهُمْ مَّا كَانُوْا يَحْذَرُوْنَ ۞ وَاَوْحَيْنَاۤ اِلٰى اُمِّ مُوْسٰۤى اَنْ اَرْضِعِيْهِ ۚ فَاِذَا خِفْتِ عَلَيْهِ فَاَلْقِيْهِ فِى الْيَمِّ وَلَا تَخَافِىْ وَلَا تَحْزَنِىْ ۚ اِنَّا رَآدُّوْهُ اِلَيْكِ وَجَاعِلُوْهُ مِنَ الْمُرْسَلِيْنَ ۞ فَالْتَقَطَهٗۤ اٰلُ فِرْعَوْنَ لِيَكُوْنَ لَهُمْ عَدُوًّا وَّحَزَنًا ط اِنَّ فِرْعَوْنَ وَهَامٰنَ وَجُنُوْدَهُمَا كَانُوْا خٰطِئِيْنَ ۞ وَقَالَتِ امْرَاَتُ فِرْعَوْنَ قُرَّتُ عَيْنٍ لِّىْ وَلَكَ ط لَا تَقْتُلُوْهُ ۖ عَسٰۤى اَنْ يَّنْفَعَنَاۤ اَوْ نَتَّخِذَهٗ وَلَدًا وَّهُمْ لَا يَشْعُرُوْنَ ۞ وَاَصْبَحَ فُؤَادُ اُمِّ مُوْسٰى فٰرِغًا ط اِنْ كَادَتْ لَتُبْدِىْ بِهٖ لَوْلَاۤ اَنْ رَّبَطْنَا عَلٰى قَلْبِهَا لِتَكُوْنَ مِنَ الْمُؤْمِنِيْنَ ۞ وَقَالَتْ لِاُخْتِهٖ قُصِّيْهِ ۖ فَبَصُرَتْ بِهٖ عَنْ جُنُبٍ

The Pharaoh claimed to be mighty, yet he didn't know that the baby in his palace will one day destroy his kingdom.

In the name of Allah, the Kind, the Caring.

[1] *Ta Sin Meem.*

Pharaoh adopts the strategy of divide and rule

[2] These are verses of the Clear Book, [3] *in which* We recite to you part of the true story of Musa and Pharaoh for those who believe. [4] Pharaoh was unjust to people, and divided them by *their* ethnicity. Oppressing one group of them by killing their sons whilst keeping their women alive, he oppressed others. [5] Our plan was to favour the victims in the land and to make them leaders and heirs; [6] to settle them in the land and, through them, to force Pharaoh, Haman[a] and their armies to face their worst fears.

The story of Musa's infancy

[7] We inspired the mother of Musa: "Breastfeed him, but when you fear for him then *put him in a basket* and let it float on the river, but don't be afraid or sad. We shall return him to you and make him a messenger. [8] *Members of* Pharaoh's household found him *by chance, little did they know* he would become their enemy and a cause of grief. Pharaoh, Haman and their armies were gravely mistaken. [9] Pharaoh's wife said, "He would be a joy to behold for me and you, so don't kill him he may be useful for us, or we could adopt him. They were unaware of its consequences." [10] By the morning Musa's mother was impatient and she nearly revealed his *identity*, if We hadn't strengthened her resolve to *remain* silent about him. [11] She told his sister: "Follow him." From the river bank she kept an eye on him without letting *the Egyptians* see her.

---

[a] Haman was the high priest of the Egyptian god Amon. Haman ranked second only to the reigning Pharaoh. (Asad)

وَهُمْ لَا يَشْعُرُونَ ﴿١١﴾ وَحَرَّمْنَا عَلَيْهِ الْمَرَاضِعَ مِن

قَبْلُ فَقَالَتْ هَلْ اَدُلُّكُمْ عَلٰى اَهْلِ بَيْتٍ يَّكْفُلُونَهُ

لَكُمْ وَهُمْ لَهٗ نٰصِحُونَ ﴿١٢﴾ فَرَدَدْنٰهُ اِلٰٓى اُمِّهٖ كَيْ تَقَرَّ

عَيْنُهَا وَلَا تَحْزَنَ وَلِتَعْلَمَ اَنَّ وَعْدَ اللّٰهِ حَقٌّ وَّلٰكِنَّ

اَكْثَرَهُمْ لَا يَعْلَمُونَ ﴿١٣﴾ وَلَمَّا بَلَغَ اَشُدَّهٗ وَاسْتَوٰٓى

اٰتَيْنٰهُ حُكْمًا وَّعِلْمًا ؕ وَكَذٰلِكَ نَجْزِى الْمُحْسِنِيْنَ ﴿١٤﴾

وَدَخَلَ الْمَدِيْنَةَ عَلٰى حِيْنِ غَفْلَةٍ مِّنْ اَهْلِهَا فَوَجَدَ

فِيْهَا رَجُلَيْنِ يَقْتَتِلٰنِ ۗ هٰذَا مِنْ شِيْعَتِهٖ وَهٰذَا

مِنْ عَدُوِّهٖ ۚ فَاسْتَغَاثَهُ الَّذِىْ مِنْ شِيْعَتِهٖ عَلَى

الَّذِىْ مِنْ عَدُوِّهٖ ۙ فَوَكَزَهٗ مُوْسٰى فَقَضٰى عَلَيْهِ ۖ قَالَ

هٰذَا مِنْ عَمَلِ الشَّيْطٰنِ ؕ اِنَّهٗ عَدُوٌّ مُّضِلٌّ مُّبِيْنٌ ﴿١٥﴾

قَالَ رَبِّ اِنِّىْ ظَلَمْتُ نَفْسِىْ فَاغْفِرْ لِىْ فَغَفَرَ لَهٗ ؕ اِنَّهٗ

هُوَ الْغَفُوْرُ الرَّحِيْمُ ﴿١٦﴾ قَالَ رَبِّ بِمَآ اَنْعَمْتَ عَلَىَّ فَلَنْ

اَكُوْنَ ظَهِيْرًا لِّلْمُجْرِمِيْنَ ﴿١٧﴾ فَاَصْبَحَ فِى الْمَدِيْنَةِ

خَآئِفًا يَّتَرَقَّبُ فَاِذَا الَّذِى اسْتَنْصَرَهٗ بِالْاَمْسِ

يَسْتَصْرِخُهٗ ؕ قَالَ لَهٗ مُوْسٰٓى اِنَّكَ لَغَوِىٌّ مُّبِيْنٌ ﴿١٨﴾

فَلَمَّآ اَنْ اَرَادَ اَنْ يَّبْطِشَ بِالَّذِىْ هُوَ عَدُوٌّ لَّهُمَا ۙ

قَالَ يٰمُوْسٰٓى اَتُرِيْدُ اَنْ تَقْتُلَنِىْ كَمَا قَتَلْتَ نَفْسًا

بِالْاَمْسِ ۖ اِنْ تُرِيْدُ اِلَّآ اَنْ تَكُوْنَ جَبَّارًا فِى

الْاَرْضِ وَمَا تُرِيْدُ اَنْ تَكُوْنَ مِنَ الْمُصْلِحِيْنَ ﴿١٩﴾ وَجَآءَ

Musa could tell the difference between the works of Allah and Satan, so he admits the mistake he made. Are you so forthcoming?

[12] We made him reject *the breast milk of* the wet nurses, so *his sister* said to them, "Shall I show you a household that will look after him for you and take good care of him?" [13] So We returned him to his mother, to be a *comforting* sight for her *sore* eyes, so she wouldn't be anxious and know that Allah's promise is true. Though most *people* don't know.

Musa attempts to sort out a racial fight

[14] When he had grown up and reached maturity, We blessed him with wisdom and knowledge; that's how We reward the righteous. [15] One day, he entered the town while people were resting[a] and found two men fighting, one from his ethnic group and the other from his enemy. The one from his ethnic group cried out to him for help against the one from his enemy's *group*; so Musa punched him, so hard that it finished him off. *Musa* said, "This is the work of Satan. He is clearly an enemy who leads *people* astray."

Musa's prayer for forgiveness

[16] *Then* he said, "My Lord, I have done wrong, so forgive me." Allah forgave him; the Forgiving, the Caring. [17] *Musa* said, "My Lord, because you gave me *favours* I will never stand up for criminals *again*." [18] From then on he became fearful in the town, *constantly* on the lookout. *Next day*, the man who previously sought his help again cried out. Musa said, "You are clearly a deceitful man." [19] *Musa* tried to grab the enemy and *the Israelite* said, "Musa, are you going to kill me like you killed someone yesterday? You want to be an oppressor in the land; you've no wish to do good."

---

[a] Another meaning could be: "when its residents no longer recognised him."

رَجُلٌ مِّنْ اَقْصَا الْمَدِيْنَةِ يَسْعٰى ۙ قَالَ يٰمُوْسٰٓى اِنَّ

الْمَلَاَ يَاْتَمِرُوْنَ بِكَ لِيَقْتُلُوْكَ فَاخْرُجْ اِنِّيْ لَكَ مِنَ

النّٰصِحِيْنَ ۲۰ فَخَرَجَ مِنْهَا خَآئِفًا يَّتَرَقَّبُ ۖ قَالَ رَبِّ

نَجِّنِيْ مِنَ الْقَوْمِ الظّٰلِمِيْنَ ۲۱ وَلَمَّا تَوَجَّهَ تِلْقَآءَ مَدْيَنَ

قَالَ عَسٰى رَبِّيْٓ اَنْ يَّهْدِيَنِيْ سَوَآءَ السَّبِيْلِ ۲۲ وَلَمَّا وَرَدَ

مَآءَ مَدْيَنَ وَجَدَ عَلَيْهِ اُمَّةً مِّنَ النَّاسِ يَسْقُوْنَ ۖ۬ وَ

وَجَدَ مِنْ دُوْنِهِمُ امْرَاَتَيْنِ تَذُوْدٰنِ ۚ قَالَ مَا خَطْبُكُمَا ۖ

قَالَتَا لَا نَسْقِيْ حَتّٰى يُصْدِرَ الرِّعَآءُ ۖ وَاَبُوْنَا شَيْخٌ

Notice Musa
volunteering to help the
stranger at the well. How
often do you volunteer?

كَبِيْرٌ ۲۳ فَسَقٰى لَهُمَا ثُمَّ تَوَلّٰٓى اِلَى الظِّلِّ فَقَالَ رَبِّ اِنِّيْ

لِمَآ اَنْزَلْتَ اِلَيَّ مِنْ خَيْرٍ فَقِيْرٌ ۲۴ فَجَآءَتْهُ اِحْدٰىهُمَا

تَمْشِيْ عَلَى اسْتِحْيَآءٍ ۖ قَالَتْ اِنَّ اَبِيْ يَدْعُوْكَ لِيَجْزِيَكَ

اَجْرَ مَا سَقَيْتَ لَنَا ؕ فَلَمَّا جَآءَهُ وَ قَصَّ عَلَيْهِ

الْقَصَصَ ۙ قَالَ لَا تَخَفْ ۣ۟ نَجَوْتَ مِنَ الْقَوْمِ

الظّٰلِمِيْنَ ۲۵ قَالَتْ اِحْدٰىهُمَا يٰٓاَبَتِ اسْتَاْجِرْهُ ۖ اِنَّ

خَيْرَ مَنِ اسْتَاْجَرْتَ الْقَوِيُّ الْاَمِيْنُ ۲۶ قَالَ اِنِّيْٓ اُرِيْدُ

اَنْ اُنْكِحَكَ اِحْدَى ابْنَتَيَّ هٰتَيْنِ عَلٰٓى اَنْ تَاْجُرَنِيْ

ثَمٰنِيَ حِجَجٍ ۚ فَاِنْ اَتْمَمْتَ عَشْرًا فَمِنْ عِنْدِكَ ۚ

وَمَآ اُرِيْدُ اَنْ اَشُقَّ عَلَيْكَ ؕ سَتَجِدُنِيْٓ اِنْ شَآءَ اللّٰهُ

مِنَ الصّٰلِحِيْنَ ۲۷ قَالَ ذٰلِكَ بَيْنِيْ وَبَيْنَكَ ؕ اَيَّمَا

الْاَجَلَيْنِ قَضَيْتُ فَلَا عُدْوَانَ عَلَيَّ ؕ وَاللّٰهُ عَلٰى مَا

[20] A man from the far side of town came running and said, "Musa, members of *Pharaoh's* court are deliberating whether to have you killed, so leave *now*. I am your well-wisher." [21] So he left *the city* in fear and remained wary, he prayed: "My Lord, save me from this nation of wrongdoers."

Musa helps two women at the well of Madyan

[22] Having set out for Madyan, he said to himself: "Maybe, My Lord will guide me on the right path."[a] [23] After he arrived at the water *well* of Madyan, he found a large crowd of people watering *their flocks*. He saw standing apart from them two women, holding *their sheep* back. He asked: "What is the matter with you?" They said, "We can't water *our sheep* until the shepherds move off, our father is an elderly man, *unable to help us*." [24] So *Musa* watered *their sheep*, then he turned *to rest* in the shade, praying: "My Lord, I am in *desperate* need of whatever good You may send down to me."

Musa accepts a marriage proposal

[25] One of *the two women* came to him, walking shyly, and said, "My father is calling you, to reward you for watering *our flock*." *Musa* went and told him the *whole* story. *He* said, "Do not be afraid. You have been saved from a nation of wrongdoers." [26] One of *them* said, "My dear father, *why not* employ him? The best person you can employ is strong and trustworthy." [27] He said, "I wish to marry you to one of the two daughters of mine, on the condition that you work for me for eight years. If you complete ten years, that will be up to you. I won't impose it on you. Allah willing, you will find me to be upright *in my dealings*." [28] *Musa* said, "That's *agreed* between you and me. Whichever of the two terms I fulfil, let there be no resentment towards me; and let Allah be a guarantor of what we *decide*."

---

[a] Madyan is the Biblical Midian, this is the area of the gulf of Aqaba and extended eastward towards the Dead Sea.

نَقُولُ وَكِيلٌ ۝ فَلَمَّا قَضَى مُوسَى الْأَجَلَ وَسَارَ بِأَهْلِهِ

اٰنَسَ مِنْ جَانِبِ الطُّورِ نَارًا ۚ قَالَ لِأَهْلِهِ امْكُثُوٓا

اِنِّيٓ اٰنَسْتُ نَارًا لَّعَلِّيٓ اٰتِيكُمْ مِّنْهَا بِخَبَرٍ أَوْ جَذْوَةٍ

مِّنَ النَّارِ لَعَلَّكُمْ تَصْطَلُونَ ۝ فَلَمَّآ أَتٰهَا نُودِيَ مِنْ

شَاطِئِ الْوَادِ الْأَيْمَنِ فِي الْبُقْعَةِ الْمُبٰرَكَةِ مِنَ

الشَّجَرَةِ أَنْ يّٰمُوسٰىٓ اِنِّيٓ أَنَا اللهُ رَبُّ الْعٰلَمِينَ ۝ وَ

أَنْ أَلْقِ عَصَاكَ ۚ فَلَمَّا رَاٰهَا تَهْتَزُّ كَأَنَّهَا جَآنٌّ وَّلّٰى

مُدْبِرًا وَّلَمْ يُعَقِّبْ ۚ يٰمُوسٰىٓ أَقْبِلْ وَلَا تَخَفْ ۖ

اِنَّكَ مِنَ الْاٰمِنِينَ ۝ اُسْلُكْ يَدَكَ فِي جَيْبِكَ تَخْرُجْ

بَيْضَآءَ مِنْ غَيْرِ سُوٓءٍ ۖ وَّاضْمُمْ اِلَيْكَ جَنَاحَكَ مِنَ

الرَّهْبِ فَذٰنِكَ بُرْهَانَانِ مِنْ رَّبِّكَ اِلٰى فِرْعَوْنَ وَ

مَلَإِيهِ ۚ اِنَّهُمْ كَانُوا قَوْمًا فٰسِقِينَ ۝ قَالَ رَبِّ

اِنِّي قَتَلْتُ مِنْهُمْ نَفْسًا فَأَخَافُ أَنْ يَّقْتُلُونِ ۝

وَأَخِي هٰرُونُ هُوَ أَفْصَحُ مِنِّي لِسَانًا فَأَرْسِلْهُ مَعِيَ

رِدْءًا يُّصَدِّقُنِيٓ ۖ اِنِّيٓ أَخَافُ أَنْ يُّكَذِّبُونِ ۝ قَالَ

سَنَشُدُّ عَضُدَكَ بِأَخِيكَ وَنَجْعَلُ لَكُمَا سُلْطٰنًا

فَلَا يَصِلُونَ اِلَيْكُمَا ۚ بِاٰيٰتِنَآ ۚ أَنْتُمَا وَمَنِ اتَّبَعَكُمَا

الْغٰلِبُونَ ۝ فَلَمَّا جَآءَهُمْ مُّوسٰى بِاٰيٰتِنَا بَيِّنٰتٍ

قَالُوا مَا هٰذَآ اِلَّا سِحْرٌ مُّفْتَرًى وَّمَا سَمِعْنَا بِهٰذَا

فِيٓ اٰبَآئِنَا الْأَوَّلِينَ ۝ وَقَالَ مُوسٰى رَبِّيٓ أَعْلَمُ

The burning bush was a milestone in Musa's life. What is the milestone in your life?

Musa moves from Madyan back to Egypt

²⁹ Once Musa had completed his term in Madyan, he set off with his family *to Egypt*. On the way he noticed a fire *burning* by the side of the mountain, he told his wife, "Wait here for a while. I've noticed a fire. Maybe I'll bring you some news from there or some embers from the fire so that you may warm yourselves." ³⁰ When he reached it, a voice called out from the tree on the right-hand side of the valley in that blessed spot: "Musa, it is I, Allah, the Lord of the worlds. ³¹ Throw down your *shepherd's* staff." When he saw it wriggling *like a snake*, he turned and fled, without looking back. "Musa, go ahead and pick it up, and don't be afraid. You are safe. ³² Put your hand inside your shirt, and it will come out *brilliant* white and unharmed, and hold it under the armpit *to rid yourself* of fear.ᵃ Here are two proofs from your Lord to show to Pharaoh and his nobles; they are sinners."

Musa asks for support

³³ *Musa* said, "My Lord, I killed one of their men, I fear they'll kill me. ³⁴ My brother, Harun, is more eloquent in speech than I am, so send him with me as a support to confirm *what I say, for* I fear they will reject me." ³⁵ *Allah* said, "We shall strengthen your arm with your brother and give you both authority, so that they don't harm you; because of Our signs,ᵇ the two of you and whoever follows you will be victorious."

Musa moves into Pharaoh's court

³⁶ When Musa came with Our clear signs to them, they said, "This is nothing but clever tricks of magic; and we never heard this *message* from our forefathers."

ᵃ Shah Waliyallah explained this idiom; "now gather your thoughts, overcome your doubts and anxiety."
ᵇ In the Arabic text, the words "because of Our signs" can go with either the phrase before, or the one after.

بِمَنْ جَآءَ بِالْهُدٰى مِنْ عِنْدِهٖ وَمَنْ تَكُوْنُ لَهٗ
عَاقِبَةُ الدَّارِ ۚ اِنَّهٗ لَا يُفْلِحُ الظّٰلِمُوْنَ ۞ وَقَالَ
فِرْعَوْنُ يٰٓاَيُّهَا الْمَلَاُ مَا عَلِمْتُ لَكُمْ مِّنْ اِلٰهٍ
غَيْرِيْ ۚ فَاَوْقِدْ لِيْ يٰهَامٰنُ عَلَى الطِّيْنِ فَاجْعَلْ لِّيْ
صَرْحًا لَّعَلِّيْٓ اَطَّلِعُ اِلٰٓى اِلٰهِ مُوْسٰى ۙ وَاِنِّيْ لَاَظُنُّهٗ
مِنَ الْكٰذِبِيْنَ ۞ وَاسْتَكْبَرَ هُوَ وَجُنُوْدُهٗ فِى الْاَرْضِ
بِغَيْرِ الْحَقِّ وَظَنُّوْٓا اَنَّهُمْ اِلَيْنَا لَا يُرْجَعُوْنَ ۞
فَاَخَذْنٰهُ وَجُنُوْدَهٗ فَنَبَذْنٰهُمْ فِى الْيَمِّ ۚ فَانْظُرْ كَيْفَ
كَانَ عَاقِبَةُ الظّٰلِمِيْنَ ۞ وَجَعَلْنٰهُمْ اَئِمَّةً يَّدْعُوْنَ
اِلَى النَّارِ ۚ وَيَوْمَ الْقِيٰمَةِ لَا يُنْصَرُوْنَ ۞ وَاَتْبَعْنٰهُمْ
فِيْ هٰذِهِ الدُّنْيَا لَعْنَةً ۚ وَيَوْمَ الْقِيٰمَةِ هُمْ مِّنَ
الْمَقْبُوْحِيْنَ ۞ وَلَقَدْ اٰتَيْنَا مُوْسَى الْكِتٰبَ مِنْ بَعْدِ
مَآ اَهْلَكْنَا الْقُرُوْنَ الْاُوْلٰى بَصَآئِرَ لِلنَّاسِ وَهُدًى
وَّرَحْمَةً لَّعَلَّهُمْ يَتَذَكَّرُوْنَ ۞ وَمَا كُنْتَ بِجَانِبِ
الْغَرْبِيِّ اِذْ قَضَيْنَآ اِلٰى مُوْسَى الْاَمْرَ وَمَا كُنْتَ
مِنَ الشّٰهِدِيْنَ ۞ وَلٰكِنَّآ اَنْشَاْنَا قُرُوْنًا فَتَطَاوَلَ
عَلَيْهِمُ الْعُمُرُ ۚ وَمَا كُنْتَ ثَاوِيًا فِيْٓ اَهْلِ مَدْيَنَ
تَتْلُوْا عَلَيْهِمْ اٰيٰتِنَا ۙ وَلٰكِنَّا كُنَّا مُرْسِلِيْنَ ۞ وَمَا
كُنْتَ بِجَانِبِ الطُّوْرِ اِذْ نَادَيْنَا وَلٰكِنْ رَّحْمَةً مِّنْ
رَّبِّكَ لِتُنْذِرَ قَوْمًا مَّآ اَتٰىهُمْ مِّنْ نَّذِيْرٍ مِّنْ قَبْلِكَ

Musa is blessed with Divine guidance and insights, a distinct way that Allah cares for His people.

³⁷ Musa said, "My Lord knows best who comes from Him with His guidance and who will *enjoy* the Final Abode; *but* the wrongdoers won't succeed." ³⁸ Pharaoh said, "*My* nobles, I know of no other god for you than myself. Haman, bake *bricks* of clay and build a tower for me, so that I may ascend to the God of Musa, though I know he's a liar." ³⁹ And *so it was that* he and his armies, were falsely arrogant in the country, thinking they would never be returned to Us. ⁴⁰ So We seized him and his armies and threw them into the sea. See the fate of the wrongdoers! ⁴¹ We made them foremost amongst those who call *others* to the Fire; and on Judgement Day, they will be helpless. ⁴² We tracked them with a curse in this world and, on Judgement Day, they will be the most despised.

Muhammad ﷺ is a sign of Allah's kindness for the Makkans

⁴³ We gave Musa the Book, after We destroyed previous *rebellious* generations, to be examples[a] for *all* people, a guidance and kindness, so they might pay heed. ⁴⁴ You were not *present* on the west side *of the mountain* when We handed down *Our* commandments to Musa, you weren't a witness. ⁴⁵ However, We raised *successive* generations, who lived long lives. Nor did you live among the people of Madyan, reciting Our verses to them, but We sent *them* messengers nonetheless. ⁴⁶ Nor were you on the mountainside when We called *Musa*, but *you have been sent* as a kindness from your Lord to warn those people to whom no warner was sent before you, so they might wake up *to the reality.*

---

[a] Literally to give them 'insights'.

لَعَلَّهُمْ يَتَذَكَّرُوْنَ ۞ وَلَوْلَا اَنْ تُصِيْبَهُمْ مُّصِيْبَةٌۢ

بِمَا قَدَّمَتْ اَيْدِيْهِمْ فَيَقُوْلُوْا رَبَّنَا لَوْلَا اَرْسَلْتَ

اِلَيْنَا رَسُوْلًا فَنَتَّبِعَ اٰيٰتِكَ وَنَكُوْنَ مِنَ الْمُؤْمِنِيْنَ ۞

فَلَمَّا جَآءَهُمُ الْحَقُّ مِنْ عِنْدِنَا قَالُوْا لَوْلَا اُوْتِيَ

مِثْلَ مَآ اُوْتِيَ مُوْسٰى ط اَوَلَمْ يَكْفُرُوْا بِمَآ اُوْتِيَ

مُوْسٰى مِنْ قَبْلُ ۚ قَالُوْا سِحْرٰنِ تَظَاهَرَا ۣقف وَّقَالُوْٓا اِنَّا

بِكُلٍّ كٰفِرُوْنَ ۞ قُلْ فَأْتُوْا بِكِتٰبٍ مِّنْ عِنْدِ اللّٰهِ هُوَ

اَهْدٰى مِنْهُمَآ اَتَّبِعْهُ اِنْ كُنْتُمْ صٰدِقِيْنَ ۞ فَاِنْ لَّمْ

The Makkans failed to
appreciate the Quran, so
they lost. How much do
you value the Quran?

يَسْتَجِيْبُوْا لَكَ فَاعْلَمْ اَنَّمَا يَتَّبِعُوْنَ اَهْوَآءَهُمْ ط وَمَنْ

اَضَلُّ مِمَّنِ اتَّبَعَ هَوٰىهُ بِغَيْرِ هُدًى مِّنَ اللّٰهِ ط اِنَّ

اللّٰهَ لَا يَهْدِي الْقَوْمَ الظّٰلِمِيْنَ ۞ وَلَقَدْ وَصَّلْنَا

لَهُمُ الْقَوْلَ لَعَلَّهُمْ يَتَذَكَّرُوْنَ ۞ اَلَّذِيْنَ اٰتَيْنٰهُمُ

الْكِتٰبَ مِنْ قَبْلِهِ هُمْ بِهٖ يُؤْمِنُوْنَ ۞ وَاِذَا يُتْلٰى

عَلَيْهِمْ قَالُوْٓا اٰمَنَّا بِهٖٓ اِنَّهُ الْحَقُّ مِنْ رَّبِّنَآ اِنَّا كُنَّا

مِنْ قَبْلِهٖ مُسْلِمِيْنَ ۞ اُولٰٓئِكَ يُؤْتَوْنَ اَجْرَهُمْ مَّرَّتَيْنِ

بِمَا صَبَرُوْا وَيَدْرَءُوْنَ بِالْحَسَنَةِ السَّيِّئَةَ وَمِمَّا

رَزَقْنٰهُمْ يُنْفِقُوْنَ ۞ وَاِذَا سَمِعُوا اللَّغْوَ اَعْرَضُوْا

عَنْهُ وَقَالُوْا لَنَآ اَعْمَالُنَا وَلَكُمْ اَعْمَالُكُمْ ۠ سَلٰمٌ

عَلَيْكُمْ ۠ لَا نَبْتَغِي الْجٰهِلِيْنَ ۞ اِنَّكَ لَا تَهْدِيْ مَنْ

اَحْبَبْتَ وَلٰكِنَّ اللّٰهَ يَهْدِيْ مَنْ يَّشَآءُ ۚ وَهُوَ

Pride prevents them pursuing the Prophet ﷺ

⁴⁷ When a disaster strikes them due to their *evil* actions they pray: "Our Lord, had You sent us a messenger, we would have followed Your verses and become believers." ⁴⁸ However, when Our truth reached them, they said, "Why wasn't he given a book like the one Musa was given?" They also denied what was given to Musa, saying, "Two competing works of magic!"^a And said, "We reject each *of them*"? ⁴⁹ Say: "So produce a book from Allah for me to follow that is a better guide than either of them, if you are telling the truth." ⁵⁰ If they fail to respond to you, then know that they are following their impulses. And who is more misguided than the one who follows his impulses without any guidance from Allah. Allah does not guide people who do wrong.

Christians and Jewish believers praised^b

⁵¹ We caused the *message* to reach them so they may pay heed. ⁵² Those given the Book previously believe in it; ⁵³ and when it is recited to them, they say: "We believe in it. It is the truth from our Lord; and *even* before this we had surrendered ourselves *to Allah's will*." ⁵⁴ Such people will be given double reward because of their patience and *secondly* they stop evil with good, and they spend *in charity* what We provided them; ⁵⁵ and when they hear idle talk they turn away from it, saying: "We have our deeds, and you have yours. Peace be upon you. We don't envy the ignorant." ⁵⁶ *Messenger,* you can't guide who you love. But Allah guides anyone He chooses. And Allah knows the guided.

---

^a The Quran and Torah.
^b This refers to the group of Jews like Abdullah ibn Salam and some Christians who became Muslims.

اَعْلَمُ بِالْمُهْتَدِيْنَ ۞ وَقَالُوْاۤ اِنْ نَّتَّبِعِ الْهُدٰى مَعَكَ

نُتَخَطَّفْ مِنْ اَرْضِنَا ؕ اَوَلَمْ نُمَكِّنْ لَّهُمْ حَرَمًا اٰمِنًا

يُّجْبٰۤى اِلَيْهِ ثَمَرٰتُ كُلِّ شَىْءٍ رِّزْقًا مِّنْ لَّدُنَّا وَ

لٰكِنَّ اَكْثَرَهُمْ لَا يَعْلَمُوْنَ ۞ وَكَمْ اَهْلَكْنَا مِنْ قَرْيَةٍ

بَطِرَتْ مَعِيْشَتَهَا ۚ فَتِلْكَ مَسٰكِنُهُمْ لَمْ تُسْكَنْ مِّنْ

بَعْدِهِمْ اِلَّا قَلِيْلًا ؕ وَكُنَّا نَحْنُ الْوٰرِثِيْنَ ۞ وَمَا

كَانَ رَبُّكَ مُهْلِكَ الْقُرٰى حَتّٰى يَبْعَثَ فِيْۤ اُمِّهَا

رَسُوْلًا يَّتْلُوْا عَلَيْهِمْ اٰيٰتِنَا ۚ وَمَا كُنَّا مُهْلِكِى الْقُرٰى

اِلَّا وَاَهْلُهَا ظٰلِمُوْنَ ۞ وَمَاۤ اُوْتِيْتُمْ مِّنْ شَىْءٍ

فَمَتَاعُ الْحَيٰوةِ الدُّنْيَا وَزِيْنَتُهَا ۚ وَمَا عِنْدَ اللّٰهِ خَيْرٌ

وَّاَبْقٰى ؕ اَفَلَا تَعْقِلُوْنَ ۞ اَفَمَنْ وَّعَدْنٰهُ وَعْدًا حَسَنًا

فَهُوَ لَاقِيْهِ كَمَنْ مَّتَّعْنٰهُ مَتَاعَ الْحَيٰوةِ الدُّنْيَا ثُمَّ

هُوَ يَوْمَ الْقِيٰمَةِ مِنَ الْمُحْضَرِيْنَ ۞ وَيَوْمَ يُنَادِيْهِمْ

فَيَقُوْلُ اَيْنَ شُرَكَآءِىَ الَّذِيْنَ كُنْتُمْ تَزْعُمُوْنَ ۞ قَالَ

الَّذِيْنَ حَقَّ عَلَيْهِمُ الْقَوْلُ رَبَّنَا هٰۤؤُلَآءِ الَّذِيْنَ

اَغْوَيْنَا ۚ اَغْوَيْنٰهُمْ كَمَا غَوَيْنَا ۚ تَبَرَّاْنَاۤ اِلَيْكَ ۫

مَا كَانُوْاۤ اِيَّانَا يَعْبُدُوْنَ ۞ وَقِيْلَ ادْعُوْا شُرَكَآءَكُمْ

فَدَعَوْهُمْ فَلَمْ يَسْتَجِيْبُوْا لَهُمْ وَرَاَوُا الْعَذَابَ ۚ لَوْ

اَنَّهُمْ كَانُوْا يَهْتَدُوْنَ ۞ وَيَوْمَ يُنَادِيْهِمْ فَيَقُوْلُ

مَا ذَاۤ اَجَبْتُمُ الْمُرْسَلِيْنَ ۞ فَعَمِيَتْ عَلَيْهِمُ الْاَنْبَآءُ

The failure to be respectful of the Divine Book led to their ruin, so let us value the Divine Book.

Flouting Allah's call due to household tasks

⁵⁷ The *Makkans* say: "If we followed your religion, then we would be unsafe in our city." Haven't We settled them in a safe and sacred place where fruits of every sort are brought, a provision from Us? Yet most don't know. ⁵⁸ How many cities have We destroyed that were disrespectful due to their *lavish* lifestyles? Their homes are there, scarcely lived in since their day, and We took them. ⁵⁹ Your Lord never destroyed cities without first sending a messenger to their affluent people, who recited to them Our verses; nor did We destroy any city unless its population were wrongdoers.

Short-lived pleasures of this life

⁶⁰ What you receive *from Allah* are the passing pleasures and attractions of this worldly life; but what Allah has stored for you is far better and long lasting. Don't you understand? ⁶¹ Is the person who We made a beautiful promise *of Paradise* the same as the person who enjoys the pleasures of worldly life? On Judgement Day he will be summoned *to account for his deeds*?

False gods are unable to help

⁶² On that Day Allah will call them: "Where are the partners you associated with Me?" ⁶³ Those questioned will say, "Our Lord, here are the ones we led astray. We led them astray since we were misguided. We declare ourselves innocent before You. They were not worshipping us." ⁶⁴ *Then* they will be told: "Call on your partners *for help*," and when they call them they will not answer. When they see the punishment *they'll wish they had*, if only they had been guided. ⁶⁵ On the Day that He calls them, saying: "How did you respond to the messengers?" ⁶⁶ They will be so confused by the events of the Day that they won't be able to consult one another.

يَوْمَئِذٍ فَهُمْ لَا يَتَسَآءَلُوْنَ ۝ فَاَمَّا مَنْ تَابَ وَاٰمَنَ
وَعَمِلَ صَالِحًا فَعَسٰۤى اَنْ يَّكُوْنَ مِنَ الْمُفْلِحِيْنَ ۝

وَرَبُّكَ يَخْلُقُ مَا يَشَآءُ وَيَخْتَارُ ط مَا كَانَ لَهُمُ
الْخِيَرَةُ ط سُبْحٰنَ اللّٰهِ وَتَعٰلٰى عَمَّا يُشْرِكُوْنَ ۝

وَرَبُّكَ يَعْلَمُ مَا تُكِنُّ صُدُوْرُهُمْ وَمَا يُعْلِنُوْنَ ۝

وَهُوَ اللّٰهُ لَاۤ اِلٰهَ اِلَّا هُوَ ط لَهُ الْحَمْدُ فِى الْاُوْلٰى
وَالْاٰخِرَةِ ز وَلَهُ الْحُكْمُ وَاِلَيْهِ تُرْجَعُوْنَ ۝ قُلْ

The complexity and the power of nature all point to Allah's creativity. Why don't you see it?

اَرَءَيْتُمْ اِنْ جَعَلَ اللّٰهُ عَلَيْكُمُ الَّيْلَ سَرْمَدًا اِلٰى
يَوْمِ الْقِيٰمَةِ مَنْ اِلٰهٌ غَيْرُ اللّٰهِ يَاْتِيْكُمْ بِضِيَآءٍ ط
اَفَلَا تَسْمَعُوْنَ ۝ قُلْ اَرَءَيْتُمْ اِنْ جَعَلَ اللّٰهُ عَلَيْكُمُ
النَّهَارَ سَرْمَدًا اِلٰى يَوْمِ الْقِيٰمَةِ مَنْ اِلٰهٌ غَيْرُ اللّٰهِ
يَاْتِيْكُمْ بِلَيْلٍ تَسْكُنُوْنَ فِيْهِ ط اَفَلَا تُبْصِرُوْنَ ۝

وَمِنْ رَّحْمَتِهٖ جَعَلَ لَكُمُ الَّيْلَ وَالنَّهَارَ لِتَسْكُنُوْا
فِيْهِ وَلِتَبْتَغُوْا مِنْ فَضْلِهٖ وَلَعَلَّكُمْ تَشْكُرُوْنَ ۝

وَيَوْمَ يُنَادِيْهِمْ فَيَقُوْلُ اَيْنَ شُرَكَآءِىَ الَّذِيْنَ
كُنْتُمْ تَزْعُمُوْنَ ۝ وَنَزَعْنَا مِنْ كُلِّ اُمَّةٍ شَهِيْدًا
فَقُلْنَا هَاتُوْا بُرْهَانَكُمْ فَعَلِمُوْۤا اَنَّ الْحَقَّ لِلّٰهِ وَ
ضَلَّ عَنْهُمْ مَّا كَانُوْا يَفْتَرُوْنَ ۝ اِنَّ قَارُوْنَ
كَانَ مِنْ قَوْمِ مُوْسٰى فَبَغٰى عَلَيْهِمْ ص وَاٰتَيْنٰهُ
مِنَ الْكُنُوْزِ مَاۤ اِنَّ مَفَاتِحَهٗ لَتَنُوْۤاُ بِالْعُصْبَةِ

There is hope for those who repent

[67] Those who repented, believed and performed good deeds will be among the successful. [68] Your Lord creates whatever He wills and *then* makes His selection; the choice is not theirs. Glory be to Allah! Far exalted is Allah above whatever they associate *with Him* as partners. [69] And your Lord knows what their hearts conceal and reveal. [70] He is Allah. There is no god but Him. All praise in this world and the next is His. The *Final* Judgement rests with Him, and to Him you will return.

Can anyone other than Allah recreate night and day?

[71] Say: "Have you considered if Allah plunged you into unending night until Judgement Day; which god beside Allah could bring you light? Do you not hear?" [72] Say: "Have you considered if Allah were to make your daylight unending until Judgement Day; which god is there beside Allah to bring you night in which to rest? Do you not see?" [73] Through His kindness, He has made for you both night and day so you may rest in one and seek his bounty *in the other*, and be thankful. [74] On the Day that He calls them, saying: "Where are the partners that you ascribed to Me?" [75] On that Day, We shall take from each community a witness and say, "Fetch *Me* your proof," so they know the truth belongs to Allah, and that whatever they invented has deserted them.

The smugness of Qarun, the rich Israelite

[76] Qarun was from Musa's people, but unkind to them[a]. We gave him so much treasure that the keys alone would have weighed down a dozen or so strong men. His people told him, "Do not be proud *of your wealth*. Allah dislikes those who brag.

---

[a]   Qarun is the Biblical Korah.

اُولِى الْقُوَّةِ ۚ اِذْ قَالَ لَهٗ قَوْمُهٗ لَا تَفْرَحْ اِنَّ اللّٰهَ

لَا يُحِبُّ الْفَرِحِيْنَ ۝ وَابْتَغِ فِيْمَاۤ اٰتٰىكَ اللّٰهُ

الدَّارَ الْاٰخِرَةَ وَلَا تَنْسَ نَصِيْبَكَ مِنَ الدُّنْيَا

وَاَحْسِنْ كَمَاۤ اَحْسَنَ اللّٰهُ اِلَيْكَ وَلَا تَبْغِ الْفَسَادَ

فِى الْاَرْضِ ؕ اِنَّ اللّٰهَ لَا يُحِبُّ الْمُفْسِدِيْنَ ۝ قَالَ

اِنَّمَاۤ اُوْتِيْتُهٗ عَلٰى عِلْمٍ عِنْدِىْ ؕ اَوَلَمْ يَعْلَمْ اَنَّ

اللّٰهَ قَدْ اَهْلَكَ مِنْ قَبْلِهٖ مِنَ الْقُرُوْنِ مَنْ

هُوَ اَشَدُّ مِنْهُ قُوَّةً وَّ اَكْثَرُ جَمْعًا ؕ وَلَا يُسْئَلُ

What stops people from believing in the Hereafter? Materialism, the pleasures of a worldly life, neglect and laziness.

عَنْ ذُنُوْبِهِمُ الْمُجْرِمُوْنَ ۝ فَخَرَجَ عَلٰى قَوْمِهٖ فِىْ

زِيْنَتِهٖ ؕ قَالَ الَّذِيْنَ يُرِيْدُوْنَ الْحَيٰوةَ الدُّنْيَا

يٰلَيْتَ لَنَا مِثْلَ مَاۤ اُوْتِىَ قَارُوْنُ ۙ اِنَّهٗ لَذُوْ حَظٍّ

عَظِيْمٍ ۝ وَقَالَ الَّذِيْنَ اُوْتُوا الْعِلْمَ وَيْلَكُمْ

ثَوَابُ اللّٰهِ خَيْرٌ لِّمَنْ اٰمَنَ وَعَمِلَ صَالِحًا ۚ وَلَا

يُلَقّٰىهَاۤ اِلَّا الصّٰبِرُوْنَ ۝ فَخَسَفْنَا بِهٖ وَبِدَارِهِ

الْاَرْضَ ۟ فَمَا كَانَ لَهٗ مِنْ فِئَةٍ يَّنْصُرُوْنَهٗ

مِنْ دُوْنِ اللّٰهِ ۖ وَمَا كَانَ مِنَ الْمُنْتَصِرِيْنَ ۝

وَاَصْبَحَ الَّذِيْنَ تَمَنَّوْا مَكَانَهٗ بِالْاَمْسِ يَقُوْلُوْنَ

وَيْكَاَنَّ اللّٰهَ يَبْسُطُ الرِّزْقَ لِمَنْ يَّشَآءُ مِنْ

عِبَادِهٖ وَيَقْدِرُ ۚ لَوْلَاۤ اَنْ مَّنَّ اللّٰهُ عَلَيْنَا لَخَسَفَ

بِنَا ۚ وَيْكَاَنَّهٗ لَا يُفْلِحُ الْكٰفِرُوْنَ ۝ تِلْكَ الدَّارُ

[77] Instead use some of what Allah has given you to secure *your place in* the Final home, at the same time not losing your share of this world. Treat *others* as well as Allah has treated you; and do not wreak havoc in the land. Allah dislikes those who wreak havoc." [78] *Qarun* said, "I've been given it because of *my expertise and* knowledge." Didn't he realise that Allah destroyed *people of* previous generations who were far stronger and wealthier than him? The guilty won't be asked about their sins.

A lesson for those who envied Qarun

[79] *So one day* he went out among his people, *dressed* in his finery; and those who yearn for this worldly life said, "Oh, if only we had been given the same as Qarun. He's most fortunate!" [80] But those who had been given knowledge said, "Woe to you! Allah's reward for believers and the righteous is better; the patient will achieve that." [81] So *it was* We made the Earth swallow him and his mansion; there was no *rescue* party to help him beside Allah, nor was he able to protect himself. [82] Those who only the other day had longed to be in his place said, "Alas! It seems Allah gives in abundance to whichever of His servants He pleases, and in strict measure. If Allah hadn't been gracious to us, He might have destroyed us *too*. Alas! It's apparent the ungrateful fail."

الْاٰخِرَةُ نَجْعَلُهَا لِلَّذِيْنَ لَا يُرِيْدُوْنَ عُلُوًّا فِی
الْاَرْضِ وَلَا فَسَادًا ؕ وَالْعَاقِبَةُ لِلْمُتَّقِيْنَ ﴿٨٣﴾ مَنْ
جَآءَ بِالْحَسَنَةِ فَلَهٗ خَيْرٌ مِّنْهَا ۚ وَمَنْ جَآءَ
بِالسَّيِّئَةِ فَلَا يُجْزَى الَّذِيْنَ عَمِلُوا السَّيِّاٰتِ
اِلَّا مَا كَانُوْا يَعْمَلُوْنَ ﴿٨٤﴾ اِنَّ الَّذِیْ فَرَضَ عَلَيْكَ
الْقُرْاٰنَ لَرَآدُّكَ اِلٰی مَعَادٍ ؕ قُلْ رَّبِّیْۤ اَعْلَمُ مَنْ
جَآءَ بِالْهُدٰی وَمَنْ هُوَ فِیْ ضَلٰلٍ مُّبِيْنٍ ﴿٨٥﴾
وَمَا كُنْتَ تَرْجُوْۤا اَنْ يُّلْقٰۤی اِلَيْكَ الْكِتٰبُ اِلَّا
رَحْمَةً مِّنْ رَّبِّكَ فَلَا تَكُوْنَنَّ ظَهِيْرًا لِّلْكٰفِرِيْنَ ﴿٨٦﴾ ز
وَلَا يَصُدُّنَّكَ عَنْ اٰيٰتِ اللّٰهِ بَعْدَ اِذْ اُنْزِلَتْ اِلَيْكَ
وَادْعُ اِلٰی رَبِّكَ وَلَا تَكُوْنَنَّ مِنَ الْمُشْرِكِيْنَ ﴿٨٧﴾ ج
وَلَا تَدْعُ مَعَ اللّٰهِ اِلٰهًا اٰخَرَ ۘ لَاۤ اِلٰهَ اِلَّا
هُوَ قف كُلُّ شَیْءٍ هَالِكٌ اِلَّا وَجْهَهٗ ؕ لَهُ الْحُكْمُ
وَاِلَيْهِ تُرْجَعُوْنَ ﴿٨٨﴾ ع

ع ٩ ٦ ١٢ الثلثة

Here is a Divine promise of victory to anyone willing to be an obedient servant.

⁸³ Such is the Final Abode; We grant it to those who desire neither grandeur nor wreak havoc in the land. And the *best* outcome is for those mindful *of Allah*. ⁸⁴ Anyone who does good deeds will be generously rewarded with something wonderful; and anyone who does evil deeds will be rewarded for what they did.

The gift of the Quran and the promise of returning home one day

⁸⁵ The Legislator of *the laws of* the Quran will return you *to Makkah*. Say: "My Lord knows who is guided and who is misguided." ⁸⁶ You weren't expecting to be given the Book, it was due to your Lord's kindness. So, don't be a helper of the disbelievers; ⁸⁷ and let no one distract you from *acting on* Allah's verses after they are revealed to you. Call *people* to your Lord, and don't be an associator of partners *with Allah*. ⁸⁸ Don't call others god beside Allah. There is no god but Him. Everything will perish except His being.^a He will make the *Final* Judgement, and to Him you will be returned.

---

^a Literally: Execpt his face.

29. Surat Al-ʿAnkabut

The Spider

Most commentators class this as the last Makkan surat. This is apparent from its confrontational character tempered by rational and historical evidence warning the people of Makkah against their folly. The intense persecution made it dangerous to be a follower of the beloved Messenger ﷺ. The surat opens with a reminder to the believers: life is full of tests and success comes by passing them. The reward for their Jihad, hard work and tireless effort is nothing less than victory; mentioned in the closing verse of the surat: "Those who strive *hard* for Our sake, We shall guide them along on Our ways. Allah is with those who do good" (69).

What lies between these two ends are details and processes for achieving success. The central theme is the constant confrontation between belief and disbelief – symbolised by the antagonism between Ibrahim ﷺ and Nimrod; the tussle between Musa ﷺ and Pharaoh, and the struggle between Nuh ﷺ and his people. So, the Prophet ﷺ is bolstered to face hostility from the likes of Abu Jahl and Abu Lahab.

The metaphor of the spider's web is used to convey the weak and fragile nature of worldly power, in contrast to the enduring nature of Allah's religion. The Quran says: "An example of those who adopt gods beside Allah is like a spider that spins a web – and a spider's web is the weakest of homes" (41). A sharp criticism of idolatry, love of the world, and denial of the truth, but what is at stake is so precious that the Quran employs such devices to awaken the dead conscience of idolaters, and people drunk with the material world.

Two instructions stand out: perform the prayer regularly, and be polite to People of The Book:

"Recite the Book revealed to you, *messenger*, and perform the prayer. Without doubt, prayer protects from indecency and evil; and to remember Allah is greater *still*; and Allah knows well what you do. *Believers*, debate courteously with People of The Book" (45–46).

بِسْمِ اللّٰهِ الرَّحْمٰنِ الرَّحِیْمِ

الٓمّٓ ۚ﴿١﴾ اَحَسِبَ النَّاسُ اَنْ یُّتْرَكُوْۤا اَنْ یَّقُوْلُوْۤا اٰمَنَّا وَهُمْ لَا یُفْتَنُوْنَ ﴿٢﴾ وَلَقَدْ فَتَنَّا الَّذِیْنَ مِنْ قَبْلِهِمْ فَلَیَعْلَمَنَّ اللّٰهُ الَّذِیْنَ صَدَقُوْا وَلَیَعْلَمَنَّ الْكٰذِبِیْنَ ﴿٣﴾ اَمْ حَسِبَ الَّذِیْنَ یَعْمَلُوْنَ السَّیِّاٰتِ اَنْ یَّسْبِقُوْنَا ؕ سَآءَ مَا یَحْكُمُوْنَ ﴿٤﴾ مَنْ كَانَ یَرْجُوْا لِقَآءَ اللّٰهِ فَاِنَّ اَجَلَ اللّٰهِ لَاٰتٍ ؕ وَهُوَ السَّمِیْعُ الْعَلِیْمُ ﴿٥﴾ وَمَنْ جَاهَدَ فَاِنَّمَا یُجَاهِدُ لِنَفْسِهٖ ؕ اِنَّ اللّٰهَ لَغَنِیٌّ عَنِ الْعٰلَمِیْنَ ﴿٦﴾ وَالَّذِیْنَ اٰمَنُوْا وَعَمِلُوا الصّٰلِحٰتِ لَنُكَفِّرَنَّ عَنْهُمْ سَیِّاٰتِهِمْ وَلَنَجْزِیَنَّهُمْ اَحْسَنَ الَّذِیْ كَانُوْا یَعْمَلُوْنَ ﴿٧﴾ وَوَصَّیْنَا الْاِنْسَانَ بِوَالِدَیْهِ حُسْنًا ؕ وَاِنْ جَاهَدٰكَ لِتُشْرِكَ بِیْ مَا لَیْسَ لَكَ بِهٖ عِلْمٌ فَلَا تُطِعْهُمَا ؕ اِلَیَّ مَرْجِعُكُمْ فَاُنَبِّئُكُمْ بِمَا كُنْتُمْ تَعْمَلُوْنَ ﴿٨﴾ وَالَّذِیْنَ اٰمَنُوْا وَعَمِلُوا الصّٰلِحٰتِ لَنُدْخِلَنَّهُمْ فِی الصّٰلِحِیْنَ ﴿٩﴾ وَمِنَ النَّاسِ مَنْ یَّقُوْلُ اٰمَنَّا بِاللّٰهِ فَاِذَاۤ اُوْذِیَ فِی اللّٰهِ جَعَلَ فِتْنَةَ النَّاسِ كَعَذَابِ اللّٰهِ ؕ وَلَئِنْ جَآءَ نَصْرٌ مِّنْ رَّبِّكَ لَیَقُوْلُنَّ اِنَّا كُنَّا مَعَكُمْ ؕ اَوَلَیْسَ اللّٰهُ بِاَعْلَمَ بِمَا فِیْ صُدُوْرِ الْعٰلَمِیْنَ ﴿١٠﴾ وَلَیَعْلَمَنَّ اللّٰهُ الَّذِیْنَ اٰمَنُوْا وَلَیَعْلَمَنَّ

After Allah's worship, caring for parents is the best deed. Do you care for your parents?

In the name of Allah, the Kind, the Caring.

¹ *Alif Lam Meem.*

Choosing to believe does not mean an instant end to sufferings

² Do people think they will be left alone because they say, "We believe," then will not be tested? ³ We tested those before them. Allah knows the truthful and the liars. ⁴ Or do evildoers think they can beat Us? How wrong they judge! ⁵ Anyone expecting to meet Allah *should know:* Allah's appointed time is *fast* approaching; and He is the Hearer, the Knower. ⁶ Whoever strives hard he strives for his benefit. Allah is Self-Sufficient, *independent* of all creation. ⁷ The believers who do good works will have their sins erased and We shall reward them *in* the best way for what they did.

Caring for parents is a socio-spiritual duty

⁸ We urged humanity to treat their parents well, but if they strive to get you to associate with Me anything you have no knowledge of, then do not obey them. You will return to Me, when I shall inform you of what you did. ⁹ The believers who do good works, We shall join them with the righteous.

Hypocrites lack resolve

¹⁰ Some people say, "We believe in Allah," but when they are persecuted for the sake of Allah, they consider people's persecution like Allah's punishment. But if help arrives from Your Lord, they say, "We were with you *all along.*" Surely Allah knows best what is in people's minds. ¹¹ Allah knows the believers and the hypocrites.

الْمُنٰفِقِيْنَ ⓫ وَقَالَ الَّذِيْنَ كَفَرُوْا لِلَّذِيْنَ اٰمَنُوا

اتَّبِعُوْا سَبِيْلَنَا وَلْنَحْمِلْ خَطٰيٰكُمْ ؕ وَمَا هُمْ بِحٰمِلِيْنَ

مِنْ خَطٰيٰهُمْ مِّنْ شَيْءٍ ؕ اِنَّهُمْ لَكٰذِبُوْنَ ⓬ وَلَيَحْمِلُنَّ

اَثْقَالَهُمْ وَاَثْقَالًا مَّعَ اَثْقَالِهِمْ ؗ وَلَيُسْـَٔلُنَّ يَوْمَ

الْقِيٰمَةِ عَمَّا كَانُوْا يَفْتَرُوْنَ ⓭ وَلَقَدْ اَرْسَلْنَا نُوْحًا

اِلٰى قَوْمِهٖ فَلَبِثَ فِيْهِمْ اَلْفَ سَنَةٍ اِلَّا خَمْسِيْنَ عَامًا ؕ

فَاَخَذَهُمُ الطُّوْفَانُ وَهُمْ ظٰلِمُوْنَ ⓮ فَاَنْجَيْنٰهُ وَ

اَصْحٰبَ السَّفِيْنَةِ وَجَعَلْنٰهَآ اٰيَةً لِّلْعٰلَمِيْنَ ⓯ وَ

Study history and you will see that evildoers always failed. Why don't we learn?

اِبْرٰهِيْمَ اِذْ قَالَ لِقَوْمِهِ اعْبُدُوا اللهَ وَاتَّقُوْهُ ؕ ذٰلِكُمْ

خَيْرٌ لَّكُمْ اِنْ كُنْتُمْ تَعْلَمُوْنَ ⓰ اِنَّمَا تَعْبُدُوْنَ مِنْ

دُوْنِ اللهِ اَوْثَانًا وَّتَخْلُقُوْنَ اِفْكًا ؕ اِنَّ الَّذِيْنَ

تَعْبُدُوْنَ مِنْ دُوْنِ اللهِ لَا يَمْلِكُوْنَ لَكُمْ رِزْقًا

فَابْتَغُوْا عِنْدَ اللهِ الرِّزْقَ وَاعْبُدُوْهُ وَاشْكُرُوْا لَهٗ ؕ

اِلَيْهِ تُرْجَعُوْنَ ⓰ وَاِنْ تُكَذِّبُوْا فَقَدْ كَذَّبَ اُمَمٌ مِّنْ

قَبْلِكُمْ ؕ وَمَا عَلَى الرَّسُوْلِ اِلَّا الْبَلٰغُ الْمُبِيْنُ ⓲ اَوَلَمْ

يَرَوْا كَيْفَ يُبْدِئُ اللهُ الْخَلْقَ ثُمَّ يُعِيْدُهٗ ؕ اِنَّ ذٰلِكَ

عَلَى اللهِ يَسِيْرٌ ⓳ قُلْ سِيْرُوْا فِى الْاَرْضِ فَانْظُرُوْا

كَيْفَ بَدَاَ الْخَلْقَ ثُمَّ اللهُ يُنْشِئُ النَّشْاَةَ الْاٰخِرَةَ ؕ

اِنَّ اللهَ عَلٰى كُلِّ شَيْءٍ قَدِيْرٌ ⓴ يُعَذِّبُ مَنْ يَّشَآءُ

وَيَرْحَمُ مَنْ يَّشَآءُ ؕ وَاِلَيْهِ تُقْلَبُوْنَ ㉑ وَمَآ اَنْتُمْ

Disbelievers make promises they cannot fulfil

¹²The disbelievers say to the believers: "Follow in our footsteps, and we will bear *the burden of* your sins," though they won't carry *the believers'* sins. They are liars. ¹³*However*, they will carry their own burdens and other burdens beside; and on Judgement Day they will be questioned about whatever *falsehoods* they made up.

Two examples of those who rejected Allah

¹⁴We sent Nuh to his people; he lived amid them for one thousand years less fifty. Then the flood destroyed them, they were still *unrepentant* wrongdoers; ¹⁵We saved him and the companions of the Ark, which We made a sign for all people. ¹⁶And Ibrahim *too*, when he said to his people: "Worship Allah and be mindful of Him. That is better for you, if only you knew. ¹⁷Whatever you worship beside Allah are nothing but idols, you create a lie.ᵃ Those you worship beside Allah have no power to provide for you; so seek provision from Allah, worship and thank Him; *eventually* you will return to Him." ¹⁸*Makkans*, if you reject *the message, you will be like* so many other nations before you. The Messenger's task is to convey *the message* clearly.

Our senses are sufficient to infer Allah's existence

¹⁹Have they not considered how Allah sets creation in motion and then *periodically* restores it? That is easy for Allah. ²⁰Say: "Wander about the land and see how He *previously* set creation in motion. Then Allah will bring into being the life of the Hereafter." Allah has power over everything. ²¹He punishes whomever He wills, and He shows kindness to whomever He wills; and *eventually* you will revert back to Him.

ᵃ The idol is a physical structure, a visible shape that the disbeliever gives to a false idea, hence "you create a lie".

بِمُعْجِزِيْنَ فِي الْأَرْضِ وَلَا فِي السَّمَاءِ ز وَمَا لَكُمْ مِّنْ دُوْنِ اللّٰهِ مِنْ وَّلِيٍّ وَّلَا نَصِيْرٍ ۚ وَالَّذِيْنَ كَفَرُوْا بِاٰيٰتِ اللّٰهِ وَلِقَآئِهٖٓ أُولٰٓئِكَ يَئِسُوْا مِنْ رَّحْمَتِيْ وَ أُولٰٓئِكَ لَهُمْ عَذَابٌ أَلِيْمٌ ۞ فَمَا كَانَ جَوَابَ قَوْمِهٖٓ إِلَّآ أَنْ قَالُوا اقْتُلُوْهُ أَوْ حَرِّقُوْهُ فَأَنْجٰهُ اللّٰهُ مِنَ النَّارِ ۚ إِنَّ فِيْ ذٰلِكَ لَاٰيٰتٍ لِّقَوْمٍ يُّؤْمِنُوْنَ ۞ وَقَالَ إِنَّمَا اتَّخَذْتُمْ مِّنْ دُوْنِ اللّٰهِ أَوْثَانًا لا مَّوَدَّةَ بَيْنِكُمْ فِي الْحَيٰوةِ الدُّنْيَا ۚ ثُمَّ يَوْمَ الْقِيٰمَةِ يَكْفُرُ بَعْضُكُمْ بِبَعْضٍ وَّيَلْعَنُ بَعْضُكُمْ بَعْضًا ز وَّمَأْوٰىكُمُ النَّارُ وَمَا لَكُمْ مِّنْ نّٰصِرِيْنَ ۞ فَاٰمَنَ لَهٗ لُوْطٌ م وَقَالَ إِنِّيْ مُهَاجِرٌ إِلٰى رَبِّيْ ط إِنَّهٗ هُوَ الْعَزِيْزُ الْحَكِيْمُ ۞ وَوَهَبْنَا لَهٗٓ إِسْحٰقَ وَيَعْقُوْبَ وَجَعَلْنَا فِيْ ذُرِّيَّتِهِ النُّبُوَّةَ وَالْكِتٰبَ وَاٰتَيْنٰهُ أَجْرَهٗ فِي الدُّنْيَا ۚ وَإِنَّهٗ فِي الْاٰخِرَةِ لَمِنَ الصّٰلِحِيْنَ ۞ وَ لُوْطًا إِذْ قَالَ لِقَوْمِهٖٓ إِنَّكُمْ لَتَأْتُوْنَ الْفَاحِشَةَ ز مَا سَبَقَكُمْ بِهَا مِنْ أَحَدٍ مِّنَ الْعٰلَمِيْنَ ۞ أَئِنَّكُمْ لَتَأْتُوْنَ الرِّجَالَ وَتَقْطَعُوْنَ السَّبِيْلَ ۙ وَتَأْتُوْنَ فِيْ نَادِيْكُمُ الْمُنْكَرَ ۚ فَمَا كَانَ جَوَابَ قَوْمِهٖٓ إِلَّآ أَنْ قَالُوا ائْتِنَا بِعَذَابِ اللّٰهِ إِنْ كُنْتَ مِنَ الصّٰدِقِيْنَ ۞ قَالَ رَبِّ انْصُرْنِيْ عَلَى الْقَوْمِ

Despite being rejected and cruelly treated, the prophets pursued their mission. How committed to Allah are you?

²²You can't defeat *Allah*, either on Earth or in the sky; you have no protector or a helper beside Allah. ²³People who deny Allah's signs and meeting Him despair of *receiving* My kindness, and they will have a painful punishment.

Makkans are invited to reflect on Ibrahim's words

²⁴The only response *Ibrahim's* people gave was: "Kill him," or "Burn him." But Allah rescued him from the fire. There are signs in that for the believers. ²⁵*Ibrahim* said, "The reason you adopted idols beside Allah is the love of this life, something that you have in common. On Judgement Day, you will disown and curse each other when *you see that* your home will be the Fire, and you will have no help."

Lut is rejected by his people

²⁶Lut believed in *Ibrahim* when he told him: "I am migrating to my Lord. He is the Almighty, the Wise." ²⁷We granted *Ibrahim* Ishaq and Yaqub, planting prophethood in his offspring and *knowledge of* the Book; and We rewarded him in this life, and in the Hereafter he will be amid the righteous. ²⁸And Lut, when he said to his people, "You approach gross indecency in a way no one in the whole world has done before you. ²⁹How can you approach men, kidnap *them*, and perform repulsive acts in the clubs where you meet?" His people's response was: "Fetch us Allah's punishment, if you are truthful." ³⁰*Lut* prayed: "My Lord, support me against people who are spoilers."ᵃ

ᵃ 'Mufsideen' here refers to people who damage human society by indulgence in evil.

المُفْسِدِيْنَ ۞ وَلَمَّا جَاۤءَتْ رُسُلُنَاۤ اِبْرٰهِيْمَ

بِالْبُشْرٰى ۙ قَالُوْۤا اِنَّا مُهْلِكُوْۤا اَهْلِ هٰذِهِ الْقَرْيَةِ ۚ

اِنَّ اَهْلَهَا كَانُوْا ظٰلِمِيْنَ ۞ قَالَ اِنَّ فِيْهَا لُوْطًا ؕ

قَالُوْا نَحْنُ اَعْلَمُ بِمَنْ فِيْهَا ۫ لَنُنَجِّيَنَّهٗ وَ اَهْلَهٗۤ

اِلَّا امْرَاَتَهٗ ۫ كَانَتْ مِنَ الْغٰبِرِيْنَ ۞ وَلَمَّاۤ اَنْ

جَاۤءَتْ رُسُلُنَا لُوْطًا سِیْۤءَ بِهِمْ وَضَاقَ بِهِمْ

ذَرْعًا وَّ قَالُوْا لَا تَخَفْ وَلَا تَحْزَنْ ۫ اِنَّا مُنَجُّوْكَ

وَاَهْلَكَ اِلَّا امْرَاَتَكَ كَانَتْ مِنَ الْغٰبِرِيْنَ ۞ اِنَّا

مُنْزِلُوْنَ عَلٰۤى اَهْلِ هٰذِهِ الْقَرْيَةِ رِجْزًا مِّنَ

السَّمَاۤءِ بِمَا كَانُوْا يَفْسُقُوْنَ ۞ وَلَقَدْ تَّرَكْنَا مِنْهَاۤ

اٰيَةًۢ بَيِّنَةً لِّقَوْمٍ يَّعْقِلُوْنَ ۞ وَ اِلٰى مَدْيَنَ

اَخَاهُمْ شُعَيْبًا ۙ فَقَالَ يٰقَوْمِ اعْبُدُوا اللّٰهَ وَارْجُوا

الْيَوْمَ الْاٰخِرَ وَلَا تَعْثَوْا فِى الْاَرْضِ مُفْسِدِيْنَ ۞

فَكَذَّبُوْهُ فَاَخَذَتْهُمُ الرَّجْفَةُ فَاَصْبَحُوْا فِيْ دَارِهِمْ

جٰثِمِيْنَ ۞ وَعَادًا وَّثَمُوْدَا۟ وَقَدْ تَّبَيَّنَ لَكُمْ مِّنْ

مَّسٰكِنِهِمْ ۫ وَزَيَّنَ لَهُمُ الشَّيْطٰنُ اَعْمَالَهُمْ فَصَدَّهُمْ

عَنِ السَّبِيْلِ وَكَانُوْا مُسْتَبْصِرِيْنَ ۞ وَقَارُوْنَ وَ

فِرْعَوْنَ وَهَامٰنَ ۫ وَلَقَدْ جَاۤءَهُمْ مُّوْسٰى بِالْبَيِّنٰتِ

فَاسْتَكْبَرُوْا فِى الْاَرْضِ وَمَا كَانُوْا سٰبِقِيْنَ ۞

فَكُلًّا اَخَذْنَا بِذَنْۢبِهٖ ۚ فَمِنْهُمْ مَّنْ اَرْسَلْنَا عَلَيْهِ

People admit their faults but many remain deceived.

Angels come as terminators

³¹ Our messengers came to Ibrahim with the good news *of a child*, then they told him, "We came to destroy the people of this city, its residents are wrongdoers." ³² He quipped, "But Lut is *living* there." They said, "We know who is *living* there. We will save him and his household, except for his wife, who will remain behind." ³³ When Our messengers came to Lut, he felt distressed since he couldn't protect them, but *the angels* said, "Don't be afraid or sad. We are *here* to save you and your household, except for your wife, who will remain behind. ³⁴ We are to bring down a plague from the sky against the residents of this city because of their habitual sinfulness." ³⁵ We have left *enough remains* of it behind to be a clear sign for people who understand.

A reminder to reflect on the ruins of early communities

³⁶ To Madyan, We sent their brother Shuʿayb, who said: "My people, worship Allah and long for the Last Day, and don't roam the land, wreaking havoc." ³⁷ Yet they rejected him, so an Earthquake took them *all of a sudden* and by the next morning they lay dead in their homes. ³⁸ Similarly, Ad and Thamud, *what happened to them* is quite clear from *the ruins of* their homes. Satan made their deeds appear attractive to them, preventing them from the path *of Allah*, though they could see *right from wrong*.

Four Earthly punishments inflicted on the arrogant

³⁹ Musa came with clear proofs to Qarun, Pharaoh and Haman, but they were arrogant in the land, they weren't the first.

حَاصِبًا ۚ وَمِنْهُمْ مَّنْ اَخَذَتْهُ الصَّیْحَةُ ۚ وَمِنْهُمْ

مَّنْ خَسَفْنَا بِهِ الْاَرْضَ ۚ وَمِنْهُمْ مَّنْ اَغْرَقْنَا ۚ

وَمَا كَانَ اللّٰهُ لِیَظْلِمَهُمْ وَلٰكِنْ كَانُوْۤا اَنْفُسَهُمْ

یَظْلِمُوْنَ ۞ مَثَلُ الَّذِیْنَ اتَّخَذُوْا مِنْ دُوْنِ

اللّٰهِ اَوْلِیَآءَ كَمَثَلِ الْعَنْكَبُوْتِ ۖ اِتَّخَذَتْ بَیْتًا ۚ

وَاِنَّ اَوْهَنَ الْبُیُوْتِ لَبَیْتُ الْعَنْكَبُوْتِ ۘ لَوْ

كَانُوْا یَعْلَمُوْنَ ۞ اِنَّ اللّٰهَ یَعْلَمُ مَا یَدْعُوْنَ

مِنْ دُوْنِهٖ مِنْ شَیْءٍ ؕ وَهُوَ الْعَزِیْزُ الْحَكِیْمُ ۞

وَتِلْكَ الْاَمْثَالُ نَضْرِبُهَا لِلنَّاسِ ۚ وَمَا یَعْقِلُهَاۤ

اِلَّا الْعٰلِمُوْنَ ۞ خَلَقَ اللّٰهُ السَّمٰوٰتِ وَالْاَرْضَ

بِالْحَقِّ ؕ اِنَّ فِیْ ذٰلِكَ لَاٰیَةً لِّلْمُؤْمِنِیْنَ ۞

اُتْلُ مَآ اُوْحِیَ اِلَیْكَ مِنَ الْكِتٰبِ وَاَقِمِ الصَّلٰوةَ ؕ

اِنَّ الصَّلٰوةَ تَنْهٰی عَنِ الْفَحْشَآءِ وَالْمُنْكَرِ ؕ وَلَذِكْرُ اللّٰهِ

اَكْبَرُ ؕ وَاللّٰهُ یَعْلَمُ مَا تَصْنَعُوْنَ ۞ وَلَا تُجَادِلُوْۤا اَهْلَ

الْكِتٰبِ اِلَّا بِالَّتِیْ هِیَ اَحْسَنُ ۖ اِلَّا الَّذِیْنَ ظَلَمُوْا

مِنْهُمْ وَقُوْلُوْۤا اٰمَنَّا بِالَّذِیْۤ اُنْزِلَ اِلَیْنَا وَاُنْزِلَ

اِلَیْكُمْ وَاِلٰهُنَا وَاِلٰهُكُمْ وَاحِدٌ وَّنَحْنُ لَهٗ مُسْلِمُوْنَ ۞

وَكَذٰلِكَ اَنْزَلْنَاۤ اِلَیْكَ الْكِتٰبَ ؕ فَالَّذِیْنَ اٰتَیْنٰهُمُ

الْكِتٰبَ یُؤْمِنُوْنَ بِهٖ ۚ وَمِنْ هٰۤؤُلَآءِ مَنْ یُّؤْمِنُ بِهٖ ؕ

وَمَا یَجْحَدُ بِاٰیٰتِنَاۤ اِلَّا الْكٰفِرُوْنَ ۞ وَمَا كُنْتَ تَتْلُوْا

Reliance on material things is compared with a cobweb; a flimsy structure. Moral and spiritual values provide a much more solid foundation.

⁴⁰ So We punished each one of them for their crime. We sent sand storms; the Blast; swallowed them *in the bowels of* the Earth; and others We drowned. Allah did not wrong any of them; rather, they wronged themselves.

The lies of idolaters are as easily destroyed as a spider's web
⁴¹ An example of those who adopt gods beside Allah is like a spider that spins a web – and a spider's web is the weakest of homes – if only they knew.ᵃ ⁴² Allah knows what they call on beside Him is nothing. He is the Almighty, the Wise. ⁴³ We give people such examples, and the knowledgeable understand them. ⁴⁴ Allah has created the Heavens and the Earth, *and* in that there is a sign for the believers.

Prayer performed properly is a shield against sinfulness
⁴⁵ Recite the Book revealed to you, *messenger*, and perform the prayer. Without doubt, prayer protects from indecency and evil; and to remember Allah is greater *still*; and Allah knows well what you do.

Advice on interfaith dialogue
⁴⁶ *Believers*, debate courteously with People of The Book – except the oppressors among them – and tell them: "We believe in what's revealed to us and what's revealed to you, Our God and your God is One, and we submit to Him." ⁴⁷ That is how We have revealed the Book to you; and those to whom We *previously* gave *a share of* the Book believe in it, just as some of them believe in it; only the disbelievers reject Our signs.

ᵃ "A symbol of false beliefs and values, which in the long run are bound to be blown away by the winds of truth." (Asad)

مِنۡ قَبۡلِهٖ مِنۡ كِتٰبٍ وَّلَا تَخُطُّهٗ بِيَمِيۡنِكَ اِذًا لَّارۡتَابَ الۡمُبۡطِلُوۡنَ ۝ بَلۡ هُوَ اٰيٰتٌۢ بَيِّنٰتٌ فِىۡ صُدُوۡرِ الَّذِيۡنَ اُوۡتُوا الۡعِلۡمَ ؕ وَمَا يَجۡحَدُ بِاٰيٰتِنَاۤ اِلَّا الظّٰلِمُوۡنَ ۝ وَقَالُوۡا لَوۡلَاۤ اُنۡزِلَ عَلَيۡهِ اٰيٰتٌ مِّنۡ رَّبِّهٖ ؕ قُلۡ اِنَّمَا الۡاٰيٰتُ عِنۡدَ اللّٰهِ ؕ وَاِنَّمَاۤ اَنَا نَذِيۡرٌ مُّبِيۡنٌ ۝ اَوَلَمۡ يَكۡفِهِمۡ اَنَّاۤ اَنۡزَلۡنَا عَلَيۡكَ الۡكِتٰبَ يُتۡلٰى عَلَيۡهِمۡ ؕ اِنَّ فِىۡ ذٰلِكَ لَرَحۡمَةً وَّذِكۡرٰى لِقَوۡمٍ يُّؤۡمِنُوۡنَ ۝

Bear with patience, the harshness and the enmity of the disbelievers, or migrate to another place.

قُلۡ كَفٰى بِاللّٰهِ بَيۡنِىۡ وَبَيۡنَكُمۡ شَهِيۡدًا ۚ يَعۡلَمُ مَا فِى السَّمٰوٰتِ وَالۡاَرۡضِ ؕ وَالَّذِيۡنَ اٰمَنُوۡا بِالۡبَاطِلِ وَكَفَرُوۡا بِاللّٰهِ ۙ اُولٰٓئِكَ هُمُ الۡخٰسِرُوۡنَ ۝ وَيَسۡتَعۡجِلُوۡنَكَ بِالۡعَذَابِ ؕ وَلَوۡلَاۤ اَجَلٌ مُّسَمًّى لَّجَآءَهُمُ الۡعَذَابُ ؕ وَلَيَاۡتِيَنَّهُمۡ بَغۡتَةً وَّهُمۡ لَا يَشۡعُرُوۡنَ ۝ يَسۡتَعۡجِلُوۡنَكَ بِالۡعَذَابِ ؕ وَاِنَّ جَهَنَّمَ لَمُحِيۡطَةٌۢ بِالۡكٰفِرِيۡنَ ۝ يَوۡمَ يَغۡشٰهُمُ الۡعَذَابُ مِنۡ فَوۡقِهِمۡ وَمِنۡ تَحۡتِ اَرۡجُلِهِمۡ وَيَقُوۡلُ ذُوۡقُوۡا مَا كُنۡتُمۡ تَعۡمَلُوۡنَ ۝ يٰعِبَادِىَ الَّذِيۡنَ اٰمَنُوۡاۤ اِنَّ اَرۡضِىۡ وَاسِعَةٌ فَاِيَّاىَ فَاعۡبُدُوۡنِ ۝ كُلُّ نَفۡسٍ ذَآئِقَةُ الۡمَوۡتِ ثُمَّ اِلَيۡنَا تُرۡجَعُوۡنَ ۝ وَالَّذِيۡنَ اٰمَنُوۡا وَعَمِلُوا الصّٰلِحٰتِ لَنُبَوِّئَنَّهُمۡ مِّنَ الۡجَنَّةِ غُرَفًا تَجۡرِىۡ مِنۡ تَحۡتِهَا الۡاَنۡهٰرُ خٰلِدِيۡنَ فِيۡهَا ؕ نِعۡمَ اَجۡرُ الۡعٰمِلِيۡنَ ۝ الَّذِيۡنَ صَبَرُوۡا وَعَلٰى رَبِّهِمۡ يَتَوَكَّلُوۡنَ ۝

⁴⁸You did not recite *any* book before, nor did you ever copy it out with your right hand; had you done so then the fault finders would have a reason to doubt. ⁴⁹On the contrary, *it contains* clear verses in the breasts of knowledgeable people. Only wrongdoers reject Our signs.

Why demand miracles when one has the Quran?

⁵⁰They say: "If only miracles were sent down to him from his Lord." Say: "Miracles come from Allah, and I am a clear warner." ⁵¹Isn't it enough that We revealed the Book to you so it may be recited to them? There's kindness and a reminder in that for people who believe. ⁵²Say: "Allah is sufficient witness between me and you. He knows whatever is in the Heavens and the Earth. As for those who believe in falsehood and reject Allah, they are the losers."

Hell has room enough for all who deserve it

⁵³They ask you to hasten the punishment, but the punishment would have already come, if the appointed time hadn't been fixed. And it will strike them suddenly, when they least expect it. ⁵⁴They ask you to hasten the punishment; but Hell is *big enough* to contain the disbelievers ⁵⁵on the Day when the punishment envelops them from above and below their feet, and *Allah* says: "Taste the fruit of your deeds."

Believers allowed to migrate

⁵⁶My believing servants, My Earth is vast, so worship Me *wherever you are.* ⁵⁷Every soul tastes death, then to Us you will be returned; ⁵⁸and *the* believers who perform good deeds shall settle in lofty homes of Paradise under which rivers flow, living there forever. What a wonderful reward for the hard workers, ⁵⁹who were patient and trusted their Lord.

وَکَاَیِّنْ مِّنْ دَآبَّةٍ لَّا تَحْمِلُ رِزْقَهَا ۖ اَللّٰهُ یَرْزُقُهَا

وَاِیَّاکُمْ ۖ وَهُوَ السَّمِیْعُ الْعَلِیْمُ ۝ وَلَئِنْ سَاَلْتَهُمْ

مَّنْ خَلَقَ السَّمٰوٰتِ وَالْاَرْضَ وَسَخَّرَ الشَّمْسَ وَالْقَمَرَ

لَیَقُوْلُنَّ اللّٰهُ ۚ فَاَنّٰی یُؤْفَکُوْنَ ۝ اَللّٰهُ یَبْسُطُ الرِّزْقَ

لِمَنْ یَّشَآءُ مِنْ عِبَادِهٖ وَیَقْدِرُ لَهٗ ؕ اِنَّ اللّٰهَ بِکُلِّ

شَیْءٍ عَلِیْمٌ ۝ وَلَئِنْ سَاَلْتَهُمْ مَّنْ نَّزَّلَ مِنَ السَّمَآءِ

مَآءً فَاَحْیَا بِهِ الْاَرْضَ مِنْ بَعْدِ مَوْتِهَا لَیَقُوْلُنَّ

اللّٰهُ ؕ قُلِ الْحَمْدُ لِلّٰهِ ؕ بَلْ اَکْثَرُهُمْ لَا یَعْقِلُوْنَ ۝

وَمَا هٰذِهِ الْحَیٰوةُ الدُّنْیَاۤ اِلَّا لَهْوٌ وَّلَعِبٌ ؕ وَاِنَّ

الدَّارَ الْاٰخِرَةَ لَهِیَ الْحَیَوَانُ ۘ لَوْ کَانُوْا یَعْلَمُوْنَ ۝

فَاِذَا رَکِبُوْا فِی الْفُلْکِ دَعَوُا اللّٰهَ مُخْلِصِیْنَ لَهُ

الدِّیْنَ ۚ فَلَمَّا نَجّٰهُمْ اِلَی الْبَرِّ اِذَا هُمْ یُشْرِکُوْنَ ۝

لِیَکْفُرُوْا بِمَاۤ اٰتَیْنٰهُمْ ۙ وَلِیَتَمَتَّعُوْا ۫ فَسَوْفَ

یَعْلَمُوْنَ ۝ اَوَلَمْ یَرَوْا اَنَّا جَعَلْنَا حَرَمًا اٰمِنًا وَّ

یُتَخَطَّفُ النَّاسُ مِنْ حَوْلِهِمْ ؕ اَفَبِالْبَاطِلِ یُؤْمِنُوْنَ

وَبِنِعْمَةِ اللّٰهِ یَکْفُرُوْنَ ۝ وَمَنْ اَظْلَمُ مِمَّنِ افْتَرٰی

عَلَی اللّٰهِ کَذِبًا اَوْ کَذَّبَ بِالْحَقِّ لَمَّا جَآءَهٗ ؕ اَلَیْسَ

فِیْ جَهَنَّمَ مَثْوًی لِّلْکٰفِرِیْنَ ۝ وَالَّذِیْنَ جَاهَدُوْا فِیْنَا

لَنَهْدِیَنَّهُمْ سُبُلَنَا ؕ وَاِنَّ اللّٰهَ لَمَعَ الْمُحْسِنِیْنَ ۝

The righteous are given a promise of final victory, with constant engagement and Divine support.

795

The contradictions of those who believe in Allah but reject His message

⁶⁰ Animals don't carry their provisions around; Allah provides for them and you. He is the Hearer, the Knower. ⁶¹ If you were to ask them: "Who created the Heavens and the Earth, and harnessed the sun and the moon?" Without doubt, they will say, "Allah!" So why do they spread lies? ⁶² Allah distributes *His* provision to anyone He wills among His servants, and He measures it out for him. Allah has knowledge of everything. ⁶³ And if you were to ask them: "Who sends water from the sky, and gives with it life to the Earth after its death?" They'll say, "Allah!" Say, "Praise be to Allah!" And most of them still don't understand.

The idolaters swing between sincerity and disbelief

⁶⁴ This worldly life is *little* but fun and games; the home of the Hereafter is *true* life[a], if they knew. ⁶⁵ When they are on board a ship, they call Allah sincerely in devotion. Then, when He brings them safely back to the land, they associate partners *with Him*, ⁶⁶ unthankful for what We gave them. Let them enjoy, soon they will realise.

Allah rewards the hard workers

⁶⁷ Haven't they considered *how* We made *Makkah* a safe place, while all around them people *live in fear of* being kidnapped. Will they *continue* believing in falsehood and deny Allah's gifts? ⁶⁸ Who is a greater sinner than someone who makes up lies about Allah or *flatly* rejects the truth when it comes to him? Isn't Hell a *fitting* home for the disbelievers? ⁶⁹ Those who strive *hard* for Our sake, We shall guide them along on Our ways. Allah is with those who do good.

---

[a] Had they used reason they would have realised the transient and fleeting nature of life.

30. Surat Ar-Rum

The Romans

This surat was revealed in the fifth or sixth year of the mission of the Prophet ﷺ, at a time when tensions between Muslims and the Quraysh were intense. The surat opens with a remarkable prediction: "The Romans were defeated in a nearby country, but within a few years of their defeat they will be victorious." (2–4) In 615 CE, the Persians defeated them. Their defeat made the Quraysh happy; they took this as an omen that the Muslims who were closer to the Christians, would be similarly defeated. The idea that the Romans would recover from this terrible defeat was not credible to them. However, the Quran predicted otherwise:

> At the time this prediction is said to have been delivered no prophecy could be more distant from its accomplishment, since the first twelve years of Heraclius announced the approaching dissolution of the Empire (E. Gibbon, *The Decline and Fall of the Roman Empire*, Vol. 4, p. 514).

The Quranic prediction was fulfilled on the same day as Battle of Badr (624 CE). The central theme of the surat is the creative power of Allah that reinforces the belief in the resurrection. It explains the underlying problem with the disbelievers' materialistic mind-set: "People know the outer nature of worldly life, but are unaware of the Hereafter" (7).

Fitrah, the natural human character, is the essence of Islamic teachings: "So set your face towards the religion *of Allah* sincerely, in accordance with human nature, which Allah shaped." (30). Islam helps it to flourish, brings out the best in it rather than crushing it. Others have translated this as "natural disposition, sound human nature", which means "man's inborn, intuitive ability to discern between right and wrong, true and false, and sense God's existence and oneness" (Asad). A positive, pure and near perfect vision of Humanity, a far cry from Hobbs (d.1679) image of beastly, brutal and selfish humanity.

We can't fail to see all around us wonderful and awesome signs that point to Allah's creative power. Seven signs are brought to our attention: the creation of humanity from elements, the love between husband and wife, differences in language and people's colour, the functions of night and day, the lightning and the winds. These natural phenomena point to their Creator, and the Quran urges readers to progress onto the next stage – that of recognising Allah as the Creator, worthy of worship.

There is another prediction in this surat: "If pollution has appeared on land and sea it's because of what people have done with their hands, it is to make them taste something of the fruits of what they have done" (41). The reference can be to the environmental catastrophe that humanity faces today. There is another remarkable prediction:

> The Day the *Final* Hour comes, the sinners will swear they lingered no more than a short while *in their graves*; that is how they were deceived. And those given knowledge and faith will say, "According to Allah's Book, you have lingered until the Day of Resurrection; and this is the Day of Resurrection" (55–56).

The prediction is: Islam will continue until the end of the time; there will always be true believers to the Last Day. This is good news: despite setbacks, the Ummah will thrive. The Messenger ﷺ is given encouraging advice: "So be patient, Allah's promise is true; and don't let the deniers frighten you" (60). The surat closes with a positive message just as it opened with a prediction.

بِسْمِ اللّٰهِ الرَّحْمٰنِ الرَّحِيْمِ

الٓمّٓ ۚ۝١ غُلِبَتِ الرُّوْمُ ۙ۝٢ فِیْۤ اَدْنَی الْاَرْضِ وَهُمْ مِّنْۢ

بَعْدِ غَلَبِهِمْ سَیَغْلِبُوْنَ ۙ۝٣ فِیْ بِضْعِ سِنِیْنَ ۬ؕ لِلّٰهِ

الْاَمْرُ مِنْ قَبْلُ وَمِنْۢ بَعْدُ ؕ وَیَوْمَئِذٍ یَّفْرَحُ

الْمُؤْمِنُوْنَ ۙ۝٤ بِنَصْرِ اللّٰهِ ؕ یَنْصُرُ مَنْ یَّشَآءُ ؕ وَهُوَ

الْعَزِیْزُ الرَّحِیْمُ ۝٥ وَعْدَ اللّٰهِ ؕ لَا یُخْلِفُ اللّٰهُ وَعْدَهٗ

وَلٰكِنَّ اَكْثَرَ النَّاسِ لَا یَعْلَمُوْنَ ۝٦ یَعْلَمُوْنَ ظَاهِرًا

مِّنَ الْحَیٰوةِ الدُّنْیَا ۪ۖ وَهُمْ عَنِ الْاٰخِرَةِ هُمْ غٰفِلُوْنَ ۝٧

اَوَلَمْ یَتَفَكَّرُوْا فِیْۤ اَنْفُسِهِمْ ۣ مَا خَلَقَ اللّٰهُ السَّمٰوٰتِ

وَالْاَرْضَ وَمَا بَیْنَهُمَاۤ اِلَّا بِالْحَقِّ وَاَجَلٍ مُّسَمًّی ؕ وَ

اِنَّ كَثِیْرًا مِّنَ النَّاسِ بِلِقَآئِ رَبِّهِمْ لَكٰفِرُوْنَ ۝٨

اَوَلَمْ یَسِیْرُوْا فِی الْاَرْضِ فَیَنْظُرُوْا كَیْفَ كَانَ

عَاقِبَةُ الَّذِیْنَ مِنْ قَبْلِهِمْ ؕ كَانُوْۤا اَشَدَّ مِنْهُمْ

قُوَّةً وَّاَثَارُوا الْاَرْضَ وَعَمَرُوْهَاۤ اَكْثَرَ مِمَّا عَمَرُوْهَا

وَجَآءَتْهُمْ رُسُلُهُمْ بِالْبَیِّنٰتِ ؕ فَمَا كَانَ اللّٰهُ لِیَظْلِمَهُمْ

وَلٰكِنْ كَانُوْۤا اَنْفُسَهُمْ یَظْلِمُوْنَ ۝٩ ثُمَّ كَانَ عَاقِبَةَ

الَّذِیْنَ اَسَآءُوا السُّوْٓاٰۤی اَنْ كَذَّبُوْا بِاٰیٰتِ اللّٰهِ وَكَانُوْا

بِهَا یَسْتَهْزِءُوْنَ ۠۝١٠ اَللّٰهُ یَبْدَؤُا الْخَلْقَ ثُمَّ یُعِیْدُهٗ

ثُمَّ اِلَیْهِ تُرْجَعُوْنَ ۝١١ وَیَوْمَ تَقُوْمُ السَّاعَةُ یُبْلِسُ

Allah asserts his authority: He will change the course of history. The defeated Romans will win once again!

In the name of Allah, the Kind, the Caring.

[1] *Alif Lam Meem.*

The power struggle between Rome and Persia

[2] The Romans were defeated [3] in a nearby land; but after their defeat, they will be victorious [4] within a few years. Whether *it occurs* sooner or later, the decision is Allah's; that day the believers will rejoice [5] at the victory *from* Allah. He grants victory to anyone He wants; the Almighty, the Caring. [6] Allah's promise; Allah never breaks His promise, but most people don't know.

The deeper meaning of life

[7] *People* know the outer nature of worldly life, but are unaware of the Hereafter. [8] Haven't they thought about themselves? Everything Allah created – in the Heavens and the Earth and what lies between them – is for a purpose and a fixed timespan. Despite this, many people are in denial about meeting their Lord. [9] Haven't they travelled around and seen what happened to those before them? They were more powerful than them; they farmed the land and populated it even more than it is now, and their messengers came to them with clear proofs. Allah did not wrong them, but they wronged themselves; [10] and the outcome of evil was bound to be evil. They rejected Allah's signs and mocked them.

People will be separated on the Last Day

[11] Allah starts the creation, then He will restore it *to its original state*, then you will be returned to Him. [12] The Day the Final Hour comes, the sinners will despair.

الْمُجْرِمُوْنَ ۞ وَلَمْ يَكُنْ لَّهُمْ مِّنْ شُرَكَآئِهِمْ شُفَعٰٓؤُا

وَكَانُوْا بِشُرَكَآئِهِمْ كٰفِرِيْنَ ۞ وَيَوْمَ تَقُوْمُ السَّاعَةُ

يَوْمَئِذٍ يَّتَفَرَّقُوْنَ ۞ فَاَمَّا الَّذِيْنَ اٰمَنُوْا وَعَمِلُوا

الصّٰلِحٰتِ فَهُمْ فِيْ رَوْضَةٍ يُّحْبَرُوْنَ ۞ وَاَمَّا الَّذِيْنَ

كَفَرُوْا وَكَذَّبُوْا بِاٰيٰتِنَا وَلِقَآئِ الْاٰخِرَةِ فَاُولٰٓئِكَ فِي

الْعَذَابِ مُحْضَرُوْنَ ۞ فَسُبْحٰنَ اللّٰهِ حِيْنَ تُمْسُوْنَ

وَحِيْنَ تُصْبِحُوْنَ ۞ وَلَهُ الْحَمْدُ فِي السَّمٰوٰتِ وَ

الْاَرْضِ وَعَشِيًّا وَّحِيْنَ تُظْهِرُوْنَ ۞ يُخْرِجُ الْحَيَّ مِنَ

الْمَيِّتِ وَيُخْرِجُ الْمَيِّتَ مِنَ الْحَيِّ وَيُحْيِ الْاَرْضَ

بَعْدَ مَوْتِهَا ط وَكَذٰلِكَ تُخْرَجُوْنَ ۞ وَمِنْ اٰيٰتِهٖۤ

اَنْ خَلَقَكُمْ مِّنْ تُرَابٍ ثُمَّ اِذَاۤ اَنْتُمْ بَشَرٌ

تَنْتَشِرُوْنَ ۞ وَمِنْ اٰيٰتِهٖۤ اَنْ خَلَقَ لَكُمْ مِّنْ

اَنْفُسِكُمْ اَزْوَاجًا لِّتَسْكُنُوْۤا اِلَيْهَا وَجَعَلَ بَيْنَكُمْ مَّوَدَّةً

وَّرَحْمَةً ط اِنَّ فِيْ ذٰلِكَ لَاٰيٰتٍ لِّقَوْمٍ يَّتَفَكَّرُوْنَ ۞ وَمِنْ

اٰيٰتِهٖ خَلْقُ السَّمٰوٰتِ وَالْاَرْضِ وَاخْتِلَافُ اَلْسِنَتِكُمْ

وَاَلْوَانِكُمْ ط اِنَّ فِيْ ذٰلِكَ لَاٰيٰتٍ لِّلْعٰلِمِيْنَ ۞ وَمِنْ

اٰيٰتِهٖ مَنَامُكُمْ بِالَّيْلِ وَالنَّهَارِ وَابْتِغَآؤُكُمْ مِّنْ

فَضْلِهٖ ط اِنَّ فِيْ ذٰلِكَ لَاٰيٰتٍ لِّقَوْمٍ يَّسْمَعُوْنَ ۞ وَمِنْ

اٰيٰتِهٖ يُرِيْكُمُ الْبَرْقَ خَوْفًا وَّطَمَعًا وَّيُنَزِّلُ مِنَ

السَّمَآءِ مَآءً فَيُحْيٖ بِهِ الْاَرْضَ بَعْدَ مَوْتِهَا ط اِنَّ فِيْ

Signs give information, the millions of signs in nature point to the Almighty Creator Allah!

[13] Their idols will not intercede for them, but reject them. [14] When the Final Hour comes, that Day *all humanity* will be divided: [15] the believers who did good deeds will be celebrating in Paradise; [16] but the disbelievers who rejected Our signs and Our meeting in the Hereafter will be in everlasting torment. [17] So *say:* "Glory be to Allah!" When you settle down for the evening and when you rise in the morning, [18] and: "Praise be to Him in the Heavens and the Earth!" At night and noon.

The growth of plants on dry land after rain; a sign of resurrection

[19] He brings the living from the dead, and He brings the dead from the living, that's how He revives the Earth after it *appears* dead. That's how you will be brought to life. [20] And among His signs is He created you from dust, and scattered you *around the world.*

The love that exists between husband and wife is Allah's sign

[21] Among His signs is He created spouses for you from your own kind, so you can live together peacefully;[a] and He commands you to love and care for each other[b], in that are signs for thinkers. [22] Among His signs is the creation of the Heavens and the Earth, and the differences in your languages and skin colour, there are signs for those who know.

Day and night, and lightning and rain as signs

[23] Among His signs is you sleep at night and *during* the day you seek His bounty. There are signs for people who hear. [24] Among His signs is that He shows you the lightning, *filling you* with fear and hope, and He sends water from the sky, reviving the Earth after it *seemed to have* died. In that there are signs for those who understand.

---

[a] '*Letaskunoo*' is derived from '*Sakana*', which means 'to live in a home'. So I have taken the literal meaning rather than the implied meaning of 'with tranquillity'.

[b] An alternative meaning is "He planted love and kindness between you."

ذٰلِكَ لَاٰیٰتٍ لِّقَوْمٍ یَّعْقِلُوْنَ ۲۴ وَمِنْ اٰیٰتِهٖۤ اَنْ تَقُوْمَ

السَّمَآءُ وَالْاَرْضُ بِاَمْرِهٖ ؕ ثُمَّ اِذَا دَعَاكُمْ دَعْوَةً ۚ

مِّنَ الْاَرْضِ ۙ اِذَاۤ اَنْتُمْ تَخْرُجُوْنَ ۲۵ وَلَهٗ مَنْ فِی

السَّمٰوٰتِ وَالْاَرْضِ ؕ كُلٌّ لَّهٗ قٰنِتُوْنَ ۲۶ وَهُوَ الَّذِیْ

یَبْدَؤُا الْخَلْقَ ثُمَّ یُعِیْدُهٗ وَهُوَ اَهْوَنُ عَلَیْهِ ؕ وَلَهُ

الْمَثَلُ الْاَعْلٰی فِی السَّمٰوٰتِ وَالْاَرْضِ ۚ وَهُوَ الْعَزِیْزُ

الْحَكِیْمُ ۲۷ ضَرَبَ لَكُمْ مَّثَلًا مِّنْ اَنْفُسِكُمْ ؕ هَلْ لَّكُمْ

مِّنْ مَّا مَلَكَتْ اَیْمَانُكُمْ مِّنْ شُرَكَآءَ فِیْ مَا رَزَقْنٰكُمْ

فَاَنْتُمْ فِیْهِ سَوَآءٌ تَخَافُوْنَهُمْ كَخِیْفَتِكُمْ اَنْفُسَكُمْ ؕ

كَذٰلِكَ نُفَصِّلُ الْاٰیٰتِ لِقَوْمٍ یَّعْقِلُوْنَ ۲۸ بَلِ اتَّبَعَ

الَّذِیْنَ ظَلَمُوْۤا اَهْوَآءَهُمْ بِغَیْرِ عِلْمٍ ۚ فَمَنْ یَّهْدِیْ

مَنْ اَضَلَّ اللّٰهُ ؕ وَمَا لَهُمْ مِّنْ نّٰصِرِیْنَ ۲۹ فَاَقِمْ

وَجْهَكَ لِلدِّیْنِ حَنِیْفًا ؕ فِطْرَتَ اللّٰهِ الَّتِیْ فَطَرَ النَّاسَ

عَلَیْهَا ؕ لَا تَبْدِیْلَ لِخَلْقِ اللّٰهِ ؕ ذٰلِكَ الدِّیْنُ الْقَیِّمُ ۙ

وَلٰكِنَّ اَكْثَرَ النَّاسِ لَا یَعْلَمُوْنَ ۳۰ مُنِیْبِیْنَ اِلَیْهِ

وَاتَّقُوْهُ وَاَقِیْمُوا الصَّلٰوةَ وَلَا تَكُوْنُوْا مِنَ الْمُشْرِكِیْنَ ۳۱

مِنَ الَّذِیْنَ فَرَّقُوْا دِیْنَهُمْ وَكَانُوْا شِیَعًا ؕ كُلُّ حِزْبٍۢ

بِمَا لَدَیْهِمْ فَرِحُوْنَ ۳۲ وَاِذَا مَسَّ النَّاسَ ضُرٌّ دَعَوْا

رَبَّهُمْ مُّنِیْبِیْنَ اِلَیْهِ ثُمَّ اِذَاۤ اَذَاقَهُمْ مِّنْهُ

رَحْمَةً اِذَا فَرِیْقٌ مِّنْهُمْ بِرَبِّهِمْ یُشْرِكُوْنَ ۳۳ لِیَكْفُرُوْا

Belief in Allah isn't myth, it's logical and reasonable! So confidently commit to Allah!

803

The universe is Allah's greatest sign

[25] Among His signs is the sky and the Earth that exist by His command. Then, when He makes the call, you shall come out of the Earth. [26] Everything in the Heavens and the Earth belong to Him; they are all obedient to Him. [27] He starts the creation, then restores it *to its original state*; and that's easy for Him. And His greatest example is the Heavens and the Earth. He is the Almighty, the Wise.

Allah is not like any of His creatures

[28] *Allah gives* you an example from yourselves. Do you take any of your slaves as your partners, in what We have provided you, so you are equal in *shares*, do you worry about them as you worry for yourselves? That's how We explain *Our* signs to people who think. [29] But those who do wrong ignorantly follow their whims. Who can guide the one whom Allah has allowed to go astray, and who has no helpers?

To be Humble is in harmony with human nature

[30] So stand firmly for the religion *of Allah* sincerely. That is the human nature, which Allah made. There is no change in *the laws of* Allah's creation. That is the upright religion, most people don't know.[a] [31] *Believers, turn* in repentance to Him, be mindful of Him, perform the prayer, and don't be an idolater. [32] Don't be like those who divided their religion and became sects, each sect happy with the *beliefs* they follow.

The reaction in good and bad times reveals character

[33] In bad times people call on their Lord, longing for Him; He treats them kindly, but a group of them continues to associate *partners* with their Lord,

---

[a] Human nature refers to our ability to distinguish good from bad, we are ever-capable of doing good. The third century Chinese sage Mencius (Mang Tzu) said "all men have a mind, which cannot bear to see the sufferings of others."

بِمَآ اٰتَيْنٰهُمْ ط فَتَمَتَّعُوْا رقفة فَسَوْفَ تَعْلَمُوْنَ ۞ اَمْ

اَنْزَلْنَا عَلَيْهِمْ سُلْطٰنًا فَهُوَ يَتَكَلَّمُ بِمَا كَانُوْا بِهٖ

يُشْرِكُوْنَ ۞ وَاِذَآ اَذَقْنَا النَّاسَ رَحْمَةً فَرِحُوْا بِهَا ط

وَاِنْ تُصِبْهُمْ سَيِّئَةٌ بِمَا قَدَّمَتْ اَيْدِيْهِمْ اِذَا هُمْ

يَقْنَطُوْنَ ۞ اَوَلَمْ يَرَوْا اَنَّ اللهَ يَبْسُطُ الرِّزْقَ لِمَنْ

يَّشَآءُ وَيَقْدِرُ ط اِنَّ فِىْ ذٰلِكَ لَاٰيٰتٍ لِّقَوْمٍ يُّؤْمِنُوْنَ ۞

فَاٰتِ ذَا الْقُرْبٰى حَقَّهٗ وَالْمِسْكِيْنَ وَابْنَ السَّبِيْلِ ط

ذٰلِكَ خَيْرٌ لِّلَّذِيْنَ يُرِيْدُوْنَ وَجْهَ اللهِ ز وَاُولٰٓئِكَ هُمُ

الْمُفْلِحُوْنَ ۞ وَمَآ اٰتَيْتُمْ مِّنْ رِّبًا لِّيَرْبُوَا۟ فِىْٓ اَمْوَالِ

النَّاسِ فَلَا يَرْبُوْا عِنْدَ اللهِ ج وَمَآ اٰتَيْتُمْ مِّنْ زَكٰوةٍ

تُرِيْدُوْنَ وَجْهَ اللهِ فَاُولٰٓئِكَ هُمُ الْمُضْعِفُوْنَ ۞

اَللهُ الَّذِىْ خَلَقَكُمْ ثُمَّ رَزَقَكُمْ ثُمَّ يُمِيْتُكُمْ ثُمَّ

يُحْيِيْكُمْ ط هَلْ مِنْ شُرَكَآئِكُمْ مَّنْ يَّفْعَلُ مِنْ ذٰلِكُمْ

مِّنْ شَىْءٍ ط سُبْحٰنَهٗ وَتَعٰلٰى عَمَّا يُشْرِكُوْنَ ۞ ظَهَرَ

الْفَسَادُ فِى الْبَرِّ وَالْبَحْرِ بِمَا كَسَبَتْ اَيْدِى النَّاسِ

لِيُذِيْقَهُمْ بَعْضَ الَّذِىْ عَمِلُوْا لَعَلَّهُمْ يَرْجِعُوْنَ ۞

قُلْ سِيْرُوْا فِى الْاَرْضِ فَانْظُرُوْا كَيْفَ كَانَ عَاقِبَةُ

الَّذِيْنَ مِنْ قَبْلُ ط كَانَ اَكْثَرُهُمْ مُّشْرِكِيْنَ ۞ فَاَقِمْ

وَجْهَكَ لِلدِّيْنِ الْقَيِّمِ مِنْ قَبْلِ اَنْ يَّاْتِىَ يَوْمٌ لَّا مَرَدَّ

لَهٗ مِنَ اللهِ يَوْمَئِذٍ يَّصَّدَّعُوْنَ ۞ مَنْ كَفَرَ فَعَلَيْهِ

Look at the pollution on land and the sea, a result of human greed. Isn't that enough for you to see the light of Allah?

805

³⁴ being ungrateful for what We gave them. So enjoy yourselves, soon you shall know *the truth*. ³⁵ Or have We sent them any authority that talks about what they associated with Him? ³⁶ When We treat people kindly they're happy; but when they fall into bad times due to what they have done, they despair. ³⁷ Haven't they considered that Allah distributes *His* provision to whomever He wills, and that He measures it out? For the believers, there are signs in that.

Zakat brings lasting benefits

³⁸ Give relatives, the needy and the travellers their due. That's a good thing to do for those who seek Allah's pleasure, and they will have *lasting* success. ³⁹ The wealth you lend people with interest for an increase^a will not increase in Allah's sight; but what you give in Zakat, seeking Allah's pleasure *will increase*, such people will be rewarded many times over. ⁴⁰ Allah created you, provided you, then will cause you to die, and then resurrect you. Which of these, if any, can your *false* idols do? Glory be to Him! He is exalted far above what they associate *with Him* as partners.

Pollution of Earth: The environmental crisis

⁴¹ Pollution has appeared on land and sea it's what people have done with their hands, it is to make them taste something of the fruits of their work, so they may turn back *from their wicked ways*.^b ⁴² Say: "Travel about the land and observe what became of those before *you*." Most of them associated *partners with Allah*. ⁴³ Stand firmly for the upright religion before a Day comes from Allah that can't be postponed; that Day, *humanity* will split in two:

---

^a　In this verse, Allah links two words that are clearly related in Arabic: 'usury', and 'increase'.

^b　*Fasad* is 'to become bad', to be spoiled, corrupt, weaken and undermine. Isn't the environmental pollution we see so wide-spread *Fasad*?

كُفْرَهٗ ۚ وَمَنْ عَمِلَ صَالِحًا فَلِاَنْفُسِهِمْ يَمْهَدُوْنَ ۙ﴿٤٤﴾

لِيَجْزِیَ الَّذِیْنَ اٰمَنُوْا وَعَمِلُوا الصّٰلِحٰتِ مِنْ فَضْلِهٖ ؕ

اِنَّهٗ لَا یُحِبُّ الْكٰفِرِیْنَ ﴿٤٥﴾ وَمِنْ اٰیٰتِهٖۤ اَنْ یُّرْسِلَ

الرِّیَاحَ مُبَشِّرٰتٍ وَّلِیُذِیْقَكُمْ مِّنْ رَّحْمَتِهٖ وَلِتَجْرِیَ

الْفُلْكُ بِاَمْرِهٖ وَلِتَبْتَغُوْا مِنْ فَضْلِهٖ وَلَعَلَّكُمْ

تَشْكُرُوْنَ ﴿٤٦﴾ وَلَقَدْ اَرْسَلْنَا مِنْ قَبْلِكَ رُسُلًا اِلٰی

قَوْمِهِمْ فَجَآءُوْهُمْ بِالْبَیِّنٰتِ فَانْتَقَمْنَا مِنَ الَّذِیْنَ

اَجْرَمُوْا ؕ وَكَانَ حَقًّا عَلَیْنَا نَصْرُ الْمُؤْمِنِیْنَ ﴿٤٧﴾ اَللّٰهُ

الَّذِیْ یُرْسِلُ الرِّیٰحَ فَتُثِیْرُ سَحَابًا فَیَبْسُطُهٗ فِی

السَّمَآءِ كَیْفَ یَشَآءُ وَیَجْعَلُهٗ كِسَفًا فَتَرَی الْوَدْقَ

یَخْرُجُ مِنْ خِلٰلِهٖ ۚ فَاِذَاۤ اَصَابَ بِهٖ مَنْ یَّشَآءُ مِنْ

عِبَادِهٖۤ اِذَا هُمْ یَسْتَبْشِرُوْنَ ﴿٤٨﴾ وَاِنْ كَانُوْا مِنْ قَبْلِ

اَنْ یُّنَزَّلَ عَلَیْهِمْ مِّنْ قَبْلِهٖ لَمُبْلِسِیْنَ ﴿٤٩﴾ فَانْظُرْ اِلٰۤی

اٰثٰرِ رَحْمَتِ اللّٰهِ كَیْفَ یُحْیِ الْاَرْضَ بَعْدَ مَوْتِهَا ؕ

اِنَّ ذٰلِكَ لَمُحْیِ الْمَوْتٰی ۚ وَهُوَ عَلٰی كُلِّ شَیْءٍ قَدِیْرٌ ﴿٥٠﴾

وَلَئِنْ اَرْسَلْنَا رِیْحًا فَرَاَوْهُ مُصْفَرًّا لَّظَلُّوْا مِنْ بَعْدِهٖ

یَكْفُرُوْنَ ﴿٥١﴾ فَاِنَّكَ لَا تُسْمِعُ الْمَوْتٰی وَلَا تُسْمِعُ الصُّمَّ

الدُّعَآءَ اِذَا وَلَّوْا مُدْبِرِیْنَ ﴿٥٢﴾ وَمَاۤ اَنْتَ بِهٰدِ الْعُمْیِ

عَنْ ضَلٰلَتِهِمْ ؕ اِنْ تُسْمِعُ اِلَّا مَنْ یُّؤْمِنُ بِاٰیٰتِنَا

فَهُمْ مُّسْلِمُوْنَ ﴿٥٣﴾ اَللّٰهُ الَّذِیْ خَلَقَكُمْ مِّنْ ضُعْفٍ

Rain falls on dry soil and a seed germinates; shoots sprout, flowers and fruits flourish. Allah's miracle! That's how you will be resurrected.

⁴⁴ the disbelievers will answer for their disbelief; and the righteous will have a comfortable place arranged for them. ⁴⁵ So He may reward with His bounty those who believed and did good deeds. *Allah* dislikes the disbelievers.

The cycle of wind and rain: Allah's bounties

⁴⁶ Among His signs is the winds bearing glad tidings, to give you a taste of His kindness, and ships that sail by His command, enabling you to seek His bounty and show gratitude. ⁴⁷ We sent messengers before you, *each* to their people, with clear proofs; and We punished the sinners and helped the believers. ⁴⁸ Allah sends the winds, which scatter clouds across the sky as He pleases; then He causes *the sky* to break so that you see rain come down; and if He makes it fall on whomever of His servants He pleases, they become happy. ⁴⁹ Before it was sent down, they were in despair. ⁵⁰ So observe the effects of Allah's kindness; the revival of the Earth after its death. *Allah* resurrects the dead. He has power over all things. ⁵¹ Had We sent wind that turned *their crops* yellow, they still wouldn't believe. ⁵² You can't make the dead hear the call any more than you can the deaf, if they turn their backs to leave; ⁵³ nor can you guide the blind to turn away from their error. The believers are the only ones who will listen to you and accept Our signs, they submit *to Our will.*

ثُمَّ جَعَلَ مِنْۢ بَعْدِ ضَعْفٍ قُوَّةً ثُمَّ جَعَلَ مِنْۢ

بَعْدِ قُوَّةٍ ضَعْفًا وَّشَيْبَةً ؕ يَخْلُقُ مَا يَشَآءُ ۚ وَهُوَ

الْعَلِيْمُ الْقَدِيْرُ ۵۴ وَيَوْمَ تَقُوْمُ السَّاعَةُ يُقْسِمُ

الْمُجْرِمُوْنَ ۙ مَا لَبِثُوْا غَيْرَ سَاعَةٍ ؕ كَذٰلِكَ كَانُوْا

يُؤْفَكُوْنَ ۵۵ وَقَالَ الَّذِيْنَ اُوْتُوا الْعِلْمَ وَالْاِيْمَانَ

لَقَدْ لَبِثْتُمْ فِیْ كِتٰبِ اللّٰهِ اِلٰی يَوْمِ الْبَعْثِ ۫ فَهٰذَا يَوْمُ

الْبَعْثِ وَلٰكِنَّكُمْ كُنْتُمْ لَا تَعْلَمُوْنَ ۵۶ فَيَوْمَىِٕذٍ لَّا يَنْفَعُ

الَّذِيْنَ ظَلَمُوْا مَعْذِرَتُهُمْ وَلَا هُمْ يُسْتَعْتَبُوْنَ ۵۷

وَلَقَدْ ضَرَبْنَا لِلنَّاسِ فِیْ هٰذَا الْقُرْاٰنِ مِنْ كُلِّ

مَثَلٍ ؕ وَلَىِٕنْ جِئْتَهُمْ بِاٰيَةٍ لَّيَقُوْلَنَّ الَّذِيْنَ كَفَرُوْۤا

اِنْ اَنْتُمْ اِلَّا مُبْطِلُوْنَ ۵۸ كَذٰلِكَ يَطْبَعُ اللّٰهُ عَلٰی

قُلُوْبِ الَّذِيْنَ لَا يَعْلَمُوْنَ ۵۹ فَاصْبِرْ اِنَّ وَعْدَ اللّٰهِ

حَقٌّ وَّلَا يَسْتَخِفَّنَّكَ الَّذِيْنَ لَا يُوْقِنُوْنَ ۷۰

As a believer be bold and assertive about your faith and be patient as you face backlash.

Human life: birth, youth, old age, death, the grave and resurrection

⁵⁴ Allah created you weak; after weakness He made you strong, and after being strong He made you weak *again* in old age. He creates whatever He pleases and He is the Knower, the Powerful. ⁵⁵ The Day the *Final* Hour comes, the sinners will swear they lingered no more than a short while *in their graves*; that is how they were deceived. ⁵⁶ And those given knowledge and faith will say, "According to Allah's Book, you have lingered until the Day of Resurrection; and this is the Day of Resurrection, but you were unaware." ⁵⁷ That Day, the wrongdoers' excuses will not benefit them, nor will they *have a chance to* beg for favours.

The Quran contains sufficient examples, even for doubters

⁵⁸ We gave people all kinds of examples in this Quran. Were you to produce a miracle for them, the disbelievers would still say, "You are fake." ⁵⁹ That is how Allah seals the hearts of those who don't know. ⁶⁰ So be patient, Allah's promise is true; and don't let the deniers frighten you.

31. Surat Luqman

Luqman the Wise

This surat was revealed in the middle Makkan period. It bears the name of the legendary sage, the wise Luqman from Southern Egypt. By narrating his polite and educational teachings, the Quran is promoting diversity of cultures, races and languages. The central theme of the surat is: be thankful to Allah for His gifts.

The surat starts with a vivid description of the "devout Muslim": he benefits from the teachings of the Quran; stays away from useless activities that distract from the worship of Allah.

Sometimes the blessed Messenger ﷺ would teach the Quran sitting around the Kaaba. A Makkan storyteller, Nadhar ibn Harith, would also gather people around himself to distract people from the Messenger ﷺ. He would tell Persian stories, and to entertain his audience he hired dancers. Verse 7 was revealed to condemn him.

Allah's visible and hidden gifts that people enjoy are mentioned, and the question is asked: "What have the idols created?" Luqman the wise teaches his son the correct beliefs about Allah: how to worship Him, how to behave justly with others, especially parents, and how to be humble. The final passage describes the natural world and several signs of Allah's creative power and contrasts it with human feebleness.

بِسۡمِ اللّٰهِ الرَّحۡمٰنِ الرَّحِیۡمِ

الٓمّٓ ۱ تِلۡكَ اٰیٰتُ الۡكِتٰبِ الۡحَكِیۡمِ ۲ هُدًی

وَّرَحۡمَةً لِّلۡمُحۡسِنِیۡنَ ۳ الَّذِیۡنَ یُقِیۡمُوۡنَ الصَّلٰوةَ

وَیُؤۡتُوۡنَ الزَّكٰوةَ وَهُمۡ بِالۡاٰخِرَةِ هُمۡ یُوۡقِنُوۡنَ ۴

اُولٰٓئِكَ عَلٰی هُدًی مِّنۡ رَّبِّهِمۡ وَاُولٰٓئِكَ هُمُ

الۡمُفۡلِحُوۡنَ ۵ وَمِنَ النَّاسِ مَنۡ یَّشۡتَرِیۡ لَهۡوَ

الۡحَدِیۡثِ لِیُضِلَّ عَنۡ سَبِیۡلِ اللّٰهِ بِغَیۡرِ عِلۡمٍ ۙ

وَّیَتَّخِذَهَا هُزُوًا ؕ اُولٰٓئِكَ لَهُمۡ عَذَابٌ مُّهِیۡنٌ ۶

وَاِذَا تُتۡلٰی عَلَیۡهِ اٰیٰتُنَا وَلّٰی مُسۡتَكۡبِرًا كَاَنۡ لَّمۡ

یَسۡمَعۡهَا كَاَنَّ فِیۡۤ اُذُنَیۡهِ وَقۡرًا ۚ فَبَشِّرۡهُ بِعَذَابٍ

اَلِیۡمٍ ۷ اِنَّ الَّذِیۡنَ اٰمَنُوۡا وَعَمِلُوا الصّٰلِحٰتِ لَهُمۡ

جَنّٰتُ النَّعِیۡمِ ۸ خٰلِدِیۡنَ فِیۡهَا ؕ وَعۡدَ اللّٰهِ حَقًّا ؕ

وَهُوَ الۡعَزِیۡزُ الۡحَكِیۡمُ ۹ خَلَقَ السَّمٰوٰتِ بِغَیۡرِ عَمَدٍ

تَرَوۡنَهَا وَاَلۡقٰی فِی الۡاَرۡضِ رَوَاسِیَ اَنۡ تَمِیۡدَ بِكُمۡ

وَبَثَّ فِیۡهَا مِنۡ كُلِّ دَآبَّةٍ ؕ وَاَنۡزَلۡنَا مِنَ السَّمَآءِ

مَآءً فَاَنۡۢبَتۡنَا فِیۡهَا مِنۡ كُلِّ زَوۡجٍ كَرِیۡمٍ ۱۰ هٰذَا خَلۡقُ

اللّٰهِ فَاَرُوۡنِیۡ مَاذَا خَلَقَ الَّذِیۡنَ مِنۡ دُوۡنِهٖ ؕ بَلِ

الظّٰلِمُوۡنَ فِیۡ ضَلٰلٍ مُّبِیۡنٍ ۱۱ وَلَقَدۡ اٰتَیۡنَا لُقۡمٰنَ

الۡحِكۡمَةَ اَنِ اشۡكُرۡ لِلّٰهِ ؕ وَمَنۡ یَّشۡكُرۡ فَاِنَّمَا یَشۡكُرُ

Doubt makes you insecure, faith gives certainty and peace of mind. How certain are you?

813

In the name of Allah, the Kind, the Caring.

¹*Alif Lam Meem.*

The glorious Quran offers guidance to believers

²These are the verses of the Book full of wisdom, ³a guidance, beneficial for the righteous; ⁴who perform the prayer, pay Zakat and believe firmly in the Hereafter. ⁵They *follow* their Lord's guidance and are the successful.

The false storyteller

⁶Some people pay for false stories *to be told* to divert *people* from Allah's way,ᵃ treating it as a joke; they will have a humiliating punishment. ⁷When Our verses are recited to him, he arrogantly turns away as though he had not heard it, as though his ears were blocked; so cheer him up with news of a painful punishment. ⁸The believers who do righteous deeds will have gardens of delight, ⁹living in them forever. Allah's promise is true; and He is the Almighty, the Wise.

What have the false gods ever created?

¹⁰*Allah* created the skies without any pillar that you can see; and has fixed mountains *like pegs* in the Earth, so you don't feel it's tremors; and spread all animals across it. And We sent rain from the sky, growing plants of every kind all over it. ¹¹This is Allah's creation. Now show me what others beside Him have created. Nothing! The wrongdoers are clearly misguided.

Luqman teaches his son to reject the false gods

¹²We gave Luqman wisdom: "Be thankful to Allah." Whoever is thankful benefits himself; and whoever is unthankful *harms himself.* Allah is Self-Sufficient, Praiseworthy.

ᵃ This refers to a Makkan, Nadhar ibn Harith, who was paid to narrate Persian stories in competition with the Quran.

لِنَفْسِهٖ ۚ وَمَنْ كَفَرَ فَاِنَّ اللّٰهَ غَنِیٌّ حَمِیْدٌ ۝ وَاِذْ
قَالَ لُقْمٰنُ لِابْنِهٖ وَهُوَ یَعِظُهٗ یٰبُنَیَّ لَا تُشْرِكْ بِاللّٰهِ ؕ
اِنَّ الشِّرْكَ لَظُلْمٌ عَظِیْمٌ ۝ وَوَصَّیْنَا الْاِنْسَانَ
بِوَالِدَیْهِ ۚ حَمَلَتْهُ اُمُّهٗ وَهْنًا عَلٰی وَهْنٍ وَّفِصٰلُهٗ
فِیْ عَامَیْنِ اَنِ اشْكُرْ لِیْ وَلِوَالِدَیْكَ ؕ اِلَیَّ الْمَصِیْرُ ۝
وَاِنْ جَاهَدٰكَ عَلٰۤی اَنْ تُشْرِكَ بِیْ مَا لَیْسَ لَكَ
بِهٖ عِلْمٌ ۙ فَلَا تُطِعْهُمَا وَصَاحِبْهُمَا فِی الدُّنْیَا
مَعْرُوْفًا ۫ وَّاتَّبِعْ سَبِیْلَ مَنْ اَنَابَ اِلَیَّ ۚ ثُمَّ اِلَیَّ
مَرْجِعُكُمْ فَاُنَبِّئُكُمْ بِمَا كُنْتُمْ تَعْمَلُوْنَ ۝ یٰبُنَیَّ
اِنَّهَاۤ اِنْ تَكُ مِثْقَالَ حَبَّةٍ مِّنْ خَرْدَلٍ فَتَكُنْ فِیْ
صَخْرَةٍ اَوْ فِی السَّمٰوٰتِ اَوْ فِی الْاَرْضِ یَاْتِ بِهَا
اللّٰهُ ؕ اِنَّ اللّٰهَ لَطِیْفٌ خَبِیْرٌ ۝ یٰبُنَیَّ اَقِمِ الصَّلٰوةَ
وَاْمُرْ بِالْمَعْرُوْفِ وَانْهَ عَنِ الْمُنْكَرِ وَاصْبِرْ عَلٰی مَاۤ
اَصَابَكَ ؕ اِنَّ ذٰلِكَ مِنْ عَزْمِ الْاُمُوْرِ ۝ وَلَا تُصَعِّرْ
خَدَّكَ لِلنَّاسِ وَلَا تَمْشِ فِی الْاَرْضِ مَرَحًا ؕ
اِنَّ اللّٰهَ لَا یُحِبُّ كُلَّ مُخْتَالٍ فَخُوْرٍ ۝ وَاقْصِدْ
فِیْ مَشْیِكَ وَاغْضُضْ مِنْ صَوْتِكَ ؕ اِنَّ اَنْكَرَ
الْاَصْوَاتِ لَصَوْتُ الْحَمِیْرِ ۝ اَلَمْ تَرَوْا اَنَّ اللّٰهَ
سَخَّرَ لَكُمْ مَّا فِی السَّمٰوٰتِ وَمَا فِی الْاَرْضِ
وَاَسْبَغَ عَلَیْكُمْ نِعَمَهٗ ظَاهِرَةً وَّبَاطِنَةً ؕ وَ

Which pieces of Luqman's advice impress you the most? Why?

¹³*Remember* when Luqman said to his son, as he advised him, "My dear son, don't associate *anything* with Allah. Associating is a major sin."

We should respect our parents

¹⁴We commanded *every* human to care for his parents; his mother carried him in pain *during pregnancy*, and breastfed him for *nearly* two years. So be thankful to Me and your parents, *your* destination is to Me. ¹⁵However, if they force you to associate something with Me of which you have no proof, then don't obey them. Despite this care for them in this life. Follow the path of those who turn to Me, eventually you will return to Me, and I shall inform you of what you did.

Luqman teaches his son: Beliefs and values

¹⁶"My dear son, *everything* – even as small as a mustard seed *hidden* inside a rock, or in the Heavens or under ground – Allah will bring out *on Judgement Day*. Allah is the *infinitely* Subtle, the All-Aware. ¹⁷"My dear son, perform the prayer regularly, enjoin good, forbid evil, and be patient in times of *hardship*; these are *the marks* of determination. ¹⁸"Don't look down on people or swagger about. Allah dislikes every rude boaster. ¹⁹Walk humbly and keep your voice down. The most disliked sound is the *braying* of the donkey."

Appreciating Allah's gifts

²⁰Haven't you considered how Allah made everything in the Heavens and the Earth serve your needs, and bestowed His gifts on you, visible and hidden? *Yet* there are people who argue about Allah without any knowledge, guidance or book to enlighten *them*.

مِنَ النَّاسِ مَنْ يُّجَادِلُ فِي اللهِ بِغَيْرِ عِلْمٍ وَّلَا

هُدًى وَّلَا كِتٰبٍ مُّنِيْرٍ ۞ وَاِذَا قِيْلَ لَهُمُ اتَّبِعُوْا

مَا اَنْزَلَ اللهُ قَالُوْا بَلْ نَتَّبِعُ مَا وَجَدْنَا عَلَيْهِ

اٰبَآءَنَا ط اَوَلَوْ كَانَ الشَّيْطٰنُ يَدْعُوْهُمْ اِلٰى عَذَابِ

السَّعِيْرِ ۞ وَمَنْ يُّسْلِمْ وَجْهَهٗٓ اِلَى اللهِ وَهُوَ

مُحْسِنٌ فَقَدِ اسْتَمْسَكَ بِالْعُرْوَةِ الْوُثْقٰى ط وَاِلَى

اللهِ عَاقِبَةُ الْاُمُوْرِ ۞ وَمَنْ كَفَرَ فَلَا يَحْزُنْكَ

The sheer power and
force of Allah's words are
incomprehensible. Have
you ever experienced
their effect?

كُفْرُهٗ ط اِلَيْنَا مَرْجِعُهُمْ فَنُنَبِّئُهُمْ بِمَا عَمِلُوْا ط اِنَّ

اللهَ عَلِيْمٌۢ بِذَاتِ الصُّدُوْرِ ۞ نُمَتِّعُهُمْ قَلِيْلًا ثُمَّ

نَضْطَرُّهُمْ اِلٰى عَذَابٍ غَلِيْظٍ ۞ وَلَئِنْ سَاَلْتَهُمْ مَّنْ

خَلَقَ السَّمٰوٰتِ وَالْاَرْضَ لَيَقُوْلُنَّ اللهُ ط قُلِ الْحَمْدُ

لِلهِ ط بَلْ اَكْثَرُهُمْ لَا يَعْلَمُوْنَ ۞ لِلهِ مَا فِي السَّمٰوٰتِ

وَالْاَرْضِ ط اِنَّ اللهَ هُوَ الْغَنِيُّ الْحَمِيْدُ ۞ وَلَوْ اَنَّ مَا

فِي الْاَرْضِ مِنْ شَجَرَةٍ اَقْلَامٌ وَّالْبَحْرُ يَمُدُّهٗ مِنْ

بَعْدِهٖ سَبْعَةُ اَبْحُرٍ مَّا نَفِدَتْ كَلِمٰتُ اللهِ ط اِنَّ

اللهَ عَزِيْزٌ حَكِيْمٌ ۞ مَا خَلْقُكُمْ وَلَا بَعْثُكُمْ اِلَّا

كَنَفْسٍ وَّاحِدَةٍ ط اِنَّ اللهَ سَمِيْعٌۢ بَصِيْرٌ ۞ اَلَمْ تَرَ اَنَّ

اللهَ يُوْلِجُ الَّيْلَ فِي النَّهَارِ وَيُوْلِجُ النَّهَارَ فِي الَّيْلِ

وَسَخَّرَ الشَّمْسَ وَالْقَمَرَ كُلٌّ يَّجْرِيْٓ اِلٰٓى اَجَلٍ مُّسَمًّى

وَّاَنَّ اللهَ بِمَا تَعْمَلُوْنَ خَبِيْرٌ ۞ ذٰلِكَ بِاَنَّ اللهَ

²¹ When they are told: "Follow what Allah has revealed," they say, "No! We follow what we found our forefathers doing." What? Even if it is Satan who is calling them to the torment of the *fiery* Blaze? ²² Whoever turns his face in submission and righteousness towards Allah has grasped an unshakable handhold. *Thereafter,* the outcome of events rests with Allah. ²³ The disbelievers' disbelief shouldn't grieve you. They will return to Us, and We'll tell them what they did. Allah knows well their innermost thoughts. ²⁴ We let them enjoy themselves a little, then force them in to a severe punishment.

Allah's words and works are limitless

²⁵ If you ask them: "Who created the Heavens and the Earth?" They will say, "Allah." Say: "Praise be to Allah!" Most don't have any knowledge. ²⁶ Whatever is in the Heavens and the Earth belongs to Allah. He is the Self-Sufficient, the Praiseworthy. ²⁷ If all the trees on Earth were pens, and the sea and seven more seas beside were ink, the words of Allah would not end. Allah is Almighty, Wise. ²⁸ *For Him*, creating and resurrecting *all of* you is just like *creating and resurrecting* a single soul. Allah is Hearing, Seeing.

Observing Allah's signs without believing

²⁹ Haven't you considered how Allah causes night to merge into day, and day to merge into night; and how He has made the sun and the moon for your benefit, each coursing *through the sky* until *their* appointed time *to set*; and how Allah is fully aware of what you do?

هُوَ الْحَقُّ وَ اَنَّ مَا يَدْعُوْنَ مِنْ دُوْنِهِ الْبَاطِلُ ۙ

وَ اَنَّ اللّٰهَ هُوَ الْعَلِىُّ الْكَبِيْرُ ۞ اَلَمْ تَرَ اَنَّ الْفُلْكَ

تَجْرِىْ فِى الْبَحْرِ بِنِعْمَتِ اللّٰهِ لِيُرِيَكُمْ مِنْ اٰيٰتِهٖ ؕ

اِنَّ فِىْ ذٰلِكَ لَاٰيٰتٍ لِّكُلِّ صَبَّارٍ شَكُوْرٍ ۞ وَ اِذَا

غَشِيَهُمْ مَّوْجٌ كَالظُّلَلِ دَعَوُا اللّٰهَ مُخْلِصِيْنَ لَهُ

الدِّيْنَ ۚ فَلَمَّا نَجّٰهُمْ اِلَى الْبَرِّ فَمِنْهُمْ مُّقْتَصِدٌ ؕ

وَ مَا يَجْحَدُ بِاٰيٰتِنَآ اِلَّا كُلُّ خَتَّارٍ كَفُوْرٍ ۞ يٰۤاَيُّهَا

النَّاسُ اتَّقُوْا رَبَّكُمْ وَ اخْشَوْا يَوْمًا لَّا يَجْزِىْ

وَالِدٌ عَنْ وَّلَدِهٖ ۫ وَ لَا مَوْلُوْدٌ هُوَ جَازٍ عَنْ وَّالِدِهٖ

شَيْئًا ؕ اِنَّ وَعْدَ اللّٰهِ حَقٌّ فَلَا تَغُرَّنَّكُمُ الْحَيٰوةُ

الدُّنْيَا ٰقفة وَ لَا يَغُرَّنَّكُمْ بِاللّٰهِ الْغَرُوْرُ ۞ اِنَّ

اللّٰهَ عِنْدَهٗ عِلْمُ السَّاعَةِ ۚ وَ يُنَزِّلُ الْغَيْثَ ۚ

وَ يَعْلَمُ مَا فِى الْاَرْحَامِ ؕ وَ مَا تَدْرِىْ نَفْسٌ

مَّاذَا تَكْسِبُ غَدًا ؕ وَ مَا تَدْرِىْ نَفْسٌ بِاَىِّ

اَرْضٍ تَمُوْتُ ؕ اِنَّ اللّٰهَ عَلِيْمٌ خَبِيْرٌ ۞

Thankfulness is key to a happy life; thanking Allah, one's parents and the people around you.

³⁰Since Allah is the Truth, while whatever *disbelievers* call beside Him is false. Allah is the Exalted, the Great. ³¹Haven't you considered how ships sail across the sea by the grace of Allah to show you *some* of His signs? In that there are signs for every patient *and* thankful person. ³²Whenever a wave covers them like shadows they call Allah, sincere in their devotion; but when He brings them safely to land, some of them hesitate *to believe*.ᵃ Anyone who disputes Our signs, is disloyal, unthankful.

Concluding thoughts

³³People, be mindful of your Lord and fear a Day when a parent will not benefit his child, nor a child benefit his parent. Allah's promise is true; so make sure this worldly life doesn't deceive you, and make sure *Satan*, the arch-deceiver, doesn't deceive you *either*. ³⁴Allah *alone* has knowledge of the Final Hour; He sends rain and He knows what is in wombs. Nobody knows what he will earn tomorrow, and nobody knows where on Earth he will die; *but* Allah is the Knower, Aware.

ᵃ   Muqtasid according to Suyuti is "someone who wavers between faith and disbelief."

32. Surat As-Sajdah
The Prostration

This surat was revealed in the middle Makkan period, when debates raged about three key beliefs of Islam: oneness of Allah, *Tawhid*; prophethood, *Risalah*; and the Hereafter, *Akhirah*. The three beliefs are interconnected and arguments for one support the other. The surat opens with a confident assertion that refutes the disbeliever's objection that Muhammad ﷺ fabricated his message: "The revelation of the Book is, without a doubt, from the Lord of the worlds" (2). It is a universal message that is not confined to the Arabian Peninsula, but will eventually reach every corner of the globe. The central theme is: Allah the Supreme Ruler, the Absolute Governor and Commander has full control.

The Quran warns the disbelievers about the punishment to be meted out to them, not only in the Hereafter but in this life. When they see Hellfire they will believe, but it will be too late then. Similarly, the unimaginable delights awaiting the believers are highlighted to motivate people: "No one knows what blissful delights have been set aside for them as a reward for what they did" (17).

Finally, the Prophet ﷺ is told that he and Musa ﷺ are alike: both are receivers of Divine Revelation. The surat returns to the repeated theme of the confrontation between truth and falsehood, and compares the glorious Quran with life-giving rain; the latter gives life to dry, parched land. Similarly, the Quran gives life to dead hearts, and the dry minds.

بِسْمِ اللّٰهِ الرَّحْمٰنِ الرَّحِیْمِ

الٓمّٓ ۞ تَنْزِیْلُ الْكِتٰبِ لَا رَیْبَ فِیْهِ مِنْ رَّبِّ الْعٰلَمِیْنَ ۞ اَمْ یَقُوْلُوْنَ افْتَرٰىهُ ۚ بَلْ هُوَ الْحَقُّ مِنْ رَّبِّكَ لِتُنْذِرَ قَوْمًا مَّاۤ اَتٰىهُمْ مِّنْ نَّذِیْرٍ مِّنْ قَبْلِكَ لَعَلَّهُمْ یَهْتَدُوْنَ ۞ اَللّٰهُ الَّذِیْ خَلَقَ السَّمٰوٰتِ وَالْاَرْضَ وَمَا بَیْنَهُمَا فِیْ سِتَّةِ اَیَّامٍ ثُمَّ اسْتَوٰى عَلَى الْعَرْشِ ۚ مَا لَكُمْ مِّنْ دُوْنِهٖ مِنْ وَّلِیٍّ وَّلَا شَفِیْعٍ ۚ اَفَلَا تَتَذَكَّرُوْنَ ۞ یُدَبِّرُ الْاَمْرَ مِنَ السَّمَآءِ اِلَى الْاَرْضِ ثُمَّ یَعْرُجُ اِلَیْهِ فِیْ یَوْمٍ كَانَ مِقْدَارُهٗۤ اَلْفَ سَنَةٍ مِّمَّا تَعُدُّوْنَ ۞ ذٰلِكَ عٰلِمُ الْغَیْبِ وَالشَّهَادَةِ الْعَزِیْزُ الرَّحِیْمُ ۙ الَّذِیْۤ اَحْسَنَ كُلَّ شَیْءٍ خَلَقَهٗ وَبَدَاَ خَلْقَ الْاِنْسَانِ مِنْ طِیْنٍ ۞ ثُمَّ جَعَلَ نَسْلَهٗ مِنْ سُلٰلَةٍ مِّنْ مَّآءٍ مَّهِیْنٍ ۞ ثُمَّ سَوّٰىهُ وَنَفَخَ فِیْهِ مِنْ رُّوْحِهٖ وَجَعَلَ لَكُمُ السَّمْعَ وَالْاَبْصَارَ وَالْاَفْئِدَةَ ؕ قَلِیْلًا مَّا تَشْكُرُوْنَ ۞ وَقَالُوْۤا ءَاِذَا ضَلَلْنَا فِی الْاَرْضِ ءَاِنَّا لَفِیْ خَلْقٍ جَدِیْدٍ ؕ بَلْ هُمْ بِلِقَآءِ رَبِّهِمْ كٰفِرُوْنَ ۞ قُلْ یَتَوَفّٰىكُمْ مَّلَكُ الْمَوْتِ الَّذِیْ وُكِّلَ بِكُمْ ثُمَّ اِلٰى رَبِّكُمْ تُرْجَعُوْنَ ۞ وَلَوْ تَرٰىۤ اِذِ الْمُجْرِمُوْنَ

Praise, glorify and sing the hymns of Allah's creativity. Why does Quran repeatedly remind one of the Creator?

In the name of Allah, the Kind, the Caring.

[1] *Alif Lam Meem.*

The Quran is revelation, not fiction

[2] The revelation of the Book free from any doubt, is from the Lord of the worlds. [3] They say: "*Muhammad* has made it up"? On the contrary, it is the truth from your Lord, *revealed* to you to warn a people to whom no warner has come before you, so they may be guided. [4] Allah created the Heavens and the Earth and what's between them in six days, and then established Himself upon the Throne *as befits Him.* You have no helper or intercessor beside Him. Will you not pay attention?

Allah governs the universe

[5] He oversees the running *of everything* from the sky to the Earth, which will then go up to Him on a Day whose extent shall be *like* a thousand years by your counting. [6] Such is the Knower of the seen and the unseen *realms*, the Almighty, the Caring, [7] He created everything perfectly; He began the creation of the *first* human from clay, [8] and then made his offspring from a drop of semen.[a] [9] Then He gave *Adam* his form, and blew into him of His spirit; and gave you hearing, sight and awareness. Little do you thank!

The evildoers will be convinced when they see Hell

[10] *The disbelievers* say: "How is it *possible* when we have decomposed in the Earth, we shall be created anew?" They are in denial of meeting their Lord. [11] Say: "The angel of death assigned to you will take your soul, and you will be returned to your Lord."

---

[a] Literally 'humble water', that interestingly contains the entire human genome.

نَا كِسُوۡا رُءُوۡسِهِمۡ عِنۡدَ رَبِّهِمۡ ط رَبَّنَاۤ اَبۡصَرۡنَا

وَ سَمِعۡنَا فَارۡجِعۡنَا نَعۡمَلۡ صَالِحًا اِنَّا مُوۡقِنُوۡنَ ۝

وَ لَوۡ شِئۡنَا لَاٰتَیۡنَا كُلَّ نَفۡسٍ هُدٰىهَا وَ لٰكِنۡ حَقَّ

الۡقَوۡلُ مِنِّیۡ لَاَمۡلَـَٔنَّ جَهَنَّمَ مِنَ الۡجِنَّةِ وَ النَّاسِ

اَجۡمَعِیۡنَ ۝ فَذُوۡقُوۡا بِمَا نَسِیۡتُمۡ لِقَآءَ یَوۡمِكُمۡ هٰذَا ۚ

اِنَّا نَسِیۡنٰكُمۡ وَ ذُوۡقُوۡا عَذَابَ الۡخُلۡدِ بِمَا كُنۡتُمۡ

تَعۡمَلُوۡنَ ۝ اِنَّمَا یُؤۡمِنُ بِاٰیٰتِنَا الَّذِیۡنَ اِذَا ذُكِّرُوۡا

بِهَا خَرُّوۡا سُجَّدًا وَّ سَبَّحُوۡا بِحَمۡدِ رَبِّهِمۡ وَ هُمۡ

لَا یَسۡتَكۡبِرُوۡنَ ۩ ۝ تَتَجَافٰی جُنُوۡبُهُمۡ عَنِ الۡمَضَاجِعِ

یَدۡعُوۡنَ رَبَّهُمۡ خَوۡفًا وَّ طَمَعًا ۪ وَّ مِمَّا رَزَقۡنٰهُمۡ

یُنۡفِقُوۡنَ ۝ فَلَا تَعۡلَمُ نَفۡسٌ مَّاۤ اُخۡفِیَ لَهُمۡ مِّنۡ

قُرَّةِ اَعۡیُنٍ ۚ جَزَآءًۢ بِمَا كَانُوۡا یَعۡمَلُوۡنَ ۝ اَفَمَنۡ كَانَ

مُؤۡمِنًا كَمَنۡ كَانَ فَاسِقًا ط لَا یَسۡتَوٗنَ ۝ اَمَّا الَّذِیۡنَ

اٰمَنُوۡا وَ عَمِلُوا الصّٰلِحٰتِ فَلَهُمۡ جَنّٰتُ الۡمَاۡوٰی ۫ نُزُلًۢا

بِمَا كَانُوۡا یَعۡمَلُوۡنَ ۝ وَ اَمَّا الَّذِیۡنَ فَسَقُوۡا فَمَاۡوٰىهُمُ

النَّارُ ط كُلَّمَاۤ اَرَادُوۡۤا اَنۡ یَّخۡرُجُوۡا مِنۡهَاۤ اُعِیۡدُوۡا فِیۡهَا

وَ قِیۡلَ لَهُمۡ ذُوۡقُوۡا عَذَابَ النَّارِ الَّذِیۡ كُنۡتُمۡ بِهٖ

تُكَذِّبُوۡنَ ۝ وَ لَنُذِیۡقَنَّهُمۡ مِّنَ الۡعَذَابِ الۡاَدۡنٰی دُوۡنَ

الۡعَذَابِ الۡاَكۡبَرِ لَعَلَّهُمۡ یَرۡجِعُوۡنَ ۝ وَ مَنۡ اَظۡلَمُ

مِمَّنۡ ذُكِّرَ بِاٰیٰتِ رَبِّهٖ ثُمَّ اَعۡرَضَ عَنۡهَا ط اِنَّا

The consequences of good and bad actions are presented in startling and shocking language. Why?

[12] If only you could see the evildoers bowing their heads before their Lord *and saying*: "Our Lord, we've seen and heard *the truth*, let us go back *to the world* and we shall do good deeds; we are convinced *now*." [13] If We had so wished, We could have given every person guidance; but My declaration will be fulfilled: "I will fill Hell with jinn and humans, [14] *so* taste *the punishment*, because you ignored the coming of this Day. We shall now ignore you. Taste this everlasting torment for what you did."

The delights of Paradise are beyond imagination

[15] When some people are reminded of Our signs they believe and fall in prostration, glorify and praise their Lord, and aren't arrogant. [16] They drag themselves out of bed to worship their Lord, with fear and hope, and they spend *in charity* from what We provided them. [17] No one knows what blissful delights have been set aside for them as a reward for what they did. [18] So, can a believer be compared to a sinner? They aren't equal. [19] Those who believed and were righteous shall be in the gardens of *Mawa*,ª hospitality for what they did.

Disbelievers will be punished in this world and the next

[20] The major sinners will have a home, the Fire; *and* every time they try to escape it, they will be thrown back, and told: "Taste the torment of the Fire you denied." [21] We'll make them taste the lesser torment *in this life*, and the greater torment *in the Hereafter*, so they may return *to the straight path*. [22] Who can do *himself* greater wrong than the one who is reminded of his Lord's verses and turns his back on them. We shall punish the evildoers.

ª   *Mawa* is the name of one of the Heavens; it means a place of refuge and perpetual rest.

مِنَ الْمُجْرِمِيْنَ مُنْتَقِمُوْنَ ۝ وَلَقَدْ اٰتَيْنَا مُوْسَى

الْكِتٰبَ فَلَا تَكُنْ فِيْ مِرْيَةٍ مِّنْ لِّقَآئِهٖ وَجَعَلْنٰهُ

هُدًى لِّبَنِيْ اِسْرَآءِيْلَ ۝ وَجَعَلْنَا مِنْهُمْ اَئِمَّةً

يَّهْدُوْنَ بِاَمْرِنَا لَمَّا صَبَرُوْا ۖ وَكَانُوْا بِاٰيٰتِنَا

يُوْقِنُوْنَ ۝ اِنَّ رَبَّكَ هُوَ يَفْصِلُ بَيْنَهُمْ يَوْمَ

الْقِيٰمَةِ فِيْمَا كَانُوْا فِيْهِ يَخْتَلِفُوْنَ ۝ اَوَلَمْ يَهْدِ

لَهُمْ كَمْ اَهْلَكْنَا مِنْ قَبْلِهِمْ مِّنَ الْقُرُوْنِ يَمْشُوْنَ

فِيْ مَسٰكِنِهِمْ ۚ اِنَّ فِيْ ذٰلِكَ لَاٰيٰتٍ ۗ اَفَلَا يَسْمَعُوْنَ ۝

اَوَلَمْ يَرَوْا اَنَّا نَسُوْقُ الْمَآءَ اِلَى الْاَرْضِ الْجُرُزِ

فَنُخْرِجُ بِهٖ زَرْعًا تَاْكُلُ مِنْهُ اَنْعَامُهُمْ وَاَنْفُسُهُمْ ۗ

اَفَلَا يُبْصِرُوْنَ ۝ وَيَقُوْلُوْنَ مَتٰى هٰذَا الْفَتْحُ اِنْ

كُنْتُمْ صٰدِقِيْنَ ۝ قُلْ يَوْمَ الْفَتْحِ لَا يَنْفَعُ الَّذِيْنَ

كَفَرُوْا اِيْمَانُهُمْ وَلَا هُمْ يُنْظَرُوْنَ ۝ فَاَعْرِضْ

عَنْهُمْ وَانْتَظِرْ اِنَّهُمْ مُّنْتَظِرُوْنَ ۝

All good things take time to mature, blossom, and give fruit. Similarly, a long-life dedicated to Allah will achieve great results. Are you ready to wait?

Muhammad's ﷺ experience of revelation is similar to Musa's

²³We gave Musa the Book; don't doubt receiving it; and We made it a guide for the Israelites. ²⁴Some of them We made leaders, guiding others patiently with Our Command; and they were convinced of Our signs. ²⁵Your Lord will judge between them on Judgement Day concerning what they differed about. ²⁶How many generations before them We destroyed in whose *former* homes they walk, isn't there a lesson for them? In that are signs. So *why* don't they listen? ²⁷Haven't they considered how We move the clouds towards dry land, thereby producing crops from which they and their livestock eat? Have they no insight?

The disbelievers' anxiety about Judgement Day

²⁸They say, "When will this judgement come to pass, if you are telling the truth?" ²⁹Say: "On Decision Day, their *new-found* faith will not benefit the disbelievers, nor will they be given time *to repent*." ³⁰So take no notice of them; wait, as they are waiting.

33. Surat Al-Ahzab
The Confederates

This surat was revealed in the fifth year of Hijrah (626 CE). After the indecisive Battle of Uhud, the Makkans wanted to defeat the Muslims, so in collaboration with the expelled Jews of Banu Nadhir, living in Khyber, they planned to attack Madinah. They gathered an army of 10,000 strong, consisting of many tribes, the confederates.

Background of The Battle of the Trench.

When the Prophet ﷺ heard about the Makkan plan, he immediately called a meeting of the disciples to discuss the impending danger. Various ideas were presented and the proposal of Salman the Persian was preferred: to dig a trench between the long stretches of fortress-like houses on the outskirts of the city, whilst in the Northwest there were high rocks that were difficult to cross. So, a trench five metres wide, five metres deep, and seven kilometres long must be dug in three weeks. The Prophet ﷺ assigned a twenty-metre stretch to a team of ten men. For three weeks, thousands of volunteers worked day and night. A daunting task, requiring camaraderie and sense of unity, this song captures their enthusiasm beautifully: "Allah! There is no life but the life Hereafter; be kind to the helpers and the migrants."

As soon as the trench was finished, the army of confederates reached the outskirts of Madinah. Abu Sufyan, the commander, was baffled when he saw the trench. He decided to camp outside the city near Uhud, and lay siege on Madinah. The only way to enter the city was if the Jews of Banu Nadhir were to attack from inside. So, the Quraysh and the Jews of Banu Qurayda put together a strategy to win over Banu Nadhir and eventually a pact was agreed; Banu Nadhir would help. The plan went horribly wrong, and the confederates received no help from them. The siege was difficult to maintain, the winter nights were long and bitterly cold, and the horsemen tried several times to cross the trench, but failed miserably. A violent sandstorm blew the tents; the camels and horses of the Makkan forces ran wildly. The besiegers, dispirited and frightened, fled, after three weeks this Divine Intervention saved the Muslims.

This was a testing time for the Muslims. It required wise and brave leadership and committed followers. A large part of the surat deals with the personal life and wonderful character of the Prophet ﷺ, and his relationships with disciples and family. He is addressed on six occasions with the refrain: "O Prophet!" To bolster his morale, reassuring him of his unique position in Allah's sight, and encouraging him to lead confidently. Also:

> In the Messenger of Allah there is a beautiful example for you … We sent you as a witness, giver of good news and a Warner, one who invites to Allah by his permission and *you are* a light-giving lamp (21–46).

True followers practise self-control, a key to success in life, so special advice is offered to the Disciples, who faced all kinds of tests: criticism from the hypocrites; the siege; lack of food and water; and the continuous threat of attack. They had to control anger, frustration and fear. The challenge was to resist Satan's whispers, and refrain from losing self-control.

The surat highlights some qualities of the believers: unwavering faith in the mission of the Prophet 舜; grateful to Allah; truthful and direct. The surat ends by clarifying the purpose and meaning of human life – proper use of "free will" and "moral responsibility". How we fulfil this responsibility will determine our eventual fate; Hell, or Heaven.

بِسْمِ اللهِ الرَّحْمٰنِ الرَّحِيْمِ

يٰٓاَيُّهَا النَّبِيُّ اتَّقِ اللهَ وَلَا تُطِعِ الْكٰفِرِيْنَ وَ

الْمُنٰفِقِيْنَ ؕ اِنَّ اللهَ كَانَ عَلِيْمًا حَكِيْمًا ۙ وَّاتَّبِعْ مَا

يُوْحٰۤى اِلَيْكَ مِنْ رَّبِّكَ ؕ اِنَّ اللهَ كَانَ بِمَا تَعْمَلُوْنَ

خَبِيْرًا ۙ وَّتَوَكَّلْ عَلَى اللهِ ؕ وَكَفٰى بِاللهِ وَكِيْلًا ۳

مَا جَعَلَ اللهُ لِرَجُلٍ مِّنْ قَلْبَيْنِ فِيْ جَوْفِهٖ ۚ وَمَا

جَعَلَ اَزْوَاجَكُمُ الّٰٓئِيْ تُظٰهِرُوْنَ مِنْهُنَّ اُمَّهٰتِكُمْ ۚ

وَمَا جَعَلَ اَدْعِيَآءَكُمْ اَبْنَآءَكُمْ ؕ ذٰلِكُمْ قَوْلُكُمْ

بِاَفْوَاهِكُمْ ؕ وَاللهُ يَقُوْلُ الْحَقَّ وَهُوَ يَهْدِى السَّبِيْلَ ۴

اُدْعُوْهُمْ لِاٰبَآئِهِمْ هُوَ اَقْسَطُ عِنْدَ اللهِ ۚ فَاِنْ لَّمْ

تَعْلَمُوْۤا اٰبَآءَهُمْ فَاِخْوَانُكُمْ فِى الدِّيْنِ وَمَوَالِيْكُمْ ؕ

وَلَيْسَ عَلَيْكُمْ جُنَاحٌ فِيْمَاۤ اَخْطَاْتُمْ بِهٖ ۙ وَلٰكِنْ مَّا

تَعَمَّدَتْ قُلُوْبُكُمْ ؕ وَكَانَ اللهُ غَفُوْرًا رَّحِيْمًا ۵

اَلنَّبِيُّ اَوْلٰى بِالْمُؤْمِنِيْنَ مِنْ اَنْفُسِهِمْ وَاَزْوَاجُهٗۤ

اُمَّهٰتُهُمْ ؕ وَاُولُوا الْاَرْحَامِ بَعْضُهُمْ اَوْلٰى بِبَعْضٍ

فِيْ كِتٰبِ اللهِ مِنَ الْمُؤْمِنِيْنَ وَالْمُهٰجِرِيْنَ اِلَّاۤ

اَنْ تَفْعَلُوْۤا اِلٰۤى اَوْلِيٰٓئِكُمْ مَّعْرُوْفًا ؕ كَانَ ذٰلِكَ

فِى الْكِتٰبِ مَسْطُوْرًا ۷ وَاِذْ اَخَذْنَا مِنَ النَّبِيّٖنَ

مِيْثَاقَهُمْ وَمِنْكَ وَمِنْ نُّوْحٍ وَّاِبْرٰهِيْمَ وَمُوْسٰى وَ

We have one mind, one heart and therefore one Lord to love.

831

In the name of Allah, the Kind, the Caring.

Be mindful of Allah

¹Prophet, be mindful of Allah, and don't listen to the disbelievers and the hypocrites. Allah is the Knower, the Wise. ²Follow what is revealed to you from your Lord. Allah is fully aware of what you do. ³Put your trust in Allah, He is a sufficient Guardian.

The false relationships of pagan times are abolished

⁴Allah has not set two hearts in any human chest; He doesn't turn your wives that were given divorce into your mothers;[a] nor does He turn your adopted sons into sons. These are *empty* words from your mouths; Allah speaks the truth, and He guides along the *straight* path. ⁵Call *the adopted children* by the names of their *biological* fathers; that is fairer in Allah's sight. And if you don't know *who* their fathers *are*, then they are your brothers in faith and your clients *deserving protection*. You won't be blamed for any mistakes you make, but only for deliberately planned activities. Allah is Forgiving, Caring.

The Prophet's ﷺ special relationship with believers

⁶The Prophet cares for the believers far more than they care for themselves, and his wives are their *spiritual* mothers. Although blood relatives are still closer to each other than are the believers and the emigrants – in Allah's Book – you should still act with common decency towards your dependants. All this is written in the Book.

---

[a] In Arabia, if a husband told his wife: "You are like my mother's back to me," that was a suspended divorce, it deprived her of sexual intimacy and the freedom to remarry. A cruel practice, also condemned in *Surat Al-Mujadilah* 58: 2.

عِيسَى ابْنَ مَرْيَمَ ۖ وَأَخَذْنَا مِنْهُم مِّيثَاقًا غَلِيظًا ۞

لِّيَسْئَلَ الصَّدِقِينَ عَن صِدْقِهِمْ ۚ وَأَعَدَّ لِلْكَفِرِينَ

عَذَابًا أَلِيمًا ۞ يَٰٓأَيُّهَا الَّذِينَ ءَامَنُوا اذْكُرُوا نِعْمَةَ

اللَّهِ عَلَيْكُمْ إِذْ جَآءَتْكُمْ جُنُودٌ فَأَرْسَلْنَا عَلَيْهِمْ

رِيحًا وَّجُنُودًا لَّمْ تَرَوْهَا ۚ وَكَانَ اللَّهُ بِمَا تَعْمَلُونَ

بَصِيرًا ۞ إِذْ جَآءُوكُم مِّن فَوْقِكُمْ وَمِنْ أَسْفَلَ

مِنكُمْ وَإِذْ زَاغَتِ الْأَبْصَارُ وَبَلَغَتِ الْقُلُوبُ الْحَنَاجِرَ

وَتَظُنُّونَ بِاللَّهِ الظُّنُونَا ۞ هُنَالِكَ ابْتُلِىَ الْمُؤْمِنُونَ

وَزُلْزِلُوا زِلْزَالًا شَدِيدًا ۞ وَإِذْ يَقُولُ الْمُنَٰفِقُونَ

وَالَّذِينَ فِى قُلُوبِهِم مَّرَضٌ مَّا وَعَدَنَا اللَّهُ

وَرَسُولُهُ إِلَّا غُرُورًا ۞ وَإِذْ قَالَت طَّآئِفَةٌ مِّنْهُمْ

يَٰٓأَهْلَ يَثْرِبَ لَا مُقَامَ لَكُمْ فَارْجِعُوا ۚ وَيَسْتَئْذِنُ

فَرِيقٌ مِّنْهُمُ النَّبِىَّ يَقُولُونَ إِنَّ بُيُوتَنَا عَوْرَةٌ ۚ وَمَا

هِىَ بِعَوْرَةٍ ۖ إِن يُرِيدُونَ إِلَّا فِرَارًا ۞ وَلَوْ دُخِلَتْ

عَلَيْهِم مِّنْ أَقْطَارِهَا ثُمَّ سُئِلُوا الْفِتْنَةَ لَأَتَوْهَا

وَمَا تَلَبَّثُوا بِهَآ إِلَّا يَسِيرًا ۞ وَلَقَدْ كَانُوا عَاهَدُوا

اللَّهَ مِن قَبْلُ لَا يُوَلُّونَ الْأَدْبَارَ ۚ وَكَانَ عَهْدُ اللَّهِ

مَسْئُولًا ۞ قُل لَّن يَنفَعَكُمُ الْفِرَارُ إِن فَرَرْتُم مِّنَ

الْمَوْتِ أَوِ الْقَتْلِ وَإِذًا لَّا تُمَتَّعُونَ إِلَّا قَلِيلًا ۞ قُلْ

مَن ذَا الَّذِى يَعْصِمُكُم مِّنَ اللَّهِ إِنْ أَرَادَ بِكُمْ

Sometimes in life everyone has to face serious life-threatening situations. That's when faith is tested. How will you fair?

[7] *Remember* when We took a contract from the prophets, and you, Nuh, Ibrahim, Musa and Isa, son of Maryam; We took a solemn contract from *all of* them: [8] He would test the claim of truthfulness of the truthful; He has prepared a painful punishment for the disbelievers.

The gathered tribes posed serious threat

[9] Believers, remember Allah's favour when the armies gathered *against* you, We sent a wind-*stoked sandstorm* against them that you couldn't see. *Meanwhile,* Allah saw whatever you did. [10] They came *against* you from above and below, *your eyes rolled*, your hearts leapt to *your* throats, and you had wild thoughts about Allah;[a] [11] the believers were tested and severely shaken.

The hypocrites lacked loyalty and courage

[12] The hypocrites and those with sickness in their hearts said, "Allah and His Messenger promised us nothing but deception." [13] A group of them said, "People of Yathrib, you will not be safe anywhere, so retreat," while another group sought the Prophet's permission *to go back*, saying, "Our homes are exposed," yet they were not exposed; they wanted to flee. [14] If *the enemy* had attacked *the city* from *all* sides, and they had been offered an incentive *to switch sides*, they would have done so without hesitation, [15] despite previously having sworn by Allah that they would not turn tail *and flee*. They will be questioned about *the* oaths sworn in Allah's name. [16] Say: "Fleeing will not benefit you, if you run away from death or fighting you will have limited enjoyment *in life*." [17] Say: "Who can hold back Allah from you, if He willed you harm or kindness?" They will not find any supporter or helper beside Allah.

---

a   "The eyes rolled, the hearts leapt and you had wild thoughts..." this is an idiom that expresses the serious life-threatening situation the disciples faced, it shook their faith.

سُوٓءًا اَوْ اَرَادَ بِكُمْ رَحْمَةً ط وَلَا يَجِدُوْنَ لَهُمْ مِّنْ

دُوْنِ اللّٰهِ وَلِيًّا وَّلَا نَصِيْرًا ۟ قَدْ يَعْلَمُ اللّٰهُ

الْمُعَوِّقِيْنَ مِنْكُمْ وَالْقَآئِلِيْنَ لِاِخْوَانِهِمْ هَلُمَّ

اِلَيْنَا ۚ وَلَا يَأْتُوْنَ الْبَأْسَ اِلَّا قَلِيْلًا ۙ اَشِحَّةً

عَلَيْكُمْ ۚ فَاِذَا جَآءَ الْخَوْفُ رَاَيْتَهُمْ يَنْظُرُوْنَ اِلَيْكَ

تَدُوْرُ اَعْيُنُهُمْ كَالَّذِىْ يُغْشٰى عَلَيْهِ مِنَ الْمَوْتِ ۚ فَاِذَا

ذَهَبَ الْخَوْفُ سَلَقُوْكُمْ بِاَلْسِنَةٍ حِدَادٍ اَشِحَّةً عَلَى

الْخَيْرِ ط اُولٰٓئِكَ لَمْ يُؤْمِنُوْا فَاَحْبَطَ اللّٰهُ اَعْمَالَهُمْ ط

وَكَانَ ذٰلِكَ عَلَى اللّٰهِ يَسِيْرًا ۟ يَحْسَبُوْنَ الْاَحْزَابَ

لَمْ يَذْهَبُوْا ۚ وَاِنْ يَّأْتِ الْاَحْزَابُ يَوَدُّوْا لَوْ اَنَّهُمْ

بَادُوْنَ فِى الْاَعْرَابِ يَسْاَلُوْنَ عَنْ اَنْبَآئِكُمْ ط وَلَوْ

كَانُوْا فِيْكُمْ مَّا قٰتَلُوٓا اِلَّا قَلِيْلًا ۟ لَقَدْ كَانَ لَكُمْ

فِىْ رَسُوْلِ اللّٰهِ اُسْوَةٌ حَسَنَةٌ لِّمَنْ كَانَ يَرْجُوا اللّٰهَ وَ

الْيَوْمَ الْاٰخِرَ وَذَكَرَ اللّٰهَ كَثِيْرًا ط وَلَمَّا رَاَ الْمُؤْمِنُوْنَ

الْاَحْزَابَ ۙ قَالُوْا هٰذَا مَا وَعَدَنَا اللّٰهُ وَرَسُوْلُهُ وَ

صَدَقَ اللّٰهُ وَرَسُوْلُهُ ۖ وَمَا زَادَهُمْ اِلَّا اِيْمَانًا

وَّتَسْلِيْمًا ط مِنَ الْمُؤْمِنِيْنَ رِجَالٌ صَدَقُوْا مَا

عَاهَدُوا اللّٰهَ عَلَيْهِ ۚ فَمِنْهُمْ مَّنْ قَضٰى نَحْبَهُ وَ

مِنْهُمْ مَّنْ يَّنْتَظِرُ ۖ وَمَا بَدَّلُوْا تَبْدِيْلًا ۙ لِّيَجْزِىَ

اللّٰهُ الصّٰدِقِيْنَ بِصِدْقِهِمْ وَيُعَذِّبَ الْمُنٰفِقِيْنَ اِنْ

The disciples were afraid, tired and hungry but they had an unwavering faith in the Messenger's ﷺ leadership. Who do you look up to?

٢
ع
١٣
١٨

The hypocrites were disloyal

¹⁸ Allah knows those who obstruct and those who said to their brothers: "Why don't you come over to our side?" They hardly entered the battlefield. ¹⁹ *They are* envious of you; and when fear strikes, you see them looking to you *for reassurance*, their eyes flitting back and forth like someone dazed by *dread of* dying. Then, when the fear ebbs, they abuse you with sharp words. They resent you, expecting to gain something good. Such people haven't believed, so Allah will render their deeds worthless *on Judgement Day*, that's easy for Allah. ²⁰ They reckon the confederates haven't gone yet; and if the confederates should return, they would then love to be mingling with the Bedouins, seeking news about you. Even if they were on your side, they would barely fight.

The Muslims were loyal and confident

²¹ You have an excellent role model in the Messenger of Allah, particularly for anyone who longs for Allah and the Last Day and remembers Him abundantly. ²² When the believers saw the confederates, they said, "This is what Allah and His Messenger promised us. Allah and His Messenger spoke the truth," and *this experience* increased their faith and submission. ²³ Amid the believers are men who fulfilled their promise to Allah, some fulfilled their vow *by dying as martyrs*, while others are waiting; they didn't change. ²⁴ So Allah will reward the truthful for their truthfulness and punish the hypocrites *for disloyalty* as He pleases, or forgive them, Allah is Forgiving, Caring.

شَاءَ اَوْ يَتُوبَ عَلَيْهِمْ ۚ اِنَّ اللّٰهَ كَانَ غَفُوْرًا رَّحِيْمًا ۲۴

وَرَدَّ اللّٰهُ الَّذِيْنَ كَفَرُوْا بِغَيْظِهِمْ لَمْ يَنَالُوْا خَيْرًا ۚ

وَكَفَى اللّٰهُ الْمُؤْمِنِيْنَ الْقِتَالَ ۗ وَكَانَ اللّٰهُ قَوِيًّا

عَزِيْزًا ۲۵ وَاَنْزَلَ الَّذِيْنَ ظَاهَرُوْهُمْ مِّنْ اَهْلِ الْكِتٰبِ

مِنْ صَيَاصِيْهِمْ وَقَذَفَ فِيْ قُلُوْبِهِمُ الرُّعْبَ فَرِيْقًا

تَقْتُلُوْنَ وَتَأْسِرُوْنَ فَرِيْقًا ۲۶ وَاَوْرَثَكُمْ اَرْضَهُمْ وَ

دِيَارَهُمْ وَاَمْوَالَهُمْ وَاَرْضًا لَّمْ تَطَئُوْهَا ۗ وَكَانَ اللّٰهُ

عَلٰى كُلِّ شَيْءٍ قَدِيْرًا ۲۷ يٰٓاَيُّهَا النَّبِيُّ قُلْ لِّاَزْوَاجِكَ

اِنْ كُنْتُنَّ تُرِدْنَ الْحَيٰوةَ الدُّنْيَا وَزِيْنَتَهَا فَتَعَالَيْنَ

اُمَتِّعْكُنَّ وَاُسَرِّحْكُنَّ سَرَاحًا جَمِيْلًا ۲۸ وَاِنْ كُنْتُنَّ

تُرِدْنَ اللّٰهَ وَرَسُوْلَهُ وَالدَّارَ الْاٰخِرَةَ فَاِنَّ اللّٰهَ اَعَدَّ

لِلْمُحْسِنٰتِ مِنْكُنَّ اَجْرًا عَظِيْمًا ۲۹ يٰنِسَاءَ النَّبِيِّ

مَنْ يَّأْتِ مِنْكُنَّ بِفَاحِشَةٍ مُّبَيِّنَةٍ يُّضٰعَفْ لَهَا

الْعَذَابُ ضِعْفَيْنِ ۗ وَكَانَ ذٰلِكَ عَلَى اللّٰهِ يَسِيْرًا ۳۰

وَمَنْ يَّقْنُتْ مِنْكُنَّ لِلّٰهِ وَرَسُوْلِهِ وَتَعْمَلْ صَالِحًا

نُّؤْتِهَآ اَجْرَهَا مَرَّتَيْنِ ۙ وَاَعْتَدْنَا لَهَا رِزْقًا كَرِيْمًا ۳۱

يٰنِسَاءَ النَّبِيِّ لَسْتُنَّ كَاَحَدٍ مِّنَ النِّسَاءِ اِنِ اتَّقَيْتُنَّ

فَلَا تَخْضَعْنَ بِالْقَوْلِ فَيَطْمَعَ الَّذِيْ فِيْ قَلْبِهِ مَرَضٌ

وَّقُلْنَ قَوْلًا مَّعْرُوْفًا ۳۲ وَقَرْنَ فِيْ بُيُوْتِكُنَّ وَلَا

تَبَرَّجْنَ تَبَرُّجَ الْجَاهِلِيَّةِ الْاُوْلٰى وَاَقِمْنَ الصَّلٰوةَ

The Messenger's ﷺ wives are mothers of the believers. They gave up their luxurious lifestyle and adopted a simple one. Are you ready for a simple life too?

²⁵ Allah turned back the disbelievers, who were furious for not achieving any material gain; and Allah was sufficient *in His support* for the believers throughout the battle. Allah is Strong, Almighty.

Jews who acted disloyally were expelled

²⁶ The People of The Book who backed *the confederates* came out of their forts, but He cast terror into their hearts, *enabling* you to kill some and take others captive, ²⁷ and made you the heirs of their homes, wealth and land, the land that you had never set foot on. Allah has power over everything.

The Prophet's ☀ wives live a simple life

²⁸ Prophet, tell your wives: "If you desire worldly life and its luxuries, then come forward, I'll ensure that you get them, and release you *from marriage* in a dignified manner. ²⁹ But if you desire Allah and His Messenger, and the home of the Hereafter, then Allah has prepared a great reward for your righteousness." ³⁰ Wives of the Prophet, if any one of you commits a flagrant act of indecency, she will suffer double the *usual* punishment. That's easy to do for Allah; ³¹ but whoever is dedicated to Allah and His Messenger and does good works shall have double the reward; and We have prepared a generous provision for her.

Advice on how to prevent gossip

³² Wives of the Prophet, you are not like other women, you are more mindful. Don't speak softly, in case someone with sickness in his heart should build up his hopes; be polite *but assertive*;

٤
ع
١

وَاٰتِيْنَ الزَّكٰوةَ وَاَطِعْنَ اللهَ وَرَسُوْلَهٗ ۗ اِنَّمَا يُرِيْدُ
اللهُ لِيُذْهِبَ عَنْكُمُ الرِّجْسَ اَهْلَ الْبَيْتِ وَيُطَهِّرَكُمْ
تَطْهِيْرًا ۚ وَاذْكُرْنَ مَا يُتْلٰى فِيْ بُيُوْتِكُنَّ مِنْ اٰيٰتِ
اللهِ وَالْحِكْمَةِ ۗ اِنَّ اللهَ كَانَ لَطِيْفًا خَبِيْرًا ۞ اِنَّ
الْمُسْلِمِيْنَ وَالْمُسْلِمٰتِ وَالْمُؤْمِنِيْنَ وَالْمُؤْمِنٰتِ
وَالْقٰنِتِيْنَ وَالْقٰنِتٰتِ وَالصّٰدِقِيْنَ وَالصّٰدِقٰتِ وَ
الصّٰبِرِيْنَ وَالصّٰبِرٰتِ وَالْخٰشِعِيْنَ وَالْخٰشِعٰتِ وَ
الْمُتَصَدِّقِيْنَ وَالْمُتَصَدِّقٰتِ وَالصّٰٓئِمِيْنَ وَالصّٰٓئِمٰتِ وَ
الْحٰفِظِيْنَ فُرُوْجَهُمْ وَالْحٰفِظٰتِ وَالذّٰكِرِيْنَ اللهَ كَثِيْرًا
وَّالذّٰكِرٰتِ ۙ اَعَدَّ اللهُ لَهُمْ مَّغْفِرَةً وَّاَجْرًا عَظِيْمًا ۞
وَمَا كَانَ لِمُؤْمِنٍ وَّلَا مُؤْمِنَةٍ اِذَا قَضَى اللهُ وَرَسُوْلُهٗۤ
اَمْرًا اَنْ يَّكُوْنَ لَهُمُ الْخِيَرَةُ مِنْ اَمْرِهِمْ ۗ وَمَنْ يَّعْصِ
اللهَ وَرَسُوْلَهٗ فَقَدْ ضَلَّ ضَلٰلًا مُّبِيْنًا ۞ وَاِذْ تَقُوْلُ
لِلَّذِيْۤ اَنْعَمَ اللهُ عَلَيْهِ وَاَنْعَمْتَ عَلَيْهِ اَمْسِكْ
عَلَيْكَ زَوْجَكَ وَاتَّقِ اللهَ وَتُخْفِيْ فِيْ نَفْسِكَ مَا اللهُ
مُبْدِيْهِ وَتَخْشَى النَّاسَ ۚ وَاللهُ اَحَقُّ اَنْ تَخْشٰىهُ ۗ
فَلَمَّا قَضٰى زَيْدٌ مِّنْهَا وَطَرًا زَوَّجْنٰكَهَا لِكَيْ لَا يَكُوْنَ
عَلَى الْمُؤْمِنِيْنَ حَرَجٌ فِيْۤ اَزْوَاجِ اَدْعِيَآئِهِمْ اِذَا قَضَوْا
مِنْهُنَّ وَطَرًا ۗ وَكَانَ اَمْرُ اللهِ مَفْعُوْلًا ۞ مَا كَانَ عَلَى
النَّبِيِّ مِنْ حَرَجٍ فِيْمَا فَرَضَ اللهُ لَهٗ ۗ سُنَّةَ اللهِ

Once you are a believer you only have one way: Islam. Submit and commit yourself to Allah! Do you do what you are told?

839

³³ stay home; don't dress to show off, like the custom of the Age of Ignorance; perform the prayer, give Zakat, and obey Allah and His Messenger. Allah wants to remove *all* blemish from you as you are the *Prophet's* household, and to purify you. ³⁴ And think about the wonderful verses of Allah recited and the Prophetic wisdom that's practiced in your homes. Allah is Subtle, Aware.

A description of the women and men of Allah

³⁵ The Men and the women who submit *to the Will of Allah* are: believers, devout, truthful, patient, humble, charitable, keep fast, are chaste and *pure* and remember Allah frequently. Allah has prepared forgiveness and a mighty reward for them.

The story of Zaynab and Zayd

³⁶ A believing man and a woman have no choice in a matter that is decided by Allah and His Messenger; and anyone who disobeys Allah and His Messenger is wrong[a]. ³⁷ *Remember* when you said to the one Allah had favoured, and you also favoured: "Remain *married* to your wife, and be mindful of Allah." You kept to yourself what Allah had made clear *to you*, because you feared people's *reaction*, though Allah is to be feared more. When Zayd formally dissolved his marriage to her, We married her to you so that believers might feel no shame regarding *marrying* the *ex*-wives of their adopted sons, if they had formally dissolved their marriages to them, so that Allah's command is fulfilled.

---

[a] When the Messenger ﷺ asked Zaynab, who was his cousin to marry Zayd ibn Harith she refused because she thought he was not her equal, however upon hearing this verse she agreed to marry him. The Messenger ﷺ had brought up Zayd like a son.

فِى الَّذِيْنَ خَلَوْا مِنْ قَبْلُ ط وَكَانَ اَمْرُ اللّٰهِ قَدَرًا

مَّقْدُوْرَاۨ ۳۸ الَّذِيْنَ يُبَلِّغُوْنَ رِسٰلٰتِ اللّٰهِ وَيَخْشَوْنَهٗ

وَلَا يَخْشَوْنَ اَحَدًا اِلَّا اللّٰهَ ط وَكَفٰى بِاللّٰهِ حَسِيْبًا ۳۹

مَا كَانَ مُحَمَّدٌ اَبَآ اَحَدٍ مِّنْ رِّجَالِكُمْ وَلٰكِنْ

رَّسُوْلَ اللّٰهِ وَخَاتَمَ النَّبِيّٖنَ ط وَكَانَ اللّٰهُ بِكُلِّ شَىْءٍ

عَلِيْمًا ۴۰ يٰٓاَيُّهَا الَّذِيْنَ اٰمَنُوا اذْكُرُوا اللّٰهَ ذِكْرًا

كَثِيْرًاۙ ۴۱ وَّسَبِّحُوْهُ بُكْرَةً وَّاَصِيْلًا ۴۲ هُوَ الَّذِىْ

يُصَلِّىْ عَلَيْكُمْ وَمَلٰٓئِكَتُهٗ لِيُخْرِجَكُمْ مِّنَ الظُّلُمٰتِ اِلَى

النُّوْرِ ط وَكَانَ بِالْمُؤْمِنِيْنَ رَحِيْمًا ۴۳ تَحِيَّتُهُمْ يَوْمَ

يَلْقَوْنَهٗ سَلٰمٌ ۚ وَاَعَدَّ لَهُمْ اَجْرًا كَرِيْمًا ۴۴ يٰٓاَيُّهَا

النَّبِىُّ اِنَّآ اَرْسَلْنٰكَ شَاهِدًا وَّمُبَشِّرًا وَّنَذِيْرًاۙ ۴۵

وَّدَاعِيًا اِلَى اللّٰهِ بِاِذْنِهٖ وَسِرَاجًا مُّنِيْرًا ۴۶ وَبَشِّرِ

الْمُؤْمِنِيْنَ بِاَنَّ لَهُمْ مِّنَ اللّٰهِ فَضْلًا كَبِيْرًا ۴۷ وَلَا

تُطِعِ الْكٰفِرِيْنَ وَالْمُنٰفِقِيْنَ وَدَعْ اَذٰهُمْ وَتَوَكَّلْ عَلَى

اللّٰهِ ط وَكَفٰى بِاللّٰهِ وَكِيْلًا ۴۸ يٰٓاَيُّهَا الَّذِيْنَ اٰمَنُوْٓا اِذَا

نَكَحْتُمُ الْمُؤْمِنٰتِ ثُمَّ طَلَّقْتُمُوْهُنَّ مِنْ قَبْلِ اَنْ

تَمَسُّوْهُنَّ فَمَا لَكُمْ عَلَيْهِنَّ مِنْ عِدَّةٍ تَعْتَدُّوْنَهَا ۚ

فَمَتِّعُوْهُنَّ وَسَرِّحُوْهُنَّ سَرَاحًا جَمِيْلًا ۴۹ يٰٓاَيُّهَا النَّبِىُّ

اِنَّآ اَحْلَلْنَا لَكَ اَزْوَاجَكَ الّٰتِىْٓ اٰتَيْتَ اُجُوْرَهُنَّ وَمَا

مَلَكَتْ يَمِيْنُكَ مِمَّآ اَفَآءَ اللّٰهُ عَلَيْكَ وَبَنٰتِ عَمِّكَ وَبَنٰتِ

The Quran gives the Messenger ﷺ hundreds of titles that show his high station and the way Allah has honoured him.

841

³⁸The Prophet should feel no embarrassment regarding what Allah has made obligatory on him. *This is* the practice *of* Allah regarding those *prophets* who lived previously – and Allah's command is fulfilled – ³⁹delivering the messages of Allah, fearing Him *alone*, and fearing no one else but Allah; and Allah is sufficient Reckoner.

Muhammad ﷺ is the last and the final Prophet

⁴⁰Muhammad is not a father of anyone of your men, he is the Messenger of Allah and the seal of the Prophets, *the final Prophet*. Allah has knowledge of all things. ⁴¹Believers, remember Allah frequently, ⁴²and glorify Him in the morning and evening. ⁴³He blesses you, His angels pray to bring you out of darkness into the light; and He cares for the believers. ⁴⁴Their greeting on the Day they meet Him will be: "Peace!" And He has prepared for them a generous reward.

The Prophet's ﷺ clear mission

⁴⁵Prophet, We sent you as a witness, a herald of good news, and a warner, ⁴⁶calling *people* to Allah by His permission, and a shinning lamp. ⁴⁷So bring the believers good news of the bounty they will receive from Allah ⁴⁸and don't follow the disbelievers and hypocrites; ignore their harassment and put your trust in Allah. Allah is a sufficient Guardian.

Divorce before consummation

⁴⁹Believers, if you marry believing women, then before the consummation of your marriage you *decide to* divorce them, there is no waiting period for them.^a Provide for them and release them *from their marriage* in a dignified manner.

Clarification on marriage to prevent malicious gossip

⁵⁰Prophet, We made lawful for you: your wives who you gave a bridal gift; a *maid* you own from what Allah allotted you; the daughters of your paternal and maternal uncles and aunts, who emigrated with you; and any believing woman who offers herself to you, *and* you also want to wed; *this last ruling is* solely in relation to you, as distinct from the *other* believers – We know what We made obligatory on *other believers* regarding their wives and what their slave maids – so that there is no embarrassment for you. Allah is Forgiving, Caring.

---

^a The waiting period before a divorcee or a widow can marry is three months, to ensure that a child born after the divorce will know its father. This doesn't apply to an unconsummated marriage.

عَمَّتِكَ وَبَنَتِ خَالِكَ وَبَنَتِ خَلَاتِكَ الَّتِىْ هَاجَرْنَ مَعَكَ

وَامْرَاَةً مُّؤْمِنَةً اِنْ وَّهَبَتْ نَفْسَهَا لِلنَّبِىِّ اِنْ اَرَادَ النَّبِىُّ

اَنْ يَّسْتَنْكِحَهَا ۚ خَالِصَةً لَّكَ مِنْ دُوْنِ الْمُؤْمِنِيْنَ ۗ قَدْ

عَلِمْنَا مَا فَرَضْنَا عَلَيْهِمْ فِىْۤ اَزْوَاجِهِمْ وَمَا مَلَكَتْ

اَيْمَانُهُمْ لِكَيْلَا يَكُوْنَ عَلَيْكَ حَرَجٌ ۗ وَكَانَ اللهُ غَفُوْرًا

رَّحِيْمًا ۞ تُرْجِىْ مَنْ تَشَآءُ مِنْهُنَّ وَتُــْٔوِىْۤ اِلَيْكَ مَنْ

تَشَآءُ ۗ وَمَنِ ابْتَغَيْتَ مِمَّنْ عَزَلْتَ فَلَا جُنَاحَ عَلَيْكَ ۗ

ذٰلِكَ اَدْنٰۤى اَنْ تَقَرَّ اَعْيُنُهُنَّ وَلَا يَحْزَنَّ وَيَرْضَيْنَ

بِمَاۤ اٰتَيْتَهُنَّ كُلُّهُنَّ ۗ وَاللهُ يَعْلَمُ مَا فِىْ قُلُوْبِكُمْ ۗ

وَكَانَ اللهُ عَلِيْمًا حَلِيْمًا ۞ لَا يَحِلُّ لَكَ النِّسَآءُ مِنْ

بَعْدُ وَلَاۤ اَنْ تَبَدَّلَ بِهِنَّ مِنْ اَزْوَاجٍ وَّلَوْ اَعْجَبَكَ

حُسْنُهُنَّ اِلَّا مَا مَلَكَتْ يَمِيْنُكَ ۗ وَكَانَ اللهُ عَلٰى كُلِّ

شَىْءٍ رَّقِيْبًا ۞ يٰۤاَيُّهَا الَّذِيْنَ اٰمَنُوْا لَا تَدْخُلُوْا بُيُوْتَ

النَّبِىِّ اِلَّاۤ اَنْ يُّؤْذَنَ لَكُمْ اِلٰى طَعَامٍ غَيْرَ نٰظِرِيْنَ

اِنٰىهُ ۙ وَلٰكِنْ اِذَا دُعِيْتُمْ فَادْخُلُوْا فَاِذَا طَعِمْتُمْ

فَانْتَشِرُوْا وَلَا مُسْتَاْنِسِيْنَ لِحَدِيْثٍ ۗ اِنَّ ذٰلِكُمْ كَانَ

يُؤْذِى النَّبِىَّ فَيَسْتَحْىٖ مِنْكُمْ ۖ وَاللهُ لَا يَسْتَحْىٖ مِنَ

الْحَقِّ ۗ وَاِذَا سَاَلْتُمُوْهُنَّ مَتَاعًا فَسْـَٔلُوْهُنَّ مِنْ وَّرَآءِ

حِجَابٍ ۗ ذٰلِكُمْ اَطْهَرُ لِقُلُوْبِكُمْ وَقُلُوْبِهِنَّ ۗ وَمَا كَانَ

لَكُمْ اَنْ تُؤْذُوْا رَسُوْلَ اللهِ وَلَاۤ اَنْ تَنْكِحُوْۤا اَزْوَاجَهٗ

The unique station of the Prophet ﷺ is revealed by having certain privileges that no one else shares. See how Allah blesses Him?

843

⁵¹ You may postpone *the turn of* whomever of *your wives* you wish and receive back *into your intimacy* whomever you wish, *including* those you had withdrawn from, there should be no blame on you. That will reassure them, not sadden them; and please them with whatever *intimacy* you *give* them. Allah knows what is in your hearts. Allah is Knowing, Gentle. ⁵² From now on, no *other* women will be lawful for you, nor can you exchange them for other wives, even if you like their beauty, except a slave maid. Allah is the Observer of all things.

How to behave in the Prophet's 🕊 house

⁵³ Believers, don't enter the Prophet's apartments to eat without permission, and don't *come early and* wait around for it *to be cooked*. However, if you are invited, then come, and once you have eaten, leave without staying on to chat. Such *behaviour* offended the Prophet, he's embarrassed to tell you; but Allah is not embarrassed of *telling* the truth. And if you ask *his wives* for something, do so from behind a curtain; that is purer for your hearts and theirs. It isn't right for you either to cause offence to the Messenger of Allah or marry his wives after him, ever; such *behaviour* would be outrageous in Allah's sight.

مِنْۢ بَعْدِهٖۤ اَبَدًا ۭ اِنَّ ذٰلِكُمْ كَانَ عِنْدَ اللّٰهِ عَظِيْمًا ۝

اِنْ تُبْدُوْا شَيْـًٔا اَوْ تُخْفُوْهُ فَاِنَّ اللّٰهَ كَانَ بِكُلِّ

شَيْءٍ عَلِيْمًا ۝ لَا جُنَاحَ عَلَيْهِنَّ فِيْۤ اٰبَآئِهِنَّ وَلَاۤ

اَبْنَآئِهِنَّ وَلَاۤ اِخْوَانِهِنَّ وَلَاۤ اَبْنَآءِ اِخْوَانِهِنَّ وَلَاۤ

اَبْنَآءِ اَخَوٰتِهِنَّ وَلَا نِسَآئِهِنَّ وَلَا مَا مَلَكَتْ اَيْمَانُهُنَّ ۚ

وَاتَّقِيْنَ اللّٰهَ ۭ اِنَّ اللّٰهَ كَانَ عَلٰى كُلِّ شَيْءٍ شَهِيْدًا ۝

اِنَّ اللّٰهَ وَمَلٰٓئِكَتَهٗ يُصَلُّوْنَ عَلَى النَّبِيِّ ۭ يٰۤاَيُّهَا

الَّذِيْنَ اٰمَنُوْا صَلُّوْا عَلَيْهِ وَسَلِّمُوْا تَسْلِيْمًا ۝ اِنَّ

الَّذِيْنَ يُؤْذُوْنَ اللّٰهَ وَرَسُوْلَهٗ لَعَنَهُمُ اللّٰهُ فِى الدُّنْيَا

وَالْاٰخِرَةِ وَاَعَدَّ لَهُمْ عَذَابًا مُّهِيْنًا ۝ وَالَّذِيْنَ

يُؤْذُوْنَ الْمُؤْمِنِيْنَ وَالْمُؤْمِنٰتِ بِغَيْرِ مَا اكْتَسَبُوْا فَقَدِ

احْتَمَلُوْا بُهْتَانًا وَّاِثْمًا مُّبِيْنًا ۝ يٰۤاَيُّهَا النَّبِيُّ قُلْ

لِّاَزْوَاجِكَ وَبَنٰتِكَ وَنِسَآءِ الْمُؤْمِنِيْنَ يُدْنِيْنَ عَلَيْهِنَّ

مِنْ جَلَابِيْبِهِنَّ ۭ ذٰلِكَ اَدْنٰٓى اَنْ يُّعْرَفْنَ فَلَا يُؤْذَيْنَ ۭ

وَكَانَ اللّٰهُ غَفُوْرًا رَّحِيْمًا ۝ لَئِنْ لَّمْ يَنْتَهِ الْمُنٰفِقُوْنَ

وَالَّذِيْنَ فِيْ قُلُوْبِهِمْ مَّرَضٌ وَّالْمُرْجِفُوْنَ فِى الْمَدِيْنَةِ

لَنُغْرِيَنَّكَ بِهِمْ ثُمَّ لَا يُجَاوِرُوْنَكَ فِيْهَاۤ اِلَّا قَلِيْلًا ۝

مَّلْعُوْنِيْنَ ۚ اَيْنَمَا ثُقِفُوْۤا اُخِذُوْا وَقُتِّلُوْا تَقْتِيْلًا ۝

سُنَّةَ اللّٰهِ فِى الَّذِيْنَ خَلَوْا مِنْ قَبْلُ ۚ وَلَنْ تَجِدَ لِسُنَّةِ

اللّٰهِ تَبْدِيْلًا ۝ يَسْـَٔلُكَ النَّاسُ عَنِ السَّاعَةِ ۭ قُلْ اِنَّمَا

Why does the Quran insist on modesty? It provides a pure attitude and pure lifestyle.

ع
۴

⁵⁴ Whether you reveal or conceal something, Allah has knowledge of everything. ⁵⁵ There is no blame on *the Prophet's wives* being visited by their fathers, or their sons, or their brothers, or the sons of their brothers and sisters, or their *servant* women, or their servants. Be mindful of Allah, Allah sees everything.

Send blessings on the Messenger ﷺ

⁵⁶ Allah and His angels *continually* bless the Messenger; *so* believers, you too bless and greet him with peace. ⁵⁷ Anyone who insults Allah and His Messenger, Allah curses them in this world and the next, and has prepared for them a humiliating punishment. ⁵⁸ Similarly, those who insult believing men and women for no reason will carry the burden of *their* slandering and sinfulness.

Women to dress modestly

⁵⁹ Prophet, tell your wives, daughters, and the believers' wives to draw their overcoats close around;ᵃ that will ensure they are recognised and will not be harmed. Allah is Forgiving, Caring. ⁶⁰ If the hypocrites and the troublemakers with sickness in their hearts don't stop *harassing women* in the city,ᵇ then We will instruct you *to act against* them, after which they won't remain your neighbours for long. ⁶¹ They are cursed, *and in the past*, wherever they were found, they were seized and slain. ⁶² *This was* the practice *laid down* by Allah regarding those who lived previously; and you will never find any change in the law of Allah.

ᵃ The *jilbab* is a loose outer garment, the overcoat draped around the body. See *Surat Al-Nur* 24: 31.
ᵇ This verse is best understood in the context of *Surat Al-Nur* 24: 33, which refers to the practice of forcing slave women into prostitution, leading some young men to harass even free women as they left their homes to answer the call of nature in the open fields at night.

عِلۡمُهَا عِنۡدَ اللّٰهِ ؕ وَمَا يُدۡرِيۡكَ لَعَلَّ السَّاعَةَ تَكُوۡنُ

قَرِيۡبًا ۝ اِنَّ اللّٰهَ لَعَنَ الۡكٰفِرِيۡنَ وَاَعَدَّ لَهُمۡ سَعِيۡرًا ۝

خٰلِدِيۡنَ فِيۡهَاۤ اَبَدًا ۚ لَا يَجِدُوۡنَ وَلِيًّا وَّلَا نَصِيۡرًا ۝ يَوۡمَ

تُقَلَّبُ وُجُوۡهُهُمۡ فِى النَّارِ يَقُوۡلُوۡنَ يٰلَيۡتَنَاۤ اَطَعۡنَا اللّٰهَ

وَاَطَعۡنَا الرَّسُوۡلَا ۝ وَقَالُوۡا رَبَّنَاۤ اِنَّاۤ اَطَعۡنَا سَادَتَنَا

وَكُبَرَآءَنَا فَاَضَلُّوۡنَا السَّبِيۡلَا ۝ رَبَّنَاۤ اٰتِهِمۡ ضِعۡفَيۡنِ

مِنَ الۡعَذَابِ وَالۡعَنۡهُمۡ لَعۡنًا كَبِيۡرًا ۝ يٰۤاَيُّهَا الَّذِيۡنَ

اٰمَنُوۡا لَا تَكُوۡنُوۡا كَالَّذِيۡنَ اٰذَوۡا مُوۡسٰى فَبَرَّاَهُ اللّٰهُ

مِمَّا قَالُوۡا ؕ وَكَانَ عِنۡدَ اللّٰهِ وَجِيۡهًا ۝ يٰۤاَيُّهَا

الَّذِيۡنَ اٰمَنُوا اتَّقُوا اللّٰهَ وَقُوۡلُوۡا قَوۡلًا سَدِيۡدًا ۝

يُّصۡلِحۡ لَكُمۡ اَعۡمَالَكُمۡ وَيَغۡفِرۡ لَكُمۡ ذُنُوۡبَكُمۡ ؕ وَمَنۡ

يُّطِعِ اللّٰهَ وَرَسُوۡلَهٗ فَقَدۡ فَازَ فَوۡزًا عَظِيۡمًا ۝

اِنَّا عَرَضۡنَا الۡاَمَانَةَ عَلَى السَّمٰوٰتِ وَالۡاَرۡضِ وَ

الۡجِبَالِ فَاَبَيۡنَ اَنۡ يَّحۡمِلۡنَهَا وَاَشۡفَقۡنَ مِنۡهَا

وَحَمَلَهَا الۡاِنۡسَانُ ؕ اِنَّهٗ كَانَ ظَلُوۡمًا جَهُوۡلًا ۝

لِيُعَذِّبَ اللّٰهُ الۡمُنٰفِقِيۡنَ وَالۡمُنٰفِقٰتِ وَالۡمُشۡرِكِيۡنَ

وَالۡمُشۡرِكٰتِ وَيَتُوۡبَ اللّٰهُ عَلَى الۡمُؤۡمِنِيۡنَ وَالۡمُؤۡمِنٰتِ ؕ

وَكَانَ اللّٰهُ غَفُوۡرًا رَّحِيۡمًا ۝

The Divine trust given to humanity was the burden of being morally upright. How well have you honoured that trust?

847

The regret of the disbelievers on Judgement Day

⁶³ *When* people ask you about *the time* of the Final Hour, say: "Allah Knows that." And who knows the Final Hour could be near? ⁶⁴ Allah cursed the disbelievers and prepared a *fiery* Blaze for them ⁶⁵ in which they will live forever, they won't find a protector or a helper. ⁶⁶ On the Day that their faces will be distorted in the Fire, they will say, "If Only we had obeyed Allah and the Messenger." ⁶⁷ And they will say, "Our Lord, we obeyed our leaders and the elders, and they led us astray. ⁶⁸ Our Lord, give them double the punishment and put a great curse on them."

Concluding instructions for the believers

⁶⁹ Believers, don't be like those who insulted Musa, yet Allah declared him innocent of what they alleged; *Musa* was honourable in Allah's sight. ⁷⁰ Believers, be mindful of Allah and speak straight to the point, ⁷¹ so Allah may improve your deeds and forgive your sins. Anyone who obeys Allah and His Messenger has won a mighty victory.

Humanity is entrusted with free will

⁷² We presented the Trust to the Heavens, the Earth and the mountains,ᵃ but they declined to carry it *since* they were fearful; but humans *decided* to carry it – humans were wrong and ignorant *of the demands* – ⁷³ Allah would punish them *for this failure, especially* the hypocrites and the idolaters, both men and women; but Allah will relent towards the believers, both men and women, *for their failures.* Allah is, Forgiving, Caring.

ᵃ This Trust is comprehensive: including faith, prayers, moral character, caring for the environment, etc. Compare with the first assembly of prophets, *Surat Al ʿImran* 3: 81, and the first assembly of human souls, *Surat Al-Aʾraf* 7: 172.

34. Surat Saba'

The Kingdom of Sheba

This surat was revealed in the middle-Makkan period, and its central theme is the evidence for resurrection. The scenes of Judgement Day are presented in vivid terms, as if they are unfolding before the reader. Allah's Glory and Power is emphasised as displayed on Judgement Day, when humanity will be held accountable for its actions.

Dawud ﷺ and Sulayman ﷺ, received many extraordinary gifts from Allah, which they appreciated. Consequently, Allah rewarded them even more. In contrast, the people of Saba' were blessed with a dam and fertile land, and the towns built in the area prospered economically. However, they were ungrateful.

The kingdom of Saba was situated in South Western Arabia, Yemen, and at the time of its greatest prosperity (the first millennium BC) comprised Yemen and a large part of Ethiopia. Its capital was Marib. The Sabaeans had built over the centuries an extraordinary system of dams and dykes, and became famous in history, with its astonishing remnants extant to this day (Asad).

This invited Divine retribution, the dam burst and the unstoppable flood destroyed everything in its wake. This devastated the agricultural land, and left them impoverished. Since the Makkans were familiar with this story, the Quran doesn't describe it in too much detail.

An outline of the conversation between disbelievers on Judgement Day shows the horrific landscape. At the end, the Messenger ﷺ is proclaimed as a prophet for all humanity: "We sent you to all the people as a messenger of good news and a warner, but most people do not know this." (28). Clearly an announcement of the universality of Islam.

بِسْمِ اللهِ الرَّحْمٰنِ الرَّحِيْمِ

اَلْحَمْدُ لِلّٰهِ الَّذِىْ لَهٗ مَا فِى السَّمٰوٰتِ وَمَا فِى الْاَرْضِ وَلَهُ الْحَمْدُ فِى الْاٰخِرَةِ ؕ وَهُوَ الْحَكِيْمُ الْخَبِيْرُ ۚ١

يَعْلَمُ مَا يَلِجُ فِى الْاَرْضِ وَمَا يَخْرُجُ مِنْهَا وَمَا يَنْزِلُ مِنَ السَّمَاءِ وَمَا يَعْرُجُ فِيْهَا ؕ وَهُوَ الرَّحِيْمُ الْغَفُوْرُ ۚ٢

وَقَالَ الَّذِيْنَ كَفَرُوْا لَا تَأْتِيْنَا السَّاعَةُ ؕ قُلْ بَلٰى وَرَبِّىْ لَتَأْتِيَنَّكُمْ عٰلِمِ الْغَيْبِ ۚ لَا يَعْزُبُ عَنْهُ مِثْقَالُ ذَرَّةٍ فِى السَّمٰوٰتِ وَلَا فِى الْاَرْضِ وَلَاۤ اَصْغَرُ مِنْ ذٰلِكَ وَلَاۤ اَكْبَرُ اِلَّا فِىْ كِتٰبٍ مُّبِيْنٍ ۙ٣

لِيَجْزِىَ الَّذِيْنَ اٰمَنُوْا وَعَمِلُوا الصّٰلِحٰتِ ؕ اُولٰٓئِكَ لَهُمْ مَّغْفِرَةٌ وَّرِزْقٌ كَرِيْمٌ ٤

وَالَّذِيْنَ سَعَوْ فِىْۤ اٰيٰتِنَا مُعٰجِزِيْنَ اُولٰٓئِكَ لَهُمْ عَذَابٌ مِّنْ رِّجْزٍ اَلِيْمٌ ٥

وَيَرَى الَّذِيْنَ اُوْتُوا الْعِلْمَ الَّذِىْۤ اُنْزِلَ اِلَيْكَ مِنْ رَّبِّكَ هُوَ الْحَقَّ ۙ وَيَهْدِىْۤ اِلٰى صِرَاطِ الْعَزِيْزِ الْحَمِيْدِ ٦

وَقَالَ الَّذِيْنَ كَفَرُوْا هَلْ نَدُلُّكُمْ عَلٰى رَجُلٍ يُّنَبِّئُكُمْ اِذَا مُزِّقْتُمْ كُلَّ مُمَزَّقٍ ۙ اِنَّكُمْ لَفِىْ خَلْقٍ جَدِيْدٍ ۚ٧

اَفْتَرٰى عَلَى اللهِ كَذِبًا اَمْ بِهٖ جِنَّةٌ ؕ بَلِ الَّذِيْنَ لَا يُؤْمِنُوْنَ بِالْاٰخِرَةِ فِى الْعَذَابِ وَالضَّلٰلِ الْبَعِيْدِ ٨

اَفَلَمْ يَرَوْا اِلٰى مَا بَيْنَ اَيْدِيْهِمْ وَمَا خَلْفَهُمْ مِّنَ السَّمَاءِ وَالْاَرْضِ ؕ اِنْ نَّشَأْ نَخْسِفْ بِهِمُ الْاَرْضَ

The Lord has complete knowledge of all things.

851

In the name of Allah, the Kind, the Caring.

Praise for Allah's knowledge and justice

[1] Praise be to Allah, everything in the Heavens and the Earth belongs to Him; and the praise will be His in the Hereafter, the Wise, the Aware. [2] He knows what goes inside the Earth and what comes out of it, and what comes down from the sky and what goes up. He is the Caring, the Forgiving. [3] The disbelievers say, "the Hour won't come for us." Say: "Not so! By my Lord the Knower of the unseen, it will strike you. Not an atom's weight in the Heavens and the Earth is hidden from Him; nor *does* anything smaller or bigger than that *exist* that is not written down in a Clear Book. [4] Allah will reward the believers who did righteous deeds, they will be forgiven and blessed with generous provision. [5] Those who tried desperately to undermine Our *Quran*[a] will be severely punished.

The disbelievers mock the resurrection

[6] Those given the knowledge *of earlier revelations* consider as the truth what is revealed to you by your Lord, and accept that it leads to the path of the Almighty, the Praiseworthy. [7] The disbelievers say, "Shall we show you a man who says, when you *die and you* are decomposed, you will be created anew? [8] He has either invented a lie about Allah, or is possessed." Not at all, those who don't believe in the Hereafter will *end up* in torment, they're wandering far *from the truth*. [9] Haven't they considered all that is around them in the Heaven and Earth. If We so wanted, We could make the Earth swallow them, or drop a chunk of the sky on them. In that are signs for the servant *of Allah* who repents.

---

[a] "Our signs" refers to the Quran (Suyuti).

اَوْ نُسْقِطْ عَلَيْهِمْ كِسَفًا مِّنَ السَّمَآءِ ط اِنَّ فِيْ ذٰلِكَ لَاٰيَةً
لِّكُلِّ عَبْدٍ مُّنِيْبٍ ۹ وَلَقَدْ اٰتَيْنَا دَاوٗدَ مِنَّا فَضْلًا ط
يٰجِبَالُ اَوِّبِيْ مَعَهٗ وَالطَّيْرَ ۚ وَاَلَنَّا لَهُ الْحَدِيْدَ ۱۰
اَنِ اعْمَلْ سٰبِغٰتٍ وَّقَدِّرْ فِي السَّرْدِ وَاعْمَلُوْا
صَالِحًا ط اِنِّيْ بِمَا تَعْمَلُوْنَ بَصِيْرٌ ۱۱ وَلِسُلَيْمٰنَ الرِّيْحَ
غُدُوُّهَا شَهْرٌ وَّ رَوَاحُهَا شَهْرٌ ۚ وَاَسَلْنَا لَهٗ عَيْنَ
الْقِطْرِ ط وَمِنَ الْجِنِّ مَنْ يَّعْمَلُ بَيْنَ يَدَيْهِ بِاِذْنِ
رَبِّهٖ ط وَمَنْ يَّزِغْ مِنْهُمْ عَنْ اَمْرِنَا نُذِقْهُ مِنْ عَذَابِ
السَّعِيْرِ ۱۲ يَعْمَلُوْنَ لَهٗ مَا يَشَآءُ مِنْ مَّحَارِيْبَ وَتَمَاثِيْلَ
وَجِفَانٍ كَالْجَوَابِ وَقُدُوْرٍ رّٰسِيٰتٍ ط اِعْمَلُوْٓا اٰلَ دَاوٗدَ
شُكْرًا ط وَقَلِيْلٌ مِّنْ عِبَادِيَ الشَّكُوْرُ ۱۳ فَلَمَّا قَضَيْنَا
عَلَيْهِ الْمَوْتَ مَا دَلَّهُمْ عَلٰى مَوْتِهٖٓ اِلَّا دَآبَّةُ الْاَرْضِ
تَأْكُلُ مِنْسَاَتَهٗ ۚ فَلَمَّا خَرَّ تَبَيَّنَتِ الْجِنُّ اَنْ لَّوْ كَانُوْا
يَعْلَمُوْنَ الْغَيْبَ مَا لَبِثُوْا فِي الْعَذَابِ الْمُهِيْنِ ۱۴ لَقَدْ
كَانَ لِسَبَاٍ فِيْ مَسْكَنِهِمْ اٰيَةٌ ۚ جَنَّتٰنِ عَنْ يَّمِيْنٍ
وَّشِمَالٍ ط كُلُوْا مِنْ رِّزْقِ رَبِّكُمْ وَاشْكُرُوْا لَهٗ ط بَلْدَةٌ
طَيِّبَةٌ وَّرَبٌّ غَفُوْرٌ ۱۵ فَاَعْرَضُوْا فَاَرْسَلْنَا عَلَيْهِمْ سَيْلَ
الْعَرِمِ وَبَدَّلْنٰهُمْ بِجَنَّتَيْهِمْ جَنَّتَيْنِ ذَوَاتَيْ اُكُلٍ خَمْطٍ وَّ
اَثْلٍ وَّشَيْءٍ مِّنْ سِدْرٍ قَلِيْلٍ ۱۶ ذٰلِكَ جَزَيْنٰهُمْ بِمَا كَفَرُوْا ط
وَهَلْ نُجٰزِيْٓ اِلَّا الْكَفُوْرَ ۱۷ وَجَعَلْنَا بَيْنَهُمْ وَبَيْنَ

The prophet Dawud and his illustrious son, Sulayman, were blessed with knowledge and worldly power. See how well they lived it.

Dawud and Sulayman's special powers

¹⁰ We gave Dawud Our favours: "Mountains and birds! Echo *My praises* with him"; and We made the iron soft to his *touch*. ¹¹ *We told him*: "Make coats of armour, and be precise with the links *of chainmail*, and do good. I see what you are doing." ¹² To Sulayman, *We gave control of* the wind, its outward and its return journey each covered the distance *of* a month; and We made a stream of molten brass to flow for him. By the authority of His Lord some jinn worked under his control, and if any one of them deviated from Our command, We punished them with the *fiery* Blaze. ¹³ They worked for *Sulayman*, building whatever he wanted: lofty chambers, statues, basins as big as water tanks, and *huge* fixed cauldrons. *We said*: "Work, children of Dawud, be thankful. Not many of My servants are thankful." ¹⁴ When We decreed *Sulayman's* death, the only way *they knew* he was dead was when the woodworm ate his staff and he tumbled *to the ground*. The jinn then realised that if they had knowledge of the unseen, they would never have continued with their demeaning, punishing *tasks*.ᵃ

The unthankful people of Saba'

¹⁵ *The dam* had gardens on both sides, the right and the left, and between them were their houses. A sign for the people of Sheba. "Eat of the provision of your Lord," *they were told*, "and be thankful to Him. *You have* a fertile country and a Forgiving Lord." ¹⁶ They turned away from Our *call*, so We sent the floodwater of the *broken* dam against them, and We turned their gardens into gardens that *now* produced bitter fruit, Tamarisks, and the sparse *thorny* Lote tree. ¹⁷ That's how We repaid their ingratitude. Would We reward anyone *in this way* except the ungrateful?

ᵃ This hints to Sulayman's death whilst sitting on his mighty throne, leaning on his staff. His death went unnoticed until his staff eaten by termites gave way and fell to the ground. An allusion to the fleeting and feeble nature of human life.

الْقُرَى الَّتِيْ بٰرَكْنَا فِيْهَا قُرًى ظَاهِرَةً وَّقَدَّرْنَا فِيْهَا
السَّيْرَ ۚ سِيْرُوْا فِيْهَا لَيَالِيَ وَاَيَّامًا اٰمِنِيْنَ ۝ فَقَالُوْا
رَبَّنَا بَاعِدْ بَيْنَ اَسْفَارِنَا وَظَلَمُوْٓا اَنْفُسَهُمْ فَجَعَلْنٰهُمْ
اَحَادِيْثَ وَمَزَّقْنٰهُمْ كُلَّ مُمَزَّقٍ ۚ اِنَّ فِيْ ذٰلِكَ لَاٰيٰتٍ
لِّكُلِّ صَبَّارٍ شَكُوْرٍ ۝ وَلَقَدْ صَدَّقَ عَلَيْهِمْ اِبْلِيْسُ
ظَنَّهٗ فَاتَّبَعُوْهُ اِلَّا فَرِيْقًا مِّنَ الْمُؤْمِنِيْنَ ۝ وَمَا كَانَ
لَهٗ عَلَيْهِمْ مِّنْ سُلْطٰنٍ اِلَّا لِنَعْلَمَ مَنْ يُّؤْمِنُ بِالْاٰخِرَةِ
مِمَّنْ هُوَ مِنْهَا فِيْ شَكٍّ ۚ وَرَبُّكَ عَلٰى كُلِّ شَيْءٍ حَفِيْظٌ ۝

Contrast Allah's knowledge and power with the helpless, dumb and deaf idols. Who should you love?

قُلِ ادْعُوا الَّذِيْنَ زَعَمْتُمْ مِّنْ دُوْنِ اللهِ ۚ لَا يَمْلِكُوْنَ
مِثْقَالَ ذَرَّةٍ فِي السَّمٰوٰتِ وَلَا فِي الْاَرْضِ وَمَا لَهُمْ
فِيْهِمَا مِنْ شِرْكٍ وَّمَا لَهٗ مِنْهُمْ مِّنْ ظَهِيْرٍ ۝ وَلَا تَنْفَعُ
الشَّفَاعَةُ عِنْدَهٗٓ اِلَّا لِمَنْ اَذِنَ لَهٗ ۚ حَتّٰٓى اِذَا فُزِّعَ عَنْ
قُلُوْبِهِمْ قَالُوْا مَاذَا ۙ قَالَ رَبُّكُمْ ۙ قَالُوا الْحَقَّ ۚ وَهُوَ الْعَلِيُّ
الْكَبِيْرُ ۝ قُلْ مَنْ يَّرْزُقُكُمْ مِّنَ السَّمٰوٰتِ وَالْاَرْضِ ۖ قُلِ
اللهُ ۙ وَاِنَّآ اَوْ اِيَّاكُمْ لَعَلٰى هُدًى اَوْ فِيْ ضَلٰلٍ مُّبِيْنٍ ۝
قُلْ لَّا تُسْئَلُوْنَ عَمَّآ اَجْرَمْنَا وَلَا نُسْئَلُ عَمَّا تَعْمَلُوْنَ ۝
قُلْ يَجْمَعُ بَيْنَنَا رَبُّنَا ثُمَّ يَفْتَحُ بَيْنَنَا بِالْحَقِّ ۚ وَهُوَ
الْفَتَّاحُ الْعَلِيْمُ ۝ قُلْ اَرُوْنِيَ الَّذِيْنَ اَلْحَقْتُمْ بِهٖ شُرَكَآءَ
كَلَّا ۚ بَلْ هُوَ اللهُ الْعَزِيْزُ الْحَكِيْمُ ۝ وَمَآ اَرْسَلْنٰكَ اِلَّا كَآفَّةً
لِّلنَّاسِ بَشِيْرًا وَّنَذِيْرًا وَّلٰكِنَّ اَكْثَرَ النَّاسِ لَا يَعْلَمُوْنَ ۝

Saba' after the flood

¹⁸ We allowed the growth of towns that were easily visible all the way from *Yemen* to *Greater Syria,* they were blessed *with fruit trees and water,* making travelling between them easy; *and We said*: "Travel this *land* in safety by night or by day." ¹⁹ Despite this they said, "Our Lord has made our journeys even longer." They were unthankful. We made them a legend, destroying them. In that are signs for the patient and thankful. ²⁰ Satan's assessment of them proved right, they followed him; except for a group of believers ²¹ over who he had no power. We will distinguish believers in the Hereafter from those who were doubtful. Your Lord is the Protector of everything.

The Messenger ﷺ tests the disbelievers

²² Say *Messenger*: "Call those you claim to be gods beside Allah. They don't control an atom's weight in the Heavens or on Earth; they have no share in them, nor do they have any helper." ²³ No intercession *by angels or others* will benefit in His presence, except for the one granted permission. Only when *the terror of Judgement Day* is released from their hearts will *the angels on high* ask: "What did your Lord say?" *Those below* will say, "The truth! And He is the Exalted, the Great." ²⁴ Ask, *Messenger*: "Who provides you *sustenance* from the Heavens and the Earth?" Say: "Allah. *It is* either you or us: since only one can be guided, the other must be misguided." ²⁵ Say: "You will not be questioned about what *you think* we are guilty of, nor shall we be questioned about what you did." ²⁶ Say: "Our Lord will gather us all, then He will judge us justly. He is the Supreme Judge, the Knower." ²⁷ Say: "Show me those you associate as partners with Allah. Never! Allah is Almighty, the Wise."

The Messenger ﷺ is sent to all of humanity

²⁸ We sent you to all the people *of the world* as a messenger of good news, and a warner; but most people don't know *this.*

وَيَقُولُونَ مَتَىٰ هَٰذَا الْوَعْدُ إِن كُنتُمْ صَٰدِقِينَ ۟۲۹

قُل لَّكُم مِّيعَادُ يَوْمٍ لَّا تَسْتَـٔخِرُونَ عَنْهُ سَاعَةً وَلَا

تَسْتَقْدِمُونَ ۟۳۰ وَقَالَ الَّذِينَ كَفَرُوا لَن نُّؤْمِنَ بِهَٰذَا

الْقُرْآنِ وَلَا بِالَّذِي بَيْنَ يَدَيْهِ ۗ وَلَوْ تَرَىٰ إِذِ الظَّٰلِمُونَ

مَوْقُوفُونَ عِندَ رَبِّهِمْ يَرْجِعُ بَعْضُهُمْ إِلَىٰ بَعْضٍ

الْقَوْلَ ۚ يَقُولُ الَّذِينَ اسْتُضْعِفُوا لِلَّذِينَ اسْتَكْبَرُوا

لَوْلَا أَنتُمْ لَكُنَّا مُؤْمِنِينَ ۟۳۱ قَالَ الَّذِينَ اسْتَكْبَرُوا

لِلَّذِينَ اسْتُضْعِفُوا أَنَحْنُ صَدَدْنَٰكُمْ عَنِ الْهُدَىٰ

بَعْدَ إِذْ جَاءَكُم ۖ بَلْ كُنتُم مُّجْرِمِينَ ۟۳۲ وَقَالَ الَّذِينَ

اسْتُضْعِفُوا لِلَّذِينَ اسْتَكْبَرُوا بَلْ مَكْرُ الَّيْلِ وَالنَّهَارِ

إِذْ تَأْمُرُونَنَا أَن نَّكْفُرَ بِاللَّهِ وَنَجْعَلَ لَهُ أَندَادًا ۚ وَ

أَسَرُّوا النَّدَامَةَ لَمَّا رَأَوُا الْعَذَابَ ۚ وَجَعَلْنَا الْأَغْلَٰلَ

فِي أَعْنَاقِ الَّذِينَ كَفَرُوا ۚ هَلْ يُجْزَوْنَ إِلَّا مَا كَانُوا

يَعْمَلُونَ ۟۳۳ وَمَا أَرْسَلْنَا فِي قَرْيَةٍ مِّن نَّذِيرٍ إِلَّا قَالَ

مُتْرَفُوهَا إِنَّا بِمَا أُرْسِلْتُم بِهِ كَٰفِرُونَ ۟۳۴ وَقَالُوا نَحْنُ

أَكْثَرُ أَمْوَٰلًا وَأَوْلَٰدًا وَمَا نَحْنُ بِمُعَذَّبِينَ ۟۳۵ قُلْ إِنَّ

رَبِّي يَبْسُطُ الرِّزْقَ لِمَن يَشَاءُ وَيَقْدِرُ وَلَٰكِنَّ أَكْثَرَ

النَّاسِ لَا يَعْلَمُونَ ۟۳۶ وَمَا أَمْوَٰلُكُمْ وَلَا أَوْلَٰدُكُم بِالَّتِي

تُقَرِّبُكُمْ عِندَنَا زُلْفَىٰ إِلَّا مَنْ آمَنَ وَعَمِلَ صَٰلِحًا فَأُولَٰئِكَ

لَهُمْ جَزَاءُ الضِّعْفِ بِمَا عَمِلُوا وَهُمْ فِي الْغُرُفَٰتِ آمِنُونَ ۟۳۷

The disbelievers will regret on Judgment Day. Why not accept the truth now?

²⁹ And they say, "When will this promise *be fulfilled*, if you are telling the truth?" ³⁰ Tell them: "You have a fixed day, which you can't delay nor bring forward even by a single hour."

The disbelievers will bicker amongst themselves

³¹ The disbelievers say, "We won't believe in this Quran, or in *the scriptures* that came before it." If only you could see the wrongdoers standing before their Lord, each criticising the other, some of the oppressed will say to the arrogant, "If it hadn't been for you, we would have been believers." ³² The arrogant will reply, "Was it really us who blocked your *path* to guidance after it came to you? Not at all, you were sinners." ³³ The oppressed will say to the arrogant, "Not so! *This is* a trick of *calling day night and* night day. *Remember* when you used to order us to disbelieve in Allah and set up rivals with Him?" They will conceal their remorse when they see the punishment, and We shall put iron collars around the necks of the disbelievers. Shouldn't We reward them for what they did?

The wealthy relied on their possessions

³⁴ Never did We send a warner to a city without the well-to-do saying, "We reject what you are sent with." ³⁵ And also added, "Because we have plenty of wealth and offspring we won't be tormented." ³⁶ Say *to them*: "My Lord is the one Who either increases or withholds the provision as He pleases," but most people don't know. ³⁷ It is neither your wealth nor your offspring that will bring you closer to Us, but belief and the righteousness; the reward of such people will be doubled due to their deeds, and they will be safe in lofty apartments.

وَالَّذِيْنَ يَسْعَوْنَ فِيْٓ اٰيٰتِنَا مُعٰجِزِيْنَ اُولٰٓئِكَ فِى الْعَذَابِ مُحْضَرُوْنَ ۝ قُلْ اِنَّ رَبِّيْ يَبْسُطُ الرِّزْقَ لِمَنْ يَّشَاۤءُ مِنْ عِبَادِهٖ وَيَقْدِرُ لَهٗ ۚ وَمَآ اَنْفَقْتُمْ مِّنْ شَىْءٍ فَهُوَ يُخْلِفُهٗ ۚ وَهُوَ خَيْرُ الرّٰزِقِيْنَ ۝ وَيَوْمَ يَحْشُرُهُمْ جَمِيْعًا ثُمَّ يَقُوْلُ لِلْمَلٰٓئِكَةِ اَهٰٓؤُلَاۤءِ اِيَّاكُمْ كَانُوْا يَعْبُدُوْنَ ۝ قَالُوْا سُبْحٰنَكَ اَنْتَ وَلِيُّنَا مِنْ دُوْنِهِمْ ۚ بَلْ كَانُوْا يَعْبُدُوْنَ الْجِنَّ ۚ اَكْثَرُهُمْ بِهِمْ مُّؤْمِنُوْنَ ۝ فَالْيَوْمَ لَا يَمْلِكُ بَعْضُكُمْ لِبَعْضٍ نَّفْعًا وَّلَا ضَرًّا ۚ وَنَقُوْلُ لِلَّذِيْنَ ظَلَمُوْا ذُوْقُوْا عَذَابَ النَّارِ الَّتِيْ كُنْتُمْ بِهَا تُكَذِّبُوْنَ ۝ وَاِذَا تُتْلٰى عَلَيْهِمْ اٰيٰتُنَا بَيِّنٰتٍ قَالُوْا مَا هٰذَآ اِلَّا رَجُلٌ يُّرِيْدُ اَنْ يَّصُدَّكُمْ عَمَّا كَانَ يَعْبُدُ اٰبَاۤؤُكُمْ ۚ وَقَالُوْا مَا هٰذَآ اِلَّآ اِفْكٌ مُّفْتَرًى ۚ وَقَالَ الَّذِيْنَ كَفَرُوْا لِلْحَقِّ لَمَّا جَاۤءَهُمْ ۙ اِنْ هٰذَآ اِلَّا سِحْرٌ مُّبِيْنٌ ۝ وَمَآ اٰتَيْنٰهُمْ مِّنْ كُتُبٍ يَّدْرُسُوْنَهَا وَمَآ اَرْسَلْنَآ اِلَيْهِمْ قَبْلَكَ مِنْ نَّذِيْرٍ ۝ وَكَذَّبَ الَّذِيْنَ مِنْ قَبْلِهِمْ ۙ وَمَا بَلَغُوْا مِعْشَارَ مَآ اٰتَيْنٰهُمْ فَكَذَّبُوْا رُسُلِيْ ۚ فَكَيْفَ كَانَ نَكِيْرِ ۝ قُلْ اِنَّمَآ اَعِظُكُمْ بِوَاحِدَةٍ ۚ اَنْ تَقُوْمُوْا لِلّٰهِ مَثْنٰى وَفُرَادٰى ثُمَّ تَتَفَكَّرُوْا ۫ مَا بِصَاحِبِكُمْ مِّنْ جِنَّةٍ ۭ اِنْ هُوَ اِلَّا نَذِيْرٌ لَّكُمْ بَيْنَ يَدَيْ عَذَابٍ شَدِيْدٍ ۝ قُلْ مَا سَاَلْتُكُمْ مِّنْ اَجْرٍ فَهُوَ لَكُمْ ۭ اِنْ اَجْرِيَ اِلَّا عَلَى اللّٰهِ ۚ وَهُوَ عَلٰى كُلِّ شَىْءٍ

The Messenger's ﷺ earnest plea was to think; about the purpose of life rather than being caught up in unimportant things.

[38] Those who tried desperately to undermine Our signs shall be tormented forever. [39] Say: "My Lord increases or withholds the provision of any one of His servants as He pleases. Whatever you spend *in charity*, He shall repay it. He is the Best Provider."

The angels deny encouraging disbelievers

[40] On the Day He gathers them together, He will ask the angels: "Are these the ones who worshipped you?" [41] *The angels* will say, "Glory be to you! Only you are our patron, not them. Rather, they worshipped the jinn, and most of them had faith in them." [42] On this Day none of you will have the power to benefit or to harm the other, and We shall say to the wrongdoers: "Taste the torment of the Fire, you denied." [43] Whenever Our clear verses are recited they say, "This man wants to stop you from worshipping what your forefathers worshipped." And they say, "This *Quran* is fabricated lies." When the truth came to them the disbelievers said, "This is clearly magic."

The only Prophet sent to the Arabs

[44] Before you We never gave them books to study, or sent them a warner. [45] Those before them also denied *the truth*, though they haven't got more than a tenth of what We gave them, still they rejected My messengers. So, *imagine* how terrible My condemnation will be. [46] Say: "I will give you one piece *of advice*: stand for Allah, whether *you are* alone or in pairs, *and* then think deeply. Your companion is not possessed; rather, he is warning you about the severe punishment about to come." [47] Say: "Whatever reward I may have asked from you, keep it; Allah will reward me. He is the Witness of everything."

Allah's truth will prevail. How much do you search for truth?

شَهِيْدٌ ۝ قُلْ اِنَّ رَبِّيْ يَقْذِفُ بِالْحَقِّ عَلَّامُ الْغُيُوْبِ ۝

قُلْ جَآءَ الْحَقُّ وَمَا يُبْدِئُ الْبَاطِلُ وَمَا يُعِيْدُ ۝ قُلْ اِنْ

ضَلَلْتُ فَاِنَّمَا اَضِلُّ عَلٰى نَفْسِيْ ۚ وَاِنِ اهْتَدَيْتُ فَبِمَا

يُوْحِيْ اِلَيَّ رَبِّيْ ؕ اِنَّهٗ سَمِيْعٌ قَرِيْبٌ ۝ وَلَوْ تَرٰٓى اِذْ فَزِعُوْا

فَلَا فَوْتَ وَاُخِذُوْا مِنْ مَّكَانٍ قَرِيْبٍ ۝ وَّقَالُوْٓا اٰمَنَّا

بِهٖ ۚ وَاَنّٰى لَهُمُ التَّنَاوُشُ مِنْ مَّكَانٍ بَعِيْدٍ ۝ وَّقَدْ

كَفَرُوْا بِهٖ مِنْ قَبْلُ ۚ وَيَقْذِفُوْنَ بِالْغَيْبِ مِنْ مَّكَانٍ

بَعِيْدٍ ۝ وَحِيْلَ بَيْنَهُمْ وَبَيْنَ مَا يَشْتَهُوْنَ كَمَا فُعِلَ

بِاَشْيَاعِهِمْ مِّنْ قَبْلُ ؕ اِنَّهُمْ كَانُوْا فِيْ شَكٍّ مُّرِيْبٍ ۝

Finding faith after one has died will be useless

[48] Say: "My Lord, the Knower of all mysteries, launched the truth." [49] Say: "The truth has come, falsehood has vanished and will not return." [50] Say: "If I went off course, then I am only leading myself astray; *however,* if I am guided, then it is due to what my Lord has revealed. He is a Hearer, near *at hand.*" [51] If only you could see *the disbelievers* in a state of terror. There will be no escape when they are snatched from nearby. [52] They will say, "We believe!" How can they *possibly* receive *faith* now, [53] when previously they had denied it? They are stabbing in the dark from far away[a], [54] and a barrier is put up between them and their desires, as happened with their type before; *because* they were deeply suspicious.

---

[a] Literally: They were throwing arrows in the dark from a long distance.

35. Surat Fatir

The Originator of the Universe

This is an early Makkan surat, revealed possibly in the third or fourth year of the Prophet's mission ﷺ. The central theme is Allah's numerous gifts: the wonders of His creation in nature is a display of his Kindness: "People, remember the gifts Allah gave you. Is there any other creator beside Allah who provides for you from the Earth and the sky?" (3). Imam Ghazali observes:

> Human beings are in urgent need of understanding this universal law of creation, since many of them are under the illusion that what nature provides bears no relation to Allah Almighty whatsoever. Some have dared to eliminate Allah from life, giving the wildest explanations of the nature and purpose of existence.[a]

But intelligent and thoughtful people can't fail to see the created world as the handiwork of Allah. For them, Allah is everywhere: "Among his servants, only the knowledgeable fear Allah. Allah is the Almighty, the Forgiver" (28).

The Makkan people were stubborn in their denial of the Prophet ﷺ, so he is reassured: "If they think you are a liar, *so what*? Those before them treated their messengers as liars when they came to them with clear signs, with writings and the enlightening Book" (25). He is told to be patient and resilient, since Allah gives respite and time for people to think. The stubborn disbelievers are given a warning; whilst He is the Kindest, He is an Avenger who takes exact retribution. "Were Allah to punish people for the wrong they did; He wouldn't have left a single creature on the surface of *the Earth*" (45).

In terms of faith and good deeds, the surat divides the believers into three grades: "Some wronged themselves, others were good and some by the grace of Allah were foremost in good works" (32). The implication is that the Ummah of Muhammad ﷺ will include a group who makes mistakes and pays no attention to their duties, here called "*zalim*", the wrongdoers. The second group are "*muqtasid*", the good: the moderates who fulfil religious obligations and avoid the forbidden, but are sluggish with regards to voluntary activities. The third group are "*al-sabiq*", who are committed to "seeking the pleasure of Allah, avoid worldly luxuries, the trappings of the world, and never forget Allah" (Ibn Kathir).

---

[a] Al-Ghazali, *A Thematic Commentary on the Quran.*

بِسْمِ اللهِ الرَّحْمٰنِ الرَّحِيْمِ

اَلْحَمْدُ لِلّٰهِ فَاطِرِ السَّمٰوٰتِ وَالْاَرْضِ جَاعِلِ الْمَلٰٓئِكَةِ

رُسُلًا اُولِيْٓ اَجْنِحَةٍ مَّثْنٰى وَثُلٰثَ وَرُبٰعَ ؕ يَزِيْدُ فِي

الْخَلْقِ مَا يَشَآءُ ؕ اِنَّ اللهَ عَلٰى كُلِّ شَيْءٍ قَدِيْرٌ ۟١ مَا يَفْتَحِ

اللهُ لِلنَّاسِ مِنْ رَّحْمَةٍ فَلَا مُمْسِكَ لَهَا ۚ وَمَا يُمْسِكْ ۙ

فَلَا مُرْسِلَ لَهٗ مِنْۢ بَعْدِهٖ ؕ وَهُوَ الْعَزِيْزُ الْحَكِيْمُ ۟٢

يٰٓاَيُّهَا النَّاسُ اذْكُرُوْا نِعْمَتَ اللهِ عَلَيْكُمْ ؕ هَلْ مِنْ

خَالِقٍ غَيْرُ اللهِ يَرْزُقُكُمْ مِّنَ السَّمَآءِ وَالْاَرْضِ ؕ لَآ اِلٰهَ

اِلَّا هُوَ ۫ۖ فَاَنّٰى تُؤْفَكُوْنَ ۟٣ وَاِنْ يُّكَذِّبُوْكَ فَقَدْ كُذِّبَتْ

رُسُلٌ مِّنْ قَبْلِكَ ؕ وَاِلَى اللهِ تُرْجَعُ الْاُمُوْرُ ۟٤ يٰٓاَيُّهَا

النَّاسُ اِنَّ وَعْدَ اللهِ حَقٌّ فَلَا تَغُرَّنَّكُمُ الْحَيٰوةُ الدُّنْيَا ۟ۖ

وَلَا يَغُرَّنَّكُمْ بِاللهِ الْغَرُوْرُ ۟٥ اِنَّ الشَّيْطٰنَ لَكُمْ عَدُوٌّ

فَاتَّخِذُوْهُ عَدُوًّا ؕ اِنَّمَا يَدْعُوْا حِزْبَهٗ لِيَكُوْنُوْا مِنْ

اَصْحٰبِ السَّعِيْرِ ؕ اَلَّذِيْنَ كَفَرُوْا لَهُمْ عَذَابٌ شَدِيْدٌ ؕ

وَالَّذِيْنَ اٰمَنُوْا وَعَمِلُوا الصّٰلِحٰتِ لَهُمْ مَّغْفِرَةٌ وَّاَجْرٌ

كَبِيْرٌ ۟٦ اَفَمَنْ زُيِّنَ لَهٗ سُوْءُ عَمَلِهٖ فَرَاٰهُ حَسَنًا ؕ

فَاِنَّ اللهَ يُضِلُّ مَنْ يَّشَآءُ وَيَهْدِيْ مَنْ يَّشَآءُ ۖ

فَلَا تَذْهَبْ نَفْسُكَ عَلَيْهِمْ حَسَرٰتٍ ؕ اِنَّ اللهَ عَلِيْمٌۢ

بِمَا يَصْنَعُوْنَ ۟٨ وَاللهُ الَّذِيْٓ اَرْسَلَ الرِّيٰحَ فَتُثِيْرُ

In the name of Allah, the Kind, the Caring.

Allah's glory, majesty and power

¹Praise be to Allah, the Originator of the Heavens and the Earth, Creator of the messenger angels with two, three and four *pairs* of wings. He adds to the creation whatever He pleases. Allah has power over everything. ²How He treats people kindly *is up to Him*, no one can withhold it; and what He withholds, no one can take it after His *decision*. He is the Almighty, the Wise. ³People, remember the gifts Allah gave you. Is there any other creator beside Allah who provides for you from the Earth and the sky? There is no god but Him. How then can you turn away *from the truth*?

Makkans accuse the Messenger ﷺ of lying

⁴If they deny you, *so what*? Messengers before you were denied *too. In the end* all matters will be returned to Allah. ⁵People, Allah's promise is true, so don't let this worldly life deceive you, and don't let *Satan*, the arch-deceiver, draw you away from Allah. ⁶Satan is your enemy, so treat him as such. He invites his followers to become companions of the *fiery* Blaze. ⁷Those who disbelieved will *suffer* severe punishment, but those who believe and do righteous deeds will be forgiven and granted great reward. ⁸Evil deeds look attractive to some people, so they like them. Allah allows some people to go astray, and He guides others as He pleases; so don't be overcome by *pity and* regret over them. Allah knows what they do.

سَحَابًا فَسُقْنٰهُ اِلٰى بَلَدٍ مَّيِّتٍ فَاَحْيَيْنَا بِهِ الْاَرْضَ
بَعْدَ مَوْتِهَا ۭ كَذٰلِكَ النُّشُوْرُ ۞ مَنْ كَانَ يُرِيْدُ
الْعِزَّةَ فَلِلّٰهِ الْعِزَّةُ جَمِيْعًا ۭ اِلَيْهِ يَصْعَدُ الْكَلِمُ
الطَّيِّبُ وَالْعَمَلُ الصَّالِحُ يَرْفَعُهُ ۭ وَالَّذِيْنَ يَمْكُرُوْنَ
السَّيِّاٰتِ لَهُمْ عَذَابٌ شَدِيْدٌ ۭ وَمَكْرُ اُولٰٓئِكَ هُوَ
يَبُوْرُ ۞ وَاللّٰهُ خَلَقَكُمْ مِّنْ تُرَابٍ ثُمَّ مِنْ نُّطْفَةٍ ثُمَّ
جَعَلَكُمْ اَزْوَاجًا ۭ وَمَا تَحْمِلُ مِنْ اُنْثٰى وَلَا تَضَعُ
اِلَّا بِعِلْمِهٖ ۭ وَمَا يُعَمَّرُ مِنْ مُّعَمَّرٍ وَّلَا يُنْقَصُ مِنْ
عُمُرِهٖ اِلَّا فِيْ كِتٰبٍ ۭ اِنَّ ذٰلِكَ عَلَى اللّٰهِ يَسِيْرٌ ۞ وَمَا
يَسْتَوِى الْبَحْرٰنِ ۚ هٰذَا عَذْبٌ فُرَاتٌ سَائِغٌ شَرَابُهٗ
وَهٰذَا مِلْحٌ اُجَاجٌ ۭ وَمِنْ كُلٍّ تَاْكُلُوْنَ لَحْمًا طَرِيًّا
وَّتَسْتَخْرِجُوْنَ حِلْيَةً تَلْبَسُوْنَهَا ۚ وَتَرَى الْفُلْكَ فِيْهِ
مَوَاخِرَ لِتَبْتَغُوْا مِنْ فَضْلِهٖ وَلَعَلَّكُمْ تَشْكُرُوْنَ ۞
يُوْلِجُ الَّيْلَ فِى النَّهَارِ وَيُوْلِجُ النَّهَارَ فِى الَّيْلِ ۙ وَ
سَخَّرَ الشَّمْسَ وَالْقَمَرَ ۖ كُلٌّ يَّجْرِيْ لِاَجَلٍ مُّسَمًّى ۭ
ذٰلِكُمُ اللّٰهُ رَبُّكُمْ لَهُ الْمُلْكُ ۭ وَالَّذِيْنَ تَدْعُوْنَ مِنْ
دُوْنِهٖ مَا يَمْلِكُوْنَ مِنْ قِطْمِيْرٍ ۞ اِنْ تَدْعُوْهُمْ
لَا يَسْمَعُوْا دُعَاءَكُمْ ۚ وَلَوْ سَمِعُوْا مَا اسْتَجَابُوْا لَكُمْ ۭ
وَيَوْمَ الْقِيٰمَةِ يَكْفُرُوْنَ بِشِرْكِكُمْ ۭ وَلَا يُنَبِّئُكَ مِثْلُ
خَبِيْرٍ ۞ يٰٓاَيُّهَا النَّاسُ اَنْتُمُ الْفُقَرَآءُ اِلَى اللّٰهِ ۚ

We are invited to observe the incredible beauty of Allah's creation. How often do you go into the countryside to observe it?

New creation is like the resurrection

⁹Allah sends winds that move the clouds, which We drive towards dead regions, and We revive dead land *with rain*. The Resurrection will be like that. ¹⁰Anyone seeking power *should know,* all power belongs to Allah, an eloquently pure speech rises up to Him, and He elevates all good deeds[a]. However, those who plot evil, theirs will be a severe punishment. Their plot will fail. ¹¹Allah created you from dust, then from a drop *of semen,* then He made you into pairs, *male and female.* No female becomes pregnant or gives birth without His knowledge, no one grows old, or has their life cut short but is written in a *celestial* Book. *All* that is easy for Allah.

Salty sea water, the cycle of night and day prove resurrection

¹²*Take* two bodies of water, *they* are not the same: one fresh, sweet and pleasant to drink, the other is salty and bitter; *from these waters,* you eat the tender flesh *of fish,* and extract pearls to wear. *Similarly,* you see ships ploughing through *the sea* to seek *a share* of His bounty, and maybe you will appreciate *Allah.* ¹³He merges night into day and day into night and has caused both the sun and the moon to travel *through the sky* for a fixed period. That's Allah, your Lord, all power belongs to Him; those you call beside Him don't possess even the tiniest amount.[b] ¹⁴If you call them they don't hear your call, and even if they were to hear they can't answer you; and on Judgement Day, *your idols* will reject your association of *partners with Allah.* So, *messenger,* no one can enlighten you *with truth* like the All-Aware.

There is no shifting of blame on Judgement Day

¹⁵People, you need Allah, and Allah is Self-Sufficient, Praiseworthy.

---

[a] This Arabic idiom in plain English means "Allah hears good words and rewards good works."
[b] Literally the thin filament covering the date pit.

وَاللّٰهُ هُوَ الْغَنِيُّ الْحَمِيدُ ۝ اِنْ يَّشَأْ يُذْهِبْكُمْ وَ

يَاتِ بِخَلْقٍ جَدِيْدٍ ۝ وَمَا ذٰلِكَ عَلَى اللّٰهِ بِعَزِيْزٍ ۝

وَلَا تَزِرُ وَازِرَةٌ وِّزْرَ اُخْرٰى ط وَاِنْ تَدْعُ مُثْقَلَةٌ

اِلٰى حِمْلِهَا لَا يُحْمَلْ مِنْهُ شَيْءٌ وَّلَوْ كَانَ ذَا قُرْبٰى ط

اِنَّمَا تُنْذِرُ الَّذِيْنَ يَخْشَوْنَ رَبَّهُمْ بِالْغَيْبِ وَاَقَامُوا

الصَّلٰوةَ ط وَمَنْ تَزَكّٰى فَاِنَّمَا يَتَزَكّٰى لِنَفْسِهٖ ط وَاِلَى

اللّٰهِ الْمَصِيْرُ ۝ وَمَا يَسْتَوِى الْاَعْمٰى وَالْبَصِيْرُ ۝

وَلَا الظُّلُمٰتُ وَلَا النُّوْرُ ۝ وَلَا الظِّلُّ وَلَا الْحَرُوْرُ ۝

وَمَا يَسْتَوِى الْاَحْيَآءُ وَلَا الْاَمْوَاتُ ط اِنَّ اللّٰهَ يُسْمِعُ

مَنْ يَّشَآءُ ج وَمَا اَنْتَ بِمُسْمِعٍ مَّنْ فِى الْقُبُوْرِ ۝ اِنْ

اَنْتَ اِلَّا نَذِيْرٌ ۝ اِنَّا اَرْسَلْنٰكَ بِالْحَقِّ بَشِيْرًا وَّنَذِيْرًا ط

وَاِنْ مِّنْ اُمَّةٍ اِلَّا خَلَا فِيْهَا نَذِيْرٌ ۝ وَاِنْ يُّكَذِّبُوْكَ

فَقَدْ كَذَّبَ الَّذِيْنَ مِنْ قَبْلِهِمْ ج جَآءَتْهُمْ رُسُلُهُمْ

بِالْبَيِّنٰتِ وَبِالزُّبُرِ وَبِالْكِتٰبِ الْمُنِيْرِ ۝ ثُمَّ اَخَذْتُ

الَّذِيْنَ كَفَرُوْا فَكَيْفَ كَانَ نَكِيْرِ ۝ اَلَمْ تَرَ اَنَّ اللّٰهَ

اَنْزَلَ مِنَ السَّمَآءِ مَآءً ج فَاَخْرَجْنَا بِهٖ ثَمَرٰتٍ مُّخْتَلِفًا

اَلْوَانُهَا ط وَمِنَ الْجِبَالِ جُدَدٌ بِيْضٌ وَّحُمْرٌ مُّخْتَلِفٌ

اَلْوَانُهَا وَغَرَابِيْبُ سُوْدٌ ۝ وَمِنَ النَّاسِ وَالدَّوَآبِّ

وَالْاَنْعَامِ مُخْتَلِفٌ اَلْوَانُهٗ كَذٰلِكَ ط اِنَّمَا يَخْشَى اللّٰهَ

مِنْ عِبَادِهِ الْعُلَمٰٓؤُا ط اِنَّ اللّٰهَ عَزِيْزٌ غَفُوْرٌ ۝ اِنَّ

The marvels of nature are shouting loud: 'glory be to our Lord!' Yet people are deaf to it.

¹⁶ If He wanted He could get rid of you and bring about a new creation; ¹⁷ that wouldn't be too difficult for Allah. ¹⁸ No one will bear another's burden. If a *person* with a heavy load were to cry out *for help*, no one – not even a close relative – would accept it. Those you can warn are fearful of their Lord without seeing Him, and they perform the prayer regularly. Anyone who purifies himself, does for his own good; and to Allah is the final return.

A reminder that Allah guides, and the Messenger ﷺ warns

¹⁹ The blind and the sighted are not the same, ²⁰ nor darkness and light, ²¹ nor *cool* shade and *sweltering* heat. ²² The living and the dead are not the same *either*. Allah lets him hear, who wants to hear; *messenger*, the one who is in the grave, you cannot make him hear.^a ²³ You are a warner. ²⁴ We sent you as a messenger of good news and a warner. No community was without *its* warner. ²⁵ If they think you are a liar, *so what*? Those before them treated their messengers as liars when they came to them with clear signs, with writings and the light giving Book. ²⁶ After that, I seized the disbelievers. So, *imagine* My terrible displeasure!

The people of true knowledge fear Allah

²⁷ Haven't you considered, how Allah sends rain from the sky, that produces fruits of different colours; *look at* the mountains with streaks of white and red *rock* of various shades, some pitch black? ²⁸ In the same way, colour differences exist among people and wild and domesticated animals. Among His servants only the knowledgeable fear Allah. Allah is Almighty, Forgiving.

---

^a Since the disbelievers refused to listen to the Messenger ﷺ they are referred to as dead, their fate is sealed.

الَّذِيْنَ يَتْلُوْنَ كِتَبَ اللهِ وَاَقَامُوا الصَّلٰوةَ وَاَنْفَقُوْا

مِمَّا رَزَقْنٰهُمْ سِرًّا وَّعَلَانِيَةً يَّرْجُوْنَ تِجَارَةً لَّنْ

تَبُوْرَ ۲۹ لِيُوَفِّيَهُمْ اُجُوْرَهُمْ وَيَزِيْدَهُمْ مِّنْ فَضْلِهٖ ط

اِنَّهٗ غَفُوْرٌ شَكُوْرٌ ۳۰ وَالَّذِيْٓ اَوْحَيْنَآ اِلَيْكَ مِنَ

الْكِتٰبِ هُوَ الْحَقُّ مُصَدِّقًا لِّمَا بَيْنَ يَدَيْهِ ط اِنَّ

اللهَ بِعِبَادِهٖ لَخَبِيْرٌ بَصِيْرٌ ۳۱ ثُمَّ اَوْرَثْنَا الْكِتٰبَ

الَّذِيْنَ اصْطَفَيْنَا مِنْ عِبَادِنَا ۚ فَمِنْهُمْ ظَالِمٌ لِّنَفْسِهٖ ۚ

وَمِنْهُمْ مُّقْتَصِدٌ ۚ وَمِنْهُمْ سَابِقٌ بِالْخَيْرٰتِ بِاِذْنِ اللهِ ط

ذٰلِكَ هُوَ الْفَضْلُ الْكَبِيْرُ ۳۲ جَنّٰتُ عَدْنٍ يَّدْخُلُوْنَهَا

يُحَلَّوْنَ فِيْهَا مِنْ اَسَاوِرَ مِنْ ذَهَبٍ وَّلُؤْلُؤًا ۚ وَلِبَاسُهُمْ

فِيْهَا حَرِيْرٌ ۳۳ وَقَالُوا الْحَمْدُ لِلهِ الَّذِيْٓ اَذْهَبَ عَنَّا

الْحَزَنَ ط اِنَّ رَبَّنَا لَغَفُوْرٌ شَكُوْرٌ ۳۴ الَّذِيْٓ اَحَلَّنَا

دَارَ الْمُقَامَةِ مِنْ فَضْلِهٖ ۚ لَا يَمَسُّنَا فِيْهَا نَصَبٌ وَّلَا

يَمَسُّنَا فِيْهَا لُغُوْبٌ ۳۵ وَالَّذِيْنَ كَفَرُوْا لَهُمْ نَارُ جَهَنَّمَ ۚ

لَا يُقْضٰى عَلَيْهِمْ فَيَمُوْتُوْا وَلَا يُخَفَّفُ عَنْهُمْ مِّنْ

عَذَابِهَا ط كَذٰلِكَ نَجْزِيْ كُلَّ كَفُوْرٍ ۳۶ وَهُمْ يَصْطَرِخُوْنَ

فِيْهَا ۚ رَبَّنَآ اَخْرِجْنَا نَعْمَلْ صَالِحًا غَيْرَ الَّذِيْ كُنَّا

نَعْمَلُ ط اَوَلَمْ نُعَمِّرْكُمْ مَّا يَتَذَكَّرُ فِيْهِ مَنْ تَذَكَّرَ وَ

جَآءَكُمُ النَّذِيْرُ ط فَذُوْقُوْا فَمَا لِلظّٰلِمِيْنَ مِنْ نَّصِيْرٍ ۳۷

اِنَّ اللهَ عٰلِمُ غَيْبِ السَّمٰوٰتِ وَالْاَرْضِ ط اِنَّهٗ عَلِيْمٌ

Three levels of a Muslim: Weak and ignorant, trying but lukewarm and the one who works hard. Which one are you?

871

²⁹ Those who recite Allah's Book, perform the prayer and spend publicly and privately from what We provided them, they long for a business that will never be in loss, ³⁰ so He will fully reward them for their *deeds*, and bless them extra from His bounty. He is Forgiving, Appreciative *of their efforts.*

Three grades of believers

³¹ What We revealed to you from the Book is the truth, it confirms what came before it. Allah is Aware *and* sees His servants' *actions.* ³² We chose some servants to inherit the Book: some wronged themselves *by ignoring its teachings, others* have good intentions, and yet others are ahead in doing good deeds by Allah's permission; that's the great favour. ³³ *These believers* will enter Gardens of Eden, where they will be decorated with bracelets of gold and pearls, and silky clothes. ³⁴ They will say, "Praise be to Allah, Who has relieved us of distress. Our Lord is Forgiving, Appreciative, ³⁵ Who by His grace has settled us in the everlasting home, here there's no hard work or weariness."

The terrible fate of disbelievers

³⁶ The disbelievers will be in the Fire of Hell, they won't die and the punishment will not be reduced for them. That is how We reward every ungrateful *person.* ³⁷ There they will cry loud, "Our Lord, let us out to do good works, not like what we used to do." *Allah will say,* "Did We not give you long enough to live? Whoever wished to reflect had enough time to do so. And the warner came to you. So, taste *the Fire of Hell.* There is no helper for the wrongdoers."

The disbelievers' claims are baseless

³⁸ Allah Knows *the* unseen in the Heavens and the Earth, He knows *people's* innermost thoughts.

بِذَاتِ الصُّدُوْرِ ۝ هُوَ الَّذِيْ جَعَلَكُمْ خَلٰٓئِفَ فِى الْاَرْضِ ۚ فَمَنْ كَفَرَ فَعَلَيْهِ كُفْرُهٗ ۚ وَلَا يَزِيْدُ الْكٰفِرِيْنَ كُفْرُهُمْ عِنْدَ رَبِّهِمْ اِلَّا مَقْتًا ۚ وَلَا يَزِيْدُ الْكٰفِرِيْنَ كُفْرُهُمْ اِلَّا خَسَارًا ۝ قُلْ اَرَءَيْتُمْ شُرَكَآءَكُمُ الَّذِيْنَ تَدْعُوْنَ مِنْ دُوْنِ اللّٰهِ ۚ اَرُوْنِيْ مَاذَا خَلَقُوْا مِنَ الْاَرْضِ اَمْ لَهُمْ شِرْكٌ فِى السَّمٰوٰتِ ۚ اَمْ اٰتَيْنٰهُمْ كِتٰبًا فَهُمْ عَلٰى بَيِّنَتٍ مِّنْهُ ۚ بَلْ اِنْ يَّعِدُ الظّٰلِمُوْنَ بَعْضُهُمْ بَعْضًا اِلَّا غُرُوْرًا ۝ اِنَّ اللّٰهَ يُمْسِكُ السَّمٰوٰتِ وَالْاَرْضَ اَنْ تَزُوْلَا ۚ وَلَئِنْ زَالَتَا اِنْ اَمْسَكَهُمَا مِنْ اَحَدٍ مِّنْ بَعْدِهٖ ۚ اِنَّهٗ كَانَ حَلِيْمًا غَفُوْرًا ۝ وَاَقْسَمُوْا بِاللّٰهِ جَهْدَ اَيْمَانِهِمْ لَئِنْ جَآءَهُمْ نَذِيْرٌ لَّيَكُوْنُنَّ اَهْدٰى مِنْ اِحْدَى الْاُمَمِ ۚ فَلَمَّا جَآءَهُمْ نَذِيْرٌ مَّا زَادَهُمْ اِلَّا نُفُوْرَا ۝ اِسْتِكْبَارًا فِى الْاَرْضِ وَمَكْرَ السَّيِّئِ ۚ وَلَا يَحِيْقُ الْمَكْرُ السَّيِّئُ اِلَّا بِاَهْلِهٖ ۚ فَهَلْ يَنْظُرُوْنَ اِلَّا سُنَّتَ الْاَوَّلِيْنَ ۚ فَلَنْ تَجِدَ لِسُنَّتِ اللّٰهِ تَبْدِيْلًا ۚ وَلَنْ تَجِدَ لِسُنَّتِ اللّٰهِ تَحْوِيْلًا ۝ اَوَلَمْ يَسِيْرُوْا فِى الْاَرْضِ فَيَنْظُرُوْا كَيْفَ كَانَ عَاقِبَةُ الَّذِيْنَ مِنْ قَبْلِهِمْ وَكَانُوْا اَشَدَّ مِنْهُمْ قُوَّةً ۚ وَمَا كَانَ اللّٰهُ لِيُعْجِزَهٗ مِنْ شَيْءٍ فِى السَّمٰوٰتِ وَلَا فِى الْاَرْضِ ۚ اِنَّهٗ كَانَ عَلِيْمًا قَدِيْرًا ۝ وَلَوْ يُؤَاخِذُ اللّٰهُ النَّاسَ بِمَا كَسَبُوْا مَا تَرَكَ عَلٰى ظَهْرِهَا مِنْ دَآبَّةٍ

*Praise the Lord, glorify
the Originator, love the
Creator.*

³⁹ He made you successors *of people* on Earth. Anyone who disbelieves must bear the consequences of his disbelief; the disbelief of disbelievers increases the dislike of their Lord; the disbelief of disbelievers only increases loss. ⁴⁰ Say: "Have you *really* thought about the *false* partners you call beside Allah? Show me what they have created on Earth. Do they have a share of the Heavens, or have We given them a book on whose guidance they rely?" On the contrary, the wrongdoers promise nothing but false hopes to each other.

What goes around comes around

⁴¹ Allah keeps the Heavens and Earth from disappearing, were they to disappear, could anyone else preserve them? He is Gentle, Forgiving. ⁴² They swore solemn oaths by Allah that if a warner came to them, they would be the most rightly guided people. When a warner came to them, it increased their hatred *of the truth*, ⁴³ behaving arrogantly in the land and plotting evil – and evil plots only ever rebound on those who devise them. So, what else can they expect but what happened in practice to the people of the past? And you will never see change in Allah's *good* practice, nor will you see a modification in Allah's *good* practice. ⁴⁴ Haven't they travelled the Earth and seen how those before them met their end, though they were far greater than them in strength? Nothing in the Heavens or the Earth can weaken Allah. He is Knowing, Powerful. ⁴⁵ Were Allah to take people to task for what wrong they did, then He wouldn't leave a single creature on the face of *the Earth*, but He grants a delay for a fixed period *for reflection*; when their time comes, *that's it*, Allah observes His servants.

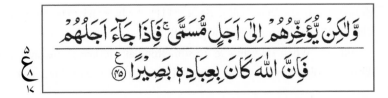

36. Surat Ya Seen

Ya Seen

This is an early Makkan surat, revealed at a time of severe tension between the Muslims and the idolaters. The Prophet 🦋 called it, "The heart of the Quran." Its central theme is convincing arguments for the doctrines of *Tawhid, Risalah* and *Akhirah.* Reading Surat Ya Seen in times of hardship calms the nerves and reassures one, restores health in sickness and at the time of death eases the pain of death.

It opens by reassuring the Messenger 🦋 of the importance of his role in guiding humanity, and laments the history of human disobedience. The story of three messengers, who were rejected by the people of the town, is told to warn the Makkans; the chief reason identified for their disbelief is arrogance, which they expressed as stubborn behaviour. The brave supporter in the story, who stands up for the messengers, symbolises the small band of Muslims in Makkah, thereby reassuring them of Divine Help. The Makkans are warned of dire consequences of the denial of truth: "Haven't they considered how many generations We destroyed before them?" (31).

The second section of the surat describes Allah's amazing creative power, and invites the reader to reflect on creation: a marvel of incredible complexity and beauty. Attention is drawn to the lifeless Earth and how it comes to life after it rains, producing lush vegetation. The lesson is Allah will bring the dead to life.

A description of Judgement Day follows: The Trumpet is blown, justice done; evidence of one's good and bad deeds won't only come from records kept by the angels, but human limbs will speak. The accuracy and veracity of this evidence will be unquestionable. A vivid account of the delights of Paradise shows how its residents will see Allah in His Glory and Majesty.

The surat opened with two claims: The Messenger 🦋 is divinely appointed to guide humanity, and the reality of resurrection. To prove this, it presented historical, rational, and moral evidence. The conceptual boundaries of the readers' mind are prompted to ponder the paradoxical: sparks of fire that come from rubbing together fresh twigs. Seven proofs are presented for Allah's amazing creative power: The wonder of dry earth becoming lush green after rainfall (33-35); the cycle of day and night (37); the orbits of Sun and Moon (38-40); the ships sailing on seas (41); the livestock (71-73); the mystery of human creation (76); fire from green twigs (80).

Indeed: "When He wants to do something all He says is 'Be,' and it is! Glory to Him Who controls everything and you shall be returned to Him" (82–83).

بِسۡمِ اللّٰهِ الرَّحۡمٰنِ الرَّحِيۡمِ

يٰسٓ ۞ وَالۡقُرۡاٰنِ الۡحَكِيۡمِ ۞ اِنَّكَ لَمِنَ الۡمُرۡسَلِيۡنَ ۞ عَلٰى

صِرَاطٍ مُّسۡتَقِيۡمٍ ۞ تَنۡزِيۡلَ الۡعَزِيۡزِ الرَّحِيۡمِ ۞ لِتُنۡذِرَ قَوۡمًا

مَّاۤ اُنۡذِرَ اٰبَآؤُهُمۡ فَهُمۡ غٰفِلُوۡنَ ۞ لَقَدۡ حَقَّ الۡقَوۡلُ عَلٰى

اَكۡثَرِهِمۡ فَهُمۡ لَا يُؤۡمِنُوۡنَ ۞ اِنَّا جَعَلۡنَا فِيۡۤ اَعۡنَاقِهِمۡ اَغۡلٰلًا

فَهِيَ اِلَى الۡاَذۡقَانِ فَهُمۡ مُّقۡمَحُوۡنَ ۞ وَجَعَلۡنَا مِنۡۢ بَيۡنِ

اَيۡدِيۡهِمۡ سَدًّا وَّمِنۡ خَلۡفِهِمۡ سَدًّا فَاَغۡشَيۡنٰهُمۡ فَهُمۡ

لَا يُبۡصِرُوۡنَ ۞ وَسَوَآءٌ عَلَيۡهِمۡ ءَاَنۡذَرۡتَهُمۡ اَمۡ لَمۡ تُنۡذِرۡهُمۡ

لَا يُؤۡمِنُوۡنَ ۞ اِنَّمَا تُنۡذِرُ مَنِ اتَّبَعَ الذِّكۡرَ وَخَشِيَ الرَّحۡمٰنَ

بِالۡغَيۡبِ ۚ فَبَشِّرۡهُ بِمَغۡفِرَةٍ وَّاَجۡرٍ كَرِيۡمٍ ۞ اِنَّا نَحۡنُ

نُحۡىِ الۡمَوۡتٰى وَنَكۡتُبُ مَا قَدَّمُوۡا وَاٰثَارَهُمۡ ۚ وَكُلَّ شَىۡءٍ

اَحۡصَيۡنٰهُ فِىۡۤ اِمَامٍ مُّبِيۡنٍ ۞ وَاضۡرِبۡ لَهُمۡ مَّثَلًا اَصۡحٰبَ

الۡقَرۡيَةِ ۘ اِذۡ جَآءَهَا الۡمُرۡسَلُوۡنَ ۞ اِذۡ اَرۡسَلۡنَاۤ اِلَيۡهِمُ

اثۡنَيۡنِ فَكَذَّبُوۡهُمَا فَعَزَّزۡنَا بِثَالِثٍ فَقَالُوۡۤا اِنَّاۤ اِلَيۡكُمۡ

مُّرۡسَلُوۡنَ ۞ قَالُوۡا مَاۤ اَنۡتُمۡ اِلَّا بَشَرٌ مِّثۡلُنَا ۙ وَمَاۤ اَنۡزَلَ

الرَّحۡمٰنُ مِنۡ شَىۡءٍ ۙ اِنۡ اَنۡتُمۡ اِلَّا تَكۡذِبُوۡنَ ۞ قَالُوۡا

رَبُّنَا يَعۡلَمُ اِنَّاۤ اِلَيۡكُمۡ لَمُرۡسَلُوۡنَ ۞ وَمَا عَلَيۡنَاۤ اِلَّا الۡبَلٰغُ

الۡمُبِيۡنُ ۞ قَالُوۡۤا اِنَّا تَطَيَّرۡنَا بِكُمۡ ۚ لَئِنۡ لَّمۡ تَنۡتَهُوۡا

لَنَرۡجُمَنَّكُمۡ وَلَيَمَسَّنَّكُمۡ مِّنَّا عَذَابٌ اَلِيۡمٌ ۞ قَالُوۡا

Allah guides but people are stubborn, unwilling to accept. How open are you to question?

In the name of Allah, the Kind, the Caring.

¹ *Ya' Seen.*

The beloved Messenger ﷺ is honoured

² By the Quran, full of wisdom. ³ You are a Messenger, ⁴ on the straight path. ⁵ *This is a Revelation from the Almighty, the Caring,* ⁶ to warn a community whose ancestors were not warned, so they're unaware.

Why is it hard for them to believe?

⁷ The sentence against most of them is justified, because they don't believe. ⁸ *As though* We've placed iron collars around their necks, right up to their chins, so their heads can't move; ⁹ and We've placed a wall in front and behind them and hooded them so that they can't see. ¹⁰ It makes no difference whether you warn them or not, they won't believe. ¹¹ You can only warn someone who follows the Reminderᵃ and fears the Most Kind, *the* Unseen. So, make him happy with the news of forgiveness and a generous reward. ¹² We will resurrect the dead and record all they achieved and the *legacies* they left behind; and We recorded everything in a Clear Book.ᵇ

The story of the three messengers

¹³ As an example, tell them about the people of the town, where the messengers came. ¹⁴ We sent two *at first*, they rejected them; so We strengthened *them* with a third; and they said, "We are messengers sent to you." ¹⁵ *They* said, "You're mortals like us. The Most Kind hasn't sent anything, you are lying." ¹⁶ *They* said, "Our Lord knows we are messengers *sent* to you, ¹⁷ and our duty is to communicate *the Message* clearly." ¹⁸ *They* said, "you are an evil omen for us. If you don't stop, we'll torture you, and punish you severely."

ᵃ In other words, the Quran.
ᵇ The word "imam" here has the meaning of a guidebook, and refers to the Divine Tablet.

طَآئِرُكُم مَّعَكُمْ ط اِن ذُكِّرْتُم ط بَلْ اَنتُمْ قَوْمٌ مُّسْرِفُونَ ۝

وَجَآءَ مِنْ اَقْصَا الْمَدِينَةِ رَجُلٌ يَّسْعٰى قَالَ يٰقَوْمِ اتَّبِعُوا

الْمُرْسَلِينَ ۝ اتَّبِعُوا مَن لَّا يَسْـَٔلُكُمْ اَجْرًا وَّهُم مُّهْتَدُونَ ۝

وَمَالِيَ لَاۤ اَعْبُدُ الَّذِى فَطَرَنِى وَاِلَيْهِ تُرْجَعُونَ ۝

ءَاَتَّخِذُ مِن دُونِهٖۤ اٰلِهَةً اِن يُّرِدْنِ الرَّحْمٰنُ بِضُرٍّ لَّا

تُغْنِ عَنِّى شَفَاعَتُهُمْ شَيْـًٔا وَّلَا يُنقِذُونِ ۝ اِنِّىۤ

اِذًا لَّفِى ضَلٰلٍ مُّبِينٍ ۝ اِنِّىۤ اٰمَنتُ بِرَبِّكُمْ فَاسْمَعُونِ ۝

قِيلَ ادْخُلِ الْجَنَّةَ ط قَالَ يٰلَيْتَ قَوْمِى يَعْلَمُونَ ۝ بِمَا

The believer, the
thoughtful and supporter
of the truth, is given
Paradise. We hope to join
Him!

غَفَرَ لِى رَبِّى وَجَعَلَنِى مِنَ الْمُكْرَمِينَ ۝ وَمَاۤ اَنزَلْنَا

عَلٰى قَوْمِهٖ مِنۢ بَعْدِهٖ مِن جُندٍ مِّنَ السَّمَآءِ وَمَا كُنَّا

مُنزِلِينَ ۝ اِن كَانَتْ اِلَّا صَيْحَةً وَّاحِدَةً فَاِذَا هُمْ

خٰمِدُونَ ۝ يٰحَسْرَةً عَلَى الْعِبَادِ ج مَا يَاْتِيهِم مِّن

رَّسُولٍ اِلَّا كَانُوا بِهٖ يَسْتَهْزِءُونَ ۝ اَلَمْ يَرَوْا كَمْ اَهْلَكْنَا

قَبْلَهُم مِّنَ الْقُرُونِ اَنَّهُمْ اِلَيْهِمْ لَا يَرْجِعُونَ ۝ وَاِن

كُلٌّ لَّمَّا جَمِيعٌ لَّدَيْنَا مُحْضَرُونَ ۝ وَاٰيَةٌ لَّهُمُ الْاَرْضُ

الْمَيْتَةُ ج اَحْيَيْنٰهَا وَاَخْرَجْنَا مِنْهَا حَبًّا فَمِنْهُ

يَاْكُلُونَ ۝ وَجَعَلْنَا فِيهَا جَنّٰتٍ مِّن نَّخِيلٍ وَّاَعْنَابٍ

وَّفَجَّرْنَا فِيهَا مِنَ الْعُيُونِ ۝ لِيَاْكُلُوا مِن ثَمَرِهٖ وَمَا

عَمِلَتْهُ اَيْدِيهِمْ ط اَفَلَا يَشْكُرُونَ ۝ سُبْحٰنَ الَّذِى خَلَقَ

الْاَزْوَاجَ كُلَّهَا مِمَّا تُنۢبِتُ الْاَرْضُ وَمِنْ اَنفُسِهِمْ وَمِمَّا

¹⁹ *The messengers* replied, "The evil omen is with you. Are you annoyed because you've been reminded? You've gone beyond the limits."

A brave man stands up for the messengers

²⁰ A man came running from the far side of the town, and said, "My people, follow the messengers. ²¹ Follow those who don't ask you for any payment, and they are guided. ²² Why shouldn't I worship the One Who created me and to Whom you will be returned? ²³ Should I take beside Him gods whose intercessionᵃ would not benefit me in the slightest if the Most Kind willed to harm me? Nor would they be able to save me. ²⁴ Obviously I would be misguided. ²⁵ I *chose to* believe in Your Lord, so *please* listen to me."

The brave man is martyred and taken to Paradise

²⁶ "Enter the Garden *of Paradise*," he was told. "If only my people knew," he said, ²⁷ "the extent to which My Lord has forgiven me and placed me among the honourable." ²⁸ Thereafter, We didn't send an army against his people from the sky, We don't do that. ²⁹ Just one Blast, *that's all*, and there they were, *lying* dead. ³⁰ What a shame, whenever a messenger came to a community, they mocked him. ³¹ Haven't they seen how many generations We destroyed before them, none will come back to them. ³² Yet they will all be presented before Us.

The wonder of the lifeless Earth; evidence of resurrection

³³ A proof *of the Resurrection* for them is the dead Earth. How We give it life and make it produce cereals, which they eat, ³⁴ and here and there We have grown palm groves and vineyards and caused *fresh water* springs to flow, ³⁵ so they might eat its fruit even though they had no hand in making it.ᵇ Won't they be grateful? ³⁶ Glory be to Him who created every variety *of living things in pairs* from the Earth: *humans* themselves, and others which they *still* don't know.ᶜ

ᵃ "Intercession" means to put in a good word for someone, or to plead on someone's behalf.

ᵇ An alternative meaning preferred is "and what their hands have produced."

ᶜ Scientists estimate there are more than twelve million living species on Earth, only two million have so far been identified; the rest remain to be discovered.

لَا يَعْلَمُونَ ۝ وَاٰيَةٌ لَّهُمُ الَّيْلُ ۚ نَسْلَخُ مِنْهُ النَّهَارَ

فَاِذَا هُمْ مُّظْلِمُونَ ۝ وَالشَّمْسُ تَجْرِيْ لِمُسْتَقَرٍّ لَّهَا ۗ

ذٰلِكَ تَقْدِيْرُ الْعَزِيْزِ الْعَلِيْمِ ۝ وَالْقَمَرَ قَدَّرْنٰهُ مَنَازِلَ

حَتّٰى عَادَ كَالْعُرْجُوْنِ الْقَدِيْمِ ۝ لَا الشَّمْسُ يَنْۢبَغِيْ

لَهَآ اَنْ تُدْرِكَ الْقَمَرَ وَلَا الَّيْلُ سَابِقُ النَّهَارِ ۗ وَكُلٌّ

فِيْ فَلَكٍ يَّسْبَحُوْنَ ۝ وَاٰيَةٌ لَّهُمْ اَنَّا حَمَلْنَا ذُرِّيَّتَهُمْ

فِى الْفُلْكِ الْمَشْحُوْنِ ۝ وَخَلَقْنَا لَهُمْ مِّنْ مِّثْلِهٖ مَا

يَرْكَبُوْنَ ۝ وَاِنْ نَّشَأْ نُغْرِقْهُمْ فَلَا صَرِيْخَ لَهُمْ وَلَا

هُمْ يُنْقَذُوْنَ ۝ اِلَّا رَحْمَةً مِّنَّا وَمَتَاعًا اِلٰى حِيْنٍ ۝

وَاِذَا قِيْلَ لَهُمُ اتَّقُوْا مَا بَيْنَ اَيْدِيْكُمْ وَمَا خَلْفَكُمْ

لَعَلَّكُمْ تُرْحَمُوْنَ ۝ وَمَا تَأْتِيْهِمْ مِّنْ اٰيَةٍ مِّنْ اٰيٰتِ

رَبِّهِمْ اِلَّا كَانُوْا عَنْهَا مُعْرِضِيْنَ ۝ وَاِذَا قِيْلَ

لَهُمْ اَنْفِقُوْا مِمَّا رَزَقَكُمُ اللّٰهُ ۙ قَالَ الَّذِيْنَ كَفَرُوْا

لِلَّذِيْنَ اٰمَنُوْٓا اَنُطْعِمُ مَنْ لَّوْ يَشَآءُ اللّٰهُ اَطْعَمَهٗ ۖ اِنْ

اَنْتُمْ اِلَّا فِيْ ضَلٰلٍ مُّبِيْنٍ ۝ وَيَقُوْلُوْنَ مَتٰى هٰذَا

الْوَعْدُ اِنْ كُنْتُمْ صٰدِقِيْنَ ۝ مَا يَنْظُرُوْنَ اِلَّا صَيْحَةً

وَّاحِدَةً تَأْخُذُهُمْ وَهُمْ يَخِصِّمُوْنَ ۝ فَلَا يَسْتَطِيْعُوْنَ

تَوْصِيَةً وَّلَآ اِلٰٓى اَهْلِهِمْ يَرْجِعُوْنَ ۝ وَنُفِخَ فِى

الصُّوْرِ فَاِذَا هُمْ مِّنَ الْاَجْدَاثِ اِلٰى رَبِّهِمْ يَنْسِلُوْنَ ۝

قَالُوْا يٰوَيْلَنَا مَنْۢ بَعَثَنَا مِنْ مَّرْقَدِنَا ۗ هٰذَا مَا

٣ ع ١٥ ٢

The precision with which the solar system runs is a testament to Allah's power.

The orbits of the sun and the moon, the sailing of ships; further evidences

³⁷ Another sign for them is the night, from which We *gradually* peel the daylight away, and there they are in pitch darkness; ³⁸ the sun travels in its orbit that is precisely determined by the Almighty, the Knower.ᵃ ³⁹ Similarly the moon, We determined its phases from *full moon* to *crescent* that is *slim* as a dry date-stalk. ⁴⁰ The sun can't overtake the moon, nor the night outpace the day; all are floating in their fixed orbits. ⁴¹ Another sign for them is *the story of* their forefathers who We carried in the heavily-laden ship,ᵇ ⁴² and We created for them similar *modes of transport* which they ride. ⁴³ If We wanted We could drown them, and they will have no help, nor will they be saved, ⁴⁴ unless – *that is* – We show kindness and give brief respite.

Disbelief: an arrogant attitude and selfish behaviour

⁴⁵ When they are told: "Be careful about your past and future *deeds* to deserve kind treatment." ⁴⁶ They turn away from every sign of their Lord that comes to them. ⁴⁷ When they are told: "Spend what Allah has provided you," the disbelievers say to the believers, "Why should we feed someone who Allah could have fed, if He wanted? You are clearly misguided." ⁴⁸ And they say, "When will this promise *be fulfilled*, if you are telling the truth?" ⁴⁹ What they are waiting for is a Blast that will seize them while they argue among themselves. ⁵⁰ Then they won't be able to make a will or return to their families.

The Trumpet is blown: Judgement begins

⁵¹ The Trumpet will be blown, and they will emerge from their graves, rushing to their Lord, ⁵² saying: "Woe to us! Who woke us up from our graves?" *They will be told* "This is what the Most Kind promised, and the messengers kept reminding you about."

ᵃ Alternatively 'Dhaalika takdirul Aziz' means: That's laid down by the Will of the Almighty.
ᵇ A reference to the Ark of Nuh ﷺ.

وَعَدَ الرَّحْمٰنُ وَصَدَقَ الْمُرْسَلُوْنَ ۵۲ اِنْ كَانَتْ اِلَّا
صَيْحَةً وَّاحِدَةً فَاِذَا هُمْ جَمِيْعٌ لَّدَيْنَا مُحْضَرُوْنَ ۵۳
فَالْيَوْمَ لَا تُظْلَمُ نَفْسٌ شَيْئًا وَّلَا تُجْزَوْنَ اِلَّا مَا
كُنْتُمْ تَعْمَلُوْنَ ۵۴ اِنَّ اَصْحٰبَ الْجَنَّةِ الْيَوْمَ فِيْ شُغُلٍ
فٰكِهُوْنَ ۵۵ هُمْ وَاَزْوَاجُهُمْ فِيْ ظِلٰلٍ عَلَى الْاَرَآئِكِ
مُتَّكِئُوْنَ ۵۶ لَهُمْ فِيْهَا فَاكِهَةٌ وَّلَهُمْ مَّا يَدَّعُوْنَ ۵۷
سَلٰمٌ قف قَوْلًا مِّنْ رَّبٍّ رَّحِيْمٍ ۵۸ وَامْتَازُوا الْيَوْمَ
اَيُّهَا الْمُجْرِمُوْنَ ۵۹ اَلَمْ اَعْهَدْ اِلَيْكُمْ يٰبَنِيْ اٰدَمَ
اَنْ لَّا تَعْبُدُوا الشَّيْطٰنَ اِنَّهٗ لَكُمْ عَدُوٌّ مُّبِيْنٌ ۶۰
وَّاَنِ اعْبُدُوْنِيْ ط هٰذَا صِرَاطٌ مُّسْتَقِيْمٌ ۶۱ وَلَقَدْ
اَضَلَّ مِنْكُمْ جِبِلًّا كَثِيْرًا ط اَفَلَمْ تَكُوْنُوْا تَعْقِلُوْنَ ۶۲
هٰذِهٖ جَهَنَّمُ الَّتِيْ كُنْتُمْ تُوْعَدُوْنَ ۶۳ اِصْلَوْهَا
الْيَوْمَ بِمَا كُنْتُمْ تَكْفُرُوْنَ ۶۴ اَلْيَوْمَ نَخْتِمُ عَلٰى
اَفْوَاهِهِمْ وَتُكَلِّمُنَا اَيْدِيْهِمْ وَتَشْهَدُ اَرْجُلُهُمْ
بِمَا كَانُوْا يَكْسِبُوْنَ ۶۵ وَلَوْ نَشَاءُ لَطَمَسْنَا عَلٰى
اَعْيُنِهِمْ فَاسْتَبَقُوا الصِّرَاطَ فَاَنّٰى يُبْصِرُوْنَ ۶۶ وَلَوْ
نَشَاءُ لَمَسَخْنٰهُمْ عَلٰى مَكَانَتِهِمْ فَمَا اسْتَطَاعُوْا مُضِيًّا
وَّلَا يَرْجِعُوْنَ ۶۷ ع وَمَنْ نُّعَمِّرْهُ نُنَكِّسْهُ فِي الْخَلْقِ ط
اَفَلَا يَعْقِلُوْنَ ۶۸ وَمَا عَلَّمْنٰهُ الشِّعْرَ وَمَا يَنْۢبَغِيْ
لَهٗ ط اِنْ هُوَ اِلَّا ذِكْرٌ وَّقُرْاٰنٌ مُّبِيْنٌ ۶۹ لِّيُنْذِرَ

The beatific vision: Allah appears to His faithful, loyal and obedient servant.

⁵³ It will be a single Blast, and quickly they will be made to stand before Us. ⁵⁴ On this day, no one will be wronged in the least; and you will only be repaid for what you did.

Separation of the righteous from the wicked

⁵⁵ Today the companions of Paradise will be enjoying themselves; ⁵⁶ sitting beside their spouses on comfortable sofas relaxing in the shade, ⁵⁷ *surrounded* with fruit they like ⁵⁸ *and the greeting*: "Peace!" Spoken by the Caring Lord.^a ⁵⁹ The evildoers" *will be told*: "Step aside today. ⁶⁰ Didn't I command you, children of Adam, not to obey Satan, he is your open enemy, ⁶¹ and worship Me? This is the straight path, ⁶² but *Satan* led masses of you astray. Didn't you think? ⁶³ This is Hell about which you were warned, ⁶⁴ burn in it today, because of your disbelief."

Allah's patience with humanity

⁶⁵ Today We shall seal their mouths; their hands will speak, and their feet will bear witness to what they did. ⁶⁶ If We wanted, We could have taken away their eyesight so how could they see it, as they struggled along the path? ⁶⁷ If We wanted, We could have paralysed them, so they wouldn't move to and fro^b. ⁶⁸ Anyone We allow to age, We reduce them in size bit by bit.^c Will you not reflect? ⁶⁹ We didn't teach *the Messenger* poetry, it isn't appropriate for him. This *Quran* is a reminder and a clear recitation.

---

^a This greeting of "Salam!" Will come directly from Allah, and will be the height of all the pleasures of Paradise.

^b "We could have blinded their eyes" is a metaphor for "We could have created them morally blind" and thus devoid of all sense of moral responsibility (Asad). This would be tantamount to human life being purposeless and empty of spiritual value.

^c An elderly person in their sixties can lose two centimetres in height.

مَنْ كَانَ حَيًّا وَّيَحِقَّ الْقَوْلُ عَلَى الْكٰفِرِيْنَ ۞

اَوَلَمْ يَرَوْا اَنَّا خَلَقْنَا لَهُمْ مِّمَّا عَمِلَتْ اَيْدِيْنَا

اَنْعَامًا فَهُمْ لَهَا مٰلِكُوْنَ ۞ وَذَلَّلْنٰهَا لَهُمْ فَمِنْهَا

رَكُوْبُهُمْ وَمِنْهَا يَاْكُلُوْنَ ۞ وَلَهُمْ فِيْهَا مَنَافِعُ وَ

مَشَارِبُ ۗ اَفَلَا يَشْكُرُوْنَ ۞ وَاتَّخَذُوْا مِنْ دُوْنِ اللّٰهِ

اٰلِهَةً لَّعَلَّهُمْ يُنْصَرُوْنَ ۞ لَا يَسْتَطِيْعُوْنَ نَصْرَهُمْ ۙ

وَهُمْ لَهُمْ جُنْدٌ مُّحْضَرُوْنَ ۞ فَلَا يَحْزُنْكَ قَوْلُهُمْ ۘ

اِنَّا نَعْلَمُ مَا يُسِرُّوْنَ وَمَا يُعْلِنُوْنَ ۞ اَوَلَمْ يَرَ

الْاِنْسَانُ اَنَّا خَلَقْنٰهُ مِنْ نُّطْفَةٍ فَاِذَا هُوَ خَصِيْمٌ

مُّبِيْنٌ ۞ وَضَرَبَ لَنَا مَثَلًا وَّنَسِيَ خَلْقَهٗ ۗ قَالَ مَنْ

يُّحْيِ الْعِظَامَ وَهِيَ رَمِيْمٌ ۞ قُلْ يُحْيِيْهَا الَّذِيْٓ اَنْشَاَهَآ

اَوَّلَ مَرَّةٍ ۗ وَهُوَ بِكُلِّ خَلْقٍ عَلِيْمٌ ۙ الَّذِيْ جَعَلَ لَكُمْ

مِّنَ الشَّجَرِ الْاَخْضَرِ نَارًا فَاِذَآ اَنْتُمْ مِّنْهُ تُوْقِدُوْنَ ۞

اَوَلَيْسَ الَّذِيْ خَلَقَ السَّمٰوٰتِ وَالْاَرْضَ بِقٰدِرٍ عَلٰٓى اَنْ

يَّخْلُقَ مِثْلَهُمْ ۗ بَلٰى ۗ وَهُوَ الْخَلّٰقُ الْعَلِيْمُ ۞ اِنَّمَآ اَمْرُهٗٓ

اِذَآ اَرَادَ شَيْئًا اَنْ يَّقُوْلَ لَهٗ كُنْ فَيَكُوْنُ ۞ فَسُبْحٰنَ

الَّذِيْ بِيَدِهٖ مَلَكُوْتُ كُلِّ شَيْءٍ وَّاِلَيْهِ تُرْجَعُوْنَ ۞

Allah's words have enormous power. They make things happen.

[70] So *he* can warn anyone who is alive, and to confirm the sentence against the disbelievers.

Evidence for resurrection from domesticated animals

[71] Haven't they considered how We created their livestock, made by Our hands; [72] and how We tamed *animals* to give in to them, so they ride some and eat some of them? [73] And they derive other benefits from them, *like milk to* drink. Won't they be grateful? [74] Yet they take *other* gods beside Allah, *hoping* to be helped *by them*. [75] But *they* are incapable of helping them, even if they were standing to attention for them, like an army. [76] So don't let what they say sadden you. We know what they do secretly and openly.

Evidence from human birth

[77] Haven't humans considered how We created them from a drop of fluid, so they openly argue *against Us*? [78] They make up comparisons about Us whilst forgetting their own creation, saying, "Who will give life to *these* bones when they have turned into dust?" [79] Say: "The one Who produced them originally will bring them back to life – and He has full knowledge of every creature – [80] *and* Who, for your *benefit*, placed *the energy of* fire in green trees, from which you get fuel?"

Allah's perfect power is limitless

[81] Isn't the Creator of the Heavens and the Earth capable of recreating the like of these *quarrelsome humans*? Of course, He is the Creator, the Knower. [82] When He wills something, His command is: "Be!" And it is![a] [83] Glory to Him Who controls everything, to Him you shall be returned.

---

[a] "It is" means it comes into being.

37. Surat As-Saffat

Arranged in Rows

This surat was revealed in the middle-Makkan period. Its central theme is proving the truthfulness of the Islamic doctrines: *Tawhid, Risalah,* and *Akhirah.* It opens with three attention-grabbing oaths that describe the mysterious and the perennial Heavenly battles between the angels and Satan, but comes back to Earthly battles of Prophets and their disobedient communities.[a] It tells the stories of six messengers, describing their heroic and courageous efforts to guide their communities. In the dream of Ibrahim 🕊 and his willingness to sacrifice, it points to the inner battle: love of children versus love of Allah.

Two scenes from Judgement Day are described: leaders and their followers are at loggerheads, blaming each other for their dreadful fate; a pious person finds his friend in Hell, and reminds him how he tried to misguide him, but failed in doing so. Zaqqum, the food of the people of Hell is described as:

A tree that grows in the middle of Hell. Its fruit is like the heads of Satan. They will eat from it to fill their bellies, then drink boiling water; their home is Hell (64–68).

The Zaqqum tree resembles the desert cactus, with a poisonous sap and a foul smell, that causes blistering and even death. The surat returns to the role of the angels and how they are organised in Paradise, and ends by stressing the significance of the beliefs of *Tawhid* and *Risalah.*

---

[a] Razi gives three other subjects of these oaths; the scholars; the soldiers conducting Jihad; and the Majestic Quran. About the Quran he says: "The verses of the Quran are arranged in an orderly way, they cover different topics; arguments for Tawhid, Divine predestination, Wisdom, Prophethood, the Resurrection, Human responsibilities, Moral virtues. These verses are arranged coherently resembling well-arranged rows of people."

بِسْمِ اللهِ الرَّحْمٰنِ الرَّحِيْمِ

وَالصّٰفّٰتِ صَفًّا ۙ﴿١﴾ فَالزّٰجِرٰتِ زَجْرًا ۙ﴿٢﴾ فَالتّٰلِيٰتِ

ذِكْرًا ۙ﴿٣﴾ اِنَّ اِلٰهَكُمْ لَوَاحِدٌ ؕ﴿٤﴾ رَبُّ السَّمٰوٰتِ وَالْاَرْضِ

وَمَا بَيْنَهُمَا وَرَبُّ الْمَشَارِقِ ؕ﴿٥﴾ اِنَّا زَيَّنَّا السَّمَآءَ الدُّنْيَا

بِزِيْنَةِ ۨالْكَوَاكِبِ ۙ﴿٦﴾ وَحِفْظًا مِّنْ كُلِّ شَيْطٰنٍ مَّارِدٍ ۚ﴿٧﴾

لَا يَسَّمَّعُوْنَ اِلَى الْمَلَاِ الْاَعْلٰى وَيُقْذَفُوْنَ مِنْ كُلِّ

جَانِبٍ ۖ﴿٨﴾ دُحُوْرًا وَّلَهُمْ عَذَابٌ وَّاصِبٌ ۙ﴿٩﴾ اِلَّا مَنْ

خَطِفَ الْخَطْفَةَ فَاَتْبَعَهٗ شِهَابٌ ثَاقِبٌ ﴿١٠﴾ فَاسْتَفْتِهِمْ

اَهُمْ اَشَدُّ خَلْقًا اَمْ مَّنْ خَلَقْنَا ؕ اِنَّا خَلَقْنٰهُمْ مِّنْ طِيْنٍ

لَّازِبٍ ﴿١١﴾ بَلْ عَجِبْتَ وَيَسْخَرُوْنَ ۪﴿١٢﴾ وَاِذَا ذُكِّرُوْا لَا

يَذْكُرُوْنَ ۪﴿١٣﴾ وَاِذَا رَاَوْا اٰيَةً يَّسْتَسْخِرُوْنَ ۪﴿١٤﴾ وَقَالُوْۤا اِنْ

هٰذَاۤ اِلَّا سِحْرٌ مُّبِيْنٌ ۚ﴿١٥﴾ ءَاِذَا مِتْنَا وَكُنَّا تُرَابًا وَّعِظَامًا

ءَاِنَّا لَمَبْعُوْثُوْنَ ۙ﴿١٦﴾ اَوَاٰبَآؤُنَا الْاَوَّلُوْنَ ؕ﴿١٧﴾ قُلْ نَعَمْ وَاَنْتُمْ

دَاخِرُوْنَ ۚ﴿١٨﴾ فَاِنَّمَا هِيَ زَجْرَةٌ وَّاحِدَةٌ فَاِذَا هُمْ يَنْظُرُوْنَ ﴿١٩﴾

وَقَالُوْا يٰوَيْلَنَا هٰذَا يَوْمُ الدِّيْنِ ﴿٢٠﴾ هٰذَا يَوْمُ الْفَصْلِ

الَّذِيْ كُنْتُمْ بِهٖ تُكَذِّبُوْنَ ۰﴿٢١﴾ اُحْشُرُوا الَّذِيْنَ ظَلَمُوْا

وَاَزْوَاجَهُمْ وَمَا كَانُوْا يَعْبُدُوْنَ ۙ﴿٢٢﴾ مِنْ دُوْنِ اللهِ

فَاهْدُوْهُمْ اِلٰى صِرَاطِ الْجَحِيْمِ ۙ﴿٢٣﴾ وَقِفُوْهُمْ اِنَّهُمْ

مَّسْئُوْلُوْنَ ۙ﴿٢٤﴾ مَا لَكُمْ لَا تَنَاصَرُوْنَ ﴿٢٥﴾ بَلْ هُمُ الْيَوْمَ

Disbelief and idolatry are the result of doubts, ignorance and the unwillingness to pay attention. So be a serious student.

In the name of Allah, the Kind, the Caring.

Heavenly battles between the angels and Satan

[1] By *the angels* – arranged in rows, [2] who stop people from evil [3] and by those who recite the word [4] that your Lord is One, [5] Lord of the Heavens and the Earth and what is between them, the Lord of the Easts. [6] We have decorated the lower sky with the stars [7] and protected it from every disobedient devil. [8] They cannot eavesdrop on the higher assembly *of angels,* they will be attacked from all sides [9] and driven out. Theirs is everlasting punishment. [10] The snatcher of information is chased by a fiery comet.

The mocking attitude of the disbelievers

[11] Ask: "Are they more difficult to create than the rest of the creation?" We created them from a sticky clay. [12] Are you surprised they mock, [13] if they are reminded they take no notice; [14] when they see a sign they poke fun at it, [15] saying, "This is magic; [16] when we are dead and become dust and bones will we [17] be raised to life with our forefathers?" [18] Say: "Yes, *and* you will be despised!"

The disbelievers blame each other on Judgement Day

[19] It will be a single blast as they look on *terrified.* [20] With regret they will say, "This is Judgement Day." [21] Indeed, the Day of Decision that you denied. [22] *The angels will be ordered*: "Gather the wicked people, *including* their spouses and whatever they worshipped [23] beside Allah, and lead them on the path to the Blazing Fire. [24] Stop them for questioning, [25] why are you not helping each other *today?*" [26] No, today is the Day that they submit fully.

مُسْتَسْلِمُوْنَ ۲۶ وَأَقْبَلَ بَعْضُهُمْ عَلٰى بَعْضٍ يَّتَسَآءَلُوْنَ ۲۷

قَالُوْٓا اِنَّكُمْ كُنْتُمْ تَأْتُوْنَنَا عَنِ الْيَمِيْنِ ۲۸ قَالُوْا بَلْ

لَّمْ تَكُوْنُوْا مُؤْمِنِيْنَ ۲۹ وَمَا كَانَ لَنَا عَلَيْكُمْ مِّنْ

سُلْطٰنٍ ۚ بَلْ كُنْتُمْ قَوْمًا طٰغِيْنَ ۳۰ فَحَقَّ عَلَيْنَا قَوْلُ

رَبِّنَآ ۖ اِنَّا لَذَآئِقُوْنَ ۳۱ فَأَغْوَيْنٰكُمْ اِنَّا كُنَّا غٰوِيْنَ ۳۲

فَاِنَّهُمْ يَوْمَئِذٍ فِي الْعَذَابِ مُشْتَرِكُوْنَ ۳۳ اِنَّا كَذٰلِكَ

نَفْعَلُ بِالْمُجْرِمِيْنَ ۳۴ اِنَّهُمْ كَانُوْٓا اِذَا قِيْلَ لَهُمْ لَاۤ اِلٰهَ

اِلَّا اللّٰهُ ۙ يَسْتَكْبِرُوْنَ ۳۵ وَيَقُوْلُوْنَ اَئِنَّا لَتَارِكُوْۤا اٰلِهَتِنَا

لِشَاعِرٍ مَّجْنُوْنٍ ۳۶ بَلْ جَآءَ بِالْحَقِّ وَصَدَّقَ الْمُرْسَلِيْنَ ۳۷

اِنَّكُمْ لَذَآئِقُوا الْعَذَابِ الْاَلِيْمِ ۳۸ وَمَا تُجْزَوْنَ

اِلَّا مَا كُنْتُمْ تَعْمَلُوْنَ ۳۹ اِلَّا عِبَادَ اللّٰهِ الْمُخْلَصِيْنَ ۴۰

اُولٰٓئِكَ لَهُمْ رِزْقٌ مَّعْلُوْمٌ ۴۱ فَوَاكِهُ ۚ وَهُمْ مُّكْرَمُوْنَ ۴۲

فِيْ جَنّٰتِ النَّعِيْمِ ۴۳ عَلٰى سُرُرٍ مُّتَقٰبِلِيْنَ ۴۴ يُطَافُ

عَلَيْهِمْ بِكَأْسٍ مِّنْ مَّعِيْنٍ ۴۵ بَيْضَآءَ لَذَّةٍ لِّلشّٰرِبِيْنَ ۴۶

لَا فِيْهَا غَوْلٌ وَّلَا هُمْ عَنْهَا يُنْزَفُوْنَ ۴۷ وَعِنْدَهُمْ

قٰصِرٰتُ الطَّرْفِ عِيْنٌ ۴۸ كَأَنَّهُنَّ بَيْضٌ مَّكْنُوْنٌ ۴۹

فَأَقْبَلَ بَعْضُهُمْ عَلٰى بَعْضٍ يَّتَسَآءَلُوْنَ ۵۰ قَالَ

قَآئِلٌ مِّنْهُمْ اِنِّيْ كَانَ لِيْ قَرِيْنٌ ۵۱ يَّقُوْلُ اَئِنَّكَ

لَمِنَ الْمُصَدِّقِيْنَ ۵۲ ءَاِذَا مِتْنَا وَكُنَّا تُرَابًا وَّعِظَامًا

ءَاِنَّا لَمَدِيْنُوْنَ ۵۳ قَالَ هَلْ اَنْتُمْ مُّطَّلِعُوْنَ ۵۴

²⁷They will confront each other, quarrelling. ²⁸"You overpowered us," ²⁹they will reply, "No! You didn't *want* to be believers; ³⁰we had no power over you, you were rebellious *anyway*. ³¹Our Lord's judgement against us is fair. We'll taste the *punishment*. ³²We misguided you since we were misguided." ³³That Day they will share the punishment; ³⁴that's Our way of dealing with sinners. ³⁵The arrogant people, when they were asked to say: "There is no God but Allah," ³⁶said, "Should we give up our gods for the sake of a mad poet?" ³⁷No, he came with the truth and confirmed the *previous* prophets. ³⁸Now taste the painful punishment. ³⁹You'll be repaid fully for what you did.

The delights of Paradise
⁴⁰The sincere servants of Allah ⁴¹will have *plenty of* provisions; fruits they were familiar with. ⁴²They shall be honoured ⁴³in Gardens of Delight, ⁴⁴sitting on comfortable sofas facing each other; ⁴⁵they shall be served *drinks* in cups filled from a flowing fountain, ⁴⁶white and delicious for the drinkers; ⁴⁷*this wine* won't cause headache or confusion; ⁴⁸sitting with their spouses of modest gaze and lovely eyes; ⁴⁹like *precious* eggs, well-preserved.

The conversation of a pious person with a disbeliever
⁵⁰They will turn to one another asking questions; ⁵¹one of them will ask, "I had a friend ⁵²who would ask me, 'Do you really believe: ⁵³when we are dead and turned to dust and bones we shall be brought back for judgement?' ⁵⁴He will say, 'Would you like to see him?'

فَٱطَّلَعَ فَرَاٰهُ فِىۡ سَوَآءِ الۡجَحِيۡمِ ۵۵ قَالَ تَٱللّٰهِ اِنۡ
كِدۡتَّ لَتُرۡدِيۡنِ ۵۶ وَلَوۡلَا نِعۡمَةُ رَبِّىۡ لَكُنۡتُ مِنَ
الۡمُحۡضَرِيۡنَ ۵۷ اَفَمَا نَحۡنُ بِمَيِّتِيۡنَ ۵۸ اِلَّا مَوۡتَتَنَا
الۡاُوۡلٰى وَمَا نَحۡنُ بِمُعَذَّبِيۡنَ ۵۹ اِنَّ هٰذَا لَهُوَ الۡفَوۡزُ
الۡعَظِيۡمُ ۶۰ لِمِثۡلِ هٰذَا فَلۡيَعۡمَلِ الۡعٰمِلُوۡنَ ۶۱ اَذٰلِكَ
خَيۡرٌ نُّزُلًا اَمۡ شَجَرَةُ الزَّقُّوۡمِ ۶۲ اِنَّا جَعَلۡنٰهَا فِتۡنَةً
لِّلظّٰلِمِيۡنَ ۶۳ اِنَّهَا شَجَرَةٌ تَخۡرُجُ فِىۡ اَصۡلِ الۡجَحِيۡمِ ۶۴
طَلۡعُهَا كَاَنَّهٗ رُءُوۡسُ الشَّيٰطِيۡنِ ۶۵ فَاِنَّهُمۡ لَاٰكِلُوۡنَ
مِنۡهَا فَمَالِئُوۡنَ مِنۡهَا الۡبُطُوۡنَ ۶۶ ثُمَّ اِنَّ لَهُمۡ
عَلَيۡهَا لَشَوۡبًا مِّنۡ حَمِيۡمٍ ۶۷ ثُمَّ اِنَّ مَرۡجِعَهُمۡ لَاۤ اِلَى
الۡجَحِيۡمِ ۶۸ اِنَّهُمۡ اَلۡفَوۡا اٰبَآءَهُمۡ ضَآلِّيۡنَ ۶۹ فَهُمۡ
عَلٰٓى اٰثٰرِهِمۡ يُهۡرَعُوۡنَ ۷۰ وَلَقَدۡ ضَلَّ قَبۡلَهُمۡ اَكۡثَرُ
الۡاَوَّلِيۡنَ ۷۱ وَلَقَدۡ اَرۡسَلۡنَا فِيۡهِمۡ مُّنۡذِرِيۡنَ ۷۲ فَٱنۡظُرۡ
كَيۡفَ كَانَ عَاقِبَةُ الۡمُنۡذَرِيۡنَ ۷۳ اِلَّا عِبَادَ اللّٰهِ
الۡمُخۡلَصِيۡنَ ۷۴ وَلَقَدۡ نَادٰنَا نُوۡحٌ فَلَنِعۡمَ الۡمُجِيۡبُوۡنَ ۷۵
وَنَجَّيۡنٰهُ وَاَهۡلَهٗ مِنَ الۡكَرۡبِ الۡعَظِيۡمِ ۷۶ وَجَعَلۡنَا
ذُرِّيَّتَهٗ هُمُ الۡبٰقِيۡنَ ۷۷ وَتَرَكۡنَا عَلَيۡهِ فِى الۡاٰخِرِيۡنَ ۷۸
سَلٰمٌ عَلٰى نُوۡحٍ فِى الۡعٰلَمِيۡنَ ۷۹ اِنَّا كَذٰلِكَ نَجۡزِى
الۡمُحۡسِنِيۡنَ ۸۰ اِنَّهٗ مِنۡ عِبَادِنَا الۡمُؤۡمِنِيۡنَ ۸۱ ثُمَّ
اَغۡرَقۡنَا الۡاٰخَرِيۡنَ ۸۲ وَاِنَّ مِنۡ شِيۡعَتِهٖ لَاِبۡرٰهِيۡمَ ۸۳

The dreadful time of Hell and the pleasant time of Paradise symbolise the difference in the fate of belief and disbelief.

ع
۵۳
۲
۶

55 So when he looked down, he saw him in the middle of the blazing Fire. 56 He said, 'By Allah, you nearly ruined me; 57 hadn't it been for the gift of my Lord, I would have been in Hell too. 58 Aren't we to die except for our first death? 59 Shall we never suffer?'" 60 This is a real victory. 61 Everyone should work for this.

The tree of Zaqqum

62 Is this better hospitality or the tree of Zaqqum? 63 We made this to chastise the wicked. 64 It is a tree that grows in the middle of Hell. 65 Its fruit is like the heads of Satan. 66 They will eat from it to fill their bellies, 67 then drink boiling water, 68 their home is Hell. 69 They found their forefathers misguided, 70 and *thoughtlessly* followed in their footsteps; 71 previously, most of them were misguided. 72 We sent *many* warners to them. 73 Look, what's the fate of those who were warned; 74 only the sincere servants of Allah *were saved.*

A tribute to Prophet Nuh

75 Remember when Nuh prayed to Us, so We responded graciously 76 and saved him and his followers from a terrible suffering. 77 We made his offspring continue *in the world,* 78 and we kept his praise in the future generations. 79 Peace be upon Nuh of all people. 80 This is how We reward the righteous. 81 He was our faithful servant. 82 The others We drowned.

Ibrahim challenged his people

83 Ibrahim was from the same group;

إِذْ جَآءَ رَبَّهُ بِقَلْبٍ سَلِيمٍ ۞ إِذْ قَالَ لِأَبِيهِ وَقَوْمِهِ مَا

ذَا تَعْبُدُونَ ۞ أَئِفْكًا آلِهَةً دُونَ اللَّهِ تُرِيدُونَ ۞

فَمَا ظَنُّكُم بِرَبِّ الْعَٰلَمِينَ ۞ فَنَظَرَ نَظْرَةً فِى النُّجُومِ ۞

فَقَالَ إِنِّى سَقِيمٌ ۞ فَتَوَلَّوْا عَنْهُ مُدْبِرِينَ ۞ فَرَاغَ إِلَىٰ

آلِهَتِهِمْ فَقَالَ أَلَا تَأْكُلُونَ ۞ مَا لَكُمْ لَا تَنطِقُونَ ۞

فَرَاغَ عَلَيْهِمْ ضَرْبًۢا بِالْيَمِينِ ۞ فَأَقْبَلُوٓا إِلَيْهِ يَزِفُّونَ ۞

قَالَ أَتَعْبُدُونَ مَا تَنْحِتُونَ ۞ وَاللَّهُ خَلَقَكُمْ وَمَا

تَعْمَلُونَ ۞ قَالُوا ابْنُوا لَهُ بُنْيَٰنًا فَأَلْقُوهُ فِى الْجَحِيمِ ۞

فَأَرَادُوا بِهِ كَيْدًا فَجَعَلْنَٰهُمُ الْأَسْفَلِينَ ۞ وَقَالَ إِنِّى

ذَاهِبٌ إِلَىٰ رَبِّى سَيَهْدِينِ ۞ رَبِّ هَبْ لِى مِنَ

الصَّٰلِحِينَ ۞ فَبَشَّرْنَٰهُ بِغُلَٰمٍ حَلِيمٍ ۞ فَلَمَّا بَلَغَ

مَعَهُ السَّعْىَ قَالَ يَٰبُنَىَّ إِنِّىٓ أَرَىٰ فِى الْمَنَامِ أَنِّىٓ

أَذْبَحُكَ فَانظُرْ مَاذَا تَرَىٰ قَالَ يَٰٓأَبَتِ افْعَلْ مَا تُؤْمَرُ

سَتَجِدُنِىٓ إِن شَآءَ اللَّهُ مِنَ الصَّٰبِرِينَ ۞ فَلَمَّآ أَسْلَمَا

وَتَلَّهُ لِلْجَبِينِ ۞ وَنَٰدَيْنَٰهُ أَن يَٰٓإِبْرَٰهِيمُ ۞ قَدْ

صَدَّقْتَ الرُّءْيَآ إِنَّا كَذَٰلِكَ نَجْزِى الْمُحْسِنِينَ ۞

إِنَّ هَٰذَا لَهُوَ الْبَلَٰٓؤُا الْمُبِينُ ۞ وَفَدَيْنَٰهُ بِذِبْحٍ

عَظِيمٍ ۞ وَتَرَكْنَا عَلَيْهِ فِى الْءَاخِرِينَ ۞ سَلَٰمٌ عَلَىٰٓ

إِبْرَٰهِيمَ ۞ كَذَٰلِكَ نَجْزِى الْمُحْسِنِينَ ۞ إِنَّهُۥ مِنْ

عِبَادِنَا الْمُؤْمِنِينَ ۞ وَبَشَّرْنَٰهُ بِإِسْحَٰقَ نَبِيًّا مِّنَ

The young Ismail willingly laid down his life to comply with Divine will; a symbol of Islam, submission and dedication. How much do we commit ourselves?

⁸⁴he turned to his Lord with a heart free of evil. ⁸⁵He asked his father and people, "What do you worship,⁸⁶do you take false gods beside Allah? ⁸⁷What do you think about the Lord of the worlds?" ⁸⁸He looked at the stars ⁸⁹and said, "I'm sick."^a ⁹⁰So people turned away and left him alone.

Ibrahim smashed the idols

⁹¹So he quietly went to *the temple full* of idols and spoke with the idols: "Don't you eat? ⁹²Why don't you speak?" ⁹³He turned on them striking them with full force.^b ⁹⁴*His people* came to him hurriedly. ⁹⁵He said to them, "Why do you worship something you shape with your hands? ⁹⁶Allah created you and all you do." ⁹⁷They decided: "Let's make a pile of wood and throw him into a blazing fire." ⁹⁸They plotted against him but We ruined their plot.

Ibrahim's scary dream

⁹⁹He said, "I'm going to my Lord, He will guide me; ¹⁰⁰Lord, give me *a pious son.*" ¹⁰¹So We gave good news of a son with strong character.^c ¹⁰²When he was old enough to work with him, *one day* he told him: "My son, I saw in a dream I'm sacrificing you; tell me what you think?" He replied, "Father, do as you were told; you'll find me patient, Allah willing." ¹⁰³When both submitted and Ibrahim laid him face down, ¹⁰⁴We called out: "Ibrahim ¹⁰⁵you have fulfilled the dream. This is how We reward the righteous." ¹⁰⁶It was a clear test *of faith.* ¹⁰⁷We saved *Ismael* in exchange for a slaughtered *ram,* ¹⁰⁸and left his tribute among future generations. ¹⁰⁹Peace be on Ibrahim. ¹¹⁰That's how We reward the righteous, ¹¹¹he was Our faithful servant. ¹¹²We *later* gave him good news of Ishaq, a righteous Prophet.

---

^a "I'm sick" of your idol worship, shows Ibrahim's annoyance that he felt ill of seeing their evil way.
^b *Bi Yameen* literally means "with the right hand", a metaphor for "with force".
^c *Haleem* means gentle, a moral virtue that represents a strong character.

الصّٰلِحِينَ ۝ وَبٰرَكْنَا عَلَيْهِ وَعَلٰى إِسْحٰقَ ط وَمِنْ

ذُرِّيَّتِهِمَا مُحْسِنٌ وَظَالِمٌ لِّنَفْسِهِ مُبِينٌ ۝ وَلَقَدْ مَنَنَّا

عَلٰى مُوسٰى وَهٰرُونَ ۝ وَنَجَّيْنٰهُمَا وَقَوْمَهُمَا مِنَ

الْكَرْبِ الْعَظِيمِ ۝ وَنَصَرْنٰهُمْ فَكَانُوا هُمُ الْغٰلِبِينَ ۝

وَآتَيْنٰهُمَا الْكِتٰبَ الْمُسْتَبِينَ ۝ وَهَدَيْنٰهُمَا الصِّرَاطَ

الْمُسْتَقِيمَ ۝ وَتَرَكْنَا عَلَيْهِمَا فِي الْاٰخِرِينَ ۝ سَلٰمٌ

عَلٰى مُوسٰى وَهٰرُونَ ۝ إِنَّا كَذٰلِكَ نَجْزِي الْمُحْسِنِينَ ۝

إِنَّهُمَا مِنْ عِبَادِنَا الْمُؤْمِنِينَ ۝ وَإِنَّ إِلْيَاسَ لَمِنَ

الْمُرْسَلِينَ ط إِذْ قَالَ لِقَوْمِهِ أَلَا تَتَّقُونَ ۝ أَتَدْعُونَ

بَعْلًا وَتَذَرُونَ أَحْسَنَ الْخَالِقِينَ ۝ اللهَ رَبَّكُمْ وَرَبَّ

آبَائِكُمُ الْأَوَّلِينَ ۝ فَكَذَّبُوهُ فَإِنَّهُمْ لَمُحْضَرُونَ ۝ إِلَّا

عِبَادَ اللهِ الْمُخْلَصِينَ ۝ وَتَرَكْنَا عَلَيْهِ فِي الْاٰخِرِينَ ۝

سَلٰمٌ عَلٰى إِلْ يَاسِينَ ۝ إِنَّا كَذٰلِكَ نَجْزِي الْمُحْسِنِينَ ۝

إِنَّهُ مِنْ عِبَادِنَا الْمُؤْمِنِينَ ۝ وَإِنَّ لُوطًا لَّمِنَ

الْمُرْسَلِينَ ط إِذْ نَجَّيْنٰهُ وَأَهْلَهُ أَجْمَعِينَ ۝ إِلَّا عَجُوزًا

فِي الْغَابِرِينَ ۝ ثُمَّ دَمَّرْنَا الْاٰخَرِينَ ۝ وَإِنَّكُمْ لَتَمُرُّونَ

عَلَيْهِمْ مُّصْبِحِينَ ۝ وَبِالَّيْلِ ط أَفَلَا تَعْقِلُونَ ۝ وَ

إِنَّ يُونُسَ لَمِنَ الْمُرْسَلِينَ ط إِذْ أَبَقَ إِلَى الْفُلْكِ

الْمَشْحُونِ ۝ فَسَاهَمَ فَكَانَ مِنَ الْمُدْحَضِينَ ۝

فَالْتَقَمَهُ الْحُوتُ وَهُوَ مُلِيمٌ ۝ فَلَوْلَا أَنَّهُ كَانَ مِن

The human history of disobedience, rejecting their prophets. How effective a warning is this?

¹¹³ We blessed him and Ishaq; some of their children were righteous, others wrongdoers.

Musa and Harun were the winners

¹¹⁴ We favoured Musa and Harun *too*; ¹¹⁵ We rescued them and their people from a dreadful suffering, ¹¹⁶ and helped them to become the winners. ¹¹⁷ We gave them the Book that explained things clearly, ¹¹⁸ We guided them on the straight path, ¹¹⁹ and left their praise among the future generations. ¹²⁰ Peace be on Musa and Harun. ¹²¹ That's how We reward the righteous, ¹²² Our faithful servants.

Tribute to Prophet Ilyas

¹²³ Ilyas was also from the messengers. ¹²⁴ He said to his people: "Won't you believe? ¹²⁵ How can you worship Baal and turn your back on the best Creator? ¹²⁶ Isn't Allah Your Lord and Lord of your forefathers?" ¹²⁷ But they denied and will be brought *before Us*, ¹²⁸ except for the devout servants of Allah. ¹²⁹ We left his praise among the later generations. ¹³⁰ Peace be on Ilyas. ¹³¹ That's how We reward the righteous, ¹³² Our faithful servants.

The Prophet Lut acknowledged

¹³³ *Similarly,* Lut was Our messenger. ¹³⁴ We saved him and all his followers, ¹³⁵ except the old lady who remained behind. ¹³⁶ Then We destroyed all others. ¹³⁷ *Quraysh!* You pass through their ruins in broad daylight, ¹³⁸ and *sometimes* at night, don't you understand?

The Prophet Yunus was forgiven

¹³⁹ Yunus was also from the messengers. ¹⁴⁰ When he fled on board the heavily-loaded ship, ¹⁴¹ they cast lots, he was the loser, thrown overboard. ¹⁴² A whale swallowed him, as he blamed himself. ¹⁴³ Had he not been among those who glorify Allah, ¹⁴⁴ he would have stayed in its belly till the Day of Resurrection. ¹⁴⁵ Eventually, We flung him out, sick, on to an empty shore.

الْمُسَبِّحِينَ ۝ لَلَبِثَ فِى بَطْنِهِ إِلَىٰ يَوْمِ يُبْعَثُونَ ۝

فَنَبَذْنَاهُ بِالْعَرَآءِ وَهُوَ سَقِيمٌ ۝ وَأَنْبَتْنَا عَلَيْهِ شَجَرَةً

مِّن يَقْطِينٍ ۝ وَأَرْسَلْنَاهُ إِلَىٰ مِائَةِ أَلْفٍ أَوْ يَزِيدُونَ ۝

فَآمَنُوا فَمَتَّعْنَاهُمْ إِلَىٰ حِينٍ ۝ فَاسْتَفْتِهِمْ أَرَبِّكَ

الْبَنَاتُ وَلَهُمُ الْبَنُونَ ۝ أَمْ خَلَقْنَا الْمَلَائِكَةَ إِنَاثًا

وَهُمْ شَاهِدُونَ ۝ أَلَا إِنَّهُم مِّنْ إِفْكِهِمْ لَيَقُولُونَ ۝

وَلَدَ اللَّهُ وَإِنَّهُمْ لَكَاذِبُونَ ۝ أَصْطَفَى الْبَنَاتِ عَلَى

الْبَنِينَ ۝ مَا لَكُمْ كَيْفَ تَحْكُمُونَ ۝ أَفَلَا تَذَكَّرُونَ ۝

أَمْ لَكُمْ سُلْطَانٌ مُّبِينٌ ۝ فَأْتُوا بِكِتَابِكُمْ إِن كُنتُمْ صَادِقِينَ ۝

وَجَعَلُوا بَيْنَهُ وَبَيْنَ الْجِنَّةِ نَسَبًا وَلَقَدْ عَلِمَتِ الْجِنَّةُ

إِنَّهُمْ لَمُحْضَرُونَ ۝ سُبْحَانَ اللَّهِ عَمَّا يَصِفُونَ ۝ إِلَّا عِبَادَ

اللَّهِ الْمُخْلَصِينَ ۝ فَإِنَّكُمْ وَمَا تَعْبُدُونَ ۝ مَا أَنتُمْ

عَلَيْهِ بِفَاتِنِينَ ۝ إِلَّا مَنْ هُوَ صَالِ الْجَحِيمِ ۝ وَمَا مِنَّا

إِلَّا لَهُ مَقَامٌ مَّعْلُومٌ ۝ وَإِنَّا لَنَحْنُ الصَّافُّونَ ۝ وَإِنَّا

لَنَحْنُ الْمُسَبِّحُونَ ۝ وَإِن كَانُوا لَيَقُولُونَ ۝ لَوْ أَنَّ عِندَنَا

ذِكْرًا مِّنَ الْأَوَّلِينَ ۝ لَكُنَّا عِبَادَ اللَّهِ الْمُخْلَصِينَ ۝

فَكَفَرُوا بِهِ فَسَوْفَ يَعْلَمُونَ ۝ وَلَقَدْ سَبَقَتْ كَلِمَتُنَا

لِعِبَادِنَا الْمُرْسَلِينَ ۝ إِنَّهُمْ لَهُمُ الْمَنصُورُونَ ۝ وَإِنَّ

جُندَنَا لَهُمُ الْغَالِبُونَ ۝ فَتَوَلَّ عَنْهُمْ حَتَّىٰ حِينٍ ۝ وَ

أَبْصِرْهُمْ فَسَوْفَ يُبْصِرُونَ ۝ أَفَبِعَذَابِنَا يَسْتَعْجِلُونَ ۝

Spiritual blindness is the result of a stubborn and quarrelsome attitude. Are you willing to listen readily? Do you quarrel?

¹⁴⁶We caused a gourd tree to grow over to shade him, ¹⁴⁷and sent him back to one hundred thousand or more people. ¹⁴⁸They believed, so We allowed them to enjoy their lives fully.

A difficult question for the disbelievers

¹⁴⁹So ask the disbelievers: "You assign daughters for your Lord and sons for yourself? ¹⁵⁰Were you witness when We created the angels?" ¹⁵¹Beware! This is another of their *concocted* lies, they say, ¹⁵²"Allah has begotten;" they are liars. ¹⁵³Did He choose daughters over sons? ¹⁵⁴What has come over you that you judge *in this way*? ¹⁵⁵Do you not pay attention? ¹⁵⁶Or do you have evidence? ¹⁵⁷Bring your book if you are truthful. ¹⁵⁸They declare a relationship between Him and the jinn, and the jinn know they will be brought *before him*. ¹⁵⁹Glory be to Allah, He is far above what they imagine. ¹⁶⁰The true servants of Allah don't do such things. ¹⁶¹Neither you nor what you worship ¹⁶²can tempt anyone away from Allah ¹⁶³except him who will burn in the Blazing Fire.

The angels arranged in rows

¹⁶⁴The angels will say, "each one of us has a role; ¹⁶⁵we are organised in ranks ¹⁶⁶and we glorify Allah. ¹⁶⁷The disbelievers used to say, ¹⁶⁸"If we had the Scripture like the past people, ¹⁶⁹we would have been like the devout servants of Allah." ¹⁷⁰So they disbelieved *the Quran*; soon they will know.

The messengers are very special

¹⁷¹Our promise to the messengers, Our servants, was fulfilled; ¹⁷²they were helped ¹⁷³and our armies were the winners. ¹⁷⁴So leave them for a while. ¹⁷⁵Watch them, they will see *the reality* soon. ¹⁷⁶Do they want our punishment to come sooner? ¹⁷⁷When it comes into their courtyards it will be a terrible morning for those warned. ¹⁷⁸Leave them for a while ¹⁷⁹and watch, soon they will see *the reality*. ¹⁸⁰Glory be to Your Lord, Lord of Might and Power far above their claims. ¹⁸¹And peace be on the Messengers ¹⁸²and all praises are for Allah, Lord of the worlds.

فَإِذَا نَزَلَ بِسَاحَتِهِمْ فَسَآءَ صَبَاحُ ٱلْمُنذَرِينَ ۝ وَتَوَلَّ عَنْهُمْ حَتَّىٰ حِينٍ ۝ وَأَبْصِرْ فَسَوْفَ يُبْصِرُونَ ۝ سُبْحَـٰنَ رَبِّكَ رَبِّ ٱلْعِزَّةِ عَمَّا يَصِفُونَ ۝ وَسَلَـٰمٌ عَلَى ٱلْمُرْسَلِينَ ۝ وَٱلْحَمْدُ لِلَّهِ رَبِّ ٱلْعَـٰلَمِينَ ۝

38. Surat Saad

The Letter Saad

This early-Makkan surat was revealed in the fourth or fifth year of the mission of the Prophet ﷺ. It opens by describing the role of the Quran as a reminder, creating awareness and consciousness of a greater reality, its central theme. This is developed by relating the stories of previous communities and the tireless efforts of prophets, starting with an account of the excellent qualities of Dawud ﷺ and his son Sulayman ﷺ. They were rulers, but also devout and pious servants of Allah. The heartbreaking story of the sufferings of Prophet Ayyub ﷺ concludes the surat.

According to Tabari, Satan surmised that Ayyub ﷺ would not remain faithful if he encountered difficulties. Allah allowed Satan to test him. So disaster struck Ayyub: his house subsided, his livestock were killed, his family were killed in an accident and he became ill with a contagious disease so people abandoned him. Satan attempted to shake Ayyub's faith through his wife: she put forward an idea that for him to recover, he must sacrifice a baby goat for Satan. Ayyub ﷺ refused to do so; he swore an oath to give her one hundred lashes for the blasphemy, once he recovered. In that despair and anguish he prayed: "Satan has brought hardship and pain" (41). Ayyub is presented as model of patience and endurance, and is honoured as "An excellent servant!" He didn't despair, he cried to Allah for relief and placed his trust in Him. This is what makes this story a lesson, *zikra*, for those with understanding (43).

This passage can be read in the wider context of the surat. In the beginning, it mentions the arrogance and the hostility of the people of Makkah to the Prophet ﷺ, resulting in the warning: "How many past generations have We destroyed before them! They cried out; there was no time for escape" (3). The surat presents other objections of the disbelievers to the message of Muhammad ﷺ. The stories of previous communities who rejected prophets alternate with passages about the Makkans, facilitating comparison between them. The surat ends as it began: "This is a reminder for all people, and after a while you will come to know its truth" (87–88).

اٰیاتُهَا ٨٨   (٣٨) سُوْرَةُ صۤ مَکِّیَّةٌ (٣٨)   رُکُوْعاتُهَا ٥

بِسْمِ اللهِ الرَّحْمٰنِ الرَّحِیْمِ

صۤ ۖ وَالْقُرْاٰنِ ذِی الذِّکْرِ ۚ بَلِ الَّذِیْنَ کَفَرُوْا فِیْ
عِزَّةٍ وَّشِقَاقٍ ۞ کَمْ اَهْلَکْنَا مِنْ قَبْلِهِمْ مِّنْ قَرْنٍ
فَنَادَوْا وَّلَاتَ حِیْنَ مَنَاصٍ ۞ وَعَجِبُوْۤا اَنْ جَآءَهُمْ
مُّنْذِرٌ مِّنْهُمْ ۫ وَقَالَ الْکٰفِرُوْنَ هٰذَا سٰحِرٌ کَذَّابٌ ۞
اَجَعَلَ الْاٰلِهَةَ اِلٰهًا وَّاحِدًا ۖ اِنَّ هٰذَا لَشَیْءٌ عُجَابٌ ۞
وَانْطَلَقَ الْمَلَاُ مِنْهُمْ اَنِ امْشُوْا وَاصْبِرُوْا عَلٰۤی اٰلِهَتِکُمْ ۖ

Evil and corrupt
leadership often destroys
a community. So, who do
you follow?

اِنَّ هٰذَا لَشَیْءٌ یُّرَادُ ۞ مَا سَمِعْنَا بِهٰذَا فِی الْمِلَّةِ
الْاٰخِرَةِ ۖ اِنْ هٰذَاۤ اِلَّا اخْتِلَاقٌ ۞ ءَاُنْزِلَ عَلَیْهِ الذِّکْرُ
مِنْۢ بَیْنِنَا ط بَلْ هُمْ فِیْ شَکٍّ مِّنْ ذِکْرِیْ ۚ بَلْ لَّمَّا
یَذُوْقُوْا عَذَابِ ۞ اَمْ عِنْدَهُمْ خَزَآئِنُ رَحْمَةِ رَبِّکَ
الْعَزِیْزِ الْوَهَّابِ ۞ اَمْ لَهُمْ مُّلْکُ السَّمٰوٰتِ وَالْاَرْضِ
وَمَا بَیْنَهُمَا ۫ فَلْیَرْتَقُوْا فِی الْاَسْبَابِ ۞ جُنْدٌ مَّا هُنَالِکَ
مَهْزُوْمٌ مِّنَ الْاَحْزَابِ ۞ کَذَّبَتْ قَبْلَهُمْ قَوْمُ نُوْحٍ وَّعَادٌ
وَّفِرْعَوْنُ ذُو الْاَوْتَادِ ۞ وَثَمُوْدُ وَقَوْمُ لُوْطٍ وَّاَصْحٰبُ
لْئَیْکَةِ ط اُولٰٓئِکَ الْاَحْزَابُ ۞ اِنْ کُلٌّ اِلَّا کَذَّبَ الرُّسُلَ
فَحَقَّ عِقَابِ ۞ وَمَا یَنْظُرُ هٰۤؤُلَآءِ اِلَّا صَیْحَةً وَّاحِدَةً
مَّا لَهَا مِنْ فَوَاقٍ ۞ وَقَالُوْا رَبَّنَا عَجِّلْ لَّنَا قِطَّنَا
قَبْلَ یَوْمِ الْحِسَابِ ۞ اِصْبِرْ عَلٰی مَا یَقُوْلُوْنَ وَاذْکُرْ

ع
١٤
١٠

In the name of Allah, the Kind, the Caring.

Divine revelation is a reminder

[1] *Sad.*[a] By the Quran full of reminders, [2] the disbelievers are haughty and hostile. [3] How many generations We destroyed before them? They all cried out *for help*, but there was no time to escape. [4] They are surprised that a warner came from them, they say, "This is a fraudulent magician. [5] He's turned *all* the gods into one god? How strange!" [6] Their leaders hastily set out *to tell people*, "Walk away and stick to your gods. That's what you must do, [7] we've not heard of this in *any* religion of recent times. This is a fabrication. [8] Did *this* reminder have to be sent down to him of all people?" So, they doubt My reminder? Then *wait* till they taste My punishment. [9] Do they hold *the keys to* the coffers of your Lord's Compassion, the Almighty, the Giver? [10] Or do they have control over the Heavens, the Earth and whatever lies in between? *So let them climb the ropes*[b].

Today's enemies of the truth will lose, like those before them

[11] The armies of the confederates that *oppose you* will be defeated. [12] Before them, the people of Nuh, Ad and Pharaoh of the columns,[c] they *all* denied *their prophets,* [13] as did Thamud, the people of Lut and the forest dwellers. Those were the confederates *of their day*; [14] they denied the messengers and so My punishment was justified. [15] And the *Makkans* can expect a single Blast that will not be postponed.

Be like Dawud in his fortitude and wisdom

[16] *Your opponents* said: "Our Lord, give us our share in advance *of either Heaven or Hell* before the Day of Reckoning." [17] Put up with what they say, and remember Our servant, the *strong*-handed Dawud: he was devout.

---

[a] The deep voiced Arabic letter '*Sad*' stands for '*As Siddiq*', the truthful friend referring to the Prophet ﷺ or human conscience that like a truthful friend tells everything, whether you like it or not. The Prophet ﷺ said "ask your heart". The voice of conscience.

[b] 'Let them climb the ropes', is an idiom meaning "allow them to continue on their course and suffer its consequences."

[c] Reference to Pharaoh's temples with massive columns.

عِبَادَنَا دَاوُدَ ذَا الْأَيْدِ ۚ اِنَّهٗٓ اَوَّابٌ ۝ اِنَّا سَخَّرْنَا
الْجِبَالَ مَعَهٗ يُسَبِّحْنَ بِالْعَشِيِّ وَالْاِشْرَاقِ ۝ وَالطَّيْرَ
مَحْشُوْرَةً ؕ كُلٌّ لَّهٗٓ اَوَّابٌ ۝ وَشَدَدْنَا مُلْكَهٗ وَاٰتَيْنٰهُ
الْحِكْمَةَ وَفَصْلَ الْخِطَابِ ۝ وَهَلْ اَتٰىكَ نَبَؤُا الْخَصْمِ ۘ اِذْ
تَسَوَّرُوا الْمِحْرَابَ ۝ اِذْ دَخَلُوْا عَلٰى دَاوُدَ فَفَزِعَ مِنْهُمْ قَالُوْا
لَا تَخَفْ ۚ خَصْمٰنِ بَغٰى بَعْضُنَا عَلٰى بَعْضٍ فَاحْكُمْ بَيْنَنَا
بِالْحَقِّ وَلَا تُشْطِطْ وَاهْدِنَآ اِلٰى سَوَآءِ الصِّرَاطِ ۝ اِنَّ هٰذَآ
اَخِيْ ۫ لَهٗ تِسْعٌ وَّتِسْعُوْنَ نَعْجَةً وَّلِيَ نَعْجَةٌ وَّاحِدَةٌ ۫
فَقَالَ اَكْفِلْنِيْهَا وَعَزَّنِيْ فِي الْخِطَابِ ۝ قَالَ لَقَدْ
ظَلَمَكَ بِسُؤَالِ نَعْجَتِكَ اِلٰى نِعَاجِهٖ ؕ وَاِنَّ كَثِيْرًا مِّنَ
الْخُلَطَآءِ لَيَبْغِيْ بَعْضُهُمْ عَلٰى بَعْضٍ اِلَّا الَّذِيْنَ اٰمَنُوْا وَعَمِلُوا
الصّٰلِحٰتِ وَقَلِيْلٌ مَّا هُمْ ؕ وَظَنَّ دَاوُدُ اَنَّمَا فَتَنّٰهُ فَاسْتَغْفَرَ
رَبَّهٗ وَخَرَّ رَاكِعًا وَّاَنَابَ ۩ ۝ فَغَفَرْنَا لَهٗ ذٰلِكَ ؕ وَاِنَّ
لَهٗ عِنْدَنَا لَزُلْفٰى وَحُسْنَ مَاٰبٍ ۝ يٰدَاوُدُ اِنَّا جَعَلْنٰكَ
خَلِيْفَةً فِي الْاَرْضِ فَاحْكُمْ بَيْنَ النَّاسِ بِالْحَقِّ وَلَا تَتَّبِعِ
الْهَوٰى فَيُضِلَّكَ عَنْ سَبِيْلِ اللّٰهِ ؕ اِنَّ الَّذِيْنَ يَضِلُّوْنَ
عَنْ سَبِيْلِ اللّٰهِ لَهُمْ عَذَابٌ شَدِيْدٌۢ بِمَا نَسُوْا يَوْمَ
الْحِسَابِ ۝ وَمَا خَلَقْنَا السَّمَآءَ وَالْاَرْضَ وَمَا بَيْنَهُمَا
بَاطِلًا ؕ ذٰلِكَ ظَنُّ الَّذِيْنَ كَفَرُوْا ۚ فَوَيْلٌ لِّلَّذِيْنَ كَفَرُوْا
مِنَ النَّارِ ۝ اَمْ نَجْعَلُ الَّذِيْنَ اٰمَنُوْا وَعَمِلُوا الصّٰلِحٰتِ

The intelligence, melodious voice, the strength and justice of Dawud are examples of the skills of a good leader.

¹⁸ We made the mountains *echo* with him, glorifying Us in the evening and in the morning, ¹⁹ and the birds in flocks, each of them obedient to *Dawud*. ²⁰ And *so* We strengthened his rule, and We gave him wisdom and *the ability to reach* decisive judgements.

In resolving dispute, Dawud realised his mistake

²¹ Has the report of the *parties to a* dispute reached you? They climbed over the wall of *his* private chamber ²² and came to Dawud, he was frightened to *see* them; they said, "Don't be afraid. We have a dispute; one *party* has wronged the other. So, judge between us without deviating and guide us towards a fair solution." ²³ *One of them said,* "This brother of mine has ninety-nine sheep, whereas I have one. He demands: 'Let me look after it,' and he's putting pressure on me." ²⁴ *Dawud* said, "He is wrong to ask for your sheep. Business partners often take advantage, one of the other – except the believers who are righteous, but they are few!" *When* Dawud realised We had tested him, he begged forgiveness of His Lord, fell in prostration and repented.ᵃ ²⁵ So We forgave him. *Dawud* will *enjoy* closeness to Us in the most beautiful of homecomings.

Lessons to learn from Dawud's story

²⁶ "Dawud, We appointed you Our vice-regent on Earth, so judge fairly between people and don't act on a whim that may lead you astray from the path of Allah. Those who wander away from the path of Allah will have severe punishment for neglecting the Day of Reckoning."

Allah's works are purposeful

²⁷ We didn't create the Heavens and the Earth and what lies between them purposeless, though the disbelievers may think so. Woe to those who disbelieve, *they will suffer* in the Fire! ²⁸ Should We put those who believe and do righteous deeds on a par with those who wreak havoc in the land, or those who are mindful *of Allah* on a par with outright sinners?

ᵃ A verse of prostration. Regarding Dawud's realisation that Allah was testing him, commentaries mention the dispute over the ewes. Dawud understood the similarity between that case and when he demanded that a man break up his engagement so he could marry his fiancée.

كَالْمُفْسِدِيْنَ فِي الْأَرْضِ أَمْ نَجْعَلُ الْمُتَّقِيْنَ كَالْفُجَّارِ ۝

كِتٰبٌ اَنْزَلْنٰهُ اِلَيْكَ مُبٰرَكٌ لِّيَدَّبَّرُوْۤا اٰيٰتِهٖ وَلِيَتَذَكَّرَ اُولُوا

الْاَلْبَابِ ۝ وَوَهَبْنَا لِدَاؤُدَ سُلَيْمٰنَ ؕ نِعْمَ الْعَبْدُ ؕ اِنَّهٗۤ

اَوَّابٌ ۝ اِذْ عُرِضَ عَلَيْهِ بِالْعَشِيِّ الصّٰفِنٰتُ الْجِيَادُ ۝

فَقَالَ اِنِّیْۤ اَحْبَبْتُ حُبَّ الْخَيْرِ عَنْ ذِكْرِ رَبِّیْ ۚ حَتّٰی

تَوَارَتْ بِالْحِجَابِ ۝ رُدُّوْهَا عَلَیَّ ؕ فَطَفِقَ مَسْحًۢا بِالسُّوْقِ

وَالْاَعْنَاقِ ۝ وَلَقَدْ فَتَنَّا سُلَيْمٰنَ وَاَلْقَيْنَا عَلٰی كُرْسِيِّهٖ

جَسَدًا ثُمَّ اَنَابَ ۝ قَالَ رَبِّ اغْفِرْ لِیْ وَهَبْ لِیْ مُلْكًا لَّا

يَنْۢبَغِیْ لِاَحَدٍ مِّنْۢ بَعْدِیْ ۚ اِنَّكَ اَنْتَ الْوَهَّابُ ۝ فَسَخَّرْنَا

لَهُ الرِّيْحَ تَجْرِیْ بِاَمْرِهٖ رُخَآءً حَيْثُ اَصَابَ ۝ وَالشَّيٰطِيْنَ

كُلَّ بَنَّآءٍ وَّغَوَّاصٍ ۝ وَّاٰخَرِيْنَ مُقَرَّنِيْنَ فِی الْاَصْفَادِ ۝

هٰذَا عَطَآؤُنَا فَامْنُنْ اَوْ اَمْسِكْ بِغَيْرِ حِسَابٍ ۝ وَاِنَّ

لَهٗ عِنْدَنَا لَزُلْفٰی وَحُسْنَ مَاٰبٍ ۝ وَاذْكُرْ عَبْدَنَاۤ اَيُّوْبَ ۘ

اِذْ نَادٰی رَبَّهٗۤ اَنِّیْ مَسَّنِیَ الشَّيْطٰنُ بِنُصْبٍ وَّعَذَابٍ ۝

اُرْكُضْ بِرِجْلِكَ ۚ هٰذَا مُغْتَسَلٌ بَارِدٌ وَّشَرَابٌ ۝ وَ

وَهَبْنَا لَهٗۤ اَهْلَهٗ وَمِثْلَهُمْ مَّعَهُمْ رَحْمَةً مِّنَّا وَذِكْرٰی

لِاُولِی الْاَلْبَابِ ۝ وَخُذْ بِيَدِكَ ضِغْثًا فَاضْرِبْ بِّهٖ وَلَا

تَحْنَثْ ؕ اِنَّا وَجَدْنٰهُ صَابِرًا ؕ نِعْمَ الْعَبْدُ ؕ اِنَّهٗۤ اَوَّابٌ ۝

وَاذْكُرْ عِبٰدَنَاۤ اِبْرٰهِيْمَ وَاِسْحٰقَ وَيَعْقُوْبَ اُولِی الْاَيْدِیْ

وَالْاَبْصَارِ ۝ اِنَّاۤ اَخْلَصْنٰهُمْ بِخَالِصَةٍ ذِكْرَی الدَّارِ ۝

The luxury and delights of Sulayman's kingdom contrasted to the suffering of Ayyub. Tell us that it's cyclical: difficult times are followed by good.

²⁹This is a Book that We sent down to you, a blessed *Book*, so *people* might think about its message, and the intelligent might pay attention.

After a lesson in mortality, Sulayman is blessed with gifts

³⁰We granted Dawud *a son*, Sulayman. What an excellent servant! Truly devout. ³¹*One evening,* when the pure-bred horses were paraded before *Sulayman*, ³²he said, "my love of fine things increased my Lord's remembrance. He watched them till they disappeared out of sight. ³³Bring *the horses* back to me." He patted their legs and necks. ³⁴We tested Sulayman with an illness, so he became thin as a skeleton sat on his throne, then turned devoutly to Us.ᵃ ³⁵He said, "My Lord, forgive me, and grant me a kingdom the like of which no one after me will ever see. *Only* You are the Giver." ³⁶So We made the winds compliant to him, blowing gently at his command wherever he wanted them *to go*; ³⁷and demons *from the jinn*, their builders, divers; ³⁸and others bound in chains. ³⁹*Allah said*: "This is Our gift *for you to* give it to *others* or withhold it as you like." ⁴⁰*Sulayman* will *enjoy* closeness to Us in the most beautiful of homecomings.

Ayyub's legendary patience is praised

⁴¹Mention Our servant, Ayyub, he cried out to his Lord: "Satan has wreaked sorrow and torment on me." ⁴²*Allah said*: "Stamp your foot *on the ground*. This is a cool place to wash and drink." ⁴³We treated him kindly and cured him, so We gave him his family *back* and an equal number of others with them, as a reminder for those gifted with understanding. ⁴⁴*Allah told him*: "Take a handful of grass and strike *your wife* with it so you don't break your oath."ᵇ We found him to be patient. What a wonderful servant! So devout.

Allah commends morally competent people

⁴⁵And mention Our servants Ibrahim, Ishaq and Yaqub; they were strong men with insight. ⁴⁶We chose them for the special task of reminding *others* of the Abode *of the Hereafter*.

ᵃ   Razi said "Sulayman became seriously ill, he lost so much weight he looked like a skeleton. The huge throne he used to sit on with splendour and authority no longer had that majesty, now he looked like a skeleton placed on a large chair".

ᵇ   When Ayyub's wife blasphemed, he swore to give her 100 lashes. He was spared from doing this and told to use a handful of grass, so she isn't physically harmed.

وَاِنَّهُمْ عِنْدَنَا لَمِنَ الْمُصْطَفَیْنَ الْاَخْیَارِ ۞ وَاذْكُرْ

اِسْمٰعِیْلَ وَالْیَسَعَ وَذَا الْكِفْلِ ۚ وَكُلٌّ مِّنَ الْاَخْیَارِ ۞

هٰذَا ذِكْرٌ ؕ وَاِنَّ لِلْمُتَّقِیْنَ لَحُسْنَ مَاٰبٍ ۞ جَنّٰتِ عَدْنٍ

مُّفَتَّحَةً لَّهُمُ الْاَبْوَابُ ۞ مُتَّكِئِیْنَ فِیْهَا یَدْعُوْنَ فِیْهَا

بِفَاكِهَةٍ كَثِیْرَةٍ وَّشَرَابٍ ۞ وَعِنْدَهُمْ قٰصِرٰتُ الطَّرْفِ

اَتْرَابٌ ۞ هٰذَا مَا تُوْعَدُوْنَ لِیَوْمِ الْحِسَابِ ۞ اِنَّ هٰذَا

لَرِزْقُنَا مَا لَهٗ مِنْ نَّفَادٍ ۚ هٰذَا ؕ وَاِنَّ لِلطّٰغِیْنَ لَشَرَّ

مَاٰبٍ ۞ جَهَنَّمَ ۚ یَصْلَوْنَهَا ۚ فَبِئْسَ الْمِهَادُ ۞ هٰذَا ۙ

فَلْیَذُوْقُوْهُ حَمِیْمٌ وَّغَسَّاقٌ ۞ وَّاٰخَرُ مِنْ شَكْلِهٖۤ اَزْوَاجٌ ۞

هٰذَا فَوْجٌ مُّقْتَحِمٌ مَّعَكُمْ ۚ لَا مَرْحَبًۢا بِهِمْ ؕ اِنَّهُمْ صَالُوا

النَّارِ ۞ قَالُوْا بَلْ اَنْتُمْ ۫ لَا مَرْحَبًۢا بِكُمْ ؕ اَنْتُمْ قَدَّمْتُمُوْهُ

لَنَا ۚ فَبِئْسَ الْقَرَارُ ۞ قَالُوْا رَبَّنَا مَنْ قَدَّمَ لَنَا هٰذَا فَزِدْهُ

عَذَابًا ضِعْفًا فِی النَّارِ ۞ وَقَالُوْا مَا لَنَا لَا نَرٰی رِجَالًا

كُنَّا نَعُدُّهُمْ مِّنَ الْاَشْرَارِ ۞ اَتَّخَذْنٰهُمْ سِخْرِیًّا

اَمْ زَاغَتْ عَنْهُمُ الْاَبْصَارُ ۞ اِنَّ ذٰلِكَ لَحَقٌّ تَخَاصُمُ

اَهْلِ النَّارِ ۞ قُلْ اِنَّمَاۤ اَنَا مُنْذِرٌ ۚ وَّمَا مِنْ اِلٰهٍ اِلَّا

اللّٰهُ الْوَاحِدُ الْقَهَّارُ ۞ رَبُّ السَّمٰوٰتِ وَالْاَرْضِ وَمَا

بَیْنَهُمَا الْعَزِیْزُ الْغَفَّارُ ۞ قُلْ هُوَ نَبَؤٌا عَظِیْمٌ ۞ اَنْتُمْ

عَنْهُ مُعْرِضُوْنَ ۞ مَا كَانَ لِیَ مِنْ عِلْمٍۢ بِالْمَلَاِ الْاَعْلٰۤی

اِذْ یَخْتَصِمُوْنَ ۞ اِنْ یُّوْحٰۤی اِلَیَّ اِلَّاۤ اَنَّمَاۤ اَنَا نَذِیْرٌ

The humble believer's fate is Paradise, the arrogant disbeliever's fate is Hell.

909

⁴⁷In Our Sight, they are the best of the chosen ones. ⁴⁸And mention Ismail, al-Yasa and Dhu'l-Kifl; they were the chosen ones. ⁴⁹This is a *brief* reminder; and for those mindful *of Allah*, there will be a beautiful homecoming, ⁵⁰the Gardens of Eden with open gates waiting for them; ⁵¹*and* reclining there *on sofas*, asking for fruits of all kind and for drinks, ⁵²and beside them *spouses* modest in their glances and of equal age. ⁵³This is what you are promised for the Day of Reckoning. ⁵⁴This provision of Ours will not end.

An example of how the people of Hell will quarrel

⁵⁵This is *for the righteous,* the tyrants will have a most terrifying of homecomings, ⁵⁶Hell, where they will burn. What a dreadful resting place! ⁵⁷Let them taste, scalding water and pus, ⁵⁸coupled with other similar *torments.* ⁵⁹This *here* is another crowd rushing headlong with you *into Hell.* No welcome for them. They will burn in the Fire. ⁶⁰*The newcomers* will say, "No! It is you, there is no welcome for you, you got us in to this. What a dreadful place to stay!" ⁶¹*Then* they will say, "Our Lord, whoever got us in to this, double his punishment in the Fire." ⁶²And they will say, "What is *happening* to us? Why don't we see *those* men whom we considered evil? ⁶³We took them as a laughing stock? Or did we overlook them?" ⁶⁴That is how the people of the Fire will quarrel among themselves.

The Messenger's ﷺ job is to warn

⁶⁵Say, *Messenger*: "I am a warner; and there is no God but Allah, the One, the Supreme, ⁶⁶the Lord of the Heavens and the Earth, and whatever lies in between, the Almighty, the Forgiving." ⁶⁷Say: "It's news of great importance ⁶⁸which you reject. ⁶⁹I have never had knowledge of the assembly on high when a dispute arose among them. ⁷⁰The revelation to me is that I am a warner."

مُّبِيۡنٌ ۞ اِذۡ قَالَ رَبُّكَ لِلۡمَلٰٓئِكَةِ اِنِّىۡ خَالِقٌۢ بَشَرًا مِّنۡ طِيۡنٍ ۞ فَاِذَا سَوَّيۡتُهٗ وَنَفَخۡتُ فِيۡهِ مِنۡ رُّوۡحِىۡ فَقَعُوۡا لَهٗ سٰجِدِيۡنَ ۞ فَسَجَدَ الۡمَلٰٓئِكَةُ كُلُّهُمۡ اَجۡمَعُوۡنَ ۞ اِلَّاۤ اِبۡلِيۡسَ ؕ اِسۡتَكۡبَرَ وَكَانَ مِنَ الۡكٰفِرِيۡنَ ۞ قَالَ يٰۤاِبۡلِيۡسُ مَا مَنَعَكَ اَنۡ تَسۡجُدَ لِمَا خَلَقۡتُ بِيَدَىَّ ؕ اَسۡتَكۡبَرۡتَ اَمۡ كُنۡتَ مِنَ الۡعَالِيۡنَ ۞ قَالَ اَنَا خَيۡرٌ مِّنۡهُ ؕ خَلَقۡتَنِىۡ مِنۡ نَّارٍ وَّخَلَقۡتَهٗ مِنۡ طِيۡنٍ ۞ قَالَ فَاخۡرُجۡ مِنۡهَا فَاِنَّكَ رَجِيۡمٌ ۙ وَّاِنَّ عَلَيۡكَ لَعۡنَتِىۡۤ اِلٰى يَوۡمِ الدِّيۡنِ ۞ قَالَ رَبِّ فَاَنۡظِرۡنِىۡۤ اِلٰى يَوۡمِ يُبۡعَثُوۡنَ ۞ قَالَ فَاِنَّكَ مِنَ الۡمُنۡظَرِيۡنَ ۙ اِلٰى يَوۡمِ الۡوَقۡتِ الۡمَعۡلُوۡمِ ۞ قَالَ فَبِعِزَّتِكَ لَاُغۡوِيَنَّهُمۡ اَجۡمَعِيۡنَ ۙ اِلَّا عِبَادَكَ مِنۡهُمُ الۡمُخۡلَصِيۡنَ ۞ قَالَ فَالۡحَقُّ ۫ وَالۡحَقَّ اَقُوۡلُ ۚ لَاَمۡلَـَٔنَّ جَهَنَّمَ مِنۡكَ وَمِمَّنۡ تَبِعَكَ مِنۡهُمۡ اَجۡمَعِيۡنَ ۞ قُلۡ مَاۤ اَسۡـَٔلُكُمۡ عَلَيۡهِ مِنۡ اَجۡرٍ وَّمَاۤ اَنَا مِنَ الۡمُتَكَلِّفِيۡنَ ۞ اِنۡ هُوَ اِلَّا ذِكۡرٌ لِّلۡعٰلَمِيۡنَ ۞ وَلَتَعۡلَمُنَّ نَبَاَهٗ بَعۡدَ حِيۡنٍ ۞

Satan's vow to mislead people and his constant effort to fulfil his vow.

Satan refused to bow, he was arrogant

⁷¹ *Remember* when your Lord said to the angels, "I am creating a human being from clay. ⁷²So once I have formed him and blown My spirit into him, prostrate before him." ⁷³So the angels prostrated all together ⁷⁴except Iblis; he was arrogant and ungrateful. ⁷⁵*Allah* said, "Iblis, what stopped you from prostrating to the one I created with My Hands? Were you arrogant then, or were you already from the haughty?" ⁷⁶*Iblis* said, "I am better than him. You created me from fire, and You created him from clay." ⁷⁷*Allah* said, "Get out of here! You are an outlaw. ⁷⁸My curse will be on you till Judgement Day."

Allah permits Satan to do his worst to lead humanity astray

⁷⁹*Iblis* said, "My Lord, give me time till the day they're resurrected." ⁸⁰*Allah* said, "You have it ⁸¹until the Day of the Appointed Hour." ⁸²*Iblis* said, "*I swear* by Your Might, I will try to mislead them, ⁸³except the devout servants of Yours." ⁸⁴Allah said, "That's right; and I too speak the truth: ⁸⁵I will fill Hell with you, *Iblis*, and those who follow you." ⁸⁶Say *messenger*: "I don't ask you for any reward for this, nor am I claiming what I'm not. ⁸⁷This is a reminder for all people; ⁸⁸and in due course you will know its *truth*."

39. Surat Az-Zumar

The Crowds

This surat was revealed in the middle Makkan period. It convincingly reinforces belief in the Oneness of Allah and the dreadful consequences of denying Him. Professor Sells eloquently captures the mood of that early time:

> What gives the early Makkan Surat's their depth, psychological subtlety, texture and tone is the way the future is collapsed into the present; the way the day of reckoning is transferred from the fear and hope of a moment in the future to a sense of reckoning in the present moment. The centrality of the day of reckoning to the early revelations is based on a prophetic impulse to remind humanity of the moment of truth.[a]

The graphic scenes of the Hereafter are presented in a variety of ways to emphasise the enormity and the terror of Judgement Day. Whilst the severity of Divine Punishment is stressed repeatedly in the surat, verse 53 helps to dispel the pessimism of the sinners: "Say, 'My servants who have wronged themselves, do not be hopeless of Allah's kindness; indeed Allah forgives all sins. He is the Forgiver, the Kind'" (53).

The surat opens with a commanding reference to Allah's Majesty, and questions how such a wonderful and generous Lord could be ignored and denied. Allah's marvellous gifts are poured on us day and night: the air we breathe, the delightful foods we enjoy and the spouses that give us friendship and comfort. "If you are unthankful, then Allah has no need of you; He is not pleased with the thanklessness of his servants. But if you are thankful, He will be pleased with you" (7). The surat identifies thankful servants and congratulates them:

> Good news for those who avoid serving evil forces and turn genuinely to Allah, so give My servants good news: *those* who listen attentively to what is said and follow the best of it, Allah has guided these and they're the understanding (17–18).

Such fortunate ones are blessed by Allah in an incredible way:

> So the one whose mind Allah opens with *the light* of Islam will have light from His

---

a   M.A. Sells, *Approaching the Qur'an: The Early Revelations*.

Lord. But those whose minds[a] are closed to the remembrance of Allah will be ruined; they are wholly misguided (22).

The ability to see, feel and speak the Truth is a great gift. The next passage again compares the person of faith to the idol worshipper (the latter could well include the modern materialist): "Can a servant devoted to many masters who are at odds with each other be the same as the one who is devoted solely to one master?" (29).

A vivid description of the unthankful person, immersed in selfishness, who follows whims and lowly desires, and as a consequence, "The evil of what they did will distress them. The sinners will suffer the distress as a result of their deeds and they will not escape" (51). The final section of the surat describes the crushing manner in which crowds of the wicked people will be hurled into Hell. The angels will ask them, "Didn't messengers from among you come to recite your Lord's verses and warn you of this Day's meeting?" (71). How they will regret that day. This is the purpose of presenting the Hereafter in the present: to jolt us, and fill us with awe. The final scene of the surat presents the serene and dignified entry of believers into Paradise, and the masses of angels praising the Lord.

---

[a] *Lil-Qasiyati Quloobhuhum* literally means their hardened hearts. The heart is a metaphor for the mind since it is the organ of both understanding and emotions.

اَیَاتُهَا ٤٥ (۳۹) سُوْرَةُ الزُّمَرِ مَكِّيَّةٌ (۵۹) رُكُوْعَاتُهَا ۸

بِسْمِ اللهِ الرَّحْمٰنِ الرَّحِيْمِ

تَنْزِيْلُ الْكِتٰبِ مِنَ اللهِ الْعَزِيْزِ الْحَكِيْمِ ۚ إِنَّا ۞

اَنْزَلْنَآ اِلَيْكَ الْكِتٰبَ بِالْحَقِّ فَاعْبُدِ اللهَ مُخْلِصًا لَّهُ

الدِّيْنَ ۚ اَلَا لِلّٰهِ الدِّيْنُ الْخَالِصُ ۚ وَالَّذِيْنَ اتَّخَذُوْا

مِنْ دُوْنِهٖٓ اَوْلِيَآءَ ۚ مَا نَعْبُدُهُمْ اِلَّا لِيُقَرِّبُوْنَآ اِلَى اللهِ

زُلْفٰى ۚ اِنَّ اللهَ يَحْكُمُ بَيْنَهُمْ فِيْ مَا هُمْ فِيْهِ

يَخْتَلِفُوْنَ ۚ اِنَّ اللهَ لَا يَهْدِيْ مَنْ هُوَ كٰذِبٌ كَفَّارٌ ۞

The idolaters are deceived, they think their idol worship will bring them closer to Allah. It's not so!

لَوْ اَرَادَ اللهُ اَنْ يَّتَّخِذَ وَلَدًا لَّاصْطَفٰى مِمَّا يَخْلُقُ

مَا يَشَآءُ ۙ سُبْحٰنَهٗ ۚ هُوَ اللهُ الْوَاحِدُ الْقَهَّارُ ۞ خَلَقَ

السَّمٰوٰتِ وَالْاَرْضَ بِالْحَقِّ ۚ يُكَوِّرُ الَّيْلَ عَلَى النَّهَارِ

وَيُكَوِّرُ النَّهَارَ عَلَى الَّيْلِ وَسَخَّرَ الشَّمْسَ وَالْقَمَرَ ۚ كُلٌّ

يَّجْرِيْ لِاَجَلٍ مُّسَمًّى ۚ اَلَا هُوَ الْعَزِيْزُ الْغَفَّارُ ۞

خَلَقَكُمْ مِّنْ نَّفْسٍ وَّاحِدَةٍ ثُمَّ جَعَلَ مِنْهَا زَوْجَهَا وَ

اَنْزَلَ لَكُمْ مِّنَ الْاَنْعَامِ ثَمٰنِيَةَ اَزْوَاجٍ ۚ يَخْلُقُكُمْ فِيْ

بُطُوْنِ اُمَّهٰتِكُمْ خَلْقًا مِّنْ بَعْدِ خَلْقٍ فِيْ ظُلُمٰتٍ

ثَلٰثٍ ۚ ذٰلِكُمُ اللهُ رَبُّكُمْ لَهُ الْمُلْكُ ۚ لَا اِلٰهَ اِلَّا هُوَ ۚ

فَاَنّٰى تُصْرَفُوْنَ ۞ اِنْ تَكْفُرُوْا فَاِنَّ اللهَ غَنِيٌّ عَنْكُمْ ۖ

وَلَا يَرْضٰى لِعِبَادِهِ الْكُفْرَ ۚ وَاِنْ تَشْكُرُوْا يَرْضَهُ لَكُمْ ۚ

وَلَا تَزِرُ وَازِرَةٌ وِّزْرَ اُخْرٰى ۚ ثُمَّ اِلٰى رَبِّكُمْ مَّرْجِعُكُمْ

In the name of Allah, the Kind and Caring.

Allah is the mighty creator

¹This Book is revealed by Allah, the Almighty, the Wise. ²We revealed to you the Book of the Truth, so worship Allah sincerely with commitment. ³Take heed! Sincere commitment should be for Allah alone. People who take protectors beside Him, *claiming that* we just worship them to achieve nearness to Allah, Allah will judge their disagreement. Allah will not guide the lying thankless person. ⁴Had Allah wanted to take a son, He would have chosen from His creation as He pleased, glory be to Him. He is Allah, the One, the Dominant. ⁵He created the Heavens and the Earth for a purpose; He merges the night into the day and the day into the night; and made the sun and the moon for a specific task,ᵃ each floating in its orbit of a fixed time. Indeed, He is the Almighty, the Forgiving.

The thankful and unthankful

⁶He created you from a single being, then made from it its spouse, and gave you eight pairs of livestock.ᵇ He creates you in the wombs of your mothers, developing stage by stage inside three layers of darkness. That is Allah your Lord, the Absolute Controller; He is the only God so how can you turn away from Him? ⁷If you are unthankful, then Allah has no need of you; He's not pleased with the unthankfulness of His servants. If you are thankful, He will be pleased with you. No one will carry the burden of another person, then to your Lord you will be returned and He shall tell you what you did. He knows *your* innermost thoughts.

ᵃ *Sakhkhara* means, "to force something to do a special task"; in this case, the moon and the sun both provide light and a means of measuring time.

ᵇ This refers to the four pairs of livestock: camels, cows, sheep and goats.

فَيُنَبِّئُكُمْ بِمَا كُنْتُمْ تَعْمَلُوْنَ ط اِنَّهٗ عَلِيْمٌۢ بِذَاتِ
الصُّدُوْرِ ۝ وَاِذَا مَسَّ الْاِنْسَانَ ضُرٌّ دَعَا رَبَّهٗ
مُنِيْبًا اِلَيْهِ ثُمَّ اِذَا خَوَّلَهٗ نِعْمَةً مِّنْهُ نَسِىَ
مَا كَانَ يَدْعُوْٓا اِلَيْهِ مِنْ قَبْلُ وَجَعَلَ لِلّٰهِ اَنْدَادًا
لِّيُضِلَّ عَنْ سَبِيْلِهٖ ط قُلْ تَمَتَّعْ بِكُفْرِكَ قَلِيْلًا ۖ
اِنَّكَ مِنْ اَصْحٰبِ النَّارِ ۝ اَمَّنْ هُوَ قَانِتٌ اٰنَآءَ
الَّيْلِ سَاجِدًا وَّقَآئِمًا يَّحْذَرُ الْاٰخِرَةَ وَيَرْجُوْا رَحْمَةَ
رَبِّهٖ ط قُلْ هَلْ يَسْتَوِى الَّذِيْنَ يَعْلَمُوْنَ وَالَّذِيْنَ
لَا يَعْلَمُوْنَ ط اِنَّمَا يَتَذَكَّرُ اُولُوا الْاَلْبَابِ ۝ قُلْ
يٰعِبَادِ الَّذِيْنَ اٰمَنُوا اتَّقُوْا رَبَّكُمْ ط لِلَّذِيْنَ اَحْسَنُوْا
فِيْ هٰذِهِ الدُّنْيَا حَسَنَةٌ ط وَاَرْضُ اللّٰهِ وَاسِعَةٌ ط
اِنَّمَا يُوَفَّى الصّٰبِرُوْنَ اَجْرَهُمْ بِغَيْرِ حِسَابٍ ۝
قُلْ اِنِّيْٓ اُمِرْتُ اَنْ اَعْبُدَ اللّٰهَ مُخْلِصًا لَّهُ
الدِّيْنَ ۝ وَاُمِرْتُ لِاَنْ اَكُوْنَ اَوَّلَ الْمُسْلِمِيْنَ ۝
قُلْ اِنِّيْٓ اَخَافُ اِنْ عَصَيْتُ رَبِّيْ عَذَابَ يَوْمٍ
عَظِيْمٍ ۝ قُلِ اللّٰهَ اَعْبُدُ مُخْلِصًا لَّهٗ دِيْنِيْ ۝
فَاعْبُدُوْا مَا شِئْتُمْ مِّنْ دُوْنِهٖ ط قُلْ اِنَّ الْخٰسِرِيْنَ
الَّذِيْنَ خَسِرُوْٓا اَنْفُسَهُمْ وَاَهْلِيْهِمْ يَوْمَ الْقِيٰمَةِ ط
اَلَا ذٰلِكَ هُوَ الْخُسْرَانُ الْمُبِيْنُ ۝ لَهُمْ مِّنْ فَوْقِهِمْ
ظُلَلٌ مِّنَ النَّارِ وَمِنْ تَحْتِهِمْ ظُلَلٌ ط ذٰلِكَ يُخَوِّفُ

The devout night worshipper, full of expectation in the Hereafter, is the winner. Do you have any of these habits?

١
٩
١٥
ع

917

[8] When a person suffers a hardship he calls His Lord devoutly, then when He eases the suffering he forgets that a short while before he had prayed to Him, and he sets up rivals with Allah which misguide him from His path. Say: "Enjoy your ungratefulness for a while; you are people of the Fire." [9] Can such a person be compared to the obedient, prostrating and standing during the night, fearful of the Hereafter and hopeful of his Lord's *kindness*? Say: "Can those who know be equal to those who don't know? Only the understanding people pay attention."

The reward for the thankful

[10] Say: "My believing servants, be mindful of Your Lord." Those who are righteous in this life will have goodness. Allah's Earth is vast; He shall fully reward the patient without limits. [11] Say: "I have been commanded to worship Allah, sincerely committed to His religion, [12] and I was ordered to be the first to submit." [13] Say: "If I disobey my Lord, I fear the punishment of a Great Day." [14] Say: "I worship Allah sincerely committing myself to Him, [15] so worship whoever you please beside Him." Say: "The losers are those who lose themselves and their families on Judgement Day. That is a big loss!" [16] Smoke of fire above and smoke beneath them; with that Allah frightens His servants, so My *sincere* servants, be fearful of Me.

اللّٰهُ بِهٖ عِبَادَهٗ ۗ يٰعِبَادِ فَاتَّقُوْنِ ۞ وَالَّذِيْنَ اجْتَنَبُوا الطَّاغُوْتَ اَنْ يَّعْبُدُوْهَا وَاَنَابُوْٓا اِلَى اللّٰهِ لَهُمُ الْبُشْرٰى ۚ فَبَشِّرْ عِبَادِ ۞ الَّذِيْنَ يَسْتَمِعُوْنَ الْقَوْلَ فَيَتَّبِعُوْنَ اَحْسَنَهٗ ۗ اُولٰٓئِكَ الَّذِيْنَ هَدٰىهُمُ اللّٰهُ وَاُولٰٓئِكَ هُمْ اُولُوا الْاَلْبَابِ ۞ اَفَمَنْ حَقَّ عَلَيْهِ كَلِمَةُ الْعَذَابِ ۗ اَفَاَنْتَ تُنْقِذُ مَنْ فِى النَّارِ ۞ لٰكِنِ الَّذِيْنَ اتَّقَوْا رَبَّهُمْ لَهُمْ غُرَفٌ مِّنْ فَوْقِهَا غُرَفٌ مَّبْنِيَّةٌ ۙ تَجْرِيْ مِنْ تَحْتِهَا الْاَنْهٰرُ ۗ وَعْدَ اللّٰهِ ۗ لَا يُخْلِفُ اللّٰهُ الْمِيْعَادَ ۞ اَلَمْ تَرَ اَنَّ اللّٰهَ اَنْزَلَ مِنَ السَّمَآءِ مَآءً فَسَلَكَهٗ يَنَابِيْعَ فِى الْاَرْضِ ثُمَّ يُخْرِجُ بِهٖ زَرْعًا مُّخْتَلِفًا اَلْوَانُهٗ ثُمَّ يَهِيْجُ فَتَرٰىهُ مُصْفَرًّا ثُمَّ يَجْعَلُهٗ حُطَامًا ۗ اِنَّ فِيْ ذٰلِكَ لَذِكْرٰى لِاُولِى الْاَلْبَابِ ۞ اَفَمَنْ شَرَحَ اللّٰهُ صَدْرَهٗ لِلْاِسْلَامِ فَهُوَ عَلٰى نُوْرٍ مِّنْ رَّبِّهٖ ۗ فَوَيْلٌ لِّلْقٰسِيَةِ قُلُوْبُهُمْ مِّنْ ذِكْرِ اللّٰهِ ۗ اُولٰٓئِكَ فِيْ ضَلٰلٍ مُّبِيْنٍ ۞ اَللّٰهُ نَزَّلَ اَحْسَنَ الْحَدِيْثِ كِتٰبًا مُّتَشَابِهًا مَّثَانِيَ ۖ تَقْشَعِرُّ مِنْهُ جُلُوْدُ الَّذِيْنَ يَخْشَوْنَ رَبَّهُمْ ۚ ثُمَّ تَلِيْنُ جُلُوْدُهُمْ وَقُلُوْبُهُمْ اِلٰى ذِكْرِ اللّٰهِ ۗ ذٰلِكَ هُدَى اللّٰهِ يَهْدِيْ بِهٖ مَنْ يَّشَآءُ ۗ وَمَنْ يُّضْلِلِ اللّٰهُ فَمَا لَهٗ مِنْ هَادٍ ۞ اَفَمَنْ يَّتَّقِيْ بِوَجْهِهٖ سُوْٓءَ الْعَذَابِ يَوْمَ الْقِيٰمَةِ ۗ

The opening of the heart and the mind to the light of Allah is a great blessing, have you experienced this?

[17] Good news for those who avoid serving the idols and turn genuinely to Allah, so give My servants good news: [18] *Those* who listen attentively to what is said and follow the best of it, Allah has guided these, the one's with understanding. [19] The one who Allah has passed sentence against, how can you rescue him? He's already in the Fire. [20] But those who fear their Lord, they will have lofty apartments luxuriously furnished and streams flowing beneath them; *this is* Allah's promise. Allah doesn't break His promise.

The mind of the thankful opens to Islam

[21] Don't you see that Allah sends rain from the sky. He lets it seep into the ground, where it forms springs. Then with it He produces plants of different colours, then they become dry, so you see them turn yellow, and then He turns it back into soil. In this are lessons for the understanding people. [22] So the one whose mind Allah opens with *the light* of Islam will have light from His Lord. But those whose minds are closed[a] to the remembrance of Allah will be ruined; they are wholly misguided.

They tremble when reading the Quran

[23] Allah has sent down a beautiful set of teachings *in* a Book that is consistent, proclaiming promises and warnings[b]. The skin shivers of those who fear their Lord. Then, their skin and hearts relax with the remembrance of Allah; that is Allah's guidance. He guides with it who He pleases. Whoever Allah allows to go astray, will have no guide. [24] So the one who must shield his face from the terrible punishment of Judgement Day, the evil, will be told: "Taste what you have earned."

---

[a] *Lil-Qasiyati Quloobhuhum*, means their hardened hearts. The heart is a metaphor for the mind, since it is the organ of both understanding and emotion.

[b] "Masani" according to Suyuti is the promises and warnings.

وَقِيلَ لِلظّٰلِمِينَ ذُوْقُوْا مَا كُنْتُمْ تَكْسِبُوْنَ ۝ كَذَّبَ الَّذِيْنَ مِنْ قَبْلِهِمْ فَاَتٰىهُمُ الْعَذَابُ مِنْ حَيْثُ لَا يَشْعُرُوْنَ ۝ فَاَذَاقَهُمُ اللهُ الْخِزْيَ فِى الْحَيٰوةِ الدُّنْيَا ۚ وَلَعَذَابُ الْاٰخِرَةِ اَكْبَرُ ۘ لَوْ كَانُوْا يَعْلَمُوْنَ ۝ وَلَقَدْ ضَرَبْنَا لِلنَّاسِ فِىْ هٰذَا الْقُرْاٰنِ مِنْ كُلِّ مَثَلٍ لَّعَلَّهُمْ يَتَذَكَّرُوْنَ ۙ ۝ قُرْاٰنًا عَرَبِيًّا غَيْرَ ذِىْ عِوَجٍ لَّعَلَّهُمْ يَتَّقُوْنَ ۝ ضَرَبَ اللهُ مَثَلًا رَّجُلًا فِيْهِ شُرَكَآءُ مُتَشٰكِسُوْنَ وَ رَجُلًا سَلَمًا لِّرَجُلٍ ۗ

*Those who follow and
support the Prophet ﷺ
will be rewarded.*

هَلْ يَسْتَوِيٰنِ مَثَلًا ۗ اَلْحَمْدُ لِلّٰهِ ۚ بَلْ اَكْثَرُهُمْ لَا يَعْلَمُوْنَ ۝ اِنَّكَ مَيِّتٌ وَّاِنَّهُمْ مَّيِّتُوْنَ ۝ ثُمَّ اِنَّكُمْ يَوْمَ الْقِيٰمَةِ عِنْدَ رَبِّكُمْ تَخْتَصِمُوْنَ ۝ فَمَنْ اَظْلَمُ مِمَّنْ كَذَبَ عَلَى اللهِ وَكَذَّبَ بِالصِّدْقِ اِذْ جَآءَهٗ ۗ اَلَيْسَ فِىْ جَهَنَّمَ مَثْوًى لِّلْكٰفِرِيْنَ ۝ وَالَّذِىْ جَآءَ بِالصِّدْقِ وَصَدَّقَ بِهٖٓ اُولٰٓئِكَ هُمُ الْمُتَّقُوْنَ ۝ لَهُمْ مَّا يَشَآءُوْنَ عِنْدَ رَبِّهِمْ ۗ ذٰلِكَ جَزٰٓؤُا الْمُحْسِنِيْنَ ۝ لِيُكَفِّرَ اللهُ عَنْهُمْ اَسْوَاَ الَّذِىْ عَمِلُوْا وَيَجْزِيَهُمْ اَجْرَهُمْ بِاَحْسَنِ الَّذِىْ كَانُوْا يَعْمَلُوْنَ ۝ اَلَيْسَ اللهُ بِكَافٍ عَبْدَهٗ ۗ وَ يُخَوِّفُوْنَكَ بِالَّذِيْنَ مِنْ دُوْنِهٖ ۗ وَمَنْ يُّضْلِلِ اللهُ فَمَا لَهٗ مِنْ هَادٍ ۝ وَمَنْ يَّهْدِ اللهُ فَمَا لَهٗ مِنْ مُّضِلٍّ ۗ اَلَيْسَ اللهُ بِعَزِيْزٍ ذِى انْتِقَامٍ ۝ وَلَئِنْ سَاَلْتَهُمْ مَّنْ خَلَقَ

²⁵Others before them also disbelieved, and they were unaware of where the punishment came from. ²⁶So Allah made them taste humiliation in this worldly life, and the punishment of the Hereafter is even greater. If only they knew.

The believers only have one Master

²⁷In this *Majestic* Quran, We give examples for people of all kinds so they pay attention, ²⁸to an Arabic Quran, free from any defect so they may be mindful *of Allah.* ²⁹Allah gives this example: can a servant devoted to many masters who are at odds with each other be the same as the one who is devoted to only one master? All the praises belong to Allah! Unfortunately, the majority don't know.

The believer in the Quran will be satisfied

³⁰You shall die, so shall they die; ³¹then on Judgement Day you will argue with one another, near Your Lord. ³²Who can be more wretched than the one who lied about Allah and denied the truth when it came to him? Isn't Hell the final home of the disbelievers? ³³The one who came with the truth and the one who accepted him, such are the mindful people. ³⁴They shall have whatever they want *from* their Lord. That is the reward of the righteous. ³⁵Allah will remove their wrongs and give them an excellent reward for what they did. ³⁶Isn't Allah enough for His servant? Yet they threaten you with *idols* they worship beside Allah; anyone Allah allows to go astray will have no guide. ³⁷And anyone Allah guides no one can misguide him, isn't Allah the Almighty, the Avenger?

السَّمٰوٰتِ وَالْأَرْضِ لَيَقُوْلُنَّ اللّٰهُ طُ قُلْ أَفَرَءَيْتُمْ مَّا تَدْعُوْنَ

مِنْ دُوْنِ اللّٰهِ إِنْ أَرَادَنِيَ اللّٰهُ بِضُرٍّ هَلْ هُنَّ كٰشِفٰتُ

ضُرِّهٖ أَوْ أَرَادَنِيْ بِرَحْمَةٍ هَلْ هُنَّ مُمْسِكٰتُ رَحْمَتِهٖ طُ قُلْ

حَسْبِيَ اللّٰهُ طُ عَلَيْهِ يَتَوَكَّلُ الْمُتَوَكِّلُوْنَ ۳۸ قُلْ يٰقَوْمِ

اعْمَلُوْا عَلٰى مَكَانَتِكُمْ إِنِّيْ عَامِلٌ فَسَوْفَ تَعْلَمُوْنَ ۳۹ مَنْ

يَّأْتِيْهِ عَذَابٌ يُّخْزِيْهِ وَيَحِلُّ عَلَيْهِ عَذَابٌ مُّقِيْمٌ ۴۰

إِنَّا أَنْزَلْنَا عَلَيْكَ الْكِتٰبَ لِلنَّاسِ بِالْحَقِّ ۚ فَمَنِ اهْتَدٰى

Allah allows people to seek favours for others.

فَلِنَفْسِهٖ ۚ وَمَنْ ضَلَّ فَإِنَّمَا يَضِلُّ عَلَيْهَا ۚ وَمَا أَنْتَ

عَلَيْهِمْ بِوَكِيْلٍ ۴۱ اللّٰهُ يَتَوَفَّى الْأَنْفُسَ حِيْنَ مَوْتِهَا وَالَّتِيْ

لَمْ تَمُتْ فِيْ مَنَامِهَا ۚ فَيُمْسِكُ الَّتِيْ قَضٰى عَلَيْهَا الْمَوْتَ

وَيُرْسِلُ الْأُخْرٰى إِلٰى أَجَلٍ مُّسَمًّى طُ إِنَّ فِيْ ذٰلِكَ لَأٰيٰتٍ

لِّقَوْمٍ يَّتَفَكَّرُوْنَ ۴۲ أَمِ اتَّخَذُوْا مِنْ دُوْنِ اللّٰهِ شُفَعَآءَ طُ

قُلْ أَوَلَوْ كَانُوْا لَا يَمْلِكُوْنَ شَيْئًا وَّلَا يَعْقِلُوْنَ ۴۳ قُلْ

لِّلّٰهِ الشَّفَاعَةُ جَمِيْعًا طُ لَهٗ مُلْكُ السَّمٰوٰتِ وَالْأَرْضِ طُ ثُمَّ

إِلَيْهِ تُرْجَعُوْنَ ۴۴ وَإِذَا ذُكِرَ اللّٰهُ وَحْدَهُ اشْمَأَزَّتْ قُلُوْبُ

الَّذِيْنَ لَا يُؤْمِنُوْنَ بِالْأٰخِرَةِ ۚ وَإِذَا ذُكِرَ الَّذِيْنَ مِنْ

دُوْنِهٖ إِذَا هُمْ يَسْتَبْشِرُوْنَ ۴۵ قُلِ اللّٰهُمَّ فَاطِرَ السَّمٰوٰتِ

وَالْأَرْضِ عٰلِمَ الْغَيْبِ وَالشَّهَادَةِ أَنْتَ تَحْكُمُ بَيْنَ

عِبَادِكَ فِيْ مَا كَانُوْا فِيْهِ يَخْتَلِفُوْنَ ۴۶ وَلَوْ أَنَّ لِلَّذِيْنَ

ظَلَمُوْا مَا فِي الْأَرْضِ جَمِيْعًا وَّمِثْلَهٗ مَعَهٗ لَافْتَدَوْا

The helplessness of idols

³⁸ If you ask them: "Who created the Heavens and the Earth?" They will say, "Allah". Say: "What do you think about those you worship beside Allah; can they relieve my distress if Allah wished to harm me, or if He wished to be kind to me could they stop Him being Kind?" Say: "Allah is enough for me, those who trust put their trust in Him." ³⁹ Say: "My people, do what you want to do and so will I; soon you will know ⁴⁰ who will be humiliated by sufferings in the world and finally thrown in an everlasting punishment."

The mystery of sleep

⁴¹ We sent down the Book for people, *it has* the truth. Whoever follows *its* guidance will benefit himself, and whoever goes astray will fail himself. You aren't their caretaker. ⁴² Allah takes away the souls of people dying and the souls of *the living* during their sleep. He keeps hold of those whose time of death has come, but sends back others, so *they will die* at their fixed time. In this are lessons for thinkers.

The idols are incapable of helping you

⁴³ Have they chosen intermediaries beside Allah? Say: "Though they haven't got power nor understanding?" ⁴⁴ Say: "Allah has complete authority for intercession." He controls the Heavens and the Earth, then to Him you shall be returned. ⁴⁵ When Allah's Oneness is declared, the disbelievers of the Hereafter hate[a] it intensely, yet when their gods beside Allah are mentioned they are thrilled. ⁴⁶ Say: "Allah, Creator of the Heavens and the Earth, Knower of the unseen and the seen worlds, You shall decide between Your servants about their differences."

---

[a] *Ishma'azzat Quloobuhum* literally means "to hate and despair."

بِهٖ مِنْ سُوْٓءِ الْعَذَابِ يَوْمَ الْقِيٰمَةِ ط وَبَدَا لَهُمْ مِّنَ

اللّٰهِ مَا لَمْ يَكُوْنُوْا يَحْتَسِبُوْنَ ۝ وَبَدَا لَهُمْ سَيِّاٰتُ مَا

كَسَبُوْا وَحَاقَ بِهِمْ مَّا كَانُوْا بِهٖ يَسْتَهْزِءُوْنَ ۝ فَاِذَا مَسَّ

الْاِنْسَانَ ضُرٌّ دَعَانَا ۪ ثُمَّ اِذَا خَوَّلْنٰهُ نِعْمَةً مِّنَّا ۙ قَالَ

اِنَّمَآ اُوْتِيْتُهٗ عَلٰى عِلْمٍ ط بَلْ هِىَ فِتْنَةٌ وَّلٰكِنَّ اَكْثَرَهُمْ

لَا يَعْلَمُوْنَ ۝ قَدْ قَالَهَا الَّذِيْنَ مِنْ قَبْلِهِمْ فَمَآ اَغْنٰى

عَنْهُمْ مَّا كَانُوْا يَكْسِبُوْنَ ۝ فَاَصَابَهُمْ سَيِّاٰتُ مَا كَسَبُوْا ط

وَالَّذِيْنَ ظَلَمُوْا مِنْ هٰٓؤُلَآءِ سَيُصِيْبُهُمْ سَيِّاٰتُ مَا كَسَبُوْا ۙ

وَمَا هُمْ بِمُعْجِزِيْنَ ۝ اَوَلَمْ يَعْلَمُوْٓا اَنَّ اللّٰهَ يَبْسُطُ الرِّزْقَ

لِمَنْ يَّشَآءُ وَيَقْدِرُ ط اِنَّ فِىْ ذٰلِكَ لَاٰيٰتٍ لِّقَوْمٍ يُّؤْمِنُوْنَ ۝

قُلْ يٰعِبَادِىَ الَّذِيْنَ اَسْرَفُوْا عَلٰٓى اَنْفُسِهِمْ لَا تَقْنَطُوْا مِنْ

رَّحْمَةِ اللّٰهِ ط اِنَّ اللّٰهَ يَغْفِرُ الذُّنُوْبَ جَمِيْعًا ط اِنَّهٗ هُوَ

الْغَفُوْرُ الرَّحِيْمُ ۝ وَاَنِيْبُوْٓا اِلٰى رَبِّكُمْ وَاَسْلِمُوْا لَهٗ مِنْ

قَبْلِ اَنْ يَّاْتِيَكُمُ الْعَذَابُ ثُمَّ لَا تُنْصَرُوْنَ ۝ وَاتَّبِعُوْٓا

اَحْسَنَ مَآ اُنْزِلَ اِلَيْكُمْ مِّنْ رَّبِّكُمْ مِّنْ قَبْلِ اَنْ يَّاْتِيَكُمُ

الْعَذَابُ بَغْتَةً وَّاَنْتُمْ لَا تَشْعُرُوْنَ ۝ اَنْ تَقُوْلَ نَفْسٌ

يّٰحَسْرَتٰى عَلٰى مَا فَرَّطْتُّ فِىْ جَنْبِ اللّٰهِ وَاِنْ كُنْتُ لَمِنَ

السّٰخِرِيْنَ ۝ اَوْ تَقُوْلَ لَوْ اَنَّ اللّٰهَ هَدٰىنِىْ لَكُنْتُ مِنَ

الْمُتَّقِيْنَ ۝ اَوْ تَقُوْلَ حِيْنَ تَرَى الْعَذَابَ لَوْ اَنَّ لِىْ

كَرَّةً فَاَكُوْنَ مِنَ الْمُحْسِنِيْنَ ۝ بَلٰى قَدْ جَآءَتْكَ اٰيٰتِىْ

Always be helpful and optimistic, and expect Allah to take care of you.

A description of an unthankful person

47 If everything on Earth plus twice as much belonged to the wicked, they would happily offer it as a ransom against the terrible punishment of Judgement Day. Allah will show them what they couldn't have imagined. 48 Their evil deeds will be disclosed, and their mocking will track them *as punishment*. 49 When people are distressed they call on Us, but when We give them Our gifts, they claim: "We've been given this because of our knowledge." No, it is a test but most do not know this. 50 Those before them said the same. Their works will not save them *that Day*. 51 The evil of what they did will distress them; the sinners will suffer the distress because of their deeds, and they will not escape. 52 Don't they know Allah provides plentifully to *some* and sparingly to *others* as He pleases. In that are lessons for the faithful.

Invitation to confess sins privately

53 Say: "My servants who wronged themselves, don't be hopeless of Allah's Kindness; Allah forgives all the sins, He is the Forgiver, the Kind." 54 Turn devoutly to your Lord, and submit to Him before the punishment overtakes you – then you shall not be helped. 55 And follow the best teachings sent down to you by your Lord before the unexpected punishment overtakes you when you are unaware 56 and a soul will cry out: "Woe to me since I disobeyed Allah and mocked *His revelations*." 57 Or he will say, "Had Allah guided me I would be among the pious," 58 or when he sees the punishment he will say, "If I could live again I would be among the righteous." 59 No, My signs came to you but you denied them; you were arrogant and among the disbelievers.

فَكَذَّبْتَ بِهَا وَاسْتَكْبَرْتَ وَكُنْتَ مِنَ الْكَفِرِينَ ۵۹ وَيَوْمَ

الْقِيَمَةِ تَرَى الَّذِينَ كَذَبُوا عَلَى اللهِ وُجُوهُهُمْ مُّسْوَدَّةٌ ط

اَلَيْسَ فِي جَهَنَّمَ مَثْوًى لِّلْمُتَكَبِّرِينَ ۶۰ وَيُنَجِّى اللهُ الَّذِينَ

اتَّقَوْا بِمَفَازَتِهِمْ لَا يَمَسُّهُمُ السُّوءُ وَلَاهُمْ يَحْزَنُونَ ۶۱ اللهُ

خَالِقُ كُلِّ شَيْءٍ وَّهُوَ عَلَى كُلِّ شَيْءٍ وَّكِيلٌ ۶۲ لَهُ مَقَالِيدُ

السَّمَوَاتِ وَالْاَرْضِ ط وَالَّذِينَ كَفَرُوا بِاَيَاتِ اللهِ اُولَئِكَ

هُمُ الْخَاسِرُونَ ۶۳ قُلْ اَفَغَيْرَ اللهِ تَامُرُوٓنِّي اَعْبُدُ اَيُّهَا

الْجَاهِلُونَ ۶۴ وَلَقَدْ اُوحِيَ اِلَيْكَ وَاِلَى الَّذِينَ مِنْ قَبْلِكَ ج

لَئِنْ اَشْرَكْتَ لَيَحْبَطَنَّ عَمَلُكَ وَلَتَكُونَنَّ مِنَ الْخَاسِرِينَ ۶۵

بَلِ اللهَ فَاعْبُدْ وَكُنْ مِّنَ الشَّاكِرِينَ ۶۶ وَمَا قَدَرُوا اللهَ

حَقَّ قَدْرِهِ صلے وَالْاَرْضُ جَمِيعًا قَبْضَتُهُ يَوْمَ الْقِيَمَةِ

وَالسَّمَوَاتُ مَطْوِيَّاتٌ بِيَمِينِهِ ط سُبْحَنَهُ وَتَعَلَى عَمَّا

يُشْرِكُونَ ۶۷ وَنُفِخَ فِي الصُّورِ فَصَعِقَ مَنْ فِي السَّمَوَاتِ وَمَنْ

فِي الْاَرْضِ اِلَّا مَنْ شَاءَ اللهُ ط ثُمَّ نُفِخَ فِيهِ اُخْرَى فَاِذَا

هُمْ قِيَامٌ يَّنْظُرُونَ ۶۸ وَاَشْرَقَتِ الْاَرْضُ بِنُورِ رَبِّهَا وَوُضِعَ

الْكِتَبُ وَجِايْءَ بِالنَّبِيِّنَ وَالشُّهَدَاءِ وَقُضِيَ بَيْنَهُمْ

بِالْحَقِّ وَهُمْ لَا يُظْلَمُونَ ۶۹ وَوُفِّيَتْ كُلُّ نَفْسٍ مَّا

عَمِلَتْ وَهُوَ اَعْلَمُ بِمَا يَفْعَلُونَ ۷۰ وَسِيقَ الَّذِينَ

كَفَرُوٓا اِلَى جَهَنَّمَ زُمَرًا ط حَتَّى اِذَا جَاءُوهَا فُتِحَتْ

اَبْوَابُهَا وَقَالَ لَهُمْ خَزَنَتُهَا اَلَمْ يَاتِكُمْ رُسُلٌ مِّنْكُمْ

We fail to recognise the true greatness of Allah. How can we be grateful?

⁶⁰ You will see on Judgement Day those who denied Allah, their faces darkened – isn't Hell the final home for the arrogant? ⁶¹ And Allah will save the pious in a safe place where they won't be harmed, nor will they worry.

Human failure to understand the greatness of Allah
⁶² Allah is the Creator and Guardian of all things. ⁶³ He has the keys to the Heavens and the Earth. Those who disbelieve in Allah's revelations will be the losers. ⁶⁴ Say: "Ignorant ones! Are you telling me to worship others beside Allah?" ⁶⁵ It was revealed to you and those before you: if you commit idolatry all your deeds will come to nothing and you will be the losers. ⁶⁶ No, worship Allah and be among the thankful ones. ⁶⁷ They don't understand Allah's true greatness; on Judgement Day, the entire Earth will be in His grip and the Heavens will be rolled up by His command^a. Glory be to Him, He is exalted above what they associate with Him.

The end of the world
⁶⁸ When the Trumpet is blown, whoever is in the Heavens and the Earth will fall unconscious, except him whom Allah wills. Then when it is blown again they will stand up looking *dazed*. ⁶⁹ The Earth will shine with the light of its Lord, the Book of Deeds will lay open, the prophets and other witnesses will be brought forward, judgement will be made, and they will not be wronged. ⁷⁰ Every soul will be fully rewarded for what it did; *Allah* knows best what they did.

Driven to Hell in crowds
⁷¹ Those who denied their Lord will be driven into Hell in crowds. When they reach it, the gates will be opened and the gatekeepers will ask them, "Didn't messengers from among you come to recite your Lord's verses and warn you of this Day's meeting?" They will say, "Yes," but the sentence of punishment will come to pass against the disbelievers.

---

^a "Biyameenhey" literally means by his right hand, however Suyuti interprets it as "by His power and command".

يَتْلُونَ عَلَيْكُمْ ءَايٰتِ رَبِّكُمْ وَيُنْذِرُونَكُمْ لِقَآءَ يَوْمِكُمْ
هٰذَا ۗ قَالُوا بَلٰى وَلٰكِنْ حَقَّتْ كَلِمَةُ الْعَذَابِ عَلَى
الْكٰفِرِينَ ﴿٧١﴾ قِيلَ ادْخُلُوٓا أَبْوَابَ جَهَنَّمَ خٰلِدِينَ فِيهَا ۖ
فَبِئْسَ مَثْوَى الْمُتَكَبِّرِينَ ﴿٧٢﴾ وَسِيقَ الَّذِينَ اتَّقَوْا رَبَّهُمْ
إِلَى الْجَنَّةِ زُمَرًا ۗ حَتّٰى إِذَا جَآءُوهَا وَفُتِحَتْ أَبْوَابُهَا
وَقَالَ لَهُمْ خَزَنَتُهَا سَلٰمٌ عَلَيْكُمْ طِبْتُمْ فَادْخُلُوهَا
خٰلِدِينَ ﴿٧٣﴾ وَقَالُوا الْحَمْدُ لِلّٰهِ الَّذِى صَدَقَنَا وَعْدَهُ
وَأَوْرَثَنَا الْأَرْضَ نَتَبَوَّأُ مِنَ الْجَنَّةِ حَيْثُ نَشَآءُ ۖ فَنِعْمَ
أَجْرُ الْعٰمِلِينَ ﴿٧٤﴾ وَتَرَى الْمَلٰٓئِكَةَ حَآفِّينَ مِنْ حَوْلِ
الْعَرْشِ يُسَبِّحُونَ بِحَمْدِ رَبِّهِمْ ۚ وَقُضِىَ بَيْنَهُمْ
بِالْحَقِّ وَقِيلَ الْحَمْدُ لِلّٰهِ رَبِّ الْعٰلَمِينَ ﴿٧٥﴾

We please Allah by prayer, glorifying Him, and thinking about His gifts.

⁷²It will be said, "Enter through the gates of Hell; remain in it forever." What a miserable home for the arrogant!

Driven to Paradise in crowds

⁷³Those who were mindful of their Lord will be led into Paradise in crowds. When they reach there, its gates will be opened, and the gatekeepers will greet them: "Peace be on you, you were good so enter it and stay here forever." ⁷⁴They will say, "All the praises are for Allah Who kept His promise for us, and gave us this place, we shall live in the Garden wherever we want." What a wonderful reward for those who worked hard. ⁷⁵You will see the angels around the Divine Throne glorifying and praising their Lord. A just judgement will be passed between them and it will be said: "All the praises are for Allah, the Lord of the worlds."

40. Surat Mu'min

The Believer

This Makkan surat was revealed around the sixth year, at a time of intense persecution of the Muslims. The name Mu'min comes from verse 28, "A believing man from Pharaoh's family who kept his faith secret...". Its other name is surat Ghafir, it is mentioned in verse 3, "the forgiver of sins...". The surat opens with a claim: "This is a revelation from Allah the Almighty, the Knower" (2). The disbelievers rejected this, so arguments from human history, experience and the natural world around them are presented. The underlying cause of their rejection is false pride in their knowledge and wealth, which leads to delusion and conceit. They mistakenly think material things will save them, and that they have no need of the Almighty: "So when Our Messengers came to them with clear signs, they smugly continued to boast about their knowledge and *eventually* were engulfed by the punishment they mocked" (83).

The central theme of the surat is false pride; humans think they're the centre of the world, they're deceived in thinking they're independent and self-sufficient. Their wealth, talents and networks make them smug and self-satisfied.

The surat opens by acknowledging the dignity of the faithful through prayer of the angels:

Our Lord, everything is under the cover of Your Kindness and Knowledge, therefore forgive those who repent and follow Your way, and protect them from the punishment of Hell (7).

Scenes from Judgement Day: Divine Justice in full swing, people's limbs testifying against them, disbelievers being hurled into Hellfire, conversations with angels and graphic depictions of Hellish torment – all combine to strike fear into hearts.

A prominent verse is: "Your Lord said, 'Call on me, and I shall answer you'"(60). Allah is Mujeeb, the Answerer, a Responder, a lovely way of encouraging us to seek His goodwill, care and friendliness. There is diversity in the stories, scenes and subjects of the surat, but the common thread running through them all is: Allah is the Almighty, able to resurrect the dead.

بِسْمِ اللّٰهِ الرَّحْمٰنِ الرَّحِیْمِ

حٰمٓ ۚ ۝ تَنْزِیْلُ الْكِتٰبِ مِنَ اللّٰهِ الْعَزِیْزِ الْعَلِیْمِ ۝

غَافِرِ الذَّنْۢبِ وَقَابِلِ التَّوْبِ شَدِیْدِ الْعِقَابِ ۙ ذِی

الطَّوْلِ ؕ لَاۤ اِلٰهَ اِلَّا هُوَ ؕ اِلَیْهِ الْمَصِیْرُ ۝ مَا یُجَادِلُ

فِیْۤ اٰیٰتِ اللّٰهِ اِلَّا الَّذِیْنَ كَفَرُوْا فَلَا یَغْرُرْكَ تَقَلُّبُهُمْ

فِی الْبِلَادِ ۝ كَذَّبَتْ قَبْلَهُمْ قَوْمُ نُوْحٍ وَّالْاَحْزَابُ مِنْۢ

بَعْدِهِمْ ۪ وَهَمَّتْ كُلُّ اُمَّةٍۭ بِرَسُوْلِهِمْ لِیَاْخُذُوْهُ

وَجَادَلُوْا بِالْبَاطِلِ لِیُدْحِضُوْا بِهِ الْحَقَّ فَاَخَذْتُهُمْ ۟

فَكَیْفَ كَانَ عِقَابِ ۝ وَكَذٰلِكَ حَقَّتْ كَلِمَتُ رَبِّكَ عَلَی

الَّذِیْنَ كَفَرُوْۤا اَنَّهُمْ اَصْحٰبُ النَّارِ ۝ اَلَّذِیْنَ یَحْمِلُوْنَ

الْعَرْشَ وَمَنْ حَوْلَهٗ یُسَبِّحُوْنَ بِحَمْدِ رَبِّهِمْ وَیُؤْمِنُوْنَ

بِهٖ وَیَسْتَغْفِرُوْنَ لِلَّذِیْنَ اٰمَنُوْا ۚ رَبَّنَا وَسِعْتَ كُلَّ شَیْءٍ

رَّحْمَةً وَّعِلْمًا فَاغْفِرْ لِلَّذِیْنَ تَابُوْا وَاتَّبَعُوْا سَبِیْلَكَ

وَقِهِمْ عَذَابَ الْجَحِیْمِ ۝ رَبَّنَا وَاَدْخِلْهُمْ جَنّٰتِ عَدْنِۨ

الَّتِیْ وَعَدْتَّهُمْ وَمَنْ صَلَحَ مِنْ اٰبَآئِهِمْ وَاَزْوَاجِهِمْ وَ

ذُرِّیّٰتِهِمْ ؕ اِنَّكَ اَنْتَ الْعَزِیْزُ الْحَكِیْمُ ۝ وَقِهِمُ السَّیِّاٰتِ ؕ

وَمَنْ تَقِ السَّیِّاٰتِ یَوْمَئِذٍ فَقَدْ رَحِمْتَهٗ ؕ وَذٰلِكَ هُوَ

الْفَوْزُ الْعَظِیْمُ ۝ اِنَّ الَّذِیْنَ كَفَرُوْا یُنَادَوْنَ لَمَقْتُ

اللّٰهِ اَكْبَرُ مِنْ مَّقْتِكُمْ اَنْفُسَكُمْ اِذْ تُدْعَوْنَ اِلَی الْاِیْمَانِ

To deny Allah is a deception. The believers are fortunate that they are blessed with the gift of faith. How much do you value it?

In the name of Allah, the Kind the Caring.

[1] *Ha Meem.*

The Forgiving and Generous Lord

[2] This is a Revelation from Allah the Almighty, the Knower, [3] the Forgiver of sins, Acceptor of repentance, Severe in punishment and the Bestower of favours.[a] There is no god but Him. To Him is the return. [4] Only the disbelievers argue about Allah's revelations, so don't be surprised by their toing and froing in the land *for trade.* [5] The people of Nuh before them and other parties after them also denied; each community tried to defeat their messenger and disputed desperately to crush the Truth with falsehood. I punished them, so look what became of them! [6] Your Lord's sentence against the disbelievers was carried out: "They are people of the Fire."

The Angels' prayer for the believers

[7] The angels who maintain the Divine Throne and those around it glorify and praise their Lord. They are faithful, and seek forgiveness for the believers; they pray: "Our Lord, all good happens because of Your Kindness and with Your Knowledge, so forgive those who repent, follow Your way and protect them from the punishment of Hell. [8] Our Lord, admit them into Everlasting Gardens, which You have promised them and anyone who reforms himself, including their forefathers, spouses and children. You are Almighty, the Wise. [9] Protect them from the consequences of evil; whoever You have protected from punishment that Day, You will be kind to them, and that's the supreme victory."

The disbelievers will confess their sins

[10] The disbelievers will be told: "When you were invited to faith you disbelieved, Allah's dislike of you was far greater than your dislike of yourselves this day.

---

[a] *Zul Fadl* shows kindness, gives gifts freely.

فَتَكْفُرُونَ ۞ قَالُوا رَبَّنَا أَمَتَّنَا اثْنَتَيْنِ وَ أَحْيَيْتَنَا

اثْنَتَيْنِ فَاعْتَرَفْنَا بِذُنُوبِنَا فَهَلْ اِلَى خُرُوجٍ مِّنْ

سَبِيلٍ ۞ ذَلِكُمْ بِأَنَّهُ اِذَا دُعِيَ اللهُ وَحْدَهُ كَفَرْتُمْ وَ

اِنْ يُّشْرَكْ بِهِ تُؤْمِنُوا فَالْحُكْمُ لِلّهِ الْعَلِيِّ الْكَبِيرِ ۞ هُوَ

الَّذِي يُرِيكُمْ اٰيٰتِهِ وَيُنَزِّلُ لَكُمْ مِّنَ السَّمَاءِ رِزْقًا

وَمَا يَتَذَكَّرُ اِلَّا مَنْ يُّنِيبُ ۞ فَادْعُوا اللهَ مُخْلِصِينَ

لَهُ الدِّينَ وَلَوْ كَرِهَ الْكٰفِرُونَ ۞ رَفِيعُ الدَّرَجٰتِ

ذُو الْعَرْشِ يُلْقِي الرُّوحَ مِنْ اَمْرِهِ عَلَى مَنْ يَّشَاءُ مِنْ

The faithful are those
who turn earnestly,
keenly and lovingly
towards Allah.

عِبَادِهِ لِيُنْذِرَ يَوْمَ التَّلَاقِ ۞ يَوْمَ هُمْ بٰرِزُونَ ۚ

لَا يَخْفَى عَلَى اللهِ مِنْهُمْ شَيْءٌ ۗ لِمَنِ الْمُلْكُ الْيَوْمَ ۗ

لِلّهِ الْوَاحِدِ الْقَهَّارِ ۞ اَلْيَوْمَ تُجْزَى كُلُّ نَفْسٍ بِمَا

كَسَبَتْ ۗ لَا ظُلْمَ الْيَوْمَ ۗ اِنَّ اللهَ سَرِيعُ الْحِسَابِ ۞

وَاَنْذِرْهُمْ يَوْمَ الْاٰزِفَةِ اِذِ الْقُلُوبُ لَدَى الْحَنَاجِرِ

كٰظِمِينَ ۚ مَا لِلظّٰلِمِينَ مِنْ حَمِيمٍ وَّلَا شَفِيعٍ

يُّطَاعُ ۞ يَعْلَمُ خَائِنَةَ الْاَعْيُنِ وَمَا تُخْفِي الصُّدُورُ ۞

وَاللهُ يَقْضِي بِالْحَقِّ ۗ وَالَّذِينَ يَدْعُونَ مِنْ دُونِهِ

لَا يَقْضُونَ بِشَيْءٍ ۗ اِنَّ اللهَ هُوَ السَّمِيعُ الْبَصِيرُ ۞

اَوَلَمْ يَسِيرُوا فِي الْاَرْضِ فَيَنْظُرُوا كَيْفَ كَانَ عَاقِبَةُ

الَّذِينَ كَانُوا مِنْ قَبْلِهِمْ ۗ كَانُوا هُمْ اَشَدَّ مِنْهُمْ قُوَّةً

وَّاٰثَارًا فِي الْاَرْضِ فَاَخَذَهُمُ اللهُ بِذُنُوبِهِمْ ۗ وَمَا كَانَ

¹¹ They will say, "Our Lord, twice you put us to death and twice you gave lifeᵃ; we now confess our sins, so is there a way out?" ¹² That is because when you were called to Allah you disbelieved but accepted idolatry, so *today* the decision is Allah's, the Exalted, the Great. ¹³ He will show you His Signs, and sends provision down from the sky for you. But only the devout pay attention. ¹⁴ So serve Allah, sincerely serving His religion, though the disbelievers dislike it.

The terrifying events of Judgement Day

¹⁵ High above all ranks is, the Lord of the *mighty* Throne. The Revelation is sent by His Command to His servants with whom He is pleased to warn *people* of the Day of Meeting. ¹⁶ The Day when they will come out and nothing of theirs will be hidden from Allah. "Whose is the *absolute power* and control today?" "Allah, the One, the Dominant." ¹⁷ Today every soul will be rewarded for what it did; there will be no injustice today. Allah is quick in reckoning. ¹⁸ Warn them of a fast-approaching Day, when hearts will come up to the throats chokingly. The evildoers will have no friend or an intercessor who will be listened to. ¹⁹ Allah knows the cheatersᵇ and what the minds conceal. ²⁰ Allah will judge justly, but those they served beside Allah will make no judgment at all; indeed Allah is the Hearing, the Seeing.

Allah is the only Protector

²¹ Haven't they travelled about in the land to see the fate of those before them? They were far stronger than them, and they left behind many remains on the land. So Allah punished them for their sins; no one can protect them from Allah.

ᵃ You were non-existent; you were dead, then Allah gave you life; you then died for a second time and you will be resurrected on Judgement Day a second time.

ᵇ *Khainat ul Ayun* literally means fraudulence of the eye: betrayal, sly, sneaky and secret.

لَهُمۡ مِّنَ ٱللَّهِ مِنۡ وَاقٍ ۝ ذَٰلِكَ بِأَنَّهُمۡ كَانَتۡ تَأۡتِيهِمۡ

رُسُلُهُم بِٱلۡبَيِّنَٰتِ فَكَفَرُوا فَأَخَذَهُمُ ٱللَّهُ ۚ إِنَّهُ قَوِىٌّ

شَدِيدُ ٱلۡعِقَابِ ۝ وَلَقَدۡ أَرۡسَلۡنَا مُوسَىٰ بِـَٔايَٰتِنَا وَ

سُلۡطَٰنٍ مُّبِينٍ ۝ إِلَىٰ فِرۡعَوۡنَ وَهَٰمَٰنَ وَقَٰرُونَ فَقَالُوا

سَٰحِرٌ كَذَّابٌ ۝ فَلَمَّا جَآءَهُم بِٱلۡحَقِّ مِنۡ عِندِنَا قَالُوا

ٱقۡتُلُوٓا أَبۡنَآءَ ٱلَّذِينَ ءَامَنُوا مَعَهُۥ وَٱسۡتَحۡيُوا نِسَآءَهُمۡ ۚ

وَمَا كَيۡدُ ٱلۡكَٰفِرِينَ إِلَّا فِى ضَلَٰلٍ ۝ وَقَالَ فِرۡعَوۡنُ

ذَرُونِىٓ أَقۡتُلۡ مُوسَىٰ وَلۡيَدۡعُ رَبَّهُۥٓ ۖ إِنِّىٓ أَخَافُ أَن

يُبَدِّلَ دِينَكُمۡ أَوۡ أَن يُظۡهِرَ فِى ٱلۡأَرۡضِ ٱلۡفَسَادَ ۝

وَقَالَ مُوسَىٰٓ إِنِّى عُذۡتُ بِرَبِّى وَرَبِّكُم مِّن كُلِّ مُتَكَبِّرٍ

لَّا يُؤۡمِنُ بِيَوۡمِ ٱلۡحِسَابِ ۝ وَقَالَ رَجُلٌ مُّؤۡمِنٌ

مِّنۡ ءَالِ فِرۡعَوۡنَ يَكۡتُمُ إِيمَٰنَهُۥٓ أَتَقۡتُلُونَ رَجُلًا أَن

يَقُولَ رَبِّىَ ٱللَّهُ وَقَدۡ جَآءَكُم بِٱلۡبَيِّنَٰتِ مِن رَّبِّكُمۡ ۖ

وَإِن يَكُ كَٰذِبًا فَعَلَيۡهِ كَذِبُهُۥ ۖ وَإِن يَكُ صَادِقًا

يُصِبۡكُم بَعۡضُ ٱلَّذِى يَعِدُكُمۡ ۖ إِنَّ ٱللَّهَ لَا يَهۡدِى

مَنۡ هُوَ مُسۡرِفٌ كَذَّابٌ ۝ يَٰقَوۡمِ لَكُمُ ٱلۡمُلۡكُ ٱلۡيَوۡمَ

ظَٰهِرِينَ فِى ٱلۡأَرۡضِ فَمَن يَنصُرُنَا مِنۢ بَأۡسِ ٱللَّهِ

إِن جَآءَنَا ۚ قَالَ فِرۡعَوۡنُ مَآ أُرِيكُمۡ إِلَّا مَآ أَرَىٰ وَمَآ

أَهۡدِيكُمۡ إِلَّا سَبِيلَ ٱلرَّشَادِ ۝ وَقَالَ ٱلَّذِىٓ ءَامَنَ يَٰقَوۡمِ

إِنِّىٓ أَخَافُ عَلَيۡكُم مِّثۡلَ يَوۡمِ ٱلۡأَحۡزَابِ ۝ مِثۡلَ دَأۡبِ

The boldness of the believer is admirable; he challenges Pharaoh: 'why do you want to kill Musa?' Just because he has faith. A man of courage.

ع ٣
٨

937

²² That *happened* because messengers came to them with clear signs, and they disbelieved, so Allah punished them; He is Strong, severe in punishment.

The Pharaoh is terrified of Musa

²³ We sent Musa with Our signs and a mandate ²⁴ to Pharaoh, Haman and Qarun. They called him, "a magician, a liar!" ²⁵ He came to them with Our Truth, and they replied, "Kill the children of the believers with him and spare their women." However, the disbelievers' plot was bound to fail. ²⁶ The Pharaoh said, "Leave me to kill Musa, and let him call upon His Lord; I fear he will change your religion or spread disorderᵃ in the land." ²⁷ Musa replied, "I seek protection from my Lord and your Lord from every haughty person who disbelieves the Day of Reckoning."

A secret believer defends Musa

²⁸ A believing man from Pharaoh's family, who had kept his faith secret, said: "Are you going to kill a man because he says Allah is my Lord, and has come with clear signs from your Lord? If he is a liar then let it fall on his head, and if he is truthful then some of what he threatens you with will fall on you." Allah does not guide the one who is a lying rebel.ᵇ ²⁹ *He continued*: "My people! Today you rule this land and have power, but who would help if Allah's punishment came on us?" The Pharaoh replied, "I have told you what I believe, and I am guiding you to the right path." ³⁰ The believer answered, "I am fearful about your fate, it will be the same as those people who opposed *the messengers*, ³¹ the fate of Nuh's people, Ad, Thamud and those after them. Allah does not want injustice for human beings.

ᵃ Cause an uprising against us.
ᵇ Literally, one who wastes Allah's gifts of guidance and witnessing His miracles.

قَوْمِ نُوحٍ وَّعَادٍ وَّثَمُوْدَ وَالَّذِيْنَ مِنْ بَعْدِهِمْ ط وَمَا

اللّٰهُ يُرِيْدُ ظُلْمًا لِّلْعِبَادِ ۞ وَيٰقَوْمِ اِنِّيْ اَخَافُ عَلَيْكُمْ

يَوْمَ التَّنَادِ ۞ يَوْمَ تُوَلُّوْنَ مُدْبِرِيْنَ ۚ مَا لَكُمْ مِّنَ اللّٰهِ

مِنْ عَاصِمٍ ۚ وَمَنْ يُّضْلِلِ اللّٰهُ فَمَا لَهٗ مِنْ هَادٍ ۞

وَلَقَدْ جَاءَكُمْ يُوْسُفُ مِنْ قَبْلُ بِالْبَيِّنٰتِ فَمَا زِلْتُمْ

فِيْ شَكٍّ مِّمَّا جَاءَكُمْ بِهٖ ط حَتّٰى اِذَا هَلَكَ قُلْتُمْ لَنْ

يَّبْعَثَ اللّٰهُ مِنْ بَعْدِهٖ رَسُوْلًا ط كَذٰلِكَ يُضِلُّ اللّٰهُ

مَنْ هُوَ مُسْرِفٌ مُّرْتَابٌ ۞ اَلَّذِيْنَ يُجَادِلُوْنَ فِيْ

اٰيٰتِ اللّٰهِ بِغَيْرِ سُلْطٰنٍ اَتٰىهُمْ ط كَبُرَ مَقْتًا عِنْدَ اللّٰهِ

وَعِنْدَ الَّذِيْنَ اٰمَنُوْا ط كَذٰلِكَ يَطْبَعُ اللّٰهُ عَلٰى كُلِّ

قَلْبِ مُتَكَبِّرٍ جَبَّارٍ ۞ وَقَالَ فِرْعَوْنُ يٰهَامٰنُ ابْنِ

لِيْ صَرْحًا لَّعَلِّيْ اَبْلُغُ الْاَسْبَابَ ۞ اَسْبَابَ السَّمٰوٰتِ

فَاَطَّلِعَ اِلٰى اِلٰهِ مُوْسٰى وَاِنِّيْ لَاَظُنُّهٗ كَاذِبًا ط وَ

كَذٰلِكَ زُيِّنَ لِفِرْعَوْنَ سُوْٓءُ عَمَلِهٖ وَصُدَّ عَنِ السَّبِيْلِ ط

وَمَا كَيْدُ فِرْعَوْنَ اِلَّا فِيْ تَبَابٍ ۞ وَقَالَ الَّذِيْ اٰمَنَ

يٰقَوْمِ اتَّبِعُوْنِ اَهْدِكُمْ سَبِيْلَ الرَّشَادِ ۞ يٰقَوْمِ اِنَّمَا

هٰذِهِ الْحَيٰوةُ الدُّنْيَا مَتَاعٌ ۫ وَّاِنَّ الْاٰخِرَةَ هِيَ دَارُ

الْقَرَارِ ۞ مَنْ عَمِلَ سَيِّئَةً فَلَا يُجْزٰى اِلَّا مِثْلَهَا ۚ

وَمَنْ عَمِلَ صَالِحًا مِّنْ ذَكَرٍ اَوْ اُنْثٰى وَهُوَ مُؤْمِنٌ

فَاُولٰٓئِكَ يَدْخُلُوْنَ الْجَنَّةَ يُرْزَقُوْنَ فِيْهَا بِغَيْرِ

Yusuf had preached to the Egyptians before Musa, but they ignored him. They're reminded of Allah's favours.

[32] My people, I fear for you the Day of Lament.[a] [33] the Day you will turn back and flee with no one to defend you against Allah's *wrath*. Whoever Allah lets go stray, will have no guide."

He reminds them of Yusuf

[34] "Previously Yusuf came to you with clear signs, but you doubted what he brought until his death, then you said, "Now Allah will not send a messenger after him." That is how Allah leaves in error the doubting rebel; [35] they dispute Allah's revelations without His endorsement. That's loathsome to Allah and the believers. So Allah closes the mind[b] of every proud tyrant. [36] The Pharaoh said, "Haman, build a tower for me, so I might find pathways reaching [37] to the skies to look for the God of Musa; I think he is a liar." That is how Pharaoh's evil deeds appeared attractive to him, and he was prevented from reaching the path – and Pharaoh's plot led him to ruin.

The believer continues to preach

[38] The believer said: "My people, follow me and I shall guide you to the right path. [39] My people, the life of this world is a brief *period of* enjoyment whilst the Hereafter is the lasting home. [40] Whoever does evil will be punished proportionally, and whoever does righteousness, whether male or female, and is a believer will enter Paradise, there they will have unlimited provision.

---

[a]   *Yaum at-Tanaad* refers to Judgement Day, literally to, "cry out to one another for help". The next verse explains it further.

[b]   Literally, "seals the heart".

النمون

حِسَابٌ ۝ وَيَٰقَوْمِ مَا لِىٓ أَدْعُوكُمْ إِلَى النَّجَوٰةِ وَ
تَدْعُونَنِىٓ إِلَى النَّارِ ۝ تَدْعُونَنِى لِأَكْفُرَ بِاللَّهِ وَ
أُشْرِكَ بِهِ مَا لَيْسَ لِى بِهِ عِلْمٌ وَأَنَا أَدْعُوكُمْ إِلَى
الْعَزِيزِ الْغَفَّارِ ۝ لَاجَرَمَ أَنَّمَا تَدْعُونَنِىٓ إِلَيْهِ لَيْسَ
لَهُ دَعْوَةٌ فِى الدُّنْيَا وَلَا فِى الْأَخِرَةِ وَ أَنَّ مَرَدَّنَآ
إِلَى اللَّهِ وَ أَنَّ الْمُسْرِفِينَ هُمْ أَصْحَٰبُ النَّارِ ۝
فَسَتَذْكُرُونَ مَآ أَقُولُ لَكُمْ ۗ وَأُفَوِّضُ أَمْرِىٓ إِلَى
اللَّهِ ۚ إِنَّ اللَّهَ بَصِيرٌۢ بِالْعِبَادِ ۝ فَوَقَىٰهُ اللَّهُ سَيِّئَاتِ
مَا مَكَرُوا۟ وَحَاقَ بِـَٔالِ فِرْعَوْنَ سُوٓءُ الْعَذَابِ ۝
النَّارُ يُعْرَضُونَ عَلَيْهَا غُدُوًّا وَّعَشِيًّا ۖ وَيَوْمَ تَقُومُ
السَّاعَةُ ۖ أَدْخِلُوٓا۟ ءَالَ فِرْعَوْنَ أَشَدَّ الْعَذَابِ ۝ وَ
إِذْ يَتَحَآجُّونَ فِى النَّارِ فَيَقُولُ الضُّعَفَٰٓؤُا۟ لِلَّذِينَ
اسْتَكْبَرُوٓا۟ إِنَّا كُنَّا لَكُمْ تَبَعًا فَهَلْ أَنتُم مُّغْنُونَ عَنَّا
نَصِيبًا مِّنَ النَّارِ ۝ قَالَ الَّذِينَ اسْتَكْبَرُوٓا۟ إِنَّا كُلٌّ
فِيهَآ إِنَّ اللَّهَ قَدْ حَكَمَ بَيْنَ الْعِبَادِ ۝ وَقَالَ الَّذِينَ
فِى النَّارِ لِخَزَنَةِ جَهَنَّمَ ادْعُوا۟ رَبَّكُمْ يُخَفِّفْ عَنَّا يَوْمًا
مِّنَ الْعَذَابِ ۝ قَالُوٓا۟ أَوَلَمْ تَكُ تَأْتِيكُمْ رُسُلُكُم
بِالْبَيِّنَٰتِ ۚ قَالُوا۟ بَلَىٰ ۚ قَالُوا۟ فَادْعُوا۟ ۚ وَمَا دُعَٰٓؤُا۟
الْكَٰفِرِينَ إِلَّا فِى ضَلَٰلٍ ۝ إِنَّا لَنَنصُرُ رُسُلَنَا وَالَّذِينَ
ءَامَنُوا۟ فِى الْحَيَوٰةِ الدُّنْيَا وَيَوْمَ يَقُومُ الْأَشْهَٰدُ ۝

The true believer assigns all matters to Allah, knowing full well that He will deal with it in the best way!

ع
١٣
١٠

⁴¹My people, how come I am calling you to salvation and you are calling me to the Fire? ⁴²You invite me to disbelieve in Allah and associate with Him what I have no knowledge of. I *will continue to* invite you to the Almighty, the Forgiver. ⁴³Undoubtedly what you call me to worship is unfit for worship here and in the Hereafter. We will all be returning to Allah, and the rebels will be the companions of the Fire. ⁴⁴Then you will soon remember what I am saying to you; I rest my case with Allah. Allah sees His servants." ⁴⁵Allah protected him from being harmed, but Pharaoh's people were overwhelmed by terrible sufferings.

The punishment of the grave

⁴⁶The Fire of Hell will be there[a] all the time[b] for them until Judgement Day, and *the angels are told*: "Enter Pharaoh's people into the severest punishment." ⁴⁷In the Fire they will quarrel with each other, and those who were oppressed will say to the arrogant leaders, "We were your followers, now save us from burning in the fire." ⁴⁸The arrogant will say, "We are all in it together; indeed Allah has decided among His servants." ⁴⁹Those in the Fire will say to the gatekeepers of Hell, "Ask your Lord to reduce our punishment *at least* for a day." ⁵⁰They will say, "Didn't your messengers come to you with clear signs?" They will answer, "Yes." They will reply, "So call them! The prayers of the disbelievers are ineffective." ⁵¹We support Our Messengers and those who believe both in this life and on the Day when witnesses will stand up *to testify* –

---

a   Literally, "The fire will be presented to them", refers to the punishment of the grave. It will be a "pit of fire or a garden of Paradise" (Hadith).

b   Literally, "evening and morning" in their graves.

يَوْمَ لَا يَنْفَعُ الظّٰلِمِيْنَ مَعْذِرَتُهُمْ وَلَهُمُ اللَّعْنَةُ

وَلَهُمْ سُوْءُ الدَّارِ ۞ وَلَقَدْ اٰتَيْنَا مُوسَى الْهُدَى

وَاَوْرَثْنَا بَنِيْ اِسْرَآءِيْلَ الْكِتٰبَ ۞ هُدًى وَّذِكْرَى

لِاُولِي الْاَلْبَابِ ۞ فَاصْبِرْ اِنَّ وَعْدَ اللّٰهِ حَقٌّ

وَّاسْتَغْفِرْ لِذَنْبِكَ وَسَبِّحْ بِحَمْدِ رَبِّكَ بِالْعَشِيِّ

وَالْاِبْكَارِ ۞ اِنَّ الَّذِيْنَ يُجَادِلُوْنَ فِيْ اٰيٰتِ اللّٰهِ بِغَيْرِ

سُلْطٰنٍ اَتٰهُمْ ۙ اِنْ فِيْ صُدُوْرِهِمْ اِلَّا كِبْرٌ مَّا هُمْ

بِبَالِغِيْهِ ۚ فَاسْتَعِذْ بِاللّٰهِ ؕ اِنَّهٗ هُوَ السَّمِيْعُ الْبَصِيْرُ ۞

لَخَلْقُ السَّمٰوٰتِ وَالْاَرْضِ اَكْبَرُ مِنْ خَلْقِ النَّاسِ وَلٰكِنَّ

اَكْثَرَ النَّاسِ لَا يَعْلَمُوْنَ ۞ وَمَا يَسْتَوِي الْاَعْمٰى

وَالْبَصِيْرُ ۙ وَالَّذِيْنَ اٰمَنُوْا وَعَمِلُوا الصّٰلِحٰتِ وَلَا

الْمُسِيْٓءُ ؕ قَلِيْلًا مَّا تَتَذَكَّرُوْنَ ۞ اِنَّ السَّاعَةَ لَاٰتِيَةٌ

لَّا رَيْبَ فِيْهَا وَلٰكِنَّ اَكْثَرَ النَّاسِ لَا يُؤْمِنُوْنَ ۞

وَقَالَ رَبُّكُمُ ادْعُوْنِيْٓ اَسْتَجِبْ لَكُمْ ؕ اِنَّ الَّذِيْنَ

يَسْتَكْبِرُوْنَ عَنْ عِبَادَتِيْ سَيَدْخُلُوْنَ جَهَنَّمَ دٰخِرِيْنَ ۞

اَللّٰهُ الَّذِيْ جَعَلَ لَكُمُ الَّيْلَ لِتَسْكُنُوْا فِيْهِ وَالنَّهَارَ

مُبْصِرًا ؕ اِنَّ اللّٰهَ لَذُوْ فَضْلٍ عَلَى النَّاسِ وَلٰكِنَّ اَكْثَرَ

النَّاسِ لَا يَشْكُرُوْنَ ۞ ذٰلِكُمُ اللّٰهُ رَبُّكُمْ خَالِقُ كُلِّ

شَيْءٍ ۖ لَّاۤ اِلٰهَ اِلَّا هُوَ ۖ فَاَنّٰى تُؤْفَكُوْنَ ۞ كَذٰلِكَ

يُؤْفَكُ الَّذِيْنَ كَانُوْا بِاٰيٰتِ اللّٰهِ يَجْحَدُوْنَ ۞ اَللّٰهُ

The final hour is about to happen, just around the corner. We think we'll live forever, but what a delusion that is. How can you take yourself out of this trap?

⁵²the Day when no excuses will benefit the wrongdoers – and they will be cursed and *given* a dreadful home.

The arrogant dispute truth and do not reflect

⁵³We gave Musa the guidance and made the Israelites heirs of the Book, ⁵⁴a guidance and a reminder for the understanding. ⁵⁵So be patient, since Allah's promise is true, seek forgiveness for the sins of your people, glorify and praise your Lord evening and morning. ⁵⁶Those who dispute the revelations of Allah without any authority given to them have only *a desire for* greatness in their hearts that they will never achieve. So seek Allah's protection, He is Hearing, Seeing. ⁵⁷The creation of the Heavens and the Earth is far greater than the creation of humans, but most people don't know. ⁵⁸The blind and the seeing are not the same; the righteous believers are not the same as the wicked. How little you reflect.

The Lord answers you

⁵⁹There is no doubt that the Final Hour will come, but most people don't believe. ⁶⁰Your Lord said: "Call on me and I will answer you." Those who are arrogant about worshipping Me will soon enter Hell disgraced. ⁶¹Allah made the night for you to rest in and the day for you to see *His bounties*; Allah is graciously generous to people, but most people are unthankful. ⁶²That is Allah your Lord, Creator of everything; there is no god but Him! So how then can you turn away from *Him*? ⁶³But that is how those who dispute Allah's Scriptures turn away.

اَلَّذِیۡ جَعَلَ لَکُمُ الۡاَرۡضَ قَرَارًا وَّالسَّمَآءَ بِنَآءً وَّ

صَوَّرَکُمۡ فَاَحۡسَنَ صُوَرَکُمۡ وَرَزَقَکُمۡ مِّنَ الطَّیِّبٰتِؕ

ذٰلِکُمُ اللّٰهُ رَبُّکُمۡ ۚ فَتَبٰرَکَ اللّٰهُ رَبُّ الۡعٰلَمِیۡنَ ۶۴ هُوَ

الۡحَیُّ لَاۤ اِلٰهَ اِلَّا هُوَ فَادۡعُوۡهُ مُخۡلِصِیۡنَ لَهُ الدِّیۡنَؕ

اَلۡحَمۡدُ لِلّٰهِ رَبِّ الۡعٰلَمِیۡنَ ۶۵ قُلۡ اِنِّیۡ نُهِیۡتُ اَنۡ اَعۡبُدَ

الَّذِیۡنَ تَدۡعُوۡنَ مِنۡ دُوۡنِ اللّٰهِ لَمَّا جَآءَنِیَ الۡبَیِّنٰتُ

مِنۡ رَّبِّیۡ ۫ وَاُمِرۡتُ اَنۡ اُسۡلِمَ لِرَبِّ الۡعٰلَمِیۡنَ ۶۶ هُوَ

The way to Allah is to call on Him sincerely, lovingly and patiently. He responds brilliantly.

الَّذِیۡ خَلَقَکُمۡ مِّنۡ تُرَابٍ ثُمَّ مِنۡ نُّطۡفَۃٍ ثُمَّ مِنۡ

عَلَقَۃٍ ثُمَّ یُخۡرِجُکُمۡ طِفۡلًا ثُمَّ لِتَبۡلُغُوۡۤا اَشُدَّکُمۡ

ثُمَّ لِتَکُوۡنُوۡا شُیُوۡخًا ۚ وَمِنۡکُمۡ مَّنۡ یُّتَوَفّٰی مِنۡ قَبۡلُ

وَلِتَبۡلُغُوۡۤا اَجَلًا مُّسَمًّی وَّلَعَلَّکُمۡ تَعۡقِلُوۡنَ ۶۷ هُوَ الَّذِیۡ

یُحۡیٖ وَیُمِیۡتُ ۚ فَاِذَا قَضٰۤی اَمۡرًا فَاِنَّمَا یَقُوۡلُ لَهٗ

کُنۡ فَیَکُوۡنُ ۶۸ اَلَمۡ تَرَ اِلَی الَّذِیۡنَ یُجَادِلُوۡنَ فِیۡۤ

اٰیٰتِ اللّٰهِؕ اَنّٰی یُصۡرَفُوۡنَ ۶۹ الَّذِیۡنَ کَذَّبُوۡا بِالۡکِتٰبِ

وَبِمَاۤ اَرۡسَلۡنَا بِهٖ رُسُلَنَا ۟ فَسَوۡفَ یَعۡلَمُوۡنَ ۷۰

اِذِ الۡاَغۡلٰلُ فِیۡۤ اَعۡنَاقِهِمۡ وَالسَّلٰسِلُؕ یُسۡحَبُوۡنَ ۷۱ فِی

الۡحَمِیۡمِ ۬ ثُمَّ فِی النَّارِ یُسۡجَرُوۡنَ ۷۲ ثُمَّ قِیۡلَ لَهُمۡ

اَیۡنَ مَا کُنۡتُمۡ تُشۡرِکُوۡنَ ۷۳ مِنۡ دُوۡنِ اللّٰهِؕ قَالُوۡا

ضَلُّوۡا عَنَّا بَلۡ لَّمۡ نَکُنۡ نَّدۡعُوۡا مِنۡ قَبۡلُ شَیۡئًاؕ

کَذٰلِکَ یُضِلُّ اللّٰهُ الۡکٰفِرِیۡنَ ۷۴ ذٰلِکُمۡ بِمَا کُنۡتُمۡ

ع
۸
۱۲

Some favours of Allah

⁶⁴Allah made the Earth for you to live on, and the sky a roof. He fashioned you in the best forms and gave you enjoyable provision. That is Allah your Lord! Blessed is Allah, the Lord of the worlds. ⁶⁵He is the Living; there is no god but Him, so worship Him sincerely, wholly committed. All praises are for Allah, the Lord of the worlds. ⁶⁶Say: "I am forbidden to worship those you pray to beside Allah, since clear signs have come to me from My Lord, and I have been commanded to submit to the Lord of the worlds."

He says: "Be," and it comes into existence

⁶⁷He created you from dust, then from semen, then from a clot of blood and then He brought you out as a baby. Then you reached maturity, eventually becoming old – though some of you will die earlier – so you reach a fixed time so you might understand. ⁶⁸He gives life and death, and when He decides an affair He says to it: "Be," and it comes *into existence.*

The disgrace and torment of disbelievers

⁶⁹Haven't you seen those who dispute Allah's revelations – how they turn away? ⁷⁰They don't believe the Book that We sent with Our Messengers – they will know *the consequences.* ⁷¹With iron collars around their necks and chains *on their feet* they will be dragged ⁷²into boiling water, then burned in the Fire. ⁷³They will be asked: "Where are those you associated with ⁷⁴beside Allah?" They will say, "They have deserted us, those we worshipped in the past were nothing." That is how Allah lets the disbelievers go astray.

تَفْرَحُوْنَ فِي الْاَرْضِ بِغَيْرِ الْحَقِّ وَبِمَا كُنْتُمْ

تَمْرَحُوْنَ ۝ اُدْخُلُوْا اَبْوَابَ جَهَنَّمَ خٰلِدِيْنَ فِيْهَا ۚ

فَبِئْسَ مَثْوَى الْمُتَكَبِّرِيْنَ ۝ فَاصْبِرْ اِنَّ وَعْدَ

اللّٰهِ حَقٌّ ۚ فَاِمَّا نُرِيَنَّكَ بَعْضَ الَّذِيْ نَعِدُهُمْ

اَوْ نَتَوَفَّيَنَّكَ فَاِلَيْنَا يُرْجَعُوْنَ ۝ وَلَقَدْ اَرْسَلْنَا

رُسُلًا مِّنْ قَبْلِكَ مِنْهُمْ مَّنْ قَصَصْنَا عَلَيْكَ

وَمِنْهُمْ مَّنْ لَّمْ نَقْصُصْ عَلَيْكَ ؕ وَمَا كَانَ لِرَسُوْلٍ

اَنْ يَّاْتِيَ بِاٰيَةٍ اِلَّا بِاِذْنِ اللّٰهِ ۚ فَاِذَا جَاءَ اَمْرُ

اللّٰهِ قُضِيَ بِالْحَقِّ وَخَسِرَ هُنَالِكَ الْمُبْطِلُوْنَ ۝

اَللّٰهُ الَّذِيْ جَعَلَ لَكُمُ الْاَنْعَامَ لِتَرْكَبُوْا مِنْهَا وَ

مِنْهَا تَاْكُلُوْنَ ۝ وَلَكُمْ فِيْهَا مَنَافِعُ وَلِتَبْلُغُوْا

عَلَيْهَا حَاجَةً فِيْ صُدُوْرِكُمْ وَعَلَيْهَا وَعَلَى الْفُلْكِ

تُحْمَلُوْنَ ۝ وَيُرِيْكُمْ اٰيٰتِهٖ ۗ فَاَيَّ اٰيٰتِ اللّٰهِ

تُنْكِرُوْنَ ۝ اَفَلَمْ يَسِيْرُوْا فِي الْاَرْضِ فَيَنْظُرُوْا

كَيْفَ كَانَ عَاقِبَةُ الَّذِيْنَ مِنْ قَبْلِهِمْ ؕ كَانُوْا اَكْثَرَ

مِنْهُمْ وَاَشَدَّ قُوَّةً وَّاٰثَارًا فِي الْاَرْضِ فَمَا اَغْنٰى

عَنْهُمْ مَّا كَانُوْا يَكْسِبُوْنَ ۝ فَلَمَّا جَاءَتْهُمْ

رُسُلُهُمْ بِالْبَيِّنٰتِ فَرِحُوْا بِمَا عِنْدَهُمْ مِّنَ الْعِلْمِ

وَحَاقَ بِهِمْ مَّا كَانُوْا بِهٖ يَسْتَهْزِءُوْنَ ۝ فَلَمَّا رَاَوْا

بَاْسَنَا قَالُوْا اٰمَنَّا بِاللّٰهِ وَحْدَهٗ وَكَفَرْنَا بِمَا كُنَّا

Faith is to acknowledge Allah's gifts. Just thank Him for all of His favours, large or small.

٨
ع
١٣

947

⁷⁵This is all because you were happy with falsehood in the Earth and lived merrily. ⁷⁶Enter through the gates of Hell to stay there forever, a terrible place for the arrogant. ⁷⁷So be patient; Allah's promise is true. Whether We let you see some of the punishment promised to them or We cause you to die *first* it does not matter; finally, they will be returned to Us.

Some more favours of Allah
⁷⁸We sent messengers before you; some We told you about and others We haven't *yet* told you about. A messenger only brings miracles by Allah's permission. When Allah's command comes on Judgement Day justice will be done; there the followers of falsehood will be losers. ⁷⁹Allah made livestock for you to ride on and to eat from, ⁸⁰there are other benefits too for you in them. You can get to any destination you wish riding on them, and ships also carry you. ⁸¹He shows you His signs, so which of Allah's signs will you deny?

Disbelievers' belief will not benefit them
⁸²Haven't they travelled about the land and seen the outcome of the deniers of past times? They were greater in numbers, mightier than them and *moreover* left behind bigger remains on the land, yet all they accomplished will not benefit. ⁸³So when Our messengers came to them with clear signs, they smugly continued with what little they knew, and were *finally* engulfed by the punishment they mocked. ⁸⁴So when they saw Our punishment they declared, "We believe in Allah; the One and we reject any partner we associated with Him." ⁸⁵Their belief won't benefit them now, since they have seen Our punishment. This was the Way of Allah among His servants in the past, the disbelievers will be *utter* losers there.

بِهٖ مُشْرِكِيْنَ ۝ فَلَمْ يَكُ يَنْفَعُهُمْ اِيْمَانُهُمْ لَمَّا رَاَوْا بَاْسَنَا ط سُنَّتَ اللّٰهِ الَّتِيْ قَدْ خَلَتْ فِيْ عِبَادِهٖ ج وَخَسِرَ هُنَالِكَ الْكٰفِرُوْنَ ۝

41. Surat Ha Meem Sajdah

Ha Meem Prostration

This surat was revealed in the middle Makkan period, a few days after Hamza, the uncle of the Messenger ﷺ, accepted Islam. Persecution against the Messenger ﷺ and his small band of followers was at its worst. The acceptance of Islam by this prominent young Qurayshi substantially strengthened the Muslims. After this momentous conversion, the Quraysh held a meeting about the growing threat from Islam. Utbah ibn Rabiah, a wealthy leader, took the responsibility of 'striking a deal' with the Messenger ﷺ, so he went and said to him:

> My nephew ... you have brought to your people something of grave concern whereby you have created a rift between the community ... here is a proposal, see if you can accept it; if it is wealth that you seek then we will put together a fortune for you ... if it is honour you seek we will make you our overlord ... and if it is that you cannot rid yourself of the spirit that appears to you we will find the best physician until you are cured (Lings).

The Prophet ﷺ replied: "Father of Walid, now listen to me," and began reciting this surat. Utbah listened attentively; he was captivated by the words of the Quran. Utbah put his finger on his mouth and requested the Prophet ﷺ to stop reciting when the Prophet ﷺ came to the line: "If they turn away say, 'I warned you of a thunderbolt like the thunderbolt of Ad and Thamud'" (13). Utbah returned to the group and told them: "I've heard some words the like of which I have never heard before. It is not poetry, by God, neither is it a sorcery nor a soothsaying ... come not between this man and what he is about, but let him be."

The central theme of the surat is the fundamental doctrines of Islam: *Tawhid*, *Risalah* and *Akhirah*. The surat opens with an introduction to the Quran: "*This is* a revelation from the Kind, the Caring; a book whose verses are clearly explained, an Arabic Quran for a people who have knowledge; it gives good news and warnings" (2–4). It then explains why the disbelievers are unable to listen and benefit from the Quran: they have locked minds and are intolerant. To open their mind, they are told to look at the wonderful signs of Allah's Majesty in nature. The power, wisdom, kindness, providence, organisation and management evident in the vast universe is a testimony that this is no drama or play of an imagined god, but the handiwork of the Almighty and the Knower.

As in other surats, a clear warning is given to the Quraysh for their rudeness and rejection of the truth by telling the stories of the past nations that behaved like them. The surat refutes recurrent objections against *Tawhid*, the Oneness of Allah, such as questions about how dead bones can be raised to life, and how a man can be Allah's messenger. The surat warns the disbelievers: their attitude to the Messenger ﷺ is a dangerous one, and the consequences will be dreadful. Even the ears, eyes and skin will bear witness against them in the Hereafter.

The early Makkan Surats are conversational and speak directly to the listeners, each listener is asked to think, reflect and interrogate himself, for example it poses questions like, "Say: "Consider *this*," or "Haven't you seen" or "Haven't you heard". This is a powerful teaching style where facts and figures aren't being taught but critical thinking is being encouraged and awareness of the Reality is being raised.

The Quraysh were prompted by the Jews to ask, "What is the need for a new revelation when the Quran already accepts the Psalms and the Gospels as divine revelations?" The Quran answered: "We gave Musa the Book, but disagreement arose about it too" (45). The Messenger ﷺ is reassured, he has a lofty, pure, beneficial, life-changing message, and if the ignorant fail to listen, then his response should be dignified, gentle and forgiving.

بِسْمِ اللهِ الرَّحْمٰنِ الرَّحِيْمِ

حٰمٓ ۝ تَنْزِيْلٌ مِّنَ الرَّحْمٰنِ الرَّحِيْمِ ۝ كِتٰبٌ

فُصِّلَتْ اٰيٰتُهٗ قُرْاٰنًا عَرَبِيًّا لِّقَوْمٍ يَّعْلَمُوْنَ ۝

بَشِيْرًا وَّ نَذِيْرًا ۚ فَاَعْرَضَ اَكْثَرُهُمْ فَهُمْ لَا

يَسْمَعُوْنَ ۝ وَ قَالُوْا قُلُوْبُنَا فِيْٓ اَكِنَّةٍ مِّمَّا تَدْعُوْنَآ

اِلَيْهِ وَ فِيْٓ اٰذَانِنَا وَقْرٌ وَّ مِنْۢ بَيْنِنَا وَ بَيْنِكَ

حِجَابٌ فَاعْمَلْ اِنَّنَا عٰمِلُوْنَ ۝ قُلْ اِنَّمَآ اَنَا

بَشَرٌ مِّثْلُكُمْ يُوْحٰٓى اِلَيَّ اَنَّمَآ اِلٰهُكُمْ اِلٰهٌ وَّاحِدٌ

فَاسْتَقِيْمُوْٓا اِلَيْهِ وَاسْتَغْفِرُوْهُ ۭ وَ وَيْلٌ لِّلْمُشْرِكِيْنَ ۝

الَّذِيْنَ لَا يُؤْتُوْنَ الزَّكٰوةَ وَ هُمْ بِالْاٰخِرَةِ هُمْ

كٰفِرُوْنَ ۝ اِنَّ الَّذِيْنَ اٰمَنُوْا وَعَمِلُوا الصّٰلِحٰتِ

لَهُمْ اَجْرٌ غَيْرُ مَمْنُوْنٍ ۝ قُلْ اَئِنَّكُمْ لَتَكْفُرُوْنَ

بِالَّذِيْ خَلَقَ الْاَرْضَ فِيْ يَوْمَيْنِ وَ تَجْعَلُوْنَ لَهٗٓ

اَنْدَادًا ۭ ذٰلِكَ رَبُّ الْعٰلَمِيْنَ ۝ وَجَعَلَ فِيْهَا

رَوَاسِيَ مِنْ فَوْقِهَا وَ بٰرَكَ فِيْهَا وَ قَدَّرَ فِيْهَآ

اَقْوَاتَهَا فِيْٓ اَرْبَعَةِ اَيَّامٍ ۭ سَوَآءً لِّلسَّآئِلِيْنَ ۝

ثُمَّ اسْتَوٰٓى اِلَى السَّمَآءِ وَ هِيَ دُخَانٌ فَقَالَ لَهَا

وَ لِلْاَرْضِ ائْتِيَا طَوْعًا اَوْ كَرْهًا ۭ قَالَتَآ اَتَيْنَا

طَآئِعِيْنَ ۝ فَقَضٰهُنَّ سَبْعَ سَمٰوٰتٍ فِيْ يَوْمَيْنِ

The vast, expanding universe of billions of stars spread over trillions of kilometres is an awesome creation of the Almighty.

In the name of Allah, the Kind, the Caring.

The Prophet ﷺ can't be accused of being power-hungry

¹*Ha Meem.* ²*This is* a Revelation from the Kind, the Caring; ³a Book whose verses are clearly explained, an Arabic Quran for people who know. ⁴It gives good news and warnings, though most of them will turn away and won't listen. ⁵They say, "Our hearts are hardy to what you invite us to; we are hard of hearing and there is a barrier between us and you, therefore do as you like, and we shall do what we like." ⁶Say: "I am a human like you; except that I receive revelation: your Lord is One God, so take the straight path to Him and seek forgiveness. Woe to the idolaters. ⁷Those who don't give charity and deny the Hereafter. ⁸But the believers who are righteous will have a never-ending reward."

The stages of the creation of the Heavens and the Earth

⁹Say: "Do you deny the one Who created the Earth in two days? You have set up rivals to the Lord of the worlds." ¹⁰He made the mountains, blessed it, and in four days determined its provisions for seekers.^a ¹¹Then He focused on the sky and it was smoke^b so He said to it and the Earth: "Come *into existence* whether willingly or unwillingly." They replied, "We shall come willingly."

---

^a Literally, "in front and behind them", but implies "all things everywhere".

^b Provisions from mountains include: gold and precious metals, minerals, marble, coal, and much more.

وَ اَوْحٰى فِىْ كُلِّ سَمَآءٍ اَمْرَهَاطْ وَ زَيَّنَّا السَّمَآءَ
الدُّنْيَا بِمَصَابِيْحَ ۚۙ وَحِفْظًاطْ ذٰلِكَ تَقْدِيْرُ الْعَزِيْزِ
الْعَلِيْمِ ۝ فَاِنْ اَعْرَضُوْا فَقُلْ اَنْذَرْتُكُمْ صٰعِقَةً
مِّثْلَ صٰعِقَةِ عَادٍ وَّثَمُوْدَ ۝ اِذْ جَآءَتْهُمُ الرُّسُلُ
مِنْۢ بَيْنِ اَيْدِيْهِمْ وَ مِنْ خَلْفِهِمْ اَلَّا تَعْبُدُوْٓا
اِلَّا اللّٰهَطْ قَالُوْا لَوْ شَآءَ رَبُّنَا لَاَنْزَلَ مَلٰٓئِكَةً
فَاِنَّا بِمَآ اُرْسِلْتُمْ بِهٖ كٰفِرُوْنَ ۝ فَاَمَّا عَادٌ
فَاسْتَكْبَرُوْا فِى الْاَرْضِ بِغَيْرِ الْحَقِّ وَ قَالُوْا
مَنْ اَشَدُّ مِنَّا قُوَّةًطْ اَوَلَمْ يَرَوْا اَنَّ اللّٰهَ
الَّذِىْ خَلَقَهُمْ هُوَ اَشَدُّ مِنْهُمْ قُوَّةًطْ وَكَانُوْا
بِاٰيٰتِنَا يَجْحَدُوْنَ ۝ فَاَرْسَلْنَا عَلَيْهِمْ رِيْحًا صَرْصَرًا
فِىْٓ اَيَّامٍ نَّحِسَاتٍ لِّنُذِيْقَهُمْ عَذَابَ الْخِزْىِ فِى
الْحَيٰوةِ الدُّنْيَاطْ وَلَعَذَابُ الْاٰخِرَةِ اَخْزٰى وَهُمْ
لَا يُنْصَرُوْنَ ۝ وَ اَمَّا ثَمُوْدُ فَهَدَيْنٰهُمْ فَاسْتَحَبُّوا
الْعَمٰى عَلَى الْهُدٰى فَاَخَذَتْهُمْ صٰعِقَةُ الْعَذَابِ
الْهُوْنِ بِمَا كَانُوْا يَكْسِبُوْنَ ۚ وَنَجَّيْنَا الَّذِيْنَ اٰمَنُوْا
وَ كَانُوْا يَتَّقُوْنَ ۝ وَيَوْمَ يُحْشَرُ اَعْدَآءُ اللّٰهِ اِلَى
النَّارِ فَهُمْ يُوْزَعُوْنَ ۝ حَتّٰٓى اِذَا مَا جَآءُوْهَا شَهِدَ
عَلَيْهِمْ سَمْعُهُمْ وَاَبْصَارُهُمْ وَجُلُوْدُهُمْ بِمَا كَانُوْا
يَعْمَلُوْنَ ۝ وَقَالُوْا لِجُلُوْدِهِمْ لِمَ شَهِدْتُّمْ عَلَيْنَاط

People who deny the truth of a Creator are severely deluded. How can you follow such ignorant people?

٢ ع
١٦

953

[12] In two days He formed them into seven skies, and to each sky He assigned its functions. We decorated the nearest sky with stars and made it safe. That's the plan[a] of the Almighty, the All-Knowing.

Divine punishment: outcome of disbelief and arrogance

[13] If they turn away say: "I warned you of a thunderbolt like the thunderbolt of Ad and Thamud." [14] When their messengers came to them from all sides *saying*,[b] "Worship Allah alone," they replied, "Had Our Lord so wanted He would have sent angels; we refuse to accept what you have been sent with." [15] The *people of* Ad behaved arrogantly and unjustly on the land, and boasted, "Who is stronger than us?" Didn't they realise Allah created them, He is stronger than them? But they still rejected Our messages. [16] So, over a few ill-fated days We sent a violent roaring wind to give them a taste of the shocking punishment in this life and an even more shameful one in the Hereafter, and they won't be helped. [17] Similarly, We gave *the people of* Thamud guidance, but they preferred blindness instead of guidance, so they were struck by a thunderbolt of a shocking punishment for what they did. [18] But, We saved the obedient believers.

Ears, eyes and skin will give evidence

[19] The Day all enemies of Allah are gathered in Hell, they will be divided into groups, and [20] when they reach it, their ears, eyes and skins will testify against them for their misdeeds. [21] They will ask their skins, "Why did you testify against us?" They will reply, "Allah is the One Who taught everything to speak and has taught us to speak too, and He created you the first time and to Him you will be returned."

---

[a] *Taqdeer* is precise calculation, accurate measurement and strategic planning.

[b] It literally means, "from the front and the behind", an idiom employed for persuading with powerful arguments from all sides.

قَالُوْۤا اَنْطَقَنَا اللهُ الَّذِیْۤ اَنْطَقَ كُلَّ شَیْءٍ وَّهُوَ خَلَقَكُمْ اَوَّلَ مَرَّةٍ وَّاِلَیْهِ تُرْجَعُوْنَ ۲۱ وَمَا كُنْتُمْ تَسْتَتِرُوْنَ اَنْ یَّشْهَدَ عَلَیْكُمْ سَمْعُكُمْ وَلَاۤ اَبْصَارُكُمْ وَلَا جُلُوْدُكُمْ وَلٰكِنْ ظَنَنْتُمْ اَنَّ اللهَ لَا یَعْلَمُ كَثِیْرًا مِّمَّا تَعْمَلُوْنَ ۲۲ وَذٰلِكُمْ ظَنُّكُمُ الَّذِیْ ظَنَنْتُمْ بِرَبِّكُمْ اَرْدٰىكُمْ فَاَصْبَحْتُمْ مِّنَ الْخٰسِرِیْنَ ۲۳ فَاِنْ یَّصْبِرُوْا فَالنَّارُ مَثْوًى لَّهُمْ ۚ وَاِنْ یَّسْتَعْتِبُوْا فَمَا هُمْ مِّنَ الْمُعْتَبِیْنَ ۲۴ وَقَیَّضْنَا لَهُمْ قُرَنَآءَ فَزَیَّنُوْا لَهُمْ مَّا بَیْنَ اَیْدِیْهِمْ وَمَا خَلْفَهُمْ وَحَقَّ عَلَیْهِمُ الْقَوْلُ فِیْۤ اُمَمٍ قَدْ خَلَتْ مِنْ قَبْلِهِمْ مِّنَ الْجِنِّ وَالْاِنْسِ ۚ اِنَّهُمْ كَانُوْا خٰسِرِیْنَ ۲۵ وَقَالَ الَّذِیْنَ كَفَرُوْا لَا تَسْمَعُوْا لِهٰذَا الْقُرْاٰنِ وَالْغَوْا فِیْهِ لَعَلَّكُمْ تَغْلِبُوْنَ ۲۶ فَلَنُذِیْقَنَّ الَّذِیْنَ كَفَرُوْا عَذَابًا شَدِیْدًا ۙ وَّلَنَجْزِیَنَّهُمْ اَسْوَاَ الَّذِیْ كَانُوْا یَعْمَلُوْنَ ۲۷ ذٰلِكَ جَزَآءُ اَعْدَآءِ اللهِ النَّارُ ۚ لَهُمْ فِیْهَا دَارُ الْخُلْدِ ۚ جَزَآءًۢ بِمَا كَانُوْا بِاٰیٰتِنَا یَجْحَدُوْنَ ۲۸ وَقَالَ الَّذِیْنَ كَفَرُوْا رَبَّنَاۤ اَرِنَا الَّذَیْنِ اَضَلّٰنَا مِنَ الْجِنِّ وَالْاِنْسِ نَجْعَلْهُمَا تَحْتَ اَقْدَامِنَا لِیَكُوْنَا مِنَ الْاَسْفَلِیْنَ ۲۹ اِنَّ الَّذِیْنَ قَالُوْا رَبُّنَا اللهُ ثُمَّ اسْتَقَامُوْا تَتَنَزَّلُ عَلَیْهِمُ الْمَلٰٓئِكَةُ

Satan whispers into people's ears and the world appears attractive and delightful to their eyes and their ego loves it all.

²²You didn't try to hide your evil deeds from your ears, your eyes and your skins. But you thought that Allah didn't know what you did. ²³That's what you imagined about your Lord and it ruined you, so you became losers. ²⁴Even if they are patient now, the Fire will be their home. No matter how much forgiveness they seek, they won't be pardoned.

Satan misleads by making things seem gratifying

²⁵We appointed companions for them that make things seem attractive for them everywhere.ᵃ Sentence was passed against them, the jinns and people before them: "They will be the losers". ²⁶The disbelievers shouted, "Don't listen to this Quran; *you can* drown it out with noisy laughter so you would prevail." ²⁷We shall give the disbelievers a taste of severe punishment and repay them for the worst deed they did. ²⁸A payback for the enemies of Allah: Hell, where they will be forever, a reward for rejecting Our messages! ²⁹The disbelievers will say, "Our Lord, show the jinn and humans who misguided us, so we may crush them under our feet to make them lowest of the low."

The angels motivate the steadfast

³⁰People who say, "Allah is Our Lord," and are steadfast are visited *and motivated* by the angels: "Don't fear nor be sad, be happy with the news of promised Paradise.

ᵃ Literally, "in front and behind them", but implies "all things everywhere".

اَلَّا تَخَافُوْا وَلَا تَحْزَنُوْا وَاَبْشِرُوْا بِالْجَنَّةِ الَّتِيْ
كُنْتُمْ تُوْعَدُوْنَ ۟ ﴿٣٠﴾ نَحْنُ اَوْلِيٰٓؤُكُمْ فِي الْحَيٰوةِ الدُّنْيَا
وَفِي الْاٰخِرَةِ ۚ وَلَكُمْ فِيْهَا مَا تَشْتَهِيْۤ اَنْفُسُكُمْ وَلَكُمْ
فِيْهَا مَا تَدَّعُوْنَ ﴿٣١﴾ نُزُلًا مِّنْ غَفُوْرٍ رَّحِيْمٍ ﴿٣٢﴾
وَمَنْ اَحْسَنُ قَوْلًا مِّمَّنْ دَعَاۤ اِلَى اللّٰهِ وَعَمِلَ
صَالِحًا وَّقَالَ اِنَّنِيْ مِنَ الْمُسْلِمِيْنَ ﴿٣٣﴾ وَلَا تَسْتَوِى
الْحَسَنَةُ وَلَا السَّيِّئَةُ ۭ اِدْفَعْ بِالَّتِيْ هِيَ اَحْسَنُ
فَاِذَا الَّذِيْ بَيْنَكَ وَبَيْنَهٗ عَدَاوَةٌ كَاَنَّهٗ وَلِيٌّ
حَمِيْمٌ ﴿٣٤﴾ وَمَا يُلَقّٰىهَاۤ اِلَّا الَّذِيْنَ صَبَرُوْا ۚ وَمَا
يُلَقّٰىهَاۤ اِلَّا ذُوْ حَظٍّ عَظِيْمٍ ﴿٣٥﴾ وَاِمَّا يَنْزَغَنَّكَ مِنَ
الشَّيْطٰنِ نَزْغٌ فَاسْتَعِذْ بِاللّٰهِ ۭ اِنَّهٗ هُوَ السَّمِيْعُ
الْعَلِيْمُ ﴿٣٦﴾ وَمِنْ اٰيٰتِهِ الَّيْلُ وَالنَّهَارُ وَالشَّمْسُ وَ
الْقَمَرُ ۭ لَا تَسْجُدُوْا لِلشَّمْسِ وَلَا لِلْقَمَرِ وَاسْجُدُوْا لِلّٰهِ
الَّذِيْ خَلَقَهُنَّ اِنْ كُنْتُمْ اِيَّاهُ تَعْبُدُوْنَ ﴿٣٧﴾ فَاِنِ
اسْتَكْبَرُوْا فَالَّذِيْنَ عِنْدَ رَبِّكَ يُسَبِّحُوْنَ لَهٗ
بِالَّيْلِ وَالنَّهَارِ وَهُمْ لَا يَسْـَٔمُوْنَ ۩ ﴿٣٨﴾ وَمِنْ اٰيٰتِهٖۤ
اَنَّكَ تَرَى الْاَرْضَ خَاشِعَةً فَاِذَاۤ اَنْزَلْنَا عَلَيْهَا
الْمَاۤءَ اهْتَزَّتْ وَرَبَتْ ۭ اِنَّ الَّذِيْۤ اَحْيَاهَا لَمُحْيِ
الْمَوْتٰى ۭ اِنَّهٗ عَلٰى كُلِّ شَيْءٍ قَدِيْرٌ ﴿٣٩﴾ اِنَّ الَّذِيْنَ
يُلْحِدُوْنَ فِيْۤ اٰيٰتِنَا لَا يَخْفَوْنَ عَلَيْنَا ۭ اَفَمَنْ يُّلْقٰى

Look at the true believers, who boldly claim their faith devoutly. Do you?

³¹ We are your friends in this life and the Hereafter, and you will have whatever your souls want in Paradise: every wish fulfilled. ³² A warm hospitality from the Forgiver, the Caring Lord."

The preachers are polite, approachable

³³ Whose speech can be better than the one who calls to Allah and acts righteously and openly says: "I am a Muslim." ³⁴ Good and evil aren't the same; counter evil with goodness, and if there was *any* enmity between you and the other, he will become a dearest friend. ³⁵ Only the patient are like this; they are fortunate. ³⁶ If Satan tempts you, seek Allah's protection. He is the Listener, the Knower.

Rain gives dry land life; Allah gives the dead life

³⁷ The night and the day, the sun and the moon are among His signs. Don't worship the sun or the moon; worship Allah their Creator, if you *truly* worship Him. ³⁸ If they are arrogant about worshipping Allah, so what, there are many in His service who glorify Him day and night, they never get tired. ³⁹ You will see among His signs a dry, barren landᵃ; when We send rain it swells and plants grow there – the One Who gives life to it will bring the dead to life. He has power over all things. ⁴⁰ Those who reject Our verses aren't hidden from Us. So how can the one thrown in the Fire be better than the one who comes safely through on Judgement Day? Do what you like; He sees what you do.

ᵃ *Khashiatan* literally means calm and serene, a metaphor applied to barren land.

فِی النَّارِ خَیرٌ اَم مَّن یَّاتِیٓ اٰمِنًا یَّومَ القِیٰمَۃِ ط

اِعمَلُوا مَا شِئتُم اِنَّهٗ بِمَا تَعمَلُونَ بَصِیرٌ ۴۰ اِنَّ

الَّذِینَ کَفَرُوا بِالذِّکرِ لَمَّا جَآءَهُم ۚ وَاِنَّهٗ لَکِتٰبٌ

عَزِیزٌ ۴۱ لَّا یَاتِیهِ البَاطِلُ مِن بَینِ یَدَیهِ وَلَا

مِن خَلفِهٖ ط تَنزِیلٌ مِّن حَکِیمٍ حَمِیدٍ ۴۲ مَا یُقَالُ

لَکَ اِلَّا مَا قَد قِیلَ لِلرُّسُلِ مِن قَبلِکَ ط اِنَّ

رَبَّکَ لَذُو مَغفِرَۃٍ وَّذُو عِقَابٍ اَلِیمٍ ۴۳ وَلَو جَعَلنٰهُ

قُراٰنًا اَعجَمِیًّا لَّقَالُوا لَولَا فُصِّلَت اٰیٰتُهٗ ط ءَ اَعجَمِیٌّ

Any good we do is for ourselves, not for Allah. We benefit from it.

وَّعَرَبِیٌّ ط قُل هُوَ لِلَّذِینَ اٰمَنُوا هُدًی وَّشِفَآءٌ ط

وَالَّذِینَ لَا یُؤمِنُونَ فِیٓ اٰذَانِهِم وَقرٌ وَّهُوَ عَلَیهِم

عَمًی ط اُولٰٓئِکَ یُنَادَونَ مِن مَّکَانٍ بَعِیدٍ ۴۴

وَلَقَد اٰتَینَا مُوسَی الکِتٰبَ فَاختُلِفَ فِیهِ ط وَلَولَا

کَلِمَۃٌ سَبَقَت مِن رَّبِّکَ لَقُضِیَ بَینَهُم ط وَاِنَّهُم

لَفِی شَکٍّ مِّنهُ مُرِیبٍ ۴۵ مَن عَمِلَ صَالِحًا فَلِنَفسِهٖ

وَمَن اَسَآءَ فَعَلَیهَا ط وَمَا رَبُّکَ بِظَلَّامٍ لِّلعَبِیدِ ۴۶

اِلَیهِ یُرَدُّ عِلمُ السَّاعَۃِ ط وَمَا تَخرُجُ مِن ثَمَرٰتٍ

مِّن اَکمَامِهَا وَمَا تَحمِلُ مِن اُنثٰی وَلَا تَضَعُ اِلَّا

بِعِلمِهٖ ط وَیَومَ یُنَادِیهِم اَینَ شُرَکَآءِی ۙ قَالُوٓا

اٰذَنّٰکَ ۙ مَا مِنَّا مِن شَهِیدٍ ۴۷ وَضَلَّ عَنهُم

مَّا کَانُوا یَدعُونَ مِن قَبلُ وَظَنُّوا مَا لَهُم مِّن

The Quran: the protected, a guidance and a healing

⁴¹ Those who deny the Quran when it comes to them *do not realise* that it is a honourable book^a ⁴² that cannot be influenced by falsehood from any angle,^b a revelation from the Wise, the Praiseworthy. ⁴³ Messenger, what is said to you was said to the messengers before you; Your Lord is the Forgiver and the Lord of a painful torment. ⁴⁴ Had We written the Quran in a foreign language they would have complained: "If only its verses were made clear." What, in a foreign language yet he is an Arab: "It is a guidance and a healing for those who believe, but those who don't believe are hard of hearing and blind to it, as *though* they are being called from far away." ⁴⁵ We gave Musa the Book, but disagreement arose about it too. If Your Lord's sentence had not been passed against them, their disagreements would have been settled. They are doubtful and distrustful.

Nothing is hidden from Allah

⁴⁶ Whoever does good does so for himself, and whoever does evil harms himself. Your Lord is not unjust to His servants. ⁴⁷ Allah alone has the knowledge of the Final Hour: no fruit comes out of its cover, neither a female conceives nor gives birth except with His knowledge. On that Day He will ask them: "Where are my partners?" They will say, "We declare *before* You we aren't their witness." ⁴⁸ Those they worshipped before will have vanished, and they will know there is no escape.

---

a   *Kitabun aziz* can also mean indomitable and unassailable, sound and irrefutable.
b   *Mimbain yadihe wa min khalfihi* means "from front and behind", an idiom for "from all angles".

مَّحِيصٍ ۞ لَا يَسْـَٔمُ الْإِنْسَانُ مِنْ دُعَاءِ الْخَيْرِ ۖ

وَإِنْ مَّسَّهُ الشَّرُّ فَيَـُٔوْسٌ قَنُوْطٌ ۞ وَلَئِنْ أَذَقْنٰهُ

رَحْمَةً مِّنَّا مِنْۢ بَعْدِ ضَرَّآءَ مَسَّتْهُ لَيَقُوْلَنَّ هٰذَا

لِىْ ۙ وَمَآ أَظُنُّ السَّاعَةَ قَآئِمَةً ۙ وَّلَئِنْ رُّجِعْتُ إِلٰى

رَبِّيْٓ إِنَّ لِيْ عِنْدَهٗ لَلْحُسْنٰى ۚ فَلَنُنَبِّئَنَّ الَّذِيْنَ

كَفَرُوْا بِمَا عَمِلُوْا ۖ وَلَنُذِيْقَنَّهُمْ مِّنْ عَذَابٍ غَلِيْظٍ ۞

وَإِذَآ أَنْعَمْنَا عَلَى الْإِنْسَانِ أَعْرَضَ وَنَاٰ بِجَانِبِهٖ ۚ

وَإِذَا مَسَّهُ الشَّرُّ فَذُوْ دُعَاءٍ عَرِيْضٍ ۞ قُلْ

أَرَءَيْتُمْ إِنْ كَانَ مِنْ عِنْدِ اللّٰهِ ثُمَّ كَفَرْتُمْ

بِهٖ مَنْ أَضَلُّ مِمَّنْ هُوَ فِيْ شِقَاقٍۭ بَعِيْدٍ ۞

سَنُرِيْهِمْ اٰيٰتِنَا فِى الْاٰفَاقِ وَفِيْٓ أَنْفُسِهِمْ حَتّٰى

يَتَبَيَّنَ لَهُمْ أَنَّهُ الْحَقُّ ۗ أَوَلَمْ يَكْفِ بِرَبِّكَ أَنَّهٗ

عَلٰى كُلِّ شَيْءٍ شَهِيْدٌ ۞ أَلَآ إِنَّهُمْ فِيْ مِرْيَةٍ

مِّنْ لِّقَآءِ رَبِّهِمْ ۗ أَلَآ إِنَّهٗ بِكُلِّ شَيْءٍ مُّحِيْطٌ ۞

The greatness and the wonder of Allah's marvellous creation is in front of us: Nanotechnology, human intelligence; all show how magnificent a creator Allah is!

ع ١

961

How quickly people's mood changes

⁴⁹ Man never tires of praying for good, but at times of difficulty he becomes hopeless and sad. ⁵⁰ When We are kind to himᵃ after a misfortune he claims, "This is all my doing, and I don't think that the Final Hour will come, and even if I'm returned to my Lord I'm sure to receive Paradise from Him."ᵇ We will tell them what they did and torment them with a severe punishment.ᶜ ⁵¹ When We are gracious to a person he turns away and stays aloof, but at times of difficulty he prays and prays.

What does the Quran expect of us?

⁵² Say: "Consider *this:* if this *Quran* is really from Allah and you deny it, who would be the biggest loser other than the one who opposed it openly?" ⁵³ Soon We shall show them Our signs in the horizons and in themselves so the Truth becomes clear to them. Isn't Your Lord enough, a witness over all things? ⁵⁴ Beware! They are in doubt about meeting Their Lord. Beware! Everything is in His grasp.

ᵃ Literally, "When We make him taste".

ᵇ *Husna* is Paradise, according to most commentators.

ᶜ Literally it is "make them taste".

42. Surat Ash-Shura

The Consultation

This surat was revealed in the middle Makkan period, at a time when the Muslims were being severely persecuted. The Makkans didn't just object to the belief in the Oneness of Allah, but denied that a human being could be a prophet. This awesome objection is refuted: "The Heavens are about to cleave" (5), so absurd and insulting was their conviction. The central theme is the truthfulness of prophethood. In describing the unique, distinctive and the otherness of Allah the Quran states: "There is nothing like Him" (11).

A list of tips for encountering the other is given: invite people to the way of Allah; be patient; don't follow others' whims; believe firmly; be just; be tolerant; be responsible; don't argue; and finally, "Allah will gather us together and all will return to Him" (15).

"You will see *the wrongdoers* in a state of terror because of what they did and its consequences will unfold before them. But the righteous believers will be in the gardens of Paradise" (22). The message is one of making the right choice: do you want the harvest of this life, or the Hereafter? The mission of the Prophet ﷺ is to help us make the right choice: "Say, 'I don't ask you for any reward for this work, except, "love one's relatives"'" (23). The next few verses explain the wisdom behind differences in human abilities and talents. Without this difference between the rich and poor and varying abilities, there would be no rank and file, no discipline and no organisation; people would be unwilling to cooperate with each other. Consequently, human civilisation wouldn't flourish. The next section (36–39) gives nine tips for social harmony; "the works one ought to do" (41): avoid major sins, indecency and anger; forgive; obey the Almighty; pray; mutual consultation; give charity; be courageous in standing up for the rights of others. A powerful appeal is made to humanity: "Come back[a] to your Lord before the Day when there will be no turning back from Allah. You will find no place to escape that Day, nor will you be able to deny your sins"[b] (47).

At the end the subject of prophethood, Allah's channel of communication, is covered briefly, dispelling the Makkans' cynicism and doubts. Since not all human beings can speak to Allah directly, He sends His prophets, with whom He communicates by revelation, from behind a screen, or by sending an angel with revelation (51).

---

[a] Literally an instruction to answer, but the implication is "come back". That's how I translated it.
[b] *Nakeer* means helper, supporter, and changer: someone who could change the punishment.

بِسْمِ اللّٰهِ الرَّحْمٰنِ الرَّحِيْمِ ۞

حٰمٓ ۞ عٓسٓقٓ ۞ كَذٰلِكَ يُوْحِىْٓ اِلَيْكَ وَ اِلَى

الَّذِيْنَ مِنْ قَبْلِكَ ۙ اللّٰهُ الْعَزِيْزُ الْحَكِيْمُ ۞

لَهٗ مَا فِى السَّمٰوٰتِ وَمَا فِى الْاَرْضِ ط وَهُوَ

الْعَلِىُّ الْعَظِيْمُ ۞ تَكَادُ السَّمٰوٰتُ يَتَفَطَّرْنَ مِنْ

فَوْقِهِنَّ وَالْمَلٰٓئِكَةُ يُسَبِّحُوْنَ بِحَمْدِ رَبِّهِمْ

وَيَسْتَغْفِرُوْنَ لِمَنْ فِى الْاَرْضِ ط اَلَآ اِنَّ اللّٰهَ هُوَ

الْغَفُوْرُ الرَّحِيْمُ ۞ وَالَّذِيْنَ اتَّخَذُوْا مِنْ دُوْنِهٖٓ

اَوْلِيَآءَ اللّٰهُ حَفِيْظٌ عَلَيْهِمْ ۚ وَمَآ اَنْتَ عَلَيْهِمْ

بِوَكِيْلٍ ۞ وَكَذٰلِكَ اَوْحَيْنَآ اِلَيْكَ قُرْاٰنًا عَرَبِيًّا

لِّتُنْذِرَ اُمَّ الْقُرٰى وَمَنْ حَوْلَهَا وَتُنْذِرَ يَوْمَ

الْجَمْعِ لَا رَيْبَ فِيْهِ ط فَرِيْقٌ فِى الْجَنَّةِ وَفَرِيْقٌ

فِى السَّعِيْرِ ۞ وَلَوْ شَآءَ اللّٰهُ لَجَعَلَهُمْ اُمَّةً

وَّاحِدَةً وَّلٰكِنْ يُّدْخِلُ مَنْ يَّشَآءُ فِىْ رَحْمَتِهٖ ط

وَالظّٰلِمُوْنَ مَا لَهُمْ مِّنْ وَّلِىٍّ وَّلَا نَصِيْرٍ ۞ اَمِ

اتَّخَذُوْا مِنْ دُوْنِهٖٓ اَوْلِيَآءَ ۚ فَاللّٰهُ هُوَ الْوَلِىُّ

وَهُوَ يُحْىِ الْمَوْتٰى ۫ وَهُوَ عَلٰى كُلِّ شَىْءٍ قَدِيْرٌ ۞

وَمَا اخْتَلَفْتُمْ فِيْهِ مِنْ شَىْءٍ فَحُكْمُهٗٓ اِلَى اللّٰهِ ط

ذٰلِكُمُ اللّٰهُ رَبِّىْ عَلَيْهِ تَوَكَّلْتُ ۚ وَاِلَيْهِ اُنِيْبُ ۞

Allah is the mighty, powerful and loving Lord. Be thankful, turn to Him and trust Him!

965

In the name of Allah, the Kind the Caring.

The Quran is Allah's Revelation
¹*Ha Meem,* ²*Ain Seen Qaaf.* ³This is what Allah the Almighty, the Wise revealed to you, and those before you. ⁴Everything in the Heavens and the Earth belongs to Him; the Exalted, the Great. ⁵The Heavens above nearly collapsed, the angels glorify and praise their Lord and seek forgiveness for those on Earth. Allah is the Forgiving, the Caring. ⁶Those who have taken lords[a] beside Allah know that He watches over them; you aren't their keeper.

The Quran cautions
⁷We revealed an Arabic Quran, so you may warn the people of Makkah[b] and its surroundings of the Day of Gathering, in which is no doubt; a group *will be* in the Garden and *another* group in the blazing Fire. ⁸Had Allah wanted He would have made them one community, but He allows into His Care whom He pleases. The disobedient have no friend, no helper. ⁹Have they taken lords or protectors beside Him? Allah is the only Lord, He gives life to the dead and controls all things. ¹⁰Whatever you disagree about, the final decision will be Allah's, that's Allah, My Lord; I trust Him, and I turn to Him *sincerely.*

---

a   *Awliya* is the plural of *wali:* near, friend and patron. Here, it means *Mutawalli li umur al alam,* "Lord of worldly affairs".
b   Literally *Umm ul Qura* refers to "mother of towns", a name for the city of Makkah.

فَاطِرُ السَّمٰوٰتِ وَالْاَرْضِ ؕ جَعَلَ لَكُمْ مِّنْ اَنْفُسِكُمْ اَزْوَاجًا وَّمِنَ الْاَنْعَامِ اَزْوَاجًا ۚ یَذْرَؤُكُمْ فِیْهِ ؕ لَیْسَ كَمِثْلِهٖ شَیْءٌ ۚ وَهُوَ السَّمِیْعُ الْبَصِیْرُ ۝ لَهٗ مَقَالِیْدُ السَّمٰوٰتِ وَالْاَرْضِ ۚ یَبْسُطُ الرِّزْقَ لِمَنْ یَّشَآءُ وَیَقْدِرُ ؕ اِنَّهٗ بِكُلِّ شَیْءٍ عَلِیْمٌ ۝ شَرَعَ لَكُمْ مِّنَ الدِّیْنِ مَا وَصّٰی بِهٖ نُوْحًا وَّالَّذِیْۤ اَوْحَیْنَاۤ اِلَیْكَ وَمَا وَصَّیْنَا بِهٖۤ اِبْرٰهِیْمَ وَمُوْسٰی وَعِیْسٰۤی اَنْ اَقِیْمُوا الدِّیْنَ وَلَا تَتَفَرَّقُوْا فِیْهِ ؕ كَبُرَ عَلَی الْمُشْرِكِیْنَ مَا تَدْعُوْهُمْ اِلَیْهِ ؕ اَللّٰهُ یَجْتَبِیْۤ اِلَیْهِ مَنْ یَّشَآءُ وَیَهْدِیْۤ اِلَیْهِ مَنْ یُّنِیْبُ ۝ وَمَا تَفَرَّقُوْۤا اِلَّا مِنْۢ بَعْدِ مَا جَآءَهُمُ الْعِلْمُ بَغْیًۢا بَیْنَهُمْ ؕ وَلَوْلَا كَلِمَةٌ سَبَقَتْ مِنْ رَّبِّكَ اِلٰۤی اَجَلٍ مُّسَمًّی لَّقُضِیَ بَیْنَهُمْ ؕ وَاِنَّ الَّذِیْنَ اُوْرِثُوا الْكِتٰبَ مِنْۢ بَعْدِهِمْ لَفِیْ شَكٍّ مِّنْهُ مُرِیْبٍ ۝ فَلِذٰلِكَ فَادْعُ ۚ وَاسْتَقِمْ كَمَاۤ اُمِرْتَ ۚ وَلَا تَتَّبِعْ اَهْوَآءَهُمْ ۚ وَقُلْ اٰمَنْتُ بِمَاۤ اَنْزَلَ اللّٰهُ مِنْ كِتٰبٍ ۚ وَاُمِرْتُ لِاَعْدِلَ بَیْنَكُمُ ؕ اَللّٰهُ رَبُّنَا وَرَبُّكُمْ ؕ لَنَاۤ اَعْمَالُنَا وَلَكُمْ اَعْمَالُكُمْ ؕ لَا حُجَّةَ بَیْنَنَا وَبَیْنَكُمُ ؕ اَللّٰهُ یَجْمَعُ بَیْنَنَا ۚ وَاِلَیْهِ الْمَصِیْرُ ۝ وَالَّذِیْنَ یُحَآجُّوْنَ

The belief in Allah is an effective shield against selfishness. Does it rebuke you when you follow your desires?

There is nothing like Allah

¹¹Creator of the Heavens and the Earth. He made the pair of you, the human species, so you may multiply *on Earth,* and a pair of each livestock. Nothing is like Him and He is the Hearing and the Seeing. ¹²The keys to the Heavens and the Earth belong to Him. He increases or decreases the provision as He pleases. He knows all things.

The unity of the Divine Message over the ages

¹³He made the *same* religion for you as for Nuh; We revealed the same to Ibrahim, Musa and Isa, to accept this religion and not be divided. What you call them to, the idolaters dislike. Allah selects and guides to Himself anyone He wants.[a] ¹⁴The conflict among people, despite having knowledge, was caused by jealousy. Had your Lord's sentence, *that* they will be given respite for a fixed term, not been passed, then the Judgment would have come *sooner.* Those who were made heirs of the Book, *Jews and Christians,* are in doubt and are making others doubt too.

Manners for interfaith dialogue

¹⁵Therefore, continue inviting *people to the truth;* remain steadfast as you have been commanded; do not follow their whims, *but* say: "I believe in what Allah has revealed from the Book; I have been commanded to be fair to you; Allah is our Lord and your Lord; our works are for us and yours for you; there is no argument between us and you; Allah will gather us all and we'll return to Him."

---

[a] Two ways in which Allah blesses people: He selects some; the prophets, truthful, and martyrs; secondly anyone who earnestly turns to Allah.

فِى اللهِ مِنْ بَعْدِ مَا اسْتُجِيْبَ لَهُ حُجَّتُهُمْ

دَاحِضَةٌ عِنْدَ رَبِّهِمْ وَعَلَيْهِمْ غَضَبٌ وَّلَهُمْ

عَذَابٌ شَدِيْدٌ ۝ اَللّٰهُ الَّذِىْ اَنْزَلَ الْكِتٰبَ

بِالْحَقِّ وَالْمِيْزَانَ ط وَمَا يُدْرِيْكَ لَعَلَّ السَّاعَةَ

قَرِيْبٌ ۝ يَسْتَعْجِلُ بِهَا الَّذِيْنَ لَا يُؤْمِنُوْنَ بِهَا ج

وَالَّذِيْنَ اٰمَنُوْا مُشْفِقُوْنَ مِنْهَا لا وَيَعْلَمُوْنَ اَنَّهَا

الْحَقُّ ط اَلَا اِنَّ الَّذِيْنَ يُمَارُوْنَ فِى السَّاعَةِ لَفِىْ

ضَلٰلٍ بَعِيْدٍ ۝ اَللّٰهُ لَطِيْفٌ بِعِبَادِهٖ يَرْزُقُ مَنْ

يَّشَاءُ ج وَهُوَ الْقَوِىُّ الْعَزِيْزُ ۝ مَنْ كَانَ يُرِيْدُ

حَرْثَ الْاٰخِرَةِ نَزِدْ لَهُ فِىْ حَرْثِهٖ ج وَمَنْ كَانَ يُرِيْدُ

حَرْثَ الدُّنْيَا نُؤْتِهٖ مِنْهَا لا وَمَا لَهُ فِى الْاٰخِرَةِ

مِنْ نَّصِيْبٍ ۝ اَمْ لَهُمْ شُرَكٰٓؤُا شَرَعُوْا لَهُمْ مِّنَ

الدِّيْنِ مَا لَمْ يَاْذَنْ بِهِ اللهُ ط وَلَوْلَا كَلِمَةُ الْفَصْلِ

لَقُضِىَ بَيْنَهُمْ ط وَاِنَّ الظّٰلِمِيْنَ لَهُمْ عَذَابٌ

اَلِيْمٌ ۝ تَرَى الظّٰلِمِيْنَ مُشْفِقِيْنَ مِمَّا كَسَبُوْا وَهُوَ

وَاقِعٌ بِهِمْ ط وَالَّذِيْنَ اٰمَنُوْا وَعَمِلُوا الصّٰلِحٰتِ فِىْ

رَوْضٰتِ الْجَنّٰتِ ج لَهُمْ مَّا يَشَاءُوْنَ عِنْدَ رَبِّهِمْ ط

ذٰلِكَ هُوَ الْفَضْلُ الْكَبِيْرُ ۝ ذٰلِكَ الَّذِىْ يُبَشِّرُ

اللهُ عِبَادَهُ الَّذِيْنَ اٰمَنُوْا وَعَمِلُوا الصّٰلِحٰتِ ط

قُلْ لَّا اَسْئَلُكُمْ عَلَيْهِ اَجْرًا اِلَّا الْمَوَدَّةَ فِى الْقُرْبٰى ط

Do you want your harvest now or do you want to keep it for the life Hereafter?

Debating about Allah is disliked

¹⁶Those who debate Allah's *being and attributes* after He has been accepted, their arguments are meaningless in the sight of their Lord, upon them is wrath, and they shall have a severe punishment. ¹⁷Allah sent down the Book with truth and scales of justice, and the Final Hour is near. ¹⁸The disbelievers want to hasten its onset, and the believers are fearful of it, since they know it's the truth. But those in doubt have gone far astray.

The Big question: harvest of this life or the Hereafter?

¹⁹Allah is most Caring to His servants, provides sustenance as He pleases, He is the Strong, the Almighty. ²⁰Those who want the harvest of the Hereafter, We shall increase its harvest for them, and those who want the harvest of this life, We shall give its harvest to them, but they won't have a share in the Hereafter.

People reap what they sow

²¹Did their idols start a religion without Allah's permission? Had the judgement not been passed, their fate would have long been sealed, and for the wrongdoers is a painful punishment. ²²You will see them in a state of terror because of what they did, as they face its consequences. But the believers who were righteous will be in the Gardens of Paradise, where their wishes will be fulfilled; they'll have whatever they wish from their Lord. What a great bounty! ²³Allah gives this good news to His believing, righteous servants. Say: "I don't ask you for any reward, except, 'love one's relatives'. And whoever does a good deed We shall increase its positive impact for him. Allah is Forgiving, Rewarding.

وَمَنْ یَّقْتَرِفْ حَسَنَةً نَّزِدْ لَهٗ فِیْهَا حُسْنًا ؕ اِنَّ
اللّٰهَ غَفُوْرٌ شَكُوْرٌ ۲۳ اَمْ یَقُوْلُوْنَ افْتَرٰی عَلَی اللّٰهِ
كَذِبًا ۚ فَاِنْ یَّشَاِ اللّٰهُ یَخْتِمْ عَلٰی قَلْبِكَ ؕ وَیَمْحُ
اللّٰهُ الْبَاطِلَ وَیُحِقُّ الْحَقَّ بِكَلِمٰتِهٖ ؕ اِنَّهٗ عَلِیْمٌۢ
بِذَاتِ الصُّدُوْرِ ۲۴ وَهُوَ الَّذِیْ یَقْبَلُ التَّوْبَةَ
عَنْ عِبَادِهٖ وَیَعْفُوْا عَنِ السَّیِّاٰتِ وَیَعْلَمُ مَا
تَفْعَلُوْنَ ۲۵ وَیَسْتَجِیْبُ الَّذِیْنَ اٰمَنُوْا وَعَمِلُوا
الصّٰلِحٰتِ وَیَزِیْدُهُمْ مِّنْ فَضْلِهٖ ؕ وَالْكٰفِرُوْنَ لَهُمْ
عَذَابٌ شَدِیْدٌ ۲۶ وَلَوْ بَسَطَ اللّٰهُ الرِّزْقَ لِعِبَادِهٖ
لَبَغَوْا فِی الْاَرْضِ وَلٰكِنْ یُّنَزِّلُ بِقَدَرٍ مَّا یَشَآءُ ؕ
اِنَّهٗ بِعِبَادِهٖ خَبِیْرٌۢ بَصِیْرٌ ۲۷ وَهُوَ الَّذِیْ یُنَزِّلُ
الْغَیْثَ مِنْۢ بَعْدِ مَا قَنَطُوْا وَیَنْشُرُ رَحْمَتَهٗ ؕ وَهُوَ
الْوَلِیُّ الْحَمِیْدُ ۲۸ وَمِنْ اٰیٰتِهٖ خَلْقُ السَّمٰوٰتِ وَالْاَرْضِ
وَمَا بَثَّ فِیْهِمَا مِنْ دَآبَّةٍ ؕ وَهُوَ عَلٰی جَمْعِهِمْ اِذَا
یَشَآءُ قَدِیْرٌ ۲۹ وَمَاۤ اَصَابَكُمْ مِّنْ مُّصِیْبَةٍ فَبِمَا
كَسَبَتْ اَیْدِیْكُمْ وَیَعْفُوْا عَنْ كَثِیْرٍ ۳۰ وَمَاۤ اَنْتُمْ
بِمُعْجِزِیْنَ فِی الْاَرْضِ ۚ وَمَا لَكُمْ مِّنْ دُوْنِ اللّٰهِ
مِنْ وَّلِیٍّ وَّلَا نَصِیْرٍ ۳۱ وَمِنْ اٰیٰتِهِ الْجَوَارِ فِی الْبَحْرِ
كَالْاَعْلَامِ ۳۲ اِنْ یَّشَاْ یُسْكِنِ الرِّیْحَ فَیَظْلَلْنَ
رَوَاكِدَ عَلٰی ظَهْرِهٖ ؕ اِنَّ فِیْ ذٰلِكَ لَاٰیٰتٍ لِّكُلِّ صَبَّارٍ

His bounties are plenty,
including forgiveness.
It's easy to get, just ask.
Try it.

ع
۳
۴

People deny and disobey but Allah is ready to forgive

²⁴ How dare they say, "He has invented a lie about Allah." In that case Allah would have sealed your heart and blotted out the falsehood, and established the truth with His Words. He knows what's in people's minds. ²⁵ He accepts the repentance of His servants, forgives evil deeds, knows what you are doing, ²⁶ answers the righteous believers, and increases His bounty for them. But for the disbelievers there is a severe punishment.

Why some people have more wealth than others

²⁷ Were Allah to give all the people same amount of sustenance in the city, they would be indifferent to each other, but Allah gives it in right measure as He pleases; He is Aware and watching His servants. ²⁸ He sends the rain when they lose hope, and spreads His kindness all around. He is the Helper, the Praiseworthy.

Humans can't disrupt Allah's plans

²⁹ Among His signs are the creation of the Heavens and the Earth, and the living things He has spread out. He will gather them together when He likes. ³⁰ The misfortune you face is due to your own fault.ᵃ However, Allah forgives much. ³¹ You can't disrupt *Allah's plan*ᵇ on Earth; you have no protector and helper beside Him. ³² Among His signs are the ships sailing on *open* seas, *appearing* like mountains. ³³ He could stop the wind blowing if He wished, so they would stand still on the surface *of the sea*. In that are signs for every patient and thankful person.

ᵃ Literally, "a result of what your hands have done".
ᵇ *Mu'jizeen* literally, to debilitate and to weaken something; escape and frustrate.

شَكُوْرٍ ۳۳ اَوْ یُوْبِقْهُنَّ بِمَا كَسَبُوْا وَ یَعْفُ عَنْ

كَثِیْرٍ ۳۴ وَّ یَعْلَمَ الَّذِیْنَ یُجَادِلُوْنَ فِیْۤ اٰیٰتِنَا مَا

لَهُمْ مِّنْ مَّحِیْصٍ ۳۵ فَمَاۤ اُوْتِیْتُمْ مِّنْ شَیْءٍ فَمَتَاعُ

الْحَیٰوةِ الدُّنْیَا وَمَا عِنْدَ اللهِ خَیْرٌ وَّ اَبْقٰی لِلَّذِیْنَ

اٰمَنُوْا وَ عَلٰی رَبِّهِمْ یَتَوَكَّلُوْنَ ۳۶ وَ الَّذِیْنَ یَجْتَنِبُوْنَ

كَبٰٓئِرَ الْاِثْمِ وَالْفَوَاحِشَ وَاِذَا مَا غَضِبُوْا هُمْ یَغْفِرُوْنَ ۳۷

وَالَّذِیْنَ اسْتَجَابُوْا لِرَبِّهِمْ وَ اَقَامُوا الصَّلٰوةَ وَاَمْرُهُمْ

شُوْرٰی بَیْنَهُمْ وَمِمَّا رَزَقْنٰهُمْ یُنْفِقُوْنَ ۳۸ وَ الَّذِیْنَ

اِذَاۤ اَصَابَهُمُ الْبَغْیُ هُمْ یَنْتَصِرُوْنَ ۳۹ وَجَزٰٓؤُا سَیِّئَةٍ

سَیِّئَةٌ مِّثْلُهَا فَمَنْ عَفَا وَاَصْلَحَ فَاَجْرُهٗ عَلَی اللهِ

اِنَّهٗ لَا یُحِبُّ الظّٰلِمِیْنَ ۴۰ وَلَمَنِ انْتَصَرَ بَعْدَ ظُلْمِهٖ

فَاُولٰٓئِكَ مَا عَلَیْهِمْ مِّنْ سَبِیْلٍ ۴۱ اِنَّمَا السَّبِیْلُ عَلَی

الَّذِیْنَ یَظْلِمُوْنَ النَّاسَ وَیَبْغُوْنَ فِی الْاَرْضِ بِغَیْرِ

الْحَقِّ اُولٰٓئِكَ لَهُمْ عَذَابٌ اَلِیْمٌ ۴۲ وَلَمَنْ صَبَرَ

وَ غَفَرَ اِنَّ ذٰلِكَ لَمِنْ عَزْمِ الْاُمُوْرِ ۴۳ وَمَنْ یُّضْلِلِ

اللهُ فَمَا لَهٗ مِنْ وَّلِیٍّ مِّنْ بَعْدِهٖ وَتَرَی الظّٰلِمِیْنَ

لَمَّا رَاَوُا الْعَذَابَ یَقُوْلُوْنَ هَلْ اِلٰی مَرَدٍّ مِّنْ

سَبِیْلٍ ۴۴ وَتَرٰىهُمْ یُعْرَضُوْنَ عَلَیْهَا خٰشِعِیْنَ مِنَ

الذُّلِّ یَنْظُرُوْنَ مِنْ طَرْفٍ خَفِیٍّ وَقَالَ الَّذِیْنَ

اٰمَنُوْۤا اِنَّ الْخٰسِرِیْنَ الَّذِیْنَ خَسِرُوْۤا اَنْفُسَهُمْ وَ

Modesty is a quality of true believers, as is shame and respect for the privacy of others. Look and see how modest you are.

[34]Or else He could wreck *their ship*, because of what they have done, but Allah forgives a lot. [35]Those who argue about[a] Our message, *let them know* there's no escape for them.

The works one ought to do; nine social and spiritual actions

[36]What you are given is passing enjoyment of the worldly life, and what Allah has is lasting and excellent; it will be given to the believers who: trust their Lord; [37]avoid major sins of indecency; forgive readily when angered; [38]respond by obeying their Lord; perform the prayer; consult each other to settle their affairs; spend what We have provided them; [39]when oppressed they defend themselves. [40]A revenge against a wrong could turn into an equal evil, therefore *be careful and* forgive and put things right through reconciliation; such a person will have his reward from Allah directly. Allah does not like the wrongdoers. [41]Anyone who defends himself against injustice mustn't be blamed; [42]the blame is on those who commit injustice and oppress people in the city. For them will be a painful punishment. [43]Whoever is patient and forgives, *now* these are things one ought to do.[b]

Disbelievers will be disgraced in dungeons

[44]Whoever Allah allows to go astray will have no helper after that, and you will see the wrongdoers when they see the punishment; they will say, "Is there any way of going back?" [45]And you will see them offered to Hell, overwhelmed and disgraced, looking around ashamedly,[c] whilst the believers will say, "Today, on Judgement Day, the losers ruined themselves and their families." Beware, the wrongdoers will have eternal punishment.

---

[a] An alternative meaning is "who question".

[b] *Azmi-l-'umuur* literally means determination and resolution; to show resolve.

[c] Or with a furtive glance.

اَهْلِیْهِمْ یَوْمَ الْقِیٰمَةِ ط اَلَاۤ اِنَّ الظّٰلِمِیْنَ فِیْ عَذَابٍ

مُّقِیْمٍ ۴۵ وَ مَا كَانَ لَهُمْ مِّنْ اَوْلِیَآءَ یَنْصُرُوْنَهُمْ

مِّنْ دُوْنِ اللّٰهِ ط وَ مَنْ یُّضْلِلِ اللّٰهُ فَمَا لَهٗ مِنْ

سَبِیْلٍ ط اِسْتَجِیْبُوْا لِرَبِّكُمْ مِّنْ قَبْلِ اَنْ یَّاْتِیَ

یَوْمٌ لَّا مَرَدَّ لَهٗ مِنَ اللّٰهِ ط مَا لَكُمْ مِّنْ مَّلْجَاٍ

یَّوْمَئِذٍ وَّ مَا لَكُمْ مِّنْ نَّكِیْرٍ ۴۷ فَاِنْ اَعْرَضُوْا

فَمَاۤ اَرْسَلْنٰكَ عَلَیْهِمْ حَفِیْظًا ط اِنْ عَلَیْكَ اِلَّا

الْبَلٰغُ ط وَ اِنَّاۤ اِذَاۤ اَذَقْنَا الْاِنْسَانَ مِنَّا رَحْمَةً فَرِحَ

بِهَا ۚ وَ اِنْ تُصِبْهُمْ سَیِّئَةٌ بِمَا قَدَّمَتْ اَیْدِیْهِمْ

فَاِنَّ الْاِنْسَانَ كَفُوْرٌ ۴۸ لِلّٰهِ مُلْكُ السَّمٰوٰتِ وَ

الْاَرْضِ ط یَخْلُقُ مَا یَشَآءُ ط یَهَبُ لِمَنْ یَّشَآءُ اِنَاثًا

وَّ یَهَبُ لِمَنْ یَّشَآءُ الذُّكُوْرَ ۴۹ اَوْ یُزَوِّجُهُمْ ذُكْرَانًا

وَّ اِنَاثًا ۚ وَّ یَجْعَلُ مَنْ یَّشَآءُ عَقِیْمًا ط اِنَّهٗ عَلِیْمٌ

قَدِیْرٌ ۵۰ وَ مَا كَانَ لِبَشَرٍ اَنْ یُّكَلِّمَهُ اللّٰهُ اِلَّا وَحْیًا

اَوْ مِنْ وَّرَآئِ حِجَابٍ اَوْ یُرْسِلَ رَسُوْلًا فَیُوْحِیَ

بِاِذْنِهٖ مَا یَشَآءُ ط اِنَّهٗ عَلِیٌّ حَكِیْمٌ ۵۱ وَ كَذٰلِكَ اَوْحَیْنَاۤ

اِلَیْكَ رُوْحًا مِّنْ اَمْرِنَا ط مَا كُنْتَ تَدْرِیْ مَا الْكِتٰبُ

وَ لَا الْاِیْمَانُ وَ لٰكِنْ جَعَلْنٰهُ نُوْرًا نَّهْدِیْ بِهٖ مَنْ

نَّشَآءُ مِنْ عِبَادِنَا ط وَ اِنَّكَ لَتَهْدِیْۤ اِلٰی صِرَاطٍ

مُّسْتَقِیْمٍ ۵۲ صِرَاطِ اللّٰهِ الَّذِیْ لَهٗ مَا فِی السَّمٰوٰتِ

Do you linger when it comes to decisions? Are you reluctant to do good? Then be decisive, hurry up and do good! You may miss the train.

975

⁴⁶ They will have no protectors beside Allah to help them, and whoever Allah allows to go astray will not find his way.

A call to come back

⁴⁷ Come back^a to your Lord before the Day when there will be no turning back from Allah. You will find nowhere to escape that Day, nor be able to deny your sins.^b ⁴⁸ If they turn away from you *Prophet!* Know, We didn't send you as their keeper; your responsibility is to deliver the Message. When We give people a taste of Our kindness they are joyful, but when times are difficult because of their fault they are ungrateful. ⁴⁹ The Heavens and the Earth belong to Allah; He creates what He pleases, He gives daughters or sons as He pleases to whom He pleases, ⁵⁰ to some He gives boys and girls and others He leaves childless as He pleases. He is the Knower, the Powerful.

The Quran gives details of faith

⁵¹ Allah doesn't speak to any human being *directly*, except by revelation from behind a screen, or an angel brings the revelation by His permission. He is the Exalted, the Wise. ⁵² So, We revealed to you the essence of Our command when you didn't know *the details of* faith or the Scripture. We made it a light and We guide with it whom We please from among Our servants. And you are guiding them to a straight path, ⁵³ the path of Allah – His is what is in the Heavens and the Earth^c – in the end, all things will return to Allah.

---

^a Literally this is an instruction to answer or respond, but the implication is "come back"; that is how it has been translated here.

^b *Nakeer* also means helper and supporter, or someone who might change the punishment.

^c *'A laa* is a participle meaning: is it not? Are they not? It implies "the fact" is and "but".

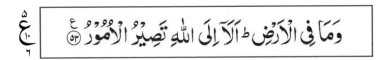

43. Surat Az-Zukhruf
The Golden Ornaments

This surat was revealed in the middle Makkan period, at the height of the tension between the Muslims and the Makkans. The darkest days of the Prophet's 鑾 struggle. It opens by demonstrating the unconditionally loving and forgiving nature of Allah: "Shall We turn away from you and deprive you of this Reminder because you are people who've gone beyond limits?" (5) No matter how heartless and unwilling people are to Allah's Message and His messenger, He continues to provide guidance.

The contradictory beliefs of the disbelievers are exposed: on one hand they believed in Allah as the Creator, but on the other they worshipped idols. "If you ask them who created the Heavens and the Earth they will certainly say they were created by the Almighty, the Knower" (9). Another one of their contradictory beliefs was the idea that the angels were Allah's daughters. They felt shamed if they had daughters, but they happily assigned angels as Allah's daughters.

They criticised the Prophet Muhammad 鑾 because he was poor and therefore unfit to lead. The Quran disproves them: "And they said, 'Why was this Quran not sent down on a famous personality from one of the two towns?" (31). Allah shows His disregard for material wealth by saying, "if it were not for the prospect of everyone becoming a disbeliever, He would have given the disbelievers so much wealth that the roofs, the staircases and the furnishing of their homes would be made of gold and silver" (33–35).

The surat also teaches the wisdom behind differences in individuals' capabilities and skills: "Do they distribute your Lord's kindness? We distribute among them their livelihoods in this worldly life, and We raise some among others in ranks so that some may take others in employment" (32). Without this there would be no rank and file to help civilisations to flourish. To illustrate how wealth and power can corrupt people, the Quran gives the example of the Pharaoh: "The Pharaoh declared to his people, 'My people, is not the country of Egypt and all these rivers flowing beneath my feet mine?" (51). The Pharaoh despised Musa 鑾 simply because the latter did not have "golden bracelets". The Quran teaches, this is a mean and miserly attitude.

Their persistent objection to the Glorious Quran is rejected: "This Quran is a great honour for you and your people; you will be questioned about it" (44). The Makkans were rude about the Prophet Isa 鑾: "Whenever the example of the son of Maryam is given, your people kick up a fuss about it, and say, 'Are our gods better or is he?'" (57–58). The

Quran goes on to praise Isa ﷺ and show that he will be one of the signs of the Final Hour.

The purpose of revelation is to caution people about the consequences of their actions in this life, and to motivate them to accept the truth. To achieve this it presents vivid descriptions of life in Paradise and life in Hell: "*They will be told,* 'Enter the Garden, you and your spouses *together* happily.' *Food and drink* in golden trays and cups shall be passed around. Everything that one desires and the eyes delight in will be there; here you will live forever. This is the Garden you are made heirs of, *a reward* for what you did. *Here* you will have plenty of fruit to eat from" (70–73). This is vividly contrasted with the misery of Hell (74–78).

The surat opened with the loving and the forgiving nature of Allah, so it ends by advising the Prophet ﷺ: "*Prophet,* forgive them and say, 'Peace'; they will come to know" (89).

۞ (٤٣) سُوۡرَةُ الزُّخۡرُفِ مَكِّيَّةٌ (٢٣) رُکُوۡعَاتُهَا ٧ اٰیَاتُهَا ٨٩ ۞

بِسۡمِ اللهِ الرَّحۡمٰنِ الرَّحِیۡمِ

حٰمٓ ۚ۝١ وَالۡكِتٰبِ الۡمُبِیۡنِ ۙ۝٢ اِنَّا جَعَلۡنٰهُ قُرۡءٰنًا

عَرَبِیًّا لَّعَلَّكُمۡ تَعۡقِلُوۡنَ ۚ۝٣ وَاِنَّهٗ فِیۡۤ اُمِّ الۡكِتٰبِ

لَدَیۡنَا لَعَلِیٌّ حَكِیۡمٌ ؕ۝٤ اَفَنَضۡرِبُ عَنۡكُمُ الذِّكۡرَ صَفۡحًا

اَنۡ كُنۡتُمۡ قَوۡمًا مُّسۡرِفِیۡنَ ۝٥ وَكَمۡ اَرۡسَلۡنَا مِنۡ نَّبِیٍّ

فِی الۡاَوَّلِیۡنَ ۝٦ وَمَا یَاۡتِیۡهِمۡ مِّنۡ نَّبِیٍّ اِلَّا كَانُوۡا بِهٖ

یَسۡتَهۡزِءُوۡنَ ۝٧ فَاَهۡلَكۡنَاۤ اَشَدَّ مِنۡهُمۡ بَطۡشًا وَّمَضٰی

مَثَلُ الۡاَوَّلِیۡنَ ۝٨ وَلَئِنۡ سَاَلۡتَهُمۡ مَّنۡ خَلَقَ السَّمٰوٰتِ

وَالۡاَرۡضَ لَیَقُوۡلُنَّ خَلَقَهُنَّ الۡعَزِیۡزُ الۡعَلِیۡمُ ۙ۝٩ الَّذِیۡ

جَعَلَ لَكُمُ الۡاَرۡضَ مَهۡدًا وَّجَعَلَ لَكُمۡ فِیۡهَا سُبُلًا

لَّعَلَّكُمۡ تَهۡتَدُوۡنَ ۚ۝١٠ وَالَّذِیۡ نَزَّلَ مِنَ السَّمَآءِ مَآءًۢ

بِقَدَرٍ ۚ فَاَنۡشَرۡنَا بِهٖ بَلۡدَةً مَّیۡتًا ؕ كَذٰلِكَ تُخۡرَجُوۡنَ ۝١١

وَالَّذِیۡ خَلَقَ الۡاَزۡوَاجَ كُلَّهَا وَجَعَلَ لَكُمۡ مِّنَ الۡفُلۡكِ

وَالۡاَنۡعَامِ مَا تَرۡكَبُوۡنَ ۙ۝١٢ لِتَسۡتَوُۥا عَلٰی ظُهُوۡرِهٖ ثُمَّ

تَذۡكُرُوۡا نِعۡمَةَ رَبِّكُمۡ اِذَا اسۡتَوَیۡتُمۡ عَلَیۡهِ وَ

تَقُوۡلُوۡا سُبۡحٰنَ الَّذِیۡ سَخَّرَ لَنَا هٰذَا وَمَا كُنَّا لَهٗ

مُقۡرِنِیۡنَ ۙ۝١٣ وَاِنَّاۤ اِلٰی رَبِّنَا لَمُنۡقَلِبُوۡنَ ۝١٤ وَجَعَلُوۡا لَهٗ

مِنۡ عِبَادِهٖ جُزۡءًا ؕ اِنَّ الۡاِنۡسَانَ لَكَفُوۡرٌ مُّبِیۡنٌ ؕ۝١٥ اَمِ

اتَّخَذَ مِمَّا یَخۡلُقُ بَنٰتٍ وَّاَصۡفٰكُمۡ بِالۡبَنِیۡنَ ۝١٦ وَاِذَا

In hot countries, when it rains, within few days the dry, dead land becomes green and lush. Similarly, the dead will be brought to life!

In the name of Allah, the Kind, the Caring

¹*Ha Meem.*

Allah will not stop guiding humanity

²By the Book whose teachings are clear, ³We sent an Arabic Quran so you may understand. ⁴Preserved in the Divine Tablet, securely with Us; it is majestic and full of wisdom. ⁵Should We turn away and deprive you[a] of this reminder because you are people who have gone beyond limits? ⁶We sent many prophets to the past generations; ⁷when a prophet came to them they mocked him, ⁸so We destroyed them. They were stronger than them, and now they are part of history.

The prayer for travelling

⁹If you ask them who created the Heavens and the Earth they will say they were created by the Almighty, the Knower, ¹⁰Who made the Earth flat[b] and in it made many paths so that you may find your way around. ¹¹He sent rain from the sky in *carefully* measured amounts; with it We bring dead land to life, similarly you will be brought out *alive from graves.* ¹²He created all kinds of things, made ships and livestock for you to ride on, ¹³sitting comfortably on their backs remembering the bounties of your Lord, and when you are mounted comfortably on them you *should* pray: "Glory to Him Who made this for our benefit; we weren't capable of controlling it, ¹⁴and we are returning to our Lord."

Disapproval of the discrimination against daughters

¹⁵Do *the idolaters* think some of His servants are *His* offspring? Humans are openly unthankful. ¹⁶So Allah chose daughters for Himself from His creation and preferred sons for you?

---

[a] *Dharabtu anho safhan*, an Arabic idiom used when someone turns away from something, ignoring it (Al-Qurtubi).

[b] *Mahdan* literally means flat and small. However, commentators say this is not contradicting the fact that the Earth is a sphere, because it is so big and vast that the roundness is not felt as far as the eye can see.

بُشِّرَ اَحَدُهُمۡ بِمَا ضَرَبَ لِلرَّحۡمٰنِ مَثَلًا ظَلَّ وَجۡهُهٗ

مُسۡوَدًّا وَّهُوَ كَظِیۡمٌ ۱۴ اَوَمَنۡ یُّنَشَّؤُا فِی الۡحِلۡیَةِ وَهُوَ

فِی الۡخِصَامِ غَیۡرُ مُبِیۡنٍ ۱۸ وَجَعَلُوا الۡمَلٰٓئِكَةَ الَّذِیۡنَ

هُمۡ عِبٰدُ الرَّحۡمٰنِ اِنَاثًا ؕ اَشَهِدُوۡا خَلۡقَهُمۡ ؕ

سَتُكۡتَبُ شَهَادَتُهُمۡ وَیُسۡـَٔلُوۡنَ ۱۹ وَقَالُوۡا لَوۡ شَآءَ

الرَّحۡمٰنُ مَا عَبَدۡنٰهُمۡ ؕ مَا لَهُمۡ بِذٰلِكَ مِنۡ عِلۡمٍ ۥ

اِنۡ هُمۡ اِلَّا یَخۡرُصُوۡنَ ۲۰ اَمۡ اٰتَیۡنٰهُمۡ كِتٰبًا مِّنۡ قَبۡلِهٖ

فَهُمۡ بِهٖ مُسۡتَمۡسِكُوۡنَ ۲۱ بَلۡ قَالُوۡۤا اِنَّا وَجَدۡنَاۤ اٰبَآءَنَا

عَلٰۤی اُمَّةٍ وَّ اِنَّا عَلٰۤی اٰثٰرِهِمۡ مُّهۡتَدُوۡنَ ۲۲ وَكَذٰلِكَ مَاۤ

اَرۡسَلۡنَا مِنۡ قَبۡلِكَ فِیۡ قَرۡیَةٍ مِّنۡ نَّذِیۡرٍ اِلَّا قَالَ

مُتۡرَفُوۡهَاۤ ۙ اِنَّا وَجَدۡنَاۤ اٰبَآءَنَا عَلٰۤی اُمَّةٍ وَّ اِنَّا عَلٰۤی

اٰثٰرِهِمۡ مُّقۡتَدُوۡنَ ۲۳ قٰلَ اَوَلَوۡ جِئۡتُكُمۡ بِاَهۡدٰی مِمَّا

وَجَدۡتُّمۡ عَلَیۡهِ اٰبَآءَكُمۡ ؕ قَالُوۡۤا اِنَّا بِمَاۤ اُرۡسِلۡتُمۡ بِهٖ

كٰفِرُوۡنَ ۲۴ فَانۡتَقَمۡنَا مِنۡهُمۡ فَانۡظُرۡ كَیۡفَ كَانَ عَاقِبَةُ

الۡمُكَذِّبِیۡنَ ۲۵ وَاِذۡ قَالَ اِبۡرٰهِیۡمُ لِاَبِیۡهِ وَقَوۡمِهٖۤ

اِنَّنِیۡ بَرَآءٌ مِّمَّا تَعۡبُدُوۡنَ ۲۶ اِلَّا الَّذِیۡ فَطَرَنِیۡ

فَاِنَّهٗ سَیَهۡدِیۡنِ ۲۷ وَجَعَلَهَا كَلِمَةً بَاقِیَةً فِیۡ

عَقِبِهٖ لَعَلَّهُمۡ یَرۡجِعُوۡنَ ۲۸ بَلۡ مَتَّعۡتُ هٰۤؤُلَآءِ

وَاٰبَآءَهُمۡ حَتّٰی جَآءَهُمُ الۡحَقُّ وَرَسُوۡلٌ مُّبِیۡنٌ ۲۹

وَلَمَّا جَآءَهُمُ الۡحَقُّ قَالُوۡا هٰذَا سِحۡرٌ وَّ اِنَّا بِهٖ

A severe warning of Divine retribution for those who ignore Him, how seriously do you take Allah?

¹⁷ When one of them is given the good news of what he ascribes to the Most Kind, his face turns dark and he is furious: ¹⁸ "What!" One who is brought up in fine jewellery and incapable of presenting a case clearly.ᵃ ¹⁹ They describe the angels who are servants of the Most Kind as females. Were they present at their creation? Their false claims are recorded and they will be questioned.

The idolaters deny free will

²⁰ They say, "If the Most Kind wanted, we wouldn't have worshipped the idols." They don't understand what they are *saying* and guessing. ²¹ Or have We given them a book before this which they follow? ²² No; they say, "We found our forefathers on this path and we are guided by their footsteps." ²³ Similarly, when We sent a Warner before you to a town, the affluent peopleᵇ said, "We found our forefathers on this path and we are followers in their footsteps." ²⁴ The Prophet said, "If I bring you a better guide than what you received from your forefathers, even then?" They said, "We are deniers of your message." ²⁵ Consequently, We punished them; look what was the fate of the deniers.

The idolaters would like a celebrity to be a prophet

²⁶ Remember when Ibrahim told his father and his people, "I reject what you worship ²⁷ and I worship the One Who created me, and He guides me." ²⁸ And he implemented *this* wordᶜ among his children so they may return *to it.* ²⁹ I let them and their forefathers enjoy life, until the truth *eventually* came to them and a noble messenger who explained clearly. ³⁰ When the truth came to them they said, "This is magic and so we deny it."

ᵃ   These are the attitudes of the Arab idolaters about women, and not the Divine Teaching.

ᵇ   *Mutraf* means "one who enjoys a life of plenty" and "indulges in pleasures".

ᶜ   *Kalimatan* here means "declaration of the unity of God".

كٰفِرُوْنَ ۝ وَقَالُوْا لَوْلَا نُزِّلَ هٰذَا الْقُرْاٰنُ عَلٰى رَجُلٍ

مِّنَ الْقَرْيَتَيْنِ عَظِيْمٍ ۝ اَهُمْ يَقْسِمُوْنَ رَحْمَتَ رَبِّكَ ط

نَحْنُ قَسَمْنَا بَيْنَهُمْ مَّعِيْشَتَهُمْ فِي الْحَيٰوةِ الدُّنْيَا

وَرَفَعْنَا بَعْضَهُمْ فَوْقَ بَعْضٍ دَرَجٰتٍ لِّيَتَّخِذَ بَعْضُهُمْ

بَعْضًا سُخْرِيًّا ط وَرَحْمَتُ رَبِّكَ خَيْرٌ مِّمَّا يَجْمَعُوْنَ ۝

وَلَوْلَا اَنْ يَّكُوْنَ النَّاسُ اُمَّةً وَّاحِدَةً لَّجَعَلْنَا لِمَنْ

يَّكْفُرُ بِالرَّحْمٰنِ لِبُيُوْتِهِمْ سُقُفًا مِّنْ فِضَّةٍ وَّمَعَارِجَ

عَلَيْهَا يَظْهَرُوْنَ ۝ وَلِبُيُوْتِهِمْ اَبْوَابًا وَّ سُرُرًا عَلَيْهَا

يَتَّكِئُوْنَ ۝ وَ زُخْرُفًا ط وَاِنْ كُلُّ ذٰلِكَ لَمَّا مَتَاعُ

الْحَيٰوةِ الدُّنْيَا ط وَالْاٰخِرَةُ عِنْدَ رَبِّكَ لِلْمُتَّقِيْنَ ۝

وَمَنْ يَّعْشُ عَنْ ذِكْرِ الرَّحْمٰنِ نُقَيِّضْ لَهُ شَيْطٰنًا فَهُوَ

لَهُ قَرِيْنٌ ۝ وَاِنَّهُمْ لَيَصُدُّوْنَهُمْ عَنِ السَّبِيْلِ وَ

يَحْسَبُوْنَ اَنَّهُمْ مُّهْتَدُوْنَ ۝ حَتّٰى اِذَا جَآءَنَا قَالَ

يٰلَيْتَ بَيْنِيْ وَبَيْنَكَ بُعْدَ الْمَشْرِقَيْنِ فَبِئْسَ الْقَرِيْنُ ۝

وَلَنْ يَّنْفَعَكُمُ الْيَوْمَ اِذْ ظَّلَمْتُمْ اَنَّكُمْ فِي الْعَذَابِ

مُشْتَرِكُوْنَ ۝ اَفَاَنْتَ تُسْمِعُ الصُّمَّ اَوْ تَهْدِي الْعُمْيَ

وَمَنْ كَانَ فِيْ ضَلٰلٍ مُّبِيْنٍ ۝ فَاِمَّا نَذْهَبَنَّ بِكَ

فَاِنَّا مِنْهُمْ مُّنْتَقِمُوْنَ ۝ اَوْ نُرِيَنَّكَ الَّذِيْ وَعَدْنٰهُمْ

فَاِنَّا عَلَيْهِمْ مُّقْتَدِرُوْنَ ۝ فَاسْتَمْسِكْ بِالَّذِيْ اُوْحِيَ

اِلَيْكَ ج اِنَّكَ عَلٰى صِرَاطٍ مُّسْتَقِيْمٍ ۝ وَاِنَّهُ لَذِكْرٌ لَّكَ

A person is recognised by his mate. Satan adopts those who forget Allah, he is their mate. Do you have good mates?

983

[31] And said, "Why was this Quran not sent down on a famous personality from one of the two towns?"[a] [32] Are they distributing your Lord's Kindness? We Ourselves distribute among them their livelihoods in this worldly life, and We raise some among others in ranks so some may take others in employment. Your Lord's Kindness is more excellent than the treasures they gather.

Houses of silver and gold

[33] And if it weren't for the prospect that people would become one *disbelieving* community, We would have made for the deniers of the Most Kind, houses with silver roofs and stairways to climb; [34] the gates of their houses and the couches on which they rest would be made of silver, [35] and they would be *surrounded* by golden ornaments. These are mere enjoyments of worldly life. *The delights* of your Lord in the Hereafter are for the pious.

Whose companion is Satan?

[36] Anyone who turns a blind eye to the Most Kind's reminder, will have a Satan appointed as their close companion. [37] They will stop them from following the straight path but they will believe they are guided. [38] Until he comes to Us and says, "Woe! I wish we were poles apart[b]" what an evil companion. [39] *This criticism* today will not benefit you at all since you have sinned and now you will share the punishment together. [40] Can you make the deaf hear or guide the blind? Or the misguided. [41] Even if We took you away We would certainly punish them, [42] or We shall show you the punishment We have promised them, and We can do so. [43] So, hold firmly what's revealed to you, since you are on the straight path.

---

a   This refers to the two towns of Makkah and Taif.
b   "There was between me and you the distance of the two Easts".

وَلِقَوْمِكَ ۚ وَسَوْفَ تُسْـَٔلُوْنَ ۞ وَسْـَٔلْ مَنْ اَرْسَلْنَا مِنْ

قَبْلِكَ مِنْ رُّسُلِنَاۤ اَجَعَلْنَا مِنْ دُوْنِ الرَّحْمٰنِ اٰلِهَةً

يُّعْبَدُوْنَ ۞ وَلَقَدْ اَرْسَلْنَا مُوْسٰى بِاٰيٰتِنَاۤ اِلٰى فِرْعَوْنَ

وَ مَلَا۟ئِهٖ فَقَالَ اِنِّيْ رَسُوْلُ رَبِّ الْعٰلَمِيْنَ ۞ فَلَمَّا

جَآءَهُمْ بِاٰيٰتِنَاۤ اِذَا هُمْ مِّنْهَا يَضْحَكُوْنَ ۞ وَمَا نُرِيْهِمْ

مِّنْ اٰيَةٍ اِلَّا هِيَ اَكْبَرُ مِنْ اُخْتِهَا ۫ وَاَخَذْنٰهُمْ بِالْعَذَابِ

لَعَلَّهُمْ يَرْجِعُوْنَ ۞ وَقَالُوْا يٰۤاَيُّهَ السّٰحِرُ ادْعُ لَنَا رَبَّكَ

بِمَا عَهِدَ عِنْدَكَ ۚ اِنَّنَا لَمُهْتَدُوْنَ ۞ فَلَمَّا كَشَفْنَا

عَنْهُمُ الْعَذَابَ اِذَا هُمْ يَنْكُثُوْنَ ۞ وَنَادٰى فِرْعَوْنُ

فِيْ قَوْمِهٖ قَالَ يٰقَوْمِ اَلَيْسَ لِيْ مُلْكُ مِصْرَ وَ هٰذِهِ

الْاَنْهٰرُ تَجْرِيْ مِنْ تَحْتِيْ ۚ اَفَلَا تُبْصِرُوْنَ ۞ اَمْ اَنَا

خَيْرٌ مِّنْ هٰذَا الَّذِيْ هُوَ مَهِيْنٌ ۙ وَّلَا يَكَادُ يُبِيْنُ ۞

فَلَوْلَاۤ اُلْقِيَ عَلَيْهِ اَسْوِرَةٌ مِّنْ ذَهَبٍ اَوْ جَآءَ مَعَهُ

الْمَلٰٓئِكَةُ مُقْتَرِنِيْنَ ۞ فَاسْتَخَفَّ قَوْمَهٗ فَاَطَاعُوْهُ ۚ

اِنَّهُمْ كَانُوْا قَوْمًا فٰسِقِيْنَ ۞ فَلَمَّاۤ اٰسَفُوْنَا انْتَقَمْنَا

مِنْهُمْ فَاَغْرَقْنٰهُمْ اَجْمَعِيْنَ ۞ فَجَعَلْنٰهُمْ سَلَفًا وَّمَثَلًا

لِّلْاٰخِرِيْنَ ۞ وَلَمَّا ضُرِبَ ابْنُ مَرْيَمَ مَثَلًا اِذَا قَوْمُكَ

مِنْهُ يَصِدُّوْنَ ۞ وَقَالُوْۤا ءَاٰلِهَتُنَا خَيْرٌ اَمْ هُوَ ۗ مَا

ضَرَبُوْهُ لَكَ اِلَّا جَدَلًا ۗ بَلْ هُمْ قَوْمٌ خَصِمُوْنَ ۞

اِنْ هُوَ اِلَّا عَبْدٌ اَنْعَمْنَا عَلَيْهِ وَ جَعَلْنٰهُ مَثَلًا

Pharaoh's arrogance prevented him from believing Musa: one way of overcoming arrogance is to sidestep luxuries. Simple enough.

⁴⁴This Quran is a great honour for you and your people; you will be questioned about it. ⁴⁵And ask Our messengers We sent before you: did We ever allow gods beside Allah to be worshipped?

Musa was similarly insulted by the Pharaoh
⁴⁶We sent Musa with Our signs to Pharaoh and his nobles. *Musa* said, "I am a messenger from the Lord of the worlds". ⁴⁷When he came to them with Our miracles they laughed at him. ⁴⁸Every miracle We showed them was greater than the previous one, and each time We punished them *for rejecting it,* hoping they might return. ⁴⁹And they kept saying, "Magician! Pray for us to your Lord through the contract you have with Him; we will certainly accept guidance." ⁵⁰However, as soon as We removed the punishment from them, they broke the promise.

The Pharaoh boasted like the Makkans
⁵¹The Pharaoh announced to his people: "My people, isn't the kingdom of Egypt and the rivers flowing under my feet mine? Can't you see? ⁵²Am I not better than this wretched person who can barely express himself? ⁵³Why hasn't he been given golden bracelets? Why are there no angels sent down with him?" ⁵⁴So he fooled his peopleᵃ and they followed him. They were a sinful people. ⁵⁵Then when they roused Our anger, We punished them by drowning them all, ⁵⁶We made them a thing of the past and an example for those coming after them.

The Prophet Isa is a sign of the Final Hour
⁵⁷Whenever the example of the son of Maryam is given, your people kick up a fuss about itᵇ ⁵⁸and say, "Are our gods better or him?" They say this just to annoy you; they really are a quarrelsome lot. ⁵⁹He was Our blessed servant who We made a model for the Israelites.

ᵃ *Fastakhaff qaumahu* can also mean: "he incited his people". It could also mean, "make a fool of someone."
ᵇ The Makkans would argue our worship of Angels is like the Christian worshipping Jesus as 'the son of God', so why do you object? Since you call them the People of the Book. Their line of reasoning is rejected.

لِبَنِیْۤ اِسْرَآءِیْلَ ۵۹ۙ وَلَوْ نَشَآءُ لَجَعَلْنَا مِنْكُمْ مَّلٰٓئِكَةً فِی الْاَرْضِ یَخْلُفُوْنَ ۶۰ وَاِنَّهٗ لَعِلْمٌ لِّلسَّاعَةِ فَلَا تَمْتَرُنَّ بِهَا وَاتَّبِعُوْنِ ؕ هٰذَا صِرَاطٌ مُّسْتَقِیْمٌ ۶۱ وَلَا یَصُدَّنَّكُمُ الشَّیْطٰنُ ؕ اِنَّهٗ لَكُمْ عَدُوٌّ مُّبِیْنٌ ۶۲ وَلَمَّا جَآءَ عِیْسٰی بِالْبَیِّنٰتِ قَالَ قَدْ جِئْتُكُمْ بِالْحِكْمَةِ وَلِاُبَیِّنَ لَكُمْ بَعْضَ الَّذِیْ تَخْتَلِفُوْنَ فِیْهِ ۚ فَاتَّقُوا اللّٰهَ وَ اَطِیْعُوْنِ ۶۳ اِنَّ اللّٰهَ هُوَ رَبِّیْ وَرَبُّكُمْ فَاعْبُدُوْهُ ؕ هٰذَا صِرَاطٌ مُّسْتَقِیْمٌ ۶۴ فَاخْتَلَفَ الْاَحْزَابُ مِنْ بَیْنِهِمْ ۚ فَوَیْلٌ لِّلَّذِیْنَ ظَلَمُوْا مِنْ عَذَابِ یَوْمٍ اَلِیْمٍ ۶۵ هَلْ یَنْظُرُوْنَ اِلَّا السَّاعَةَ اَنْ تَاْتِیَهُمْ بَغْتَةً وَّهُمْ لَا یَشْعُرُوْنَ ۶۶ اَلْاَخِلَّآءُ یَوْمَئِذٍ بَعْضُهُمْ لِبَعْضٍ عَدُوٌّ اِلَّا الْمُتَّقِیْنَ ۶۷ؕۧ یٰعِبَادِ لَاخَوْفٌ عَلَیْكُمُ الْیَوْمَ وَلَاۤ اَنْتُمْ تَحْزَنُوْنَ ۶۸ۚ اَلَّذِیْنَ اٰمَنُوْا بِاٰیٰتِنَا وَكَانُوْا مُسْلِمِیْنَ ۶۹ۚ اُدْخُلُوا الْجَنَّةَ اَنْتُمْ وَاَزْوَاجُكُمْ تُحْبَرُوْنَ ۷۰ یُطَافُ عَلَیْهِمْ بِصِحَافٍ مِّنْ ذَهَبٍ وَّاَكْوَابٍ ۚ وَفِیْهَا مَا تَشْتَهِیْهِ الْاَنْفُسُ وَتَلَذُّ الْاَعْیُنُ ۚ وَاَنْتُمْ فِیْهَا خٰلِدُوْنَ ۷۱ۚ وَتِلْكَ الْجَنَّةُ الَّتِیْۤ اُوْرِثْتُمُوْهَا بِمَا كُنْتُمْ تَعْمَلُوْنَ ۷۲ لَكُمْ فِیْهَا فَاكِهَةٌ كَثِیْرَةٌ مِّنْهَا تَاْكُلُوْنَ ۷۳ اِنَّ الْمُجْرِمِیْنَ فِیْ عَذَابِ جَهَنَّمَ خٰلِدُوْنَ ۷۴ۚ لَا یُفَتَّرُ عَنْهُمْ وَهُمْ فِیْهِ مُبْلِسُوْنَ ۷۵ۚ وَمَا ظَلَمْنٰهُمْ وَلٰكِنْ

٦
١١
١٢
ع

987

⁶⁰ Had We wanted, We could have made angels on Earth to succeed you. ⁶¹ He is indeed a sign of the Final Hour, so don't doubt it and follow me; this is the straight path, ⁶² let not the Satan stop you, since he is your open enemy. ⁶³ When Isa came with clear signs he said, "I have come with wisdom to you and to clarify for you those things in which you differ, so be mindful of Allah and obey me; ⁶⁴ indeed Allah is Mine and Your Lord, worship Him. This is the straight path." ⁶⁵ Then groups began bickering amongst themselves. So woe to the wrongdoers when they will suffer the punishment of a painful Day. ⁶⁶ Are they waiting for the sudden coming of the Final Hour when they are unaware? ⁶⁷ Even best friends on that Day will be each other's enemies – but not the pious.

The delights of Paradise

⁶⁸ My servants, today don't fear nor worry. ⁶⁹ Those who believed in our Scriptures and were true Muslims, ⁷⁰ *they will be told*: "Enter the Garden; you and your spouses *together* happily." ⁷¹ *Food and drink* in golden trays and cups shall be passed around. Everything that one desires and the eyes delight in will be there; here you will live forever. ⁷² This is the Garden you are made heirs of, *a reward* for your works. ⁷³ *Here* you will have plenty of fruit to eat from.

The wicked will stay in Hell forever

⁷⁴ The wicked will be punished in Hell forever. ⁷⁵ It will not be lightened for them, so they will lose all hope. ⁷⁶ We didn't wrong them, they wronged themselves.

كَانُوا هُمُ الظّٰلِمِيْنَ ۞ وَنَادَوْا يٰمٰلِكُ لِيَقْضِ عَلَيْنَا

رَبُّكَ ط قَالَ اِنَّكُمْ مّٰكِثُوْنَ ۞ لَقَدْ جِئْنٰكُمْ بِالْحَقِّ

وَلٰكِنَّ اَكْثَرَكُمْ لِلْحَقِّ كٰرِهُوْنَ ۞ اَمْ اَبْرَمُوْٓا اَمْرًا

فَاِنَّا مُبْرِمُوْنَ ۞ اَمْ يَحْسَبُوْنَ اَنَّا لَا نَسْمَعُ سِرَّهُمْ

وَنَجْوٰىهُمْ ط بَلٰى وَرُسُلُنَا لَدَيْهِمْ يَكْتُبُوْنَ ۞ قُلْ اِنْ

كَانَ لِلرَّحْمٰنِ وَلَدٌ ۖ فَاَنَا اَوَّلُ الْعٰبِدِيْنَ ۞ سُبْحٰنَ

رَبِّ السَّمٰوٰتِ وَالْاَرْضِ رَبِّ الْعَرْشِ عَمَّا يَصِفُوْنَ ۞

فَذَرْهُمْ يَخُوْضُوْا وَيَلْعَبُوْا حَتّٰى يُلٰقُوْا يَوْمَهُمُ

الَّذِىْ يُوْعَدُوْنَ ۞ وَهُوَ الَّذِىْ فِى السَّمَآءِ اِلٰهٌ

وَّفِى الْاَرْضِ اِلٰهٌ ط وَهُوَ الْحَكِيْمُ الْعَلِيْمُ ۞ وَتَبٰرَكَ

الَّذِىْ لَهٗ مُلْكُ السَّمٰوٰتِ وَالْاَرْضِ وَمَا بَيْنَهُمَا ۚ

وَعِنْدَهٗ عِلْمُ السَّاعَةِ ۚ وَاِلَيْهِ تُرْجَعُوْنَ ۞ وَلَا

يَمْلِكُ الَّذِيْنَ يَدْعُوْنَ مِنْ دُوْنِهِ الشَّفَاعَةَ اِلَّا

مَنْ شَهِدَ بِالْحَقِّ وَهُمْ يَعْلَمُوْنَ ۞ وَلَئِنْ سَاَلْتَهُمْ

مَّنْ خَلَقَهُمْ لَيَقُوْلُنَّ اللّٰهُ فَاَنّٰى يُؤْفَكُوْنَ ۞ وَقِيْلِهٖ

يٰرَبِّ اِنَّ هٰٓؤُلَآءِ قَوْمٌ لَّا يُؤْمِنُوْنَ ۞ فَاصْفَحْ عَنْهُمْ

وَقُلْ سَلٰمٌ ط فَسَوْفَ يَعْلَمُوْنَ ۞

⁷⁷ "Angel," they will call out, "If only your Lord would finish us off ." He will reply, "You are here to stay forever!" ⁷⁸ We brought the truth to you, but most of you disliked the truth. ⁷⁹ Yes, if they have made a final decision, let them know We have also made a final decision. ⁸⁰ Or do they think We don't hear their secret chats and private discussions? No, Our messengers *standing* by their sides are recording them. ⁸¹ Say: "If the most Kind had a son, I would be *his* first worshipper. ⁸² Glory be to the Lord of the Heavens and the Earth, the Lord of the Throne, from what they ascribe to Him." ⁸³ Leave them in idle talk and amusement until they meet their Day, which they have been promised.

Only the truthful are allowed to intercede

⁸⁴ He is the only God in the sky, and He is the only God on Earth, the Wise, the Knower. ⁸⁵ Blessed is He to Whom the Heavens and the Earth belongs and all that is between them, and He knows the coming of the Final Hour and to Him you will be returned. ⁸⁶ Those they worship beside Him have no right of intercession; only those who bear witness to the truth will have the right to intercession, and they know that. ⁸⁷ If you ask them: "Who created them?" They will certainly say, "Allah," so why are they deceived? ⁸⁸ And I swear by what He says, "My Lord, these are a people who don't believe." ⁸⁹ *Prophet* forgive them and say: "Peace," they will come to know *the reality*.

44. Surat Ad-Dukhan

The Smoke

According to some commentators, this Makkan surat was revealed after a famine struck Makkah; the dust blew, and Makkah was covered with a cloud of dust. The Makkans came to the Prophet ﷺ and asked him to pray for relief from the famine, they promised to believe if they were relieved. He ﷺ prayed and it rained, but the Makkans didn't keep their word, like the people of Pharaoh they broke their promise. The Quran tells the story as a deterrent. Some commentators believe the smoke cloud refers to a catastrophe that will occur near the Final Hour, possibly a nuclear explosion.

The surat paints a frightening picture of the people of Hell; fed from the tree known as Zaqqum, when its fruit enters the stomach, it boils. What a contrast to the delights that await the pious people of Paradise. The purpose of the Quran is to awaken God-consciousness in people: "So wait, they *the disbelievers* are also waiting" (59).

بِسْمِ اللهِ الرَّحْمٰنِ الرَّحِیْمِ

حٰمٓ ۟ وَالْكِتٰبِ الْمُبِیْنِ ۟ۙ اِنَّاۤ اَنْزَلْنٰهُ فِیْ لَیْلَةٍ

مُّبٰرَكَةٍ اِنَّا كُنَّا مُنْذِرِیْنَ ۟ فِیْهَا یُفْرَقُ كُلُّ اَمْرٍ

حَكِیْمٍ ۟ۙ اَمْرًا مِّنْ عِنْدِنَا ؕ اِنَّا كُنَّا مُرْسِلِیْنَ ۟ۚ

رَحْمَةً مِّنْ رَّبِّكَ ؕ اِنَّهٗ هُوَ السَّمِیْعُ الْعَلِیْمُ ۟ۙ

رَبِّ السَّمٰوٰتِ وَالْاَرْضِ وَمَا بَیْنَهُمَا ۚ اِنْ

كُنْتُمْ مُّوْقِنِیْنَ ۟ لَاۤ اِلٰهَ اِلَّا هُوَ یُحْیٖ وَیُمِیْتُ ؕ

رَبُّكُمْ وَرَبُّ اٰبَآئِكُمُ الْاَوَّلِیْنَ ۟ بَلْ هُمْ فِیْ شَكٍّ

یَّلْعَبُوْنَ ۟ فَارْتَقِبْ یَوْمَ تَاْتِی السَّمَآءُ بِدُخَانٍ

مُّبِیْنٍ ۟ۙ یَّغْشَی النَّاسَ ؕ هٰذَا عَذَابٌ اَلِیْمٌ ۟

رَبَّنَا اكْشِفْ عَنَّا الْعَذَابَ اِنَّا مُؤْمِنُوْنَ ۟ اَنّٰی

لَهُمُ الذِّكْرٰی وَقَدْ جَآءَهُمْ رَسُوْلٌ مُّبِیْنٌ ۟ۙ

ثُمَّ تَوَلَّوْا عَنْهُ وَقَالُوْا مُعَلَّمٌ مَّجْنُوْنٌ ۟ اِنَّا

كَاشِفُوا الْعَذَابِ قَلِیْلًا اِنَّكُمْ عَآئِدُوْنَ ۟ۘ یَوْمَ

نَبْطِشُ الْبَطْشَةَ الْكُبْرٰی ۚ اِنَّا مُنْتَقِمُوْنَ ۟

وَلَقَدْ فَتَنَّا قَبْلَهُمْ قَوْمَ فِرْعَوْنَ وَجَآءَهُمْ

رَسُوْلٌ كَرِیْمٌ ۟ۙ اَنْ اَدُّوْۤا اِلَیَّ عِبَادَ اللهِ ؕ اِنِّیْ

لَكُمْ رَسُوْلٌ اَمِیْنٌ ۟ۙ وَّاَنْ لَّا تَعْلُوْا عَلَی اللهِ ۚ

اِنِّیْۤ اٰتِیْكُمْ بِسُلْطٰنٍ مُّبِیْنٍ ۟ۚ وَاِنِّیْ عُذْتُ

Eleventh-hour belief is worthless when you are ill, facing immanent death. Believe now!

993

In the name of Allah, the Kind, the Caring.

¹ *Ha Meem.*

The Quran was revealed on a blessed night
² By the clear readable book, ³ We revealed it on a blessed night and have been warning *humanity.* ⁴ In it every matter is decided wisely; ⁵ all the commands come from Ourselves, We send *Message and messengers,* ⁶ a favour from Your Lord – the Hearer, the Knower, ⁷ the Lord of the Heavens and the Earth and what is between them – if only you are firm believers.

Makkans' are tested by a famine
⁸ There is no god but Him, He gives life and death, Your Lord and the Lord of your forefathers. ⁹ *Unfortunately,* they are in doubt, dilly-dallying.ᵃ ¹⁰ So wait for a Day when the sky brings clouds of smoke ¹¹ that will cover up people *and they will cry:* "This is painful punishment! ¹² Our Lord, relieve us, and we will believe." ¹³ They will not learn a lesson even when a Messenger has come to them, ¹⁴ they turn away from him and say, "He's been taught by someone and is possessed!" ¹⁵ Shortly We shall remove the punishment, but they will turn back *to their disbelief.* ¹⁶ The Day We seize them brutally, We shall take full revenge.

The Makkans are reminded of Pharaoh's fate
¹⁷ Long ago We tested Pharaoh's people, when a noble messenger came saying to them, ¹⁸ "Hand over to me the servants of Allah; I am a trustworthy messenger sent to you. ¹⁹ Don't regard yourself greater than Allah; I've come with distinct authority to you. ²⁰ I've sought protection from my Lord and your Lord from your abuse;ᵇ

ᵃ *Fee shakkin yal'abun* literally means "toying with doubt".
ᵇ *Tarjumun* literally means to stone, abuse and expel.

بِرَبِّىْ وَرَبِّكُمْ اَنْ تَرْجُمُوْنِ ﴿٢٠﴾ وَاِنْ لَّمْ تُؤْمِنُوْا
لِىْ فَاعْتَزِلُوْنِ ﴿٢١﴾ فَدَعَا رَبَّهٗۤ اَنَّ هٰۤؤُلَآءِ قَوْمٌ
مُّجْرِمُوْنَ ﴿٢٢﴾ فَاَسْرِ بِعِبَادِىْ لَيْلًا اِنَّكُمْ مُّتَّبَعُوْنَ ﴿٢٣﴾ الثلثة
وَاتْرُكِ الْبَحْرَ رَهْوًا ؕ اِنَّهُمْ جُنْدٌ مُّغْرَقُوْنَ ﴿٢٤﴾
كَمْ تَرَكُوْا مِنْ جَنّٰتٍ وَّعُيُوْنٍ ﴿٢٥﴾ وَّزُرُوْعٍ وَّ
مَقَامٍ كَرِيْمٍ ﴿٢٦﴾ وَّنَعْمَةٍ كَانُوْا فِيْهَا فٰكِهِيْنَ ﴿٢٧﴾
كَذٰلِكَ قف وَاَوْرَثْنٰهَا قَوْمًا اٰخَرِيْنَ ﴿٢٨﴾ فَمَا
بَكَتْ عَلَيْهِمُ السَّمَآءُ وَالْاَرْضُ وَمَا كَانُوْا
ع ١ ٢٩ ١٤ مُنْظَرِيْنَ ﴿٢٩﴾ ع وَلَقَدْ نَجَّيْنَا بَنِىْۤ اِسْرَآءِيْلَ مِنَ
الْعَذَابِ الْمُهِيْنِ ﴿٣٠﴾ مِنْ فِرْعَوْنَ ؕ اِنَّهٗ كَانَ عَالِيًا
مِّنَ الْمُسْرِفِيْنَ ﴿٣١﴾ وَلَقَدِ اخْتَرْنٰهُمْ عَلٰى عِلْمٍ
عَلَى الْعٰلَمِيْنَ ﴿٣٢﴾ وَاٰتَيْنٰهُمْ مِّنَ الْاٰيٰتِ مَا فِيْهِ
بَلٰٓؤٌا مُّبِيْنٌ ﴿٣٣﴾ اِنَّ هٰۤؤُلَآءِ لَيَقُوْلُوْنَ ﴿٣٤﴾ اِنْ هِىَ
اِلَّا مَوْتَتُنَا الْاُوْلٰى وَمَا نَحْنُ بِمُنْشَرِيْنَ ﴿٣٥﴾
فَاْتُوْا بِاٰبَآىِٕنَاۤ اِنْ كُنْتُمْ صٰدِقِيْنَ ﴿٣٦﴾ اَهُمْ
خَيْرٌ اَمْ قَوْمُ تُبَّعٍ ۙ وَّالَّذِيْنَ مِنْ قَبْلِهِمْ ؕ
اَهْلَكْنٰهُمْ ز اِنَّهُمْ كَانُوْا مُجْرِمِيْنَ ﴿٣٧﴾ وَمَا خَلَقْنَا
السَّمٰوٰتِ وَالْاَرْضَ وَمَا بَيْنَهُمَا لٰعِبِيْنَ ﴿٣٨﴾ مَا
خَلَقْنٰهُمَاۤ اِلَّا بِالْحَقِّ وَلٰكِنَّ اَكْثَرَهُمْ لَا يَعْلَمُوْنَ ﴿٣٩﴾
اِنَّ يَوْمَ الْفَصْلِ مِيْقَاتُهُمْ اَجْمَعِيْنَ ﴿٤٠﴾ يَوْمَ

There were strong communities and empires before you, where are they now? Gone! You too will be gone – so get ready!

²¹ if you don't believe me then leave me alone." ²² Musa called out to His Lord, "These are wicked people." ²³ So *We ordered him*: "Take my servants by night, *though* you will be chased, ²⁴ *after crossing* the sea leave it parted,^a they will be a drowned army." ²⁵ They, *the Pharaoh's lot,* left behind many gardens, springs, ²⁶ cornfields and spacious homes and ²⁷ clubs where they had fun. ²⁸ We raised other people to inherit them, ²⁹ neither the Heavens nor the Earth wept over them, they weren't given respite.

Allah favoured the Israelites

³⁰ We delivered the Israelites from the shameful punishment ³¹ of the Pharaoh; he was arrogant and had gone beyond limits. ³² We knowingly favoured them above other people *of their time.* ³³ We showed them many miracles; in them was a clear test.

Life has a purpose

³⁴ These *Makkans* say: ³⁵ "There is only one death for us; we won't be resurrected. ³⁶ Why don't you bring to life our forefathers if you are truthful." ³⁷ Are they better, or the people of Tubba^b and the people before them? We destroyed them since they were wicked. ³⁸ We didn't create the Heavens and the Earth and what is between them as an amusement *park.* ³⁹ We created them for a purpose, but most don't know. ⁴⁰ The Day of Decision is the fixed time for all of them,

---

^a *Rahwan* according to Al-Qurtubi means cleft or parted.
^b *Tubba* is the historic title of the Kings of Yemen of southern Arabia.

لَا يُغْنِىْ مَوْلًى عَنْ مَّوْلًى شَيْئًا وَّ لَا هُمْ يُنْصَرُوْنَ ۞ۙ اِلَّا مَنْ رَّحِمَ اللهُ ط اِنَّهٗ هُوَ الْعَزِيْزُ الرَّحِيْمُ ۞ع اِنَّ شَجَرَتَ الزَّقُّوْمِۙ ۞ طَعَامُ الْاَثِيْمِۚۛ ۞ كَالْمُهْلِۚۛ يَغْلِىْ فِى الْبُطُوْنِۙ ۞ كَغَلْىِ الْحَمِيْمِ ۞ خُذُوْهُ فَاعْتِلُوْهُ اِلٰى سَوَآءِ الْجَحِيْمِۖ۟ ۞ ثُمَّ صُبُّوْا فَوْقَ رَاْسِهٖ مِنْ عَذَابِ الْحَمِيْمِؕ ۞ ذُقْۚ اِنَّكَ اَنْتَ الْعَزِيْزُ الْكَرِيْمُ ۞ اِنَّ هٰذَا مَا كُنْتُمْ بِهٖ تَمْتَرُوْنَ ۞ اِنَّ الْمُتَّقِيْنَ فِىْ مَقَامٍ اَمِيْنٍۙ ۞ فِىْ جَنّٰتٍ وَّ عُيُوْنٍۚۙ ۞ يَلْبَسُوْنَ مِنْ سُنْدُسٍ وَّ اِسْتَبْرَقٍ مُّتَقٰبِلِيْنَۚۙ ۞ كَذٰلِكَۛ وَ زَوَّجْنٰهُمْ بِحُوْرٍ عِيْنٍؕ ۞ يَدْعُوْنَ فِيْهَا بِكُلِّ فَاكِهَةٍ اٰمِنِيْنَۙ ۞ لَا يَذُوْقُوْنَ فِيْهَا الْمَوْتَ اِلَّا الْمَوْتَةَ الْاُوْلٰىۚ وَ وَقٰىهُمْ عَذَابَ الْجَحِيْمِۙ ۞ فَضْلًا مِّنْ رَّبِّكَؕ ذٰلِكَ هُوَ الْفَوْزُ الْعَظِيْمُ ۞ فَاِنَّمَا يَسَّرْنٰهُ بِلِسَانِكَ لَعَلَّهُمْ يَتَذَكَّرُوْنَ ۞ فَارْتَقِبْ اِنَّهُمْ مُّرْتَقِبُوْنَ ۞ع

Life is a serious gift of the Lord. Don't waste it by indulging in worldly delights and pleasures!

997

[41] a Day when no friend will benefit a friend in the slightest, nor will they be helped, [42] except anyone Allah wants to be kind to. He is the Mighty, the Caring.

The sinners' punishment in Hell

[43] The tree of Zaqqum [44] will be the sinners' food, [45] like molten copper that boils in the stomach, [46] bubbling like boiling water. [47] It will be said: "Seize him and drag him to the middle of Hell! [48] Then pour the punishment of boiling water over his head. [49] Taste it! You were the honourable influential one![a] [50] This is what you doubted!"

The pious will enjoy Paradise

[51] The pious will *live* in a safe place; [52] of gardens and water fountains, [53] wearing embroidered silken dress enjoying each other's company. [54] That's how it will be, We shall wed them with pure spouses with gorgeous eyes. [55] Safe and satisfied, they will enjoy every kind of fruit. [56] They will taste death only once and will be protected from the punishment of Hell, [57] a bounty from your Lord! That is the supreme victory. [58] We made the Quran easy to understand in your language, so they may pay attention. [59] So wait, they're waiting *too*.

---

[a]   This is irony and an example of covert contempt for them.

45. Surat Al-Jathiyah

Kneeling

The central theme of this Makkan surat is to acknowledge *Tawhid*, the Unity of Allah, and depose idols. This seminal teaching of the Quran sums up the mission of Islam. A passage about nature opens the surat: marvellous signs in the creation clearly point to a Creator, from the plant kingdom to animals, the celestial bodies and the rain cycle. Attention is drawn to Divine creativity, and the idolaters are invited to reflect on the helplessness of their idols: "This Quran is full of insights for humanity, a guidance and beneficial for faithful people" (20).

The leaders of Quraysh vehemently opposed the Messenger ﷺ because he was too radical, and posed a serious threat to their status, wealth and belief systems. They opposed him to preserve their hegemony and customs: they sought to defend their gods, protect the status quo and the wealth they earned from pilgrims who visited the shrines. They weren't prepared to accept the Sovereignty and the Oneness of the God of Muhammad ﷺ. Too much was at stake; loss of status and power.

The disbelievers are warned of the consequences of their rebellion: "When you will see all the communities kneeling down. Today, each community will be summoned to its Book of Deeds" (28). They "mocked Allah's verses and were deceived by worldly life" (35) to their own detriment. The surat ends as it began, by emphasising the greatness of Allah.

بِسْمِ اللهِ الرَّحْمٰنِ الرَّحِيْمِ

حٰمٓ ۚ ۱ تَنْزِيْلُ الْكِتٰبِ مِنَ اللهِ الْعَزِيْزِ الْحَكِيْمِ ۲

اِنَّ فِى السَّمٰوٰتِ وَ الْاَرْضِ لَاٰيٰتٍ لِّلْمُؤْمِنِيْنَ ۳

وَ فِىْ خَلْقِكُمْ وَ مَا يَبُثُّ مِنْ دَآبَّةٍ اٰيٰتٌ لِّقَوْمٍ يُّوْقِنُوْنَ ۴ وَ اخْتِلَافِ الَّيْلِ وَ النَّهَارِ وَ مَاۤ اَنْزَلَ اللهُ مِنَ السَّمَآءِ مِنْ رِّزْقٍ فَاَحْيَا بِهِ الْاَرْضَ بَعْدَ مَوْتِهَا وَ تَصْرِيْفِ الرِّيٰحِ اٰيٰتٌ لِّقَوْمٍ يَّعْقِلُوْنَ ۵ تِلْكَ اٰيٰتُ اللهِ نَتْلُوْهَا عَلَيْكَ بِالْحَقِّ ۚ فَبِاَىِّ حَدِيْثٍۭ بَعْدَ اللهِ وَ اٰيٰتِهٖ يُؤْمِنُوْنَ ۶ وَيْلٌ لِّكُلِّ اَفَّاكٍ اَثِيْمٍ ۷

يَّسْمَعُ اٰيٰتِ اللهِ تُتْلٰى عَلَيْهِ ثُمَّ يُصِرُّ مُسْتَكْبِرًا كَاَنْ لَّمْ يَسْمَعْهَا ۚ فَبَشِّرْهُ بِعَذَابٍ اَلِيْمٍ ۸ وَ اِذَا عَلِمَ مِنْ اٰيٰتِنَا شَيْئًا ۨ اتَّخَذَهَا هُزُوًا ۙ اُولٰٓئِكَ لَهُمْ عَذَابٌ مُّهِيْنٌ ۹ مِنْ وَّرَآئِهِمْ جَهَنَّمُ ۚ وَ لَا يُغْنِىْ عَنْهُمْ مَّا كَسَبُوْا شَيْئًا وَّلَا مَا اتَّخَذُوْا مِنْ دُوْنِ اللهِ اَوْلِيَآءَ ۚ وَ لَهُمْ عَذَابٌ عَظِيْمٌ ۱۰ هٰذَا هُدًى ۚ وَ الَّذِيْنَ كَفَرُوْا بِاٰيٰتِ رَبِّهِمْ لَهُمْ عَذَابٌ مِّنْ رِّجْزٍ اَلِيْمٌ ۱۱ اَللهُ الَّذِىْ سَخَّرَ لَكُمُ الْبَحْرَ لِتَجْرِىَ الْفُلْكُ

The vast, complex, expansive and awesome universe is inviting you to bow before its Creator. So bow!

1001

In the name of Allah, the Kind, the Caring.

¹ *Ha Meem.*

Signs of Allah's greatness in nature

² This *Majestic* Book is revealed by Allah, the Almighty, the Wise. ³ There are *plenty* of signs for the believers in the Heavens and the Earth; ⁴ and in your creation and the way creatures have been dispersed *around the globe, there* are signs for people of firm faith. ⁵ In the alternation of the night and the day, and *the rain* which He sends from the sky and the blowing winds, *a* delivery that brings the dead Earth to life. These are signs for intelligent people, ⁶ *clear* signs *of* Allah's *creative power;* We described them exactly as they are. So what kind of message will they believe in once Allah has explained His Signs?

Signs of Allah's greatness in the Scripture

⁷ Woe to every liar and sinner ⁸ who hears the verses of Allah recited in front of him, but remains stubbornly arrogant as though he hasn't heard them. So give him the good news of a painful punishment. ⁹ When he hears something about Our Scripture he mocks it. They deserve a humiliating punishment. ¹⁰ Hell is waiting for them – nothing they did nor those who they took as friends beside Allah will benefit them – they will have a painful punishment. ¹¹ A painful punishment for those who deny *this Quran,* a guidance, the Scripture of their Lord.

Allah created nature for human benefit

¹² Allah laid open the sea for you, so ships sail in it by His command, making it possible for you to seek His bounty and be thankful.

فِيهِ بِأَمْرِهِ وَلِتَبْتَغُوا مِنْ فَضْلِهِ وَلَعَلَّكُمْ

تَشْكُرُونَ ۝ وَسَخَّرَ لَكُمْ مَّا فِي السَّمٰوٰتِ وَمَا

فِي الْأَرْضِ جَمِيعًا مِّنْهُ ۚ إِنَّ فِي ذٰلِكَ لَأَيٰتٍ

لِّقَوْمٍ يَّتَفَكَّرُونَ ۝ قُلْ لِّلَّذِينَ اٰمَنُوا يَغْفِرُوا

لِلَّذِينَ لَا يَرْجُونَ أَيَّامَ اللّٰهِ لِيَجْزِيَ قَوْمًا

بِمَا كَانُوا يَكْسِبُونَ ۝ مَنْ عَمِلَ صَالِحًا

فَلِنَفْسِهِ ۚ وَمَنْ أَسَاءَ فَعَلَيْهَا ۖ ثُمَّ إِلَىٰ رَبِّكُمْ

تُرْجَعُونَ ۝ وَلَقَدْ اٰتَيْنَا بَنِيٓ إِسْرَآءِيلَ

الْكِتٰبَ وَالْحُكْمَ وَالنُّبُوَّةَ وَرَزَقْنٰهُمْ مِّنَ

الطَّيِّبٰتِ وَفَضَّلْنٰهُمْ عَلَى الْعٰلَمِينَ ۝ وَاٰتَيْنٰهُمْ

بَيِّنٰتٍ مِّنَ الْأَمْرِ ۚ فَمَا اخْتَلَفُوٓا إِلَّا مِنْ بَعْدِ

مَا جَآءَهُمُ الْعِلْمُ ۙ بَغْيًا بَيْنَهُمْ ۚ إِنَّ رَبَّكَ

يَقْضِي بَيْنَهُمْ يَوْمَ الْقِيٰمَةِ فِيمَا كَانُوا فِيهِ

يَخْتَلِفُونَ ۝ ثُمَّ جَعَلْنٰكَ عَلَىٰ شَرِيعَةٍ مِّنَ الْأَمْرِ

فَاتَّبِعْهَا وَلَا تَتَّبِعْ أَهْوَآءَ الَّذِينَ لَا يَعْلَمُونَ ۝

اِنَّهُمْ لَنْ يُّغْنُوا عَنْكَ مِنَ اللّٰهِ شَيْئًا ۚ وَاِنَّ

الظّٰلِمِينَ بَعْضُهُمْ أَوْلِيَآءُ بَعْضٍ ۚ وَاللّٰهُ وَلِيُّ

الْمُتَّقِينَ ۝ هٰذَا بَصَآئِرُ لِلنَّاسِ وَهُدًى

وَّرَحْمَةٌ لِّقَوْمٍ يُّوقِنُونَ ۝ أَمْ حَسِبَ الَّذِينَ

اجْتَرَحُوا السَّيِّئَاتِ أَنْ نَّجْعَلَهُمْ كَالَّذِينَ

The good we do benefits us, not Allah. Its benefit to others in the end comes back to us. So do good all the time.

¹³ *As a favour,* He has subjected everything for your benefit in the Heavens and the Earth; there are signs for reflective people. ¹⁴ Say to the believers: "Pardon those who have no hope of Allah's days," Allah will reward people for what they earned. ¹⁵ Whoever does good deeds will benefit himself and whoever does evil will harm himself. Then, you will be returned to Your Lord.

The Israelites also disagreed

¹⁶ We gave the Book, the law, prophethood, and plenty of wealth to the Israelites, and *furthermore* favoured them over other folks. ¹⁷ We gave them clear proofs for the law, and though they had knowledge they still disagreed among themselves, they were jealous of each other. On Judgement Day, Your Lord will make the judgement about their disagreement.

The Quran gives enlightenment to the faithful

¹⁸ *Prophet,* We established a Shariah for you,ᵃ so follow it and don't follow the whims of those who don't know. ¹⁹ They won't benefit you in the slightest against the Will of Allah. The wrongdoers are each other's helpers while Allah is the helper of the pious. ²⁰ This Quran is full of insights for humanity,ᵇ and a guidance and other benefits for faithful people. ²¹ Or do evildoers think We will make them like the righteous believers, so they are like them in their living and dying? They've made a bad judgement.

ᵃ *Shariah* literally means "the path to a watering hole", and technically refers to the system of Islamic law, moral values, social manners, and spiritual principles.

ᵇ *Basaa'ir* literally means insights, understanding underlying truths and meanings; seeing beyond the visible and being able to understand the character and the context.

أَمَنُوْا وَ عَمِلُوا الصَّلِحْتِ لا سَوَآءً مَّحْیَاهُمْ
وَمَمَاتُهُمْ ط سَآءَ مَا یَحْكُمُوْنَ ع ۲۱ وَ خَلَقَ اللهُ
السَّمٰوٰتِ وَالْاَرْضَ بِالْحَقِّ وَلِتُجْزٰى كُلُّ نَفْسٍ
بِمَا كَسَبَتْ وَ هُمْ لَا یُظْلَمُوْنَ ۲۲ اَفَرَءَیْتَ
مَنِ اتَّخَذَ اِلٰهَهٗ هَوٰهُ وَ اَضَلَّهُ اللهُ عَلٰی
عِلْمٍ وَّ خَتَمَ عَلٰی سَمْعِهٖ وَقَلْبِهٖ وَجَعَلَ
عَلٰی بَصَرِهٖ غِشَاوَةً ط فَمَنْ یَّهْدِیْهِ مِنْ بَعْدِ
اللهِ ط اَفَلَا تَذَكَّرُوْنَ ۲۳ وَ قَالُوْا مَا هِیَ اِلَّا
حَیَاتُنَا الدُّنْیَا نَمُوْتُ وَنَحْیَا وَمَا یُهْلِكُنَا اِلَّا
الدَّهْرُ ج وَمَا لَهُمْ بِذٰلِكَ مِنْ عِلْمٍ ج اِنْ هُمْ
اِلَّا یَظُنُّوْنَ ۲۴ وَاِذَا تُتْلٰى عَلَیْهِمْ اٰیٰتُنَا بَیِّنٰتٍ
مَّا كَانَ حُجَّتَهُمْ اِلَّا اَنْ قَالُوا ائْتُوْا بِاٰبَآئِنَآ
اِنْ كُنْتُمْ صٰدِقِیْنَ ۲۵ قُلِ اللهُ یُحْیِیْكُمْ ثُمَّ
یُمِیْتُكُمْ ثُمَّ یَجْمَعُكُمْ اِلٰی یَوْمِ الْقِیٰمَةِ لَا
رَیْبَ فِیْهِ وَلٰكِنَّ اَكْثَرَ النَّاسِ لَا یَعْلَمُوْنَ ۲۶
وَلِلّٰهِ مُلْكُ السَّمٰوٰتِ وَالْاَرْضِ ط وَیَوْمَ تَقُوْمُ
السَّاعَةُ یَوْمَئِذٍ یَّخْسَرُ الْمُبْطِلُوْنَ ۲۷ وَتَرٰى
كُلَّ اُمَّةٍ جَاثِیَةً قف كُلُّ اُمَّةٍ تُدْعٰى اِلٰى
كِتٰبِهَا ط اَلْیَوْمَ تُجْزَوْنَ مَا كُنْتُمْ تَعْمَلُوْنَ ۲۸
هٰذَا كِتٰبُنَا یَنْطِقُ عَلَیْكُمْ بِالْحَقِّ ط اِنَّا

When the shameful ego, pleasure and passion becomes one's god, and he adores and loves his wealth, body, home and children, he becomes forgetful of Allah.

Their desires are their gods

²² Allah created the Heavens and the Earth for a purpose: to reward each person for what they did and they won't be wronged. ²³ Have you seen him who made desire his god despite knowing otherwise? Allah let him go astray, sealed his hearing and heart and covered his eyes. Who will guide him now beside Allah? Don't you pay attention? ²⁴ They say, "There is no life except our worldly life, we die, we live and *eventually*, time will kill us." They have no understanding of the reality, and they are merely guessing.

The Book of Deeds will be presented

²⁵ When our clear verses are recited before them they're unable to *find* proofs against them, but they still say, "Bring back to life our forefathers if you are truthful." ²⁶ Tell them: "Allah gave you life, then will let you die and then gather you on Judgement Day, there is no doubt in that. But most people don't know." ²⁷ The control of the Heavens and the Earth belongs to Allah. When the Final Hour comes the followers of falsehood will be the losers that Day. ²⁸ You will see all communities kneeling. Today, each community will be summoned to its Book of Deeds, and told: "You shall be rewarded for what you did, ²⁹ this is Our record, it speaks the truth, everything you did We wrote down."

كُنَّا نَسۡتَنۡسِخُ مَا كُنۡتُمۡ تَعۡمَلُوۡنَ ﴿۲۹﴾ فَاَمَّا

الَّذِیۡنَ اٰمَنُوۡا وَ عَمِلُوا الصّٰلِحٰتِ فَیُدۡخِلُهُمۡ

رَبُّهُمۡ فِیۡ رَحۡمَتِهٖ ؕ ذٰلِكَ هُوَ الۡفَوۡزُ الۡمُبِیۡنُ ﴿۳۰﴾

وَ اَمَّا الَّذِیۡنَ كَفَرُوۡا ۟ اَفَلَمۡ تَكُنۡ اٰیٰتِیۡ تُتۡلٰی

عَلَیۡكُمۡ فَاسۡتَكۡبَرۡتُمۡ وَ كُنۡتُمۡ قَوۡمًا مُّجۡرِمِیۡنَ ﴿۳۱﴾

وَ اِذَا قِیۡلَ اِنَّ وَعۡدَ اللّٰهِ حَقٌّ وَّ السَّاعَةُ لَا رَیۡبَ

فِیۡهَا ۙ قُلۡتُمۡ مَّا نَدۡرِیۡ مَا السَّاعَةُ ۙ اِنۡ نَّظُنُّ

اِلَّا ظَنًّا وَّ مَا نَحۡنُ بِمُسۡتَیۡقِنِیۡنَ ﴿۳۲﴾ وَ بَدَا لَهُمۡ

سَیِّاٰتُ مَا عَمِلُوۡا وَ حَاقَ بِهِمۡ مَّا كَانُوۡا بِهٖ

یَسۡتَهۡزِءُوۡنَ ﴿۳۳﴾ وَ قِیۡلَ الۡیَوۡمَ نَنۡسٰكُمۡ كَمَا نَسِیۡتُمۡ

لِقَآءَ یَوۡمِكُمۡ هٰذَا وَ مَاۡوٰىكُمُ النَّارُ وَ مَا لَكُمۡ

مِّنۡ نّٰصِرِیۡنَ ﴿۳۴﴾ ذٰلِكُمۡ بِاَنَّكُمُ اتَّخَذۡتُمۡ اٰیٰتِ

اللّٰهِ هُزُوًا وَّ غَرَّتۡكُمُ الۡحَیٰوةُ الدُّنۡیَا ۚ فَالۡیَوۡمَ

لَا یُخۡرَجُوۡنَ مِنۡهَا وَ لَا هُمۡ یُسۡتَعۡتَبُوۡنَ ﴿۳۵﴾ فَلِلّٰهِ

الۡحَمۡدُ رَبِّ السَّمٰوٰتِ وَ رَبِّ الۡاَرۡضِ رَبِّ

الۡعٰلَمِیۡنَ ﴿۳۶﴾ وَ لَهُ الۡكِبۡرِیَآءُ فِی السَّمٰوٰتِ وَ

الۡاَرۡضِ ۫ وَ هُوَ الۡعَزِیۡزُ الۡحَكِیۡمُ ﴿۳۷﴾

The Day of Judgement will wake them all up, but that will be too late. Let's turn to Him now! Right now!

³⁰ So those who believed and did righteous deeds, their Lord will be kind to them; that will be the clear victory. ³¹ Those who disbelieved will be asked: "Were My verses not recited to you? No, you were arrogant and a wicked lot."

The life of the world deceived them

³² When it was said: "Allah's promise is true and there is no doubt *in the coming of the Final Hour,*" you replied, "We don't know what the Final Hour is; we assumed it's an idea, and we weren't convinced at all". ³³ The evil consequences of their deeds will become clear to them as they are tracked by what they mocked. ³⁴ They will be told: "Today We'll abandon you since you forgot the meeting of this Day of yours; this is your destination – Hell. You have no helpers. ³⁵ That is because you mocked Allah's verses and were deceived by worldly life." So today they won't be taken out of it, nor given an opportunity to explain themselves.ᵃ ³⁶ All the praises are for Allah; the Lord of the Heavens, the Lord of the Earth and Lord of the worlds. ³⁷ All greatness in the Heavens and the Earth is His and He is the Almighty, the Wise.

ᵃ   *Yusta'thabun* literally means "to demand repentance from a sinner". Here it means, on Judgement Day, when the reality dawns on them and they see Hell, they will want to repent, but that won't happen.

46. Surat Al-Ahqaf

The Sand Dunes

This surat was revealed before the migration of the Prophet ﷺ to Madinah, the tone and tenor of the surat makes this clear. The Prophet ﷺ is advised: "be patient like the strong-willed messengers" (35). The boycott faced by the Muslims in the valley of Abu-Talib for three years had been lifted. Here they had languished in abject poverty and starvation, which left them with physical and psychological scars.

A group of jinn visited the Prophet ﷺ on his return from the torturous journey to Taif. If so, then this surat would have been revealed in the tenth or eleventh year of his mission in Makkah. The opening describes the helplessness of the idols, and contrasts it with the creative power of Allah. Then it explains how Allah's channel of communication was always open with humanity through His messengers, therefore the coming of Prophet Muhammad ﷺ was nothing new or odd. In fact, his coming was foreseen by Musa ﷺ:

> An Israelite witness has already testified to the coming of one like him, and has believed, why are you being arrogant? Allah does not guide the wrongdoers (10).

This refers to Deuteronomy 18, verses 15–18. The Quran comments on the suspicious mind of the disbelievers: "The disbelievers say to the believers, 'If this *religion* was any good then you wouldn't have believed in it before us'" (11).

Verses 15–19 encourage the development of parent-child relationships, by describing how the mother bears the child and then suckles and rears it until the child becomes strong and mature. Just as we should be grateful to our parents and appreciative of what they have blessed us with, we should be thankful to Allah, our Lord and Creator. The surat goes on to warn the Makkans of the demise of the People of the Sand Dunes, who were rebellious, and then towards the closing of the surat relates the story of a band of jinn who visited the Prophet ﷺ as an encouragement to believe in him: the loyalty and submission of the jinn is a mark of being Muslims among the invisible creatures of Allah.

بِسْمِ اللهِ الرَّحْمٰنِ الرَّحِيْمِ

حٰمٓ ۚ ١ تَنْزِيْلُ الْكِتٰبِ مِنَ اللهِ الْعَزِيْزِ الْحَكِيْمِ ٢

مَا خَلَقْنَا السَّمٰوٰتِ وَالْاَرْضَ وَمَا بَيْنَهُمَآ اِلَّا بِالْحَقِّ وَاَجَلٍ مُّسَمًّى ۗ وَالَّذِيْنَ كَفَرُوْا عَمَّآ اُنْذِرُوْا مُعْرِضُوْنَ ٣ قُلْ اَرَءَيْتُمْ مَّا تَدْعُوْنَ مِنْ دُوْنِ اللهِ اَرُوْنِيْ مَا ذَا خَلَقُوْا مِنَ الْاَرْضِ اَمْ لَهُمْ شِرْكٌ فِى السَّمٰوٰتِ ۗ اِيْتُوْنِيْ بِكِتٰبٍ مِّنْ قَبْلِ هٰذَآ اَوْ اَثٰرَةٍ مِّنْ عِلْمٍ اِنْ كُنْتُمْ صٰدِقِيْنَ ٤

وَمَنْ اَضَلُّ مِمَّنْ يَّدْعُوْا مِنْ دُوْنِ اللهِ مَنْ لَّا يَسْتَجِيْبُ لَهٗٓ اِلٰى يَوْمِ الْقِيٰمَةِ وَهُمْ عَنْ دُعَآئِهِمْ غٰفِلُوْنَ ٥ وَاِذَا حُشِرَ النَّاسُ كَانُوْا لَهُمْ اَعْدَآءً وَّكَانُوْا بِعِبَادَتِهِمْ كٰفِرِيْنَ ٦ وَاِذَا تُتْلٰى عَلَيْهِمْ اٰيٰتُنَا بَيِّنٰتٍ قَالَ الَّذِيْنَ كَفَرُوْا لِلْحَقِّ لَمَّا جَآءَهُمْ ۙ هٰذَا سِحْرٌ مُّبِيْنٌ ٧ اَمْ يَقُوْلُوْنَ افْتَرٰىهُ ۗ قُلْ اِنِ افْتَرَيْتُهٗ فَلَا تَمْلِكُوْنَ لِيْ مِنَ اللهِ شَيْئًا ۗ هُوَ اَعْلَمُ بِمَا تُفِيْضُوْنَ فِيْهِ ۗ كَفٰى بِهٖ شَهِيْدًۢا بَيْنِيْ وَبَيْنَكُمْ ۗ وَهُوَ الْغَفُوْرُ الرَّحِيْمُ ٨

قُلْ مَا كُنْتُ بِدْعًا مِّنَ الرُّسُلِ وَمَآ اَدْرِيْ مَا يُفْعَلُ بِيْ وَلَا بِكُمْ ۗ اِنْ اَتَّبِعُ اِلَّا مَا يُوْحٰىٓ اِلَيَّ

The material world is attractive, useful and honours power, but don't make it God! For many, material things are idols that they worship.

In the name of Allah, the Kind, the Caring.

¹ *Ha Meem.*

The helplessness of idols

² This glorious Book is sent down by Allah, the Almighty, the Wise. ³ We created Heavens and the Earth and what lies between them with a purpose only, for a fixed term. The disbelievers turn away from the warning given to them. ⁴ Say: "Have you seriously considered those you worship beside Allah? Show me what they have created on Earth, or were they partners in *the creation* of Heavens? Bring me a book from the past or any remnants of knowledgeᵃ if you are truthful." ⁵ Who is more misguided than the one who worships things that don't answer him beside Allah, till Judgement Day they will be unaware of their worship. ⁶ When they're gathered they will be their enemies, and will reject their worship.

The coming of Prophet Muhammad ﷺ is not a new thing

⁷ When Our verses are recited before the disbelievers, they speak about the truth *saying*, "This is plain magic!" ⁸ Or they say, "he has made this up." Say: "If I made it up you can't save me from Allah; He knows very well what you say about it. He is a sufficient witness between me and you. He is Forgiving and Most Caring." ⁹ Say: " I am not the first of the messengers nor *do I claim* that I know what will happen to me and you, I only follow what is revealed to me and I am a clear warner."

ᵃ *Asaratam min ilm* is an idiom for "knowledge that has been handed down by scholars and the sages" (Ibn Hayyan Undlasi).

وَمَاۤ اَنَا اِلَّا نَذِيْرٌ مُّبِيْنٌ ۟ قُلْ اَرَءَيْتُمْ اِنْ كَانَ
مِنْ عِنْدِ اللّٰهِ وَكَفَرْتُمْ بِهٖ وَشَهِدَ شَاهِدٌ مِّنْ
بَنِيْۤ اِسْرَآءِيْلَ عَلٰى مِثْلِهٖ فَاٰمَنَ وَاسْتَكْبَرْتُمْ ۚ
اِنَّ اللّٰهَ لَا يَهْدِى الْقَوْمَ الظّٰلِمِيْنَ ۟ وَقَالَ
الَّذِيْنَ كَفَرُوْا لِلَّذِيْنَ اٰمَنُوْا لَوْ كَانَ خَيْرًا مَّا
سَبَقُوْنَاۤ اِلَيْهِ ؕ وَاِذْ لَمْ يَهْتَدُوْا بِهٖ فَسَيَقُوْلُوْنَ
هٰذَاۤ اِفْكٌ قَدِيْمٌ ۟ وَمِنْ قَبْلِهٖ كِتٰبُ مُوْسٰۤى اِمَامًا
وَّرَحْمَةً ؕ وَهٰذَا كِتٰبٌ مُّصَدِّقٌ لِّسَانًا عَرَبِيًّا
لِّيُنْذِرَ الَّذِيْنَ ظَلَمُوْا ۖ وَبُشْرٰى لِلْمُحْسِنِيْنَ ۟ اِنَّ
الَّذِيْنَ قَالُوْا رَبُّنَا اللّٰهُ ثُمَّ اسْتَقَامُوْا فَلَا خَوْفٌ
عَلَيْهِمْ وَلَا هُمْ يَحْزَنُوْنَ ۟ اُولٰٓئِكَ اَصْحٰبُ الْجَنَّةِ
خٰلِدِيْنَ فِيْهَا ۚ جَزَآءًۢ بِمَا كَانُوْا يَعْمَلُوْنَ ۟ وَ
وَصَّيْنَا الْاِنْسَانَ بِوَالِدَيْهِ اِحْسَانًا ؕ حَمَلَتْهُ اُمُّهٗ
كُرْهًا وَّوَضَعَتْهُ كُرْهًا ؕ وَحَمْلُهٗ وَفِصٰلُهٗ ثَلٰثُوْنَ
شَهْرًا ؕ حَتّٰۤى اِذَا بَلَغَ اَشُدَّهٗ وَبَلَغَ اَرْبَعِيْنَ
سَنَةً ۙ قَالَ رَبِّ اَوْزِعْنِيۤ اَنْ اَشْكُرَ نِعْمَتَكَ الَّتِيْۤ
اَنْعَمْتَ عَلَيَّ وَعَلٰى وَالِدَيَّ وَاَنْ اَعْمَلَ صَالِحًا
تَرْضٰهُ وَاَصْلِحْ لِيْ فِيْ ذُرِّيَّتِيْ ؕ اِنِّيْ تُبْتُ
اِلَيْكَ وَاِنِّيْ مِنَ الْمُسْلِمِيْنَ ۟ اُولٰٓئِكَ الَّذِيْنَ
نَتَقَبَّلُ عَنْهُمْ اَحْسَنَ مَا عَمِلُوْا وَنَتَجَاوَزُ عَنْ

The thankful, obedient and hardworking person prays for inspiration to really appreciate the gifts of Allah. Learn the prayer and open your mind.

¹⁰ Say: "Have you considered: if this was from Allah and you denied it, *what would be the consequences?* A witness from the Israelites testified to the coming of one like himself and has believed, yet you are being arrogant.^a Allah does not guide the wrongdoers.

Contrasting attitudes of believers and disbelievers

¹¹ The disbelievers say to the believers, "If this *religion* was good, then you couldn't have believed it before we did." Since they didn't get any guidance from the Quran, they say, "This is an old lie," ¹² although before this Musa's Book came as a guide and a useful manual; and this Book too confirms it in the Arabic language to warn the wicked people, and to give good news to the righteous. ¹³ The people who say, "Our Lord is Allah," remain steadfast without fear, without worry – ¹⁴ these are people of Paradise, where they will live forever, a reward for what they did.

Importance of caring for parents

¹⁵ We advised humanity to care for parents; in pregnancy, his mother carried him with difficulty, and with greater difficulty she gave him birth. The pregnancy and the weaning took thirty months; when he reached his full maturity and *the* fortieth year, he prayed: "My Lord, inspire me to thank You for the gifts that You have blessed me and my parents with, and give me the ability to be righteous, to please You; make my children righteous, too. I turn towards You, and I am a Muslim." ¹⁶ These are the people whose good deeds We shall accept and forgive their sins, and they shall be people of Paradise. This is a true promise, Allah made with the faithful.

---

^a This refers to Musa ﷺ forecasting the coming of Prophet Muhammad ﷺ in Deuteronomy 18:18: "I will raise up for them a prophet like you from among their own people; I will put My words in the mouth of the Prophet, he shall speak to them everything that I command. Anyone who does not heed the words that the prophet shall speak in My name I Myself will hold accountable."

سَيِّاٰتِهِمْ فِىْ اَصْحٰبِ الْجَنَّةِؕ وَعْدَ الصِّدْقِ الَّذِىْ

كَانُوْا يُوْعَدُوْنَ ۝ وَالَّذِىْ قَالَ لِوَالِدَيْهِ اُفٍّ

لَّكُمَاۤ اَتَعِدٰنِنِىْۤ اَنْ اُخْرَجَ وَقَدْ خَلَتِ الْقُرُوْنُ

مِنْ قَبْلِىْۚ وَهُمَا يَسْتَغِيْثٰنِ اللهَ وَيْلَكَ اٰمِنْؕ اِنَّ

وَعْدَ اللهِ حَقٌّۚ فَيَقُوْلُ مَا هٰذَاۤ اِلَّاۤ اَسَاطِيْرُ

الْاَوَّلِيْنَ ۝ اُولٰٓئِكَ الَّذِيْنَ حَقَّ عَلَيْهِمُ الْقَوْلُ فِىْۤ

اُمَمٍ قَدْ خَلَتْ مِنْ قَبْلِهِمْ مِّنَ الْجِنِّ وَالْاِنْسِؕ

اِنَّهُمْ كَانُوْا خٰسِرِيْنَ ۝ وَلِكُلٍّ دَرَجٰتٌ مِّمَّا عَمِلُوْاۚ

وَلِيُوَفِّيَهُمْ اَعْمَالَهُمْ وَهُمْ لَا يُظْلَمُوْنَ ۝ وَيَوْمَ

يُعْرَضُ الَّذِيْنَ كَفَرُوْا عَلَى النَّارِؕ اَذْهَبْتُمْ طَيِّبٰتِكُمْ

فِىْ حَيَاتِكُمُ الدُّنْيَا وَاسْتَمْتَعْتُمْ بِهَاۚ فَالْيَوْمَ

تُجْزَوْنَ عَذَابَ الْهُوْنِ بِمَا كُنْتُمْ تَسْتَكْبِرُوْنَ فِى

الْاَرْضِ بِغَيْرِ الْحَقِّ وَبِمَا كُنْتُمْ تَفْسُقُوْنَ ۝ وَاذْكُرْ

اَخَا عَادٍؕ اِذْ اَنْذَرَ قَوْمَهٗ بِالْاَحْقَافِ وَقَدْ خَلَتِ

النُّذُرُ مِنْۢ بَيْنِ يَدَيْهِ وَمِنْ خَلْفِهٖۤ اَلَّا تَعْبُدُوْۤا

اِلَّا اللهَؕ اِنِّىْۤ اَخَافُ عَلَيْكُمْ عَذَابَ يَوْمٍ عَظِيْمٍ ۝

قَالُوْۤا اَجِئْتَنَا لِتَاْفِكَنَا عَنْ اٰلِهَتِنَاۚ فَاْتِنَا بِمَا

تَعِدُنَاۤ اِنْ كُنْتَ مِنَ الصّٰدِقِيْنَ ۝ قَالَ اِنَّمَا

الْعِلْمُ عِنْدَ اللهِۖ وَاُبَلِّغُكُمْ مَّاۤ اُرْسِلْتُ بِهٖ وَلٰكِنِّىْۤ

اَرٰىكُمْ قَوْمًا تَجْهَلُوْنَ ۝ فَلَمَّا رَاَوْهُ عَارِضًا مُّسْتَقْبِلَ

The prodigal son;
reckless, uncaring and
unthankful. A wretch.
Are you like him?

A disobedient son denies resurrection

¹⁷ *There's the one who angrily* said to his parents, "How come! You threaten me with being brought out *of the grave,* yet generations have passed away before me." Both parents beg Allah for help and say to *the son,* "Woe to you! Believe in Allah's true promise." He replies by saying, "These are stories of the ancient." ¹⁸ These are the ones who justly deserve the fate of the bygone nations of jinn and humans. They were losers. ¹⁹ People will have rank according to their works, and will get full reward for their works, and they won't be deprived *of their rights.* ²⁰ The Day when the disbelievers will be brought in front of the Fire *it will be said*: "You wasted the precious gifts of worldly life and indulged in pleasures, so today you will be rewarded with a humiliating punishment for your arrogance without any right on Earth, and for your disobedience.

The People of the Sand Dunes rejected the message

²¹ And remember *Prophet* Hud of the tribe of Ad. When he warned his people living near the sand dunes[a] – and many messengers had come to them before and after him – telling them, "Do not worship anyone except Allah. I fear for you the punishment of a mighty Day," ²² they said, "Have you come to turn us away from our gods? If that is so, then bring upon us what you threaten us with, if you are truthful." ²³ Prophet Hud said, "Allah alone knows *it's time*; however, I will keep delivering what message is given to me, but you are stubbornly ignorant people." ²⁴ When they saw the punishment coming, *it was* a cloud moving towards their valleys; they said, "This cloud will bring us rain." *Hud said,* "Yes, it's what you eagerly wanted, a sandstorm carrying painful torment.

---

[a] *Ahqaf,* from which the surat takes its name, refers to the sand dunes in the southern part of the Arabian Peninsula, where the empty quarter is north of Yemen. The modern cities of Tarim and Hadramaut are in this area.

أَوْدِيَتِهِمْ ۙ قَالُوْا هٰذَا عَارِضٌ مُّمْطِرُنَا ۚ بَلْ هُوَ مَا

اسْتَعْجَلْتُمْ بِهٖ ۗ رِيْحٌ فِيْهَا عَذَابٌ اَلِيْمٌ ۙ ۝ تُدَمِّرُ كُلَّ

شَىْءٍۢ بِاَمْرِ رَبِّهَا فَاَصْبَحُوْا لَا يُرٰٓى اِلَّا مَسٰكِنُهُمْ ۗ

كَذٰلِكَ نَجْزِى الْقَوْمَ الْمُجْرِمِيْنَ ۝ وَلَقَدْ مَكَّنّٰهُمْ

فِيْمَآ اِنْ مَّكَّنّٰكُمْ فِيْهِ وَجَعَلْنَا لَهُمْ سَمْعًا وَّاَبْصَارًا وَّ

اَفْـِٔدَةً ۖ فَمَآ اَغْنٰى عَنْهُمْ سَمْعُهُمْ وَلَآ اَبْصَارُهُمْ

وَلَآ اَفْـِٔدَتُهُمْ مِّنْ شَىْءٍ اِذْ كَانُوْا يَجْحَدُوْنَ ۙ بِاٰيٰتِ

اللّٰهِ وَحَاقَ بِهِمْ مَّا كَانُوْا بِهٖ يَسْتَهْزِءُوْنَ ۝ وَلَقَدْ

اَهْلَكْنَا مَا حَوْلَكُمْ مِّنَ الْقُرٰى وَصَرَّفْنَا الْاٰيٰتِ

لَعَلَّهُمْ يَرْجِعُوْنَ ۝ فَلَوْلَا نَصَرَهُمُ الَّذِيْنَ اتَّخَذُوْا

مِنْ دُوْنِ اللّٰهِ قُرْبَانًا اٰلِهَةً ۗ بَلْ ضَلُّوْا عَنْهُمْ ۚ

وَذٰلِكَ اِفْكُهُمْ وَمَا كَانُوْا يَفْتَرُوْنَ ۝ وَاِذْ صَرَفْنَآ

اِلَيْكَ نَفَرًا مِّنَ الْجِنِّ يَسْتَمِعُوْنَ الْقُرْاٰنَ ۚ فَلَمَّا

حَضَرُوْهُ قَالُوْٓا اَنْصِتُوْا ۚ فَلَمَّا قُضِىَ وَلَّوْا اِلٰى

قَوْمِهِمْ مُّنْذِرِيْنَ ۝ قَالُوْا يٰقَوْمَنَآ اِنَّا سَمِعْنَا

كِتٰبًا اُنْزِلَ مِنْۢ بَعْدِ مُوْسٰى مُصَدِّقًا لِّمَا بَيْنَ

يَدَيْهِ يَهْدِيْٓ اِلَى الْحَقِّ وَاِلٰى طَرِيْقٍ مُّسْتَقِيْمٍ ۝

يٰقَوْمَنَآ اَجِيْبُوْا دَاعِىَ اللّٰهِ وَاٰمِنُوْا بِهٖ يَغْفِرْ لَكُمْ

مِّنْ ذُنُوْبِكُمْ وَيُجِرْكُمْ مِّنْ عَذَابٍ اَلِيْمٍ ۝ وَمَنْ

لَّا يُجِبْ دَاعِىَ اللّٰهِ فَلَيْسَ بِمُعْجِزٍ فِى الْاَرْضِ

The Jinn's, the invisible intelligent creation of Allah. The Quran reminds us of other intelligent beings in the universe.

٣
ع
٤

²⁵ It will destroy everything in its path by the Lord's command." Next morning, there was nothing to see except their ruined homes. That is how We repay the sinners.

The Makkans are warned

²⁶ We made them stronger than you, and gave them ears, eyes and hearts, yet they didn't benefit the slightest from their ears, their eyes and their hearts, since they denied Allah's verses. What they used to mock overwhelmed them as punishment. ²⁷ We destroyed many towns that once flourished around you, and made clear to them the Scripture, so they may return. ²⁸ So why weren't they helped by the idols they took for nearness to gods beside Allah? In fact they deserted them, and this was the lie they invented.

Jinn converted to Islam

²⁹ Remember when We sent a group of jinnᵃ, they came and listened to the Quran, and said, "Listen silently." When the recitation had finished, they returned to their people to warn them. ³⁰ They told them, "Our people! We have heard a Book revealed after Musa, confirming previous Scriptures, and it guides to the truth and to the straight path. ³¹ They *continued,* "Accept the invitation of the one who calls you to Allah, and believe him and Allah will forgive your sins and save you from a painful punishment." ³² Whoever does not answer the one who summons to Allah, cannot escape the plan of Allah on Earth, and will have no helpers. They are clearly misguided.

ᵃ Abdullah ibn Masud said "the Prophet was reading the Quran at Batan-Nakhla when a group of Jinn came; they listened quietly" (Jalalain). Batan-Nakhla is a place south of Makka near Taif.

وَلَيْسَ لَهٗ مِنْ دُوْنِهٖٓ اَوْلِيَآءُ ۚ اُولٰٓئِكَ فِيْ ضَلٰلٍ
مُّبِيْنٍ ۞ اَوَلَمْ يَرَوْا اَنَّ اللّٰهَ الَّذِيْ خَلَقَ السَّمٰوٰتِ
وَالْاَرْضَ وَلَمْ يَعْىَ بِخَلْقِهِنَّ بِقٰدِرٍ عَلٰٓى اَنْ
يُّحْيِۦَ الْمَوْتٰى ۚ بَلٰٓى اِنَّهٗ عَلٰى كُلِّ شَيْءٍ قَدِيْرٌ ۞
وَيَوْمَ يُعْرَضُ الَّذِيْنَ كَفَرُوْا عَلَى النَّارِ ۗ اَلَيْسَ
هٰذَا بِالْحَقِّ ۗ قَالُوْا بَلٰى وَرَبِّنَا ۗ قَالَ فَذُوْقُوا
الْعَذَابَ بِمَا كُنْتُمْ تَكْفُرُوْنَ ۞ فَاصْبِرْ كَمَا صَبَرَ
اُولُوا الْعَزْمِ مِنَ الرُّسُلِ وَلَا تَسْتَعْجِلْ لَّهُمْ ۗ
كَاَنَّهُمْ يَوْمَ يَرَوْنَ مَا يُوْعَدُوْنَ ۙ لَمْ يَلْبَثُوْٓا
اِلَّا سَاعَةً مِّنْ نَّهَارٍ ۚ بَلٰغٌ ۚ فَهَلْ يُهْلَكُ
اِلَّا الْقَوْمُ الْفٰسِقُوْنَ ۞

Patiently advise, invite and preach. But don't give up! That's the way of the prophets of Allah.

Disbelievers will accept the truth

³³ Don't they see that Allah created Heavens and the Earth, and its creation didn't tire Him out, and He is capable of giving life to the dead. Yes, He has control over all things. ³⁴ The Day when the disbelievers will be brought in front of the Fire, it will be said: "Isn't this the truth?" They will say, "By our Lord, this is truth." Allah will say, "Taste the punishment for your disbelief."

The Prophet ﷺ is advised to be patient

³⁵ Be patient, like the strong-willed messengers[a] were patient, and don't wish to hasten *the punishment* for them. The day they see the punishment they were warned about, they will think they only lived an hour of the day. *This is* a true message. Only the disobedient will be destroyed!

---

[a] *Ulul azm* literally means "people of determination and resolve", referring to the resilience and the patience of the prophets in response to fierce persecution.

47. Surat Muhammad

The Beloved Messenger Muhammad ﷺ

Muslims were persecuted and oppressed in Makkah for thirteen years, and even after the migration to Madinah they were attacked. So, in the second year of Hijra Muslims were given formal permission to take up arms against oppressors: "Permission to fight is given to those who were attacked and oppressed" (*Surat al-Hajj*: 39). Muslim scholars' unanimous opinion about war is: it is only permissible in defence. Offensive invasions are not permitted in special circumstances. *Surat Muhammad* was revealed in Madinah, before the Battle of Badr. It reflects the new era of hostility, at the threshold of war, and its other name is "fighting".

The surat opens by describing the perennial conflict between truth and falsehood and urges believers to be steadfast, since the life of a believer is, in one way or another a constant battle. The surat makes clear that Islam does not surrender to oppressors, and urges its followers to stand up against oppression and support the victims. War becomes necessary to defend people's rights and freedoms, and to defeat evil. "When you encounter the disbelievers *in battle* beat their necks ... Allah will never let the works of those killed in his way go to waste" (4). This is followed by images of the luxuries of Paradise: "rivers of water with never-changing taste and smell; rivers of milk whose taste never changes; rivers of wine that give pleasure to their drinkers; and rivers of pure honey; for them are all kinds of fruits" (15).

The surat alludes to the signs of the final hour, many Ahadith give lists of these signs; the Prophet ﷺ said: "people will distribute booty among themselves, things in trust will be misused, the Zakah will be regarded as a tax, knowledge will be learnt for worldly purposes, a husband obedient to wife but disobedient to his mother; a person will be closer to his friend than father; mosques will be noisy places; wicked persons will be leaders; people will be respected to escape their harm; singers will be popular; alcohol common; people will curse ancestors; storms and Earthquakes common" (Tirmidhi).

In Madinah there were many new Muslims. There was a group that was confused, unsure and disliked the new community of believers: these were the hypocrites. In the next few passages their malicious plots, attitudes and disgraceful behaviour is exposed: they are cynical about the Prophet ﷺ and terrified of fighting for the truth. The Prophet ﷺ is warned about them and they are identified for him, so he was aware of these dangerous people, although he did not name or shame them until after the Battle of Tabuk in the eighth year of Hijra.

Just as the surat opened by highlighting the human tendency to war, it closes by encouraging the faithful to be ever-vigilant, willing and prepared to defend themselves against tyranny. This is a costly business, so they are urged to spend in the path of Allah to defend their rights. Miserliness, selfishness and self-centeredness is sternly condemned.

بِسْمِ اللهِ الرَّحْمٰنِ الرَّحِيْمِ

اَلَّذِيْنَ كَفَرُوْا وَصَدُّوْا عَنْ سَبِيْلِ اللهِ اَضَلَّ

اَعْمَالَهُمْ ۝ وَالَّذِيْنَ اٰمَنُوْا وَعَمِلُوا الصّٰلِحٰتِ وَاٰمَنُوْا

بِمَا نُزِّلَ عَلٰى مُحَمَّدٍ وَّهُوَ الْحَقُّ مِنْ رَّبِّهِمْ ۙ كَفَّرَ

عَنْهُمْ سَيِّاٰتِهِمْ وَاَصْلَحَ بَالَهُمْ ۝ ذٰلِكَ بِاَنَّ الَّذِيْنَ

كَفَرُوا اتَّبَعُوا الْبَاطِلَ وَاَنَّ الَّذِيْنَ اٰمَنُوا اتَّبَعُوا الْحَقَّ

مِنْ رَّبِّهِمْ ؕ كَذٰلِكَ يَضْرِبُ اللهُ لِلنَّاسِ اَمْثَالَهُمْ ۝

فَاِذَا لَقِيْتُمُ الَّذِيْنَ كَفَرُوْا فَضَرْبَ الرِّقَابِ ؕ حَتّٰى

اِذَآ اَثْخَنْتُمُوْهُمْ فَشُدُّوا الْوَثَاقَ ۙ فَاِمَّا مَنًّا بَعْدُ

وَاِمَّا فِدَآءً حَتّٰى تَضَعَ الْحَرْبُ اَوْزَارَهَا ۛ۬ ذٰلِكَ ؕ

وَلَوْ يَشَآءُ اللهُ لَانْتَصَرَ مِنْهُمْ ۙ وَلٰكِنْ لِّيَبْلُوَا

بَعْضَكُمْ بِبَعْضٍ ؕ وَالَّذِيْنَ قُتِلُوْا فِيْ سَبِيْلِ اللهِ فَلَنْ

يُّضِلَّ اَعْمَالَهُمْ ۝ سَيَهْدِيْهِمْ وَيُصْلِحُ بَالَهُمْ ۝ وَ

يُدْخِلُهُمُ الْجَنَّةَ عَرَّفَهَا لَهُمْ ۝ يٰاَيُّهَا الَّذِيْنَ اٰمَنُوْٓا

اِنْ تَنْصُرُوا اللهَ يَنْصُرْكُمْ وَيُثَبِّتْ اَقْدَامَكُمْ ۝ وَ

الَّذِيْنَ كَفَرُوْا فَتَعْسًا لَّهُمْ وَاَضَلَّ اَعْمَالَهُمْ ۝ ذٰلِكَ

بِاَنَّهُمْ كَرِهُوْا مَآ اَنْزَلَ اللهُ فَاَحْبَطَ اَعْمَالَهُمْ ۝

اَفَلَمْ يَسِيْرُوْا فِي الْاَرْضِ فَيَنْظُرُوْا كَيْفَ كَانَ عَاقِبَةُ

الَّذِيْنَ مِنْ قَبْلِهِمْ ؕ دَمَّرَ اللهُ عَلَيْهِمْ ۫ وَلِلْكٰفِرِيْنَ

What is the meaning of helping Allah? Believing, practising Divine teachings and spreading them.

In the name of Allah, the Kind, the Caring.

Believing in the truth

¹The works of the disbelievers - who obstruct people *from accepting* Allah's religion - are wasted, ²but the believers who are righteous and convinced of the truth revealed to Muhammad from His Lord, will be forgiven their sins, and Allah will improve their current situation. ³This is because the disbelievers follow falsehood and the believers follow their Lord's truth. This is how Allah presents examples for people.

Permission to fight the aggressors

⁴When you encounter the disbelievers *in battle* beat their necks until they are thoroughly weakened, then tie them up with ropes as captives. Afterwards, you can release them gracefully or take a ransom from them, but they must have surrendered their weapons. That is an order[a]. Had Allah wanted, He could have taken revenge Himself from them, but he wishes to test some of you with others. Allah will never let the deeds of those killed go to waste. ⁵He will guide and improve their situation. ⁶And He shall admit them into the Paradise He guided them to.

Believers urged to help Allah's religion

⁷Believers, if you help Allah's *religion* then he will help you and make you firm and strong-minded. ⁸On the other hand, the disbelievers will be ruined and their works will go to waste; ⁹this is because they dislike what Allah reveals and wasted their works. ¹⁰Haven't they travelled about in the land so they may see the fate of those people before them? Allah destroyed them and the same fate awaits *these* disbelievers.

---

[a] Literally: This is it!

أَمْثَالُهَا ۞ ذَلِكَ بِأَنَّ اللهَ مَوْلَى الَّذِيْنَ اٰمَنُوْا وَاَنَّ

الْكٰفِرِيْنَ لَا مَوْلَى لَهُمْ ۞ اِنَّ اللهَ يُدْخِلُ الَّذِيْنَ

اٰمَنُوْا وَعَمِلُوا الصّٰلِحٰتِ جَنّٰتٍ تَجْرِيْ مِنْ تَحْتِهَا

الْاَنْهٰرُ ط وَالَّذِيْنَ كَفَرُوْا يَتَمَتَّعُوْنَ وَيَأْكُلُوْنَ كَمَا

تَأْكُلُ الْاَنْعَامُ وَالنَّارُ مَثْوًى لَّهُمْ ۞ وَكَاَيِّنْ مِّنْ

قَرْيَةٍ هِيَ اَشَدُّ قُوَّةً مِّنْ قَرْيَتِكَ الَّتِيْ اَخْرَجَتْكَ ۚ

اَهْلَكْنٰهُمْ فَلَا نَاصِرَ لَهُمْ ۞ اَفَمَنْ كَانَ عَلٰى بَيِّنَةٍ مِّنْ

رَّبِّهٖ كَمَنْ زُيِّنَ لَهُ سُوْٓءُ عَمَلِهٖ وَاتَّبَعُوْٓا اَهْوَآءَهُمْ ۞

مَثَلُ الْجَنَّةِ الَّتِيْ وُعِدَ الْمُتَّقُوْنَ ط فِيْهَآ اَنْهٰرٌ مِّنْ

مَّآءٍ غَيْرِ اٰسِنٍ ۚ وَاَنْهٰرٌ مِّنْ لَّبَنٍ لَّمْ يَتَغَيَّرْ طَعْمُهٗ ۚ وَ

اَنْهٰرٌ مِّنْ خَمْرٍ لَّذَّةٍ لِّلشّٰرِبِيْنَ ۚ٥ وَاَنْهٰرٌ مِّنْ عَسَلٍ

مُّصَفًّى ط وَلَهُمْ فِيْهَا مِنْ كُلِّ الثَّمَرٰتِ وَمَغْفِرَةٌ

مِّنْ رَّبِّهِمْ ط كَمَنْ هُوَ خَالِدٌ فِي النَّارِ وَسُقُوْا مَآءً

حَمِيْمًا فَقَطَّعَ اَمْعَآءَهُمْ ۞ وَمِنْهُمْ مَّنْ يَّسْتَمِعُ

اِلَيْكَ ۚ حَتّٰى اِذَا خَرَجُوْا مِنْ عِنْدِكَ قَالُوْا لِلَّذِيْنَ

اُوْتُوا الْعِلْمَ مَا ذَا قَالَ اٰنِفًا قف اُولٰٓئِكَ الَّذِيْنَ

طَبَعَ اللهُ عَلٰى قُلُوْبِهِمْ وَاتَّبَعُوْٓا اَهْوَآءَهُمْ ۞ وَ

الَّذِيْنَ اهْتَدَوْا زَادَهُمْ هُدًى وَّاٰتٰهُمْ تَقْوٰىهُمْ ۞

فَهَلْ يَنْظُرُوْنَ اِلَّا السَّاعَةَ اَنْ تَأْتِيَهُمْ بَغْتَةً ۚ

فَقَدْ جَآءَ اَشْرَاطُهَا ۚ فَاَنّٰى لَهُمْ اِذَا جَآءَتْهُمْ

The four streams in Paradise: sweet as honey, tasty, fresh and healthy.

¹¹ This is because Allah is the protector of believers, but the disbelievers have no protector. ¹² Allah will admit the righteous believers into Paradise, with running streams. The disbelievers today are enjoying themselves and eating like cattle, although the Fire is their final home. ¹³ There were many towns more powerful than the town that expelled you, yet We destroyed their residents and they had no helper.

The four rivers of Paradise

¹⁴ Is the one who accepted the Lord's clear arguments like the one whose evil deeds seem attractive and he follows his desires? ¹⁵ The Paradise promised to the Allah-conscious will have: rivers of water whose taste and smell never changes; rivers of milk whose taste never changes; rivers of wine that give pleasure to their drinkers; and rivers of pure honey; for them are all kinds of fruits as well as forgiveness from their Lord. Can these be like those who will be in the Fire forever, given boiling water to drink that cuts through their bowels?

The hypocrites pretend to listen

¹⁶ Some of them listen carefully to you until they leave you, and say to those who were given knowledge,^a "What was he saying just now?" These are people whose hearts Allah sealed and they followed their desires. ¹⁷ Those who followed the straight path, Allah increased their guidance and blessed them with piety. ¹⁸ So are they waiting for the Final Hour to overwhelm them suddenly? Its signs have already appeared, so what use will it be to pay attention then?^b

---

^a "Those given knowledge" refers to the true believers, the practising Muslims.
^b See introduction to Surat.

ذِكْرٰهُمْ ۱۸ فَاعْلَمْ اَنَّهٗ لَاۤ اِلٰهَ اِلَّا اللّٰهُ وَاسْتَغْفِرْ

لِذَنْۢبِكَ وَلِلْمُؤْمِنِيْنَ وَالْمُؤْمِنٰتِ ۗ وَاللّٰهُ يَعْلَمُ

مُتَقَلَّبَكُمْ وَمَثْوٰىكُمْ ۱۹ وَيَقُوْلُ الَّذِيْنَ اٰمَنُوْا

لَوْلَا نُزِّلَتْ سُوْرَةٌ ۚ فَاِذَاۤ اُنْزِلَتْ سُوْرَةٌ مُّحْكَمَةٌ

وَّذُكِرَ فِيْهَا الْقِتَالُ ۙ رَاَيْتَ الَّذِيْنَ فِيْ قُلُوْبِهِمْ

مَّرَضٌ يَّنْظُرُوْنَ اِلَيْكَ نَظَرَ الْمَغْشِيِّ عَلَيْهِ مِنَ

الْمَوْتِ ۗ فَاَوْلٰى لَهُمْ ۲۰ طَاعَةٌ وَّقَوْلٌ مَّعْرُوْفٌ ۟

فَاِذَا عَزَمَ الْاَمْرُ ۟ فَلَوْ صَدَقُوا اللّٰهَ لَكَانَ خَيْرًا

لَّهُمْ ۲۱ فَهَلْ عَسَيْتُمْ اِنْ تَوَلَّيْتُمْ اَنْ تُفْسِدُوْا

فِى الْاَرْضِ وَتُقَطِّعُوْۤا اَرْحَامَكُمْ ۲۲ اُولٰٓئِكَ الَّذِيْنَ

لَعَنَهُمُ اللّٰهُ فَاَصَمَّهُمْ وَاَعْمٰۤى اَبْصَارَهُمْ ۲۳ اَفَلَا

يَتَدَبَّرُوْنَ الْقُرْاٰنَ اَمْ عَلٰى قُلُوْبٍ اَقْفَالُهَا ۲۴ اِنَّ

الَّذِيْنَ ارْتَدُّوْا عَلٰۤى اَدْبَارِهِمْ مِّنْۢ بَعْدِ مَا تَبَيَّنَ

لَهُمُ الْهُدَى ۙ الشَّيْطٰنُ سَوَّلَ لَهُمْ ۗ وَاَمْلٰى لَهُمْ ۲۵

ذٰلِكَ بِاَنَّهُمْ قَالُوْا لِلَّذِيْنَ كَرِهُوْا مَا نَزَّلَ اللّٰهُ

سَنُطِيْعُكُمْ فِيْ بَعْضِ الْاَمْرِ ۚ وَاللّٰهُ يَعْلَمُ اِسْرَارَهُمْ ۲۶

فَكَيْفَ اِذَا تَوَفَّتْهُمُ الْمَلٰٓئِكَةُ يَضْرِبُوْنَ وُجُوْهَهُمْ

وَاَدْبَارَهُمْ ۲۷ ذٰلِكَ بِاَنَّهُمُ اتَّبَعُوْا مَاۤ اَسْخَطَ اللّٰهَ

وَكَرِهُوْا رِضْوَانَهٗ فَاَحْبَطَ اَعْمَالَهُمْ ۲۸ اَمْ حَسِبَ

الَّذِيْنَ فِيْ قُلُوْبِهِمْ مَّرَضٌ اَنْ لَّنْ يُّخْرِجَ اللّٰهُ

[19] Know, there is no God but Allah, and pray that Allah protects your people from sins,[a] and seek forgiveness for the sins of all believing men and women. Allah knows your places of work and rest.

The hypocrites are terrified of fighting

[20] And the believers say, "Why hasn't a surat been revealed *about fighting*?" When a decisive surat is revealed that mentions fighting, you will see people with a disease in their hearts looking at you like the one who is in death throes. It would be far better for them [21] to obey and to say a good thing when the commandment came to pass. If only they were sincere about Allah, that would be far better for them. [22] So if you turn away now perhaps you would create corruption on the land and sever your blood ties. [23] Allah cursed these people, made them deaf, and blinded their eyes. [24] Haven't they reflected on the Quran? Or are there locks on their minds?

The hypocrites have false hopes

[25] Those who turn their backs after the truth was made clear to them have been fooled[b] by Satan, and given false long hopes. [26] That is because they say to those who hate what Allah has revealed, "We will follow you in some things only." Allah knows their secrets. [27] What will it be like when the angels take their souls at the time of death, and they will be striking them on their faces and backs. [28] That *punishment* will be because they followed what angers Allah, and they disliked *seeking divine* pleasure, so their works are now worthless.

The hypocrites are full of hatred

[29] Or do those with disease in their heart think Allah will never expose their hatred?

---

[a]   Al-Qurtubi says this means, "ask Allah to protect you from sins". I have translated accordingly, since the Prophet 襲 we believe is always free from sins.

[b]   *Sawwal* also means to deceive, dupe and trick.

أَضْغَانَهُمْ ۝ وَلَوْ نَشَآءُ لَأَرَيْنٰكَهُمْ فَلَعَرَفْتَهُمْ بِسِيْمٰهُمْ ط وَلَتَعْرِفَنَّهُمْ فِىْ لَحْنِ الْقَوْلِ ط وَاللّٰهُ يَعْلَمُ اَعْمَالَكُمْ ۝ وَلَنَبْلُوَنَّكُمْ حَتّٰى نَعْلَمَ الْمُجٰهِدِيْنَ مِنْكُمْ وَالصّٰبِرِيْنَ لا وَنَبْلُوَا اَخْبَارَكُمْ ۝ اِنَّ الَّذِيْنَ كَفَرُوْا وَصَدُّوْا عَنْ سَبِيْلِ اللّٰهِ وَشَآقُّوا الرَّسُوْلَ مِنْ بَعْدِ مَا تَبَيَّنَ لَهُمُ الْهُدٰى لا لَنْ يَّضُرُّوا اللّٰهَ شَيْئًا ط وَسَيُحْبِطُ اَعْمَالَهُمْ ۝ يٰاَيُّهَا الَّذِيْنَ اٰمَنُوْٓا اَطِيْعُوا اللّٰهَ وَ اَطِيْعُوا الرَّسُوْلَ وَلَا تُبْطِلُوْٓا اَعْمَالَكُمْ ۝ اِنَّ الَّذِيْنَ كَفَرُوْا وَصَدُّوْا عَنْ سَبِيْلِ اللّٰهِ ثُمَّ مَاتُوْا وَهُمْ كُفَّارٌ فَلَنْ يَّغْفِرَ اللّٰهُ لَهُمْ ۝ فَلَا تَهِنُوْا وَتَدْعُوْٓا اِلَى السَّلْمِ ۖ وَ اَنْتُمُ الْاَعْلَوْنَ ۖ وَاللّٰهُ مَعَكُمْ وَلَنْ يَّتِرَكُمْ اَعْمَالَكُمْ ۝ اِنَّمَا الْحَيٰوةُ الدُّنْيَا لَعِبٌ وَّلَهْوٌ ط وَ اِنْ تُؤْمِنُوْا وَتَتَّقُوْا يُؤْتِكُمْ اُجُوْرَكُمْ وَلَا يَسْئَلْكُمْ اَمْوَالَكُمْ ۝ اِنْ يَّسْئَلْكُمُوْهَا فَيُحْفِكُمْ تَبْخَلُوْا وَيُخْرِجْ اَضْغَانَكُمْ ۝ هٰٓاَنْتُمْ هٰٓؤُلَآءِ تُدْعَوْنَ لِتُنْفِقُوْا فِىْ سَبِيْلِ اللّٰهِ ۚ فَمِنْكُمْ مَّنْ يَّبْخَلُ ۚ وَمَنْ يَّبْخَلْ فَاِنَّمَا يَبْخَلُ عَنْ نَّفْسِهٖ ط وَاللّٰهُ الْغَنِيُّ وَاَنْتُمُ الْفُقَرَآءُ ۚ وَ اِنْ تَتَوَلَّوْا يَسْتَبْدِلْ قَوْمًا غَيْرَكُمْ ۙ ثُمَّ لَا يَكُوْنُوْٓا اَمْثَالَكُمْ ۝

Miserliness is the unwillingness to spend for the sake of Allah: a deadly sin. To avoid it be generous.

[30] If We wanted we can show them to you, and you will *easily* recognise them from their faces and from the tone of their speech. Allah knows your works. [31] We shall test you in order to see who among you strives hard and is patient and test *the sincerity* of your claims. [32] The disbelievers who stop others from Allah's way and oppose the Messenger after the truth is made clear to them are incapable of harming Allah in the slightest. And their works will be worthless.

Believers will be influential and prevail

[33] Believers! Obey Allah and obey the Messenger and don't ruin your works. [34] Surely, the disbelievers who stop others from Allah's way will not be forgiven if they die as disbelievers. [35] *Believers!* Never lose heart nor beg for peace; you shall be dominant and Allah will be with you, and He will not deprive you of *the reward* for your works.

Miserliness condemned

[36] Indeed, the life of this world is an amusement and pleasant pastime. However, if you believe and are mindful, you will be have rewards, and He will not ask you to give all of your wealth. [37] Were He to demand from you to spend all of your wealth, you would be miserly and your dislike to spend would then be exposed. [38] You are called upon to spend some of it in Allah's way, but some of you are miserly, and whoever is miserly deprives himself *of goodness*. Allah is Self-Sufficient, whereas you are in need of Him. And if you turn away, He will bring others in your place, and they will not be the likes of you.

48. Surat Al-Fath
The Victory

This surat was revealed in the sixth year of Hijra, just after the Treaty of Hudaibiyah. The Prophet ﷺ had a dream, he was performing Umrah, and the next day he informed the disciples of this. The central theme of the surat is this dream of the Prophet ﷺ. There was lot of excitement, and preparations began for the sacred journey. The Prophet ﷺ also invited some new Muslims and Bedouins from around Madinah to join, though only a few joined him. Nearly 1,400 devotees participated, with their sacrificial animals that had clear marks on their flanks and garlands around their necks. Men wore two-piece unstitched uniforms and carried only a sheathed sword. They left Madinah in Dhul-Qada. When the Makkans heard of this they were bewildered, and suspicious of the Muslims. They faced the dilemma of whether to violate the time-honoured Arabian custom of allowing anyone to enter Makkah for the pilgrimage, or to stop them entering the city. When the Muslims reached Hudaibiyah, 13 km outside the city, they were stopped by the Makkan army led by Khalid ibn Waleed. This was an unprecedented move in their history.

The Quraysh sent their envoy, Urwah, to negotiate with the Muslims. This is what he reported back:

> O people, I have been sent as envoy to kings, the Caesar, Chosreo of Persia, and Negus, but I have not seen a king whose men so honour him as the disciples of Muhammad honour him. If he gives a command they almost outstrip his words in fulfilling it; when he washes himself they compete for the water that falls off his hands; when he speaks their voices are hushed in his presence; nor will they look him full in the face; [they] lower their eyes and [display] reverence for him. He has offered you a goodly concession; therefore, accept from him. [M. Lings]

In the meantime, the Prophet ﷺ also dispatched his envoy, his son-in-law Usman ibn Affan ؓ, to seek the Quraysh's permission to perform the Umrah. Usman made it clear that Muslims came only to perform their religious duty, and were not armed nor willing to fight. However, they refused to listen and held him captive. During this tense period of negotiation, a rumour spread that he was martyred. When the Prophet ﷺ heard this, he announced the Muslims would not leave until they had avenged the blood of Usman. Sitting under a green acacia tree full of fresh spring foliage, the Prophet ﷺ took a pledge of loyalty from everyone present. They pledged to die for the blood of Usman. A few days later the rumour proved to be false, and Usman safely returned to the Muslim camp.

However, the Quraysh soon realised their mistake, and sent their envoy to conclude the negotiation with a peace treaty. The salient features of this were:

- The two parties will not engage in any kind of warfare for the next ten years
- The Muslims must return this year, and will be allowed to come back next year for three days to perform the Umrah.

The Muslims were furious with these conditions. However, the Prophet ﷺ signed the treaty. He ordered the disciples to rise and sacrifice their animals, and to shave their heads. After this, many set off to return to Madinah. This surat was revealed during this journey, and announcing the expedition was a great victory. Mohammed Asad summed up the benefits of this victory:

> The truce of Hudaibiyah proved to be beneficial for to the future of Islam; for the first time in six years peaceful contacts were established ... Thus the way was open to the penetration of Islamic ideas into the citadel of Arabian paganism ... As soon as the perennial warfare came to an end and people of both sides could meet freely, new converts rallied around the Prophet, first in tens, then in hundreds, then in thousands – so much so that when the pagan Koresh broke the truce two years after its conclusion, the Prophet could occupy Makkah almost without resistance. Thus the truce of Hudaibiyah ushered in the moral and political victory of Islam over all Arabia (*The Message of the Quran*).

بِسْمِ اللهِ الرَّحْمٰنِ الرَّحِيْمِ

اِنَّا فَتَحْنَا لَكَ فَتْحًا مُّبِيْنًا ۟ۙ لِّيَغْفِرَ لَكَ اللهُ

مَا تَقَدَّمَ مِنْ ذَنْۢبِكَ وَمَا تَاَخَّرَ وَيُتِمَّ نِعْمَتَهٗ

عَلَيْكَ وَيَهْدِيَكَ صِرَاطًا مُّسْتَقِيْمًا ۟ۙ وَّيَنْصُرَكَ

اللهُ نَصْرًا عَزِيْزًا ۟ هُوَ الَّذِىْٓ اَنْزَلَ السَّكِيْنَةَ فِىْ

قُلُوْبِ الْمُؤْمِنِيْنَ لِيَزْدَادُوْٓا اِيْمَانًا مَّعَ اِيْمَانِهِمْ ؕ

وَلِلّٰهِ جُنُوْدُ السَّمٰوٰتِ وَالْاَرْضِ ؕ وَكَانَ اللهُ عَلِيْمًا

حَكِيْمًا ۟ۙ لِّيُدْخِلَ الْمُؤْمِنِيْنَ وَالْمُؤْمِنٰتِ جَنّٰتٍ

تَجْرِىْ مِنْ تَحْتِهَا الْاَنْهٰرُ خٰلِدِيْنَ فِيْهَا وَيُكَفِّرَ

عَنْهُمْ سَيِّاٰتِهِمْ ؕ وَكَانَ ذٰلِكَ عِنْدَ اللهِ فَوْزًا

عَظِيْمًا ۟ۙ وَّيُعَذِّبَ الْمُنٰفِقِيْنَ وَالْمُنٰفِقٰتِ وَ

الْمُشْرِكِيْنَ وَالْمُشْرِكٰتِ الظَّآنِّيْنَ بِاللهِ ظَنَّ

السَّوْءِ ؕ عَلَيْهِمْ دَآئِرَةُ السَّوْءِ ۚ وَغَضِبَ اللهُ

عَلَيْهِمْ وَلَعَنَهُمْ وَاَعَدَّ لَهُمْ جَهَنَّمَ ؕ وَسَآءَتْ

مَصِيْرًا ۟ وَلِلّٰهِ جُنُوْدُ السَّمٰوٰتِ وَالْاَرْضِ ؕ وَ

كَانَ اللهُ عَزِيْزًا حَكِيْمًا ۟ اِنَّآ اَرْسَلْنٰكَ شَاهِدًا

وَّمُبَشِّرًا وَّنَذِيْرًا ۟ۙ لِّتُؤْمِنُوْا بِاللهِ وَرَسُوْلِهٖ

وَتُعَزِّرُوْهُ وَتُوَقِّرُوْهُ ؕ وَتُسَبِّحُوْهُ بُكْرَةً وَّ

اَصِيْلًا ۟ اِنَّ الَّذِيْنَ يُبَايِعُوْنَكَ اِنَّمَا يُبَايِعُوْنَ

All victories, success and achievements are from Allah, He gives them pleasure. So please Him!

In the name of Allah, the Kind, the Caring.

The peace treaty was a victory

[1] Indeed, We opened up a *path to* a clear victory for you [2] in order that Allah may forgive the past and the future sins of your people,[a] and perfect His favours on you, and guide you to the straight path; [3] and Allah will help you in a mighty way. He gave the believers' hearts an inner peace so their faith grew ever stronger. [4] The forces of the Heavens and the Earth belong to Allah, the Knower, the Wise. [5] Believing men and women's sins will be deleted, and admitted to Paradise, beneath which rivers flow, to live there forever. This is a great achievement from Allah.

Fate of those who think ill of Allah

[6] The hypocrites: men and women, and idolatrous men and women, who think wrong thoughts about Allah will be overwhelmed by Allah's wrath and curse, and evil from all sides; and He has prepared Hell for them; a miserable place of no return. [7] The forces of Heaven and the Earth are Allah's, the Almighty, Wise.

Believers support and honour the Messenger ﷺ

[8] We sent you as a witness, a giver of good news and a warner, [9] so you *people* will believe in Allah and His Messenger, and support him and honour him. And glorify Allah morning and evening. [10] Those who took your pledge of loyalty, really took Allah's pledge of loyalty, since Allah's Hand of power is over their hands. Anyone who breaks his pledge will face dreadful consequences. And whoever fulfils his pledge, He will richly reward him.

---

[a] Since the Messenger ﷺ is sinless and protected from all sins, the only appropriate translation is to assume there is an ellipsis: your people. For further discussion see the introduction to the surat.

اللّٰهِ ۖ یَدُ اللّٰهِ فَوْقَ اَیْدِیْهِمْ ۚ فَمَنْ نَّکَثَ فَاِنَّمَا

یَنْکُثُ عَلٰی نَفْسِہٖ ۚ وَمَنْ اَوْفٰی بِمَا عٰہَدَ

عَلَیْہُ اللّٰہَ فَسَیُؤْتِیْہِ اَجْرًا عَظِیْمًا ۟ سَیَقُوْلُ

لَکَ الْمُخَلَّفُوْنَ مِنَ الْاَعْرَابِ شَغَلَتْنَاۤ اَمْوَالُنَا

وَاَہْلُوْنَا فَاسْتَغْفِرْ لَنَا ۚ یَقُوْلُوْنَ بِاَلْسِنَتِہِمْ

مَّا لَیْسَ فِیْ قُلُوْبِہِمْ ؕ قُلْ فَمَنْ یَّمْلِکُ لَکُمْ

مِّنَ اللّٰہِ شَیْئًا اِنْ اَرَادَ بِکُمْ ضَرًّا اَوْ اَرَادَ بِکُمْ

نَفْعًا ؕ بَلْ کَانَ اللّٰہُ بِمَا تَعْمَلُوْنَ خَبِیْرًا ۟ بَلْ

ظَنَنْتُمْ اَنْ لَّنْ یَّنْقَلِبَ الرَّسُوْلُ وَالْمُؤْمِنُوْنَ اِلٰۤی

اَہْلِیْہِمْ اَبَدًا وَّ زُیِّنَ ذٰلِکَ فِیْ قُلُوْبِکُمْ وَظَنَنْتُمْ

ظَنَّ السَّوْءِ ۚ وَکُنْتُمْ قَوْمًۢا بُوْرًا ۟ وَمَنْ لَّمْ

یُؤْمِنْ بِاللّٰہِ وَرَسُوْلِہٖ فَاِنَّاۤ اَعْتَدْنَا لِلْکٰفِرِیْنَ

سَعِیْرًا ۟ وَلِلّٰہِ مُلْکُ السَّمٰوٰتِ وَالْاَرْضِ ؕ یَغْفِرُ

لِمَنْ یَّشَآءُ وَیُعَذِّبُ مَنْ یَّشَآءُ ؕ وَکَانَ اللّٰہُ

غَفُوْرًا رَّحِیْمًا ۟ سَیَقُوْلُ الْمُخَلَّفُوْنَ اِذَا انْطَلَقْتُمْ

اِلٰی مَغَانِمَ لِتَاْخُذُوْہَا ذَرُوْنَا نَتَّبِعْکُمْ ۚ

یُرِیْدُوْنَ اَنْ یُّبَدِّلُوْا کَلٰمَ اللّٰہِ ؕ قُلْ لَّنْ تَتَّبِعُوْنَا

کَذٰلِکُمْ قَالَ اللّٰہُ مِنْ قَبْلُ ۚ فَسَیَقُوْلُوْنَ بَلْ

تَحْسُدُوْنَنَا ؕ بَلْ کَانُوْا لَا یَفْقَہُوْنَ اِلَّا قَلِیْلًا ۟

قُلْ لِّلْمُخَلَّفِیْنَ مِنَ الْاَعْرَابِ سَتُدْعَوْنَ اِلٰی قَوْمٍ

We can make many excuses for not being active and engaged in the work of Allah. Do you make excuses when invited to do work?

The hypocrites stayed behind

¹¹ The Bedouins who stayed behind *in Madinah* will come and say to you, "We were busy with our jobs and families, ask Allah to forgive us." But they say things with their mouths that aren't from their hearts. Say: "Who can intervene for you if Allah wanted to harm you or to benefit you?" Indeed, Allah is fully aware of what you do. ¹² You thought the Messenger and the believers will never return to their families, and you were delighted with this thought, and you kept thinking these evil thoughts. You are wicked losers.ᵃ ¹³ The ones who did not believe in Allah and his Messenger – We have prepared for such disbelievers a blazing Fire. ¹⁴ Allah has the control of the Heavens and the Earth, and forgives and punishes who He pleases. And Allah is Forgiving, Caring.

The hypocrites are challenged

¹⁵ Those who stayed behind will say, "When you go somewhere *next time* which promises rich booty, do let us follow you." They want to change Allah's words. Say: "You will never follow us; that is what Allah has told beforehand." They will say, "You are jealous of us." They understand very little.

ᵃ *Qaumum boura* literally means ruined person who has not a speck of goodness in him or her.

اُولِیْ بَاْسٍ شَدِیْدٍ تُقَاتِلُوْنَهُمْ اَوْ یُسْلِمُوْنَ ۚ

فَاِنْ تُطِیْعُوْا یُؤْتِکُمُ اللّٰهُ اَجْرًا حَسَنًا ۚ وَ اِنْ

تَتَوَلَّوْا کَمَا تَوَلَّیْتُمْ مِّنْ قَبْلُ یُعَذِّبْکُمْ عَذَابًا

اَلِیْمًا ۞ لَیْسَ عَلَی الْاَعْمٰی حَرَجٌ وَّلَا عَلَی الْاَعْرَجِ

حَرَجٌ وَّلَا عَلَی الْمَرِیْضِ حَرَجٌ ؕ وَمَنْ یُّطِعِ اللّٰهَ

وَرَسُوْلَهٗ یُدْخِلْهُ جَنّٰتٍ تَجْرِیْ مِنْ تَحْتِهَا

الْاَنْهٰرُ ۚ وَمَنْ یَّتَوَلَّ یُعَذِّبْهُ عَذَابًا اَلِیْمًا ۞

لَقَدْ رَضِیَ اللّٰهُ عَنِ الْمُؤْمِنِیْنَ اِذْ یُبَایِعُوْنَکَ

تَحْتَ الشَّجَرَةِ فَعَلِمَ مَا فِیْ قُلُوْبِهِمْ فَاَنْزَلَ

السَّکِیْنَةَ عَلَیْهِمْ وَاَثَابَهُمْ فَتْحًا قَرِیْبًا ۞ وَّمَغَانِمَ

کَثِیْرَةً یَّاْخُذُوْنَهَا ؕ وَکَانَ اللّٰهُ عَزِیْزًا حَکِیْمًا ۞

وَعَدَکُمُ اللّٰهُ مَغَانِمَ کَثِیْرَةً تَاْخُذُوْنَهَا فَعَجَّلَ

لَکُمْ هٰذِهٖ وَکَفَّ اَیْدِیَ النَّاسِ عَنْکُمْ ۚ وَلِتَکُوْنَ

اٰیَةً لِّلْمُؤْمِنِیْنَ وَیَهْدِیَکُمْ صِرَاطًا مُّسْتَقِیْمًا ۞

وَّاُخْرٰی لَمْ تَقْدِرُوْا عَلَیْهَا قَدْ اَحَاطَ اللّٰهُ بِهَا ؕ

وَکَانَ اللّٰهُ عَلٰی کُلِّ شَیْءٍ قَدِیْرًا ۞ وَلَوْ قَاتَلَکُمُ

الَّذِیْنَ کَفَرُوْا لَوَلَّوُا الْاَدْبَارَ ثُمَّ لَا یَجِدُوْنَ وَلِیًّا

وَّلَا نَصِیْرًا ۞ سُنَّةَ اللّٰهِ الَّتِیْ قَدْ خَلَتْ مِنْ

قَبْلُ ۚ وَلَنْ تَجِدَ لِسُنَّةِ اللّٰهِ تَبْدِیْلًا ۞ وَهُوَ

الَّذِیْ کَفَّ اَیْدِیَهُمْ عَنْکُمْ وَاَیْدِیَکُمْ عَنْهُمْ

Loyalty is a mark of honest, friends who stand up at time of need. The disciples showed their loyalty to the Messenger ﷺ at a time of need.

1037

¹⁶Tell those Bedouins who stayed behind: "Soon you will be called upon to face people of great prowess in war; *you may* fight or they may surrender. If you obey, then Allah will give you a wonderful reward, but if you turn away as you turned away before, He will punish you with painful punishment. ¹⁷It is not a sin for the blind, the lame and the sick to stay behind. Anyone who obeys Allah and His Messenger will be admitted into Paradise, beneath which rivers flow, and anyone who turns away will be punished with painful punishment.

The pledge of loyalty under the tree

¹⁸Allah was pleased with the believers when they took a pledge of loyalty with you under the tree, and He knew what was in their hearts, so He gave them inner peace, and as a reward will give them a victory soon,ᵃ ¹⁹and in the near future they'll have many rich booties. Allah is Almighty, Wise. ²⁰Allah promised you many rich booties, which you will have in the future. He quickly gave you *this victory* and protected you from the harm of others,ᵇ so this becomes a sign of help for the believers and they can be guided on the straight path. ²¹Many other victories await you are not yet capable of, but Allah has control over them; Allah has power over all things.

Allah doesn't want people to fight

²²Had the disbelievers fought you, they would have turned their backs *and fled*, then they would have found no protector and helper. ²³This was Allah's practice in the past; *truth will succeed* and you will never find Allah's practice changing. ²⁴He stopped them attacking you, and you from attacking them, in the valley of Makkah after giving you capability to conquer them. Allah sees all you do.

ᵃ This predicts the victory of Khybar that occurred immediately after this. (Ibn Abbas)
ᵇ Literally this means, "he held back people's hands from you", simply put this means "protected you".

بِبَطْنِ مَكَّةَ مِنْ بَعْدِ اَنْ اَظْفَرَكُمْ عَلَيْهِمْ ۖ وَكَانَ اللّٰهُ بِمَا تَعْمَلُوْنَ بَصِيْرًا ۝ هُمُ الَّذِيْنَ كَفَرُوْا وَصَدُّوْكُمْ عَنِ الْمَسْجِدِ الْحَرَامِ وَالْهَدْيَ مَعْكُوْفًا اَنْ يَّبْلُغَ مَحِلَّهٗ ۚ وَلَوْلَا رِجَالٌ مُّؤْمِنُوْنَ وَنِسَآءٌ مُّؤْمِنٰتٌ لَّمْ تَعْلَمُوْهُمْ اَنْ تَطَئُوْهُمْ فَتُصِيْبَكُمْ مِّنْهُمْ مَّعَرَّةٌ بِغَيْرِ عِلْمٍ ۚ لِيُدْخِلَ اللّٰهُ فِيْ رَحْمَتِهٖ مَنْ يَّشَآءُ ۚ لَوْ تَزَيَّلُوْا لَعَذَّبْنَا الَّذِيْنَ كَفَرُوْا مِنْهُمْ عَذَابًا اَلِيْمًا ۝ اِذْ جَعَلَ الَّذِيْنَ كَفَرُوْا فِيْ قُلُوْبِهِمُ الْحَمِيَّةَ حَمِيَّةَ الْجَاهِلِيَّةِ فَاَنْزَلَ اللّٰهُ سَكِيْنَتَهٗ عَلٰى رَسُوْلِهٖ وَعَلَى الْمُؤْمِنِيْنَ وَاَلْزَمَهُمْ كَلِمَةَ التَّقْوٰى وَكَانُوْا اَحَقَّ بِهَا وَاَهْلَهَا ۚ وَكَانَ اللّٰهُ بِكُلِّ شَيْءٍ عَلِيْمًا ۝ لَقَدْ صَدَقَ اللّٰهُ رَسُوْلَهُ الرُّءْيَا بِالْحَقِّ ۚ لَتَدْخُلُنَّ الْمَسْجِدَ الْحَرَامَ اِنْ شَآءَ اللّٰهُ اٰمِنِيْنَ مُحَلِّقِيْنَ رُءُوْسَكُمْ وَمُقَصِّرِيْنَ لَا تَخَافُوْنَ ۚ فَعَلِمَ مَا لَمْ تَعْلَمُوْا فَجَعَلَ مِنْ دُوْنِ ذٰلِكَ فَتْحًا قَرِيْبًا ۝ هُوَ الَّذِيْ اَرْسَلَ رَسُوْلَهٗ بِالْهُدٰى وَدِيْنِ الْحَقِّ لِيُظْهِرَهٗ عَلَى الدِّيْنِ كُلِّهٖ ۚ وَكَفٰى بِاللّٰهِ شَهِيْدًا ۝ مُحَمَّدٌ رَّسُوْلُ اللّٰهِ ۚ وَالَّذِيْنَ مَعَهٗ اَشِدَّآءُ عَلَى الْكُفَّارِ رُحَمَآءُ بَيْنَهُمْ تَرٰىهُمْ رُكَّعًا سُجَّدًا يَّبْتَغُوْنَ

Dream! The prophet ﷺ dreamed, and see how Allah fulfilled his dreams. But its hard work.

²⁵ The disbelievers stopped you from entering the Sacred Mosque, and your sacrificial animals from reaching their place of sacrifice. If it were not for the believing men and women *in Makkah – about* whom you were unaware – you may have trampled them, thereby unwittingly incurring guilt.[a] So Allah may admit in to His kindness who He pleases. Had *the believers* separated themselves from *the Makkans* then We would have severely punished the disbelievers.

The Makkans' stubborn disdain

²⁶ While stubborn disdain filled the disbelievers' hearts, their superiority complex, Allah gave inner peace to His Messenger and the believers, and made them firm in the word of Allah-consciousness,[b] which they rightly deserved and were worthy of it. Allah knows all things.

The Prophet's ﷺ dream was true

²⁷ Allah fulfilled His Messenger's true dream; by the Will of Allah, you will enter the Sacred Mosque in peace with your heads shaven or hair trimmed, fearing no one. You don't know what he knows; soon beside this you will have a near victory.[c] ²⁸ He sent His Messenger with guidance and a true religion to override all religions. And Allah is a sufficient witness.

---

[a] Otherwise Allah would have allowed you to fight them.

[b] *Kalimat tutaqwa* means "there is no God but Allah and Muhammad is the messenger of Allah" according to Imam Ali.

[c] This may refer to either victory in Tabuk, which took place a few months after this or the victory of Makkah.

فَضْلًا مِّنَ اللّٰهِ وَرِضْوَانًا ۚ سِيْمَاهُمْ فِیْ وُجُوْهِهِمْ

مِّنْ اَثَرِ السُّجُوْدِ ؕ ذٰلِكَ مَثَلُهُمْ فِی التَّوْرٰىةِ ۚ وَ

مَثَلُهُمْ فِی الْاِنْجِيْلِ ۚ كَزَرْعٍ اَخْرَجَ شَطْئَهٗ فَاٰزَرَهٗ

فَاسْتَغْلَظَ فَاسْتَوٰى عَلٰى سُوْقِهٖ يُعْجِبُ الزُّرَّاعَ

لِيَغِيْظَ بِهِمُ الْكُفَّارَ ؕ وَعَدَ اللّٰهُ الَّذِيْنَ اٰمَنُوْا وَ

عَمِلُوا الصّٰلِحٰتِ مِنْهُمْ مَّغْفِرَةً وَّ اَجْرًا عَظِيْمًا ۟ ۲۹

Strong faith is likened to a firm plant stalk: standing tall and proudly displaying its leaves and flowers. Let others eat the fruits of your labour.

ع
۱۲

The disciples are praised

²⁹Muhammad is the Messenger of Allah, and those with him are tough with the disbelievers and caring among themselves; you will see them bowing and prostrating, seeking the grace of Allah and His pleasure. They bear marks on their faces, an effect of their prostration. These qualities of theirs are mentioned in the Torah and the Gospels; they are like a seed from which a shoot sprouts. He strengthens it so it rises stout and stands straight on its stem. The sower loves it, but the disbelievers become enraged. Allah promised the believers and the righteous among them forgiveness, and a great reward.

49. Surat Al-Hujurat

The Living Quarters

This Madinan surat was revealed in the ninth year of Hijra, following two events: a delegation of new Muslims from the Bedouin tribe of Bani Tamim visited the Prophet ﷺ, they called out to him from outside his living room. The surat disapproved of their behaviour, and laid out simple rules for respecting the leader. The second event concerned the misinformation given to the Prophet ﷺ by one of the Zakat collectors about the tribe of Bani Mustalaq (verses 6–8). He wrongly informed the Messenger ﷺ that the tribe was unwilling to pay the Zakat. However, upon investigation, this turned out to be untrue. This kind of behaviour was condemned.

This surat is also called the "surat of morals and manners," since it offers moral guidance for living in the community: how to develop trust and overcome suspicions. In verse 13, the unity of humanity is stressed, uprooting any kind of discrimination based on colour, creed and caste. It points out our common origin: Adam and Eve. It teaches that honour and nobility is achieved through being Allah-conscious, mindful of Him, and having a strong character. This is the foundation that creates equality and fairness in a society. It is these values that lead to peace and trust among people.

The last passage of the surat returns to the ill-mannered Bedouins, and seeks to clarify the difference between true faith and mere ritual formalities of religion, urging them to acknowledge Allah's favour. Faith is a special favour of Allah.

بِسْمِ اللهِ الرَّحْمٰنِ الرَّحِيْمِ

يٰۤاَيُّهَا الَّذِيْنَ اٰمَنُوْا لَا تُقَدِّمُوْا بَيْنَ يَدَىِ اللهِ وَرَسُوْلِهٖ وَاتَّقُوا اللهَ ؕ اِنَّ اللهَ سَمِيْعٌ عَلِيْمٌ ۚ ١

يٰۤاَيُّهَا الَّذِيْنَ اٰمَنُوْا لَا تَرْفَعُوْۤا اَصْوَاتَكُمْ فَوْقَ صَوْتِ النَّبِيِّ وَلَا تَجْهَرُوْا لَهٗ بِالْقَوْلِ كَجَهْرِ بَعْضِكُمْ لِبَعْضٍ اَنْ تَحْبَطَ اَعْمَالُكُمْ وَاَنْتُمْ لَا تَشْعُرُوْنَ ۚ ٢ اِنَّ الَّذِيْنَ يَغُضُّوْنَ اَصْوَاتَهُمْ عِنْدَ رَسُوْلِ اللهِ اُولٰۤئِكَ الَّذِيْنَ امْتَحَنَ اللهُ قُلُوْبَهُمْ لِلتَّقْوٰى ؕ لَهُمْ مَّغْفِرَةٌ وَّاَجْرٌ عَظِيْمٌ ۚ ٣ اِنَّ الَّذِيْنَ يُنَادُوْنَكَ مِنْ وَّرَآءِ الْحُجُرٰتِ اَكْثَرُهُمْ لَا يَعْقِلُوْنَ ۚ ٤ وَلَوْ اَنَّهُمْ صَبَرُوْا حَتّٰى تَخْرُجَ اِلَيْهِمْ لَكَانَ خَيْرًا لَّهُمْ ؕ وَاللهُ غَفُوْرٌ رَّحِيْمٌ ۚ ٥

يٰۤاَيُّهَا الَّذِيْنَ اٰمَنُوْۤا اِنْ جَآءَكُمْ فَاسِقٌۢ بِنَبَاٍ فَتَبَيَّنُوْۤا اَنْ تُصِيْبُوْا قَوْمًاۢ بِجَهَالَةٍ فَتُصْبِحُوْا عَلٰى مَا فَعَلْتُمْ نٰدِمِيْنَ ۚ ٦ وَاعْلَمُوْۤا اَنَّ فِيْكُمْ رَسُوْلَ اللهِ ؕ لَوْ يُطِيْعُكُمْ فِيْ كَثِيْرٍ مِّنَ الْاَمْرِ لَعَنِتُّمْ وَلٰكِنَّ اللهَ حَبَّبَ اِلَيْكُمُ الْاِيْمَانَ وَزَيَّنَهٗ فِيْ قُلُوْبِكُمْ وَكَرَّهَ اِلَيْكُمُ الْكُفْرَ وَالْفُسُوْقَ وَالْعِصْيَانَ ؕ اُولٰۤئِكَ هُمُ الرّٰشِدُوْنَ ۙ ٧ فَضْلًا مِّنَ اللهِ وَ

The Quran gives insights into the mysterious unseen world, and it's a powerful reminder.

In the name of Allah, the Kind, the Caring.

Manners of meeting and greeting the Messenger ﷺ
[1] Believers, do not put yourselves ahead of Allah and His Messenger; be fearful of Allah. Indeed, Allah is the Hearer, the Knower. [2] Believers, don't raise your voices above the voice of the Prophet, nor talk loudly with him as you might talk loudly with each other, your deeds will be ruined without you knowing. [3] Those who lower their voices in the presence of the Messenger of Allah are the ones whose hearts Allah has selected[a] for piety. Forgiveness and a great reward awaits them. [4] Most of those who called out to you from outside your home[b] don't understand. [5] It would have been far better for them had they waited patiently till you came out. Allah is Forgiving, Caring.

When you hear news, check the facts
[6] Believers, if a discredited person[c] brings you news, then check *it* in case you cause harm to others ignorantly, and then later regret what you did. [7] Remember, the Messenger of Allah is among you. If he frequently followed your wishes then you would suffer *badly*; however, Allah has made faith beloved and highly attractive for your hearts, and made disbelief, sin and disobedience dislikeable to you. These are the rightly guided, [8] *given* grace as a gift from Allah, the Knower, Wise.

---

[a] *Imtahana Allahu* literally means "Allah has tested", in other words proved that they are fit and deserving to be selected. I have accordingly translated it.

[b] The living quarters, means the Prophet's ﷺ home.

[c] *Fasiq* means a transgressor who commits major sins, is uncouth, and a mischievous law breaker.

نِعْمَةً ط وَ اللهُ عَلِيْمٌ حَكِيْمٌ ۞ وَ اِنْ طَآئِفَتٰنِ

مِنَ الْمُؤْمِنِيْنَ اقْتَتَلُوْا فَاَصْلِحُوْا بَيْنَهُمَا ج

فَاِنْ بَغَتْ اِحْدٰىهُمَا عَلَى الْاُخْرٰى فَقَاتِلُوا الَّتِيْ

تَبْغِيْ حَتّٰى تَفِيْٓءَ اِلٰٓى اَمْرِ اللهِ ج فَاِنْ فَآءَتْ

فَاَصْلِحُوْا بَيْنَهُمَا بِالْعَدْلِ وَ اَقْسِطُوْا ط اِنَّ

اللهَ يُحِبُّ الْمُقْسِطِيْنَ ۞ اِنَّمَا الْمُؤْمِنُوْنَ اِخْوَةٌ

فَاَصْلِحُوْا بَيْنَ اَخَوَيْكُمْ وَ اتَّقُوا اللهَ لَعَلَّكُمْ

تُرْحَمُوْنَ ۞ يٰٓاَيُّهَا الَّذِيْنَ اٰمَنُوْا لَا يَسْخَرْ قَوْمٌ

مِّنْ قَوْمٍ عَسٰٓى اَنْ يَّكُوْنُوْا خَيْرًا مِّنْهُمْ وَ لَا

نِسَآءٌ مِّنْ نِّسَآءٍ عَسٰٓى اَنْ يَّكُنَّ خَيْرًا مِّنْهُنَّ ج

وَ لَا تَلْمِزُوْٓا اَنْفُسَكُمْ وَ لَا تَنَابَزُوْا بِالْاَلْقَابِ ط

بِئْسَ الِاسْمُ الْفُسُوْقُ بَعْدَ الْاِيْمَانِ ج وَ مَنْ

لَّمْ يَتُبْ فَاُولٰٓئِكَ هُمُ الظّٰلِمُوْنَ ۞ يٰٓاَيُّهَا

الَّذِيْنَ اٰمَنُوا اجْتَنِبُوْا كَثِيْرًا مِّنَ الظَّنِّ ز اِنَّ

بَعْضَ الظَّنِّ اِثْمٌ وَّ لَا تَجَسَّسُوْا وَ لَا يَغْتَبْ

بَّعْضُكُمْ بَعْضًا ط اَيُحِبُّ اَحَدُكُمْ اَنْ يَّاْكُلَ لَحْمَ

اَخِيْهِ مَيْتًا فَكَرِهْتُمُوْهُ ط وَ اتَّقُوا اللهَ ط اِنَّ اللهَ

تَوَّابٌ رَّحِيْمٌ ۞ يٰٓاَيُّهَا النَّاسُ اِنَّا خَلَقْنٰكُمْ

مِّنْ ذَكَرٍ وَّ اُنْثٰى وَ جَعَلْنٰكُمْ شُعُوْبًا وَّ قَبَآئِلَ

لِتَعَارَفُوْا ط اِنَّ اَكْرَمَكُمْ عِنْدَ اللهِ اَتْقٰكُمْ ط

Beware of satanic attacks; weird, strange and evil thoughts and imaginations, wicked dreams and visions. Seek Allah's protection.

Standing up for justice and creating peace

⁹If two groups of believers fight, then *you must* make peace between them. If one of them is unjust to the other, then fight the unjust until he accepts Allah's judgement. If he accepts it then make peace between them fairly, and be just. Indeed, Allah loves the just. ¹⁰The believers are brothers,[a] so make peace between your two brothers; be mindful of Allah so you might be cared for.

Behaviours that lead to conflict

¹¹Believers! Let no man make fun of another,[b] he might be better than him; no woman should make fun of other women, they may be better than them; nor speak ill, nor use offensive nicknames for one another. How bad it is to be called "a trouble maker," after accepting faith. Those who don't turn away from such behaviour are wicked.

Suspicions undermine relationships

¹²Believers, do not be suspicious, since some suspicions[c] are sins. Neither spy on one another nor backbite about each other. Would anyone of you like to eat the meat of his dead brother? Never! You would hate it. So be fearful of Allah. Allah is indeed Forgiving, Caring.

Our common humanity

¹³People, We created you from a male and female; *then* made you into different races and tribes so you may know each other. The most honourable in the sight of Allah is the most mindful of Allah, the Knower, the Aware.

---

[a] Also sisters to each other.
[b] *Quamun* here means a group of men.
[c] *Zann* means to suspect and to assume about others: to be inclined to accuse others, and doubt their innocence.

إِنَّ اللّٰهَ عَلِيمٌ خَبِيرٌ ۩ قَالَتِ الْأَعْرَابُ اٰمَنَّا ۚ

قُلْ لَّمْ تُؤْمِنُوْا وَلٰكِنْ قُوْلُوْٓا اَسْلَمْنَا وَلَمَّا

يَدْخُلِ الْإِيْمَانُ فِيْ قُلُوْبِكُمْ ۚ وَاِنْ تُطِيْعُوا

اللّٰهَ وَرَسُوْلَهُ لَا يَلِتْكُمْ مِّنْ اَعْمَالِكُمْ شَيْـًٔا ۚ

اِنَّ اللّٰهَ غَفُوْرٌ رَّحِيْمٌ ۩ اِنَّمَا الْمُؤْمِنُوْنَ

الَّذِيْنَ اٰمَنُوْا بِاللّٰهِ وَرَسُوْلِهٖ ثُمَّ لَمْ يَرْتَابُوْا

وَجَاهَدُوْا بِاَمْوَالِهِمْ وَاَنْفُسِهِمْ فِيْ سَبِيْلِ اللّٰهِ ۚ

اُولٰٓئِكَ هُمُ الصّٰدِقُوْنَ ۩ قُلْ اَتُعَلِّمُوْنَ اللّٰهَ

بِدِيْنِكُمْ ۚ وَاللّٰهُ يَعْلَمُ مَا فِي السَّمٰوٰتِ وَمَا

فِي الْأَرْضِ ۚ وَاللّٰهُ بِكُلِّ شَيْءٍ عَلِيْمٌ ۩

يَمُنُّوْنَ عَلَيْكَ اَنْ اَسْلَمُوْا ۚ قُلْ لَّا تَمُنُّوْا عَلَيَّ

اِسْلَامَكُمْ ۚ بَلِ اللّٰهُ يَمُنُّ عَلَيْكُمْ اَنْ هَدٰىكُمْ

لِلْإِيْمَانِ اِنْ كُنْتُمْ صٰدِقِيْنَ ۩ اِنَّ اللّٰهَ يَعْلَمُ

غَيْبَ السَّمٰوٰتِ وَالْأَرْضِ ۚ وَاللّٰهُ بَصِيْرٌ بِمَا

تَعْمَلُوْنَ ۩

Your toolkit against Satan must have 'patience'.

The true nature of faith

¹⁴The Bedouins say, "We believe," tell them: "You haven't believed yet, you should say, 'We have surrendered.'" Faith hasn't fully entered their hearts. Had they obeyed Allah and His Messenger, none of their deeds would be lost. Indeed, Allah is Forgiving, the Caring. ¹⁵The true believers are those who believed in Allah and His Messenger, and have no doubts. They strive with their wealth and their lives in Allah's way. They are the truthful. ¹⁶Are you teaching Allah your religion? Allah knows what is in the Heavens and the Earth; Allah knows all things. ¹⁷They think they have done you a favour by embracing Islam; say: "By embracing Islam you haven't done me any favour; *in fact* Allah has done you a favour. He has guided you to the faith, if you are true in faith." ¹⁸Allah knows the secrets of Heaven and the Earth, and Allah sees all you do.

50. Surat Qaf

The Arabic Letter Qaf

This surat was revealed in the middle Makkan period, and this is apparent in its subject matter: arguments for Resurrection and Divine Judgement. The sceptics are surprised by the idea of new life after death. The Quran responds to them by providing visible evidence from nature, the creation of the Heavens and the Earth, and the mountains and date groves from which they eat. This is followed by another line of visible evidence from human history with which Makkans were familiar: the ruins of previous rebellious nations. The surat eloquently asks: "Has the first creation tired Us out? Not at all, but they are doubtful about *the possibility* of a new creation" (15).

The next section makes reference to the ego and lower self of human consciousness: "We created man, and We know exactly what his desires are urging him *to do*;[a] in fact, We are nearer to him than his jugular vein" (16). The surat warns: everything humans say and do is accurately recorded, and on Judgement Day this will lead either to Paradise or Hell. Here, the surat vividly paints contrasting scenes from Paradise and Hell. In the end is a reminder of Allah's creative power. Humanity is advised to celebrate the glory and praise of Allah. The Prophet ﷺ is reminded: continue to remind people, and you can't force religion into people's hearts.

---

[a] The literal meaning is "what his soul whispers to him".

بِسْمِ اللهِ الرَّحْمٰنِ الرَّحِیْمِ

قٓ ۟ وَالْقُرْاٰنِ الْمَجِیْدِ ۟۱ بَلْ عَجِبُوْۤا اَنْ جَآءَهُمْ

مُّنْذِرٌ مِّنْهُمْ فَقَالَ الْكٰفِرُوْنَ هٰذَا شَیْءٌ

عَجِیْبٌ ۟۲ ءَاِذَا مِتْنَا وَكُنَّا تُرَابًا ۚ ذٰلِكَ رَجْعٌ

بَعِیْدٌ ۟۳ قَدْ عَلِمْنَا مَا تَنْقُصُ الْاَرْضُ مِنْهُمْ ۚ

وَعِنْدَنَا كِتٰبٌ حَفِیْظٌ ۟۴ بَلْ كَذَّبُوْا بِالْحَقِّ لَمَّا

جَآءَهُمْ فَهُمْ فِیْۤ اَمْرٍ مَّرِیْجٍ ۟۵ اَفَلَمْ یَنْظُرُوْۤا

اِلَى السَّمَآءِ فَوْقَهُمْ كَیْفَ بَنَیْنٰهَا وَزَیَّنّٰهَا وَمَا لَهَا

مِنْ فُرُوْجٍ ۟۶ وَالْاَرْضَ مَدَدْنٰهَا وَاَلْقَیْنَا فِیْهَا

رَوَاسِیَ وَاَنْۢبَتْنَا فِیْهَا مِنْ كُلِّ زَوْجٍۭ بَهِیْجٍ ۟۷

تَبْصِرَةً وَّ ذِكْرٰى لِكُلِّ عَبْدٍ مُّنِیْبٍ ۟۸ وَنَزَّلْنَا

مِنَ السَّمَآءِ مَآءً مُّبٰرَكًا فَاَنْۢبَتْنَا بِهٖ جَنّٰتٍ وَّحَبَّ

الْحَصِیْدِ ۟۹ وَالنَّخْلَ بٰسِقٰتٍ لَّهَا طَلْعٌ نَّضِیْدٌ ۟۱۰

رِّزْقًا لِّلْعِبَادِ ۙ وَاَحْیَیْنَا بِهٖ بَلْدَةً مَّیْتًا ؕ كَذٰلِكَ

الْخُرُوْجُ ۟۱۱ كَذَّبَتْ قَبْلَهُمْ قَوْمُ نُوْحٍ وَّاَصْحٰبُ

الرَّسِّ وَثَمُوْدُ ۟۱۲ وَّعَادٌ وَّفِرْعَوْنُ وَاِخْوَانُ لُوْطٍ ۟۱۳ وَّ

اَصْحٰبُ الْاَیْكَةِ وَقَوْمُ تُبَّعٍ ؕ كُلٌّ كَذَّبَ الرُّسُلَ فَحَقَّ

وَعِیْدِ ۟۱۴ اَفَعَیِیْنَا بِالْخَلْقِ الْاَوَّلِ ؕ بَلْ هُمْ فِیْ لَبْسٍ

مِّنْ خَلْقٍ جَدِیْدٍ ۟۱۵ وَلَقَدْ خَلَقْنَا الْاِنْسَانَ وَنَعْلَمُ

The Quran gives insights into the mysterious unseen world, and it's a powerful reminder.

In the name of Allah, the Kind, the Caring.

¹*Qaf.*

The Resurrection will be a shock for disbelievers

By the Majestic Quran. ²How is it that they are surprised that a warner has come from among them? The disbelievers say, "This is a strange thing! ³When we are dead and turned into dust will we be returned; a far-fetched *idea*." ⁴Indeed, We know what the Earth consumes of their bodies.ᵃ We have a Book in which everything is carefully recorded. ⁵In fact, they denied the truth when it came to them because they are confused.

Allah's creative power in nature

⁶Haven't they looked at the sky above them, how We made it beautiful and flawless, ⁷and the Earth how We spread it out and firmly set mountains on it, and produced all kinds of beneficial plants there? ⁸They offer an insightful lesson and a reminder for every human being who willingly turns to Allah. ⁹And how We sent down blessed water from the sky, and with it We grow gardens and crops that are harvested, ¹⁰and tall palm trees loaded with clusters of dates – ¹¹a sustenance for people, and that is how We bring a dead place back to life with rain. The coming out *of graves* will be like that too!

Allah never gets tired

¹²Previously the truth was denied by the people of Nuh, the Rass, Thamud, ¹³Ad, Pharaoh and the brothers of Lut, ¹⁴the people of Iekah and Tubba. All of them denied the messengers, and so what they were threatened with actually happened to them. ¹⁵Has the first creation tired Us out? Not at all, but they are doubtful about *the possibility* of a new creation.

ᵃ   Literally this means "we know what the Earth diminishes of them".

مَا تُوَسْوِسُ بِهٖ نَفْسُهٗ ۚ وَ نَحْنُ اَقْرَبُ اِلَيْهِ مِنْ

حَبْلِ الْوَرِيْدِ ۞ اِذْ يَتَلَقَّى الْمُتَلَقِّيٰنِ عَنِ الْيَمِيْنِ وَ

عَنِ الشِّمَالِ قَعِيْدٌ ۞ مَا يَلْفِظُ مِنْ قَوْلٍ اِلَّا لَدَيْهِ

رَقِيْبٌ عَتِيْدٌ ۞ وَ جَآءَتْ سَكْرَةُ الْمَوْتِ بِالْحَقِّ ۗ

ذٰلِكَ مَا كُنْتَ مِنْهُ تَحِيْدُ ۞ وَ نُفِخَ فِى الصُّوْرِ ۗ ذٰلِكَ

يَوْمُ الْوَعِيْدِ ۞ وَ جَآءَتْ كُلُّ نَفْسٍ مَّعَهَا سَآئِقٌ

وَّ شَهِيْدٌ ۞ لَقَدْ كُنْتَ فِىْ غَفْلَةٍ مِّنْ هٰذَا فَكَشَفْنَا

عَنْكَ غِطَآءَكَ فَبَصَرُكَ الْيَوْمَ حَدِيْدٌ ۞ وَ قَالَ

قَرِيْنُهٗ هٰذَا مَا لَدَىَّ عَتِيْدٌ ۗ اَلْقِيَا فِىْ جَهَنَّمَ

كُلَّ كَفَّارٍ عَنِيْدٍ ۞ مَّنَّاعٍ لِّلْخَيْرِ مُعْتَدٍ مُّرِيْبِ ۞

الَّذِىْ جَعَلَ مَعَ اللّٰهِ اِلٰهًا اٰخَرَ فَاَلْقِيٰهُ فِى الْعَذَابِ

الشَّدِيْدِ ۞ قَالَ قَرِيْنُهٗ رَبَّنَا مَاۤ اَطْغَيْتُهٗ وَ لٰكِنْ

كَانَ فِىْ ضَلٰلٍۭ بَعِيْدٍ ۞ قَالَ لَا تَخْتَصِمُوْا لَدَىَّ وَ قَدْ

قَدَّمْتُ اِلَيْكُمْ بِالْوَعِيْدِ ۞ مَا يُبَدَّلُ الْقَوْلُ لَدَىَّ

وَ مَاۤ اَنَا بِظَلَّامٍ لِّلْعَبِيْدِ ۞ يَوْمَ نَقُوْلُ لِجَهَنَّمَ

هَلِ امْتَلَاْتِ وَ تَقُوْلُ هَلْ مِنْ مَّزِيْدٍ ۞ وَ اُزْلِفَتِ

الْجَنَّةُ لِلْمُتَّقِيْنَ غَيْرَ بَعِيْدٍ ۞ هٰذَا مَا تُوْعَدُوْنَ

لِكُلِّ اَوَّابٍ حَفِيْظٍ ۞ مَنْ خَشِىَ الرَّحْمٰنَ بِالْغَيْبِ

وَ جَآءَ بِقَلْبٍ مُّنِيْبِ ۞ ادْخُلُوْهَا بِسَلٰمٍ ۗ ذٰلِكَ يَوْمُ

الْخُلُوْدِ ۞ لَهُمْ مَّا يَشَآءُوْنَ فِيْهَا وَ لَدَيْنَا مَزِيْدٌ ۞

Beware of satanic attacks; weird, strange and evil thoughts and imaginations, wicked dreams and visions. Seek Allah's protection.

Guardian angels record

¹⁶ We created humans, and know exactly what their desires urge them *to do*; in fact, We are nearer to them than their jugular vein. ¹⁷ When the two recording angels, one sitting on their right and the other on their left, record. ¹⁸ Not a word they speak goes *unrecorded* by a vigilant observer. ¹⁹ Death throes will bring the truth with it: "This is what you tried to escape." ²⁰ The Trumpet will be blown; that is the Day you were warned about. ²¹ Everyone will be escorted by an angel and a witness. ²² *They will be told*: "You paid no attention to this Day, and We removed your veil, so today your sight is razor-sharp." ²³ Their lifelong companion will say, "I prepared, this *file of yours*."

Who will be thrown into Hell?

²⁴ "Throw him into Hell,^a every rebellious disbeliever, ²⁵ everyone who obstructed others from good, every aggressor, every doubter ²⁶ who had set up other gods with Allah. So throw him into the terrible punishment." ²⁷ His devil companion will say, "Our Lord, I didn't lead him to evil; he had already gone far astray." ²⁸ Allah will say to them, "Do not squabble in My presence; I sent you a warning. ²⁹ My Word does not change, and I am not unjust to any creature." ³⁰ Remember the Day I shall ask Hell, "Are you full?" It will reply, "Are there more?"

Who will enter Paradise?

³¹ Paradise will be brought near the righteous; it won't be far away from them. ³² This is what you were promised; it is for the one who turned to Allah, and was ever mindful of Him. ³³ The one who feared Al-Rahman without ever seeing Him and came with a devout heart, ³⁴ *he shall be told*: "Enter Paradise peacefully, for this is the Everlasting Day." ³⁵ They will have anything they want there, and We will have much more for them.

---

^a This address is to the angels.

وَكَمْ اَهْلَكْنَا قَبْلَهُمْ مِّنْ قَرْنٍ هُمْ اَشَدُّ مِنْهُمْ

بَطْشًا فَنَقَّبُوْا فِى الْبِلَادِ ؕ هَلْ مِنْ مَّحِيْصٍ ۝ اِنَّ

فِىْ ذٰلِكَ لَذِكْرٰى لِمَنْ كَانَ لَهٗ قَلْبٌ اَوْ اَلْقَى

السَّمْعَ وَهُوَ شَهِيْدٌ ۝ وَلَقَدْ خَلَقْنَا السَّمٰوٰتِ وَ

الْاَرْضَ وَمَا بَيْنَهُمَا فِىْ سِتَّةِ اَيَّامٍ ۚ وَّمَا مَسَّنَا

مِنْ لُّغُوْبٍ ۝ فَاصْبِرْ عَلٰى مَا يَقُوْلُوْنَ وَسَبِّحْ بِحَمْدِ

رَبِّكَ قَبْلَ طُلُوْعِ الشَّمْسِ وَقَبْلَ الْغُرُوْبِ ۝ وَمِنَ

الَّيْلِ فَسَبِّحْهُ وَ اَدْبَارَ السُّجُوْدِ ۝ وَاسْتَمِعْ يَوْمَ

يُنَادِ الْمُنَادِ مِنْ مَّكَانٍ قَرِيْبٍ ۝ يَّوْمَ يَسْمَعُوْنَ

الصَّيْحَةَ بِالْحَقِّ ؕ ذٰلِكَ يَوْمُ الْخُرُوْجِ ۝ اِنَّا نَحْنُ

نُحْىٖ وَنُمِيْتُ وَاِلَيْنَا الْمَصِيْرُ ۝ يَوْمَ تَشَقَّقُ

الْاَرْضُ عَنْهُمْ سِرَاعًا ؕ ذٰلِكَ حَشْرٌ عَلَيْنَا يَسِيْرٌ ۝

نَحْنُ اَعْلَمُ بِمَا يَقُوْلُوْنَ وَمَا اَنْتَ عَلَيْهِمْ

بِجَبَّارٍ ۫ فَذَكِّرْ بِالْقُرْاٰنِ مَنْ يَّخَافُ وَعِيْدِ ۝

Your toolkit against Satan must have the virtue of 'patience'.

1057

To witness Allah's power requires senses and feelings

³⁶ We destroyed people in the past who were far stronger than them; they used to travel everywhere – did they escape? ³⁷ In this is a reminder for anyone who has a heart, or listens attentively. ³⁸ We created the Heavens and the Earth and what lies between them in six days only, and We were not tired. ³⁹ So bear patiently what they say. Glorify and praise your Lord before the sunrise and sunset, ⁴⁰ and during the night, and glorify him after the *set* prayers *too*.

The Day people come out of graves

⁴¹ Listen carefully about the Day when the caller from nearby will call out, ⁴² when people hear a Blast. That shall be the Day of the coming out *of graves*. ⁴³ We give life and death, and the Final Return will be to Us. ⁴⁴ The Day when the Earth will split open, letting them rush out, that gathering will be easy for Us. ⁴⁵ We know well what they say, and you can't force them *to believe*. So keep reminding through the Quran anyone who fears My Warning.

51. Surat Adh-Dhariyat
Gale-force Winds

A series of oaths referring to the wind opens this surat. Wind is a fundamental element of life on Earth. Its function is the maintenance of the water cycle. The sun heats the oceans, and water evaporates into the air as vapour. With rising height, the air temperature falls and water vapour condenses into tiny droplets. These droplets over a large area join to form clouds. The winds blow them towards the land, where they fall as rain. The implied question is: since wind is life-giving and is created by Allah, why can't the disbelievers accept Allah's power to bring back the dead to life?

The surat reveals two more facts: "And in the sky is your promised sustenance" (22); and secondly, "We built the universe with *our creative* power, and We are ever expanding it (47). The sun provides all the energy for photosynthesis for plants to grow, which becomes human food. Astronomers believe the universe is expanding, so how could the Prophet Muhammad ﷺ, who lived in seventh-century Arabia, know this extraordinary fact? Isn't this evidence that the Quran is God's Word?

The Makkans are reminded about their forefather Ibrahim عليه السلام, blessed with a child in his old age, so He can give life to an infertile couple. Another instance of the Quran challenging conceptual boundaries, which made belief in the Resurrection difficult for them. Then a reminder of the fate of those who denied; a warning to them that their fate could be the same if they persist in their denial. At the end, the Messenger ﷺ is encouraged: "Reminder benefits the believers" (55), so carry on reminding humanity of the purpose of their creation: "I created jinn and human beings only to worship Me" (56).

بِسْمِ اللهِ الرَّحْمٰنِ الرَّحِيْمِ

وَالذّٰرِيٰتِ ذَرْوًا ۙ١ فَالْحٰمِلٰتِ وِقْرًا ۙ٢ فَالْجٰرِيٰتِ يُسْرًا ۙ٣ فَالْمُقَسِّمٰتِ اَمْرًا ۙ٤ اِنَّمَا تُوْعَدُوْنَ لَصَادِقٌ ۙ٥ وَّاِنَّ الدِّيْنَ لَوَاقِعٌ ؕ٦ وَالسَّمَاءِ ذَاتِ الْحُبُكِ ۙ٧ اِنَّكُمْ لَفِيْ قَوْلٍ مُّخْتَلِفٍ ۙ٨ يُّؤْفَكُ عَنْهُ مَنْ اُفِكَ ؕ٩ قُتِلَ الْخَرّٰصُوْنَ ۙ١٠ الَّذِيْنَ هُمْ فِيْ غَمْرَةٍ سَاهُوْنَ ۙ١١ يَسْــَٔلُوْنَ اَيَّانَ يَوْمُ الدِّيْنِ ؕ١٢ يَوْمَ هُمْ عَلَى النَّارِ يُفْتَنُوْنَ ١٣ ذُوْقُوْا فِتْنَتَكُمْ ؕ هٰذَا الَّذِيْ كُنْتُمْ بِهٖ تَسْتَعْجِلُوْنَ ١٤ اِنَّ الْمُتَّقِيْنَ فِيْ جَنّٰتٍ وَّعُيُوْنٍ ۙ١٥ اٰخِذِيْنَ مَاۤ اٰتٰىهُمْ رَبُّهُمْ ؕ اِنَّهُمْ كَانُوْا قَبْلَ ذٰلِكَ مُحْسِنِيْنَ ؕ١٦ كَانُوْا قَلِيْلًا مِّنَ الَّيْلِ مَا يَهْجَعُوْنَ ١٧ وَبِالْاَسْحَارِ هُمْ يَسْتَغْفِرُوْنَ ١٨ وَفِيْۤ اَمْوَالِهِمْ حَقٌّ لِّلسَّاۤئِلِ وَالْمَحْرُوْمِ ١٩ وَفِي الْاَرْضِ اٰيٰتٌ لِّلْمُوْقِنِيْنَ ۙ٢٠ وَفِيْۤ اَنْفُسِكُمْ ؕ اَفَلَا تُبْصِرُوْنَ ٢١ وَفِي السَّمَاءِ رِزْقُكُمْ وَمَا تُوْعَدُوْنَ ٢٢ فَوَرَبِّ السَّمَاءِ وَالْاَرْضِ اِنَّهٗ لَحَقٌّ مِّثْلَ مَاۤ اَنَّكُمْ تَنْطِقُوْنَ ٢٣ هَلْ اَتٰىكَ حَدِيْثُ ضَيْفِ اِبْرٰهِيْمَ الْمُكْرَمِيْنَ ۘ٢٤ اِذْ دَخَلُوْا عَلَيْهِ فَقَالُوْا سَلٰمًا ؕ قَالَ سَلٰمٌ ۚ قَوْمٌ مُّنْكَرُوْنَ ۚ٢٥ فَرَاغَ اِلٰۤى اَهْلِهٖ فَجَاۤءَ بِعِجْلٍ سَمِيْنٍ ۙ٢٦ فَقَرَّبَهٗۤ اِلَيْهِمْ

The mindful are the faithful who do honourable works and give generously.

ع
۲۳
۱۸

In the name of Allah, the Kind, the Caring.

The life giving wind

¹By the gale-force winds that scatter dust; ²by the winds that carry heavily-laden clouds; ³by the winds that sail ships with ease; ⁴by the winds that distribute rain as commanded; ⁵no doubt, what you have been promised is true; ⁶the *Day of Judgement* will certainly come. ⁷By the sky with its paths.ᵃ

Fate of the deniers of the Quran

⁸You have different views about *this Quran*. ⁹Those who turn away from *the Quran* are deceived. ¹⁰The liars are ruined, ¹¹who are numb and unaware *of reality*. ¹²They ask, "When will the Judgement Day come?" ¹³That Day they shall be punished with Fire. ¹⁴"Taste your punishment; this is what you were so impatient for."

Fate of the believers of the Quran

¹⁵The mindful will be in Gardens with flowing fountains; ¹⁶they will take what their Lord gives them. In the *world,* they were gracious; ¹⁷they slept little at night, ¹⁸and at dawn sought Allah's forgiveness. ¹⁹They set aside a share in their wealth for beggars, and the needy. ²⁰And for those who believe firmly there are signs in the Earth ²¹and in themselves. Don't you see? ²²And in the sky is your promised sustenance. ²³By the Lord of the Heavens and the Earth, this is as true as what you speak.

Ibrahim is visited by angels

²⁴Did you hear the story of Ibrahim's honourable guests? ²⁵They came and said, "Peace;" he replied, "Peace." *He thought,* "these are strangers." ²⁶He quietly slipped away to his family and brought a *roasted* fat calf ²⁷which he placed before them, and said, "Won't you eat?"

ᵃ   *Hubuk* also means ripples, waves and trails (Zia-ul-Quran).

قَالَ اِنِّىٓ اَلَّا تَاْكُلُوْنَ ۝ فَاَوْجَسَ مِنْهُمْ خِيْفَةً ط قَالُوْا

لَا تَخَفْ ط وَبَشَّرُوْهُ بِغُلٰمٍ عَلِيْمٍ ۝ فَاَقْبَلَتِ امْرَاَتُهٗ

فِيْ صَرَّةٍ فَصَكَّتْ وَجْهَهَا وَقَالَتْ عَجُوْزٌ عَقِيْمٌ ۝

قَالُوْا كَذٰلِكِ ۙ قَالَ رَبُّكِ ط اِنَّهٗ هُوَ الْحَكِيْمُ الْعَلِيْمُ ۝

قَالَ فَمَا خَطْبُكُمْ اَيُّهَا الْمُرْسَلُوْنَ ۝ قَالُوْٓا اِنَّآ

اُرْسِلْنَآ اِلٰى قَوْمٍ مُّجْرِمِيْنَ ۝ لِنُرْسِلَ عَلَيْهِمْ حِجَارَةً

مِّنْ طِيْنٍ ۝ مُّسَوَّمَةً عِنْدَ رَبِّكَ لِلْمُسْرِفِيْنَ ۝

فَاَخْرَجْنَا مَنْ كَانَ فِيْهَا مِنَ الْمُؤْمِنِيْنَ ۝ فَمَا

وَجَدْنَا فِيْهَا غَيْرَ بَيْتٍ مِّنَ الْمُسْلِمِيْنَ ۝ وَتَرَكْنَا

فِيْهَآ اٰيَةً لِّلَّذِيْنَ يَخَافُوْنَ الْعَذَابَ الْاَلِيْمَ ۝ وَ

فِيْ مُوْسٰٓى اِذْ اَرْسَلْنٰهُ اِلٰى فِرْعَوْنَ بِسُلْطٰنٍ مُّبِيْنٍ ۝

فَتَوَلّٰى بِرُكْنِهٖ وَقَالَ سٰحِرٌ اَوْ مَجْنُوْنٌ ۝ فَاَخَذْنٰهُ

وَجُنُوْدَهٗ فَنَبَذْنٰهُمْ فِى الْيَمِّ وَهُوَ مُلِيْمٌ ط وَفِيْ

عَادٍ اِذْ اَرْسَلْنَا عَلَيْهِمُ الرِّيْحَ الْعَقِيْمَ ۝ مَا تَذَرُ

مِنْ شَيْءٍ اَتَتْ عَلَيْهِ اِلَّا جَعَلَتْهُ كَالرَّمِيْمِ ط وَفِيْ

ثَمُوْدَ اِذْ قِيْلَ لَهُمْ تَمَتَّعُوْا حَتّٰى حِيْنٍ ۝ فَعَتَوْا عَنْ

اَمْرِ رَبِّهِمْ فَاَخَذَتْهُمُ الصّٰعِقَةُ وَهُمْ يَنْظُرُوْنَ ۝

فَمَا اسْتَطَاعُوْا مِنْ قِيَامٍ وَّمَا كَانُوْا مُنْتَصِرِيْنَ ۝

وَقَوْمَ نُوْحٍ مِّنْ قَبْلُ ط اِنَّهُمْ كَانُوْا قَوْمًا فٰسِقِيْنَ ۝

وَالسَّمَآءَ بَنَيْنٰهَا بِاَيْدٍ وَّاِنَّا لَمُوْسِعُوْنَ ۝ وَالْاَرْضَ

The history of human disobedience; look how people of Nuh, Lut and Pharaoh denied the eternal truths. Let's repent and be obedient.

²⁸He felt afraid of them, and they replied, "Don't be afraid." They gave him good news of a knowledgeable son. ²⁹His wife stepped forward and struck her face *at this news,* she was amazed and said, "*Who me? A barren old woman!*" ³⁰They said, "That's how your Lord has decreed. Indeed, He is Wise, the Knower."

The angels disclose their assignment

³¹Ibrahim asked, "What's the purpose of your coming, messengers?" ³²They replied, "We've been sent to the wicked people,ᵃ ³³to pelt them with clay stones ³⁴marked by your Lord for those who've gone beyond limits." ³⁵We rescued the believers from there; ³⁶We only found a single household of believers. ³⁷And We left behind a sign for those who fear the painful punishment.

Examples of other people who were destroyed

³⁸Also in the story of Musa *is a sign,* when We sent him with a clear authority to Pharaoh. ³⁹He turned away because of his military mightᵇ and said, "Musa is a magician or a madman." ⁴⁰So We seized him and his army and threw them into the sea; he was guilty. ⁴¹And in the story of Ad *is a lesson* too, when we sent devastating wind upon them. ⁴²In its wake it left behind everything crushed and torn up. ⁴³And in the story of Thamud when it was said to them: "Enjoy yourselves for a while." ⁴⁴They disobeyed the Lord's command, so were seized by a blast as they watched. ⁴⁵Neither could they bear the punishment nor defend themselves against Us. ⁴⁶The people of Nuh before *them faced a similar fate.* They too were sinners.

The expanding universe

⁴⁷We built the universeᶜ with *our creative* power and We are ever expanding it.ᵈ

ᵃ   This refers to the people of Lut ﷺ, who lived in the towns of Sodom and Gomorrah.

ᵇ   *Rukn* means army, bureaucrats and citizens.

ᶜ   *Al sama* literally means the sky, the Heavens, including all stars and galaxies, i.e. the cosmos or the universe.

ᵈ   Astronomers now believe that the universe is expanding. It is very interesting to note the Quran described Allah as the expander of the universe.

فَرَشْنٰهَا فَنِعْمَ الْمٰهِدُوْنَ ۞ وَمِنْ كُلِّ شَىْءٍ خَلَقْنَا زَوْجَيْنِ لَعَلَّكُمْ تَذَكَّرُوْنَ ۞ فَفِرُّوْا إِلَى اللهِ ط إِنِّى لَكُمْ مِّنْهُ نَذِيْرٌ مُّبِيْنٌ ۞ وَلَا تَجْعَلُوْا مَعَ اللهِ إِلٰهًا اٰخَرَ ط إِنِّى لَكُمْ مِّنْهُ نَذِيْرٌ مُّبِيْنٌ ۞ كَذٰلِكَ مَآ أَتَى الَّذِيْنَ مِنْ قَبْلِهِمْ مِّنْ رَّسُوْلٍ إِلَّا قَالُوْا سَاحِرٌ أَوْ مَجْنُوْنٌ ۞ أَتَوَاصَوْا بِهٖ ج بَلْ هُمْ قَوْمٌ طَاغُوْنَ ۞ فَتَوَلَّ عَنْهُمْ فَمَآ أَنْتَ بِمَلُوْمٍ ۞ وَّذَكِّرْ فَإِنَّ الذِّكْرٰى تَنْفَعُ الْمُؤْمِنِيْنَ ۞ وَمَا خَلَقْتُ الْجِنَّ وَالْإِنْسَ إِلَّا لِيَعْبُدُوْنِ ۞ مَآ أُرِيْدُ مِنْهُمْ مِّنْ رِّزْقٍ وَّمَآ أُرِيْدُ أَنْ يُّطْعِمُوْنِ ۞ إِنَّ اللهَ هُوَ الرَّزَّاقُ ذُو الْقُوَّةِ الْمَتِيْنُ ۞ فَإِنَّ لِلَّذِيْنَ ظَلَمُوْا ذَنُوْبًا مِّثْلَ ذَنُوْبِ أَصْحٰبِهِمْ فَلَا يَسْتَعْجِلُوْنِ ۞ فَوَيْلٌ لِّلَّذِيْنَ كَفَرُوْا مِنْ يَّوْمِهِمُ الَّذِىْ يُوْعَدُوْنَ ۞

Sincere advice: good words always strike a chord with the believer and they benefit from them.

⁴⁸ And the Earth We spread out and levelled it smoothly. ⁴⁹ We created everything in pairs so that you may reflect. ⁵⁰ So come to Allah quickly. I am a clear Warner to you. ⁵¹ Don't set up gods beside Allah, I am a clear Warner to you. ⁵² This is exactly what previous people did when a messenger was sent, they called him "a magician or a mad man." ⁵³ Did they tell one another to do this? No. They were transgressors.

Purpose of human creation

⁵⁴ So ignore them, you are not to blame; ⁵⁵ continue reminding, a reminder benefits the believers. ⁵⁶ I created jinn and human beings only to worship Me. ⁵⁷ I don't want any sustenance from them nor for them to feed Me. ⁵⁸ Allah is surely the Sustainer, the Superpower and strong. ⁵⁹ The wrongdoers will have the punishment like their ancestors, so they shouldn't ask Me to hasten it. ⁶⁰ It will be too bad for the disbelievers that Day, which they've been promised.

52. Surat At-Tur

The Mountain

This is a late Makkan surat that emphatically provides evidence from both nature and human history for the truthfulness of Islamic beliefs: the Oneness of Allah, the messengership of Muhammad ﷺ, and Resurrection. It opens with five powerful oaths as witnesses of the message of the Prophet ﷺ, and threatens the disbelievers of Makkah, warning them of the consequences of their persistent denials: "Your Lord's punishment will certainly come to pass" (7), followed by a description of the luxuries of Paradise. Verse 21 lends some credence to a common proverb: you reap what you sow. "Each person is answerable for his deeds". However, a concession is made for righteous people: their faithful children will join them in Paradise, despite not being as righteous as their parents.

This is followed by a passage that poses ten challenging questions. These range from challenging the mistaken notion about the Prophet ﷺ being a poet and soothsayer, to the question of who holds the treasures of Allah. The Quran masterly asks tag questions: Questions at the end of a statement in a way that invites agreement. By asking several questions in a row, where the reader gets used to answering in agreement, so this makes it easy for them to agree to the next suggestion or order.

The surat concludes: the Makkans are a stubborn bunch of people, intolerant and close-minded. The Prophet ﷺ is urged to continue his mission despite their rejection and hostility: "Therefore wait patiently for your Lord's judgement; you are *always* in Our Eyes, and glorify and praise your Lord whenever you stand *for the prayer*" (48).

بِسْمِ اللهِ الرَّحْمٰنِ الرَّحِيْمِ

وَالطُّوْرِ ۙ۱ وَكِتٰبٍ مَّسْطُوْرٍ ۙ۲ فِيْ رَقٍّ مَّنْشُوْرٍ ۙ۳ وَّالْبَيْتِ الْمَعْمُوْرِ ۙ۴ وَالسَّقْفِ الْمَرْفُوْعِ ۙ۵ وَالْبَحْرِ الْمَسْجُوْرِ ۙ۶ اِنَّ عَذَابَ رَبِّكَ لَوَاقِعٌ ۙ۷ مَّا لَهٗ مِنْ دَافِعٍ ۙ۸ يَّوْمَ تَمُوْرُ السَّمَآءُ مَوْرًا ۙ۹ وَّتَسِيْرُ الْجِبَالُ سَيْرًا ۱۰ فَوَيْلٌ يَّوْمَئِذٍ لِّلْمُكَذِّبِيْنَ ۙ۱۱ الَّذِيْنَ هُمْ فِيْ خَوْضٍ يَّلْعَبُوْنَ ۱۲ يَوْمَ يُدَعُّوْنَ اِلٰى نَارِ جَهَنَّمَ دَعًّا ۱۳ هٰذِهِ النَّارُ الَّتِيْ كُنْتُمْ بِهَا تُكَذِّبُوْنَ ۱۴ اَفَسِحْرٌ هٰذَآ اَمْ اَنْتُمْ لَا تُبْصِرُوْنَ ۱۵ اِصْلَوْهَا فَاصْبِرُوْٓا اَوْ لَا تَصْبِرُوْا ۚ سَوَآءٌ عَلَيْكُمْ ۚ اِنَّمَا تُجْزَوْنَ مَا كُنْتُمْ تَعْمَلُوْنَ ۱۶ اِنَّ الْمُتَّقِيْنَ فِيْ جَنّٰتٍ وَّنَعِيْمٍ ۙ۱۷ فٰكِهِيْنَ بِمَآ اٰتٰىهُمْ رَبُّهُمْ ۚ وَوَقٰىهُمْ رَبُّهُمْ عَذَابَ الْجَحِيْمِ ۱۸ كُلُوْا وَاشْرَبُوْا هَنِيْٓئًا ۢ بِمَا كُنْتُمْ تَعْمَلُوْنَ ۙ۱۹ مُتَّكِئِيْنَ عَلٰى سُرُرٍ مَّصْفُوْفَةٍ ۚ وَزَوَّجْنٰهُمْ بِحُوْرٍ عِيْنٍ ۲۰ وَالَّذِيْنَ اٰمَنُوْا وَاتَّبَعَتْهُمْ ذُرِّيَّتُهُمْ بِاِيْمَانٍ اَلْحَقْنَا بِهِمْ ذُرِّيَّتَهُمْ وَمَآ اَلَتْنٰهُمْ مِّنْ عَمَلِهِمْ مِّنْ شَيْءٍ ۚ كُلُّ امْرِئٍ ۢ بِمَا كَسَبَ رَهِيْنٌ ۲۱ وَاَمْدَدْنٰهُمْ بِفَاكِهَةٍ وَّلَحْمٍ مِّمَّا يَشْتَهُوْنَ ۲۲ يَتَنَازَعُوْنَ فِيْهَا كَأْسًا لَّا لَغْوٌ فِيْهَا وَلَا تَأْثِيْمٌ ۲۳

The children of the people of Paradise will be allowed to join them even though they are not of the same calibre in terms of faith and action.

1069

In the name of Allah, the Kind, the Caring.

The certainty of suffering and punishment of Hell

[1] By the mountain, [2] and by a Book written down [3] on open pages, [4] and by the visited house,[a] [5] and by the soaring roof, [6] and by the over-full, ferocious sea – [7] your Lord's punishment will come to pass; [8] no power can stop it! [9] Even the sky will shudder and judder that Day, [10] and the mountains will float. [11] Ruined that Day will be the deniers, [12] who were absorbed in useless projects. [13] That Day they will be thrust into the fire of Hell. [14] "This is the Fire you use to deny. [15] Is this magic? Or do you not see? [16] Burn in it! Whether you are patient or not it is the same; you are being rewarded for what you did."

The righteous will enjoy the luxuries of Paradise

[17] The righteous will be in Gardens full of luxuries, [18] enjoying what the Lord gave them, and protected them from the punishment of Hell. [19] *They shall be told:* "Eat, drink and be merry, a reward for what you did." [20] *They will* rest on *comfortable* sofas *gracefully* arranged in rows, and We shall marry them with spouses with beautiful eyes.[b]

Children of righteous parents join them in Paradise

[21] The believers whose children followed them in faith will be united with them in Paradise without their parents' good deeds being diminished in value. Each person is answerable[c] for his deeds. [22] We shall feed them with all the kinds of fruits and meat they desire. [23] A cup of *wine* passed around will not cause drunken uproar or a sin.

---

[a] The visited house is *Al Bait al Ma'mur,* refers to the Kaaba of the angels in the Heavens, visited by 70,000 angels morning and evenings (Bukhari).

[b] *Hurin ein* literally means "an eye that has a black iris and large white eyeball" (Qamus). According to Hassan al-Basri, it simply refers to "righteous women" (Tabari).

[c] *Raheen*: pawned, mortgaged, given as security. Implying that the person is responsible for his deeds.

وَيَطُوفُ عَلَيْهِمْ غِلْمَانٌ لَّهُمْ كَأَنَّهُمْ لُؤْلُؤٌ مَّكْنُونٌ ۞

وَأَقْبَلَ بَعْضُهُمْ عَلَى بَعْضٍ يَتَسَاءَلُونَ ۞ قَالُوٓا إِنَّا

كُنَّا قَبْلُ فِىٓ أَهْلِنَا مُشْفِقِينَ ۞ فَمَنَّ اللَّهُ عَلَيْنَا

وَوَقَىٰنَا عَذَابَ السَّمُومِ ۞ إِنَّا كُنَّا مِن قَبْلُ نَدْعُوهُ ۗ

إِنَّهُ هُوَ الْبَرُّ الرَّحِيمُ ۞ فَذَكِّرْ فَمَآ أَنتَ بِنِعْمَتِ رَبِّكَ

بِكَاهِنٍ وَّلَا مَجْنُونٍ ۞ أَمْ يَقُولُونَ شَاعِرٌ نَّتَرَبَّصُ

بِهِ رَيْبَ الْمَنُونِ ۞ قُلْ تَرَبَّصُوا فَإِنِّى مَعَكُم مِّنَ

الْمُتَرَبِّصِينَ ۞ أَمْ تَأْمُرُهُمْ أَحْلَامُهُم بِهَٰذَآ أَمْ هُمْ

قَوْمٌ طَاغُونَ ۞ أَمْ يَقُولُونَ تَقَوَّلَهُ ۚ بَل لَّا يُؤْمِنُونَ ۞

فَلْيَأْتُوا بِحَدِيثٍ مِّثْلِهِ إِن كَانُوا صَادِقِينَ ۞ أَمْ

خُلِقُوا مِنْ غَيْرِ شَىْءٍ أَمْ هُمُ الْخَالِقُونَ ۞ أَمْ

خَلَقُوا السَّمَاوَاتِ وَالْأَرْضَ ۚ بَل لَّا يُوقِنُونَ ۞ أَمْ

عِندَهُمْ خَزَائِنُ رَبِّكَ أَمْ هُمُ الْمُصَيْطِرُونَ ۞

أَمْ لَهُمْ سُلَّمٌ يَّسْتَمِعُونَ فِيهِ ۖ فَلْيَأْتِ مُسْتَمِعُهُم

بِسُلْطَانٍ مُّبِينٍ ۞ أَمْ لَهُ الْبَنَاتُ وَلَكُمُ الْبَنُونَ ۞

أَمْ تَسْئَلُهُمْ أَجْرًا فَهُم مِّن مَّغْرَمٍ مُّثْقَلُونَ ۞ أَمْ

عِندَهُمُ الْغَيْبُ فَهُمْ يَكْتُبُونَ ۞ أَمْ يُرِيدُونَ

كَيْدًا ۖ فَالَّذِينَ كَفَرُوا هُمُ الْمَكِيدُونَ ۞ أَمْ لَهُمْ

إِلَٰهٌ غَيْرُ اللَّهِ ۚ سُبْحَانَ اللَّهِ عَمَّا يُشْرِكُونَ ۞ وَإِن

يَّرَوْا كِسْفًا مِّنَ السَّمَاءِ سَاقِطًا يَّقُولُوا سَحَابٌ

Idols will be of no avail to them on Judgement Day.

²⁴Serving them will be young people as *beautiful* as hidden pearls. ²⁵Turning to each other, they will ask, ²⁶"were we not fearful about the fate of our families? ²⁷Allah has favoured us and spared us the punishment of the Intense Fire. ²⁸We used to pray to Him; the Good, the Caring."

Ten challenging questions for the disbelievers

²⁹So, remind them, by the grace of your Lord; you aren't a soothsayer nor a madman. ³⁰They call you, "A poet, and we are waiting to see what time will do to him."ᵃ ³¹Tell them: "Wait if you wish, and I shall wait with you." ³²Or do their minds tell them to say this? Or are they simply a *bunch of* unruly people? ³³Or they say, "He has made it up." Never will they believe. ³⁴So let them bring a book like it if they are truthful. ³⁵Were they created without a creator? Or are they themselves creators? ³⁶Or did they create the Heavens and the Earth? No, they will never be convinced. ³⁷Or is it that they possess the treasures of your Lord, or have control over them? ³⁸Or do they have a ladder that allows them to eavesdrop on *the secrets of the Heavens*? Let their eavesdropper bring clear proof. ³⁹Or is it that He has daughters and you have sons? ⁴⁰Or do you ask them for a wage *for this guidance* that would make them heavily indebted? ⁴¹Or do they have the knowledge *of the unseen* they write down? ⁴²Or do they want to deceive you? The disbelievers only deceive themselves. ⁴³Or do they have a god besides Allah? Glory be to Allah; He is far above what they associate with Him.

The disbelievers have no answers, and they are stubborn

⁴⁴Even if they saw a part of the sky fall, they would say, "It's merely heaps of cloud."

ᵃ *Raib el manun* is an Arabic idiom which means, "evil happenings of time" (Zia-ul-Quran).

مَّرْكُوْمٌ ۞ فَذَرْهُمْ حَتّٰى يُلٰقُوْا يَوْمَهُمُ الَّذِىْ فِيْهِ

يُصْعَقُوْنَ ۞ يَوْمَ لَا يُغْنِىْ عَنْهُمْ كَيْدُهُمْ شَيْئًا وَّلَا

هُمْ يُنْصَرُوْنَ ۞ وَاِنَّ لِلَّذِيْنَ ظَلَمُوْا عَذَابًا دُوْنَ

ذٰلِكَ وَلٰكِنَّ اَكْثَرَهُمْ لَا يَعْلَمُوْنَ ۞ وَاصْبِرْ لِحُكْمِ

رَبِّكَ فَاِنَّكَ بِاَعْيُنِنَا وَسَبِّحْ بِحَمْدِ رَبِّكَ حِيْنَ

تَقُوْمُ ۞ وَمِنَ الَّيْلِ فَسَبِّحْهُ وَاِدْبَارَ النُّجُوْمِ ۞

Look how the Lord gazes at His beloved when he worships Him.

⁴⁵ So leave them till they encounter the Day they'll die.^a ⁴⁶ A Day when their plots will not benefit them at all, neither will they be helped. ⁴⁷ For the evildoers there is another punishment *in this world* before that one, but most of them don't know.

Allah watches His beloved Messenger ﷺ

⁴⁸ Therefore, wait patiently for your Lord's judgement; you are *always* in Our sight, so glorify and praise your Lord whenever you stand *for the prayer*, ⁴⁹ *and also* at night glorify Him till the stars fade away.

---

^a   *Sa'aqa* has two meanings: to become unconscious or to die. This translation uses the latter.

53. Surat An-Najm
The Star

This surat was revealed in the late Makkan period. When the Messenger ﷺ recited this surat to the Quraysh near the Kaaba, they were mesmerised by its tempo and fell in prostration. The surat opens by rejecting the Quraysh's allegation that the Messenger ﷺ was misguided.

According to the commentators verses 1-18 are descriptions of the Messenger's ﷺ vertical phase of the ascension. The Messenger ﷺ goes beyond the celestial realm into the Divine presence, he ﷺ is honoured, he ﷺ sees the Divine Majesty.

Detailed narratives of the ascension are found in Hadith books. The Messenger ﷺ said, "One night I was asleep, in the Haram near the Kaaba, I was woken by Jibreel, he informed me of the Divine plan and took me to the well of Zam Zam, and opened my chest and filled it with wisdom and faith. Afterwards a beautiful Buraq was presented: an animal larger than a mule but smaller than a horse. I mounted it. Soon the Messenger ﷺ was at the Masjid al-Aqsa in Jerusalem. Here prophets were eagerly waiting for him. He led them in congregational prayer. This marked the end of the horizontal part of the journey. From here, accompanied by Jibreel, the Messenger ﷺ travelled on the Buraq ascending the heavens. In the first heaven, He met Adam; in the second Isa and Yahya; in the third Yusuf; the fourth Idris; in the fifth Harun; and in the sixth Musa; and in the seventh Ibrahim. The journey continued beyond the heavens until He reached the Bait al-Mamur - The Kaaba of the Angels, from where He ﷺ ascended to the Lote tree (Sidratul Muntaha) of the uttermost boundary. Surat Al-Najm describes this mysterious part of the journey: "Then he drew near, very near, like two bows lengths or even closer (Al-Najm: 8).

The Prophet ﷺ witnessed the delights of Paradise and the Punishments of Hell during his celestial journey, he ﷺ saw the grandeur and the Majesty of his Lord. For more read my book "Isra wal Miraj."

The disbelievers are challenged; they're irrational, lack historical evidence, and consequently sceptical. The Quran, on the other hand, provides knowledge from the Divine, and its arguments are rational that appeal to common sense. The surat distils the meaning of previous Scriptures in a pithy verse: "Each person will have what he has worked towards" (39), thus refuting the Quraysh's belief in intercession by idols.

It ends with a warning: "The Judgement Day is near and draws ever nearer ... Are you surprised about this? Laughing at it rather than crying?" (58–60).

سُوْرَةُ النَّجْمِ مَكِّيَّةٌ (٢٣) رُكُوْعُهَا ٣ (٥٣) اٰيَاتُهَا ٦٢

بِسْمِ اللهِ الرَّحْمٰنِ الرَّحِيْمِ

وَالنَّجْمِ اِذَا هَوٰى ۞ مَا ضَلَّ صَاحِبُكُمْ وَمَا غَوٰى ۞

وَمَا يَنْطِقُ عَنِ الْهَوٰى ۞ اِنْ هُوَ اِلَّا وَحْىٌ يُّوْحٰى ۞

عَلَّمَهٗ شَدِيْدُ الْقُوٰى ۞ ذُوْمِرَّةٍ ۖ فَاسْتَوٰى ۞ وَهُوَ

بِالْاُفُقِ الْاَعْلٰى ۞ ثُمَّ دَنَا فَتَدَلّٰى ۞ فَكَانَ قَابَ

قَوْسَيْنِ اَوْ اَدْنٰى ۞ فَاَوْحٰى اِلٰى عَبْدِهٖ مَا اَوْحٰى ۞ مَا

كَذَبَ الْفُؤَادُ مَا رَاٰى ۞ اَفَتُمٰرُوْنَهٗ عَلٰى مَا يَرٰى ۞

وَلَقَدْ رَاٰهُ نَزْلَةً اُخْرٰى ۞ عِنْدَ سِدْرَةِ الْمُنْتَهٰى ۞

عِنْدَهَا جَنَّةُ الْمَاْوٰى ۞ اِذْ يَغْشَى السِّدْرَةَ مَا يَغْشٰى ۞

مَا زَاغَ الْبَصَرُ وَمَا طَغٰى ۞ لَقَدْ رَاٰى مِنْ اٰيٰتِ رَبِّهِ

الْكُبْرٰى ۞ اَفَرَءَيْتُمُ اللّٰتَ وَالْعُزّٰى ۞ وَمَنٰوةَ الثَّالِثَةَ

الْاُخْرٰى ۞ اَلَكُمُ الذَّكَرُ وَلَهُ الْاُنْثٰى ۞ تِلْكَ اِذًا قِسْمَةٌ

ضِيْزٰى ۞ اِنْ هِيَ اِلَّا اَسْمَاءٌ سَمَّيْتُمُوْهَا اَنْتُمْ وَ

اٰبَاؤُكُمْ مَّا اَنْزَلَ اللهُ بِهَا مِنْ سُلْطٰنٍ ۚ اِنْ يَّتَّبِعُوْنَ

اِلَّا الظَّنَّ وَمَا تَهْوَى الْاَنْفُسُ ۚ وَلَقَدْ جَاءَهُمْ مِّنْ

رَّبِّهِمُ الْهُدٰى ۞ اَمْ لِلْاِنْسَانِ مَا تَمَنّٰى ۞ فَلِلّٰهِ الْاٰخِرَةُ

وَالْاُوْلٰى ۞ وَكَمْ مِّنْ مَّلَكٍ فِى السَّمٰوٰتِ لَا تُغْنِى

شَفَاعَتُهُمْ شَيْئًا اِلَّا مِنْ بَعْدِ اَنْ يَّاْذَنَ اللهُ لِمَنْ

يَّشَاءُ وَيَرْضٰى ۞ اِنَّ الَّذِيْنَ لَا يُؤْمِنُوْنَ بِالْاٰخِرَةِ

The mysterious celestial world, the beloved Messenger's ﷺ faculties see either the Lord Almighty or Jibreel.

In the name of Allah, the Kind, the Caring.

The Prophet's ﷺ ascension: The celestial journey

[1] By the *shining* star when it came down, [2] your master[a] is neither misguided nor deluded. [3] He doesn't speak from his desire. [4] This is a Revelation sent down [5] and taught to him by the most powerful, [6] the most wise. When he appeared *to him,* [7] He was on the uppermost horizon. [8] Then they drew near, very near. [9] The distance between two bows held together.[b] [10] So He revealed to His servant what He revealed. [11] His heart didn't deny what he saw. [12] So why are you disputing what he saw? [13] And on another occasion he saw him coming down [14] near the far side of the Lote Tree, [15] nearby was the Paradise of *Mawa.*[c] [16] The Lote Tree was covered with *indescribable* splendour;[d] [17] his eyes didn't wander nor turn to the side [18] as he witnessed the greatest signs of His Lord.

The idols are the products of materialist minds

[19] *Disbelievers!* Have you thought about Al-Lat, Al-Uzza [20] and Al-Manat, the third of them? [21] *You chose* sons for yourselves and daughters for Allah, why? [22] How unfair is this division! [23] These are merely names you and your forefathers gave them; Allah hasn't given them any authority. They are following suspicions and their whims. The Lord's guidance has come to them. [24] Does a person always get his wish? [25] Both the Hereafter and this world belong to Allah.

Intercession is by Allah's permission only

[26] There are many angels in Heaven, their intercession cannot benefit anyone, except after Allah allows it for anyone He wants. [27] The disbelievers of the Hereafter give the angels female names.

---

[a]   *Sahib* means companion, master and owner, since this refers to the beloved Messenger ﷺ I translated it as master.

[b]   Literally "the distance between two bows held together". When two Arab chiefs agreed a treaty they would hold their bows together and then release a single arrow from it. An expression that the two chiefs were united. This expression is used now to convey this sense of closeness.

[c]   *Mawa* is the name of one of the seven Paradises it means "a restful place".

[d]   A description of "the inconceivable Majesty and splendour attaching to this symbol of Paradise, which no description can picture and no definition can embrace" (Asad).

لَيُسَمُّوْنَ الْمَلٰٓئِكَةَ تَسْمِيَةَ الْاُنْثٰى ۲۷ وَمَا لَهُمْ بِهٖ

مِنْ عِلْمٍ ط اِنْ يَّتَّبِعُوْنَ اِلَّا الظَّنَّ ج وَاِنَّ الظَّنَّ لَا

يُغْنِيْ مِنَ الْحَقِّ شَيْئًا ۲۸ فَاَعْرِضْ عَنْ مَّنْ تَوَلّٰى ۵

عَنْ ذِكْرِنَا وَلَمْ يُرِدْ اِلَّا الْحَيٰوةَ الدُّنْيَا ۲۹ ذٰلِكَ

مَبْلَغُهُمْ مِّنَ الْعِلْمِ ط اِنَّ رَبَّكَ هُوَ اَعْلَمُ بِمَنْ ضَلَّ

عَنْ سَبِيْلِهٖ وَهُوَ اَعْلَمُ بِمَنِ اهْتَدٰى ۳۰ وَلِلّٰهِ مَا فِى

السَّمٰوٰتِ وَمَا فِى الْاَرْضِ لِيَجْزِيَ الَّذِيْنَ اَسَاءُوْا

بِمَا عَمِلُوْا وَيَجْزِيَ الَّذِيْنَ اَحْسَنُوْا بِالْحُسْنٰى ۳۱

اَلَّذِيْنَ يَجْتَنِبُوْنَ كَبٰٓئِرَ الْاِثْمِ وَالْفَوَاحِشَ اِلَّا اللَّمَمَ ط

اِنَّ رَبَّكَ وَاسِعُ الْمَغْفِرَةِ ط هُوَ اَعْلَمُ بِكُمْ اِذْ اَنْشَاَكُمْ

مِّنَ الْاَرْضِ وَاِذْ اَنْتُمْ اَجِنَّةٌ فِيْ بُطُوْنِ اُمَّهٰتِكُمْ ج

فَلَا تُزَكُّوْٓا اَنْفُسَكُمْ ط هُوَ اَعْلَمُ بِمَنِ اتَّقٰى ۳۲ اَفَرَءَيْتَ

الَّذِيْ تَوَلّٰى ۳۳ وَاَعْطٰى قَلِيْلًا وَّاَكْدٰى ۳۴ اَعِنْدَهٗ عِلْمُ

الْغَيْبِ فَهُوَ يَرٰى ۳۵ اَمْ لَمْ يُنَبَّأْ بِمَا فِيْ صُحُفِ مُوْسٰى ۳۶

وَاِبْرٰهِيْمَ الَّذِيْ وَفّٰٓى ۳۷ اَلَّا تَزِرُ وَازِرَةٌ وِّزْرَ اُخْرٰى ۳۸

وَاَنْ لَّيْسَ لِلْاِنْسَانِ اِلَّا مَا سَعٰى ۳۹ وَاَنَّ سَعْيَهٗ

سَوْفَ يُرٰى ۴۰ ثُمَّ يُجْزٰىهُ الْجَزَآءَ الْاَوْفٰى ۴۱ وَاَنَّ

اِلٰى رَبِّكَ الْمُنْتَهٰى ۴۲ وَاَنَّهٗ هُوَ اَضْحَكَ وَاَبْكٰى ۴۳

وَاَنَّهٗ هُوَ اَمَاتَ وَاَحْيَا ۴۴ وَاَنَّهٗ خَلَقَ الزَّوْجَيْنِ

الذَّكَرَ وَالْاُنْثٰى ۴۵ مِنْ نُّطْفَةٍ اِذَا تُمْنٰى ۴۶ وَاَنَّ عَلَيْهِ

People reap what they sow; Allah's reward will be fair and generous.

²⁸ They have no knowledge but follow speculation, and speculation is no substitute for the truth. ²⁹ So pay no attention to the one who has turned away from Our remembrance and pursues only the life of this world. ³⁰ This is the sum total of their knowledge. Indeed, your Lord knows who strayed from His path and who is guided.

Why a person surrenders to desires?

³¹ Everything in the Heavens and the Earth belongs to Allah. He shall punish the evil, and richly reward the righteous: ³² who avoid major sins and shameful deeds, but *may* stumble *into minor sins*. Your Lord is infinite in forgiveness. He knows you from the time He created you from the Earth, and when you were a foetus in your mothers' wombs, so don't admire yourselves too much.ᵃ He knows well who is mindful.

Each person will have what he worked towards

³³ Have you seen him who turned away? ³⁴ He gives little *anyway* then becomes more stingy. ³⁵ Does he know the Unseen? Is he seeing it? ³⁶ Does he know what's in the Scriptures of Musa, ³⁷ and Ibrahim? He fulfilled *his responsibility of preaching*. ³⁸ No one bears the burden of another, ³⁹ and each person will have what he strived for. ⁴⁰ Soon *the outcome* of his work will be shown, ⁴¹ and will be fully rewarded. ⁴² The Final Destination is to your Lord.

The one who makes you laugh

⁴³ He makes you laugh and cry, ⁴⁴ He gives death and life, ⁴⁵ He created the male and the female, ⁴⁶ from a drop of spurted semen. ⁴⁷ He is responsible for the second creation,

---

ᵃ *Falatazaku anfusakum* means don't claim to be pure, it's an idiom for "don't flatter yourself, don't justify yourself".

النَّشْاَةَ الْاُخْرٰى ۞ وَاَنَّهٗ هُوَ اَغْنٰى وَاَقْنٰى ۞ وَاَنَّهٗ

هُوَ رَبُّ الشِّعْرٰى ۞ وَاَنَّهٗ اَهْلَكَ عَادَاۨ الْاُوْلٰى ۞

وَثَمُوْدَا فَمَاۤ اَبْقٰى ۞ وَقَوْمَ نُوْحٍ مِّنْ قَبْلُ ۗ اِنَّهُمْ

كَانُوْا هُمْ اَظْلَمَ وَاَطْغٰى ۞ وَالْمُؤْتَفِكَةَ اَهْوٰى ۞

فَغَشّٰىهَا مَا غَشّٰى ۞ فَبِاَيِّ اٰلَآءِ رَبِّكَ تَتَمَارٰى ۞

هٰذَا نَذِيْرٌ مِّنَ النُّذُرِ الْاُوْلٰى ۞ اَزِفَتِ الْاٰزِفَةُ ۞

لَيْسَ لَهَا مِنْ دُوْنِ اللّٰهِ كَاشِفَةٌ ۗ اَفَمِنْ هٰذَا

الْحَدِيْثِ تَعْجَبُوْنَ ۞ وَتَضْحَكُوْنَ وَلَا تَبْكُوْنَ ۞

وَاَنْتُمْ سٰمِدُوْنَ ۞ فَاسْجُدُوْا لِلّٰهِ وَاعْبُدُوْا ۩ ۞

Don't doubt nor be surprised. Just have faith and worship Him!

⁴⁸who gives wealth and poverty.ᵃ ⁴⁹The Lord of the star Sirius!ᵇ ⁵⁰He destroyed the first Ad ⁵¹and Thamud, and didn't leave a single one of them, ⁵²and the people of Nuh before *that since* they were evildoers and rebellious. ⁵³He destroyed the Mu'tafikkahᶜ ⁵⁴and covered them *with rubble* so they're hidden from sight. ⁵⁵So which favours of your Lord will you doubt?

Pay attention to the Messenger ﷺ

⁵⁶This warner is like the previous warners. ⁵⁷The *Judgement Day* is near, and draws ever nearer, ⁵⁸there is no one beside Allah who can disclose *its time.* ⁵⁹Are you surprised about this? ⁶⁰Would you laugh and not cry? ⁶¹You are careless and ignorant.ᵈ ⁶²Prostrate before Allah and worship Him.

ᵃ   *Aqna* has several meanings, I have followed the meaning given in Zia-ul-Quran.
ᵇ   Sirius is the 'dog star' that appears in springtime and was worshipped by the pagan Arabs.
ᶜ   This refers to the city of the Prophet Lut, Sodom and Gomorrah.
ᵈ   *Samidun* means "a person who is neglectful and carelessly walks with his head high" (Raghib); someone not bothered about anything.

54. Surat Al-Qamar

The Moon

One night on the plains of Mina outside Makkah, the Prophet 🌼 was with a group of Quraysh, and they demanded a miracle: "split the moon in two parts, and we'll believe". Abdullah ibn Masood reports that the Prophet 🌼 raised his hands and pointed at the moon with his index finger, and lo and behold, it split into two parts. The Makkans were stunned, and the Prophet 🌼 called out to each one of them by their names: you have now seen the miracle with your eyes, so be a witness. Unfortunately, instead of believing they retorted, "This is a powerful magic" (2).

The miracle of splitting of the moon took place in the seventh year of the mission of the Prophet 🌼. The Makkans are warned about the dire consequences of their stubbornness, disbelief and foolishness. The stories of four ancient people are presented to drive the point home; those who oppose God's prophets always lose. Each story ends with the refrain, "How terrible were My punishment and warnings? We made the Quran easy to learn, so will anyone pay attention?"

بِسْمِ اللهِ الرَّحْمٰنِ الرَّحِيْمِ

اِقْتَرَبَتِ السَّاعَةُ وَانْشَقَّ الْقَمَرُ ۚ۝ وَاِنْ يَّرَوْا اٰيَةً يُّعْرِضُوْا وَيَقُوْلُوْا سِحْرٌ مُّسْتَمِرٌّ ۝ وَكَذَّبُوْا وَاتَّبَعُوْٓا اَهْوَآءَهُمْ وَكُلُّ اَمْرٍ مُّسْتَقِرٌّ ۝ وَلَقَدْ جَآءَهُمْ مِّنَ الْاَنْبَآءِ مَا فِيْهِ مُزْدَجَرٌ ۝ حِكْمَةٌ بَالِغَةٌ فَمَا تُغْنِ النُّذُرُ ۙ۝ فَتَوَلَّ عَنْهُمْ ۘ يَوْمَ يَدْعُ الدَّاعِ اِلٰى شَیْءٍ نُّكُرٍ ۙ۝ خُشَّعًا اَبْصَارُهُمْ يَخْرُجُوْنَ مِنَ الْاَجْدَاثِ كَاَنَّهُمْ جَرَادٌ مُّنْتَشِرٌ ۙ۝ مُّهْطِعِیْنَ اِلَى الدَّاعِ ؕ يَقُوْلُ الْكٰفِرُوْنَ هٰذَا يَوْمٌ عَسِرٌ ۝ كَذَّبَتْ قَبْلَهُمْ قَوْمُ نُوْحٍ فَكَذَّبُوْا عَبْدَنَا وَقَالُوْا مَجْنُوْنٌ وَّازْدُجِرَ ۝ فَدَعَا رَبَّهٗٓ اَنِّیْ مَغْلُوْبٌ فَانْتَصِرْ ۝ فَفَتَحْنَآ اَبْوَابَ السَّمَآءِ بِمَآءٍ مُّنْهَمِرٍ ۫ۖ۝ وَّفَجَّرْنَا الْاَرْضَ عُيُوْنًا فَالْتَقَى الْمَآءُ عَلٰٓى اَمْرٍ قَدْ قُدِرَ ۝ وَحَمَلْنٰهُ عَلٰى ذَاتِ اَلْوَاحٍ وَّدُسُرٍ ۝ تَجْرِیْ بِاَعْيُنِنَا ۚ جَزَآءً لِّمَنْ كَانَ كُفِرَ ۝ وَلَقَدْ تَّرَكْنٰهَآ اٰيَةً فَهَلْ مِنْ مُّدَّكِرٍ ۝ فَكَيْفَ كَانَ عَذَابِیْ وَنُذُرِ ۝ وَلَقَدْ يَسَّرْنَا الْقُرْاٰنَ لِلذِّكْرِ فَهَلْ مِنْ مُّدَّكِرٍ ۝ كَذَّبَتْ عَادٌ فَكَيْفَ كَانَ عَذَابِیْ وَنُذُرِ ۝ اِنَّآ اَرْسَلْنَا عَلَيْهِمْ رِيْحًا صَرْصَرًا فِیْ يَوْمِ نَحْسٍ مُّسْتَمِرٍّ ۙ۝ تَنْزِعُ النَّاسَ ۙ

A warning of severe punishment for the stubborn refusers.

1085

In the name of Allah, the Kind, the Caring

Makkans deny the miracle

[1]The Final Hour[a] is drawing near and the moon has split into two. [2]And after seeing the miracle they turned away saying, "This is a powerful magic." [3]They denied and followed their whims. For every action produces a specific outcome. [4]The reports *of ancient people* have come to them containing lessons [5]with far-reaching wisdom, but those warnings didn't benefit them. [6]*Messenger,* turn away from them, one Day a caller will call them to something terrible; [7]with eyes lowered they will exit their graves like swarms of locusts, [8]rushing in terror towards the caller, and the disbelievers will say, "This is a difficult Day."

The people of Nuh rejected him: So they drowned

[9]Previously, the people of Nuh denied Our servant, and called him a mad man and severely scolded him. [10]He cried out to His Lord: "I am weak and beaten, so help me!" [11]So We opened the sky's floodgates with torrential rain, [12]and caused the Earth's springs to surge, and the two waters met as pre-designed. [13]We carried him on a *boat* made of wooden planks *held together with* nails, [14]floating under our watchful gaze. A *magnificent* reward for the one denied. [15]We left that as a sign; will anyone pay attention? [16]How terrible were My punishments and warnings? [17]We made the Quran easy to learn and understand,[b] so will anyone pay attention?

The people of Ad face are punished with a storm

[18]The people of Ad also denied, so how terrible were My punishment and warnings? [19]We sent a howling storm wind on a Day of bitter misfortune, [20]which blew people away like uprooted palm trunks.

كَاَنَّهُمْ اَعْجَازُ نَخْلٍ مُّنْقَعِرٍ ۝ فَكَيْفَ كَانَ عَذَابِيْ

وَنُذُرِ ۝ وَلَقَدْ يَسَّرْنَا الْقُرْاٰنَ لِلذِّكْرِ فَهَلْ مِنْ

مُّدَّكِرٍ ۝ كَذَّبَتْ ثَمُوْدُ بِالنُّذُرِ ۝ فَقَالُوْٓا اَبَشَرًا مِّنَّا

وَاحِدًا نَّتَّبِعُهٗٓ ۙ اِنَّآ اِذًا لَّفِيْ ضَلٰلٍ وَّسُعُرٍ ۝ ءَاُلْقِيَ

الذِّكْرُ عَلَيْهِ مِنْۢ بَيْنِنَا بَلْ هُوَ كَذَّابٌ اَشِرٌ ۝

سَيَعْلَمُوْنَ غَدًا مَّنِ الْكَذَّابُ الْاَشِرُ ۝ اِنَّا مُرْسِلُوا

النَّاقَةِ فِتْنَةً لَّهُمْ فَارْتَقِبْهُمْ وَاصْطَبِرْ ۝ وَنَبِّئْهُمْ

اَنَّ الْمَآءَ قِسْمَةٌۢ بَيْنَهُمْ ۚ كُلُّ شِرْبٍ مُّحْتَضَرٌ ۝ فَنَادَوْا

صَاحِبَهُمْ فَتَعَاطٰى فَعَقَرَ ۝ فَكَيْفَ كَانَ عَذَابِيْ وَ

نُذُرِ ۝ اِنَّآ اَرْسَلْنَا عَلَيْهِمْ صَيْحَةً وَّاحِدَةً فَكَانُوْا

كَهَشِيْمِ الْمُحْتَظِرِ ۝ وَلَقَدْ يَسَّرْنَا الْقُرْاٰنَ لِلذِّكْرِ

فَهَلْ مِنْ مُّدَّكِرٍ ۝ كَذَّبَتْ قَوْمُ لُوْطٍۭ بِالنُّذُرِ ۝

اِنَّآ اَرْسَلْنَا عَلَيْهِمْ حَاصِبًا اِلَّآ اٰلَ لُوْطٍ ۗ نَجَّيْنٰهُمْ

بِسَحَرٍ ۝ نِّعْمَةً مِّنْ عِنْدِنَا ۗ كَذٰلِكَ نَجْزِيْ مَنْ

شَكَرَ ۝ وَلَقَدْ اَنْذَرَهُمْ بَطْشَتَنَا فَتَمَارَوْا بِالنُّذُرِ ۝

وَلَقَدْ رَاوَدُوْهُ عَنْ ضَيْفِهٖ فَطَمَسْنَآ اَعْيُنَهُمْ فَذُوْقُوْا

عَذَابِيْ وَنُذُرِ ۝ وَلَقَدْ صَبَّحَهُمْ بُكْرَةً عَذَابٌ

مُّسْتَقِرٌّ ۝ فَذُوْقُوْا عَذَابِيْ وَنُذُرِ ۝ وَلَقَدْ يَسَّرْنَا

الْقُرْاٰنَ لِلذِّكْرِ فَهَلْ مِنْ مُّدَّكِرٍ ۝ وَلَقَدْ جَآءَ اٰلَ

فِرْعَوْنَ النُّذُرُ ۝ كَذَّبُوْا بِاٰيٰتِنَا كُلِّهَا فَاَخَذْنٰهُمْ

The Quran is easy to read, memorise and understand. How much do you know?

[21] How terrible were My punishment and warnings. [22] We have made the Quran easy to learn and understand, so will anyone pay attention?

The Prophet Salih was denied: People blasted

[23] The people of Thamud also denied Our warnings. [24] They said, "We must be misguided and mad people if we follow one man from among us. [25] How could he be given a Revelation? He is a big-headed liar." [26] Tomorrow they shall know who is a big-headed liar. [27] We shall send a she-camel to test them, so patiently watch over them. [28] And tell them, the water shall be divided equally among them, and each will come to it when it's their turn. [29] So they called for their leader who cut the hamstrings of the she-camel. [30] How terrible were My punishment and warnings? [31] We sent a single blast to destroy them, and they were like the scattered sticks of a broken fence. [32] Indeed We made the Quran easy to learn and understand, so will anyone pay attention?

The people of Lut are punished with a sand storm

[33] The people of Lut denied the warnings. [34] We sent a sandstorm of stones; the only exception was the family of Lut, We saved them at dawn, [35] a favour from Us. This is how We reward the thankful. [36] He warned them clearly about Our punishment, but they doubted the warnings. [37] They also demanded from him his guests, so We blinded them and told them, "Taste My punishment and the warnings." [38] So early one morning, a lasting punishment seized them. [39] *It was said:* "Taste My punishment and warnings." [40] We made the Quran easy to learn and understand; so will anyone pay attention?

The Quraysh are warned: Listen to the Messenger ﷺ

[41] Warners came to the people of Pharaoh, [42] but they denied all Our signs, so We grabbed them with force and power.

Once again, the mindful are promised the delights of Paradise. Are you yearning for them?

اَخْذَ عَزِيْزٍ مُّقْتَدِرٍ ۞ اَكُفَّارُكُمْ خَيْرٌ مِّنْ اُولٰئِكُمْ

اَمْ لَكُمْ بَرَآءَةٌ فِي الزُّبُرِ ۞ اَمْ يَقُوْلُوْنَ نَحْنُ

جَمِيْعٌ مُّنْتَصِرٌ ۞ سَيُهْزَمُ الْجَمْعُ وَيُوَلُّوْنَ الدُّبُرَ ۞

بَلِ السَّاعَةُ مَوْعِدُهُمْ وَالسَّاعَةُ اَدْهٰى وَاَمَرُّ ۞

اِنَّ الْمُجْرِمِيْنَ فِيْ ضَلٰلٍ وَّسُعُرٍ ۞ يَوْمَ يُسْحَبُوْنَ

فِي النَّارِ عَلٰى وُجُوْهِهِمْ ط ذُوْقُوْا مَسَّ سَقَرَ ۞ اِنَّا

كُلَّ شَيْءٍ خَلَقْنٰهُ بِقَدَرٍ ۞ وَمَاۤ اَمْرُنَاۤ اِلَّا وَاحِدَةٌ

كَلَمْحٍ بِالْبَصَرِ ۞ وَلَقَدْ اَهْلَكْنَاۤ اَشْيَاعَكُمْ فَهَلْ

مِنْ مُّدَّكِرٍ ۞ وَكُلُّ شَيْءٍ فَعَلُوْهُ فِي الزُّبُرِ ۞ وَكُلُّ

صَغِيْرٍ وَّكَبِيْرٍ مُّسْتَطَرٌ ۞ اِنَّ الْمُتَّقِيْنَ فِيْ جَنّٰتٍ

وَّنَهَرٍ ۞ فِيْ مَقْعَدِ صِدْقٍ عِنْدَ مَلِيْكٍ مُّقْتَدِرٍ ۞

⁴³ Are your disbelievers, *the Quraysh*, stronger than them, or have they been promised protection in Divine Scriptures? ⁴⁴ Or do they say: "We are a united people bound to be victorious." ⁴⁵ Soon they will be defeated, and they will turn their backs and flee. ⁴⁶ The Judgement Day is their appointed time, and it will be a terrifying and most difficult *Day*. ⁴⁷ The sinners are indeed misguided and foolish. ⁴⁸ The Day when they are dragged on their faces and thrown into Hell, *it will be said*: "Taste the burning of Hellfire."

Allah's creative and precise power over all

⁴⁹ We created everything in a precisely-measured way. ⁵⁰ Our order is carried out instantly, like the blink of an eye. ⁵¹ We destroyed the likes of you, so is there anyone who will pay attention? ⁵² Everything they did is in the Records – ⁵³ whether big or small – all was written down. ⁵⁴ The righteous will be in Paradise with *flowing* streams, ⁵⁵ a delightful place in the presence of the All-Powerful King.

55. Surat Ar-Rahman

The Most Kind

This Makkan surat begins with the most beautiful name of Allah: Al-Rahman, the Kind. The beautiful names of Allah are word-portraits of the loving and caring Lord. Each portrays an aspect of majesty. Al-Rahman as a word-portrait shows countless gifts, bounties and favours of Allah and asks a simple question: "So which favours of your Lord will you deny?" This refrain is repeated thirty-one times after mentioning two favours, so effectively sixty-two favours of Allah are listed in this surat. People are challenged about how they deny the Majestic, Creative, Almighty and Powerful Lord. Sells hints to the mystery of the refrain, which "resounds through the surat each time as a reminder of the creative re-duplication of compassion, tying that core message into the morphology and the acoustics of language itself" (*Approaching the Quran*).

This refrain is in a form of a question, but at a deeper level it's a command. This is the Quranic style, which avoids giving direct instruction but makes the reader think; can you imagine that? Or have you seen that? Do you know? The question also invites agreement, since who can deny the obvious gifts of the Lord.

The first section of the surat draws attention to universal spiritual principles that underpin the existence of the universe, and maintain, control and regulate it. Just as the orbits of the moon and the sun are determined by Allah, so are the colours of flowers and the flavours of fruits. The farthest stars and planets in space are firmly under His control: "The sun and the moon move in exactly measured *orbits,* and plants and trees bow before Him" (5–6). Everywhere in the universe, there is symmetry and balance. In human society, balance can take the form of just dealings with each other, family relations, business dealings, and transactions where everything must be weighed and measured accurately.

The second section presents a frightening and terrifying picture of Judgement Day, and the punishment meted to disbelievers and those who deny the favours of Allah. The tenor of this passage is harsh and terrifying, reflecting Divine Anger. The image is a contrasting one to the luxuries, cool shade, delightful foods and flowing streams of Paradise. This is followed by another section that describes a further two gardens for ordinary believers. So, ranks will exist among the people of Paradise, as they will among the people of Hell.

بِسْمِ اللهِ الرَّحْمٰنِ الرَّحِيْمِ

اَلرَّحْمٰنُ ۙ١ عَلَّمَ الْقُرْاٰنَ ؕ٢ خَلَقَ الْاِنْسَانَ ۙ٣ عَلَّمَهُ

الْبَيَانَ ٤ اَلشَّمْسُ وَالْقَمَرُ بِحُسْبَانٍ ۙ٥ وَّالنَّجْمُ وَالشَّجَرُ

يَسْجُدٰنِ ٦ وَالسَّمَآءَ رَفَعَهَا وَوَضَعَ الْمِيْزَانَ ۙ٧ اَلَّا

تَطْغَوْا فِي الْمِيْزَانِ ٨ وَاَقِيْمُوا الْوَزْنَ بِالْقِسْطِ وَلَا

تُخْسِرُوا الْمِيْزَانَ ٩ وَالْاَرْضَ وَضَعَهَا لِلْاَنَامِ ۙ١٠

The perfect, complex and
lovely universe offers
glimpses into the future
life of the believer and
the disbeliever.

فِيْهَا فَاكِهَةٌ ۖ وَّالنَّخْلُ ذَاتُ الْاَكْمَامِ ۖ١١ وَالْحَبُّ

ذُو الْعَصْفِ وَالرَّيْحَانُ ۚ١٢ فَبِاَيِّ اٰلَآءِ رَبِّكُمَا

تُكَذِّبٰنِ ١٣ خَلَقَ الْاِنْسَانَ مِنْ صَلْصَالٍ كَالْفَخَّارِ ۙ١٤

وَخَلَقَ الْجَآنَّ مِنْ مَّارِجٍ مِّنْ نَّارٍ ۚ١٥ فَبِاَيِّ اٰلَآءِ

رَبِّكُمَا تُكَذِّبٰنِ ١٦ رَبُّ الْمَشْرِقَيْنِ وَرَبُّ الْمَغْرِبَيْنِ ۚ١٧

فَبِاَيِّ اٰلَآءِ رَبِّكُمَا تُكَذِّبٰنِ ١٨ مَرَجَ الْبَحْرَيْنِ

يَلْتَقِيٰنِ ١٩ بَيْنَهُمَا بَرْزَخٌ لَّا يَبْغِيٰنِ ۚ٢٠ فَبِاَيِّ

اٰلَآءِ رَبِّكُمَا تُكَذِّبٰنِ ٢١ يَخْرُجُ مِنْهُمَا اللُّؤْلُؤُ وَ

الْمَرْجَانُ ۚ٢٢ فَبِاَيِّ اٰلَآءِ رَبِّكُمَا تُكَذِّبٰنِ ٢٣ وَلَهُ

الْجَوَارِ الْمُنْشَئٰتُ فِي الْبَحْرِ كَالْاَعْلَامِ ۚ٢٤ فَبِاَيِّ اٰلَآءِ

رَبِّكُمَا تُكَذِّبٰنِ ٢٥ كُلُّ مَنْ عَلَيْهَا فَانٍ ۚ٢٦ وَّيَبْقٰى

وَجْهُ رَبِّكَ ذُو الْجَلٰلِ وَالْاِكْرَامِ ۚ٢٧ فَبِاَيِّ اٰلَآءِ

رَبِّكُمَا تُكَذِّبٰنِ ٢٨ يَسْئَلُهٗ مَنْ فِي السَّمٰوٰتِ وَالْاَرْضِ ؕ

In the Name of Allah, the Kind, the Caring.

His favours come from the Heavens

¹The Most Kind ²taught *the beloved Messenger* the *Majestic* Quran. ³He created human beings ⁴*and* taught them the *art of* communication. ⁵The sun and the moon *orbit* in set paths, ⁶plants and trees bow before Him. ⁷He raised the sky and finely balanced everything, ⁸so don't disturb the fine balance. ⁹Give due weight and *measure,* don't short change *one another.*

His favours are everywhere on Earth

¹⁰He created the Earth for living creatures, ¹¹fruits and date trees with sheathed bunches, ¹²husked grains and fragrant flowers. ¹³So which favours of your Lord will you deny? ¹⁴He created human beings from oven-baked clay, ¹⁵and created jinn from smokeless flame. ¹⁶So which favours of your Lord will you deny? ¹⁷He is the Lord of two risings and settings.^a ¹⁸So which favours of your Lord will you deny?

His favours also lie in the sea

¹⁹He combined the seawater and the freshwater, ²⁰there's an invisible barrier between them which stops them mixing. ²¹So which favours of your Lord will you deny? ²²Pearls large and small come from there. ²³So which favours of your Lord will you deny? ²⁴The ships sail on the seas looming high like mountains. ²⁵So which favours of your Lord will you deny?

How Allah is involved in human life

²⁶All things on Earth will perish; ²⁷all that will remain is your Lord,^b the Majestic and the Giver of honour. ²⁸So which favours of your Lord will you deny? ²⁹All those in the Heavens and the Earth depend on Him; every day He appears in *wondrous* ways^c.

---

^a "Two risings and settings" refers to the rising of the Sun and the Moon.

^b *Wajhu rabika* literally means "your Lord's face", obviously a metonym for Allah; the face refers to "the self", the whole being of a person.

^c He is engaged in the running of the affairs of the world e.g. creating new life, causing death, honouring or humiliating, giving and responding to the seekers (Jalalain).

كُلَّ يَوْمٍ هُوَ فِىْ شَانٍ ۞ فَبِاَىِّ اٰلَآءِ رَبِّكُمَا

تُكَذِّبٰنِ ۞ سَنَفْرُغُ لَكُمْ اَيُّهَ الثَّقَلٰنِ ۞ فَبِاَىِّ

اٰلَآءِ رَبِّكُمَا تُكَذِّبٰنِ ۞ يٰمَعْشَرَ الْجِنِّ وَالْاِنْسِ

اِنِ اسْتَطَعْتُمْ اَنْ تَنْفُذُوْا مِنْ اَقْطَارِ السَّمٰوٰتِ وَ

الْاَرْضِ فَانْفُذُوْا ۫ لَا تَنْفُذُوْنَ اِلَّا بِسُلْطٰنٍ ۞ فَبِاَىِّ

اٰلَآءِ رَبِّكُمَا تُكَذِّبٰنِ ۞ يُرْسَلُ عَلَيْكُمَا شُوَاظٌ مِّنْ

نَّارٍ ەۙ وَّنُحَاسٌ فَلَا تَنْتَصِرٰنِ ۞ فَبِاَىِّ اٰلَآءِ رَبِّكُمَا

تُكَذِّبٰنِ ۞ فَاِذَا انْشَقَّتِ السَّمَآءُ فَكَانَتْ وَرْدَةً

كَالدِّهَانِ ۞ فَبِاَىِّ اٰلَآءِ رَبِّكُمَا تُكَذِّبٰنِ ۞

فَيَوْمَئِذٍ لَّا يُسْئَلُ عَنْ ذَنْبِهٖٓ اِنْسٌ وَّلَا جَآنٌّ ۞

فَبِاَىِّ اٰلَآءِ رَبِّكُمَا تُكَذِّبٰنِ ۞ يُعْرَفُ الْمُجْرِمُوْنَ

بِسِيْمٰهُمْ فَيُؤْخَذُ بِالنَّوَاصِىْ وَالْاَقْدَامِ ۞ فَبِاَىِّ

اٰلَآءِ رَبِّكُمَا تُكَذِّبٰنِ ۞ هٰذِهٖ جَهَنَّمُ الَّتِىْ يُكَذِّبُ بِهَا

الْمُجْرِمُوْنَ ۞ يَطُوْفُوْنَ بَيْنَهَا وَ بَيْنَ حَمِيْمٍ

اٰنٍ ۞ فَبِاَىِّ اٰلَآءِ رَبِّكُمَا تُكَذِّبٰنِ ۞ وَلِمَنْ خَافَ

مَقَامَ رَبِّهٖ جَنَّتٰنِ ۞ فَبِاَىِّ اٰلَآءِ رَبِّكُمَا تُكَذِّبٰنِ ۞

ذَوَاتَآ اَفْنَانٍ ۞ فَبِاَىِّ اٰلَآءِ رَبِّكُمَا تُكَذِّبٰنِ ۞

فِيْهِمَا عَيْنٰنِ تَجْرِيٰنِ ۞ فَبِاَىِّ اٰلَآءِ رَبِّكُمَا

تُكَذِّبٰنِ ۞ فِيْهِمَا مِنْ كُلِّ فَاكِهَةٍ زَوْجٰنِ ۞

فَبِاَىِّ اٰلَآءِ رَبِّكُمَا تُكَذِّبٰنِ ۞ مُتَّكِئِيْنَ عَلٰى فُرُشٍ

The exquisite secrets of Paradise, with the comforts of its mansions and the efficiency of the service given, is indescribable.

١٢

ع
٢

³⁰So which favours of your Lord will you deny? ³¹We'll give you attention, humans and jinn^a. ³²So which favours of your Lord will you deny?

Space travel is possible

³³Humans and jinn! If you have the capability of passing beyond the regions of Heaven and the Earth then do so; but, you won't be able to pass without authority.^b ³⁴So which favours of your Lord will you deny? ³⁵Flames of fire will lash at you, cover you with smoke, and leave you defenceless.^c ³⁶So which favours of your Lord will you deny?

The frightening scene of Judgement Day

³⁷When the sky splits up it will be *bright* red, like red leather. ³⁸So which favours of your Lord will you deny? ³⁹That Day neither human nor jinn will be asked about their sins. ⁴⁰So which favours of your Lord will you deny? ⁴¹The sinners will be recognised by the marks *on their faces,* and they shall be grabbed by their forelocks and feet. ⁴²So which favours of your Lord will you deny? ⁴³This is Hell that the sinners denied. ⁴⁴Here they will wander *aimlessly* between Hell and *cauldrons of* boiling water. ⁴⁵So which favours of your Lord will you deny?

The two splendid gardens for the most pious

⁴⁶The person who feared standing before his Lord will have two gardens. ⁴⁷So which favours of your Lord will you deny? ⁴⁸Both with thick foliage. ⁴⁹So which favours of your Lord will you deny? ⁵⁰Both with two flowing fountains. ⁵¹So which favours of your Lord will you deny? ⁵²Both with fruits of two kinds. ⁵³So which favours of your Lord will you deny? ⁵⁴Sitting relaxed on sofas lined with brocade, with their low-hanging fruit gardens.

---

^a So you can carry out your work.
^b *Sultanin* is also translated as "my power"; perhaps referring to the power of a space rocket?
^c This seems like the description of a space rocket hurtling through the stratosphere into space.

بَطَآئِنُهَا مِنْ اِسْتَبْرَقٍ ۚ وَجَنَا الْجَنَّتَيْنِ دَانٍ ﴿٥٤﴾

فَبِاَيِّ اٰلَآءِ رَبِّكُمَا تُكَذِّبٰنِ ﴿٥٥﴾ فِيْهِنَّ قٰصِرٰتُ

الطَّرْفِ ۙ لَمْ يَطْمِثْهُنَّ اِنْسٌ قَبْلَهُمْ وَلَا جَآنٌّ ﴿٥٦﴾

فَبِاَيِّ اٰلَآءِ رَبِّكُمَا تُكَذِّبٰنِ ﴿٥٧﴾ كَاَنَّهُنَّ الْيَاقُوتُ

وَالْمَرْجَانُ ﴿٥٨﴾ فَبِاَيِّ اٰلَآءِ رَبِّكُمَا تُكَذِّبٰنِ ﴿٥٩﴾

هَلْ جَزَآءُ الْاِحْسَانِ اِلَّا الْاِحْسَانُ ﴿٦٠﴾ فَبِاَيِّ

اٰلَآءِ رَبِّكُمَا تُكَذِّبٰنِ ﴿٦١﴾ وَمِنْ دُوْنِهِمَا جَنَّتٰنِ ﴿٦٢﴾

فَبِاَيِّ اٰلَآءِ رَبِّكُمَا تُكَذِّبٰنِ ﴿٦٣﴾ مُدْهَآمَّتٰنِ ﴿٦٤﴾

فَبِاَيِّ اٰلَآءِ رَبِّكُمَا تُكَذِّبٰنِ ﴿٦٥﴾ فِيْهِمَا عَيْنٰنِ

نَضَّاخَتٰنِ ﴿٦٦﴾ فَبِاَيِّ اٰلَآءِ رَبِّكُمَا تُكَذِّبٰنِ ﴿٦٧﴾

فِيْهِمَا فَاكِهَةٌ وَّنَخْلٌ وَّرُمَّانٌ ﴿٦٨﴾ فَبِاَيِّ اٰلَآءِ

رَبِّكُمَا تُكَذِّبٰنِ ﴿٦٩﴾ فِيْهِنَّ خَيْرٰتٌ حِسَانٌ ﴿٧٠﴾

فَبِاَيِّ اٰلَآءِ رَبِّكُمَا تُكَذِّبٰنِ ﴿٧١﴾ حُوْرٌ مَّقْصُوْرٰتٌ

فِي الْخِيَامِ ﴿٧٢﴾ فَبِاَيِّ اٰلَآءِ رَبِّكُمَا تُكَذِّبٰنِ ﴿٧٣﴾

لَمْ يَطْمِثْهُنَّ اِنْسٌ قَبْلَهُمْ وَلَا جَآنٌّ ﴿٧٤﴾

فَبِاَيِّ اٰلَآءِ رَبِّكُمَا تُكَذِّبٰنِ ﴿٧٥﴾ مُتَّكِئِيْنَ عَلٰى

رَفْرَفٍ خُضْرٍ وَّعَبْقَرِيٍّ حِسَانٍ ﴿٧٦﴾ فَبِاَيِّ اٰلَآءِ

رَبِّكُمَا تُكَذِّبٰنِ ﴿٧٧﴾ تَبٰرَكَ اسْمُ رَبِّكَ ذِى الْجَلٰلِ

وَالْاِكْرَامِ ﴿٧٨﴾

The fabulous gardens of Paradise, the attractive habitat, and Divine splendour will make future life a true Paradise.

⁵⁵ So which favours of your Lord will you deny? ⁵⁶ In them will be ladies with lowered gazes who no man or jinn would have touched. ⁵⁷ So which favours of your Lord will you deny? ⁵⁸ Like *glamorous* rubies and pearls. ⁵⁹ So which favours of your Lord will you deny? ⁶⁰ What's the reward for kindness except kindness? ⁶¹ So which favours of your Lord will you deny?

The two other gardens for ordinary believers

⁶² Beside these there are two other gardens. ⁶³ So which favours of your Lord will you deny? ⁶⁴ Both with deep green *foliage.* ⁶⁵ So which favours of your Lord will you deny? ⁶⁶ Both have two gushing fountains. ⁶⁷ So which favours of your Lord will you deny? ⁶⁸ Both gardens will have plenty of fruit dates and pomegranates. ⁶⁹ So which favours of your Lord will you deny? ⁷⁰ In them will be ladies with *charming* character and beauty.ᵃ ⁷¹ So which favours of your Lord will you deny? ⁷² With beautiful eyes living in *tall* tents. ⁷³ So which favours of your Lord will you deny? ⁷⁴ Never touched before by a human or a jinn. ⁷⁵ So which favours of your Lord will you deny? ⁷⁶ Sitting relaxed on green cushions and fine carpets. ⁷⁷ So which favours of your Lord will you deny? ⁷⁸ Blessed is the name of your Lord, Most Majestic and Giver of Honours.

ᵃ *Khayrat,* interpreted as strong character; and *Hisan,* as pretty face (Zia-ul-Quran).

56. Surat Al-Waqi'ah
The Inevitable Event

This Makkan surat is paired with the previous surat, which described two kinds of Paradise; here more details are provided. The Quraysh are challenged and warned of the dire consequences of their denial. After describing the cataclysmic events of the Final Hour and the coming to pass of Judgement Day, it describes the three groups into which humanity will be divided. The rest of the surat deals with each one of them: the group blessed with the highest level of Paradise, people who struggled and strived with all their might to achieve the nearness of Allah; the group of the right hand, living in a delightful Paradise, but a rank below the first – their Paradise will be lesser compared to that of the foremost; and the third group, the people of the left hand, living in Hell.

Followed by questions about the beginning and ending of life, they expose the folly of those who deny Resurrection, and urge the reader to examine closely some powerful phenomena. Who makes the semen? Who grows the seed when it is in the depths of the soil? Who sends the rain down? Who made the fire? The surat teaches that human resurrection is similar to the birth of a baby created from a spermatozoon, nutritious cereals growing from a dead seed, flames of fire coming from wood, and rain from clouds enabling so much to live. Behind them all is the power of Allah. He creates and destroys what He wills. The frequent reference to Resurrection in the Quran is to remind people of the purpose of their lives, and to protect them from the deception of the fleeting world. The Quran wants to save humanity from falling into its trap. The rampant selfishness and individualism common in our society today can only be corrected by accepting resurrection. The belief that your actions bear consequences. One day you will have to face your evil deeds. This gives life meaning and purpose. The lack of this belief has made modern society nihilistic; aimless and purposeless, that's causing so much misery and pain.

The surat ends with the frightening scene of a person in death throes; can anyone prevent his death? After reminding humanity of their helplessness in such situations, "This is the certain truth, Messenger! Glorify the name of your Mighty Lord" (95–96).

بِسْمِ اللّٰهِ الرَّحْمٰنِ الرَّحِيمِ

اِذَا وَقَعَتِ الْوَاقِعَةُ ۙ لَيْسَ لِوَقْعَتِهَا كَاذِبَةٌ ۘ

خَافِضَةٌ رَّافِعَةٌ ۙ اِذَا رُجَّتِ الْاَرْضُ رَجًّا ۙ

وَّبُسَّتِ الْجِبَالُ بَسًّا ۙ فَكَانَتْ هَبَآءً مُّنْۢبَثًّا ۙ

وَّكُنْتُمْ اَزْوَاجًا ثَلٰثَةً ؕ فَاَصْحٰبُ الْمَيْمَنَةِ ۙ

مَآ اَصْحٰبُ الْمَيْمَنَةِ ؕ وَاَصْحٰبُ الْمَشْـَٔمَةِ ۙ

مَآ اَصْحٰبُ الْمَشْـَٔمَةِ ؕ وَالسّٰبِقُوْنَ السّٰبِقُوْنَ ۙ

On Judgment Day people will be divided into three groups. Which group will you be in? Do you have any idea how you could know that?

اُولٰٓئِكَ الْمُقَرَّبُوْنَ ۚ فِيْ جَنّٰتِ النَّعِيْمِ ؕ ثُلَّةٌ

مِّنَ الْاَوَّلِيْنَ ۙ وَقَلِيْلٌ مِّنَ الْاٰخِرِيْنَ ؕ عَلٰى

سُرُرٍ مَّوْضُوْنَةٍ ۙ مُّتَّكِئِيْنَ عَلَيْهَا مُتَقٰبِلِيْنَ

يَطُوْفُ عَلَيْهِمْ وِلْدَانٌ مُّخَلَّدُوْنَ ۙ بِاَكْوَابٍ

وَّاَبَارِيْقَ ۙ وَكَأْسٍ مِّنْ مَّعِيْنٍ ۙ لَّا يُصَدَّعُوْنَ

عَنْهَا وَلَا يُنْزِفُوْنَ ۙ وَفَاكِهَةٍ مِّمَّا يَتَخَيَّرُوْنَ ۙ

وَّلَحْمِ طَيْرٍ مِّمَّا يَشْتَهُوْنَ ؕ وَحُوْرٌ عِيْنٌ ۙ

كَاَمْثَالِ اللُّؤْلُؤِ الْمَكْنُوْنِ ۚ جَزَآءً ۢ بِمَا كَانُوْا

يَعْمَلُوْنَ ؕ لَا يَسْمَعُوْنَ فِيْهَا لَغْوًا وَّلَا تَأْثِيْمًا ۙ

اِلَّا قِيْلًا سَلٰمًا سَلٰمًا ؕ وَاَصْحٰبُ الْيَمِيْنِ ۙ مَآ

اَصْحٰبُ الْيَمِيْنِ ؕ فِيْ سِدْرٍ مَّخْضُوْدٍ ۙ وَّطَلْحٍ

مَّنْضُوْدٍ ۙ وَّظِلٍّ مَّمْدُوْدٍ ۙ وَّمَآءٍ مَّسْكُوْبٍ ۙ

In the Name of Allah, the Kind, the Caring.

The three groups of people on Judgement Day
[1] When the Inevitable Event[a] happens, [2] no one will be a denier. [3] Some will be humiliated, others honoured. [4] When the Earth trembles violently, [5] the mountains will crumble [6] and become scattered dust. [7] That Day you will be sorted out into three lots: [8] *first* will be people of the right hand; how wonderful will be those of the right hand! [9] *Second* will be people of the left hand; how wretched will be those of the left hand! [10] And *third* will be in the first rank, the foremost; [11] closest to Allah. [12] They will enjoy the delights of Paradise. [13] Many from the earlier generations, [14] but a few from the later generations.[b]

The foremost in a luxurious Paradise
[15] Resting on couches decked with jewels, [16] they will *enjoy each other's company* face to face. [17] Served by young people of timeless youth [18] carrying glasses and jugs full of the purest wine, [19] which doesn't give headache nor drunkenness, [20] they will choose *to eat* fruit of all kinds [21] and relish *roasted* bird's meat. [22] Their spouses will be beautiful, [23] like hidden pearls. [24] A reward for what they used to do. [25] They will hear neither idle talk, nor sinful conversation, [26] only the greetings of peace!

The people of the right hand in a delightful Paradise
[27] And the people of the right hand, how wonderful are the *people* of the right hand, [28] living among thornless cedar trees, [29] bunches of bananas, [30] widely-spread cool shade, [31] water fountains,

---

[a] *Al-Waqiʿah*, the inevitable event, refers to Judgement Day
[b] The fact that "the foremost people" of Paradise will mostly be from the earlier generations of the faithful and only a few from the later generations hints to the progressive decline in human moral and spiritual intelligence.

وَّفَاكِهَةٍ كَثِيرَةٍ ۙ۳۲ لَّا مَقْطُوعَةٍ وَّلَا مَمْنُوعَةٍ ۙ۳۳

وَّفُرُشٍ مَّرْفُوعَةٍ ؕ۳۴ اِنَّآ اَنْشَاْنٰهُنَّ اِنْشَآءً ۙ۳۵

فَجَعَلْنٰهُنَّ اَبْكَارًا ۙ۳۶ عُرُبًا اَتْرَابًا ۙ۳۷ لِّاَصْحٰبِ

الْيَمِيْنِ ؕ۳۸ ثُلَّةٌ مِّنَ الْاَوَّلِيْنَ ۙ۳۹ وَثُلَّةٌ مِّنَ

الْاٰخِرِيْنَ ؕ۴۰ وَاَصْحٰبُ الشِّمَالِ ۙۙ مَاۤ اَصْحٰبُ

الشِّمَالِ ؕ۴۱ فِيْ سَمُوْمٍ وَّحَمِيْمٍ ۙ۴۲ وَّظِلٍّ مِّنْ

يَّحْمُوْمٍ ۙ۴۳ لَّا بَارِدٍ وَّلَا كَرِيْمٍ ؕ۴۴ اِنَّهُمْ كَانُوْا

قَبْلَ ذٰلِكَ مُتْرَفِيْنَ ۚ۴۵ وَكَانُوْا يُصِرُّوْنَ عَلَى

الْحِنْثِ الْعَظِيْمِ ۚ۴۶ وَكَانُوْا يَقُوْلُوْنَ ۙ اَىِٕذَا مِتْنَا

وَكُنَّا تُرَابًا وَّعِظَامًا ءَاِنَّا لَمَبْعُوْثُوْنَ ۙ۴۷

اَوَ اٰبَآؤُنَا الْاَوَّلُوْنَ ۴۸ قُلْ اِنَّ الْاَوَّلِيْنَ

وَالْاٰخِرِيْنَ ۙ۴۹ لَمَجْمُوْعُوْنَ ۙ اِلٰى مِيْقَاتِ

يَوْمٍ مَّعْلُوْمٍ ۵۰ ثُمَّ اِنَّكُمْ اَيُّهَا الضَّآلُّوْنَ

الْمُكَذِّبُوْنَ ۙ۵۱ لَاٰكِلُوْنَ مِنْ شَجَرٍ مِّنْ زَقُّوْمٍ ۙ۵۲

فَمَالِؤُوْنَ مِنْهَا الْبُطُوْنَ ۚ۵۳ فَشٰرِبُوْنَ عَلَيْهِ

مِنَ الْحَمِيْمِ ۚ۵۴ فَشٰرِبُوْنَ شُرْبَ الْهِيْمِ ؕ۵۵ هٰذَا

نُزُلُهُمْ يَوْمَ الدِّيْنِ ؕ۵۶ نَحْنُ خَلَقْنٰكُمْ فَلَوْلَا

تُصَدِّقُوْنَ ۵۷ اَفَرَءَيْتُمْ مَّا تُمْنُوْنَ ؕ۵۸ ءَاَنْتُمْ

تَخْلُقُوْنَهٗۤ اَمْ نَحْنُ الْخٰلِقُوْنَ ۵۹ نَحْنُ قَدَّرْنَا

بَيْنَكُمُ الْمَوْتَ وَمَا نَحْنُ بِمَسْبُوْقِيْنَ ۙ۶۰ عَلٰٓى اَنْ

The group you yearn to join will enjoy the delights of Paradise, Comforts that are unimaginable and company that is sublime.

³²lots of fruit ³³ never ending, never out of reach. ³⁴They will have the most beautiful partners ³⁵We *especially* created for them, ³⁶made them virgins, ³⁷passionately loving and young – ³⁸especially for the people of the right-hand. ³⁹Many from the earlier generations, ⁴⁰and many from later generations.

The people of the left hand in a blazing Hellfire

⁴¹The people of the left hand, how wretched will be those of the left hand. ⁴²*They will be* living in *surroundings of* scorching winds and boiling water ⁴³in the shadow of dark smoke, ⁴⁴neither cool nor comforting. ⁴⁵In the past life they lived in luxury, ⁴⁶and kept committing *the* grave sin *of idolatry.*ᵃ ⁴⁷And said, "What, when we are dead and turned to dust and bones, will we be resurrected? ⁴⁸And our forefathers too?" ⁴⁹Tell them: "Those of the past and the later generations ⁵⁰will be gathered together at a fixed time on a known Day. ⁵¹Then, you the misled and the deniers, ⁵²you will be forced to eat *fruit* from *the* Zaqqum tree,ᵇ ⁵³filling your bellies with it, ⁵⁴forced to drink boiling water, ⁵⁵you'll drink it like thirsty camels." ⁵⁶This is their hospitality, on Judgement Day!

The beginnings; semen, seed, water and fire

⁵⁷We created you, why don't you accept this? ⁵⁸Haven't you considered the semen you emit? ⁵⁹Did you create it yourselves, or are We its Creator? ⁶⁰We decreed, death will surround you, and nothing can stop Us

---

ᵃ *Hinsil azeem* refers to idolatry; this is the biggest sin of all major sins.
ᵇ *Zaqqum* refers to one of the trees of Hell, resembling a thorny cactus.

نُبَدِّلَ اَمْثَالَكُمْ وَنُنْشِئَكُمْ فِيْ مَا لَا تَعْلَمُوْنَ ۝

وَلَقَدْ عَلِمْتُمُ النَّشْاَةَ الْاُوْلٰى فَلَوْلَا تَذَكَّرُوْنَ ۝

اَفَرَءَيْتُمْ مَّا تَحْرُثُوْنَ ۝ ءَاَنْتُمْ تَزْرَعُوْنَهٗٓ اَمْ

نَحْنُ الزّٰرِعُوْنَ ۝ لَوْ نَشَآءُ لَجَعَلْنٰهُ حُطَامًا

فَظَلْتُمْ تَفَكَّهُوْنَ ۝ اِنَّا لَمُغْرَمُوْنَ ۝ بَلْ نَحْنُ

مَحْرُوْمُوْنَ ۝ اَفَرَءَيْتُمُ الْمَآءَ الَّذِيْ تَشْرَبُوْنَ ۝

ءَاَنْتُمْ اَنْزَلْتُمُوْهُ مِنَ الْمُزْنِ اَمْ نَحْنُ الْمُنْزِلُوْنَ ۝

The questions about the creation invite us to their Creator. So, reflect …

لَوْ نَشَآءُ جَعَلْنٰهُ اُجَاجًا فَلَوْلَا تَشْكُرُوْنَ ۝

اَفَرَءَيْتُمُ النَّارَ الَّتِيْ تُوْرُوْنَ ۝ ءَاَنْتُمْ اَنْشَأْتُمْ

شَجَرَتَهَآ اَمْ نَحْنُ الْمُنْشِئُوْنَ ۝ نَحْنُ جَعَلْنٰهَا

تَذْكِرَةً وَّمَتَاعًا لِّلْمُقْوِيْنَ ۝ فَسَبِّحْ بِاسْمِ

رَبِّكَ الْعَظِيْمِ ۝ فَلَآ اُقْسِمُ بِمَوٰقِعِ النُّجُوْمِ ۝

وَاِنَّهٗ لَقَسَمٌ لَّوْ تَعْلَمُوْنَ عَظِيْمٌ ۝ اِنَّهٗ لَقُرْاٰنٌ

كَرِيْمٌ ۝ فِيْ كِتٰبٍ مَّكْنُوْنٍ ۝ لَّا يَمَسُّهٗٓ اِلَّا

الْمُطَهَّرُوْنَ ۝ تَنْزِيْلٌ مِّنْ رَّبِّ الْعٰلَمِيْنَ ۝

اَفَبِهٰذَا الْحَدِيْثِ اَنْتُمْ مُّدْهِنُوْنَ ۝ وَتَجْعَلُوْنَ

رِزْقَكُمْ اَنَّكُمْ تُكَذِّبُوْنَ ۝ فَلَوْلَآ اِذَا بَلَغَتِ

الْحُلْقُوْمَ ۝ وَاَنْتُمْ حِيْنَئِذٍ تَنْظُرُوْنَ ۝ وَنَحْنُ

اَقْرَبُ اِلَيْهِ مِنْكُمْ وَلٰكِنْ لَّا تُبْصِرُوْنَ ۝ فَلَوْلَآ

اِنْ كُنْتُمْ غَيْرَ مَدِيْنِيْنَ ۝ تَرْجِعُوْنَهَآ اِنْ

⁶¹from changing you and recreating you anew, something you don't know. ⁶²Since you know well your first creation *in the mother's womb*, why don't you pay attention? ⁶³Haven't you considered what you sow? ⁶⁴Do you make it grow, or are We its growers? ⁶⁵If We wanted, We could have turned it into a stubble *after harvest*, and you would be left to wonder: ⁶⁶"Why are we debtors! ⁶⁷No, in fact we have been robbed." ⁶⁸Haven't you considered the water that you drink? ⁶⁹Do you send the rain from clouds or are We the senders? ⁷⁰If We wanted we could make it bitter, so why don't you thank *Allah*? ⁷¹Have you considered the fire you light? ⁷²Did you make the wood or are We its makers? ⁷³We made fire a reminder of Hell and a beneficial thing for the traveller. ⁷⁴So glorify the Name of your Mighty Lord.

The special status of the Majestic Quran

⁷⁵I swear by the positions of the stars, ⁷⁶if only you knew, this is indeed a mighty oath. ⁷⁷Indeed this is a Majestic Quran, ⁷⁸*stored* in a hidden Book; ⁷⁹only the clean ones can touch it.ᵃ ⁸⁰A Revelation from the Lord of the worlds. ⁸¹So how can you disrespect Scripture like this? ⁸²And *from its blessings* all you could receive is denying it? ⁸³

The final destination

Why, then, when *a dying person's* last breath comes to the throat, you can't return it? ⁸⁴You watch *helplessly*? ⁸⁵Though We are closer to him than you, though you can't see. ⁸⁶Why do you think that you are not dependent on Us? ⁸⁷If you are truthful, why can't you cause that ebbing life to return?

ᵃ   An order to be in pure state i.e. to wash oneself before touching the Quran.

كُنْتُمْ صٰدِقِينَ ۝ فَأَمَّا إِنْ كَانَ مِنَ الْمُقَرَّبِينَ ۝

فَرَوْحٌ وَّرَيْحَانٌ ۙ وَّجَنَّتُ نَعِيمٍ ۝ وَأَمَّا إِنْ كَانَ

مِنْ أَصْحٰبِ الْيَمِينِ ۝ فَسَلٰمٌ لَّكَ مِنْ أَصْحٰبِ

الْيَمِينِ ۝ وَأَمَّا إِنْ كَانَ مِنَ الْمُكَذِّبِينَ

الضَّآلِّينَ ۝ فَنُزُلٌ مِّنْ حَمِيمٍ ۝ وَّتَصْلِيَةُ

جَحِيمٍ ۝ إِنَّ هٰذَا لَهُوَ حَقُّ الْيَقِينِ ۝ فَسَبِّحْ

بِاسْمِ رَبِّكَ الْعَظِيمِ ۝

Those closest to Allah glorify Him now and in the Hereafter.

The final destination

⁸⁸ So *the dying person if they were* from the closest to Allah, ⁸⁹ they shall be comfortable in fragrant and blissful Paradise. ⁹⁰ And if they are from the people of the right hand, ⁹¹ they shall be greeted with: "Peace be with you from people of the right hand." ⁹² But if they happen to be one of the deniers, misguided, ⁹³ their welcome will be boiling water, ⁹⁴ a blazing fire of Hell! ⁹⁵ This is the convincing truth, ⁹⁶ *Messenger*; glorify the Name of Your Mighty Lord.

57. Surat Al-Hadid

The Iron

This Madinan surat was revealed in 8 AH, before the victory of Makkah. The previous surat divided humanity into three groups: the companions of the right hand, companions of the left hand, and the foremost. The central theme of this surat is encouragement to become the foremost, achieving higher status and nearness of Allah through spending in Allah's path. The surat outlines the importance and the rewards of charity. Wealth has been granted as a trust; it is natural that we should spend it in Allah's way. It demonstrates a person's faith in Allah, and acknowledgment of His kindness. Charity is a mark of faith, it is likened to giving a loan to Allah. In the Hereafter, charity will be the light that will lead the believers into Paradise. Charity givers are given the honorific titles of the "truthful" and the "martyrs".

Next the issue of the hypocrites, those in two minds, an uncharitable bunch neither with Muslims nor with non-Muslims; neither here nor there.

Believers are challenged: "Hasn't the time come for the believers, that their hearts humbly submit to Allah's remembrance and the revealed truth?" (16) The sense of urgency imparted by this verse encourages the giving of charity without delay. A major hindrance to giving in charity is love of the world, so the next section describes the fleeting and short-lived nature of worldly life, and cautions: don't be tempted by the world. The image used to describe the fleeting nature of life is that of a plant; it grows, dries, and withers away becoming dry stubble. Similarly, human life has its blossoming period, a vibrant youth, old age, a time of decline and finally death.

The theme of spiritual development is continued by revealing another divine principle: predestination. Whatever happens in the world, or to people, is all written down by Allah. Its purpose is to help people to persevere, endure difficulties and show patience at times of difficulty. The surat ends with how Allah will reward the generous.

The question of predestination

The knowledge that whatever happened, had to happen - nothing could stop it from happening since Allah willed it - That's His plan for us. This ought to enable us to face the reality of good and evil. This is predestination; *Taqdeer*, the relationship between Allah's knowledge of human actions and human free-will. On the face they seem to be contradictory but that's not so.

Allah is the Knower, who has given humans free-will. But with this free-will He gave them the huge responsibility of being His representative (*Khalifa*). He gave them a moral choice: to be good or bad. Allah could have made all good or all bad, but He chose to give us free-will so we become masters of our destiny, so we can choose to do good. This now gives human life a meaning and a purpose, it is a probationary period, preparation to meet the Kind Lord. In addition to this moral discretion, He gave us the revelation to enable us to live "a good life". Furthermore, He has blessed us with the ability to use natural resources. The best example of this is the Iron; the strength of the iron enables engineers to make vehicles, build one hundred storey buildings, weapons and tools of all kinds.

How did the Iron come down?

Interestingly, the Quran mentioned the scriptures were sent down, '*Anzalna*' and so was the Iron. Traditional commentators translated this as "We made the Iron", however, astro-physicists believe that all the elements including Iron 'came down' from the stars, they are 'stardust'. The Quran's choice of '*Anzalna*' we sent down Iron is not accidental. It shows it's from the Lord who created the stars and the universe. Here the Quran is inviting us to use the spiritual (scripture) and the material (iron) to succeed. One without the other would be disorder.

بِسْمِ اللهِ الرَّحْمٰنِ الرَّحِيْمِ

سَبَّحَ لِلهِ مَا فِى السَّمٰوٰتِ وَالْاَرْضِ ۚ وَهُوَ الْعَزِيْزُ
الْحَكِيْمُ ۞ لَهٗ مُلْكُ السَّمٰوٰتِ وَالْاَرْضِ ۚ يُحْيٖ وَ
يُمِيْتُ ۚ وَهُوَ عَلٰى كُلِّ شَىْءٍ قَدِيْرٌ ۞ هُوَ الْاَوَّلُ
وَالْاٰخِرُ وَالظَّاهِرُ وَالْبَاطِنُ ۚ وَهُوَ بِكُلِّ شَىْءٍ
عَلِيْمٌ ۞ هُوَ الَّذِىْ خَلَقَ السَّمٰوٰتِ وَالْاَرْضَ فِىْ
سِتَّةِ اَيَّامٍ ثُمَّ اسْتَوٰى عَلَى الْعَرْشِ ۚ يَعْلَمُ مَا
يَلِجُ فِى الْاَرْضِ وَمَا يَخْرُجُ مِنْهَا وَمَا يَنْزِلُ
مِنَ السَّمَآءِ وَمَا يَعْرُجُ فِيْهَا ۚ وَهُوَ مَعَكُمْ اَيْنَ
مَا كُنْتُمْ ۚ وَاللهُ بِمَا تَعْمَلُوْنَ بَصِيْرٌ ۞ لَهٗ
مُلْكُ السَّمٰوٰتِ وَالْاَرْضِ ۚ وَاِلَى اللهِ تُرْجَعُ الْاُمُوْرُ ۞
يُوْلِجُ الَّيْلَ فِى النَّهَارِ وَيُوْلِجُ النَّهَارَ فِى الَّيْلِ ۚ
وَهُوَ عَلِيْمٌ بِذَاتِ الصُّدُوْرِ ۞ اٰمِنُوْا بِاللهِ وَ
رَسُوْلِهٖ وَاَنْفِقُوْا مِمَّا جَعَلَكُمْ مُّسْتَخْلَفِيْنَ
فِيْهِ ۚ فَالَّذِيْنَ اٰمَنُوْا مِنْكُمْ وَاَنْفَقُوْا لَهُمْ اَجْرٌ
كَبِيْرٌ ۞ وَمَا لَكُمْ لَا تُؤْمِنُوْنَ بِاللهِ ۚ وَالرَّسُوْلُ
يَدْعُوْكُمْ لِتُؤْمِنُوْا بِرَبِّكُمْ وَقَدْ اَخَذَ مِيْثَاقَكُمْ
اِنْ كُنْتُمْ مُّؤْمِنِيْنَ ۞ هُوَ الَّذِىْ يُنَزِّلُ عَلٰى
عَبْدِهٖ اٰيٰتٍۭ بَيِّنٰتٍ لِّيُخْرِجَكُمْ مِّنَ الظُّلُمٰتِ اِلَى

Spending in Allah's way is proof of faith in the Divine Majesty.

1111

In the name of Allah, the Kind, the Caring.

A majestic description of Allah

[1] All things in the Heavens and the Earth glorify Allah; the Almighty, the Wise. [2] The Heavens and the Earth are in His control; He gives life, death and has absolute control over all things. [3] He is the First and the Last, the Evident and the Unseen and the Knower of all things. [4] He created Heavens and the Earth in six days, then established Himself on His Throne *as befits Him*. He knows what goes inside the Earth and what comes out from it, and what comes down from the sky, and what goes up. He is with you wherever you are, and sees whatever you do. [5] He has the control of the Heavens and the Earth and all things will return to Allah. [6] He extends the night into the day, and the day into the night, *so varying the length of day and night*. He is the Knower of the secrets of the mind.

Encouragement to give charity

[7] Believe in Allah and His Messenger, and spend from what He has handed over to you. The believers who spend in Allah's way will have a great reward. [8] What is the matter with you that you don't believe in Allah, when the Messenger calls you so that you may believe in your Lord? He has already taken a pledge from you, if you are believers. [9] He reveals clear teachings to His servant, to take you out of darkness into light, and treats you kindly.

النُّوْرِ ط وَاِنَّ اللهَ بِكُمْ لَرَءُوْفٌ رَّحِيْمٌ ۚ وَمَا

لَكُمْ اَلَّا تُنْفِقُوْا فِيْ سَبِيْلِ اللهِ وَلِلّٰهِ مِيْرَاثُ

السَّمٰوٰتِ وَالْاَرْضِ ط لَا يَسْتَوِيْ مِنْكُمْ مَّنْ اَنْفَقَ

مِنْ قَبْلِ الْفَتْحِ وَقٰتَلَ ط اُولٰٓئِكَ اَعْظَمُ دَرَجَةً

مِّنَ الَّذِيْنَ اَنْفَقُوْا مِنْ بَعْدُ وَقٰتَلُوْا ط وَكُلًّا

وَّعَدَ اللهُ الْحُسْنٰى ط وَاللهُ بِمَا تَعْمَلُوْنَ خَبِيْرٌ ۚ

مَنْ ذَا الَّذِيْ يُقْرِضُ اللهَ قَرْضًا حَسَنًا فَيُضٰعِفَهُ

لَهُ وَلَهٗٓ اَجْرٌ كَرِيْمٌ ۚ يَوْمَ تَرَى الْمُؤْمِنِيْنَ وَ

الْمُؤْمِنٰتِ يَسْعٰى نُوْرُهُمْ بَيْنَ اَيْدِيْهِمْ وَبِاَيْمَانِهِمْ

بُشْرٰىكُمُ الْيَوْمَ جَنّٰتٌ تَجْرِيْ مِنْ تَحْتِهَا الْاَنْهٰرُ

خٰلِدِيْنَ فِيْهَا ط ذٰلِكَ هُوَ الْفَوْزُ الْعَظِيْمُ ۚ يَوْمَ

يَّقُوْلُ الْمُنٰفِقُوْنَ وَالْمُنٰفِقٰتُ لِلَّذِيْنَ اٰمَنُوا

انْظُرُوْنَا نَقْتَبِسْ مِنْ نُّوْرِكُمْ ۚ قِيْلَ ارْجِعُوْا

وَرَآءَكُمْ فَالْتَمِسُوْا نُوْرًا ط فَضُرِبَ بَيْنَهُمْ بِسُوْرٍ لَّهٗ

بَابٌ ط بَاطِنُهٗ فِيْهِ الرَّحْمَةُ وَظَاهِرُهٗ مِنْ قِبَلِهِ

الْعَذَابُ ط يُنَادُوْنَهُمْ اَلَمْ نَكُنْ مَّعَكُمْ ط قَالُوْا

بَلٰى وَلٰكِنَّكُمْ فَتَنْتُمْ اَنْفُسَكُمْ وَتَرَبَّصْتُمْ وَارْتَبْتُمْ

وَغَرَّتْكُمُ الْاَمَانِيُّ حَتّٰى جَآءَ اَمْرُ اللهِ وَغَرَّكُمْ

بِاللهِ الْغَرُوْرُ ۚ فَالْيَوْمَ لَا يُؤْخَذُ مِنْكُمْ فِدْيَةٌ

وَّلَا مِنَ الَّذِيْنَ كَفَرُوْا ط مَاْوٰىكُمُ النَّارُ ط هِيَ

What stops one from faith? Getting trapped in the affairs of the world, doubts and long hopes of worldly achievements. Can you get around them?

¹⁰Why don't you spend in Allah's way? All *things* in the Heavens and the Earth belong to Allah. None of you can be equal to him who spent and fought before the victory *of Makkah*. Their status is far higher than those who spent and fought afterwards. However, Allah promised to be generous to all. He is fully aware of what you do.

Charity will be light in the Hereafter

¹¹Who will give Allah a beautiful loan so that He may multiply it for him, and reward him generously? ¹²On that Day you will see believing men and women with their lights shining ahead of them, and on their right-hand side. *Believers! Here is good* news for you today: *a home in* Paradise with streams running beneath it, where you will live forever. This is the supreme victory. ¹³That Day, hypocrite men and women will ask the believers, "Wait a moment, let us benefit from your light." They will be told, "Go back and get the light." Then a wall with a gate will be put up between the believers and them. Inside *the wall* is *divine* benevolence and comfort, outside is pain and suffering.

The weaknesses of uncharitable hypocrites

¹⁴The hypocrites will then call *to the believers*: "Weren't we with you?" "*Yes*, but you succumbed to your temptations, you were hesitant to believe, full of doubts, and you were deceived by false hopes until the Divine Command came. The deceiver deceived you! ¹⁵Today, no ransom will be accepted from you or from the disbelievers. Your home will be the Hellfire; that will be your residence, and a wretched destination."

مَوْلٰىكُمْ ط وَبِئْسَ الْمَصِيْرُ ۞ اَلَمْ يَاْنِ لِلَّذِيْنَ

اٰمَنُوْۤا اَنْ تَخْشَعَ قُلُوْبُهُمْ لِذِكْرِ اللّٰهِ وَ مَا

نَزَلَ مِنَ الْحَقِّ لا وَلَا يَكُوْنُوْا كَالَّذِيْنَ اُوْتُوا

الْكِتٰبَ مِنْ قَبْلُ فَطَالَ عَلَيْهِمُ الْاَمَدُ فَقَسَتْ

قُلُوْبُهُمْ ط وَكَثِيْرٌ مِّنْهُمْ فٰسِقُوْنَ ۞ اِعْلَمُوْۤا اَنَّ

اللّٰهَ يُحْيِ الْاَرْضَ بَعْدَ مَوْتِهَا ط قَدْ بَيَّنَّا لَكُمُ

الْاٰيٰتِ لَعَلَّكُمْ تَعْقِلُوْنَ ۞ اِنَّ الْمُصَّدِّقِيْنَ وَ

الْمُصَّدِّقٰتِ وَاَقْرَضُوا اللّٰهَ قَرْضًا حَسَنًا يُّضٰعَفُ

لَهُمْ وَلَهُمْ اَجْرٌ كَرِيْمٌ ۞ وَالَّذِيْنَ اٰمَنُوْا بِاللّٰهِ

وَ رُسُلِهٖۤ اُولٰٓئِكَ هُمُ الصِّدِّيْقُوْنَ ۚ وَالشُّهَدَآءُ

عِنْدَ رَبِّهِمْ ط لَهُمْ اَجْرُهُمْ وَنُوْرُهُمْ ط وَالَّذِيْنَ

كَفَرُوْا وَكَذَّبُوْا بِاٰيٰتِنَآ اُولٰٓئِكَ اَصْحٰبُ الْجَحِيْمِ ۞

اِعْلَمُوْۤا اَنَّمَا الْحَيٰوةُ الدُّنْيَا لَعِبٌ وَّ لَهْوٌ وَّ

زِيْنَةٌ وَّ تَفَاخُرٌۢ بَيْنَكُمْ وَ تَكَاثُرٌ فِي الْاَمْوَالِ

وَالْاَوْلَادِ ط كَمَثَلِ غَيْثٍ اَعْجَبَ الْكُفَّارَ نَبَاتُهٗ

ثُمَّ يَهِيْجُ فَتَرٰىهُ مُصْفَرًّا ثُمَّ يَكُوْنُ حُطَامًا ط

وَ فِي الْاٰخِرَةِ عَذَابٌ شَدِيْدٌ لا وَّمَغْفِرَةٌ مِّنَ

اللّٰهِ وَ رِضْوَانٌ ط وَمَا الْحَيٰوةُ الدُّنْيَآ اِلَّا

مَتَاعُ الْغُرُوْرِ ۞ سَابِقُوْۤا اِلٰى مَغْفِرَةٍ مِّنْ

رَّبِّكُمْ وَ جَنَّةٍ عَرْضُهَا كَعَرْضِ السَّمَآءِ وَ

Giving in charity is giving a loan to Allah that will be returned multiplied. What an honour!

Lack of charity and Hardness of the heart

[16] Hasn't the time come for the believers, that their hearts submit humbly to Allah's remembrance and the revealed truth? Don't be like the ancients, who were given the Scripture, and with passing of time their hearts hardened; they were mostly lawbreakers. [17] Know, Allah gave life to Earth when it was lifeless, that's how We explain for you the signs, so you may understand.

Charitable people are truthful and martyrs

[18] Men and women who gave charity as a beautiful loan to Allah will have it multiplied for them, and will be generously rewarded by Allah. [19] The believers in Allah and His messenger are the truthful and the martyrs in the Sight of Allah.[a] They will have a *special* reward and a light. The deniers of Our Scripture are the people of Hell.

The short-lived nature of worldly life

[20] *You should* know, the worldly life is a sport and an amusement, an attraction, showing off among yourselves and wanting more wealth and children. The rain is an illustration of it; the farmer delights in the *rapid* growth of his crops, then they dry and he sees them turning yellow, then turn into *dry* stubble. In the Hereafter there will be severe punishment *for the disbelievers, but for the believers* forgiveness and His Divine pleasure. The life of this world is a provision that deceives.

---

[a] *Shuhada* means witnesses. Here I've used the technical meaning, "martyrs", those killed in the path of Allah.

الْاَرْضِ لَا اُعِدَّتْ لِلَّذِیْنَ اٰمَنُوْا بِاللّٰهِ وَ

رُسُلِهٖ ط ذٰلِكَ فَضْلُ اللّٰهِ یُؤْتِیْهِ مَنْ یَّشَآءُ ط

وَ اللّٰهُ ذُو الْفَضْلِ الْعَظِیْمِ ۲۱ مَآ اَصَابَ مِنْ

مُّصِیْبَةٍ فِی الْاَرْضِ وَ لَا فِیْۤ اَنْفُسِكُمْ اِلَّا

فِیْ كِتٰبٍ مِّنْ قَبْلِ اَنْ نَّبْرَاَهَا ط اِنَّ ذٰلِكَ

عَلَی اللّٰهِ یَسِیْرٌ ۲۲ لِّكَیْلَا تَاْسَوْا عَلٰی مَا

فَاتَكُمْ وَ لَا تَفْرَحُوْا بِمَاۤ اٰتٰىكُمْ ط وَ اللّٰهُ لَا

یُحِبُّ كُلَّ مُخْتَالٍ فَخُوْرِ ۲۳ الَّذِیْنَ یَبْخَلُوْنَ

وَ یَاْمُرُوْنَ النَّاسَ بِالْبُخْلِ ط وَ مَنْ یَّتَوَلَّ

فَاِنَّ اللّٰهَ هُوَ الْغَنِیُّ الْحَمِیْدُ ۲۳ لَقَدْ اَرْسَلْنَا

رُسُلَنَا بِالْبَیِّنٰتِ وَ اَنْزَلْنَا مَعَهُمُ الْكِتٰبَ

وَ الْمِیْزَانَ لِیَقُوْمَ النَّاسُ بِالْقِسْطِ ج وَ اَنْزَلْنَا

الْحَدِیْدَ فِیْهِ بَاْسٌ شَدِیْدٌ وَّ مَنَافِعُ لِلنَّاسِ

وَ لِیَعْلَمَ اللّٰهُ مَنْ یَّنْصُرُهٗ وَ رُسُلَهٗ بِالْغَیْبِ ط

اِنَّ اللّٰهَ قَوِیٌّ عَزِیْزٌ ۲۵ وَ لَقَدْ اَرْسَلْنَا نُوْحًا وَّ

اِبْرٰهِیْمَ وَ جَعَلْنَا فِیْ ذُرِّیَّتِهِمَا النُّبُوَّةَ وَ الْكِتٰبَ

فَمِنْهُمْ مُّهْتَدٍ ج وَ كَثِیْرٌ مِّنْهُمْ فٰسِقُوْنَ ۲۲ ثُمَّ

قَفَّیْنَا عَلٰۤی اٰثَارِهِمْ بِرُسُلِنَا وَ قَفَّیْنَا بِعِیْسَی ابْنِ

مَرْیَمَ وَ اٰتَیْنٰهُ الْاِنْجِیْلَ ۙ۬ وَ جَعَلْنَا فِیْ قُلُوْبِ

الَّذِیْنَ اتَّبَعُوْهُ رَاْفَةً وَّ رَحْمَةً ط وَ رَهْبَانِیَّةَ

The miserly and the unwilling to share with others are disliked by Allah.

²¹ Therefore, compete with each other for Your Lord's forgiveness and Paradise, its breadth is like the breadth of the Heavens and the Earth, prepared for the believers of Allah and His messengers. That's Allah's grace; He gives it to who He pleases. And Allah is the Most Gracious.

Belief in predestination prevents hopelessness

²² Any disaster on Earth or to yourselves is written down before it happens; this is easy for Allah. ²³ Its purpose: to *ensure* you don't become hopeless because of your loss, nor boast about your gain. Allah doesn't like the show-offs, ²⁴ or those who are miserly and tell others to be miserly. If anyone turns away, *remember* Allah is Self-Sufficient, deserving of all Praise. ²⁵ We sent our messengers with clear proofs, the Book, and Scales of Justice so people may establish justice. We sent down iron; a strong *metal* with many benefits for people, to see who uses this to help Allah and His messengers, without seeing *Him*. Indeed, Allah is the Strong, Almighty.

The Christians innovated self-denial

²⁶ We sent Nuh and Ibrahim, and blessed their children with prophethood and the Book; some of them were guided, but most were lawbreakers. ²⁷ We sent more messengers in their footsteps, including Isa son of Maryam, to whom We gave the Gospel. We filled his follower's hearts with compassion, and they invented self-denial,[a] which We hadn't prescribed for them. They *invented* this to seek Allah's pleasure, but failed to fulfil its requirements. Those who believed, We rewarded them, but many were lawbreakers.

---

[a] *Rahbaniyat*, asceticism, monkhood, retreat from worldly activities. An innovation by the fathers of early Christianity, the Quran doesn't disapprove of it, an evidence for permissibility of good innovations in Muslim culture and society.

اِبْتَدَعُوْهَا مَا كَتَبْنٰهَا عَلَيْهِمْ اِلَّا ابْتِغَآءَ رِضْوَانِ

اللّٰهِ فَمَا رَعَوْهَا حَقَّ رِعَايَتِهَا ۚ فَاٰتَيْنَا الَّذِيْنَ

اٰمَنُوْا مِنْهُمْ اَجْرَهُمْ ۚ وَكَثِيْرٌ مِّنْهُمْ فٰسِقُوْنَ ۝

يٰۤاَيُّهَا الَّذِيْنَ اٰمَنُوا اتَّقُوا اللّٰهَ وَاٰمِنُوْا بِرَسُوْلِهٖ

يُؤْتِكُمْ كِفْلَيْنِ مِنْ رَّحْمَتِهٖ وَيَجْعَلْ لَّكُمْ نُوْرًا

تَمْشُوْنَ بِهٖ وَيَغْفِرْ لَكُمْ ۚ وَاللّٰهُ غَفُوْرٌ رَّحِيْمٌ ۝

لِئَلَّا يَعْلَمَ اَهْلُ الْكِتٰبِ اَلَّا يَقْدِرُوْنَ عَلٰى شَیْءٍ ۙ

مِّنْ فَضْلِ اللّٰهِ وَاَنَّ الْفَضْلَ بِيَدِ اللّٰهِ يُؤْتِيْهِ

مَنْ يَّشَآءُ ۚ وَاللّٰهُ ذُو الْفَضْلِ الْعَظِيْمِ ۝

Those who do new and bold things for the love of Allah are honoured.

Double reward for the charitable

²⁸ Believers, be mindful of Allah and believe in His Messenger, so you are given a double share of His Kindness. He will offer you a light to walk in, and forgiveness. Allah is the Forgiving, the Caring. ²⁹ Let the People of The Book know, they don't control Allah's grace, that's in Allah's hand; He gives it to anyone He wants. Allah's grace is vast.

58. Surat Al-Mujadilah

The Woman at Odds

This Madinan surat is entitled Al-Mujadilah as well as Al-Mujadilah. Aisha (Allah be pleased with her) reported that Khawla bint Sa'laba came to the Messenger ﷺ, and pleaded with him about the injustice her husband had done to her. He divorced her by the Arabian custom of *Zihar*, when the husband tells his wife: "You are to me like the back of my mother." This declaration could not be revoked, so the woman would be left in limbo, in an indeterminate state – neither married, nor divorced. So Khawla appealed to the Messenger ﷺ: he told her that until Allah revealed a new law about *Zihar*, it remained normative. She was disappointed and continued to argue with him, she said, "When Aws married me, I was young and wealthy, and my parents were alive. Now that I am old, my parents dead, and my wealth finished – now he divorced me. Is there any room for us to live together?" The Prophet ﷺ said, "Until I receive revelation, this is the normative." She kept complaining, until finally this surat was revealed to provide a way out for her from this difficult situation. This story reminds us that Allah is deeply engaged with His people. It shows that Allah's speech can be elicited by anyone who earnestly pleads to Him.

The surat offers instruction on the manners of having private conversations. The secret conversations of the hypocrites and Jews alarmed the Muslims, unaware of what they were plotting. So they complained to the Messenger ﷺ, and these verses were revealed as a warning. Another social manner highlighted is how to make room for others in gatherings. The surat ends by describing the dedication and loyalty of true believers.

بِسْمِ اللّٰهِ الرَّحْمٰنِ الرَّحِيْمِ

قَدْ سَمِعَ اللّٰهُ قَوْلَ الَّتِيْ تُجَادِلُكَ فِيْ زَوْجِهَا وَ تَشْتَكِيْ اِلَى اللّٰهِ وَ اللّٰهُ یَسْمَعُ تَحَاوُرَكُمَا ط اِنَّ اللّٰهَ سَمِیْعٌ بَصِیْرٌ ۞ اَلَّذِیْنَ یُظٰهِرُوْنَ مِنْكُمْ مِّنْ نِّسَآئِهِمْ مَّا هُنَّ اُمَّهٰتِهِمْ ط اِنْ اُمَّهٰتُهُمْ اِلَّا الّٰٓئِیْ وَلَدْنَهُمْ ط وَ اِنَّهُمْ لَیَقُوْلُوْنَ مُنْكَرًا مِّنَ الْقَوْلِ وَ زُوْرًا ط وَ اِنَّ اللّٰهَ لَعَفُوٌّ غَفُوْرٌ ۞ وَ الَّذِیْنَ یُظٰهِرُوْنَ مِنْ نِّسَآئِهِمْ ثُمَّ یَعُوْدُوْنَ لِمَا قَالُوْا فَتَحْرِیْرُ رَقَبَةٍ مِّنْ قَبْلِ اَنْ یَّتَمَآسَّا ط ذٰلِكُمْ تُوْعَظُوْنَ بِهٖ ط وَ اللّٰهُ بِمَا تَعْمَلُوْنَ خَبِیْرٌ ۞ فَمَنْ لَّمْ یَجِدْ فَصِیَامُ شَهْرَیْنِ مُتَتَابِعَیْنِ مِنْ قَبْلِ اَنْ یَّتَمَآسَّا فَمَنْ لَّمْ یَسْتَطِعْ فَاِطْعَامُ سِتِّیْنَ مِسْکِیْنًا ط ذٰلِكَ لِتُؤْمِنُوْا بِاللّٰهِ وَ رَسُوْلِهٖ ط وَ تِلْكَ حُدُوْدُ اللّٰهِ ط وَ لِلْکٰفِرِیْنَ عَذَابٌ اَلِیْمٌ ۞ اِنَّ الَّذِیْنَ یُحَآدُّوْنَ اللّٰهَ وَ رَسُوْلَهٗ کُبِتُوْا کَمَا کُبِتَ الَّذِیْنَ مِنْ قَبْلِهِمْ وَ قَدْ اَنْزَلْنَاۤ اٰیٰتٍ بَیِّنٰتٍ ط وَ لِلْکٰفِرِیْنَ عَذَابٌ مُّهِیْنٌ ۞ یَوْمَ یَبْعَثُهُمُ اللّٰهُ جَمِیْعًا فَیُنَبِّئُهُمْ بِمَا عَمِلُوْا ط اَحْصٰهُ اللّٰهُ وَ نَسُوْهُ ط وَ اللّٰهُ عَلٰى کُلِّ شَیْءٍ شَهِیْدٌ ۞ اَلَمْ تَرَ اَنَّ اللّٰهَ یَعْلَمُ مَا فِی السَّمٰوٰتِ وَ مَا فِی الْاَرْضِ ط مَا یَکُوْنُ مِنْ نَّجْوٰى ثَلٰثَةٍ اِلَّا هُوَ رَابِعُهُمْ وَ لَا خَمْسَةٍ اِلَّا هُوَ

Just think how loving Allah is. He hears the painful complaint of a wife, those who have been abused, and the abuser will pay a penalty. This is talking about domestic violence.

In the Name of Allah, the Kind, the Caring.

The woman who pleaded
[1] Allah heard the woman who pleaded with you about her husband and complained to Allah, and Allah heard your conversation. Allah is the Hearer, the Seeing. [2] Those of you who divorce their wives by Zihar[a] *should know* that they are not their mothers. Their mothers are those who gave birth to them; they are saying something horrible and false. Indeed, Allah is Pardoner and Forgiver. [3] Those who divorce their wives by Zihar, and then *decide* to take back what they have said, must free a slave before they sleep together. This is what you have been ordered to do. Allah is fully aware of what you do. [4] Anyone who can't do this must fast for two consecutive months, before sleeping together. If he is unable to do that, then he should feed sixty needy people. This will be a proof of your faith[b] in Allah and His Messenger. These are the boundaries of Allah. And for the disbelievers is painful punishment.

The disbelievers will be humiliated
[5] Those people who opposed Allah and his Messenger have been disgraced, like those disgraced before them. We sent clear signs, and for the disbelievers is humiliating punishment. [6] The Day Allah raises them up they will be told what they did. Allah has taken account of all *they did,* but they forgot it. And Allah is Witness of all things.

Rules about secret talks
[7] Don't you realise Allah knows what is in the Heavens and the Earth? There is no private conversation between three people but He is their fourth, if five He is their sixth; whether they are few or more, He is with them wherever they are. Then, on Judgement Day, He will tell them what they did. Indeed, Allah knows all things.

---

[a] This refers to the pagan Arab custom of rejecting a wife. See, the Introduction.
[b] According to Al-Qurtubi, "to believe" here means to confirm.

سَادِسُهُمْ وَلَا أَدْنَى مِن ذَلِكَ وَلَا أَكْثَرَ إِلَّا هُوَ مَعَهُمْ
أَيْنَ مَا كَانُوا ۖ ثُمَّ يُنَبِّئُهُم بِمَا عَمِلُوا يَوْمَ الْقِيَامَةِ ۚ
إِنَّ اللَّهَ بِكُلِّ شَيْءٍ عَلِيمٌ ٧ أَلَمْ تَرَ إِلَى الَّذِينَ نُهُوا
عَنِ النَّجْوَى ثُمَّ يَعُودُونَ لِمَا نُهُوا عَنْهُ وَيَتَنَاجَوْنَ
بِالْإِثْمِ وَالْعُدْوَانِ وَمَعْصِيَتِ الرَّسُولِ ۖ وَإِذَا جَاءُوكَ
حَيَّوْكَ بِمَا لَمْ يُحَيِّكَ بِهِ اللَّهُ وَيَقُولُونَ فِي أَنْفُسِهِمْ
لَوْلَا يُعَذِّبُنَا اللَّهُ بِمَا نَقُولُ ۚ حَسْبُهُمْ جَهَنَّمُ يَصْلَوْنَهَا ۖ

Plotting against others is condemnable. Always wish well for others and never cause harm. Have you ever plotted against anyone?

فَبِئْسَ الْمَصِيرُ ٨ يَا أَيُّهَا الَّذِينَ آمَنُوا إِذَا تَنَاجَيْتُمْ فَلَا
تَتَنَاجَوْا بِالْإِثْمِ وَالْعُدْوَانِ وَمَعْصِيَتِ الرَّسُولِ
وَتَنَاجَوْا بِالْبِرِّ وَالتَّقْوَى ۖ وَاتَّقُوا اللَّهَ الَّذِي إِلَيْهِ
تُحْشَرُونَ ٩ إِنَّمَا النَّجْوَى مِنَ الشَّيْطَانِ لِيَحْزُنَ
الَّذِينَ آمَنُوا وَلَيْسَ بِضَارِّهِمْ شَيْئًا إِلَّا بِإِذْنِ اللَّهِ ۗ
وَعَلَى اللَّهِ فَلْيَتَوَكَّلِ الْمُؤْمِنُونَ ١٠ يَا أَيُّهَا الَّذِينَ آمَنُوا
إِذَا قِيلَ لَكُمْ تَفَسَّحُوا فِي الْمَجَالِسِ فَافْسَحُوا يَفْسَحِ
اللَّهُ لَكُمْ ۖ وَإِذَا قِيلَ انْشُزُوا فَانْشُزُوا يَرْفَعِ اللَّهُ
الَّذِينَ آمَنُوا مِنكُمْ وَالَّذِينَ أُوتُوا الْعِلْمَ دَرَجَاتٍ ۚ
وَاللَّهُ بِمَا تَعْمَلُونَ خَبِيرٌ ١١ يَا أَيُّهَا الَّذِينَ آمَنُوا
إِذَا نَاجَيْتُمُ الرَّسُولَ فَقَدِّمُوا بَيْنَ يَدَيْ نَجْوَاكُمْ
صَدَقَةً ۚ ذَلِكَ خَيْرٌ لَّكُمْ وَأَطْهَرُ ۚ فَإِن لَّمْ تَجِدُوا
فَإِنَّ اللَّهَ غَفُورٌ رَّحِيمٌ ١٢ أَأَشْفَقْتُمْ أَن تُقَدِّمُوا

⁸Haven't you seen those who were forbidden to hold private conversations, yet they return *again and again* to do what they were forbidden? When they talk privately, they conspire to do that which is sinful, hostile and disobedient to the Prophet. When they come to you, they greet you with what Allah doesn't greet you with, and they tell themselves: "Why doesn't Allah punish us for what we said?" Hell will be sufficient for them; they will burn in it. What a wretched place of rest. ⁹Believers, when you talk in private, do not plot to sin, *create* hostility towards, or disobedience of the Messenger, but talk about goodness and being mindful of Allah. Be aware of Allah; you shall be gathered before Him. ¹⁰Any other kind of private conversations are the works of Satan, *which* makes the believers unhappy; he can't harm them except by the Will of Allah. So the believers should put their trust in Allah.

Humility and kindness

¹¹Believers, when you are asked to make room in congregations then do so, Allah will make it spacious for you. If you are told to get up *from your place* then do so; Allah will raise the ranks of the believers among you, *particularly* those who have knowledge. Allah is aware of what you do.

Paying charity as a consultation fee to the Messenger ﷺ

¹²Believers, before you consult the Messenger privately, offer charity for the consultation. That's a good practice and purification for you. If you can't offer anything, then you *will still find* Allah Most Forgiving, Most Kind[a].

---

[a] When people began to demand private audience with the Messenger ﷺ too frequently, this order was given. However, it was quickly abrogated within a short time (Al Sabuni).

بَيْنَ يَدَيْ نَجْوَاكُمْ صَدَقَاتٍ ۚ فَاِذْ لَمْ تَفْعَلُوْا وَتَابَ
اللهُ عَلَيْكُمْ فَاَقِيْمُوا الصَّلٰوةَ وَاٰتُوا الزَّكٰوةَ وَاَطِيْعُوا
اللهَ وَرَسُوْلَهٗ ۚ وَاللهُ خَبِيْرٌۢ بِمَا تَعْمَلُوْنَ ۞ اَلَمْ
تَرَ اِلَى الَّذِيْنَ تَوَلَّوْا قَوْمًا غَضِبَ اللهُ عَلَيْهِمْ ۗ
مَا هُمْ مِّنْكُمْ وَلَا مِنْهُمْ وَيَحْلِفُوْنَ عَلَى الْكَذِبِ وَ
هُمْ يَعْلَمُوْنَ ۞ اَعَدَّ اللهُ لَهُمْ عَذَابًا شَدِيْدًا ۗ اِنَّهُمْ
سَآءَ مَا كَانُوْا يَعْمَلُوْنَ ۞ اِتَّخَذُوْا اَيْمَانَهُمْ جُنَّةً فَصَدُّوْا
عَنْ سَبِيْلِ اللهِ فَلَهُمْ عَذَابٌ مُّهِيْنٌ ۞ لَنْ تُغْنِيَ
عَنْهُمْ اَمْوَالُهُمْ وَلَا اَوْلَادُهُمْ مِّنَ اللهِ شَيْئًا ۗ اُولٰٓئِكَ
اَصْحٰبُ النَّارِ ۗ هُمْ فِيْهَا خٰلِدُوْنَ ۞ يَوْمَ يَبْعَثُهُمُ
اللهُ جَمِيْعًا فَيَحْلِفُوْنَ لَهٗ كَمَا يَحْلِفُوْنَ لَكُمْ وَ
يَحْسَبُوْنَ اَنَّهُمْ عَلٰى شَيْءٍ ۗ اَلَآ اِنَّهُمْ هُمُ الْكٰذِبُوْنَ ۞
اِسْتَحْوَذَ عَلَيْهِمُ الشَّيْطٰنُ فَاَنْسٰهُمْ ذِكْرَ اللهِ ۗ اُولٰٓئِكَ حِزْبُ
الشَّيْطٰنِ ۗ اَلَآ اِنَّ حِزْبَ الشَّيْطٰنِ هُمُ الْخٰسِرُوْنَ ۞ اِنَّ
الَّذِيْنَ يُحَآدُّوْنَ اللهَ وَرَسُوْلَهٗٓ اُولٰٓئِكَ فِى الْاَذَلِّيْنَ ۞
كَتَبَ اللهُ لَاَغْلِبَنَّ اَنَا وَرُسُلِيْ ۗ اِنَّ اللهَ قَوِيٌّ عَزِيْزٌ ۞
لَا تَجِدُ قَوْمًا يُّؤْمِنُوْنَ بِاللهِ وَالْيَوْمِ الْاٰخِرِ يُوَآدُّوْنَ مَنْ
حَآدَّ اللهَ وَرَسُوْلَهٗ وَلَوْ كَانُوْٓا اٰبَآءَهُمْ اَوْ اَبْنَآءَهُمْ اَوْ
اِخْوَانَهُمْ اَوْ عَشِيْرَتَهُمْ ۗ اُولٰٓئِكَ كَتَبَ فِيْ قُلُوْبِهِمُ الْاِيْمَانَ
وَاَيَّدَهُمْ بِرُوْحٍ مِّنْهُ ۗ وَيُدْخِلُهُمْ جَنّٰتٍ تَجْرِيْ مِنْ

Here is emphasis to stay clear of evil people who harm others. Even if they're relatives.

1127

¹³ Are you afraid of offering charity before your private consultation? If you haven't done so, Allah has forgiven you; so perform the prayer, and pay the Zakat and obey Allah and his Messenger. Allah is fully aware of what you do.

The hypocrites use oaths as shields

¹⁴ Have you seen those who befriend a group with whom Allah is angry? They are neither from you nor from them, and knowingly take false oaths. ¹⁵ Allah has prepared a severe punishment for them. What they are doing is evil. ¹⁶ They take their oaths as shields, so they can stop people from the path of Allah; for them is a humiliating punishment. ¹⁷ Neither their wealth nor their children will benefit them in the slightest against Allah. These are people of the Fire; they shall live there forever. ¹⁸ The Day Allah raises them up, they will swear before Him as they swear before you now, thinking it will help them. Be aware, they are liars. ¹⁹ Satan has control over them, and has made them forget the remembrance of Allah. They are the party of Satan. Be aware, these are party of the Satan, they are the losers. ²⁰ Those who opposed Allah and his Messenger are the most despised.

True believers are dedicated to Allah and his Messenger ﷺ

²¹ Allah has declared: "I and My messengers will always be the winners." Allah is Strong and Almighty. ²² You won't find those who believe in Allah and the Last Day dedicated to those who oppose Allah and His Messenger, even if they are their parents, or children, or brothers or relatives. These are the ones whose hearts Allah has strengthened with faith, and helped them with a spirit from Himself. He will take them into gardens with rivers flowing beneath them, where they will live forever. Allah is pleased with them, and they are pleased with Him. These are the party of Allah. Be aware, the party of Allah will win.

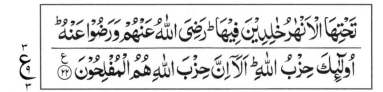

59. Surat Al-Hashr

The Gathering of the Forces

This Madinan surat was revealed after the Battle of Uhud, in the fourth year after Hijra. The central theme is the expulsion of the tribe of Banu al-Nadir from their fortresses, in the south of the city. Historians believe the Jewish tribes settled in Madinah after the sacking of Jerusalem in 587 BCE by Ebenezer. The two Arab tribes of Aws and Khazraj are thought to have moved to Madinah centuries later, following a flood in Yemen.

When the Messenger ﷺ arrived in Madinah, he created a bond of brotherhood between the Arab tribes, through their faith in Islam. The Treaty of Madinah was also made with the three Jewish tribes of Banu al-Nadir, Qaynuqa and Quraza:

> The aim was to create a single community of believers but allowing for the differences between the two religions. Muslims and Jews were to have equal status ... In case of war against them they must all fight as one people ... There was no express stipulation that the Jews should formally recognise Muhammad ﷺ as the Messenger of God, though he was referred to as such throughout the document.[a]

The Jews welcomed this new arrangement, which guaranteed them peace. However, some elders found this treaty frustrating, and took every opportunity to create discord among the two communities. They were joined in their intrigues and conspiracies by Abdullah ibn Ubayy, the leader of the hypocrites in Madinah.

A Muslim woman selling her goods at the market was insulted by a Jewish goldsmith. A young Muslim stood up for her and in the scuffle that ensued he killed the offender. Rather than referring the case to the Messenger ﷺ, the Jews took the matter into their own hands and killed him. The Messenger ﷺ asked them for the payment of blood money. Instead of honouring the treaty, Banu al-Nadir conspired to kill the Messenger ﷺ. The Angel Jibreel عليه السلام informed him of their plot, so he immediately left their castle. This was a clear violation of the treaty, so the Messenger ﷺ gave them ten days to leave. Most of the tribe began preparing to leave, however Ibn Ubayy came to them promising them help if they were attacked. So, they refused to leave their fortresses. This was a declaration of war. The Muslims marched and laid siege, then the Messenger ﷺ ordered the cutting of palm trees, a signal that they will be attacked, so they agreed to leave. The Prophet ﷺ allowed

---

[a] M. Lings, *Muhammad: His Life Based on the Earliest Sources.*

them to carry as much as they could on their camels. What they left behind was taken as spoils of war. The Messenger ﷺ gave the palm groves, land, homes and other possessions to the emigrants. The Helpers' were happy with this distribution. The Quran comments on the generosity and sacrifice in these glowing words:

> In fact, they give them preference over themselves, even though they are poor too: whoever is saved from the greed of his selfish *desires,* those are *amongst* the successful (9).

The helpers were given the glad tidings: future generations will remember them in their prayers. The surat then returns to the story of Banu al-Nadir, pointing to how they were betrayed by the hypocrites, who had promised to help them. The hypocrites are compared to Satan, who will also relinquish responsibility for those he misled.

This surat contains twenty-two beautiful Names of Allah. Eighteen of them are mentioned at its close.

بِسْمِ اللهِ الرَّحْمٰنِ الرَّحِيْمِ

سَبَّحَ لِلّٰهِ مَا فِي السَّمٰوٰتِ وَمَا فِي الْأَرْضِ ۚ وَهُوَ
الْعَزِيْزُ الْحَكِيْمُ ١ هُوَ الَّذِيْ أَخْرَجَ الَّذِيْنَ كَفَرُوْا مِنْ
أَهْلِ الْكِتٰبِ مِنْ دِيَارِهِمْ لِأَوَّلِ الْحَشْرِ ۚ مَا ظَنَنْتُمْ أَنْ
يَّخْرُجُوْا وَظَنُّوْا أَنَّهُمْ مَّانِعَتُهُمْ حُصُوْنُهُمْ مِّنَ اللهِ
فَأَتٰىهُمُ اللهُ مِنْ حَيْثُ لَمْ يَحْتَسِبُوْا وَقَذَفَ فِيْ قُلُوْبِهِمُ
الرُّعْبَ يُخْرِبُوْنَ بُيُوْتَهُمْ بِأَيْدِيْهِمْ وَأَيْدِي الْمُؤْمِنِيْنَ ۚ
فَاعْتَبِرُوْا يٰأُولِي الْأَبْصَارِ ٢ وَلَوْلَا أَنْ كَتَبَ اللهُ عَلَيْهِمُ
الْجَلَاءَ لَعَذَّبَهُمْ فِي الدُّنْيَا ۖ وَلَهُمْ فِي الْأٰخِرَةِ عَذَابُ
النَّارِ ٣ ذٰلِكَ بِأَنَّهُمْ شَاقُّوا اللهَ وَرَسُوْلَهُ ۚ وَمَنْ
يُّشَاقِّ اللهَ فَإِنَّ اللهَ شَدِيْدُ الْعِقَابِ ٤ مَا قَطَعْتُمْ
مِّنْ لِّيْنَةٍ أَوْ تَرَكْتُمُوْهَا قَائِمَةً عَلٰى أُصُوْلِهَا فَبِإِذْنِ
اللهِ وَلِيُخْزِيَ الْفٰسِقِيْنَ ٥ وَمَا أَفَاءَ اللهُ عَلٰى رَسُوْلِهٖ
مِنْهُمْ فَمَا أَوْجَفْتُمْ عَلَيْهِ مِنْ خَيْلٍ وَّلَا رِكَابٍ
وَّلٰكِنَّ اللهَ يُسَلِّطُ رُسُلَهُ عَلٰى مَنْ يَّشَاءُ ۗ وَاللهُ عَلٰى
كُلِّ شَيْءٍ قَدِيْرٌ ٦ مَا أَفَاءَ اللهُ عَلٰى رَسُوْلِهٖ مِنْ
أَهْلِ الْقُرٰى فَلِلّٰهِ وَلِلرَّسُوْلِ وَلِذِي الْقُرْبٰى وَالْيَتٰمٰى
وَالْمَسٰكِيْنِ وَابْنِ السَّبِيْلِ ۙ كَيْ لَا يَكُوْنَ دُوْلَةً بَيْنَ
الْأَغْنِيَاءِ مِنْكُمْ ۚ وَمَا أٰتٰىكُمُ الرَّسُوْلُ فَخُذُوْهُ ۚ وَمَا

Our worldly powers cannot save us from the Divine wrath, particularly when we have been unfair to others.

In the name of Allah, the Kind, the Caring.

The Banu al-Nadir are expelled from Madinah

[1] All things in the Heavens and Earth glorify Allah, He is the Almighty, the Wise. [2] He is the One Who drove out the disbelievers of the People of The Book from their homes, by the forces gathered, for the first time. You thought they would never leave, since they believed their fortresses would protect them from Allah. But Allah came upon them from where they didn't expect, and put fear into their hearts, and they destroyed their homes with their hands and by the hands of the believers. So, learn a lesson from this, people of insight! [3] Had Allah not decreed exile for them, He would have severely punished them *in some other way* in the world. In the Hereafter, they will have the punishment of the Fire. [4] That is because they opposed Allah and His Messenger, and whoever opposes Allah *should know* that Allah's punishment is severe. [5] The palm trees you cut down or left standing on their roots was done by the permission of Allah, to humiliate guilty people.

The Messenger's ﷺ authority to make laws

[6] Whatever Allah returned *of the booty* to His Messenger from them *wasn't due to* your swift horses or camels, but Allah gave authority to His Messengers to overwhelm anyone He wills. Allah has control over all things. [7] So whatever Allah returned to His Messenger from the *booty* of the townspeople really belongs to Allah; the Messenger, *his* relatives; the orphans; the needy; and the travellers. This is *to ensure* wealth does not circulate among your wealthy *only*. Whatever the Messenger gives you take it, and whatever he forbids you avoid it; be mindful of Allah, His punishment is severe.[a]

---

[a] This gives the beloved Messenger ﷺ the mandate to make laws and whatever he ﷺ says has Divine authority. Thus, his Sunnah, his way, is being endorsed.

نَهٰكُمْ عَنْهُ فَانْتَهُوْا ۚ وَاتَّقُوا اللهَ ۗ اِنَّ اللهَ شَدِيْدُ
الْعِقَابِ ۞ لِلْفُقَرَآءِ الْمُهٰجِرِيْنَ الَّذِيْنَ اُخْرِجُوْا
مِنْ دِيَارِهِمْ وَاَمْوَالِهِمْ يَبْتَغُوْنَ فَضْلًا مِّنَ اللهِ
وَرِضْوَانًا وَّيَنْصُرُوْنَ اللهَ وَرَسُوْلَهٗ ۗ اُولٰٓئِكَ هُمُ
الصّٰدِقُوْنَ ۞ وَالَّذِيْنَ تَبَوَّؤُ الدَّارَ وَالْاِيْمَانَ
مِنْ قَبْلِهِمْ يُحِبُّوْنَ مَنْ هَاجَرَ اِلَيْهِمْ وَلَا يَجِدُوْنَ
فِيْ صُدُوْرِهِمْ حَاجَةً مِّمَّآ اُوْتُوْا وَيُؤْثِرُوْنَ عَلٰٓى
اَنْفُسِهِمْ وَلَوْ كَانَ بِهِمْ خَصَاصَةٌ ۗ وَمَنْ يُّوْقَ شُحَّ
نَفْسِهٖ فَاُولٰٓئِكَ هُمُ الْمُفْلِحُوْنَ ۞ وَالَّذِيْنَ جَآءُوْ
مِنْ بَعْدِهِمْ يَقُوْلُوْنَ رَبَّنَا اغْفِرْ لَنَا وَلِاِخْوَانِنَا
الَّذِيْنَ سَبَقُوْنَا بِالْاِيْمَانِ وَلَا تَجْعَلْ فِيْ قُلُوْبِنَا
غِلًّا لِّلَّذِيْنَ اٰمَنُوْا رَبَّنَآ اِنَّكَ رَءُوْفٌ رَّحِيْمٌ ۞
اَلَمْ تَرَ اِلَى الَّذِيْنَ نَافَقُوْا يَقُوْلُوْنَ لِاِخْوَانِهِمُ الَّذِيْنَ
كَفَرُوْا مِنْ اَهْلِ الْكِتٰبِ لَئِنْ اُخْرِجْتُمْ لَنَخْرُجَنَّ
مَعَكُمْ وَلَا نُطِيْعُ فِيْكُمْ اَحَدًا اَبَدًا ۙ وَّاِنْ قُوْتِلْتُمْ
لَنَنْصُرَنَّكُمْ ۗ وَاللهُ يَشْهَدُ اِنَّهُمْ لَكٰذِبُوْنَ ۞ لَئِنْ
اُخْرِجُوْا لَا يَخْرُجُوْنَ مَعَهُمْ ۚ وَلَئِنْ قُوْتِلُوْا لَا
يَنْصُرُوْنَهُمْ ۚ وَلَئِنْ نَّصَرُوْهُمْ لَيُوَلُّنَّ الْاَدْبَارَ ۫ ثُمَّ
لَا يُنْصَرُوْنَ ۞ لَاَنْتُمْ اَشَدُّ رَهْبَةً فِيْ صُدُوْرِهِمْ
مِّنَ اللهِ ۗ ذٰلِكَ بِاَنَّهُمْ قَوْمٌ لَّا يَفْقَهُوْنَ ۞ لَا

Preferring others over yourself is a sign of a good character. Help others in need. Have you done this?

1133

The self-sacrifice of the Helpers of Madinah is praised

⁸ *This booty* is for the poor *Makkan* emigrants, who were expelled from their homes, and their wealth *confiscated;* they are seeking the bounty and pleasure of Allah, and are helping Allah and His Messenger. These are honest people. ⁹ The settled people of Madinah have firm faith, love the emigrants who came to them, and they don't envy what was given to the emigrants. *In fact,* they give them preference over themselves, yet they are poor themselves: anyone who is saved from the greed of his selfish *desires,* is successful.

The prayer of forgiveness for past generations

¹⁰ People who come afterwards will pray for them: "Our Lord, forgive us and our brothers in faith who passed away, and don't leave any hatred in our hearts of the believers. Our Lord, you are the Compassionate, the Kind."

The hypocrites' false promises

¹¹ Haven't you seen the hypocrites saying to their disbelieving brothers among the People of The Book, "If you are expelled, we will also leave with you, and we shall not obey anyone else. If you are attacked, we will help you." Allah is a witness, they are liars. ¹² If they are expelled, neither will they leave with them, nor help them if they are attacked. If they came to help them, they would soon turn their backs and flee, they wouldn't be helped. ¹³ They really fear you more than they fear Allah; that's because they are a people who don't understand.

يُقَاتِلُوْنَكُمْ جَمِيْعًا اِلَّا فِيْ قُرًى مُّحَصَّنَةٍ اَوْ مِنْ وَّرَآءِ
جُدُرٍ ط بَأْسُهُمْ بَيْنَهُمْ شَدِيْدٌ ط تَحْسَبُهُمْ جَمِيْعًا
وَّ قُلُوْبُهُمْ شَتّٰى ط ذٰلِكَ بِاَنَّهُمْ قَوْمٌ لَّا يَعْقِلُوْنَ ۝
كَمَثَلِ الَّذِيْنَ مِنْ قَبْلِهِمْ قَرِيْبًا ذَاقُوْا وَبَالَ
اَمْرِهِمْ ۚ وَلَهُمْ عَذَابٌ اَلِيْمٌ ۝ كَمَثَلِ الشَّيْطٰنِ اِذْ
قَالَ لِلْاِنْسَانِ اكْفُرْ ۚ فَلَمَّا كَفَرَ قَالَ اِنِّيْ بَرِيْٓءٌ مِّنْكَ
اِنِّيْٓ اَخَافُ اللّٰهَ رَبَّ الْعٰلَمِيْنَ ۝ فَكَانَ عَاقِبَتَهُمَآ
اَنَّهُمَا فِى النَّارِ خَالِدَيْنِ فِيْهَا ط وَ ذٰلِكَ جَزٰٓؤُا
الظّٰلِمِيْنَ ۝ يٰٓاَيُّهَا الَّذِيْنَ اٰمَنُوا اتَّقُوا اللّٰهَ وَلْتَنْظُرْ
نَفْسٌ مَّا قَدَّمَتْ لِغَدٍ ۚ وَ اتَّقُوا اللّٰهَ ط اِنَّ اللّٰهَ
خَبِيْرٌۢ بِمَا تَعْمَلُوْنَ ۝ وَ لَا تَكُوْنُوْا كَالَّذِيْنَ نَسُوا
اللّٰهَ فَاَنْسٰهُمْ اَنْفُسَهُمْ ط اُولٰٓئِكَ هُمُ الْفٰسِقُوْنَ ۝
لَا يَسْتَوِيْٓ اَصْحٰبُ النَّارِ وَاَصْحٰبُ الْجَنَّةِ ط اَصْحٰبُ
الْجَنَّةِ هُمُ الْفَآئِزُوْنَ ۝ لَوْ اَنْزَلْنَا هٰذَا الْقُرْاٰنَ عَلٰى
جَبَلٍ لَّرَاَيْتَهٗ خَاشِعًا مُّتَصَدِّعًا مِّنْ خَشْيَةِ اللّٰهِ ط
وَ تِلْكَ الْاَمْثَالُ نَضْرِبُهَا لِلنَّاسِ لَعَلَّهُمْ
يَتَفَكَّرُوْنَ ۝ هُوَ اللّٰهُ الَّذِيْ لَآ اِلٰهَ اِلَّا هُوَ ۚ
عٰلِمُ الْغَيْبِ وَ الشَّهَادَةِ ۚ هُوَ الرَّحْمٰنُ الرَّحِيْمُ ۝
هُوَ اللّٰهُ الَّذِيْ لَآ اِلٰهَ اِلَّا هُوَ ۚ اَلْمَلِكُ الْقُدُّوْسُ
السَّلٰمُ الْمُؤْمِنُ الْمُهَيْمِنُ الْعَزِيْزُ الْجَبَّارُ الْمُتَكَبِّرُ ط

How are you affected by reading the Quran? Moved? Afraid? Thoughtful? Reflective?

¹⁴ Even if they were all together, they would not fight you except in fortified settlements or behind *strong* walls. You would think they are united, but their hearts are divided; they are an unreasonable people.

Hypocrites compared with Satan

¹⁵ Their example is like the people who were recently punished;ᵃ they tasted the consequences of their *bad* behaviour, and for them is a painful punishment *in the Hereafter.* ¹⁶ Another comparison *of the hypocrites* is Satan; he says to man, "Don't believe," and when he disbelieves, Satan says to him, "I disown you, I fear Allah, the Lord of the worlds." ¹⁷ The punishment for both is the Fire where they will live forever, the reward for the wrongdoers.

The believers prepare for Paradise

¹⁸ Believers, be mindful of Allah, and let everyone consider *carefully* what they carry forward for tomorrow. Fear Allah! He is fully aware of what you do. ¹⁹ Don't be like those who forgot Allah so He made them forget themselves. Those are the sinners. ²⁰ The companions of the Fire and the companions of Paradise are not alike; the companions of Paradise will be the winners. ²¹ Had We revealed this Quran on a mountain, you would have seen it humble itself and turn to dust out of fear of Allah. We give these examples so people may reflect.

Eighteen beautiful names of Allah

²² He is Allah: there is no God but Him. He is the Knower of the hidden and the open, the Kind, the Caring. ²³ He is Allah, there is no God but Him, the Sovereign, the Holy, the Peace Giver, Security Giver, the Guardian, the Almighty, the Compeller, the Greatest. Allah is far above the partners they ascribe to Him. ²⁴ He is Allah: the Creator, the Originator and the Fashioner. He has beautiful Names, all things in the Heavens and the Earth glorify Him, the Almighty, the Wise.

ᵃ This could refer to the Jewish tribe of Banu Qaynuqa, who were banished after the battle of Badr for their betrayal of the treaty.

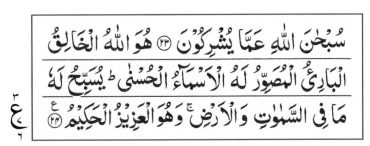

60. Surat Al-Mumtahinah

The Woman Investigated

This surat was revealed in the eighth year after Hijra, well after the Treaty of Hudaibiyah. The practice of the Prophet ﷺ was to keep his expeditions and campaigns secret, to prevent information leaking to enemies. The Prophet ﷺ planned action against the Quraysh leaders. However, a companion by the name of Hatib ibn Balata sent a letter via a woman who was travelling to Makkah to disclose the plan to the Quraysh. Hatib ibn Balata's family was under the control of the Makkans, and he engaged in this information leak in an attempt to secure their safety. When the Prophet ﷺ learnt about this he sent some disciples to find her and confiscate the letter. They found her and seized the letter which Hatib had given her. The Prophet ﷺ summoned Hatib and asked for an explanation. He admitted his mistake, but declared his strong and true faith in Islam. His excuse was to win favour from the Quraysh so that his family was not harmed. Since Hatib had fought in the Battle of Badr, the Prophet ﷺ forgave him. We learn a few important lessons from this incident: do not base judgements on guesswork; the forgiving nature of Allah; the need to be loyal to one's community.

The central theme of the surat is the relationship between the Muslims and non-Muslims. The Quran teaches diplomacy: If attacked defend yourself, but strive for peace and friendship with them, "Allah will make friendship between you and your current enemies one day" (7). The beautiful example is given of Prophet Ibrahim ﷺ who lived in a multi-faith society. However, faith will make us different and we must accept this difference so we can live in peace and harmony.

بِسْمِ اللهِ الرَّحْمٰنِ الرَّحِيْمِ

يٰۤاَيُّهَا الَّذِيْنَ اٰمَنُوْا لَا تَتَّخِذُوْا عَدُوِّيْ وَعَدُوَّكُمْ

اَوْلِيَآءَ تُلْقُوْنَ اِلَيْهِمْ بِالْمَوَدَّةِ وَقَدْ كَفَرُوْا بِمَا

جَآءَكُمْ مِّنَ الْحَقِّ ۚ يُخْرِجُوْنَ الرَّسُوْلَ وَاِيَّاكُمْ

اَنْ تُؤْمِنُوْا بِاللهِ رَبِّكُمْ ۗ اِنْ كُنْتُمْ خَرَجْتُمْ جِهَادًا فِيْ

سَبِيْلِيْ وَابْتِغَآءَ مَرْضَاتِيْ ۖ تُسِرُّوْنَ اِلَيْهِمْ بِالْمَوَدَّةِ ۖ

وَاَنَا اَعْلَمُ بِمَاۤ اَخْفَيْتُمْ وَمَاۤ اَعْلَنْتُمْ ۗ وَمَنْ يَّفْعَلْهُ

مِنْكُمْ فَقَدْ ضَلَّ سَوَآءَ السَّبِيْلِ ۝ اِنْ يَّثْقَفُوْكُمْ

يَكُوْنُوْا لَكُمْ اَعْدَآءً وَّيَبْسُطُوْۤا اِلَيْكُمْ اَيْدِيَهُمْ وَ

اَلْسِنَتَهُمْ بِالسُّوْٓءِ وَوَدُّوْا لَوْ تَكْفُرُوْنَ ۝ لَنْ تَنْفَعَكُمْ

اَرْحَامُكُمْ وَلَاۤ اَوْلَادُكُمْ ۚ يَوْمَ الْقِيٰمَةِ ۚ يَفْصِلُ

بَيْنَكُمْ ۗ وَاللهُ بِمَا تَعْمَلُوْنَ بَصِيْرٌ ۝ قَدْ كَانَتْ

لَكُمْ اُسْوَةٌ حَسَنَةٌ فِيْۤ اِبْرٰهِيْمَ وَالَّذِيْنَ مَعَهٗ ۚ

اِذْ قَالُوْا لِقَوْمِهِمْ اِنَّا بُرَءٰٓؤُا مِنْكُمْ وَمِمَّا تَعْبُدُوْنَ

مِنْ دُوْنِ اللهِ ۫ كَفَرْنَا بِكُمْ وَبَدَا بَيْنَنَا وَبَيْنَكُمُ

الْعَدَاوَةُ وَالْبَغْضَآءُ اَبَدًا حَتّٰى تُؤْمِنُوْا بِاللهِ وَحْدَهٗۤ

اِلَّا قَوْلَ اِبْرٰهِيْمَ لِاَبِيْهِ لَاَسْتَغْفِرَنَّ لَكَ وَمَاۤ

اَمْلِكُ لَكَ مِنَ اللهِ مِنْ شَيْءٍ ۗ رَبَّنَا عَلَيْكَ تَوَكَّلْنَا

وَاِلَيْكَ اَنَبْنَا وَاِلَيْكَ الْمَصِيْرُ ۝ رَبَّنَا لَا تَجْعَلْنَا

Never wish to bump into the enemy. Be truthful and honest with your own people.

1139

In the name of Allah, the Kind, the Caring.

The obligation to be loyal and faithful

¹Believers, don't take as allies those who are Mine and your enemies. How can you fondly send reports about Muslims to them? Yet they disbelieved the truth that came to you; they expelled the Messenger and you because you believed in Allah, your Lord. If you truly emigrated in My path seeking My pleasure, then how can you correspond secretly with them? I know well what you have concealed and what you have revealed. Whoever did so has lost the straight path. ²If they could suppress you, they would be your bitter enemies who would stretch out their hands and tongues to destroy you, and they wish you would disbelieve. ³Neither your relatives nor your children will benefit you on Judgement Day. There, Allah will separate you out. Allah sees what you do.

Ibrahim and his followers are role models

⁴There is a beautiful role model for you in Ibrahim and those with him; when they said to their people, "We disown you and those you worship beside Allah; we reject you; there will be hostility and hatred between us until you believe in Allah alone." Except for what Ibrahim said to his father: "I will seek forgiveness for you, although I can't protect you from Allah in the slightest. Our Lord, we rely on You, and we turn devoutly to You, and the final return is to You.

فِتْنَةً لِّلَّذِيْنَ كَفَرُوْا وَاغْفِرْ لَنَا رَبَّنَا ۚ اِنَّكَ اَنْتَ الْعَزِيْزُ الْحَكِيْمُ ۞ لَقَدْ كَانَ لَكُمْ فِيْهِمْ اُسْوَةٌ حَسَنَةٌ لِّمَنْ كَانَ يَرْجُوا اللّٰهَ وَالْيَوْمَ الْاٰخِرَ ۚ وَمَنْ يَّتَوَلَّ فَاِنَّ اللّٰهَ هُوَ الْغَنِيُّ الْحَمِيْدُ ۞ عَسَى اللّٰهُ اَنْ يَّجْعَلَ بَيْنَكُمْ وَبَيْنَ الَّذِيْنَ عَادَيْتُمْ مِّنْهُمْ مَّوَدَّةً ۗ وَاللّٰهُ قَدِيْرٌ ۗ وَاللّٰهُ غَفُوْرٌ رَّحِيْمٌ ۞ لَا يَنْهٰىكُمُ اللّٰهُ عَنِ الَّذِيْنَ لَمْ يُقَاتِلُوْكُمْ فِي الدِّيْنِ وَلَمْ يُخْرِجُوْكُمْ مِّنْ دِيَارِكُمْ اَنْ تَبَرُّوْهُمْ وَتُقْسِطُوْٓا اِلَيْهِمْ ۗ اِنَّ اللّٰهَ يُحِبُّ الْمُقْسِطِيْنَ ۞ اِنَّمَا يَنْهٰىكُمُ اللّٰهُ عَنِ الَّذِيْنَ قَاتَلُوْكُمْ فِي الدِّيْنِ وَاَخْرَجُوْكُمْ مِّنْ دِيَارِكُمْ وَظَاهَرُوْا عَلٰٓى اِخْرَاجِكُمْ اَنْ تَوَلَّوْهُمْ ۚ وَمَنْ يَّتَوَلَّهُمْ فَاُولٰٓئِكَ هُمُ الظّٰلِمُوْنَ ۞ يٰٓاَيُّهَا الَّذِيْنَ اٰمَنُوْٓا اِذَا جَآءَكُمُ الْمُؤْمِنٰتُ مُهٰجِرٰتٍ فَامْتَحِنُوْهُنَّ ۗ اَللّٰهُ اَعْلَمُ بِاِيْمَانِهِنَّ ۚ فَاِنْ عَلِمْتُمُوْهُنَّ مُؤْمِنٰتٍ فَلَا تَرْجِعُوْهُنَّ اِلَى الْكُفَّارِ ۗ لَا هُنَّ حِلٌّ لَّهُمْ وَلَا هُمْ يَحِلُّوْنَ لَهُنَّ ۗ وَاٰتُوْهُمْ مَّآ اَنْفَقُوْا ۗ وَلَا جُنَاحَ عَلَيْكُمْ اَنْ تَنْكِحُوْهُنَّ اِذَآ اٰتَيْتُمُوْهُنَّ اُجُوْرَهُنَّ ۗ وَلَا تُمْسِكُوْا بِعِصَمِ الْكَوَافِرِ وَسْئَلُوْا مَآ اَنْفَقْتُمْ وَلْيَسْئَلُوْا مَآ اَنْفَقُوْا ۗ ذٰلِكُمْ حُكْمُ اللّٰهِ ۗ يَحْكُمُ بَيْنَكُمْ ۗ وَاللّٰهُ عَلِيْمٌ حَكِيْمٌ ۞ وَاِنْ فَاتَكُمْ

Be willing to forgive, so eventually it will revert to friendship once more – flexibility in mood.

⁵Our Lord, do not make us a prey^a for the disbelievers; forgive us our Lord. Our Lord, You are the Almighty, the Wise." ⁶What a beautiful role model they are for you *and in fact* for anyone who hopes to meet Allah on the Last Day. Anyone turning away *should know* Allah is Self-Sufficient, Praiseworthy.

Friendship with non-Muslims isn't forbidden

⁷Allah will make friendship between you and your current enemies *one day*; Allah is Powerful, Forgiving, Caring. ⁸Allah does not forbid you from being good and just to those who have not fought against you due to religion, nor expelled you from your houses. Allah loves the just people. ⁹However, Allah does forbid you from befriending those who fought against you due to religion, expelled you from your houses and helped to drive you out *of Makkah.* Those who befriend them are wrong.

Kindness to migrant women

¹⁰Believers, when believing migrant women come to you, investigate them. Allah knows well their faith. If you find them to be believers, then don't return them to the disbelievers. Neither are they lawful for them, nor *believing women* lawful for them. Give the disbelievers what they have spent *on them.*^b There *would be* nothing wrong if you were to marry them after giving their bridal gift. You should not hold on to marriage ties with disbelieving women; ask for what you have spent on them, just as *the Makkan disbelievers* will ask for what they have spent on them.^c That is Allah's judgement. Allah makes *fair* judgements between you, and Allah is the Knower, the Wise.

---

^a   *Fitna* literally means a test; here it is used metaphorically, hence my translation, "prey", a victim.
^b   The bridal gift.
^c   When a woman seeks divorce, the man can demand back the bridal gift he gave at the time of marriage.

شَىْءٌ مِّنْ اَزْوَاجِكُمْ اِلَى الْكُفَّارِ فَعَاقَبْتُمْ فَاٰتُوا

الَّذِيْنَ ذَهَبَتْ اَزْوَاجُهُمْ مِّثْلَ مَآ اَنْفَقُوْا ط

وَاتَّقُوا اللهَ الَّذِىٓ اَنْتُمْ بِهٖ مُؤْمِنُوْنَ ⑪ يٰٓاَيُّهَا النَّبِىُّ

اِذَا جَآءَكَ الْمُؤْمِنٰتُ يُبَايِعْنَكَ عَلٰٓى اَنْ لَّا يُشْرِكْنَ

بِاللهِ شَيْئًا وَّلَا يَسْرِقْنَ وَلَا يَزْنِيْنَ وَلَا يَقْتُلْنَ

اَوْلَادَهُنَّ وَلَا يَأْتِيْنَ بِبُهْتَانٍ يَّفْتَرِيْنَهٗ بَيْنَ اَيْدِيْهِنَّ

وَاَرْجُلِهِنَّ وَلَا يَعْصِيْنَكَ فِىْ مَعْرُوْفٍ فَبَايِعْهُنَّ وَ

اسْتَغْفِرْ لَهُنَّ اللهَ ط اِنَّ اللهَ غَفُوْرٌ رَّحِيْمٌ ⑫ يٰٓاَيُّهَا

الَّذِيْنَ اٰمَنُوْا لَا تَتَوَلَّوْا قَوْمًا غَضِبَ اللهُ عَلَيْهِمْ قَدْ يَئِسُوْا

مِنَ الْاٰخِرَةِ كَمَا يَئِسَ الْكُفَّارُ مِنْ اَصْحٰبِ الْقُبُوْرِ ⑬

Being an optimist, hopeful and upbeat is the way to finish a day.

[11] If any of your wives went *back* to the disbelievers *in Makkah,* and afterwards you gained victory over them, pay those whose wives fled the equivalent of the bridal gift they had given them. Fear Allah, the One you believe.

Women's oath of allegiance

[12] Prophet! When believing women come to you to take an oath of allegiance, accept their oath: they will not associate any partner with Allah, nor steal, nor commit adultery, nor murder their children, nor lie about who has fathered their children, nor disobey you in common good. And seek Allah's forgiveness for them. Allah is the Forgiving, the Caring. [13] Believers, don't befriend a people with whom Allah was angry; they are hopeless of *success* in the Hereafter, just like the disbelievers are hopeless about the dead people in the graves.

61. Surat As-Saff

The Rows

This short Madinan surat motivates the believers to be brave: to practice what they say, and not be like the hypocrites who say one thing and do another. It encourages them to stand up for justice when called to do so, and not to shy away from the momentous responsibility of defending the truth. The hypocrites who had deserted the Muslims in the battle of Uhud are reprimanded.

The central theme of the surat is to encourage Muslims to keep their word; a unity between professed faith and practical life. The believers are warned of the vicious intentions of the Makkan disbelievers to extinguish Allah's light. However, Allah promises that Islam's light will prevail and spread. There is nothing that the disbelievers can do to stop this religion of truth being triumphant. A Divine promise and good news of victory to encourage them to continue with the struggle in Allah's path. Naturally, the Prophet was disheartened by the hypocrites' actions, but the Quran comforted him by giving examples of two great Prophets: Musa and Isa, who were similarly let down.

By giving the example of Musa عليه السلام and Isa عليه السلام, the surat challenges Jews and Christians to examine their heritage and conscience: their prophets had already predicted the coming of Muhammad ﷺ as the final Messenger. In the Gospel of John 14: 15, Jesus speaks to the Disciples and tells them, "If you love me keep my commands, and I will ask the Father to give you another advocate to help you and be with you forever." Who was this advocate? We believe it is our beloved Prophet Muhammad ﷺ.

The next section gives a method of achieving salvation: faith and Jihad, firm belief in Allah and His Messenger ﷺ, and practical and persistent efforts to obey them. Those who do so are honoured with the title, "the helpers of Allah."

اَيَاتُهَا ۱۴ (۶۱) سُوْرَةُ الصَّفِّ مَدَنِيَّةٌ (۱۰۹) رُكُوْعَاتُهَا ۲

بِسْمِ اللّٰهِ الرَّحْمٰنِ الرَّحِيْمِ

سَبَّحَ لِلّٰهِ مَا فِى السَّمٰوٰتِ وَمَا فِى الْاَرْضِ ۚ وَهُوَ الْعَزِيْزُ الْحَكِيْمُ ۝ يٰٓاَيُّهَا الَّذِيْنَ اٰمَنُوْا لِمَ تَقُوْلُوْنَ مَا لَا تَفْعَلُوْنَ ۝ كَبُرَ مَقْتًا عِنْدَ اللّٰهِ اَنْ تَقُوْلُوْا مَا لَا تَفْعَلُوْنَ ۝ اِنَّ اللّٰهَ يُحِبُّ الَّذِيْنَ يُقَاتِلُوْنَ فِى سَبِيْلِهٖ صَفًّا كَاَنَّهُمْ بُنْيَانٌ مَّرْصُوْصٌ ۝ وَاِذْ قَالَ مُوْسٰى لِقَوْمِهٖ يٰقَوْمِ لِمَ تُؤْذُوْنَنِيْ وَقَدْ تَّعْلَمُوْنَ اَنِّيْ رَسُوْلُ اللّٰهِ اِلَيْكُمْ ۚ فَلَمَّا زَاغُوْٓا اَزَاغَ اللّٰهُ قُلُوْبَهُمْ ۚ وَاللّٰهُ لَا يَهْدِى الْقَوْمَ الْفٰسِقِيْنَ ۝ وَاِذْ قَالَ عِيْسَى ابْنُ مَرْيَمَ يٰبَنِيْٓ اِسْرَآءِيْلَ اِنِّيْ رَسُوْلُ اللّٰهِ اِلَيْكُمْ مُّصَدِّقًا لِّمَا بَيْنَ يَدَيَّ مِنَ التَّوْرٰىةِ وَمُبَشِّرًا بِرَسُوْلٍ يَّاْتِيْ مِنْ بَعْدِى اسْمُهٗٓ اَحْمَدُ ۚ فَلَمَّا جَآءَهُمْ بِالْبَيِّنٰتِ قَالُوْا هٰذَا سِحْرٌ مُّبِيْنٌ ۝ وَمَنْ اَظْلَمُ مِمَّنِ افْتَرٰى عَلَى اللّٰهِ الْكَذِبَ وَهُوَ يُدْعٰىٓ اِلَى الْاِسْلَامِ ۚ وَاللّٰهُ لَا يَهْدِى الْقَوْمَ الظّٰلِمِيْنَ ۝ يُرِيْدُوْنَ لِيُطْفِئُوْا نُوْرَ اللّٰهِ بِاَفْوَاهِهِمْ ۚ وَاللّٰهُ مُتِمُّ نُوْرِهٖ وَلَوْ كَرِهَ الْكٰفِرُوْنَ ۝ هُوَ الَّذِيْٓ اَرْسَلَ رَسُوْلَهٗ بِالْهُدٰى وَدِيْنِ الْحَقِّ لِيُظْهِرَهٗ عَلَى الدِّيْنِ كُلِّهٖ ۙ وَلَوْ كَرِهَ الْمُشْرِكُوْنَ ۝ يٰٓاَيُّهَا الَّذِيْنَ

Practice what you preach: this is a sign of strong character. Do you tell just others to do good and forget yourself?

ع
۹

In the name of Allah, the Kind, the Caring.

Do as you say

[1] All things in the Heavens and the Earth glorify Allah, He is the Almighty, the Wise. [2] Believers, why do you say things that you don't do? [3] It's disliked by Allah that you say things that you don't do. [4] Allah loves the ones who fight in His way in rows upon rows, *standing* like a solid building.

Denouncing hypocrites who offended Messengers

[5] Remember when Musa said to his people, "My people, why do you insult me? Yet you know I am the messenger of Allah *sent* to you." When they deviated from the path, Allah lets them go astray[a]. Allah doesn't guide the sinful people. [6] Also remember when Isa, son of Maryam, said, "Israelites, I am Allah's messenger *sent* to you confirming the Torah that you already have, and I give you good news of a messenger who will come after me; his name will be Ahmad." Isa showed them clear signs, but they said, "This is wizardry."

The truth of Allah's religion will prevail

[7] Who can be more wicked than the one who invents lies against Allah, whilst he is invited to embrace Islam? Allah doesn't guide the wrongdoers. [8] They want to extinguish Allah's light with their propaganda, but Allah will spread His light everywhere,[b] no matter how much the disbelievers dislike it. [9] He is the One Who sent His Messenger with guidance and the religion of truth, so it will prevail over other religions, no matter how much the idolaters dislike it.

---

[a] Literally this means, "Allah led their hearts astray."
[b] Literally this means, "will complete or perfect."

اٰمَنُوْا هَلْ اَدُلُّكُمْ عَلٰى تِجَارَةٍ تُنْجِيْكُمْ مِّنْ عَذَابٍ اَلِيْمٍ ۝ تُؤْمِنُوْنَ بِاللهِ وَرَسُوْلِهٖ وَتُجَاهِدُوْنَ فِيْ سَبِيْلِ اللهِ بِاَمْوَالِكُمْ وَ اَنْفُسِكُمْ ۭ ذٰلِكُمْ خَيْرٌ لَّكُمْ اِنْ كُنْتُمْ تَعْلَمُوْنَ ۝ يَغْفِرْ لَكُمْ ذُنُوْبَكُمْ وَ يُدْخِلْكُمْ جَنّٰتٍ تَجْرِيْ مِنْ تَحْتِهَا الْاَنْهٰرُ وَمَسٰكِنَ طَيِّبَةً فِيْ جَنّٰتِ عَدْنٍ ۭ ذٰلِكَ الْفَوْزُ الْعَظِيْمُ ۝ وَ اُخْرٰى تُحِبُّوْنَهَا ۭ نَصْرٌ مِّنَ اللهِ وَفَتْحٌ قَرِيْبٌ ۭ وَ بَشِّرِ الْمُؤْمِنِيْنَ ۝ يٰٓاَيُّهَا الَّذِيْنَ اٰمَنُوْا كُوْنُوْٓا اَنْصَارَ اللهِ كَمَا قَالَ عِيْسَى ابْنُ مَرْيَمَ لِلْحَوَارِيّٖنَ مَنْ اَنْصَارِيْٓ اِلَى اللهِ ۭ قَالَ الْحَوَارِيُّوْنَ نَحْنُ اَنْصَارُ اللهِ فَاٰمَنَتْ طَّآئِفَةٌ مِّنْۢ بَنِيْٓ اِسْرَآءِيْلَ وَ كَفَرَتْ طَّآئِفَةٌ ۚ فَاَيَّدْنَا الَّذِيْنَ اٰمَنُوْا عَلٰى عَدُوِّهِمْ فَاَصْبَحُوْا ظٰهِرِيْنَ ۝

Faith is the most valuable bargain you can get – so value it.

Success lies in faith and action

¹⁰Believers, shall I show you a course of action[a] that will save you from a painful punishment? ¹¹*It is:* you believe in Allah and His Messenger, and strive in His path with your wealth and lives. This is good for you. ¹²Allah will forgive your sins and take you into gardens beneath which rivers flow, and into wonderful mansions in the gardens of Eden. That is the greatest achievement. ¹³*You will also get* something else that you dearly love: help from Allah and a speedy victory. Give good news to the believers.

Believers are urged to become helpers of Allah

¹⁴Believers, become helpers of Allah, like Isa son of Maryam invited his disciples: "Who will be my helper for Allah's sake?" The disciples replied, "We are Allah's helpers." So, one group of the Israelites believed and another denied. We helped the believers against their enemies, so they prevailed over them.

---

a   *Tijara* literally means "business, commerce, bargain and transaction".

62. Surat Al-Jumuʿah

The Day of Congregation

This is a Madinan surat, revealed after the Treaty of Hudaibiyah in the sixth year after Hijra. It opens with the glorification of Allah and four important roles of the Prophet ﷺ: teaching; recitation of the verses of the Quran; purification and development of the character of his followers; and explaining the Book with wisdom. The Arabs are referred to as "*Ummiyeen*," unlettered people, as opposed to the literate Jews and Christians who were People of Scripture. The Quran is critical of the Jewish Rabbis who regarded themselves above others because they were literate, People of The Book, and the children of prophets. The question is, what is the point of being literate if you don't read and follow the instructions of the Torah. This is not merely a criticism of the Rabbis of Madinah, but a clear message to Muslims: if you don't read and follow the message of the Quran, you are like "a donkey carrying books."

The central theme of the surat is the importance of the Friday prayer, a way of glorifying Allah. It was revealed to reprimand those people who had rushed out during the Friday sermon when they saw a caravan carrying grain arrive in Madinah. The surat urges Muslims to attend the Friday prayer promptly. "*Fasʿaw*" means running; the use of it here imparts a sense of urgency and importance to the call for prayer, stressing the significance of the weekly learning time, the sermon. The Friday prayer is not only devotion, but an important socio-political gathering where the leader of the community addresses the congregation. The tone of this passage makes clear that a true believer will always give precedence to worship of Allah over worldly things. The Prophet ﷺ said:

"When one of you takes a bath on Friday, brushes their teeth, wears beautiful clothes, puts on perfume and then attends the Masjid and prays there until the Imam begins the sermon, all these things will be an atonement for his sins from the previous to this Friday". (Abu Dawud)

بِسْمِ اللَّهِ الرَّحْمٰنِ الرَّحِيمِ

يُسَبِّحُ لِلَّهِ مَا فِى السَّمٰوٰتِ وَمَا فِى الْأَرْضِ الْمَلِكِ الْقُدُّوسِ الْعَزِيزِ الْحَكِيمِ ١ هُوَ الَّذِى بَعَثَ فِى الْأُمِّيِّنَ رَسُولًا مِنْهُمْ يَتْلُوا عَلَيْهِمْ اٰيٰتِهِ وَ يُزَكِّيهِمْ وَ يُعَلِّمُهُمُ الْكِتٰبَ وَالْحِكْمَةَ وَ اِنْ كَانُوا مِنْ قَبْلُ لَفِى ضَلٰلٍ مُبِينٍ ٢ وَّاٰخَرِينَ مِنْهُمْ لَمَّا يَلْحَقُوا بِهِمْ وَ هُوَ الْعَزِيزُ الْحَكِيمُ ٣ ذٰلِكَ فَضْلُ اللَّهِ يُؤْتِيهِ مَنْ يَّشَاءُ وَاللَّهُ ذُو الْفَضْلِ الْعَظِيمِ ٤ مَثَلُ الَّذِينَ حُمِّلُوا التَّوْرٰةَ ثُمَّ لَمْ يَحْمِلُوهَا كَمَثَلِ الْحِمَارِ يَحْمِلُ أَسْفَارًا بِئْسَ مَثَلُ الْقَوْمِ الَّذِينَ كَذَّبُوا بِاٰيٰتِ اللَّهِ وَاللَّهُ لَا يَهْدِى الْقَوْمَ الظّٰلِمِينَ ٥ قُلْ يٰأَيُّهَا الَّذِينَ هَادُوا اِنْ زَعَمْتُمْ أَنَّكُمْ أَوْلِيَاءُ لِلَّهِ مِنْ دُونِ النَّاسِ فَتَمَنَّوُا الْمَوْتَ اِنْ كُنْتُمْ صٰدِقِينَ ٦ وَ لَا يَتَمَنَّوْنَهُ أَبَدًا بِمَا قَدَّمَتْ أَيْدِيهِمْ وَاللَّهُ عَلِيمٌ بِالظّٰلِمِينَ ٧ قُلْ اِنَّ الْمَوْتَ الَّذِى تَفِرُّونَ مِنْهُ فَاِنَّهُ مُلٰقِيكُمْ ثُمَّ تُرَدُّونَ اِلٰى عٰلِمِ الْغَيْبِ وَالشَّهَادَةِ فَيُنَبِّئُكُمْ بِمَا كُنْتُمْ تَعْمَلُونَ ٨ يٰأَيُّهَا الَّذِينَ اٰمَنُوا اِذَا نُودِىَ لِلصَّلٰوةِ مِنْ يَّوْمِ الْجُمُعَةِ فَاسْعَوْا اِلٰى ذِكْرِ اللَّهِ وَ ذَرُوا

Knowledge and wisdom are taught by the Messenger ﷺ but must be practised, not merely for learning.

In the name of Allah, the Kind, the Caring.

The Messenger's ﷺ responsibility to unite humanity

¹ All things in the Heavens and the Earth glorify Allah, the Sovereign, the Holy, the Almighty, the Wise. ² He sent a Messenger to the unlettered people. He recites His verses to them, purifies them, teaches them the Book and the wisdom. Before that they were misguided. ³ *He has been sent* to them and others[a] who haven't yet joined them, and He is the Almighty, the Wise. ⁴ That is Allah's grace;[b] He gives it to whom He pleases, and Allah possesses immense grace.

Act on the teachings of Allah's Books

⁵ *Look at* the example of the people who were burdened with the Torah but didn't practise its *teachings; they* are like a donkey carrying books. Shameful is the example of the people who deny Allah's revelations. Allah doesn't guide the wrongdoers. ⁶ Say: "Israelites, if you claim sincerely that you alone out of all the people are the friends of Allah, then you should wish to die." ⁷ But they will never wish death, because what their hands have sent before, and Allah knows the wrongdoers. ⁸ Say: "The death you are running away from will soon catch up with you, and you will be returned to the One Who knows the seen and the unseen. Then He will inform you of what you did."

The Friday prayer is a compulsory weekly assembly

⁹ Believers, when the call for the prayer is made on Friday, come hurriedly to Allah's remembrance and stop all work.[c] That certainly is good for you.

---

a   "Others" refers to all non-Arabs (Ibn Kathir); the Messenger ﷺ came to unite all humanity.

b   *Fadhl* in Arabic means grace, undeserved, unearned and unmerited reward.

c   This verse makes Friday prayer compulsory for all believers. However, there are some exemptions to this: women, travellers and the sick. The *Dhikr-Allah* here is interpreted as the Friday sermon, not the usual remembrance.

البَيْعُ ط ذٰلِكُمْ خَيْرٌ لَّكُمْ اِنْ كُنْتُمْ تَعْلَمُوْنَ ۞ فَاِذَا

قُضِيَتِ الصَّلٰوةُ فَانْتَشِرُوْا فِى الْاَرْضِ وَابْتَغُوْا

مِنْ فَضْلِ اللهِ وَاذْكُرُوا اللهَ كَثِيْرًا لَّعَلَّكُمْ

تُفْلِحُوْنَ ۞ وَ اِذَا رَاَوْا تِجَارَةً اَوْ لَهْوَاۨ انْفَضُّوْٓا

اِلَيْهَا وَتَرَكُوْكَ قَآئِمًا ط قُلْ مَا عِنْدَ اللهِ خَيْرٌ مِّنَ

اللَّهْوِ وَمِنَ التِّجَارَةِ ط وَاللهُ خَيْرُ الرّٰزِقِيْنَ ۞

The Friday prayer is the making of a believer; the Messenger ﷺ said: 'whoever misses three Friday prayers is not from us!'

¹⁰ When the prayer is finished, then disperse in the city, seeking Allah's grace, and frequently remember Allah so you may be successful. ¹¹ When they saw a *commercial* bargain or entertainment, they rushed towards it and left you standing. Tell them: "What Allah has is far better than the entertainment and the bargain." Allah is the Best Provider.

63. Surat Al-Munafiqun

The Hypocrites

This surat was revealed in Madinah after the campaign of Banu Mustalaq in the sixth year of Hijra. It is a commentary on an incident that took place after this campaign. The Muslims were camped in an oasis near a well. A fight between two men broke out. One of them called out: 'Ansar! Come to my help!' The other called out: 'Emigrants! Come to my help!' Both sides responded, swords were drawn out and a battle about to follow. The Prophet ﷺ rushed to the site and cautioned them: "Why have you started shouting the slogans of the Age of Ignorance? After embracing Islam, this is criminal behaviour." The Prophet ﷺ calmed the belligerents, and everyone dispersed. However, the hypocrites were annoyed by this. They were jealous of Muslim unity and began to scheme. Abdullah ibn Ubayy, the leader of the hypocrites stated: "When we get back to Madinah, the strong will expel the weak," meaning his forces were the strong, and would expel "the weak" Muslims. Some Muslims heard this insulting threat, the Helpers in particular were furious. They went to Abdullah ibn Ubayy and asked him to retract his words and apologise to the Messenger ﷺ. Instead, he responded angrily: "You told me to believe in him, so I believed in him. You said pay Zakat and I donated money. What do you want me to do now – prostrate before him?" When he approached Madinah, his son stood tall with his sword drawn out in front of his father, and stopped him from entering. He swore an oath: "I will not let you enter Madinah until the Messenger ﷺ allows you." Upon hearing this, the Prophet ﷺ said, "Let him enter Madinah."

The Muslims are warned about the appalling behaviour of the hypocrites, their insults, betrayals and plots to create conflict among Muslims. Hypocrisy is vehemently condemned in the Quran on numerous occasions, because it smacks of an unprincipled attitude, indecisiveness and disloyalty. The final section of the surat provides a powerful antidote to hypocrisy: give charity, and seek closeness to the Divine before time passes away.

۞ آیاتها ۱۱ ۞ (۲۳) سُوْرَةُ الْمُنٰفِقُوْنَ مَدَنِیَّةٌ (۱۰۴) ۞ رُكُوْعَاتُها ۲ ۞

بِسْمِ اللَّهِ الرَّحْمٰنِ الرَّحِيمِ

اِذَا جَآءَكَ الْمُنٰفِقُوْنَ قَالُوْا نَشْهَدُ اِنَّكَ لَرَسُوْلُ اللَّهِ ؕ

وَاللَّهُ يَعْلَمُ اِنَّكَ لَرَسُوْلُهُ ؕ وَاللَّهُ يَشْهَدُ اِنَّ

الْمُنٰفِقِيْنَ لَكٰذِبُوْنَ ۙ اِتَّخَذُوْۤا اَيْمَانَهُمْ جُنَّةً

فَصَدُّوْا عَنْ سَبِيْلِ اللَّهِ ؕ اِنَّهُمْ سَآءَ مَا كَانُوْا

يَعْمَلُوْنَ ۞ ذٰلِكَ بِاَنَّهُمْ اٰمَنُوْا ثُمَّ كَفَرُوْا فَطُبِعَ عَلٰى

قُلُوْبِهِمْ فَهُمْ لَا يَفْقَهُوْنَ ۞ وَاِذَا رَاَيْتَهُمْ تُعْجِبُكَ

اَجْسَامُهُمْ ؕ وَاِنْ يَّقُوْلُوْا تَسْمَعْ لِقَوْلِهِمْ ؕ كَاَنَّهُمْ

خُشُبٌ مُّسَنَّدَةٌ ؕ يَحْسَبُوْنَ كُلَّ صَيْحَةٍ عَلَيْهِمْ ؕ هُمُ

الْعَدُوُّ فَاحْذَرْهُمْ ؕ قَاتَلَهُمُ اللَّهُ ۫ اَنّٰى يُؤْفَكُوْنَ ۞

وَاِذَا قِيْلَ لَهُمْ تَعَالَوْا يَسْتَغْفِرْ لَكُمْ رَسُوْلُ اللَّهِ

لَوَّوْا رُءُوْسَهُمْ وَرَاَيْتَهُمْ يَصُدُّوْنَ وَهُمْ مُّسْتَكْبِرُوْنَ۞

سَوَآءٌ عَلَيْهِمْ اَسْتَغْفَرْتَ لَهُمْ اَمْ لَمْ تَسْتَغْفِرْ لَهُمْ ؕ

لَنْ يَّغْفِرَ اللَّهُ لَهُمْ ؕ اِنَّ اللَّهَ لَا يَهْدِى الْقَوْمَ

الْفٰسِقِيْنَ ۞ هُمُ الَّذِيْنَ يَقُوْلُوْنَ لَا تُنْفِقُوْا عَلٰى

مَنْ عِنْدَ رَسُوْلِ اللَّهِ حَتّٰى يَنْفَضُّوْا ؕ وَلِلّٰهِ خَزَآئِنُ

السَّمٰوٰتِ وَالْاَرْضِ وَلٰكِنَّ الْمُنٰفِقِيْنَ لَا يَفْقَهُوْنَ ۞

يَقُوْلُوْنَ لَئِنْ رَّجَعْنَاۤ اِلَى الْمَدِيْنَةِ لَيُخْرِجَنَّ

الْاَعَزُّ مِنْهَا الْاَذَلَّ ؕ وَلِلّٰهِ الْعِزَّةُ وَلِرَسُوْلِهٖ وَ

Hypocrisy is the disease of mind; it creates doubts, fear, suspicions and mistrust – bordering on insanity. So, keep away from the hypocrites.

In the name of Allah, the Kind, the Caring.

The contradictory beliefs and behaviour of the hypocrites

¹When the hypocrites come to you they say, "We bear witness you are truly the Messenger of Allah." *Of course,* Allah knows you are His Messenger, and Allah bears witness that the hypocrites are the liars. ²They take their oaths as a shield, then they stop others from *coming to the* path of Allah. What they are doing is evil. ³*First* they believed, then they denied, therefore their hearts are sealed so they *no longer* understand. ⁴When you see them their outward appearances please you, when they speak, you listen to them, but *in reality,* they are like propped-up wooden posts. They think any outcry is against them. They are the enemy, so be careful of them. May Allah destroy them; they are utterly lost!

The hypocrites are arrogant and mischievous

⁵When it is said to them, "Come so the Messenger of Allah so he may ask forgiveness for you," they shake their heads and you see them turn away arrogantly. ⁶Whether you seek forgiveness for them or not it is the same; Allah will not forgive them. Indeed, Allah does not guide disobedient people. ⁷They say, "Don't spend on those who are with the Messenger of Allah until they leave *him.*" The treasures of the Heavens and the Earth belong to Allah, but the hypocrites don't understand. ⁸They claim: "When we return to Madinah, the strong will expel the weak." All strength belongs to Allah, His Messenger and the believers, but the hypocrites don't understand *this.*

The antidote for hypocrisy: Charity! Spend in the way of Allah for others.

لِلْمُؤْمِنِيْنَ وَلٰكِنَّ الْمُنٰفِقِيْنَ لَا يَعْلَمُوْنَ ۝ يٰۤاَيُّهَا

الَّذِيْنَ اٰمَنُوْا لَا تُلْهِكُمْ اَمْوَالُكُمْ وَلَاۤ اَوْلَادُكُمْ

عَنْ ذِكْرِ اللهِۚ وَمَنْ يَّفْعَلْ ذٰلِكَ فَاُولٰٓئِكَ هُمُ

الْخٰسِرُوْنَ ۝ وَاَنْفِقُوْا مِنْ مَّا رَزَقْنٰكُمْ مِّنْ قَبْلِ

اَنْ يَّاْتِيَ اَحَدَكُمُ الْمَوْتُ فَيَقُوْلَ رَبِّ لَوْلَاۤ

اَخَّرْتَنِيْۤ اِلٰۤى اَجَلٍ قَرِيْبٍ فَاَصَّدَّقَ وَاَكُنْ مِّنَ

الصّٰلِحِيْنَ ۝ وَلَنْ يُّؤَخِّرَ اللهُ نَفْسًا اِذَا جَاۤءَ اَجَلُهَاؕ

وَاللهُ خَبِيْرٌۢ بِمَا تَعْمَلُوْنَ ۝

1161

The antidote to hypocrisy: give charity

⁹Believers, don't let your wealth and children turn you away from the remembrance of Allah; those who do so are the losers. ¹⁰Spend from the provisions We gave you before death comes, and you say, "My Lord, if you delay my death for a little while I will *go and* spend in charity and become righteous." ¹¹Allah won't delay death for anyone once its time has come. Allah is aware of what you do.

64. Surat At-Taghabun

The Gain and Loss

The central theme of this Madinan surat are Islamic beliefs, especially the life Hereafter. The majesty and grandeur of Allah's power opens the surat. It points out the benefits of faith: believers will be successful, whilst disbelievers will be ruined, as is apparent in the fates of past generations. The believers are directed to carry out duties that will lead them to success: being charitable, obedient and ever mindful of Allah. It also warns how wealth, spouses and children can be a temptation that can lead to breaking Divine laws: "Whoever can save themselves from greed, then those are the successful ones" (16).

Al-Taghabun means mutual loss and cheating. Perhaps the former translation refers to the sense of loss that the disbelievers will feel when they are deprived of Paradise, and some believers also may feel upon realising that they could have worked harder for the Hereafter. The latter meaning, cheating, is also implied. The noun *ghibn* means, "to take something without paying its price." In other words, to cheat.[a] So the world and its trappings cheat those who pour themselves into it, but get nothing in return.

---

[a] M.A. Sabuni, *Safwat al-Tafsir*.

بِسْمِ اللّٰهِ الرَّحْمٰنِ الرَّحِيْمِ

يُسَبِّحُ لِلّٰهِ مَا فِي السَّمٰوٰتِ وَمَا فِي الْاَرْضِ ۚ لَهُ الْمُلْكُ وَلَهُ الْحَمْدُ ۫ وَهُوَ عَلٰى كُلِّ شَيْءٍ قَدِيْرٌ ۝ هُوَ الَّذِيْ خَلَقَكُمْ فَمِنْكُمْ كَافِرٌ وَّمِنْكُمْ مُّؤْمِنٌ ۗ وَاللّٰهُ بِمَا تَعْمَلُوْنَ بَصِيْرٌ ۝ خَلَقَ السَّمٰوٰتِ وَالْاَرْضَ بِالْحَقِّ وَصَوَّرَكُمْ فَاَحْسَنَ صُوَرَكُمْ ۚ وَاِلَيْهِ الْمَصِيْرُ ۝ يَعْلَمُ مَا فِي السَّمٰوٰتِ وَالْاَرْضِ وَيَعْلَمُ مَا تُسِرُّوْنَ وَمَا تُعْلِنُوْنَ ۗ وَاللّٰهُ عَلِيْمٌ بِذَاتِ الصُّدُوْرِ ۝ اَلَمْ يَاْتِكُمْ نَبَؤُا الَّذِيْنَ كَفَرُوْا مِنْ قَبْلُ ۫ فَذَاقُوْا وَبَالَ اَمْرِهِمْ وَلَهُمْ عَذَابٌ اَلِيْمٌ ۝ ذٰلِكَ بِاَنَّهُ كَانَتْ تَّاْتِيْهِمْ رُسُلُهُمْ بِالْبَيِّنٰتِ فَقَالُوْا اَبَشَرٌ يَّهْدُوْنَنَا ۫ فَكَفَرُوْا وَتَوَلَّوْا وَّاسْتَغْنَى اللّٰهُ ۗ وَاللّٰهُ غَنِيٌّ حَمِيْدٌ ۝ زَعَمَ الَّذِيْنَ كَفَرُوْا اَنْ لَّنْ يُّبْعَثُوْا ۗ قُلْ بَلٰى وَرَبِّيْ لَتُبْعَثُنَّ ثُمَّ لَتُنَبَّؤُنَّ بِمَا عَمِلْتُمْ ۗ وَذٰلِكَ عَلَى اللّٰهِ يَسِيْرٌ ۝ فَاٰمِنُوْا بِاللّٰهِ وَرَسُوْلِهِ وَالنُّوْرِ الَّذِيْ اَنْزَلْنَا ۗ وَاللّٰهُ بِمَا تَعْمَلُوْنَ خَبِيْرٌ ۝ يَوْمَ يَجْمَعُكُمْ لِيَوْمِ الْجَمْعِ ذٰلِكَ يَوْمُ التَّغَابُنِ ۗ وَمَنْ يُّؤْمِنْ بِاللّٰهِ وَيَعْمَلْ صَالِحًا يُّكَفِّرْ عَنْهُ سَيِّاٰتِهِ

Allah created beautiful humans, both outwardly and inwardly, but they fail to see that. Do you appreciate your beauty?

1165

In the name of Allah, the Kind, the Caring.

Human creation has a purpose

¹ All things in the Heavens and the Earth glorify Allah. He rules over all things and all praise is for Him. He has control over all things. ² He is the One Who created you; but some of you chose to be disbelievers, and others choose to be believers, and Allah sees what you do. ³ He created the Heavens and the Earth for a true purpose and shaped you, then He perfected your forms, and to Him is the final return. ⁴ He knows what is in the Heavens and the Earth, and He knows what you conceal and what you reveal. Allah knows what lies in *people's* minds.

The life of the Hereafter is humanity's final destination

⁵ Hasn't the news of the disbelievers of the past reached you? They tasted the consequences of their deeds, and for them is a painful punishment. ⁶ That was because when their messengers with miracles used to come to them, they *disapprovingly* said, "How can *mere* humans guide us?" So, they denied and turned away. Allah has no need of them. Allah is Independent and Praiseworthy. ⁷ The disbelievers claimed they will not be resurrected; say *to them*: "Of course My Lord will resurrect you, and then you will be told what you did." That is easy for Allah. ⁸ So believe in Allah and His Messenger, and the light that We have sent down. Allah is aware of what you do.

Some will gain, others will face loss on Judgement Day

⁹ He will assemble you on the Day of Gathering, that's the Day of gain and loss. Whoever believed in Allah and did righteous deeds, He will erase his sins and take him into gardens with rivers flowing beneath them, to live there forever – the great success.

وَيُدْخِلْهُ جَنّٰتٍ تَجْرِيْ مِنْ تَحْتِهَا الْاَنْهٰرُ
خٰلِدِيْنَ فِيْهَا اَبَدًا ۗ ذٰلِكَ الْفَوْزُ الْعَظِيْمُ ۹ وَ
الَّذِيْنَ كَفَرُوْا وَكَذَّبُوْا بِاٰيٰتِنَا اُولٰٓئِكَ اَصْحٰبُ
النَّارِ خٰلِدِيْنَ فِيْهَا ۗ وَبِئْسَ الْمَصِيْرُ ۱۰ مَآ اَصَابَ
مِنْ مُّصِيْبَةٍ اِلَّا بِاِذْنِ اللّٰهِ ۗ وَمَنْ يُّؤْمِنْ بِاللّٰهِ
يَهْدِ قَلْبَهٗ ۗ وَاللّٰهُ بِكُلِّ شَيْءٍ عَلِيْمٌ ۱۱ وَاَطِيْعُوا
اللّٰهَ وَاَطِيْعُوا الرَّسُوْلَ ۚ فَاِنْ تَوَلَّيْتُمْ فَاِنَّمَا عَلٰى
رَسُوْلِنَا الْبَلٰغُ الْمُبِيْنُ ۱۲ اَللّٰهُ لَاۤ اِلٰهَ اِلَّا هُوَ ۗ وَ
عَلَى اللّٰهِ فَلْيَتَوَكَّلِ الْمُؤْمِنُوْنَ ۱۳ يٰۤاَيُّهَا الَّذِيْنَ
اٰمَنُوْۤا اِنَّ مِنْ اَزْوَاجِكُمْ وَاَوْلَادِكُمْ عَدُوًّا لَّكُمْ
فَاحْذَرُوْهُمْ ۚ وَاِنْ تَعْفُوْا وَتَصْفَحُوْا وَتَغْفِرُوْا
فَاِنَّ اللّٰهَ غَفُوْرٌ رَّحِيْمٌ ۱۴ اِنَّمَاۤ اَمْوَالُكُمْ وَ
اَوْلَادُكُمْ فِتْنَةٌ ۗ وَاللّٰهُ عِنْدَهٗۤ اَجْرٌ عَظِيْمٌ ۱۵
فَاتَّقُوا اللّٰهَ مَا اسْتَطَعْتُمْ وَاسْمَعُوْا وَاَطِيْعُوْا
وَاَنْفِقُوْا خَيْرًا لِّاَنْفُسِكُمْ ۗ وَمَنْ يُّوْقَ شُحَّ
نَفْسِهٖ فَاُولٰٓئِكَ هُمُ الْمُفْلِحُوْنَ ۱۶ اِنْ تُقْرِضُوا
اللّٰهَ قَرْضًا حَسَنًا يُّضٰعِفْهُ لَكُمْ وَيَغْفِرْ لَكُمْ ۗ
وَاللّٰهُ شَكُوْرٌ حَلِيْمٌ ۱۷ عٰلِمُ الْغَيْبِ وَالشَّهَادَةِ
الْعَزِيْزُ الْحَكِيْمُ ۱۸

The way to escape the quagmire and trapping of the world is to be selfless – not self-centred. Are you selfless or selfish?

¹⁰ But the ones who disbelieved and rejected our revelations, will be people of the Fire, to live therein forever. What an evil place!

How to avoid loss

¹¹ No misfortune befalls anyone except by the permission of Allah. Whoever believes in Allah, Allah will guide his heart, and Allah knows all things. ¹² *Therefore* obey Allah, and obey the Messenger; were you to turn away *you would lose,* since Our Messenger's responsibility is only to deliver the message clearly. ¹³ There is no god but Him, so let the believers put trust in Allah alone.

How to achieve success

¹⁴ Believers, some of your spouses and your children could be enemies, so beware of them! However, if you forgive, tolerate and pardon *their conduct* then *you will find* Allah too is Forgiving, Caring. ¹⁵ Your wealth and children are a test; with Allah is a great reward. ¹⁶ So be mindful of Allah as much as you can, and listen, obey, and give in charity; that is good for you. Whoever can save themselves from greed, then those are the successful ones. ¹⁷ If you lend Allah a beautiful loan, He will multiply it for you, and forgive you. Allah is Most Appreciative, Gentle, ¹⁸ Knower of the unseen world and the seen, the Almighty, the Wise.

65. Surat At-Talaq

The Divorce

This Madinan surat deals with the subject of divorce: proper method, prescribed waiting term, maintenance expense, the custody and breastfeeding of the child. It was revealed after *Surat Al-Baqarah's* passage on family law (222–242). The blessed Messenger ﷺ described divorce as, "the most abhorrent of permissible things" (Abu Dawud). Ali, the fourth caliph, said, "The Divine Throne trembles when someone gives divorce." Islam allows divorce only when life as husband and wife becomes unbearable and could lead to damaging welfare and the quality of life. The Islamic divorce as described here specifies that divorce should be given at the end of the menstruation period. Once the husband has given the notice of divorce to his wife, in the presence of two just witnesses, she must stay in her home and must not leave. This is not the end of the marriage. What happened during the heat of the moment in a state of anger may dissipate; reconciliation may occur. The prescribed waiting time of three menstruation periods is effectively a cooling-off period. This is the revocable divorce, and husband and wife can resume their marital life without a new wedding contract (*Nikah*) within the waiting term.

The divorce according to Shariah is a simple, straightforward, short and equitable procedure compared to the complicated , expensive and torturous procedure in other legal systems. It's good to notice how the recent changes in British Law are catching up with the Shariah.

Further rules for pregnant women are outlined: prohibiting divorce during pregnancy, the prescribed waiting term is the end of her pregnancy and the birth of the child. Every opportunity is being provided to help keep the family together, and several warnings are given: "Those are Allah's boundaries; whoever exceeds the boundaries of Allah has wronged himself" (1). People going through divorce are reminded, "Be mindful of Allah." He shall provide them a means out of this dreadful situation, and He will provide for them sustenance. The final section of the surat warns against disobeying Allah's commands. It cites the example of previous communities who disobeyed and were severely punished.

بِسْمِ اللّٰهِ الرَّحْمٰنِ الرَّحِيْمِ

يٰٓاَيُّهَا النَّبِيُّ اِذَا طَلَّقْتُمُ النِّسَآءَ فَطَلِّقُوْهُنَّ لِعِدَّتِهِنَّ وَاَحْصُوا الْعِدَّةَ ۚ وَاتَّقُوا اللّٰهَ رَبَّكُمْ ۚ لَا تُخْرِجُوْهُنَّ مِنْ بُيُوْتِهِنَّ وَلَا يَخْرُجْنَ اِلَّآ اَنْ يَّاْتِيْنَ بِفَاحِشَةٍ مُّبَيِّنَةٍ ۚ وَتِلْكَ حُدُوْدُ اللّٰهِ ۚ وَمَنْ يَّتَعَدَّ حُدُوْدَ اللّٰهِ فَقَدْ ظَلَمَ نَفْسَهٗ ۚ لَا تَدْرِيْ لَعَلَّ اللّٰهَ يُحْدِثُ بَعْدَ ذٰلِكَ اَمْرًا ۝ فَاِذَا بَلَغْنَ اَجَلَهُنَّ فَاَمْسِكُوْهُنَّ بِمَعْرُوْفٍ اَوْ فَارِقُوْهُنَّ بِمَعْرُوْفٍ وَّاَشْهِدُوْا ذَوَيْ عَدْلٍ مِّنْكُمْ وَاَقِيْمُوا الشَّهَادَةَ لِلّٰهِ ۚ ذٰلِكُمْ يُوْعَظُ بِهٖ مَنْ كَانَ يُؤْمِنُ بِاللّٰهِ وَالْيَوْمِ الْاٰخِرِ ۚ وَمَنْ يَّتَّقِ اللّٰهَ يَجْعَلْ لَّهٗ مَخْرَجًا ۙ ۝ وَّيَرْزُقْهُ مِنْ حَيْثُ لَا يَحْتَسِبُ ۚ وَمَنْ يَّتَوَكَّلْ عَلَى اللّٰهِ فَهُوَ حَسْبُهٗ ۚ اِنَّ اللّٰهَ بَالِغُ اَمْرِهٖ ۚ قَدْ جَعَلَ اللّٰهُ لِكُلِّ شَيْءٍ قَدْرًا ۝ وَالّٰٓئِيْ يَئِسْنَ مِنَ الْمَحِيْضِ مِنْ نِّسَآئِكُمْ اِنِ ارْتَبْتُمْ فَعِدَّتُهُنَّ ثَلٰثَةُ اَشْهُرٍ ۙ وَّالّٰٓئِيْ لَمْ يَحِضْنَ ۚ وَاُولَاتُ الْاَحْمَالِ اَجَلُهُنَّ اَنْ يَّضَعْنَ حَمْلَهُنَّ ۚ وَمَنْ يَّتَّقِ اللّٰهَ يَجْعَلْ لَّهٗ

Be mindful of Allah and be concerned for people; simply pay attention to them, worship Allah, and serve people.

In the name of Allah, the Kind, the Caring.

Safety measures when divorcing
¹Prophet, when someone *intends to* divorce a woman, let *him* divorce her at a time when their waiting term[a] can begin, and accurately count the waiting term. Fear Allah, your Lord. Do not drive them out of their houses, nor should they leave *by themselves* except if they had committed a shameless indecency. Those are Allah's boundaries; whoever exceeds the boundaries of Allah has wronged himself. You don't know what new circumstances Allah may bring about after that. ²So when they have completed their waiting term, you may keep them honourably, or let them go honourably. *On this occasion* appoint two just witnesses amongst you, and establish witnesses for the sake of Allah. A guidance *for* believers in Allah and the Final Day. Whoever is mindful of Allah, He shall make a way out for him, ³and provide him sustenance from where he wouldn't expect. Whoever puts trust in Allah is enough for him. Allah will complete His task. Allah has made a precise amount *of sustenance* for all things.

Rules about divorce during pregnancy
⁴Your older women in menopause should complete the *waiting* term of three months if you are in doubt. The same applies to those who aren't menstruating. The prescribed term for pregnant women is the end of their pregnancy. Whoever fears Allah, He will make his circumstances easy.

---

[a] *'Idda* is the legal waiting term. It is three menstruation periods, or the end of pregnancy, or three months and ten days for a widow.

مِنْ اَمْرِهٖ يُسْرًا ۞ ذٰلِكَ اَمْرُ اللّٰهِ اَنْزَلَهٗ

اِلَيْكُمْ ط وَمَنْ يَّتَّقِ اللّٰهَ يُكَفِّرْ عَنْهُ سَيِّاٰتِهٖ

وَيُعْظِمْ لَهٗ اَجْرًا ۞ اَسْكِنُوْهُنَّ مِنْ حَيْثُ

سَكَنْتُمْ مِّنْ وُّجْدِكُمْ وَلَا تُضَآرُّوْهُنَّ لِتُضَيِّقُوْا

عَلَيْهِنَّ ط وَاِنْ كُنَّ اُولَاتِ حَمْلٍ فَاَنْفِقُوْا عَلَيْهِنَّ

حَتّٰى يَضَعْنَ حَمْلَهُنَّ ۚ فَاِنْ اَرْضَعْنَ لَكُمْ فَاٰتُوْهُنَّ

اُجُوْرَهُنَّ ۚ وَاْتَمِرُوْا بَيْنَكُمْ بِمَعْرُوْفٍ ۚ وَاِنْ

تَعَاسَرْتُمْ فَسَتُرْضِعُ لَهٗۤ اُخْرٰى ۞ لِيُنْفِقْ ذُوْ سَعَةٍ

مِّنْ سَعَتِهٖ ط وَمَنْ قُدِرَ عَلَيْهِ رِزْقُهٗ فَلْيُنْفِقْ

مِمَّاۤ اٰتٰىهُ اللّٰهُ ط لَا يُكَلِّفُ اللّٰهُ نَفْسًا اِلَّا مَاۤ

اٰتٰىهَا ط سَيَجْعَلُ اللّٰهُ بَعْدَ عُسْرٍ يُّسْرًا ۞ وَكَاَيِّنْ

مِّنْ قَرْيَةٍ عَتَتْ عَنْ اَمْرِ رَبِّهَا وَرُسُلِهٖ

فَحَاسَبْنٰهَا حِسَابًا شَدِيْدًاۙ وَّعَذَّبْنٰهَا عَذَابًا

نُّكْرًا ۞ فَذَاقَتْ وَبَالَ اَمْرِهَا وَكَانَ عَاقِبَةُ

اَمْرِهَا خُسْرًا ۞ اَعَدَّ اللّٰهُ لَهُمْ عَذَابًا شَدِيْدًاۙ

فَاتَّقُوا اللّٰهَ يٰۤاُولِى الْاَلْبَابِ ۛۚۙ الَّذِيْنَ اٰمَنُوْا ط

قَدْ اَنْزَلَ اللّٰهُ اِلَيْكُمْ ذِكْرًاۙ ۞ رَّسُوْلًا يَّتْلُوْا

عَلَيْكُمْ اٰيٰتِ اللّٰهِ مُبَيِّنٰتٍ لِّيُخْرِجَ الَّذِيْنَ

اٰمَنُوْا وَعَمِلُوا الصّٰلِحٰتِ مِنَ الظُّلُمٰتِ

اِلَى النُّوْرِ ط وَمَنْ يُّؤْمِنْۢ بِاللّٰهِ وَيَعْمَلْ

١
ع
١٨

Even when severing the ties of a relationship like marriage, be aware and be thoughtful, don't be unfair and angry.

1173

⁵That is the command of Allah, which He has sent down to you. Whoever is mindful of Allah, He will forgive his evil deeds, and increase for him *his* reward. ⁶House them *during the waiting period* where you live, according to your *financial* means, and do not harass them in order to make their lives miserable. If they are pregnant, then spend *generously* on them until they have delivered the newborn. If they breastfeed *the child* for you, then give them a payment *for that*. Deal in a good way with each other. If you find yourselves in difficulty, then let another woman breastfeed the child for him.ᵃ ⁷Let the wealthy man spend according to his wealth, and let the one whose income is limited spend from what Allah has given him. Allah doesn't burden anyone except with what He has given him. Allah will soon make ease after hardship.

Severe punishment for those who disobey Allah's rules

⁸How many cities have rebelled against its Lord and His messengers' command? We sternly brought them to account, and severely punished them. ⁹So they tasted the evil effects of their disobedience, and their works finally came to nothing. ¹⁰Allah has prepared a severe punishment for them. So be mindful of Allah, understanding people who believe! Allah has sent down a reminder to you, ¹¹a Messenger who recites Allah's clear verses to you, to take those who believe and do good deeds out of the layers of darkness into the light. Whoever believes in Allah and does righteous deeds, He will admit him into gardens beneath which rivers flow; they will live therein forever. Allah has perfected for them *their* provisions.

ᵃ The time of childbirth marks the end of the prescribed waiting term for a divorced pregnant woman. She is now free to marry and therefore will be like a stranger to her former husband. It is the duty of the father to make the arrangements for the newborn; that is why she can negotiate in maintenance fees.

صَالِحًا يُّدْخِلْهُ جَنّٰتٍ تَجْرِىْ مِنْ تَحْتِهَا

الْاَنْهٰرُ خٰلِدِيْنَ فِيْهَآ اَبَدًا ۚ قَدْ اَحْسَنَ

اللّٰهُ لَهٗ رِزْقًا ۝ اَللّٰهُ الَّذِىْ خَلَقَ سَبْعَ

سَمٰوٰتٍ وَّ مِنَ الْاَرْضِ مِثْلَهُنَّ ۗ يَتَنَزَّلُ

الْاَمْرُ بَيْنَهُنَّ لِتَعْلَمُوْٓا اَنَّ اللّٰهَ عَلٰى كُلِّ

شَىْءٍ قَدِيْرٌ ۙ وَّ اَنَّ اللّٰهَ قَدْ اَحَاطَ بِكُلِّ

شَىْءٍ عِلْمًا ۝

Put trust in Allah; don't rely on others alone.

¹²Allah is the One Who created the seven Heavens and the Earth in a similar *number* to them. *His* commandments come down between them, so that you may come to know that Allah has control over all things, and that Allah's knowledge encompasses all things.

66. Surat At-Tahrim

The Prohibition

This Madinan surat was revealed in the eighth year of Hijra. There are differing reports surrounding the circumstances of its revelation. The most likely is the following story: One day, Zainab, the wife of the Prophet 🌸, offered him some honey. She knew he was very fond of it, and thoroughly enjoyed it. As a consequence, he spent extra time with her. Later that night, he 🌸 met Aisha, who felt upset and complained that his breath smelled of *Maghafir*, a wild tree on which bees feed. The Prophet 🌸 was disappointed, and promised to refrain from eating honey, and that they should keep this a secret. However, Aisha disclosed it to Hafsah.

Whatever the circumstances here, the Quran teaches five general principles: not to make unlawful that which Allah has made lawful; how to amend and atone for vows; not to betray trusts and give away secrets; the whole family should work together to save themselves from the Hellfire; and seeking repentance for sins committed intentionally or unintentionally.

The solution given for the human condition of sinning is *"Taubatan Nasuhan"* (8) – sincere and genuine repentance. This means regretting the sin, feeling ashamed of it, resolving not to repeat it, and then asking for Allah's forgiveness.

The wives of the Prophet 🌸 are gently reprimanded here for this marital tiff, a petty quarrel. They are asked to be more caring and considerate towards each other. There is possibly a warning implied in the mention of the wives of two other prophets, Nuh 🌸 and Lut 🌸: if they are to be disobedient and unmindful of Allah and the Messenger 🌸, they will be the losers like those two women. Finally, it gives them the example of two wonderful women; Asiya, the wife of the Pharaoh, and Maryam the Virgin 🌸, the mother of Isa 🌸.

بِسۡمِ اللَّهِ الرَّحۡمَٰنِ الرَّحِيمِ

يَٰٓأَيُّهَا النَّبِيُّ لِمَ تُحَرِّمُ مَآ أَحَلَّ اللَّهُ لَكَ

تَبۡتَغِي مَرۡضَاتَ أَزۡوَٰجِكَۚ وَاللَّهُ غَفُورٌ رَّحِيمٌ ١

قَدۡ فَرَضَ اللَّهُ لَكُمۡ تَحِلَّةَ أَيۡمَٰنِكُمۡۚ وَاللَّهُ

مَوۡلَىٰكُمۡۖ وَهُوَ الۡعَلِيمُ الۡحَكِيمُ ٢ وَإِذۡ أَسَرَّ

النَّبِيُّ إِلَىٰ بَعۡضِ أَزۡوَٰجِهِ حَدِيثࣰاۖ فَلَمَّا نَبَّأَتۡ

بِهِ وَأَظۡهَرَهُ اللَّهُ عَلَيۡهِ عَرَّفَ بَعۡضَهُ وَ

أَعۡرَضَ عَن بَعۡضࣲۖ فَلَمَّا نَبَّأَهَا بِهِ قَالَتۡ

مَنۡ أَنۢبَأَكَ هَٰذَاۖ قَالَ نَبَّأَنِيَ الۡعَلِيمُ الۡخَبِيرُ ٣

إِن تَتُوبَآ إِلَى اللَّهِ فَقَدۡ صَغَتۡ قُلُوبُكُمَاۖ

وَإِن تَظَٰهَرَا عَلَيۡهِ فَإِنَّ اللَّهَ هُوَ مَوۡلَىٰهُ

وَجِبۡرِيلُ وَصَٰلِحُ الۡمُؤۡمِنِينَۖ وَالۡمَلَٰٓئِكَةُ

بَعۡدَ ذَٰلِكَ ظَهِيرٌ ٤ عَسَىٰ رَبُّهُۥ إِن طَلَّقَكُنَّ

أَن يُبۡدِلَهُۥٓ أَزۡوَٰجًا خَيۡرࣰا مِّنكُنَّ مُسۡلِمَٰتࣲ

مُّؤۡمِنَٰتࣲ قَٰنِتَٰتࣲ تَٰٓئِبَٰتٍ عَٰبِدَٰتࣲ سَٰٓئِحَٰتࣲ

ثَيِّبَٰتࣲ وَأَبۡكَارࣰا ٥ يَٰٓأَيُّهَا الَّذِينَ ءَامَنُوا قُوٓا

أَنفُسَكُمۡ وَأَهۡلِيكُمۡ نَارࣰا وَقُودُهَا النَّاسُ

وَالۡحِجَارَةُ عَلَيۡهَا مَلَٰٓئِكَةٌ غِلَاظࣱ شِدَادࣱ

لَّا يَعۡصُونَ اللَّهَ مَآ أَمَرَهُمۡ وَيَفۡعَلُونَ مَا

Notice how careful the Messenger ﷺ was towards his wives? He didn't want to upset them.

In the name of Allah, the Kind, the Caring.

The importance of keeping secrets

¹Prophet, why do you – desiring to please your wives – avoidᵃ things that Allah has made lawful for you? Allah is Forgiving, Caring. ²Allah has ordered for you that you make up for your *unfulfilled* oaths. Allah is your Master; He is the Knower, the Wise. ³Remember when the Prophet shared a secret with one of his wives, and when she disclosed it *to another* Allah informed him about it; he confirmed part of it and kept the other secret. So when he informed her about this she said, "Who has told you this?" He replied, "The Knower, the Aware told me." ⁴Both of you *wives* should repent before Allah; your hearts have *already* inclined towards *seeking forgiveness*. Were you to assist one another against him, *remember* that Allah is his Protector, so is Jibreel; the righteous believers and *all* the angels after that are *his* helpers. ⁵Were he to divorce you, his Lord would give him better wives in your place, those who are submitting, believers, obedient, repentant, devout, fasting, and *some* previously married and *others* virgins.

The responsibility of saving one's family from Hellfire

⁶Believers, protect yourselves and your families from a fire whose fuel is humanity and *their* stone *idols*; *it will be* controlled by fierce, stern angels who don't disobey Allah in what He commands them to do, and they do what they are told to do.

ᵃ *Al-Tahreem* literally means "to prohibit and make unlawful". However, here it refers to the Prophet ﷺ avoiding eating honey, rather than regarding it as unlawful.

يُؤْمَرُوْنَ ۞ يٰٓاَيُّهَا الَّذِيْنَ كَفَرُوْا لَا تَعْتَذِرُوا

الْيَوْمَ ط اِنَّمَا تُجْزَوْنَ مَا كُنْتُمْ تَعْمَلُوْنَ ۞

يٰٓاَيُّهَا الَّذِيْنَ اٰمَنُوْا تُوْبُوْٓا اِلَى اللّٰهِ تَوْبَةً

نَّصُوْحًا ط عَسٰى رَبُّكُمْ اَنْ يُّكَفِّرَ عَنْكُمْ سَيِّاٰتِكُمْ

وَيُدْخِلَكُمْ جَنّٰتٍ تَجْرِيْ مِنْ تَحْتِهَا الْاَنْهٰرُ

يَوْمَ لَا يُخْزِى اللّٰهُ النَّبِيَّ وَالَّذِيْنَ اٰمَنُوْا

مَعَهٗ ۚ نُوْرُهُمْ يَسْعٰى بَيْنَ اَيْدِيْهِمْ وَ

بِاَيْمَانِهِمْ يَقُوْلُوْنَ رَبَّنَآ اَتْمِمْ لَنَا نُوْرَنَا

وَاغْفِرْ لَنَا ۚ اِنَّكَ عَلٰى كُلِّ شَيْءٍ قَدِيْرٌ ۞

The example of two: disobedient and loyal women; good humans and bad humans.

يٰٓاَيُّهَا النَّبِيُّ جَاهِدِ الْكُفَّارَ وَالْمُنٰفِقِيْنَ وَاغْلُظْ

عَلَيْهِمْ ط وَمَاْوٰىهُمْ جَهَنَّمُ ط وَبِئْسَ الْمَصِيْرُ ۞

ضَرَبَ اللّٰهُ مَثَلًا لِّلَّذِيْنَ كَفَرُوا امْرَاَتَ نُوْحٍ

وَّامْرَاَتَ لُوْطٍ ط كَانَتَا تَحْتَ عَبْدَيْنِ مِنْ

عِبَادِنَا صَالِحَيْنِ فَخَانَتٰهُمَا فَلَمْ يُغْنِيَا

عَنْهُمَا مِنَ اللّٰهِ شَيْئًا وَّقِيْلَ ادْخُلَا النَّارَ

مَعَ الدّٰخِلِيْنَ ۞ وَضَرَبَ اللّٰهُ مَثَلًا لِّلَّذِيْنَ

اٰمَنُوا امْرَاَتَ فِرْعَوْنَ ۘ اِذْ قَالَتْ رَبِّ ابْنِ لِيْ

عِنْدَكَ بَيْتًا فِى الْجَنَّةِ وَنَجِّنِيْ مِنْ فِرْعَوْنَ

وَعَمَلِهٖ وَنَجِّنِيْ مِنَ الْقَوْمِ الظّٰلِمِيْنَ ۞ وَ

مَرْيَمَ ابْنَتَ عِمْرٰنَ الَّتِيْٓ اَحْصَنَتْ فَرْجَهَا

7 Disbelievers, don't make excuses today; you will only be repaid for what you used to do. 8 Believers, turn to Allah in sincere repentance. Your Lord may forgive your sins, and admit you into gardens with rivers flowing beneath them, the Day that Allah will neither humiliate the Prophet nor those who believed. Their light will be beaming in front of them and on their right, and they will pray: "Our Lord, perfect our light for us and forgive us, You control all things."

The two disobedient wives

9 Prophet, strive against the disbelievers and the hypocrites, and deal with them firmly. Hell is their resting place; what a terrible home! 10 Allah gives an example to the disbelievers of the wife of *the Prophet* Nuh and the wife of *the Prophet* Lut; both *women* were married to two of our devout and righteous servants, but they betrayed them. *So* their husbands couldn't save them from Allah at all. It will be said, "Both of you enter into the Fire along, with the other entrants."

The example of two pious women

11 Allah gives an example to the believers of Pharaoh's wife, when she said, "My Lord, build for me a house near you in Paradise, and save me from Pharaoh and his works, and save me from the evildoers." 12 And *the second* example is of Maryam, the daughter of Imran, who protected her chastity, and We blew in her Our spirit, and she accepted the truth of Her Lord's Words and the Scriptures, and she was an obedient woman.

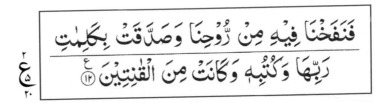

67. Surat Al-Mulk

The Control

The central theme of this surat is the purpose of life: an opportunity to earn Allah's pleasure, falling in love with Him, and doing good works. The surat points to a common failure to understand this simple fact, for which desperate regret will be felt on Judgement Day by the negligent: "If only we had listened or understood *the message,* we would not be among the companions of the Blazing Hell" (10). The surat effectively draws our attention to Divine Power as displayed in the splendour of nature, affirming the existence of the spiritual reality beyond the material world. A stern warning is given against failing to see beyond the material world: "Which forces beside the Most Kind can possibly help you? The disbelievers are only deceived" (20). The surat opened with the purpose of human life, and ends by pointing out that human life is dependent upon water. To emphasise Allah's control over all, it poses a question: "Have you considered: if your *drinking* water level went low, who could bring back running water for you?" (30)

بِسۡمِ اللّٰهِ الرَّحۡمٰنِ الرَّحِيۡمِ

تَبٰرَكَ الَّذِىۡ بِيَدِهِ الۡمُلۡكُ وَهُوَ عَلٰى كُلِّ شَىۡءٍ

قَدِيۡرُ ۙ الَّذِىۡ خَلَقَ الۡمَوۡتَ وَالۡحَيٰوةَ لِيَبۡلُوَكُمۡ

اَيُّكُمۡ اَحۡسَنُ عَمَلًا ؕ وَهُوَ الۡعَزِيۡزُ الۡغَفُوۡرُ ۙ الَّذِىۡ

خَلَقَ سَبۡعَ سَمٰوٰتٍ طِبَاقًا ؕ مَا تَرٰى فِىۡ خَلۡقِ الرَّحۡمٰنِ

مِنۡ تَفٰوُتٍ ؕ فَارۡجِعِ الۡبَصَرَ ۙ هَلۡ تَرٰى مِنۡ فُطُوۡرٍ ۙ

ثُمَّ ارۡجِعِ الۡبَصَرَ كَرَّتَيۡنِ يَنۡقَلِبۡ اِلَيۡكَ الۡبَصَرُ

خَاسِئًا وَّهُوَ حَسِيۡرٌ ۙ وَلَقَدۡ زَيَّنَّا السَّمَآءَ الدُّنۡيَا

بِمَصَابِيۡحَ وَجَعَلۡنٰهَا رُجُوۡمًا لِّلشَّيٰطِيۡنِ وَاَعۡتَدۡنَا لَهُمۡ

عَذَابَ السَّعِيۡرِ ۙ وَلِلَّذِيۡنَ كَفَرُوۡا بِرَبِّهِمۡ عَذَابُ

جَهَنَّمَ ؕ وَبِئۡسَ الۡمَصِيۡرُ ۙ اِذَآ اُلۡقُوۡا فِيۡهَا سَمِعُوۡا

لَهَا شَهِيۡقًا وَّهِىَ تَفُوۡرُ ۙ تَكَادُ تَمَيَّزُ مِنَ الۡغَيۡظِ ؕ

كُلَّمَآ اُلۡقِىَ فِيۡهَا فَوۡجٌ سَاَلَهُمۡ خَزَنَتُهَآ اَلَمۡ يَاۡتِكُمۡ

نَذِيۡرٌ ۙ قَالُوۡا بَلٰى قَدۡ جَآءَنَا نَذِيۡرٌ ۙ فَكَذَّبۡنَا

وَقُلۡنَا مَا نَزَّلَ اللّٰهُ مِنۡ شَىۡءٍ ۙ اِنۡ اَنۡتُمۡ اِلَّا فِىۡ

ضَلٰلٍ كَبِيۡرٍ ۙ وَقَالُوۡا لَوۡ كُنَّا نَسۡمَعُ اَوۡ نَعۡقِلُ مَا كُنَّا

فِىۡٓ اَصۡحٰبِ السَّعِيۡرِ ۙ فَاعۡتَرَفُوۡا بِذَنۡۢبِهِمۡ ۚ فَسُحۡقًا

لِّاَصۡحٰبِ السَّعِيۡرِ ۙ اِنَّ الَّذِيۡنَ يَخۡشَوۡنَ رَبَّهُمۡ

بِالۡغَيۡبِ لَهُمۡ مَّغۡفِرَةٌ وَّاَجۡرٌ كَبِيۡرٌ ۙ وَاَسِرُّوۡا قَوۡلَكُمۡ

On Judgement Day the losers will regret; why didn't we listen and pay attention? How much do you listen to Allah?

1185

In the name of Allah, the Kind, the Caring.

The purpose of human life

[1] The Blessed One has authority, *complete* control, and power over all things. [2] He created death and life to test you – who among you is best in good works. He is the Almighty, the Forgiver; [3] He created the Seven Heavens, layer upon layer. You will not see the slightest defect in the creation of the Most Kind. Look *at it* again; do you see anything wrong? [4] Then look once more; your sight will come back weary and fatigued. [5] We decorated the lowest sky with stars,[a] and made them projectiles hurled at the devils. We have prepared the punishment of Blazing Hell for them.

The disbelievers' regret for not heeding the Message

[6] The disbelievers of the Lord will have the punishment of Hell, a miserable home! [7] When they are thrown into it, they will hear roaring as *Hell* boils bubbling noisily, [8] about to explode with rage. Every group thrown into it will be asked by its guards: "Didn't any warner come to you?" [9] They will say, "Yes, a warner came to us, but we denied and told them, 'Allah hasn't revealed anything, you are grossly misguided." [10] They will *regretfully* reply, "If only we had listened or understood *the Message,* we wouldn't be among the companions of Blazing Hell." [11] So they will confess their sins; away with the companions of Blazing Hell. [12] The people who feared their Lord without seeing Him will be forgiven, and have a great reward.

---

[a] Literally "lamps", but denotes stars. It can also refer to the shooting stars, which act like missiles against the devils.

اَوِ اجْهَرُوْا بِهٖ ط اِنَّهٗ عَلِيْمٌۢ بِذَاتِ الصُّدُوْرِ ۱۳ اَلَا

يَعْلَمُ مَنْ خَلَقَ ط وَهُوَ اللَّطِيْفُ الْخَبِيْرُ ع ۱۴ هُوَ الَّذِيْ

جَعَلَ لَكُمُ الْاَرْضَ ذَلُوْلًا فَامْشُوْا فِيْ مَنَاكِبِهَا وَ

كُلُوْا مِنْ رِّزْقِهٖ ط وَاِلَيْهِ النُّشُوْرُ ۱۵ ءَاَمِنْتُمْ مَّنْ فِي

السَّمَآءِ اَنْ يَّخْسِفَ بِكُمُ الْاَرْضَ فَاِذَا هِيَ تَمُوْرُ ۱۶

اَمْ اَمِنْتُمْ مَّنْ فِي السَّمَآءِ اَنْ يُّرْسِلَ عَلَيْكُمْ

حَاصِبًا ط فَسَتَعْلَمُوْنَ كَيْفَ نَذِيْرِ ۱۷ وَلَقَدْ كَذَّبَ

الَّذِيْنَ مِنْ قَبْلِهِمْ فَكَيْفَ كَانَ نَكِيْرِ ۱۸ اَوَلَمْ يَرَوْا

اِلَى الطَّيْرِ فَوْقَهُمْ صٰٓفّٰتٍ وَّيَقْبِضْنَ ط مَا يُمْسِكُهُنَّ

اِلَّا الرَّحْمٰنُ ط اِنَّهٗ بِكُلِّ شَيْءٍ بَصِيْرٌ ۱۹ اَمَّنْ هٰذَا

الَّذِيْ هُوَ جُنْدٌ لَّكُمْ يَنْصُرُكُمْ مِّنْ دُوْنِ الرَّحْمٰنِ ط

اِنِ الْكٰفِرُوْنَ اِلَّا فِيْ غُرُوْرٍ ۲۰ اَمَّنْ هٰذَا الَّذِيْ

يَرْزُقُكُمْ اِنْ اَمْسَكَ رِزْقَهٗ ۚ بَلْ لَّجُّوْا فِيْ عُتُوٍّ

وَّنُفُوْرٍ ۲۱ اَفَمَنْ يَّمْشِيْ مُكِبًّا عَلٰى وَجْهِهٖ اَهْدٰى

اَمَّنْ يَّمْشِيْ سَوِيًّا عَلٰى صِرَاطٍ مُّسْتَقِيْمٍ ۲۲ قُلْ هُوَ

الَّذِيْ اَنْشَاَكُمْ وَجَعَلَ لَكُمُ السَّمْعَ وَالْاَبْصَارَ

وَالْاَفْـِٔدَةَ ط قَلِيْلًا مَّا تَشْكُرُوْنَ ۲۳ قُلْ هُوَ الَّذِيْ

ذَرَاَكُمْ فِي الْاَرْضِ وَاِلَيْهِ تُحْشَرُوْنَ ۲۴ وَيَقُوْلُوْنَ

مَتٰى هٰذَا الْوَعْدُ اِنْ كُنْتُمْ صٰدِقِيْنَ ۲۵ قُلْ

اِنَّمَا الْعِلْمُ عِنْدَ اللّٰهِ ۪ وَاِنَّمَا اَنَا نَذِيْرٌ مُّبِيْنٌ ۲۶

Allah has full control of all things. Are you aware of this reality? How good is your seeing, hearing and perception?

Allah's punishment can strike at any moment

¹³Whether you hide your words or make them public, He is the Knower of what is in *your* innermost thoughts. ¹⁴Does He not know who He created? He is the Subtle, the Aware. ¹⁵He made the Earth accessible for you, so you could travel through its vast expanses, and eat from His provision, and before Him you will be gathered, alive. ¹⁶Do you feel safe from the One in the Heaven that He wouldn't command the Earth to swallow you up when it shakes violently? ¹⁷Or do you feel safe from the One in the Heaven that He wouldn't send a sandstorm *to destroy* you? Then you will soon know *the seriousness of* My Warning! ¹⁸Those before them also denied, so how terrible My Condemnation!

Arrogance leads to denial of Divine gifts

¹⁹Have they not seen the birds flying over their heads arranged in rows, flapping their wings in harmony? It is the Most Kind Who holds them there; indeed He sees all things. ²⁰Which forces beside the Most Kind can possibly help you? The disbelievers are only deceived. ²¹Who can give you provision if He withholds His provision? *Unfortunately,* they persist in *their* arrogance and hostility. ²²Who is more guided: the one who walks grovelling, *looking down* and falls flat on his face, or the one who walks upright on a straight path? ²³Say: "He created you and made hearing, sight and intellect for you; how little you thank!" ²⁴Say: "He dispersed you throughout the Earth, and you will be gathered before him."

Disbelievers will be grief-striken

²⁵They ask, "When will this promise be *fulfilled*, if you are telling the truth?" ²⁶Say: "Only Allah knows it's *timing*, and I am a clear warner."

فَلَمَّا رَاَوْهُ زُلْفَةً سِيَّتْ وُجُوهُ الَّذِيْنَ كَفَرُوْا

وَقِيْلَ هٰذَا الَّذِىْ كُنْتُمْ بِهٖ تَدَّعُوْنَ ۝ قُلْ

اَرَءَيْتُمْ اِنْ اَهْلَكَنِىَ اللّٰهُ وَمَنْ مَّعِىَ اَوْ رَحِمَنَا لَا

فَمَنْ يُّجِيْرُ الْكٰفِرِيْنَ مِنْ عَذَابٍ اَلِيْمٍ ۝ قُلْ هُوَ

الرَّحْمٰنُ اٰمَنَّا بِهٖ وَعَلَيْهِ تَوَكَّلْنَا ۚ فَسَتَعْلَمُوْنَ مَنْ

هُوَ فِىْ ضَلٰلٍ مُّبِيْنٍ ۝ قُلْ اَرَءَيْتُمْ اِنْ اَصْبَحَ

مَاؤُكُمْ غَوْرًا فَمَنْ يَّاْتِيْكُمْ بِمَآءٍ مَّعِيْنٍ ۝

Let's put trust in Allah the absolute controller.

27 When they see *Hell* come close, the disbelievers' faces will be grief-stricken, and it will be said, "This is what you used to ask for." 28 Say: "Consider this – whether Allah destroys me and those with me or He treats us kindly, *the question is*: so who will save the disbelievers from a painful punishment?"

Believers accept Allah controls everything

29 Say: "He is the Most Kind; We believe in Him and we put trust in Him, and soon you will know who is misguided." 30 Say: "Have you considered: if your *underground* water level went low, who could bring back running water for you?"

68. Surat Al-Qalam

The Pen

The central theme of this early Makkan surat is a warning to the people of Makkah: if you refuse to believe in the Messenger ﷺ, then be prepared to face severe consequences like previous disobedient nations did. To affirm that the Messenger ﷺ is trustworthy, and that his Message should be accepted by the Makkans, the surat opens by acknowledging the beautiful character of Prophet Muhammad ﷺ. He possesses truthfulness, kindness, generosity, patience, forgiveness, humility, justice, modesty and thankfulness. This is contrasted with the vices of al-Walid ibn al-Mughira, a ruthless opponent of the Messenger ﷺ.

The story of the owners of the orchard highlights how much miserliness is disliked by Allah. The gross injustice of the owners of the orchard is contrasted with the arguably smaller error of Prophet Yunus ﷺ, who left the city of Nineveh without Divine permission, and was reprimanded severely. The suggestion is that Allah will not tolerate even minor misdemeanours from His chosen, let alone those who openly oppose Allah and the Messenger ﷺ.

The final verse gives us an idea of the dislike with which the Makkans listened to the Majestic Quran. The beloved Prophet ﷺ is consoled: their evil eye will not impact him. According to a saying of the Prophet ﷺ: "If there is anything that can overcome destiny, it is the evil eye" (Tirmidhi).

بِسْمِ اللهِ الرَّحْمٰنِ الرَّحِيْمِ

نۤ وَالْقَلَمِ وَمَا يَسْطُرُوْنَ ۝ مَاۤ أَنْتَ بِنِعْمَةِ رَبِّكَ بِمَجْنُوْنٍ ۝ وَإِنَّ لَكَ لَأَجْرًا غَيْرَ مَمْنُوْنٍ ۝ وَإِنَّكَ لَعَلٰى خُلُقٍ عَظِيْمٍ ۝ فَسَتُبْصِرُ وَيُبْصِرُوْنَ ۝ بِأَيِّكُمُ الْمَفْتُوْنُ ۝ إِنَّ رَبَّكَ هُوَ أَعْلَمُ بِمَنْ ضَلَّ عَنْ سَبِيْلِهِ وَهُوَ أَعْلَمُ بِالْمُهْتَدِيْنَ ۝ فَلَا تُطِعِ الْمُكَذِّبِيْنَ ۝ وَدُّوْا لَوْ تُدْهِنُ فَيُدْهِنُوْنَ ۝ وَلَا تُطِعْ كُلَّ حَلَّافٍ مَهِيْنٍ ۝ هَمَّازٍ مَشَّاءٍ بِنَمِيْمٍ ۝ مَنَّاعٍ لِّلْخَيْرِ مُعْتَدٍ أَثِيْمٍ ۝ عُتُلٍّ بَعْدَ ذٰلِكَ زَنِيْمٍ ۝ أَنْ كَانَ ذَا مَالٍ وَبَنِيْنَ ۝ إِذَا تُتْلٰى عَلَيْهِ اٰيٰتُنَا قَالَ أَسَاطِيْرُ الْأَوَّلِيْنَ ۝ سَنَسِمُهُ عَلَى الْخُرْطُوْمِ ۝ إِنَّا بَلَوْنٰهُمْ كَمَا بَلَوْنَاۤ أَصْحٰبَ الْجَنَّةِ إِذْ أَقْسَمُوْا لَيَصْرِمُنَّهَا مُصْبِحِيْنَ ۝ وَلَا يَسْتَثْنُوْنَ ۝ فَطَافَ عَلَيْهَا طَاۤئِفٌ مِّنْ رَّبِّكَ وَهُمْ نَاۤئِمُوْنَ ۝ فَأَصْبَحَتْ كَالصَّرِيْمِ ۝ فَتَنَادَوْا مُصْبِحِيْنَ ۝ أَنِ اغْدُوْا عَلٰى حَرْثِكُمْ إِنْ كُنْتُمْ صٰرِمِيْنَ ۝ فَانْطَلَقُوْا وَهُمْ يَتَخَافَتُوْنَ ۝ أَنْ لَّا يَدْخُلَنَّهَا الْيَوْمَ عَلَيْكُمْ مِّسْكِيْنٌ ۝ وَّغَدَوْا عَلٰى حَرْدٍ قٰدِرِيْنَ ۝ فَلَمَّا رَأَوْهَا قَالُوْۤا إِنَّا لَضَاۤلُّوْنَ ۝ بَلْ

Allah defends His friends from the critics and enemies. He despises them and puts them to shame.

In the name of Allah, the Kind, the Caring.

¹*Noon.*

The Messenger's ﷺ strong character is a proof of his truthfulness

By the pen and everything they write. ²By the grace of your Lord, *Prophet*, you aren't possessed. ³Indeed, you shall have an everlasting reward, ⁴and you have a strong character.

The evil character of the opponents of the Messenger ﷺ

⁵Soon you will see, and so will they, ⁶who is really demented. ⁷Your Lord knows best who strayed from His path, and He knows best who are the guided. ⁸So don't compromise with the deniers; ⁹they would love to see you compromise with them so that they may compromise. ¹⁰Don't yield to every[a] despicable swearer of oaths – ¹¹a fault-finder, dashing around backbiting, ¹²obstructing the common good, an aggressor, a sinner, ¹³an oppressor, and moreover of doubtful birth. ¹⁴He has plenty of wealth and children. ¹⁵When Our verses are recited to him he says, "These are ancient stories." ¹⁶We shall soon put a mark on his nose.[b]

The story of the miserly landlords of the orchard

¹⁷We test them as We tested the owners of the orchard, when they promised they would pick the fruits early in the morning ¹⁸and they made no exceptions.[c] ¹⁹While they slept, a disaster from your Lord struck *the orchard*, ²⁰so by the morning it was a desolate place. ²¹They woke up in the morning and called out to each other, ²²"Hurry to your harvest, if you are going to pick its fruits." ²³So off they went, whispering to each other, ²⁴"Absolutely no needy person will enter it today and bother you." ²⁵They went early, purposefully and determined. ²⁶However, when they reached there they saw it *utterly desolate*, they said, "We are lost, ²⁷rather we are prevented *from picking the fruit!*"

---

[a]   This refers primarily to al-Walid ibn al-Mughira, a leader of the Quraysh and a staunch opponent of the Prophet ﷺ.

[b]   To disgrace him.

[c]   Either they failed to say "if Allah wills," or they promised not to leave any fruits hanging on the trees for the poor.

نَحْنُ مَحْرُومُونَ ۞ قَالَ أَوْسَطُهُمْ أَلَمْ أَقُلْ لَّكُمْ

لَوْلَا تُسَبِّحُونَ ۞ قَالُوا سُبْحَانَ رَبِّنَا إِنَّا كُنَّا

ظَالِمِينَ ۞ فَأَقْبَلَ بَعْضُهُمْ عَلَىٰ بَعْضٍ يَتَلَاوَمُونَ ۞

قَالُوا يَا وَيْلَنَا إِنَّا كُنَّا طَاغِينَ ۞ عَسَىٰ رَبُّنَا أَن

يُبْدِلَنَا خَيْرًا مِّنْهَا إِنَّا إِلَىٰ رَبِّنَا رَاغِبُونَ ۞ كَذَٰلِكَ

الْعَذَابُ ۗ وَلَعَذَابُ الْآخِرَةِ أَكْبَرُ ۚ لَوْ كَانُوا

يَعْلَمُونَ ۞ إِنَّ لِلْمُتَّقِينَ عِندَ رَبِّهِمْ جَنَّاتِ

النَّعِيمِ ۞ أَفَنَجْعَلُ الْمُسْلِمِينَ كَالْمُجْرِمِينَ ۞

مَا لَكُمْ كَيْفَ تَحْكُمُونَ ۞ أَمْ لَكُمْ كِتَابٌ فِيهِ

تَدْرُسُونَ ۞ إِنَّ لَكُمْ فِيهِ لَمَا تَخَيَّرُونَ ۞ أَمْ لَكُمْ

أَيْمَانٌ عَلَيْنَا بَالِغَةٌ إِلَىٰ يَوْمِ الْقِيَامَةِ ۙ إِنَّ لَكُمْ

لَمَا تَحْكُمُونَ ۞ سَلْهُمْ أَيُّهُم بِذَٰلِكَ زَعِيمٌ ۞

أَمْ لَهُمْ شُرَكَاءُ فَلْيَأْتُوا بِشُرَكَائِهِمْ إِن كَانُوا

صَادِقِينَ ۞ يَوْمَ يُكْشَفُ عَن سَاقٍ وَيُدْعَوْنَ

إِلَى السُّجُودِ فَلَا يَسْتَطِيعُونَ ۞ خَاشِعَةً أَبْصَارُهُمْ

تَرْهَقُهُمْ ذِلَّةٌ ۖ وَقَدْ كَانُوا يُدْعَوْنَ إِلَى السُّجُودِ

وَهُمْ سَالِمُونَ ۞ فَذَرْنِي وَمَن يُكَذِّبُ بِهَٰذَا

الْحَدِيثِ ۖ سَنَسْتَدْرِجُهُم مِّنْ حَيْثُ لَا يَعْلَمُونَ ۞

وَأُمْلِي لَهُمْ ۚ إِنَّ كَيْدِي مَتِينٌ ۞ أَمْ تَسْأَلُهُمْ أَجْرًا

فَهُم مِّن مَّغْرَمٍ مُّثْقَلُونَ ۞ أَمْ عِندَهُمُ الْغَيْبُ

The evildoer's friends and gods will abandon them on Judgement Day. What could they do anyway.

²⁸The middle one said, "Didn't I tell you to glorify Allah?" ²⁹They replied, "Glory be to Our Lord, we were wicked!" ³⁰So they turned to one other and began blaming each other. ³¹They cried, "Woe to us! We were shamelessly disobedient, ³²perhaps Our Lord will give us something better in exchange for the orchard; we turn genuinely in hope to Our Lord." ³³Such was the punishment, *but* the punishment of the Hereafter is even greater. If only they knew.

The punishment of Hell will be severe

³⁴The righteous will have attractive Gardens near their Lord. ³⁵So are We to treat those who have submitted themselves like the sinners? ³⁶What is the matter with you; what makes you judge in this way? ³⁷Or do you have a book from where you have learnt ³⁸that you will get whatever you choose? ³⁹Or do you have solemn oaths with Us that are binding till Judgement Day – you will have whatever you decide? ⁴⁰Ask them: "Who will guarantee this? ⁴¹Or do they have partners *beside Allah*?" So let them bring their partners if they are truthful. ⁴²The Day things will be extremely difficult, they will be invited to prostrate, but they won't be able to do so, ⁴³their eyes lowered and *faces* covered with humiliation. They were invited to prostrate when they were safe and sound. ⁴⁴So leave those to Me who deny this Revelation. So gradually We shall lead them to their ruin, and they will not know it, ⁴⁵and We shall give them more time. My plan will work.

They want to harm the Messenger ﷺ with their evil eyes

⁴⁶Or do you ask them for a wage, which will burden them heavily with debt? ⁴⁷Or do they have knowledge of the unseen that they write down?

فَهُمْ يَكْتُبُونَ ۞ فَاصْبِرْ لِحُكْمِ رَبِّكَ وَلَا تَكُنْ

كَصَاحِبِ الْحُوتِ ۖ إِذْ نَادَىٰ وَهُوَ مَكْظُومٌ ۞ لَوْلَا

أَن تَدَارَكَهُ نِعْمَةٌ مِّن رَّبِّهِ لَنُبِذَ بِالْعَرَآءِ وَهُوَ

مَذْمُومٌ ۞ فَاجْتَبَٰهُ رَبُّهُ فَجَعَلَهُ مِنَ الصَّٰلِحِينَ ۞

وَإِن يَّكَادُ الَّذِينَ كَفَرُوا لَيُزْلِقُونَكَ بِأَبْصَارِهِمْ

لَمَّا سَمِعُوا الذِّكْرَ وَيَقُولُونَ إِنَّهُ لَمَجْنُونٌ ۞

وَمَا هُوَ إِلَّا ذِكْرٌ لِّلْعَٰلَمِينَ ۞

The messenger ﷺ must preach and teach no matter how badly they treat him. And don't do what prophet Yunus did; he left the city in anger without Allah's permission.

[48] So wait patiently for your Lord's judgement and do not be like the companion in the *belly of the* whale[a] who prayed whilst in distress. [49] Hadn't a blessing from His Lord reached him, he would have been abandoned on the barren shore, condemned forever. [50] So His Lord *accepted his plea and* selected him, and He made him among the righteous. [51] They wish to strike you down with their *evil* eyes; when the disbelievers hear the Reminder they say, "He is mad!" [52] This is a clear Reminder for all people.

---

[a] This refers to the Prophet Yunus ﷺ.

بِسْمِ اللهِ الرَّحْمٰنِ الرَّحِيْمِ

اَلْحَاقَّةُ ۞ مَا الْحَاقَّةُ ۞ وَمَا اَدْرٰىكَ مَا الْحَاقَّةُ ۞

كَذَّبَتْ ثَمُوْدُ وَعَادٌ بِالْقَارِعَةِ ۞ فَاَمَّا ثَمُوْدُ فَاُهْلِكُوْا

بِالطَّاغِيَةِ ۞ وَاَمَّا عَادٌ فَاُهْلِكُوْا بِرِيْحٍ صَرْصَرٍ

عَاتِيَةٍ ۞ سَخَّرَهَا عَلَيْهِمْ سَبْعَ لَيَالٍ وَّثَمٰنِيَةَ

اَيَّامٍ حُسُوْمًا فَتَرَى الْقَوْمَ فِيْهَا صَرْعٰى كَاَنَّهُمْ

اَعْجَازُ نَخْلٍ خَاوِيَةٍ ۞ فَهَلْ تَرٰى لَهُمْ مِّنْ

The Hereafter is a reality; but it seems virtual, an unreal dream. Is this surat knocking sense into you?

بَاقِيَةٍ ۞ وَجَاءَ فِرْعَوْنُ وَمَنْ قَبْلَهُ وَالْمُؤْتَفِكٰتُ

بِالْخَاطِئَةِ ۞ فَعَصَوْا رَسُوْلَ رَبِّهِمْ فَاَخَذَهُمْ اَخْذَةً

رَّابِيَةً ۞ اِنَّا لَمَّا طَغَا الْمَاءُ حَمَلْنٰكُمْ فِي الْجَارِيَةِ ۞

لِنَجْعَلَهَا لَكُمْ تَذْكِرَةً وَّتَعِيَهَا اُذُنٌ وَّاعِيَةٌ ۞

فَاِذَا نُفِخَ فِي الصُّوْرِ نَفْخَةٌ وَّاحِدَةٌ ۞ وَّحُمِلَتِ

الْاَرْضُ وَالْجِبَالُ فَدُكَّتَا دَكَّةً وَّاحِدَةً ۞ فَيَوْمَئِذٍ

وَّقَعَتِ الْوَاقِعَةُ ۞ وَانْشَقَّتِ السَّمَاءُ فَهِيَ

يَوْمَئِذٍ وَّاهِيَةٌ ۞ وَّالْمَلَكُ عَلٰى اَرْجَائِهَا وَيَحْمِلُ

عَرْشَ رَبِّكَ فَوْقَهُمْ يَوْمَئِذٍ ثَمٰنِيَةٌ ۞ يَوْمَئِذٍ

تُعْرَضُوْنَ لَا تَخْفٰى مِنْكُمْ خَافِيَةٌ ۞ فَاَمَّا مَنْ اُوْتِيَ

كِتٰبَهُ بِيَمِيْنِهِ فَيَقُوْلُ هَاؤُمُ اقْرَءُوْا كِتٰبِيَهْ ۞

اِنِّيْ ظَنَنْتُ اَنِّيْ مُلٰقٍ حِسَابِيَهْ ۞ فَهُوَ فِيْ عِيْشَةٍ

69. Surat Al-Haqqah

The Reality

The core teaching of the Majestic Quran is: Hereafter is the reality, and worldly life is a mere shadow of it. The physical world is the apparent, and the underlying reality is the Hereafter. Some have translated the title of this surat as the inevitable hour, referring to the Final Hour. The Quran, in its inimitable style, presents it as "here and now". The central theme of the surat is the question: what is the reality of human life? The surat is a direct challenge to human materialist tendencies, and invites the reader to consider the horrors and reckoning of Judgment Day. By offering examples of previous disobedient communities, the Quran warns the neglectful and belligerent Makkans that it would be wise to accept the reality.

In the name of Allah, the Kind, the Caring.

The Hereafter is the ultimate reality

¹The ultimate reality – ²what is the ultimate reality? ³What could explain to you what is the ultimate reality? ⁴ *The people of* Thamud and Ad both denied that the striking blow *would ever happen.* ⁵ *The people of* Thamud, they were destroyed by the thunderous storm. ⁶And as for *the people of* Ad, they were destroyed by a violent and furious cold wind, ⁷which He forced against them for seven nights and eight days in succession. So you would have seen the people therein dead, lying prostrate as if they were like the hollow trunks of palm trees. ⁸Do you see their remains *today?* ⁹Then the Pharaoh and those before him brought habitual sin from the overturned cities,ᵃ committed great sin. ¹⁰So they disobeyed the Messenger of their Lord, and He seized them with a punishment. ¹¹When the floodwater rose high, We carried you in the sailing ship ¹²to make it a lasting reminder for you, and so attentive ears may understand it.

The events of the Final Hour

¹³So when the Trumpet is blown, it will be a single blast, ¹⁴the Earth and the mountains will be raised high and crushed to powdered dust; ¹⁵on that Day, the Inevitable Event will happen; ¹⁶the sky will be split apart, looking flimsy. ¹⁷On that Day, *a group of* eight angels *standing* along its edges will carry your Lord's Throne

---

ᵃ 'Overturned cities' could refer to Sodom and Gomorrah where the prophet Lut 🕊 preached.

رَاضِيَةٍ ۝ فِىْ جَنَّةٍ عَالِيَةٍ ۝ قُطُوْفُهَا دَانِيَةٌ ۝

كُلُوْا وَاشْرَبُوْا هَنِيْئًا بِمَا أَسْلَفْتُمْ فِى الْاَيَّامِ

الْخَالِيَةِ ۝ وَاَمَّا مَنْ أُوْتِىَ كِتٰبَهُ بِشِمَالِهٖ ۬

فَيَقُوْلُ يٰلَيْتَنِىْ لَمْ أُوْتَ كِتٰبِيَهْ ۝ وَلَمْ اَدْرِ مَا

حِسَابِيَهْ ۝ يٰلَيْتَهَا كَانَتِ الْقَاضِيَةَ ۝ مَا اَغْنٰى

عَنِّىْ مَالِيَهْ ۝ هَلَكَ عَنِّىْ سُلْطٰنِيَهْ ۝ خُذُوْهُ

فَغُلُّوْهُ ۝ ثُمَّ الْجَحِيْمَ صَلُّوْهُ ۝ ثُمَّ فِىْ سِلْسِلَةٍ

ذَرْعُهَا سَبْعُوْنَ ذِرَاعًا فَاسْلُكُوْهُ ۝ اِنَّهٗ كَانَ

لَا يُؤْمِنُ بِاللهِ الْعَظِيْمِ ۝ وَلَا يَحُضُّ عَلٰى طَعَامِ

الْمِسْكِيْنِ ۝ فَلَيْسَ لَهُ الْيَوْمَ هٰهُنَا حَمِيْمٌ ۝

وَّلَا طَعَامٌ اِلَّا مِنْ غِسْلِيْنٍ ۝ لَّا يَاْكُلُهٗ اِلَّا

الْخَاطِئُوْنَ ۝ فَلَا أُقْسِمُ بِمَا تُبْصِرُوْنَ ۝ وَمَا لَا

تُبْصِرُوْنَ ۝ اِنَّهٗ لَقَوْلُ رَسُوْلٍ كَرِيْمٍ ۝ وَّمَا

هُوَ بِقَوْلِ شَاعِرٍ ط قَلِيْلًا مَّا تُؤْمِنُوْنَ ۝ وَلَا

بِقَوْلِ كَاهِنٍ ط قَلِيْلًا مَّا تَذَكَّرُوْنَ ۝ تَنْزِيْلٌ

مِّنْ رَّبِّ الْعٰلَمِيْنَ ۝ وَلَوْ تَقَوَّلَ عَلَيْنَا بَعْضَ

الْاَقَاوِيْلِ ۝ لَاَخَذْنَا مِنْهُ بِالْيَمِيْنِ ۝ ثُمَّ

لَقَطَعْنَا مِنْهُ الْوَتِيْنَ ۝ فَمَا مِنْكُمْ مِّنْ اَحَدٍ

عَنْهُ حٰجِزِيْنَ ۝ وَاِنَّهٗ لَتَذْكِرَةٌ لِّلْمُتَّقِيْنَ ۝

وَاِنَّا لَنَعْلَمُ اَنَّ مِنْكُمْ مُّكَذِّبِيْنَ ۝ وَاِنَّهٗ

The reality of Judgement Day is brought to the forefront; presented as Fire, chains, and the pain of Hell, as compared to the fruits and joy of Heaven.

above them. ¹⁸On that Day, you will be brought *for Judgement,* and nothing of your deeds will remain hidden.

The delightful life of the people of Paradise

¹⁹The one given the Book *of Deeds* in his right hand, will say, "Here, take it and read my Book! ²⁰I believed that I would be held accountable." ²¹So he will have a happy life, ²²in a lofty garden, ²³with its low-hanging bunches of fruits, easily *plucked.* ²⁴*He will be told*: "Eat, drink and be merry for what you did in the days gone by."

A portrait of wasted life

²⁵*However*, the one given the Book *of Deeds* in his left hand, will say, "I am ruined! I wish that I had not been given my Book, ²⁶and I never knew I would be held accountable; ²⁷how I wish death would have ended this. ²⁸My wealth hasn't benefited me ²⁹and my influence has disappeared." ³⁰Seize him, handcuff him, ³¹then let him burn in Hell ³²and drag him with a seventy-metre long chain! ³³He didn't believe in Allah, the Almighty, ³⁴nor would he encourage others to feed the needy. ³⁵Today, he has no close friend here, ³⁶neither any food except from filthy bodily discharges, ³⁷that only the sinners will eat.

The glorious Quran is Allah's Revelation

³⁸No, I swear by what you can see ³⁹and what you can't see. ⁴⁰*The Majestic Quran* is the speech of a noble Messenger; ⁴¹not the speech of a poet, little do you believe! ⁴²Neither is it the speech of a soothsayer, little do you reflect! ⁴³A Revelation from the Lord of the worlds. ⁴⁴Had *the Prophet* made up a lie against Us, ⁴⁵We would have seized him by the right hand, ⁴⁶and then cut the major artery *in his heart,* ⁴⁷so none of you would have been able to stop *Us* from him. ⁴⁸Indeed *the Quran* is a reminder for the pious. ⁴⁹We know some of you will deny *it,* ⁵⁰and it will be *a source of* severe regret for the disbelievers. ⁵¹*The Quran* is the absolute truth, ⁵²so glorify the name of your Lord, the Almighty.

لَحَسْرَةٌ عَلَى الْكَافِرِينَ ۞ وَإِنَّهُ لَحَقُّ الْيَقِينِ ۞

فَسَبِّحْ بِاسْمِ رَبِّكَ الْعَظِيمِ ۞

70. Surat Al-Ma'arij

The Stairways to Heaven

This surat was revealed in the middle Makkan period, and its central theme is criticism of the Makkan sceptics who wanted punishment to come sooner. According to Ibn Kathir, the Messenger ﷺ once warned a Makkan storyteller, Nadhr ibn Harith, of the punishment of Hell. He mockingly demanded, "Why don't you bring a sandstorm that will destroy us?" The surat was revealed in response to his tactless demand.

The surat opens with a critical reprimand of the questioner who makes such a foolish request. It reminds him of Allah's Power, Majesty and the stairways leading to the Heavens that can take people to their spiritual heights. The section vividly captures the terrifying moments of the end of time: the sky turning red, mountains hanging like fluffed tufts of wool, and the Day when everyone will be anxious. The next section praises the person who accepts Judgement Day; he is described as a dutiful worshipper who has a good moral character. He cares for others, spends generously, and controls his sexual appetite. The final section questions why disbelievers are unable to believe in the Creator, and gives a stern warning.

بِسْمِ اللهِ الرَّحْمٰنِ الرَّحِيْمِ

سَاَلَ سَآئِلٌۢ بِعَذَابٍ وَّاقِعٍۙ ۱ لِّلْكٰفِرِيْنَ لَيْسَ لَهٗ دَافِعٌۙ ۲ مِّنَ اللهِ ذِى الْمَعَارِجِؕ ۳ تَعْرُجُ الْمَلٰٓئِكَةُ وَالرُّوْحُ اِلَيْهِ فِىْ يَوْمٍ كَانَ مِقْدَارُهٗ خَمْسِيْنَ اَلْفَ سَنَةٍۚ ۴ فَاصْبِرْ صَبْرًا جَمِيْلًا ۵ اِنَّهُمْ يَرَوْنَهٗ بَعِيْدًاۙ ۶ وَّنَرٰىهُ قَرِيْبًاؕ ۷ يَوْمَ تَكُوْنُ السَّمَآءُ كَالْمُهْلِۙ ۸ وَتَكُوْنُ الْجِبَالُ كَالْعِهْنِۙ ۹ وَلَا يَسْـَٔلُ حَمِيْمٌ حَمِيْمًاۚ ۱۰ يُّبَصَّرُوْنَهُمْؕ يَوَدُّ الْمُجْرِمُ لَوْ يَفْتَدِىْ مِنْ عَذَابِ يَوْمِئِذٍۢ بِبَنِيْهِۙ ۱۱ وَصَاحِبَتِهٖ وَاَخِيْهِۙ ۱۲ وَفَصِيْلَتِهِ الَّتِىْ تُـٔوِيْهِۙ ۱۳ وَمَنْ فِى الْاَرْضِ جَمِيْعًاۙ ثُمَّ يُنْجِيْهِۙ ۱۴ كَلَّاؕ اِنَّهَا لَظٰىۙ ۱۵ نَزَّاعَةً لِّلشَّوٰىۚ ۱۶ تَدْعُوْا مَنْ اَدْبَرَ وَتَوَلّٰىۙ ۱۷ وَجَمَعَ فَاَوْعٰى ۱۸ اِنَّ الْاِنْسَانَ خُلِقَ هَلُوْعًاۙ ۱۹ اِذَا مَسَّهُ الشَّرُّ جَزُوْعًاۙ ۲۰ وَّاِذَا مَسَّهُ الْخَيْرُ مَنُوْعًاۙ ۲۱ اِلَّا الْمُصَلِّيْنَۙ ۲۲ الَّذِيْنَ هُمْ عَلٰى صَلَاتِهِمْ دَآئِمُوْنَۙ ۲۳ وَالَّذِيْنَ فِىْ اَمْوَالِهِمْ حَقٌّ مَّعْلُوْمٌۙ ۲۴ لِّلسَّآئِلِ وَالْمَحْرُوْمِۙ ۲۵ وَالَّذِيْنَ يُصَدِّقُوْنَ بِيَوْمِ الدِّيْنِۙ ۲۶ وَالَّذِيْنَ هُمْ مِّنْ عَذَابِ رَبِّهِمْ مُّشْفِقُوْنَۚ ۲۷ اِنَّ عَذَابَ رَبِّهِمْ غَيْرُ مَاْمُوْنٍۙ ۲۸

Humans have a tendency to be anxious and afraid of the future. But believers, they look forward to it.

In the name of Allah, the Kind, the Caring

The end of time

[1]A *sceptical* questioner demanded a punishment to fall [2]upon the disbelievers; nothing can ward it off *once it comes* [3]from Allah, the Lord of the spiritual stairways to the Heavens, [4]by which the angels and the *Noble* Spirit ascend to Him on a Day with a time-span of fifty thousand years. [5]So *Messenger!* Be patient in a beautiful manner! [6]Indeed, they consider it a long way off, [7]*yet* We know it is near. [8]The Day when the sky will be like molten brass, [9]and the *hanging* mountains will be like masses of *fluffed* wool.

The day of sorrow, dread and regret

[10]*It will be a Day* when no close friend will bother to ask *anything of* his close friend, [11]yet they will be within sight of one another. The wicked person will wish to give away everything to save himself from punishment that Day, even his children, [12]his spouse, his brother, [13]his blood relatives who sheltered him, [14]and everyone on Earth, to save his own skin. [15]That will not *happen!* There will be a raging flame [16]that peels away the skin. [17]*Hell* shall call out to all who turned their backs and turned away, [18]the one who gathered *wealth* and hoarded it.

A glowing description of worshippers

[19]Humans were created anxious; [20]when misfortune befalls them, they are impatient, [21]and when good fortune befalls them, they are selfish; [22]except the worshippers, [23]who perform their prayer constantly, [24]in whose wealth is a due share [25]for the beggar and the deprived, [26]who believe in Judgement Day, [27]who are fearful of their Lord's punishment, [28]their Lord's punishment from which no one is safe.

وَالَّذِیْنَ هُمْ لِفُرُوْجِهِمْ حٰفِظُوْنَ ۟﴿٢٩﴾ اِلَّا عَلٰۤى

اَزْوَاجِهِمْ اَوْ مَا مَلَكَتْ اَیْمَانُهُمْ فَاِنَّهُمْ غَیْرُ

مَلُوْمِیْنَ ۟﴿٣٠﴾ فَمَنِ ابْتَغٰى وَرَآءَ ذٰلِكَ فَاُولٰٓئِكَ هُمُ

الْعٰدُوْنَ ۟﴿٣١﴾ وَالَّذِیْنَ هُمْ لِاَمٰنٰتِهِمْ وَعَهْدِهِمْ

رٰعُوْنَ ۟﴿٣٢﴾ وَالَّذِیْنَ هُمْ بِشَهٰدٰتِهِمْ قَآئِمُوْنَ ۟﴿٣٣﴾

وَالَّذِیْنَ هُمْ عَلٰى صَلَاتِهِمْ یُحَافِظُوْنَ ۟﴿٣٤﴾ اُولٰٓئِكَ

فِیْ جَنّٰتٍ مُّكْرَمُوْنَ ۟﴿٣٥﴾ فَمَالِ الَّذِیْنَ كَفَرُوْا قِبَلَكَ

مُهْطِعِیْنَ ۟﴿٣٦﴾ عَنِ الْیَمِیْنِ وَعَنِ الشِّمَالِ عِزِیْنَ ۟﴿٣٧﴾

اَیَطْمَعُ كُلُّ امْرِئٍ مِّنْهُمْ اَنْ یُّدْخَلَ جَنَّةَ نَعِیْمٍ ۟﴿٣٨﴾

كَلَّا ؕ اِنَّا خَلَقْنٰهُمْ مِّمَّا یَعْلَمُوْنَ ۟﴿٣٩﴾ فَلَاۤ اُقْسِمُ

بِرَبِّ الْمَشٰرِقِ وَالْمَغٰرِبِ اِنَّا لَقٰدِرُوْنَ ۟﴿٤٠﴾ عَلٰۤى

اَنْ نُّبَدِّلَ خَیْرًا مِّنْهُمْ ۙ وَمَا نَحْنُ بِمَسْبُوْقِیْنَ ۟﴿٤١﴾

فَذَرْهُمْ یَخُوْضُوْا وَیَلْعَبُوْا حَتّٰى یُلٰقُوْا یَوْمَهُمُ

الَّذِیْ یُوْعَدُوْنَ ۟﴿٤٢﴾ یَوْمَ یَخْرُجُوْنَ مِنَ الْاَجْدَاثِ

سِرَاعًا كَاَنَّهُمْ اِلٰى نُصُبٍ یُّوْفِضُوْنَ ۟﴿٤٣﴾ خَاشِعَةً

اَبْصَارُهُمْ تَرْهَقُهُمْ ذِلَّةٌ ؕ ذٰلِكَ الْیَوْمُ الَّذِیْ

كَانُوْا یُوْعَدُوْنَ ۟﴿٤٤﴾

The respected humans have seven qualities. Can you list them?

1207

²⁹ Who guard their sexual purity, ³⁰ except from their spouses, or their slave maids; for that they can't be blamed. ³¹ But those whose lustful desires go beyond that, they are the transgressors. ³² Who fulfil their trusts and promises, ³³ who give honest testimonies, ³⁴ who are focused and regular in their prayers. ³⁵ They will be honoured in *delightful* gardens.

Why are the disbelievers surprised?

³⁶ What is the matter with the disbelievers? They all stare at you *Prophet*, ³⁷ from the right and the left. ³⁸ Does each one of them expect to be admitted into a Garden of Delight? ³⁹ *That will* never happen; We created them from something they know. ⁴⁰ So I swear by the Lord of the Eastern and the Western horizons, indeed We are fully capable ⁴¹ of replacing them with people better than them, and no one can stop Us. ⁴² So leave them *pandering* to their idle talk and playing *games*, until they face *Judgement Day*, which they are promised. ⁴³ The Day they will quickly come out of the graves, as if racing towards goal posts, ⁴⁴ their eyes cast down and *faces* covered with humiliation. That is the Day, which they were promised.

بِسْمِ اللهِ الرَّحْمٰنِ الرَّحِیْمِ

اِنَّاۤ اَرْسَلْنَا نُوْحًا اِلٰی قَوْمِهۤ اَنْ اَنْذِرْ قَوْمَكَ مِنْ

قَبْلِ اَنْ یَّاْتِیَهُمْ عَذَابٌ اَلِیْمٌ ۞ قَالَ یٰقَوْمِ اِنِّیْ

لَكُمْ نَذِیْرٌ مُّبِیْنٌ ۞ اَنِ اعْبُدُوا اللهَ وَ اتَّقُوْهُ

وَ اَطِیْعُوْنِ ۞ یَغْفِرْ لَكُمْ مِّنْ ذُنُوْبِكُمْ وَ یُؤَخِّرْكُمْ

اِلٰۤی اَجَلٍ مُّسَمًّی ؕ اِنَّ اَجَلَ اللهِ اِذَا جَآءَ لَا یُؤَخَّرُ ۘ

لَوْ كُنْتُمْ تَعْلَمُوْنَ ۞ قَالَ رَبِّ اِنِّیْ دَعَوْتُ قَوْمِیْ

لَیْلًا وَّ نَهَارًا ۞ فَلَمْ یَزِدْهُمْ دُعَآءِیْۤ اِلَّا فِرَارًا ۞

وَ اِنِّیْ كُلَّمَا دَعَوْتُهُمْ لِتَغْفِرَ لَهُمْ جَعَلُوْۤا اَصَابِعَهُمْ

فِیْۤ اٰذَانِهِمْ وَ اسْتَغْشَوْا ثِیَابَهُمْ وَ اَصَرُّوْا وَ اسْتَكْبَرُوا

اسْتِكْبَارًا ۞ ثُمَّ اِنِّیْ دَعَوْتُهُمْ جِهَارًا ۞ ثُمَّ اِنِّیْۤ

اَعْلَنْتُ لَهُمْ وَ اَسْرَرْتُ لَهُمْ اِسْرَارًا ۞ فَقُلْتُ

اسْتَغْفِرُوْا رَبَّكُمْ ؕ اِنَّهٗ كَانَ غَفَّارًا ۞ یُّرْسِلِ السَّمَآءَ

عَلَیْكُمْ مِّدْرَارًا ۞ وَّ یُمْدِدْكُمْ بِاَمْوَالٍ وَّ بَنِیْنَ وَ

یَجْعَلْ لَّكُمْ جَنّٰتٍ وَّ یَجْعَلْ لَّكُمْ اَنْهٰرًا ؕ مَا لَكُمْ

لَا تَرْجُوْنَ لِلهِ وَقَارًا ۞ وَ قَدْ خَلَقَكُمْ اَطْوَارًا ۞

اَلَمْ تَرَوْا كَیْفَ خَلَقَ اللهُ سَبْعَ سَمٰوٰتٍ طِبَاقًا ۞

وَّ جَعَلَ الْقَمَرَ فِیْهِنَّ نُوْرًا وَّ جَعَلَ الشَّمْسَ سِرَاجًا ۞

وَ اللهُ اَنْۢبَتَكُمْ مِّنَ الْاَرْضِ نَبَاتًا ۙ ثُمَّ یُعِیْدُكُمْ

Nuh preached with a heroic effort, passion and wisdom. He invited them to see the truth of religion but people ignored, ridiculed and threatened him. Can you stand up for Allah like that?

71. Surat Nuh

Noah

This Makkan surat sketches the life and works of one of the great prophets of Allah, Nuh ﷺ. The archaeologists of the Bible believe he lived approximately 10,000 years ago, on the Southern shores of the Black Sea. Its central theme is his struggle against unbelievers. The story comes as a reassurance for the Prophet Muhammad ﷺ and the early Muslims: they would be saved and their enemies destroyed, as happened with the people of Nuh ﷺ in the past.

For nine and a half centuries, Nuh ﷺ preached bravely in a variety of ways, with determination. He presented convincing evidence from their lives, the natural world around them, and from history, but his words fell on deaf ears. They were stubborn, materialistic idolaters who could not see beyond the physical realm. The surat presents a heartrending prayer, his moving sermon, and finally his prayer of desperation in the final section.

In the name of Allah, the Kind, the Caring.

Nuh warned his people

¹Indeed, We sent Nuh to his people *with a message*: "Warn your people before a painful punishment comes to them." ²He told them, "My people! I am a clear warner to you, ³so worship Allah, be mindful of Him and obey me, ⁴then He will forgive your sins and spare you until your appointed time. When Allah's deadline comes, it cannot be delayed, I *wish* you understood."

Nuh's heartrending prayer

⁵He prayed: "My Lord, I called my people day and night, ⁶my calling has only increased them in fleeing further and further away. ⁷Each time I invited them to Your forgiveness, they put their fingers into their ears, covered themselves up with their garments, persisted *in their disbelief* and were thoroughly arrogant. ⁸I invited them openly, ⁹then in public, and in private with the utmost discretion.

Nuh's commanding sermon to his people

¹⁰I told them, 'Seek your Lord's forgiveness; He is Most Forgiving.¹¹He will send plenty of rain for you from the sky, ¹²and bless you with wealth, children, provide for you gardens, and provide for you rivers. ¹³What's the matter with you that you don't fear the Majesty of Allah? ¹⁴Yet He created you in stages. ¹⁵Haven't

فِيهَا وَيُخْرِجُكُمْ إِخْرَاجًا ۝ وَاللَّهُ جَعَلَ لَكُمُ
الْأَرْضَ بِسَاطًا ۝ لِّتَسْلُكُوا مِنْهَا سُبُلًا فِجَاجًا ۝

قَالَ نُوحٌ رَّبِّ إِنَّهُمْ عَصَوْنِي وَاتَّبَعُوا مَن لَّمْ
يَزِدْهُ مَالُهُ وَوَلَدُهُ إِلَّا خَسَارًا ۝ وَمَكَرُوا
مَكْرًا كُبَّارًا ۝ وَقَالُوا لَا تَذَرُنَّ آلِهَتَكُمْ وَلَا
تَذَرُنَّ وَدًّا وَّلَا سُوَاعًا ۝ وَّلَا يَغُوثَ وَيَعُوقَ
وَنَسْرًا ۝ وَقَدْ أَضَلُّوا كَثِيرًا ۚ وَلَا تَزِدِ
الظَّالِمِينَ إِلَّا ضَلَالًا ۝ مِّمَّا خَطِيئَاتِهِمْ أُغْرِقُوا
فَأُدْخِلُوا نَارًا ۖ فَلَمْ يَجِدُوا لَهُم مِّن دُونِ
اللَّهِ أَنصَارًا ۝ وَقَالَ نُوحٌ رَّبِّ لَا تَذَرْ عَلَى
الْأَرْضِ مِنَ الْكَافِرِينَ دَيَّارًا ۝ إِنَّكَ إِن
تَذَرْهُمْ يُضِلُّوا عِبَادَكَ وَلَا يَلِدُوا إِلَّا
فَاجِرًا كَفَّارًا ۝ رَّبِّ اغْفِرْ لِي وَلِوَالِدَيَّ وَلِمَن
دَخَلَ بَيْتِيَ مُؤْمِنًا وَّلِلْمُؤْمِنِينَ وَالْمُؤْمِنَاتِ ۖ
وَلَا تَزِدِ الظَّالِمِينَ إِلَّا تَبَارًا ۝

Even a great prophet like Nuh cursed his people for their persistent denial and disobedience of Allah.

you considered how Allah created the Seven Heavens one above the other? ¹⁶He placed the moon as a light, and the sun as a lamp. ¹⁷Allah produced you from the Earth *like* plants, ¹⁸then He will return you to it, and will bring you out *from it.* ¹⁹And Allah spread out the Earth for you, ²⁰so you may travel over its broad paths and valleys."

Nuh's prayer of desperation

²¹*Eventually* Nuh prayed: "My Lord, they disobeyed me and followed those whose wealth and children increased them in loss. ²²They devised a scheme of great magnitude: ²³*they* tell them, 'Don't abandon your gods and don't abandon Wadd, Suwa', Yaghuth, Ya'uq or Nasr.'ᵃ ²⁴They have misled many; *My Lord,* do not increase the wicked except from going further and further astray *from the Truth.*" ²⁵Due to their sins, they were drowned and then thrown into Hell; they couldn't find any helper for them against Allah. ²⁶Nuh prayed: "My Lord, don't leave any disbelievers on Earth; ²⁷if you left them, they will misguide Your servants, and breed *more* wicked disbelievers. My Lord, forgive me and my parents and whoever enters my house as a believer, believing men and women. Don't increase the wicked except in utter destruction."

ᵃ   These were five idols they used to worship.

72. Surat Al-Jinn

Jinn

According to Ibn 'Abbas, a group of jinn visited the Prophet ﷺ after he returned from his journey to Taif, in which case, the surat was revealed in the tenth or eleventh year of his mission in Makkah. The central theme is challenging the stubbornness and disbelief of the Quraysh. By telling the story of a group of jinn who believed in the Messenger ﷺ, the Quraysh are made to feel jealous of them. The surat presented a direct report from the mouth of a jinn accepting faith in the Messenger ﷺ and the Revelation, whilst the materialistic disbelievers think the Quran is merely poetry, or the words of a soothsayer or madman. It also reassured the Messenger ﷺ of the truthfulness of his message, building his confidence and self-esteem, so that he isn't upset.

The jinn are an invisible and intelligent creation of Allah, made from smokeless fire, a high-energy form. Like humans, they can be either believers or disbelievers. The surat outlines some of their characteristics, and some similarities and differences to human beings. It reveals their amazement and surprise at the inability of Makkans to believe in the Majestic Quran. Finally, it shows the humility of the Messenger ﷺ who proclaims: "I have no control over harming or benefiting you" (21). Allah is protective of His messengers by providing them with guardians, who look after them all the time.

بِسْمِ اللهِ الرَّحْمٰنِ الرَّحِيْمِ

قُلْ اُوْحِيَ اِلَيَّ اَنَّهُ اسْتَمَعَ نَفَرٌ مِّنَ الْجِنِّ فَقَالُوْا

اِنَّا سَمِعْنَا قُرْاٰنًا عَجَبًا ۱ يَّهْدِيْ اِلَى الرُّشْدِ

فَاٰمَنَّا بِهٖ ط وَلَنْ نُّشْرِكَ بِرَبِّنَا اَحَدًا ۲ وَّاَنَّهٗ

تَعٰلٰى جَدُّ رَبِّنَا مَا اتَّخَذَ صَاحِبَةً وَّلَا وَلَدًا ۳ وَّاَنَّهٗ

كَانَ يَقُوْلُ سَفِيْهُنَا عَلَى اللهِ شَطَطًا ۴ وَّاَنَّا ظَنَنَّآ

اَنْ لَّنْ تَقُوْلَ الْاِنْسُ وَالْجِنُّ عَلَى اللهِ كَذِبًا ۵

وَّاَنَّهٗ كَانَ رِجَالٌ مِّنَ الْاِنْسِ يَعُوْذُوْنَ بِرِجَالٍ

مِّنَ الْجِنِّ فَزَادُوْهُمْ رَهَقًا ۶ وَّاَنَّهُمْ ظَنُّوْا كَمَا

ظَنَنْتُمْ اَنْ لَّنْ يَّبْعَثَ اللهُ اَحَدًا ۷ وَّاَنَّا لَمَسْنَا

السَّمَآءَ فَوَجَدْنٰهَا مُلِئَتْ حَرَسًا شَدِيْدًا وَّشُهُبًا ۸

وَّاَنَّا كُنَّا نَقْعُدُ مِنْهَا مَقَاعِدَ لِلسَّمْعِ ط فَمَنْ

يَّسْتَمِعِ الْاٰنَ يَجِدْ لَهٗ شِهَابًا رَّصَدًا ۹ وَّاَنَّا لَا

نَدْرِيْ اَشَرٌّ اُرِيْدَ بِمَنْ فِى الْاَرْضِ اَمْ اَرَادَ بِهِمْ

رَبُّهُمْ رَشَدًا ۱۰ وَّاَنَّا مِنَّا الصّٰلِحُوْنَ وَمِنَّا دُوْنَ

ذٰلِكَ ط كُنَّا طَرَآئِقَ قِدَدًا ۱۱ وَّاَنَّا ظَنَنَّآ اَنْ لَّنْ

نُّعْجِزَ اللهَ فِى الْاَرْضِ وَلَنْ نُّعْجِزَهٗ هَرَبًا ۱۲ وَّاَنَّا

لَمَّا سَمِعْنَا الْهُدٰى اٰمَنَّا بِهٖ ط فَمَنْ يُّؤْمِنْ بِرَبِّهٖ

فَلَا يَخَافُ بَخْسًا وَّلَا رَهَقًا ۱۳ وَّاَنَّا مِنَّا الْمُسْلِمُوْنَ

The Jinns are invisible creatures with intellect; they believed the Messenger ﷺ, they could see the reality far clearer then humans.

In the name of Allah, the Kind, the Caring.

A group of faithful jinn

¹ Say *Prophet*: "It was revealed to me that a group of jinn listened *to the Quran* and said *to their people*, 'We heard an amazing recitation, ²which guides to the right path and we believed it, and will not associate anyone with Our Lord.' ³Our Lord's majesty is exalted and He hasn't taken a wife nor a child, ⁴as some fools claimed such an outrageous lie against Allah. ⁵We never thought human beings and jinn would utter *such* lies against Allah.'

What do jinns believe and do? How powerful are they?

⁶'Men used to seek protection from male jinn, but all they have done is increased them in evil practices, ⁷and they believed as you believed that Allah will not resurrect anyone. ⁸When we snooped at the secrets of the sky, we found it was full of powerful guards and comets.ᵃ ⁹We sat in there waiting to eavesdrop, but now whoever listens in will have comets lying in wait for him. ¹⁰So we don't know whether it is evil that is intended for those on Earth, or if their Lord wishes to guide them. ¹¹Some of us righteous and others not so, we follow many different paths, ¹²and we know we won't frustrate Allah on the Earth, nor manage to run away from Him.'

The jinn are surprised at the Makkans' attitude toward the Prophet

¹³'When we heard the guidance, we instantly believed it, and whoever believes in His Lord need not fear loss nor oppression. ¹⁴Some of us have submitted, and others are unjust. So the one who submits *to Him*, has received true guidance.

ᵃ *Shihab* means a shooting star, flaming fires and a luminous meteor.

وَّمِنَّا الْقَسِطُوْنَ ط فَمَنْ اَسْلَمَ فَاُولٰٓئِكَ تَحَرَّوْا
رَشَدًا ۝ وَ اَمَّا الْقَسِطُوْنَ فَكَانُوْا لِجَهَنَّمَ حَطَبًا ۝
وَّاَنْ لَّوِ اسْتَقَامُوْا عَلَى الطَّرِيْقَةِ لَاَسْقَيْنٰهُمْ مَّآءً
غَدَقًا ۝ لِّنَفْتِنَهُمْ فِيْهِ ط وَمَنْ يُّعْرِضْ عَنْ ذِكْرِ
رَبِّهِ يَسْلُكْهُ عَذَابًا صَعَدًا ۝ وَّاَنَّ الْمَسٰجِدَ لِلّٰهِ فَلَا
تَدْعُوْا مَعَ اللّٰهِ اَحَدًا ۝ وَّاَنَّهُ لَمَّا قَامَ عَبْدُ اللّٰهِ
يَدْعُوْهُ كَادُوْا يَكُوْنُوْنَ عَلَيْهِ لِبَدًا ۝ قُلْ اِنَّمَآ
اَدْعُوْا رَبِّىْ وَلَآ اُشْرِكُ بِهٖٓ اَحَدًا ۝ قُلْ اِنِّىْ
لَآ اَمْلِكُ لَكُمْ ضَرًّا وَّلَا رَشَدًا ۝ قُلْ اِنِّىْ
لَنْ يُّجِيْرَنِىْ مِنَ اللّٰهِ اَحَدٌ ۙ وَّلَنْ اَجِدَ مِنْ
دُوْنِهٖ مُلْتَحَدًا ۝ اِلَّا بَلٰغًا مِّنَ اللّٰهِ وَرِسٰلٰتِهٖ ط
وَمَنْ يَّعْصِ اللّٰهَ وَرَسُوْلَهُ فَاِنَّ لَهُ نَارَ جَهَنَّمَ
خٰلِدِيْنَ فِيْهَآ اَبَدًا ط حَتّٰى اِذَا رَاَوْا مَا يُوْعَدُوْنَ
فَسَيَعْلَمُوْنَ مَنْ اَضْعَفُ نَاصِرًا وَّاَقَلُّ عَدَدًا ۝
قُلْ اِنْ اَدْرِىْٓ اَقَرِيْبٌ مَّا تُوْعَدُوْنَ اَمْ يَجْعَلُ
لَهٗ رَبِّىْٓ اَمَدًا ۝ عٰلِمُ الْغَيْبِ فَلَا يُظْهِرُ عَلٰى
غَيْبِهٖٓ اَحَدًا ۙ اِلَّا مَنِ ارْتَضٰى مِنْ رَّسُوْلٍ فَاِنَّهٗ
يَسْلُكُ مِنْ بَيْنِ يَدَيْهِ وَمِنْ خَلْفِهٖ رَصَدًا ۝
لِّيَعْلَمَ اَنْ قَدْ اَبْلَغُوْا رِسٰلٰتِ رَبِّهِمْ وَاَحَاطَ
بِمَا لَدَيْهِمْ وَاَحْصٰى كُلَّ شَىْءٍ عَدَدًا ۝

The Jinns eloquently presented their faith in the Lord and why they accept the beloved Messenger ﷺ. Can you talk about the truth like that?

¹⁵The unjust shall be fuel for Hell." ¹⁶Had they remained steadfast on the straight path, We would have given them plenty of water to drink, ¹⁷so that We could test them regarding it. Whoever turns away from his Lord's remembrance, He will thrust him into ever-increasing difficulties. ¹⁸The places of worship are for Allah, so don't worship anyone beside Allah. ¹⁹When the servant of Allah stood up to worship Him, they packed around him in crowds.

The Messenger ﷺ humbles himself before Allah

²⁰Say: "I worship my Lord, and I don't associate anyone with Him." ²¹Say: "I have no control over hurting or benefiting you." ²²Say: "No one will save me from Allah, nor will I find a refuge beside Him; ²³my mission is only to deliver His Messages. Whoever disobeys Allah and His Messenger will be in the fire of Hell forever." ²⁴Eventually, when they see what they are promised, they will instantly know who is the weakest helper and the smallest in number. ²⁵Say: "I don't know whether *the scourage* you are promised is near, or if My Lord has postponed it.

Allah protects His Messengers from all harm

²⁶He is the Knower of the unseen and doesn't reveal His secrets to anyone, ²⁷except the messengers of His choosing. To protect *the messengers,* He sends guardians who walk in front and behind them, ²⁸to ensure they *can freely* deliver the messages of their Lord. Allah knows what they have, and He keeps an exact count of all things."

بِسۡمِ اللّٰهِ الرَّحۡمٰنِ الرَّحِیۡمِ

یٰۤاَیُّهَا الۡمُزَّمِّلُ ۙ١ قُمِ الَّیۡلَ اِلَّا قَلِیۡلًا ۙ٢ نِّصۡفَهٗۤ

اَوِ انۡقُصۡ مِنۡهُ قَلِیۡلًا ۙ٣ اَوۡ زِدۡ عَلَیۡهِ وَ رَتِّلِ

الۡقُرۡاٰنَ تَرۡتِیۡلًا ؕ٤ اِنَّا سَنُلۡقِیۡ عَلَیۡكَ قَوۡلًا ثَقِیۡلًا٥

اِنَّ نَاشِئَةَ الَّیۡلِ هِیَ اَشَدُّ وَطۡاً وَّ اَقۡوَمُ قِیۡلًا٦

اِنَّ لَكَ فِی النَّهَارِ سَبۡحًا طَوِیۡلًا ؕ٧ وَ اذۡكُرِ اسۡمَ رَبِّكَ

وَ تَبَتَّلۡ اِلَیۡهِ تَبۡتِیۡلًا ؕ٨ رَبُّ الۡمَشۡرِقِ وَ الۡمَغۡرِبِ

لَاۤ اِلٰهَ اِلَّا هُوَ فَاتَّخِذۡهُ وَكِیۡلًا٩ وَ اصۡبِرۡ عَلٰی

مَا یَقُوۡلُوۡنَ وَ اهۡجُرۡهُمۡ هَجۡرًا جَمِیۡلًا١٠ وَ ذَرۡنِیۡ

وَ الۡمُكَذِّبِیۡنَ اُولِی النَّعۡمَةِ وَ مَهِّلۡهُمۡ قَلِیۡلًا١١ اِنَّ

لَدَیۡنَاۤ اَنۡكَالًا وَّجَحِیۡمًا ۙ١٢ وَّطَعَامًا ذَا غُصَّةٍ وَّعَذَابًا

اَلِیۡمًا ۬ ١٣ یَوۡمَ تَرۡجُفُ الۡاَرۡضُ وَ الۡجِبَالُ وَكَانَتِ

الۡجِبَالُ كَثِیۡبًا مَّهِیۡلًا١٤ اِنَّاۤ اَرۡسَلۡنَاۤ اِلَیۡكُمۡ

رَسُوۡلًا ۬ شَاهِدًا عَلَیۡكُمۡ كَمَاۤ اَرۡسَلۡنَاۤ اِلٰی فِرۡعَوۡنَ

رَسُوۡلًا ؕ١٥ فَعَصٰی فِرۡعَوۡنُ الرَّسُوۡلَ فَاَخَذۡنٰهُ اَخۡذًا

وَّبِیۡلًا١٦ فَكَیۡفَ تَتَّقُوۡنَ اِنۡ كَفَرۡتُمۡ یَوۡمًا یَّجۡعَلُ

الۡوِلۡدَانَ شِیۡبَا۟ۨ ١٧ۚۖ السَّمَآءُ مُنۡفَطِرٌۢ بِهٖ ؕ كَانَ

وَعۡدُهٗ مَفۡعُوۡلًا١٨ اِنَّ هٰذِهٖ تَذۡكِرَةٌ ۚ فَمَنۡ شَآءَ

اتَّخَذَ اِلٰی رَبِّهٖ سَبِیۡلًا١٩ اِنَّ رَبَّكَ یَعۡلَمُ اَنَّكَ

The Messenger's ﷺ night vigil and devotions are highlighted, as well as his daytime activities. What are your devotions like?

١٩ع
١٣

1219

73. Surat Al-Muzammil

The Enwrapped

This is an early Makkan surat, possibly the second after *Surat Al-'Alaq*. The first part of the surat highlights the worries of the Prophet ﷺ about his mission, and his devoutness. The final long verse was revealed in Madinah. This final verse came as a concession to the Prophet ﷺ and the companions with regards to the length of their night vigils. The surat opens by describing the devotion of the Messenger ﷺ, his longing for Allah, and his recitation of the Quran. He is urged to read the Quran slowly, and articulate each letter clearly in a rhythmic and beautiful tone. The Prophet ﷺ used to say, "Beautify the Quran with your voices" (Al-Hakim). The surat illustrates that the blessed Messenger ﷺ is a beautiful example of the ultimate worshipper of Allah, who stands all night in worship, whilst others sleep.

The final lengthy verse gives instructions with regards to night vigils. The Quran is relaxing previous, more demanding instructions, since the situation of the Muslims in Madinah demanded they engage in carrying out other tasks during the day, including those concerned with their livelihoods, preaching and spreading Islam, and protecting their land.

In the name of Allah, the Kind, the Caring.

The Messenger's ﷺ night worship is exemplary
¹The Enwrapped! ²Pray standing during the night for a little while; ³half the night or even less; ⁴or a bit more, and read the Quran with clear pronunciation.ª ⁵Soon, We will send you a weighty Revelation. ⁶*Prayer* during the night makes a strong impact on the mind and makes the speech effective, ⁷since all day long you remain busy; ⁸remember the Name of your Lord and wholly devote yourself to Him. ⁹The Lord of the East and the West, there is no god but Him, so take Him as *your* Protector.

The Makkans are warned of a punishment
¹⁰And bear patiently what they say, and avoid them in a goodly manner. ¹¹Leave Me to deal with the deniers who selfishly enjoy comfort, and bear with them for a little while. ¹²Indeed, We have prepared chains, a blazing Fire, ¹³food that chokes

---

ª Ali defined *Tarteel* as pronouncing clearly each letter of the words of the glorious Quran.

In addition to worshipping, we must give charity, and spend our wealth, talents and time for His sake.

تَقُوْمُ اَدْنٰی مِنْ ثُلُثَیِ الَّیْلِ وَ نِصْفَهٗ وَ ثُلُثَهٗ

وَ طَآئِفَةٌ مِّنَ الَّذِیْنَ مَعَكَ ؕ وَ اللّٰهُ یُقَدِّرُ الَّیْلَ

وَ النَّهَارَ ؕ عَلِمَ اَنْ لَّنْ تُحْصُوْهُ فَتَابَ عَلَیْكُمْ

فَاقْرَءُوْا مَا تَیَسَّرَ مِنَ الْقُرْاٰنِ ؕ عَلِمَ اَنْ سَیَكُوْنُ

مِنْكُمْ مَّرْضٰی ۙ وَ اٰخَرُوْنَ یَضْرِبُوْنَ فِی الْاَرْضِ

یَبْتَغُوْنَ مِنْ فَضْلِ اللّٰهِ ۙ وَ اٰخَرُوْنَ یُقَاتِلُوْنَ فِیْ

سَبِیْلِ اللّٰهِ ۖ فَاقْرَءُوْا مَا تَیَسَّرَ مِنْهُ ۙ وَ اَقِیْمُوا

الصَّلٰوةَ وَ اٰتُوا الزَّكٰوةَ وَ اَقْرِضُوا اللّٰهَ قَرْضًا حَسَنًا ؕ

وَ مَا تُقَدِّمُوْا لِاَنْفُسِكُمْ مِّنْ خَیْرٍ تَجِدُوْهُ عِنْدَ

اللّٰهِ هُوَ خَیْرًا وَّ اَعْظَمَ اَجْرًا ؕ وَ اسْتَغْفِرُوا اللّٰهَ ؕ

اِنَّ اللّٰهَ غَفُوْرٌ رَّحِیْمٌ ۠ ۲۰

۲
ع
۱۴

and a painful punishment. [14] The Day when the Earth and the mountains will shake violently, then turn into heaps of sand.

Children's hair will turn grey

[15] Indeed, We sent to you a *noble* Messenger, *who is* a witness for you, like We sent a messenger to Pharaoh. [16] *But* Pharaoh disobeyed the messenger, so We punished him severely. [17] So how will you protect yourself *from the suffering* of a Day which will turn children's hair grey, how can you deny it? [18] The sky will be torn into pieces, and His promise fulfilled. [19] This is a reminder, so anyone who wants to take a path to his Lord, let him do so.

The night worship; the Messenger ﷺ permitted to relax his worship

[20] Your Lord knows, you stay awake worshipping Him with a group of *disciples*, sometimes for nearly two-thirds of the night and *other times* half of it or a third of it. *It is* Allah Who determines the length of the night and the day. He knows you won't be able to keep this *practice* up for too long, so He is kind to you: from now on, recite the Quran as much as you are able to with ease. He knows there are some who are ill, others travelling on business trips,[a] and others fighting in Allah's path. So recite from the Quran what is easy for you. *Furthermore*, establish the prayer regularly, pay the Zakat and give Allah a beautiful loan. *Remember*, whatever good you stock up is for yourselves; *in the Hereafter* you will find it with Allah. You will be greatly rewarded. Seek Allah's forgiveness; Allah is Forgiving, Caring.

---

[a] *Fadhu-l-Allah*, or "Allah's grace", is a metaphor for business.

74. Surat Al-Muddathir

The Cloaked One

After the first revelation of *surat Al-'Alaq* the Angel Jibreel ﷺ stopped coming to the Prophet ﷺ. This break in revelation may have lasted for a year, and this surat was the first to be revealed after the break. In this case it's a significant revelation. The Prophet ﷺ is reminded of his important position and crucial role in transforming humanity. The opening verses clearly instruct him to be energetic and forthright in preaching the Message, without fear of anyone.

> However, it also contains scores of new constructions, expressions, linguistic patterns, metaphors, statements that allow multiple interpretations, and elegantly concise turns of phrase, not to mention the new intellectual and cultural dimensions that intersect with *this* linguistic and rhetorical development.[a]

The Messenger ﷺ is being prepared for the hostility he will face, and Walid ibn al-Mughira, his opponent, is severely criticised, and his gloomy future in Hellfire vividly described. The proverb, "You reap what you sow" is mentioned in this context. The Quran also presents this principle: "Every person is endangered by the evil he has done, except the companions of the right hand" (38). In other words, every person is held hostage by the wrong they do; evil leads to evil results, vice creates vice, and wrong actions lead to wrong outcomes. An empowering verse; people can touch their own destiny. At the end the Messenger ﷺ is reassured and cautioned that the jealousy of some will prompt their opposition to him.

---

[a] B. Saeh, *The Miraculous Language of the Qur'an: Evidence of Divine Origin.*

بِسْمِ اللّٰهِ الرَّحْمٰنِ الرَّحِيْمِ

یٰۤاَیُّهَا الْمُدَّثِّرُ ۙ قُمْ فَاَنْذِرْ ۙ وَرَبَّكَ فَكَبِّرْ ۙ

وَثِیَابَكَ فَطَهِّرْ ۙ وَالرُّجْزَ فَاهْجُرْ ۙ وَلَا تَمْنُنْ

تَسْتَكْثِرُ ۙ وَلِرَبِّكَ فَاصْبِرْ ؕ فَاِذَا نُقِرَ فِی النَّاقُوْرِ ۙ

فَذٰلِكَ یَوْمَئِذٍ یَّوْمٌ عَسِیْرٌ ۙ عَلَی الْكٰفِرِیْنَ غَیْرُ

یَسِیْرٍ ؕ ذَرْنِیْ وَمَنْ خَلَقْتُ وَحِیْدًا ۙ وَّجَعَلْتُ

لَهٗ مَالًا مَّمْدُوْدًا ۙ وَّبَنِیْنَ شُهُوْدًا ۙ وَّمَهَّدْتُّ

لَهٗ تَمْهِیْدًا ۙ ثُمَّ یَطْمَعُ اَنْ اَزِیْدَ ۗ كَلَّا ؕ اِنَّهٗ

كَانَ لِاٰیٰتِنَا عَنِیْدًا ؕ سَاُرْهِقُهٗ صَعُوْدًا ؕ اِنَّهٗ

فَكَّرَ وَقَدَّرَ ۙ فَقُتِلَ كَیْفَ قَدَّرَ ۙ ثُمَّ قُتِلَ كَیْفَ

قَدَّرَ ۙ ثُمَّ نَظَرَ ۙ ثُمَّ عَبَسَ وَبَسَرَ ۙ ثُمَّ اَدْبَرَ

وَاسْتَكْبَرَ ۙ فَقَالَ اِنْ هٰذَاۤ اِلَّا سِحْرٌ یُّؤْثَرُ ۙ اِنْ

هٰذَاۤ اِلَّا قَوْلُ الْبَشَرِ ؕ سَاُصْلِیْهِ سَقَرَ ۙ وَمَاۤ

اَدْرٰىكَ مَا سَقَرُ ؕ لَا تُبْقِیْ وَلَا تَذَرُ ۚ لَوَّاحَةٌ

لِّلْبَشَرِ ۖ عَلَیْهَا تِسْعَةَ عَشَرَ ؕ وَمَا جَعَلْنَاۤ اَصْحٰبَ

النَّارِ اِلَّا مَلٰٓئِكَةً ۪ وَّمَا جَعَلْنَا عِدَّتَهُمْ اِلَّا فِتْنَةً

لِّلَّذِیْنَ كَفَرُوْا ۙ لِیَسْتَیْقِنَ الَّذِیْنَ اُوْتُوا الْكِتٰبَ

وَیَزْدَادَ الَّذِیْنَ اٰمَنُوْۤا اِیْمَانًا وَّلَا یَرْتَابَ الَّذِیْنَ

اُوْتُوا الْكِتٰبَ وَالْمُؤْمِنُوْنَ ۙ وَلِیَقُوْلَ الَّذِیْنَ

In the name of Allah, the Kind, the Caring.

The Messenger ﷺ is instructed to preach openly

[1] *Messenger,* the cloaked one, [2] stand up and warn *people,* [3] and magnify *the praise* of Your Lord. [4] Keep your clothes clean, [5] and steer clear of evil. [6] Don't expect any gains in return for the favours you do, [7] and be patient for the sake of Your Lord. [8] When the Trumpet is blown, [9] it will be a difficult Day, [10] not at all easy for the disbelievers.

A stubborn opponent is condemned for disbelieving

[11] Let me deal with the one I created a lone child;[a] [12] I gave him lots of wealth, [13] many sons around him, [14] and I made his *material* progress smooth. [15] He is full of hopes that I shall increase *it.* [16] No! He is a determined opponent of Our Revelations. [17] I shall soon lay upon him increasing punishment. [18] He thought and plotted. [19] He is ruined for what he plotted. [20] Again, he is ruined for what he plotted. [21] Then he looked, [22] then he frowned and scowled, [23] then he turned his back and was arrogant, [24] declaring: "This is magic of the ancients; [25] the speech of a mere mortal!"

The misguided is punished

[26] I shall burn him in Hellfire. [27] What will explain to you the Hellfire? [28] It neither spares nor leaves anyone, [29] constantly scorching the skin; [30] there are nineteen *guards* over it. [31] We appointed the angels over the inmates of Hell, and made their number only as a test for the disbelievers and to assure the ones who were given the Book, and to increase the faith of the believers. So, the believers and those given the Book will have no doubt about your truthfulness.

---

[a]   This is al-Walid ibn al-Mughira, a staunch opponent of the Messenger ﷺ.

فِى قُلُوبِهِم مَّرَضٌ وَّالكٰفِرُونَ مَاذَآ اَرَادَ اللهُ بِهٰذَا مَثَلًا ۚ كَذٰلِكَ يُضِلُّ اللهُ مَن يَّشَآءُ وَ يَهدِى مَن يَّشَآءُ ۚ وَمَا يَعلَمُ جُنُودَ رَبِّكَ اِلَّا هُوَ ۚ وَمَا هِىَ اِلَّا ذِكرٰى لِلبَشَرِ ﴿٣١﴾ كَلَّا وَالقَمَرِ ﴿٣٢﴾ وَالَّيلِ اِذ اَدبَرَ ﴿٣٣﴾ وَالصُّبحِ اِذَآ اَسفَرَ ﴿٣٤﴾ اِنَّهَا لَاِحدَى الكُبَرِ ﴿٣٥﴾ نَذِيرًا لِّلبَشَرِ ﴿٣٦﴾ لِمَن شَآءَ مِنكُم اَن يَّتَقَدَّمَ اَو يَتَاَخَّرَ ﴿٣٧﴾ كُلُّ نَفسٍ بِمَا كَسَبَت رَهِينَةٌ ﴿٣٨﴾ اِلَّآ اَصحٰبَ اليَمِينِ ﴿٣٩﴾ فِى جَنّٰتٍ يَتَسَآءَلُونَ ﴿٤٠﴾ عَنِ المُجرِمِينَ ﴿٤١﴾ مَا سَلَكَكُم فِى سَقَرَ ﴿٤٢﴾ قَالُوا لَم نَكُ مِنَ المُصَلِّينَ ﴿٤٣﴾ وَلَم نَكُ نُطعِمُ المِسكِينَ ﴿٤٤﴾ وَكُنَّا نَخُوضُ مَعَ الخَآئِضِينَ ﴿٤٥﴾ وَكُنَّا نُكَذِّبُ بِيَومِ الدِّينِ ﴿٤٦﴾ حَتّٰى اَتَانَا اليَقِينُ ﴿٤٧﴾ فَمَا تَنفَعُهُم شَفَاعَةُ الشّٰفِعِينَ ﴿٤٨﴾ فَمَا لَهُم عَنِ التَّذكِرَةِ مُعرِضِينَ ﴿٤٩﴾ كَاَنَّهُم حُمُرٌ مُّستَنفِرَةٌ ﴿٥٠﴾ فَرَّت مِن قَسوَرَةٍ ﴿٥١﴾ بَل يُرِيدُ كُلُّ امرِئٍ مِّنهُم اَن يُّؤتٰى صُحُفًا مُّنَشَّرَةً ﴿٥٢﴾ كَلَّا ۚ بَل لَّا يَخَافُونَ الاٰخِرَةَ ﴿٥٣﴾ كَلَّآ اِنَّهُ تَذكِرَةٌ ﴿٥٤﴾ فَمَن شَآءَ ذَكَرَهُ ﴿٥٥﴾ وَمَا يَذكُرُونَ اِلَّآ اَن يَّشَآءَ اللهُ ۚ هُوَ اَهلُ التَّقوٰى وَاَهلُ المَغفِرَةِ ﴿٥٦﴾

The believers are certain and convinced about the reality of Judgement Day. Therefore, they worship the Lord and spend in charity.

But the disbelievers and the ones in whose hearts there is a sickness will say, "What does Allah mean by this example *of the nineteen angels*?" That is how Allah allows some to be misguided and others to be guided. No one knows the forces of your Lord except Him. It is a *Majestic* reminder for humanity.

Why people will end up in Hell

³²Yes, by the moon, ³³by the night as it fades away, ³⁴by the morning as it shines! ³⁵It's a great thing; ³⁶a warner for humanity, ³⁷for those wanting to progress *spiritually* and those who wish to stay behind. ³⁸Every person is held hostageᵃ by the evil he does, ³⁹except the companions of the right hand ⁴⁰*living* in gardens; they will ask each other ⁴¹about the sinners: ⁴²"What *deeds* brought you into Hellfire?" ⁴³They will answer, "We neither worshipped, ⁴⁴nor fed the needy, ⁴⁵busy doing evil and friends of those who were frivolous. ⁴⁶We denied Judgement Day ⁴⁷until the inevitable, certain, *death* came to us." ⁴⁸The intercession of the intercessors, *the idols,* won't benefit them.

Wild frightened donkeys

⁴⁹So what's the matter with them, they turn away from the Reminder? ⁵⁰Like frightened donkeys ⁵¹fleeing from a lioness. ⁵²Rather, each man among them wants a revelation to be rolled out and handed over to him. ⁵³No! They don't fear the Hereafter. ⁵⁴No! This is a Reminder, ⁵⁵so let him who wishes to listen to it do so. ⁵⁶They will listen if Allah wills. He alone should be feared, the Lord of forgiveness.

ᵃ *Rahina* literally means "to be held in pledge" or "hostage". I have translated it accordingly.

بِسْمِ اللهِ الرَّحْمٰنِ الرَّحِيْمِ

لَاۤ اُقْسِمُ بِيَوْمِ الْقِيٰمَةِ ۙ١ وَلَاۤ اُقْسِمُ بِالنَّفْسِ

اللَّوَّامَةِ ؕ٢ اَيَحْسَبُ الْاِنْسَانُ اَلَّنْ نَّجْمَعَ عِظَامَهٗ ؕ٣

بَلٰى قٰدِرِيْنَ عَلٰۤى اَنْ نُّسَوِّيَ بَنَانَهٗ ٤ بَلْ يُرِيْدُ

الْاِنْسَانُ لِيَفْجُرَ اَمَامَهٗ ۚ٥ يَسْـَٔلُ اَيَّانَ يَوْمُ الْقِيٰمَةِ ؕ٦

فَاِذَا بَرِقَ الْبَصَرُ ۙ٧ وَخَسَفَ الْقَمَرُ ۙ٨ وَجُمِعَ الشَّمْسُ

وَالْقَمَرُ ۙ٩ يَقُوْلُ الْاِنْسَانُ يَوْمَئِذٍ اَيْنَ الْمَفَرُّ ۚ١٠

كَلَّا لَا وَزَرَ ؕ١١ اِلٰى رَبِّكَ يَوْمَئِذِ الْمُسْتَقَرُّ ؕ١٢ يُنَبَّؤُا

الْاِنْسَانُ يَوْمَئِذٍ بِمَا قَدَّمَ وَاَخَّرَ ؕ١٣ بَلِ الْاِنْسَانُ

عَلٰى نَفْسِهٖ بَصِيْرَةٌ ۙ١٤ وَّلَوْ اَلْقٰى مَعَاذِيْرَهٗ ؕ١٥ لَا

تُحَرِّكْ بِهٖ لِسَانَكَ لِتَعْجَلَ بِهٖ ؕ١٦ اِنَّ عَلَيْنَا جَمْعَهٗ

وَقُرْاٰنَهٗ ۚ١٧ فَاِذَا قَرَاْنٰهُ فَاتَّبِعْ قُرْاٰنَهٗ ۚ١٨ ثُمَّ اِنَّ

عَلَيْنَا بَيَانَهٗ ؕ١٩ كَلَّا بَلْ تُحِبُّوْنَ الْعَاجِلَةَ ۙ٢٠ وَ

تَذَرُوْنَ الْاٰخِرَةَ ؕ٢١ وُجُوْهٌ يَّوْمَئِذٍ نَّاضِرَةٌ ۙ٢٢ اِلٰى

رَبِّهَا نَاظِرَةٌ ۚ٢٣ وَوُجُوْهٌ يَّوْمَئِذٍ بَاسِرَةٌ ۙ٢٤ تَظُنُّ

اَنْ يُّفْعَلَ بِهَا فَاقِرَةٌ ؕ٢٥ كَلَّاۤ اِذَا بَلَغَتِ التَّرَاقِيَ ۙ٢٦

وَقِيْلَ مَنْ ٚرَاقٍ ۙ٢٧ وَّظَنَّ اَنَّهُ الْفِرَاقُ ۙ٢٨ وَالْتَفَّتِ

السَّاقُ بِالسَّاقِ ۙ٢٩ اِلٰى رَبِّكَ يَوْمَئِذِ الْمَسَاقُ ؕ٣٠

فَلَا صَدَّقَ وَلَا صَلّٰى ۙ٣١ وَلٰكِنْ كَذَّبَ وَتَوَلّٰى ۙ٣٢

The Day of Resurrection is presented, and Allah is the Judge. Its imminent, so stop postponing it.

1229

75. Surat Al-Qiyamah

The Day of Judgement

This is an early Makkan surat with the central theme of the Day of Judgement. It describes some of the scenes from that Day: disintegrated human bones will be brought to life, a lunar eclipse will occur, people will be astonished and confused. It will dawn upon them that they are standing in front of the Mighty Lord Who will do justice. They will see their whole life unfold before them like a film, and they will make excuses for their wretched behaviour.

Abu Jahl, the Makkan leader, bitterly opposed the Prophet ﷺ. He would bring decaying bones to the Prophet ﷺ and ask, "Can this be brought back to life?" The surat answers that query, and further explains Abu Jahl's problem: "You love the fleeting world *dearly*" (20). His other problems include his disbelief, lack of worship, and arrogance (31–33). He is warned about his death throes, when he will be dying and no one will be able to cure him. Finally, the Quran asks, "Isn't He capable of bringing life to the dead?" (40).

In the name of Allah, the Kind, the Caring.

The horrors of Judgement Day

[1] I swear by the Day of Judgement, [2] and I swear by the self-critical soul! [3] Do people think We won't put together their *disintegrated* bones? [4] Of course, We are capable of restoring even their fingertips. [5] Yet they openly commit evil in front of Him, [6] and *mockingly* ask: "When will Judgement Day come?" [7] *When it comes* eyes will be dazzled, [8] the moon eclipsed, [9] the sun and the moon *will appear to* be joined together, [10] and man will ask that Day: "Where can we flee to?" [11] No, there is no safe place. [12] That Day, *you will* be brought before your Lord: [13] people will learn what they achieved and what they failed to do. [14] They will have evidence against themselves, [15] but still offer excuses.

The preservation of the Quran is the concern of Allah

[16] *Messenger*, don't read *the Quran* too fast to *memorise* it. [17] We are responsible for its compilation and recital. [18] So when We recite it, then follow its recitation. [19] It is also Our responsibility to explain it clearly *to you.*

ثُمَّ ذَهَبَ اِلٰٓى اَهْلِهٖ يَتَمَطّٰى ۞ اَوْلٰى لَكَ فَاَوْلٰى ۞ ثُمَّ

اَوْلٰى لَكَ فَاَوْلٰى ۞ اَيَحْسَبُ الْاِنْسَانُ اَنْ يُّتْرَكَ

سُدًى ۞ اَلَمْ يَكُ نُطْفَةً مِّنْ مَّنِيٍّ يُّمْنٰى ۞ ثُمَّ كَانَ

عَلَقَةً فَخَلَقَ فَسَوّٰى ۞ فَجَعَلَ مِنْهُ الزَّوْجَيْنِ الذَّكَرَ

وَالْاُنْثٰى ۞ اَلَيْسَ ذٰلِكَ بِقٰدِرٍ عَلٰٓى اَنْ يُّحْيِۦَ الْمَوْتٰى ۞

The fool thinks he will stay here forever.

ع
٢
١٨

1231

Love of the world makes people forget the Hereafter

[20] You love the fleeting world, [21] and dislike the Hereafter. [22] That Day, some faces will be shining, [23] *happily* watching their Lord. [24] That Day, other faces will be gloomy and grave, [25] sensing the occurrence of a back-breaking sufferings. [26] No, when the soul reaches the breastbone, [27] it will be said, "Where's the charmer *doctor who can heal?*" [28] He will know it's time to leave, [29] the legs will be straightened and brought together;[a] [30] then that Day he will be driven toward Your Lord.

Allah will resurrect

[31] He didn't believe or pray,[b] [32] instead he denied and turned his back, [33] walked arrogantly amid his people. [34] Yet, *the Hereafter* is drawing closer and closer to you, [35] and even more and more closer to you. [36] Do people think they aren't *answerable to Allah*? [37] Weren't they a drop of emitted semen? [38] Then a germ cell that *Allah* created and perfected? [39] Then He made from it the pair: the male and the female. [40] Isn't He *the One Who did* that? So, isn't He capable of bringing back to life the dead?

---

[a]   When a person is dead, the legs are straightened before rigor mortis sets in.
[b]   This refers to a bitter opponent of the Prophet 鐤, Abu Jahl, and describes his arrogance and disbelief.

بِسْمِ اللّٰهِ الرَّحْمٰنِ الرَّحِيْمِ

هَلْ اَتٰى عَلَى الْاِنْسَانِ حِيْنٌ مِّنَ الدَّهْرِ لَمْ يَكُنْ شَيْئًا مَّذْكُوْرًا ۝ اِنَّا خَلَقْنَا الْاِنْسَانَ مِنْ نُّطْفَةٍ اَمْشَاجٍ ۖ نَّبْتَلِيْهِ فَجَعَلْنٰهُ سَمِيْعًۢا بَصِيْرًا ۝ اِنَّا هَدَيْنٰهُ السَّبِيْلَ اِمَّا شَاكِرًا وَّ اِمَّا كَفُوْرًا ۝ اِنَّاۤ اَعْتَدْنَا لِلْكٰفِرِيْنَ سَلٰسِلَا۟ وَ اَغْلٰلًا وَّ سَعِيْرًا ۝ اِنَّ الْاَبْرَارَ يَشْرَبُوْنَ مِنْ كَأْسٍ كَانَ مِزَاجُهَا كَافُوْرًا ۝ عَيْنًا يَّشْرَبُ

What a vivid description of the delights and joys of Paradise. A reward for your effort, love of Allah and service to humanity.

بِهَا عِبَادُ اللّٰهِ يُفَجِّرُوْنَهَا تَفْجِيْرًا ۝ يُوْفُوْنَ بِالنَّذْرِ وَ يَخَافُوْنَ يَوْمًا كَانَ شَرُّهٗ مُسْتَطِيْرًا ۝ وَ يُطْعِمُوْنَ الطَّعَامَ عَلٰى حُبِّهٖ مِسْكِيْنًا وَّ يَتِيْمًا وَّ اَسِيْرًا ۝ اِنَّمَا نُطْعِمُكُمْ لِوَجْهِ اللّٰهِ لَا نُرِيْدُ مِنْكُمْ جَزَآءً وَّلَا شُكُوْرًا ۝ اِنَّا نَخَافُ مِنْ رَّبِّنَا يَوْمًا عَبُوْسًا قَمْطَرِيْرًا ۝ فَوَقٰىهُمُ اللّٰهُ شَرَّ ذٰلِكَ الْيَوْمِ وَ لَقّٰىهُمْ نَضْرَةً وَّ سُرُوْرًا ۝ وَ جَزٰىهُمْ بِمَا صَبَرُوْا جَنَّةً وَّ حَرِيْرًا ۝ مُّتَّكِئِيْنَ فِيْهَا عَلَى الْاَرَآئِكِ ۚ لَا يَرَوْنَ فِيْهَا شَمْسًا وَّلَا زَمْهَرِيْرًا ۝ وَ دَانِيَةً عَلَيْهِمْ ظِلٰلُهَا وَ ذُلِّلَتْ قُطُوْفُهَا تَذْلِيْلًا ۝ وَ يُطَافُ عَلَيْهِمْ بِاٰنِيَةٍ مِّنْ فِضَّةٍ وَّ اَكْوَابٍ كَانَتْ قَوَارِيْرَا۠ ۝ قَوَارِيْرَ مِنْ فِضَّةٍ قَدَّرُوْهَا

76. Surat Ad-Dahr
The Time

According to some commentators this is a Madinan surat. Its central theme is: humanity is blessed with the ability to intelligently distinguish between right and wrong, and therefore will be held accountable; a terse reminder of the purpose and meaning of human life. These introductory comments are followed by a lively description of the good people: they fulfil their vows, fear Judgement Day, are generous and selfless, and take care of the needy and the poor. For these wonderful works, they will have the delights of Paradise. The surat makes it clear that this is a reward for their patience and hard work. Finally, the Messenger ﷺ is reminded to continue his work patiently and diligently.

In the name of Allah, the Kind, the Caring.

The purpose of human creation
¹Hasn't there been a phase *in human history* when humans were nothing worthy of mention? ²We created human – from a drop of mixed fluid – to test. We gave them hearing and sight; ³We showed the straight path, *to see* whether they would be thankful, or an unthankful denier. ⁴For the disbelievers We've prepared chains, iron collars and a Blazing Fire. ⁵The righteous will drink wine mixed with fragrant herbs,ª ⁶a drink from a freely-flowing spring, *made for* the servants of Allah.

Who are the righteous?
⁷They fulfil *their* vows, fear a Day whose horror is widespread, ⁸they feed the needy, the orphan and the prisoner for the love *of Allah,* ⁹*saying,* "We feed you for His sake; we don't want some payment or thanks from you. ¹⁰We fear a Day of calamity and destruction, coming from Our Lord." ¹¹Allah will protect them from the distress of that Day, their faces will shine with joy.

A glowing description of the delights of Paradise
¹²He rewarded them with *breathtaking* Gardens and silk *clothing* for the patience they showed; ¹³*they will* rest on *comfortable* sofas and they won't have extreme heat or bitter cold; ¹⁴low-hanging *branches* will give them shade and clusters of fruits will be close at hand. ¹⁵They will be served in crystal-like silver cups, ¹⁶selecting the size of the cups to drink from. ¹⁷They will have a drink mixed with

---

ª *Kafur* literally means camphor and fragrance.

تَقۡدِیۡرًا ۞ وَیُسۡقَوۡنَ فِیۡهَا كَاۡسًا كَانَ مِزَاجُهَا

زَنۡجَبِیۡلًا ۞ عَیۡنًا فِیۡهَا تُسَمّٰی سَلۡسَبِیۡلًا ۞ وَ

یَطُوۡفُ عَلَیۡهِمۡ وِلۡدَانٌ مُّخَلَّدُوۡنَ ۚ اِذَا رَاَیۡتَهُمۡ

حَسِبۡتَهُمۡ لُؤۡلُؤًا مَّنۡثُوۡرًا ۞ وَاِذَا رَاَیۡتَ ثَمَّ رَاَیۡتَ

نَعِیۡمًا وَّمُلۡكًا كَبِیۡرًا ۞ عٰلِیَهُمۡ ثِیَابُ سُنۡدُسٍ

خُضۡرٌ وَّاِسۡتَبۡرَقٌ ۚ وَّحُلُّوۡۤا اَسَاوِرَ مِنۡ فِضَّةٍ ۚ

وَسَقٰىهُمۡ رَبُّهُمۡ شَرَابًا طَهُوۡرًا ۞ اِنَّ هٰذَا كَانَ لَكُمۡ

جَزَآءً وَّكَانَ سَعۡیُكُمۡ مَّشۡكُوۡرًا ۞ اِنَّا نَحۡنُ نَزَّلۡنَا

عَلَیۡكَ الۡقُرۡاٰنَ تَنۡزِیۡلًا ۞ فَاصۡبِرۡ لِحُكۡمِ رَبِّكَ وَلَا

تُطِعۡ مِنۡهُمۡ اٰثِمًا اَوۡ كَفُوۡرًا ۞ وَاذۡكُرِ اسۡمَ رَبِّكَ

بُكۡرَةً وَّاَصِیۡلًا ۞ وَمِنَ الَّیۡلِ فَاسۡجُدۡ لَهٗ وَسَبِّحۡهُ

لَیۡلًا طَوِیۡلًا ۞ اِنَّ هٰۤؤُلَآءِ یُحِبُّوۡنَ الۡعَاجِلَةَ وَ

یَذَرُوۡنَ وَرَآءَهُمۡ یَوۡمًا ثَقِیۡلًا ۞ نَحۡنُ خَلَقۡنٰهُمۡ

وَشَدَدۡنَاۤ اَسۡرَهُمۡ ۚ وَاِذَا شِئۡنَا بَدَّلۡنَاۤ اَمۡثَالَهُمۡ

تَبۡدِیۡلًا ۞ اِنَّ هٰذِهٖ تَذۡكِرَةٌ ۚ فَمَنۡ شَآءَ اتَّخَذَ

اِلٰی رَبِّهٖ سَبِیۡلًا ۞ وَمَا تَشَآءُوۡنَ اِلَّاۤ اَنۡ

یَّشَآءَ اللّٰهُ ط اِنَّ اللّٰهَ كَانَ عَلِیۡمًا حَكِیۡمًا ۞

یُّدۡخِلُ مَنۡ یَّشَآءُ فِیۡ رَحۡمَتِهٖ ط وَالظّٰلِمِیۡنَ

اَعَدَّ لَهُمۡ عَذَابًا اَلِیۡمًا ۞

Success in the Hereafter is a result of your effort and Divine grace.

1235

ginger, ¹⁸from the spring of Salsabilᵃ. ¹⁹Eternal youth will serve them, and when you see them you will think they are pearls; ²⁰when you look around these delightful scenes, you will see an immense *blissful* kingdom. ²¹Their *fine clothes* will be made of green silk and brocade; they will be adorned with silver bracelets, and their Lord will give them pure drinks. ²²*It will be said:* "This is the reward for you, and today your *tireless* efforts are gratefully acknowledged."

The Messenger ﷺ is urged to be patient

²³We gradually revealed the Majestic Quran to you, ²⁴so wait patiently for the judgement of Your Lord, and don't obey any of them: the sinner or the ungrateful person. ²⁵Remember the Name of your Lord in the morning and evening, ²⁶and prostrate to Him, and glorify him throughout the night. ²⁷These *people* love the *short-lived* world, and dislike a Weighty Day ahead of them. ²⁸We created them, and strengthened their ligaments and joints; if We wanted, We could have totally replaced the likes of them. ²⁹This is a Reminder for anyone who wants to take the road to his Lord. ³⁰You can't have it unless Allah wills to show you that way,ᵇ and Allah is Knowing, Wise. ³¹He cares for anyone He wants, and for the wrongdoers He has prepared a painful punishment.

ᵃ *Salsabil* is the fountain in paradise (Suyuti).

ᵇ This means you have it because Allah wanted to guide you. He has given you reason and revelation to see the truth. This means that humans have the choice to willingly accept the guidance or reject it.

بِسْمِ اللّٰهِ الرَّحْمٰنِ الرَّحِيْمِ

وَالْمُرْسَلٰتِ عُرْفًا ۙ ١ فَالْعٰصِفٰتِ عَصْفًا ۙ ٢

وَّالنّٰشِرٰتِ نَشْرًا ۙ ٣ فَالْفٰرِقٰتِ فَرْقًا ۙ ٤

فَالْمُلْقِيٰتِ ذِكْرًا ۙ ٥ عُذْرًا اَوْ نُذْرًا ۙ ٦ اِنَّمَا

تُوْعَدُوْنَ لَوَاقِعٌ ؕ ٧ فَاِذَا النُّجُوْمُ طُمِسَتْ ۙ ٨

وَاِذَا السَّمَآءُ فُرِجَتْ ۙ ٩ وَّاِذَا الْجِبَالُ نُسِفَتْ ۙ ١٠

وَاِذَا الرُّسُلُ اُقِّتَتْ ؕ ١١ لِاَيِّ يَوْمٍ اُجِّلَتْ ؕ ١٢

لِيَوْمِ الْفَصْلِ ۚ ١٣ وَمَآ اَدْرٰىكَ مَا يَوْمُ الْفَصْلِ ؕ ١٤

وَيْلٌ يَّوْمَىِٕذٍ لِّلْمُكَذِّبِيْنَ ١٥ اَلَمْ نُهْلِكِ الْاَوَّلِيْنَ ؕ ١٦

ثُمَّ نُتْبِعُهُمُ الْاٰخِرِيْنَ ١٧ كَذٰلِكَ نَفْعَلُ

بِالْمُجْرِمِيْنَ ١٨ وَيْلٌ يَّوْمَىِٕذٍ لِّلْمُكَذِّبِيْنَ ١٩

اَلَمْ نَخْلُقْكُّمْ مِّنْ مَّآءٍ مَّهِيْنٍ ۙ ٢٠ فَجَعَلْنٰهُ فِيْ

قَرَارٍ مَّكِيْنٍ ۙ ٢١ اِلٰى قَدَرٍ مَّعْلُوْمٍ ۙ ٢٢ فَقَدَرْنَا ۖ

فَنِعْمَ الْقٰدِرُوْنَ ٢٣ وَيْلٌ يَّوْمَىِٕذٍ لِّلْمُكَذِّبِيْنَ ٢٤

اَلَمْ نَجْعَلِ الْاَرْضَ كِفَاتًا ۙ ٢٥ اَحْيَآءً وَّاَمْوَاتًا ۙ ٢٦

وَّجَعَلْنَا فِيْهَا رَوَاسِيَ شٰمِخٰتٍ وَّاَسْقَيْنٰكُمْ

مَّآءً فُرَاتًا ؕ ٢٧ وَيْلٌ يَّوْمَىِٕذٍ لِّلْمُكَذِّبِيْنَ ٢٨ اِنْطَلِقُوْۤا

اِلٰى مَا كُنْتُمْ بِهٖ تُكَذِّبُوْنَ ۚ ٢٩ اِنْطَلِقُوْۤا اِلٰى

ظِلٍّ ذِيْ ثَلٰثِ شُعَبٍ ۙ ٣٠ لَّا ظَلِيْلٍ وَّلَا يُغْنِيْ

The refrain, "a day of great loss for the deniers", is repeated ten times. A stress on the need to beware of Judgement Day.

1237

77. Surat Al-Mursalat

The Winds

Five oaths open the surat: the first four refer to the incredible power of the wind, its movement of the air, that it is an amazing natural phenomenon: from the calm and pleasant morning breeze, to the gale-force winds that create storms on land to sea, and the gusty winds that move the clouds to become hurricanes and cyclones. The fifth refers to the angels responsible for the Divine Revelation. The phrase, "That will be a Day of big loss for the deniers!" Is repeated ten times. Such refrains warn stubborn people and open their eyes, so they can overcome their ignorance and egoism. Threats are employed, warning the disbelievers of the consequences of their disbelief. This is a powerful rhetorical device for conveying the message. The first time it occurs is after warning the disbelievers of "the Day of Distinction".

The surat points out the humble beginnings of a human being: from a sperm and an egg a human baby is produced. The One Who can perform this can also resurrect the dead: "Didn't We make the Earth a place for holding back the living and the dead?" (25–26)

In the name of Allah, the Kind, the Caring.

The immense power of the wind is testimony to Allah's creative powers
¹By the winds that blow non-stop,ᵃ ²the strong gusty winds, ³the scattering winds, ⁴the shearing winds that forcefully separate, ⁵and I swear by the angels who deliver a reminder, ⁶sometimes a prayer and sometimes a warning, ⁷what you've been promised will happen.

The Day of Decision; the winners and the losers are separated
⁸When the stars' light is faded, ⁹when the sky is split, ¹⁰when the mountains are crumbled to dust, ¹¹when the appointed term for the messengers *finally* comes – ¹²for which Day has this been set for? ¹³The Day of Decision. ¹⁴What will explain to you what the Day of Decision is? ¹⁵A Day of great loss for the deniers!

Lessons from history and nature
¹⁶Didn't We destroy the previous generations? ¹⁷We shall do the same to this one; ¹⁸Our way of dealing with the sinners. ¹⁹A Day of great loss for the deniers! ²⁰Didn't We create you out of an embarrassing fluid? ²¹That We lodged in the womb ²²for

---

ᵃ Literally "that which is sent forth".

1238

مِنَ اللَّهَبِ ۞ اِنَّهَا تَرْمِى بِشَرَرٍ كَالْقَصْرِ ۞

كَاَنَّهٗ جِمٰلَتٌ صُفْرٌ ۞ وَيْلٌ يَّوْمَئِذٍ لِّلْمُكَذِّبِيْنَ ۞

هٰذَا يَوْمُ لَا يَنْطِقُوْنَ ۞ وَلَا يُؤْذَنُ لَهُمْ

فَيَعْتَذِرُوْنَ ۞ وَيْلٌ يَّوْمَئِذٍ لِّلْمُكَذِّبِيْنَ ۞ هٰذَا

يَوْمُ الْفَصْلِ جَمَعْنٰكُمْ وَالْاَوَّلِيْنَ ۞ فَاِنْ كَانَ لَكُمْ

كَيْدٌ فَكِيْدُوْنِ ۞ وَيْلٌ يَّوْمَئِذٍ لِّلْمُكَذِّبِيْنَ ۞

اِنَّ الْمُتَّقِيْنَ فِيْ ظِلٰلٍ وَّعُيُوْنٍ ۞ وَّفَوَاكِهَ مِمَّا

Their real problem was reluctance to worship and bow before Allah

يَشْتَهُوْنَ ۞ كُلُوْا وَاشْرَبُوْا هَنِيْئًا بِمَا كُنْتُمْ

تَعْمَلُوْنَ ۞ اِنَّا كَذٰلِكَ نَجْزِى الْمُحْسِنِيْنَ ۞

وَيْلٌ يَّوْمَئِذٍ لِّلْمُكَذِّبِيْنَ ۞ كُلُوْا وَتَمَتَّعُوْا

قَلِيْلًا اِنَّكُمْ مُّجْرِمُوْنَ ۞ وَيْلٌ يَّوْمَئِذٍ

لِّلْمُكَذِّبِيْنَ ۞ وَاِذَا قِيْلَ لَهُمُ ارْكَعُوْا لَا

يَرْكَعُوْنَ ۞ وَيْلٌ يَّوْمَئِذٍ لِّلْمُكَذِّبِيْنَ ۞

فَبِاَيِّ حَدِيْثٍ بَعْدَهٗ يُؤْمِنُوْنَ ۞

a fixed period, ²³ precisely determined by Us; we are excellent at determining its length. ²⁴ A Day of great loss for the deniers! ²⁵ Didn't We make the Earth a place for holding back ²⁶ the living and the dead? ²⁷ *Didn't We* make lofty fixed mountains and give you sweet water to drink? ²⁸ A Day of great loss for the deniers!

The losers driven to burning flames

²⁹ "Go to the place, you used to deny! ³⁰ Go in to the shade of the smoke that rises in three columns!" ³¹ *This will provide* neither cool shade nor safety from the heat of the flames. ³² It throws out columns of sparks like tall towers, ³³ like *pieces of* copper. ³⁴ A Day of great loss for the deniers! ³⁵ Today, they won't speak, ³⁶ nor be allowed to make excuses for themselves. ³⁷ A Day of great loss for the deniers. ³⁸ This is the Day of Decision, We'll gather you and all the previous generations. ³⁹ If you've devised a plot against Me then try it! ⁴⁰ A Day of great loss for the deniers!

The winners in the cool shade of Paradise

⁴¹ The righteous will enjoy themselves in *cool* shade and *gushing* springs, ⁴² and their favourite fruits. ⁴³ *They will be told*: "Eat, drink and be merry for what you did." ⁴⁴ That's how We reward the righteous people. ⁴⁵ A Day of great loss for the deniers! ⁴⁶ *Tell the disbelievers*: "Eat and enjoy yourselves for a while; you are sinners". ⁴⁷ A Day of great loss for the deniers! ⁴⁸ When they were told, "Bow for prayer," they didn't bow. ⁴⁹ A Day of great loss for the deniers! ⁵⁰ So which revelation after this will they believe?

بِسْمِ اللهِ الرَّحْمٰنِ الرَّحِيْمِ

عَمَّ يَتَسَآءَلُوْنَ ۟١ عَنِ النَّبَاِ الْعَظِيْمِ ۟٢ الَّذِیْ
هُمْ فِیْهِ مُخْتَلِفُوْنَ ۟٣ كَلَّا سَيَعْلَمُوْنَ ۟٤ ثُمَّ كَلَّا
سَيَعْلَمُوْنَ ۟٥ اَلَمْ نَجْعَلِ الْاَرْضَ مِهٰدًا ۟٦ وَّالْجِبَالَ
اَوْتَادًا ۟٧ وَّخَلَقْنٰكُمْ اَزْوَاجًا ۟٨ وَّجَعَلْنَا نَوْمَكُمْ
سُبَاتًا ۟٩ وَّجَعَلْنَا الَّيْلَ لِبَاسًا ۟١٠ وَّجَعَلْنَا النَّهَارَ
مَعَاشًا ۟١١ وَّبَنَيْنَا فَوْقَكُمْ سَبْعًا شِدَادًا ۟١٢ وَّجَعَلْنَا
سِرَاجًا وَّهَّاجًا ۟١٣ وَّاَنْزَلْنَا مِنَ الْمُعْصِرٰتِ مَآءً
ثَجَّاجًا ۟١٤ لِّنُخْرِجَ بِهٖ حَبًّا وَّنَبَاتًا ۟١٥ وَّجَنّٰتٍ اَلْفَافًا ۟١٦
اِنَّ يَوْمَ الْفَصْلِ كَانَ مِيْقَاتًا ۟١٧ يَّوْمَ يُنْفَخُ فِی
الصُّوْرِ فَتَاْتُوْنَ اَفْوَاجًا ۟١٨ وَّفُتِحَتِ السَّمَآءُ فَكَانَتْ
اَبْوَابًا ۟١٩ وَّسُيِّرَتِ الْجِبَالُ فَكَانَتْ سَرَابًا ۟٢٠ اِنَّ
جَهَنَّمَ كَانَتْ مِرْصَادًا ۟٢١ لِّلطَّاغِيْنَ مَاٰبًا ۟٢٢ لّٰبِثِيْنَ
فِیْهَآ اَحْقَابًا ۟٢٣ لَا يَذُوْقُوْنَ فِیْهَا بَرْدًا وَّلَا شَرَابًا ۟٢٤
اِلَّا حَمِيْمًا وَّغَسَّاقًا ۟٢٥ جَزَآءً وِّفَاقًا ۟٢٦ اِنَّهُمْ كَانُوْا
لَا يَرْجُوْنَ حِسَابًا ۟٢٧ وَّكَذَّبُوْا بِاٰيٰتِنَا كِذَّابًا ۟٢٨ وَكُلَّ
شَیْءٍ اَحْصَيْنٰهُ كِتٰبًا ۟٢٩ فَذُوْقُوْا فَلَنْ نَّزِيْدَكُمْ
اِلَّا عَذَابًا ۟٣٠ اِنَّ لِلْمُتَّقِيْنَ مَفَازًا ۟٣١ حَدَآئِقَ وَ
اَعْنَابًا ۟٣٢ وَّكَوَاعِبَ اَتْرَابًا ۟٣٣ وَّكَاْسًا دِهَاقًا ۟٣٤

The disbelievers are sceptical and confused about the reality and Hereafter. They will pay a heavy price for this delusional state.

78. Surat An-Naba'

The News

This early Makkan surat is critical of the Arab pagans who believed in the Almighty God, Allah, yet worshipped many idols. They did not believe in life after death, so they questioned the Prophet ﷺ again and again about the life Hereafter, and bitterly disagreed with him. Unfortunately, they didn't see the importance of this belief in ensuring a peaceful, just and purposeful life on Earth. What they could not comprehend was how the dead can be brought back to life. The Quran continually reminds them about Allah's creative power. The surat opens with a rich description of the natural world: vast landmasses and oceans, lofty mountains, pairs of living things, the mysteries of sleep and nightfall, and so on. After mentioning these eleven pieces of evidence of Allah's creativity, people are warned about the Day of Judgement: the Day of Distinction; the Day when justice will be done and people will be rewarded according to how they lived. Then follows a description of the horrors and pain of Hell. The final section beautifully captures the delights and pleasures of Paradise.

In the name of Allah, the Kind, the Caring.

The incredible Divine creative power

¹What are they questioning one another about? ²Is it the awesome news ³that they are disputing? ⁴No, soon they will know, ⁵indeed very soon they will know. ⁶Didn't We make the Earth a vast expanse, ⁷the mountains *like* mighty stakes? ⁸*Didn't We* create you in pairs, ⁹made your sleep for resting, ¹⁰made the night a covering, ¹¹and made the day for earning a livelihood? ¹²*Didn't* We build seven durable *skies* over your head, ¹³*the sun* a brightly burning lamp, ¹⁴and sent down abundant rain pouring from storm clouds? ¹⁵So We produced cereals, plants, ¹⁶and gardens of dense greenery.

A shocking description of the punishment of Hell

¹⁷The *time for the* Day of Distinction is fixed; ¹⁸the Trumpet will be blown that day and you will come in crowds; ¹⁹when the sky is opened becoming a gateway, ²⁰and the mountains will move as if they were a mirage. ²¹Hell lies in waiting, ²²to receive the disobedient, *their* home; ²³they will live there for ages and ages. ²⁴There will be nothing cool to taste, nor anything to drink ²⁵except boiling water and a dark foul fluid; ²⁶a fitting reward! ²⁷Since they never expected any kind of

لَا يَسْمَعُوْنَ فِيْهَا لَغْوًا وَّلَا كِذّٰبًا ۞ جَزَآءً مِّنْ

رَّبِّكَ عَطَآءً حِسَابًا ۞ رَّبِّ السَّمٰوٰتِ وَالْأَرْضِ وَمَا

بَيْنَهُمَا الرَّحْمٰنِ لَا يَمْلِكُوْنَ مِنْهُ خِطَابًا ۞ يَوْمَ يَقُوْمُ

الرُّوْحُ وَالْمَلٰٓئِكَةُ صَفًّا ۗ لَّا يَتَكَلَّمُوْنَ اِلَّا مَنْ اَذِنَ

لَهُ الرَّحْمٰنُ وَقَالَ صَوَابًا ۞ ذٰلِكَ الْيَوْمُ الْحَقُّ ۚ فَمَنْ

شَآءَ اتَّخَذَ اِلٰى رَبِّهٖ مَاٰبًا ۞ اِنَّآ اَنْذَرْنٰكُمْ عَذَابًا

قَرِيْبًا ۙ يَّوْمَ يَنْظُرُ الْمَرْءُ مَا قَدَّمَتْ يَدٰهُ وَيَقُوْلُ

الْكٰفِرُ يٰلَيْتَنِيْ كُنْتُ تُرٰبًا ۞

The believers will relish the delights of Paradise: a reward for their faith.

accounting, ²⁸ and denied our Scriptures. ²⁹ Yet We took account of everything in a Book, ³⁰ so it will be said to them: "Taste *the punishment*. We won't add anything except punishment for you!"

The righteous in the gardens

³¹ The mindful will have a splendid success: ³² gardens, vineyards, ³³ beautiful young companions of similar ages ³⁴ and an overflowing cup. ³⁵ They won't hear idle talk or lies, ³⁶ a *fitting* reward and a gift from Your Lord, ³⁷ Lord of the Heavens and the Earth and what is between the two. The Most Kind will not allow them to speak ³⁸ on the Day when the Spirit *Jibreel* and the *other* angels will stand in rows, they won't speak either without the Most Kind's permission, and they will speak the truth. ³⁹ That's the *Day of* Truth! So, anyone who wishes, let him take the road leading to His Lord. ⁴⁰ We certainly warned you of a punishment so near, the Day when every person will see what their own hands have produced, and the disbeliever will say, "Oh, I wish I were dust!"

بِسْمِ اللّٰهِ الرَّحْمٰنِ الرَّحِيْمِ

وَالنّٰزِعٰتِ غَرْقًا ۙ١ وَّالنّٰشِطٰتِ نَشْطًا ۙ٢ وَّالسّٰبِحٰتِ سَبْحًا ۙ٣ فَالسّٰبِقٰتِ سَبْقًا ۙ٤ فَالْمُدَبِّرٰتِ اَمْرًا ۘ٥ يَوْمَ تَرْجُفُ الرَّاجِفَةُ ۙ٦ تَتْبَعُهَا الرَّادِفَةُ ؕ٧ قُلُوْبٌ يَّوْمَئِذٍ وَّاجِفَةٌ ۙ٨ اَبْصَارُهَا خَاشِعَةٌ ۘ٩ يَقُوْلُوْنَ ءَاِنَّا لَمَرْدُوْدُوْنَ فِي الْحَافِرَةِ ؕ١٠ ءَاِذَا كُنَّا عِظَامًا نَّخِرَةً ؕ١١ قَالُوْا تِلْكَ اِذًا كَرَّةٌ خَاسِرَةٌ ۘ١٢ فَاِنَّمَا هِيَ زَجْرَةٌ وَّاحِدَةٌ ۙ١٣ فَاِذَا هُمْ بِالسَّاهِرَةِ ؕ١٤ هَلْ اَتٰىكَ حَدِيْثُ مُوْسٰى ۘ١٥ اِذْ نَادٰىهُ رَبُّهٗ بِالْوَادِ الْمُقَدَّسِ طُوًى ۚ١٦ اِذْهَبْ اِلٰى فِرْعَوْنَ اِنَّهٗ طَغٰى ١٧ فَقُلْ هَلْ لَّكَ اِلٰى اَنْ تَزَكّٰى ۙ١٨ وَاَهْدِيَكَ اِلٰى رَبِّكَ فَتَخْشٰى ۚ١٩ فَاَرٰىهُ الْاٰيَةَ الْكُبْرٰى ۖ٢٠ فَكَذَّبَ وَعَصٰى ۖ٢١ ثُمَّ اَدْبَرَ يَسْعٰى ۖ٢٢ فَحَشَرَ فَنَادٰى ۖ٢٣ فَقَالَ اَنَا رَبُّكُمُ الْاَعْلٰى ۖ٢٤ فَاَخَذَهُ اللّٰهُ نَكَالَ الْاٰخِرَةِ وَالْاُوْلٰى ؕ٢٥ اِنَّ فِيْ ذٰلِكَ لَعِبْرَةً لِّمَنْ يَّخْشٰى ۗ٢٦ ءَاَنْتُمْ اَشَدُّ خَلْقًا اَمِ السَّمَآءُ ۚ بَنٰهَا ؕ٢٧ رَفَعَ سَمْكَهَا فَسَوّٰىهَا ۙ٢٨ وَاَغْطَشَ لَيْلَهَا وَاَخْرَجَ ضُحٰىهَا ۪٢٩ وَالْاَرْضَ بَعْدَ ذٰلِكَ دَحٰىهَا ؕ٣٠ اَخْرَجَ مِنْهَا مَآءَهَا وَمَرْعٰىهَا ۪٣١ وَالْجِبَالَ اَرْسٰىهَا ۙ٣٢ مَتَاعًا لَّكُمْ

These verses give an 'electric shock' to the deluded human mind. Wake up to the reality of the Mighty, Majestic and Caring Lord.

79. Surat An-Nazi'at

The Snatchers

This is an early Makkan surat; its central theme is the Resurrection. The story of Pharaoh highlights why some people don't believe: because of pride, selfishness and love of the world (15). The surat opens with five oaths – five descriptive active participles that are enigmatic and unclear, making them difficult to translate. However, commentators have variously interpreted them as referring to warhorses, different winds, various stars, the souls of the righteous, and the angels. The evidence invoked here leads to the conclusion, "You will certainly be resurrected."

In the name of Allah, the Kind, the Caring.

Resurrection is a grand plan with far-reaching outcomes
¹By the angels who snatch *human* souls, ²the angels who take away human souls nimbly, ³the angels floating naturally, ⁴the angels speeding ahead, ⁵the Angels managing Heavenly affairs. *You will certainly be resurrected,*ᵃ ⁶on the Day the Trumpet is sounded for the first time, ⁷then followed by the second blast. ⁸Hearts will beat fast that Day, ⁹their eyes downcast. ¹⁰*Today* they ask, "Will we be returned to *our* previous state, ¹¹when we are rotten bones?" ¹²Commenting on it *they say,* "That would be a useless exercise!"ᵇ ¹³It will only take a single *Trumpet* blast, ¹⁴and they will be back on open ground.

Take lessons from the story of the Pharaoh
¹⁵Has the story of Musa reached you? ¹⁶When His Lord called out to him in the blessed valley of Tuwa: ¹⁷"Go to the Pharaoh, he is arrogant, ¹⁸and say *to him,* 'Would you like to purify yourself *spiritually*? ¹⁹I shall guide you to your Lord so that you may be mindful.'" ²⁰So he showed him the greatest miracle, ²¹but he denied and disobeyed; ²²then turned his back and rushed ²³to gather together *the magicians,* and announced: ²⁴"I am your highest lord". ²⁵So, Allah punished him by making an example of him in this world and the Hereafter. ²⁶There are lessons for the one who fears *His Lord.*

ᵃ This is the implied conclusion, in italics, of the five oaths or the evidences presented in verses 1 to 5.
ᵇ Literally "a purposeless return".

وَلِاَنْعَامِكُمْ ۝ فَاِذَا جَآءَتِ الطَّآمَّةُ الْكُبْرٰى ۝

يَوْمَ يَتَذَكَّرُ الْاِنْسَانُ مَا سَعٰى ۝ وَبُرِّزَتِ الْجَحِيْمُ

لِمَنْ يَّرٰى ۝ فَاَمَّا مَنْ طَغٰى ۝ وَاٰثَرَ الْحَيٰوةَ

الدُّنْيَا ۝ فَاِنَّ الْجَحِيْمَ هِيَ الْمَاْوٰى ۝ وَاَمَّا مَنْ

خَافَ مَقَامَ رَبِّهٖ وَنَهَى النَّفْسَ عَنِ الْهَوٰى ۝

فَاِنَّ الْجَنَّةَ هِيَ الْمَاْوٰى ۝ يَسْئَلُوْنَكَ عَنِ السَّاعَةِ

اَيَّانَ مُرْسٰهَا ۝ فِيْمَ اَنْتَ مِنْ ذِكْرٰهَا ۝ اِلٰى رَبِّكَ

مُنْتَهٰهَا ۝ اِنَّمَآ اَنْتَ مُنْذِرُ مَنْ يَّخْشٰهَا ۝ كَاَنَّهُمْ

يَوْمَ يَرَوْنَهَا لَمْ يَلْبَثُوْۤا اِلَّا عَشِيَّةً اَوْ ضُحٰهَا ۝

Those aware of the Hereafter who are fearful of the Lord will be in Paradise. How fearful of the Lord are you?

Invitation to reflect upon nature

²⁷ Are you more difficult to create, or the sky, which He raised up? ²⁸ He raised and perfected its canopy, ²⁹ and darkened its night and brought about bright morning light, ³⁰ and the Earth after that, which He spread out. ³¹ He produced its spring water and its green pastures. ³² He fixed the mountains in their place; ³³ *all this is* a provision for you and your animals. ³⁴ So when the mighty catastrophe comes, ³⁵ that Day humans will remember what they accomplished, ³⁶ when they will see the Blazing Flames clearly – ³⁷ *then the* one who was disobedient, ³⁸ and preferred the worldly life, ³⁹ the Blazing Fire will be *his* home. ⁴⁰ But the one who feared standing before His Lord and stopped himself from following his lusts, ⁴¹ he will be at home, in Paradise. ⁴² They ask you *Prophet* about the Hour: "What is its fixed time?" ⁴³ What can you tell them about that? ⁴⁴ Only your Lord knows its fixed time. ⁴⁵ You are a warner for the one who fears it. ⁴⁶ The Day they see it, they'll realise, *the worldly life* was only an evening, or a morning.

80. Surat ʿAbasa

Frowning

One day, the Messenger ﷺ was preaching to the leaders of Makkah, hopeful they would accept his message. He was extremely concerned to bringing them into the fold of Islam, and saving them from the Hellfire. However, Abdullah ibn Umm-al Maktum, a blind Muslim, came unexpectedly and wanted the attention of the Prophet ﷺ, saying: "Messenger! Teach me what Allah has taught you." The Messenger ﷺ did not like this interruption and frowned at him, turning away from him and towards the Makkans leaders. The surat commented on this incident, and thereafter the Messenger ﷺ used to say to him, "You are the man for whom my Lord censured me." It is obvious that Abdullah was in error when he interrupted the Messenger ﷺ, who was conveying the Message. So why does the Quran censure him? A closer look at the passage reveals that the Quran wants to remove the Makkan leaders' misunderstanding; they thought Islam needed them. However, the Quran tells them they are wrong, Islam doesn't need them. On the other hand, it appreciates sincere people like the blind man. Whenever the Prophet ﷺ left Madinah, he would appoint Ibn Maktum as the governor. The Quran teaches respect and equality for the blind and disabled.

The next section highlights how Allah has blessed humanity with life, food, and a rich land, but unfortunately people fail to thank Him for His generosity.

بِسْمِ اللّٰهِ الرَّحْمٰنِ الرَّحِيْمِ

عَبَسَ وَتَوَلّٰى ۙ١ اَنْ جَآءَهُ الْاَعْمٰى ؕ٢ وَمَا يُدْرِيْكَ

لَعَلَّهٗ يَزَّكّٰى ۙ٣ اَوْ يَذَّكَّرُ فَتَنْفَعَهُ الذِّكْرٰى ؕ٤ اَمَّا

مَنِ اسْتَغْنٰى ۙ٥ فَاَنْتَ لَهٗ تَصَدّٰى ؕ٦ وَمَا عَلَيْكَ اَلَّا

يَزَّكّٰى ؕ٧ وَاَمَّا مَنْ جَآءَكَ يَسْعٰى ۙ٨ وَهُوَ يَخْشٰى ۙ٩

فَاَنْتَ عَنْهُ تَلَهّٰى ؕ١٠ كَلَّا ٓ اِنَّهَا تَذْكِرَةٌ ۚ١١ فَمَنْ شَآءَ

ذَكَرَهٗ ۘ١٢ فِيْ صُحُفٍ مُّكَرَّمَةٍ ۙ١٣ مَّرْفُوْعَةٍ مُّطَهَّرَةٍ ۙ١٤

بِاَيْدِيْ سَفَرَةٍ ۙ١٥ كِرَامٍ بَرَرَةٍ ؕ١٦ قُتِلَ الْاِنْسَانُ

مَآ اَكْفَرَهٗ ؕ١٧ مِنْ اَيِّ شَيْءٍ ۪ خَلَقَهٗ ؕ١٨ مِنْ نُّطْفَةٍ ؕ

خَلَقَهٗ فَقَدَّرَهٗ ۙ١٩ ثُمَّ السَّبِيْلَ يَسَّرَهٗ ۙ٢٠ ثُمَّ

اَمَاتَهٗ فَاَقْبَرَهٗ ۙ٢١ ثُمَّ اِذَا شَآءَ اَنْشَرَهٗ ؕ٢٢ كَلَّا

لَمَّا يَقْضِ مَآ اَمَرَهٗ ؕ٢٣ فَلْيَنْظُرِ الْاِنْسَانُ اِلٰى

طَعَامِهٖٓ ۙ٢٤ اَنَّا صَبَبْنَا الْمَآءَ صَبًّا ۙ٢٥ ثُمَّ شَقَقْنَا

الْاَرْضَ شَقًّا ۙ٢٦ فَاَنْبَتْنَا فِيْهَا حَبًّا ۙ٢٧ وَّعِنَبًا

وَّقَضْبًا ۙ٢٨ وَّزَيْتُوْنًا وَّنَخْلًا ۙ٢٩ وَّحَدَآئِقَ غُلْبًا ۙ٣٠

وَّفَاكِهَةً وَّاَبًّا ؕ٣١ مَّتَاعًا لَّكُمْ وَلِاَنْعَامِكُمْ ؕ٣٢ فَاِذَا

جَآءَتِ الصَّآخَّةُ ۫٣٣ يَوْمَ يَفِرُّ الْمَرْءُ مِنْ اَخِيْهِ ۙ٣٤

وَاُمِّهٖ وَاَبِيْهِ ۙ٣٥ وَصَاحِبَتِهٖ وَبَنِيْهِ ؕ٣٦ لِكُلِّ

امْرِئٍ مِّنْهُمْ يَوْمَئِذٍ شَأْنٌ يُّغْنِيْهِ ؕ٣٧ وُجُوْهٌ

The Messenger's ﷺ passion and intense zeal to invite non-believers to faith should motivate you to do the same. The rewards are marvellous.

In the name of Allah, the Kind, the Caring.

Who is most deserving of the Prophet's attention?
¹He frowned and turned away ²because the blind man came to him. ³For all you know, he might have developed *spiritually*, ⁴or listened, and the Reminder benefitted him. ⁵*But* as for the one who *thinks he* is self-sufficient, ⁶you paid special attention. ⁷You aren't responsible if he fails to purify himself *spiritually*. ⁸*But* as for the one who came rushing to you, ⁹whilst fearful *of his Lord*, ¹⁰you ignored him. ¹¹Indeed *the Quran* is a Reminder, ¹²for the one who wants to be reminded; ¹³*it is kept* in scrolls, which are honoured, ¹⁴raised and purified, ¹⁵*written* by the hands of angels ¹⁶who are noble and righteous.

How can people be so ungrateful?
¹⁷Humans have ruined themselves by being unthankful. ¹⁸What sort of thing did He create them from? ¹⁹A drop of semen, He created them then assigned their destiny,ᵃ ²⁰then by making their way smooth *in life* enabled them. ²¹Then He lets them die and be buried. ²²Then when He wants, He shall resurrect them. ²³Unfortunately, they didn't do what Allah commanded them. ²⁴So let humans look at the food they eat *closely*; ²⁵We let the rain pour down, ²⁶then We split open the ground ²⁷to produce cereals, ²⁸grapes, vegetation, ²⁹olives, date palms, ³⁰densely-populated orchards, ³¹fruits and fodder ³²what a sustenance for you and your animals.

A warning for the unthankful
³³When the Deafening Blast comes, ³⁴that Day a person will flee from his brother, ³⁵mother, father, ³⁶spouse and children. ³⁷That Day, everyone will be concerned just about themselves. ³⁸Some faces that Day will be shining, ³⁹laughing and rejoicing. ⁴⁰*But other* faces that Day will be covered with dust, ⁴¹darkness restricting them. ⁴²The darkened *faces of* the disobedient disbelievers.

ᵃ Razi interprets *Qaddara* as: his provision, span of life, accomplishments in worldly life.

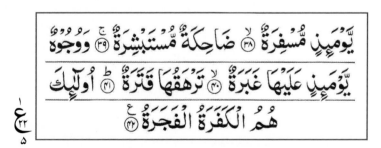

اَيَاتُهَا ٢٩ (٨١) سُوْرَةُ التَّكْوِيرِ مَكِّيَّةٌ (٧) رُكُوْعُهَا ١

بِسْمِ اللهِ الرَّحْمٰنِ الرَّحِيمِ

اِذَا الشَّمْسُ كُوِّرَتْ ۞ وَاِذَا النُّجُوْمُ انْكَدَرَتْ ۞ وَاِذَا الْجِبَالُ سُيِّرَتْ ۞ وَاِذَا الْعِشَارُ عُطِّلَتْ ۞ وَاِذَا الْوُحُوْشُ حُشِرَتْ ۞ وَاِذَا الْبِحَارُ سُجِّرَتْ ۞ وَاِذَا النُّفُوْسُ زُوِّجَتْ ۞ وَاِذَا الْمَوْءٗدَةُ سُئِلَتْ ۞ بِاَيِّ ذَنْبٍ قُتِلَتْ ۞ وَاِذَا الصُّحُفُ نُشِرَتْ ۞ وَاِذَا السَّمَآءُ كُشِطَتْ ۞ وَاِذَا الْجَحِيْمُ سُعِّرَتْ ۞ وَاِذَا الْجَنَّةُ اُزْلِفَتْ ۞ عَلِمَتْ نَفْسٌ مَّآ اَحْضَرَتْ ۞ فَلَآ اُقْسِمُ بِالْخُنَّسِ ۞ الْجَوَارِ الْكُنَّسِ ۞ وَالَّيْلِ اِذَا عَسْعَسَ ۞ وَالصُّبْحِ اِذَا تَنَفَّسَ ۞ اِنَّهٗ لَقَوْلُ رَسُوْلٍ كَرِيْمٍ ۞ ذِيْ قُوَّةٍ عِنْدَ ذِي الْعَرْشِ مَكِيْنٍ ۞ مُّطَاعٍ ثَمَّ اَمِيْنٍ ۞ وَمَا صَاحِبُكُمْ بِمَجْنُوْنٍ ۞ وَلَقَدْ رَاٰهُ بِالْاُفُقِ الْمُبِيْنِ ۞ وَمَا هُوَ عَلَى الْغَيْبِ بِضَنِيْنٍ ۞ وَمَا هُوَ بِقَوْلِ شَيْطٰنٍ رَّجِيْمٍ ۞ فَاَيْنَ تَذْهَبُوْنَ ۞ اِنْ هُوَ اِلَّا ذِكْرٌ لِّلْعٰلَمِيْنَ ۞ لِمَنْ شَآءَ مِنْكُمْ اَنْ يَّسْتَقِيْمَ ۞ وَمَا تَشَآءُوْنَ اِلَّآ اَنْ يَّشَآءَ اللهُ رَبُّ الْعٰلَمِيْنَ ۞

Do the shocking events of the Day of Judgement make you realise the transient and fleeting nature of worldly life?

81. Surat At-Takwir
The Shrouding

The central theme of this early Makkan surat is the truthfulness of the Majestic Quran and the validity of its teachings. It opens with twelve oaths, each signifying one of the cataclysmic events prior to the Day of Resurrection. In the second section, another set of oaths about time of celestial bodies is presented. I translated *Wal-Kunnas* (Verse 16) as, "By the dying stars", this is a star whose light is diminishing – astrophysicists call this a dying star.

The Quran is keen to stress the truthfulness of the Messenger ﷺ and the source of his message, so it describes the power, authority and reliability of the Angel Jibreel عليه السلام, responsible for bringing the Divine Message. Finally, it challenges its audience with this verse: "So where are you going?" (26).

In the name of Allah, the Kind, the Caring.

The occurrence of overwhelming events before Judgement Day

¹When the sun is covered, ²when the stars are dimmed, ³when the mountains are moved, ⁴when pregnant camels are left untended, ⁵when wild beasts are gathered, ⁶when the seas boil, ⁷when the souls are paired, ⁸when the baby girl buried alive is asked ⁹for which crime she was murdered, ¹⁰when the scrolls *of deeds* are unrolled, ¹¹and when *a layer of* the sky is peeled, ¹²when Hell is set ablaze, ¹³when Paradise is brought near – ¹⁴*then* everyone will know what they achieved *or failed to achieve in life.*

The Angel Jibreel brings the revelation

¹⁵So, I swear by the shining stars,ᵃ ¹⁶by the dying stars, ¹⁷by the fall of the night, ¹⁸by the morning breeze.ᵇ ¹⁹Certainly, *the Quran* is the recitation of a noble Angel, ²⁰who possesses *immense* power, and has a firmly-established rank with the Possessor of the Divine Throne, ²¹who is obeyed *by other angels* and is trustworthy. ²²Your companion isn't mad; ²³he saw him clearly on the horizon. ²⁴He doesn't hide *the news of* the Unseen. ²⁵It isn't the word of a rejected devil. ²⁶So where are you going? ²⁷It's a reminder for all people, ²⁸*especially* for the one who longs to be *guided* on the straight path. ²⁹But how can you long for it unless Allah, the Lord of the worlds, so wills, to show you that way.

ᵃ *Khunas* literally means stars that shine brightly at night but are invisible in the daytime. They can also refer to five planets: Saturn, Jupiter, Mars, Venus and Mercury.

ᵇ Literally this means, "breath", however metaphorically it refers to morning breeze.

بِسْمِ اللهِ الرَّحْمٰنِ الرَّحِيمِ

اِذَا السَّمَآءُ انْفَطَرَتْ ۞ وَاِذَا الْكَوَاكِبُ انْتَثَرَتْ ۞

وَاِذَا الْبِحَارُ فُجِّرَتْ ۞ وَاِذَا الْقُبُورُ بُعْثِرَتْ ۞

عَلِمَتْ نَفْسٌ مَّا قَدَّمَتْ وَاَخَّرَتْ ۞ يٰٓاَيُّهَا الْاِنْسَانُ

مَا غَرَّكَ بِرَبِّكَ الْكَرِيمِ ۞ الَّذِيْ خَلَقَكَ فَسَوّٰىكَ

فَعَدَلَكَ ۞ فِيْٓ اَيِّ صُوْرَةٍ مَّا شَآءَ رَكَّبَكَ ۞ كَلَّا بَلْ

تُكَذِّبُوْنَ بِالدِّيْنِ ۞ وَاِنَّ عَلَيْكُمْ لَحٰفِظِيْنَ ۞

كِرَامًا كَاتِبِيْنَ ۞ يَعْلَمُوْنَ مَا تَفْعَلُوْنَ ۞ اِنَّ

الْاَبْرَارَ لَفِيْ نَعِيْمٍ ۞ وَاِنَّ الْفُجَّارَ لَفِيْ جَحِيْمٍ ۞

يَصْلَوْنَهَا يَوْمَ الدِّيْنِ ۞ وَمَا هُمْ عَنْهَا بِغَآئِبِيْنَ ۞

وَمَآ اَدْرٰىكَ مَا يَوْمُ الدِّيْنِ ۞ ثُمَّ مَآ اَدْرٰىكَ مَا

يَوْمُ الدِّيْنِ ۞ يَوْمَ لَا تَمْلِكُ نَفْسٌ لِّنَفْسٍ شَيْئًا

وَالْاَمْرُ يَوْمَئِذٍ لِّلّٰهِ ۞

Why are people deceived about their generous Lord; who gives them everything? How thankful are you?

1255

82. Surat Al-Infitar

The Cleaving

This is an early Makkan surat. Its central theme is self-deception that turns a person away from Allah. After taking the oaths of the events leading to Judgement Day, a question is gently asked: "people, what deceived *and misled* you from your generous Lord?" (6) The qualities of the Lord Who created are recalled to prick the conscience. Humanity is warned: you are monitored by the Angels who record your every move. On Judgement Day, all will give an account.

In the name of Allah, the Kind, the Caring.

Why are you deceived?

¹When the sky is cleaved, ²when the stars are scattered, ³when the oceans surge and merge, ⁴when the graves are turned inside out – ⁵*that Day*, every person will know what it did and what it failed to do. ⁶People, what deceived you from your generous Lord? ⁷He created you, assigned you a provision, and perfected you ⁸with *a beautifully*-shaped physical appearance as He pleased. ⁹Yet, you still deny the Judgement. ¹⁰The guardians standing over you are ¹¹the noble scribes, ¹²who know what you do.

The terrible fate of self-deception

¹³The righteous will enjoy the delights *of Paradise*, ¹⁴whilst the wicked will be *damned* in Hell. ¹⁵They will enter in it on Judgement Day, ¹⁶and they won't ever be able to leave. ¹⁷What can explain to you the reality of the Day of Judgement? ¹⁸Again, what can explain to you the reality of Judgement Day? ¹⁹The Day when no one will be able to do anything for another person; only Allah's command will prevail that Day.

(٨٣) سُورَةُ الْمُطَفِّفِينَ مَكِّيَّةٌ (٨٦)

بِسْمِ اللهِ الرَّحْمٰنِ الرَّحِيمِ

وَيْلٌ لِّلْمُطَفِّفِينَ ۞ الَّذِينَ إِذَا اكْتَالُوا عَلَى النَّاسِ يَسْتَوْفُونَ ۞ وَإِذَا كَالُوهُمْ اَوْ وَّزَنُوهُمْ يُخْسِرُونَ ۞ اَلَا يَظُنُّ اُولٰٓئِكَ اَنَّهُمْ مَّبْعُوثُونَ ۞ لِيَوْمٍ عَظِيمٍ ۞ يَّوْمَ يَقُومُ النَّاسُ لِرَبِّ الْعٰلَمِينَ ۞ كَلَّا اِنَّ كِتٰبَ الْفُجَّارِ لَفِى سِجِّينٍ ۞ وَمَآ اَدْرٰىكَ مَا سِجِّينٌ ۞ كِتٰبٌ مَّرْقُومٌ ۞ وَيْلٌ يَّوْمَئِذٍ لِّلْمُكَذِّبِينَ ۞ الَّذِينَ يُكَذِّبُونَ بِيَوْمِ الدِّينِ ۞ وَمَا يُكَذِّبُ بِهٖٓ اِلَّا كُلُّ مُعْتَدٍ اَثِيمٍ ۞ اِذَا تُتْلٰى عَلَيْهِ اٰيٰتُنَا قَالَ اَسَاطِيرُ الْاَوَّلِينَ ۞ كَلَّا بَلْ ران عَلٰى قُلُوبِهِمْ مَّا كَانُوا يَكْسِبُونَ ۞ كَلَّا اِنَّهُمْ عَنْ رَّبِّهِمْ يَوْمَئِذٍ لَّمَحْجُوبُونَ ۞ ثُمَّ اِنَّهُمْ لَصَالُوا الْجَحِيمِ ۞ ثُمَّ يُقَالُ هٰذَا الَّذِى كُنْتُمْ بِهٖ تُكَذِّبُونَ ۞ كَلَّا اِنَّ كِتٰبَ الْاَبْرَارِ لَفِى عِلِّيِّينَ ۞ وَمَآ اَدْرٰىكَ مَا عِلِّيُّونَ ۞ كِتٰبٌ مَّرْقُومٌ ۞ يَّشْهَدُهُ الْمُقَرَّبُونَ ۞ اِنَّ الْاَبْرَارَ لَفِى نَعِيمٍ ۞ عَلَى الْاَرَآئِكِ يَنْظُرُونَ ۞ تَعْرِفُ فِى وُجُوهِهِمْ نَضْرَةَ النَّعِيمِ ۞ يُسْقَوْنَ مِنْ رَّحِيقٍ مَّخْتُومٍ ۞ خِتٰمُهُ مِسْكٌ وَفِى ذٰلِكَ فَلْيَتَنَافَسِ الْمُتَنَافِسُونَ ۞ وَمِزَاجُهُ مِنْ تَسْنِيمٍ ۞ عَيْنًا يَّشْرَبُ بِهَا الْمُقَرَّبُونَ ۞ اِنَّ الَّذِينَ اَجْرَمُوا

The cheaters swindle others, but the disbeliever is cheating him/herself by short-changing.

83. Surat Al-Mutaffifin

The Cheats

This is a late Makkan surat, condemning cheating traders and shopkeepers who were dishonest in their dealings with others. This picture of a dishonest person isn't limited to commercial transactions, but is also relevant to people who are dishonest in other aspects of life, both in seventh-century Arabia and today.

The surat, interestingly, doesn't mention the rope makers, tanners and perfume sellers working in Hijaz. Why does it single out the merchants, bankers and bookkeepers? Possibly because they have more opportunities to cheat, exploit the weak and perpetrate injustices. Recall the financial crisis of 2008, which affected economies around the world. Who was responsible for the that? Such injustices are committed by those who deny Judgment Day, and feel they can swindle and cheat without consequence. "Don't they believe they will be resurrected on a Grand Day?" (4–5) The surat speaks of the effects of such conduct on hearts and minds: "their hearts are coated *with rust*, because of what they did" (14). The Messenger ﷺ said, "When a person commits a sin, a black spot appears on the heart. If he repents it will be removed, but if he continues doing evil, more spots appear until the entire heart is covered" (Ibn Majah). This encrusted, rust-coated, stained heart will lead to dishonesty and evil actions. The consequences in the Hereafter will be dire: those guilty of such crimes will burn in Hell. These are contrasted with people of faith and honest behaviour, who will enjoy the delights of Paradise.

In the name of Allah, the Kind, the Caring.

Observation on the behaviour of the cheats

¹Woe to the cheats; ²the ones who demand full measure from people, ³but when they measure and weigh for others, they give less. ⁴Don't those *double dealers* believe they will be resurrected ⁵on a Grand Day? ⁶The Day when people will stand before the Lord of the worlds.

How evil deeds harden the heart

⁷The written record of the wicked is in Sijjeen – ⁸and what can explain Sijjeen to you? ⁹*It's* a written document. ¹⁰It will be too bad for the deniers that Day, ¹¹who deny Judgment Day. ¹²Only the wicked transgressor denies it. ¹³When Our Scriptures are read to him, he says, "*These are* fables of the ancients!" ¹⁴Moreover, their hearts are coated *with rust* because of what they did. ¹⁵Never! On that Day,

كَانُوْا مِنَ الَّذِيْنَ اٰمَنُوْا يَضْحَكُوْنَ ۞ وَاِذَا مَرُّوْا بِهِمْ

يَتَغَامَزُوْنَ ۞ وَاِذَا انْقَلَبُوْۤا اِلٰۤى اَهْلِهِمُ انْقَلَبُوْا

فَكِهِيْنَ ۞ وَاِذَا رَاَوْهُمْ قَالُوْۤا اِنَّ هٰۤؤُلَآءِ لَضَآلُّوْنَ ۞

وَمَاۤ اُرْسِلُوْا عَلَيْهِمْ حٰفِظِيْنَ ۞ فَالْيَوْمَ الَّذِيْنَ اٰمَنُوْا

مِنَ الْكُفَّارِ يَضْحَكُوْنَ ۞ عَلَى الْاَرَآئِكِ يَنْظُرُوْنَ ۞

هَلْ ثُوِّبَ الْكُفَّارُ مَا كَانُوْا يَفْعَلُوْنَ ۞

They mock true believers yet will be the laughing stock in the Hereafter.

they will be shut out from *seeing* their Lord, ¹⁶then they will enter Hell. ¹⁷It will be said *to them*: "This is what you used to deny."

Faithful people in the serene surroundings of Paradise
¹⁸The written record of the righteous is *kept* in 'Illiyeen. ¹⁹What can explain 'Illiyeen to you? ²⁰*It's* a written record, ²¹which is witnessed by those brought close *to Allah*. ²²The righteous will be enjoying *the delights of* Paradise, ²³sitting *relaxed* on sofas watching *the tranquil scenery*; ²⁴you will see brightness on their faces in Paradise. ²⁵They will be served sealed wine, pure ²⁶musk its aftertaste – let the competitors compete for that – ²⁷mixed with *the water of* Tasneem, ²⁸a spring from which those brought close *to Allah* will drink.

A warning to the disbelievers who mock others
²⁹The wicked used to laugh at the believers ³⁰when they passed by them, they would wink at each other teasingly. ³¹Back with their families they made fun of them ³²and when they saw them, they would say, "These are misguided!" ³³They weren't sent as their guardians. ³⁴But today, the believers are laughing at the disbelievers, ³⁵sitting on the sofas watching *them in misery*: ³⁶"Have the disbelievers *not* been repaid for what they used to do?"

بِسْمِ اللهِ الرَّحْمٰنِ الرَّحِيمِ

اِذَا السَّمَآءُ انْشَقَّتْ ۝ وَاَذِنَتْ لِرَبِّهَا وَحُقَّتْ ۝ وَاِذَا

الْاَرْضُ مُدَّتْ ۝ وَاَلْقَتْ مَا فِيهَا وَتَخَلَّتْ ۝ وَاَذِنَتْ

لِرَبِّهَا وَحُقَّتْ ۝ يٰٓاَيُّهَا الْاِنْسَانُ اِنَّكَ كَادِحٌ اِلٰى رَبِّكَ

كَدْحًا فَمُلٰقِيهِ ۝ فَاَمَّا مَنْ اُوْتِيَ كِتٰبَهُ بِيَمِيْنِهِ ۝

فَسَوْفَ يُحَاسَبُ حِسَابًا يَّسِيْرًا ۝ وَّيَنْقَلِبُ اِلٰٓى اَهْلِهِ

مَسْرُوْرًا ۝ وَاَمَّا مَنْ اُوْتِيَ كِتٰبَهُ وَرَآءَ ظَهْرِهِ ۝ فَسَوْفَ

يَدْعُوْا ثُبُوْرًا ۝ وَّيَصْلٰى سَعِيْرًا ۝ اِنَّهُ كَانَ فِيْٓ اَهْلِهِ

مَسْرُوْرًا ۝ اِنَّهُ ظَنَّ اَنْ لَّنْ يَّحُوْرَ ۝ بَلٰٓى اِنَّ رَبَّهُ

كَانَ بِهِ بَصِيْرًا ۝ فَلَآ اُقْسِمُ بِالشَّفَقِ ۝ وَالَّيْلِ وَمَا

وَسَقَ ۝ وَالْقَمَرِ اِذَا اتَّسَقَ ۝ لَتَرْكَبُنَّ طَبَقًا عَنْ طَبَقٍ ۝

فَمَا لَهُمْ لَا يُؤْمِنُوْنَ ۝ وَاِذَا قُرِئَ عَلَيْهِمُ الْقُرْاٰنُ

لَا يَسْجُدُوْنَ ۝ بَلِ الَّذِيْنَ كَفَرُوْا يُكَذِّبُوْنَ ۝ وَاللهُ

اَعْلَمُ بِمَا يُوْعُوْنَ ۝ فَبَشِّرْهُمْ بِعَذَابٍ اَلِيْمٍ ۝ اِلَّا

الَّذِيْنَ اٰمَنُوْا وَعَمِلُوا الصّٰلِحٰتِ لَهُمْ اَجْرٌ غَيْرُ مَمْنُوْنٍ ۝

A lament on wasted human lives: by ignoring faith, Allah and the teachings of the Quran. A wakeup call!

84. Surat Al-Inshiqaq

The Splitting Open

This is a late Makkan surat, of which the central theme is the connection between actions and consequences. It opens by stressing the instinctive obedience of the inanimate; the Sky and the Earth. An indirect disapproval of the Makkans, who refused to obey their Lord despite having intelligence.

Working hard for one's livelihood is a universal human value. However, to limit life to this is a folly; the workaholic is being challenged in this surat. He is advised not to forget the Hereafter and the meeting with the Lord Who is the true Sustainer and Provider. However, those who work hard for their Hereafter are guaranteed progress: "You will develop stage by stage." (19)

In the name of Allah, the Kind, the Caring.

What are you striving for?

¹When the sky splits open, ²duly obeying its Lord; ³when the Earth is flattened ⁴and throws out its contents and becomes empty, ⁵duly obeying its Lord. ⁶People, you strive and struggleᵃ *gradually moving* towards your Lord; finally you'll meet Him! ⁷So anyone given the written record in his right hand ⁸will have an easy reckoning, ⁹and will return happily to his family. ¹⁰But anyone who is given the written record from behind his back ¹¹will cry out for death, ¹²and will go in the Blazing Fire. ¹³He used to be happy amid his family. ¹⁴He was convinced he wouldn't return *to His Lord*. ¹⁵Yes, His Lord was watching him.

Progress in life is guaranteed to hard workers

¹⁶So, I swear by the red horizon *at sunset,* ¹⁷and by the night and all that it covers up, ¹⁸and by the full moon: ¹⁹you will develop stage by stage. ²⁰What's the matter with them that they don't believe, ²¹and when the Quran is recited to them they don't prostrate. ²²The disbelievers deny. ²³Allah knows best what they hide *in their minds,* ²⁴so give them good news of a painful punishment, ²⁵except for those who believe and do righteous deeds; for them, there is a never-ending reward.

ᵃ Strive and struggle may refer to the worries, anxieties, happiness and the drudgery of daily life.

بِسْمِ اللهِ الرَّحْمٰنِ الرَّحِيمِ

وَالسَّمَآءِ ذَاتِ الْبُرُوجِ ۟ وَالْيَوْمِ الْمَوْعُودِ ۟ وَشَاهِدٍ وَّ

مَشْهُودٍ ط قُتِلَ اَصْحٰبُ الْاُخْدُودِ ۟ النَّارِ ذَاتِ الْوَقُوْدِ ۟

اِذْ هُمْ عَلَيْهَا قُعُوْدٌ ۟ وَّهُمْ عَلٰى مَا يَفْعَلُوْنَ بِالْمُؤْمِنِيْنَ

شُهُودٌ ط وَمَا نَقَمُوْا مِنْهُمْ اِلَّا اَنْ يُّؤْمِنُوْا بِاللهِ الْعَزِيْزِ

الْحَمِيْدِ ۙ الَّذِىْ لَهٗ مُلْكُ السَّمٰوٰتِ وَالْاَرْضِ ط وَاللهُ

عَلٰى كُلِّ شَيْءٍ شَهِيْدٌ ط اِنَّ الَّذِيْنَ فَتَنُوا الْمُؤْمِنِيْنَ

وَالْمُؤْمِنٰتِ ثُمَّ لَمْ يَتُوبُوْا فَلَهُمْ عَذَابُ جَهَنَّمَ وَلَهُمْ

عَذَابُ الْحَرِيْقِ ط اِنَّ الَّذِيْنَ اٰمَنُوْا وَعَمِلُوا الصّٰلِحٰتِ لَهُمْ

جَنّٰتٌ تَجْرِىْ مِنْ تَحْتِهَا الْاَنْهٰرُ ط ذٰلِكَ الْفَوْزُ الْكَبِيْرُ ۟

اِنَّ بَطْشَ رَبِّكَ لَشَدِيْدٌ ط اِنَّهٗ هُوَ يُبْدِئُ وَيُعِيْدُ ۟

وَهُوَ الْغَفُوْرُ الْوَدُوْدُ ۟ ذُو الْعَرْشِ الْمَجِيْدُ ۟ فَعَّالٌ لِّمَا

يُرِيْدُ ط هَلْ اَتٰىكَ حَدِيْثُ الْجُنُوْدِ ۟ فِرْعَوْنَ وَثَمُوْدَ ۟

بَلِ الَّذِيْنَ كَفَرُوْا فِىْ تَكْذِيْبٍ ۟ وَّاللهُ مِنْ وَّرَآئِهِمْ

مُّحِيْطٌ ۟ بَلْ هُوَ قُرْاٰنٌ مَّجِيْدٌ ۟ فِىْ لَوْحٍ مَّحْفُوْظٍ ۟

The Divine punishment is severe and his grip tight. So beware.

85. Surat Al-Buruj
The Constellations

This Makkan surat marks the beginning of the second phase of the mission of the Prophet ﷺ, around the third year; the start of tensions. Its central theme is the support of the faithful. The story of the "diggers of the trench" (4) is recounted in the Hadith collection of Muslim, where the Jewish King of Yemen burnt the Christians of Najran in a trench. This story would have given reassurance to the believers, and a clear warning to the Quraysh, the persecutors.

The surat opens with a series of oaths, "By the sky full of constellations." A constellation is a recognisable group of stars which appear to be located close together in the sky, and form a picture of imaginary lines that connect them. Constellations are usually named after an animal, a character from mythology, or a common object. Muslim astronomers discovered several constellations and named them in Arabic, such as Ursa Major, and Ursa Minor.

In the name of Allah, the Kind, the Caring.

Believers face persecution
¹By the sky full of constellations, ²by the promised Day, ³by a witness and what is witnessed. ⁴Cursed are the diggers of the trench, ⁵*who lit* the well-fuelled fire; ⁶ when they sat around it, ⁷watching what they were doing to the believers. ⁸They punished them because they believed in Allah, the Almighty, the Praiseworthy, ⁹the One Who controls *all things in the* Heavens and the Earth, and Allah is the witness of everything. ¹⁰The persecutors of the believing men and women didn't repent, so they will be punished in Hell, in the Burning Flames.

The persecutors cannot escape the punishment
¹¹The believers who were righteous will have gardens *of Paradise,* beneath which rivers flow. That will be the great achievement. ¹²Your Lord's punishment will be severely harsh. ¹³He started the creation and will reproduce it once more, ¹⁴He is the Forgiving, the most Loving, ¹⁵Possessor of the Majestic Throne, ¹⁶the Most Able to carry out what He pleases. ¹⁷Has the story of the armies reached you? ¹⁸*About* the Pharaoh and Thamud? ¹⁹Yet the disbelievers are *still* in denial, ²⁰while Allah surrounds them from all sides. ²¹But this is a Majestic reading, ²²in the Protected Tablet.

The mystery of life is complex, therefore don't be dramatic and put up with others amiably!

﷽

(٨٦) سُوْرَةُ الطَّارِقِ مَكِّيَّةٌ (٣٦)   اٰيَاتُهَا ١٤   رُكُوْعُهَا ١

بِسْمِ اللهِ الرَّحْمٰنِ الرَّحِيْمِ

وَالسَّمَآءِ وَالطَّارِقِ ۙ﴿١﴾ وَمَآ اَدْرٰىكَ مَا الطَّارِقُ ۙ﴿٢﴾ النَّجْمُ الثَّاقِبُ ۙ﴿٣﴾ اِنْ كُلُّ نَفْسٍ لَّمَّا عَلَيْهَا حَافِظٌ ؕ﴿٤﴾ فَلْيَنْظُرِ الْاِنْسَانُ مِمَّ خُلِقَ ؕ﴿٥﴾ خُلِقَ مِنْ مَّآءٍ دَافِقٍ ۙ﴿٦﴾ يَّخْرُجُ مِنْۢ بَيْنِ الصُّلْبِ وَالتَّرَآئِبِ ؕ﴿٧﴾ اِنَّهٗ عَلٰى رَجْعِهٖ لَقَادِرٌ ؕ﴿٨﴾ يَوْمَ تُبْلَى السَّرَآئِرُ ۙ﴿٩﴾ فَمَا لَهٗ مِنْ قُوَّةٍ وَّلَا نَاصِرٍ ؕ﴿١٠﴾ وَالسَّمَآءِ ذَاتِ الرَّجْعِ ۙ﴿١١﴾ وَالْاَرْضِ ذَاتِ الصَّدْعِ ۙ﴿١٢﴾ اِنَّهٗ لَقَوْلٌ فَصْلٌ ۙ﴿١٣﴾ وَّمَا هُوَ بِالْهَزْلِ ؕ﴿١٤﴾ اِنَّهُمْ يَكِيْدُوْنَ كَيْدًا ۙ﴿١٥﴾ وَّاَكِيْدُ كَيْدًا ۖ﴿١٦﴾ فَمَهِّلِ الْكٰفِرِيْنَ اَمْهِلْهُمْ رُوَيْدًا ۠﴿١٧﴾

ع
١١

86. Surat At-Tariq

The Night Visitor

A Makkan surat with a central theme about the truthfulness of Judgement Day. After taking the oath of the shining stars, people are reminded, "There is a keeper over you" (4). Those who denied the Judgement Day are invited to reflect about their humble beginnings. Where do you come from? The evidence from the shooting stars, the spurted semen and the blooming plants and flowers are perfect illustrations of Allah's ability to bring the living from the dead; a proof of resurrection. The next important question for the thoughtful is, "Where are we going?" A simple statement contains the answer: "Indeed Allah is fully able to return him *to life*" (8). Finally, the Makkans, who were busy insulting the beloved Messenger ﷺ are warned, "I too have a plan" (16). In the final verse, the Prophet ﷺ is gently instructed to relax.

In the name of Allah, the Kind, the Caring.

Where do you come from?

¹By the sky and the night visitor^a – ²what can explain the night visitor to you? ³A piercing comet. ⁴There is a keeper over every person. ⁵Let humans look at what they were created from; ⁶they were created from spurted semen ⁷that comes from *bodily organs* in the torso.^b

Where are you going?

⁸Allah is fully able to return them *to life,* ⁹on the Day when secrets will be exposed; ¹⁰they won't have any power and no helper. ¹¹By the sky and its repeated *rain cycle,* ¹²and the Earth splitting open with *new growth.* ¹³Indeed, this *Majestic Quran* is a decisive speech; ¹⁴no joking matter. ¹⁵They are continually plotting, ¹⁶and I have a plan too. ¹⁷*Messenger,* put up with the disbelievers; let them off for a short while.

---

^a *Al-tariq* is the comet or shooting star, a meteor that burns up on entering the Earth's atmosphere forming a bright streak in the night sky. They were considered as supernatural omens by the Makkans.
^b Literally, "the backbone [or] the loins and the breastbones."

بِسْمِ اللهِ الرَّحْمٰنِ الرَّحِیْمِ

سَبِّحِ اسْمَ رَبِّكَ الْاَعْلَی ۱ الَّذِیْ خَلَقَ فَسَوّٰی ۲

وَالَّذِیْ قَدَّرَ فَهَدٰی ۳ وَالَّذِیْۤ اَخْرَجَ الْمَرْعٰی ۴

فَجَعَلَهٗ غُثَآءً اَحْوٰی ۵ سَنُقْرِئُكَ فَلَا تَنْسٰۤی ۶

اِلَّا مَا شَآءَ اللهُ ط اِنَّهٗ یَعْلَمُ الْجَهْرَ وَمَا یَخْفٰی ۷

وَنُیَسِّرُكَ لِلْیُسْرٰی ۸ فَذَكِّرْ اِنْ نَّفَعَتِ الذِّكْرٰی ۹

سَیَذَّكَّرُ مَنْ یَّخْشٰی ۱۰ وَیَتَجَنَّبُهَا الْاَشْقَی ۱۱ الَّذِیْ

یَصْلَی النَّارَ الْكُبْرٰی ۱۲ ثُمَّ لَا یَمُوْتُ فِیْهَا وَلَا

یَحْیٰی ۱۳ قَدْ اَفْلَحَ مَنْ تَزَكّٰی ۱۴ وَذَكَرَ اسْمَ رَبِّهٖ

فَصَلّٰی ۱۵ بَلْ تُؤْثِرُوْنَ الْحَیٰوۃَ الدُّنْیَا ۱۶ وَالْاٰخِرَۃُ

خَیْرٌ وَّاَبْقٰی ۱۷ اِنَّ هٰذَا لَفِی الصُّحُفِ الْاُوْلٰی ۱۸

صُحُفِ اِبْرٰهِیْمَ وَمُوْسٰی ۱۹

Real success lies in self-purification; a clean mind, pure thoughts and performance of honourable works.

87. Surat Al-Aʻla

The Highest

An early Makkan surat, its central theme is the role of the Majestic Quran and the Messenger as reminders. By referring to the early Scriptures of Musa ﷺ and Ibrahim ﷺ, the Quran makes it clear that this is a continuation of the same mission of past prophets. What blinds humanity to this reality? The answer is love of worldly life. These verses express contempt for love of material world, since it distracts people from their Lord.

In the name of Allah, the Kind, the Caring.

Praise and glorify your Lord

¹Glorify the Name of your Lord, the Most High. ²Who created and made *you* complete; ³Who fixed destiny^a and gave guidance, ⁴Who produced green pasture, ⁵then turned it into dry dusty debris.

The journey of spiritual growth

⁶We will teach you *the Quran* so you will not forget *it*, ⁷except what Allah may wish. He knows the open and the hidden. ⁸We shall make your *journey* easy, ⁹so give a reminder; the reminder is beneficial. ¹⁰The one in awe *of his Lord* will listen, ¹¹but the wicked will ignore, ¹²he will enter the Great Fire, ¹³no dying and no living. ¹⁴Successful indeed is the one who purifies himself, ¹⁵and remembers the Name of his Lord, and performs the prayer *regularly*. ¹⁶You prefer the worldly life, ¹⁷yet the Hereafter is far better and everlasting. ¹⁸This fact is also *mentioned* in the previous Scriptures, ¹⁹*and in* the Scriptures of Ibrahim and Musa.

---

^a *Qaddara* refers to the sustenance, life span, choices and lifestyle of the individual (Razi).

بِسْمِ اللهِ الرَّحْمٰنِ الرَّحِيمِ

هَلْ اَتٰىكَ حَدِيْثُ الْغَاشِيَةِ ۙ۱ وُجُوْهٌ يَّوْمَئِذٍ

خَاشِعَةٌ ۙ۲ عَامِلَةٌ نَّاصِبَةٌ ۙ۳ تَصْلٰى نَارًا حَامِيَةً ۙ۴

تُسْقٰى مِنْ عَيْنٍ اٰنِيَةٍ ؕ۵ لَيْسَ لَهُمْ طَعَامٌ اِلَّا مِنْ

ضَرِيْعٍ ۙ۶ لَّا يُسْمِنُ وَلَا يُغْنِيْ مِنْ جُوْعٍ ؕ۷ وُجُوْهٌ

يَّوْمَئِذٍ نَّاعِمَةٌ ۙ۸ لِّسَعْيِهَا رَاضِيَةٌ ۙ۹ فِيْ جَنَّةٍ

عَالِيَةٍ ۙ۱۰ لَّا تَسْمَعُ فِيْهَا لَاغِيَةً ؕ۱۱ فِيْهَا عَيْنٌ

جَارِيَةٌ ۘ۱۲ فِيْهَا سُرُرٌ مَّرْفُوْعَةٌ ۙ۱۳ وَّ اَكْوَابٌ

مَّوْضُوْعَةٌ ۙ۱۴ وَّ نَمَارِقُ مَصْفُوْفَةٌ ۙ۱۵ وَّ زَرَابِيُّ

مَبْثُوْثَةٌ ؕ۱۶ اَفَلَا يَنْظُرُوْنَ اِلَى الْاِبِلِ كَيْفَ خُلِقَتْ ۟۱۷

وَ اِلَى السَّمَآءِ كَيْفَ رُفِعَتْ ۟۱۸ وَ اِلَى الْجِبَالِ كَيْفَ

نُصِبَتْ ۟۱۹ وَ اِلَى الْاَرْضِ كَيْفَ سُطِحَتْ ۟۲۰ فَذَكِّرْ ؕ

اِنَّمَآ اَنْتَ مُذَكِّرٌ ؕ۲۱ لَسْتَ عَلَيْهِمْ بِمُصَۜيْطِرٍ ۙ۲۲ اِلَّا

مَنْ تَوَلّٰى وَكَفَرَ ۙ۲۳ فَيُعَذِّبُهُ اللهُ الْعَذَابَ الْاَكْبَرَ ؕ۲۴

اِنَّ اِلَيْنَآ اِيَابَهُمْ ۙ۲۵ ثُمَّ اِنَّ عَلَيْنَا حِسَابَهُمْ ۟۲۶

Faith in Allah is supported, strengthened and nurtured by reason and nature.

88. Surat Al-Ghashiyah
The Awe-inspiring Event

This surat was revealed in the middle Makkan period. The three fundamental doctrines of Islam are emphasised. The Day of Judgement is introduced in an unusual manner: "Has the news of the Overwhelming Event reached you?" This is followed by a harrowing account of what will happen to the disbeliever who toiled, struggled and worked hard in his life but ignored Allah, and never thought about the Hereafter. This is contrasted with the fate of a believer who worked to please his Lord. Humanity is invited to enjoy the delights of Paradise, its elegant surroundings, its comforts and luxuries. The price is strong faith. To conclude, the surat comforts the Prophet ﷺ by telling him not to worry, since he cannot compel people to believe. His mission is to remind: "To Us is their final return, then it will be up to Us to call them to account" (25–26).

In the name of Allah, the Kind, the Caring.

The miserable fate of disbelieving hard workers
¹Has news of the Awe-inspiring Event reached you? ²*Some* faces that Day will be humbled, ³*looking* tired and exhausted. ⁴They will walk in to an intensely-hot Fire, ⁵and drink from a boiling water spring. ⁶They will have no food except bitter thorns, ⁷which won't nourish or satisfy *their* hunger.

The delights of Paradise
⁸*Some* faces that Day will be beautiful and bright, ⁹well-pleased with their efforts, ¹⁰*living* in an elegant Garden, ¹¹where they won't hear any idle chat, ¹²*watered by* a flowing spring, ¹³*furnished with* raised and comfortable sofas, ¹⁴ wine glasses *gracefully* arranged, ¹⁵*silken* cushions set in rows, ¹⁶and *luxurious* soft carpets laid all around.

Invitation to observe the world around us
¹⁷Don't they see the camels, how they were created? ¹⁸And the sky, how it was raised? ¹⁹And the mountains, how they were fixed? ²⁰And at the Earth, how it was spread out? ²¹So remind, *Prophet*, your job is to remind. ²²You aren't their controller. ²³The one who turned away and disbelieved, ²⁴Allah will give him terrible punishment. ²⁵They will finally return to Us, ²⁶and We will call them to account.

89. Surat Al-Fajr

The Dawn

The surat begins by taking four oaths to draw our attention: the dawn, the time when the first light appears, the ten sacred nights of the twelfth lunar month of Dhu'l-Hijja, the month of pilgrimage, and the mystery of odd and even numbers. The odd may hint to Allah, who is the One, the Unique and cannot be compared with anything. In contrast, the even reminds how creation is not singular or one, only Allah is One. The surat reassures the Messenger ﷺ after mentioning these awesome phenomena: what you face in Makkah is what earlier prophets faced, so be patient. Reference is made to the ancient cities of Iram in the Arabian desert, Petra in modern-day Jordan, and the splendid temples of ancient Egypt with their tall columns. The city of Iram, deep in the Arabian desert, was discovered in the early 1990s by a group of archaeologists. Their ruins demonstrate that these were master masons who had fantastic advanced technology to build enormous buildings. However, their arrogance and denial of Allah brought them to ruin.

The surat points out how humans are unthankful to their Lord. At the slight loss of wealth or pain, they grumble and become impatient. They are sternly warned, and told to renounce their bad habits. However, those who are mindful of Allah are promised a welcome of utter bliss.

بِسْمِ اللهِ الرَّحْمٰنِ الرَّحِيْمِ

وَالْفَجْرِ ۱ وَلَيَالٍ عَشْرٍ ۲ وَّالشَّفْعِ وَالْوَتْرِ ۳ وَالَّيْلِ اِذَا يَسْرِ ۴ هَلْ فِیْ ذٰلِكَ قَسَمٌ لِّذِیْ حِجْرٍ ۵ اَلَمْ تَرَ كَيْفَ فَعَلَ رَبُّكَ بِعَادٍ ۶ اِرَمَ ذَاتِ الْعِمَادِ ۷ الَّتِیْ لَمْ يُخْلَقْ مِثْلُهَا فِی الْبِلَادِ ۸ وَثَمُوْدَ الَّذِیْنَ جَابُوا الصَّخْرَ بِالْوَادِ ۹ وَفِرْعَوْنَ ذِی الْاَوْتَادِ ۱۰ الَّذِیْنَ طَغَوْا فِی الْبِلَادِ ۱۱ فَاَكْثَرُوْا فِيْهَا الْفَسَادَ ۱۲ فَصَبَّ عَلَيْهِمْ رَبُّكَ سَوْطَ عَذَابٍ ۱۳ اِنَّ رَبَّكَ لَبِالْمِرْصَادِ ۱۴ فَاَمَّا الْاِنْسَانُ اِذَا مَا ابْتَلٰهُ رَبُّهُ فَاَكْرَمَهُ وَنَعَّمَهٗ ۵ فَيَقُوْلُ رَبِّیْ اَكْرَمَنِ ۱۵ وَاَمَّا اِذَا مَا ابْتَلٰهُ فَقَدَرَ عَلَيْهِ رِزْقَهٗ ۵ فَيَقُوْلُ رَبِّیْ اَهَانَنِ ۱۶ كَلَّا بَلْ لَّا تُكْرِمُوْنَ الْيَتِيْمَ ۱۷ وَلَا تَحٰضُّوْنَ عَلٰی طَعَامِ الْمِسْكِيْنِ ۱۸ وَتَاْكُلُوْنَ التُّرَاثَ اَكْلًا لَّمًّا ۱۹ وَّتُحِبُّوْنَ الْمَالَ حُبًّا جَمًّا ۲۰ كَلَّا اِذَا دُكَّتِ الْاَرْضُ دَكًّا دَكًّا ۲۱ وَّجَاءَ رَبُّكَ وَالْمَلَكُ صَفًّا صَفًّا ۲۲ وَّجِایْءَ يَوْمَئِذٍ بِجَهَنَّمَ ۵ يَوْمَئِذٍ يَّتَذَكَّرُ الْاِنْسَانُ وَاَنّٰی لَهُ الذِّكْرٰی ۲۳ يَقُوْلُ يٰلَيْتَنِیْ قَدَّمْتُ لِحَيَاتِیْ ۲۴ فَيَوْمَئِذٍ لَّا يُعَذِّبُ عَذَابَهٗ اَحَدٌ ۲۵ وَّلَا يُوْثِقُ وَثَاقَهٗ اَحَدٌ ۲۶ يٰۤاَيَّتُهَا النَّفْسُ الْمُطْمَئِنَّةُ ۲۷ ارْجِعِیْ اِلٰی رَبِّكِ رَاضِيَةً

The devout care for needy and weak. What's your attitude?

In the name of Allah, the Kind, the Caring.

Reminders from past civilisations

¹By the dawn, ²by the ten *holy* nights, ³by the even and the odd *numbers*, ⁴and by the night as it slips away! ⁵Isn't there a *convincing* oath for an intelligent person? ⁶Haven't you considered how your Lord dealt with *the people of* Ad; ⁷*of* Iram with *its* lofty pillars, ⁸the likes of which haven't existed in *other* lands; ⁹and *the people of* Thamud who carved *homes out of* rocks in the valley; ¹⁰and the Pharaoh, *his temples* with massive columns? ¹¹Those who transgressed in the lands, ¹²who brought about havoc throughout them – ¹³Your Lord let loose a scourge of suffering against them. ¹⁴Your Lord is ever watchful.

Ingratitude and disbelief are linked

¹⁵The *mortal* man, when His Lord tests him with honour and blessings says, "My Lord has honoured me." ¹⁶However, when He tests him by lessening his provision he says, "My Lord has shamed me."¹⁷On the contrary, it is you *Makkans* who don't honour orphans, ¹⁸and don't urge others to feed the needy, ¹⁹while you consume the whole of the *orphans'* inheritance ²⁰with your insatiable love of wealth.

The harshest of harsh punishments

²¹So, how will you fare when the Earth is ground to dust, ²²and Your Lord's command comes, and the angels *stand* in rows upon rows. ²³That Day Hell will be brought close, people will then remember. But how will remembering *benefit* them now? ²⁴They will say, "If only We had something to show for our lives!" ²⁵Then on that Day, He will punish as no one will ever punish, ²⁶and He will chain them as no one will ever chain.

A joyous welcome from the Lord

²⁷Allah will say: O happy soul! ²⁸Return to Your Lord cheerfully and loved; ²⁹now join *the company of* My servants ³⁰and come into My Paradise.

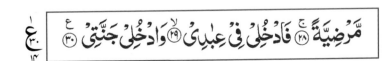

بِسْمِ اللهِ الرَّحْمٰنِ الرَّحِيمِ

لَآ أُقْسِمُ بِهٰذَا الْبَلَدِ ۙ وَأَنتَ حِلٌّۢ بِهٰذَا الْبَلَدِ ۙ

وَوَالِدٍ وَّمَا وَلَدَ ۙ لَقَدْ خَلَقْنَا الْإِنسَانَ فِى كَبَدٍ ۙ

أَيَحْسَبُ أَن لَّن يَّقْدِرَ عَلَيْهِ أَحَدٌ ۚ يَقُولُ أَهْلَكْتُ

مَالًا لُّبَدًا ۚ أَيَحْسَبُ أَن لَّمْ يَرَهُۥٓ أَحَدٌ ۚ أَلَمْ نَجْعَل لَّهُۥ

عَيْنَيْنِ ۙ وَلِسَانًا وَّشَفَتَيْنِ ۙ وَهَدَيْنٰهُ النَّجْدَيْنِ ۚ

فَلَا اقْتَحَمَ الْعَقَبَةَ ۖ وَمَآ أَدْرَىٰكَ مَا الْعَقَبَةُ ۖ فَكُّ

Sincere practise of Islam is difficult but rewarding, like climbing a mountain.

رَقَبَةٍ ۙ أَوْ إِطْعَٰمٌ فِى يَوْمٍ ذِى مَسْغَبَةٍ ۙ يَتِيمًا

ذَا مَقْرَبَةٍ ۙ أَوْ مِسْكِينًا ذَا مَتْرَبَةٍ ۚ ثُمَّ كَانَ مِنَ

الَّذِينَ آمَنُوا وَتَوَاصَوْا بِالصَّبْرِ وَتَوَاصَوْا بِالْمَرْحَمَةِ ۚ

أُو۟لٰٓئِكَ أَصْحٰبُ الْمَيْمَنَةِ ۚ وَالَّذِينَ كَفَرُوا بِآيٰتِنَا

هُمْ أَصْحٰبُ الْمَشْـَٔمَةِ ۚ عَلَيْهِمْ نَارٌ مُّؤْصَدَةٌ ۚ

90. Surat Al-Balad

The City

The mountain is a permanent feature of our landscape, an effective metaphor for the smallness of humans. The Majestic Quran uses the mountains to provide a dramatic setting: "Had We revealed this Quran on a mountain, you would have seen it humble itself and turn to dust out of fear of Allah." (*Surat Al-Hashr* 59: 21). The Prophet ﷺ lived in a city surrounded by black rugged mountains, so here is an oath of a city of mountains. The metaphor of the steep mountainous track describes the difficulties of life: a constant Jihad, "Every human We created *experiences* hardship." This might refer both to people in general, or to Usaid ibn Kalda, a famous wrestler. When he stood on a leather hide and men tried to pull it away from under his feet, it would tear into pieces, but he would not budge an inch.

Here Divine Dislike is expressed for people who are deceived by their strength and influence. Usaid thought no one had power over him, not even the angel of death. The Quran warns against such delusions, life is symbolised by a steep path. Following the story of Usaid, this would imply this foolish man made no effort to obey the Lord, the steep path; he hadn't gone beyond physical existence and failed to understand the higher purpose of life.

In the name of Allah, the Kind, the Caring.

People experience hardships

¹I swear by this city, ²where you, live freely? ³And by a father, and all his offspring! ⁴Every human We created *experiences* hardship. ⁵Does he *really* think no one has control over him? ⁶He boasts, "I have spent a huge amount of wealth!" ⁷Does he *really* think no one has seen him? ⁸Haven't We given him two eyes, ⁹a tongue and two lips? ¹⁰We showed him the two steep paths *of good and evil*?

The way to success is hard

¹¹He hasn't yet set foot on the steep mountain track. ¹²What can explain to you the mountain track? ¹³*It is* to free a slave, ¹⁴to feed on a day of severe hunger ¹⁵an orphan relative, ¹⁶or a penniless and distressed person. ¹⁷Only they are believers, who instruct each other to be patient and kind. ¹⁸They *will get their Book of Deeds* in the right hand. ¹⁹But those who denied Our signs, *will get it* in the left hand, ²⁰ the Fire closing in around them.

بِسْمِ اللهِ الرَّحْمٰنِ الرَّحِيْمِ

وَالشَّمْسِ وَضُحٰىهَا ۞ وَالْقَمَرِ اِذَا تَلٰىهَا ۞ وَالنَّهَارِ

اِذَا جَلّٰىهَا ۞ وَالَّيْلِ اِذَا يَغْشٰىهَا ۞ وَالسَّمَآءِ وَمَا

بَنٰىهَا ۞ وَالْاَرْضِ وَمَا طَحٰىهَا ۞ وَنَفْسٍ وَّمَا

سَوّٰىهَا ۞ فَاَلْهَمَهَا فُجُوْرَهَا وَتَقْوٰىهَا ۞ قَدْ اَفْلَحَ

مَنْ زَكّٰىهَا ۞ وَقَدْ خَابَ مَنْ دَسّٰىهَا ۞ كَذَّبَتْ

ثَمُوْدُ بِطَغْوٰىهَآ ۞ اِذِ انْۢبَعَثَ اَشْقٰىهَا ۞ فَقَالَ

لَهُمْ رَسُوْلُ اللهِ نَاقَةَ اللهِ وَسُقْيٰهَا ۞ فَكَذَّبُوْهُ

فَعَقَرُوْهَا ۞ فَدَمْدَمَ عَلَيْهِمْ رَبُّهُمْ بِذَنْۢبِهِمْ

فَسَوّٰىهَا ۞ وَلَا يَخَافُ عُقْبٰهَا ۞

Good and bad are inside us; we can bring out one or the other.

91. Surat Ash-Shams

The Sun

This early Makkan surat opens with ten oaths. The first four relate to the sun and the last six to the sky, the Earth and the human soul. The purpose of these oaths is to support the claim, "Then He inspired it to follow *either* its vice or virtue" (8). The central theme is developing human potential, either to be conscious of Allah or remain unaware of Him. "He inspired" means that the human conscience has been endowed with the ability to distinguish between right and wrong, between good and evil. The one who develops the moral values, spiritual beliefs and social norms presented in the Quran will flourish, and the one who disregards them will inevitably fail.

This is further proved by reference to the tribe of Thamud. The Makkans often went past their ruins in the old city of Petra on the southern border of Jordan. They called it a "red rose city". The surat points out that just as an individual may deny and ignore the Divine Commandments, similarly whole communities can deny the truth. They refused to listen to their prophet and that led to their ultimate destruction. They killed a she-camel; an outrage in Bedouin culture. This surat has a beautiful rhyme – "ha" at the end of each verse, making it lyrical and poetic.

In the name of Allah, the Kind, the Caring.

Powerful oaths

¹ By the sun and by the morning brightness, ² by the moon that follows it, ³ by the day that it brightens up, ⁴ by the night that covers it. ⁵ By the sky and by Him who designed it, ⁶ by the Earth and by Him who levelled it out. ⁷ By the human and by Him who perfected him; ⁸ so inspired him to follow *either* its vice or virtue.

Success and failure is in human hands

⁹ Whoever purified himself succeeded, ¹⁰ and whoever was immoral failed himself. ¹¹ The *people of* Thamud cruelly treated *their Messenger*. ¹² When the most wicked among them was dispatched *against him*. ¹³ Allah's Messenger told him, "Let Allah's she-camel have her share of the water." ¹⁴ But they denied him, and hamstrung her, so due to this crime their Lord destroyed them. ¹⁵ He didn't fear its consequences.

بِسْمِ اللهِ الرَّحْمٰنِ الرَّحِيمِ

وَالَّيْلِ اِذَا يَغْشٰى ۞ وَالنَّهَارِ اِذَا تَجَلّٰى ۞ وَمَا

خَلَقَ الذَّكَرَ وَالْاُنْثٰى ۞ اِنَّ سَعْيَكُمْ لَشَتّٰى ۞ فَاَمَّا

مَنْ اَعْطٰى وَاتَّقٰى ۞ وَصَدَّقَ بِالْحُسْنٰى ۞ فَسَنُيَسِّرُهٗ

لِلْيُسْرٰى ۞ وَاَمَّا مَنْ بَخِلَ وَاسْتَغْنٰى ۞ وَكَذَّبَ

بِالْحُسْنٰى ۞ فَسَنُيَسِّرُهٗ لِلْعُسْرٰى ۞ وَمَا يُغْنِيْ عَنْهُ

مَالُهٗٓ اِذَا تَرَدّٰى ۞ اِنَّ عَلَيْنَا لَلْهُدٰى ۞ وَاِنَّ

لَنَا لَلْاٰخِرَةَ وَالْاُوْلٰى ۞ فَاَنْذَرْتُكُمْ نَارًا تَلَظّٰى ۞

لَا يَصْلٰىهَآ اِلَّا الْاَشْقَى ۞ الَّذِيْ كَذَّبَ وَتَوَلّٰى ۞

وَسَيُجَنَّبُهَا الْاَتْقَى ۞ الَّذِيْ يُؤْتِيْ مَالَهٗ يَتَزَكّٰى ۞

وَمَا لِاَحَدٍ عِنْدَهٗ مِنْ نِّعْمَةٍ تُجْزٰى ۞ اِلَّا ابْتِغَآءَ

وَجْهِ رَبِّهِ الْاَعْلٰى ۞ وَلَسَوْفَ يَرْضٰى ۞

A successful person is a giver who likes others and loves Allah. On the other hand, an unsuccessful person is miserly, hates others, and is full of himself.

92. Surat Al-Layl

The Night

This is an early Makkan surat with the central theme of diversity in human endeavours, enterprises and efforts. However, the primary choice confronting people is between good or evil, and practising moral values. The surat identifies righteous people as those who have three outstanding qualities: generosity, mindfulness of Allah, and appreciation for the good – the three inner dimensions of human life: the moral, spiritual and social, respectively. As a reward for goodness, "We shall soon make his work easy" (8). This is the Quranic hero, the champion and Beloved ﷺ of Allah. In contrast, the miserly, the forgetful, and the denier of good. For such a wretch, "We shall make his work hard" (10).

These two contrasting statements, "We shall make his work easy" and "We shall make his work hard," clearly show that Allah has given free will to humanity. However, He aids and supports those who wish to do good, and hinders those who do wrong. Once a habit is developed that brings pleasure or material gains, many become comfortable with it and adopt it as a way of life. The same applies to being mindful of Allah. The more the worship, the easier the way to Allah.

In the name of Allah, the Kind, the Caring.

Diversity and differences in creation

¹By the night as it conceals; ²by the day as it reveals; ³by the male and the female He created! ⁴Indeed your works are different *from each other's*: ⁵so the one who gives, is mindful *of Allah* ⁶and believes in common good, ⁷We shall make his work easy. ⁸But for the miserly, who thinks he is self-sufficient ⁹and denies common good, ¹⁰We shall make his work difficult. ¹¹His wealth will not benefit him when he falls *into Hell.*

Humans are spoilt for choice

¹²Our role is to provide guidance; ¹³the Hereafter and the world are Ours. ¹⁴I have warned you about a raging Fire; ¹⁵where the wicked will go, ¹⁶who denied and turned away. ¹⁷*But* the one who was mindful will be kept away from it, ¹⁸he gave his wealth *in charity* to purify himself. ¹⁹Not as a payment for favours received, ²⁰but because he longed for the pleasure of His Lord, the Highest, ²¹and he will be pleased *with the outcome.*

بِسْمِ اللهِ الرَّحْمٰنِ الرَّحِيْمِ

وَالضُّحٰى ۟١ وَالَّيْلِ اِذَا سَجٰى ۟٢ مَا وَدَّعَكَ رَبُّكَ وَمَا

قَلٰى ؕ٣ وَلَلْاٰخِرَةُ خَيْرٌ لَّكَ مِنَ الْاُوْلٰى ؕ٤ وَلَسَوْفَ

يُعْطِيْكَ رَبُّكَ فَتَرْضٰى ۟٥ اَلَمْ يَجِدْكَ يَتِيْمًا فَاٰوٰى ۪٦

وَوَجَدَكَ ضَآلًّا فَهَدٰى ۪٧ وَوَجَدَكَ عَآئِلًا فَاَغْنٰى ؕ٨

فَاَمَّا الْيَتِيْمَ فَلَا تَقْهَرْ ؕ٩ وَاَمَّا السَّآئِلَ فَلَا تَنْهَرْ ؕ١٠

وَاَمَّا بِنِعْمَةِ رَبِّكَ فَحَدِّثْ ۠١١

Overcome stress by trusting Allah. Be positive about a better future, remember past successes and take action.

ع
٨
١٩

93. Surat Ad-Duha

The Morning Brightness

This is an early Makkan surat. According to Suyuti, there was a short period when the revelation stopped and the Messenger ﷺ did not preach, prompting the Makkans to say mockingly, "Your Satan has deserted you." The Messenger ﷺ was upset, and the surat was revealed to reassure him. To cope with this stressful personal experience, he is given a four-point strategy to overcome stress and sorrow: get rid of negative thoughts, be determined that you will succeed, recall your past successes and set yourself clear targets. The basic message it contains is an amazing force field of energy, which can heal our anxieties. Furthermore, it gives a snapshot of the orphan life of the Messenger ﷺ, his dire poverty, deep spiritual experience, and marriage with a wonderful lady, Khadija the Great [Allah be pleased with Her].

In the name of Allah, the Kind, the Caring.

Oaths highlighting Allah's loving care of the Prophet
¹By the *brightness of* mid-morning, ²by the night's darkness. ³Your Lord hasn't deserted you, nor is He displeased with you. ⁴Your future will be better than the past. ⁵And your Lord will give you so much that you will be well-pleased.

Past favours guide the way
⁶Didn't He find you an orphan and shelter you? ⁷*Didn't He* find you absorbed in Divine love, and guide you? ⁸And *didn't* He find you needy and made you prosperous? ⁹So, don't be harsh with the orphan, ¹⁰nor chase away the beggar, ¹¹and speak positively about the gifts of your Lord.

Life is a continuous cycle of winning and losing; happiness and sadness, honour and humiliation.

سُوْرَةُ الْاِنْشِرَاح مَكِّيَّةٌ (١١٢)   رُكُوْعُهَا ١   اٰيَاتُهَا ٨ (٩٤)

بِسْمِ اللّٰهِ الرَّحْمٰنِ الرَّحِيْمِ

اَلَمْ نَشْرَحْ لَكَ صَدْرَكَ ۙ١ وَوَضَعْنَا عَنْكَ وِزْرَكَ ۙ٢

الَّذِيْۤ اَنْقَضَ ظَهْرَكَ ۙ٣ وَرَفَعْنَا لَكَ ذِكْرَكَ ؕ٤ فَاِنَّ

مَعَ الْعُسْرِ يُسْرًا ۙ٥ اِنَّ مَعَ الْعُسْرِ يُسْرًا ؕ٦ فَاِذَا

فَرَغْتَ فَانْصَبْ ۙ٧ وَاِلٰى رَبِّكَ فَارْغَبْ ٨

١٩
ع
٨

١

94. Surat Al-Inshirah

The Expansion

This Makkan surat builds on the previous surat's consolation of the Messenger ﷺ in a tone that displays friendship and love. The opening, or expansion, of the chest of the Prophet ﷺ occurred twice: once in his childhood, and again at the start of the Night Journey, his Ascension. The Angel Jibreel ﷺ carried out a remarkable procedure in which the heart of the Prophet ﷺ was taken out, purified, filled with wisdom, and put back in his noble chest. This miracle prepared it to be the container of Divine Revelation. The surat expresses the incredibly elevated position of the Messenger ﷺ, but despite this honour he is told to strive enthusiastically in Allah's worship.

In the name of Allah, the Kind, the Caring.

Gain after strain

¹Didn't We expand your chest, ²and lift your burden, ³which was breaking your back. ⁴We raised high your honour. ⁵Indeed, *every* hardship is followed by ease, ⁶indeed, *every* hardship is followed by ease.ᵃ ⁷Once you finish your daily chores, ⁸seek your Lord passionately in worship.

ᵃ *Inna maʿ-al-ʿusr yusran* could also mean, "Gain after strain", and "The storm before the calm".

Realise your inner goodness through faith and virtue.

95. Surat At-Tin

The Fig

This Makkan surat opens with four oaths: two of the valuable trees and two sacred places. These splendid symbols are used as a testimony to the truthfulness of its theme: the 'inherent goodness' of human nature, and how this is ruined. This vivid description of the splendour of Allah's creation and the nobility of humanity is an elegant piece of rhetoric. The reference to human nature being as the "most beautiful" (4) is an important Quranic teaching, which offers hope in a world ravaged by wars and human greed. It refers to the upright and beautiful human figure, possessing beneficial intelligence, moral goodness and yearnings for the Divine. In other words, humans have the potential to be good, kind and generous, but can easily be ruined by disregarding faith in the Hereafter. This "most beautiful" nature can be easily damaged. The concept of *Din* (creed) or Judgement Day acts as a deterrent.

In the name of Allah, the Kind, the Caring

How wonderful is the human physique?

¹By the fig, by the olive, ²by Mount Sinai ³and this safe city. ⁴We created humans in the most beautiful form, ⁵then reduced them to the lowest of the lows, *due to disobedience*, ⁶except those who believed and performed honourable deeds; they shall have a never-ending reward. ⁷So after *knowing this* what makes you deny Judgement Day? ⁸Isn't Allah the most Just Judge?

Fear is a powerful emotion that the Quran uses to correct our neglect of the Lord and the Hereafter.

سُوْرَةُ الْعَلَق مَكِّيَّةٌ (١)   (٩٦)   اٰیٰاتُهَا ١٩   رُكُوْعُهَا ١

بِسْمِ اللّٰهِ الرَّحْمٰنِ الرَّحِيْمِ

اِقْرَاْ بِاسْمِ رَبِّكَ الَّذِیْ خَلَقَ ۞ خَلَقَ الْاِنْسَانَ مِنْ

عَلَقٍ ۞ اِقْرَاْ وَرَبُّكَ الْاَكْرَمُ ۞ الَّذِیْ عَلَّمَ بِالْقَلَمِ ۞

عَلَّمَ الْاِنْسَانَ مَا لَمْ يَعْلَمْ ۞ كَلَّا اِنَّ الْاِنْسَانَ

لَيَطْغٰی ۞ اَنْ رَّاٰهُ اسْتَغْنٰی ۞ اِنَّ اِلٰی رَبِّكَ الرُّجْعٰی ۞

اَرَءَيْتَ الَّذِیْ يَنْهٰی ۞ عَبْدًا اِذَا صَلّٰی ۞ اَرَءَيْتَ

اِنْ كَانَ عَلَی الْهُدٰی ۞ اَوْ اَمَرَ بِالتَّقْوٰی ۞ اَرَءَيْتَ

اِنْ كَذَّبَ وَتَوَلّٰی ۞ اَلَمْ يَعْلَمْ بِاَنَّ اللّٰهَ يَرٰی ۞ كَلَّا

لَئِنْ لَّمْ يَنْتَهِ ۙ لَنَسْفَعًۢا بِالنَّاصِيَةِ ۞ نَاصِيَةٍ كَاذِبَةٍ

خَاطِئَةٍ ۞ فَلْيَدْعُ نَادِيَهٗ ۞ سَنَدْعُ الزَّبَانِيَةَ ۞ كَلَّا

لَا تُطِعْهُ وَاسْجُدْ وَاقْتَرِبْ ۞

96. Surat Al-'Alaq

The Clot of Blood

The Messenger ﷺ used to take spiritual retreat in the cave of Hira, seven kilometres south-west of the Kaaba. Here, in the stillness and solitude of the Mountain of Light, far away from the hustle and bustle of a busy city, he had ample opportunity to meditate on his Lord and reflect on the waywardness of his fellow citizens. He loathed their idolatry, corrupt business practices, uncaring behaviour towards the poor and needy. It was during one such moment that the Holy Spirit, Jibreel ﷺ, brought him the first revelation, comprising the first five verses of this surat, commanding him to recite in Allah's name. The second part of the surat comes as a clear warning to all disbelievers, but in particular to one of his staunchest opponents, Abu Jahl, since he frequently mistreated the Messenger ﷺ verbally and physically.

In the name of Allah, the Kind, the Caring

The first revelation
¹Recite in the name of your Lord Who created, ²created humans from clustered germ-cells.ᵃ ³Recite! "Your Lord is the most Generous", ⁴Who taught with the Pen, ⁵He taught humans what they didn't know.

Abu Jahl is warned of dreadful consequences
⁶But humans go beyond *boundaries of Allah*, ⁷considering themselves to be self-sufficient. ⁸*Yet* the *final* return is to your Lord. ⁹Have you seen the one who stops ¹⁰a servant *of Ours* from praying? ¹¹Don't you realise he is rightly guided, ¹²and issues commands based on fear *of Allah*? ¹³Have you considered, when he denies *the truth* and turns away, ¹⁴doesn't he know Allah sees *everything*? ¹⁵No! If he doesn't end *this behaviour*, We shall drag him by the forelock, ¹⁶*that* lying and sinful forelock.ᵇ ¹⁷So let him call out to his supporters; ¹⁸We shall summon the angel guards *at the gates* of Hell *to take care of him*. ¹⁹No! Don't follow him, *Prophet*, but prostrate *before Us* and draw *ever* closer.ᶜ

ᵃ The word in Arabic literally means "congealed blood", and it is used figuratively as a label for the early embryonic stage in the womb.

ᵇ The "forelock" is the hair of the forehead that some vain people, when they choose to grow it long, are constantly tossing or pushing back, typically with extravagant and self-conscious gestures, in order to distract others and draw attention to themselves.

ᶜ This is the last of the Verses of Prostration in the Quran.

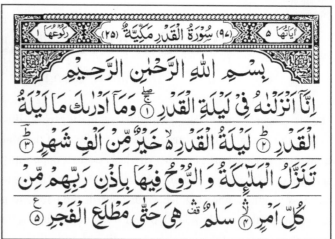

بِسْمِ اللّٰهِ الرَّحْمٰنِ الرَّحِیْمِ

اِنَّاۤ اَنْزَلْنٰهُ فِیْ لَیْلَةِ الْقَدْرِ ۚ ۝ وَمَاۤ اَدْرٰىكَ مَا لَیْلَةُ الْقَدْرِ ۭ ۝ لَیْلَةُ الْقَدْرِ ۙ خَیْرٌ مِّنْ اَلْفِ شَهْرٍ ۭ ۝ تَنَزَّلُ الْمَلٰٓئِكَةُ وَ الرُّوْحُ فِیْهَا بِاِذْنِ رَبِّهِمْ مِّنْ كُلِّ اَمْرٍ ۙ ۝ سَلٰمٌ ۛ هِیَ حَتّٰی مَطْلَعِ الْفَجْرِ ۝

Majestic and magnificent is the Night of Power. Stay awake, worship and receive peace.

١ع
٥
٢٢

97. Surat Al-Qadr

The Night of Destiny

This early Makkan surat praises the splendour of the night on which the Majestic Quran was revealed, a night in the blessed month of Ramadan. On this night of power, glory and splendour, the Quran was transferred from the Protected Tablet in the upper Heaven to the lower Heaven, from which it was gradually and in piecemeal fashion revealed to the Messenger ﷺ over a period of twenty-three years. This explains why this night is very special. Three things come down during the night: angels, human destiny and peace.

In the name of Allah, the Kind, the Caring.

The Night of Power

¹We sent down *the Quran* on the Night of Destiny, ²and what can explain the Night of Destiny to you? ³The Night of Destiny is better than one thousand months;ᵃ ⁴the angels and the Spirit, *Jibreel*, come down by the order of their Lord, bringing with them *each person's* destiny. ⁵Peace *descends everywhere* until the break of the dawn.

ᵃ This means that worship during this night is more valuable than the worship of over a thousand months, a lifetime of worship.

بِسْمِ اللّٰهِ الرَّحْمٰنِ الرَّحِيْمِ

لَمْ يَكُنِ الَّذِيْنَ كَفَرُوْا مِنْ اَهْلِ الْكِتٰبِ وَالْمُشْرِكِيْنَ مُنْفَكِّيْنَ حَتّٰى تَاْتِيَهُمُ الْبَيِّنَةُ ۙ١ رَسُوْلٌ مِّنَ اللّٰهِ يَتْلُوْا صُحُفًا مُّطَهَّرَةً ۙ٢ فِيْهَا كُتُبٌ قَيِّمَةٌ ؕ٣ وَمَا تَفَرَّقَ الَّذِيْنَ اُوْتُوا الْكِتٰبَ اِلَّا مِنْۢ بَعْدِ مَا جَآءَتْهُمُ الْبَيِّنَةُ ؕ٤ وَمَآ اُمِرُوْٓا اِلَّا لِيَعْبُدُوا اللّٰهَ مُخْلِصِيْنَ لَهُ الدِّيْنَ ۙ۬ حُنَفَآءَ وَيُقِيْمُوا الصَّلٰوةَ وَيُؤْتُوا الزَّكٰوةَ وَذٰلِكَ دِيْنُ الْقَيِّمَةِ ؕ٥ اِنَّ الَّذِيْنَ كَفَرُوْا مِنْ اَهْلِ الْكِتٰبِ وَالْمُشْرِكِيْنَ فِيْ نَارِ جَهَنَّمَ خٰلِدِيْنَ فِيْهَا ؕ اُولٰٓئِكَ هُمْ شَرُّ الْبَرِيَّةِ ؕ٦ اِنَّ الَّذِيْنَ اٰمَنُوْا وَعَمِلُوا الصّٰلِحٰتِ ۙ اُولٰٓئِكَ هُمْ خَيْرُ الْبَرِيَّةِ ؕ٧ جَزَآؤُهُمْ عِنْدَ رَبِّهِمْ جَنّٰتُ عَدْنٍ تَجْرِيْ مِنْ تَحْتِهَا الْاَنْهٰرُ خٰلِدِيْنَ فِيْهَآ اَبَدًا ؕ رَضِيَ اللّٰهُ عَنْهُمْ وَرَضُوْا عَنْهُ ؕ ذٰلِكَ لِمَنْ خَشِيَ رَبَّهٗ ؕ٨

The believers are praised, honoured and rewarded by the Mighty Lord.

ع
٨
٢٣

1291

98. Surat Al-Bayyinah

The Clear Proof

This is a late Makkan surat, and the central theme is how to deal with the scepticism, resistance and disbelief of the Makkan idolaters, as well as the Christians and the Jews. The Messenger ﷺ initially thought that the People of The Book would readily accept Islam. However, they resisted his call, except for a few. In many ways, this surat was a consolation to the Prophet ﷺ and his followers: they need not be disappointed at such reactions from the People of The Book. The Jews did the same to the Prophet Jesus عليه السلام, when they refused to acknowledge his prophethood and handed him over to the Romans, accusing him of treason.

In the name of Allah, the Kind, the Caring

People are given an opportunity before being condemned

¹The disbelievers among the People of the Book and the idolaters were not condemned until the clear proof had come to them[a] – ²the Messenger of Allah recited pages of pure teachings *from the Quran,* ³containing clear commandments. ⁴Those given the Book became divided after the clear proof had come to them. ⁵They were commanded: worship Allah sincerely, turn away from false gods, establish the prayer, and pay the Zakat. That is the religion of truth. ⁶The disbelievers from the People of The Book and the idolaters will be in the Hell-Fire forever. These are the worst of the creatures.

Believers are richly rewarded

⁷The believers who did righteous works are the best of the creatures. ⁸Their reward is with the Lord: Gardens of Eden beneath which rivers flow; *they will live* there forever. Allah is pleased with them, and they're pleased with Him. That's for the one who fears His Lord.

---

[a] Then they knowingly reject it.

99. Surat Al-Zilzal

The Earthquake

This is an early Madinan surat, its central theme is accountability on the Day of Resurrection. The surat opens with the advent of the Day of Resurrection, marked by a devastating Earthquake that will flatten the Earth; mountains will turn into rubble, and the seas will surge and merge as described elsewhere. However, the focus in this surat is the Earth, and what it will reveal of its history. The mindless human will spend his life without a thought for the Hereafter, indulging in evil. The surat reminds that on Judgement Day, he must stand before his Lord and give an account. It transplants you into another age, you're fired up and deeply inspired.

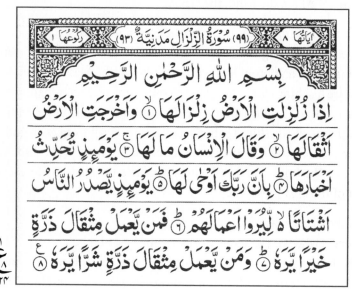

In the name of Allah, the Kind, the Caring.

The Divine Justice

[1] When the Earth is shaken violently, [2] it *will* throw up its burden; [3] people will ask, "What's the matter with her?" [4] That Day, it will tell all its news, [5] inspired by her Lord. [6] That Day, people will come separately in groups to be shown their deeds. [7] So, anyone who did an atom's weight of good will see it. [8] And anyone who did an atom's weight of evil will see it *too*.

100. Surat Al-'Adiyat

The War Horses

This is a late Makkan surat that concisely describes the human condition of thankless-ness. The Arabic is *Kufr*, a key theme in the Quran, as it often warns people of the dread-ful consequences of human ingratitude. A *Kafir* is an unthankful person, who fails to acknowledge the gifts of the Generous Lord. The *Kafir*, the disbeliever, is condemned for this ingratitude. Hell is the only place that will cleanse humanity of the filth of this sin. The surat strongly condemns unthankfulness, and reminds people of the Day when everything will be revealed, and no secrets will remain.

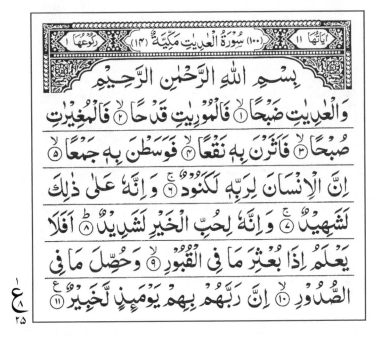

In the name of Allah, the Kind, the Caring.

The ungratefulness of humans

[1] By the snorting war horses, [2] *their hooves* striking sparks, [3] charging in dawn raids [4] scattering dust *clouds* [5] then dashing into the centre *of the enemy*. [6] Human beings are most unthankful to His Lord. [7] He is a witness to this, [8] and passionately loves wealth. [9] Doesn't he know everything in the graves will be thrown out, [10] and the *secrets* of hearts will be revealed? [11] That Day their Lord will be aware of them.

101. Surat Al-Qariʿah
The Sudden Calamity

This is a Makkan surat that starts with a question about Judgement Day in order to open our eyes to the reality of it. It describes the momentous events of that Day and then points out the root of a successful life: good deeds, a guarantee for success. Those who lack good deeds will have "a blazing fire" (11).

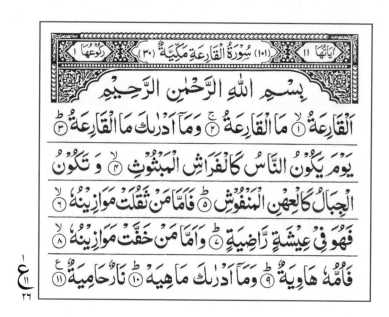

In the name of Allah, the Kind, the Caring.

Good deeds are the basis of success
[1] The Sudden Calamity! [2] What is the Sudden Calamity? [3] What can explain the reality of the Sudden Calamity to you? [4] The Day when people will *look lost*, like scattered moths, [5] and the mountains *will sway* like fluffy wool. [6] So the one who has heavy scale of deeds [7] will have a happy life. [8] But the one who has light scale of deeds [9] his home will be a bottomless Pit[a]. [10] What can explain what it *looks like* to you? [11] A Blazing Fire!

---

[a] *Hawiya* is one of the names of Hell, and means a bottomless pit.

102. Surat At-Takathur

The Competition for More and More

This is a Makkan surat that concisely highlights human greed and obsession with material things. It is trying to shock that person who is deeply immersed in love of the world. Therefore, particularly relevant for our affluent societies. It lays bare the fact that this diversion and distraction from the reality of the Hereafter cannot save us from dying and going into graves. The solution is simple: believe in the Resurrection and Divine Justice. Such moving revelation can awaken readers to the dangers of worldliness and forgetfulness of the Hereafter.

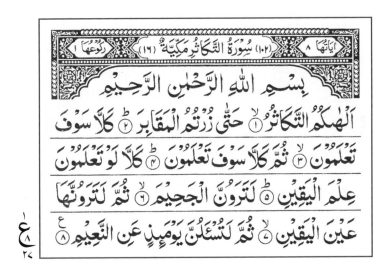

In the name of Allah, the Kind, the Caring.

Human greed

[1] The competition for more and more *wealth* preoccupied you,[a] [2] until you went down into your graves. [3] Surely, you will know; [4] Eventually you will understand. [5] If only you had knowledge of certainty. [6] You will certainly see Hell; [7] you will see it with the eye of certainty; [8] that Day, you will be questioned about all the gifts.

---

[a] From the worship of Allah, being kind to others and mindful of reality.

103. Surat Al-ʿAsr

The Age

The short and pithy message of this Makkan surat is moving description of those who are mindful. Imam Shafie (d.820 AH) expressed this eloquently: "If people thought deeply just about this one surat, it would be enough for them." This is because it simply states the obvious: as time passes, man is at loss, except those blessed ones who do four things: believe, act righteously and encourage each other to be truthful and patient.

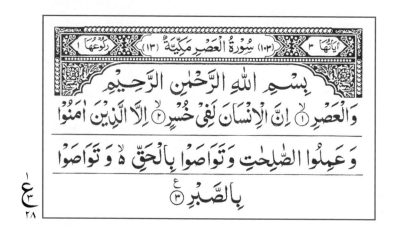

In the name of Allah, the Kind, the Caring.

Humans are at a loss unless they are righteous
[1] By the age,[a] [2] humans are at a loss, [3] except the believers who are righteous, and encourage each other to be truthful and patient.

---

[a] ʿAsr also means evening time, and the twilight hours of the day. It may also refer to the age of the beloved Messenger, how incredibly blessed it was.

104. Surat Al-Humazah

The Faultfinder

This is a Makkan surat that condemns people who have a negative attitude towards others, and are obsessed with wealth. The belief that money can give them health, longevity, happiness and freedom from difficulties is a delusion. Many wealth-obsessed people are so out of touch with reality that they forget their mortality. The only fitting place for such people is what the surat calls "the Crusher" (*al-Hutama*), Hell, described as a vault of fire. That will be an agonising realisation of a wasted life.

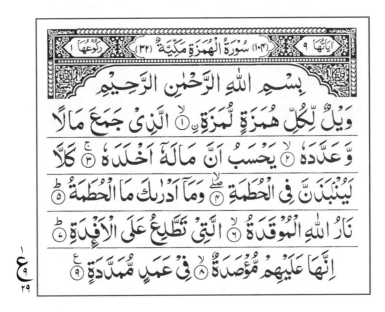

In the name of Allah, the Kind, the Caring

Beware of the idolisation of wealth

[1] Wretched is every backbiting fault-finder, [2] who gathers wealth and counts it over and over, [3] thinking his wealth will make him live forever. [4] No, he will be thrown into the Crusher! [5] And what can explain to you what the Crusher is? [6] Allah's blazing Fire, [7] which rises over *their* hearts. [8] Indeed, it is closed over them from all sides, [9] *flames* stretching out in columns.

105. Surat Al-Fil

The Elephant

This is an early Makkan surat, which reminds the people of Makkah how they were saved from the army of Abraha. He was a Yemenite Christian king, whose capital Sana housed a magnificent cathedral. The only rival to this cathedral in the Arabian Peninsula was the Kaaba in Makkah. Abraha was enthusiastic about spreading Christianity throughout the Arabian Peninsula, so Makkah was his natural target. He decided to attack it in 570 CE, but his plan went badly wrong, as described by this surat. This was also the year the Messenger ﷺ was born. The defeat of Abraha was a wonderful sign that marked the beginning of a new era of spiritual change, and the coming of the Messenger ﷺ.

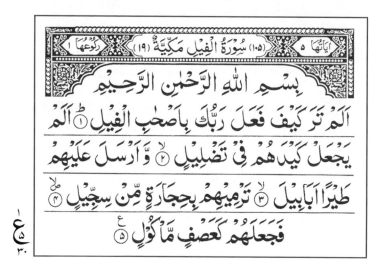

In the name of Allah, the Kind, the Caring

The defeat of Abraha

[1] Have you not seen how your Lord dealt with the army of the elephant? [2] Didn't He smash their plan? [3] When He sent a flock of birds against them, [4] they pelted them with flint-stones. [5] So, He turned them into *what looked like* chewed hay.

106. Surat Al-Quraysh

The Tribe of Quraysh

This Makkan surat highlights another favour given to the Quraysh: a good livelihood through trading. The Quraysh are reminded they can travel safely to Yemen with their caravans laden with expensive cargo during the winter months, and to Syria in the summer, and this is indeed a Divine favour on them.

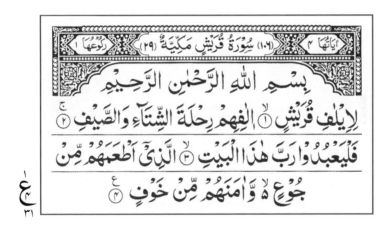

In the name of Allah, the Kind, the Caring.

The Quraysh were safe
[1] For the Quraysh's feeling of security – [2] their security in the winter and summer journeys. [3] So, they should worship the Lord of this house, *the Kaaba,* [4] Who feeds them, protects from famine and gives them safety from fear.

107. Surat Al-Ma'un

Small Kindness

This is an early Makkan surat that opens with a description of the character of a Qurayshi leader: unwilling to accept Judgement Day and its justice, unkind to the weak, indifferent to the welfare of the needy, and so mean-spirited that he doesn't lend even small tools or utensils to his neighbours. The Qurayshi leader hinted at could be Abu Lahab, the uncle of the Prophet ﷺ, he was also the keeper of the Kaaba, taking care of its maintenance and income. Worship, which is supposed to be from the depths of one's heart, became a show rather than a symbol of true faith and genuine longing for the Divine. The surat gives a powerful message that a person with such a wretched character can never give even "small kindnesses" (7).

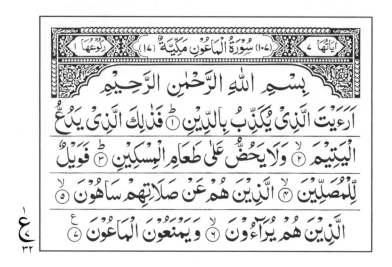

In the name of Allah, the Kind, the Caring.

Small kindnesses

[1] Have you seen him who denies the *Divine* Judgement? [2] He treats the orphan roughly, [3] nor encourages the feeding of the needy. [4] So, ruined are the worshippers [5] who are daydreaming whilst praying, [6] they just show off, [7] and stop others from doing small kindness.[a]

---

[a] *Al-Ma'un* are small tools and utensils, implying that such people are so miserly that they cannot even lend these items to their close neighbours.

108. Surat Al-Kawthar

The Abundance

This is a Makkan surat. When the Prophet ﷺ lost both of his baby sons, Qasim and Abdullah, the Qurayshi leaders, including Abu Lahab, were jubilant and called the Prophet *Abtar*: a pejorative term meaning cut off, i.e. sonless. In other words, the taunt was that the Prophet ﷺ had no surviving male heirs, therefore his mission and campaign would come to end with his demise. The Messenger ﷺ was naturally hurt by these callous comments, so Allah consoled His beloved Messenger ﷺ and promised him abundant success, bliss and never-ending Divine favours. The Kawthar, abundance could be his beautiful qualities, masses and masses of followers and the lake of sweet water on Judgement Day.

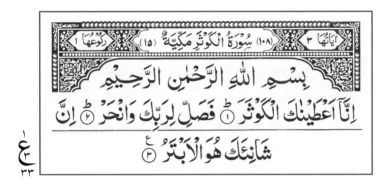

In the name of Allah, the Kind, the Caring.

The Prophet will not be cut off; his enemies will
¹We gave *everything in* abundance to you, ²so, pray to your Lord and make a sacrifice. ³Your enemy will be finished, cut off.ᵃ

ᵃ Literally childless, "finished" in the sense that he will have no surviving male heirs.

109. Surat Al-Kafirun

The Disbelievers

This surat was revealed in the middle Makkan period, when a group of Qurayshi leaders came to the Messenger ﷺ with a proposal: "If you worship our idols for one year, we shall worship your God for one year. This way we will keep our people united." The surat was revealed to reject this nonsensical proposal. It clearly condemns compromising with idolatry. True believers have never done so in the past; they will not do it now, nor in the future. The final verse: "For you is your religion, and for me is my religion," (6) points to the fundamental human right of religion. Despite this uncompromising tone, the surat lays down the principle of a pluralistic, diverse society. It stresses freedom of religion, and teaches about the coexistence of different religions and ideologies. Islam does not believe in destroying other religions; instead, it preaches living alongside others in a peaceful way.

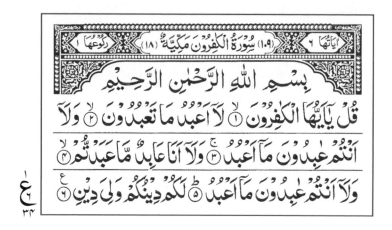

In the name of Allah, the Kind, the Caring.

Co-existence of religions

¹Say: "Disbelievers, ²I don't worship what you worship, ³neither are you worshippers of what I worship. ⁴Nor will I be a worshipper of what you worship, ⁵neither will you be worshippers of what I worship. ⁶For you is your religion, and for me is mine."

110. Surat An-Nasr

The Help

This is a Madinan surat that forecasts the victory of Makkah and the ultimate success of
the Messenger ﷺ, hinting his mission is nearly complete. According to some scholars, this
was revealed on the occasion of the 'farewell pilgrimage', in the final year of the life of the
Prophet ﷺ (622 CE). It beautifully encapsulates the humble attitude of the Prophet ﷺ to
worldly victories and successes: in times of affluence and power, we must be modest.

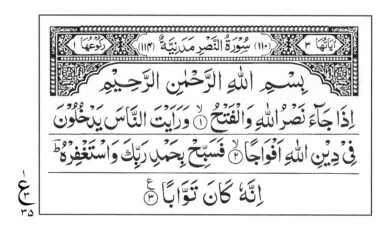

In the name of Allah, the Kind, the Caring.

Be grateful in times of success
¹When Allah's help and the victory comes ²and you see masses of people entering
Allah's religion, ³then glorify and praise Your Lord, and seek His forgiveness. He
is ever ready to accept repentance.

111. Surat Al-Lahab

The Flames

This is a Makkan surat. Abu Lahab was the uncle of the Prophet ﷺ but a bitter enemy. He had considerable influence in the city. One day, the Prophet ﷺ was preaching on Mount Safa near the Kaaba to an attentive crowd. He was inviting them to believe in one God, and to accept him as the Messenger ﷺ. Abu Lahab could not contain himself and shouted, "Damn you! Is this what you wanted to tell us?" This surat, in contrast to other Quranic surats, was revealed to condemn his outrageous behaviour. In other places, the Prophet ﷺ and the Muslims are instructed to be patient, but here Allah directly confronts this abuser of His beloved Messenger ﷺ, and by naming him, shames him. Unfortunately, Abu Lahab and his wife continued their animosity until the end. Here Allah is showing His support for the Messenger ﷺ and severely condemning his enemies. Abu Lahab's 'hands are broken' is an idiom for "his hands are paralysed so he will not be able to confront."

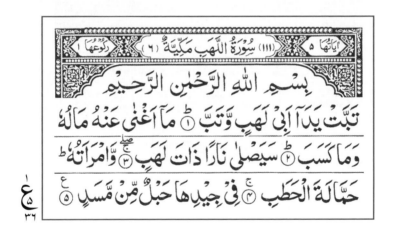

In the name of Allah, the Kind, the Caring.

Abu Lahab will be punished

[1] Abu Lahab's hands are broken, he's ruined. [2] Neither his wealth nor his achievements will help him. [3] Soon he will enter the Flaming Fire; [4] so will his wife, the firewood-carrier – [5] *she* will have a rope of palm-fibre around her neck.

112. Surat Al-Ikhlas

Sincere Faith

This Makkan surat succinctly summarises Quranic teachings about *Tawhid*, the Oneness of Allah and the core of Islamic faith: all power, glory and control is in the hands of the Almighty Lord. I have translated *Al-Samad* as "The Eternal". He is the aim and goal of everything, since He is the Master of all and the final refuge. Everything depends upon Him, but He is independent of all, and He is the final cause of all causes. The surat concisely conveys this message in four points: unique, Eternal, He is not a father nor a son. A brief but an effective refutation of idolatry.

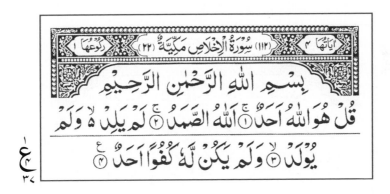

In the name of Allah, the Kind, the Caring.

Allah, the One

¹Say: "He is Allah, the One, ²Allah the Eternal. ³He is not a father nor a son. ⁴None is equal to Him."

113. Surat Al-Falaq

The Daybreak

These last two surats of the glorious Quran (*Surat Al-Falaq* and *Surat Al-Nas*) were revealed together in Makkah. *Surat Al-Falaq* describes four sources of possible physical and psychological harm: from creation, including visible creatures and the invisible; darkness and what is hidden in it; the witches and their witchcraft; and jealousy. Allah is the only true Protector Who can shield and prevent harm from them. Aisha [Allah be pleased with Her], the wife of the Messenger ﷺ reported: "When the Messenger lay down to sleep, he would recite *Surat al-Ikhlas* and these two surats, and blow on his palms, then wipe over his entire body" (Bukhari).

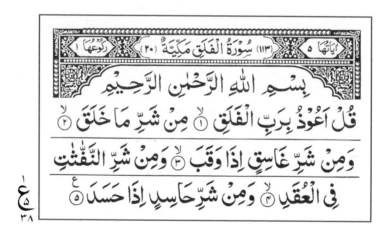

In the name of Allah, the Kind, the Caring.

Seek refuge with Allah

[1] Say: "I seek refuge in the Lord of the daybreak, [2] from the harm of all His creation, [3] from the harm of the ever-darkening night, [4] from the harm of witches who blow on knots, [5] and from the harm of a jealous person when jealous."

114. Surat An-Nas

The People

Whilst the previous surat described sources of physical and psychological harm, this surat focuses on harm from our archenemy, Satan. This surat tells us how he tries to influence our hearts and minds. Protection lies in turning to Allah for refuge, shield and shelter.

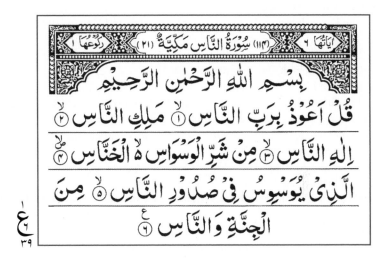

In the name of Allah, the Kind, the Caring.

Seek Allah's refuge from evil

¹Say: "I seek refuge in the Lord of the people, ²the King of the people, ³the God of the people, ⁴from the evil of the sneaking whisperer, ⁵who whispers into people's hearts *and minds*, ⁶from among the jinn or the people."

Bibliography

Abdel Haleem, M.A.S., *The Quran: A New Translation* (Oxford: Oxford University Press, 2004).

Ahsan Islahi, A., *Taddabur-e-Quran*, 9 volumes (Lahore: Faran Foundation, 1983).

Al-Ghazali, M., *A Thematic Commentary on the Quran* (Kuala Lumpur: Islamic Book Trust, 2000).

Al-Mu'jam al-Wasit, fifth edition, (Cairo, Egypt: Dar al-Shruq al-Dawliyya, 2011).

Al-Razi, M., ibn Umar al-Hussain Fakhraudin, *Mafateehal Ghayb*, 16 volumes (Beirut: Dar al-Kutub al-Ilmiyyah, n.d.).

Arberry, A.J., *The Koran Interpreted* (London: George Allen and Unwin, 1980).

Asad, M., *The Message of The Qur'an* (Gibraltar: Dar al-Andalus, 1980).

Hussain, M., *The Five Pillars of Islam: Laying the Foundations of Divine Love and Service to Humanity* (Markfield: Kube Publications, 2012).

Irving, T.B., *The Qur'an* (New Delhi: Goodword Books, 2009).

Ismail ibn Kathir, *Tafsir ibn Kathir*, 3 volumes (Beirut: Dar al-Quran, n.d.).

Lane, E.W., *Arabic-English lexicon* (Beirut: Librairie du Liban, 1968).

Lings, M., *Muhammad: His Life Based on the Earliest Sources* (Rochester, VT: Inner Traditions – Bear & Company, 2006).

Al-Nasafi, Abdullah ibn Ahmed (d.710 AH), *Tafseer al-Madarik*, 3 volumes (Karachi: Qadimi Kutub Khana, n.d.).

Mazhari, Qazi Sanaullah Panipathi, *Tafsir Mazhari*, (Lahore: Zia ul-Quran Publications, 2002).

Penrice, J., *Dictionary and Glossary of the Kor-an* (Beirut: Librairie du Liban, 1873).

Al-Sabuni, M.A., *Safwat al-Tafasir*, 3 volumes (Halb: Dar al-Qalam al-Arabi, 1994).

Saeh, B., *The Miraculous Language of the Qur'an: Evidence of Divine Origin* (London: IIIT, 2015).

Shah, P.M.K., *Tafsir Zia ul-Quran* (Lahore: Zia ul-Quran Publications, 1978).

Al-Suyuti, J.A.R., *Al-Itqan fi ulum al-Quran*, 2 volumes (Beirut: Dar Ihya al-Ulum, 1996).

Al-Suyuti, *Tafsir al-Jalalayn* (Mansoura: Dar al Ghadd, 2002).

Von Denffer, H., *Ulum al-Qur'an: An Introduction to the Sciences of the Qur'an* (Leicester: The Islamic Foundation, 1999).

Wehr, H., *A Dictionary of Modern Written Arabic* (Beirut: Librairie du Liban, 1980).

Yusuf Ali, A., *The Holy Qur'an* (Madinah: King Fahd Holy Qur'an Printing Complex, 1990).

General Index

closeness of, 2:186

creating of, 6:95-99, 13:1-4

debating about, as disliked, 42:16

does not have children, 2:116, 19:88-92, 23:91, 43:15-19, 112:1-4

everything as belonging to, 4:131-34

first assembly of souls before, 7:172-74

inventing lies about, 6:93

Jews asking to see, 4:153

love of, 2:165, 3:28-32, 5:54, 9:23-24

making oaths in the name of, 2:224-27

making up lies against, 3:93

Musa asking to see, 7:143

Names of, 7:180, 17:110-11, 20:8, 17:110-11, 59:22-24

not perceived by sight, 6:103

nothing concealed from, 11:5

oneness of, 112:1-4

purchase of believers, 9:111-12

remembrance of (See remembrance)

to Him we belong, 2:156

ultimate sovereignty of, 6:14-18

Al-Lat (idol), 53. 19

allegiance, pledge of, 48:10, 48:18-21

of believing women, 60:12-13

alliances with disbelievers, 3:28

angel of death, 32:11

angels

appearing in human form, 6:8-9

around the throne, 39:75, 40:7

arranged in rows, 37:164-69

as motivating the righteous, 41:30-32

as prostrating to Allah, 16:49-50

assigned to watch over each person, 13:11

at battle of Badr, 8:12, 8:49-54

at battle of Uhud, 3:124-29

belief in, 2:177

descent on Night of Power, 97:4

eavesdropping on, 37:8-9

given female names by disbelievers,

A

ablution

obligation of, 4:43

performing, 5:6

abrogation of verses, 2:106

actions, recording of, 10:61

'Ad, people of

rejection of Hud, 7:65-72, 11:50-58, 26:123-40, 46:21-25

thunderbolt of, 41:13-16

destruction of, 50:13, 51:41-42, 53:50, 54:18-22, 69:1-7

adoption, 33:4

marrying ex wife of adopted child, 33:36-37

adultery

penalty for, 4:15

prohibition of, 17:32

See also fornication; sexual relations

afterlife

disbelievers' rejection of, 27:67-73

rejection of, 23:35-43

aging, 36:68, 103:1-2

Alast, day of, 7:172-74

alcohol

drinking, as sinful, 2:219

prohibition of praying under influence of, 4:43

prohibition of, 5:90-93

Allah

absoluteness of, 6:59-62, 11:6-7, 27:62-66

as answering prayers, 40:60

as declaring war on usurers, 2:279

as decreeing mercy over Himself, 6:54

as friend of the believers, 2:257

as giver of life and death, 2:28

as light of heavens and earth, 24:35-38

attributes of, 57:1-6

beautiful names, calling by, 7:180

calling on, in secret, 7:55

armour, 21:80, 34:11

arrogance
  as disliked, 4:37
  as preventing entrance to Paradise, 7:40-41
  avoiding, 31:18
  of disbelief, 23:75-80
  of Satan, 2:31
  rejecting revelation as, 16:23-29
ascension, 53:1-18
ashes, parable of, 14:18-20
associating others with Allah. See idolatry
atonement for breaking oaths, 5:89
awliya. See friends of Allah,
Azar, 6:74

B

Baal, 37:125
backbiting, wretchedness of, 104:1-8
banditry, punishment for, 5:33-34
Banu al-Nadir, expulsion from Medina, 59:1-5
barren land, metaphor of, 41:39
bath, ritual, 5:6
battle. See warfare; jihad
beast, emergence of, 27:82
Bedouins
  as submitting, but not believing, 49:14-18
  seeking exemption from Tabuk, 9:90
  sincerity and hypocrisy amongst, 9:97-99, 9:101
bees, 16:68-69
belief, as accepting the Messenger as arbiter, 4:65
believers
  Allah is friend of, 2:257
  angels taking souls of at death, 16:32
  as belonging to Allah, 9:111-12
  as best community from humanity, 3:110
  attitude in battle, 3:146-51, 8:45-48, 8:64-66
  attributes of, 2:2-5
  Christians as closest to, 5:82-86

53:27
  glorifying Allah, 13:13
  greeting believers in Paradise, 13:23
  guests of Ibrahim, 15:51-59
  idolaters' view of, 43:15-19
  Malik (angel at gates of Hell), 43:77
  nineteen, 74:31
  on Judgement Day, 78:38
  only sent to destroy a people, 15:7-8
  prostration to Adam, 17:61
  questioning of on Judgement Day, 34:40-43
  questioning the creation of Adam, 2:30
  Quraysh view as daughters of Allah, 37:149-62
  recording of deeds, 50:17, 82:10-12
  sending blessings on the believers, 33:42
  sent to people of Lut, 11:70-83, 29:31-35
  snatching of souls, 79:1-5
  taking souls of believers at death, 16:32
  visit to Ibrahim, 11:69-76, 51:24-37
  wings of, 35:1
anger, forgiving while in, 42:37
animals
  Allah provides for, 29:60
  as a sign of Allah, 36:71-73
  as prostrating to Allah, 16:49-50
  created from water, 24:45
  living in communities, 6:38
  proliferation of as a sign of Allah, 2:164
  shades of colour in, 35:28
  skins of, 16:80
  slaughter of, 5:3
  See also livestock
ants, valley of, 27:18-19
anxiousness of man, 70:19
apes, transmogrification into, 7:166
apostasy, 3:86-91
apostates, works of as fruitless, 2:216
argumentation
  avoiding, 22:67-70
  in the best way, 29:46-49
ark. See ship of Nuh.
Ark of the Covenant, 2:248. See also covenant

C

calf, worship of Israelites of, 2:51, 2:54, 2:92-93

call to prayer, mocking, as censured, 5:58-60

camels
  superstitions surrounding, 5:103-105
  sacrificing, 22:36-37

captives, in war, 8:67-71, 47:4-6

carrion, prohibition of, 5:3

cattle
  pagan customs regarding, 6:138, 6:142-47
  slitting ears of, 4:119

cave, one of two in, 9:40

cave, sleepers of
  supplication of, 18:10
  awakening of, 18:19-21
  numbers of, 18:22
  years spent asleep, 18:25-27

change, comes from within, 13:11

character, people acting according to, 17:84

charity
  as attribute of the believer, 2:3
  as not decreasing wealth, 2:268
  as righteous, 2:177
  encouragement to spend in, 51:19, 57:7-10, 57:18
  forgiveness as, 5:45
  giving in secret, 2:270-71
  giving the best of one's possessions, 2:267, 3:92
  giving to atone for leaving ihram due to illness, 2:196
  giving with humility, 2:262-64
  giving before consulting with the Messenger, 58:12-13
  hypocrites mocking of generosity, 9:77-80
  of the disbelievers, 3:117
  parable of grain of wheat, 2:261
  parable of orchard, 2:215, 2:265
  recipients of, 9:60
  recognising the needy, 2:273-74

compared with disbelievers, 11:15-24

described, 7:157, 8:2-4, 9:71-72, 23:1-11, 25:63-73, 27:2-3, 70:22-35, 76:7-11

fearing Allah, 3:102

half-heartedness in, 22:11-16

keeping the company of the devout, 6:51-55

love of Allah, 2:165, 5:54, 9:23-24

mocking of, 83:30-35

pardoning and overlooking faults of, 24:22

penalty for murdering, 4:92-93

praise of, 48:29

preference for marriage, 4:25

Quran as healing for, 17:82

Qur'an as soothing to, 10:57-60

reward of, 22:23-24

saving of, from Hell, 19:71-72

victory promised to, 24:55-57

will be tested, 29:2-5

bequests, 4:12

big bang, 21:30-35

birds
  flight of, 16:79, 67:19
  hunting with, 5:4
  language of, given to Sulayman, 27:15
  living in communities, 6:38
  obedient to Dawud, 38:19
  praise alongside Dawud, 21:79

blindness, on Judgement Day, 20:102, 20:124-25

blood
  as forbidden food, 2:173
  prohibition of consuming, 5:3

boastfulness, as disliked, 4:37, 19:77-83. See also arrogance; showing off

boat, Khidr's damaging of, 18:71

Book. See Scripture

booty, 59:6-8

boy, Khidr's killing of, 18:74

breastfeeding, after divorce, 2:233

bribes, prohibition of, 2:188

coming face to face with, 3:143
delaying repentance till, 23:99-100
disbelievers in throes of, 6:93-94
every soul shall taste, 21:35
everything on earth will perish, 55:26
fear of, 2:243-45
in disbelief, 2:161-62
in state of purity, 16:30-32
last moments before, 56:83-85
leaving a will, 2:180-81
no escape from, 4:78-80
no one knows their place of, 31:34
parable of rain, 7:57-58
relation with sleep, 39:42
repentance at point of, 4:18
seeking, 2:94
unavoidability of, 39:30
debating about Allah, as disliked, 42:16
debt
    receiving zakat to pay, 9:60
    settling after death, 4:12
deception, of hypocrisy, 2:9
deeds
    atom's weight will be seen, 99:7-8
    Illiyeen, book of, 83:18-28
    recording of, 50:17, 82:10-12
    Sijjeen, book of, 83:7-16
defensive war, 22:38-41
demons
    as assigned to be enemy of each
        prophet, 6:112-13
    Qur'an protected from, 26:210-13
    seeking refuge from, 113:1-5, 114:1-6
desertion, prohibition of, 8:15-16
despair, avoiding, 39:53
destiny
    everything written in a book, 35:11
    tied to necks of man, 17:13-14
devil. See Satan; demons; evil
dietary laws
    eating of the good, 2:168, 2:172
    forbidden food, 2:173
    invoking Allah's name over meat, 6:118-
        21
    livestock, as lawful, 5:1

D

date tree, at birth of Isa, 19:23-25
daughters
    ingratitude for, 16:57-60
    negative attitudes towards, as
        disapproved, 43:15-19
    See also children; family
day
    alternation with night, as a sign of
        Allah, 2:164
    as a blessing, 16:12, 30:23
    as a sign, 17:12, 41:37
    only Allah changes to night, 28:71-75
Day of Judgement
    arguments among disbelievers, 34:31-33
    as day of loss, 64:9
    assembly of believers and disbelievers
        contrasted, 19:84-87
    bewilderment of disbelievers on, 14:42-
        45
    blindness of sinners on, 20:102, 20:124-
        25
    bright and darkened faces on, 3:106
    described, 14:46-51, 18:99-108, 70:1-18,
        75:7-15, 79:1-13
    disbelievers blaming each other on,
        37:19-39
    division of people into two groups,
        11:104-109
    idolaters on, 16:86-88
    Isa as sign of, 43:57-67
    opening of personal records on, 18:47-
        49
    questioning about, 7:187-88
    questioning of idols on, 25:17-19
    severity and shock of, 22:1-4
    summoning of communities on, 45:27-
        31
    terror of, 80:33-42
    testimony of idols on, 28:62-66
    time for, as fixed, 78:17
    wasted lives on, 6:27-32
    weighing of scales on, 7:8-9
death
    as from Allah, 2:28

excuses, made by hypocrites, 9:43-49
eye for an eye, 5:45
eyes, testimony of, 41:20-22

F
factionalism, 30:32
fairness, standing up for, 4:135-36. See
    also justice
faith
    arguments against rejection of, 2:28-29
    articles of, 2:177, 2:284-85
    as accepting the Messenger as arbiter,
      4:65
    as innate trait , 10:21-23
    described, 2:3-4
    migration for the sake of, 4:97-100
    of sleepers of cave, 18:13-16
    requires conviction, 5:61-63
    success through, 2:62
    true nature of, 49:14-18
false oaths, 58:14-20
falsehood, vanquished by truth, 34:48-49
family
    adopted children, 33:4-5
    caring for parents, 29:8-9, 46:15-16
    categories of relatives forbidden from
      marriage, 4:22-23
    disobedient son, 46:17-20
    dissolution of kinship on day of
      judgement, 23:101
    giving charity to parents, 2:215
    grieving for an absent child, 12:84-87
    love between spouses, 30:21
    love for relatives, 42:23
    marrying disbelievers, 2:221
    protecting from the fire, 66:6
    rights of relatives, 33:6
    sowing discord between man and wife,
      2:102
    supplication for, 25:74
    teaching to perform the prayer, 20:132
    See also marriage; divorce; children.
famine
    in Makkah, 44:8-16
    relaxation of dietary laws during, 5:3

zihar, 33:4, 58:1-4
dog
    of sleepers of cave, 18:18
    parable of, 7:176
dowry, 5:5
    giving, 4:24
    in divorce settlements, 2:236-37
    obtaining divorce by returning, 2:229
    retaking, prohibition of, 4:20
dreams
    fulfilment of Yusuf's, 12:99-100
    of the Prophet, 48:27
    of Yusuf, 12:4-6
    Yusuf's interpretation of, 12:41-49
dua'. See supplications

E
ears, testimony of, 41:20-22
earth
    on Judgement Day, 14:46-51
    righteous inherit, 21:105
    travelling to see the consequence of
      disbelief, 3:137
ease and hardship, 94:5-6
eating together, 24:61
Eden, Gardens of, 35:33
Egypt, flight of Israelites from, 26:52-59
elephant, companions of, 105:1-4
emigration, 8:72-75, 29:56
end of time, emergence of beast, 27:82.
    See also Day of Judgement
envy
    as breeding double standards, 2:89
    of disbelievers, 4:54-55
    seeking refuge from, 113:5
Eve
    deception of Satan, 7:19-22
    temptation of, 2:35
evil
    protection from through worship of
      Allah, 2:21
    forbidding, 3:104, 3:110
    attractiveness of, 6:122-24
    seeking refuge from, 113:1-5, 114:1-6
evil eye, avoiding, 12:67-68

for idolaters, prohibition of seeking, 9:113-16

hypocrites cannot avail themselves of, 9:80

never despairing of, 39:53

not available to disbelievers, 47:34

of Adam and Eve, 7:23-25

of minor sins, 53:32

of those who delayed joining Tabuk expedition, 9:117-18

of those who have wronged one, as charity, 5:45

on Hajj, 2:199

prayer for past generations, 59:10

racing towards, 57:21

seeking at dawn, 51:18

seeking, as means of warding off punishment, 8:33

seeking, by coming to the Mesenger, 4:64

supplication for, 3:16, 28:16

through giving charity, 2:268

through repentance, 6:54

towards People of the Book, 2:109

while angry, 42:37

See also repentance

fornication

accusations of, 24:4-10

penalty for, 4:16

punishment for, 24:2

See also adultery; sexual relations

fortune telling, prohibition of, 5:90-93

foster mothers, 2:233

foul word, parable of tree, 14:26-27

fraud, 11:85-86

free will

idolaters' arguments on, 43:20-25

trust of, 33:72-73

freedom of worship, 2:114

Friday prayers, 62:9-10

friends, choosing wisely, 3:118-20

friends of Allah, described, 10:62-65

frog plague, 7:133

fruit tree, parable of, 14:24-27

funeral prayer, of hypocrites, 9:84

fasting

as compensation for zihar divorce, 58:4

in atonement for leaving ihram due to illness, 2:196

laws of, 2:183-87

Ramadan, 2:185

fathers, providing for children, 2:233. See also family; children; marriage

fault-finders, 68:11

female infanticide, 16:56-60, 81:8-9

fickle nature of man, 41:49-51

fighting, in sacred months, 2:216

Final Hour. See Day of Judgement,

financial matters

compound interest, prohibition of, 3:130-32

loans, 2:282-83

mingling of orphan's and guardian's wealth, 2:220

prohibition of usury, 2:275-81

witnessing commercial transactions, 2:282

See also commerce

fraud, 11:85-86

fire, as sign of Allah, 56:71-74

fishing, lawfulness of while on pilgrimage, 5:96

flash flood, parable of, 13:17-18

flight of birds, 16:79, 67:19

flood

of Egypt, 7:133

of people of Nuh, 11:40-44, 29:14-15, 37:75-82

parable of, 13:17-18

fly, parable of, 22:73-76

foetus, development of , 23:12-16, 39:6

followers, as disowned by their leaders, 2:166-67

food. See dietary laws

forbidding evil, 3:104

foremost inhabitants of Paradise, 56:10-26

forest, companions of, 26:176

forgiveness

acceptance of, 42:25

for all sins except polytheism, 4:116

See also mankind

humility

calling on Allah in secret, 7:55

of the Messenger, 6:48-50

through suffering, 6:42-47

wisdom of, 18:37-38

Hunain, battle of, 9:25-28

hunting

while on pilgrimage, as unlawful, 5:1,
5:94-97

with birds of prey, 5:4

husbands, inheriting from, 4:12

hypocrites

as waiting for victor to emerge, 4:137-41

attempts to cause splits among
believers, 9:61-66

attributes of, 2:8-20

compared with Satan, 59:15-17

deceptions of, 4:60-63

excuses made by, 9:43-49, 48:11-14

false promises of, 59:11-14

false witness of, 63:1-4

gloating at other's misfortune, 9:50-55

in bottommost pit of Hell, 4:144-47

lack of loyalty in battle of the Trench,
33:12

lack of resolve, 29:10-11

Messenger prohibited from praying
over, 9:84-88

misquoting the Quran, 5:41

objecting to the judgement of Allah and
His Messenger, 24:46-50

response to order to march on Tabuk,
9:41-42

rules of engagement with, 4:88-91

sealed hearts of, 47:16

searching for light on Judgement Day,
57:13-15

tendency to look for loopholes, 4:81-82

trouble makers, 2:204-206

warning to, 48:6-7

I

iddah. See waiting period

idolaters

loving this world more than, 2:92-95

harvest of, 42:20

hijab, 24:31, 24:60

hoarding, among rabbis and monks, 9:34-
35

Holy Land, reluctance of Israelites to
enter, 5:20-26

holy spirit, as strengthening Jesus, 2:87

home

blessing of, 16:80

light of Allah in, 24:36

returning to, 28:85

seeking permission to enter, 24:27-29

homicide, penalty for, 4:92-93

homosexuality, 7:81, 27:55, 29:29

honesty, in trade, 26:181-84

honey, blessing of, 16:68-69

hoopoe, 27:20-23

hopelessness, avoiding, 39:53

horses, paraded before Sulayman, 38:30-
33

houses

entering from the back, 2:189

light of Allah in, 24:36

seeking permission to enter, 24:27-29

Hudaybiyyah, treaty of, 48:1-5

human beings, duty of, 2:21

humanity

accepted trust of free will, 33:72-73

Allah easing burden of, 4:26-28

creation of, 32:7-9

differences among peoples, 10:19-20

differences in colour and language,
30:22

divided, on Day of Judgement, 30:11-18

enmity with Satan, 18:50-53

honouring of, 17:70-72

Messengers sent to, 2:213

miserliness of, 17:99-100

momentousness of life of, 5:32

need for messengers, 17:94-98

purpose of creation of, 51:56

quarrelsomeness of, 18:54-56

races and tribes, 49:13

when giving charity, 2:262-64

loopholes, 4:81-82
Lote tree, 53:14-16
loudness, avoiding, 31:19
love
    as a sign of Allah, 30:21
    between spouses, 30:21
    for relatives, 42:23
    obeying the Messenger as, 3:28-32
    of Allah, 2:165, 5:54, 9:23-24
    victory for lovers of Allah, 5:54-56
loyalty
    importance of, 60:1-3
    pledge of, 48:10, 48:18-21
    retaining, even after victory, 8:26-29
lying
    being wary of, 2:76
    to avoid punishment, as sinful, 4:110-12

M

magic, 2:102
magicians
    acknowledgement of Musa, 7:113-26,
      20:71-76
    contest with Musa, 10:79-82, 20:65-70,
      26:43-51
Magog, 18:92-98
maintenance, after divorce, 2:241
Malik (angel at gates of Hell), 43:77
mankind
    Allah does not speak to directly, 42:51
    as at a loss, 103:2
    as fickle, 41:49-51
    as hasty and impatient, 21:37
    as vice-regents on earth, 35:39
    blessings of Allah on, 14:31-34
    created anxious, 70:19
    created from a pair, 42:11
    created from water, 25:54
    creation of Adam, 15:26-40
    creation of, 40:67, 55:14
    development in womb, 23:12-16
    differences among peoples, 10:19-20
    divided, on Day of Judgement, 30:11-18
    division into two groups, 11:104-109
    enmity with Satan, 17:53, 17:61-65,

leather, blessing of, 16:80
left hand, people of, 56:41-56, 69:25-37,
    84:10-15
lice, plague of, 7:133
life
    as from Allah, 2:28
    brevity of, 57:20-21
    greed for, 2:96
    killing, as killing all humanity, 5:32
    not created without a purpose, 21:16-
      21, 23:115-18
    sanctity of, 17:33
    seven stages of, 22:5-7
    wasting, 6:27-32
lifespan of nations, 10:47-52
light
    Allah as, 24:35-38
    hypocrites searching for on Judgement
      Day, 57:13-15
    idolaters unable to stop spread of, 61:7-
      9
    of Islam, opening mind to, 39:22
    Qur'an as, 14:1
lighting, 13:13
listening, 8:20-25
livestock
    as a sign of Allah, 36:71-73
    as lawful to consume, 5:1
    blessing of milk, 16:66
    blessing of wool and skins of, 16:80
    blessing of, 16:5-8, 23:21-22
    lawfulness of, 22:30
    pagan customs regarding, 6:138, 6:142-
      47
    sending of eight kinds of, 39:6
    slaughtering, 5:3
    See also animals
loan
    allowing people time to repay, 2:280
    giving to Allah, 64:17
    prohibition of usury, 2:275-81
    witnesses, presence of, 2:283
    writing terms of contract, necessity of,
      2:282
locust plague, 7:133

prostration of to Allah, 22:18

refused trust of free will, 33:72-73

shades of colour in, 35:27

turned to dust on Judgement Day, 20:105-107

would crumble under the Quran, 59:21

murder

of Habil (Abel), 5:27-31

of one life, as killing all humanity, 5:32

penalty for, 4:92-93

prohibition of, 6:151, 17:33

retaliation for, 2:178

Muslims

as best community from humanity, 3:110

as following religion of Ibrahim, 2:135-36

unity, command for, 3:103

See also believers

mutilation, of nature, 4:119

N

Names of Allah, 7:180, 17:110-11, 20:8, 17:110-11, 59:22-24

nations, as allotted a lifespan, 10:47-52

nature

mutilation of, 4:119

reflecting on signs of, 79:27-46

signs in, 45:3-6

neighbours, kindness to, 4:36

new moon, 2:189

news, checking facts of, 49:6-8

nicknames, 49:11

night, alternation with day, as a sign of Allah, 2:164

night

as a blessing, 30:23

as a sign, 17:12, 36:37, 41:37

as rest, 6:95

blessing of, 16:12

only Allah changes to day, 28:71-75

prayer at, 17:79, 51:17, 52:49, 73:2-4

Night Journey, 17:1, 53:1-18

Night of Power, 97:1-5

nineteen angels, 74:31

mischief makers, 2:204-206

miserliness

avoiding, 17:29-30

as despised, 57:24

condemnation of, 47:36-37

of humankind, 17:99-100

wealth of no benefit, 92:8-11

See also charity; wealth

misfortune

as from yourself, 4:78

avoiding, 64:11-13

gloating at, as hypocrisy, 9:50-55

mockery of religion, 5:57-60

modesty

dressing with, 33:59-62

lowering the gaze, 24:30-31

monasticism, 57:27

months, number of, 9:36

moon

as sign of Allah, 2:189, 41:37

journey through the sky, 35:13

phases of, as a sign, 36:39

prostration of to Allah, 22:18

rejection of worship of, 6:74-79

morning prayer, 17:78

mosques. See masajid

mothers, breastfeeding children after divorce, 2:233

Mount Sinai

Musa's forty nights, 7:142-45

Musa's return to, 7:154-56

olives on, 23:17-22

mountain track, 90:11-20

mountains

as pegs, 31:10

blessing of, 16:15

creation of, 41:10

crumbling at manifestation of Allah, 7:143

disappearance of on Judgement Day, 78:20

glorifying Allah with Dawud, 21:79, 34:10, 38:18

like mighty columns, 78:7

looking over the Israelites, 7:171

of the flood, 13:17-18
of the fly, 22:73-76
of the tree, 14:24-25
of those who reject faith, 2:170
Paradise
  angels greeting those who enter, 13:23
  arrogant denied entry to, 7:40-41
  believers led to in crowds, 39:73
  children in, 52:21-28
  delights of, 44:51-59
  described, 2:25, 35:33, 37:40-48, 47:14-
    15, 52:17-20, 55:46-78, 76:12-22,
    77:41-50, 88:8-16
  ejection of Satan from, 7:11-18
  entering, 43:68-73
  for adhering to the boundaries of Allah,
    4:13
  foremost inhabitants of, 56:10-26
  hardship as means to enter, 2:214
  Jewish and Christian claims to, 2:111
  racing towards, 57:21
  right hand, people of, 56:27-40
  Satan's ejection from, 17:61-64
  Satan's tricking of Adam, 20:115-23
  those who enter, 50:31-35
parents
  caring for, 17:23-25, 29:8-9, 31:14-15,
    46:15-16
  disobedient son, 46:17-20
  kindness to, 4:36
  spending on, 2:215
  See also family; children
patience
  as a gift from Allah, 16:125-27
  as righteous, 2:177
  of the strong-willed messengers, 46:35
  on being separated from a child, 12:18
  seeking help with, 2:45, 2:153-57
peace, greeting of, from angels to believers
  in Paradise, 13:23
pearls, 55:22
penal law, retaliation, 2:178
People of the Book
  arguing with in the best way, 29:46-49
  arguments over Ibrahim, 3:65-68

non-Muslims
  friendships with, 60:7-9
  prohibition of insulting beliefs of,
    6:106-108

O

oaths
  atonement for breaking, 5:89
  false, punishment for, 58:14-20
  law of fulfilling, 2:224-27, 16:90-94
  making up for unfulfilment of, 66:2
obedience
  avoiding cherry picking
    commandments, 4:150-52
  reward for, 4:69
  to Allah and His Messenger, 24:51-54
old age, 16:70
olive trees, 23:20
oneness of Allah, as self evident, 6:19-21
oppression, as worse than bloodshed,
  2:216
orchards
  landlords in, 68:17-33
  parable of, 2:215, 2:265, 18:32-44
Original Decree (Umm al-Kitab), 13:39
orphans
  calling by their real names, 33:4-5
  guarding property of, obligation of,
    6:151
  kindness to, 4:36
  mingling wealth of with one's own,
    2:220
  safeguarding, 4:127
  spending on, 2:177, 2:215
  taking care of wealth of, 17:34

P

pairs, creation of things in, 42:11, 51:49
parables
  of ashes, 14:18-20
  of dog, 7:176
  of grain of wheat, 2:261
  of orchard, 2:215, 2:265, 18:32-44
  of rain, 7:57-58
  of rich man, 18:32-44

as righteous, 2:177
as shield against sinfulness, 29:45
direction. (See Qibla)
dressing well for, 7:29-32
Friday prayer, 62:9-10
in battle, 2:238-39, 4:102-104
in secret, 7:54-56
laziness in, as mark of hypocrisy, 4:142-43
neglecting, danger of, 19:59-60
of disbelievers as ineffective, 13:14
steadfastness in, 2:110
teaching family to perform, 20:132
times for, 11:114, 17:78-79
while travelling, 4:101
See also supplications
pregnancy, divorce during, 65:4
Preserved Tablet (Lawh Mahfuz), 13:39
previous generations, destruction of, 25:35-40
priesthood, taking as lords besides Allah, 9:31-33
prison, Yusuf's time in, 12:36-42
prophets
  as assigned an enemy, 6:112-13
  belief in, 2:135-36, 2:177
  covenant of, 33:7-8
  killing of, 3:21
  mocking of, 43:7-8
  pledge of, 3:81-82
  ranks among, 2:253
  revelations to, 4:163-66
  showing enmity to, 2:98
  test for validity of, 3:79-80
  See also messengers; and under
    individual names in people and places
prostration
  of all creation to Allah, 16:48-52
  of sun, moon and mountains, 22:18
  of those who recognise the Quran,
    17:105-109
Protected Tablet, 85:22
protection from tyrants, supplication for,
  40:27
protection of the Qur'an, 15:9

as not wishing good from God for the
  Prophet, 2:105
as rejecting the Book, 2:101-102
curse of disbelief, 4:47
denying Allah's signs, 3:98-101
disagreement about the Qur'an, 98:1-7
envy of, 2:109
marrying, 5:5
Qibla of, 2:145
recognition of the Quran, 17:105-109
righteous amongst, 3:113-15
stratagems of against the believers,
  3:69-74
See also Christians; Jews; Israelites
people. See humanity
persecution, as worse than bloodshed,
  2:191, 2:216
piety
  as best clothing, 7:26
  how to gain, 2:42
  See also righteousness
pilgrimage. See Hajj
pious, rank of, 2:212. See also believers.
plagues, on Pharaoh's people, 7:130-36
plants, 23:17-20, 39:21
pledge of loyalty to the Messenger, 48:10,
  48:18-21, 60:12-13
pledges, law of fulfilling, 16:90-94. See
  also oaths
poets, misguidance of, 26:224-25
pollination, 15:22
polygamy, being just with wives, 4:129
polytheism. See idolatry
poor, the, recipients of zakat, 9:60. See
  also charity
pork, as forbidden food, 2:173, 5:3
poverty, killing children for fear of, 17:31.
  See also charity
power (worldly)
  cannot guarantee victory, 3:10-13
  quest for, 2:102-103
prayer
  as attribute of the believer, 2:3
  ablution before, 4:43, 5:6
  absentmindedness in, 107:5

miraculousness of, 13:30-31

misquoting, 5:41

nature of, 17:105-109

obligation of listening to when recited, 7:204

protection of, 26:210-13

purpose of, 14:52

reciting in the morning, 17:78

searching for hidden meanings in, 3:7-9

seeking protection from Satan when reading, 16:98-104

seven oft-recited verses, 15:87

touching while clean, 56:79

trembling when reading, 39:23

turning one's back to verses of, 23:66

varying reactions to, 13:36-37

veil over heart prevents understanding of, 6:25-26

R

Rabbinate

taking as lords besides Allah, 9:31-33

hoarding of wealth among, 9:34-35

races and tribes among mankind, 49:13

Al-Rahman, taught the Qur'an, 55:1-2

rain

as a sign of Allah, 2:164, 15:22, 39:21, 41:39

blessing of, 16:10-12

parable of raising the dead, 7:57-58

Ramadan, fast of, 2:185

ransom, for war captives, 47:4

Rass, 50:12

rebellion, prohibition of, 7:33

reconciliation, in marital disputes, 4:35, 4:128-30

recording angels, 50:17

refugees, prohibition of exiling people, 2:84

regret, on Judgement Day, 15:2

relatives

categories forbidden in marriage, 4:22-23

kindness to, 4:36

love for, 42:23

Psalms of Dawud, 4:163, 17:55, 21:105

punishment

delay of, 16:61-65

no escape from, 16:45-47

of disbelievers in this life, 13:34

warnings before, 7:94-99

Q

Qibla

change of, 2:142, 2:144

Ka'ba as, 2:142, 2:144, 2:149-50

of People of the Book, 2:145

quarrelsomeness of man, 18:54-56

questions, avoiding being excessive in, 5:101

Quran

acceptance of, among people of the Book, 28:51-56

as a reminder for those who fear, 20:3, 38:1, 50:45, 80:11

as containing guidance, 2:2

as containing wisdom, 10:1-2

as good news, 17:9-10

as healing, 17:82

as made easy, 19:96, 54:17

as protected, 15:9

as revelation, 69:38-52

as soothing to believers, 10:57-60

as standard for goodness, 3:3-4

as warning and reminder, 7:1-3

avoiding asking questions in revelation of, 5:101-102

avoiding those who mock, 6:66-70

challenge of, 2:23, 10:36-40, 11:12-14, 17:88

described, 41:2-4

disbelievers as screened from, 17:45-48

disbelievers ask to change text of, 10:15-18

disbelievers attempt to distract people from, 41:26

enlightenment through, 45:20-21

immensity of would crumble mountains, 59:21

Jewish rejection of, 2:89-92

revelation
    abrogation of, 2:106
    as same for all prophets, 4:163-66
    as sent to men, 21:7
    changing, enormity of, 2:79-81
    false claims to , 6:93
    of the Qur'an, 26:192-99
    reality of, 6:91-92
    three modes of, 42:51-53
    to Musa, 2:54
revenge, avoiding acting on, 5:1-2, 42:40
rich man, parable of, 18:32-44
right hand, people of, 56:27-40, 69:19-24, 84:7-9
righteousness
    defined, 2:177, 4:36-38
    rank of the pious, 2:212
    reward of, 2:25
    women, 4:34
    worship as route to, 2:21
rocks, shades of colour in, 35:27
Romans, 30:2-6
rope of Allah, 3:103, 3:112
rumours
    dismissing, 49:6-8
    of Yusuf, 12:30
    prohibition of spreading, 4:83, 24:14-18

S

Sabbath, punishment for breaking, 2:65, 7:163-66
Sabians, 2:62, 5:69, 22:17
sacred months, 2:194
    fighting in, 2:216
    desecrating, as unlawful, 5:2
    fighting after, 9:5-11
    prohibition of fighting in, 9:36-37
Sacred Mosque
    preventing access to, 2:216
    violating sanctity of, 22:25
    See also Kaba; Qibla; Makka
sacrificial offerings
    camels, 22:39-37
    on Hajj, 22:34
    piety of reaches Allah, 22:37

    rights of, 33:6
    spending on, 2:215
    See also family
religion
    as submission to Allah, 3:19-20
    avoiding those who mock, 6:66-70
    basis of, 4:36-38
    differences in, 5:48, 11:118
    freedom of, 2:114, 2:256
    mockery of, warning about, 5:57-60
    sectarianism in, 30:32
    staying behind from jihad to study, 9:122
    submission to Allah as the only form of, 3:83-85
    taking as amusement, 7:51
remembrance of Allah
    Allah remembering you, 2:152
    being frequent in, 33:41
    finding peace in, 13:28
    keeping company of those who engage in, 18:28
    times of the day for, 20:130
repentance
    acceptance of, 9:104-106
    after behaving indecently, 3:133-38
    criterion for acceptability, 4:17-18
    from banditry, 5:34
    from evil, 6:54
    from hypocrisy, 4:146
    from theft, 5:39
    of Adam, 2:37
    of those who conceal the clear signs, 2:159
    of those who delayed joining Tabuk expedition, 9:117-18
    success of, 28:67
    See also forgiveness
resurrection
    denial of, 17:49-52
    example of revived land, 35:9, 36:33-36
    surprise of, to disbelievers, 50:1-5
retaliation
    law of, 2:178, 5:45
    for murder, 17:33

miserliness

storytellers, 31:6-7

straight path, 15:41

submission to Allah, 3:19-20, 3:26
  as the only true religion, 3:83-85
  all creation in, 16:48-52

sun
  rejection of worship of, 6:74-79, 27:24
  journey through the sky, 35:13, 36:38
  as a sign, 41:37
  wrapped up on Judgement Day, 81:1
  prostration of to Allah, 22:18

superstition
  censure of, 5:103-105
  pagan customs, 6:136-47

supplications, Dua
  as answered, 2:186, 40:60, 42:26
  for entering and leaving, 17:80
  for forgiveness, 2:286, 3:16, 7:23, 28:16
  for good in both worlds, 2:201
  for gratitude at age 40, 46:15
  for guidance, 1:1-6, 3:8-9, 39:46
  for increasing knowledge, 20:114
  for lightening of burdens, 2:286
  for parents, 17:24
  for past generations, 59:10
  for protection from Hell, 25:65-66
  for spouses and children, 21:89, 25:74
  for travelling, 43:13-14
  for true judgement, 21:112
  for upright offspring, 3:38
  of Adam, for forgiveness, 7:23
  of Ayyub, 38:41
  of Dhan Nun in the whale, 21:87-88
  of gratitude, 27:19
  of Ibrahim, 2:126-29, 14:35-41, 26:83-89, 60:4-5
  of Lut, 26:169
  of Musa for mercy, 7:151
  of Musa for protection, 40:27
  of Musa, when invested in prophethood, 20:25-36
  of Nuh, 71:5-9, 71:21-24, 71:26-27, 26:117-18, 54:10
  of people on the heights, 7:47

Allah and His Messenger, 24:46-50

Sirius (star), 53:49

skies, creation of, 41:11-12

skin, testimony of, 41:20-22

sky
  human sustenance from, 51:20-23
  rolling up of, 21:104

slander
  to avoid punishment, as sinful, 4:110-12
  demons descend upon, 26:221-23

slaves
  emancipating on demand, 24:33
  freeing as compensation for zihar divorce, 58:3
  marrying, 4:25
  setting free, as righteousness, 2:177
  using zakat to buy freedom for, 9:60
  Yusuf sold as, 12:19-22

sleep
  before battle of Badr, 8:11, 8:43
  removal of soul during, 39:42
  sleepers of the cave. See cave.

soul
  as by Lord's command, 17:85
  death of, 21:35
  first assembly before Allah, 7:172-74
  not given task beyond its capacity, 23:62
  removal of during sleep, 39:42

speech, saying that which you do not do, 61:1-3

spoils of war, distribution of, 8:41

spouses, love between, 30:21. See also marriage

spying, avoiding, 49:12

staff of Musa, 20:17-21, 27:10

stars
  constellations of, 15:16-19, 25:61
  decoration of lower sky with, 67:5
  dimming of on Judgement Day, 81:2
  rejection of worship of, 6:74-79

Station of Abraham, 2:125

stick of Musa, 20:17-21, 27:10

stillness (sakinah), descent of in battle of Hunain, 9:26

stinginess, parable of, 2:266. See also

5:46
eye for an eye, 5:45
revelation of, 3:3-4
using to judge in disputes, 5:42-43
trade. See commerce.
travel; travellers; travelling
as recipients of zakat, 9:60
giving charity to, 2:215
prayer while, 4:101
purification for prayer while, 4:43
spending on, as righteous, 2:177
supplication for, 43:13-14
to see the consequences of disbelief,
3:137
treachery, sin of, 4:105-109, 8:55-58
treaties
breaking, enormity of, 8:55-58
punishing those who break, 9:12-16
with idolaters, annulment of, 9:1-4
treaty of Hudaybiyyah, 48:1-5
tree of Zaqqum, 37:62-65
tree, pledge of loyalty under, 48:18-21
trees, parable of, 14:24-27
Trench, battle of
lack of loyalty of the hypocrites, 33:12
test of the believers on, 33:9-11
trench, companions of, 85:4-8
trials, as means to Paradise, 2:214
tribes and races among mankind, 49:13
tribulation, as means to Paradise, 2:214
trinity
censure of, 4:170-71
irrationality of divinity of Jesus, 5:17,
5:72-77
nature of Isa son of Maryan, 3:59-60
witness of Isa against, 5:116-19
troublemakers, 2:204-206
trumpet
blowing of, 36:51
on Judgement Day, 27:87
people falling unconscious at, 39:68
trusts, returning to their owners, 4:58
truth
obstructing others from, 4:167-69
pretending not to know, 2:97-101

of sleepers of cave, 18:10
of the Israelites after repenting, 7:149
of the queen of Sheba, 27:44
of the righteous, as answered, 42:26
of utter submission to Allah, 3:26
of Yusuf, 12:101, 12:33
of Zakariyya for a child, 21:89
protection from Satan, 23:97-98
when in desperate need, 28:24
suspicion, avoiding, 49:12
sustenance, as from the sky, 51:20-23
sword verse, 9:5
symbols of Allah, 5:2

T
table, miracle of, 5:111-15
Tablet, Protected, 85:22
tablets of Musa, revelation of, 7:145
tahajjud prayer, 17:79, 32:16, 51:17, 52:49
command to the Messenger to perform,
73:2-4
talk, saying that which you do not do,
61:1-3
tashriq, days of, 2:203
Tasneem, water of, 83:27-28
taxes, of non-Muslim citizens, 9:29-30
tayammum, 4:43, 5:6
teasing each other, 49:11
Ten Commandments, 17:23-40
Quranic version, 6:151-53
tests,
of the believers, 2:214, 29:2-5
of humility, 6:5
thankfulness. See gratitude
thieves, punishment and repentance,
5:38-40
threefold divorce, 2:230
Throne
angels around, 39:75, 40:7
establishment of Allah on, 32:4
verse of, 2:255
thunder, glorifying Allah, 13:13
tight-fistedness, 5:46. See also miserliness
Torah
as confirmed by Isa son of Maryam,

rules for, 65:4-7
walking stick of Musa, 20:17-21
wall, Khidr's building of, 18:77
warfare
    attitude of the believer in battle, 3:146-51, 8:45-48, 8:64-66
    being prepared for, 8:59-63
    bloodshed among the Israelites, 2:84
    captives in, 8:67-71
    desertion, prohibition of, 8:15-16
    facing an army, 8:45-48
    in sacred months, 2:191, 2:194, 9:36-37
    in self defence, 22:38-41
    martyrs as alive, 2:154
    necessity of fighting, 2:216
    permission to engage in, 47:4-6
    prohibition of transgressing in, 2:190
    self-defence, 42:39-42
    spoils of war, 8:1, 59:6-8, 8:41
wastefulness, 17:26-28
water
    as sign of Allah, 56:68-70
    creatures created from, 24:45, 25:54
    forms of, 25:48-50
    people of Hell asking for, 7:50-51
wealth
    and forgetting Allah's gifts, 16:112-13
    as a test, 64:15
    as decoration of this life, 18:46
    cannot guarantee victory, 3:10-13
    distracting from remembrance of Allah, 63:9-11
    distraction of, 102:1-8
    distribution of, 16:71
    hoarding, among rabbis and monks, 9:34-35
    increased by zakat, not interest, 30:39
    no one knows what they will earn, 31:34
    of no avail on Day of Judgement, 5:35
    of no benefit to misers, 92:8-11
    of others, misusing, as unlawful, 4, 29
    of the disbelievers, 3:116-17
    parable of rich man, 18:32-44
    rejection of prophets because of, 34:34-39

vanquishes falsehood, 17:81, 34:48-49
twelve springs of the Israelites, 2:60
twelve tribes of Israel, 7:159-62
tyranny
    punishment for tyrants, 14:15-17
    supplication for protection from, 40:27

U
Uhud, battle of
    angels at, 3:124-29
    hard lessons from, 3:139-43
    help of Allah at, 3:121-23
Ummah
    as balanced, 2:143
    as best community from humanity, 3:110
Umra
    Safa and Marwa as signs of Allah, 2:158
    being unable to complete, 2:196
unbelievers, attributes of, 2:6-7
unity, 3:103
universe
    creation of, 10:3-6, 21:30-35
    expansion of, 51:47
    in submission to Allah, 16:48-52
    not created without a purpose, 15:85, 21:16-21
unseen, belief in, 2:3
usury
    prohibition of, 2:275-81, 3:130-32
    does not increase wealth, 30:39
Al-Uzza (idol), 53:19

V
vice-regent on earth, 35:39
victory
    for lovers of Allah, 5:54-56
    promise of, at Badr, 8:9-14
    promised to the believers, 24:55-57
voluntary prayers, 17:79

W
waiting period
    after divorce, 2:228, 2:231-32
    for widows, 2:234

womb, development of foetus in, 23:12-16, 39:6

women
difference in inheritance from men, 4:34
obtaining divorce by returning dowry, 2:229
older, concessions on dress for, 24:60
treating well, 4:19-21
See also mothers; wives; marriage

wool, blessing of, 16:80

words of Allah
infinitude of, 18:109-110
will never run dry, 31:27

words, good and foul, 14:24-27

world; worldliness
allure of, 2:212
as motivation for jihad, condemned, 4:71-74
as wasting life, 6:27-32
asking for good of, 2:200-201
brevity of this life, 57:20-21
comparison with Paradise, 3:14-18
disbelievers satisfied with, 10:7
distraction of, 21:1-5
fate of those who indulge in, 17:16-22
parable of rain, 18:45-46
quest for, 2:102-103
simile of ruined crops, 10:24-26
those who love more than Hereafter, 2:92-95
See also wealth

worship
as route to righteousness, 2:21
as thankfulness, 2:21
half-heartedness in, 22:11-16
purpose of, 2:21
pitfalls of, 107:4-7

wrongdoers, destruction of, 7:4-5

Z

zakat
eight recipients of, 9:60
giving, 2:110
increases wealth, 30:39

showing off with, as disliked, 4:38
spending in order to misguide people, 8:36-37
uneven distribution of, 42:27
wastefulness and miserliness, 17:26-30
See also charity; miserliness; worldliness

widows
maintenance for, 2:240
marrying, 2:235
waiting period and remarriage, 2:234

will of Allah, importance of acknowledging, 18:23-24

wills
being content with one's share, 4:32-33
disputes about, 2:182
leaving, 2:180
provisions for widows, 2:240
tampering with, 2:181
witnessing of, 5:106-108

winds
as a sign of Allah, 2:164, 30:46-55
control of, 34:12
under Sulayman's orders, 21:81, 38:36

wine
drinking, as sinful, 2:219
prohibition of, 5:90-93

wisdom
and humility, 18:37-38
as an immense good, 2:269
in inviting people to Allah, 16:125-27
of Luqman, 31:12-13

witnesses
in loans and commercial transactions, 2:282-83
on Judgement Day, 16:84-89
to one's last will, 5:106-108

wives
ill-conduct in, 4:34
inheriting from, 4:12
See also marriage; divorce

wives of the Prophet
as mothers of the believers, 33:6
choice between this world and next, 33:28-31

Index of Names and Places

irrationality of belief in divinity of, 5:17, 5:72-77

miracles of, 2:253, 5:109-115

nature of, as like Adam, 3:59-60

prayer for banquet, 5:

raising of, before crucifixion, 4:157-59

refuge of, 23:50-52

speaking of, in cradle, 19:27-33

tidings of a Messenger, 61:6

Ishaq (Isaac)
  as great leader, 21:72-73
  good news of, 37:112-13
  guidance of, 6:84
  prayer for, 14:35-41

Ismail (Ishmael)
  as man of his word, 19:54-55
  guidance of, 6:84
  prayer for, 14:35-41
  sacrifice of, 37:99-113

J

Jalut, (Goliath) 2:249-51

Jesus. *See* Isa

Jibreel (Gabriel)
  descent of, 19:64-65
  descent on Night of Power, 97:4
  on Judgement Day, 78:38
  revelation of the Qur'an through, 81:15-21
  showing enmity to, 2:97-98

K

Ka'ba
  as place of assembly, 2:125
  avoiding war in, 2:191
  construction of, 2:127
  establishment of as Qibla, 2:142, 2:144, 2:149-50
  establishment of rites at, 22:26-29
  Safa and Marwa as signs of Allah, 2:158
  sanctity of, 5:97
  See also Makka

Khidr, and Musa, story of, 18:60-82

coolness of fire , 21:68-69

dead birds fly again, 2:260

debate with Namrood, 2:258

debate with people of, 6:80-83

describing Allah, 26:75-82

dream of, to sacrifice son, 37:99-113

guidance of, against worshipping stars, moon and sun , 6:74-79

prayer for children of, 14:35-41

prayer for a special prophet, 2:127-29

prayers of, 2:126-29, 26:83-89

preaches to his people, 29:16-17

questioning beliefs of his people, 26:69-74

rejection of idolatry, 19:41-50, 21:51-70, 37:91-96

religion of, 2:135-36

safety from fire, 29:24-25

sincere heart of, 37:83-90

submission of, 2:131

trial of, 2:124

visit of angels, 11:69-76, 15:51-59, 51:24-37

Idris, as raised to high rank, 19:56-57

Iekah, destruction of, 50:14

Ilyas
  guidance of, 6:84
  rejection of Baal, 37:123-32

Isa (Jesus)
  as a sign, 21:91-93
  as confirming the Torah, 5:46
  as servant of Allah, 4:172
  as sign of Final Hour, 43:57-67
  as strengthened by Holy Spirit, 2:87
  as witness against those who deified him, 5:116-19
  birth of, 19:16-21, 19:22-26
  calling of disciples, 3:52-53
  curse on disbelievers among Israelites, 5:78
  deniers of, 3:54-58
  excessive claims about, 4:170-71
  glad tidings of to Maryam, 3:45-51
  guidance of, 6:84
  helpers of Allah, 61:14

Muhammad. *See* Prophet Muhammad

Musa (Moses)

Allah speaking to, 4:164

and Khidr, story of, 18:60-82

anger with Harun, 20:92-95

Ark of the Covenant, 2:248

as guiding his people out of darkness, 14:5-8

asked to pray to life punishment, 43:46-50

asks to see Allah, 7:143

beginning of prophethood, 28:29-32

Book revealed to, 6:154

childhood of, 20:38-41

confrontation with Pharaoh, 10:75-82, 20:49-56, 26:23-51, 28:36-42

contest with magicians, 7:113-26, 10:79-82, 20:65-76, 26:43-51

forty nights in Mount Sinai, 2:51, 7:142-45

given the standard, 21:47-50

guidance of, 6:84

helping women at Madyan, 28:22-24

in court of the Pharaoh, 20:42-48

on mount Sinai, 19:51-53

in valley of Tuwa, 20:9-16

infancy of, 28:7-13

Jews asking to see Allah, 4:153

Kills a man , 28:14-21

leads Israelites out of Egypt, 20:77-82

marriage of, 28:25-28

miracles of, 7:103-12, 17:101-104

nine signs of, 27:7-13

on reluctance of Israelites to enter Holy Land, 5:20-26

parting of seas, 2:50, 26:60-68

questioning, 2:108

scrolls of, 6:91

sent to Pharaoh, 26:10-22

sign of story of, 51:38-40

prayer for opening of the mind, 20:25-36

prayer in state of desperation, 40:27

twelve springs of the Israelites, 2:60

Muzdalifa, 2:198

L

Luqman, wisdom of, 31:12-13, 31:16-18

Lut (Lot)

angels visit to, 11:70-83, 15:59-66

destruction of people of, 15:67-76, 27:54-58, 54:33-39

guidance of, 6:84

prayer of, 26:169

rejection of message of, 7:80-84, 29:26-30

rescue of, 21:71, 21:74-75

wife of, 66:10

M

Madyan

destruction of people of, 15:78-80

Musa helping women at, 20:40, 28:22-24

rejection of Shu'ayb, 7:85-93, 29:36-38

warning of Shu'ayb, 11:84-87

Makka

as first place of worship, 3:96-97

avoiding war in, 2:191

famine in, 44:8-16

Ibrahim's supplication for, 2:126

promise to return to, 28:85

Safa and Marwa as signs of Allah, 2:158

safety of, 29:67

stubbornness of people of, 48:26

See also Ka'ba

Malik (angel at gates of Hell), 43:77

Marut, 2:102

Marwa, as sign of Allah, 2:158

Maryam (Mary)

Allah's choosing of, 3:42-44

birth of Isa, 19:22-26

birth of, 3:35-36

chastity of, 21:91

slander against, 4:156

tidings of Isa, 3:45-51

visitation of an angel, 19:16-21

Medina

expulsion of Banu al-Nadir from, 59:1-5

rudeness of some Jews in, 4:44-46

Mikaeel, showing enmity to, 2:98

Index of Introductions

seven deadly, 547
slander, 687
slavery, 688
sleepers of the cave, 569
social manners, 687
Sodom and Gomorrah, 423
stairways to Heavens, 1203
Subhan, 547
Sulayman, 741-42, 849, 901
Suyuti, 1282

T
tablets, 759
Tabuk, campaign of, 355, 1021
Taif, 491, 1009, 1213
ten commandments, 547
Thamud, people of, 423, 505, 1278
thankfulness, 517, 913-14
Torah, 759
trees, 491, 1286
Trench, battle of, 829
trials of life, 452
Trinity, criticism of doctrine of, 200, 593

U
Uhud, battle of, 91-92, 143, 829, 1129, 1145
Umm al-Quran, 1
universe, expanding, 1059
Urf, 286
Urwah, 1031
Usaid ibn Kalda, 1276
Usman ibn Affan, 1031-32
Utbah ibn Rabiah, 949

V
visiting people, manners for, 687

W
waiting term (after divorce), 1169
al-Walid ibn al-Mughira, 1191, 1223
warfare
    permissibility of defending oneself, 3
    jihad carried out for justice, 143
    Battle of Badr (*See under* Badr)

distinct language of, 285
lyricism of, 1278
mocking, 999
pause in revelation of, 1223, 1282
revelation of, 1290
style of Makkan Surahs, 950
truthfulness of, 1254
Quraysh, 949-50, 999, 1300, 1301

R
Al-Rahman (name of Allah), 1091
rain, 1059
Ramadan, obligation to fast, 2
Ramses II, 759
Razi, 286
recitation of Quran, 1220
religion, diversity in, 649, 1303
repentance, 931, 1177
resurrection, 671, 1246
revelation
    of the Quran, 1290
    purpose of, 491
Romans, 355, 797

S
Saba, kingdom of, 849
Safa (mount), 1305
Salman the Persian, 829
Sana (city), 423
Sand Dunes, People of, 1009
Satan, 285, 569, 570, 901, 1308
scepticism, 1292
self deception, 1256
Sells, M. A., 913
sentences in the Quran, 285
seven deadly sins, 547
seven stages of life, 649
Sheba, Queen of, 741-42
she-camel, 1278
al-Shifa (the healing), 1
Shu'ayb, 722
signs of Allah's power, 707
sincere repentance, 1177
sins
    effect of on heart, 1258